The SAGE Handbook of
Sociolinguistics

SAGE has been part of the global academic community since 1965, supporting high quality research and learning that transforms society and our understanding of individuals, groups, and cultures. SAGE is the independent,
innovative, natural home for authors, editors and societies who share our
commitment and passion for the social sciences.

Find out more at: www.sagepublications.com

The SAGE Handbook of
Sociolinguistics

Edited by
Ruth Wodak,
Barbara Johnstone
and Paul Kerswill

Los Angeles • London • New Delhi • Singapore • Washington DC

SAGE Publications Ltd
1 Oliver's Yard
55 City Road
London EC1Y 1SP

SAGE Publications Inc.
2455 Teller Road
Thousand Oaks, California 91320

SAGE Publications India Pvt Ltd
B 1/I 1 Mohan Cooperative Industrial Area
Mathura Road, Post Bag 7
New Delhi 110 044

SAGE Publications Asia-Pacific Pte Ltd
3 Church Street
10-04 Samsung Hub
Singapore 049483

Library of Congress Control Number 2009939335

British Library Cataloguing in Publication data

A catalogue record for this book is available from the British Library

ISBN 978-1-84787-095-7
ISBN 978-1-4462-7059-2 (pbk)

Typeset by Glyph International, Bangalore, India

Contents

List of Contributors

Peter Auer received his academic training at the universities of Cologne, Manchester and Constance, where he also worked as an Assistant Professor of General Linguistics. From 1992 to 1998, he was Professor of German Linguistics at the University of Hamburg. Since 1998, he has held a Chair of German Linguistics at the University of Freiburg (Germany). He is currently one of the directors of the Freiburg Institute for Advanced Studies. Auer has done extensive research on bilingualism, phonology and dialectology, prosody, interaction and spoken language from a syntactic point of view. With Li Wei, he is joint editor of *The Handbook of Multilingualism and Multilingual Communication* (de Gruyter, 2007). Among his recent publications on bilingualism are 'Bilingual conversation', in Nikolas Coupland and Adam Jaworski (eds), *The New Sociolinguistics Reader* (Palgrave Macmillan, 2009) and 'The monolingual bias in bilingualism research, or: why bilingualism is (still) a challenge for linguistics', in Monica Heller (ed.), *Bilingualism: A Social Approach* (Palgrave Macmillan, 2007).

David Barton is Professor of Language and Literacy in the Department of Linguistics at Lancaster University and Director of the Lancaster Literacy Research Centre. Current interests include the changing nature of literacy in contemporary society, literacy and social justice, research methodologies, and reading and writing. His main publications have been concerned with rethinking the nature of literacy (e.g. *Literacy*, Blackwell, *The Anthropology of Writing*, Continuum), carrying out detailed studies of everyday literacies (*Local Literacies*, Routledge; *Situated Literacies*, Routledge; *Letter Writing as a Social Practice*, John Benjamins) and the relations of literacy and learning (*Beyond Communities of Practice*, Cambridge University Press; *Literacy, Lives and Learning*, Routledge; *Improving Learning in College*, Routledge).

Tim Berard is Associate Professor of Sociology at Kent State University, Ohio, USA. His research draws on ethnomethodology and membership categorization analysis, and addresses a constellation of issues including relations between micro practices and macro social structures, group relations such as race relations and gender relations, and substantive issues of crime and law including hate crimes, racial/ethnic profiling, and institutions' disparate impact on minorities. His publications include: 'From concepts to methods: on the observability of inequality', *Journal of Contemporary Ethnography*, 35(3): 236–56 (2006); 'Rethinking practices and structures', *Journal for the Philosophy of the Social Sciences*, 35(2): 196–230 (2005); and 'On multiple identities and educational contexts: remarks on the study of inequalities and discrimination', *Journal of Language, Identity and Education*, 4(1): 67–76 (2005).

Anne-Claude Berthoud is Full Professor of Linguistics, Head of the Linguistics Department, and Chair of the Language Policy Committee at the University of Lausanne. She is coordinator of the European DYLAN project (2006–11), President of the Swiss Academy of Humanities, Vice-president of the Swiss Research Foundation and Vice-president of the European Language Council. Her main research fields are pragmatics, interactional linguistics, second language learning and multilingualism. She has conducted several research projects on interaction and second language learning and acted as an expert for national research programmes. Her publications include 'Le projet DYLAN "Dynamiques des langues et gestion de la diversité": Un aperçu', *Sociolinguistica*, 22: 171–85 (2008); 'Regards croisés sur un plurilinguisme à inventer', *Cahiers de l'ILSL*, 23 (Université de Lausanne, 2008); 'Mehrsprachigkeit als Kaleidoskop des Wissens', in Georges Lüdi, Kurt Seelmann and Beat Sitter-Liver (eds), *Sprachminderheit – Einsprachigkeit – Mehrsprachigkeit*; and *Probleme und Chancen sprachlicher Vielfalt* (Freiburg: Paulus-Verlag/Academic Press, and Stuttgart: Kohlhammer Verlag).

Brigitta Busch is Professor for Applied Linguistics in the Institute of Linguistics at the University of Vienna. She is also a researcher and teacher in the PRAESA Centre at the University of Cape Town. From 1999 to 2003, she was head of the Centre for Intercultural Studies at the University of Klagenfurt. During her work as an expert for the Council of Europe's Confidence-Building Measures Programme, she was involved in a number of intercultural projects in Eastern and South-Eastern Europe. Her main research interests focus on sociolinguistics (multilingualism), discourse analysis, media policies and intercultural communication. Recent publications include 'Reflecting social heteroglossia and accommodating diverse audiences: a challenge to the media', in Michal Krzyżanowski and Aleksandra Galasińska (eds), *Discourse and Transformation in Central and Eastern Europe*. Basingstoke: Palgrave. pp. 43–59 (2009); 'Changing media spaces: the transformative power of heteroglossic practices', in Clare Mar-Molinero and Patrick Stevenson (eds), *Language Ideologies, Policies and Practices: Language and the Future of Europe*. pp. 206–20 (Basingstoke: Palgrave, 2006); and *Sprachen im Disput. Medien und Öffentlichkeit in multilingualen Gesellschaften*. (Klagenfurt, Celovec: Drava, 2004).

Malcolm Coulthard is Professor of Forensic Linguistics and Director of the Centre for Forensic Linguistics at the University of Aston in Birmingham, England. He is probably still best known for his work on the analysis of spoken and written discourse, but since the late 1980s he has become increasingly involved with forensic applications of linguistics. He has written expert reports in over 200 cases and given evidence on author identification three times in the Courts of Appeal in London, as well as in lower courts in England, Germany, Hong Kong and Northern Ireland. Recent publications include (with Alison Johnson) *An Introduction to Forensic Linguistics: Language in Evidence* (2007); and *A Handbook of Forensic Linguistics* (2010).

Robin Dodsworth is Assistant Professor of English at North Carolina State University. She received a PhD in Linguistics from the Ohio State University in 2005, and held the position of Assistant Research Scientist at the University of Maryland before moving to NC State in 2007. Her research focuses on linguistic variation, social class, networks and sociophonetics. She is currently investigating front vowel systems in Raleigh, NC. Publications include 'Modeling social class in variationist sociolinguistics', *Language and Linguistics Compass* (forthcoming); and (with Christine Mallinson) 'Revisiting the need for new approaches to social class in variationist sociolinguistics', Special issue of *Sociolinguistic Studies*, 'Analysing language to understand social phenomena' (2009).

Susan Ehrlich is a Professor of Linguistics at York University, Toronto, Canada. She works in the areas of discourse analysis, language and gender, and language and the law. She is the author of *Representing Rape: Language and Sexual Consent* (London: Routledge 2001) and is the editor of *Language and Gender: Major Themes in English Studies*. (London: Routledge 2008) and (with Alice Freed) *'Why Do You Ask?': The Function of Questions in Institutional Discourse*. (New York: Oxford University Press 2009).

José Antonio Flores Farfán studied linguistics at the University of Amsterdam, where he defended his dissertation on Nahuatl-Spanish contact sociolinguistics. His research interests include the pragmatics of indigenous languages, discourse analysis, language ideologies, language planning and educational linguistics, and especially the revitalization of endangered languages. Together with local speakers he has produced materials in different formats, especially for children, including DVDs, videos, audio and books, which are disseminated at the community level in workshops oriented to empowering the use of endangered languages and their speakers. His publications include: *Variación, Ideologías y Purismo Lingüístico. El caso del mexicano o náhuatl.* (forthcoming); 'Sociolinguistics in Mexico: defining new agendas', in Martin Ball (ed.), *Sociolinguistics Around the World. A Handbook* (forthcoming); and 'Early and contemporary Nahuatl texts in sociolinguistic perspective', *Sociolinguistic Studies*, (1–3): 415–33 (2007).

Robert Garot is an Assistant Professor of Sociology at John Jay College in New York. His research focuses on the dilemmas of the poor and those who funnel their access to needed goods and services. Currently he is studying how undocumented immigrants in Italy cope with living outside the law. He was the recipient of a Calandra Institute Fellowship for the study of Italian society for autumn, 2009. His book *Who You Claim: Performing Gang Identity in School and on the Streets*, has been recently published by New York University Press.

Alexandra Georgakopoulou is Professor of Discourse Analysis & Sociolinguistics at King's College London. She has (co-)authored 8 books in the areas of conversational storytelling, language and identities, and language and new media. She has recently developed small stories research as a new way of doing narrative analysis, a detailed discussion of which can be found in her monograph *Small Stories, Interaction and Identities* (2007, John Benjamins).

Cynthia Gordon is Assistant Professor of Communication and Rhetorical Studies at Syracuse University. She uses theories and methods of discourse analysis, especially of interactional sociolinguistics, to investigate how meanings, relationships, and identities are created in everyday family talk. Her current research interests include family-based reality television programmes and everyday family health communication. She is the author of *Making Meanings, Creating Family: Intertextuality and Framing in Family Interaction* (Oxford: Oxford University Press, 2009) and (with Deborah Tannen and Shari Kendall) editor of *Family Talk: Discourse and Identity in Four American Families* (Oxford: Oxford University Press, 2007).

Tim Grant is Deputy Director of the Centre for Forensic Linguistics at Aston University. His consultancy primarily involves authorship analysis and he has worked in many different contexts including investigations into sexual assault, murder and terrorist offences. His research into text messaging analysis was awarded the 2008 Joseph Lister Prize by the British Science Association. He publishes on forensic linguistics and forensic psychology.

Gregory R. Guy has been Professor of Linguistics at New York University since 2001, following previous appointments at Sydney, Cornell, Stanford and York. His research interests include language variation and change, language and social class, and theoretical models of linguistic variation. He has done original sociolinguistic research in Argentina, Australia, Brazil, Canada, the Dominican Republic, New Zealand and the United States. Publications include (co-author) *Sociolingüística Quantitativa* (São Paulo: Parábola), (lead editor) *Towards a Social Science of Language* (Amsterdam: Benjamins), and a series of papers in *Language Variation and Change* dealing with formal models of sociolinguistic variation.

Kirk Hazen is Professor in the Department of English at West Virginia University. He focuses his research on language variation in American English, primarily writing about Southern US varieties and English in Appalachia. He promotes sociolinguistic goals by presenting dialect diversity programs to numerous communities, including future health professionals, social workers, and service organizations. Recent publications include a history of variationist sociolinguistics (in Bayley and Lucas (2007) *Sociolinguistic Variation: Theory, Methods, and Application*), an analysis of (ING) variation in Appalachia (*American Speech* 83:2), and an overview of sociolinguistics in the United States of America (in Ball (2010), *Sociolinguistics Around the World*).

Marlis Hellinger is Professor Emerita of English Linguistics at Johann Wolfgang Goethe University, Frankfurt am Main, Germany. Her main research interests are in language and gender, contrastive linguistics, contact linguistics, applied linguistics and pidgin and creole linguistics. Among her publications are three volumes (with Hadumod Bussmann) on *Gender Across Languages: The Linguistic Representation of Women and Men* (Amsterdam: Benjamins 2001, 2002, 2003) and (with Anne Pauwels) *Language and Communication: Diversity and Change* (Berlin: de Gruyter, 2007).

Anna Holzscheiter is a Postdoctoral Fellow at the London School of Hygiene and Tropical Medicine, carrying out a research project on the power of discourses in global HIV/AIDS policymaking. She is also Lecturer in International Relations at Freie Universität Berlin, where she is currently on study leave. Her research interests include discourse analysis in international political studies, multi-dimensional power theories and discourse, the role of non-state actors in world politics, global childhood politics and children's rights, and HIV/AIDS. She is author of 'Discourse as capability: non-state actors' capital in global governance', *Millennium*, 33(3): 723–46 (2005) and *The Transformative Power of Transnational Discourse: Children's Rights in International Politics* (Basingstoke: Palgrave Macmillan, forthcoming).

Anthea Irwin is Programme Leader of the BA (Hons.) Media & Communication degree at Glasgow Caledonian University. She researches discourse reproduction and identity construction in both conversational and media data. Her publications include 'London adolescents reproducing power/knowledge: "you know" and "I know"', *Language in Society*, 35:4 (2006); 'Now you see me, now you don't: adolescents exploring deviant positions', in P. Pichler and E. Eppler (eds), *Gender and Spoken Interaction* (Palgrave Macmillan 2009) and 'Race and ethnicity', in N. Blain and D. Hutchison (eds), *The Media in Scotland* (Edinburgh: Edinburgh University Press 2008).

Gabrielle Ivinson is a Senior Lecturer in the School of Social Sciences, Cardiff University. Her doctoral thesis brought together Bernstein's sociology of pedagogy with Moscovici's theory of social representations. With Gerard Duveen, she has written a number of papers on Bernstein's work as it applies to the primary school classroom, including 'Classroom structuration and the development of representations of the curriculum', *British Journal of Sociology of Education*, 26(5): 627–42, (2005); and 'Children's recontextualisations of pedagogy', in R. Moore et al., (eds), *Knowledge, Power and Educational Reform: Applying the Sociology of Basil Bernstein* (London, New York: Routledge Taylor Francis Group, 2006). With Patricia Murphy, she wrote *Rethinking Single Sex Teaching* (McGraw Hill, Open University, 2007), which uses a socio-cultural approach to investigate how gender emerges in everyday classroom practice.

Barbara Johnstone is Professor of Rhetoric and Linguistics at Carnegie Mellon University and editor of *Language in Society*. Her recurrent interests have to do with how people evoke and shape places in talk and with what can be learned by taking the perspective of the individual on language and discourse. Her current work is about dialect and locality in the Pittsburgh (USA) area. She is the author of *Repetition in Arabic Discourse* (Benjamins 1990); *Stories, Community, and Place: Narratives from Middle America* (Indiana UP 1990); *The Linguistic Individual* (Oxford 1996); two textbooks, *Qualitative Methods in Sociolinguistics* (Oxford 2001) and *Discourse Analysis* (Blackwell 2008) and many articles and book chapters.

Shari Kendall is Associate Professor of Linguistics in the Department of English at Texas A&M University. Her research addresses the discursive construction of gendered, professional and parental identities in work and family discourse; the constitution of gender and sexuality in legal contexts, the media, and everyday contexts; and the theoretical frameworks of framing, positioning and interactional sociolinguistics. Recent publications include 'The balancing act: framing gendered parental identities at dinnertime' in *Language in Society* and 'Father as breadwinner/mother as worker: Discursively positioning parental and professional identities' in *Family Talk: The Discourse of Four American Families*.

Paul Kerswill is Professor of Sociolinguistics at Lancaster University, and has a special interest in dialect contact and new dialect formation. He became interested in dialectology while working on a farm in Norway, and subsequently directed projects in Bergen, Durham, Cambridge, Milton Keynes, Reading and Hull. His current and most recent projects are on the emergence of new varieties among young people in inner-city London: *Linguistic Innovators: The English of Adolescents in London* and *Multicultural London English: The Emergence, Acquisition and Diffusion of a New Variety*, both funded by the Economic and Social Research Council and with Jenny Cheshire as Co-Investigator. Recent publications include the edited volume (with Peter Auer and Frans Hinskens) *Dialect Change: Convergence and Divergence in European Languages* (Cambridge: Cambridge University Press 2005) and (with Eivind Torgersen and Sue Fox) 'Reversing 'drift': innovation and diffusion in the London diphthong system', *Language Variation and Change* (2008).

Paul Kockelman is Assistant Professor of Anthropology at Barnard College, Columbia University, New York. Recent publications include: 'Meaning and time: translation and exegesis of a Q'eqchi'-Maya Myth', *Anthropological Linguistics*, 49(3/4): 308–87 (2009), 'Inalienable possession as grammatical category and discourse pattern', *Studies in Language*, 31(1): 25–68 (2009) and 'A semiotic ontology of the commodity', *Journal of Linguistic Anthropology*, 16(1): 76–102 (2006).

Helga Kotthoff is Professor in the Department of German Linguistics at Freiburg University in Germany. She has worked in the fields of applied, German and anthropological linguistics, primarily on questions of interaction analysis, gender studies, sociolinguistics and ethnography of communication. Her current research includes interactional sociolinguistics, German as a foreign language, conversational humour and irony, second language acquisition and gender and intercultural communication studies. She teaches and publishes on all these subjects.

Krzysztof Kredens received his MA in English Studies and PhD in English Linguistics from the University of Łódź, Poland. He is a Lecturer in Applied Linguistics in the School of Languages and Social Sciences at Aston University, UK. His academic interests include corpus linguistics, translation studies and social applications of linguistics, particularly in legal and forensic contexts. His main interest lies with the linguistics of the individual speaker and its implications for forensic authorship analysis. He is a practising public service interpreter. Recent publications include the edited volume (with Stanisław Goźdź-Roszkowski) *Language and the Law: International Outlooks* (Frankfurt am Main: Peter Lang

2007) and (with Ruth Morris) "A Shattered Mirror?" Interpreting in legal contexts outside the courtrooom', in M. Coulthard and A. Johnson (eds.), *The Routledge Handbook of Forensic Linguistics.*

Tore Kristiansen is Professor of Sociolinguistics at Copenhagen University's Department of Scandinavian Research, Section of Dialectology, and its Centre for Studies of Language Change in Real Time (LANCHART). His main research interest lies in the ideological and social psychological aspects of language contact situations (dialects or accents vs standards in particular, but also national languages vs English). His most recent work in this field is 'The macro-social meanings of late-modern Danish accents', *Acta Linguistica Hafniensia*, 41 (2009). His (co-)edited books and journal issues include (with Peter Garrett and Nikolas Coupland) 'Subjective processes in language variation and change', *Acta Linguistica Hafniensia*, 37 (2005) and (with Lars Vikør) *Nordiske språkhaldningar: Ei meiningsmåling* [*Nordic Language Attitudes: An Opinion Poll*] (Oslo: Novus, 2006).

Carmen Lee is Assistant Professor in the Department of English at the Chinese University of Hong Kong. Her research interests include social aspects of language and literacy, linguistic practices on the Internet, and multilingual identities. Over the past few years, she has published book chapters and journal articles on literacy practices in various digital media, including electronic mail, instant messaging and mobile phone texting. She is currently carrying out a research project on the literacies in Web 2.0 writing spaces such as weblogs and Facebook.

Constant Leung is Professor of Educational Linguistics in the Department of Education and Professional Studies at King's College London. He is Director of two MA programmes: MA English Language Teaching and Applied Linguistics, and MA Assessment in Education. He is also Deputy Head of Department. His research interests include additional/second language education in ethnically and linguistically diverse societies, English as an Additional Language in school contexts, content and language integration, language assessment, language policy and teacher professional development. Recent publications include 'Convivial communication: recontextualizing communicative competence', *International Journal of Applied Linguistics*, 15(2), 119–44; 'Integrating school-aged ESL learners into the mainstream curriculum', in J. Cummins and C. Davison (eds), *The International Handbook of English Language Teaching.* pp. 249–69 (New York: Springer, 2007) and (with J. Lewkowicz) 'Expanding horizons and unresolved conundrums: language testing and assessment', *TESOL Quarterly*, 40(1), 211–34 (2006).

Georges Lüdi is Full Professor of French Linguistics, Head of the French Department and past Dean of the Faculty of Arts at Basel University. He has conducted several third-party financed research projects with a focus on forms of (emergent) multilingualism and language contact in Switzerland, using both qualitative and quantitative methods; currently he acts as deputy coordinator of the European DYLAN project (2006–11). He has chaired a group of experts mandated to propose a whole language policy for Switzerland (1997–8), the Swiss Linguistic Society, and the Swiss Association for Applied Linguistics; he has also served as a Member of the Executive Board of the International Association for Applied Linguistics, AILA, and been awarded the distinction of Officer in the *Ordre National du Mérite*, by the French Government. He has authored numerous scientific publications on linguistic aspects of migration, multilingualism, second language teaching and learning, and workplace communication, including 'Multilingual repertoires and the consequences for linguistic theory', in Kristin Bührig and Jan D. ten Thije (eds), *Beyond Misunderstanding: Linguistic Analyses of Intercultural Communication*, pp. 11–42 (Amsterdam: John Benjamins, 2006), 'The Swiss model of plurilingual communication', in Jan D. ten Thije and Ludger Zeevaert (eds), *Receptive Multilingualism: Linguistic Analyses, Language Policies and Didactic Concepts* pp. 159–78 (Amsterdam: John Benjamins, 2007) and (with Bernard Py) 'To be or not to be ... a plurilingual speaker', *International Journal of Multilingualism*, 6(2):154–67 (2009).

Christine Mallinson is Assistant Professor in the Language, Literacy and Culture Program and Affiliate Assistant Professor in the Gender and Women's Studies Program at the University of Maryland, Baltimore County. Her research investigates English language variation, region, class, race/ethnicity, gender and education, focusing in particular on how these factors intersect in the lives and experiences of speakers of African American English and Southern US English. Her recent publications include 'Sociolinguistics and sociology: Current directions, future partnerships', in *Language and Linguistics Compass* (2009). She is also the co-author (with Anne H. Charity Hudley) of a forthcoming book on language variation for K-12 educators (Multicultural Education Series, Teachers College Press).

William M. Marcellino is a PhD student in Rhetoric at Carnegie Mellon University. He is interested in military discourse, in particular how US military members make use of discourse in ways different from civilians. His work combines ethnographic method with theoretical models of the emergence of grammar and culture.

Luisa Martín Rojo is Full Professor of Linguistics at the Universidad Autónoma (Madrid, Spain), Member of the International Pragmatic Association Consultation Board (2006–11), and Member of the Scientific Board of the CRITICS Foundation (Centre for Research into Text/Talk, Information, and Communication in Society). Her current work is focused on the management of cultural and linguistic diversity in Madrid schools, analysing how inequality is constructed, naturalized and legitimized through discursive practices. In this field, she heads the following projects: 'A socio-pragmatic analysis of inter-cultural communication in education: towards integration in schools' and 'Multilingualism in schools: a critical sociolinguistic analysis of educational linguistics programs in the Madrid region'. Dr. Martín Rojo is also a member of the editorial boards of *Discourse & Society* and *Spanish in Context*, among other international academic journals. Recent publications include *Constructing inequality in multilingual classrooms* (Mouton de Gruyter 2010).

Christian M. I. M. Matthiessen is Chair Professor and Head of the Department of English and Associate Dean of the Faculty of Humanities at the Hong Kong Polytechnic University. He has degrees in linguistics from Lund University (BA) and UCLA (MA, PhD), where he became familiar with ethnomethodology and conversation analysis, and he has been involved in major text-based research projects since 1980. His research has covered a wide range of areas, including analysis of many kinds of discourse, register analysis and description, the development of Rhetorical Structure Theory (with Bill Mann and Sandy Thompson), the description of English and other languages spoken around the world, language typology and comparison, translation studies, 'institutional linguistics', computational linguistics, the evolution of language, and systemic functional theory. His books include (with John Bateman) *Systemic Linguistics and Text Generation: Experiences from Japanese and English* (1991), *Lexicogrammatical Cartography: English Systems* (1995); (with J. R. Martin and Clare Painter) *Working with Functional Grammar* (1997), (with M. A. K. Halliday) *Construing Experience: A Language-Based Approach to Cognition* (1999), (with M. A. K. Halliday) *Introduction to Functional Grammar* (revised version of Halliday's book, 2004), and (with M. A. K. Halliday) *Systemic Functional Grammar: A First Step into the Theory* (2009). Edited volumes include (with Alice Caffarel and J. R. Martin) *Functional Typology* (2004) and (with Ruqaiya Hasan and Jonathan Webster,) *Continuing Discourse on Language* (2005 and 2007).

Norma Mendoza-Denton is Associate Professor of Linguistic Anthropology at the University of Arizona-Tucson in the Departments of Anthropology and Linguistics. Her research interests include sociophonetics, language and ethnicity, language and gender, language and gesture, migration, youth subcultures and video ethnography. Recent publications include: *Homegirls: Language and Cultural Practice among Latina Youth Gangs* (Wiley-Blackwell, 2008) and 'Sociolinguistic extensions of exemplar theory', in J. Cole and J. Hualde (eds), *Laboratory Phonology 9* (Mouton de Gruyter, 2007).

Florian Menz is Professor of Applied Linguistics and Sociolinguistics at the University of Vienna. Combining CDA with sociological systemic approaches, his main research interests include organizational language use, with a focus on medical and business institutions, gender and power-related aspects of interaction, and interactional representations of pain. Recent publications include (with Johanna Lalouschek) "I just can't tell you how much it hurts." Gender-relevant differences in the description of chest pain', in Françoise Salager-Meyer and Maurizio Gotti (eds), *Medical discourse*. Lang 2006. pp. 135–54, (with Johanna Lalouschek and Andreas Gstettner) *Effiziente ärztliche Gesprächsführung. Optimierung kommunikativer Kompetenz in der ambulanten medizinischen Versorgung. Ein gesprächs-analytisches Trainingskonzept* (Münster: Lit-Verlag, 2008) and (with Ali Al-Roubaie) 'Interruptions, status, and gender in medical interviews: the harder you brake, the longer it takes', *Discourse & Society*, 19(5): 645–66 (2008).

Terttu Nevalainen is Professor and Chair of English Philology at the University of Helsinki and the Director of the Research Unit for Variation, Contacts and Change in English, a National Centre of Excellence funded by the Academy of Finland. Her research interests include historical sociolinguistics, corpus linguistics and language change. She is the author (with H. Raumolin-Brunberg) of *Historical Sociolinguistics: Language Change in Tudor and Stuart England* Published by Pearson Education, (2003) and a co-editor of *Types of Variation* Published by Benjamins, (2006) and *The Dynamics of Linguistic*

Variation Published by Benjamins, (2008). Dr. Nevalainen is one of the compilers of the Helsinki Corpus of English Texts and the director of the project 'Sociolinguistics and Language History', which has produced the Corpus of Early English Correspondence. She also has some eighty publications on English historical sociolinguistics.

Theodossia-Soula Pavlidou is Professor of Linguistics (with specialization in pragmatics and sociolinguistics) at the Aristotle University of Thessaloniki, where she has held numerous offices, including a long-standing directorship of the Post-Graduate Studies Programme of the School of Philology. Her interest in language and gender, and women/gender studies, goes back to the late 1970s. Her research also focuses on telephone talk, classroom interaction, politeness and other topics in cross-cultural pragmatics and conversation analysis. She is one of the editors of the *Journal of Pragmatics*. Recent publications pertaining to gender include two edited volumes (in Greek) *Language-Grammatical Gender-Social Gender*, 2nd edn. (2006) and *Gender Studies: Trends/Tensions in Greece and Other European Countries* (2006); also the chapter (in Greek) '"We" and the construction of (gendered) collectivities', in M. Theodoropoulou (ed.), *Light and Warmth: In Memory of A.-Ph. Christidis*. pp. 437–53 (2008).

Alastair Pennycook is Professor of Language Studies at the University of Technology, Sydney. He is interested in how we understand language in relation to globalization, colonial history, identity, popular culture and pedagogy. Publications include *The Cultural Politics of English as an International Language* (Longman, 1994), *English and the Discourses of Colonialism* (Routledge, 1998), *Critical Applied Linguistics: A Critical Introduction* (Lawrence Erlbaum, 2001), and *Global Englishes and Transcultural Flows* (Routledge, 2007). Two recent edited books are (with Sinfree Makoni) *Disinventing and Reconstituting Languages*. (Multilingual Matters, 2007) and (with Samy Alim and Awad Ibrahim) *Global Linguistic Flows: Hip Hop Cultures, Youth Identities, and the Politics of Language* (Routledge, 2009). His most recent book, *Language as a Local Practice*, was published by Routledge in 2010.

Petra Pfisterer is currently a PhD candidate and works as a researcher at the Institute of Applied Linguistics at the University of Vienna. Her research interests concern sociolinguistics and the media; she has conducted research on minority language media, community radio and multilingualism. Recent publications include (with Judith Purkarthofer and Brigitta Busch) '10 Jahre Freies Radio in Österreich. Offener Zugang, Meinungsvielfalt und soziale Kohäsion – Eine explorative Studie', in RTR (ed.), *Nichtkommerzieller Rundfunk in Österreich und Europa*, pp. 111–13 (Vienna: Schriftenreihe der Rundfunk und Telekom Regulierungs-GmbH 2009), and (with Sabine Humer) 'Médias en contexte plurilingue', in Zohra Bouchentouf-Siagh and Peter Cichon (eds), *Le Sénégal - Un Modèle de gestion et de Promotion des Langues Nationales, Pour l'Afrique? Quo Vadis Romania. Schriften für eine moderne Romanistik.* pp. 52–63 (Vienna, University of Vienna, 2003).

Ingrid Piller (PhD, Dresden 1995) is Professor of Applied Linguistics at Macquarie University, Sydney, Australia, where she directed the Adult Migrant English Program Research Centre (AMEP RC) from 2007 to 2008. She is also affiliated with the languages programme at Zayed University, Abu Dhabi, UAE. Her research interests are in intercultural communication, language learning, multilingualism, and how they intersect with social inclusion and justice. She is currently writing a textbook on *intercultural communication* for Edinburgh University Press, which aims to provide a critical introduction to the field from a sociolinguistic and discourse-analytic perspective. She is the co-founder, together with Kimie Takahashi, of the sociolinguistics portal Language on the Move at www.languageonthemove.org.

Julia Sallabank is Lecturer in Language Support and Revitalisation in the Endangered Languages Academic Programme at the School of Oriental and African Studies, University of London. She has been conducting language documentation and sociolinguistic research in Guernsey, Channel Islands since 2000, and is currently comparing language policies in small island states. Her research interests focus on language policy for endangered and minority languages, language pedagogy for endangered languages and language revitalisation. Her publications include: 'Guernsey French, identity issues and language endangerment', in Tope Ominiyi and Goodith White (eds), *The Sociolinguistics of Identity* (Continuum, 2006) and 'Prestige from the bottom up: a review of language planning in Guernsey', in A. J. Liddicoat and R. B. Baldauf Jr. (eds), *Language Planning in Local Contexts* (Multilingual Matters, 2008). She is co-editor (with Peter Austin) of *The Cambridge Handbook of Endangered Languages* (2011).

Mark Sebba is Reader in Sociolinguistics and Language Contact in the Department of Linguistics and English Language at Lancaster University. His research interests are in bilingualism, language contact and multilingual literacies, in particular in language mixing in written media. He has written on code-switching from both a societal and syntactic point of view. His recent book *Spelling and Society: The Culture and Politics of Orthography Around the World* (Cambridge University Press, 2007) develops a view of orthography as social practice, in which bilingualism and language contact are also centrally involved. Recent publications include 'Discourses in transit', in Adam Jaworski and Crispin Thurlow (eds), *Semiotic Landscapes: Language, Image, Space* (Continuum, 2010), 'Spelling as a social practice', in Janet Maybin and Joan Swann (eds), *Routledge Companion to the English Language* (Routledge, 2009) and 'On the notions of congruence and convergence in code-switching', in Barbara E. Bullock and Almeida Jacqueline Toribio (eds). *The Cambridge Handbook of Linguistic Code-Switching* (Cambridge University Press, 2009).

Diana Slade is Professor of Applied Linguistics at the University of Technology, Sydney (UTS). Her PhD research was on the analysis of English casual conversation. Diana has over 20 years experience in researching, teaching and publishing in applied linguistics, linguistics and organizational communication. Her major research focus now is on developing and extending theoretical work in these three areas, with a particular focus on the analysis and description of spoken English. Her current research is on emergency communication, describing clinician/patient communication in hospital emergency departments. Her books include (with Scott Thornbury) *Conversation: From Description to Pedagogy* (Cambridge University Press, 2006), (with Suzanne Eggins) *Analysing Casual Conversation* (Equinox, UK, 1997) and (with Kalantzis and Cope) *Minority Languages and Dominant Culture: Issues of Equity, Education and Assessment* (Falmer Press, 1990). She has published extensively in the area of discourse analysis of conversational English and spoken communication in workplace contexts.

Stef Slembrouck is Professor of English Linguistics and Discourse Analysis at Ghent University. With Mike Baynham, he co-convenes the AILA Research Network on Language and Migration. He has published mainly on the role of socio-discursive processes in the construction of institutional identities (bureaucracy, child protection and health), including the implications of migration-connected multilingualism on the working of institutions. Slembrouck's publications include (with J. Collins and M. Baynham), *Globalization and Language in Contact: Scale, Migration, and Communicative Practices* (Continuum, 2009), (with C. Hall and S. Sarangi) *Language Practices in Social Work: Categorisation and Accountability in Child Welfare* (Routledge, 2006) and (with S. Sarangi) *Language, Bureaucracy and Social Control* (Longman, 1996).

Bernard Spolsky is Professor Emeritus in the English Department at Bar-Ilan University. Since his retirement in 2000, he has published two monographs, *Language policy* (2004) and *Language Management* (2009), both with Cambridge University Press, for whom he is currently editing a 32-chapter *Handbook of Language Policy*. With Francis Hult, he has also published an edited collection, *The Blackwell Handbook of Educational Linguistics* (2008). He also edited the 2009 volume of *Annual Review of Applied Linguistics*, on the topic of 'Language Policy and Language Assessment'. He received an Honorary Doctorate of Literature from Victoria University of Wellington in 2008.

Kimie Takahashi is a Postdoctoral Research Fellow in Linguistics Department at Macquarie University, Australia. Her research examines the relationship between bilingualism, second language learning and gender, particularly in the contexts of study overseas, migration and employment. She is currently involved in a multi-site ethnography of the role of multilingualism and language learning in tourism between Australia and Japan (funded by Macquarie University and directed by Ingrid Piller). Her work has appeared in edited volumes and she is the author of *Language Desire* (Multilingual Matters, forthcoming). She is the co-founder, together with Ingrid, Piller, of the sociolinguistics portal Language on the Move at www.languageonthemove.org.

Peter Trudgill is Adjunct Professor of Sociolinguistics at the University of Agder, Kristiansand, Norway. He has carried out research on dialects of English, Norwegian, Greek, Albanian and Spanish and has published more than 30 books on sociolinguistics and dialectology. Recent publications include 'Sociolinguistic typology and complexification', in G. Sampson, D. Gil and P. Trudgill (eds), *Language Complexity as an Evolving Variable* (Oxford) and 'Contact and sociolinguistic typology', in R. Hickey (ed.). *Handbook of Language Contact* (Blackwell). He is currently writing a book entitled *Language in Contact and Isolation: On the Social Determinants of Linguistic Structure*.

Eva Vetter currently works in research and teaching at the University of Vienna (applied linguistics, language didactics and francophone civilisation) and in the EU-funded multilingualism Network LINEE (Languages in a Network of European Excellence). Her research in social networks relates to her interest in linguistic minorities. She critically reflects on and applies the network approach in her doctoral thesis: *Nicht mehr Bretonisch? Sprachkonflikt in der ländlichen Bretagne* (Frankfurt: Lang, 1997), in French *Plus de Breton? Conflit linguistique en Bretagne rurale* (Brest: An Here, 1999). Beyond the focus on regional minorities, her research concerns language teaching and learning, discourse analysis, multilingualism and language policy. Recent publications include (with Rindler Schjerve) 'Linguistic diversity in Habsburg Austria as a model for modern European language policy', in ten Thije, Zeevaert (eds.) (2007) *Receptive Multilingualism: Linguistic Analyses, Language Policies and Didactic Concepts.* Benjamins, pp. 49–70; (with Frings) (eds.) (2008) *Mehrsprachigkeit als Schlüsselkompetenz.* ibidem and forthcoming: *Sprachenbewusstheit von FremdsprachenlehrerInnen: Chance oder Hindernis für einen mehrsprachigkeitsorientierten Unterricht?* Schneider.

Ruth Wodak is Distinguished Professor of Discourse Studies at Lancaster University and has remained affiliated with the University of Vienna, where she became Full Professor of Applied Linguistics in 1991. Besides various other prizes, she was awarded the Wittgenstein Prize for Elite Researchers in 1996. Her research interests focus on discourse studies, gender studies, language and/in politics, prejudice and discrimination, and ethnographic methods in linguistic field work. She is a member of the editorial board of a range of linguistics journals, co-editor of the journals *Discourse and Society, Critical Discourse Studies*, and *Language and Politics*, and co-editor of the book series *Discourse Approaches to Politics, Society and Culture* (DAPSAC). Recent book publications include (with R. de Cillia) *Ist Österreich ein 'deutsches' Land?* (2006), (with M. Krzyżanowski), *Qualitative Discourse Analysis in the Social Sciences* (2008), (with G. Delanty and P. Jones), *Migration, Identity and Belonging* (2008), (with H. Heer, W. Manoschek and A. Pollak) *The Discursive Construction of History: Remembering the Wehrmacht's War of Annihilation* (2008), (with M. Krzyżanowski) *The Politics of Exclusion: Debating Migration in Austria* (2009), (with R. de Cillia) *Gedenken im Gedankenjahr* (2009) and *The Discourse of Politics in Action: 'Politics as Usual'* (2009).

Walt Wolfram is William C. Friday Distinguished University Professor at North Carolina State University, where he also directs the North Carolina Language and Life Project. He has pioneered research on social and ethnic dialects since the 1960s, and he and his staff have conducted more than 3000 sociolinguistic interviews in more than 20 different research communities. Professor Wolfram is particularly interested in the practice of linguistic gratuity, which requires linguists to give back to the communities that fuel their research. He is also concerned with the dissemination of knowledge about language diversity to the public, including the production of television documentaries, the construction of museum exhibits and the development of dialect awareness curricula. Significant publications on fieldwork include (with Reaser and Vaughn) 'Operationalizing linguistic gratuity: from principle to practice', *Linguistic and Language Compass* 3 pp.1109–34 (2008) and (with R. Fasold) *The Study of Social Dialects in American English* (1974).

Introduction

Ruth Wodak, Barbara Johnstone
and Paul Kerswill

(RE)DEFINING THE FIELD

Editing a new handbook for an established field like sociolinguistics presents a huge challenge. Such a handbook should contribute novel perspectives on present knowledge; and – possibly – add new knowledge and new insights. But many excellent handbooks already exist;[1] moreover, sociolinguistics has had an enormous impact on linguistics and its neighbouring fields and has become an integral part of almost every curriculum in linguistics. Thus, one might be justifiably sceptical whether anything innovative could be found.

We confronted this challenge with much reflection. Of course, we are aware that we cannot cover this enormous field in all its complexity. We have decided to start by situating sociolinguistics in its historical and theoretical contexts, introducing the founders of the discipline and focusing on major theoretical themes which have influenced sociolinguistic research at both the macro and micro levels. We then present major foundational issues and approaches which, while being constitutive of sociolinguistic research, frequently remain implicit and unspecified or even naive (such as theories of power, interaction, social practice, and so forth). Finally, we are concerned with the application of sociolinguistics in language teaching, forensics, the struggle for human rights, and so on.

Because sociolinguistics has become such a large field in its own right (the *Sociolinguistics Symposium* started out in 1976 in Birmingham with fewer than 50 participants, whereas recent conferences have gathered around 800, with up to 15 parallel sessions), boundaries between it and other subdomains in linguistics have become blurred. Do gender studies belong within sociolinguistics? What about aspects of discourse analysis or pragmatics (such as research on organizations)?

How much sociological theory is necessarily part of sociolinguistic research? And what about the traditional dichotomy between quantitative and qualitative research? Apart from these salient questions, new important themes have emerged due to recent socio-political developments which we necessarily cover in this handbook, such as research on discursive practices resulting from new streams of migration and other impacts of globalization.

In inviting contributions, we have also attempted to transcend the Anglo-American bias that can be seen in some handbooks,[2] although we were, unfortunately, not as successful as we would have wished in getting authors from all continents on board. Nevertheless, authors were strongly encouraged to discuss research published in languages other than English and from beyond the anglophone world. As editors originating from three different countries, we ourselves represent a variety of research traditions in sociolinguistics, and have different areas of expertise. Inclusiveness and the acknowledgement of difference therefore became important principles for this book.

SOCIOLINGUISTICS AS WE SEE IT

The field of sociolinguistics started in the 1960s, arising out of the work particularly of the American scholars William Labov, Joshua Fishman, Charles Ferguson, John Gumperz and Dell Hymes, and the British scholar Basil Bernstein. This new linguistic paradigm endorsed the view that language could not be adequately understood without taking many layers of social context into account, be it the situational context of utterances, the geographical origin of the speakers, their age, gender, social class, ethnicity, and so forth. The fundamental framing question which was asked is the following:[3] *'Who speaks where, in what way, why and with what kind of impact, and how do these aspects of context shape the linguistic resources available to speakers?'*

Sociolinguistics could be seen as having its roots in Ludwig Wittgenstein's (1967) 'language games' notion and his theory of meaning as 'constantly created in use', as well as in the anthropology, symbolic interactionism and dialectology of the 1950s. By the 1930s, anthropologists such as Bronislav Malinowski recognized that language was not only a tool for referring to the world but also had functions relating to social rituals and other aspects of social life in every culture they had investigated. Erving Goffman and other qualitative sociologists had started studying language in context without having at their disposal the linguistic theories, methodologies and tools to analyse language in use in detail. Dialectologists such as Kurath, Bloch and Hansen (1939), Allen (1973), McDavid (1976), McDavid and O'Cain (1980) and Pederson, McDavid and Leas (1986) in the USA and Orton, Sanderson and Widdowson (1962–78) in England investigated regional dialects and, to a certain extent, situational styles using interviews and other kinds of fieldwork. These dialectologists and others laid the groundwork for subsequent, sometimes more theoretically sophisticated, work in variationist sociolinguistics.

One of the most important triggers for a 'different' linguistics was the conflict between Chomskyan *Transformational Grammar* and other views of language and meaning (Chomsky, 1957, 1965). The linguistic 'competence' studied by transformational, and later generative Grammarians involves the ability of idealized speaker-hearers to produce isolated sentences, and their data often consist of hypothetical sentences constructed to test their model. Beginning in the 1960s and 1970s, Jürgen Habermas, Dell Hymes, and other critics proposed a different approach. With their interest in language in use and viewing language as social practice, they proposed the concepts of *language as action* and *communicative competence* (following John Austin's (1962) and John Searle's (1969) *Speech Act Theory*[4]). Thus, they re-imagined linguists' object of study as verbal utterances in context, be they oral conversations or written documents (e.g. Habermas, 1981).

'Language in use' was labelled as (mere) 'performance' by Chomsky and perceived as unsystematic and irrelevant for scientific investigation. Sociolinguists, on the other hand, hold the contrary view: conversations and everyday interactions are to be studied for their inherent rules and norms; they also have their own systems and rules, and

are predictably shaped by social variables, on all levels of language, from phonetics and phonology to syntax and discourse/text (Panagl and Wodak, 2004; van Dijk, 2008, 2009).

Because of their roots in the social sciences and in empirical research, sociolinguists deal with different data sets and apply different methods of analysis from those of formal linguists, studying a range of genres and using quantitative and qualitative methods, ethnography, and so on (Johnstone, 2008; Gobo, 2008). Their aim is to uncover systematic relationships between language, often in the context of language change or language shift, and social phenomena. Language in use can manifest social phenomena, but language in use can also produce and reproduce social phenomena. Attention to this fundamental dialectic is a central characteristic of sociolinguistics.

By the 1970s, several different objects of investigation and levels of analysis were being developed. On the one hand, issues of language planning, diglossia and bilingualism were at the centre of attention (e.g. Charles Ferguson, Joshua Fishman; see chapters by Auer, Berthoud and Lüdi, Sallabank, Sebba and Spolsky); on the other hand, two theoretical approaches at the micro level dominated the scientific debate. The *code theory* put forward by Basil Bernstein in 1960 claimed that children from the working class in the United Kingdom were discriminated against because of the way they were socialized into language use, which resulted in a different linguistic 'code'. He coined the term *restricted code* for this. Middle class children, by contrast, were socialized differently and acquired an *elaborated code* which enabled them to succeed much better in schools and also in other socially relevant institutions. Bernstein, coming from education, integrated theoretical approaches from pedagogy with sociology (such as the Systems Theory of Talcott Parsons) and linguistics (see chapters by Ivinson and Martín Rojo).

The *variationist* school of sociolinguistics typified by William Labov is centrally concerned with linguistic structure (and thus shares an agenda with structural/generative linguistics) and, more specifically still, language change. For example, in his seminal research on linguistic variation in New York City, published in 1966, Labov demonstrated that patterns of variation leading to language change (on the phonological level) were correlated with the age and social class of the speakers, as well as how self-consciously they were speaking. Applying his notion of the 'linguistic variable', his statistical results from stratified random samples of speakers enabled him to draw up an explicit, testable model of how linguistic change moves through a speech community. Labov's work in the realm of education is a manifestation of *difference theory*. Using the methods he had developed for studying language change, he was able to show that speakers of non-standard English were just as systematic in their use of language for the expression of rational thought as speakers of standard English, provided the context was right. Thus, an African-American interviewer was able to use features of Bernstein's elaborated code with African-American children, while the latter remained almost totally silent when a white interviewer asked questions. Labov was therefore able to refute the deficit theory (see chapters by Dodsworth, Hazen and Mallinson).

Variation studies developed quickly, mostly in the USA and UK, but also in central and northern Europe (e.g. Dittmar, 1973; Nordberg, 1970; Dressler and Wodak, 1982). Difference theory had implications for social practice as well. Labov and others were asked officially for their expertise in issues of language education in the USA. Labov was an expert witness in a key court case which allowed for the recognition of, and support for, African-American children's vernacular (Whiteman, 1980). The 'Ebonics' controversy of the mid-1990s is another example of the application of variationist sociolinguistics to educational debates (Baugh, 2000).

From the outset of sociolinguistics, we can discern a distinction between *macro- and micro-sociolinguistics*. Macro-sociolinguists study issues of language planning, languages in contact, diglossia and bilingualism, intercultural communication and language policies. The practical application of results is a major goal of such investigations. Thus, language planning in countries such as Israel and South Africa, and in transnational entities such as the European Union, was and is hugely influenced by sociolinguists (see chapters by Spolsky, Berthoud and Lüdi, and Sallabank).

Micro-sociolinguists, on the other hand, focus on the study of conversations, narratives, language use in everyday life and institutions, as well as the linguistic variable in variationist sociolinguistics (see chapters by Hazen, Johnstone and Marcellino, Ivinson, Gordon, Kotthoff, Matthiessen and Slade, Georgakopolou, Ehrlich, Menz, Martin Rojo and Kerswill). Much empirical research has succeeded in illustrating basic differences between institutional, formal contexts, and everyday life. In addition, linguistic variables were found to be important in indexing specific codes, registers, styles and variants, such as gender, 'belonging' (in the sense of group membership), local and regional identities and ethnicity (see chapters by Pavlidou, Hellinger and Slembrouck). Variationist sociolinguistics started to take into account this expanded set of explanatory variables (so-called *third-wave variationist sociolinguistics* – see Eckert (2005) and Kerswill, this volume), though sometimes

(but usually with good reason) viewing them as static, presupposed at the outset without taking a specific setting or context into account (*second-wave*, represented by, e.g., Milroy (1987)).

More recent theoretical approaches propose units of investigation other than the speech community, such as *communities of practice* and *social networks*, and view social variables such as gender and ethnicity as flexible and constructed in interaction. Communities of practice are defined by similar socialization modes and social practices. Social networks represent the frequency and quality of interactions in groups or larger communities, as well as the structural properties of a person's network (key authors are Penelope Eckert, Sally McConnell-Ginet, James Milroy and Lesley Milroy; see chapters by Vetter and Mendoza-Denton). Research applying these concepts takes the view that interaction modes and dynamics as well as individual speaker differences are more relevant to an understanding of language use than are the above-mentioned static variables. Gender studies is now a field in its own right, but it is always represented at major conferences on sociolinguistics (see chapters by Hellinger and Pavlidou).

Micro-sociolinguistics has added to the micro level of phonology, morphology, syntax, and the conversational turn in the level of texts: conversations and narratives are analysed while focusing on gender-specific or class-specific differences. Labov and Waletzky proposed a model of the structure of conversational narratives, in 1967, which is still highly regarded. Another influential strand of work focusing on how understanding is negotiated in conversation is interactional sociolinguistics, associated with anthropologist John J. Gumperz (see chapters by Gordon and Kendall). Conversation analysis, arising from ethnomethodological theory in sociology, has also been widely adopted in studies of how meaning and form emerge in interaction (see chapters by Garot and Berard, Kotthoff, and Matthiessen and Slade). The methods of interactional sociolinguistics and conversation analysis have been used in studies of institutional discourse such as doctor–patient communication, therapeutic communication, communication in business, and so on (e.g. Wodak, 1996; see chapters by Martín Rojo, Menz, Ehrlich, and Georgakopolou). Often enough, the macro and micro levels overlap: for example, intercultural communication can be studied in organizational settings; language planning for educational purposes has to consider many different genres (see chapter by Leung).

In the 21st century, new challenges confront sociolinguistics: new media, new technologies of communication, and new social issues, such as the impact of globalization, the fluidity of borders and mobility as well as migration. All these new and very complex issues demand more interdisciplinary research in sociolinguistics and the development of new methodologies and new tools for language analysis (see, in this volume, chapters by Slembrouck; Piller and Takahashi; Busch and Pfisterer; Barton and Lee; Coulthard, Grant and Kredens; Pennycook).

OUTLINE OF VOLUME

History of sociolinguistics

Sociolinguistics originated in the 1960s and 1970s, when linguists, anthropologists and sociologists became interested in how the structure of language was shaped by the contexts of its use, and how language use shaped social relations and culture. In the USA, many of the key figures came together at the American Anthropological Association's 1963 Annual Meeting and the 1964 Linguistic Society of America Summer Institute. Through detailed treatments of the early work of some of the founders of the field and sketches of its subsequent influence, chapters in this section (Part I) trace the historical development of five subfields that emerged from this period of innovation and point to the subsequent influence of each. Chapters 1–5, respectively, thus examine: Joshua Fishman, Charles Ferguson and other important early figures in sociolinguistics and the sociology of language (Spolsky); William Labov and his variationist approach to the study of language change (Hazen); Basil Bernstein's work on social class and linguistic 'codes' in the context of educational research (Ivinson); Dell Hymes and the development of the ethnography of communication and ethnopoetics (Johnstone and Marcellino); and John J. Gumperz and interactional sociolinguistics (Gordon).

Sociolinguistics and social theory

The chapters in this section (Part II) treat theories of social identity and interaction, and the methods for their study, that are drawn on in contemporary sociolinguistic research.

A Chapter 6 on social stratification (Mallinson) treats the theories of social class and social hierarchy that underpin much early work in sociolinguistics. Beginning in the 1960s, under the influence of Foucault, Rorty and others, the social phenomena shaping language, such as class, gender and ethnicity, were increasingly seen as constructed in social interaction. The body of theory known as social constructionism (also sometimes called social constructivism) is the topic of Chapter 7 (Irwin). Sociologist Erving Goffman, working in the sociological framework known as symbolic interactionism, proposed that interactants draw on cultural 'frames' and adopt interactional 'footings' to shape understandings of what is going on as they talk. Kendall discusses framing in Chapter 8. Chapter 9 (Garot and Berard) deals with ethnomethodology and conversation analysis, focusing in particular on membership categorization analysis, which has been taken up by many sociolinguists. They provide an overview of the work of Garfinkel, Sacks and others concerning how meaning and social order are created in interaction. Chapter 10 (Farfán and Holzscheiter) deals with a variety of ways of theorizing power and its relationships with talk and with patterns of variation in language. Theorists examined include Habermas, Foucault and Bourdieu, and topics include domination, resistance, agency and hegemony. Chapter 11 on globalization and migration (Slembrouck) deals with theorists such as Anthony Giddens, Arjun Appadurai, Scott Lash and John Urry, David Harvey, Immanuel Wallerstein and others, and raises issues such as speech community in multilingual settings, geographical mobility and language change, and ethnolinguistic identity in cyberspace. In Chapter 12, Paul Kockelman discusses semiotic theory in the tradition of Charles Sanders Peirce, and how his work has been taken up in sociolinguistics.

Language variation and change

'Language variation and change' (LVC) is usually taken to be synonymous with 'variationist sociolinguistics'; it deals with variation within a language as opposed to the alternation of codes (bilingualism/code-switching). Variation is seen as inextricably linked to language change; hence, much work in LVC is on the linguistics of variation. The linguistic model espoused is broadly structuralist (and not, say, generative – notwithstanding the initial use of Chomsky and Halle-style rule notation), because the unit of analysis, the 'linguistic variable', is most easily reconcilable with this model. Social factors are brought to bear to account for variation and patterns of change. At the same time, social correlations potentially tell us something about society: linguistic variation, to the extent that it is socially governed, should mirror in some way the social parameters (class, gender, etc.) which have been marshalled.

It is then only a short step to claiming that linguistic variation, as manifested by speakers in particular interactions, is actually constitutive of those social parameters and also serves to define the context of speech. Exploring this dialectic is, however, not usually seen as falling within the domain of LVC. From the point of view of language in use (rather than language change agenda), the focus that LVC places on macrosocial structure and on quantitative variation means that it deals with the language–society relationship at a different level of abstraction from interactional sociolinguistics, with the ability of language use to construct social reality being backgrounded. However, as noted, 'third-wave' variationist sociolinguistics bridges this divide.

This Section (Part III) starts with Chapter 14, which addresses a central concern for LVC: how to characterize the relationship between the individual and society, so as to enable the analyst to model the patterns of variation (Mendoza-Denton). This leads directly to Chapters 14 and 15 by Dodsworth and Vetter, who deal with social class and social networks, respectively. Chapter 16 by Kerswill deals with the central concern of LVC: language change. The manner in which macrosocial structures affect language change is singled out by Trudgill in Chapter 17. In Chapter 18 Guy situates the field within formal linguistics, finding the latter wanting because of its insistence on invariant categories, while noting a new willingness in both the 'variationist' and 'theoretical' camps to engage with each other's concerns. Chapter 19 by Kristiansen deconstructs the notions of awareness, attitude and ideology in LVC, particularly the notion 'change from below'. In Chapter 20 Nevalainen shows how the sociolinguistic understandings of contemporary speech communities can be projected onto historical data.

Finally in this section, in Chapter 21, Wolfram critically outlines the range of methodologies which are available to variationists and other sociolinguists, showing how the orientation of a particular study is reflected in the *fieldwork methods* adopted. Methods are located along several dimensions, especially perhaps qualitative/quantitative, micro/macro and interactional/non-interactional. Usually more than one method is used, allowing different insights to be gained (triangulation).

Interaction

This section (Part IV) summarizes the most important research on everyday and organizational interactions. Studies in this field draw mainly on symbolic interactionism (Erving Goffman) and ethnomethodology (Harold Garfinkel). In addition, the sociological traditions of phenomenology (Alfred Schütz), anthropological approaches (Raymond William Firth, Bronislaw Malinowski, George Herbert Mead, and others) and cultural studies frameworks (Stuart Hall, Raymond Williams) have also been influential.

Chapter 22 (Kotthoff) is dedicated to spontaneous interaction and conversation (e.g. research into everyday interactions among friends, dinner table conversations, family interactions). There are various theoretical and methodological approaches involved in such studies, ranging from more discourse-analytical and conversation-analytical investigations to interactive, sociolinguistically informed ones. Cross-cultural aspects come into play as well as explicit and latent conventions and rules which exist in various subgroups, communities of practice, public spheres, cultures or even countries. Research to date includes communication in hospitals, schools, courtrooms, bureaucracies and international organizations, and these are covered in Chapters 23–25 by Menz, Martín Rojo, and Ehrlich. Chapter 26 addresses registers and conversational styles which are chosen in relation to the specific context of interaction. Styles can be analysed on multiple linguistic dimensions, ranging from prosody and intonation to semantics, text-grammar and discourse (Matthiessen and Slade).

Chapter 27 on narratives in various interactional settings is included (Georgakopolou), as narrative analysis offers a unique way to study beliefs and experiences of individuals as well as the construction of identities. Examples include both formal and informal settings, spontaneous and interview data. In Chapter 28, aspects of gender and social class are salient when studying microinteractions (Pavlidou); and finally, Chapter 29, which considers the representations of interactions in the (new) media (Busch and Pfisterer) points to the impact of the field of media for all domains of our society.

Multilingualism and contact

Multilingualism and language contact have been investigated from three main perspectives: the descriptive/theoretical linguistic (for example, the work of Sarah G. Thomason and Terrence Kaufman, or Shona Poplack, on the consequences of contact for the linguistic system); the functional (Susan Gal, Peter Auer); and the sociological (Joshua Fishman). Here, we deal mainly but not exclusively with the functional and sociological strands. Unlike in LVC, there is no unifying theory, due to the disparate nature of the phenomena and the approaches taken. Several major themes emerge, however, often in conjunction: interaction, function, power, ideology, intervention and globalization.

Societal bilingualism refers to the functional distribution of languages or language varieties across a given population, usually along ethnic lines and often reflecting past migrations. Functional divisions may also reflect differences in power among social groups (social classes, or religious or aristocratic oligarchies), with the dominant variety sometimes becoming highly differentiated (*diglossia*). This is the subject matter of the Chapter 30 (Sebba), the first chapter in this section (Part V). Code-switching, the individual reflection of societal bilingualism and a strategic resource in conversation, is dealt with in the Chapter 31 (Auer).

Chapters 32 and 33 (Berthoud and Lüdi, Sallabank) deal with public and private ideologies and their links with language policy, planning and endangerment. Berthoud and Lüdi, writing on policy and planning, consider the what, how and why of deliberate intervention through educational policy, language choice in government and commerce, and corpus and status planning. Languages come to be endangered for a variety of reasons. These are considered in the chapter by Sallabank, as are the effects of intervention on the revitalization and revival of languages. Finally, in Chapter 34, Pennycook deals with the unique position that English has in the world (for good or ill), critically considering notions such as 'World Englishes' and the 'circles' of English.

Applications

This section (Part VI) presents some applications of basic sociolinguistic research. We have selected four areas where sociolinguists have already been successful in their work in collaboration with practitioners or when informing practitioners.

Forensic (socio)linguistics is a relatively new area of application and has helped solve major court cases where voice recognition, for example, played a significant role. Detecting authors of anonymous letters or leaflets and providing expert opinions on implicitly discriminatory texts and discourses have recently become areas of sociolinguistic expertise. This field has been institutionalized through conferences and journals as well as MA modules and programmes. Interdisciplinary teams (sociolinguists and legal experts) have also reformulated legal texts (laws) and provided criteria for improving the comprehensibility of texts. Questions of multilingualism and translation need to be integrated as recent research on the drafting of European Union (EU) legislation has illustrated (Coulthard, Grant and Kredens, in Chapter 35).

Although language teaching and language testing belong to a much more broadly defined Applied Linguistics, some specific issues are inherently of a sociolinguistic nature. These relate to language teaching for migrants or the development of sociolinguistic criteria for the recently introduced citizenship tests in EU member states. Tests are frequently developed without taking relevant sociolinguistic research on gender, class, communities of practice or ethnicity into account (Leung, Chapter 36). Moreover, in many areas, guidelines for non-discriminatory language use have been or are being developed. For example, these have been introduced in many languages and countries to ensure the visibility of women in formal contexts such as the media, bureaucracies, publishing and so forth. Without taking sociolinguistic research on gender, race, ethnicity, age and social class into account, such guidelines cannot be adequately formulated (Hellinger; Piller and Takahashi, Chapter 37 and 38).

Finally, we focus on literacy, one of the most important skills in modern times to gain access to relevant domains in our complex societies. Through the rapid development of new media and related genres (email, synchronous online chat, text messaging, and so on), new forms of social inclusion and exclusion have been created. Access to literacy in the new media makes participation in many organizations and contribution to important debates (via, for instance, the Internet, instant messaging and blogs) possible. New forms of 'gate-keeping', which can be observed worldwide, are addressed throughout this section (Barton and Lee, Chapter 39). The authors contend that school education has to address related forms of inclusion and exclusion in new and creative ways.

NOTES

1 See, for example: Ammon et al., 2006/7; Chambers et al., 2002/4; Coulmas, 1999; Llamas et al., 2007; Mesthrie, 2001.

2 For example, of the 29 chapters in the Blackwell *Handbook of Language Variation and Change*, only three are written by authors originating from non-anglophone countries.

3 The development of Communication Studies after World War II was first in posing the 'famous' 6 W Question: 'Who speaks to whom, when, where, and why, and with which effect?' (e.g. Lasswell and Leites, 1949).

4 See Schiffrin (1994), Renkema (2004) for extensive summaries.

REFERENCES

Allen, H. B. (1973–76). *The linguistic atlas of the Upper Midwest.* Minneapolis: University of Minnesota Press,

Ammon, U., Dittmar, N., Mattheier, K. J. and Trudgill, P. (eds) (2006-7) *Sociolinguistics/Soziolinguistik*. 3 vols. 2nd edn. Berlin: De Gruyter.

Austin, J. L. (1962). *How to do things with words: the William James lectures delivered at Harvard University in 1955*. London: Clarendon.

Baugh, J. (2000) *Beyond Ebonics: linguistic pride and racial prejudice*. New York: Cambridge University Press.

Chambers, J. K., Trudgill, P. and Schilling-Estes, N. (eds) (2002–04) *The Handbook of Language Variation and Change*. 2nd edn. Oxford: Blackwell.

Chomsky, N. (1957) *Syntactic structures*. Berlin, New York: Mouton.

Chomsky, N. (1965) *Aspects of a theory of syntax*. Cambridge, MA: MIT Press.

Coulmas, F. (ed.) (1999) *Handbook of sociolinguistics*. Oxford: Blackwell.

Dittmar, N. (1973) *Soziolinguistik*. Frankfurt, Main: Fischer Verlag.

Dressler, W. and Wodak, R. (1982) 'Sociophonological methods in the study of sociolinguistic variation in Viennese German', *Language in Society*: 239–70.

Eckert, Penelope (2005) 'Variation, convention, and social meaning'. Paper presented at the annual meeting of the Linguistic Society of America, Oakland, California. Accessed 22 April 2009 at http://www.stanford.edu/~eckert/EckertLSA2005.pdf.

Gobo, G. (2008) *Doing ethnography*. London: Sage.

Habermas, J. (1981) *Theorie des kommunikativen Handelns*. Frankfurt, Main: Suhrkamp.

Johnstone, B. (2008). *Discourse Analysis*. 2nd edn. Oxford: Blackwell.

Kurath, H., Bloch, B. and Hansen, M. L. (1939) *Linguistic atlas of New England*. Providence, RI: Brown University Press.

Labov, W. and Waletzky, J. (1967) 'Narrative analysis: Oral versions of personal experience', in J. Helms (ed.), *Essays on the verbal and visual arts*. Seattle: University of Washington Press. pp. 12–44.

Lasswell, H. D. and Leites, N. C. (1949) *Language of politics: studies in quantitative semantics*. New York: G. W. Stewart.

Llamas, C., Mullany, L. and Stockwell, P. (eds) (2007) *Routledge Companion to Sociolinguistics*. London: Routledge.

McDavid, R. I. (1976) *The linguistic atlas of the North-Central states: Basic materials*. Chicago: Joseph Regenstein Library, University of Chicago.

McDavid, R. I. and O'Cain, R. K. (1980) *Linguistic atlas of the Middle and South Atlantic states*. Chicago: University of Chicago Press.

Mesthrie, R. (ed.) (2001) *Concise encyclopedia of sociolinguistics*. New York: Pergamon Press.

Milroy, L. (1987) *Language and social networks*. Oxford: Basil Blackwell.

Nordberg, Bengt (1970) 'The urban dialect of Eskilstuna: methods and problems', in Benediktsson, Hreinn (ed.), *The Nordic languages and modern linguistics*. Reykjavík: Vísindafélag Íslendinga. pp. 426–43.

Orton, H., Sanderson, S. and Widdowson, J. D. A. (1978) *The linguistic atlas of England*. London: Croon Helm.

Panagl, O. and Wodak, R. (eds) (2004) *Text und Kontext: Theoriemodelle und methodische Verfahren im transdisziplinären Vergleich*. Würzburg: Königshausen and Neumann.

Pederson, L., McDavid, R. I. and Leas, S. (1986–92) *Linguistic atlas of the Gulf States*. Tuscaloosa, AL: The University of Alabama Press.

Renkema, J. (2004). *Introduction to discourse studies*. Amsterdam: Benjamins.

Schiffrin, D. (1994). *Approaches to discourse*. Oxford: Blackwell.

Searle, J. R. (1969) *Speech acts: an essay in the philosophy of language*. Cambridge: Cambridge University Press.

Van Dijk, T. A. (2008) *Discourse and context: a sociocognitive approach*. Cambridge: Cambridge University Press.

Van Dijk, T. A. (2009) *Society and discourse: how social contexts influence text and talk*. Cambridge: Cambridge University Press.

Wittgenstein, L. (1967) *Philosophische Untersuchungen. Philosophical investigations*, 2nd edn. Tr. G. E. M. Anscombe. Oxford: Blackwell.

Whiteman, M. F. (1980) *Reactions to Ann Arbor: vernacular Black English and education*. Arlington, VA: Center for Applied Linguistics.

Wodak, R. (1996) *Disorders of discourse*. London: Longman.

PART 1

History of Sociolinguistics

Ferguson and Fishman: Sociolinguistics and the Sociology of Language

Bernard Spolsky

1.1 INTRODUCTION

To introduce this handbook, the editors map out the gestation of sociolinguistics by focusing on six of the 'founding fathers': William Labov, who pioneered a school devoted to showing the relevance of social determinants of variation for linguistic theory; Basil Bernstein, the British sociologist whose work on class-related 'codes' led to a brief flirtation with American sociolinguists; Dell Hymes, whose adaptation of Roman Jakobson's theory of communication (Jakobson, 1960) shaped the ethnography of communication and educational linguistics and who molded sociolinguistics by editing several pioneering volumes and the flagship journal *Language in Society*; John Gumperz, founder of interactional sociolinguistics; and Charles Ferguson and Joshua Fishman. All except Bernstein (although he was invited) attended the Linguistic Institute in Bloomington in the summer of 1964, the landmark event that launched the field. All (except Bernstein again) served on the Committee on Sociolinguistics of the Social Sciences Research Council, established in 1963 to plan the 1964 seminar and that operated until the early 1970s. All participated in the many conferences and publications which fashioned sociolinguistics in those years, and each continued to publish for the next 30 years, expanding their own interpretations of the field. My task in this chapter is to describe and assess the specific contribution of Ferguson and Fishman to the 'study of language in

its social context', and to explore the nature of the discipline that emerged, trying to explain why it is sometimes called 'sociolinguistics' and sometimes 'the sociology of language', terms occasionally used interchangeably (Paulston and Tucker, 1997)[1] though elsewhere (Bright, 1992; Gumperz, 1971) clearly distinguished.

I shall also mention founders omitted from the selected six, such as William Bright, Allen Grimshaw, Einar Haugen, Uriel Weinreich and Sue Ervin-Tripp[2] who were also pioneers. Haugen was, by 1963, a senior scholar: after 30 years as chair of Scandinavian Studies at the University of Wisconsin, he was about to take up a chair in Scandinavian and Linguistics at Harvard. He had taught a course on bilingualism at the 1948 Linguistic Institute, and his book on the Norwegian language in America (Haugen, 1953) established him as the leading authority on bilingualism and language shift. He was the first linguist to write about the ecology of language, the title of his 1972 collected papers (Haugen, 1972). His study of Norwegian language planning (Haugen, 1966) was a groundbreaking work.

A second major publication in 1953 was that of Uriel Weinreich (1953a), a seminal work that is still regularly cited as the basis for understanding language contact. Fishman (1997c), a friend of his[3] from Yiddish youth movement days, summarizes his work in sociolinguistics, starting with an undergraduate paper in Yiddish on Welsh language revival (U. Weinreich, 1944), his doctoral dissertation on Swiss bilingualism, a study of the Russian treatment of minority languages (U. Weinreich, 1953b), and the beginning of the language and culture atlas of Ashkenazic Jewry published a quarter of a century after his premature death. Fishman recalls a paper that the two of them did not write in 1954 on the societal nature of language; Weinreich's draft was too linguistic and Fishman's too sociological to negotiate a common version. Weinreich visited the 1964 Linguistic Institute, delivering four lectures on semantic theory (U. Weinreich, 1966). His theory of semantics, Fishman suggested, was 'profoundly cultural and socio-situational', and so a comforting antidote to the anti-sociolinguistic theory that Chomsky was establishing.[4] Weinreich had a strong influence on many of the founders, not least on his student William Labov. Labov (1997: 147) stresses the contribution to his own development made by a teacher not much older than him and especially the importance of Weinreich's part in writing a paper which explained the relevance of sociolinguistics to the understanding of language change (U. Weinreich, Labov and Herzog, 1968).

A third founder was Susan Ervin-Tripp who joined the Committee on Psycholinguistics as a graduate assistant. Her distinction between compound and coordinate bilingualism (Osgood, 1954) led to much research and controversy. Based at Berkeley after 1958, her interest in child language acquisition cross-culturally brought her naturally into sociolinguistics (Ervin-Tripp, 1973). She also joined the Committee on Sociolinguistics in 1966 (Ervin-Tripp, 1997).

The task I have been set in this chapter is made more complex by the need to distinguish individual contributions from joint work and both from the working of the *Zeitgeist*,[5] the difficultly to document formation of a consensus on next steps in a scientific field. All of the scholars I have named were already actively engaged in what is now describable as sociolinguistic research and publication before 1964. Shuy (1997) notes that Fishman first taught a course called 'Sociology of Language' at the University of Pennsylvania in 1956 and continued to teach it at Yeshiva University. Huebner (1996) believes that the term 'sociolinguistics' was first used by Currie (1952) and picked up by Weinreich (U. Weinreich 1953a: 99) and in articles in *Word* which Weinreich edited.[6] The classic paper on diglossia (Ferguson, 1959) appeared there. At the 1962 LSA Linguistic Institute, Ferguson taught a course with the simple title 'Sociolinguistics' and repeated it the following summer and in the 1965 academic year at Georgetown University. In 1964, Fishman had just completed his pioneering study of language loyalty in the USA (Fishman, 1966).[7] Labov had published his Martha's Vineyard study (Labov, 1962) and was completing the New York dissertation

(Labov, 1966) that continues to encourage study of socially-explainable language variation. Gumperz and Hymes were editing the papers from the 1963 American Association of Anthropology meeting (Gumperz and Hymes, 1972), which remains a foundation text. Even without the seminar, research and publication in the field were by then well underway. Bloomington 1964 was a milestone rather than a starting point, but a significant one.

1.2 FISHMAN MEETS FERGUSON

In his introduction to the festschrift for Ferguson's 65th birthday (Fishman, Tabouret-Keller, Clyne, Krishnamurti and Abdulaziz 1986: v), Fishman[8] recalls his first contact with Ferguson: 'It took almost a month for Charles Ferguson and me to realize that we were living next door to each other during the Summer Linguistic Institute of 1964 at Indiana University.' They had communicated briefly before that; during the summer, both in the seminar that Ferguson chaired 'primus inter pares', and with Fishman taking Ferguson's course (101 Introduction to Linguistics), and they became 'neighbors, colleagues, students (each acknowledging the other as teacher) and close friends, roles we have enacted, either repeatedly or continuously ...'

In May 1963, Fishman was not on the original list of scholars to be invited to Bloomington, which included Gumperz, Haugen, Immanuel Wallerstein[9] or Paul Friedrich, Steven E. Deutsch[10] and Dell Hymes. In December, William Labov and William Stewart,[11] both about to finish their degrees, were added; a month later, Fishman was also invited (as were Heinz Kloss[12] and Basil Bernstein, all three considered sociologists rather than linguists) (Committee on Sociolinguistics 1963–). Fishman had not been sure that he would be included – his only relevant publication was an article on the Whorfian hypothesis (Fishman, 1960), although he had earlier published articles on Yiddish bilingualism, pluralism and minorities, and was just finishing his first major **opus** (Fishman, 1966) which was to set the path for the host of studies of minority language maintenance and loss that now dominate the sociolinguistic research field. He later (Fishman, 1997a) recalled that he was at Stanford rewriting Fishman (1966) when he first heard about the 1964 seminar and was encouraged to apply by Einar Haugen, also a fellow at the Center for Advanced Studies in the Behavioral Sciences. He phoned Ferguson whose article on diglossia he knew; Ferguson 'seemed a little cool on the phone' but accepted the application. Ferguson quickly came to appreciate

Fishman's potential contribution: in a letter written in 1965 trying unsuccessfully to persuade Fishman to stay on the Committee of Sociolinguistics, he wrote, 'Of all the members, you are most probably the only one whose primary interest is in the field of sociolinguistics, and your publications in the field have been the most extensive. You are concerned with both "macro" and "micro" and with relating the two' (Committee on Sociolinguistics 1963–) (letter from Ferguson in Ethiopia dated 25 November 1965).

Fishman did not know what the seminar was going to be like, but he was willing to put up with a hot uncomfortable summer in Bloomington in order to be with 'a community of like-minded scholars'. When the seminar began, Fishman found the sociologists – including himself, 'a refurbished social psychologist' as he noted (Fishman, 1997a: 88) – to be in a weak position because they did not know each other and did not have strong interests in common. Only Fishman, Kloss and Lieberson had published or were ready to publish about language. The anthropologists and linguists had met before, most recently at the 1963 AAA meeting and at the May UCLA meeting. There was a major gap between the two groups and, partly because of that, Fishman returned to his earlier preference for calling the field the sociology of language.[13] He complained that social problems were not emphasized in Bloomington, and that only annoyance greeted his reference to 'the fact that people were willing to kill and be killed for their beloved language was being completely overlooked' (Fishman, 1997a: 93).[14]

At Bloomington and after, a close personal and academic relationship quickly developed between Ferguson and Fishman. Fishman's statement about their friendship has been cited: Ferguson (1997: 80) respected not just Fishman's extensive empirical studies but his potential for theory-building:

> I tend to be pessimistic about formulating a basic theory of sociolinguistics; possibly I am unduly pessimistic. I would think that if Fishman put his mind to it, he could probably come up with a kind of theory. Of course, it would tend to focus on macrosociolinguistics (sociology of language), like the books he has written on ethnicity and nationalism and so forth ...

For Fishman, Ferguson remained his main teacher of linguistics.[15] While their research paths diverged, with Ferguson firmly on the linguistic and Fishman firmly on the sociological side, their early conversations and continuing association had a major influence on the growth and shape of the field.

1.3 ORGANIZING A NEW FIELD

Left to work alone, there is little doubt that the founders of sociolinguistics would have continued their individual scholarly paths investigating the complex relations between language and society, and the structure and interplay of the two systems evolved to deal with the evolutionary inadequacies of human physiology, rejecting the ideology established in mainstream linguistics by Chomsky's lack of interest in meaning and his focus on the competence of an 'idealized monolingual'. Each of them had come with a different goal and was attracted by a different inspiration. William Bright, for instance, had been trained in American Indian linguistics by M. B. Emeneau and Mary Haas, both of whom continued the interest of Edward Sapir in language in culture; he was thus open to influence in writing his first published paper on lexical innovation in Karuk by a lecture on bilingualism from Einar Haugen in 1949 (Bright, 1997: 53). In India on a two-year post-doctoral Rockefeller fellowship, in the course of conversations with Ferguson and John Gumperz, he 'became aware that a field of sociolinguistics might be developed' (Bright, 1997: 54). In her obituary of Bright in *Language*, Jane Hill (2007) cites Murray (1998) as believing that Bright, Gumperz and Ferguson were all influenced by the multilingual patterns they discovered in India when visiting Deccan College in Pune in the mid-1950s. John Gumperz (1997) had been trained in dialectology, wrote a dissertation on the Swabian dialects of Michigan, and then spent two years studying village dialects in a Northern Indian community. There, he worked with many Indian linguists and an interdisciplinary team. He taught at the Indian summer Linguistic Institutes in Pune in 1955 and 1956 alongside American structural linguists and South Asia scholars, some trained by J. R. Firth of the School of Oriental and African Studies (Gumperz, 1997). This combination of fieldwork in complex multilingual communities and the opportunity to discuss his work with a diverse group of scholars was, he believes, critical.[16]

There were further discussions at the Foreign Service Institute of the US Department of State where both Ferguson and Bright worked in the 1950s. But it was in the early 1960s that formal activity began. In the late 1950s, the Association of Asian Studies formed a Committee on South Asian Languages, which brought together at various meetings Ferguson, Bright, Gumperz and Uriel Weinreich and produced a 1960 special issue of the *International Journal of American Linguistics* on linguistic diversity in South Asia (Ferguson and Gumperz, 1960). In 1959, Ferguson became a full-time organizer[17] when he was appointed director of the new Center for Applied Linguistics, a position he held for seven years. With support from several foundations, the Ford Foundation leading (Fox, 2007; Fox and Harris, 1964), the Center made major contributions to the development of the International Association of Teachers of English to Speakers of Other Languages (Alatis and LeClair, 1993), the Test of English as a Foreign Language (Spolsky, 1995), and American Indian education. It also organized several linguistic surveys (Ohannessian, Ferguson and Polomé, 1975), including the Ethiopian study (Bender, Bowen, Cooper and Ferguson, 1976) which Ferguson directed, spending two periods of four months each in the field in 1968–69.

Impressed by the successful model of the SSRC Committee on Psycholinguistics (Osgood, 1954), Ferguson proposed in early 1963 holding a seminar on sociolinguistics at the summer Linguistic Institute planned for Indiana University. Through the SSRC, he obtained a grant of $54,800 from the National Science Foundation to help pay the salaries of senior and junior participants. The summer seminar, building on an earlier May 1964 UCLA meeting to which Bright had invited "the usual suspects": Haugen, Ferguson, Gumperz, Hymes, Labov and others' (Bright, 1997: 55) and whose papers were later published (Bright, 1966), pinpointed according to Shuy[18] (1997: 30) 'the creation of modern sociolinguistics'.

Thom Huebner (1996)[19] summarizes the major activities of the Committee after 1964. In 1966, there was a conference on the language problems of developing nations which established language policy and management as a major component of sociolinguistics (Fishman, Ferguson and Das Gupta, 1968). In the opening paper, Fishman starts with a discussion of 'sociolinguistics': 'Interest in the sociology of language can be traced back quite far … '. Modern sociolinguistics was not the direct heir, but 'a byproduct of very recent and still ongoing developments in its two parent disciplines, linguistics and sociology' (Fishman, 1968b: 3). The stronger interest had come from linguistics. Fishman's own approach becomes clear in the concluding essay (Fishman, 1968a) in which he explored the relationship between such issues as selection of a national language, adoption of a language of wider communication, language planning concerns, and goals for bilingualism and biculturalism. In his own contribution, Ferguson recognized that many of the topics discussed could be dealt with 'by the conceptual frameworks used in the study of social organization, political systems, or economic processes' (Ferguson, 1968: 27), but they depended on understanding of language, such as the questionable belief that a language is backward or needs purifying or modernizing.

In 1966, the Committee supported a workshop on teaching sociolinguistics and a project on the acquisition of communicative competence. The manual for cross-cultural study of child language (Slobin, 1967) that resulted has guided much international research (Ervin-Tripp, 1997: 73). In 1968, Dell Hymes organized a conference on pidginization and later published a collection of papers on pidgins and creoles (Hymes, 1971). The following year, Grimshaw (1969) arranged a meeting to look at language as sociological data as an obstacle in cross-cultural sociological research. Continuing work on child language, in 1974 the Committee sponsored a conference on language input and acquisition (Snow and Ferguson, 1977) which led to extensive and continuing research on language socialization (Ervin-Tripp, 1997: 74).

The Committee and Ferguson also supported the foundation of the journal *Language in Society* edited by Dell Hymes in 1972; he was succeeded as editor by William Bright. Ferguson (1997: 86) confessed that he had opposed Fishman's plan to start his own journal, but admitted he was wrong, as *Language in Society* and *The International Journal of the Sociology of Language* have both been productive but different. Ferguson did not found a new organization for sociolinguists,[20] and the two major annual conferences NWAV[21] and the Sociolinguistics Symposium[22] came later; but his organizational work in the 1960s played a major role in forming, consolidating and publicizing what is clearly one of the more fruitful fields for the study of language.

Fishman too was an organizer, but one who did not like meetings: his main managerial activities were the planning, direction and interpretation of major research projects, and the encouragement of an impressive body of publication by scholars throughout the world. I have already mentioned the language loyalty study whose publication paralleled the burst of research in the early 1960s. Shortly after, he started work (with funding from the US Office of Education) on the equally influential study of bilingualism in a New Jersey barrio completed in 1968 and published three years later (Fishman, Cooper and Ma, 1971); among his colleagues were Robert L. Cooper and for a year John Gumperz. In the 1970s, while he was in Jerusalem, he conducted a study of bilingual education for the US Office of Education (Fishman, 1976). Also while he was in Israel, with a Ford grant and the help of Robert Cooper and others, he prepared his pioneering study of the spread of English (Fishman, Cooper and Conrad, 1977). During this time, in cooperation with Charles Ferguson and a number of international scholars, he was working on what is still the only major empirical study of the effectiveness of language planning processes (Rubin, Jernudd, Das Gupta, Fishman and Ferguson, 1977).

Apart from significant funded research projects, Fishman's most important organizational activity has been as an editor. The first venture was a collection of readings on the sociology of language (Fishman, 1968c) which marked out his claim to be the prime exponent and arbiter of the field. Noting the success of this volume, a leading European linguistics publishing house, Mouton of The Hague (now Mouton de Gruyter of Berlin), invited him to start a journal and an associated book series. *The International Journal of the Sociology of Language (IJSL)* first appeared in 1973, celebrated its centenary issue 20 years later, and has reached 194 issues in 2009. While about one out of six are 'singles' issues, the main feature of the journal is the breadth of its internationally edited thematic issues, ranging from the sociology of language in Israel (the first issue celebrating Fishman's time in Jerusalem) to the latest, a double issue on the sociolinguistics of Spanish. *IJSL* has served as a powerful instrument for encouraging international study of sociolinguistic issues, and constitutes an unmatched library of descriptions of sociolinguistic situations all around the world. There have been innovative approaches, including the 'focus' issues in which a scholar is invited to present a long paper on a controversial topic, such as bilingualism and schooling in the USA or the origin of Yiddish, and a number of other scholars are invited to write comments.[23] The journal, like all the other journals in the field is publisher-sponsored and susceptible to marketing pressure: Fishman (1997b: 239) interprets the absence of organizational support as evidence of the 'professional marginalization and tentativeness of the field' although one may hope that as a result of technological developments, producing the 'long tail' that Anderson (2004, 2006) described, if publishers were to drop the journals, there would be web-based alternatives to fill the gaps. Paralleling the enormous contribution of *IJSL* to sociolinguistics has been the related book series edited by Fishman: some 96 volumes published by Mouton now carry the 'Contributions to the Sociology of Language' imprimatur.

In addition to these two major projects, Fishman has planned and edited a distinguished body of edited collections. Macnamara (1997: 175) testifies that the special issue of *The Journal of Social Issues* that he edited on 'Problems of Bilingualism' in 1967 was largely the work of Fishman, who asked him to be editor 'mainly to give a beginner a leg up'. There are many other volumes giving evidence of Fishman's work as organizer and developer: two follow-up volumes to the *Readings* (Fishman, 1968c, 1971) and its companion Fishman (1972b); one on language planning (Fishman, 1974); another

on writing systems (Fishman, 1978a); one on societal multilingualism (Fishman, 1978b); a bilingual volume on Yiddish (Fishman, 1981); a second on language planning (again shared with a more junior colleague) (Cobarrubias and Fishman, 1983); an innovative collection of papers on the first congresses of language revival movements (Fishman, 1993b); a significant collection dealing with post-imperial English (Fishman, Rubal-Lopez and Conrad, 1996); and, most recently, a collection on the sociology of language and religion[24] (Omoniyi and Fishman, 2006).

While their contributions to the field were different, it is easy to see how impoverished sociolinguistics would have been without the organizational work of Charles Ferguson and Joshua Fishman. If each of them had been willing to sit quietly in his office, conduct and publish his individual research, and ignore the challenges and efforts of providing leadership and encouragement to others, their individual scholarship would still have had a considerable effect, but their extensive work as organizers of meetings and publishers of other people's research played a major role in shaping the field as we know it.

1.4 SEEKING A COMMUNITY OF LIKE-MINDED SCHOLARS

The terms *sociolinguistics* and *sociology of language* both suggest a bidisciplinary approach, a blending of sociologists and linguists in a combined effort to see how language and society are related. In spite of his early failure to write a joint paper with Uriel Weinreich, Fishman still believed in the 'community of like-minded scholars' (Fishman, 1997a: 88) that he hoped to find in Bloomington who could rescue him from the isolation he had felt working between the disciplines. He was soon disappointed. He knew only two participants from before, Einar Haugen and Leonard Savitz, a sociologist he had known at the University of Pennsylvania. He knew of Kloss (whose address he was able to give to Ferguson), Gumperz (whom he had met and read), Labov (whose papers Uriel Weinreich had given him), and Stewart (he had read his paper on multilingual typology – a 1962 paper he reprinted as Stewart (1968)). The sociologists were not just outnumbered (eight to five), but, except for Kloss, had not yet published anything that could be considered sociolinguistics, hardly knew each other, and did not have strong interests in common; the anthropologists[25] and the linguists had interacted before and were more at home in a seminar conducted as part of a major linguistics event. All knew linguistic theory, while none of the sociologists did.

The two groups thus formed 'two cultures'; Fishman (1997a: 91) refers specifically to methodological gaps, as when he was asked for his corpus (and quipped in return that you don't need phonology to explain the causes of World War II), and Gumperz, presenting his pioneering paper on code switching (Blom and Gumperz, 1972) in Hemnesberget that highlighted a conversation he had heard at a party, was asked why he had not carried out statistical tests.

Of the sociologists, Lieberson, who was about to publish a paper on a bilingual city (Lieberson, 1965, 1997), edited an early journal issue with important papers on sociolinguistics (Lieberson, 1966) and continued to carry out research and publish in sociolinguistics for some years (Lieberson, 1981). He writes (Lieberson, 1997: 164) that he was particularly influenced by Ferguson, who had 'a passionate commitment to the field ... labels were irrelevant'. He believes that 'few could match Ferguson in the breath of this overview'. Eventually, he 'drifted away' from sociolinguistics which he felt unlikely to be of much interest to sociology. He suspected that the work of Joshua Fishman was having less influence on American sociologists than on sociologists overseas or on other disciplines.

Leonard Savitz had been a fellow-student of Allen Grimshaw at the University of Pennsylvania, and Fishman (1997a) reports he met him there and suggested to him that they produce a set of 'sociological readings' concerned with language. His field was criminology and the sociology of crime, so that the suggestion was not taken up.[26] Chester L. Hunt was a sociologist who had carried out research in the Philippines and who wrote a paper at the seminar (Hunt, 1966). Neither continued to work in sociolinguistics.

Heinz Kloss considered himself not as a sociolinguist but rather an 'authority on ethnic law' (Mackey and McConnell, 1997: 301). Fishman, who found his interest in language, nationality and minorities very appealing, included a chapter (Kloss, 1966) in his book, and was a member of the board that recommended appointing him to the staff of the International Center for Research on Bilingualism at the University of Laval. Many of his proposals, such as the distinction between status and corpus planning, have become key concepts in sociolinguistics.

There was another sociologist who must have provided Fishman with more support. He refers to Allen Grimshaw as 'in a special category by himself', not a member of the seminar but attending it regularly. Grimshaw (1997) says that his initiation to language science was through Savitz. Grimshaw had become interested in language and social contexts during a visit to India in 1961. He writes: 'I was an informal participant in many of the activities of the seminar and gave a talk to the group about ways in which knowledge about language might eliminate sociological questions; it was not long before I became more closely involved' (1997: 101). This involvement included membership and later chairmanship of the Committee on Sociolinguistics, organization of a conference (Grimshaw, 1969), and publication of a number of papers that were later collected by Dill (Grimshaw, 1981).

Ferguson (1997: 78) acknowledges that the sociologists made important contributions to the Bloomington seminar but on the whole left it to anthropologists and linguists to develop the field. The participants each had different points of view: Labov wanted to make linguistics more relevant while Fishman wanted to improve sociology. For Ferguson himself, 'sociolinguistics was just a loose label for phenomena relating language to society'. Over the years, most did not change their opinions.

Looking back, one can speculate that it was not just lack of knowledge of each other's methodologies that kept the fields apart, but a fundamental gap between the issues that concerned them. I recall that in the 1960s, Noam Chomsky would regularly dismiss an argument as 'not interesting'. With rare exceptions, the topics that interested the linguists did not interest the sociologists, and vice versa. One solution was to train 'real' sociolinguists. In his analysis of the interdisciplinary problem, Shuy (1997: 18) notes the problem of training new scholars in two fields: 'Social scientists did not want to give up anything to get linguistics. Nor did linguists want to give up anything to get social science'. Appended to two of Fishman's edited volumes (Fishman, 1978a; 1978b), there is a description of 'A graduate program in the sociology of language', with equal number of courses and credit in linguistics, sociology of language, and sociology. It describes the kind of programme he hoped to build at Yeshiva University and proposed at the Hebrew University, combining the new field with a solid basis in the two parent disciplines. It just didn't happen – at Yeshiva, the Language Behavior Program chaired by Vera John-Steiner lasted 10 years, and at the Hebrew University it never started – and in a later paper, Fishman (1991b)[27] once again makes a convincing case for the need for sociolinguists to know sociology and sociologists to respect the significance of language. He puts it strikingly: 'Sociology, too, although far less messianic in its promise, is chained and waiting, somewhere in its own disciplinary provincialism, waiting to come to sociolinguistics, to broaden and deepen it somewhat and to enable it to live up to its name' (1991b: 67).

One sociologist who did appreciate Fishman's work was Kjolseth (1997: 145) who reports that

Fishman, in 1966, organized a one-day meeting on sociolinguistics after the sixth World Congress of Sociology, which led to the formation of the Research Committee on Sociolinguistics of the International Sociological Association.[28] Kjolseth was president until 1974 and other members of the board were Fishman and Kloss, 'If I had to select one outstanding figure from among the several true giants in our field, I would point to Joshua Fishman'. The 1992 conference was to discuss the 'interface between sociology and linguistics'.

But the gap between sociology and linguistics has remained much as noted by Fishman at a meeting in Bright's home in the summer of 1966: sociologists were interested in linguistic variables, but not linguistics, while linguists were interested in broad social contextualization, but not in sociology. Shuy (1997: 15) cites this from Hymes (1966) and remarks that it was still true. Fishman (1992: viii) characterized sociolinguistics after three decades as 'a province of linguistics and anthropology, and a rather provincial province as well'. In spite of this, Mallinson (2009), who was trained in both sociolinguistics and sociology, has traced parallels between studies in the two disciplines and outlined ways in which they might collaborate.

How should we define the field that has emerged? One approach might be a content analysis of the more than 300 papers and posters accepted for the 2008 Sociolinguistics Symposium in Amsterdam, but the great variety makes clear the wisdom of Ferguson's belief that no single theory is likely to emerge. There is not even a clear distinction possible between the macro and the micro – in fact, SS17 set its theme as 'micro and macro connections'.

The lines were already drawn at Bloomington in 1964: Labov trying to explore what social elements needed to be added to linguistic theory to account for variation and language change; Gumperz seeking to analyse discourse in social contexts to establish the nature of social interaction; Hymes and his followers exploring communicative competence and sociolinguistic ecology and its educational implications. Where do Ferguson and Fishman fit into this picture?

1.5 FERGUSON AND FISHMAN AS SOCIOLINGUISTS/SOCIOLOGISTS OF LANGUAGE

Ferguson was a brilliant linguist, applying his keen analytical abilities to discover and explore a variety of systematic connections of language to society. In an autobiographical sketch (Ferguson, 1995), he explained how he came into linguistics

and the 'constructive tension between academic and activist activities'. He grew up with a strong interest in languages, encouraged in part by his German-speaking grandmother who lived with his family, the various languages associated with his religious upbringing, and his school teachers. He learned Latin, French and German at high school. At the University of Pennsylvania, he added Greek, Modern Hebrew and Old English. Completing a BA in philosophy, his graduate major was Oriental Studies; he studied Moroccan Arabic verbs and the phonology and morphology of Bengali. Zellig Harris was his graduate adviser. With support from the Intensive Language Program of the American Council of Learned Societies, he continued to study Moroccan Arabic and developed teaching materials for spoken Arabic. Inspired by a visit of Roman Jakobson, he saw the value of uniting psychological and linguistic approaches to the study of child language. In 1947, he accepted a position at the Foreign Service Institute working with Henry Lee Smith. While there, he wrote an unpublished paper on Arabic politeness formulas in 1955 and published an article on Arabic baby talk (Ferguson, 1956). However, it was his classic paper on diglossia (Ferguson, 1959) that was his first major contribution to sociolinguistics, and, according to Huebner (1999), his best-known work. There have been several reprints and translations into Italian, Spanish, Romanian, German and Portuguese. In the article, he suggested that a full explanation of these special situations would help 'in dealing with problems in linguistic description, in historical linguistics, and in language typology' (Ferguson, 1956: 2). Since then, a retrospective paper (Ferguson, 1991) notes, there have been hundreds of articles and a score of books on the topic, most of them referring directly to the paper; a review (Hudson, 1992) lists over 1000 items. In revisiting that classic work after some 3000 items had been published (Fernández, 1993), illustrating and applying and manipulating and modifying and confirming the original model, Ferguson (1991) clarified his original intention: his goal was to describe a particular language situation that was just one slot in a fairly elaborate taxonomy of language situations. From that taxonomy, principles and a theory would emerge. He could have chosen other 'clear cases' such as the creole continuum or the standard language with dialects but chose diglossia. In confessing weaknesses in the paper, the first that he mentions is his failure to specify that he was talking about speech communities. He could have been more precise in explaining what the term variety meant. Nor did he explain fully the notion of linguistic distance. He should also have recognized that these cases of diglossia existed in a larger situation, as described by Stewart (1968). He did not describe the existence of attitudes to intermediate varieties, nor did he clarify the importance of the power differential in the choice of varieties. This first major paper and the clarification 30 years later help us to understand Ferguson's view of sociolinguistics: namely, the identification of mutually-illuminating aspects of language and society.

In later papers, he studied other language situations: he identified and analysed genres such as baby talk and sports announcer talk and politeness; he studied variation and change in a number of languages; and he wrote on important aspects of language planning. Thus, while his primary concern was with the micro, linguistic end of the continuum, his involvement with social concerns led to work relevant to language management concerns. As Huebner (1996: 7) notes, he was not constrained by a single theory but open to constant revision on the basis of new data and was eclectic in data collection and analysis. Huebner describes Ferguson's favourite approach as starting with a small piece of language in a social context, or with a small case study, and building gradually with additional examples a more comprehensive theory. His special quality was a consistent search for relationships between language change and language development, between language universals and individual differences, and a study of the process of conventionalization that build language systems. All this tends to place him at the micro or sociolinguistic end of the continuum, but he recognized and worked at the macro end too: his work on the Ethiopian survey (Bender et al., 1976) involved him in the study of sociolinguistic situations, and his papers on language and religion and on language policy and planning clearly could be defined as sociology of language.

By his own account, Fishman's motivation was narrower than Ferguson's although the way he pursued his goals led him into wider areas and encouraged a broad range of research. His language loyalty volume (Fishman et al., 1964) was completed before the Bloomington seminar. He discussed the ideas behind it with Haugen, who wrote the introduction to the printed version (Fishman, 1966) and praised the book for its positive approach to the immigrant, welcomed the introduction of the concept of ethnicity, and hoped that there would continue to be studies of 'language shifts and resistance to them' in other parts of the world. In the preface to a book (Fishman, 1991c) a quarter of a century later whose title echoes Haugen's words and ably meets his challenge, Fishman recalls a conversation in which Haugen asked if he did not find working with minority languages to be 'full of sadness'. Fishman replied by referring to the job of doctors, who treat patients even though they understand all will

eventually die. Now, after a decade of teaching medical anthropology, he recognized that his answer to Haugen had been inadequate: modern medicine aims not just to combat illness, but to cultivate 'wellness', and to do this with the understanding that it depends on the patient's cultural view of wellness; in the same way, he had come to believe that a sociology of language must aim at ethnolinguistic wellness, depending for this on theoretical knowledge based on the preferences of specific ethnolinguistic speech communities.

Minority and endangered languages were at the core of his work. In an autobiographical essay, Fishman (1991a) notes that he grew up in a typical sociolinguistic setting in Philadelphia, the elder child of Yiddish-speaking immigrants.[29] What was not typical was that his parents were language activists deeply committed to Yiddish and successful in transferring their zeal to Fishman and to his sister.[30] He started writing for Yiddish youth journals, publishing his first story at the age of 12; two years later he became editor and publisher of his own journal. At school, he learned Spanish and became a passionate stamp-collector which stimulated his interest in other countries. He had been, he claims, a sociolinguist 'unwittingly' for 30 years before he went to Indiana, and suggested the term, on the model of psycholinguistics, as early as 1953–54. Roger Brown rejected the term, so he continued to refer to his work as the sociology of language: he taught a course with that name in 1960. At Pennsylvania, he majored in history with a minor in Spanish; at Columbia, he was persuaded to complete a doctorate in social psychology. He returned to teach at the University of Pennsylvania in 1958 as an associate professor of psychology and human relations. Two years later, he was awarded a long-term research grant by the Office of Education to study the 'Non-English Language Resources of the United States'; he took the grant with him to Yeshiva University, his lifetime academic home. His personal goal, at the 'supra-rational level', was to find out if any languages were in a stronger state of preservation than Yiddish. He feels his work in sociolinguistics to be peripheral: it is 'either macro-sociological, historical or quantitative' and with no concern for 'corpus (phonology, syntax, discourse etc.)'. It is at the same time 'Yiddish-centric' with conscious efforts to maintain a scientific perspective by studying other cases and languages. Apart from Yiddish, his main topical centres have been minority communities and languages, ideological, emotional and political expressions of ethnolinguistic cultures, and applied aspects of language maintenance and ideology, concentrating mainly on status planning, although he has recently reiterated strong support of efforts to maintain the purity of a language (Fishman, 2006).

Conscious all the time of a possible bias that his love for Yiddish might produce, he spent his career learning about other languages and their situations, whether by visits which took him (commonly supported by his wife, Gella Schweid Fishman, a scholar of Yiddish education in her own right) from the Arctic[31] to the Antipodes,[32] lecturing and establishing close personal relations with the language activists whose languages he wanted to see preserved, or by his extensive career of editing. Thus, he endeavoured to avoid 'a Yiddish-centric view of the sociolinguistic enterprise' (Fishman, 1991a).

1.6 CONCLUSION

Summing up, in addition to their unmatched organizational contributions to the development of sociolinguistics and the sociology of language, Charles Ferguson and Joshua Fishman have each staked out pioneering claims to major sectors of the study of language in its social context. How important are they to contemporary sociolinguistics? A citation search using Google Scholar shows that Fishman has many more hits than Ferguson, mainly for books (*Reversing Language Shift* tops the list; among his papers, a 2007 paper on Whorf is the most cited, with over 100 hits). Most of Ferguson's hits are papers, starting with over 1000 for diglossia, followed by 260 for baby talk, 140 for foreigner talk, and 100 for politeness. Fishman's topics and methods have perhaps produced more followers, in particular with the political relevance of language loyalty and loss. Many scholars working on these topics are in the field of education, while Ferguson's followers are more strictly in the narrower field of sociolinguistics. Additionally, the strength of Fishman's following is shown in the large number of tributes in festschrifts and birthday celebratory conferences. Perhaps this is a mark of his longer publication list; it also reflects the fact that he has continued to develop his ideas and approach, while Ferguson's strength was in innovative recognition of topics of sociolinguistic relevance. Obviously, there is no point in trying to award grades; each has made (and Fishman continues to make) major contributions to studies of language in society. Without their scholarship and leadership, the field would have been thinner and weaker.

NOTES

1 Paulston and Tucker (1997) is a wonderful treasure for students of sociolinguistics, preserving the 'memories and reflections' of the scholars who were involved in the early years.

2 One founding mother at least then; Paulston (1997: 3) called attention to the 'appalling dearth of women in the early days of sociolinguistics' which has now been rectified, in part in language and gender studies. She also recognized that most of the scholars involved in the first years were American; this too has changed, as could be seen by anyone attending the 2008 Sociolinguistics Symposium in Amsterdam.

3 Fishman was also a student of Uriel's father, Max Weinreich, and translated his major study of the Yiddish language (M. Weinreich, 1980).

4 I recall Weinreich's presentation as the most polished of the half dozen sets of plenary lectures given at Bloomington. Fishman (1997a,b: 310) recounts that Weinreich met the members of the sociolinguistic seminar and remarked on their variety of approaches: he believed the new field would "have to contend with at least as great a diversity of topics as he and I had unsuccessfully tried to contend with a decade earlier."

5 Tucker (1997: 320) uses this term and notes two characteristics of the climate of the period which contributed to the growth of sociolinguistics: a sense of the social justice aspect, and a view of its relevance to politics and government. Both led to an insistence on the importance of language in use.

6 Paulston and Tucker (2003: 1) reports that Nida (1949:152) was the first linguist to use the term 'sociolinguistics'.

7 The Preface to Fishman (1966) was written by Einar Haugen in July 1964 and dated at Bloomington Indiana. The report was first available as Fishman, Nahirny, Hofman and Hayden (1964).

8 Fishman is one scholar who has not hidden his personal views or the personal history that lay behind his research, as will become clear.

9 Then a professor of sociology at McGill University.

10 A sociologist at the University of Oregon.

11 Stewart (1930–2002) worked at the Center for Applied Linguistics in the 1960s, when his major contribution to sociolinguistics was a study of Gullah, an Afro-American variety of English, which established the Creole base for Afro-American vernacular English. He was on the faculty of the City University of New York for 25 years, and continued studies of Creoles and the implications of his findings for the teaching of reading to black children.

12 Kloss (1924–87) was a regularly-cited German scholar, the knowledge of whose Nazi past, recently disclosed (Hutton, 1999), shocked those who had known him and admired his work: see the loose-leaf addendum to *The Early Days of Sociolinguistics* (Paulston and Tucker, 1997) written by the editors and by Fishman and also the footnote (1) to Fishman (2008): 25.

13   He published two introductory readers with the same publisher, one with 'sociolinguistics' in the title (Fishman, 1970) and two years later, a revision with the 'sociology of language' (Fishman, 1972a). In later correspondence with Eldridge Sibley, SSRC staff for the committee, he said he'd rather it be named 'committee on language and behavior in social contexts' (Committee on Sociolinguistics 1963–). The program he set up at Yeshiva University with Vera John-Steiner and Vivian Horner was called the Language and Behavior Program.

14   A contrasting view was presented by Friedrich (1997: 98), for whom a strong memory is the acceptance by sociolinguists of the fact that 'language forms and patterns are always politically charged and are always ensconced in sociopolitical contexts that should not be avoided by a scientific fiction', in contrast to the ironic fact that Chomsky's 'linguistics and that of his immediate followers has remained by and large deaf and mute to the political'.

15   The other two significant teachers he mentions are Irving Lorge for quantitative studies and Max Weinreich for Jewish folklore.

16   Allen Grimshaw (1997) also reports that his interest in sociolinguistics dates from a visit to India in 1961.

17   Fishman (2001a: 864) notes Ferguson's 'unusually broad range of well-developed interests and a highly significant number of organizational accomplishments'.

18   Roger Shuy (like me) was at Bloomington in a post-doctoral seminar on Computation in Linguistics directed by Paul Garvin (Garvin and Spolsky, 1966), but because he had been trained in dialectology was, I am confident, aware of the sociolinguistic seminar; he later directed the first major sociolinguistic program at Georgetown University.

19   Ferguson's articles are easily available thanks to the work of two scholars who edited collections, Anwar Dil (Ferguson, 1971) and Thomas Huebner (Ferguson, 1996).

20   He was President of the Linguistic Society of America in 1970 and of the International Association for the Study of Child Language from 1973 to 1975.

21   The 36th annual conference of NWAV (New Ways of Analyzing Variation) was in Philadelphia in 2007.

22   The first meeting of the Sociolinguistics Symposium in the 1970s in the UK marks the growth of sociolinguistics in Europe; after 2002, the Symposium began to meet elsewhere in Europe and met in Amsterdam in 2008, with over 300 contributors.

23   Fishman is singularly open to inviting comments on his own work too. In one book (Fishman, 1991c), he presented a complex and original theory of language maintenance and loss that has been widely discussed; 10 years later, he updated his own theory (Fishman, 2001b) and published comments

and criticisms from 16 scholars with knowledge of the cases he had studied in the 1991 book.

24   The important place religion plays in their work and their lives is another connection between Ferguson and Fishman, distinguishing them from the secularism common in Western scholars.

25   American anthropology, it should be noted, included linguistics as one of its four main fields alongside ethnography, archaeology and physical anthropology, which meant that anthropologists were trained in general linguistics.

26   His obituary notes:

At times, however, his consuming intellectual curiosity led him **far afield**. To note only one example, he was a pioneer in sociological interest in language and in what came to be called sociolinguistics. He gave a paper on the sociology of language in 1963; the following year he was a participant in the SSRC-sponsored seminar held in conjunction with the Summer Linguistic Institute of the Linguistic Society of America. (emphasis added)

27   The paper is reprinted in Hornberger and Pütz (2006).

28   This continues and was renamed as the RS25 Language and Society of the ISA in 2007. Jenny Perry, current secretary of the RC wrote to me (personal communication):

We decided on a change of name because we felt that 'Sociolinguistics' might sound a bit limiting as far as prospective new members were concerned. We conducted an online vote on the five most popular suggested names for change from all our members. Since the name change we have captured a more diverse membership.

29   Ferguson was also born in Philadelphia. His maternal grandparents were German speakers, and he would hear his grandmother speaking a variety of it with an elderly neighbour (Ferguson, 1995).

30   In turn, Joshua Fishman and his wife Gella have devoted much time and effort to passing on their enthusiasm for Yiddish to their children and grandchildren.

31   One paper (Fishman, 1993a) was presented at a conference in Tromsø.

32   His book (Fishman, 1991c) includes a chapter on Māori.

REFERENCES

Alatis, J. E. and LeClair, C. (1993) 'Building an association: TESOL's first quarter century', in S. Silberstein (ed.), *State of the Art TESOL Essays: Celebrating 25 Years of the*

Discipline: Alexandria VA: Teachers of English to Speakers of Other Languages. pp. 382–413.

Anderson, C. (2004) 'The long tail', *Wired,* October. Available at http://www.wired.com/wired/archive/12.10/tail.html

Anderson, C. (2006) *The Long Tail: Why the Future of Business is Selling Less of More.* New York: Hyperion.

Bender, M. L., Bowen, J. D., Cooper, R. L. and Ferguson, C. A. (eds) (1976) *Language in Ethiopia.* London: Oxford University Press.

Blom, J.-P. and Gumperz, J. J. (1972) 'Social meaning in linguistic structures: Code switching in Northern Norway', in J. J. Gumperz and D. Hymes (eds), *Directions in Sociolinguistics.* New York: Holt Rinehart and Winston. pp. 407–34.

Bright, W. (1997) 'Reminiscences: beginnings of sociolinguistics', in C. B. Paulston and G. R. Tucker (eds), *The Early Days of Sociolinguistics: Memories and Reflections.* Dallas, TX: The Summer Institute of Linguistics. pp. 53–60.

Bright, W. (ed.) (1966) *Sociolinguistics: Proceedings of the UCLA Sociolinguistics Conference, 1964.* The Hague: Mouton.

Bright, W. (ed.) (1992) *International Encyclopedia of Linguistics.* New York: Oxford University Press.

Cobarrubias, J. and Fishman, J. A. (eds) (1983) *Progress in Language Planning: International Perspectives.* The Hague: Mouton.

Committee on Sociolinguistics (1963–1973) Archives. Tarrytown, NY: Social Sciences Research Council.

Currie, H. C. (1952) 'A projection of sociolinguistics: the relationship of speech to social status', *Southern Speech Journal,* 18: 28–37.

Ervin-Tripp, S. (1973) *Language Acquisition and Communicative Choice; essays by Susan M. Ervin-Tripp. Selected and introduced by Anwar S. Dil.* Stanford, CA: Stanford University Press.

Ervin-Tripp, S. (1997) 'The development of sociolinguistics', in C. B. Paulston and G. R. Tucker (eds), *The Early Days of Sociolinguistics: Memories and Reflections.* Dallas, TX: The Summer Institute of Linguistics. pp. 61–76.

Ferguson, C. A. (1956) 'Arabic baby talk', in M. Halle (ed.), *For Roman Jakobson.* The Hague: Mouton. pp. 121–8.

Ferguson, C. A. (1959) 'Diglossia', *Word,* 15: 325–40.

Ferguson, C. A. (1968) 'Language development', in J. A. Fishman, C. A. Ferguson and J. D. Gupta (eds), *Language Problems of Developing Nations.* New York: John Wiley and Sons. pp. 27–35.

Ferguson, C. A. (1971) *Language Structure and Use: Essays by Charles A. Ferguson,* in Anwar S. Dil (ed.), Stanford, CA: Stanford, University Press. p. 328.

Ferguson, C. A. (1991) 'Epilogue: diglossia revisited', *Southwest Journal of Linguistics,* 10(1): 214–34.

Ferguson, C. A. (1995) 'Long-term commitment and lucky events', in J. E. Alatis (ed.), *Linguistics and the Education of Language Teachers: Ethnolinguistic, Psycholinguistic, and Sociolinguistic Aspects (GURT 1995).* Washington, DC: Georgetown University Press. pp. 10–24.

Ferguson, C. A. (1996) 'Sociolinguistic perspectives: Papers on language in society, 1959–1994', in T. Huebner (ed.), New York: Oxford University Press. p. 348.

Ferguson, C. A. (1997) 'History of sociolinguistics', in C. B. Paulston and G. R. Tucker (eds), *The Early Days of Sociolinguistics: Memories and Reflections.* Dallas, TX: The Summer Institute of Linguistics. pp. 77–95.

Ferguson, C. A. and Gumperz, J. J. (eds) (1960) *Linguistic Diversity in South Asia.* Bloomington, IN: Research Center in Anthropology, Folklore and Linguistics, Indiana University.

Fernández, M. (1993) *Diglossia: A Comprehensive Bibliography 1960–1990.* Amsterdam: John Benjamins.

Fishman, J. A. (1960) A systematization of the Whorfian hypothesis. *Behavioral Science,* 5: 323–39.

Fishman, J. A. (1968a) 'Language problems and types of political and sociocultural integration: a conceptual post-script', in J. A. Fishman, C. A. Ferguson and J. D. Gupta (eds), *Language Problems of Developing Nations.* New York: John Wiley and Sons. pp. 491–8.

Fishman, J. A. (1968b) 'Sociolinguistics and the language problems of the developing countries', in J. A. Fishman, C. A. Ferguson and J. D. Gupta (eds), *Language Problems of Developing Nations.* New York: John Wiley and Sons. pp. 3–16.

Fishman, J. A. (1970) *Sociolinguistics: A Brief Introduction.* Rowley, MA: Newbury House.

Fishman, J. A. (1972a) *The Sociology of Language: An Interdisciplinary Social Science Approach to Language in Society.* Rowley, MA: Newbury House.

Fishman, J. A. (1976) *Bilingual Education: An International Sociological Perspective.* Rowley, MA: Newbury House.

Fishman, J. A. (1991a) 'My life through my work; my work through my life', in K. Koerner (ed.), *First Person Singular: Autobiographies by North American Scholars in the Language Sciences.* Vol. 2. Amsterdam and Philadelphia: John Benjamins. pp. 105–24.

Fishman, J. A. (1991b) 'Putting the "socio" back into the sociolinguistic enterprise', *International Journal of the Sociology of Language,* 92: 127–38.

Fishman, J. A. (1991c) *Reversing Language Shift: Theoretical and Empirical Foundations of Assistance to Threatened Languages.* Clevedon, Avon: Multilingual Matters.

Fishman, J. A. (1992) 'Foreword', in G. Williams (ed.), *Sociolinguistics: A Sociological Critique.* London: Routledge. pp. vii–ix.

Fishman, J. A. (1993a) 'Reversing language shift: successes, failures, doubts and dilemmas', in Ernst H. Jahr (ed.), *Language Conflict and Language Planning.* Berlin: Mouton de Gruyter. pp. 69–81.

Fishman, J. A. (1997a) 'Bloomington, summer 1964: the birth of American sociolinguistics', in C. B. Paulston and G. R. Tucker (eds), *The Early Days of Sociolinguistics: Memories and Reflections.* Dallas, TX: The Summer Institute of Linguistics. pp. 87–100.

Fishman, J. A. (1997b) 'Reflection about (or prompted by) *International Journal of the Sociology of Language (IJSL)*', in C. B. Paulston and G. R. Tucker (eds), *The Early Days of Sociolinguistics: Memories and Reflections.* Dallas, TX: The Summer Institute of Linguistics. pp. 237–41.

Fishman, J. A. (1997c) 'Uriel Weinreich (1926–1967): A sociolinguistic appreciation', in C. B. Paulston and G. R. Tucker (eds), *The Early Days of Sociolinguistics: Memories and Reflections*. Dallas, TX: The Summer Institute of Linguistics. pp. 307–13.

Fishman, J. A. (2001a) 'Ferguson, Charles A. (1921–98)', in R. Mesthrie (ed.), *Concise Encyclopedia of Sociolinguistics*. Amsterdam: Elsevier. pp. 864–5.

Fishman, J. A. (2006) *Do Not Leave Your Language Alone: The Hidden Status Agendas Within Corpus Planning in Language Policy*. Mahwah, NJ: Lawrence Erlbaum.

Fishman, J. A. (2008) 'Rethinking the *Ausbau–Abstand* dichotomy into a continuous and multivariate system', *International Journal of the Sociology of Language*, 191: 17–26.

Fishman, J. A. (ed.) (1966) *Language Loyalty in the United States: The Maintenance and Perpetuation of Non-English Mother Tongues by American Ethnic and Religious Groups*. The Hague: Mouton.

Fishman, J. A. (ed.) (1968c) *Readings in the Sociology of Language*. The Hague: Mouton.

Fishman, J. A. (ed.) (1971) *Advances in the Sociology of Language*. Vol. 1. The Hague: Mouton.

Fishman, J. A. (ed.) (1972b) *Advances in the Sociology of Language*. Vol. 2. The Hague: Mouton.

Fishman, J. A. (ed.) (1974) *Advances in Language Planning*. The Hague: Mouton.

Fishman, J. A. (ed.) (1978a) *Advances in the Creation and Revision of Writing Systems*. The Hague: Mouton.

Fishman, J. A. (ed.) (1978b) *Advances in the Study of Societal Multilingualism*. The Hague: Mouton.

Fishman, J. A. (ed.) (1981) *Never Say Die! A Thousand Years of Yiddish in Jewish Life and Letters*. Hague: Mouton.

Fishman, J. A. (ed.) (1993b) *The Earliest Stage of Language Planning: the "First Congress" Phenomenon*. Berlin: Mouton de Gruyter.

Fishman, J. A. (ed.) (2001b) *Can Threatened Languages be Saved? Reversing Language Shift, Revisited: a 21st century perspective*. Clevedon, Avon: Multilingual Matters.

Fishman, J. A., Cooper, R. L. and Conrad, A. W. (1977) *The Spread of English: the Sociology of English as an Additional Language*. Rowley, MA.: Newbury House.

Fishman, J. A., Cooper, R. L. and Ma, R. (1971) *Bilingualism in the Barrio*. Bloomington, IN: Research Center for the Language Sciences, Indiana University.

Fishman, J. A., Ferguson, C. A. and Das Gupta, J. (eds) (1968) *Language Problems of Developing Nations*. New York: John Wiley and Sons.

Fishman, J. A., Nahirny, V. C., Hofman, J. E. and Hayden, R. G. (1964) *Language Loyalty in the United States*. Mimeographed report in 3 volumes. New York: Yeshiva University.

Fishman, J. A., Rubal-Lopez, A. and Conrad, A. W. (eds) (1996) *Post-Imperial English*. Berlin: Mouton de Gruyter.

Fishman, J. A., Tabouret-Keller, A., Clyne, M., Krishnamurti, B. and Abdulaziz, M. H. (eds) (1986) *The Fergusonian Impact: in Honor of Charles A. Ferguson on the occasion of his 65th Birthday*. Vol. 2, Sociolinguistics and the Sociology of Language. Berlin: Mouton de Gruyter.

Fox, M. J. (2007) 'Ford Foundation: personal reflection', in C. B. Paulston and G. R. Tucker (eds), *The Early Days of Sociolinguistics*. Dallas, TX: The Summer Institute of Linguistics. pp. 271–2.

Fox, M. J. and Harris, D. (1964) *English as a Second Language: Development and Testing*. New York: Ford Foundation.

Friedrich, P. (1997) 'Memories', in C. B. Paulston and G. R. Tucker (eds), *The Early Days of Sociolinguistics: Memories and Reflections*. Dallas, TX: The Summer Institute of Linguistics. pp. 97–100.

Garvin, P. and Spolsky, B. (eds) (1966) *Computation in Linguistics: A Case Book*. Bloomington, IN: Indiana University Press.

Grimshaw, A. D. (1969) 'Language as obstacle and as data in sociological research', *Items*, 23(2): 17–21.

Grimshaw, A. D. (1981) *Language as Social Resource: Essays by Allen D. Grimshaw, Selected and Introduced by Anwar S. Dil*. Stanford, CA: Stanford University Press.

Grimshaw, A. D. (1997) 'Origins and milestones', in C. B. Paulston and G. R. Tucker (eds), *The Early Days of Sociolinguistics: Memories and Reflections*. Dallas, TX: The Summer Institute of Linguistics. pp. 101–12.

Gumperz, J. J. (1971) *Language in Social Groups*. Stanford, CA: Stanford University Press.

Gumperz, J. J. (1997) 'Some comments on the origin and development of sociolinguistics: conversation with John Gumperz', in C. B. Paulston and G. R. Tucker (eds), *The Early Days of Sociolinguistics: Memories and Reflections*. Dallas, TX: The Summer Institute of Linguistics. pp. 113–20.

Gumperz, J. J. and Hymes, D. (eds) (1972) *Directions in Sociolinguistics: The Ethnography of Communication*. New York: Holt.

Haugen, E. (1953) *The Norwegian Language in America: a Study in Bilingual Behavior*. Philadelphia, PA: University of Pennsylvania Press.

Haugen, E. (1966) *Language Conflict and Language Planning: the Case of Modern Norwegian*. Cambridge, MA: Harvard University Press.

Haugen, E. (1972) *The Ecology of Language: Essays by Einar Haugen Edited by Anwar S. Dil*. Stanford, CA: Stanford University Press.

Hill, J. H. (2007) 'Obituary: William Oliver Bright', *Language*, 83(3): 628–41.

Hornberger, N. and Pütz, M. (eds) (2006) *Language Loyalty, Language Planning and Language Revitalization: Recent Writings and Reflections from Joshua A. Fishman*. Clevedon, Avon: Multilingual Matters Ltd.

Hudson, A. (1992) 'Diglossia: a bibliographic review', *Language in Society*, 21: 611–74.

Huebner, T. (1996) 'Introduction', in T. Huebner (ed.), *Sociolinguistic Perspectives: Papers on Language in Society by Charles A. Ferguson, 1959–1994*. New York: Oxford University Press. pp. 3–15.

Huebner, T. (1999) 'Obituary: Charles Albert Ferguson', *Language and Society*, 28(3): 431–7.

Hunt, C. L. (1966) 'Language choice in a multilingual society', *Sociological Inquiry*, 36(2): 240–53.

Hutton, C. M. (1999) *Linguistics and the Third Reich: Mother-Tongue Fascism, Race and the Science of Language*. London: Routledge.

Hymes, D. (1966) 'Teaching and training in sociolinguistics', report to Social Science Research Council.

Hymes, D. (ed.) (1971) *Pidginisation and Creolization of Languages: Proceedings of a Conference Held at the University of the West Indies, April 1968*. New York: Cambridge University Press.

Jakobson, R. (1960) 'Closing statement: linguistics and poetics', in T. A. Sebeok (ed.), *Style in Language*. Cambridge, MA: The Technology Press of MIT and John Wiley and Sons. pp. 350–77.

Kjolseth, R. (1997) 'Sociolinguistics: birth of a revolution', in C. B. Paulston and G. R. Tucker (eds), *The Early Days of Sociolinguistics: Memories and Reflections* Dallas TX: Summer Institute of Linguistics. pp. 139–46.

Kloss, H. (1966) 'German-American language maintenance efforts', in J. Fishman (ed.), *Language Loyalty in the United States*. The Hague: Mouton. pp. 206–52.

Labov, W. (1962) 'The social motivation of a sound change', *Word*, 19: 273–309.

Labov, W. (1966) *The Social Stratification of English in New York City*. Washington, DC: Center for Applied Linguistics.

Labov, W. (1997) 'Sociolinguistic patterns', in C. B. Paulston and G. R. Tucker (eds), *The Early Days of Sociolinguistics: Memories and Reflections*. Dallas, TX: The Summer Institute of Linguistics. pp. 147–58.

Lieberson, S. J. (1965) 'Bilingualism in Montreal: a social demographic analysis', *American Journal of Sociology*, 71: 10–25.

Lieberson, S. J. (1981) *Language Diversity and Language Contact: Essays by Stanley Lieberson; Selected and Introduced by Anwar S. Dil*. Stanford, CA: Stanford University Press.

Lieberson, S. J. (1997) 'Early developments in sociolinguistics', in C. B. Paulston and G. R. Tucker (eds), *The Early Days of Sociolinguistics: Memories and Reflections*. Dallas, TX: The Summer Institute of Linguistics. pp. 159–69.

Lieberson, S. J. (ed.) (1966) 'Explorations in Sociolingustics', *Special Issue of Sociolinguistic Inquiry*.

Mackey, W. and McConnell, G. D. (1997) 'Heinz Kloss and the study of language in society', in C. B. Paulston and G. R. Tucker (eds), *The Early Days of Sociolinguistics: Memories and Reflection*. Dallas TX: The Summer Institute of Linguistics. pp. 301–6.

Macnamara, J. (1997) 'Early developments in sociolinguistics', in C. B. Paulston and G. R. Tucker (eds), *The Early Days of Sociolinguistics: Memories and Reflections*. Dallas, TX: The Summer Institute of Linguistics. pp. 171–6.

Mallinson, C. (2009) 'Sociolinguistics and Sociology: Current directions, future partnerships.' *Language and Linguistics Compass*, 3(4), 1034–51.

Murray, S. O. (1998) *American Sociolinguistics: Theorists and Theory Groups*. Amsterdam: John Benjamins.

Nida, Eugene (1949) *Morphology: The Descriptive Analysis of Words*. Ann Arbor, MI: University of Michigan Press.

Ohannessian, S., Ferguson, C. A. and Polomé, E. C. (eds) (1975) *Language Surveys in Developing Nations: Papers and Reports on Sociolinguistic Surveys*. Arlington, VA: Center for Applied Linguistics.

Omoniyi, T. and Fishman, J. A. (eds) (2006) *Explorations in the Sociology of Language and Religion*. Amsterdam: John Benjamins.

Osgood, C. E. (ed.) (1954) *Psycholinguistics: a Survey of Theory and Research Problems; Report of the 1953 Summer Seminar Sponsored by the Committee on Linguistics and Psychology of the Social Science Research Council*. Baltimore: Waverly Press.

Paulston, C. B. (1997) 'Introduction', in C. B. Paulston and G. R. Tucker (eds), *The Early Days of Sociolinguistics: Memories and Reflections*. Dallas, TX: The Summer Institute of Linguistics. pp. 3–9.

Paulston, C. B. and Tucker, G. R. (eds) (1997) *The Early Days of Sociolinguistics: Memories and Reflections*. Dallas, TX: The Summer Institute of Linguistics.

Paulston, C. B. and Tucker, G. R. (2003) *Sociolinguistics: The Essential Readings*. Malden MA and Oxford UK: Blackwell Publishing.

Rubin, J., Jernudd, B., Das Gupta, J., Fishman, J. A. and Ferguson, C. A. (1977) *Language Planning Processes*. The Hague: Mouton.

Shuy, R. W. (1997) 'A brief history of American Sociolinguistics: 1949–1989', in C. B. Paulston and G. R. Tucker (eds), *The Early Days of Sociolinguistics: Memories and Reflections*. Dallas, TX: The Summer Institute of Linguistics. pp. 11–32.

Slobin, D. I. (ed.) (1967) *A Field Manual for Cross-Cultural Study of the Acquisition of Communicative Competence*. Berkeley, CA: Institute of Human Learning.

Snow, C. A. and Ferguson, C. A. (eds) (1977) *Talking to Children: Language Input and Acquisition*. Cambridge: Cambridge University Press.

Spolsky, B. (1995) *Measured Words: The Development of Objective Language Testing*. Oxford: Oxford University Press.

Stewart, W. (1968) 'A sociolinguistic typology for describing national multilingualism', in Joshua A. Fishman (ed.), *Readings in the Sociology of Language*. The Hague: Mouton. pp. 531–45.

Tucker, G. R. (1997) 'The development of sociolinguistics as a field of study: Concluding observations', in Paulston, C. B. and G. R. Tucker (eds), *The Early Days of Sociolinguistics: Memories and Reflections*. Dallas, TX: The Summer Institute of Linguistics. pp. 317–24.

Weinreich, M. (1980) *History of the Yiddish language*. Tr. J. A. Fishman and N. Shlomo. Chicago: University of Chicago Press.

Weinreich, U. (1944) 'Di velshishe shprakh in kampf far ir kiyem', *Yivo-bletter*, 23: 225–48.

Weinreich, U. (1953a) *Languages in Contact: Findings and Problems*. New York: Linguistic Circle of New York.

Weinreich, U. (1953b) 'The Russification of Soviet minority languages', *Problems of Communism*, 2: 46–57.

Weinreich, U. (1966) 'Explorations in semantic theory', in T. A. Sebeok (ed.), *Current Trends in Linguistics*. Vol. 3: Theoretical Foundations. The Hague: Mouton. pp. 395–477.

Weinreich, U., Labov, W. and Herzog, M. I. (1968) 'Empirical foundations for a theory of language change', in W. P. Lehmann and Y. Malkiel (eds), *Directions for Historical Linguistics: A Symposium*. Austin, TX: University Press pp. 95–195.

Labov: Language Variation and Change

Kirk Hazen

2.1 INTRODUCTION

The full impact of a scholar like William Labov (pronounced [ləbov]) is beyond the scope of a handbook chapter. The entire *Handbook of Language Variation and Change* (Chambers, Trudgill and Schilling-Estes, 2002) should be seen as part of Labov's scholarly impact, and even that one volume does not comprehensively capture every aspect of his work. His publications are voluminous, their range is broad, and their effects on current scholars continue. This chapter focuses primarily, although not exclusively, on the early works of Labov. At points, I also trace the connections of Labov's scholarship to that of his intellectual predecessors, illustrating his motivations for scholarship. The chapter is divided into sections on Labov's education and personal background, the intellectual influences on his scholarship, the confluence of academic fields around the beginnings of sociolinguistics, an overview of Labov's work, and a conclusion.[1]

2.2 LABOV'S TRAJECTORY TO GRADUATE SCHOOL

William Labov was born 4 December 1927 in Rutherford, NJ (USA). When he was 12 years old, he moved to Fort Lee, NJ, where he encountered a different dialect area and all kinds of conflict (Labov, 1997): he recounts getting into verbal and physical fights with local kids. From these encounters, he sharpened his argumentative skills, learned to take note of what was around him, and kept swinging at what he was good at – winning verbal arguments. He later studied at Harvard and majored in English and philosophy, graduating in 1948. In 'How I got into linguistics', Labov (1997) writes about his advisor's comments at Harvard: 'When he learned that I was taking one course in chemistry (inorganic), he sucked on his pipe, smoothed out his cord trousers, and said, "Just where did you get this idolatry of science?"' These scientific leanings fostered Labov's efforts to make language study an empirical enterprise.

Labov (1997) reports that he held several writing jobs after college, then went to work as an industrial chemist and ink-maker in the laboratory of the Union Ink Co. in Ridgefield, NJ, between 1949 and 1960. There he interacted with a wide diversity of company workers, from millhands to truck drivers and sales crew, figuring out how much everyone knew, learning how they argued, and studying their narratives years before he thought of writing about them.

In 1961, aged 34, he went back to graduate school at Columbia University in New York City with an idea to study English. Allen Walker Read was Labov's first linguistics teacher, and Labov argues (2006: 16) that Read's papers on *OK* (Read, 2002) 'stand as a progenitor of socio-historical work'. He was intrigued with linguistics because of the vibrancy of the field and linguists' propensity for open argument. What dismayed

Labov was that the 'evidence' for linguistics at the time came from the linguists' self-generated sentences, which restricted both the educational and class range of the data. He figured he could up the ante and produce studies based on richer data. With this turn towards more diverse data, he also fostered study of the working class. He earned his MA in 1963 and his PhD in 1964, both from Columbia University. He taught at Columbia (1964–70) before becoming a professor of linguistics at the University of Pennsylvania (1971), where he has remained ever since.

2.3 THE INTELLECTUAL CLIMATE: LABOV AS A LINGUIST

As Labov remembers (Gordon, 2006), there were two substantial roadblocks in linguistics when he entered graduate school to his intended field of study. First, synchronic linguistics held that a speaker's idiolect was sufficient to account for the qualities of a language. Second, since the methodology of the time went no further than the study of a few idiolects, diachronic linguistics was not able to account for how people used language if it was continually changing. In Gordon (2006), Labov discloses that he was never interested in categoricity (Chambers, 2003); his professional career has focused on principles underwritten by probabilities and swayed by social pressures.

The relationship between the speech community and the individual has been in question throughout the modern linguistic period (see also Kerswill, this volume). Since the middle of the twentieth century, this distinction has been cast often in the terms 'idiolect'[2] (the grammar of an individual) and 'dialect' (the grammar of a speech community). In order to position himself as a linguistic researcher, yet study speech communities, Labov had to establish theoretically the relation between language, the individual and the community. He writes (Labov, 1966a: 6):

> It is generally considered that the most consistent and coherent system is that of an *idiolect* ... . We find an increasing number of alternations which are due to stylistic or cultural factors, or changes in time – and these are external to language, not a part of linguistic structure.
>
> The present study adopts an entirely opposite view of the relative consistency of idiolect and dialect in the structure of New York City English.

The clearest statement Labov provides concerning the relation of idiolects and dialects would be in the new chapter in the second edition of his dissertation, where Labov (2006: 380) writes: 'Drawing upon the larger perspective set forth by Weinreich, Labov, and Herzog (1968), we can say that the linguistic behavior of individuals cannot be understood without knowledge of the communities that they belong to'. Labov acknowledges the abstract nature of speech communities and dialects but finds the data provided by idiolects to be insufficient to accurately describe, let alone explain, language change:

> The idea is that language is an abstract object, and it has to be treated with abstractions. So the question is, on what database do you form your conclusions? How do you know when you're right and how do you know when you're wrong? ... So I thought that it was possible to move this field into a more scientific basis by grounding it on the use of language in everyday life (Gordon, 2006: 333).

Labov has stated his argument on this issue repeatedly for over four decades: 'We study individuals because they give us the data to describe the community, but the individual is not really a linguistic unit' (Gordon, 2006: 341). Labov realizes that many people in sociolinguistics disagree with him on this point; they argue instead that the 'reality' is best found in the individual speaker. He takes the inverse position, that there are 'no individuals from the linguistic point of view' (Gordon, 2006: 341).

Although he did not accept the linguistics of idiolects, Labov did not forsake all theoretical linguistic concerns of the 1960s. Instead, he developed them as part of the foundation of his studies. For example, he writes (1966a: 5): 'The one point of view which would probably meet with general approval from all linguists today, is that the prime object of linguistics is the structure of language, not its elements ... '. However, despite such points of agreement, Labov did critique contemporary linguistics on several grounds.

To establish where his own work fell in linguistic history and to emphasize the theoretical issues he was critiquing, in the publication of his dissertation, Labov (1966a) lists four assumptions of linguistics which he found problematic: synchronic language systems must be studied separately from diachronic systems; sound change cannot be directly observed; feelings about language are inaccessible; and the use of non-linguistic data to explain linguistic change is prohibited. Labov lays the theoretical foundation for his empirical work by attacking the first two assumptions. He attributes the privileging of synchronic systems over diachronic systems to Saussure and instead argues that each synchronic state is marked as to its direction and rate of change, and thus the two areas of study are not so cleanly separable.

As for the second assumption, Labov deemed Bloomfield's statement about the unobservability of language change (1933: 347) as supporting the Neo-Grammarian argument for the absolute regularity of sound change (see also Labov, 1994). Bloomfield supposed that irregular linguistic processes, such as borrowing or analogy, would always disrupt, in the synchronic view, any possible observation of sound change. The data would always be too messy to draw reasonable conclusions about directions and rates of change. Labov viewed this intellectual step as '... remov[ing] the empirical study of linguistic change from the program of twentieth-century linguistics' (Labov, 1966a: 11). Labov put empirical study back on the programme for the study of language change. Labov found the explanatory power of empirical synchronic observations in the correlations between social structures and linguistic structures.[3]

With regard to the third assumption, Bloch and Trager (1942) argued that the speakers' feelings about sounds should remain off limits to linguists because that is not what linguists do, and although such psychological correlates may be important, the linguist (as linguist) has no methodology for assessing them. Labov counters (1966a: 12) that such purism gets in the way of '... one's view of language as it is spoken'. The fourth basic assumption in linguistics at the time was that linguists should not use non-linguistic information to solve linguistic problems. The intent was to strengthen linguistic argument by excluding such explanations for language change as climate or inherited differences in physiology (cf. Hock and Joseph, 1996; Labov, 2001). Labov critiques Antoine Martinet's stringent adherence to this prohibition, especially since Martinet himself had identified the potential for the study of language in social context. Martinet argued that the linguist could be excused '... if, in his capacity as a linguist, he declines the invitation to investigate sociological conditioning' (Labov 1966a: 13). Labov argues instead that the role of language in self-identification[4] is important for phonological change.

Labov was not alone in his critiques of the canonical linguistics of the late 1950s and 1960s. William Bright (1966) had criticized linguists' classifications of intralanguage diversity as 'free variation'. Labov successfully argued that most 'free variation' has systematic linguistic and social constraints. In the same vein, Labov (1969c: 15) cites Edward Klima's (1964) analysis of differences between dialects and asserts that underlying grammatical differences, such as the ordering of rules, cannot account for the differences between standard and nonstandard dialects in a systematic manner. Labov has argued that much of modern linguistics, since the Chomskyan revolution (e.g. Chomsky, 1965), concerns those aspects of language which are stable. In contrast, 'We've been involved in a complementary study

of everything that does and can change' (Gordon, 2006: 338).

To describe correlations between patterns of linguistic behaviour and social identities in as objective a way as possible, Labov focuses on phonological variation involving variants that are (or are treated as) discrete and thus quantifiable, and borrows from Parsonian sociology a way of describing social facts about speakers in quantifiable terms. In a pioneering study of variation from classroom to playground, Fischer (1958) had introduced the quantification of language data and the range of social variation to be found in that data. Fischer studied a variable – the velar vs alveolar pronunciations of the English suffix –*ing* – which sociolinguistics have continued to study for 50 years, in part because its variants are discrete rather than scalar (Campbell-Kibler, 2007; Hazen, 2008). However, not all language traits are as open to quantification. As Labov notes:

> In many areas of generative syntax, quantifications of everyday speech may not be appropriate – the data are not frequent enough. It's not as if every aspect of our field is open to quantification. Your concepts have to become clear and solid and countable. There are areas, not only abstract arenas of grammar but areas of discourse analysis, where the attempts at quantification may be quite premature (Gordon, 2006: 334).

Some syntactic variables are open to Labovian exploration, however, and Labov has also been part of the effort to quantify previously unquantifiable areas of grammar. For example, Labov directed Lavandera's 1975 University of Pennsylvania dissertation on *si*-clauses in Buenos Aires, which employed a database of 1587 tokens gathered from spontaneous speech.[5] Lavandera was able to elicit this many tokens through carefully directing the casual conversation towards the syntactic contexts most favourable to producing the *si*-clauses.

Another previous assumption Labov reassessed is the independence of variation based on social stratification and variation based on situational style. Labov (1969c: 22) draws upon John Kenyon's (1948) '... distinction between *cultural levels* and *functional varieties* of English'. Kenyon argued that '... style and class stratification of language are actually independent'. Labov counters that this arrangement would be convenient for identifying speakers, but it is not true, since the same variables are used for both style and social stratification, as demonstrated in his work in New York City. This issue would recur in Labov's work and that of other sociolinguists (Rickford and Eckert, 2001). Such research topics have been investigated repeatedly over the last four decades, including by Labov himself. Labov demonstrates consistency in his research topics over the decades of his work: for example, Labov (2008) is an enhanced and revised version of the questions first raised and explored in Labov (1966a, 1966b).

Along with these critiques of basic assumptions, Labov took note of the changing theoretical positions motivating linguistic study. In *The Study of Nonstandard English*, he writes (1969c: 40):

> Not many years ago, linguists tended to emphasize the differences among the languages of the world and to assert that there was almost no limit to the ways in which languages could differ from each other. Dialectologists concentrated upon the features which differentiated their dialects – naturally, for these are the features which define their object of study.
>
> However, the opposing trend is strong in linguistics today – there is a greater interest in the ways in which languages resemble each other and how they carry out the same functions with similar rules.

In line with this trend, in his outreach work with minority dialects in schools, Labov emphasized the similarities between vernacular varieties and standard varieties. He intended to convince educational professionals to accept the legitimacy of the vernacular varieties. But Labov's underlying interest in diversity resonates with the work of anthropological linguists in the earlier periods of the twentieth century, when descriptive work on Native American languages revealed tremendous diversity, and scholars celebrated this diversity.

With increasing awareness of diversity in language, scholars throughout the twentieth century had noted social correlates of language usage. Studies working towards the aims of sociolinguistics existed decades before the term 'sociolinguistics' appeared.[6] For example, Gesinus Gerardus Kloecke published *De Hollandsche Expansie* in 1927 where he combines language geography, sociology and history. Leonard Bloomfield (1933) relied on this work when crafting his chapter on dialectology. Koerner (1991) presents several other early works that touch upon both language change and society (e.g. Joseph Vendryes, 1925).

But while knowledge from anthropological linguistics has certainly influenced the field of linguistics, and sociolinguistics in particular, Labov does not describe anthropological linguistics as one of the sources of his approach to language change. Labov recognizes the impact and influence of anthropologists like John J. Gumperz (1958) and Dell Hymes (1962), but he identifies his work with linguistics proper.

Clearly, William Labov has worked as a linguist in linguistics. In his publications, he did not attempt to forge a new field. Rather, a new field emerged around him as a result of the political pressures internal to the linguistics at that time. The formalist methodology of syntacticians led to ever more esoteric writings and a continued reliance on extremely small data sets, mostly drawn from data derived by intuitions (Labov, 1996a). These data sets were subject to a linguistic calculus (cf. Port and Leary, 2005) that did not allow for discussion about changes to methodology in data collection or analysis. For this reason, Labov's approach to language change – long a key component of disciplinary linguistics – has come to be known as 'sociolinguistics' rather than simply 'linguistics', as Labov would have preferred.

2.4 THE INTELLECTUAL CLIMATE: LABOV AS A SOCIOLINGUIST

The debate about 'sociolinguistics' as a term was not about the label, but rather about the data, theory and goals to be reached. In the preface to Labov (1966a: v–vi), he writes:

> In the past few years, there has been considerable programmatic discussion of *sociolinguistics* at various meetings and symposia. If this term refers to the use of data from the speech community to solve problems of linguistic theory, then I would agree that it applies to the research described here. But *sociolinguistics* is more frequently used to suggest a new interdisciplinary field – the comprehensive description of the relations of language and society. This seems to me an unfortunate notion, foreshadowing a long series of purely descriptive studies with little bearing on the central theoretical problems of linguistics or of sociology. My own intention was to solve linguistic problems, bearing in mind that these are ultimately problems in the analysis of social behavior: the description of continuous variation, of overlapping and multi-layered phonemic systems; the subjective correlates of linguistic variation; the causes of linguistic differentiation and the mechanism of linguistic change.

Two problems arose in the 1960s related to the term 'sociolinguistics'. First, scholars debated whether the study of language and society should be primarily cast as a field of anthropology, sociology or linguistics. Labov took a clear and unequivocal stance: he studied linguistics, and the term 'sociolinguistics' was not necessary to label the kind of work he did. The second issue with sociolinguistics in the 1960s was that, if it were to be an interdisciplinary field, then how would future students be trained for it? Would anthropology and sociology departments be willing to sacrifice the graduate hours needed to train students in linguistics to produce the scholars required to follow in the footsteps of Dell Hymes, John Gumperz, Emmanuel Schegloff and Erving Goffman (Shuy, 1990: 187)? The divide between academic disciplines can be seen in the names *the sociology of language* and *sociolinguistics*, where *the sociology of language* denoted sociology done through the means of language and *sociolinguistics* denoted linguistics done while maintaining a focus on social factors. Such distinctions were present at the time Labov was entering graduate school: For example, Shuy (1990: 188) reports that Joshua Fishman first taught a Sociology of Language course in 1956 at the University of Pennsylvania.

Labov originally argued against the name 'sociolinguistics', but he recognizes the utility of the term today (Gordon, 2006: 335): '... it turns out that it's useful to approach the field through a subfield; most linguists want to have some form of sociolinguistics taught in their department'. Although the term 'sociolinguistics' is no longer a point of objection for Labov, he reserves the label 'variation and change' for the type of linguistics he practices:

> But today, it seems the actual field we're talking about is best called the study of variation and change. Sociolinguistics is a large and unformed area with many different ways of approaching the subject that aren't necessarily linguistic, whereas the study of variation and change describes pretty well the enterprise we're engaged in.

This differentiation can at times be seen in the subjects of study for summary reference works: the contrast between Blackwell's *The Handbook of Sociolinguistics* and Blackwell's *The Handbook of Language Variation and Change* reveals not only different authors but also different topics and different foci, even within the same topics.

Trudgill (1978: 1) takes the opinion that '... whether you call something sociolinguistics or not does not, in the last analysis, matter very much.' He notes that *sociolinguistics* '... means many different things to many different people.' For Trudgill, the term *sociolinguistics* applies to three different disciplines, each containing different methodologies and objectives (1978: 2): '... those where the objectives are purely sociological or social-scientific; those where they are partly sociological and partly linguistic; and those where the objectives are wholly linguistic.' For Labov and Trudgill (1978: 11), *sociolinguistics* is '... a way of doing linguistics.'

Shuy (1990: 195) pinpoints the creation of sociolinguistics as a scholarly field to 1964 (see, e.g., Bright, 1966; Spolsky this volume).

However, Malkiel (1976: 80 fn. 11) puts the date a decade earlier, arguing for the early 1950s. In any case, the confluence of sociology, anthropology and linguistics, along with realms such as language and education (Hazen, 2007a), developed the topics and methodologies which have now become common for sociolinguistics. For modern sociolinguists who might be dismayed by the unreconciling diversity of sociolinguistic goals, methodologies and cliques, the intellectual atmosphere of this earlier time should be juxtaposed with the scholarly background of the participants. These were scholars from distinct fields who wanted to learn from each other but not become each other. From the beginning of the term 'sociolinguistics', the field has not been unified and was mostly likely at the time not a single field but instead a set of subfields of separate disciplines.

As a named discipline, sociolinguistics was new at the time Labov was conducting his dissertation as a linguist on language change in New York City. The selected proceedings and discussions from a 1964 Conference on Sociolinguistics were published with William Bright as editor (1966). In it, a wide range of language scholars came together from fields including folklore, anthropology, linguistics, dialectology and sociology. The conference showcased renowned scholars such as Henry Hoenigswald, John J. Gumperz, Raven I. McDavid Jr., Dell Hymes, John L. Fischer, William Samarin and Charles Ferguson. Included in this august group was one graduate student, a linguist, William Labov. In editing the proceedings, and as a conference participant, William Bright sets the scene for sociolinguistic research and characterizes several areas still relevant today. Bright (1966: 11) remarks that the term 'sociolinguistics' is not new and that it is hard to precisely define. Bright argues that it is 'excessively vague' to cast the field as dealing with language and society, but that in light of 'modern' linguistics, researchers do view language as well as society to be a structure: 'The sociolinguist's task is then to show the systematic covariance of linguistic structure and social structure – and perhaps even to show a causal relationship in one direction or the other'. Bright also cites as 'pernicious' the traditional linguistic emphasis on the homogeneity of language, opting instead for diversity as the subject matter of sociolinguistics. He reflects on the applications of sociolinguistic work, one of these being within historical linguistics, which is where Bright put Labov's work (Labov, 1966b). Hence, Bright sees Labov's earliest work as the study of language variation and change drawn from descriptive sociolinguistic accounts. At the conclusion of his introduction, Bright (1966: 15) optimistically forecasts that, 'It seems likely that sociolinguistics is entering an era of rapid developments; we may expect that linguistics, sociology, and anthropology will all show the effects'. It is a safe assessment to note that linguistics has had significant programmatic effects from this rapid development. For example, it is now common for major review panels to include a sociolinguist: the advisory panel for the National Science Foundation linguistics programme has a sociolinguistic seat, as does the editorial panel for the Linguistic Society of America's journal *Language*.

At the 1964 Sociolinguistics Conference, McDavid also presented on dialect differences in urban society in general, and Greenville, SC, and Chicago, IL, specifically. A perusal of McDavid's paper and Labov's paper of the same volume provides a succinct comparison of the methodological and rhetorical changes made in the transition from traditional dialectology to variationist sociolinguistics. McDavid's paper is a dialectological narrative, highlighting his own personal judgments of the varieties in question; Labov's paper is based on an empirically-driven statistical analysis. Even though they appear adjacent to each other in print, the two papers seem to be from different decades. Like McDavid, others were concerned with urban dialects before Labov. Pederson (1964) had investigated Chicago using dialectologist methods as used by Kurath and McDavid, but Labov's method for integrating social information and linguistic analysis ultimately resonated more deeply with a wider scholarly audience.

Early commentators noted that Labov's approaches covered numerous fields. In regard to his work with English in the schools, A. Hood Roberts comments that 'his work combines the insights offered by linguistics as well as sociology, pedagogy, and psychology' (Labov, 1969c: iii). Linguists interested in the language of 'real people' and the accountability of theory to data hailed Labov's work and followed suit. The intellectual environment in which Labov presented his version of linguistics was ready for change. Labov comments:

> I found that there were many people who were ready for this approach, not only the quantitative approach but were ready to take social context into effect. That doesn't mean that it suddenly became the mainstream of linguistics, far from it. The approach that we follow in NWAV is still only a part and not at all the dominant part of linguistic studies (Gordon, 2006: 335).

In 1972, the first NWAVE ('New Ways of Analyzing Variation in English') colloquium was held at Georgetown University, in conjunction with the eighth Southeastern Conference on Linguistics, and 64 papers were presented. The resulting volume is dedicated to William Labov:

'who freed us from static analysis' (Bailey and Shuy, 1973). From the early NWAVE proceedings (later changed to NWAV as languages other than English came to be studied), it is clear the variationist enterprise was a call for all linguists interested in variation to come together around a common approach to empirical data, and not necessarily a common area of linguistics. These linguists included semanticians, syntacticians, phonologists, creolists and dialectologists. A separate linguistic profession of 'variationist' does not appear to have been a goal, although it was a term from the outset.

Modern students in linguistics may view Labov's early works as creating sociolinguistics. It would be better to characterize Labov as a linguist whose revision of the study of language change coalesced well with the institutionalization of sociolinguistics into academic organizations such as journals and departments. Sociolinguistics has never been a discrete field of study with a coherent methodology, but instead an academic place to meet, where scholars gather to have worthwhile conversations about society and language. Labov has presented numerous papers to diverse audiences where he made intriguing observations about society. However, for Labov himself, these were by-products of his research on language change.

2.5 LABOV'S PREDECESSORS IN THE STUDY OF VARIATION AND CHANGE

Labov's connection to past scholars who studied language change is strong since he views the problems and solutions of his work as being an organic component of this scholarly history (2001: 10). When he cites Edward Sapir, Franz Bopp and Max Müller, Labov places himself in the tradition of the scholarship they established. In a more connected genealogy, Konrad Koerner (1991) elucidates a lineage between William Dwight Whitney (1827–1894) who influenced Ferdinand de Saussure (1857–1913), who taught Antoine Meillet (1866–1936), who taught André Martinet (1908–1999), who directed at Columbia the MA and PhD theses of Uriel Weinreich (1926–1967), who did the same for William Labov (1927–) at Columbia.

Although Whitney may seem far removed from Labov, Whitney became the major proponent of the uniformitarian principle in linguistics. Borrowed from geology, where it had been influential since 1833, the uniformitarian principle basically states that 'knowledge of processes that operated in the past can be inferred by observing ongoing processes in the present' (from Christy, 1983 cited in Labov, 2001: 21). Whitney, whose brother was a geologist, had argued for the principle in *Language and the Study of Language* (1867), and it is this principle which allowed Labov to study language synchronically and derive diachronic inferences from the data.

Perhaps the best scholarly work to explore Labov's academic roots openly is the coauthored work by Uriel Weinreich, William Labov and Marvin Herzog (1968), *Empirical Foundations for a Theory of Language Change*. In it, the authors project the foundational problems of constraints on language change, transitions of the change through older to younger speakers, embedding of the change in linguistic and social structure, evaluation of social awareness of the change, and the actuation of the change. To tackle language change and move its study towards scientifically-processed empirical foundations, Weinreich, Labov and Herzog had to overthrow revered assumptions of renowned linguists, such as Hermann Paul (1891) and Ferdinand de Saussure (1916 [1972]). Paul had argued for the language of the individual to be the basis for analysis;[7] Paul himself was reacting against *Völkerpsychologie* which took up an ethos of community to be the controlling entity for social action, including language change. Saussure argued for a strict dichotomy between synchronic and diachronic linguistics, with the purpose of establishing synchronic study as the centrepiece of language scholarship. Saussure was reacting against his Neogrammarian predecessors, such as Paul, in an attempt to turn the focus of scholars to language structures as exemplified in the community of speakers. Weinreich, Labov and Herzog argued that these assumptions, especially Paul's isolation of the individual from the group, created paradoxes in the twentieth century about language change.

In this foundational essay, Weinreich, Labov and Herzog also react against the foundational work of generative phonology, e.g. Morris Halle (1962), and argue that '... the generative model for the description of language as a homogenous object is needlessly unrealistic, and we contend that it is quite pointless to construct a theory of change which accepts as input descriptions of language states that are contrary to fact and unnecessarily idealized'. While Noam Chomsky and Halle were publishing *The Sound Pattern of English* in 1968, the branches of linguistics were advancingly rapidly and in quantum leaps; however, the expanding technical machinery of Chomsky and Halle's work did not address the arguments of Weinreich, Labov and Herzog. Scholars in these branches of linguistics made little attempt to reconcile for years to come.

Labov has demonstrated, since this early period, the connection between social factors and language change, but he was not the first to propose this link. Meillet (1905, 1921) had explicated the idea of motivation of language change through social factors, although he and his contemporaries were unable to provide empirical proof of such effects on language change. Shuy (1990: 185) argues that the actual theoretical context of linguistics during the late nineteenth and early twentieth centuries hampered the investigation of social influences. With the advent of linguistic structuralism, the development of systems for linguistic structure allowed for the inclusion of social factors in linguistic analysis, as a place to attach the social meaning found so important in even the most casual of social studies. Labov (1966a: 14) positions Meillet as presenting the right goals for an empirical linguistics in 1905, before others adopted Saussure's exclusive focus on synchronic abstractions after 1913.[8] Koerner (1991: 64) argues that

> Labov's work constitutes a synthesis of earlier attempts at a sociological approach to questions of language change, beginning with Meillet's paper of 1905 (if not much earlier) and dialectological research done in the United States since the 1930s, which in turn goes back to European traditions established during the last quarter of nineteenth century.

Labov also was not the first to combine dialect geography with diachronic analysis: Yakov Malkiel (1976) points out that Jakob Jud, in 1914, wrote of the diffusion of the Latin lexicon, and Ramón Menéndez Pidal, in 1926, combined archival-paleographic research with spatial analysis to investigate primarily phonological and morphological data. Malkiel (1976: 60) also notes that a 'gradual rapprochement' between dialectology and ethnography occurred throughout the twentieth century. Labov does takes his scholarship into one area where Malkiel (1976: 61) criticizes early 'cultural history' language scholars: Labov avoids theoretical weakness and participates in the scholarly '... discussion of what advanced historical research is or should be ...'. Methodological topics were debated between 1920–1950 and became regular benchmarks in Labov's work: the desire for vernacular spontaneity, the value of urban dialects, the network required to capture dialect nuances, the value of different types of speakers (e.g. other than 'pure' dialect speakers), and the expectation of gruelling and time-consuming extensive data collection for the language scholar.

Other linguists who influenced Labov worked on connections between dialectology and structural linguistics. Martinet (1952, 1955) worked towards a programme of structural dialectology. Weinreich (1954) questioned this effort since such a system arrayed discrete structures over an empirical base with much more fluid data (see Port and Leary (2005) for a modern comparison). However, Moulton (1960, 1962) enacted this programme in the description of the geographic distribution of structural variations in the dialects of Swiss German. Moulton's use of structural-dialect geography employed the structures of the phonology, such as phonological gaps, to explain language changes. However, some scholars treated dialectology as if it were exempt from this trend in empirical science: Labov criticizes (1966a: 27) Herbert Pilch (1955) for his lack of empirical data, an 'a-historical' approach, in the historical account of the American vowel system.

From such critiques, the range of ideas and effort needed to drive forward the cross-sectional study of language change became wider as the twentieth century progressed. In reference to Romance language scholarship, Malkiel (1976: 68–9) writes:

> Reconciling large-scale dialectology with the sweeping scope of a full-bodied historical grammar ... and, at the same time, with the tenets of structuralism would, by 1950, have involved a three-way venture far too complex and far too demanding to be undertaken by any individual of lesser status than a genius. Unfortunately, no genius from the ranks of Romance scholars appeared on the scene when one was so desperately needed.

When Labov began his graduate work, in 1961, he faced the kind of triangulation of fields Malkiel notes was so daunting. His success in concurrently tackling academic debates in dialectology, synchronic linguistics and diachronic linguistics is a testament to his genius and determination.

As with other early scholars associated with the foundation of sociolinguistics, such as Roger Shuy for the USA and John Gumperz for India,[9] Labov commanded extensive knowledge of dialectology. His mentor, Uriel Weinreich, directed the project on the *Language and Culture Atlas of Ashkenazic Jewry*.[10] Weinreich (1953, 1954) had also wrestled with how to integrate traditional dialectology with structural linguistics, where he argued that the chasm between structural and dialectological studies was deeper than it ever had been. Yet, Weinreich sees them both as components of linguistics. It is not clear that formal generative grammarians in the next decade would have made the same assumption of the shared basis for those two fields.[11] Labov adopted and modified dialectological interview techniques for his master's thesis about Martha's Vineyard and

his dissertation on the Lower East Side of New York City. Labov states:

> There's no question that the sociolinguistic interview as we practice it today comes out of dialect geography and dialectology. As I listen to the early interviews in Martha's Vineyard, I find a lot of emphasis upon individual words and asking people direct questions about language which came from dialect geography. That's true of the New York City study too. A lot of time was wasted asking people about crullers and pot cheese and other local terms (Gordon, 2006: 336).

Labov's renunciation of some dialectological techniques, while not abandoning dialectology overall, resulted in a changed discipline (see also Labov, 1984). Weinreich himself (1951), in his Columbia dissertation a decade earlier, had initiated his own set of changes in methods which Labov adopted. These changes involved the direct observation of synchronic language and interactions with native experts for Romance, German and Swiss dialects, in order better to understand language change in this area.

Milroy (1980, 1987) argues that Labov's modifications of traditional twentieth century dialectology do not go far enough to document accurately the social influences on language variation patterns (see Vetter, this volume). Specifically, she incorporates social network analysis to study maintenance of vernacular features, demonstrating strong correlations of network quality and vernacular language variation patterns. Embracing the value of this approach, Labov (2001) incorporates these social network analyses into his description of the effects of social factors on language variation.

2.6 LABOV'S CONTRIBUTIONS

Variation, social identity and language change

Labov's 1963 publication of *The social motivation of a sound change*, based on his MA thesis, marked a turning point in the study of language change. Labov began with Sturtevant's (1907) argument that sound change starts in a few words and may then spread by analogy to others of the same class. The change may progress slowly and only end up appearing as a regular process. Labov investigated the variation of the vowels /ay/ and /aw/ and their raised and centralized variants, [ðy] and [ðw], on Martha's Vineyard, an island off the coast of Massachusetts, USA. Labov knew about the history of these vowels and other features of the area from the *Linguistic Atlas of New England* (LANE), and a previous study of some families on the island, hence incorporating dialect study into the study of language change. On this island, the rapidly-changing local economy, from fishing to tourism, strengthened the differentiation of pre-existing social divisions. The native up-islanders resented the outsiders for overshadowing the traditional industry of fishing, in contrast to the down-islanders, who supported the tourists. Labov implemented the apparent-time construct, assessing the percentage of raised, centralized vowels variants against age groups, finding that centralization corresponded with certain age groups. As importantly, he found that positive orientation towards Martha's Vineyard corresponded strongly with centralization: those with positive orientation had a rate of centralized vowel nuclei over 50 per cent higher than those with a negative orientation to the island.

The import from this study was at least two-fold: first, Labov demonstrated that sound change, long assumed to be either cataclysmic or glacially slow, was observable in synchronic variation; second, sound changes were connected to the social forces in a community. These were conceptual turning points in the scientific study of language. These issues continue to resonate with researchers and later studies have re-evaluated the progress of language change on Martha's Vineyard (Blake and Josey, 2003; Pope, Meyerhoff and Ladd, 2007).

Because Labov's doctoral dissertation about variation and change in the Lower East Side of New York City (NYC) (1966a, 2006) was so well designed, it continues to yield a series of compelling arguments about the nature of language variation and change, as well as the methodology for studying it. It marked a turning point in the study of dialects (Becker and Coggshall, 2009). A tremendous wealth of material unfolds from the NYC study. For one thing, it operationalized social categories in new ways. For example, social class is treated in this study as a composite of education and occupation. As a result of this study, the bar for planning a dialect study was set higher than it had ever been before. The NYC study demonstrates how to research linguistic patterns rigorously through empirical observation and analysis. It shows how social factors, such as social class and style shifting, affect language patterns in structured ways. It is characterized by rigorous systematicity in the definition of every variable under study: the phonological variables and their variants; careful delineation of socioeconomic class and the use of information from the Mobilization For Youth survey on education, income and occupation; and the exacting delineation of style, whereby different portions of the

interview are labelled according to channel cues of the speakers. Labov is also concerned with the best representation of his findings in tables and graphs.

The NYC study established the theoretical concept of the 'linguistic variable' (Wolfram, 1991), although the term had been used in Labov (1963). The linguistic variable was originally conceived as a set of semantically-equivalent variants which alternated with each other in the production of a variable context: a variable such as (r) could have two variants, constricted and unconstricted [r], which would be in competition with each other. The benefit of the linguistic variable as a conceptual entity was that variation could be handled in a systematic manner by quantitatively tracking the production of variants in different social and linguistic contexts. The linguistic variable as a theoretical innovation also permitted multivariate quantitative models of language variation, first implemented by Cedergren (1973) (see Tagliamonte (2006) for further discussion).

In the NYC study, Labov attended both to the speech community and to individuals whose linguistic behaviour departed from that of the group. In fact, Labov writes (2006: 157) that one effect that he has hoped for from the NYC study was the inclusion of individuals (such as Nathan B. and Josephine P., both subjects of analysis in the study) in other sociolinguistic analyses. However, most sociolinguistic studies have shied away from thorough studies of individuals. Following his own advice, in Labov (2001) he searched for the leaders of language change (2001: 500) as one approach to understanding the causes and motivations for language change. Of these leaders, he writes, 'The history of our leaders of linguistic change is a history of nonconformity, and their sociolinguistic position is a display of nonconformity' (2001: 410).

The thoroughness of Labov's work is reflected in the appendices to his published dissertation. For most sociolinguists, if potential subjects say they do not want to be interviewed, that is the end of their role in the study. Labov persisted beyond these initial rejections. Under a different guise, he conducted telephone interviews with 33 subjects who had refused to be interviewed in person: Out of a total of 195 potential subjects for the American Language Survey (ALS) study,[12] 122 were interviewed; of the 73 refusals, 33 were called on the telephone and surveyed about their TV reception in the area, gathering data on the variables in question. Labov presents the results from an analysis of these 33 speakers' language in Appendix D (Labov, 2006). In another appendix, Labov presents results from 37 ALS interviews with non-native New Yorkers. For Labov, they were another opportunity to view the speech community, and hence language, from a new perspective. Additionally, Labov provides the results from experiments designed to assess the social evaluation of language by NYC residents. Labov emphasizes that experiments are needed to study normative behaviour, necessary to understand the grammar of the speech community in an effort to study language change.

The linguistic variable and the variable rule

The variable rule was officially introduced in Labov (1969a), but the machinery for it, the linguistic variable,[13] was theoretically integrated into the study of language in Weinreich, Labov and Herzog (1968: 167).[14] Earlier scholars (e.g. Harris, 1951) had discussed 'variants', but these were not seen as part of a coherent system regulated by a linguistic module in the mental grammar (i.e. a variable). In the NYC study, Labov (1966a) analyzed five variables, orthographically distinguished from phonemes via parentheses: (r), (æh), (oh), (th), (dh). Although the term 'linguistic variable' was used in Labov (1963), the notations for it were still represented as phonemes (e.g. /ay/) and the variants as allophones [ay].

Labov's 1969a article on copula deletion used the formal logic of contemporary generative grammar and helped to bring variable rules into mainstream linguistics. Labov (1969a: 737 fn. 20) describes the advantage of variable rules over the concept of free variation. Hazen (2007b), Green (2007) and Guy (2007) highlight a few of the areas of more traditional linguistic fields where quantitative formalizations of empirical observations have become a standard for evaluating the validity of scholarship. Labov (1969a) applied the concept of the variable rule to the copula absence described in Labov et al. (1968). Notably, social factors did not play a role but were separately considered in Labov (1969a), in contrast to Weinreich et al. (1968: 170) where the formula for the linguistic variable included '... linguistic or extralinguistic ...' factors. Fasold (1991) argues that Labov's theoretical choice to consider linguistic factors separately from social factors is the most productive manner for analyzing linguistic variation. In addition, one of the initial stipulations of variable rules was that categorical application of a regular linguistic rule was constrained by variable input (1969a: 738). However, the variable rule has fallen out of favour since that time. Fasold (1991) notes that scholars have largely abandoned variable rules as a descriptive mechanism, although the construct of the variable is widely used.

Perhaps the most accepted and lasting import of the variable rule is the principle of accountability

(Labov 1969). Labov (1969a: fn20; 1972b: 72) states (small caps removed):

> That any variable form (a member of a set of alternative ways of 'saying the same thing') should be reported with the proportion of cases in which the form did occur in the relevant environment, compared to the total number of cases in which it might have occurred.

This principle is a basic, and unquestioned, part of variationist methodology today, but at the time, Labov was guarding against scholars picking and choosing data to conveniently (retro)fit their theories.

Another significant work in this regard, and one of the ones which placed nonstandard dialects in the focus of linguistic analysis, was Labov's work on negation. Labov (1972d) compares the standard English negation of *any* with three kinds of negative transfer in Black English: negative attraction to subject *any* (e.g. **Anybody doesn't go → Nobody goes*), negative postposing to indeterminates (e.g. *She doesn't like anything → He likes nothing*), and negative concord (e.g. *They don't like anything → They don't like nothing*). Labov's paper is an analysis of data drawn from Labov et al. (1968),[15] working from contemporary assumptions about deep and surface structure, and even incorporating the formal linguistic methods of abstracted intuitions and grammaticality judgments with variationist methodology: 'In this and other studies, we combine the abstract analysis of our intuitive data with naturalistic observation of language in use, and supplement this with experimental tests of well-defined variables' (Labov, 1972d: 775). Although he does bring some diachronic concerns into play, his main focus is the morphological realm of the synchronic state of Black English. Buchstaller (2009) discusses updates and current debates about Labov's methods for quantifying the variable with variation beyond phonology: 'In variationist sociolinguistics, this procedure is referred to as 'clos[ing] the set that defines the variable' (Labov 1996a: 78), which is especially important when working with more complex variables, which (morpho-) syntactic variables and discourse variables often are.

After Labov (1966a), scholars empirically studying language variation and change have conceptualized variation in terms of sociolinguistic variables. For Labov, the search for variables was not the cumulative goal, however. Labov (2006: 32) decries the 'peculiar practice' of dissertating students searching for a variable to study, rather than attempting to study the synchronic variation and ongoing diachronic variation of a speech community. For Labov, the exacting empirical description of the speech community's linguistic system was the main point. The variables were only means to that end.

Labov's work in education

Reflecting the educational concerns and larger social troubles of the 1960s, A. Hood Roberts, in Labov (1969c: iii), notes that '... the urgency of the need for a new research approach and solutions became prominent during the last decade as a result of massive social problems'. The motivation for defending minority varieties of English came from attacks on these varieties by educational scholars who promoted '... the explicit assumption that 'the language of culturally deprived children ... is not merely an underdeveloped version of standard English, but is basically a non-logical mode of expressive behavior' (Labov 1969c: 47). The subtlety of Labov's linguistic assessment combined with his sociopolitical critique established him as the linguist with the final word: minority dialects are both logical and fully developed forms of language.

Much of Labov's educational writing was based on work done in Harlem by a collaborative team he directed. This work was one of the first scholarly efforts to describe minority speech communities in the USA. As Lavandera (1989: 4) notes, numerous scholars, including Dell Hymes (see Johnstone and Marcellino, this volume), were calling for a socially-realistic linguistics at the time. The research team of William Labov, Paul Cohen, Clarence Robins and John Lewis undertook such a project between 1965 and 1967 with the goals being

> ... to determine (1) differences in the structure of non-standard Negro English (NNE) and standard English (SE), and (2) differences in the ways in which speakers of these dialects use language, with emphasis on the speech events, verbal skills, and social controls which govern the development of the vernacular (Labov et al., 1968).

With this study, they were directly providing an empirical argument against the widespread educational belief in the 'culturally deprived' child. The basic premise was that children who did not receive cultural enrichment similar to (white) middle-class families were not able to handle the requirements of school and therefore were destined to failure. For example, Fred M. Hechinger, the Education Editor of the *New York Times*, wrote, 'All the evidence today indicates that children from a home background that not only is economically and socially at the lowest level but lacks family orientation toward formal learning

are virtually excluded from success in school' (1966: 2).

The main area of deprivation on which scholars focused was language. Scholars in education did not believe that either the language or the social environment fostering language worked well or at all: '... the slum home is a place of little opportunity for infants to talk, question, and seek answers' (Hechinger, 1966). Carl Bereiter, Siegfried Engelman, Jean Osborn and Philip A. Reidford presented a study, based on assumptions from two works – *Negro Intelligence and Selective Migration* (Lee, 1951) and *Early Education of the Mentally Retarded* (Kirk, 1958) – where they argue that 'culturally deprived' children did not think because their language was so deprived that they could not think. Their solution was for the preschool to lay the foundations of language logic directly. They write (Hechinger, 1966: 105), '... culturally deprived children do not just think at an immature level: many of them do not think at all'. It is clear, in Bereiter et al.'s article, that the narrative categorization of speech is essential to distinguish thought from 'non-thought' (Hechinger, 1966: 107):

> They are oblivious of even the most extreme discrepancies between their actions and statements as they follow one another in a series. They do not just give bad explanations. They can not give explanations at all, nor do they seem to have any idea of what it is to explain an event. The question and answer process which is the core of orderly thinking is completely foreign to most of them.

In reaction to such opinions, Labov, Cohen, Robins and Lewis (1968) presented a two-volume report (732 pages) empirically refuting the foundational assumptions of the culturally-deprived view of language. From this work came Labov's *Logic of Nonstandard English* (1969b; see also Labov, 1972a), which presented Labov's view to a greatly expanded audience.

Labov's interest in narrative was fuelled in part by educational scholars' ignorance about the systematic nature of spontaneous, vernacular talk.[16] In Labov and Waletsky (1967), republished in 1997, Labov set out to provide a formal characterization of personal experience narratives, using narratives collected on Martha's Vineyard and in New York in the course of his sociolinguistic interviews. Labov's study of narrative tried to understand vernacular speakers in context. In a very influential paper called 'The Logic of Non-Standard English', Labov (1969b: 54) describes narrative interactions between students and teachers. The narratives of the non-standard speakers, often seen by educators as illogical or incoherent, are recast by Labov as clear expressions in a rule-governed system. Using the logical formalizations of the linguistics of the time, he argues for the legitimacy of non-standard English, by showing that African-American students' narratives are in some ways more logical than those of White adults (Labov 1969b: 55).

2.7 REFINING HIS RESEARCH

Since 1994, Labov has published two tomes in the three-volume set entitled *Principles of Linguistic Change* (Labov 1994, 2001). Volume I[17] deals with internal factors, predominantly drawing from work begun for Labov, Yaeger and Steiner (1972), the Linguistic Change and Variation project conducted in Philadelphia and eastern Pennsylvania from 1973 to 1979, and the work of Herold (1990) and Poplack (1979, 1980a, 1980b). Volume I predominantly explores the linguistic mechanics of vowel mergers and chain shifts. Volume II[18] deals with social factors, incorporating the findings of the internal factors developed in Volume I. Volume II explores stable and changing linguistic variables, neighbourhoods and ethnicity, gender, age and social class, while portraying the leaders of linguistic change and charting their defining characteristics. It also explores how scholars solve the problems of transmission, incrementation and continuation of linguistic change.[19]

In 2006, Labov, Sharon Ash and Charles Boberg published *The Atlas of North American English*.[20] The authors and a team of researchers collected data from 762 speakers over the telephone in reading passages, word lists and more casual interviews. Four hundred and thirty-nine of the interviews underwent acoustic analysis. Their major goals were to delimit the dialect areas of North America, primarily on the basis of speakers' vowel systems, and to take account of the 'mechanism, the causes, and the consequences of linguistic change' (Labov et al., 2006: v). This atlas takes up boundaries of perception as well as production in its search for sound changes in progress. Vowels had been part of traditional dialectology's repertoire of tools for deciding dialect boundaries, but Labov and his colleagues have greatly enhanced the acoustic analysis of vowel systems in dialectological work.[21] By analysing the entire orchestra of vowels, their movements and pressures, Labov, Ash and Boberg describe fine linguistic distinctions amongst large geographic regions. Their work represents a comprehensive sketch of English in North America, and they encourage other scholars to complete their sketch with studies of local communities.

2.8 CONCLUSION

As seen in his most recent interview (Gordon, 2006: 338), Labov continues to search for the comprehensive principles he can find for language: for example, principles of chain shifting (Labov, 1994: 116) or social principles such as the Nonconformity Principle (Labov, 2001: 516). The impact of Labov's efforts should also be assessed by their effect on how linguistic scholarship is conducted. Perhaps the most rewarding component of his legacy has been his impact on his students at the University of Pennsylvania and the many students he has assisted from around the world. Labov's former students are themselves highly productive and innovative language scholars.

Despite his sweeping influence as teacher and scholar, the conglomerate field of sociolinguistics is not uniformly a Labovian field. In the introduction to Volume I of the *Principles of Linguistic Change*, Labov remarks that his view of theorizing may not be in line with that of other students of sociolinguistics who argue for a 'sociolinguistic theory'. Labov (1994: 4) does not attempt to model all possible relations between past and present language systems, but leans towards approaches in sciences like biology and geology, proceeding '... steadily from the known to the unknown, enlarging the sphere of our knowledge on the foundation of observation and experiment in a cumulative manner' (1994: 5). This approach is in contrast to making more general statements (theories) and then **deducing** from them expectations of what can be found in certain communities. Labov instead works towards finding an explanation based on internal factors of linguistic change, an explanation which must ultimately '... find its causes in a domain outside of linguistics: in physiology, acoustic phonetics, social relations, perceptual or cognitive capacities' (1994: 5). It is towards this end of explanation that Labov has guided his work for over four decades.

NOTES

1   As with any historical view of an ongoing academic endeavor (Hazen, 2007a, 2007b), this chapter is one scholar's perspective. It should therefore be read as an interpretation and, accordingly, part of a larger conversation about how the fields analyzing language in society have developed.

2   Labov cites for the 'precise statement' concerning 'idiolects' Zellig Harris's (1951: 9) *Methods in Structural Linguistics*: 'These investigations are carried out for the speech of one particular person,

or one community of dialectally identical persons, at a time ... '.

3   As part of this debate, Uriel Weinreich wrote a review of Hockett's (1958) *A Course in Modern Linguistics* where Hockett creatively reiterated Bloomfield's view. Weinreich argued that a view which holds up changes in the past as theoretically interesting in contrast to current change is neither sufficient nor necessary (Weinreich, 1959).

4   Although perhaps not a direct influence, the work of Kenneth Burke (1969) on identification should be part of future scholarship on the history of the study of language and self since that work has connections with Labov's on several levels.

5   Lavandera (1988) asserts that Labov (1969a) and (1972g) focus on the systematicity of performance in contrast to the systematicity of competence. I disagree with that assertion. I suspect Labov viewed the boundary between the two as illusory and as simply a fabrication to allow for weak data. Labov's search for robust data in the speech community (abstracted from the grammar of the individual and hence not the grammar of an idiolect) does not fit the profile of performance as Chomsky (1965) describes it (cf. also Jackendoff 2002 for a critique of Chomskyan performance).

6   Most assessors of linguistic history (e.g. Koerner, 1991: 65) put the first use of the English term *sociolinguistics* at 1952 by Haver C. Curie (1952).

7   Weinreich, Labov and Herzog use the term 'idiolect' throughout the chapter, but the term 'idiolect' was not in print until 1948 (Hazen, 2006).

8   Labov at times contextualizes previous scholars in his own line of thought through his translations of their work. For example, he translates (2006: 11) the following line to have **variables** as the noun whereas Meillet has **variable conditions**: 'car il resterait à découvrir les conditions variables qui permettent ou provoquent la réalization des possiblités ainsi reconnues' (Meillet, 1921: 16–17).

9   Although Gumperz is renowned for his work with dialects of India, his dissertation focused on a Swabian dialect (German) of third-generation farmers in Michigan. Hence, Gumperz, who studied at the University of Michigan, has his roots, in part, in American dialectology.

10   Labov, in Gordon (2006: 334), argues that 'If Weinreich had lived, I think two things would have happened. Studies of languages in contact would be pursued much more vigorously as a part of sociolinguistics. And, most important, dialect geography would have advanced much more strongly in the past forty years'.

11   Although the contrast between 'generative grammarians' and sociolinguists is sometimes made, many scholars of language variation and change also assume that a mental grammar generates a potentially infinite set of utterances. Variationists just

contest the assumptions of categoricity and the resulting methodological choices (see Chambers, 2003).

12   The American Language Survey was the basis for Labov (1966a).

13   Weinreich et al. (1968: 167) write: 'To account for such intimate variation, it is necessary to introduce another concept into the mode of orderly heterogeneity which we are developing here: the "linguistic variable"– a variable element within the system controlled by a single rule'. The term 'variable rule' does come up in footnote 56 on page 170, but it is presented without comment.

14   Although, in section 3.21 on Coexistent Systems, Weinreich, Labov and Herzog (1968: 159) discuss forms from different language systems (in one speaker):

> In terms of the model of a differentiated language system that we are developing, such forms share the following properties: (1) They offer alternative means of 'saying the same thing': that is, for each utterance in *A* there is a corresponding utterance in *B* which provides the same referential information (is synonymous) and cannot be differentiated except in terms of the over-all significance which marks the use of *B* as against *A*.

15   Labov's (1972d) paper had first been presented in 1968 at the LSA winter meeting.

16   Labov and Fanshel (1977) take up a different track of narrative analysis by analysing a psychologist's doctor–patient relations.

17   Reviewed by Kretzschmar (1996).

18   Reviewed by Kretzschmar (2005).

19   Volume III is in progress at the time of writing. The draft chapters are available at: http://www.ling.upenn.edu/phonoatlas/PLC3/PLC3.html.

20   This book is reviewed in Bailey (2007). Some critics view this work as a return to traditional dialectology, with a lack of representative sampling in any one area.

21   See Thomas (2001) for a discussion of Labov's influence.

REFERENCES

Bailey, R. W. (2007) 'The greatest atlas ever', *American Speech*, 82(4): 292–300.

Bailey, C.-J. N. and Shuy, R. W. (eds) (1973) *New Ways of Analyzing Variation in English*. Washington, DC: Georgetown University Press.

Bamberg, M. G. W. (ed.) (1997) 'Oral versions of personal experience: three decades of narrative analysis', *Journal of Narrative and Life History*, (7): 1–4.

Becker, K. and Coggshall, E. (2009) 'The Sociolinguistics of Ethnicity in New York City'. *Language and Linguistics Compass* 3/3 751–766, 10.1111/j.1749-818x.2009.00138.x

Bereiter, C., Engelman, S., Osborn, J. and Reidford, P. A. (1966) 'An academically oriented pre-school for culturally deprived children', in F. M. Hechinger (ed.), *Pre-school Education Today*. Garden City, NY: Doubleday. pp. 105–36.

Blake, R. and Josey, M. (2003) 'The layl diphthong in a Martha's Vineyard community: What can we say 40 years after Labov?' *Language in Society*, 32: 451–85.

Bloch, B. and Trager, G. L. (1942) *Outline of Linguistic Analysis*. Baltimore: Linguistic Society of America.

Bloomfield, L. (1933) *Language*. New York: Holt, Rinehart, and Winston.

Bright, W. (ed.) (1966) *Sociolinguistics: Proceedings of the UCLA Sociolinguistics Conference, 1964*. The Hague: Mouton.

Buchstaller, I. (2009) 'The Quantitative Analysis of Morpho-syntactic Variation: Constructing and Quantifying the Denominator'. *Language and Linguistics Compass* 3/4: 1010–33, 10.1111/j.1749-818x.2009.00142.x

Burke, K. (1969) *A Grammar of Motives*. Berkeley, CA: University of California Press.

Campbell-Kibler, K. (2007) 'Accent, (ING), and the social logic of listener perceptions', *American Speech*, 82: 32–64.

Cedergren, H. J. (1973) 'On the nature of variable constraints', in C-J. N. Bailey and R. W. Shuy (eds), *New Ways of Analyzing Variation in English*. Washington, DC: Georgetown University Press. pp. 13–22.

Chambers, J., Trudgill, P. and Schilling-Estes, N. (eds.) (2002) *The Handbook of Language Variation and Change*. Malden, MA: Blackwell.

Chambers, J. K. (2003) *Sociolinguistic Theory*. 2nd edn. Malden, MA: Blackwell.

Chomsky, N. (1965) *Aspects of the Theory of Syntax*. Cambridge, MA: MIT Press.

Chomsky, N. and Halle, M. (1968) *The Sound Pattern of English*. New York: Harper and Row.

Curie, H. C. (1952) 'A projection of socio-linguistics: the relationship of speech to social status', *Southern Speech Journal*, (18): 28–37.

Fasold, R. W. (1991) 'The quiet demise of variable rules', *American Speech*, 66: 3–21.

Fischer, J. L. (1958) 'Social influence on the choice of a linguistic variant', *Word*, 14: 47–56.

Gordon, M. J. (2006) 'Interview with William Labov', *Journal of English Linguistics*, 34(4): 332–51.

Green, L. J. (2007) 'Syntactic Variation', in R. Bayley and C. Lucas (eds), *Sociolinguistic Variation*. New York: Cambridge University Press. pp. 24–44.

Gumperz, J. J. (1958) 'Dialect differences and social stratifica-tion in a North Indian village', *American Anthropologist*, 60: 668–82.

Guy, G. R. (2007) 'Variation and phonological theory', in R. Bayley and C. Lucas (eds), *Sociolinguistic Variation*. New York: Cambridge University Press. pp. 5–23.

Hagen, A. M. (1988a) 'Dutch dialectology: the national and the international perspective', *Historiographia Linguistica*, 15: 263–87.

Hagen, A. M. (1988b) 'Sociolinguistic aspects in dialectology', in U. Ammon, D. Norbert and K. J. Mattheier (eds), *Sociolinguistics/soziolinguistik: an International Handbook of the Science of Language and Society*. Berlin: Mouton de Gruyter.

Halle, M. (1962) 'Phonology in generative grammar', *Word*, 18: 54–72.

Harris, Z. (1951) *Methods in Structural Linguistics*. Chicago: University of Chicago Press.

Hazen, K. (2006) 'IN/ING Variable', in K. Brown (ed.), *Encyclopedia of Language and Linguistics*. 2nd edn. Oxford: Elsevier. pp. 581–4.

Hazen, K. (2007a) 'Variationist approaches to language & edu-cation', in N. Hornberger and K. King (eds), *The Encyclopedia of Language and Education. Volume 10: Research Methods in Language and Education*. 2nd edn. pp. 85–98.

Hazen, K. (2007b) 'The study of variation in historical perspective', in R. Bayley and C. Lucas (eds), *Sociolinguistic Variation*. New York: Cambridge University Press. pp. 70–89.

Hazen, K. (2008) '(ING): a vernacular baseline for English in Appalachia', *American Speech*, 83(2): 116–40.

Hechinger, F. M. (ed.) (1966) 'An academically oriented pre-school for culturally deprived children', in *Pre-school Education Today*. Garden City, NY: Doubleday.

Herold, R. (1990) 'Mechanisms of merger: the implementation and distribution of the low back merger in Eastern Pennsylvania'. University of Pennsylvania dissertation.

Hock, H. H. and Joseph, B. D. (1996) *Language History, Language Change, and Language Relationship*. New York: Mouton de Gruyter.

Hymes, D. (1962) 'The ethnography of speaking', in T. Gladwin and W. C. Sturtevant (eds), *Anthropology and Human Behavior*. Washington, DC: Anthropological Society of Washington. pp. 13–53.

Jackendoff, R. (2002) *Foundations of Language*. New York: Oxford University Press.

Kenyon, J. (1948) 'Cultural levels and functional varieties of English', *College English*, 10: 31–6.

Kirk, S. A. (1958) *Early Education of the Mentally Retarded*. Urbana, IL: University of Illinois Press.

Klima, E. (1964) 'Relatedness between grammatical systems', *Language*, 40: 1–30.

Kloecke, G. G. (1927) *De Hollandsche expansie in de zestiende en zeventiende eeuw en haar weerspiegeling in de hedendaagsche Nederlandsche dialecten*. The Hague: Nijhoff.

Koerner, K. (1991) 'Toward a history of modern sociolinguistics', *American Speech*, 66(1): 57–70.

Kretzschmar, W. A., Jr. (1996) 'A glass half empty, a glass half full', *American Speech*, 71(2): 198–205.

Kretzschmar, W. A., Jr. (2005) 'The Philadelphia story', *American Speech*, 80(3): 321–30.

Labov, W. (1963) 'The social motivation of language change', *Word*, 19: 273–309.

Labov, W. (1966a) *The Social Stratification of English in New York City*. Washington, DC: Center for Applied Linguistics.

Labov, W. (1966b) 'Hypercorrection by the lower middle class as a factor in linguistic change', in W. Bright (ed.), *Sociolinguistics: Proceedings of the UCLA Sociolinguistics Conference, 1964*. The Hague: Mouton. pp. 84–101.

Labov, W. (1969a) 'Contraction, deletion, and inherent variability of the English copula', *Language*, 45: 715–62.

Labov, W. (1969b) 'The logic of non-standard English', in
J. Alatis (ed.), *Linguistics and the Teaching of Standard
English to Speakers of Other Languages and Dialects.
Georgetown University Round Table on Languages and
Linguistics 1969*. Washington, DC: Georgetown University
Press. pp. 1–44.

Labov, W. (1969c) *The Study of Nonstandard English*.
Washington, DC: Center for Applied Linguistics.

Labov, W. (1972a) 'Academic ignorance and Black intelligence', *The Atlantic Monthly*, 229: 59–67.

Labov, W. (1972b) *Language in the Inner City: Studies in the
Black English vernacular*. Philadelphia: University of
Pennsylvania Press.

Labov, W. (1972c) 'The linguistic consequences of being a
lame', in *Language in the Inner City*. Philadelphia: University
of Pennsylvania Press. pp. 255–92.

Labov, W. (1972d) 'Negative attraction and negative concord
in English grammar', *Language*, 48: 773–818.

Labov, W. (1972e) 'Rules for ritual insults', in T. Kochman
(ed.), *Rappin' and Stylin' Out: Communication in Urban
Black America*. Champaign-Urbana, IL: University of Illinois
Press. pp. 265–314.

Labov, W. (1972f) 'The social stratification of (r) in New York
City department stores', in William Labov, *Sociolinguistic
Patterns*. Philadelphia: University of Pennsylvania Press.
pp. 43–69.

Labov, W. (1972g) *Sociolinguistic Patterns*. Philadelphia:
University of Pennsylvania Press.

Labov, W. (1972h) 'Some principles of linguistic methodology',
Language in Society, 1: 97–120.

Labov, W. (1972i) 'The study of language in its social context',
in W. Labov (ed.), *Sociolinguistic Patterns*. Philadelphia:
University of Pennsylvania Press. pp. 183–259.

Labov, W. (1980) 'The social origins of sound change', in
W. Labov (ed.), *Locating Language in Time and Space*.
New York: Academic Press. pp. 251–65.

Labov, W. (1982) 'Objectivity and commitment in linguistic
science', *Language in Society*, 11: 165–201.

Labov, W. (1984) 'Field methods of the project on linguistic
change and variation', in J. Baugh and J. Sherzer (eds),
Language in Use: Readings in Sociolinguistics. Englewood
Cliffs, NJ: Prentice Hall. pp. 28–53.

Labov, W. (1988) 'The judicial testing of linguistic theory', in D.
Tannen (ed.), *Linguistics in Context: Connecting Observation
and Understanding*. Norwood, NJ: Ablex. pp. 159–82.

Labov, W. (1989) 'The child as linguistic historian', *Language
Variation and Change*, 1: 85–97.

Labov, W. (1990) 'The intersection of sex and social class in
the course of linguistic change', *Language Variation and
Change*, 2: 205–54.

Labov, W. (1991) 'The three dialects of English', in P. Eckert
(ed.), *New Ways of Analyzing Sound Change*. New York:
Academic Press. pp. 1–44.

Labov, W. (1994) *Principles of Linguistic Change*, Vol. 1:
Internal factors. Oxford: Blackwell.

Labov, W. (1996) 'When intuitions fail', in L. McNair,
K. Singer, L. Dolbrin and M. Aucon (eds), *Papers from the
Parasession on Theory and Data in Linguistics*. Chicago:
Chicago Linguistic Society 32. pp. 77–106.

Labov, W. (1997) 'How I got into linguistics'. http://www.ling.
upenn.edu/~wlabov/Howlgot.html

Labov, W. (1998) 'Co-existent systems in African-American
English', in S. Mufwene, J. R. Rickford, G. Bailey and
J. Baugh (eds), *African-American English*. London:
Routledge.

Labov, W. (2001) *Principles of Linguistic Change*, Vol 2:
External factors. Oxford: Blackwell.

Labov, W. (2006) *The Social Stratification of English in New
York City*. 2nd edn. New York: Cambridge University Press.

Labov, W. (2008) 'Transmission and diffusion', *Language*,
83(2): 344–87.

Labov, W. and Ash, S. (1997) 'Understanding Birmingham', in
C. Bernstein, T. Nunnally and R. Sabino (eds), *Language
Variety in the South Revisited*. Tuscaloosa, AL: University of
Alabama Press. pp. 508–73.

Labov, W. and Fanshel, D. (1977) *Therapeutic Discourse:
Psychotherapy as Conversation*. New York: Academic Press.

Labov, W. and Waletsky, J. (1967) 'Narrative analysis: oral
versions of personal experience', in J. Helm (ed.), *Essays on
the Verbal and Visual Arts: Proceedings of the 1966 Annual
Spring Meeting of the American Ethnological Society*.
Seattle: University of Washington Press. pp. 12–44.

Labov, W., Ash, S. and Boberg, C. (2006) *The Atlas of North
American English: Phonetics, Phonology, and Sound
Change*. New York: Mouton de Gruyter.

Labov, W., Cohen, P., Robins, C. and Lewis, J. (1968) *A study
of Non-Standard English of Negro and Puerto Rican
speakers in New York City*. 2 vols. Philadelphia: US
Regional Survey.

Labov, W., Karen, M. and Miller, C. (1991) 'Near-mergers and
the suspension of phonemic contrast', *Language Variation
and Change*, 3: 33–74.

Labov, W., Yaeger, M. and Steiner, R. (1972) *A Quantitative
Study of Sound Change in Progress*. Philadelphia: US
Regional Survey.

Lavandera, B. R. (1975) 'Linguistic structure and sociolinguis-
tic conditioning in the use of verbal endings in "si" Clauses
(Buenos Aires Spanish)'. PhD dissertation, University of
Pennsylvania.

Lavandera, B. R. (1989) 'The study of language in its sociocultural context,' in Frederick J. Newmeyer (ed.), *Linguistics:
the Cambridge Survey: Vol. 4, Language: The Socio-
Cultural Context*. Cambridge: Cambridge University Press.
pp. 1–13.

Lee, E. S. (1951) 'Negro intelligence and selective migration: a
Philadelphia test of the Klineberg hypothesis', *American
Sociological Review*, 16: 227–33.

Kirk, S. A. (1958) *Early Education of the Mentally Retarded*.
Urbana, IL: University of Illinois Press.

McDavid, R. I., Jr. (1966) 'Dialect differences and social differences in an urban society', in W. Bright (ed.), *Sociolinguistics:
Proceedings of the UCLA Sociolinguistics Conference,
1964*. The Hague: Mouton. pp. 72–83.

Malkiel, Y. (1976) 'From romance philology through dialect
geography to sociolinguistics', *International Journal of the
Sociology of Language*, 9: 59–84.

Martinet, A. (1952) 'Function, structure, and sound change', *Word*, 8: 1–32.

Martinet, A. (1955) *Economie des Changements Phonétiques*. Berne: Francke.

Meillet, A. (1905) 'Comment les mots changent de sens', *Année Sociologique*, 9: 1–38.

Meillet, A. (1921) *Linguistique Histoire et Linguistique Générale*. 2 vols. Paris: Société de Linguistique.

Milroy, L. (1980) *Language and Social Networks*. Oxford: Basil Blackwell.

Milroy, L. (1987) *Observing and Analysing Natural Language*. Oxford: Blackwell.

Moulton, W. G. (1960) 'The short vowel system of Northern Switzerland: a study in structural dialectology', *Word*, 16: 155–83.

Moulton, W. G. (1962) 'Dialect geography and the concept of phonological space', *Word*, 18: 23–32.

Paul, H. (1891) *Principles of the History of Language*. (Revised and translated by Herbert A. Strong from the 1890 edition). New York: Longman, Green.

Pederson, L. (1964) 'The pronunciation of English in Chicago: consonants and vowels'. PhD dissertation, University of Chicago.

Pilch, H. (1955) 'The rise of the American English vowel pattern', *Word*, 11: 57–93.

Pope, J., Meyerhoff, M. and Ladd, D. R. (2007) 'Forty years of language change on Martha's Vineyard', *Language*, 83(3): 615–27.

Poplack, S. (1979) 'Function and process in a variable phonology'. PhD dissertation, University of Pennsylvania.

Poplack, S. (1980a) 'Deletion and disambiguation in Puerto Rican Spanish', *Language*, 56: 371–85.

Poplack, S. (1980b) 'The notion of plural in Puerto Rican Spanish: competing constraints on /s/ deletion', in W. Labov (ed.), *Locating language in Time and Space*. New York: Academic Press. pp. 55–68.

Port, R. F. and Leary, A. P. (2005) 'Against formal phonology', *Language*, 81(4): 927–64.

Read, A. W. (2002) 'Milestones in the history of English in America', in R. W. Bailey (ed.), *Publications of the American Dialect Society 86*. Durham, NC: Duke University Press.

Rickford, J. R. and Eckert, P. (2001) *Style and Sociolinguistic Variation*. New York: Cambridge UP.

Sapir. E. (1921) *Language, an Introduction to the Study of Speech*. New York: Harcourt, Brace, and Company.

Saussure, F. (1972 [1916]) *Cours de linguistique générale*. Paris: Payot.

Shuy, R. W. (1965) *Social Dialects and Language Learning*. Champaign, IL: NCTE.

Shuy, R. W. (1990) 'A brief history of American Sociolinguistics, 1949–1989', in F. P. Dinneen and E. F. K. Koerner (eds), *North American Contributions to the History of Linguistics*. Philadelphia: Benjamins. pp. 183–209.

Tagliamonte, S. (2006) *Analysing Sociolinguistic Variation*. New York. Cambridge University Press.

Thomas, E. (2001) *An Acoustic Analysis of Vowel Variation in New World English*. Publication of the American Dialect Society 85. Durham, NC: Duke University Press.

Trudgill, P. (ed.) (1978) *Sociolinguistic Patterns in British English*. London: Edward Arnold.

Vendryes, J. (1925) *Language: A Linguistic Introduction to History*. Tr. P. Radin. London: Routledge.

Weinreich, U. (1951) 'Research problems in bilingualism, with special regard to Switzerland'. PhD dissertation. Columbia University.

Weinreich, U. (1953) *Languages in Contact: Problems and Findings*. New York: Linguistic Circle of New York.

Weinreich, U. (1954) 'Is a structural dialectology possible?', *Word*, 10: 388–400.

Weinreich, U. (1959) Review of Charles F. Hockett's *A Course in Modern Linguistics. Romance Philology*, XIII: 329–32.

Weinreich, U., Labov, W. and Herzog, M. (1968) *Empirical Foundations for a Theory of Language Change*, in W. P. Lehmann and Y. Malkiel (eds), *Directions for Historical Linguistics: A Symposium*. Austin, TX: University of Texas Press.

Whitney, W. D. (1867) *Language and the Study of Language*. New York: Scribner.

Wolfram, W. (1991) 'The linguistic variable: fact and fantasy', *American Speech*, 66: 22–32.

3

Bernstein: Codes and Social Class[1]

Gabrielle Ivinson

3.1 INTRODUCTION

Basil Bernstein introduced the origins of his lifetime's work as a sociologist in the first volume of *Class, Codes and Control* (CCC), published in 1971. His personal history begins with mention of the period 1939–45, alluding to his Jewish background and immigrant status. He started his career as a resident worker at the Bernhard Baron Settlement in Stepney, London (1971: 2) where he ran clubs for boys aged between 9 and 18 years old. Bernstein noted that the boys in the club often held values that were in conflict to those held by more senior members of staff in the Settlement. He also noted the differences between Reform Judaism that informed practices within the Settlement and Orthodox Judaism practised by members of the community that the Settlement served. Bernstein became interested in the ways factions within what may appear to be homogeneous groups maintained contrasting values and how these were passed down across time as a social 'genetic code'. His experiences in the Settlement gave him a strong insight into 'the structure and process of cultural transmission' and particularly inter-generational transmission (ibid.). Bernstein stated:

> Thus the settlement introduced me to the inter-relationships between social class and religious belief within the context of an apparently distinct and homogeneous group (1971: 3).

In 1947, while studying for a BSc degree in Economics in Sociology at the London School of Economics, Bernstein read widely in sociology and psychology and was inspired by Durkheim's description of the social bond and the structuring of experience. After further study he received a postgraduate certificate of education and started teaching at Kingsway Day College in London. Here again, Bernstein's personal experiences provided insights into issues that remained central to his theoretical work. For example, many who attended the college were on day release from various industries such as the General Post Office and London docks, and Bernstein noted how difficult it was to motivate the boys to learn in class, in comparison to outside the college. The boys he taught were enrolled on a course in elementary vehicle maintenance. Outside college the boys listened with rapt interest to 50-minute lectures on topics such as 'the internal combustion engine, the general mechanics and electrics of the car and advanced study of road safety' (ibid.: 4). In order to try to motivate them inside college, he used the topic of car mechanics to instruct them in English, arithmetic, general science and civics. At the end of the course the boys received a 'printed and embossed' (ibid.) certificate in elementary car maintenance. Bernstein described how the credibility of the whole course was thrown into jeopardy when one of the boys asked, 'What do I do with this guv?' He explained:

> With my heart in my mouth I replied, 'Send it to your insurance firm, they might do something about your premium.' About a month later the same student came up to me with a broad grin and said, 'It worked. They've reduced it!' We were in business both metaphorically and materially (ibid.: 5).

The formative experience of striving to make learning meaningful to boys who had been written off by their earlier experiences of schooling gave Bernstein an abiding interest in the way groups invest in and are positioned by institutions and especially schools and families.

Bernstein's sociological endeavour has been to describe and explain pedagogic practice: a practice which almost invariably decontextualizes meanings from the situated contexts of everyday life and recontextualizes them within abstract, text-based symbolic codes which appear to have no connection or relevance to social functions. Bernstein became fascinated with the use of abstract codes and asked why some groups were motivated to preserve and pass these on while other groups in the same society ascribed them little or no value at all. The boys following the vehicle maintenance course initially saw no reason for the academic certificates handed out by the college because they appeared to have no economic or practical function. However, such institutions distributed the accolades that are used to guarantee access to well-paid, stable, professional jobs. As his work developed, Bernstein drew upon Foucauldian (1977) notions of dominant discourse to capture the values maintained by groups hierarchically positioned within societies. However, in contrast to Foucault, Bernstein retained a strong sense that power is hierarchically structured. In a neo-Marxian sense, he recognized that groups closer to the apparatus of governance or with access to the tools of production have greater control than other groups over the discourses that carry influence and legitimacy. He was particularly interested in which groups have wrestled for control of educational systems and the knowledge, codes and discourse that they reward. Towards the end of his life, Bernstein warned that we were beginning to see a new social order which does not reproduce the division of labour based along class lines filtered via education systems. The control of the highly valued symbolic codes and their distribution had begun to shift away from academia. This veritable crisis at the heart of education is not only a crisis about the inheritability of social codes and access to professional jobs but it also has implications for subjectivity. The other theme that has dominated Bernstein's work is the relationship between social organization and the formation of consciousness. Consciousness relates to subjectivity, which is influenced by access to, and familiarity with, specific groups and institutions that provide the tools for thought, and therefore the possibility to reflect on one's position in society and in the world.

During his early teaching experience, Bernstein noted a great discrepancy between the oral and written accomplishments of the boys following the elementary course in motor mechanics. During lessons, he explored language with the boys by taking apart lines of poetry and rearranging them on the page while discussing with them the changes afforded by words in space. Bernstein noted that:

> The space between the lines was the listener or reader's space out of which he [sic] created a unique, unspoken, personal meaning (ibid.: 6).

The linguistic strand of his work can be seen in embryonic form in this example and provides a hint that Bernstein was primarily interested in meaning and only secondarily interested in the formal structures of language such as syntax. His interest in meaning relates to what kinds of symbolic tools groups in society have for reflecting on life and on themselves. His early interest in the symbolic resources provided by language was illuminated by reading Sapir (1921), Whorf (1956) and especially Cassirer's *Philosophy of Symbolic Forms*. In exploring the relationship between consciousness and social organization, he developed an interest in speech codes inspired to some extent by Vygostsky's psychology, and although the book, *Thought and Language*, had not been translated in 1958, Bernstein found an article translated by Luria in *Psychiatry*, II, 1939. He also found an article on speech, used by working-class men and women to describe their experience of a tornado in Arkansas, by Strauss and Schatzman, that explored social class and forms of communication. His early attempts to characterize speech codes according to syntactical differences has to be seen within this broader picture. He later abandoned his early attempts to differentiate working- and middle-class speech codes in terms of syntax, admitting that they were not significant features and did not help him to understand the formation of consciousness. Even so, much of the criticism levelled at Bernstein, especially by Labov, focused on his early attempts to differentiate social-class codes in terms of syntax. It has to be remembered that he was primarily interested in what meanings can be created in the spaces between the words arranged on a page, or more generally, between language and the social contexts experienced by groups. His fundamental question has always been, 'Which groups are afforded the symbolic tools to recognise how they have been positioned within society?' Therefore much of his sociological work has scrutinized academic institutions where, traditionally, abstract rather than context-dependent symbolic codes have been created, maintained and passed down.

Bernstein's early interests in social organization, social-class groups, meaning, speech forms and consciousness were reworked numerous times throughout the development of the theory. At the heart of his work was a striving to understand how meanings come to be formed and how different groups value and protect their own meanings. The description of Bernstein's theoretical work will therefore start with meaning.

3.2 THE CENTRAL PROBLEMATICS OF BERNSTEIN'S *OEUVRE*

Central to Bernstein's sociology of knowledge and pedagogy is the status of meaning. In every aspect of a social problem that we may choose to think about, Bernstein insists on asking whose meanings are recognized and legitimated in this context and whose are not. What are the social forces or power dynamics that allow one group's meanings to be taken seriously while other groups' meanings are not? Bernstein sums it up beautifully as 'What meaning and where?' Practically everything else I shall describe in relation to this complex theory comes back to these questions. In his sociological reach he was interested in which groups manage to be the ones who impose meaning on others, how they mobilize and create institutional structures to maintain their powerful positions and, further, what invisible, unintended or defensive structures allow dominant social norms or discourses to be re-imagined, reinstated and reproduced. He was also interested in change in social norms across a long historical trajectory from the Hellenistic era to the present and, indeed, the future. Once we have the central problematic of **meaning** in place it becomes easier to understand the way Bernstein took some concepts from sociolinguistics and not others, and how he was happy to adapt, extend and transform what look like linguistic concepts in non-linguistic ways. Bernstein's work has in turn influenced the field of sociolinguistics to provide new inspiration to contemporary theorists such as Halliday, Hasan and Kress. The conversation between Hasan and Bernstein is deep-rooted and ongoing (cf. Hasan, 1989, 1992a, 1992b, 1995, 1996, 2002, 2006; Hasan et al., 2005). The most well-known aspect of Bernstein's sociological work is the quasi-linguistic notion of 'code'.

3.3 CODE: AN INITIAL OVERVIEW

Bernstein developed the notion of code in order to differentiate between groups within the same society in the spirit of Marx, Gramsci and Foucault (cf. Hymes, 1995: 4). In the 1960s and 1970s, this project ran counter to movements within linguistics

in which Chomsky's search for a universal grammar was influencing the field in ways which played down difference and inequality. For Chomsky, in the USA, the fundamental basis of language was innate and language was acquired rather than learned; the drive towards a universal grammar, even a universal language, aimed to provide all groups with equal access to the linguistic resources required to participate in society. In contrast, in pointing out difference, Bernstein in the UK was attempting to demonstrate the role of social institutions, such as family and school, in the perpetuation of social-class inequality. For Bernstein the fundamental basis of language was the 'real' (Kress, 2001), active, everyday experience and behaviour of children, young people and adults involved in specific family and school settings that made up their daily lives, placing emphasis on social structuration of the environment rather than biological substrates. Bernstein became branded in the USA as the person who aligned minority groups of class and, by implication, race/ethnicity with a deficit, or 'restricted code' and this dominated many people's reading of his work. While we might say that Chomsky's Language Acquisition Device pointed to a, hopefully, more egalitarian future, the Pedagogic Device that Bernstein developed around the end of the 1980s aimed to uncover the roots of present social inequality.

In this chapter my primary aim will be to introduce the reader to Bernstein's notion of 'code' in a way which gets beyond simplistic understanding of 'restricted' and 'elaborate' forms by paying attention to the theoretical influences that inspired his work. To do this I am going to take advantage of the way Bernstein's work developed across a 40-year span and reflect on **code** as he constantly revisited and reflected upon it to provide it with a depth that it did not have initially (cf. Note Vol. 1, Introduction, 1971: 1–20). This approach will help to contextualize some of the early formulations of code and recognize the depth and richness that it acquired as the theory evolved.

Broadly, Bernstein was interested in how human consciousness was formed in relation to changes in social organization across the long historical trajectory from the Greeks and Romans, through the medieval era, to the hyper-individualism of neo-liberalism.[2] In brief, he made a connection between social organization and consciousness via a particular kind of engagement with language which does not quite align with the systems and structures that make up linguistics. Between social relations and consciousness there are many kinds of mediation: '(B)etween language and speech is social structure' (Bernstein 1990: 95). While initially code was characterized in terms of syntactic features, later Bernstein changed this to express them in terms of semantic features. The form of mediation that Bernstein developed to accommodate his interest in meaning was speech forms. The concept of 'speech form' provided a way to capture something of the ways different groups are oriented to meanings, depending on their exposure to and experience of specific kinds of social relationships. In particular, he focused on relationships between children and parents in their homes and teachers and pupils in schools, so that his work could be characterized as a sociology of pedagogy in the broadest sense. He was not concerned with linguistic performance or ability, instead studying and describing the implicit meanings that align with speech forms. When he wrote about language he was not referring to systems of grammar, syntax and vocabulary, the structures of language systems, but to the social relationships that make up institutions, such as families. He was interested in the way social relationships align and order ideas, characterized as the grammar of the social in contradistinction to the grammar of linguistics. He argued that working-class children participate in different kinds of social interaction with parents than do middle-class children and, even more importantly, that fractions within the middle classes are oriented to meaning in different ways, his later work becoming particularly concerned with the latter as social changes take place within organic solidarity.

From the 1980s he became interested in changes in symbolic control relating to late capitalism. In a series of papers, especially Chapter 4 of Vol. IV and Chapter 4 of Vol. V, Bernstein addressed the limits of what can be thought across a vast historical canvas in which he identified dominant shifts in the way knowledge has been and is imagined. The kind of knowledge that has been given high status and recognized as sacred rather than profane, esoteric rather than mundane, or scientific rather than common sense, has changed across epochs from the Hellenistic era, through the Middle Ages, to the Enlightenment and into late capitalism. He pointed to the turning points, brought about through cultural shifts based on the dominance of, for example, Christianity, then science and, presently, the market, across Western societies. Such shifts are rare, yet their implications are great because they realign boundaries between high- and low-status knowledge and change its ideological underpinning. They also change how subjectivity is imagined across eras. Bernstein used the quasi-linguistic conception of code to capture these shifts, suggesting that code regulates relations between state and citizen, education policymaker and teacher and, at another level, teacher and pupil. Bernstein's theory is based on a distinction between code and its realizations, which are 'a function of the culture acting

through social relations in specific contexts' (Bernstein, 1974: 173–4). Codes operate at the level of culture and his theory sought to explain how some codes and not others come to dominate in society.

The latest shift that captured Bernstein's attention in the mid 1980s related to late capitalism. While the logic of free-market economics has come to dominate public life, there is an internal contradiction at the heart of *globalization*. While it purports to support a free-market principle in the global circulation of good and services, 'non-discrimination is discriminatory' (Hasan, 2006: 213) because free trade, such as *'the policy of non-discrimination in recruiting labour'* (ibid. original emphasis) actually imposes restrictions. Ironically, discourses of decentred state control in terms of the free market have created excessive state control, which Bernstein characterized as 'a totally pedagogised society' (Bernstein 2001: 377). This social shift has fundamental consequences for knowledge and pedagogy:

Today led by the U.S.A. and the U.K., there is a new principle guiding the latest transition of capitalism. The principles of the market and its managers are more and more the managers of the policy and practices of education. Market relevance is becoming the key orienting criterion for the selection of discourses, their relations to each other, their forms and their research [...] Knowledge, after nearly a thousand years is *divorced from the inwardness and literally dehumanized* (Bernstein, 2000: 86; emphasis Hasan's, cited in Hasan, 2006: 212).

Speech forms: elaborated and restricted codes

Clarifying the fundamental consequences of a totally-pedagogized society requires description of a range of concepts, starting with 'speech forms', which dominated Bernstein's work up to the mid 1970s. They capture something of the way different, usually social-class, groups are oriented to meaning. Using the language of semiotics, Bernstein attempted to capture the distinct signification that governs the relationship between signifier and signified for different class groups within society and connect this to their differential positioning in relation to the economic base of material and symbolic production, the latter relating to who has control of what can be thought in society. Across his large historical canvas, who controlled the thinkable and unthinkable shifted from priests in the church, to scientists in universities and, latterly, to managers of markets. Each of these groups has had varying amounts of influence on schools and teachers, who differentially distribute access to codes used by those who have control over symbolic production and so over what can be thought in each era. Traditionally, working-class groups have had less access to schooling and have performed less well than their middle- and upper-class counterparts since schooling became compulsory for all. Bernstein set out to investigate social-class speech codes and the codes through which subject knowledge, such as science or art, is transmitted in schools.

Explanation for working-class children's lower educational achievement appeared to be located in the mismatch between the speech codes acquired in their families and those used for instruction in schools. Bernstein (1971) attempted to classify the speech forms found in families with different orientations to space, time and authority, initially in terms of two, inter-dependent problems: the empirical explanation of class-regulated, differentiated school success; and the more general one of what, in the 1950s, was termed the 'process of socialization'. In the introduction to Vol. I CCC, Bernstein described how the concepts of code came about in his work. Initially they were defined in terms of the ease or difficulty of predicting the syntactic alternatives taken up to organize meaning. However, Bernstein was heavily criticized for using the terms 'public' and 'formal language', which became identified with non-standard and standard (English) use respectively. Between 1958 and 1961, Bernstein admitted to having used a range of 'unreliable features in an initial attempt at a description' of forms of speech (1990: 95). These included using terms like 'short', 'simple, often with unfinished sentences' and 'poor syntactic structure,' to characterize public language use. This became confused with dialect so that even when he refined the features of these two speech forms and called them 'restricted' and 'elaborated' codes, the charge of aligning working-class speech forms with a deficit model of language was still made. These were unfortunate times and the main issue that Bernstein was trying to focus on – social relationships – was lost for many audiences and especially for those in the USA where Labov (e.g. Labov, 1970) was developing descriptions for Black-American speech.

Elaborated and restricted codes were aimed at capturing something fundamental about groups' orientation to meaning. 'Elaborated codes were considered to regulate a greater range of combinatory possibilities than restricted codes and their syntactic alternatives were considered less predictable' (1990: 96). Bernstein stressed that he was not attempting to capture anything relating to linguistic competence that would allow the charge of a deficit model of language use for some groups to stand up. Instead, what he had differentiated was,

'how sets of social relationships in which people were embedded acted selectively on what was chosen from common linguistic resources' (ibid.). He was concerned with the organization of social contexts and how these organizations oriented groups to different ranges and different kinds of meanings.

Research projects investigated interaction between mothers and children from different social-class backgrounds, for which Bernstein and his researchers designed projects to investigate the contextual constraints on their speech (Bernstein, 1971, 1973; Cook-Gumperz, 1973). Bernstein identified 'positional' and 'personal' family types. In **positional** families, role relations and procedures of social control were characterized by strong boundaries regulating spatial and temporal features and roles were specialized and segregated. In effect, hierarchy between children and parents was made explicit in interactions. For example, a parent might say to a child, 'Do this because I say so'. In **personal** family types, social control was achieved through 'complex forms of interpersonal communication' and the boundaries between roles were blurred. Here a parent might typically say to a child, 'Maybe we could find another way to do that dear, what do you think?' While both types of family would be found in working-class and middle-class groups, Bernstein suggested that there would be more positional types in working-class groups as was borne out to some extent by later empirical studies (Cook-Gumperz, 1973; Robinson, 1973; Turner, 1973; Aggleton, 1984, 1987; Wells, 1985; Hasan, 1989). However, he was particularly interested in different forms of organic solidarity engendered by corporate capitalism, differentiating an 'old' middle class as **positional** and a new middle class as **personal**.

The forms of symbolic control, boundary maintenance and orientations to meaning that characterized family types were later worked out with great sophistication using Halliday's systematic grammar (Halliday, 1973, 1978). Instead of trying to describe codes in terms of the predictability of their syntax, as he had originally attempted, Bernstein turned to semantic features and identified forms of regulation that took place in four contexts: a moral system of regulation, often associated with the family; an instructional system, often associated with learning subject principles in schools where children were required to manage objects and people; an 'inter-personal'; and an 'imaginative' context. In this manner, by the end of the 1960s, Bernstein had a way to distinguish codes and speech variants. A code was deemed restricted or elaborated depending on the extent to which speech in each of these four contexts was context-dependent or context-independent. Stressing that speech is always to some extent context-dependent, he was interested in the degree to which its form did not rely on immediately present, visual, and/or auditory clues for it to make sense to another person. This distinction has come to have a central place in many other socio-cultural theoretical approaches which refer to the extent to which meanings are de-contextualized, abstract or rely on propositional rather than empirical clues for sense to be made (e.g. Luria, 1976; Scribner and Cole, 1981; Wertsch, 1985a, 1985b; Vygotsky, 1986).

The important transition from a syntactical description of a speech form in his earlier formulation of code to a semantic description allowed greater depth of distinction and aligned Bernstein's work with other traditions, allowing the concept of code to escape the charge levelled against his early work as constituting a deficit model of language relating to class. Codes regulated relationships both between and within contexts. As the theory developed, the principles of classification and frame were developed to translate codes between different levels of analysis. Along with Whorf (1956), Bernstein was interested in 'the connection of language to social life in terms of constraint' (Hymes, 1995: 5), the way language acts as a constraint on what is thought and done which is a sociolinguistic rather than a linguistic endeavour. 'Class mediates between institutional culture and local personnel – class is an active specifiable force' (ibid.: 21–2). To get a grip on this we must recognize the important influence of Durkheim on Bernstein's lifelong endeavour.

Durkheim's problematization

The problem addressed by Durkheim's sociology of knowledge was about the nature and origins of rationality. Kant held that the basic categories of time and space could not be derived from individual experience but exist *a priori* in the structure of the human mind. Durkheim recognized that this effectively removed the study of these basic categories from the field of scientific enquiry and objected that, in deriving universal categories from the rational quality of the human mind, cultural variability in the conception of categories, such as time and space, could not be accounted for. Durkheim aimed to show that the genesis and, consequently, the functioning of logical operations could be problematized as a function of social relations. He suggested that basic categories were *collective representations* and his mission was to identify collective features of representations as distinct from features of individuals.

First, Durkheim defined social facts as *sui generis* (unique) and, secondly, maintained that social facts were not reducible to facts about individuals.

Social aspects of representations were considered to be relatively stable, giving them objectivity over individuals. Collective representations were conceptualized as having a 'life of their own', with 'the powers to attract and repel one another and form syntheses of all kinds' (Lukes, 1973).[3] The dimensions and dynamics of social facts became the preserve of sociology and the subsequent dichotomy between social psychology and sociology could be said to stem from this definition. It has to be recognized that the nature of Durkheim's mission meant that he neglected the psychic aspects of collective representations (Moscovici, 1984).

In *The Division of Labour*, Durkheim used a distinction between traditional and modern cultures to outline two forms of social relationship that gave rise to different forms of consciousness. However, his distinction between mechanical and organic solidarity has too often been interpreted as a straightforward difference between so-called 'primitive' and 'modern' solidarities. This simplistic reading neglects the point that primitive societies had elaborate cosmologies and that social groups were positioned differently within them (Lévi-Brühl, 1925/1926). Both mechanical and organic solidarities were present in traditional societies. One fundamental difficulty with the problematics posed by Durkheim was that he did not provide the conceptual tools to demonstrate explicitly the presence of both organic and mechanical solidarity in complex societies while Bernstein's work, as it has evolved over at least 40 years, specifically addressed this theoretical lacuna. He suggested that because Durkheim was interested in the emergence of **individualism**, his concern was with only one main form of solidarity:

> Durkheim's organic solidarity refers to *individuals* in privatised class relationships; the second form of organic solidarity refers to persons in privatised class relationships. The second form of organic solidarity celebrates the apparent release, not of the individual, but of the persons and *new* forms of social control. Thus, we can distinguish *individualised* and *personalised* forms of organic solidarity *within* the m.c. [middle class] (Bernstein 1978; reprinted 1997: 62, emphasis in original).

Bernstein made a distinction between 'individualised' and 'personalised' forms of organic solidarity, arguing that new forms of the division of labour in modern societies created fractions within class divisions: for example, he differentiated an 'old' middle class and a 'new' middle class. The old middle class sought to retain its position of privilege within society by focusing on cultural reproduction, seeking to educate through explicit forms of instruction. The new middle class represented a change in habitus, educating by making the mode of socialization, rather than the mode of instruction, explicit:

> In the new m.c., socialisation is into weak classification and weak frames, which promote, through the explicitness of the communication code, far greater ambiguity and drive this class to make visible the ideology of socialisation; crucial to its ideology is the concept of the *person* not of the *individual* (Bernstein, 1997: 62).

The two modes of communication employed by the new and the old middle class can be viewed as two codes, Jenkin's (1990) historical analysis showing that progressive pedagogies were created and maintained by a faction of the new middle class.

Bernstein's main concern was with principles of social control, his secondary focus on distinct forms of experience. When he wrote about children, teachers or others he did not refer to the 'embodied' child or teacher within a phenomenological account of their specific actions, but to general patterns of intentionality and motivation that arise due to the common experiences of the group as they experience forms of social control within institutions. As Jenks points out, children (and/or other groups, such as teachers) act as 'metaphors for the different forms of consciousness within different realizations of solidarity' (Jenks, 1995: 175). Bernstein was dealing with 'both the structural constituents and the social bond' (ibid) [...] where 'normative expectations arise' (Jenks, ibid.: 177). In particular, he has been concerned with forms of social control in education, with the 'languages' used in schools and class cultures, and how these differentially position and structure pupils' experience of schooling. The languages that children acquire within their homes are influenced by how families are located within a class structure and culture. Congruence or clash between home and school codes was used to explain the relative educational success of middle-class in comparison with working-class children.[4]

Bernstein wished to be able to apply the notion of code to multiple levels of analysis, from micro-interactional processes to social-organizational parameters for what can be thought and not thought in societies across vast time frames, using his concepts of classification and frame. As it is easier to demonstrate how classification and frame work in relation to school than it is to families, partly because schools have patterns of practice that are more visible and amenable to description than those within families, which are hugely variable and more difficult to access,

I shall therefore describe them in relation to the former.

Classification and framing

The principles of classification and framing are used to identify different forms of social organization which are realized, for example, in kinds of curriculum structure and pedagogic practice.

> Classification, here, does not refer to *what* is classified, but to the *relationships* between contents. Classification refers to the nature of the differentiation between contents. Where classification is strong, contents are well insulated from each other by strong boundaries. Where classification is weak, there is reduced insulation between contents, for the boundaries between contents are weak or blurred. *Classification thus refers to the degree of boundary maintenance between contents* (Bernstein 1971: 205, emphasis in original).

Classification and framing are related dialectically, such that, although connected, they vary independently of one another within certain limitations. Framing was defined as the degree of control teachers and pupils have over the transmission of knowledge:

> Framing refers to the form of the *context* in which knowledge is transmitted and received. Frame refers to the specific pedagogic relationship between teacher and taught. In the same way as classification does not refer to contents, so frame does not refer to contents of pedagogy. Frame refers to the strength of the boundary between what may be transmitted and what may not be transmitted, in the pedagogic relationship. Where frame is strong, there is a sharp boundary, where frame is weak, a blurred boundary, between what may and may not be transmitted. Frame refers us to the range of options available to teachers and taught in the *control* of what is transmitted and received in the context of the pedagogical relationship. Strong framing entails reduced options; weak framing entails a range of options. *Thus frame refers to the degree of control teacher and pupil possess over the selection, organization, and pacing of the knowledge transmitted and received in the pedagogic relationship* (Bernstein 1971: 205–6 emphasis in original).

The first kind of boundary that may be considered is between school knowledge and everyday knowledge, or between what children may bring with them from outside school and what they have to leave at the school door. This might refer to behaviours and artefacts but more specifically it refs to what can literally be said and not said in school contexts. For example, Singh (1993) described how girls struggled to stifle their competence in information and communication technology (ICT) to conform to the dominant representation of technocratic masculinity that was being maintained by the male ICT teacher in their primary school classroom. Local school cultures and the curriculum that they maintain will determine the nature of this boundary.

The curriculum becomes apparent at the level of the school as unspecified contents, 'defined in terms of the principle by which certain periods of time and their contents are brought into a special relation with each other' (Bernstein, 1977: 79). Such periods of time may be relatively long or short. High-status categories are insulated from other contents, standing in a 'closed' relationship with each other, thus avoiding 'pollution': those less well-insulated stand in a mutually 'open' relationship. Within a curriculum, high-status subjects will be recognizable by having more time allocated to them than other subjects and being closed to the influence of others: they will have their own curriculum space and specialist teachers. In such terms, a *collection-type curriculum* is characterized as having strong classification and framing, its elements having strong boundaries distinguished as subjects, such as English, mathematics, geography, and so on, with recognizable periods of time allocated to them. Subjects or specialized discourses have their own curriculum space and internal logic insulated from everyday discourses. Schools with collection-type curricula provide pupils with strong educational identities based on visible criteria specified by the inner logic of school subjects.

Students who fail to demonstrate adequate competence are identified and 'carefully screened' to prevent them from polluting the 'pure' categories of educational knowledge. In contrast, an *integration-type curriculum* is defined through weaker forms of boundary maintenance, and contents are said to be in relatively open relation to each other, 'The various contents are subordinated to some idea which reduces their isolation from one another. Where we have integration, the various contents become part of a greater whole' (Bernstein, 1977: 80). The discrete elements of the curriculum associated with the collection type are organized according to superordinate categories which were for some time called themes or topics in British state primary schools. In them, because aspects of different subjects are taught through themes, the criteria relating to them tend not to be made explicit to children. In such child-centred curricula where subject principles were taught through topics or themes, such as those documented in the Plowden Report of 1969, there was emphasis upon **ways of knowing** rather than forms of knowledge. They required teachers to reach consensus concerning the underlying **idea** around which integration is organized and to enter into a different kind of social relationship. In schools with integration-type curricula, power relations between pupils and the teacher were thought to shift toward pupils who might exercise greater control over the production of school knowledge. In sum, differences in such pedagogic practices were to be located in the '*manner* in which criteria are transmitted' (Bernstein, 1978, reprinted 1997: 59).

In later reworking his theory, Bernstein changed its emphasis and orientation from 'contents' to 'specialist discourse', as outlined in *Class and Pedagogies: Visible and Invisible* (1978, reprinted in 1997) in which visible pedagogies realized through strong classification and strong framing, and invisible pedagogies realized through weak classification and weak framing, were contrasted. Insulation between contents was said to determine the space between one category and another: the greater the space, the more explicit the separation and the more likely that the distinction between them will be recognized. If there is little insulation, there will be little space and contents are likely to be confounded. Recognition and realization rules refer to what is made explicit to children in classroom practice and provide the clues, signals or messages that children require when trying to work out what is and is not legitimate practice within it. Daniels (1988) showed that in schools with different classification and framing practices, children used different recognition and realization rules to distinguish science and art texts. Morais and her colleagues in Portugal (Domingos, 1984; Morias, Fontinhas and Neve, 1993; Morais and Antunes, 1994; Morais and Neves, 2001) used classification and framing to describe different kinds of science classrooms in middle schools. They have shown that when teachers are taught how to manipulate classification and framing by making instructional discourses more explicit, working-class children have a better chance of accessing science, though not all children who recognize the codes for science in classrooms can necessarily realize legitimate science in their own answers and texts.

Schools do not reflect social structures – they mediate them via the curriculum. Bernstein made a distinction between subject 'voice' and 'message' to emphasize the process of mediation. The site of production and maintenance of specialist discourses or subject disciplines is usually the university. They emerge here as subject 'voice', policed by peer review through publications in professional journals. Teachers make subjects available to children according to their own values, beliefs and representation, allowing ideology to exert influence in a process which transforms knowledge as it moves between sites. Thus, a subject's 'voice' appears in classroom practice as its 'message'. Such recontextualization is, in Bernstein's theory, a form of mediation which points to the transformation of knowledge as it moves between sites. The curriculum determines how knowledge will be reconfigured in schools.

In his later work, Bernstein (1996) defined the kinds of practice projected by two opposing 'competence' and 'performance' models of recontextualized knowledge (ibid., 58) viewed as the 'poles of choice' from which a range of pedagogic practice can be described. Competence is practice which is not constrained by power relationships, 'intrinsically creative, informally, tacitly acquired, in non-formal interactions' (ibid. 55). Competence relates to behaviour which is manifest in cooperative social relations. Performance, on the other hand, is produced within hierarchical social relations.

Bernstein outlined three different modes of competence and performance models, each entailing different recognition and realization rules. Broadly, competence models are characterized by weak classification and framing and result in few explicit instructional structures, such that teachers are less able to appeal to criteria derived from specialist discourses in their efforts to control children. Children's behaviour and the products of their behaviour, their texts, are more likely to be interpreted as manifestations of inner competence, rather than as manifestations of specialist subject discourse. Performance models are characterized by explicit instructional structures and strong classification. The relation between teacher and child is mediated by specialist discourses, and surveillance within these contexts focuses on the realization of subject-discipline criteria. The criteria for achieving legitimate texts are made relatively explicit to children within local classroom cultures. Success relies less on producing personal or original texts and more on reproducing specialist-subject criteria. Although fewer of children's personal attributes, intentions and styles are used as criteria for control, they become easily classified as successful and less successful, precisely because subject-discipline criteria are publicly available. Surveillance of knowledge recontextualized according to competence criteria is centred more directly on the intentions, attributes and individuality of children and less on those attributable to specialist discourses. These models can, therefore, be seen as opposing forms of power (classification) and control (framing), and within any school or any classroom we would expect to find a patterning of practice which might tend more towards one of these poles rather than the other.

Within any society the curriculum is highly contested. The pedagogic modalities or discourses originating from it influence who has access to what kind of knowledge and when. At classroom level, it distributes legitimate and non-legitimate action and discourse within specialist contexts, some forms of action coming under scrutiny while others do not, determined by the curriculum type. Concern for this became more explicit in Bernstein's later work on the pedagogic device, where framing acquired both an internal and external dimension, the latter being concerned with how much and what kinds of attributes children could legitimately bring to and express in classrooms (cf. Bernstein, 1995: 395). Underlying these opposing pedagogic modes are competing notions of the person and the purposes of education (Ivinson and Duveen, 2006). As has already been noted:

> In the new m.c., socialisation is into weak classification and weak frames, which promote, through the explicitness of the communication code, far greater ambiguity and drive this class to make visible the ideology of socialisation; crucial to its ideology is the concept of the *person* not of the *individual* (Bernstein, 1978, reprinted 1997: 62).

Towards the end of his life Bernstein had envisioned the next social shift beyond these of the second half of the twentieth century, to what some refer to as the knowledge-based economy in which class divisions are subordinated to new social arrangements, such as 'network-based solidarities' or 'neo tribes' (Chisholm, 2001: 45).

3.4 THE PEDAGOGIC DEVICE

Much of Bernstein's theory provides conceptual tools for tracing the movement of knowledge through complex processes of recontextualization from sites where knowledge originates, often the higher agencies of education such as universities, via the state, through policies and legislation, to institutional practice. The pedagogic device determines what is made thinkable or communicable at various levels of analysis, described according to how esoteric and mundane discourses spread across groups, in terms of: 'distributive rules' as to who may transmit what to whom; 'recontextualisation rules' and how these are instantiated in classroom practice; and 'evaluation rules' (for a full description of these principles see Vol. 5, 1996: 42–53). These concepts allow researchers to trace the range of influences across agents and agencies and to study whose discourse is given weight. Bernstein's notion of discourse bears strong resemblances to what Foucauldian scholars refer to as 'strategic fictions' or 'truths'. Dominant discourses fuse and eventually can be found echoing in teachers' pedagogic discourse. For example, currently-competing discourses might be neoliberal or 'retrospective' versions of the Right, emphasizing 'nation, family and individual responsibility' (Beck, 2006: 185), managerial discourses which emphasize 'new entrepreneurialism and its instrumentalism' (Bernstein, 2000: 61, cited in Beck, 2006: 185), or discourse about the innate ability, increasingly being fused with discourses about genetics manifested in discourses of learning styles (e.g. Bourne, 2000; Moss, 2001, 2002, 2004). Within all modalities of the pedagogic device regulating the communication that takes place in classrooms between teachers and children, their instructional discourse (ID) is always embedded within the regulative (RD).

Although pedagogy can be viewed as an 'empty discourse' rather than one in its own right, it is crucially the relay for power relationships outside itself, a 'principle by which other discourses are appropriated and brought into a special relationship with each other' (Bernstein 1996: 47). In the process of dislocation from their original site of effectiveness to the pedagogic site, a gap opens up, a space in which 'ideology can play' (ibid.). All discourses project an interlocutor to whom the discourse is addressed (Bakhtin, 1981) and Bernstein refers to the interlocutor projected by pedagogic discourse as the *imaginary subject* (Ivinson and Duveen, 2006). Pedagogic discourses selectively create *imaginary subjects*, teachers make school knowledge available to children, exerting ideological influence in a process which transforms knowledge. Subsumed within the imaginary subjects projected by teachers' pedagogic discourse are ideological views about how children are imagined and the ideal persons, citizens and/or workers they ought to become. As children encounter instructional discourses they also come to recognize themselves, or not, in their teachers' discourse as imaginary subjects. 'While teaching involves fostering skills, practices and knowledge, at the same time pedagogic discourse inducts children into becoming particular kinds of moral agent' (Ivinson and Duveen, 2006: 110). 'However, moral induction is not easy to justify, and different pedagogic modes make the regulative discourses (in comparison to the instructional discourse) more or less explicit' (ibid.). Teachers as well as children are controlled by pedagogic modes, though teachers have far greater control. Weakly-classified competence modes have allowed historically-rooted social representations of gender, class and age, if not uniquely, to dominate pedagogic discourse (c.f Sharp and Green, 1975; Walkerdine, 1988, 1998), whereas, in performance modes, teachers tend to

be more constrained by dominant representations of knowledge that circulate in society and in schools. For example, recent, official Literacy and Numerous pedagogic strategies in England were experienced by some teachers as oppressive (Moss, 2002, 2004).

Such ideas allow macro relations (social structures) to be recovered from micro interaction (classroom practice and discourses) and vice versa, providing rules which link descriptions of the surface structure of classroom organization to models of social relations. When knowledge is recontextualized according to a performance model, teacher–student relationships will be explicitly hierarchical or vertical, and when a competence model is evident, teacher–student relationships will appear flatter or horizontal. Students will be controlled in different ways according to which model dominates in a specific classroom. Codes can now be specified at various levels of analysis, and which children come to be recognized as legitimate actors in classroom contexts depends on whether or not they possess codes, which usually relate back to their family type and social-class positioning, that are recognized by their teachers.

The implications for the way children are able to access knowledge in schools have long been generally argued in terms of school practices and specialist curriculum subjects, such as Science or Art having languages, vocabularies and logics that were presented to children by teachers in classroom instruction using largely middle-class codes. Given that most professionals were either middle class or had been socialized into using middle-class codes, it was held that, generally, though not at the level of all individuals, working-class children encountered a double burden in accessing curriculum subject knowledge. They had to decode both what teachers where saying in pedagogic discourse and the specialist 'scientific' discourse of the subject before **realizing** knowledge through responses, texts and other productions that were expected, recognized and legitimated by teachers. Much empirical work testifies to the usefulness of this aspect of code theory by demonstrating that non-white, middle-class children and sometimes girls (e.g. Singh, 1993) have difficulty, for example, telling stories in classrooms according to the code recognized by teachers (Heath, 1983; Michaels, 1986; Filer, 1997).

3.5 RELATIONSHIPS BETWEEN CODES AND LINGUISTICS

Bernstein's concept of 'code' has a distinctive sociological flavour and yet, as Kress points out, it highlights things about language that linguists have admired, revered, even sometimes derided but have not managed to dismiss. Kress has suggested that Bernstein made the often abstract nature of linguistics 'real':

> Users of language, in their everyday actions, organize the resources of language to achieve the ends posed by the demands of their social life. These demands follow the lines and principles of the organization of the social groups in which their everyday lives have their location. Hence the organization of language as *code* both as the expression of the real actions of individuals in their social places, and as the expression of the organisation of their social groups (Kress, 2001: 64) [italics in original].

The elaborate theoretical superstucture that became Bernstein's theory of pedagogy unpacks again and again aspects that Kress so succinctly draws our attention to in the above quotation, particularly that social life is organized in hierarchical ways, that people live their daily life mediated by their experiences within social groups, and that these experiences position them in specific ways within the world. In Bernstein's words, 'Code Theory is based on a distinction between code and its realisations, in which realisations are "a function of the culture acting through social relations in specific contexts"' (Bernstein, 1971: 173–4).

Code theory has been elaborated most fully as pedagogic practices that take place within bounded and explicitly-regulated environments, such as schools (Bernstein, 1971, 1978, 1981, 1990, 1996). Even so, as a sociological account of the hierarchical nature of the social categories which give rise to differential power relations, the theory can be adapted to a wide range of social settings in which pedagogic practices are evidenced: for example, between parents and children, between priest and laity, between manager and worker and between expert and novice. The notion of code as it relates to socialization has retained its influence, even if the empirical work on which it has been based has rarely been given the credit it should. Kress (2001: 65) has been impressed with the stability of code orientation across time, suggesting that social realities that have informed such work have informed linguistics and forced them to move away from abstract structures and towards the messy interface with the 'real'.

Individuals meet language not as a clear-cut system or systems but through practices in everyday life, and the experiences of ordinary daily life influence the way people come to concepts, meanings and the relationships between them. Code orientation adds something beyond a neat description of language systems to suggest that, even when gaining access to the same language, children, by virtue of their movement and contacts in everyday life, where they go and to what range of daily experiences they have access, come to it with different 'orientations'. It is not that their access to language is different but to **meanings**. Language acts back on users and enfolds them within the orientations to meaning that they learn though experience. Altering or breaking out of these orientations can be done through education in school and classroom contexts:

> The significance for both learning and for what is learned is clear. What it is to be learner will have specific form depending on its representation through codes of different kinds. These codes will also shape how what is to be learned will be learned: habits of conceptual engagement leading to habits of cognitive work. Above all, the realist notions of signs – to put this now semiotically – the codal arrangements as signs having the form they do because of the meanings that they realise, bestows agency on learners (Kress, 2001: 65).

The descriptive language of the theory can specify in general terms the kinds of recognition and realization rules which teachers make available to children in schools with different types of curriculum. However, the theory does not predict how individual children will read these rules. Daniels (1994: 65) has indicated that there is a need to describe the semiotic relays maintained by different schools and to investigate how these relate to cognition:

> If progress is to be made towards the construction of a system of semiotic analysis of schooling that understands individual learning within activities that are organized acts of cultural transmission then at least two levels of development are required. At a theoretical level there is a need to refine and develop models of socio-institutional organization in such a way that allows for the empirical investigation of individual positioning. Similarly social models of learning require balanced accounts of the effects of the semiotic mediation of the organization of activity (Daniels, 1994: 65).

Without this kind of work, links between micro-interactional processes and social structures remains problematic. Kress et al.'s (2001) work on multimodality is opening up new ways to identify values in classification and framing according to a multiplicity of modes of communication that are active in classrooms. Language becomes one of the several modes through which codes are instantiated in everyday classroom practice.

Bernstein's theory influenced sociolinguistic theory across the globe due to its strong relationship with systemic functional linguistics (e.g. Halliday, 1978, 1994; Hasan, 1992a, 1992b, 1996, 2006; Halliday and Hasan, 1989), which provides the potential to connect language analysis with sociological analysis (Atkinson, 1985; Chouliaraki and Fairclough, 1999). Bernstein's work has had considerable influence in sociolinguistics in Germany (c.f Leodolter, 1975; Oeverman, 1972; Wodak, 1986a, 1986b, 1996; Wodak and Shultz, 1986). The concept of recontextualization has become a major concept in discourse analysis (cf. Chouliaraki and Fairclough, 1999; Iedema, 1999; Wodak, 2000). Within Critical Discourse Analysis, the concept of recontextualization is useful in describing hybridity (Haraway, 1988). Recontextualization also captures some of the properties of discourse as condensations in time-space involving disembedding and re-embedding (Chouliaraki and Fairclough, 1999: 110). In Europe, Bernsteinian sociolinguistics has focused on inequality and class struggle and had an enormous impact on the post-1968 movement and school reforms. Bernstein's work has inspired educationalists in many countries across the world, especially in South Africa and Chile, as part of the struggle for equality.

3.6 SOME LIMITS TO CODE THEORY

Children have to recognize the messages relayed by pedagogic practices and realize these as texts that will be recognized by teachers as legitimate forms of knowledge. Such notions allow researchers to analyse classrooms, identifying which kinds of pedagogic practice are present, locating them within poles of choice of models for recontextualizing knowledge. Information about children's social-class background then allows prediction concerning their achievement in given classrooms. A great deal of empirical work testifies to the usefulness of the theory. However, social-class divisions and differences are becoming less easy to define and identify as relatively homogeneous experiences, especially when ethnic, race and gender differences are taken into account. Furthermore, the growth of new social groupings, such as network-based solidarities, neo-tribes and immigration are changing family structures and forcing children into new family groupings, raising questions about social class as the primary shaper of experience from which consciousness arises.

Bernstein's theory suggests that different forms of consciousness or, we could say, different

forms of logical thinking, arise from the practices, interaction and discourse experienced by children brought up in families of different social-class backgrounds. His theories describe how to map the social ground of classrooms in order to identify the social codes underlying practice and discourse. Instead of assuming that children recognize classroom codes according to their social-class background, there is a need to ask a preliminary question: how does the classroom code shape consciousness? There has been little empirical work that has set out to investigate the way in which classroom practices shape children's understandings that has not relied on categories of gender, ethnicity or social class to classify responses. The descriptive language of the theory can specify, in general terms, the kinds of recognition and realization rules which teachers make available to children in schools with different types of curriculum. However, the theory does not predict how children will read these rules, except at the general level of social class.

Without this kind of work the link between micro-interactional processes and social structures remains problematic. Given that socialization is a function of social context, we set out to investigate the effect of different classroom cultures on children's developing understanding of the curriculum by devising psychological instruments to investigate children's social representations of the curriculum and found that children reconstructed the social order available to them in schools with different modes of curriculum (Ivinson, 1998a, 1998b; Ivinson and Duveen, 2005, 2006). The study drew attention to the need to consider a level of mediation that has not been fully articulated in Code Theory, namely the constructive efforts of children themselves. Children reconstruct social structuration according to the socio-cognitive resources that they have available to them: they do not simply reproduce or reflect the adult order. It could be argued that classroom contexts are the primary socialization sites for understandings of the curriculum because these are the places where children experience the curriculum firsthand. Our work represents only one of the many developments to Bernstein's work, which also includes work on the Epistemic Device (Moore and Maton, 2001; Maton, 2004) and on the Corporeal Device (Evans et al., 2008). I wish to finish by returning to the dire predictions that Bernstein made in relation to the totally pedagogized society identified as the code shift of late capitalism. The prediction that knowledge has become divorced from the knower rests on the extraordinary richness of the way Bernstein worked the distinction between esoteric and mundane knowledge referred to earlier.

3.7 THE RULER OF CONSCIOUSNESS: THE POWER OF IDEAS

Distinctions between realms, such as the sacred and the profane, the public and the private, the esoteric and the mundane, and the moral and the amoral, have a long history. Scientific and commonsense knowledge are often viewed as an opposition between abstract and concrete thinking (cf. Dowling, 1998). This distinction implies a hierarchy in which abstract thinking is privileged above concrete thinking and it is this hierarchical valuation that has caused many writers, and not just Bernstein, to be accused of elitism. Lévy-Brühl's (1925/1926) distinction between pre-logical and logical thought conceptualized them as two distinct patterns of ideas but not hierarchical universes. In Bernstein's work, the **thinkable** and **unthinkable** relate to two classes of knowledge, the **esoteric** and the **mundane** (Bernstein, 1996: 43). Bernstein calls also on the esoteric realm when he explores the limits and possibilities to thinking in his last work, pointing to a dislocation between the esoteric and commonsense realms. In Bernstein's terminology, control of the unthinkable in simple, non-literate societies rests with their 'religious systems, agencies, agents, practices and the cosmologies to which they give rise' (ibid.). In complex, modern societies this control lies with the 'higher agencies of education' (ibid.). He stressed that this does not mean that the unthinkable can never take place elsewhere, for it does not relate to the unconscious or to the inaccessible, but to sociogenesis which takes place at the interface between these two types of knowledge which relate to the material and immaterial world or to the everyday, mundane and the transcendental world. Within each world, knowledge has a different relationship to a specific material base:

> If meanings have a direct relation to a material base, these meanings are wholly consumed by the context. These meanings are so embedded in the context that they have no reference outside that context. These meanings are not simply context dependent, they are necessarily context bound: and meanings which are context bound can not unite anything other than themselves. They lack the power of relation outside a context because they are totally consumed by that context (Bernstein, 1996: 44).

For meanings to unite two worlds they can never be tied to a specific material base. The indirect nature of the relation between these types of meanings and a specific material base requires a 'specific social division of labour and a specific set of social relationships within that division of

labour', opening up what Bernstein calls a 'potential discursive gap'. He stresses that this is not a 'dislocation of meaning, it is a gap' (ibid.).

The 'discursive gap' described by Bernstein outlines the social grounds from which change and therefore sociogenesis become possible. However, I think it is fair to say that Bernstein's predictions for the future were bleak, especially concerning control over symbolic resources in higher education. While traditionally the university has been seen as the site where knowledge is produced, increasingly the technologies of the free market and strong forms of accountability are being used to regulate universities. This represents a shift from a time when knowledge and education were valued for their own sakes towards a representation of knowledge as a commodity valued only for its economic output. Accordingly, knowledge has come to be thought of as economic capital:

> Knowledge should flow like money to wherever it can create advantage and profit. Indeed, knowledge is not just like money: it is money. Knowledge is divorced from persons, their commitments, their personal dedication, for these become impediments, restrictions on flow, and introduce deformities in the working of the market. Moving knowledge about, or even creating it, should not be more difficult than moving and regulating money … . Once knowledge is separated from inwardness, commitment and personal dedication, then people may be moved about, substituted for each other, and excluded from the market (Bernstein, 1990: 135 cited in Bourne, 2000: 42).

When knowledge is viewed as a commodity it seems to have the flexibility to circulate like money, 'dislocated from the knower' (Bernstein 1996: 4) and people can be substituted and dispensed with. This shift effectively obscures the process through which knowledge is created involving personal effort, repeated practice and commitment. Bernstein argued that as the state increasingly controls social space we move towards a 'totally pedagogised society'. He suggested that the last time we had a 'totally pedagogised society was in the medieval period, when the Catholic Church created this seamless, coherent, systematic society, in which people's positions and powers were known and understood and developed' (Bernstein, 2001: 377). Bernstein stated 'It's the first time that pedagogic panic has masked moral panic' (ibid.). He also suggested the possibility that pedagogy has been reduced to technology in which learning is completely decontextualized from the rest of the acquirer's life span, leading him to say that 'what I fear most of all is the "emptying out of the self", such as is found in the neo-liberal notion of trainability' (Bernstein, 2001: 366). There is a growing concern within education that vocational courses dominated by the 'new adaptability, flexibility, creativity' will become cheap training grounds in which those less well-off will be prepared not for work but for lifelong training (Bernstein, 1990; Bourne, 2000). If young people cannot recognize themselves in the **imaginary subjects** projected by pedagogic discourses, then they will have no resources with which to engage in education.

This shift in code recalibrates the relationship between the individual and the state. In schools it is still working-class groups who have less access to academic codes who are likely to be funnelled into vocational courses consisting of watered-down, basic skills rather than being given access to the codes required to gain professional jobs. Bernstein reminds us that pedagogy needs to be **meaningful** as well as relevant. The challenge, therefore, as Erica McWillian (1995, cited in Bourne, 2000: 43) has suggested that it is time to shift the way we talk about education from the 'safe terrain of quality, effectiveness, and learner-centredness' to 'an engagement somebody has with other bodies in institutional spaces' (cited in Bourne, 2000: 43). Bourne challenges us to take seriously the commitment that teachers need to be able to teach and the desires of people who want to learn. She draws attention to the effort, affect and embodied practice of both teachers and learners, as well as the inter-class negotiations and complex role-taking that goes on in classroom settings, areas seriously underplayed in recent years. By paying attention to the **effort** of teaching and learning it might be possible to make visible the point stressed by Evans et al. (2008) in relation to the Corporeal Device and described by Bourne, 'bodies are socially positioned, and pleasure constituted through the historical formations of class, gender, and race' (Bourne, 2000: 44). On a hopeful note, there may be some solace to be drawn from the notion that symbolic control, always a condition for someone else's order, carries within itself the potential for transforming the order of the imposing other (Bernstein, 1990: 159 cited in Bourne, 2000: 44).

NOTES

1   There seems to be similarity here between the scale at which Bernstein is operating when he identifies shifts across eras and Lacan's notion of a signifying cut. Lacan characterized signification in terms of S/s, where S is the signifier and s below is the signified. A shift in the large S brings about a

'discontinuity in the real', relationships between the economic base and individuals undergoing Marxist transformation. For Bernstein it is **code** that regulates the relationship between S and s; after 'the cut' meanings for people change and those of all significations shift. His identification of shifts in knowledge across eras seems to signal the same kind of shift in meaning as Lacan's cuts. Bernstein was concerned both with dominant and distinct cuts across time and within societies. Signification that dominates in one class group differs from another depending on how they are positioned with respect to the economic base of production. I am indebted to Janell Watson for drawing my attention to Lacan's signifying cut when she gave a keynote paper at the First Deleuze Studies Conference, Cardiff, 11–13 August 2008.

2   See also Bernstein: 1996 (Chapter 4); 2001 (Introduction).

3   Lukes 1973: 8; Durkheim 1924a (1951 edn): 34: tr. 1953b: 24.

4   For recent empirical work on middle-class experiences of schooling in the UK, see Power and Whitty (2002) and Power (2006).

REFERENCES

Aggleton, P. (1984) 'Reproductive resistances: a study of origins and effect of youth sub-culture style amongst a group of new middle-class students in a college of further education'. PhD thesis, University of London.

Aggleton, P. (1987) *Rebels Without a Cause? Middle-Class Youth and the Transition from School to Work.* Lewis: Falmer Press.

Atkinson, P. (1985) *Language, Structure and Reproduction: An Introduction to the Sociology of Basil Bernstein.* London: Methuen.

Atkinson, P., Davies, B. and Delamont, S. (1995) *Discourse and Reproduction: Essays in Honour of Basil Bernstein.* Cresskill, NJ: Hampton Press.

Bakhtin, M. M. (1981) *The Dialogic Imagination: Four Essays by M. M. Bakhtin.* Edited by M. Holquist, translated by C. Emerson and M. Holquist. Austin, TX: University of Texas Press.

Beck, J. (2006) '"Directed time": identity and time in New Right and New Labour policy discourse' in R. Moore, M. Arnot, J. Beck and H. Daniels (eds), *Knowledge, Power and Educational Reform: Applying the Sociology of Basil Bernstein.* London: Routledge Taylor Francis Group.

Bernstein, B. (1971b) 'On the classification and framing of educational knowledge', in M. F. D. Young (ed.), *Knowledge and Control.* London: Collier-Macmillan.

Bernstein, B. (1971a) *Class, Codes and Control 1, Theoretical Studies Towards a Sociology of Language.* London: Routledge.

Bernstein, B. (1972) 'A sociolinguistic approach to socialization; with some reference to educability', in J. J. Gumperz and D. Hymes (eds), *Directions in Sociolinguistics.* [Oxford: Blackwell] New York; London: Holt, Rinehart and Winston, 1972.

Bernstein, B. (ed.) (1973) *Class, Codes and Control 2, Applied Studies Towards a Sociology of Language.* 2nd revised edn. London: Routledge.

Bernstein, B. (1974) *Class, Codes and Control 1, Theoretical Studies Towards a Sociology of Language.* 2nd revised edn. London: Routledge.

Bernstein, B. (1977) *Class, Codes and Control 3, Towards a Theory of Educational Transmission.* 2nd revised edn. London: Routledge.

Bernstein, B. (1978) 'Class and pedagogies: visible and invisible', in J. Karabel and A. H. Halsey (eds). *Power and Ideology in Education.* Oxford: Oxford University Press. [Reprinted in (1997) A. H. Halsey, H. Lauder, P. Brown, A. Stuart Wells (eds) *Education, Culture, Economy, Society.* Oxford: Oxford University Press.]

Bernstein, B. (1981) 'Codes, modalities and the process of cultural reproduction: a model', *Language and Society,* 10: 327–63.

Bernstein, B. (1990) *The Structuring of Pedagogic Discourse. Volume IV Class, Codes and Control.* London: Routledge.

Bernstein, B. (1995) 'Response', in A. R. Sadovnick (ed.), *Pedagogy and Knowledge: The Sociology of Basil Bernstein.* Norwood, NJ: Ablex.

Bernstein, B. (1996) *Pedagogy Symbolic Control and Identity Theory, Research, Critique.* London: Taylor and Francis.

Bernstein, B. (2001) 'Video conference with Basil Bernstein', in A. Morais, I. Neves, B. Davies and H. Daniels (eds), *Towards a Sociology of Pedagogy: The Contribution of Basil Bernstein to Research,* New York: Peter Lang.

Bourne, J. (2000) 'New imaginings of reading for a new moral order: a review of the production, transmission and acquisition of a new pedagogic culture in the UK', *Linguistic and Education,* 11(1): 31–45.

Chisholm, L. (2001) 'Thinking about education and power in knowledge societies: what are the implications for contemporary social change?', in S. Power, P. Aggleton, J. Brannen, A. Brown, L. Chisholm and J. Mace (eds), *A Tribute To Basil Bernstein 1924–2000.* London: Institute of Education, University of London.

Chouliaraki, L. and Fairclough, N (1999) *Discourse in Late Modernity; Rethinking Critical Discourse Analysis.* Edinburgh: Edinburgh University Press.

Cook-Gumperz, J. (1973) *Social Control and Socialization: A Study of Class Difference in the Language of Maternal Care.* London: Routledge and Kegan Paul.

Daniels, H. R. J. (1988) *An Enquiry into Different Forms of Special School Organisation, Pedagogic Practice and Pupil Discrimination.* C.O.R. E. 12, (2).

Daniels, H. R. J. (1994) 'The individual and the organization', in H. R. J. Daniels (ed.), *Charting the Agenda.* London: Routledge.

Davies, B. (1994) 'Durkheim and the sociology of education in Britain', *British Journal of Sociology of Education,* 15(1): 3–25.

Diaz, M. (1984) 'A model of pedagogic discourse with special application to Colombian primary level'. PhD dissertation, University of London.

Domingos, A. M. (1984) 'Social class, pedagogic practice and achievement in science: a study of secondary schools in Portugal'. PhD dissertation, University of London.

Domingos, A. M. (now Morais) (1992) 'Recognition and realisation rules in acquiring school science – the contribution of pedagogy and social background of students', *British Journal of Education,* 13(2): 247–70.

Dowling, P. (1998) *The Sociology of Mathematics Education: Mathematical Myths/Pedagogic Texts.* London: Falmer.

Evans, J., Rich, E., Davies, B. and Allwood, R. (2008) *Education, Disordered Eating and Obesity Discourse: Fat Fabrication.* London: Routledge Taylor Francis Group.

Filer, A. (1997) ' "At least they were laughing": assessment and the functions of children's language in their "news" sessions', in A. Pollard, D. Thiessen and A. Filer (eds), *Children and their Curriculum. the Perspectives of Primary and Elementary School Children.* London: Falmer Press.

Foucault, M. (1977) *Discipline and Punish: The Birth of the Prison.* New York: Pantheon.

Halliday, M. A. K. (1973) *Exploration in the Function of Language.* London: Edward Arnold.

Halliday, M. A. K. (1978) *Language as Social Semiotic. The Social Interpretation of Language and Meaning.* London: Edward Arnold.

Halliday, M. and Hasan, R. (1989) *Language, context and text. Aspects of Language in a Social Semiotic Perspective.* Oxford: Oxford University Press.

Halliday, M. (1994) *Introduction to Functional Grammar,* (2nd ed), London: Edward Arnold.

Haraway, D. (1988) 'Situated knowledges: the science question in feminism and the privilege of partial perspectives', *Feminist Studies,* 14(3): 575–99.

Hasan, R. (1989) 'Semantic variation and sociolinguistics', *Australian Journal of Linguistics,* 9(2): 221–75.

Hasan, R. (1992a) 'Speech genre, semiotic mediation and the development of higher mental functions', *Language Science,* 14(4): 489–528.

Hasan, R. (1992b) 'Meaning in Sociolinguistic Theory', in K. Bolton and H. Kwok (eds), *Sociolinguistic Today: International Perspectives.* London: Routledge.

Hasan, R. (1995) 'On social conditions for semiotic mediation: the genesis of mind in society', in A. Sadovnik (ed.), *Knowledge and Pedagogy: The Sociology of Basil Bernstein.* Norwood, NJ: Ablex.

Hasan, R. (1996) 'Literacy, everyday talk and society', in R. Hasan and G. Williams (eds), *Literacy in Society.* London: Longman.

Hasan, R. (2002) 'Ways of meaning, ways of learning: code as an explanatory concept', *British Journal of Sociology of Education,* 23(4): 537–48.

Hasan, R. (2006) 'Literacy, pedagogy and social change: directions from Bernstein's sociology', in R. Moore, M. Arnot, J. Beck and H. Daniels (eds), *Knowledge, Power and Educational Reform: Applying the Sociology of Basil Bernstein.* London: Routledge Taylor Francis Group

Hasan, R., Matthiessen, C. and Webster, J. (eds) (2005) *Continuing Discourse on Language: A Functional Perspective.* Vol. I. London: Oakville.

Heath, S. B. (1983) *Ways with Words: Language, Life and Work in Communities and Classrooms*. Cambridge, MA: Cambridge University Press.

Hymes, D. (1995) 'Bernstein and poetics', in P. Atkinson, B. Davies, S. Delamont (eds), *Discourse and Reproduction; Essays in Honour of Basil Bernstein*. Cresskill, NJ: Hampton Press.

Iedema, R. (1999) 'Formalizing organizational meaning, *Discourse and Society*, 10: 49–65.

Ivinson, G. (1998a) 'The construction of the curriculum'. PhD dissertation, Cambridge University.

Ivinson, G. (1998b) 'The child's construction of the curriculum', *Papers on Social Representations: Threads and Discussions. Special Issue: The Development of Knowledge*, 7(1–2): 21–40.

Ivinson, G. and Duveen, G. (2005) 'Classroom structuration and the development of representations of the curriculum', *British Journal of Sociology of Education*, 26(5): 627–42.

Ivinson, G. and Duveen, G. (2006) 'Children's recontextualisations of pedagogy' in R. Moore, M. Arnot, J. Beck and H. Daniels (eds), *Knowledge, Power and Educational Reform: Applying the Sociology of Basil Bernstein*. London: Routledge Taylor Francis Group.

Jenkins, C. (1990) 'The professional middle class and the origins of progressivism: a case study of the New Education Fellowship 1920–1950', CORE 14, (1).

Jenks, C. (1995) 'Decoding childhood', in P. Atkinson, B. Davies and S. Delamont (eds), *Discourse and Reproduction: Essays in Honour of Basil Bernstein*. Cresskill, NJ: Hampton Press.

Kress, G. (2001) 'A tribute', in S. Power, P. Aggleton, J. Brannen, A. Brown, L. Chisholm and J. Mace (eds), *A Tribute to Basil Bernstein 1924–2000*. London: Institute of Education, University of London.

Labov, W. (1969) 'The logic of non-standard English', in J. E. Alacis (ed.), *Report of the Twentieth Round Table Meeting on Linguistics and Language Studies*, Georgetown Monograph Series in Language and Linguistics No. 22. Washington, DC: Georgetown University Press, 1970. pp. 1–29.

Leodolter (Wodak), R. (1975) *Das Sprachverhalten von Angeklagten bei Gericht*. Stuttgart: Scriptor Verlag.

Lévy-Brühl, L. (1925/1926) *How Natives Think*, trans. Lillian Clare. London: George Allen & Unwin.

Lukes, S. (1973) Emile Durkheim, His Life and Works: A historical perspective Harmonsworth: Penguin.

Luria, A. R. (1976) *Cognitive Development: Its Cultural and Social Functions*. Cambridge, MA: Harvard University Press.

Maton, K. (2004) 'The wrong kind of knower: education, expansion and the epistemic device', in J. Muller, B. Davies and A. Morais (eds.), *Reading Bernstein, Researching Bernstein*. London: Routledge Falmer.

Michaels, S. (1986) 'Narrative presentations: an oral preparation for literacy', in J. Cook-Gumperz (ed.), *The Social Construction of Literacy*. Cambridge: Cambridge University Press.

Moore, R and Maton, K. (2001) 'Founding the sociology of knowledge: Basil Bernstein, epistemic fields and the epistemic device', in A. Morais, I. Neves, B. Davies and H. Daniels (eds), *Towards a Sociology of Pedagogy: The Contributions of Basil Bernstein to Research*. New York: Peter Lang.

Morais, A. M. and Antunes, H. (1994) 'Students' differential text production in the regulative contexts of the classroom', *British Journal of the Sociology of Education*, 15(2): 243–63.

Morais, A. M. and Neves, I. (2001) 'Pedagogic social contexts: studies for a sociology of learning', in A. Morais, I. Neves, B. Davies and H. Daniels (eds), *Towards a Sociology of Pedagogy: The Contribution of Basil Bernstein to Research*. New York: Peter Lang. pp. 185–212.

Morais, A. M., Fontinhas, F. and Neve, I. P. (1993) 'Recognition and realisation rules in acquiring school science: contribution of pedagogy and social background of pupils', *British Journal of the Sociology of Education*, 13(2): 247–70.

Moscovici, S. (1984) 'The phenomenon of social representations', in R. M. Farr and S. Moscovici (eds), *Social Representations*. Cambridge: Cambridge University Press.

Moss, G. (2001) 'Bernstein's language of description: some generative principles', *International Journal of Social Research Methodology*, 4(1): 17–19.

Moss, G. (2002) 'Literacy and pedagogy in flux: constricting the object of study from a Bernsteinian perspective', *British Journal of Sociology of Education*, 23(4): 549–58.

Moss, G. (2004) 'Changing practice: the NLS and the politics of literacy policy', *Literacy*, 38(3): 126–33.

Oeverman, U. (1972) *Sprache und soziale Herkunft*. Frankfurt/Main: Suhrkamp.

Plowden Report (1969) *Children: Their Primary Schools*. London: HMSO.

Power, S. (2006) 'Disembodied middle-class pedagogic identities', in R. Moore, M. Arnot, J. Beck and H. Daniels (eds), *Knowledge, Power and Educational Reform: Applying the Sociology of Basil Bernstein*. London: Routledge Taylor Francis Group.

Power, S. and Whitty, G. (2002) 'Bernstein and the middle classes', *British Journal of Sociology of Education*, 23(4): 595–606.

Robinson, W. P. (1973) 'Where do children's answers come from?', in B. Bernstein (ed.), *Class, Codes and Control 2*. London: Routledge. pp. 202–34.

Sapir, E. (1921) *Language, an Introduction to the Study of Speech*. Oxford: E. Sapir.

Scribner, S. and Cole, M. (1981) *The Psychology of Literacy*. Cambridge, MA; London: Howard University Press.

Sharp, R. and Green, R. (1975) *Education and Social Control*. London: Routledge and Kegan Paul.

Singh, P. (1993) 'Instructional discourse: a case study of the social construction of technical competence in the primary classroom', *British Journal of Sociology of Education*, 13(1): 189–206.

Turner, G. J. (1973) 'Social class and children's language of control at age five and age seven', in B. Bernstein (ed.), *Class, Codes and Control 2*. London Routledge. pp. 135–201.

Vygotsky, L. (1986) *Thought and Language*. Cambridge, MA: MIT Press.

Walkerdine, V. (1988) *The Mastery of Reason*. London: Routledge.

Walkerdine, V. (1998) *Counting Girls Out; Girls and Mathematics*. new edn. London: Falmer Press.

Wells, G. (1985) *Language, Learning and Education: Selected Papers from the Bristol Study: Language at Home and at School*. 2nd edn. Windsor: NFER-Nelson, 1985.

Wertsch, J. V. (1985a) (ed.) *Culture, Communication and Cognition*. Cambridge: Cambridge University Press.

Wertsch, J. V. (1985b) *Vygotsky and the Social Formation of Mind*. Cambridge, MA: Havard University Press.

Whorf, B. L. (1956) *Language, Thought and Reality*. New York: B. L. Whorf.

Wodak, R. (1986a) 'Normal and deviant texts. The sociopsychological theory of textplanning', in Y. Tobin (ed.), *From Sign to Text: A Semiotic View of Communication*. Amsterdam: Benjamins. pp. 333–55.

Wodak, R. (1986b) *Language Behaviour in Therapy Groups*. Los Angeles: University of California Press.

Wodak, R. (1996) *Disorders of Discourse*. New York: Addison Wesley Longman.

Wodak, R. and Schulz, M. (1986) *The Language of Love and Guilt*, Amsterdam: Benjamins.

4

Dell Hymes and the Ethnography of Communication

Barbara Johnstone and William M. Marcellino

4.1 INTRODUCTION

Dell Hymes' formative role in the ethnography of communication, ethnopoetics and educational ethnography alone merit him biographic attention. In addition, though, tracing out Dell Hymes' career arc offers a window on the birth and development of sociolinguistics as a whole. The particular cluster of early influences on Hymes – Franz Boas, Edward Sapir, Roman Jakobson and Kenneth Burke – as well as Hymes' resulting resistance to Chomskyan linguistics, are representative of the sources of impetus for sociolinguistics in general. Hymes had an abiding personal and scholarly interest in American Indians in all their linguistic and cultural diversity. He argued for a widened scope for linguistics, which started with diversity rather than in a search for the universal. In particular, he wanted linguists to pay attention to the poetic, aesthetic, reflexive aspects of discourse through which cultural knowledge is circulated. His interest in diversity has always been linked with a concern for the sources and consequences of inequality, and much of his work has taken place in the context of educational research. In Hymes' interests, we can see sociolinguistics' recurring concerns. If we want to understand how sociolinguistics grew out of linguistics, understanding Dell Hymes' life and career is a good place to start.

4.2 LIFE AND INTELLECTUAL BIOGRAPHY

Hymes was born in Portland, Oregon in 1927. He grew up there, attending Reed College as an undergraduate, and began graduate work in anthropology at Indiana University in 1950, eventually receiving a doctorate instead in linguisticsm in 1955, with minors in anthropology and folklore. This constellation of interests would stay with Hymes throughout his career. C. F. Voegelin, Hymes' dissertation advisor at Indiana, described Hymes as 'a literary critic and minor poet who surprised us at Indiana when shifting from very general cultural interests to linguistics' (Murray, 1998: 100). For Hymes, though, these interests were naturally allied, allowing him to explore 'the use of language, oral narrative and poetry, the history of anthropology and linguistics, Native Americans, theology' (Hymes, n.d.). While at Indiana, Hymes began his association with Roman Jakobson, whose 'crucial contribution was to introduce a "functionalist" perspective and to do so in a way that suggested an empirical, manageable way of dealing with speech functions' (Hymes, 1975: 364), quoted in (Murray, 1998: 100). That functionalist concern with how humans actually use language would steer Hymes' work and presages sociolinguistics' concern for contextualized language use.

From Indiana, Hymes became an assistant professor of linguistics at Harvard University, but was denied tenure in 1960. Hymes was then offered a position at Berkeley, in both anthropology and linguistics. This was a fortuitous appointment. While other American linguistics departments were beginning to focus increasingly on transformational-generative grammar and other abstract models of linguistic competence, Berkeley's department remained focused on descriptive work on non-English languages, and the 'social and cultural determinants of language' (Murray, 1998: 101). Murray characterizes Berkeley as being split between an old guard of linguists interested in fieldwork, resulting in descriptions of languages, and a younger generation interested in developing theoretical frameworks for studying language use. That younger generation, which included founding sociolinguists like Hymes, Erving Goffman, John Gumperz and Susan Ervin-Tripp, grounded their work in the Sapirian tradition, but expanded their concerns with language beyond description.

Although their concern for the functions of language in social life represented a break from structural linguistics, there was clearly collegial respect between the emerging sociolinguists at Berkeley and the previous generation. Murray (1998: 131–3) points out that Hymes produced a rhetoric of continuity with the Sapirian and structuralist traditions in American linguistic anthropology, in part by including work by scholars such as Haas, Emeneau and Hockett in the anthology *Language in Culture and Society* (Hymes, 1964), and that the older and younger generations were always respectful of each other in their writing. This mutual respect, however, has historically occluded a very strong divide between their approaches to language. However much Hymes grounded his work in the past, he still demanded a break from prior linguistic study. Hymes advocated a shift in focus away from linguistic code *'la langue'* to actual speech, *'la parole'*. He argued for the primacy of language function, and for a shift from imagining the referential function of language as the primary one to seeing it as one of many. He saw the organizing principles of language as derived from language functions, and social appropriateness as essential criterion for the 'rightness' of utterances. He was fundamentally concerned with linguistic diversity, and so, perhaps most importantly, he demanded that language study be grounded in ethnographic observation rather than introspective theorizing.

In 1965, Hymes moved to the University of Pennsylvania, where he joined the faculty of the Department of Anthropology and trained what Murray (1998: 133) has called the 'second generation' of ethnographers of communication, whose work is represented in the influential anthology *Explorations in the Ethnography of Communication*, co-edited by two of Hymes' students (Bauman and Sherzer, 1974). During this period, Hymes worked with other sociolinguists to create a new journal devoted to 'the means of speech in human communities, and their meanings to those who use them' (Hymes, 1972a: 2). The first issue of *Language in Society* appeared in 1972, published by Cambridge University Press, with Hymes as editor. At the University of Pennsylvania, Hymes was also affiliated with the Departments of Folklore and Folklife and Sociology, and with the faculty in education.

Hymes became Dean of the University's College of Graduate Studies in Education in 1975. In 1987 he moved to the Department of Anthropology at the University of Virginia, from which he retired in 2000.

The generational shift from descriptive linguistics into sociolinguistics was contemporaneous with the Chomskyan shift to transformational-generative grammar. The sociolinguistics movement expressed continuity with prior generations of scholars, in contrast to the acrimony surrounding transformational grammarians' split with structural linguistics. But both represented fundamental changes in linguists' understanding of language. Hymes was particularly critical of Chomsky's idea of linguistic competence and his failure to account for linguistic variation. Locating language within an *a priori* mental grammar does not account for or even acknowledge the enormous role of the socially-contextualized ways we use language in determining the shape of utterances. We do more than construct grammatically possible linguistic utterances, and, as Hymes frequently noted, ungrammatical utterances may be socially appropriate, just as grammatical utterances can be socially inappropriate (Hymes, 1972b, 1989). Hymes objected to Chomsky's definition of linguistic competence in the strongest terms, saying that 'a child from whom any and all the grammatical sentences of a language might come with equal likelihood would be a social monster. Within the social matrix in which it acquires a system of grammar, a child acquires also a system of its use' (Hymes, 1974: 75). The system of use children acquire within a social matrix of language is 'communicative competence', Hymes' alternative to Chomsky's 'linguistic competence'. While, for Chomskyans, humans are born with the capacity for acquiring linguistic competence, communicative competence is learned and thus can be more or less complete or flexible. This shift in understanding competence reflects Hymes' concern for disadvantaged children who do not have equal access to the sociolinguistic resources they need (Hymes, 1971).

Hymes also took Chomsky to task for the failure of transformational-generative grammar to account for linguistic variation. Chomskyan linguistics focuses on the aspects of language that are uniform across speakers, ruling variation off the field of study by stipulating idealized speaker/hearers in completely homogeneous communities as its research object. Hymes is concerned with actual linguistic variety as found in speech and therefore calls for 'concepts and methods that enable us to deal with diversity … . [T]he great stumbling block is that the kinds of organization most developed by linguists presuppose the grammar as their frame of reference, [because they are concerned with the] analysis of a single, more or less homogenous, norm' (Hymes, 1989: 433). The concepts and methods for linguistic investigation that resulted from Hymes' concern with actual language use in social contexts would be 'the ethnography of communication'.

4.3 THE ETHNOGRAPHY OF COMMUNICATION

Hymes is best known for his founding role in the ethnography of communication. Hymes proposed the term 'ethnography of speaking', later amended to 'ethnography of communication', to describe a new approach to understanding language in use (Hymes, 1962, 1964). In doing this, Hymes aimed to move away from considering speech as an abstract model and toward investigating the diversity of speech as it is encountered in ethnographic fieldwork. Essentially, Hymes argues:

... that the study of language must concern itself with describing and analyzing the ability of the native speakers to use language for communication in real situations (communicative competence) rather than limiting itself to describing the potential ability of the ideal speaker/listener to produce grammatically correct sentences (linguistic competence). Speakers of a language in particular communities are able to communicate with each other in a manner which is not only correct but also appropriate to the socio-cultural context. This ability involves a shared knowledge of the linguistic code as well as of the socio-cultural rules, norms and values which guide the conduct and interpretation of speech and other channels of communication in a community … . [T]he ethnography of communication … is concerned with the questions of what a person knows about appropriate patterns of language use in his or her community and how he or she learns about it (Farah, 1998: 125).

The object of study Hymes proposes for linguistics is 'ways of speaking' (Hymes, 1989). The idea of language as a set of ways of speaking is an alternative to the idea of language as grammar, an abstracted set of rules or norms. Under the rubric of ways of speaking, Hymes offers a bipartite conception of speech that encompasses both the 'means of speech' available to speakers, and the 'speech economy' these speakers participate in. Thus Hymes offers a theoretical basis for language study that accounts for both linguistic variation from individual to individual and relative linguistic coherence across the social realm, while also offering a methodological heuristic for

investigating communication, often represented in terms of the SPEAKING mnemonic.

This bipartite understanding of language is important because it equally foregrounds two aspects of speaking that Hymes feels cannot be separated: what speakers can and do say, and the communal context such speech occurs in. Speech does not occur in a vacuum, but rather within a specific context, and 'when the meaning of speech styles are analyzed, we realize that they entail dimensions of participant, setting, channel, and the like, which partly govern their meanings' (Hymes, 1989: 444). For Hymes, speech cannot be considered separate from the sociological and cultural factors that help shape linguistic form and create meaning, and so the frame he offers in place of grammar gives equal place to both aspects of speech: speech and the entailments that give meaning to speech cannot be considered in isolation. Hymes is thus adamant that any terminology adopted must treat both aspects of speech equally, discarding both 'speech styles and their contexts' and 'means of speech and their meanings' as being insufficient (Hymes, 1989: 446). Hymes points out that 'contexts' and 'meaning' fail to evoke 'the norms of interaction that go beyond choice and style, and the attitudes and beliefs that underlie both' as well as 'leav[ing] the focus on "styles" and "means"' (Hymes, 1989: 446). The solution is to separate *means of speech* (comprising the features that enter into styles, as well as the styles themselves), and *speech economy* (Hymes, 1989: 446).

Hymes offers an explicit definition of means of speech as 'the features that enter into styles, as well as the styles themselves', but he does not do the same for economy of speech. Hymes does, however, talk about speech economy in such a way as to outline its major facets, and his choice of metaphor is instructive as well. Speech economy is a set of relationships within a speech community, the marketplace in which participants in speech use their means of speech, and those means of speech are in turn a constituent element of the speech economy. Means of speech and speech economy are conceptually distinct as elements of ways of speaking, but 'the two concepts are of course interrelated, even interdependent (as said, meanings lie in relationships), and from a thoroughgoing standpoint, the speech economy of a community includes its means of speech as one of the components that enter into its pattern of relationships' (Hymes, 1989: 446).

As have other language theorists (Saussure, Austin, Bourdieu), Hymes uses an economic metaphor as part of his articulation of how speech works. In addition to using the word 'economy', Hymes also uses economic terms when he justifies his partitioning of ways of speaking into two parts as reflecting 'the major *division of labor* in our society between those who study verbal means and those who study conduct' (Hymes, 1989: 447, emphasis added). Hymes' economic analogy is useful: much as individuals use their means of production to produce goods and services, and then exchange these products in an economy, so too do speakers use their means of speech to produce discourse that is exchanged within a speech economy.

This idea of speakers acting in a speech economy accounts for the contextual, relational and socially-judged aspects of speech. By according speech economy equal status with means of speech, Hymes can frame utterances as being meaningless outside of a particular macro-social context and set of relationships, subject not just to decoding but also to aesthetic judgment from members of the speech economy. In this sense, ethnopoetics – culturally-relative aesthetic sensibility – enters into Hymes' conception of language. Hymes illustrates this through Stanley Newman's research on the Indian Yokuts language. Newman's research allowed him to construct grammatically possible utterances that were, however, ineffective, either inadvertently humorous or pompous (Hymes, 1989: 447). That is to say: **within Yokuts means of speech were possible utterances that had no purchase in the Yokuts speech economy**. This is the 'economic' aspect of speech, where the community makes judgments about how we may traffic in speech. As Hymes puts it, 'grammatical Yokuts is not what is possible to the grammar ... but what is possible according to Yokuts norms ... . [W]e have a normative definition of possible Yokuts that is best described as aesthetic or stylistic in nature' (Hymes, 1989: 448). This is communicative competence visible in a specific example – grammar fails to account for rightness in Yokuts utterances, which hinge instead on context (the social) and aesthetics (ethnopoetics).

In addition to making visible the communally-judged aspect of speech, the idea of speech economy serves an important conceptual function in maintaining a balance between an understanding of language as communally shared and a way of accounting for individual choice and variation in speech. Hymes makes clear that he wants a reference frame beyond the abstracted norms of a grammar, and that 'we have reached a point at which the concept of grammar itself is that which needs to be transcended' (Hymes, 1989: 434). Hymes argues for an understanding of speech that includes the diversity of the particular, not just the structured norms of an abstraction. Ultimately, Hymes rejects an understanding of language where it is permissible 'to speak of the great role of language in general, but never language in

particular,' which leads to 'a tendency to treat some linguistic particularities as inferior' (Hymes 1989: 450). The idea of speech economy is significant in dealing with this tension between general models of language and language particularities because the metaphor of economy carries with it notions of the specific and general, the individual and the community. Conceptually, economy accounts for both individual actors and their aggregate conduct, and so the terms 'speech economy' and 'means of speech' maintain and make visible the tension between the particular speech of the individual and the aggregate speech economy. In this conception of ways of speaking, Hymes offers a theoretical basis for approaching language through the ethnography of communication.

Hymes proposes a general method of ethnographic investigation through taxonomic, descriptive fieldwork (Hymes, 1972b). He is careful to point out, however, that 'sociolinguistic fieldwork is not an end in itself', but rather 'a necessary part of the progress towards models (structural and generative) of sociolinguistic description, formulation of universal sets of features and relations, and explanatory theories' (1972b: 43). Hymes advocates comparative, ethnographic taxonomies as the only way to explore and understand language systematically, because

> ... communities differ significantly in the ways of speaking, in patterns of repertoire and switching, in the roles and meanings of speech. They indicate differences with regard to beliefs, values, reference groups, norms, and the like ... . [I]ndividual accounts that individually pass without notice ... leap out when juxtaposed, as contrasts that require explanation (Hymes, 1972b: 42).

Descriptive and taxonomical ethnographic work that allows for comparison between speech communities allows for systemic classification of ways of speaking in four traditional areas: 'genetic classification' of language descent; 'areal classification' of features spread through an area; 'typological classification' of structural features independent of genetic or areal nature; and usage/role classification (i.e. as a pidgin, trade language, etc.).

The sort of fieldwork Hymes advocates – ethnographies of communication – must 'discover and explicate the competence that enables members of a community to conduct and interpret speech' (Hymes, 1972b: 52). The exploration and documentation of communicative competence within a speech community is the essence of the ethnography of communication. As a means to this end, Hymes defines the social units and units of analysis for ethnographies of communication and proposes an etic heuristic for their analysis.

The social unit proper to sociolinguistics is the 'speech community'. By speech community, Hymes does not mean a community defined by common language, but rather by common linguistic norms: 'a community sharing rules for the conduct and interpretation of speech, and rules for the interpretation of at least one linguistic variety' (Hymes, 1972b: 54). This definition moves the ethnographer away from questions of grammar, and grammatically possible utterances, to questions of coherence and efficacy in the socially-situated use of language. The question for Hymes is not only whether speakers have a common understanding of syntax and semantics but also whether or not they share ideas about the use of silence, ideas about the meaning of irony or emphasis, speech taboos, ways of formulating requests or statements, and so on.

Within speech communities, ethnographers must look for 'speech situations', 'speech events' and 'speech acts'. By speech situations, Hymes means socially contextual situations like 'ceremonies, fights, hunts, meals, lovemaking, and the like' (Hymes, 1972b: 56). Speech events occur within speech situations: so, for example, the exchange of vows is a speech event occurring within a wedding (a speech situation). Speech acts are the individual utterances that form the minimal unit of analysis for ethnographies of communication. Hymes offers the example of 'a party (speech situation), a conversation during the party (speech event), a joke within the conversation (speech act)' to illustrate the three terms (Hymes, 1972b: 54). Hymes distinguishes speech acts from grammatical conceptions like sentences, because the meaning, status and function of a speech act are not solely dependent upon grammatical form. The interpretation of speech acts is equally (at times more) dependent upon the social status and relationship of participants, as well as the immediate context of the utterance, and so 'the level of speech acts mediates immediately between the usual levels of grammar and the rest of a speech event or situation in that it implicates both linguistic form and social norms' (Hymes, 1972b: 57).

To help ethnographers of communications frame their investigation of speech acts and events, Hymes offers the mnemonic device of the SPEAKING grid as a heuristic. Though it is by no means his most significant contribution to sociolinguistics, the SPEAKING grid is perhaps the artefact most associated with Hymes as his popular legacy. The SPEAKING grid has been widely accepted in the ethnography of communication, and has been further developed into discrete research questions by Hymes' students, Joel Sherzer and Regna Darnell (Sherzer and Darnell, 1972). The eight components of the SPEAKING mnemonic are:

(S) Setting including the time and place, physical aspects of the situation such as arrangement of furniture in the classroom; (P) participant identity including personal characteristics such as age and sex, social status, relationship with each other; (E) ends including the purpose of the event itself as well as the individual goals of the participants; (A) act, sequence or how speech acts are organized within a speech event and what topic/s are addressed; (K) key or the tone and manner in which something is said or written; (I) instrumentalities or the linguistic code i.e. language, dialect, variety and channel i.e. speech or writing; (N) norm or the standard socio-cultural rules of interaction and interpretation; and (G) genre or type of event such as lecture, poem, letter (Farah, 1998: 126).

Ultimately, this list of components of speech acts is meant to explore and explain human, social purposes in language. Like all taxonomies, the SPEAKING grid is not an end in itself, but rather a means: 'the formal analysis of speaking is a means to the understanding of human purposes and needs, and their satisfaction' (Hymes, 1972b: 70), as well as a way of understanding how language works.

The ethnography of communication is thus not just a method but a coherent theoretical approach to language. Hymes provides a theoretical basis for language in ways of speaking, which accounts for the diversity and efficacy of actual human communication in terms of the ideas of means of speech and speech economy. Hymes also offers a justification for ethnographic methods, because it is linguistic differences, the contrastive juxtaposition of different ways of speaking, which allows for classification and systematic analysis of language. In turn, Hymes offers a specific set of terminology ('speech community', 'situation', 'event' and 'act') and a suggested method for the conduct of the ethnography of communication (the SPEAKING mnemonic), with a specific unit of analysis in the speech act. Hymes has had an enormous impact in sociolinguistics by helping steer linguistic work toward human communication as it occurs in use: socially.

4.4 NARRATIVE AND ETHNOPOETICS

As we have seen, Hymes's ethnography of communication provides both a theoretical basis and a methodological heuristic for exploring how language is embedded and enacted in discourse. Doing this kind of work requires paying attention to linguistic interaction in context. Ethnographers of communication explore the physical setting, the participants, their goals; the media and modes of communication; and the norms that guide interpretation. In fact, sometimes the actual words are relatively unimportant. This concern for the whole of communication, instead of just grammatical form, has implications for Hymes in his study of American Indian languages.

Like many other US anthropological linguists, Hymes has always been a student of American Indian languages, and by the time he began his doctoral dissertation fieldwork in the 1950s, many of these languages were dying out. In the Pacific Northwest, Hymes's field site, Native American speech events could no longer be observed in their original contexts. Many of the Indians along the Columbia River had assimilated to European-American culture, moved, or died; if there were native speakers of some of the varieties of Chinook and Sahaptin spoken there, they were elderly and isolated, no longer part of a community of speakers. In some languages, Native American speech could no longer be recorded at all, since there were no longer any speakers of these languages. All that was available, in many cases, were versions of tales and myths that had been written down by earlier anthropologists, usually in ways that conformed to the anthropologists' expectations about how folk tales and myths should look on the page. They were inert, decontextualized, interesting in content but disconnected from the speech events that called them forth and shaped them, which could no longer be observed ethnographically.

Hymes's 'ethnopoetic' approach to this material was a theoretical framework and a set of methods for putting these tales and myths back into something like their original contexts. Like the literary theorists of his generation, Hymes believed in the value of close reading that is attentive to all the syntactic and semantic details of texts that constrain how readers can interpret texts' meaning. Following linguist Edward Sapir and literary theorist Kenneth Burke, with whom Hymes regularly corresponded (Jordan, 2005), Hymes saw language as a 'terministic screen' through which we see our world. Hymes also viewed narrative as a universal genre, centrally involved in the speech events in which culture is recreated and transmitted. By reading closely, Hymes proposed to reveal the implicit structure of traditional Indian narratives. This implicit structure would reveal much about how the narratives were embedded in and reflective of their cultural context. Particularly by looking at what happened when narrators 'broke through' into full performances, an analyst could see something of what made things coherent in the culture – its aesthetic system, in other words, or its native ('ethno') poetics. Ethnopoetic work could both show the rest of the world what Native American verbal art was like and help recover lost knowledge about languages and cultures that had died out (Blommaert, 2006).

In Vain I Tried to Tell You: Essays in Native American Ethnopoetics (1981, 2nd edn. 2004) is a collection of Hymes's work in this area. Hymes sets out to show 'how appreciation and interpretation of performances as unique events can be united with analysis of the underlying rules and regularities which make performances possible and intelligible' (Hymes, 1981: 79). (All references to *In Vain I Tried to Tell You* are to the 1981 University of Pennsylvania Press edition.) Hymes situates performance in the range of abilities that characterize cultural competence vis-à-vis behaviours: being able to **interpret** behaviour, being able to **report** on behaviour, and being able to *repeat* behaviour. For cultural insiders, these three types of knowledge are in an implicational relationship: people can interpret more behaviour than they can report and report less than they can repeat. In other words, we can sometimes understand what is going on in a situation without being able to say why, and we can talk about some culturally meaningful behaviours without being able to do them. Behaviour that can be repeated (a prayer, a dance step, a ritual) can be repeated simply as a way of reporting on its existence or commenting on it, or, at the other end of the axis, it can be **performed**: i.e. done in such a way as to show that one means it and intends it to accomplish something. A person who is performing 'assumes responsibility to an audience' (Hymes, 1981: 84).

Finding truly performed speech is crucial for the analyst who wants to find evidence about culture in discourse, because 'performance is a mode of existence and realization that is partly *constitutive* of what the tradition is. The tradition itself exists partly for the sake of performance; performance is itself partly an end' (Hymes, 1981: 86). Hymes's discussion of the relation between performance and tradition draws on Roman Jakobson's (Jakobson, 1960, 1968) formulation of the functions utterances serve. For Jakobson, utterances always have multiple functions, though one or another can be the focus in a particular situation. Utterances can be more or less 'referential' (aimed at making a claim about the world), more or less 'conative' (aimed at getting an interlocutor to behave in a certain way), more or less 'expressive' (calling attention to the speaker), more or less 'metalingual' (about the language or other system in which they are encoded), and more or less 'phatic' (aimed at establishing contact among interlocutors). Most importantly for our purposes here, utterances can be more or less 'poetic': that is, more or less aimed at calling attention to patterns of similarity and difference in their own structure. Poetic utterances, in this sense (which is somewhat different from everyday uses of the term), are ones that make visible normally invisible, implied categories and relationships. They do this by juxtaposing co-members of a category in repeated structural or semantic patterns.

For Hymes, only fully-performed speech is fully poetic. The poetic features of performance, those that distinguish it from non-performed speech, are thus designed to put tradition (linguistic and cultural) on display, to **present** it rather than just to describe it. These features include iteration on various levels (repeated words, repeated structural patterns, repeated incidents in stories), quotation (which is another form of repetition), the repeated use of various initial particles roughly similar to the English word *now*, and the grouping of lines into sets with predictable numbers of lines in each. (In the Chinookan narratives Hymes studies, there are often sets of three and five.) Hymes's method for analysing Native American texts is complex and not easy to systematize. 'In short', says Hymes:

A satisfactory solution emerges only after several tries. One plunges *in media res*, making trial segmentation by hand, and reconsiders and adjusts it in the light of the principles of consistent structure and form-meaning covariation. As one gets more deeply into a text, one gains a deeper sense of its inner logic and form, its particular integration of content and expression, and one's sense of inconsistency or arbitrariness of analysis grows firmer (Hymes, 1981: 151).

Because ethnopoetic analysis, as Hymes practices it, is hard to teach or learn, Hymes's methods have not been taken up widely. However, the idea that language and culture emerge in performance (and that performance is thus a crucial site for sociolinguistic analysis) has continued to resonate among North American linguistic anthropologists. Hymes's student Richard Bauman (1977) first described linguistic and paralinguistic 'keys to performance' in relatively canonical, formal speech events like myth-telling. More recently, in keeping with theorists who talk about the ways in which all language is self-referential, Bauman and Charles Briggs (1990) broaden the notion of performance to include talk that is less 'fully performed', in Hymes's sense, but which still can be said to enact and recirculate culture. Another student, Joel Sherzer, has carried forward the idea that the language used in certain Native American speech events is best described in terms of lines, verses and stanzas (Sherzer, 1975, 1981).

The influence of Hymesian ethnopoetics is also evident in the work of Michael Silverstein

(1985) and his students (e.g. Mannheim, 1986). In keeping with the field of sociolinguistics as a whole, the focus has shifted from monologic discourse to interaction, and from 'culture' as an abstraction to the processes by which people coordinate understandings of the world in real time. Silverstein, Asif Agha (2006), and others (e.g. Lempert, 2008) talk about 'interactional text' and about how patterns of repetition and variation (now called 'text metricality' rather than 'poetic structure') knit together interactants' words, gestures and prosody into an emergent set of meanings, personas and relationships.

4.5 VOICE AND EDUCATIONAL ETHNOGRAPHY

We have focused so far on the theoretical side of the ethnography of communication and ethnopoetics, and on Hymes's theoretical contributions to sociolinguistics as a whole. His work has always had applied goals as well, however, having to do with making unheard voices and ways of speaking hearable. This is particularly explicit in his work in ethnopoetics, and it is alluded to in the title of his collected essays in ethnopoetics: *In Vain I Tried to Tell You*. In the introduction to the volume, Hymes characterizes it as 'devoted to the first literature of North America' (1981: 5). He explains its title by saying:

If we refuse to consider and interpret the surprising facts of device, design, and performance inherent in the words of the texts, the Indians who made the texts, and those who preserved what they made, we will have worked in vain. We will be telling the texts not to speak. We will mistake, perhaps to our cost, the nature of the power of which they speak (Hymes 1981: 5–6).

Hymes' work has always been linked with social activism, and the need for linguists to be able to integrate their 'scientific and social goals' (Hymes, 1996: 26) is the basis for one of his critiques of abstract, universalizing, asocial approaches to language.

The major themes in Dell Hymes' explicitly educational writings are the same as those in his work as a whole: the need for a view of language and linguistics broad enough that it has something to say and do about inequality, the significance and ubiquity of narrative poetics in the circulation of knowledge, and the importance of understanding linguistic behaviour in its ethnographic context. Hymes' contribution to educational sociolinguistics is centred in particular on the concept of 'narrative voice'.

The goal of Hymes's Native American ethno-poetics, as discussed above, was to reconstruct or 'salvage' the sociolinguistic and cultural frameworks in which Chinookan stories made sense, frameworks that were on the verge of disappearing. Only these frameworks made the texts Hymes studied fully and authentically interpretable; only these frameworks gave their tellers voice. By the same token, if not always for the same reasons, there are many children in the USA and around the world who lack voice, children who cannot be heard because educators do not understand the frameworks in which their stories make sense. In his writing about language and education, Hymes hoped:

> to show ... that aesthetic shape is normal, and probably universal, something that comes with language itself, ... that the possibility of narrative voice is given with the possibility of language, but at the same time, that its realization is partly at the mercy of others (Hymes, 1996: xi).

Hymes' commitment to the application of sociolinguistic work in the world arises, arguably, out of his generally leftist, egalitarian, activist political stance (Blommaert, 2009). He positions himself against scholars who look for the universal in language and ignore the diversity among ways of speaking, because while diversity can be a resource, it can also be the basis for inequality.

In 'Speech and language: On the origins and foundations of inequality among speakers' (Hymes, 1996: 25,–62), based on a paper published in 1972, Hymes points out that linguistic diversity has always seemed problematic to Westerners, who have repeatedly proposed intellectual solutions involving original unity (from the Tower of Babel story to comparative searches for proto-languages to universal grammar) and practical solutions involving the privileging of a single language or variety. That diversity should pose a problem, however, or that original unity should be its solution, is not self-evident. For the Busama of New Guinea and the Quileute of Washington State, Hymes says, 'originally each person had a separate language, and ... community of language was a subsequent development' (Hymes, 1996: 28). What would a linguistics be like that took that view? Perhaps it would see, in the many languages and varieties that exist, evidence that social and historical adaptation is a stronger influence than shared roots or cognitive predisposition. Perhaps it would focus not on languages or dialects but on speech communities or ways of speaking.

Hymes also critiques other mainstream ideas about language: the idea that different linguistic channels (speaking, writing and signing) are simply different ways of encoding the same messages, the idea that language and reality are ideally in one-to-one correspondence and the idea that languages and varieties are thus potentially equivalent for practical purposes. In another essay, he argues that language study 'must overcome the separation between questions of language and questions of value that has characterized the development of modern linguistics in the United States' (Hymes, 1996: 100–1). The very adaptability of language implies maladaptation as well: resources suited to some purposes are unsuited to others. For linguists to continue to act as if the **potential** equality of languages (the fact that all are structurally complex, that lexica grow easily, that change is natural) were equivalent to **actual** equality is to sidestep some of the most important social issues to which linguistics is relevant. With Basil Bernstein, whose work Hymes takes seriously, he argues that while different ways of speaking may be equivalent from a linguistic perspective, '[s]ome discrimination among verbal abilities and products is not prejudice, but accurate judgment. The transformation of society to a juster, more equal way of life requires transformation of genuine equalities in verbal resource' (Hymes, 1996: 46).

Contra Bernstein, however, Hymes objects to binary divisions of styles into 'restricted' and 'elaborated' or, in Habermas' formulation of the nature of linguistic inequality, distorted communication versus the 'ideal speech situation'. While 'both Bernstein and Habermas are important in their pioneering efforts to analyze the problems of linguistic and communicative equality[,] both fall back on a cognitive ideal to which the absence of restriction, hence "more is better", is intrinsic' (Hymes, 1996: 55; see also Ivinson, this volume). Since human life is always lived under cultural constraints, such theorists are unable to propose alternatives.

Hymes' proposal begins in arguing for narrative as a way of knowing. Because teaching and learning through stories has traditionally been devalued in American educational culture, in favour of 'rational' modes of information-processing, it is easy to fail to notice how the poetic patterning of traditional tales can help socialize children to see the world as patterned in certain ways, or to miss seeing that children's writing or oral storytelling is richly structured. In several essays Hymes proposes reanalyses, his or Virginia Hymes's, of other people's data, that uncover patterns of lines and stanzas. Hymes follows Roman Jakobson and is in line with most linguists in holding the assumption that makes decontextualized reanalyses of this sort possible: that structure inheres in texts, available for discovery to anyone who looks systematically. The fact that different analysts analyse texts differently suggests, though, that structuring may be an aspect of interpretation as well as an aspect of expression.

In talks and essays addressed to ethnographers of education, Hymes also talks about field methods. He reminds them that participant observation does not in itself constitute ethnography. He discusses what makes ethnography systematic and how it differs in fundamental epistemological ways from experimental research, ways that make it potentially empowering and democratizing. He compares the study of schools with ethnology, especially the study of Native American kinship, arguing that educational research should be more cumulative, more comparative, and more cooperative.

4.6 DISCUSSION

Hymes' foundational works in sociolinguistics are still being read. They are included in collections of essential readings for anthropology and sociolinguistics (Duranti, 2009; Paulston and Tucker, 2003). His ethnopoetic work has also been recently republished (Hymes, 2003, 2004), and until recently, Hymes was still publishing in this area (Hymes, 2006). Although the concept of the speech community has been displaced to some degree by the community of practice (Wenger 1998), it remains one of several possible analytical frameworks, more or less appropriate based on analytical purpose (Gee, 2005: 593; Holmes and Meyerhoff, 1999: 182).

Hymes is one of the most important figures in sociolinguistics: a founding member of the sociolinguistics movement, the originator of the ethnography of communication, a pioneer in ethnopoetics, and a champion in linguistics for those who have been unvoiced in Western educational, anthropological and linguistic traditions. It is in this last set of concerns, where Hymes was an advocate, doing truly applied linguistic work, that we can see the coherence in his work. The repeated theme of Hymes' scholarship is his insistence that linguistic theory and practice account for the individual, the particular and the actual. In countering Chomskyan linguistics, in proposing the ethnography of communication, and in his ethnopoetic approach to Native American texts, Hymes has always centred his theory and practice on what real human beings do with language. This insistence on the rich, socially contextualized reality of human communication creates a particular affordance: the ability to apply sociolinguistic research to real-world problems of disadvantage and inequity. The ethnography of communication forces the sociolinguist to describe speech communities on their terms, sensitive to their norms of communication. Ethnopoetics forces readers to decentre themselves and interpret a text within its original context: the communication norms of the speech community that produced it. Hymes' work in voice and education has been marked by an insistence on meeting the unvoiced – socioeconomically disadvantaged children, American Indian speech communities within the larger US speech community – on their terms, within their context, and using their norms. Because Hymes resists the Western tendency to look only for the universal in language, he has been able to apply sociolinguistic research to the diverse, varied and local voices that have not received the ear they deserved. If we are sensitive to this coherency in Hymes work, the title of his ethnopoetics volume, *In Vain I Tried to Tell You*, takes on additional meaning. Hymes' significant contributions to sociolinguistics have helped make the discipline more aware of and accountable to multiple speech communities.

REFERENCES

Agha, A. (2006) *Language and Social Relations*. New York: Cambridge University Press.

Bauman, R. (1977) *Verbal Art as Performance*. Rowley, MA: Newbury House.

Bauman, R. and Briggs, C. (1990) 'Poetics and performance as critical perspectives on language and social life', *Annual Review of Anthropology*, 19: 59–88.

Bauman, R. and Sherzer, J. (eds) (1974) *Explorations in the Ethnography of Communication*. Cambridge: Cambridge University Press.

Blommaert, J. (2006) 'Ethnopoetics as functional reconstruction: Dell Hymes' narrative view of the world (Review article)', *Functions of Language*, 13: 229–49.

Blommaert, J. (2009) 'Ethnography and democracy: Hymes' political theory of language', *Text & Talk*, 29(2): 257–76.

Duranti, A. (2009) *Linguistic Anthropology: A Reader*. 2nd edn. Malden, MA: Blackwell.

Farah, I. (1998) 'The ethnography of communication', in N. H. Hornberger and P. Corson (eds), *Encyclopedia of Language and Education: Volume 8: Research Methods in Language and Education*. Dordrecht: Kluwer. pp. 125–7.

Gee, J. (2005) 'Meaning making, communities of practice, and analytical toolkits', *Journal of Sociolinguistics*, 9(4): 590–4.

Holmes, J. and Meyerhoff, M. (1999) 'The community of practice: theories and methodologies in language and gender research', *Language in Society*, 28: 173–83.

Hymes, D. (n.d.) Dell H. Hymes personal web page. Retrieved 16 January 2009, from http://www.virginia.edu/anthropology/dhymes.html.

Hymes, D. H. (1962) 'The ethnography of speaking', in T. Gladwin and W. Sturtevant (eds.), *Anthropology and*

Human Behavior. Washington, DC: The Anthropological Society of Washington. pp. 13–35.

Hymes, D. H. (ed.) (1964) *Language in Culture and Society: a Reader in Linguistics and Anthropology*. New York: Harper & Row.

Hymes, D. H. (ed.) (1971) *Pidginization and Creolization of Languages*. Proceedings of a conference held at the University of the West Indies, Mona, Jamaica, April 1968. Cambridge: Cambridge University Press.

Hymes, D. H. (1972a) 'Editorial introduction to "Language in Society"', *Language in Society*, 1(1): 1–14.

Hymes, D. H. (1972b) 'Models of the interaction of language and social life', in J. J. Gumperz and D. Hymes (eds), *Directions in Sociolinguistics: The Ethnography of Communication*. New York: Holt, Rinehart and Winston. pp. 35–71.

Hymes, D. H. (1974) *Foundations in Sociolinguistics: An Ethnographic Approach*. Philadephia: University of Pennsylvania Press.

Hymes, D. H. (1975) 'Pre-war Prague School and post-war American anthropological linguistics', in E. Koerner (ed.), *The Transformational-Generative Paradigm and Modern Linguistic Theory*. Amsterdam: John Benjamins. pp. 359–80.

Hymes, D. H. (1981) *In Vain I Tried to Tell You: Essays in Native American Ethnopoetics*. Philadelphia: University of Pennsylvania Press.

Hymes, D. H. (1989) 'Ways of speaking', in R. Bauman and J. Sherzer (eds), *Explorations in the Ethnography of Speaking*. 2nd edn. Cambridge: Cambridge University Press. pp. 433–51.

Hymes, D. H. (1996) *Ethnography, Linguistics, Narrative Inequality: Toward an Understanding of Voice*. 1st edn. London: Taylor & Francis.

Hymes, D. H. (2003) Now I know only so far: essays in ethnopoetics. Lincoln, NE: University of Nebraska Press.

Hymes, D. H. (2004) 'In vain I tried to tell you': essays in Native American Ethnopoetics. Lincoln, NE, University of Nebraska Press.

Hymes, D. H. (2006) 'Ethnopoetics', *Theory Culture Society*, 23: 67–9.

Jakobson, R. (1960) 'Concluding statement: linguistics and poetics', in T. Sebeok (ed.), *Style in Language*. Cambridge, MA: MIT Press. pp. 350–77.

Jakobson, R. (1968) 'Poetry of grammar and grammar of poetry', *Lingua*, 21: 597–609.

Jordan, J. (2005) 'Dell Hymes, Kenneth Burke's "identification," and the birth of sociolinguistics', *Rhetoric Review*, 24: 264–79.

Lempert, M. (2008) 'The poetics of stance: text-metricality, epistemicity, interaction', *Language in Society*, 37: 569–92.

Mannheim, B. (1986) 'Popular song and popular grammar, poetry and metalanguage', *Word*, 37: 45–75.

Murray, S. O. (1998) *American Sociolinguistics: Theorists and Theory Groups*. Amsterdam/Philadelphia: John Benjamins.

Paulston, C. B. and Tucker, G. R. (2003) *Sociolinguistics: the Essential Readings*. Malden, MA: Blackwell.

Sherzer, J. (1975) 'Semantic systems, discourse structures, and the ecology of language', in R. W. Shuy (ed.), *Studies in Language Variation*. Washington, DC: Georgetown University Press. pp. 283–93.

Sherzer, J. (1981) 'The interplay of structure and function in Kuna narrative, or: How to grab a snake in the Darien', in *Georgetown University Round Table on Languages and Linguistics, 1981*. Washington DC: Georgetown University Press. pp. 306–22.

Sherzer, J. and Darnell, R. (1972) 'Outline field guide for the ethnographic study of speech use', in J. J. Gumperz and D. H. Hymes (eds), *Directions in Sociolinguistics: The Ethnography of Communication*. New York: Holt, Rinehart, and Winston. pp. 548–54.

Silverstein, M. (1985) 'On the pragmatic 'poetry' of prose: parallelism, repetition, and cohesive structure in the time course of dyadic conversation', in D. Schiffrin (ed.), Meaning, form, and use in context: linguistic application. Georgetown University Round Table on Language and Linguistics. Washington, DC: Georgetown University Press. pp. 181–98.

Wenger, E. (1998) Communities of practice. Cambridge & New York: Cambridge University Press.

5

Gumperz and Interactional Sociolinguistics

Cynthia Gordon

5.1 INTRODUCTION AND OVERVIEW

Interactional sociolinguistics is a qualitative, interpretative approach to the analysis of social interaction that developed at the intersection of linguistics, anthropology and sociology. It emerged primarily out of the work of anthropological linguist John J. Gumperz, who, in his field research in the tradition of the ethnography of communication in the 1960s and 1970s, observed immense linguistic and cultural diversity in everyday talk, and sought to devise a method for analysing and understanding this diversity, and for testing hypotheses gained from doing ethnography through the collection and analysis of actual texts. Its development was also motivated by Gumperz's interest in investigating intercultural encounters characteristic of many modern urban areas, as well as by his concern for social justice.

As an 'approach to discourse' (Schiffrin, 1994), interactional sociolinguistics (IS) offers theories and methods that enable researchers to explore not only how language works but also to gain insights into the social processes through which individuals build and maintain relationships, exercise power, project and negotiate identities, and create communities. IS methodology involves an ethnographic component (observations of speakers in naturally-occurring contexts and participant-observation), audio- and/or video-recording of interactions, detailed linguistic transcription of recorded conversations, careful micro-analysis of conversational features in the context of the information gained through ethnography, and sometimes, post-recording interviews. The key theoretical contributions of IS are to explain how

speakers use signalling mechanisms, or 'contextualization cues' (Gumperz, 1978, 1982a, 1982b, 1992a, 1992b, 1999b, 2001), often prosodic (like intonation, stress, pitch register) or paralinguistic (like tempo, pausing, hesitation) in nature, to indicate how they mean what they say, and how listeners, through a nuanced, context-bound process Gumperz calls 'conversational inference', recognize and interpret contextualization cues through their own culturally-shaped background knowledge. In a foundational book investigating linguistic diversity in interaction, *Discourse Strategies*, Gumperz (1982a) suggests that communicative experiences lead to expectations regarding how to use contextualization cues; this study also demonstrates how members of diverse cultural groups often understand and employ these cues differently. Importantly, when interactional participants have dissimilar 'contextualization conventions' (Gumperz, 1982a) – that is, different ways of conventionally using and interpreting contextualization cues – misunderstandings and conversational breakdown can occur. Such breakdowns, Gumperz suggests, ultimately can contribute to larger social problems such as ethnic stereotyping and differential access to information and opportunities.

Conversational inference and the related notion of contextualization cues constitute an interactive theory of meaning-making that was designed to investigate intercultural communication and conflict based on cultural differences; in fact it has been suggested that the approach pioneered by Gumperz 'provides the most systematic investigations of such conflict' (Maynard, 1988: 315). It also offers a means of performing microanalysis of interaction in light of macro-societal issues like institutional discrimination, thus taking part in an ongoing quest in sociolinguistics to link the 'micro' and the 'macro' in meaningful ways (e.g. Erickson, 2004; Scollon and Scollon, 2004). Furthermore, IS offers a linguistic approach to the contemporary, constructionist understanding of identity put forth by researchers from a range of disciplinary perspectives (Goffman, 1959; Berger and Luckmann, 1966; Ochs, 1993; Holstein and Gubrium, 2007; see also Chapter 7 this volume). It has also made important contributions to the social scientific study of language in general, complementing other approaches aimed at understanding language from both structural and functional perspectives, such as conversation analysis and linguistic pragmatics. Additionally, IS has reached beyond the 'ivory tower' to offer non-academics a means of understanding the role of language in social relationships, ways of identifying causes of miscommunication, and strategies for improving communication. Gumperz, for instance, served as a consultant for an educational BBC television programme called *Crosstalk* (Twitchin, 1979) which addressed the subtleties of intercultural communication in multicultural workplaces in London; in addition, his work inspired other scholars to share, with non-academic audiences, sociolinguistic insights into everyday interactional dynamics.

This chapter presents an historical overview of IS, focusing on the research of Gumperz as well as of other scholars who have made significant contributions to the development of the approach. It outlines IS's primary inspirations, goals, topical foci, theoretical constructs, and methods. It also describes contemporary research in IS, identifying it as topically diverse, theoretically rich, and poised to address increasingly interdisciplinary research questions.

The main section of this paper traces the development of IS in detail, focusing primarily on the work of its founder, John Gumperz, and highlighting how, in formulating the key concepts and methodological frameworks of IS, he incorporated insights from scholars who examine interaction and meaning from a range of disciplinary perspectives (Section 5.2). I focus in particular on the methodological insights Gumperz developed in collaboration with Dell Hymes and through exposure to conversation analysis; the theoretical insights he gleaned from scholars such as Erving Goffman, Harold Garfinkel, and H. P. Grice; and IS theory developments contributed by Gumperz's student Deborah Tannen in light of Robin Lakoff's work. I also situate Gumperz's work in larger research trajectories in the field of linguistics. Next, I give a brief overview of five major research trajectories to which Gumperz's research

in IS has contributed substantially: code-switching and language contact; intercultural communication; language and gender; discursive identity construction; and language, power and institutions (Section 5.3). Finally, I discuss possible future directions of IS, in particular in the context of growing interests in interdisciplinary research (Section 5.4).

5.2 JOHN J. GUMPERZ AND THE DEVELOPMENT OF INTERACTIONAL SOCIOLINGUISTICS

Academic biography[1]

John J. Gumperz was born in 1922 in Germany; fleeing Germany pre-Holocaust, he came to the United States in 1939. He served in the US Army; it has been suggested that his later academic interests in intercultural communication and social justice may have taken root in part as a result of his emigration and military experiences. Gumperz received his bachelor's degree in science from the University of Ohio, Cincinnati in 1947, but after attending Linguistic Institute lectures as a graduate student in chemistry at the University of Michigan, he redirected his studies to linguistics. Gumperz received his PhD in Germanic Linguistics in 1954 from the University of Michigan, where he studied with Kenneth Pike and Hans Kurath. His dissertation examined variables of a German dialect spoken by third-generation immigrants in southeastern Michigan and linked these variables to social and religious groupings of individuals, setting the scene for his later research.

Gumperz went to Cornell University to teach as an instructor before finishing his degree. After receiving his PhD, Gumperz was invited to serve as the head of Cornell's Hindi language training programme; he subsequently went to India to do postdoctoral research in sociolinguistics as part of an interdisciplinary research team. In 1956, he began collaborating with linguist Charles Ferguson at Deccan College (in India) on language diversity issues when both were visiting faculty there. Ferguson and Gumperz (1960) co-edited *Linguistic Diversity in South Asia*, a special issue of the *International Journal of American Linguistics*, which, in William Labov's (2003: 5) words, provides 'the most important general statement' of the principles of the then young field of sociolinguistics. Gumperz gained more fieldwork experience in Norway in the 1960s, further fuelling his interests in linguistic diversity. The Norway study also resulted in a publication on code-switching

(Blom and Gumperz, 1972) in which forms and functions of code-switching are investigated in a novel way – as tied to situation (**situational switching**) and as tied to participants' relationships and their signalling of how the listener should interpret what the speaker says (**metaphorical switching**). As Kathryn Woolard (2004: 75), a student of Gumperz, remarks, his work 'has had not only seminal but enduring influence on the accepted anthropological view on codeswitching'. Importantly, the Norway study also proved foundational for Gumperz's development of the notion of contextualization cues in the IS framework: code-switching, like uses of pitch, intonation, pausing, gesture, and other contextualization cues, can be used to signal how verbal messages should be interpreted.

After his research in India, Gumperz was invited to design a Hindi-Urdu programme at the University of California, Berkeley. A number of his studies around that time focused specifically on conversational Hindi-Urdu (Gumperz, 1958, 1960, 1963; Gumperz and Naim, 1960; Gumperz and Rumery, 1962), but he increasingly grew interested in sociolinguistic aspects of language use across different cultural groups. At Berkeley, Gumperz served as chairperson for South and South-East Asian Studies (from 1968 to 1971); he also served as a faculty member in the Department of Anthropology, becoming a full professor in Anthropology in 1965. While affiliated with Berkley, Gumperz has taken opportunities to cultivate connections with scholars in Europe, especially in Austria, Germany, and the UK, as well as with scholars in the United States. He is currently an emeritus professor at Berkeley, and is affiliated with the University of California Santa-Barbara as a faculty member of an interdisciplinary research group with a PhD emphasis called Language, Interaction and Social Organization (LISO).

In establishing IS as an approach, Gumperz has explored topics as varied as language diversity, language contact, bilingualism, language and educational issues, and interethnic communication. With Dell Hymes, Gumperz co-edited two volumes key to the ethnography of communication (Gumperz and Hymes, 1964, 1972). His book *Discourse Strategies* (Gumperz, 1982a) and its companion edited volume, *Language and Social Identity* (Gumperz, 1982b), are viewed as groundbreaking in the study of issues of language and culture and as foundational IS texts. *Discourse Strategies* marks the beginning of Gumperz's current, ongoing research looking at interethnic and intercultural communication, communication and social background, and the social significance of details of communication (Prevignano and di Luzio, 2003). *Language and Social Identity*

consists of essays by students and postdoctoral researchers working with Gumperz – among them Monica Heller, Daniel Maltz, Ruth Borker, Celia Roberts, T.C. Jupp and Deborah Tannen – and by his spouse, and frequent co-author, Jenny Cook-Gumperz.

In the 1990s, Gumperz continued to refine his approach, linking conversational inference to Michael Silverstein's (1992, 1993) work on indexicality and conceptualizing contextualization cues as a class of indexicals (Gumperz, 2003), while also applying it to new institutional contexts in collaborative work (Cook-Gumperz and Gumperz, 1996, 1997, 2002) and furthering investigation of contextualization processes (as seen in Gumperz's contributions to two key IS edited volumes: Auer and di Luzio's *The Contextualization of Language*, and Duranti and Goodwin's *Rethinking Context*, both published in 1992). In conjunction with his former student Stephen Levinson, Gumperz co-edited a volume reexamining the influential 'Whorf hypothesis' (Gumperz and Levinson, 1996). In recent years, Gumperz (1999b, 2001) has taken opportunities to write reflective essays about IS. Additionally, he discusses his approach in *Language and Interaction: Discussions with John J. Gumperz* (Eerdmans, Prevignano and Thibault, 2003). This book includes two interviews with Gumperz (Prevignano and di Luzio, 2003; Prevignano and Thibault, 2003) in which he talks about the motivations of his work, explains in detail his conceptualization of contextualization cues, and outlines connections he sees between his approach and others, such as conversation analysis and Silverstein's semiotics. It also includes commentaries on Gumperz's work by researchers such as Levinson (2003). In a response essay, Gumperz (2003) addresses issues brought up by these commentaries.

In total, Gumperz has more than 100 published books, chapters and articles over the span of his career. He has also received many academic accolades, has served on the editorial boards of numerous academic journals, and is founding editor of the influential *Studies in Interactional Sociolinguistics* book series (in which *Discourse Strategies* is the first volume). Through his classes at Berkeley and visits to other universities in both the United States and abroad, Gumperz has introduced IS and issues of language and communication to students of interaction around the world. His approach is viewed as a key part of sociolinguistic research programmes in various European countries, such as Greece (Tsitsipis, 2006) and the UK (Rampton, 2007). Gumperz has been identified not only as the founder of IS but also as 'one of the foundational spirits in the broader field of sociolinguistics itself' (Levinson, 2003: 43).

Social and moral motivations in the development of interactional sociolinguistics

Interactional sociolinguistics emerged as Gumperz was developing 'replicable methods of qualitative analysis that account for our ability to interpret what participants intend to convey in everyday communicative practice' (Gumperz, 2001: 215). However, although as an approach to discourse IS gives insight into conversation as an entity in general, and into meaning-making processes in particular, it did not develop out of an interest in 'interaction in the abstract', but rather as a means of exploring linguistic and cultural diversity in everyday talk (Gumperz, 2003: 105). As Duranti and Goodwin (1992a: 229–30) note, 'Gumperz'[s] work is unique for his ability to merge intellectual, social, and moral considerations within his analytical apparatus'; that is, Gumperz developed IS as a way of not only explicating the interpretive procedures underlying talk but also to address the consequences of real-life, everyday conversational misunderstandings between members of different cultural groups.

The 'social' considerations of IS emerge through Gumperz's interest in understanding and explaining instances of miscommunication he observed in various fieldwork studies he undertook in India, Europe and the United States, and in trying to contribute to improving intercultural communication in increasingly diverse areas, particularly urban areas. For instance, in a now classic case-study example, Gumperz was invited to observe interactions between members of two groups suffering strained interactions and feelings of ill-will at work: native British cargo handlers and the Indian and Pakistani staff cafeteria workers who served their meals at a major British airport (Gumperz, 1982a, Chapter 8). Gumperz observed cultural differences in uses of – and expectations regarding – intonation, a key contextualization cue. When the Indian and Pakistani cafeteria workers offered a serving of gravy, for instance, they did not use rising intonation as most native British English speakers would. Instead, they uttered 'gravy' with a flat intonation because, to them, this was a culturally polite way of offering something. To native British English speakers, who had different expectations regarding intonation, this sounded rude; they thus misinterpreted the cafeteria workers' intentions. Calling into attention this seemingly minor difference in intonation usage and discussing it with members of both groups actually improved communication and inter-group perceptions. In this way, IS research clearly has practical social implications; it 'may lead to an explanation for the endemic and increasingly serious communication problems that

affect private and public affairs in our society' (Gumperz, 1982a: 172). This is particularly important as workplaces – and nations – become increasingly diverse.

The 'moral' considerations Duranti and Goodwin (1992a) mention relate to social injustices. Gumperz's work explores issues such as misattribution of intent, stereotyping, and discrimination in the context of interaction, in particular against ethnic minorities. Following the work of Frederick Erickson (1975), Gumperz investigates the role of language in enacting discrimination in 'gatekeeping encounters'; these are encounters in which 'two persons meet, usually as strangers, with one of them having authority to make decisions that affect the other's future' (Erickson and Schultz, 1982: xi). In such encounters, the consequences of misunderstandings can be very serious, especially for the person not in the authority position. In many of Gumperz's case studies, the participants have different expectations about contextualization conventions and/or mismatches regarding the nature of the institutional encounter in which they are involved. Thus, miscommunication does occur, and the person seeking access, usually an individual from an ethnic minority group, risks being denied material goods, a job prospect, or some other resource. For example, in a tape-recorded interview-counselling session that Gumperz (1982a, Chapter 8) analyses, a Pakistani teacher who has been unable to secure permanent employment in London has an unsuccessful exchange with the native British staff counsellor whose job it is to help him, largely due to different expectations about what needs to be said in the session and to different uses of prosodic and paralinguistic features like rhythm and intonation. Careful turn-by-turn analysis of the recording reveals that their interaction is rhythmically asynchronous and the speakers never achieve a joint understanding of where the interaction is going at any given time. In other words, they seem to be 'on parallel tracks which don't meet' (Gumperz and Roberts, 1980; as cited in Gumperz, 1982a: 185). Thus, the teacher does not receive the support he needs and the staff counsellor is not able to do her job effectively. One motivation of many IS studies, including many by Gumperz, is the belief that by uncovering cultural differences and by educating people about them, some such misunderstandings can be circumvented, thereby decreasing the likelihood of unintentional discrimination or denial of resources based on misinterpretation of culture-specific uses of contextualization cues.

In line with this belief, Gumperz has participated in public educational efforts. As mentioned, he served as a consultant on an educational programme called *Crosstalk*, which was broadcast on

BBC television in 1979. As part of a 10-part series called *Multi-Racial Britain*, *Crosstalk* aimed to help develop awareness of possible causes of intercultural miscommunication in workplaces, as well as to draw attention to the role of language in stereotyping and discrimination. Written materials were also prepared by Gumperz and his colleagues to accompany the programme (Gumperz et al., 1979, 1980). *Crosstalk*, while serving as a useful tool for educating the general public at the time it was aired, has applications for formal educational contexts too, such as for teaching English as a foreign language and for teacher training (Baxter and Levine, 1982), as well as for courses in intercultural communication (Kiesling and Paulston, 2005: 2). It also inspired later work aimed at general audiences, such as an educational video focused on communication between Native Alaskans and non-Natives called *Interethnic Communication* (Scollon and Jones, 1979), and, more famously, general audience books by Tannen (1986, 1990) that examine various kinds of cross-cultural and cross-subcultural communication.

The development of interactional sociolinguistics: Gumperz and his major intellectual influences

The research programme of Gumperz and his development of IS grew not only out of interest in the social issues facing diversifying societies but also out of Gumperz's training in structural linguistics; his contact with scholars from various fields interested in interaction, qualitative methodologies, and meaning-making; and broader movements in linguistics in the 1960s through to the 1980s. Gumperz's linguistics background; contacts with anthropologists, sociologists, language philosophers and other linguists; and participation in larger language debates contributed substantially to the development of IS.

A starting point: Bloomfield and structural linguistics

Gumperz's linguistic training was in the tradition of Saussure, Sapir and Bloomfield (Prevignano and di Luzio, 2003: 8); Gumperz specifically recognizes Leonard Bloomfield's (1933) book *Language*, a pioneering work in American structural linguistics, as having influenced and motivated some of his early reflections. As linguistic anthropologist (and Gumperz's student) Michael Agar (1994: 16) notes, structural linguistics 'puts a circle' around language, meaning that it separates grammar from its cultural context. However, Gumperz observes that structuralists' 'basic insights into linguistic, that is, phonological and

syntactic competence and their approach to speaking as a partially subconscious process, continue to be useful' despite shortcomings of the approach (Prevignano and di Luzio, 2003: 20). As we will see, Gumperz utilizes the notion of 'competence' in a similar sense to Hymes's 'communicative competence'. He also draws on a view of speaking as a partially 'subconscious' or 'automatic' phenomenon in examining how interpretations are actually made in interaction (see, e.g. Gumperz, 1982a). Thus he extends basic ideas from structural linguistics into social and cultural realms.

Structural linguistics also motivated Gumperz's research in a more specific way: Gumperz cites as a starting point for him Bloomfield's thinking on regional linguistic diversity as it is interconnected with patterning of interpersonal contacts. Bloomfield's work offered 'an initial outline of a theory of diversity that rests on human interaction as an analytical prime, and does not rely on *a priori* assumptions about ethnic, class or group identity' (Gumperz, 2003: 106). Gumperz (2003: 107) reports that a common assumption in the 1950s and 1960s was that communication between members of different social groups was problematic, yet, frustratingly, there was a lack of empirical evidence supporting this assumption. Therefore, he 'set out to explore the validity of the interactional approach to diversity' that he saw seeds of in Bloomfield's work (Gumperz, 2003: 107). Building on this, in research over the course of his career, Gumperz would move to erase 'the circle' that disconnects language from social life.

An anthropological perspective: Hymes and the ethnography of communication

In order to investigate diversity in interaction, in the 1960s Gumperz turned to anthropological methods while collaborating with Dell Hymes, who was then developing the ethnography of communication (see Gumperz and Hymes 1964, 1972; Chapter 4, this volume). In fact, Gumperz's use of ethnographic methods goes further back, at least to his time in India: Ferguson and Gumperz (1960), for example, undertook an exploration of language contact 'through qualitative methods involving work with informants, informal observations, and (sometimes) questionnaires' (Duranti, 2001: 5). The ethnography of communication, however, provided a systematic set of qualitative methodologies offering a means of analysing 'patterns of communication as part of cultural knowledge and behavior' (Schiffrin, 1994: 137). Importantly, ethnographic methods differ greatly from those of structural linguistics: rather than contrasting formal units, such as sounds or sentence structures, across languages, ethnographers undertake in-depth fieldwork, usually involving participant-observation and interviewing. From relatively long-term observation and engagement with the community under study, ethnographers learn things about people and the diverse ways in which they use language that can only be discovered and understood over time. To use Pike's (1967) terms, ethnographers of communication are interested in viewing data from both *etic* and *emic* perspectives (see Carbaugh and Hastings, 1992). In other words, analysis needs to go beyond a general perspective and occur 'in terms of categories which account for native perceptions of significance' (Gumperz, 1982a: 15). This is important because it extends beyond describing grammatical structures to the more problematic – and, for Gumperz, more consequential – task of identifying culturally meaningful categories, the relationships between them, and how language plays into their creation and maintenance.

This kind of anthropological 'thick description' (Geertz, 1973) can be said to characterize Gumperz's research, even during the early formation of IS. In Rampton's (2007: 597) words, 'Gumperz's work stands out for its empirical reconciliation of linguistics and ethnography'. For example, Gumperz's fieldwork in a caste-stratified North Indian village and a small, homogeneous town in northern Norway led to the development of means of exploring language diversity as firmly embedded in specific aspects of sociocultural life, giving an emic understanding of the data (see Gumperz, 1971). His findings indicated that social interaction – frequency and quality of interaction among individuals, specifically – explained the linguistic distinctions he observed. Category labels put on people like 'touchable' and 'untouchable' (terms of social categorization then used in many Indian communities) were not sufficient to explain what was going on. In addition, ideologies of interpersonal relations – who should interact with whom, and in what way – further explicated patterns of language use in these two locales. Gumperz thus discovered information about what Hymes (1972: 277) refers to as speakers' 'communicative competence', which includes information such as 'when to speak, when not' and 'what to talk about with whom, when, where, in what manner', going far beyond the grammatical knowledge described by structuralists.

Studying interaction and conceptualizing knowledge: Goffman and Garfinkel

The notion of 'communicative competence' suggests that in interacting, speakers follow not only grammatical rules, but also social rules, such as regarding what kinds of conversational topics are appropriate for what kinds of situations. In order to get at social rules in a meaningful way,

Gumperz reached beyond linguistics and anthropology to build into IS elements of sociologist Erving Goffman's work on the 'interaction order' and ethnomethodologist Harold Garfinkel's interest in the interpretive processes and background knowledge needed to keep interaction going. In fact, Gumperz has commented, 'In my approach to interaction, I take a position somewhat between that of Erving Goffman and Harold Garfinkel' (Prevignano and di Luzio, 2003: 8).

Although Goffman 'does not analyze language *per se*' (Schiffrin, 1994: 102), Gumperz views him as a 'sociological predecessor' of his own work (Gumperz, 2001: 216). Goffman (1967, 1974, 1981) contemplates face-to-face interaction with a focus on how it is that social encounters are constructed. In other words, he recognizes the 'interaction order' – how people behave in one another's co-presence and co-construct their social worlds in everyday encounters – as a legitimate area of study. Like Goffman, Gumperz views everyday interaction as worthy of study; furthermore, Goffman and Gumperz were both on the faculty at Berkeley – Gumperz in Anthropology, and Goffman in Sociology – for a number of overlapping years (1960–1968). Gumperz also finds inspiration in Goffman's work in that the notion of 'interaction order' provides 'a distinct level of discursive organization bridging the linguistic and the social' (Gumperz, 2001: 216). However, whereas Goffman does not focus on the details of language in his work, Gumperz, with his concept of contextualization cues, does.

Moreover, Goffman's observations and theorizing uncover many interesting – and often taken-for-granted – phenomena that occur in everyday encounters; IS is able to investigate these phenomena from a perspective that highlights the role of linguistic features and investigates conversation as a collaborative endeavour. For example, identity presentation, considered in Goffman's (1959) *The Presentation of Self in Everyday Life*, is examined from an IS perspective in *Language and Social Identity* (Gumperz, 1982b). Additionally, identity presentation and construction continues to be a topic of interest for IS scholars. For example, Tannen (1999), Kotthoff (2000), Kendall (2007) and others have drawn on IS to examine the linguistic creation of gendered identities. Framing, or how people establish and negotiate 'definitions of a situation' (Goffman, 1974: 11), relates to a central part of IS: invoking Silverstein's (1992, 1993) discussions of indexicality, Gumperz remarks that 'Contextualization cues, along with other indexical signs, serve to retrieve the frames (in Goffman's sense of the term) that channel the interpretive process' (Prevignano and di Luzio, 2003: 10). In other words, using a speaker's contextualization cues as guidelines, a listener imagines himself or herself to be in a particular kind of situation; this enables a listener to assess what the speaker intends. Thus, contextualization cues are a means of collaboratively accomplishing framing in discourse. Numerous IS scholars have demonstrated how this occurs and continue to develop a theory of framing in the context of sociolinguistics by integrating and extending Goffman's and Gumperz's theorizing (e.g. Tannen, 1993a). Frames theory has been used to investigate a host of contexts, ranging from everyday family interactions (e.g. Gordon, 2002, 2008; Kendall, 2006), to medical encounters (e.g. Ribeiro, 1994; Tannen and Wallat, 1993; Pinto, Ribeiro and Dantas, 2005), to moments of conversational humour (e.g. Kotthoff, 2000, 2002; Davies, 2003). Additionally, research has incorporated Goffman's (1967) work on face-saving and Brown and Levinson's (1987) work on face and linguistic politeness into IS analyses, such as by Kendall (2004), Kotthoff (2000) and Tannen (2005[1984]). Building on Goffman (1981), research in the IS tradition has also considered how alignments or 'footings' are linguistically created and managed (e.g. Couper-Kuhlen, 1996; Davies, 2003; Gordon, 2003; Tannen, 2003).

Gumperz also cites the work of Garfinkel as instrumental in his thinking about the nature of social interaction, as well as the knowledge required to participate in it. Garfinkel (1967) developed an approach within sociology known as ethnomethodology, which focuses on the interactive processes by which people create social organization and the knowledge needed to do this. Research in the IS tradition is able to examine the linguistic means by which social organization is accomplished. In addition, Garfinkel's (1967) experiments – usually known as 'breaching' or 'Garfinkeling' experiments – caught Gumperz's attention; these involved breaking social norms as a means of uncovering often unnamed social rules as well as people's knowledge and expectations about situations. Furthermore, Garfinkel made the insightful observation that interactants can never be detailed enough in talk to convey every aspect of meaning; thus some combination of 'practical reasoning' and 'unstated, taken-for-granted background knowledge' is needed to fill in what is left unsaid (Gumperz, 2001: 216). For Gumperz, Garfinkel's observations brought to light the role of sociocultural background knowledge in interpretation, a critical component of his theory of conversational inference. In the IS framework, and in the spirit of Hymes (1972), researchers argue that speakers gain sociocultural knowledge from having been acculturated in a community. In other words, knowledge about how to use language in culturally apt ways – how to use pitch, intonation and other contextualization cues, including those that are non-verbal – comes from

a speaker's collection of cultural experiences. It is this knowledge base that participants rely on too as they interpret contextualization cues. The nature and functioning of this knowledge – what exactly it encompasses, and how people access and activate the appropriate knowledge at a given conversational moment – is still under investigation in IS and related areas of research.

Micro-analysis of talk: conversation analysis

Garfinkel and Goffman also influenced Gumperz in a more indirect way: conversation analysis (CA) (see Chapter 26, this volume), which proved influential to Gumperz's research, grew out of the work of two of Goffman's students at Berkeley in the 1960s: Harvey Sacks and Emanuel Schegloff. In collaboration with Sacks's student Gail Jefferson, Sacks and Schegloff applied Garfinkel's ethnomethodology specifically to conversation (see Sacks, Schegloff and Jefferson, 1974). CA is interested in how conversation represents and creates social organization among participants; its focus on conversational discourse – both face-to-face and over the phone – as a research site and on the details of language provided inspiration for Gumperz's focus on talk and on the micro features of interaction (Gumperz, 1999b, 2001; Prevignano and di Luzio, 2003).

Both IS and CA examine actual social encounters, and their methods both involve recording, a form of careful linguistic transcription, and analysis of interaction. Key CA notions and conceptualizations of interaction are also central to IS. For example, Sacks, Schegloff and Jefferson (1974), in a seminal CA study, outline a 'systematics' for conversation based on the basic organizational unit of the conversational turn. This study views conversation as a sequentially organized event; in Heritage's (1984: 242) words, each utterance is 'context-shaped' (shaped by the prior utterance) and 'context-renewing' (creating a context for the next utterance). IS researchers consider this sense of context (discourse context) in their analyses; however, IS also takes a broader perspective on what constitutes context and its effect on conversation.[2] For example, whereas CA researchers tend to claim it is 'the independence of the turn-taking system from various aspects of the socio-cultural context of speech' such as the speakers' ethnicity, gender, or socioeconomic class (Duranti, 1989: 222), IS scholars consider such aspects to be central to how interaction unfolds, and indeed are interested in exploring diversity of turn-taking patterns across cultural groups (e.g. Tannen, 2005[1984]). In other words, whereas 'the CA view of interaction is a structural view' (Schiffrin, 1994: 236), IS shows a more social and cultural emphasis. Thus, for instance, CA research has examined assessments from the perspective of conversational structure (Pomerantz, 1984), and research growing out of IS builds on this to demonstrate how two parents use assessments as a means of presenting different kinds of identities in interaction (Gordon, 2007).

In part, based on these different conceptualizations of what constitutes an utterance's context, IS and CA differ in another regard: Gumperz adopted playback, used in early sociolinguistic work by William Labov (Labov and Fanshel, 1977; see also Fanshel and Moss, 1971), as a means of testing analyst interpretations. Playback involves playing recordings of the interaction for those who participated in it, or for other insiders to the language variety and/or community, and asking for impressions in an open-ended way. It therefore provides multiple perspectives on interaction, which can be particularly insightful in cases of cross-cultural (mis)communication, where analysts might have native speaker insights into one side of the conversation, but not the other, based on his or her own cultural and linguistic background, as in Gumperz (1982a) and Tannen (2005[1984]).

CA and IS continue to exist, side-by-side, as approaches to discourse analysis. Although they both investigate conversational discourse as what Schegloff (1982) calls 'an interactional achievement', i.e. as something 'incrementally accomplished' via collaboration, CA and IS examine different aspects of the achievement. Sharing an interest in the micro features of conversation, they continue to influence and complement each other mutually, for example by offering different perspectives on similar kinds of social interaction, as in Tannen and Goodwin's (2006) co-edited *Text and Talk* special issue on family interaction. Furthermore, some scholars, like Goodwin (1990), have integrated CA methods with ethnographic fieldwork, blurring the distinction between the approaches and demonstrating that integrated perspectives are often especially revealing.

Inference: Berkeley scholars – Grice and Lakoff

A number of scholars who interacted with Gumperz at Berkeley during the formulation of IS also influenced its development in meaningful ways. Levinson (2003: 32), who was then Gumperz's graduate student, describes the intellectual environment in which the approach developed:

> In Berkeley at that time there was a rare and wonderful confluence of ideas from different disciplines concerning the study of meaning – in philosophy, Grice and Searle were expounding the ideas about implicature and speech acts now

associated with them, Fillmore was preoccupied with indexicality in language, Kay with its sociological import, Robin Lakoff with contextual meaning, and George Lakoff was attempting to wrap it all up in a unified theory of generative semantics.

This intellectual milieu seems to have shaped Gumperz's thinking in multiple ways.

First, Gumperz's theory of conversational inference, which explains how people assess what others say to create meaning in conversation and what is required for this to occur, is related to language philosopher H. P. Grice's (1975) discussion of conversational cooperation, intention and implicature (Gumperz, 2001: 216; see also Gumperz, 1982a: 202). Grice's (1975: 47) influential Cooperative Principle (CP) states: 'Make your contribution such as is required, at the stage at which it occurs, by the accepted purpose of the talk exchange in which you are engaged'. This principle, essentially, explains why conversation works at all, in particular at the level of information exchange. The CP includes four maxims which indicate that a speaker should be as (but not more) informative than required, tell the truth, contribute relevant remarks, and be orderly and clear. Within this framework, Grice suggests that speakers send certain meanings intentionally through **implicatures** sent by following or breaking ('flouting') maxims. An implicature is 'an inference about speaker intention that arises from a recipient's use of both semantic (i.e. logical) meanings and conversational principles' (Schiffrin, 1994: 193); it refers to 'something which is implied in conversation, that is, something which is left implicit in actual language use' (Mey, 1993: 99). Thus, if a man asks a woman where he can buy a cup of coffee, and she says, 'there's a place around the corner called Joe's', based on the CP maxims of truth and relevance, the man infers that coffee is for sale by the cup at Joe's.[3] These maxims play into an IS understanding of how meaning-making works as well.

Secondly, Grice's (1975) and Searle's (1975) discussions of 'the semantic basis of indirect conversational inference' (Gumperz, 1982a: 202) link to Gumperz's exploration of the indirect means by which speakers signal how utterances are to be interpreted. One way of thinking about contextualization cues is as indirect signals for interpretation: rather than saying, for example, 'I'm mad that you didn't invite me for coffee', a speaker might furrow his brow and say, in a whiney tone of voice, 'You didn't invite me for coffee', thus indirectly indicating how the listener should interpret his meaning. The impact of Robin Lakoff's (1973, 1975) work on indirectness and linguistic politeness fits into this area as well, and it is formally incorporated into IS by Tannen (2005[1984]).

Lakoff (1973) notes that people regularly do not explicitly say what they mean in conversation for social reasons – to be nice, to respect another person's space, to leave interpretation options open, and so on. Importantly, research in IS shows that conceptualizations of how to be conventionally polite differ across cultural and subcultural groups (e.g. Scollon and Scollon, 2001[1995]; Tannen, 2005[1984]; Rogerson-Revell, 2007).

Conversational style and conversational involvement: Tannen

While at Berkeley, Gumperz also collaborated with Tannen, who had a significant impact on IS, although she is perhaps best known for her work on language and gender. When Tannen was Gumperz's student, they co-authored a foundational IS paper, 'Individual and social differences in language use' (Gumperz and Tannen, 1979) which introduced the notion of contextualization cues and provides material that would later be incorporated into a central chapter of *Discourse Strategies* entitled 'Contextualization Conventions'. Tannen's first book, *Conversational Style* (2005[1984]), provides an important case study of cross-subcultural communication, introduces the key IS notion of 'conversational style' and a new understanding of what Gumperz (1982a) called 'conversational involvement', while also serving as an excellent example and overview of IS methodology.

'Conversational style' refers to an individual's way of speaking, including decisions about rate of speaking, pitch and amplitude, and the 'countless other choices' speakers make that affect an utterance's interpretation (Tannen, 2005[1984]: 14). In broad terms, a person's conversational style encompasses how he or she uses various contextualization cues. Drawing on the IS idea that a person's contextualization conventions grow out of interactive experiences, Tannen suggests that conversational style can be influenced by a range of factors, including where a person grew up and his or her cultural background, race and ethnicity, and gender and sexual orientation. Tannen's case study of six speakers – three New York Jewish speakers, two Californians, and one speaker from England – uncovers a style continuum. Her analysis, building on not only Gumperz's research but also Hymes's (1974) on style and Lakoff's on politeness (1973) and communicative style (1979), shows that features of the 'high-involvement style' characteristic of New Yorkers – such as talking along with other people and asking questions in a 'machine gun' fashion – have a positive affect when used among those who share the style; these features create 'rapport'. In contrast, as in Gumperz's examples of mismatches in contextualization conventions, aspects of high-involvement style have negative affects when used with speakers exhibiting a style characterized by 'high-considerateness' (see also Tannen, 1981).

A concept from Gumperz that Tannen extended and made even more central to IS is 'conversational involvement' (Tannen, 2005[1984], 2007[1989]). Gumperz (1982a: 1) used this notion in a very basic way, equating sustaining conversational involvement to participating in verbal exchanges; Tannen (2007[1989]: 13) develops involvement further: it is the 'internal, even emotional connection individuals feel which binds them to other people as well as to places, things, activities, ideas, memories and words'. She suggests that when aspects of style are shared, interacting serves as a means of building coherence and of bringing people together, the inverse of how clashing styles can drive wedges between them. In *Talking Voices*, Tannen (2007[1989]) uses IS to examine both conversational and literary texts and focuses on repetition, the creation of dialogue ('constructed dialogue'), and details as linguistic strategies that seem to be especially productive in creating involvement.

Tannen (1986, 2005[1984]) also argues in her work that, through contextualization cues, participants send what Bateson (1972) calls 'metamessages', or messages about how to interpret messages (e.g. 'this is play'). In other words, Tannen develops the idea that participants use contextualization cues to negotiate both the nature of a given situation and aspects of interpersonal relationships. For example, through 'mutual revelation', where participants reciprocally share personal experiences with one another, participants are able to signal indirectly something to the effect of: 'We are intimate; we both tell about ourselves; we are both interested in hearing about the other's experience' (Tannen, 2005[1984]: 101).

Another contribution of Tannen to IS is bringing IS notions and their roles in interpersonal communication to broader audiences. Through popular books like *That's Not What I Meant!* (1986) and the best-selling *You Just Don't Understand* (1990), academic ideas about language and communication are shown to have, in the spirit of Gumperz's interests in social issues, practical applicability to everyday life.[4]

Chomsky and Labov

When Gumperz was formulating and developing IS, other theories of language were being cultivated by Noam Chomsky and William Labov, and these influenced IS through providing approaches with which it could be compared and contrasted. In the early years of IS, Gumperz was considering language and social networks (Gumperz, 1971, 1976), the sociolinguistics of bilingualism and code-switching (Gumperz 1964a, 1964b; Blom and Gumperz, 1972; Gumperz and Cook-Gumperz, 1974) and language use in a variety of institutional contexts, including educational environments (Gumperz and Hernandez-Chavez, 1972; Gumperz and Cook-Gumperz, 1974), job interviews and counselling sessions (Gumperz et al., 1979; Gumperz, 1982a), committee meetings (Gumperz and Cook-Gumperz, 1982), and legal contexts (Gumperz, 1982c). In such studies, Gumperz's approach, in his own words, reworks 'the established traditions that continue to follow structuralist practices of separating the linguistic from the social' (Prevignano and di Luzio, 2003:10). It thus stands in contrast with descendents of Saussure's structuralist approach to linguistics, including alternatives to it, the most notable being generative grammar, pioneered by Chomsky beginning in the late 1950s. For Gumperz (1982a: 19), although generative grammar has 'theoretical significance', it also 'clearly has only limited relevance for the study of verbal interaction processes'. Chomsky's work focuses on the knowledge an ideal speaker needs to produce grammatical sentences ('linguistic competence'); it does not 'attempt to account for the problem of cultural diversity' (Gumperz, 1974: 789). In contrast, Gumperz focuses on utterances produced and interpreted in context, and the knowledge – linguistic, social, and cultural – that participants use in so doing. He thus moves to erase the metaphorical 'circle' that Agar (1994) has written about that disconnects language from social life, whereas Chomsky maintains the circle. Indeed, a major division that exists in contemporary linguistics is the division between Chomskyan linguistics and sociolinguistics. Thus, IS continues to develop itself – at least implicitly – in contrast to generative grammar.

During the time of IS's development, 'the circle' was also being erased by other scholars, such as Charles Ferguson (1959), who was examining diglossia; indeed, Ferguson's work provided a foundation for Gumperz's (1977) work on conversational code-switching (see also Blom and Gumperz, 1972). In addition, Labov was developing a quantitative sociolinguistics that linked linguistic variables to social categories (see Labov, 1966, 1972; see also Chapter 2, this volume). In a spirit similar to Gumperz, Labov's research focuses on language as a social entity. However, as Gumperz notes, 'important as quantitative sociolinguistics is' for the study of language variation and change, 'its applicability to the analysis of actual processes of face to face communication ... is limited' (Gumperz, 1982a: 26). This is so because Labovian sociolinguistics traditionally focuses on the quantitative analysis of linguistic variables at the social group level, whereas IS focuses on individuals' language use. Furthermore, the statistical analyses of variationist

sociolinguistics do not give insight into meaning-making as it happens moment-by-moment; in contrast, IS offers a view of language as 'activity in a particular context, co-evolving along with that context, in part constitutive of it' (Becker, 1995[1984]: 73). Because IS gives a nuanced analysis of individuals communicating in unfolding interactive sequences, it provides what Becker (1995[1984]) might call a 'linguistics of particularity', which we need to achieve a more complete understanding of how language works generally.

Just as there are theoretical and methodological tensions between generative grammar and sociolinguistics, so there are tensions between quantitative and qualitative sociolinguistics. As Tannen (2005[1984]: 11–12) points out, it might be easy to dismiss a qualitative approach like IS due to its interpretive analytical procedures – with 'interpretive' 'wielded as a damning epithet'. Analysing talk in the IS tradition is necessarily interpretive in that researchers must weigh multiple possibilities – in terms of speaker intentions, listener interpretations, and so on – as they grapple with different levels of linguistic structure, the delicate twists and turns of social encounters, and the fact that there is no one-to-one correspondence between form and meaning. However, as Johnstone (2000: 36) notes, 'sociolinguistic work is always "interpretive," whether the interpretation involves numbers or results of some other kind. ... Only with interpretation does an analysis have a point'. And, although there will always be difficulties in uncovering speaker intent, the theory developed by Gumperz addresses these difficulties by taking an interactive approach that captures the use of (para) linguistic features in contextualized utterances as well as the listener's reaction to these. In addition, examination of negotiations and repairs occurring in discourse can aid in analyst interpretations of speaker intent (Prevignano and di Luzio, 2003).

Although Gumperz's IS is markedly different from variationist sociolinguistics, it can also be viewed as developing in complementary fashion and contributing complementary insights into language and social life. Indeed, a growing number of scholars now view quantitative and ethnographic perspectives on language as usefully applied in tandem to explore issues like identity construction (e.g. Eckert, 2000; Schilling-Estes, 2004).

5.3 KEY RESEARCH TRAJECTORIES IN INTERACTIONAL SOCIOLINGUISTICS

We have seen that IS as an approach to the analysis of discourse grew primarily out of Gumperz's work and multifaceted interests, as well as his incorporation of insights from a range of fields.

This formed a coherent framework of how meaning-making occurs in interaction that has propelled numerous research trajectories both within and beyond IS. These include studies related to code-switching and language contact, intercultural communication, language and gender, identity construction, and language, power and institutions. Note that as more and more scholars are using integrated methods – combining ideas and methods from IS and CA and social psychology, for example – it has become more and more difficult (if not impossible) to identify a 'purely' IS study.

Code-switching and language contact

Many studies in code-switching and language contact have built on Gumperz's early and groundbreaking work on linguistic diversity in speech communities, his scholarship on conversational code-switching, and his identification of code-switching as fundamentally similar to style-shifting and as a contextualization cue. In the 1980s and 1990s, Gumperz's students drew on his framework to study language choice and language rights (e.g. Heller, 1982, 1985; Woolard, 1985), and colleagues in Europe (e.g. Auer and di Luzio 1984, 1992) provided insights into code-switching, language socialization, and issues related to language and migration, while also contributing to the development of IS as an 'interpretative' sociolinguistics (see also earlier work, published in German, by Kallmeyer and Schütze, 1977).

Code-switching continues to be a topic of interest in sociolinguistic research (see Chapter 31, this volume). Code-switching has recently been examined in a number of vital everyday contexts, among them families (e.g. Wei, 1994; Blum-Kulka, 1997), informal gatherings among friends (e.g. Hinnenkamp, 2003; Kallmeyer and Keim, 2003; Keim, 2003), courtrooms (e.g. Gumperz, 1999a; Jacquemet, 1996), workplaces (e.g. Holmes and Stubbe, 2004; Prego-Vazquez, 2007), educational contexts (e.g. Rampton, 1995; Bailey, 2000), and email discourse (e.g. Georgakopoulou, 1997). It has also been investigated as a resource in discursive identity construction (e.g. Rampton, 1995; Bailey, 2000; Holmes and Stubbe, 2004; Auer, 2007) and for enacting societal ills such as racism (e.g. Hill, 1995). Indeed, much of this body of research, in the spirit of Gumperz, investigates code-switching and language contact as related to issues of social inequality.

Intercultural communication

As mentioned previously, Tannen's (2005[1984]) work on 'conversational style' advanced IS by providing a discussion of, and developing, the theoretical underpinnings of IS as an approach to cross-(sub)cultural communication. Tannen's (1986) *That's Not What I Meant!* covers similar ground for non-academic audiences, while Agar's (1994) *Language Shock* offers non-academic audiences an anthropological perspective on issues of communication and culture.

Given our continually globalizing world, there is continued interest in intercultural communication, especially between 'East' and 'West', and IS is being used productively to explore it. For example, Haru Yamada (1997) investigates Japanese–American discourse, with a focus on workplace settings, while Linda W. L. Young (1994) considers Chinese–American interaction. Yuling Pan, Suzanne Wong Scollon and Ron Scollon's more comprehensive *Professional Communication in International Settings* (2002) considers a range of cultural groups and discourse types and incorporates multiple approaches, and is also aimed at general audiences, while Scollon and Scollon's (2001[1995]) *Intercultural Communication: A Discourse Approach* provides a thorough, more academic introduction to the topic. Donal Carbaugh (2005) integrates IS and ethnography in his book *Cultures in Conversation* to consider a variety of issues related to communication and culture. Such studies, building on Gumperz's work, provide insight into various kinds of intercultural miscommunication; they identify a range of causative factors, including uses of address terms, the structuring of information in discourse, and uses of pacing and pausing; some also give practical suggestions for improving communication. Many are important not only because they contribute to a more nuanced understanding of cultural differences and how these manifest interactionally but also because they aim to educate the public about cultural aspects of communication.

Language and gender

Interactional sociolinguistics serves as one of many theoretical orientations that have been drawn on to investigate gender and communication. The pioneering study of Maltz and Borker (1982) provided a starting point for Tannen's (1990, 1994, 1996, 1999) writing on language and gender in which Tannen investigates interactions between women and men as a kind of cross-cultural communication and firmly establishes IS as a useful approach to gendered interaction. Her general audience book *You Just Don't Understand* (Tannen, 1990) offers insights into everyday communication rituals of speakers of both genders. Much like Lakoff's (1975) *Language and Woman's Place*, Tannen's work has fuelled both academic and popular interest in the topic. In fact, language and gender research 'exploded' in the 1990s and continues to be a topic receiving a great deal of attention from researchers using various theoretical and methodological perspectives (Kendall and Tannen, 2001; see also Chapter 28, this volume). IS continues to be – implicitly or explicitly – important among these (see e.g. Tannen, 1993b; Hall and Bucholtz, 1995; Kotthoff and Wodak, 1997; Wodak, 1997b, 1997c; Bucholtz, Liang and Sutton, 1999).

Discursive identity construction

In the tradition established by *Language and Social Identity* (Gumperz, 1982b), IS has been used to examine how people create and negotiate identities in interaction. Contexts explored include workplaces (e.g. Kendall, 2003; Holmes and Stubbe, 2004), educational settings (e.g. Cook-Gumperz and Gumperz, 1996; Bailey, 2000; Wortham, 2006), families (e.g. Gordon, 2004; Tannen, Kendall and Gordon, 2007), and other social groups (e.g. Hamilton, 1998; Kiesling, 2001). Gendered identities are of particular interest, as are identities related to changing ethnic landscapes, especially in Europe (e.g. Auer, 2007). Such studies reveal the various linguistic means by which identities are constructed, make efforts at linking linguistic features with broader ideologies, and in general contribute to our understanding of how individuals use language to accomplish social goals.

Language, power, and institutions

A thread of research known as critical discourse analysis (CDA) addresses social inequalities through academic research in a spirit akin to the goals of Gumperz's IS approach (see for instance Chouliaraki and Fairclough, 1999); CDA shares with IS 'the interest in looking at language as a means of illuminating social problems' (Gumperz, personal communication). CDA studies draw on a number of approaches to discourse, among them IS, but focus more explicitly on issues of dominance and inequality. For example, Scollon and Scollon (2001[1995]) integrate IS methodologies with a CDA focus on ideologies in *Intercultural Communication*, while Wodak (1997b, 1997c) does so to examine issues of language and gender.

Institutional encounters in which power is negotiated and exercised, like academic assessments (Cook-Gumperz and Gumperz, 1997), medical encounters (Tannen and Wallat, 1993; Wodak, 1997a), and courtroom interactions (Jacquemet, 1996; Eades, 2003, 2005) have also been examined by drawing on IS, although the focus of such analyses is not necessarily power. While some researchers have criticized IS for examining how members of different groups use language (the 'difference' approach) to the exclusion of considering larger power structures, like institutional discrimination (the 'dominance' approach) (Singh, Lele and Martohardjono, 1988), linking macro (sociopolitical forces and cultural discourses) and micro (conversational features) has actually been identified as a strength of IS (Levinson, 2003: 37). Furthermore, recent research by Eades (2005) explores difficulties in the difference/dominance dichotomy and explains strengths and weaknesses of each, suggesting we need a 'discourse' approach to go beyond these two perspectives. In addition, Gumperz has answered some criticisms of IS by addressing larger cultural forces like gender discrimination in his research in more explicit ways; for example, Cook-Gumperz and Gumperz (1996) uncover a subtle subtext of gender discrimination in a PhD defence by analysing contextualization cues like prosody in the context of the unfolding interaction, the interpersonal relationships among participants, the content of the talk, and the socio-historical roots of the defence as an event. Whether such efforts convince critics or not, interests in learning more about ways to link micro and macro in analyses of social interaction persist (e.g. Al Zidjaly, 2006; Wortham, 2006), and much research in this area is inspired in some way by Gumperz's approach.

5.4 SUMMARY AND FUTURE DIRECTIONS

We have seen that, since its inception, interactional sociolinguistics has been interdisciplinary. Its founder, John Gumperz, is an anthropological linguist (or a linguistic anthropologist – see Gumperz 2003: 117); other scholars contributing concepts, theories, and methodological perspectives hail from sociology (Garfinkel and Goffman), anthropology (Hymes), philosophy (Searle and Grice), and linguistics (Lakoff and Tannen). Many of these scholars, like Gumperz himself, have stretched the boundaries of their respective disciplines; their scholarship connects what is 'inside the circle' of their field with that which lies outside. Growing from these interdisciplinary roots are numerous examples of studies using IS that involve scholars from multiple, and quite disparate, backgrounds and perspectives. For instance, genetic counsellors and linguists have collaboratively examined how prenatal genetic counsellors interact with their clients (e.g. Benkendorf et al., 2001; Gordon et al., 2002); linguists and medical professionals have explored doctor–patient talk (e.g. Hamilton et al., 2008); and anthropologists, linguists, and communication studies scholars have addressed various facets of family discourse (e.g. Tannen and Goodwin, 2006). Given recent calls for moves toward interdisciplinarity in medical communication research (by Sarangi, 2004), in studies of the family (by Schneider and Waite, 2005), and in CDA (by Wodak and Chilton, 2005), and given the current academic climate in which interdisciplinary and multidisciplinary research is valued and encouraged, IS will surely continue to play a leading role in investigations of social interaction across a range of contexts.

ACKNOWLEDGEMENTS

I thank Najma Al Zidjaly, Richard Buttny, Donal Carbaugh, Deborah Tannen, and Alla Tovares for their helpful comments on earlier drafts of this chapter. I am especially grateful to John Gumperz for commenting on an earlier draft and for taking the time to talk with me about his work. I also thank Barbara Johnstone and Ruth Wodak for their valuable comments and suggestions.

NOTES

1 Biographical information was gleaned from the following sources: biographical overviews by Dil (1971) and Berenz (2001); a short 'bionote' written by Eerdmans, Prevignano and Thibault in their edited volume *Language and Interaction: Discussions with John J. Gumperz* (2003), as well as a short introduction of Gumperz (di Luzio, 2003), an interview with him (Prevignano and di Luzio, 2003), and an essay by Gumperz (2003) in the same volume; an unpublished biographical introduction and interview by Tannen conducted at Georgetown University in spring 2001; and personal communication between Gumperz and me (23 July 2008).

2 See Duranti and Goodwin (1992b) for a collection of essays – including one by Gumperz – critically examining the notion of context.

3 This example is adapted from Bergmann et al. (2007: 80).

4 *You Just Don't Understand* spent nearly four years on the *New York Times* bestseller list.

REFERENCES

Agar, M. (1994) *Language Shock: Understanding the Culture of Conversation*. New York: Quill.

Al Zidjaly, N. (2006) 'Disability and anticipatory discourse: the interconnectedness of local and global aspects of talk', *Communication and Medicine*, 3(2): 101–12.

Auer, P. (2007) (ed.) *Style and Social Identities: Alternative Approaches to Linguistic Heterogeneity*. Berlin and New York: Walter de Gruyter.

Auer, P. and di Luzio, A. (1984) *Interpretive Sociolinguistics*. Tübingen: Narr.

Auer, P. and di Luzio, A. (1992) *The Contextualization of Language*. Amsterdam: John Benjamins.

Bailey, B. (2000) 'The language of multiple identities among Dominican Americans', *Journal of Linguistic Anthropology*, 10(2): 190–223.

Bateson, G. (1972) *Steps to an Ecology of Mind*. New York: Ballantine Books.

Baxter, J. and Levine, D. (1982) 'Review of *Crosstalk* by John Twitchen', *TESOL Quarterly*, 16(2): 245–53.

Becker, A. L. (1995[1984]) 'The linguistics of particularity: interpreting superordination in a javanese text', in *Beyond Translation: Essays Toward a Modern Philology*. Ann Arbor, MI: University of Michigan Press. pp. 71–87.

Benkendorf, J. L., Prince, M. B., Rose, M. A., De Fina, A. and Hamilton, H. E. (2001) 'Does indirect speech promote nondirective genetic counseling? Results of a sociolinguistic investigation', *American Journal of Medical Genetics (Seminars in Medical Genetics)*, 106: 199–207.

Berenz, N. (2001) 'Gumperz, John J.', in Rajend Mesthrie (ed.), *Concise Encyclopedia of Sociolinguistics*. Amsterdam: Elsevier. p. 875.

Berger, P. L. and Luckmann, T. (1966) *The Social Construction of Reality: A Treatise in the Sociology of Knowledge*. Garden City, NY: Doubleday.

Bergmann, A., Hall, Kathleen, C. and Ross, S. M. (2007) *Language Files: Materials for an Introduction to Language and Linguistics*. 10th edn. Columbus, OH: the Ohio State University Press.

Blom, J.-P. and Gumperz, J. J. (1972) 'Social meaning in linguistic structure: code-switching in Norway', in J. J. Gumperz and D. Hymes (eds), *Directions in Sociolinguistics*. New York: Holt, Rinehart and Winston. pp. 407–34.

Bloomfield, L. (1933) *Language*. New York: Holt, Rinehart and Winston.

Blum-Kulka, S. (1997) *Dinner Talk: Cultural Patterns of Sociability and Socialization in Family Discourse*. Mahwah, NJ: Erlbaum.

Brown, P. and Levinson, S. (1987) *Politeness: Some Universals in Language Usage*. Cambridge: Cambridge University Press.

Bucholtz, M., Liang, A. C. and Sutton, L. A. (eds) (1999) *Reinventing Identities: The Gendered Self in Discourse*. Oxford: Oxford University Press.

Carbaugh, D. (2005) *Cultures in Conversation*. Mahwah, NJ: Lawrence Erlbaum Publishers.

Carbaugh, D. and Hastings, S. O. (1992) 'A role for communication theory in ethnography and cultural analysis', *Communication Theory*, 2: 156–65.

Chouliaraki, L. and Fairclough, N. (1999) *Discourse in Late Modernity: Rethinking Critical Discourse Analysis*. Edinburgh: Edinburgh University Press.

Cook-Gumperz, J. and Gumperz, J. J. (1996) 'Treacherous words: gender and power in academic assessment', *Folia Linguistica*, 30(3–4): 167–88.

Cook-Gumperz, J. and Gumperz, J. J. (1997) 'Narrative explanations: accounting for past experience in interviews', *Journal of Narrative and Life History*, 7(1–4): 291–8.

Cook-Gumperz, J. and Gumperz, J. J. (2002) 'Narrative accounts in gatekeeping interviews: Intercultural differences or common misunderstandings?', *Language and Intercultural Communication*, 2(1): 25–36.

Couper-Kuhlen, E. (1996) 'The prosody of repetition: on quoting and mimicry', in E. Couper-Kuhlen and M. Selting (eds), *Prosody in Conversation*. Cambridge: Cambridge University Press. pp. 367–405.

Davies, C. E. (2003) 'How English-learners joke with native speakers: an interactional sociolinguistic perspective on humor as collaborative discourse across cultures', *Journal of Pragmatics*, 35: 1361–85.

di Luzio, A. (2003) 'Presenting John J. Gumperz', in S. L. Eerdmans, C. L. Prevignano and P. J. Thibault (eds), *Language and Interaction: Discussions with John J. Gumperz*. Amsterdam: John Benjamins. pp. 1–6.

Dil, A. S. (1971) 'A biographical sketch of John J. Gumperz to 1971', in A. S. Dil (ed.), *Language in Social Groups: Essays by John J. Gumperz*. Stanford, CA: Stanford University Press. pp. xi–xiv.

Duranti, A. (1989) 'Ethnography of speaking: toward a linguistics of the praxis', in F. J. Newmeyer (ed.), *Language: The Cambridge Survey. Vol. IV, Language: The Socio-Cultural Context*. Cambridge: Cambridge University Press. pp. 210–28.

Duranti, A. (2001) 'Linguistic anthropology: history, ideas, and issues', in A. Duranti (ed.), *Linguistic Anthropology: A Reader*. Malden, MA: Blackwell. pp. 1–38.

Duranti, A. and Goodwin, C. (1992a) 'Editor's introduction to "Contextualization and understanding" by John J. Gumperz', in A. Duranti and C. Goodwin (eds), *Rethinking Context: Language as an Interactive Phenomenon*. Cambridge: Cambridge University Press. pp. 229–30.

Duranti, A. and Goodwin, C. (1992b) (eds), *Rethinking Context: Language as an Interactive Phenomenon*. Cambridge: Cambridge University Press.

Eades, D. (2003) 'Participation of second language and second dialect speakers in the legal system', *Annual Review of Applied Linguistics*, 23: 113–33.

Eades, D. (2005) 'Beyond difference and domination? Intercultural communication in legal contexts', in S. F. Kiesling and C. B. Paulston (eds), *Intercultural Discourse and Communication: The Essential Readings*. Malden, MA: Blackwell. pp. 304–16.

Eckert, P. (2000) *Linguistic Variation as Social Practice*. Malden, MA: Blackwell.

Eerdmans, S. L., Prevignano, C. L. and Thibault, P. J. (eds) (2003) *Language and Interaction: Discussions with John J. Gumperz*. Amsterdam: John Benjamins.

Erickson, F. (1975) 'Gatekeeping and the melting pot: interaction in counseling encounters', *Harvard Educational Review*, 45(1): 44–70.

Erickson, F. (2004) *Talk and Social Theory: Ecologies of Speaking and Listening in Everyday Life*. Cambridge: Polity Press.

Erickson, F. and Shultz, J. (1982) *The Counselor as Gatekeeper: Social Interaction in Interviews*. New York: Academic Press.

Fanshel, D. and Moss, F. (1971) *Playback: A Marriage in Jeopardy Examined*. New York: Columbia University Press.

Ferguson, C. (1959) 'Diglossia', *Word*, 15: 325–40.

Ferguson, C. A. and Gumperz, J. J. (eds) (1960) 'Linguistic diversity in South Asia: studies in regional, social and functional variation', *International Journal of American Linguistics*, 26: 3 (part 3).

Garfinkel, H. (1967) *Studies in Ethnomethodology*. Englewood Cliffs, NJ: Prentice-Hall.

Geertz, C. (1973) *The Interpretation of Cultures*. New York: Basic Books.

Georgakopoulou, A. (1997) 'Self-presentation and interactional alliances in e-mail discourse: the style- and code-switches of Greek messages', *International Journal of Applied Linguistics*, 7(2): 141–64.

Goffman, E. (1959) *The Presentation of Self in Everyday life*. New York: Anchor Books.

Goffman, E. (1967) *Interaction Ritual: Essays on Face-To-Face Behavior*. New York: Pantheon Books.

Goffman, E. (1974) *Frame Analysis*. New York: Harper and Row.

Goffman, E. (1981) *Forms of Talk*. Philadelphia: University of Pennsylvania Press.

Goodwin, M. H. (1990) *He-Said-She-Said: Talk as Social Organization Among Black Children*. Bloomington, IN: Indiana University Press.

Gordon, C. (2002) '"I'm Mommy and you're Natalie": role-reversal and embedded frames in mother–child discourse', *Language in Society*, 31(5): 679–720.

Gordon, C. (2003) 'Aligning as a team: forms of conjoined participation in (stepfamily) interaction', *Research on Language and Social Interaction*, 36(4): 395–431.

Gordon, C. (2004) '"Al Gore's our guy": linguistically constructing a family political identity', *Discourse and Society*, 15(4): 607–31.

Gordon, C. (2007) '"I just feel horribly embarrassed when she does that": constituting a mother's identity', in D. Tannen, S. Kendall and C. Gordon (eds), *Family Talk: Discourse and Identity in Four American Families*. Oxford: Oxford University Press. pp. 71–101.

Gordon, C. (2008) 'A(p)parent play: blending frames and reframing in family talk', *Language in Society*, 37(3): 319–49.

Gordon, C., Prince, M. B., Benkendorf, J. L. and Hamilton, H. E. (2002) '"People say it's a little uncomfortable": Prenatal genetic counselors' use of constructed dialogue to reference procedural pain', *Journal of Genetic Counseling*, 11(2): 245–63.

Grice, H. P. (1975) 'Logic and conversation', in P. Cole and J. L. Morgan (eds), *Speech Acts*. New York: Academic Press. pp. 41–58.

Gumperz, J. J. (1958) 'Phonological differences in three Hindi dialects', *Language*, 34(2): 212–24.

Gumperz, J. J. (1960) *Hindi Reader*, Vol. 1. Berkeley, CA: Center for South Asian Studies, University of California.

Gumperz, J. J. (1963) *Conversational Hindi-Urdu*, Vol. 2. Berkeley, CA: ASUC Bookstore, University of California.

Gumperz, J. J. (1964a) 'Hindi–Punjabi code-switching in Delhi', in H. G. Lunt (ed.), *Proceedings of the Ninth International Congress of Linguistics*. The Hague: Mouton. pp. 1115–24.

Gumperz, J. J. (1964b) Linguistic and social interaction in two communities', *American Anthropologist*, 66(6):II. pp. 137–53.

Gumperz, J. J. (1971) *Language in Social Groups*. Stanford, CA: Stanford University Press.

Gumperz, J. J. (1974) 'Linguistic anthropology in society', *American Anthropologist*, 76(4): 785–98.

Gumperz, J. J. (1976) 'The sociolinguistic significance of conversational code-switching,' in J. Cook-Gumperz and J. J. Gumperz (eds), *Papers on Language and Context, Working Paper No. 46*. Berkeley, CA: Language Behavior Research Laboratory, University of California.

Gumperz, J. J. (1977) 'The sociolinguistic significance of conversational code-switching', *RELC Journal*, 8(1): 1–34.

Gumperz, J. J. (1978) 'The conversational analysis of interethnic communication', in E. Lamar Ross (ed.), *Interethnic Communication* (Proceedings of the Southern Anthropological Society). Athens: University of Georgia Press. pp.13–31.

Gumperz, J. J. (1982a) *Discourse Strategies*. Cambridge: Cambridge University Press.

Gumperz, J. J. (1982b) (ed.) *Language and Social Identity*. Cambridge: Cambridge University Press.

Gumperz, J. J. (1982c) 'Fact and inference in courtroom testimony', in J. J. Gumperz (ed.), *Language and Social Identity*. Cambridge: Cambridge University Press. pp. 163–95.

Gumperz, J. J. (1992a) 'Contextualization and understanding', in A. Duranti and C. Goodwin (eds), *Rethinking Context: Language as an Interactive Phenomenon*. Cambridge: Cambridge University Press. pp. 229–52.

Gumperz, J. J. (1992b) 'Contextualization revisited', in P. Auer and A. di Luzio (eds), *The Contextualization of Language*. Amsterdam: John Benjamins. pp. 39–53.

Gumperz, J. J. (1999a) 'Culture in the cultural defense', in M. Brody, G. Liebscher and H. Ogren (eds), *Proceedings of the Sixth Annual Symposium about Language and Society (1998)*. Austin, TX: The Department of Linguistics, University of Texas. pp. 91–121.

Gumperz, J. J. (1999b) 'On interactional sociolinguistic method', in S. Sarangi and C. Roberts (eds), *Talk, Work and Institutional Order: Discourse in Medical, Mediation and Management Settings*. Berlin: Mouton de Gruyter. pp. 453–71.

Gumperz, J. J. (2001) 'Interactional sociolinguistics: a personal perspective,' in D. Schiffrin, D. Tannen and H. Hamilton (eds), *The Handbook of Discourse Analysis*. Malden, MA: Blackwell. pp. 215–28.

Gumperz, J. J. (2003) 'Response essay', in S. L. Eerdmans, C. L. Prevignano and P. J. Thibault (eds), *Language and Interaction: Discussions with John J. Gumperz*. Amsterdam: John Benjamins. pp. 105–26.

Gumperz, J. J. and Cook-Gumperz, Jenny (1974) 'The communicative basis of language problems in education', in *Sociolinguistics*. Central Institute of Indian Languages, Mysore, India.

Gumperz, J. J. and Cook-Gumperz, Jenny (1982) 'Interethnic communication in committee negotiations', in J. J. Gumperz (ed.), *Language and Social Identity*. Cambridge: Cambridge University Press. pp. 145–62.

Gumperz, J. J. and Hernandez-Chavez, E. (1972) 'Bilingualism, bidialectalism and classroom interaction,' in C. B. Cazden, V. P. John and D. Hymes (eds), *Functions of Language in the Classroom*. New York: Teachers College Press. pp. 84–110.

Gumperz, J. J. and Hymes, D, (eds) (1964) 'The ethnography of communication', Special issue of *American Anthropologist*, 66(6): II.

Gumperz, J. J. and Hymes, D. (eds) (1972) *Directions in Sociolinguistics: The Ethnography of Communication*. New York: Holt, Rinehart and Winston.

Gumperz, J. J. and Levinson, S. C. (eds) (1996) *Rethinking Linguistic Relativity*. Cambridge: Cambridge University Press.

Gumperz, J. J. and Naim, C. M. (1960) *Urdu Reader*. Berkeley, CA: Center for South Asia Studies, University of California.

Gumperz, J. J. and Roberts, C. (1980) 'Developing awareness skills for inter-ethnic communication', *Occasional Papers*, no. 12. Seameo Regional Language Center, Singapore.

Gumperz, J. J. and Rumery, J. (1962) *Conversational Hindi–Urdu*. Vol. 1: parts 1 and 2. Berkeley: University of California.

Gumperz, J. J. and Tannen, D. (1979) 'Individual and social differences in language use', in C. J. Fillmore, D. Kempler and W. S.-Y. Wang (eds), *Individual Differences in Language Ability and Language Behavior*, New York: Academic Press. pp. 305–25.

Gumperz, J. J., Jupp, T. C. and Roberts, C. (1979) *Crosstalk, a Study of Cross-Cultural Communication*. Background material and notes to accompany the BBC film. Southall: National Centre for Industrial Language Training.

Gumperz, J. J., Jupp, T. C. and Roberts, C. (1980) *Crosstalk – the Wider Perspective*. Southall: National Centre for Industrial Language Training.

Hall, K. and Bucholtz, M. (eds) (1995) *Gender Articulated: Language and the Socially Constructed Self*. New York: Routledge.

Hamilton, H. E. (1998) 'Reported speech and survivor identity in on-line bone marrow transplantation narratives', *Journal of Sociolinguistics*, 2(1), 53–67.

Hamilton, H. E., Gordon, C., Nelson, M., Cotler, S. J. and Martin, P. (2008) 'How physicians describe outcomes to HCV therapy: prevalence and meaning of "cure" during provider–patient in-office discussions of HCV', *Journal of Clinical Gastroenterology*, 42(4): 419–24.

Heller, M. S. (1982) 'Negotiations of language choice in Montreal', in J. J. Gumperz (ed.), *Language and Social Identity*. Cambridge: Cambridge University Press. pp. 108–18.

Heller, M. (1985) 'Ethnic relations and language use in Montréal', in N. Wolfson and J. Manes (eds), *Language of Inequality*. Berlin: Mouton de Gruyter. pp. 75–90.

Heritage, J. (1984) *Garfinkel and Ethnomethodology*. Oxford: Blackwell.

Hill, J. (1995) 'Junk Spanish, covert racism and the (leaky) boundary between public and private spheres', *Pragmatics*, 5(2): 197–212.

Hinnenkamp, V. (2003) 'Mixed language varieties of migrant adolescents and the discourse of hybridity', *Journal of Multilingual and Multicultural Development*, 24(1, 2): 12–41.

Holmes, J. and Stubbe, M. (2004) 'Strategic code-switching in New Zealand workplaces: scaffolding, solidarity and identity construction', in J. House and J. Rehbein (eds), *Multilingual Communication*. Amsterdam: John Benjamins. pp. 133–54.

Holstein, J. A. and Gubrium, J. F. (eds) (2007) *Handbook of Constructionist Research*. New York: Guilford Press.

Hymes, D. (1972) 'On communicative competence', in J. B. Pride and J. Holmes (eds), *Sociolinguistics*. Harmondsworth: Penguin. pp. 269–93.

Hymes, D. (1974) 'Ways of speaking', in R. Bauman and J. Sherzer (eds), *Explorations in the Ethnography of Speaking*. Cambridge: Cambridge University Press. pp. 433–51.

Jacquemet, M. (1996) *Credibility in Court: Communicative Practices in the Camorra Trials*. Cambridge: Cambridge University Press.

Johnstone, B. (2000) *Qualitative Methods in Sociolinguistics*. Oxford: Oxford University Press.

Kallmeyer, W. and Keim, I. (2003) 'Linguistic variation and the construction of social identity in a German–Turkish setting. A case study of an immigrant youth group in Mannheim, Germany', in J. Androutsopoulos and A. Georgakopoulou (eds), *Discourse Constructions of Youth Identities*. Amsterdam: John Benjamins. pp. 29–46.

Kallmeyer, W. and Schütze, F. (1977) 'Zur Konstitution von Kommunikationsschemata der Sachverhaltsdarstellung', in Dirk Wegner (ed.), *Gesprächsanalysen. IKP-Forschungsberichte*. Series I, Vol. 65. Hamburg: Helmut Buske Verlag. pp. 159–274.

Keim, I. (2003) 'Social style of communication and bilingual speech practices: case study of three migrant youth groups of Turkish origin in Mannheim, Germany', *Turkic Languages*, 6(2): 284–300.

Kendall, S. (2003) 'Creating gendered demeanors of authority at work and at home,' in J. Holmes and M. Meinhoff (eds), *Handbook of Language and Gender*. Malden, MA: Blackwell. pp. 600–23.

Kendall, S. (2004) 'Framing authority: gender, face and mitigation at a radio network', *Discourse and Society*, 15(1): 55–79.

Kendall, S. (2006) '"Honey, I'm home!": framing in family dinnertime homecomings', *Text and Talk*, 26(4–5): 411–41.

Kendall, S. (2007) 'Father as breadwinner, mother as worker: gendered positions in feminist and traditional discourses of work and family', in D. Tannen, S. Kendall and C. Gordon (eds), *Family Talk*. Oxford: Oxford University Press. pp. 123–63.

Kendall, S. and Tannen, D. (2001) 'Discourse and gender', in D. Schiffrin, D. Tannen and H. E. Hamilton (eds), *The Handbook of Discourse Analysis*. Malden, MA: Blackwell. pp. 548–67.

Kiesling, S. F. (2001) ' "Now I gotta watch what I say": shifting constructions of masculinity in discourse', *Journal of Linguistic Anthropology*, 11(2): 250–73.

Kiesling, S. F. and Paulston, C. B. (2005) 'Introduction to Part I: approaches to intercultural discourse', in S. F. Kiesling and C. B. Paulston (eds), *Intercultural Discourse and Communication: The Essential Readings*. Malden, MA: Blackwell. pp. 1–3.

Kotthoff, H. (2000) 'Gender and joking: on the complexities of women's image politics in humorous narratives', *Journal of Pragmatics*, 32: 55–80.

Kotthoff, H. (2002) 'Irony, quotation and other forms of staged intertextuality: double or contrastive perspectivation in conversation', in C. F. Graumman and W. Kallmeyer (eds), *Perspective and Perspectivation in Discourse*. Amsterdam: John Benjamins. pp. 201–29.

Kotthoff, H. and Wodak, R. (1997) *Communicating Gender in Context*. Amsterdam: John Benjamins.

Labov, W. (1966) *The Social Stratification of English in New York City*. Washington, DC: Center for Applied Linguistics.

Labov, W. (1972) *Sociolinguistic Patterns*. Philadelphia: University of Pennsylvania Press.

Labov, W. (2003) 'Thinking about Charles Ferguson', *International Journal of the Sociology of Language*, 163: 5–7.

Labov, W. and Fanshel, D. (1977) *Therapeutic Discourse: Psychotherapy as Conversation*. New York: Academic Press.

Lakoff, R. (1973) 'The logic of politeness, or minding your p's and q's', in C. Corum, T. C. Smith-Clark and A. Weiser (eds), *Papers from the Ninth Regional Meeting of the Chicago Linguistics Society*. Chicago: University of Chicago Department of Linguistics. pp. 292–305.

Lakoff, R. (1975) *Language and Woman's Place*. New York: Harper and Row.

Lakoff, R. (1979) 'Stylistic strategies within a grammar of style', in J. Orasanu, M. Slater and L. L. Adler (eds), *Language, Sex and Gender. Annals of the New York Academy of Science*, 327: 53–78.

Levinson, S. C. (2003) 'Contextualizing "contextualization cues"', in S. L. Eerdmans, C. L. Prevignano and P. J. Thibault (eds), *Language and Interaction: Discussions with John J. Gumperz*. Amsterdam: John Benjamins. pp. 31–9.

Maltz, D. N. and Borker, R. A. (1982) 'A cultural approach to male–female miscommunication', in J. Gumperz (ed.), *Language and Social Identity*. Cambridge: Cambridge University Press. pp. 195–216.

Maynard, D. W. (1988) 'Language, interaction and social problems', *Social Problems*, 35(4): 311–34.

Mey, J. L. (1993) *Pragmatics: An Introduction*. Malden, MA: Blackwell.

Ochs, E. (1993) 'Constructing social identity: a language socialization perspective', *Research on Language and Social Interaction*, 26(3): 287–306.

Pan, Y., Scollon, S. W. and Scollon, R. (2002) *Professional Communication in International Settings*. Malden, MA: Blackwell.

Pike, K. L. (1967) *Language in Relation to a Unified Theory of the Structure of Human Behavior*. The Hague: Mouton.

Pinto, D., Ribeiro, B. T. and Dantas, M. T. Lopes (2005) ' "Let the heart speak out" – interviewing practices by psychiatrists from two different traditions', *Communication and Medicine*, 2(2): 177–88.

Pomerantz, A. (1984) 'Agreeing and disagreeing with assessments: some features of preferred/dispreferred turn shapes', in J. M. Atkinson and J. Heritage (eds), *Structures of Social Action: Studies in Conversation Analysis*. Cambridge: Cambridge University Press. pp. 57–101.

Prego-Vazquez, G. (2007) 'Frame conflict and social inequality in the workplace: professional and local discourse struggles in employee/customer interactions', *Discourse and Society*, 18(3): 295–335.

Prevignano, C. L. and di Luzio, A. (2003) 'A discussion with John J. Gumperz', in S. L. Eerdmans, C. L. Prevignano and P. J. Thibault (eds), *Language and Interaction: Discussions with John J. Gumperz*. Amsterdam: John Benjamins. pp. 7–29.

Prevignano, C. L. and Thibault, P. J. (2003) 'Continuing the discussion with John J. Gumperz', in S. L. Eerdmans, C. L. Prevignano and P. J. Thibault (eds), *Language and Interaction: Discussions with John J. Gumperz*. Amsterdam: John Benjamins. pp. 149–61.

Rampton, B. (1995) *Crossing: Language and Ethnicity Among Adolescents*. London: Longman.

Rampton, B. (2007) 'Neo-Hymsian linguistic ethnography in the United Kingdom', *Journal of Sociolinguistics*, 11(5): 584–607.

Ribeiro, B. T. (1994) *Coherence in Psychotic Discourse*. New York: Oxford University Press.

Rogerson-Revell, P. (2007) 'Humor in business: a double-edged sword. A study of humor and style shifting in intercultural business meetings', *Journal of Pragmatics*, 39: 4–28.

Sacks, H., E. A. Schegloff and G. Jefferson (1974) 'A simplest systematics for the organization of turn-taking in conversation', *Language*, 50: 696–735.

Sarangi, S. (2004) 'Editorial: towards a communicative mentality in medical and healthcare practice', *Communication and Medicine*, 1(1): 1–11.

Schegloff, E. A. (1982) 'Discourse as an interactional achievement: some uses of "uh huh" and other things that come between sentences', in D. Tannen (ed.), *Analyzing Discourse: Text and Talk* (Georgetown University Round Table on Languages and Linguistics, 1981). Washington, DC: Georgetown University Press. pp. 71–93.

Schiffrin, D. (1994) *Approaches to Discourse*. Malden, MA: Blackwell.

Schilling-Estes, N. (2004) 'Constructing ethnicity in interaction', *Journal of Sociolinguistics*, 8(2): 163–95.

Schneider, B. and Waite, L. J. (2005) *Being Together, Working Apart: Dual-Career Families and the Work–Life Balance*. Cambridge: Cambridge University Press.

Scollon, R. and Jones, E. (1979) *Interethnic Communication*. Video presentation, *Talking Alaska* series, No. 5. Fairbanks, AK: Alaska Native Language Center.

Scollon, R. and Scollon, S. W. (2001[1995]) *Intercultural Communication: A Discourse Approach*. 2nd edn. Malden, MA: Blackwell.

Scollon, R. and Scollon, S. W. (2004) *Nexus Analysis: Discourse and the Emerging Internet*. New York: Routledge.

Searle, J. R. (1975) 'Indirect speech acts,' in P. Cole and J. L. Morgan (eds), *Syntax and Semantics*. Vol. 3. New York: Academic Press. pp. 59–82.

Silverstein, M. (1992) 'The indeterminacy of contextualization: When is enough enough?', in P. Auer and A. di Luzio (eds), *The Contextualization of Language*. Amsterdam: John Benjamins. pp. 55–76.

Silverstein, M. (1993) 'Metapragmatic discourse and metapragmatic function', in J. A. Lucy (ed.), *Reflexive Language: Reported Speech and Metapragmatics*. Cambridge: Cambridge University Press. pp. 33–58.

Singh, R., Lele, J. and Martohardjono, G. (1988) 'Communication in a multilingual society: some missed opportunities', *Language in Society*, 17(1): 43–59.

Tannen, D. (1981) 'New York Jewish conversational style', *International Journal of the Sociology of Language*, 30: 133–49.

Tannen, D. (1986) *That's not What I Meant!: How Conversational Style Makes or Breaks Relationships*. New York: Ballantine Books.

Tannen, D. (1990) *You Just Don't Understand: Women and Men in Conversation*. New York: Ballantine Books.

Tannen, D. (1993a) (ed.) *Framing in Discourse*. Oxford: Oxford University Press.

Tannen, D. (1993b) (ed.) *Gender and Conversational Interaction*. Oxford: Oxford University Press.

Tannen, D. (1994) *Gender and Discourse*. Oxford: Oxford University Press. (Reprinted with an added chapter in 1996.)

Tannen, D. (1996) 'The relativity of linguistic strategies: rethinking power and solidarity in gender and dominance', in *Gender and Discourse*. Oxford: Oxford University Press. pp. 19–52.

Tannen, D. (1999) 'The display of (gendered) identities in talk at work', in M. Bucholtz, A. C. Liang and L. A. Sutton (eds), *Reinventing Identities: The Gendered Self in Discourse*. New York and Oxford: Oxford University Press. pp. 221–40.

Tannen, D. (2003) 'Power maneuvers or connection maneuvers? Ventriloquizing in family interaction', in D. Tannen and J. E. Alatis (eds), *Linguistics, Language and the Real World: Discourse and Beyond* (Georgetown University Round Table on Languages and Linguistics, 2001). Washington, DC: Georgetown University Press. pp. 50–62.

Tannen, D. (2005[1984]) *Conversational Style: Analyzing Talk Among Friends*. Oxford: Oxford University Press.

Tannen, D. (2007[1989]) *Talking Voices: Repetition, Dialogue and Imagery in Conversational Discourse*. New York: Cambridge University Press.

Tannen, D. and Goodwin, M. H. (eds) (2006) 'Family discourse, framing family', special issue of *Text and Talk*, 26(4, 5): 407–9.

Tannen, D. and Wallat, C. (1993) 'Interactive frames and knowledge schemas in interaction: examples from a medical examination/interview', in D. Tannen (ed.), *Framing in Discourse*. New York: Oxford University Press. pp. 57–76.

Tannen, D., Kendall, S. and Gordon, C. (eds) (2007) *Family Talk: Discourse and Identity in Four American families.* New York: Oxford University Press.

Tsitsipis, L. D. (2006) 'Report on sociolinguistic research in Greece', *Sociolinguistica*, 20: 183–7.

Twitchin, J. (director) (1979) *Crosstalk.* (Film/video) BBC.

Wei, L. (1994) *Three Generations, Two Languages, One Family: Language Choice and Language Shift in a Chinese Community in Britain.* Clevedon: Multilingual Matters Ltd.

Wodak, R. (1997a) 'Critical Discourse Analysis and the study of doctor–patient interaction', in B.-L. Gunnarsson, P. Linell and B. Nordberg (eds), *The Construction of Professional Discourse.* London: Longman. pp. 173–200.

Wodak, R. (ed.) (1997b) *Gender and Discourse.* London: Sage.

Wodak, R. (1997c) ' "I know, we won't revolutionize the world with it, but ... ": Styles of female leadership in institutions', in H. Kotthoff and R. Wodak (eds), *Communicating Gender in Context.* Amsterdam: John Benjamins. pp. 335–71.

Wodak, R. and Chilton, P. (2005) *A New Agenda in (Critical) Discourse Analysis: Theory, Methodology and Interdisciplinarity.* Amsterdam: John Benjamins.

Woolard, K. A. (1985) 'Catalonia: the dilemma of language rights', in N. Wolfson and J. Manes (eds), *Language of Inequality.* The Hague: Mouton. pp. 91–109.

Woolard, K. A. (2004) 'Codeswitching', in A. Duranti (ed.), *A Companion to Linguistic Anthropology.* Malden, MA: Blackwell. pp. 73–94.

Wortham, S. (2006) *Learning Identity: The Joint Emergence of Social Identification and Academic Learning.* Cambridge: Cambridge University Press.

Yamada, H. (1997) *Different Games, Different Rules: Why Americans and Japanese Misunderstand Each Other.* New York: Oxford University Press.

Young, L. W. L. (1994) *Crosstalk and Culture in Sino–American Communication.* Cambridge: Cambridge University Press.

PART 2

Sociolinguistics and Social Theory

6

Social Stratification

Christine Mallinson

6.1 INTRODUCTION

It is fitting that 'social stratification' is the first entry in Part II, sociolinguistics and social theories, of this new *SAGE Handbook of Sociolinguistics*. One of the first and most famous sociolinguistic studies, Labov's (1966) *The Sociolinguistic Stratification of New York City*, explicitly engaged the topic of social stratification and its patterned relationship with language. Labov posited that if the dialect of individual New York City speakers was studied in the larger context of the speech community, it could be seen 'as an element in a highly systematic structure of social and stylistic stratification' (1966: vii). In short, Labov contended that processes of social stratification produce social divisions, evidence of which can be seen when examining the social distribution of sensitive linguistic forms.

Indeed, the social differentiation of languages and/or linguistic features within or across communities and/or societies is generally what sociolinguists mean when they talk about stratification. Only within or across socially-stratified speech communities, and within or across different interaction or contextually-variable stylistic contexts, can socially-sensitive linguistic features be found. Thus, stratification has come to play a central role in defining sociolinguistic concerns. Section 6.2 of this chapter presents an overview of studies in the areas of variationist sociolinguistics and the sociology of language that investigate how languages and/or language features are employed by speakers who belong to social groups that are hierarchically arranged within a given society.

Stratification still remains a concept, however, that has tended more to underlie various sociolinguistic theories, methods, and analyses than exist as an object of theoretical and analytic inquiry in and of itself. Sustained interdisciplinary scholarship and collaboration would provide an avenue for sociolinguists and sociologists of language to explore new ways of thinking about and measuring the relationship between language and social stratification. Section 6.3 of this chapter thus provides some background on sociological approaches to social stratification, while Section 6.4 reviews some contemporary empirical research on social stratification that is likely to be of interest to sociologists, sociolinguists/sociologists of language, and scholars from related fields.

Section 6.5 explores challenges and new directions for interdisciplinary research on social stratification. On the one hand, sociolinguistics may have yet fully to benefit from sociological perspectives on social stratification and social inequality. On the other hand, in future interdisciplinary collaboration, the use of sociolinguistic data may be able to shed light on debates about the nature and processes of stratification in ways that will be innovative and applicable to theory building in sociology. The conclusions of this chapter consider some of these possibilities.

6.2 SOCIAL STRATIFICATION: SOCIOLINGUISTIC STUDIES

Modern sociolinguistics is generally said to have originated in the 1960s as an interdisciplinary subfield, a unique intersection of the troika of sociology, anthropology and linguistics (Shuy, 2003). A 1964 seminar was held at the LSA Summer Linguistics Institute, and a 1966 session was organized at the Ohio Valley Sociological Society's annual meeting – each on the topic of sociolinguistics (see Fishman, 1997; Shuy, 2003). Among those in attendance were prominent sociologists Garfinkel, Goffman, Gumperz, Hymes, Sacks and Schegloff, and up-and-coming sociolinguists, such as William Labov, among others. Around the same time, university courses were beginning to be developed in the sociology of language and sociolinguistics, and new and important works in the field were beginning to be published.

Over time, sociolinguistics crystallized into a diverse field of study. Some areas of sociolinguistics, such as conversation analysis and discourse analysis, tend to analyze the finer patterns of language in use. The work of early scholars Hymes, Gumperz and Goffman, as well as other research from conversation analysis and ethnomethodology, are reviewed elsewhere in this handbook (see, for example, Chapters 3, 4, 9, 27 and related chapters in this handbook).

This chapter centers primarily on the investigation of social stratification and social inequality as manifested in the traditions of variationist sociolinguistics and the sociology of language. First is a review of key research in the sociology of language that explores language and social stratification, typically in the form of society-level studies of language contact, language planning and policy, and language attitudes. Following is a review of some key stratification-oriented variationist research. Variationist sociolinguistics, known for studies of dynamics within and across speech communities, has perhaps most overtly claimed to investigate language and social stratification. Critiques are also offered with respect to how each tradition has engaged with the theory, methods and analysis of social stratification.

Sociology of language

The title of an early article by Fishman (1965) asked, 'Who speaks what language to whom and when?' – basic questions that the sociology of language has since pursued in depth. As Hellinger (2005: 1117) put it, sociolinguistics and the sociology of language lie along a 'continuum', with language structure and function, influenced by social forces at one end of the continuum ('sociolinguistics') and sociopolitical issues related to language at the other ('sociology of language'). Though such a continuum is idealized and the relationship between such poles is more fuzzy than fixed, the questions that are at the heart of the

sociology of language are those of power, inequality and social stratification. The sociology of language is covered more thoroughly elsewhere in this handbook (see Chapter 5); thus, only a brief review of some trends in the sociology of language is given here, with respect to social stratification.

Some of the earliest compilations – *Toward a Sociology of Language* (Hertzler, 1953), *The Sociology of Language* (Hertzler, 1965), and *Readings in the Sociology of Language* (Fishman, 1968) – set the tone for research that explores how language may reflect, signal, support or challenge unequal relations of power within societies, and also what consequences arise out of conflicting relationships with language(s) in different societies. Since that time, much work in the sociology of language has examined how languages are treated, politically and culturally, in given societies, at specific periods and over time. For example, what economic, political and cultural processes have fostered the spread of powerful languages such as English, in its many global varieties (Brutt-Griffler, 2002; Crystal, 2003)? Other work has investigated language policies and language planning endeavors with an eye to power dynamics and inequality (e.g. Haugen, 1985; Tollefson, 1991; Myers-Scotton, 1993; Wright, 2004). Much of the research in the sociology of language is based on data collected via censuses, language surveys and fieldwork (Chen, 1997).

Complementary to studies of powerful languages and/or language practices are myriad studies of languages that are threatened or endangered, as well as those that analyze how speakers of underprivileged language(s) resist linguistic and cultural subordination. The theory of Bourdieu (1991) on language and symbolic power is particularly applicable to understanding how speakers, particularly in educational situations, may resist efforts at language planning and language standardization. Other work explores the social conditions under which speakers of minority languages may or may not view language as a marker of ethnonational identity, as well as what attitudes they may hold toward the standard and their vernacular (e.g. Rickford, 1985; Heller, 2003; see also articles in the *International Journal of the Sociology of Language* and in the book series *Contributions to the Sociology of Language*).

Within the tradition of the sociology of language, some studies deal more overtly and some more indirectly with aspects of social stratification. Sociology of language research tends to analyze, on individual, group and national levels, how speakers operate in multilingual societies, how societies react to multilingualism in the form of policy and planning efforts, and how language relates to social identity. In each case, issues of self-interest, prestige, status, power and inequality are emphasized. While this type of work is clearly seen as falling within the general scope of the socio-linguistic discipline, theoretical and methodological connections between the sociology of language and the broader discipline of sociology remain more tenuous. As a founder of this area of study, Fishman has been particularly outspoken on this disconnect between sociology, the sociology of language, and sociolinguistics. On the one hand, he argues, sociolinguists have 'created their sociology as they went along', resulting in 'self-imposed underexposure to serious sociological stimulation' (Fishman, 1991: 130, 132). On the other hand, sociologists have been equally inattentive, such that 'only a small proportion of the worldwide sociolinguistic literature is getting through to sociology' (Fishman, 1991: 131) (see also Rickford, 1986; Chen, 1997). Currently, of the constituent parts of the American Sociological Association listed on its website (http://asanet.org), three relate most directly to language: *Communication and Information Technologies, Ethnomethodology and Conversation Analysis*, and *Sociology of Culture*, which includes a subsidiary network on *Language and Culture*. There is currently no section on the sociology of language.

Like much research from the sociology of language approach, variationist sociolinguistic research can be subject to similar critiques regarding its lack of sustained engagement with sociology, including sociological literature on social stratification. Following is a review of some key studies from the variationist perspective, which also, some more overtly and some more indirectly, deal with aspects of social inequality and stratification.

Variationist sociolinguistics

As modern sociolinguistics developed in the United States, considerable attention was directed toward solving language-related social problems: namely, the educational inequalities facing the underclass, whose language patterns are stigmatized in the US educational system. Early variationist sociolinguists began to address these concerns, in part, by quantitatively investigating how linguistic variables are patterned by linguistic and social factors (see also Chapters 1 and 21, in this handbook). The quantitative findings helped build the case that dialects, including stigmatized varieties of English spoken by socially disfavoured groups, are rule-governed and patterned systems.

In the first systematic investigation of an urban speech community, Labov (1966) investigated how language related to social stratification. By 'social stratification', as defined in a later work (1972: 43–4), Labov meant that 'the normal workings of society have produced systematic differences between certain institutions or people, and that these differentiated forms have been ranked in status or prestige by general agreement'. Thus, he analyzed how language features varied by specific social structures, most notably social class (see also Chapter 19, in this handbook). For nearly all the variables Labov studied, individuals who were deemed to have high 'social status' typically used the most 'prestigious' and the least stigmatized linguistic forms. Furthermore, this pattern persisted even across speech style (or register): within each class-based group, speakers used stigmatized variants most often in casual conversation and least often when reading word lists or set passages.

There were a few exceptions to these overarching patterns. Occasionally, despite what would have been expected by their social class position, speakers in the middle ranges of the lower socioeconomic class produced the standard (non-stigmatized or prestigious) form. In more formal styles, the lower middle class also tended to use a higher percentage of standard forms than did the higher classes. Labov explained these 'crossover effects' as being a connection between speakers' class location, social/self-consciousness, and language variation.

Labov also observed that linguistic patterns related to class seemed to vary by gender, with the middle-class women generally using more standard forms than other women or men. Another seemingly contradictory pattern was that women, in the 1966 study, showed greater stylistic variation in their language than men, in two regards. Women in every class used prestigious forms more often in formal styles than men did. In casual styles, however, women used stigmatized forms more often than men. Yet not all women who showed the first pattern necessarily also showed the second.

Labov (2001: 292–3) later called the fact that women can be both more **and** less linguistically conservative the 'gender paradox': women conform more closely than men to sociolinguistic norms that are overtly prescribed, but conform less than men when they are not, as in the case of innovative forms that have not yet been socially evaluated by wider society. Other sociolinguists have critiqued the idea of the gender paradox, however, noting that it may simply result from the fact that researchers often group speakers according to gender and then examine group-level data for potential gender-based patterns (Eckert, 1989; Eckert and McConnell-Ginet, 1992, 1999; Meyerhoff, 2007). (There have been similar critiques of how sociolinguists group speakers by race and ethnicity.)

Another early, large-scale sociolinguistic study revealed similar patterns in the social and stylistic patterning of linguistic variables in an urban centre of the USA. Wolfram (1969) analyzed data from 728 interviews, each lasting over an hour, with 48 African-Americans from the general urban population in Detroit. For eight different linguistic variables, all of the African-American women used more standard forms than the African-American men. Still, not all the African-American women behaved in the same way. Like Labov (1966), Wolfram found that middle-class African-American women used non-stigmatized features much more than either the upper-class or the lower-class African-American women.

Like Labov's and Wolfram's research, Trudgill's (1974) study investigated patterns of social and stylistic variation of linguistic features in Norwich English. In Trudgill's study, speakers moved closer to the prestigious forms of speech as the formality of the speech situation increased. At the same time, the higher social status a person was deemed to have, the more likely they were to use prestigious forms. Cedergren (1973) conducted a similar variationist study of Spanish in Panama City, Panama. Much like Labov (1966), Wolfram (1969) and Trudgill (1974), she found a curvilinear pattern of linguistic change, in which the upper working-class and lower middle-class speakers were more likely to use innovative variants than speakers from other social classes. Other social factors correlated with the use of innovative variants as well: gender, age, and rural versus urban residence.

Since these early studies, sociolinguistic research has continued to explore which social variables are the most important in modeling language variation and change in a given speech community. Now, however, considerably more attention is given to how a broader set of social factors influence language in contexts around the world. Whereas early research mainly focused on class, gender, age and race/ethnicity, sociolinguists have increasingly begun to focus on how locally salient factors (which are simultaneously affected by broader societal forces like economics and urbanization) also condition language variation. For example, Nichols (1983) examined language variation among lower-class African-American women and men in rural, coastal South Carolina. Her study revealed that even in a small community, gender and class affect linguistic behavior across segments of the population, along dimensions of social capital. While some of the women used more standardized English forms than the men, older women actually used the most vernacular, using more than twice as many non-standard Gullah features as either the younger women or all of the men. Nichols explained these language

choices by pointing to key structural effects: educational attainment, job opportunities, and social networks.

Other studies have also investigated interactions between language use and speakers' place, social networks, and social locations. Gal's (1979) study of language shift among Hungarian speakers in the town of Oberwart, Austria was one of the first to analyze language use in relation to social networks. As the town faced increased urbanization, the choice to use either Hungarian or German or to code-switch signaled speakers' affiliations with either a less prestigious peasant status or a more prestigious worker/urbanite status. In a similar study in Australia, Schmidt (1985) studied the Jambun Aboriginal community's use of the language Dyirbal. In general, younger speakers were shifting away from the use of Dyirbal and increasingly using English. When younger speakers did use Dyirbal, however, the choice was dependent upon social networks, with some younger speakers using Dyirbal with family members, some using it with older members of the Jambun community, and others using it with peers in certain in-groups.

In England, Li (1994) analyzed language choice in the Tyneside Chinese community. Findings revealed that the intersecting factors of age and social network were the strongest predictors of whether a given speaker would be Chinese monolingual/dominant, Chinese–English bilingual, or English dominant, because the combination of age and social network reflected the degree to which a given speaker was socially integrated into the Tyneside community. The oldest members of the community tended to have networks made up of people who were their kin and/or Chinese; these speakers were largely Chinese monolingual/dominant. The youngest members of the community, who tended to have intragenerational, non-kin, and non-Chinese networks, were largely English dominant. The study revealed how patterns of language choice are formulated in relation to, and carried out within, a local social matrix, rather than simply being the result of the singular or combinatory effects of any individual social or linguistic factors. In a similar, larger-scale study in England, sociolinguists have investigated whether dialects in the towns of Milton Keynes, Reading and Hull are becoming more or less alike over time (Kerswill, 1996; Cheshire et al., 1999; Williams and Kerswill, 1999; Kerswill and Williams, 2000). Findings also point to the complexity and interconnected nature of social and linguistic factors in processes of language change. In this study, how and how much this linguistic process took place was closely tied to several social and stylistic factors, including speaker's location, age, class, gender, social network and contextual style.

In another approach that examined communities of practice, rather than social networks, Mallinson (2006; see also Mallinson and Childs, 2007) examined language variation among two groups of women in Texana, a small rural community in the southern USA. The 'church ladies' and the 'porch sitters', though they had nearly the same educational attainment, had occupational and lifestyle differences that distinguished them as discrete communities of practice. The church ladies adhered to a much more standard variety of English than the porch sitters, who, among other features, used more forms characteristic of African-American English. For these women, language use was one of many intersecting symbols and practices that constructed class-related social divisions within the US stratification system.

Other sociolinguistic studies have investigated how and why notions of prestige vary and change over time in various communities. Rickford (1986) found no singular notion of prestige among speakers in a Guyanese community, and his informants did not value standardized English forms across the board. Rather, speakers who valued local practices also tended to value the vernacular (that is, creole forms), which they used to manifest solidarity with their class and to express their connections to the local place. Haeri's (1997) study of Cairo, Egypt, also examined how social and stylistic factors affect the use of Classical Standard Arabic and Non-classical Standard Arabic (urban Cairene). She found that men of all educational levels and from all social classes were more conservative speakers, using significantly more Classical Standard features than women from the same cohorts. She attributes women's less frequent use of Classical Arabic features to the fact that Classical Arabic is a particularly gendered language in the domain of religion (e.g. men pray aloud, women pray in silence). In addition, in the Cairene speech community, Classical Standard Arabic was not the only prestige variety; rather, English and French were also valuable. Similarly, Jourdan (2008) examined generational language shift in Honiara, the capital of the Solomon Islands. Investigating the effects of urbanization in this tourist center, she found middle-class speakers (particularly younger middle-class speakers) increasingly using Pijin exclusively as their primary language, rather than English or one of 64 different vernacular varieties, to index an urban affiliation.

The studies reviewed above represent only a small portion of significant variationist sociolinguistic research surrounding social stratification, but they share some common elements. Each of these studies centers largely on studying the relationship between language and social class,

because class is a central pillar of the hierarchical arrangements that are found in stratified societies (see Chapter 19, in this handbook). At the same time, these studies also go beyond class to theorize and analyze how linguistic features are distributed in a stratified speech community along a range of relevant social dimensions – not only class but also age, race, gender and more.

Variationist sociolinguistics has been subject to some significant critiques. For example, scholars including Romaine (1984), Cameron (1990) and Williams (1992) have contended that variationist theory and analysis do not actually explain the relationship between language and society; rather, they reflect sets of assumptions about the nature of society and about the nature of social factors. Variationists have made tremendous strides in analyzing the nuances of variation, drawing from and contributing to formal linguistic theory, but a similar pace has not been kept with social and sociological theory. One long-standing hindrance is the fact that collaboration between sociolinguists and sociologists has generally been more sporadic than sustained. Some variationists, particularly recently, have lamented how this disjuncture affects understandings of specific forms of stratification, especially social class and social status (e.g. Rickford, 1986; Mallinson, 2006, 2009; Dodsworth, 2008; Mallinson and Dodsworth, 2009).

Another critique is that most variationists analyzing the social distribution of linguistic features tend only to wrestle with questions of how social structures like class, gender, race/ethnicity and age are observable **forms** or aspects of stratification and leave undertheorized and underanalyzed how such forms are part of stratification **processes** that build **systems** of social stratification. As a result, variationists may miss the opportunity to theorize more fully how stratification relates to sociolinguistic concerns on broader and interconnected levels.

To summarize, this section has observed that, in research from both the sociology of language and variationist sociolinguistics traditions, stratification has tended to exist more as a background concept rather than an object of theoretical and analytic inquiry. Certainly, sociolinguists' ways of thinking about and analyzing the relationship between language and social stratification would benefit from sustained collaboration with sociologists, and vice versa. As Fishman (1991) argued, sociolinguists and sociologists need comprehensive training in each other's fields. For sociolinguists, Fishman said he was 'not really advocating any particular brand or school of sociology or any particular "all purpose" research methodology or data collection and analysis technique'; instead, he advocated 'a disciplined, hard-nosed grounding in

any major substantive segment and data-collecting and analyzing method among all those that sociology has to offer, so that one can both criticize it and select from it knowingly' (1991: 132). To this end, Section 6.3 aims to bridge some of the disjuncture between sociology and sociolinguistics by exploring how social stratification has been theorized and analyzed within sociology.

6.3 SOCIAL STRATIFICATION: SOCIOLOGICAL STUDIES

For sociolinguists to engage more fully with sociological perspectives on social stratification, it is important to explore what the term 'social stratification' typically means in sociology, in addition to what it typically means in sociolinguistics. As expounded in the previous section, stratification research by sociolinguists tends to focus on how and to what extent linguistic variables pattern by social factors in a given speech community. In sociology, the term 'social stratification' refers to the hierarchical arrangement of groups within a society, and the term can be used in both broad and narrow senses. In a narrow sense, stratification 'can imply a commitment to a particular way of thinking about inequality, as seeing society as structured layers. ... In the increasingly used wider meaning, stratification is concerned with all facets, mechanisms and processes that generate, sustain, and describe social inequalities' (Savage, 2005: 250).

Sociological studies of social stratification tend to investigate systematic, structured inequality along a few different dimensions. A first major concern is how to identify the different forms of stratification that are found in a society and how they are organized. For example, achieved characteristics such as power, wealth and prestige play a significant role in dividing people into hierarchically-ranked social groups, but so do ascribed characteristics like race and gender. In a given society, which of these forms are found and which are most relevant? Other aspects of this first major concern surround how social classes or castes, etc., should be labeled and imposed (e.g. upper-middle class, lower-working class).

A second major concern is how conceptually to approach social stratification, to develop various theories about its forms, to compare stratification across societies, and to examine how stratification changes over time. For example, Marx traced the history of various modes of production in different societies and, as a result of his study, predicted the collapse of the capitalist system. Finally, a third major concern in studies of social stratification deals with the processes and conditions of

stratification – in short, how groups in power maintain their privileges, how disadvantaged groups try to get ahead, and the consequences of cohesive or conflicting social relationships in any given society. The remainder of this section investigates these major concerns in tandem, giving examples of how stratification theories relate to sociolinguistic research.

Some sociological theories of stratification

Most accounts of sociological theories of stratification begin with Karl Marx and Max Weber, both of whom adopt a broadly **relational** view of class, wherein class is defined by people's relationships to various income-generating resources or assets. Less space will be devoted to giving the details of these theories, as they are carefully articulated in many volumes on social stratification; see, for example, Grusky (2001), from which the following overviews of Marxian and Weberian theories are summarized.

In brief, Marx argued that human history unfolds through conflict between social classes over economic inequalities. The most powerful class rules both materially and intellectually (that is, they appropriate not only material goods but also ruling ideas). In a capitalist system, the powerful actors are capitalists, and the deprivation/ exclusion of resources and the garnering of surplus value from surplus labor that are inherent in exploitation constitute a specific type of class relations. Differences in class interest – that is, who exploits versus who gets exploited – generate class conflict. In the class struggle, rewards at the top are extracted from the surplus labor generated at the bottom, which leads to alienation for the workers (see summary in Grusky, 2001: 87–102).

Marx further argued that the ideology best expressing the interests of the ruling class always prevails in social institutions such as religion, economics, education, law and politics. The ideologies are necessarily pervasive because they must convince the elite as well as the rest of society that the rule of the dominant class is legitimate and justified. Thus, both the powerful elite and the proletariat are influenced by the overarching ideology that determines mass belief. Standard languages and language ideologies may accordingly be seen as a product of social stratification, as a site of conflict between the norms of the privileged and those of the non-elite.

Weber, like Marx, believed that the basic categories of all class situations derive from owning property versus not owning property. At the same time, he also believed that the stratification system is complicated by status groupings that can compete, coexist or overlap with class-based groupings. Unlike classes, status groups are normally communities that recognize each other as having more or less social honor, which affects the organization of everyday life. For example, a specific lifestyle is expected from those who wish to belong to the elite, and restrictions are placed on social interactions with undesirable others; language use may be one way that groups create and signal status distinctions. Thus, for Weber, the development of status was essentially a question of stratification (see summary in Grusky, 2001: 132–49).

Most sociological thought since the time of Marx and Weber has also tended to see social relationships as fundamentally unequal, though still recognizing functionalist perspectives, which can be traced back to Durkheim (for a review, see Grusky, 2001). Many sociological methods were pioneered as ways of understanding social inequality, including community studies and the development of class mobility surveys in the UK and the USA (Savage, 2005: 236). In the USA, Blau and Duncan (1967) introduced the status attainment model of inequality. They viewed occupational position and mobility as the single best indicators of class differentiation and thereby of social stratification. In their model, stratification occurs through a process of intergenerational status transmission that depends on a person's father's educational attainment and occupational status in combination with the person's own educational attainment, status of their first job, and status of their current occupation. These and similar indices have found considerable utility in variationist sociolinguistic research (see Chapter 19, in this handbook, for a review).

Since the development of Blau and Duncan's model and their attendant socioeconomic scales, some scholars have critiqued a lack of theory behind how the scales are conceived, and others have raised issues of validity, such as posited male/Eurocentric biases inherent in the scales (see Warren, Sheridan and Hauser, 1998). Such assessments have helped refine sociological thinking about the causal processes that generate social stratification in two main ways. First, sociologists are paying more attention to context: the fact that parents' education, income and occupation, and a person's own mental ability and aspirations are not the only factors that account for how much educational and occupational status people achieve in their lifetimes. Secondly, sociologists are increasingly attuned to how social structures like race, gender, sexuality, region of origin and more are imbricated in systems of social stratification. These and other avenues are explored in the remainder of this section.

Contemporary directions in sociological theories of social stratification

With each critique of older approaches have arisen new, more complex questions in the sociological study of social stratification. The current dilemma is how to develop sociological theory that looks much more carefully at how contemporary and changing social relations have affected social stratification – particularly with regard to how major societal forces, like race/ethnicity, gender and others, generate inequality (Savage, 2005: 237–9). Historically, factors like race and gender have been, in Grusky's words, 'relegated to the sociological sidelines by class theorists of both Marxist and non-Marxist persuasion' (2001: 28). Feminist sociologists (including Acker, 1973, 1988) critiqued this perspective, however, and sparked much controversy over how to incorporate women in class analysis and stratification research. Since that time, many other sociologists have made clear that class is not the only significant form of social stratification, arguing that it is necessary to consider how men and women, as well as members of racial/ethnic groups, sexual groups, age cohorts, etc., are differently located in the class system (e.g. Fraser, 2000; Anthias, 2001; Crompton, 2003; Malesevic and Hall, 2005).

This perspective has generally caught on in sociological research. Indeed, as Savage (2005: 245) pronounced, stratification theories that do not successfully incorporate identity and agency can only reach 'something of a dead end', because they fail to make clear the theoretical linkages between class position, class consciousness and class action. Instead, more pluralistic theories of social stratification are needed to address contemporary conditions of inequality.

Savage (2005: 245–9) finds particularly promising the work of French sociologist Pierre Bourdieu. Bourdieu is relatively well known among sociolinguists, since much of his own work centers on language (e.g. Bourdieu, 1991), and many of his theories have already been used in much contemporary sociolinguistic scholarship (see, e.g., Haeri, 1997; Myles, 1999; Pujolar, 2000; Goldstein, 2003, and many more; for a review, see also Hanks, 2005). Bourdieu was a forerunner in implicating different types of capital in the process of status attainment. His work distinguished cultural, social, economic and symbolic capitals as objectified or embodied forms that accumulate over time (Bourdieu, 1986). As a result of accumulating capitals, he theorized, advantage and privilege also accumulate for certain social groups over time, which produces social stratification.

In comparison to traditional theories of social stratification, Bourdieu's theory is particularly innovative in two regards, as discussed in detail by Savage (2005: 245–9). First, Bourdieu's theory recognizes agency, identity and subjectivity. The approach thus 'allows a way of relating stratification theory to issues of identity and subjectivity that do not rely on the problematic baggage of a class formation approach, which assumes that identities are linked to an awareness of group membership and identification' (Savage, 2005: 248). Secondly, Bourdieu's theory focuses sociological attention on processes of accumulation of resources (rather than merely on a person's relationship to income-generating resources, as in a Marxian perspective). This aspect 'allows the sociology of stratification to connect with current debates about socio-cultural change in ways that can challenge simple accounts of change and have the potential to offer more nuanced insights into persistence and the remaking of privilege' (Savage, 2005: 249).

Another aspect of Bourdieu's theory that is particularly relevant to sociolinguists is the view of language as integral to creating status distinctions that center on cultural capital. Bourdieu (1984) defined cultural capital as tools legitimated and valued by the dominant culture. Cultural capital is signaled to others via symbols in ways that are recognizable to the dominant class, by having 'good' manners, 'proper' language, and other behaviors. These status markers then serve as the criteria that élites use to select others to join them in social interaction and receive the benefits of association with them or limit access for those deemed undesirable. For example, the use of standardized English is a major component of cultural capital, and it influences material outcomes via increasing access to educational opportunities, job opportunities, and income and wealth.

At the same time, Bourdieu's theories are not without critique. For one, although he recognizes gender oppression as symbolic violence, he also pays little attention to how race/ethnicity structures social inequalities (Acker, 2006: 35). Moreover, Bourdieu (as with many other theorists) tended not to suggest how to test his theory; for example, his concept of 'habitus' can be critiqued on the grounds that he undertheorizes how agents acquire habitus and gives researchers little guidance for how to operationalize it.

One contemporary sociological approach that is similar to Bourdieu's theory is that of feminist sociologist Joan Acker, although her approach pays more explicit attention to how class, race and gender relations are interlocking and co-constitutive. In Acker's framework, '"class" stands for practices and relations that provide differential access to and control over the means of provisioning and survival' (2006: 68). In terms of empirical correlates of class, Acker prioritizes observable norms, lifestyle, status displays and consumption habits.

These divisions are reinforced by images and symbols, which include language. With these various data, researchers can study how class-related social divisions are created, how they change over time, and how they connect to extralocal social relations (other social structures) that shape social practices and social identities. For an example of how Acker's theory can be used in variationist sociolinguistic research, see Mallinson and Dodsworth (2009).

The view that Acker takes enables a study of stratification as the social process through which rewards and resources are systematically and unequally allocated within societies. This perspective 'suggests a shift in terminology – we are enmeshed in class relations, not located in class structures' (Acker, 2006: 47). Because specific processes of inequality supplant rigid boundaries and positions in Acker's model, the ways inequality is perpetuated locally must therefore be examined. This focus on the relations of distribution (the allocation of economic resources) may have more explanatory utility for sociolinguists than one that focuses primarily on the means of production, to which it may be more difficult to relate and isolate differences in patterns of linguistic variables. With respect to these and other characteristics, Acker's theory is fully compatible with identity-based approaches to linguistic variation that recognize important intersections between gender and class and also emphasize local social distinctions and the practices that index and construct them (Mallinson and Dodsworth, 2009).

The theories of Bourdieu and Acker are just two contemporary sociological approaches to social stratification that have found some utility within sociolinguistics. Section 6.4 builds upon this discussion to examine some empirical research that may be of interest to scholars from both fields. In each of these studies, language is prioritized as being a key element in the study of social stratification.

6.4 EMPIRICAL CONNECTIONS BETWEEN SOCIOLINGUISTICS AND SOCIOLOGY IN THE STUDY OF SOCIAL STRATIFICATION

Both sociologists and sociolinguists share a common perspective on language as being a primary and overt marker of social identities and a constituent of the dominant social ideologies that influence agents in the social world. Whereas there are many areas of scholarship in which sociolinguists and sociologists can overlap productively, this section highlights empirical work on educational and occupational attainment, a hallmark area in the study of social stratification (particularly in the USA). The reason for highlighting educational and occupational attainment here is largely because while there are many directions for interdisciplinary collaboration along these lines, sociolinguists and sociologists have not generally connected in this endeavor.

Studies of status attainment are particularly relevant to sociolinguists and sociologists because they often implicate standard language ideologies, which privilege the use of standard language forms, as being a primary mechanism in the perpetuation of advantage and disadvantage in culturally-hegemonic school and workplace reward systems. In broad perspective, Lippi-Green (1997) reviewed the ways in which ideologies about language variation, which surface in the United States' educational system, the judicial system, in organizations, and in the media, perpetuate discrimination and social inequality. Similarly, Bonfiglio (2002) explored how standard language ideologies that developed in America are tinged with xenophobia and racism.

Particularly in educational contexts, recent sociological and sociolinguistic studies have shown how family class resources, race, language and other factors intertwine to generate inequality. Lovaglia et al. (1998) found that deprivation of resources over time can have negative effects on self-esteem, and these psychological factors can affect minority students' motivation as well as their results on already culturally-biased tests, which are written in the language that white middle-class people know best (Fischer et al., 1996; Feagin, 2000: 169; Royster, 2003). In another example, the disproportionate allocation of wealth in US society to whites (Oliver and Shapiro, 1995) allows élite parents to send their children to better, often private schools, where resources are more concentrated and classes are smaller (Fischer et al., 1996; Roscigno, 1998; Charity Hudley and Mallinson, forthcoming).

Similarly, Farkas (1996) conducted an empirical study of group differences in school outcomes, in which he studied cultural background as being a resource that is central to educational outcomes and cognitive development. Farkas showed how teachers judge students on non-cognitive traits that may or may not be related to cognitive performance, such as homework, disruptiveness and facility in standardized English. If learners 'sound better' to their teachers, then teachers often treat them better as well. Such cultural/ideological factors are hugely determinative of minority students' success in schools, and schools remain a cultural battleground where minority/poor children are fundamentally disadvantaged.

In 2007, Durham et al., a team of sociologists, speech pathologists and educators, also studied why some children perform better than others in elementary school, since elementary school performance strongly determines a person's educational attainment later in life and since educational attainment is one of the key factors in social mobility – and therefore in social stratification. When they examined language data from white, low-socioeconomic-status children from the Midwestern region of the USA, they found that the oral language skills the children had when they entered kindergarten (before they had much formal education) explained most of the effect of family socioeconomic status on the children's elementary school performance. Presumably, the stigmatization of these speakers at school only goes to reinforce their initial disadvantage.

Other studies have also explored a range of sociological and linguistic factors in affecting the educational attainment of minority US youth. Fernandez et al. (1989) and Warren (1996) both examined Latino/a students' rates of high school attrition, focusing on factors that include family socioeconomic status, parental education, school attendance, self-esteem and English-language ability. Van Hofwegen and Wolfram (2008) similarly explored the acquisition and development of African-American English among eight African-American youths; their research was part of a larger longitudinal study, conducted by a team of linguists, psychologists and educators, that examined factors influencing African-American youths' literacy skills and overall school success.

Myriad other sociolinguistic and sociological studies have examined identity practices, language use, literacy and status attainment: for example, the educational and job attainment of the 'lads' and the 'ear'oles' in the UK (Willis, 1977); the educational and job attainment of the white 'Hallway Hangers' and the African-American 'Brothers' (MacLeod, 1995); the different linguistic and identity practices of white American working- and middle-class 'Jocks' and 'Burnouts' (Eckert, 2000); the educational experiences of African-American youths (Fordham, 1996; Smitherman, 2000; Ferguson, 2001; Ogbu, 2003); Latina American high school students' discourse about education, class, and gender (Bettie, 2003); and more.

All of these studies are just a few examples of how sociolinguistic and sociological perspectives dovetail in research on social stratification. Each study theorizes and analyzes how the élite create a status culture and control access to their rewards and privileges on the basis of who possesses and uses these cultural tools. Once it is in place, the status culture affects the opportunities of those individuals and groups who are in advantaged and disadvantaged social positions. As these studies have shown, the accumulation of capitals (i.e. cultural, social, economic, symbolic) is a primary mechanism in status attainment within a stratified society.

At the same time, while capitals operate interdependently, it is also important not to assume they interact with each other in linear ways. Class-advantaged people are not necessarily cultural-capitally advantaged, and factors like racial and gender segregation may override the influence of capitals. For example, tests of 'literacy', in combination with other measures, disproportionately disqualified African-Americans from voting in the early history of the United States (Feagin, 2000). Recently, Baugh (2007) found that even if prospective African-American or Latino/a tenants have more than enough money to rent an apartment (a question of economic capital), they still may be 'linguistically profiled' over the phone if they speak a stigmatized variety of English (a question of cultural capital). Language thus can perpetuate racially-based housing discrimination, which affects residential segregation (Massey and Lundy, 2001). In turn, residential segregation perpetuates rates of unemployment, high crime and poverty, which, together with underfunded schools, constrain the educational success of children who live in US inner cities (Labov, 2008).

This section has briefly reviewed some sociological and sociolinguistic studies that view language as one of many unequal rewards and resources that operate in processes of stratification. More interdisciplinary collaboration along these lines would complement and broaden sociolinguists' and sociologists' understandings of how patterns of language variation and change, literacy, language attitudes and more are interconnected in systems of inequality within and across societies. Section 6.5 thus concludes by exploring other avenues in the study of stratification that are complementary to both sociolinguistics and sociology.

6.5 NEW DIRECTIONS, INTERDISCIPLINARY QUESTIONS

In considering the future of the sociolinguistic study of stratification alongside the future of the sociological study of stratification, some challenges and possibilities are common to both fields. In *Social Stratification*, Grusky (2001: 1–36) contemplated the future of stratification research in sociology, theoretically and analytically. For example, he asked sociologists to consider how the class standing of modern individuals is changing. If class is becoming divorced from its historic relationship to kinship and property, then what principal stratifying forces are replacing economic capital? Like Savage (2005), Grusky argued that

sociologists must increasingly consider how class is complexly interrelated with individuals' lifestyles, consumption practices and identities.

These questions are also central to sociolinguists. If the principal stratifying forces are changing, how might sociolinguists need to adapt their theories about language variation and change? For example, do we need to revisit our theories about where and how language change originates by social class, in the light of increasing rates of extreme poverty and the recent explosive growth of the hyper-rich around the world (Pieterse, 2005)? Or, in another example, Smith, Durham and Fortune (2007) found that language change was affected by the ways that primary caregivers talked to children. In what ways might other linguistic effects arise as a result of occupational stratification, particularly the gender and/or racial segregation of occupations and jobs – a condition that is entrenched and found worldwide (Wharton, 2004)? And what, if any, sociolinguistic consequences arise from the diversification of workers, work groups and organizations?

Other salient questions concern dynamics of urbanity and rurality. For the first time in the world's history, our population is now more urban than rural (Wimberley, Morris and Fulkerson, 2007). What are the linguistic effects of increasing urbanization? Social and linguistic issues related to conditions of poverty remain poignant, even in wealthy countries: for example, the steepest inequality is not the largest in poor countries, but rather within the UK and the United States (Pieterse, 2005). In the US context in particular, many large urban centres are plagued by poverty, and minority youths face language discrimination, language prejudice and extreme gaps in the quality of their education (see Section 6.4, in this chapter). In other parts of the world, however, linguistic and educational inequality is particularly high in rural and/or developing areas and particularly for women (Kristof and WuDunn, 2009). For example, rates of female illiteracy are nearly double those of men in African and Latin American countries; minority women (Kristof and WuDunn, 2009) often face discrimination in educational and job opportunities, especially if they were raised in rural areas speaking an indigenous language (Tiano, 1987). As dynamics of rurality and urbanity change around the globe, the intersection of literacy, education and status attainment will persist as a central arena in research on social stratification.

This entry on social stratification has reviewed just some of the possibilities for sociolinguists and sociologists to work together, in mutually beneficial ways, to explore the nature of stratification and its relationship to language variation and change. Brainstorming about potential interdisciplinary avenues in the study of stratification inevitably raises more questions than answers.

At the same time, given the inherently complex social and linguistic dynamics of contemporary global societies, sociolinguists must increasingly reach across disciplinary boundaries. By joining forces with sociologists and other like-minded scholars to cultivate further the territory of social stratification research, sociolinguists may examine in new and interdisciplinary ways how patterns of language variation and change, literacy, language attitudes and more are intertwined in systems of inequality within and across societies.

REFERENCES

Acker, J. (1973) 'Women and social stratification: a case of intellectual sexism', *American Journal of Sociology*, 78: 936–45.

Acker, J. (1988) 'Class, Gender, and the Relations of distribution', *Signs*, 13: 473–97.

Acker, J. (2006) *Class Questions: Feminist Answers*. New York: Rowman and Littlefield.

Anthias, F. (2001) 'The material and the symbolic in theorizing social stratification', *British Journal of Sociology*, 52: 367–90.

Baugh, J. (2007) 'Linguistic contributions to the advancement of racial justice within and beyond the African diaspora', *Language and Linguistics Compass*, 1: 331–49.

Bettie, J. (2003) *Women Without Class: Girls, Race, and Identity*. Berkeley, CA: University of California Press.

Blau, P. M. and Duncan, O. D. (1967) *The American Occupational Structure*. New York: Free Press.

Bonfiglio, T. P. (2002) *Race and the rise of standard American*. Berlin: Mouton de Gruyter.

Bourdieu, P. (1984) *Distinction: A Social Critique of the Judgement of Taste*. President and Fellows of Harvard University Press and Routledge and Kegan Paul, Ltd.

Bourdieu, P. (1986) 'The forms of capital', in A. H. Halsey, H. Lauder, P. Brown and A. S. Wells (eds), *Education: Culture, Economy, and Society*. Oxford: Oxford University Press. pp. 46–68.

Bourdieu, P. (1991) *Language and Symbolic Power*. Cambridge, MA: Harvard University Press.

Brutt-Griffler, J. (2002) *World English: A Study of its Development*. Clevedon, UK: Multilingual Matters.

Cameron, D. (1990) 'Demythologizing sociolinguistics: why language does not reflect society', in J. E. Joseph and T. J. Taylor (eds), *Ideologies of Language*. London: Routledge. pp. 79–93.

Cedergren, H. (1973) 'The interplay of social and linguistic factors in Panama'. PhD dissertation, Cornell University.

Charity Hudley, A. H., and Mallinson, C. (Forthcoming) *Valuable Voices: Understanding English Language Variation in American Schools*. New York: Teachers College Press.

Chen, S. (1997) 'Sociology of language', in N. H. Hornberger and D. Corson (eds), *Research Methods in Language and Education*. New York: Springer. pp. 1–14.

Cheshire, J., Gillett, A., Kerswill, P. and Williams, A. (1999) 'The role of adolescents in dialect levelling'. *Final Report Submitted to the Economic and Social Research Council*, June 1999.

Crompton, R. (2003) 'Class and gender beyond the "cultural turn" ', Sociologica, *Problemas e Práticas*, 42: 9–24.

Crystal, D. (2003) *English as a Global Language*. Cambridge: Cambridge University Press.

Dodsworth, R. (2008) 'Sociological consciousness as a component of linguistic variation', *Journal of Sociolinguistics*, 12: 34–57.

Durham, R. E., Farkas, G., Hammer, C., et al. (2007) 'Kindergarten oral language skill: a key variable in the intergenerational transmission of socioeconomic status', *Research in Social Stratification and Mobility*, 25: 294–305.

Eckert, P. (1989) 'The whole woman: sex and gender differences in variation', *Language Variation and Change*, 1: 245–67.

Eckert, P. (2000) *Linguistic Variation as Social Practice*. Malden, MA: Blackwell.

Eckert, P. and McConnell-Ginet, S. (1992) 'Think practically and look locally: language and gender as community-based practice', *Annual Review of Anthropology*, 21: 461–90.

Eckert, P. and McConnell-Ginet, S. (1999) 'New generalizations and explanations in language and gender research', *Language in Society*, 28: 185–201.

Farkas, G. (1996) *Human Capital or Cultural Capital: Ethnicity and Poverty Groups in An Urban School District*. New York: Aldine de Gruyter.

Feagin, J. R. (2000) *Racist America*. New York: Routledge.

Ferguson, A. A. (2001) *Bad Boys: Public Schools in the Making of Black Masculinity*. Ann Arbor, MI: University of Michigan Press.

Fernandez, R. M., Paulsen, R. and Hirano-Nakanishi, M. (1989) 'Dropping out among Hispanic youth', *Social Science Research*, 18(1): 21–52.

Fischer, C. S., Hour, M., Jankowski, M. S., et al. (1996) *Inequality by Design*. Princeton, NJ: Princeton University Press.

Fishman, J. A. (1965) 'Who speaks what language to whom and when?', *La Linguistique*, 2: 67–88.

Fishman, J. A. (ed.) (1968) *Readings in the Sociology of Language*. The Hague, Paris: Mouton de Gruyter.

Fishman, J. A. (1991) 'Putting the "socio" back into the sociolinguistic enterprise', *International Journal of the Sociology of Language*, 92: 127–38.

Fishman, J. A. (1997) 'Bloomington, summer of 1964: the birth of American sociolinguistics', in C. B. Paulston and G. R. Tucker (eds), *The Early Days of Sociolinguistics: Memories and Reflections*. Dallas, TX: Summer Institute of Linguistics. pp. 87–95.

Fordham, S. (1996) *Blacked Out: Dilemmas of Race, Identity, and Success at Capital High*. Chicago: University of Chicago Press.

Fraser, N. (2000) 'Rethinking recognition', *New Left Review*, 3: 107–20.

Gal, S. (1979) *Language Shift: Social Determinants of Linguistic Change in Bilingual Austria*. New York: Academic Press.

Goldstein, T. (2003) 'Contemporary bilingual life at a Canadian high school: Choices, risks, tensions, and dilemmas', *Sociology of Education*, 76: 247–64.

Grusky, D. B. (ed.) (2001) *Social Stratification: Class, Race, and Gender in Sociological Perspective*. 2nd edn. Boulder, CO: Westview Press.

Haeri, N. (1997) *The Sociolinguistic Market in Cairo: Gender, Class and Education*. New York: Columbia University Press.

Hanks, W. F. (2005) 'Pierre Bourdieu and the practices of language', *Annual Review of Anthropology*, 34: 67–83.

Haugen, E. (1985) 'The language of imperialism: unity or pluralism?', in N. Wolfson and J. Manes (eds), *Language of inequality*. Berlin: Mouton de Gruyter. pp. 3–17.

Heller, M. (2003) 'Globalization, the new economy, and the commodification of language and identity', *Journal of Sociolinguistics*, 7: 473–92.

Hellinger, M. (2005) 'Contrastive sociolinguistics', in U. Ammon, N. Dittmar, K. J. Mattheier and P. Trudgill (eds), *Sociolinguistics: An International Handbook of the Science of Language and Society*. Vol. 2. Berlin: Walter de Gruyter. pp. 1117–26.

Hertzler, J. (1953) 'Toward a sociology of language,' *Social Forces*, 32: 109–19.

Hertzler, J. (1965) *The Sociology of Language*. New York: Random House.

Jourdan, C. (2008) 'Language repertoires and the middle class in urban Solomon Islands'. in M. Meyerhoff and N. Nagy (eds), *Social lives in language – Sociolinguistics and multilingual speech communities: Celebrating the work of Gillian Sankoff*. Philadelphia: John Benjamins pp. 43–67.

Kerswill, P. E. (1996) 'Milton Keynes and dialect levelling in south-eastern British English', in D. Graddol, J. Swann and D. Leith (eds), *English: History, Diversity and Change*. London: Routledge. pp. 292–300.

Kerswill, P. and Williams, A. (2000) 'Creating a new town Koiné: children and language change in Milton Keynes', *Language in Society*, 29: 65–115.

Kristof, N., and WuDunn, S. (2010) *Half the Sky: Turning Oppression into Opportunity for Women Worldwide*. New York: Alfred A. Knopf.

Labov, W. (1966) *The Social Stratification of New York City*. Washington, DC: Center for Applied Linguistics.

Labov, W. (1972) *Language in the Inner City: Studies in the Black English Vernacular*. Philadelphia: University of Pennsylvania Press.

Labov, W. (2001) *Principles of Linguistic Change: Social Factors*. Malden, MA: Blackwell.

Labov, W. (2008) 'Unendangered dialects, endangered people', in K. A. King, N. Schilling-Estes, L. Fogle, J. J. Lou and B. Soukup (eds), *Sustaining Linguistic Diversity: Endangered and Minority Languages and Language Varieties: Defining, Documenting, and Developing*. Washington, DC: Georgetown University Press. pp. 219–38.

Li, W. (1994) *Three generations, Two Languages, One Family: Language Choice and Language Shift in a Chinese Community in Britain*. Clevedon, UK: Multilingual Matters.

Lippi-Green, R. (1997) *English With an Accent: Language Ideology and Discrimination in the United States*. New York: Routledge.

Lovaglia, M., Lucas, J., Houser, J., Thye, S. and Markovsky, B. (1998) 'Status processes and mental ability test scores', *American Journal of Sociology*, 104(1): 195–228.

MacLeod, J. (1995) *Ain't No Makin' It*. Boulder, CO: Westview Press.

Malesevic, S. and Hall, J. A. (2005) 'Citizenship, ethnicity, and nation-states', in C. Calhoun, C. Rojek and B. Turner (eds), *The Sage Handbook of Sociology*. Newbury Park, CA: Sage. pp. 561–78.

Mallinson, C. (2006) The dynamic construction of race, class, and gender through linguistic practice among women in a Black Appalachian community'. PhD dissertation, North Carolina State University.

Mallinson, C. (2009) 'Sociolinguistics and sociology: current directions, future partnerships', *Language and Linguistics Compass* 3: 1034–51.

Mallinson, C., and Childs, B. (2007) 'Communities of practice in sociolinguistic description: Analyzing language and identity practices among Black women in Appalachia', *Gender and Language*, 1: 173–206.

Mallinson, C., and Dodsworth, R. (2009) 'Revisiting the need for new approaches to social class in variationist sociolinguistics', *Sociolinguistic Studies*, 3(2): 253–78.

Massey, D. S. and Lundy, G. (2001) 'Use of Black English and racial discrimination in urban housing markets: new methods and findings', *Urban Affairs Review*, 36(4): 452–69.

Meyerhoff, M. (2006) *Introducing Sociolinguistics*. New York: Routledge.

Myers-Scotton, C. (1993) 'Elite closure as a powerful language strategy: the African case', *International Journal of the Sociology of Language*, 103: 149–63.

Myles, J. (1999) 'From habitus to mouth: language and class in Bourdieu's sociology of language', *Theory and Society*, 28: 879–901.

Nichols, P. (1983) 'Linguistic options and choices for Black women in the rural South', in B. Thorne, C. Kramerae and N. Henley (eds), *Language, Gender, and Society*. Boston: Heinle and Heinle. pp. 54–68.

Ogbu, J. U. (2003) *Black American Students in an Affluent Suburb: A Study of Academic Disengagement*. Mahwah, NJ: Lawrence Erlbaum.

Oliver, M. L., and Shapiro, T. (1995) *Black Wealth/White Wealth: A New Perspective on Racial Inequality*. New York: Routledge.

Pieterse, J. N. (2005) 'Global inequality: bringing politics back in', in C. Calhoun, C. Rojek and B. Turner (eds), *The Sage Handbook of Sociology*. Newbury Park, CA: Sage. pp. 423–41.

Pujolar, J. (2000) *Gender, Heteroglossia and Power: A Sociolinguistic Study of Youth Culture*. London: Mouton de Gruyter.

Rickford, J. R. (1985) 'Standard and non-standard language attitudes in a creole continuum', in N. Wolfson and J. Manes (eds), *Language of Inequality*. Berlin: Mouton de Gruyter. pp. 145–60.

Rickford, J. R. (1986) 'The need for new approaches to social class analysis in sociolinguistics', *Journal of Communication*, 6: 215–21.

Romaine, S. (1984) 'The status of sociological models and categories in explaining linguistic variation', *Linguistische Berichte,* 90: 25–38.

Roscigno, V. J. (1998) 'Race and the reproduction of educational disadvantage', Social Forces, 76: 1033–60.

Royster, D. A. (2003) *Race and the Invisible Hand: How White Networks Exclude Black Men From Blue-Collar Jobs.* Berkeley, CA: University of California Press.

Savage, M. (2005) 'Class and stratification: current problems and revival prospects', in C. Calhoun, C. Rojek and B. Turner (eds), *The Sage Handbook of Sociology.* Newbury Park, CA: Sage. pp. 236–53.

Schmidt, A. (1985) *Young People's Dyirbal: An Example of Language Death From Australia.* Cambridge: Cambridge University Press.

Shuy, R. W. (2003) 'A brief history of American sociolinguistics 1949–1989', in C. Paulston and G. R. Tucker (eds), *Sociolinguistics: The Essential Readings.* Malden, MA: Blackwell. pp. 4–16.

Smith, J., Durham, M. and Fortune, L. (2007) '"Mam, my trousers is fa'in doon!": community, caregiver and child in the acquisition of variation in a Scottish dialect', *Language Variation and Change,* 19: 63–99.

Smitherman, G. (2000) *Talkin That Talk: Language, Culture and Education in African America.* New York: Routledge.

Tiano, S. (1987) 'Gender, work, and world capitalism: Third World women's role in world development', in B. B. Hess and M. M. Ferree (eds), *Analyzing Gender: A Handbook of Social Science Research.* Newbury Park, CA: Sage. pp. 216–43.

Tollefson, J. W. (1991) *Planning Language, Planning Inequality: Language Policy in the Community.* London: Longman.

Trudgill, P. (1974) *The social differentiation of English in Norwich.* Cambridge: Cambridge University Press.

van Hofwegen, J. and Wolfram, W. (2008) 'Coming of age in African American English: a longitudinal study', paper presented at the NWAV 37 Conference, Houston, TX.

Warren, J. R. (1996) 'Educational inequality among white and Mexican-origin adolescents in the American Southwest: 1990', *Sociology of Education,* 69(2): 142–58.

Warren, J. R., Sheridan, J. T. and Hauser, R. M. (1998) 'Choosing a measure of occupational standing', *Sociological Methods and Research,* 27: 3–76.

Wharton, A. (2004) 'Gender inequality', in G. Ritzer (ed.), *The Handbook of Social Problems: A Comparative International Perspective.* Newbury Park, CA: Sage. pp. 156–71.

Williams, A. and Kerswill, P. (1999) 'Dialect levelling: change and continuity in Milton Keynes, Reading and Hull', in P. Foulkes and G. Docherty (eds), *Urban Voices: Accent Studies in the British Isles.* London: Edward Arnold. pp. 141–62.

Williams, G. (1992) *Sociolinguistics: A Sociological Critique.* London: Routledge.

Willis, P. (1977) *Learning to Labour: How Working-Class Kids Get Working-Class Jobs.* Farnborough: Saxon House.

Wimberley, R., Morris, L. and Fulkerson, G. (2007) 'World population takes a turn', *The News and Observer* (Raleigh, NC, USA) (23 May): 15A.

Wolfram, W. (1969) *A Sociolinguistic Description of Detroit Negro Speech.* Washington, DC: Center for Applied Linguistics.

Wright, S. (2004) *Language Policy And Language Planning: From Nationalism to Globalisation.* New York: Palgrave Macmillan.

Social Constructionism

Anthea Irwin

7.1 INTRODUCTION

Consider sociolinguistics. Where did it come from? Why is it called what it's called? How come courses in sociolinguistics appear on many different types of degree programme: for example, Linguistics, (English) Language, Sociology, Cultural Studies and so on? An academic did not suddenly come upon a subject and know by observing something about its 'nature' that it was sociolinguistics. It is not an entity with discrete boundaries, just as the subjects I've listed above are not entities with discrete boundaries. Universities over the years have decided on the distinctions between the disciplines via discussion and debate, and what constitutes sociolinguistics has gone through a similar process.

The key word here is process. Social constructionism (SC) does not take as its starting point entities or states such as sociolinguistics, or motherhood, or government, or manners; rather, it argues that these have been constructed in particular ways by the societies in which they appear. SC looks beyond, and indeed challenges, taken-for-granted notions such as 'it is natural for every woman to have a maternal instinct'; or 'governments represent the societies that elect them'; or 'it is rude to speak with your mouth full' and says 'Who says?' SC wants to look back and above and beyond to the processes that have caused these things to become taken-for-granted 'knowledge': Who has said what, when, to whom, and how, to get us to where we are on any one topic?

This is not to say, it should be pointed out, that SC is all about **critiquing** the taken-for-granted: often the processes that are observed will involve some element of power and therefore potentially inequality, and in such cases there is often rightful critique; but in other cases it is simply a case of identifying and observing a social process. These two different approaches are sometimes known as macro and micro, weak and strong, or dark and light SC (although each of these sets of labels could be accused of being unnecessarily evaluative) (Burr, 1995). The macro, weak, or dark form asserts that we engage in construction that is informed by, or at least linked to, wider economic and social processes; the micro, or strong, or light form allows the individuals involved a good deal more 'agency', a concept to which I will return later, that broadly refers to acting independently and making one's own choices.

While we should not lump all SC together as negative social critique, neither should we think of the macro and micro versions as two distinct schools of thought. It is probably more useful to consider it like a continuum as regards the extent to which what is constructed has been regularized and in turn institutionalized, and there is no reason why analysis cannot take account of 'macro' elements in analysing 'micro' texts in detail.

The interactional nature of what I have been discussing above has probably already suggested that language would be a key element in SC. Wilson and Stapleton (2007: 393) point out that the obvious synergies between the two have not always been acted upon when they claim that 'modern social theory highlights the role of language in social change/reproduction, yet rarely draws on actual linguistic resources or theory. Equally, sociolinguistics situates linguistic practice within the social domain, but only weakly makes links to social theory'. They recognize the potential for sociolinguistics to both inform and be informed by social theory, and the latter part of this chapter will show that there is a growing body of work that we could refer to as social constructionist sociolinguistics.

I will, for the remainder of the chapter, attempt to position sociolinguistics in relation to SC. I will start by situating SC itself within social theory more broadly by giving an overview of key developments and shifts, particularly over the last three decades or so, but with some material from considerably earlier than that when contextually useful. I will go on to discuss in some detail the work of Berger and Luckmann, to whom SC is generally traced back. Next, I will discuss other social theorists upon whom work in the social constructionist area of contemporary sociolinguistics has drawn. Of these, Goffman is the closest to the tradition of Berger and Luckmann. Foucault, too, would be explicitly labelled a social constructionist. Others would not be so explicitly labelled, but are worthy of inclusion as their shift away from the structural to engage more fully with agency makes them important precursors or adjuncts to SC per se: for example, Bakhtin, Bourdieu and Said. Finally, I will review what I consider to be key social constructionist sociolinguistic work, highlighting the types of data and, by extension, the areas of society, which it has sought to explore.

7.2 HISTORICAL CONTEXT

To begin to situate SC, it is useful to consider the shift in thinking that is referred to as postmodernism and, in turn, to situate that we need to go much further back, starting with the Enlightenment, with the caveat that this is by necessity a bit of a 'potted history'. The Enlightenment is so called because it marks a shift from medieval ways of thinking which saw things as divinely ordained, and from a feudal power structure that consisted of a very thin pyramid with the divinely ordained king at the top and a great many serfs, the vast majority of the population, at the bottom, with very few others in between. With the Enlightenment came a focus on rationality. Big advances were made in the scientific world, and it began to be suggested that there might be universal ways of categorizing everything and suggesting how they might develop, for example Darwin's theory of evolution. Things were now viewed not as individual entities but as related to other entities. Marx's theories (e.g. Marx and Engels, 1970, 1992) suggested a process of development for the socio-political sphere too. The world could be seen as, at least potentially, progressing, moving forward towards something greater. The development of chaos theory and the fall of Communism in the Soviet Union and Eastern Europe suggested, for some, the point at which any universality of thought no longer applied (this has been challenged by many saying that the fall of Stalinism is not the same thing as the unworkability of socialism).

In any case, postmodernism developed as a way of viewing the world that rejected any form of 'grand narrative', that is, anything that purported to have all the answers, to be a 'theory of everything' (in the way that Darwinism and Marxism appeared to provide a template for the potential development of the whole natural and socio-political worlds, respectively). The world began to be viewed as fragmented, and thus it became as important to look at the little things as well as the big things, as important to look at the local as well as the global. The evaluative distinction between high culture and popular culture became blurred, and with that came a focus on the 'ordinary' or 'everyday'. And the idea that 'everything is relative' (albeit a rather simplistic way of putting it) challenged the very notion of 'truth'. And with no universal structure, the agency of the individual is paramount.

In the academic sphere, the development of postmodernism was accompanied by, or perhaps preceded by, what is sometimes referred to as 'the linguistic turn': i.e., a recognition that our experience of the world is very much bound up with the language that we hear, read and use. Early engagement with this came from the structuralists, and in particular from Ferdinand de Saussure (1983). He claimed that the meaning of particular linguistic terms did not come from some inherent nature, but instead from their relationship to other terms, a relationship of difference: things 'mean' as much because of what they are **not** as what they **are**. As an illustration, when we are acquiring language as children, our understanding of different animals develops the more animals we are aware of: we get to know that a dog is not a cat, but also that it is not a cow nor a fish nor a bird either. And what it means to be a man (at least in dominant Western culture) is as much bound up with not being a woman, not being feminine, as it is with any essential element of masculinity; one cannot be understood without the other. The relational aspect of de Saussure's work challenged earlier ideas of the essentialism of meaning. Debates were also had over which direction this understanding moves in, about the extent to which the language we acquire has implications for the way we see, experience and categorize the world. Do we experience things and then, having made sense of them perceptively, acquire ways to talk about them (the kind of view psychologists like Piaget (1954) would have taken)? Or is it impossible for us to even begin to make sense of the world until we acquire a language, a lens to view it through, as in the view taken by Sapir (1921) and Whorf (1956)? This again is a matter of degree. The debates about language and culture moved the discussions on further, but structure was still key, regardless of whether we consider that societal structure led to the development of language or vice versa. This focus on structure was challenged by poststructuralists who wanted to examine not the structures per se, but where the structures had come from, what processes had occurred to lead to things being structured as they are.

7.3 KEY THINKERS

Peter Berger and Thomas Luckmann

Social constructionism can be traced back to Berger and Luckmann. It is a phenomenological approach that contrasts with traditional positivist approaches, and which sought to analyse individuals in society in a scientific manner, thus positioning them as passive objects, 'vessels' from which 'static' information could be collected or gleaned. The phenomenological approach, on the other hand, concerns itself with human consciousness and 'common sense' and how the world is understood and structured from individuals' and groups' points of view as **subjects**.

More specifically, Berger and Luckmann work within the area of the 'sociology of knowledge'. They suggest that it was necessary to look not just comparatively at differences between what is taken as 'knowledge' in different societies, but also at how things come to be taken as knowledge; in their words, 'not only ... the empirical variety of knowledge in human societies, but also ... the processes by which *any* body of knowledge comes to be socially established *as* 'reality' (1966: 15). They draw on historicist work, which claims situations can only be understood on their own terms (1966: 19). Marxist and Nietzschean work, too, provide useful context for Berger and Luckmann's development of the sociology of knowledge. Marxist thinking sees human consciousness as brought about by activity, and more specifically labour, and the social relationships that arise in and from this activity. It tends to focus on ideology as a weapon of the powerful and as encouraging a 'false consciousness' among workers (1966: 18). Nietzschean thinking, too, talks of the 'art of mistrust' (1966: 19). It is fair to say that their contribution is to shift the focus of the social construction of reality from the highbrow to the everyday and from power struggle between groups to the interpersonal.

In shifting to the everyday context, Berger and Luckmann refer to Mannheim, who suggested that ideology is just as much a factor of an individual's thought as of their opponent's or oppressor's

thought (1966: 21), and that reality could only be got at by analysing any situation from as many positions as possible (1966: 22). Mannheim, however, focused on the intelligentsia, because he believed this group could most easily transcend the ideological nature of their thought, and the sociology of knowledge has thus tended to focus on intellectual or theoretical thought; Berger and Luckmann stress instead that 'common-sense "knowledge" rather than "ideas" must be the central focus for the sociology of knowledge. It is precisely this "knowledge" that constitutes the fabric of meanings without which no society could exist' (1966: 27).

Drawing on Durkheim and Weber, Berger and Luckmann place, at the centre of the sociology of knowledge, the subjective/objective duality of society, and, more precisely, the ways in which 'subjective meanings *become* objective facticities' (1966: 30). They observe that the world originates in individuals' thoughts and actions, but is then, on a separate level, objectified and 'maintained as real by these [thoughts and actions]' (1966: 33). Life is arranged in patterns and categories that exist before the individual comes along but are also affected or reproduced by that individual, and it is language that gives us access to the objectifications arising from these patterns and categories (1966: 35).

They differentiate between the world of dreams and the world of reality in the sense that the latter is intersubjective and that the 'here' and the 'now' that we experience in the world of reality have to be continuously negotiated through interaction (1966: 37). Furthermore, they see the world of dreams, along with other contexts such as theoretical thought, and play, as 'enclaves' which are 'enveloped' by the broader, everyday reality that is recognized as the norm, and that shifts into one or more of these other contexts are treated by us as 'excursions' (1966: 39). We can here hear distinct echoes of Goffman's notion of 'framing'.

Berger and Luckmann spend some time thinking about the importance of 'the other' for individuals' knowledge of themselves, in that this is only fully available via 'the other's' attitude towards the self (1966: 44). 'Others', just like the world of reality in general, are categorized, or 'typified', by language and 'dealt with' in those terms, and this is reciprocal in how the 'others' 'deal with' the self (1966: 45). There is an element of 'I know that you know that I know ...', and so on, in our shared use of language and the 'social stock of knowledge' that it objectifies for us (1966: 60); at the same time, however, this social stock of knowledge is distributed in various ways, and we know this, but not fully, which plays a big part in how we negotiate meanings and relationships in everyday life (1966: 61). This negotiation of meanings happens at various levels: 'habitualisation', when repeated actions take on a pattern and then meaning; 'institutionalisation', when different actors recognize and reproduce the typifications of these habitualized actions; and 'legitimation', where social reality is invested with meaning and thus becomes plausible (1966: 94).

Erving Goffman

Of all the theorists discussed here, Goffman is the one who is most roundly positioned in the social constructionist camp. Goffman's (1959) focus is very much on the individual in interaction with other individuals, and on agency, and as such he could be described as the most 'micro' of the theorists we have discussed so far. Goffman talks about the 'presentation of self', but for him it encompasses much more than incidental performances of identity. He describes all social interaction in terms of a dramatic performance and as such highlights that identity (or 'the self' as he terms it) is an ongoing interactive construction rather than something 'given'. He says, 'a correctly staged and performed scene leads the audience to impute a self to a performed character, but this imputation – this self – is a *product* of a scene that comes off, and is not a *cause* of it' (1959: 244–5). He thus clearly provides a social development of the notion of a dialectic between self and other.

The correct staging and performance of which he speaks have several components. For every interaction there is a 'front' (scenery and props) and each participant utilizes a 'personal front' consisting of 'appearances' (social statuses) and 'manner' (interactional role) (1959: 35). He distinguishes 'front region' from 'back region' or 'backstage', and says that 'suppressed facts' will make an appearance backstage. He further observes that 'impression management' often occurs in teams which do not exist in relation to a structure, but rather in relation to the impression they construct. So, although **membership** of some 'teams', for example in workplaces, is determined by the 'structure' of the company, this does not determine the team **identity**, which rather comes from interpersonal dynamics which construct and uphold the 'impression'.

Goffman does not see society as random and structureless; he accepts that structures come into existence, but only because of the repetitive reinforcing behaviour of **individuals**. For Goffman, as a result of numerous specific interactions played out in it, any particular front may in time take on a meaning of its own and become 'a 'collective representation' and 'a fact in its own right' (Goffman 1959: 34).

A particularly relevant aspect of Goffman's work for sociolinguistics is his notion of 'footing' (Goffman 1981), which illustrates well the social construction of identity by separating out individuals from the role(s) they play in conversational interaction. The notion of footing deconstructs the relationship between speaker and utterance and claims that there is not a one-to-one relationship between the two. There are three voices involved in any utterance: first, there is the animator, the person that utters the words; secondly, there is the author, the person that originated the beliefs; and thirdly, there is the principal, the person whose viewpoint is currently being expressed. The only role that is entailed by speaking an utterance is that of animator. Regarding the other two roles, put simply, speakers takes on the role of author if they use their own words; and they take on the role of principal if they speak sincerely. Conversely, the role of author may be attributed to someone else by quoting another speaker; and the role of principal may be revoked by speaking ironically, or in other words 'saying what you don't mean'. In this case, the role of principal is not attributed to anyone else: it is simply avoided altogether.

The roles of author and principal are complex, however. Regarding the author, the distinction between quoting and not quoting another speaker is not a simple one. Speakers may consciously invoke another speaker when they speak, either explicitly, by directly quoting from them, or implicitly, by appropriating a voice. Invoking another speaker may also happen unconsciously: if we accept that identity and knowledge are constructed in interaction, we would expect speakers to allude to previous exchanges in present ones, sometimes unconsciously. Indeed, given the degree of intertextuality in language use (cf. Bakhtin, 1986), it is very rare that any utterance will be entirely new and original. The invoked exchanges and other speakers will not necessarily be from the current speaker's local context, but may also be from wider public life or the media. Regarding the role of principal, again the distinction between sincerity and insincerity or irony is not a simple one. If we accept that certain discourses become dominant in society and are consequently taken as 'given' or 'the norm', a speaker drawing on these may unconsciously act as the principal of particular positions.

Michel Foucault

Foucault focuses on the relationship between interactions between individuals and wider relations of power, placing a greater degree of focus on agency than structure. Foucault suggests that we view power as ascending. There are power relations in every personal interaction we take part in but 'these (micro-level) mechanisms of power have been "invested, colonised, utilised, involuted, transformed, displaced, extended" (1980: 99) by more general forms, and these are what we tend to see as forms of social power'.

Foucault sees 'objects' as 'discursively produced' rather than having an intrinsic meaning. For any one topic, there are multiple discourses (ways of speaking about something). However, this does not mean that we can make the world into anything we want simply by speaking, writing or thinking in a certain way. Foucault shows us that there are multiple discourses but some are more highly valued or 'dominant' than others and these tend to form an accepted 'system'. All of the discourses may, however, vie for these dominant positions. For example, in the UK, there are competing discourses about asylum. One discourse would say things like 'they're coming over here and taking our homes and our jobs and there's nothing left for us', while another would say things like 'of course we should welcome people who are fleeing persecution – our foreign policy has created some of their situations'. These vie for dominance on the pages of the UK press and, in turn, in everyday discussion. There is a certain amount of input from political figures, and arguably their discourse is more likely to be considered to be dominant, but actually the vast majority of this discursive reproduction happens at the level of individual interactions. While more traditional Marxist thinking would claim that there is only one dominant ideology and it is that which positions us, Foucault believes that we, as interacting individuals, uphold the system and so it follows that we can subvert it. He claims it is possible for the dominant discourses to be subverted and the marginalized ones voiced.

Foucault coins the term 'power/knowledge' (1980) to illustrate how close he believes the relationship between the two concepts to be. For Foucault, knowledge gives you power; but on the other hand, those who have power are more likely to have their discourse accepted as knowledge. It is clear that, like Bourdieu, Foucault does not see the material and the ideological as completely discrete aspects of life. It is also clear that his ideas begin to question the very notion of 'truth'. So, his notion of knowledge does **not** correlate with ideology: what is central are the **procedures** by which something comes to be considered knowledge and, by extension, 'truth'. He is not claiming that we can never 'get at' the material reality of an event; he is simply pointing out that there may be considerable struggle over what constitutes the 'taken-for-granted' truth of that event.

Dominant discourses and systems of power by definition create categories of 'deviants', which are seen as being in opposition to 'the norm'. (See Foucault (1977) for Foucault's discussion of how sexual deviance and criminality have been constructed in the Western world. The 'norms' are maintained by 'surveillance'; Foucault uses the panopticon, designed by Jeremy Bentham, as a metaphor for this (Foucault, 1977)). The panopticon is a concrete mode of surveillance whereby the architecture of a prison allows the prison guard to see all of the prisons but none of the prisoners can see the guard. Foucault argues that this works on an abstract level too; due to these material manifestations of surveillance, the notion enters the psyche of individuals in a society to the extent that the material forms are no longer required: individuals begin to self-monitor from the point of view of the powerful.

Pierre Bourdieu

Bourdieu too focuses on the relationship between interactions between individuals and wider relations of power; he places a greater degree of focus on structure than does Foucault, however. We could therefore label him a 'structural constructionist', displaying characteristics of SC, but inhabiting a position on the continuum closer to structure than agency, and differing from Goffman and Foucault in this regard. Bourdieu moves beyond the traditional Marxist counterposing of the material and the ideological, by revisiting the Marxist notion of 'capital' in ways that suggest significant overlap between the two, and which move away from a deterministic view of identity towards a constructionist one, in which individuals use these various 'forms of capital' as resources with which to construct their identities, albeit within limits imposed by wider structures.

Traditional Marxism focuses on economic capital, something that has been produced, been assigned a value, and can be exchanged in pursuit of profit. Bourdieu (1986) suggests, however, that it is not only material entities that should be defined as 'capital'; the label for him can and should also be applied to certain 'symbolic' aspects of life. 'Social capital' applies to the networks and relationships that might be of value to a person as regards their 'social standing'; 'cultural capital' applies to accumulating valuable forms of knowledge (which might differ depending on the type of schooling one has for example); 'physical capital' applies to one's presence, the way one moves, the physical tasks one can carry out, the way one 'handles oneself'; 'linguistic capital' applies to the way one speaks.

What is notable about Bourdieu's 'forms of capital' is that, although there are overarching norms, dictated by the power-holders, regarding the value attributed to each of these forms of capital, and different subtypes within them, these values may differ at a more local level, particularly as regards social class. So, for example, speaking a marked form of the local dialect (a specific type of linguistic capital (cf. Bourdieu and Thompson 1991)) and being strong and tough (a specific type of physical capital) may be highly valued within the working class (cf. Labov's (1972) work on 'lames' being excluded from peer groups because they did not display 'core' linguistic behaviour). This type of capital, while locally valuable however, may preclude social mobility: it may be relatively more difficult, or at least less comfortable, for a core member of a working-class community to enter a professional career, with its focus on speaking standard English and acting in a 'refined' manner, regardless of whether that person has gained the relevant qualifications or 'cultural capital'. This questions further the idea that society is a 'meritocracy'.

Bourdieu's theory of capital offers us a picture of free-thinking agents who can consciously attempt to acquire particular forms of capital to exchange for particular kinds of experience, status or indeed other forms of capital. For Bourdieu, this is very much agency within limits however: societal structure is very real, and ultimately society will tend to reproduce itself in a similar form. His concept of 'habitus' is useful here (Bourdieu, 1984). It is via the habitus that objective material conditions become translated into subjective human dispositions; individuals carry out certain practices relative to structural aspects of their lives, such as family, schooling and social class, and to their experiences within certain 'fields' of activity, and as such come to embody and play these out.

Mikhail Bakhtin

Bakhtin was primarily a literary theorist, but some of his key ideas can be applied equally well to spoken language, and indeed in his later work he began to engage with this. Probably his most famous work is his analysis of the work of the novelist Dostoyevsky (Bakhtin, 1984a). In it, he introduced three key concepts: the unfinalizability of the self, the inseparability of the self and the other, and polyphony, i.e. many voices. He related the concept of polyphony to truth: whereas a traditional view might suggest that two separate accounts that differ entails that one of them is untrue, Bakhtin suggested that it was only in polyphony, and the engagement and dialogue that it presupposed, that truth could be found.

Bakhtin's later work (Bakhtin, 1986) engaged more with everyday spoken language, and the key concepts of this work were genre and intertextuality. Whereas it is usual to think of genre as an attribute of written language, Bakhtin said that spoken language also displayed this. He differentiated between primary genres, which structured what was acceptable in everyday language, and secondary genres, which dealt with specialist discourse such as legal and scientific. With intertextuality, he claimed that no utterance is unique, that the making of an utterance involves 'appropriat[ing] the words of others and populat[ing] them with one's own intention'. This can be seen to develop further his notion of the relationship between the self and the other.

Bakhtin took a particular interest in ritual and the carnivalesque (Bakhtin, 1984b), particularly in their liminal nature; that is, that they are ambiguous spaces 'between worlds' in which societal norms do not apply. An example of liminality is the ritual of 'kissing under the mistletoe' found in certain Western cultures around the Christmas period. Mistletoe is usually placed on a threshold (e.g. the entrance to a home), and the ritualistic nature of the kisses means that they are not viewed as moral transgressions. Carnival similarly allows individuals to construct alternative identities in a non-judgmental space. Rites of passage are sometimes considered liminal; in fact it can be useful to view the whole period of adolescence as a liminal time and space in which adolescents can experiment with the threshold between childhood and adulthood. Liminality has interesting applications in sociolinguistics in that language allows us to shift between different contexts and rules with simple changes to discourse, tone and so on.

Edward Said

On the topic of 'othering' and 'deviance', it is important to consider the work of Edward Said (1978) on 'Orientalism'. The theorists we have considered thus far have generally discussed the ways in which they see identities and relationships being constructed **within** specific societies, albeit with power differentials, for example social class. Said takes a more global approach and engages with power relationships **between** 'West' and 'East', and by extension between individuals and groups of different ethnicities. He analyses the notion of 'the Orient' as being an object of Western construction which arises from a set of categories, images and classifications held by Westerners.

Through reinforcement, these representations come to be viewed as reality to the point that 'the Orient' as an entity is seen to exist. It does not, however, have a status equal to that of its creator. Because the West has constructed this entity, it sees itself as active and 'the Orient' as passive. The former automatically feels it 'knows' and can master the latter, and therefore a relation of power (which appears natural) comes into play. Thus, political motives are forgotten as this definition of the entity comes to be seen as 'truth'.

Furthermore, it is through this creation of an 'other' that the West constructs an identity for itself. 'The West' and 'the Orient' do not **mean** anything intrinsically, but are defined through the differences between them.

7.3 SOCIAL CONSTRUCTIONIST SOCIOLINGUISTICS

This section will explore a range of sociolinguistic work that draws on and develops the SC tradition, in some cases as a general approach and in other cases by applying the work of a particular social theorist to spoken interaction. Not surprisingly, identity is a common theme throughout this work, shifting the sociolinguistic focus from language system to speaker(s), and from structure to performance and later construction. In what follows, I sketch work on themes including constructions of gender; constructions of ethnicity, national identity and minority languages; constructions of childhood and adolescent identity (and often gendered and ethnicicized aspects of these); mediated constructions of political relations; and constructions and reproduction within the legal system. It should be noted that I can discuss only a very small fraction of the research in sociolinguistics that draws, in one way or another, on SC.

Gender

Milroy (1992: 215) writes of meaning becoming 'gendered': certain forms become symbolically associated with masculine or feminine norms through regular use by, and in turn association with, particular groups. Lavandera (1982, cited in Milroy, 1992: 175) claims that patterns of sounds (because they are inherently meaningless) acquire 'social significance', whereas patterns in discourse acquire 'social meaning'. Holmes claims that these two can interact, however: forms with social meaning may acquire social significance because a particular group favours them; forms with social significance may have social meaning attributed to them by being seen to carry a particular value of the community that habitually uses them. Thus, in certain contexts, 'the use of phonetic variation and the construction of identities are inseparable'

(Eckert and McConnell-Ginet, 1995: 503, cited in Holmes).

Holmes (1997) further challenges traditional notions of particular linguistic features being 'women's' or 'men's' features. She highlights the problem that arises from simply counting pragmatic particles and concluding questions of identity from the results: such particles are interactive and so will serve particular (not necessarily identical) social functions for their speakers. She identifies four different functions of tag questions: facilitative, softening, epistemic modal (expressing uncertainty or tentativeness) and challenging. Similarly, 'I think' and 'you know' can function either as hedges or as boosters (Holmes, 1985, 1986).

Coates (1999) uses Goffman's notions of front and backstage to explore UK women 'behaving badly', as she terms it: in the contexts in which they are most relaxed, they report behaviour and fantasies that do not fit with the norms of femininity. Coates claims that, while there is an opportunity for subversion here, because it is 'backstage', a less dominant arena, it must be recognized that it also upholds the dominant order.

Kiesling (1998) analyses US college fraternity men's contextual variation in the use of the variable pronunciation of the English suffix spelled '-ing'. Most of the men use less of the vernacular ('dropped–g') form in fraternity meetings but some use more. He claims that all the men are constructing powerful identities (they are encouraged to do so by the norm of hegemonic masculinity), but that the working-class men's identities are based on physical rather than structural power, the latter of which they have less access to than middle-class men. He claims that they show more than just a resistant solidarity: their solidarity is bound up with hegemonic masculinity to create what Kiesling calls 'camaraderie'. The men identify themselves with certain prototypes ('alignment roles') within the confines of hegemonic masculinity, and thus their language use is bound up with physical power and serves to construct identity rather than simply produce context-specific interactional patterns (e.g. the resistance of one group to another). Through this evidence of alignment to prototypical roles, Kiesling claims that social interactive sense-making can be viewed in a similar way to other cognitive capacities.

Kiesling (2005) exemplifies the ways in which a group of (heterosexual) men in the United States discursively negotiate closeness, which is constructed by the dominant discourses of their culture as being in opposition to heterosexuality. They do this via indirectness, which again reminds us of the importance of considering form as well as function when considering construction of discourses.

Cameron (1997) highlights the importance of considering both form and content of conversation when identifying multiple discourses or discursive struggle. In her data, young men use an apparently cooperative **style** of talk but the **content** consists of 'the same old gendered script' (1997: 64).

Ethnicity

Menard-Warwic's (2005) work on what she calls 'trangression narratives' reminds us that the 'other' involved in our negotiation of identity may not in fact be a physically different person; dialogical positioning can also be employed where we need to negotiate between contradictory positions, in this case in terms of how the speaker orients towards a relative who she values highly while distancing herself from this violation of traditional family values.

Schilling-Estes (2004), in a discussion of a sociolinguistic interview from a tri-ethnic rural community in the USA, shows how speakers of different ethnicities tend to highlight ethnic components of their speech when talking about (local) race relations, but do not do this when they are talking about family and friends, or about race relations on a national level. This highlights the fact that the relationship between the 'self' and the 'other' is dynamic and continuously negotiated. All of this is done within ethnolinguistic patterns, however, which reminds us of the constant interplay between structure and agency. By applying Bakhtin's notion of 'dialogicality', Schilling-Estes also provides us with an insightful way to look at the role that researchers play in the construction of those they research.

Plas (2007) provides a fascinating demonstration of how social constructionist analysis can allow us to reassess historical accounts. He focuses on a north Dalmatian ethnographic account from the end of the nineteenth century in the context of early Croatian institutional-ethnographic practice and demonstrates that unpicking the dialogical aspects of this account, and ethnographic accounts in general, is essential in constructing reliable histories. The account shows respondents a questionnaire orienting to their own rather than the questionnaire's categories and themes, and the dialogic activity between author and editor as result of this shows a renegotiation of the identities discussed. This can be read as ideologically problematic given the cultural and national categories and themes that are dealt with.

Jaworski et al.'s (2003) analysis of British holiday programmes' construction of the local contains interesting echoes of Said's notion of 'Orientalism'. Although the presenters–tourists construct their relationship with local people as one of 'closeness' and 'friendship', and thus by extension as equals, close discourse analysis reveals that they are constructed as 'helpers'/ 'servants' or 'experts', thus 'othering' them (even in the second example which could be likened to Said's notion of 'exoticisation', whereby an overwhelmingly positive stereotype still serves to marginalize the 'other'). Local people often subvert these roles, however, by constructing themselves as, for example, 'cosmopolitan' and as such equal to those who are 'othering' them.

Childhood and adolescence

Björk-Willén (2007) exemplifies, in her study of children in a multilingual pre-school play setting in Sweden, that very young children also engage in 'crossing' for the negotiation of individual and group identities. She shows the ways in which a young speaker secures her own participation in the play by replicating the utterances of her co-interlocutors, not as a direct imitation, but as her own contributions, evident for example by being multimodally linked to a different non-vocal action. Her co-interlocutors speak Spanish while she does not. Where the replication is in English, Björk-Willén terms the utterance 'shadowing' and where it is in Spanish, she terms it 'crossing'.

Ardington (2006) exemplifies how preadolescent Australian girls employ framing, and specifically shifting between play and non-play frames, to negotiate identities and boundaries. It is no accident that shifting between these frames is a key site for negotiation, as the girls are in an in-between stage, drawing on both childhood and adolescent/adult types of talk. Unlike in documented talk of adult women, the girls use playful confrontation such as reciprocal name-calling and insulting as well as supportive behaviour to build alliances. It is notable that preadolescent talk often accompanies activity, and Ardington finds that a thematic activity can both be a springboard into language play and a frame that the girls can easily switch back to should their play frame become problematic, a useful strategy given the in-between stage of the girls and thus their experimental construction of identity.

Fraser and Cameron (1989) highlight apparent contradictions in the input of individual adolescent speakers into conversation but challenge definition of these as contradictions, analysing them instead in terms of the young women's attempts to make sense of society via the interplay of various discourses (1989: 32).

Adolescence and gender

Coates (1999) observes that the adolescent girls in her data use various discourses to position themselves as women: liberal, patriarchal, pseudo-scientific and so on. At the age of about 14 years old, a change in linguistic features suggests the advent of a new discourse that she calls the 'discourse of consciousness raising'. However, this discourse is in competition with the fact that the content of what the girls say often comes from a patriarchal, repressive discourse.

Eckert (1993) describes the discourse strategies used by the adolescent girls she studies as 'co-operative competition', thus challenging the polar opposition which sees men as competitive and women as cooperative, and highlighting the necessity of analysing function. The girls compete and negotiate agreement on trivial issues (which is easier and less threatening) and these have a cumulative effect. She claims that both gender and age account for why the girls use such discourse. Historically, men have inhabited the marketplace and women the domestic sphere, which has made it necessary for women to accumulate 'symbolic capital' (Bourdieu, 1986) to override the fact that they lack economic capital (which was at that time the most highly valued form of capital). This involved proving the whole self to be worthy of authority. The entrance of women into the marketplace has brought with it a contradictory situation for women: competition in the marketplace violates men's cultural prerogative, and competition in the personal realm contradicts the underlying definition of personal worth.

Adolescence and ethnicity

Hewitt (1986) identifies a need to redefine the term 'code-switching' to encompass what the adolescents in his UK study were doing. Code-switching had been seen to involve 'two or more fixed and discrete linguistic systems', between which speakers alternate either randomly (Labov, 1971) or in ways that show meaningful patterning (Gumperz, 1982). However, Hewitt suggests, following Le Page's (1985) theory, that speakers exist in a 'linguistic space' made up of 'acts of identity' which provides a less structuralist, more speaker-centred definition of code-switching.

The Black adolescents in Hewitt's study report creole use mainly in relation to lower-class life and conflict, especially with the police. Within this, its use can be triggered by competitive topics or situations or an antagonistic relationship with one's interlocutor (Hewitt, 1986: 108). This could be interpreted as the young people 'doing' conflict in a certain way, at the local level, which relates to and helps them to understand and deal with it at a more global level. Indeed, Hewitt saw the possibility for transformation of the social order (albeit cultural and partial) through transformation of symbolic forms. He claimed therefore that Black/White speech **relations** were important as they explored the local interactive order and, by extension, wider social relationships (ibid.: 124).

Hewitt observes the use of Jamaican creole by White adolescents with their Black peers. Although he accepts that such creole use often constitutes racial abuse (1986: 135), he claims that it also occurs in friendship situations as the playful ritualistic employment of terms of abuse. This expresses 'both a cultural self-contextualising and a *positioning* through the rivalries of verbal and other forms of play. Its reference is not simply that of cultural position but of personal position, with the emphasis on individual competitive relations' (ibid.: 136). It serves to negotiate relationships between the young White person and their Black friends.

Rampton (1995) coined the term 'language crossing', which he differentiated from code-switching by saying that the former involves 'the use of language varieties associated with social or ethnic groups that the speaker does not normally belong to' (1995: 17). Rampton's case in point is young White speakers' use of Stylished Asian English: they employ certain explicit lexical and phonological traits, but not the more implicit grammatical structure. Here we can see the importance of the 'other' in constructing one's own identity. There is the potential for challenge to structures here too, as the 'crossing' often marks a challenge to adult stereotypes of the 'other'. That said, Rampton makes it clear that most of this work is done in 'liminal' spaces, which lessens the potential of any material challenge.

Rampton's work, like Hewitt's (1986) work before it, involves young White people **with their Asian friends**; some of the more recent observations of 'crossing', however (Bucholtz, 1999; Cutler, 1999), illustrate young White people who rarely come into contact with ethnic minority communities still making a conscious choice to employ the language of these communities. This is very much a case of style over structure, and indeed Bucholtz concludes that the young White boys in her data are able to 'disclaim their structural advantage' (1999: 455), thus actually masking structural inequality rather than challenging it.

Jaworski et al. (2003) apply the notion of liminality to adolescents' 'gossipy' talk. The adolescents construct their own orientation to certain norms by way of gossiping, mostly about 'others', but sometimes about themselves in a process that Jaworski et al. term 'self-othering'. They shift between keying their talk seriously and playfully, and thus between constructing approval or disapproval of the behaviour about which they talk. This ambiguity allows for a state of constant liminality and thus constant negotiation of identities.

Adolescence and social class

My own work (Irwin, 2006) links the use of *you know* in a group of mostly working-class London adolescents (WCG) and *I know* in a mostly middle-class group (MCG) to Foucault's notion of power/knowledge and, by extension, to group-specific (re)production of dominant discourses and power relations. Speakers in WCG use *you know* clause-finally to mark the information in that clause, which tends to be about the deviance of others, as dominant. Speakers in MCG use *I know* either clause-initially or as a stand-alone item in reaction to the previous speaker's utterance and to mark that utterance as dominant. Thus, the use of *you know* shows relatively active identity construction, while the use of *I know* shows relatively reactive identity construction, but both groups construct their identities indirectly: WCG because they talk about others, and MCG because they react to others.

My work on the same groups of adolescents negotiating deviant positions (Irwin, 2008) employs Goffman's concept of footing to explore the ways in which speakers either shift positions or only partially inhabit them, thus allowing them to engage with deviance without being fully positioned as deviant. The adolescents in WCG give deviant positions a voice in two ways: by saying an utterance and then retracting it with the phrase 'only joking' and, on one occasion, by shifting positions. In terms of footing, the speaker thus withdraws the claim to have been the principal of the previous utterance. This gives the adolescents the opportunity to explore alternative discourses and positionings while still marking their knowledge of and adherence to the dominant discourse.

The adolescents in MCG, on the other hand, voice deviant positions but avoid inhabiting them until such time as they have been communally evaluated. The linguistic strategies they use include: switching between possible and actual worlds, a marked shift of framing that problematizes the extent to which a speaker is viewed as the principal of an utterance; switching between the grammatically general (e.g. general 'you') and the grammatically specific (e.g. 'I' or 'we'), which problematizes authorship; and switching between questions and statements, which at the question stage renders principal irrelevant or at most suggested.

Ethnicity, national identity and minority languages

Sandel (2003) employs Bourdieu's notion of linguistic capital to the linguistic context in Taiwan, where for many years the nationalist government forbade the speaking of local languages and dialects, whereas more recently the policy has been reversed and local varieties are being accepted and taught in schools. The Bourdieuian perspective is a useful one here as it takes us beyond the public/private binary and suggests that there has been a complex interplay between the public and private as regards the linguistic capital value of different language varieties to both policymakers and communities.

Budach et al. (2003) analyse a discursal shift around minority languages to which aspects of both Foucault's and Bourdieu's theories are applicable. They recognize that the dominant discourses around minority languages have traditionally linked language with community, and they observe a recent shift which they exemplify via data from literacy centres and a call centre in francophone Canada. Given the ongoing commodification taking place in the globalized market, they suggest that 'community' is now being treated as a commodity that can be exchanged for linguistic and cultural resources, thus echoing notions of the complex interplay of linguistic, social, symbolic and economic capital.

Messing (2007) explores language shift in the Malintzi region of central Mexico, and argues for the importance of focusing on individuals and communities in order to gain a clearer picture of the specific ways in which such shifts occur. Her data exemplify Mexican (Nahuatl) speakers negotiating their orientation towards and against various identities via their use of three key, somewhat competing, discourses: the pro-development metadiscourse of *salir adelante*, 'forging ahead' and improving one's socioeconomic position; the discourse of *menosprecio*, denigration of indigenous identity; and the *pro-indígena* or pro-indigenous discourse that promotes a positive attitude toward indigenous identity.

A theme of co-option and related disempowerment beneath superficial celebration of diversity can be found in Stroud's (2004) work on Rinkeby Swedish, a specific form of Swedish spoken by immigrant communities. By labelling and thus recognizing this unique form of Swedish, the authorities may on the surface be recognizing heterogeneity and giving voice to minority communities, but Stroud claims that this is subverted by the fact that the way in which Rinkeby Swedish is talked about and positioned devalues the linguistic capital of the immigrants who speak it.

'Othering' in the legal system

Although Baker (2004) does not explicitly describe himself as taking a Foucauldian approach, his work on the UK House of Lords' debate on lowering the age of sexual consent for gay men provides an insightful example of competing discourses being constructed 'via chains of argumentation'. In the debates, the word 'homosexual' was associated with acts, whereas the word 'gay' was associated with identities, and the discourses that were constructed around the former linked it to danger, crime and ill health, whereas the discourses that were constructed around the latter focused on equality and tolerance.

D'hondt (2009) highlights a contradiction in Belgian courtroom practice relating to the acceptability of constructing a defendant as a cultural 'other'. Attorneys will regularly provide a 'cultural defence' in the sense that they do not deny the facts of the case, but argue that it is mitigated by the effects of the defendant's cultural background on their actions. This 'othering' strategy, although its relevance is regularly challenged by the prosecution, does not detrimentally affect relations within the courtroom. If, on the other hand, the defendant highlights his or her 'otherness' in drawing attention to perceived mistreatment by the authorities, the tendency is for the interjection to be ignored by the defence or rejected by the judge. D'hondt identifies the key difference between the two examples to be that, in the first, the context of the 'otherness' is external to Belgium, whereas, in the second, the context is discrimination within Belgium. This challenges the very heart of the legal system as a system that should treat all defendants equally, and any challenges to this are silenced.

Ethnicity, national identity and policing

Wilson and Stapleton's (2007) work on discourses of policing in Northern Ireland draws both on (Foucauldian) notions of discourse and Bourdieu's concept of habitus. They point out the contentious nature of policing for the nationalist community in Northern Ireland, even given the development from the Royal Ulster Constabulary to the new Police Service of Northern Ireland. By using the concept of 'habitus' the paper engages with the fact that discourses are not stand-alone entities, but are in fact very much tied up with the material world, in particular the context and interactional practices of those who (re)produce them. They exemplify this via the 'discourse of resistance' reproduced by a group of nationalist women in Belfast.

Mediated (political) discourse

O'Malley (2009) uses frame analysis to explore an Irish radio programme that claims to be 'for and about disabled people', and challenges that

claim by exemplifying how the complexity of the disabled person's experience tends to, as she puts it, 'fall between frames'. She draws on Scannell's (1991) notion of the 'double articulation' of radio talk: i.e. it is at once an interaction between the co-interlocutors on the radio programme, and oriented towards the listening audience. In this context, part of the 'presenter frame' is to introduce the participants to the audience in a 'relevant' way, but perhaps not the way they would have introduced themselves, and the 'Interview frame' consists of a question and answer format that elicits factual answers; this facticity tends towards a medical construction of disability that loses sight of each participant's complex identity and experience.

Clayman (1992) develops Goffman's concept of footing in order to analyse how neutrality and drama are achieved simultaneously by political interviewers. They can introduce to their interviewees opposing points of view and challenges from other people (authors), while at the same time leaving their own position ambiguous (i.e. whether or not they are the principal of the utterance). In this way, utterances are marked as controversial, while at the same time speakers avoid the potential results of voicing such controversial material.

Weizman's (2006) discussion of media talk in the Israeli context draws on Goffman's (1974) notion of the multiplicity of roles and the person-role continuum to show how social roles (e.g. politician, journalist, show host), interactional roles (e.g. interviewer, interviewee) and personal identities are differentiated in meta-talk **about** news interviews, and are negotiated **within** news interviews. Such orientation to these roles by participants provides evidence of participants' construction of their reality. Situations may be evaluated by politicians in terms of both their personal identity and their social role, and these may be marked as being at odds with each other, or indeed as being in correlation: for example, where a politician constructs themselves as a 'pleasant' individual in terms of personal identity and not just because of their professional ability to come across as such. The constriction of interactional roles may be used as a mitigating factor for aggressive behaviour as well as a means to avoid it, but at the same time show hosts may be criticized when they blur the boundaries of interactional roles because this is seen not to remove constriction but remove neutrality. Thus, these roles and their negotiation are oriented to by participants throughout media talk.

The relevance of Goffman for the analysis of political discourse is also picked up on by Lauerbach (2006), who analyses television interviews with politicians of the UK Conservative and Labour Parties on Election Night, 1997. Lauerbach finds that the 'voicing' within the interviews with members of the two parties differed. The Conservatives, who lost, were presented with opposing 'voices' from within their own party, in the sense that the interviewer animated utterances that had been authored by someone else. There were no dissenting voices within the Labour Party to present to their politicians, so instead interviewers 'ventriloquised': i.e. they put (their own) discourse into the mouths of others to surmise what might happen in the future. In this way, debate was constructed but neutrality maintained in the sense that in neither case was the voice directly or fully that of the interviewer, and it also served to dramatize the proceedings.

7.4 CONCLUDING REMARKS

It is clear, then, that social constructionist sociolinguistics has emerged as a key aspect of our field, which has drawn on the fruitful link between language and social theory. Two main things strike me about the themed areas into which the work falls. First, SC is particularly helpful in illustrating transitional and liminal spaces as we see from discussions of ethically-diverse contexts and minority language debates as well as illustrations of the linguistic behaviour of preadolescents and adolescents. Secondly, it is clear that social constructionist work can provide relevant insights into everything from one-to-one interactions to constructions of power structures at the highest levels, and indeed to illustrate the latter in the former. As such, its potential to marry the 'micro' and the 'macro' has been and continues to be developed in interesting and important ways by sociolinguists.

REFERENCES

Althusser, L. (2001) *Lenin and Philosophy and Other Essays.* Monthly Review Press.

Ardington, A. (2006) 'Playfully negotiated activity in girls' talk', *Journal of Pragmatics,* 38(1): 73–95.

Baker, P. (2004) '"Unnatural acts": discourses of homosexuality within the House of Lords debates on gay male law reform', *Journal of Sociolinguistics,* 8(2): 88–106.

Bakhtin, M. M. (1981) *The Dialogic Imagination.* Austin, TX: University of Texas Press.

Bakhtin, M. M. (1984a) *Problems of Dostoevsky's Poetics.* Edited and translated by C. Emerson. Minneapolis: University of Minnesota Press.

Bakhtin, M. M. (1984b) *Rabelais and His World.* Bloomington, IN: University of Indiana Press.

Bakhtin, M. M. (1986) 'The problem of speech genres', in *Speech Genres and Other Late Essays.* Austin, TX: University of Austin Press.

Berger, P. L. and Luckmann, T. (1966) *The Social Construction of Reality: A Treatise in the Sociology of Knowledge.* New York: Anchor.

Björk-Willén, P. (2007) 'Participation in multilingual preschool play: shadowing and crossing as interactional resources', *Journal of Pragmatics,* 39(12): 2133–58.

Bourdieu, P. (1984) *Distinction: A Social Critique of the Judgement of Taste.* Cambridge, MA: Harvard University Press.

Bourdieu, P. (1986) 'The forms of capital' in Richardson, J. (ed.), *Handbook of Theory and Research for the Sociology of Education.* New York: Greenwood Press.

Bourdieu, P. and Thompson, J.B. (1991) *Language and Symbolic Power.* Cambridge, MA: Polity Press.

Bruner, J. (1990) *Acts of Meaning.* Cambridge, MA: Harvard University Press.

Bucholtz, M. (1999) 'You da man: narrating the racial other in the production of white masculinity', *Journal of Sociolinguistics,* 3(4): 443–60.

Budach, G., Roy, S. and Heller, M. (2003) 'Community and commodity in French Ontario', *Language in Society,* 32(5): 603–27.

Burr, V. (1995) *An Introduction to Social Constructionism.* London: Routledge.

Buttny, R. and Cohen, Jodi R. (2007) 'Drawing on the words of others at public hearings: Zoning, Wal-Mart, and the threat to the aquifer', *Language in Society,* 36(5): 735–56.

Cameron, D. (1997) 'Performing gender identity: young men's talk and the construction of heterosexual masculinity', in S. Johnson, and U. Meinhof (eds), *Hanna Language and Masculinity.* Oxford: Blackwell. pp. 47–64.

Clayman, S. E. (1992) 'Footing in the achievement of neutrality: the case of news interview discourse', in J. Heritage, and P. Drew (eds), *Talk at Work: Interaction in Institutional Settings.* Cambridge: Cambridge University Press. pp. 163–98.

Coates, J. (1999) 'Changing femininities: the talk of teenage girls', in M. Bucholtz, A. C. Liang, and L. A. Sutton (eds), *Reinventing Identities: The Gendered Self in Discourse.* Oxford: Oxford University Press.

Cutler, C. (1999) 'Yorkville crossing: White teens, hip hop and African American English', *Journal of Sociolinguistics,* 3(4): 428–42.

de Saussure, F. (1983) *Course in General Linguistics.* London: Duckworth.

D'hondt, S. (2009) 'Others on trial: the construction of cultural otherness in Belgian first instance criminal hearings', *Journal of Pragmatics,* 41(4): 806–28.

Eckert, P. (1993) 'Co-operative competition in adolescent "girl talk"', in D. Tannen (ed.), *Gender and Conversational Interaction.* Oxford: Oxford University Press. pp. 32–61.

Foucault, M. (1977) *Discipline and Punish: The Birth of the Prison.* London: Allen Lane.

Foucault, M. (1980) *Power/knowledge: Selected Interviews and Other Writings 1972–1977.* London: Harvester Press.

Fraser, E. and Cameron, D. (1989) 'Knowing what to say: the construction of gender in linguistic practice', in R. Grillo (ed.), *Social Anthropology and the Politics of Language*. London: Routledge.

Goffman, E. (1959) *The Presentation of Self in Everyday Life*. London: Penguin.

Goffman, E. (1974) *Frame Analysis*. New York: Harper.

Goffman, E. (1981) *Footing. Forms of talk*. Philapdelphia: University of Pennsylvania Press. pp.124–59.

Gramsci, A. (1983) *Selections from the Prison Notebooks*. London: Sage.

Gumperz, J. J. (ed.) (1982) *Language, Society and Identity*. Cambridge: Cambridge University Press.

Hewitt, R. (1986) *White Talk Black Talk: Inter-Racial Friendship and Communication Among Adolescents*. Cambridge: Cambridge University Press.

Holmes, J. (1985) 'Sex differences and miscommunication: some data from New Zealand', in J. B. Pride (ed.), *Cross-Cultural Encounters: Communication and Miscommunication*. Melbourne: River Seine. pp. 24–43.

Holmes, J. (1986) 'Functions of "you know" in women's and men's speech', *Language in Society*, 15: 1–22.

Holmes, J. (1997) 'Women, language and identity', *Journal of Sociolinguistics*, 1(2): 195–223.

Irwin, A. (2006) 'London adolescents (re)producing power/ knowledge: *you know* and *I know* ', *Language in Society*, 35: 499–528.

Irwin, A. (2008) 'Now you see me, now you don't: adolescents exploring deviant positions', in E. Eppler, and P. Pichler (eds), *Gender in Spontaneous Interaction*. Basingstoke: Palgrave Macmillan.

Jaworski, A. and Coupland, J. (2005) 'Othering in gossip: "you go out you have a laugh and you can pull yeah okay but like ... "', *Language in Society*, 34(5): 667–94.

Jaworski, A., Ylänne-McEwen, V., Thurlow, C. and Lawson, S. (2003) 'Social roles and negotiation of status in host– tourist interaction: a view from British television holiday programmes', *Journal of Sociolinguistics*, 7(2): 135–64.

Kiesling, S. F. (1998) 'Men's identities and sociolinguistic variation: the case of fraternity men', *Journal of Sociolinguistics*, 2(1): 69–99.

Kiesling, S. F. (2005) 'Homosocial desire in men's talk: balancing and re-creating cultural discourses of masculinity', *Language in Society*, 34(5): 695–726.

Labov, W. (1971) 'The notion of 'system' in Creole languages'. In D. Hymes (ed.), *Pidginization and Creolization of Languages*. Cambridge: Cambridge University Press. pp. 447–472.

Labov, W. (1972) *Language in the Inner City*. Philadelphia: University of Pennsylvania Press.

Lauerbach, G. (2006) 'Discourse representation in political interviews: the construction of identities and relations through voicing and ventriloquizing', *Journal of Pragmatics*, 38(2): 196–215.

Le Page, R. B. (1985) *Acts of Identity*. Cambridge: Cambridge University Press.

McHoul, A. and Grace, W. (1997) *A Foucault Primer: Discourse, Power and the Subject*. New York: New York University Press.

Marx, K. and Engels, F. (1970) *The German Ideology*. New York: International Publishers.

Marx, K. and Engels F. (2002) *The Communist Manifesto*. London: Penguin Classics.

Menard-Warwick, J. (2005) 'Transgression narratives, dialogic voicing, and cultural change', *Journal of Sociolinguistics*, 9(4): 533–56.

Messing, J. (2007) 'Multiple ideologies and competing discourses: language shift in Tlaxcala, Mexico', *Language in Society*, 36(4): 555–77.

Milroy, L. (1992) *Linguistic Variation and Change*. Oxford: Blackwell.

Norrick, N. (1997) 'Twice-told tales: collaborative narration of familiar stories', *Language in Society*, 26.

O'Malley, M. (2009) 'Falling between frames: institutional discourse and disability in radio', *Journal of Pragmatics*, 41(2): 346–56.

Piaget, J. (1954) *The Construction of Reality in the Child*. Tr. M. Cook. New York: Basic Books.

Plas, P. (2007) 'Voicing folk for the academy: interdiscursivity and collective identity in a north Dalmatian ethnography, 1899–1900', *Journal of Pragmatics*, 39(12): 2244–72.

Rampton, B. (1995) *Crossing: Language and Ethnicity Among Adolescents*. London: Longman.

Said, E. (1978) *Orientalism*. New York: Random House.

Sandel, T. L. (2003) 'Linguistic capital in Taiwan: the KMT's Mandarin language policy and its perceived impact on language practices of bilingual Mandarin and Tai-gi speakers', *Language in Society*, 32(4): 523–51.

Sapir, E. (1921) *Language: An Introduction to the Study of Speech*. New York: Harcourt, Brace.

Scannell, P. and David, C. (1991) *A Social History of British Broadcasting*, vol. 1:1922–1939. Oxford: Basil Blackwell.

Schiffrin, D. (1996) 'Narrative as self-portrait: sociolinguistic constructions of identity', *Language in Society*, 25(2): 167–203.

Schilling-Estes, N. (2004) 'Constructing ethnicity in interaction', *Journal of Sociolinguistics*, 8(2): 163–195.

Stroud, C. (2004) 'Rinkeby Swedish and semilingualism in language ideological debates: a Bourdieuean perspective', *Journal of Sociolinguistics*, 8(2): 196–214.

Taylor, C. (1991) 'Language and society', in A. Honneth, and H. Joas, (eds.), *Communicative Action*. Cambridge, MA: MIT Press. pp. 23–35.

Weizman, E. (2006) 'Roles and identities in news interviews: the Israeli context', *Journal of Pragmatics*, 38(2): 154–79.

Whorf, B. L. (1956) *Language, Thought, and Reality: Selected Writings*, Cambridge, MA: MIT Press.

Wilson, J. and Stapleton, K. (2007) 'The discourse of resistance: social change and policing in Northern Ireland', *Language in Society*, 36: 393–425.

Wolfson, N. (1978) 'A feature of performed narrative: the conversational historical present', *Language in Society*, 7(2): 215–37.

8

Symbolic Interactionism, Erving Goffman, and Sociolinguistics

Shari Kendall

8.1 INTRODUCTION

Sociologist Erving Goffman (1922–82) devoted his career to exploring the nuances of face-to-face interaction to discover and describe the underlying interaction order. From his early ethnographies of a small island community – hospitals, prisons, and casinos (1959, 1961, 1963a, 1963b, 1967, 1971), to his later works highlighting language (1974, 1981a, 1983), his work has inspired scholars throughout the social sciences and influenced several interactional approaches to language: ethnomethodology (Garot and Berard, in this volume), conversation analysis (Matthiessen and Slade, in this volume), and, especially, interactional sociolinguistics (Gordon, in this volume; Schiffrin, 1994). Within sociology, Goffman remains an enigma, as his work is not easily classified and does not reflect the wider perspectives or debates (Kim, 2003; Smith, 1999). A student at the University of Chicago in the 1940s, Goffman is most accurately classified as belonging to the Chicago school, first formally recognized as an approach to sociology in textbooks by Krueger and Reckless (1931) and Karpf (1932). Some scholars, such as Denzin (1992) and Joas (1987), refer to all members of the Chicago school as symbolic interactionists. Likewise, Plummer (2000: 200) observes, 'For the first four decades of the twentieth century, Chicago sociology dominated North American sociology;

and symbolic interactionism was its implicit theory'.

Goffman himself rejected the symbolic interactionist label on the grounds that it does not accurately capture the variety of work accomplished during this period,[1] nor does it effectively incorporate structure into the emergent view of interaction (Scheff, 2005; Verhoeven, 1993: 334–5). The latter criticism is aimed primarily at the form of symbolic interactionism developed by Herbert Blumer (1969), who coined the term in 1937. Within the Chicago school, Blumer's approach was only one strand of interactionism that developed (Verhoeven, 1993, 1995). In a 1980 interview, Goffman classified those scholars following in the tradition of Blumer and Louis Wirth to be symbolic interactionists, including Gregory Stone, Bernard Meltzer and, 'to a degree', Anselm Strauss (Verhoeven, 1993: 318). Goffman, in contrast, was most influenced by Everett Hughes who developed, in Goffman's words, 'a sort of occupational Sociology and basically Urban Ethnography'. Accordingly, he observes, 'what I did up to a few years ago before I got somewhat more interested in Sociolinguistics was a version of Urban Ethnography with Meadian Social Psychology' (318).[2]

However classified,[3] Goffman's work shares many of the principles that define symbolic interactionism, and he was influenced by scholars seminal to its inception, especially those associated with pragmatism: the philosophers Charles Sanders Peirce,

John Dewey, William James, George Herbert Mead and the American sociologist Charles Horton Cooley. In addition, he was influenced by the phenomenology of William James and Alfred Schütz, and the formalism of social anthropologists A. R. Radcliffe-Brown, Emile Durkheim and Georg Simmel. These influences contribute to Goffman's distinctive style and, coupled with his unique and inspirational perspective, underlie his ability to show us 'more of humanity than we could otherwise see' (Friedsen, 1983: 362). This chapter first introduces the principles of symbolic interactionism as applied to the work of Goffman and others who participated in the Chicago school, and then traces his conceptions that have most influenced scholarship on language – society and self, face, framing and footing – to those scholars that most influenced him in the areas of pragmatism, phenomenology, formalism and sociolinguistics.

8.2 SYMBOLIC INTERACTIONISM

Symbolic interactionism is a sociological perspective founded on the basis of the 'interpretive, subjective study of human experience' within 'an objective science of human conduct' (Denzin, 1992: 2). According to Plummer (2000), symbolic interactionism is characterized by four interweaving themes. First, the primary concern is not with the individual or society but with the 'joint acts through which lives are organized and societies assembled' (195). The 'self' emerges through interaction with the 'other', making interactionism fundamentally concerned with 'how people do things together' (Becker, 1986). Second, human worlds are not merely material or objective, but semiotic and symbolic. Thus, a major concern is with the process through which human beings 'go about the task of assembling meaning' through interaction with others, including 'how we define ourselves' and 'the situations we are in' (Plummer, 2000: 194). In this process, symbolic resources, both verbal and non-verbal, play a central role (Smith, 1999). Third, symbolic interactionism is an active view of the social world 'in which human beings are constantly going about their business, piecing together joint lines of activity, and constituting society through these interactions' (Plummer, 2000: 194). Fourth, and finally, the method of symbolic interactionism is fundamentally 'direct examination of the empirical world' (Blumer, 1969: 147). McCall and Becker (1990) observe, 'The ultimate interactionist test of concepts is whether they make sense of particular situations known in great detail through detailed observation' (5).

8.3 PRAGMATISM: PERFORMANCE AND IMPRESSION MANAGEMENT

Symbolic interactionism traces its roots to the American philosophical movement of pragmatism that emerged in the late nineteenth and early twentieth centuries, particularly the work of George Herbert Mead. Pragmatism posed epistemological questions about knowledge: how we acquire it, the form it takes, and how we can judge its validity. It rejected the dominant philosophical paradigm's 'quest for fundamental, foundational truths' and its emphasis on intellectual theorizing; instead, it posited 'a plurality of shifting truths grounded in concrete experiences and language, in which a truth is appraised in terms of its consequences' rather than its conformity to abstract theories (Plummer, 2000: 197). The empirical basis of symbolic interactionism stems from Mead and Dewey who, in the early twentieth century, 'transformed philosophical arguments into empirically oriented theoretical inquiries' (Cohen, 2000: 74). Dewey (1896) broke from the dominant theory of behaviorism to argue that 'the organism is not a passive receiver of stimuli, but an active perceiver of the situations it confronts' and whose behavior 'must be seen as a constant adaptation to the environment' (Denzin, 1992: 5). Mead (1934) opposed psychological behaviorism by developing 'social behaviorism', in which the self is a social object that could be studied objectively rather than through introspection (Denzin, 1992: 4). Mead offered a new understanding of the self as intersubjective, constructed in interaction with others. His theory of 'how the mind and self emerge from the social process of communication by signs' is viewed as founding the symbolic interactionist school (Delanty, 2000: 41).

The influence of pragmatism appears throughout Goffman's work, particularly in his conception of the 'self' as a collaborative, face-to-face achievement. In the 1980 interview, when asked about 'the main explanatory paradigm of symbolic interactionism', Goffman stated, 'you should go back to George Herbert Mead and *Mind, Self, and Society* ([1934] 1974), and the issue about the way we are constructed socially as individuals by taking to ourselves the opinion and attitude of the other' (Verhoeven, 1993: 336). Mead's conception of self originated with Cooley's (1922: 184) 'looking-glass self', the idea that the self is a reflected appraisal of the reactions of others (Denzin, 1992: 4). People 'see themselves reflected back in the moral judgments of others, and their sense of moral worth is largely determined by this reflected self' (Atkinson et al., 2007: 186). Like Cooley, Mead viewed the self as structured by the principle of sociality, or the taking of the attitude of the other in a social situation. As Cooley (1922) put it, we 'live in the minds of others without knowing it' (208).[4] However, whereas Cooley advocated a phenomenological, introspective approach to study the internal worlds of the self (Manning, 2005), Mead ([1934] 1974) advocated an empirical approach to explain how the self is intersubjective and achieved through social engagement.

For Mead, the individual develops a self synchronically and diachronically. In early socialization, the individual takes the role – i.e. mentally projects how others will react to one's actions – of specific others and, later, gains the ability to take the role of the 'generalized other', imagining the reactions of a group, community or society. Through this process, the individual acquires the conventional meanings of symbols and the values and norms of a society. Whereas Cooley conceived of 'communication as originating in the consciousness', Mead viewed consciousness as developing gradually through communication, particularly language (Mortensen, 2000: 114).

The reciprocal self of Cooley and Mead underlies Goffman's framework of impression management and his dramaturgical metaphor for face-to-face interaction. In *The Presentation of Self in Everyday Life*, Goffman (1959: xi) explains that he will employ 'the perspective … of the theatrical performance' to consider the way in which the individual 'presents himself [sic] and his activity to others, the ways in which he guides and controls the impressions they form of him, and the kinds of things he may or may not do while sustaining his performance before them'. Throughout this process, the individual guides the behavior of the other and is guided in turn. In *Behavior in Public Places*, Goffman (1963a) refers to this collaboration as the 'special mutuality of immediate social interaction' (16).

In the dramaturgical framework, Goffman conceives of the 'self' as a performance tailored to the audience and the situation. Because the individual has multiple audiences, he or she will display multiple selves. Goffman (1959: 48) quotes the pragmatist William James ([1890] 1925: 128–9) regarding the relation between self and other: 'we may practically say that [an individual] has as many social selves as there are distinct groups of persons about whose opinion he [or she] cares'. In addition, this 'performance' includes Mead's (1934) conceptualization of the 'generalized other' in the individual's acquisition of society's values and norms. Goffman (1959) observes that 'when the individual presents himself [sic] before others, his performance will tend to incorporate and exemplify the officially accredited values of the society, more so, in fact, than does his behavior as a whole' (35).

Unlike Mead, however, Goffman recognizes two selves, neither of which is the 'real' self. In *Presentation of Self*, the first is a 'character', a 'dramatic effect arising diffusely from a scene that is presented', and the second is 'a harried fabricator of impressions involved in the all-too-human task of staging a performance' (1959: 252, 253). In his description of deference and demeanor (1956/1967), one self is a social product, an 'image' that is 'pieced together' from the expressive implications of the encounter, and the other is an agent, 'a kind of player in a ritual game' (1967: 31). In *Frame Analysis*, Goffman (1974) acknowledges the biological being or 'relatively identifiable organism' (519) engaged in an interaction but clarifies that there is no 'perduring self' who is 'present behind the particular roles he [or she] plays at any particular moment'. The self is 'not an entity half-concealed behind events, but a changeable formula for managing oneself during them' (573).

Atkinson et al. (2007: 187) suggest that, 'if we take Goffman's own analyses seriously, then we conclude that social life is not *like* a performance, but that it *is* a performance' (italics in original). This perspective is supported by Goffman's (1981a) comment, in *Forms of Talk*, that 'I make no large literary claim that social life is but a stage, only a small technical one: that deeply incorporated into the nature of talk are the fundamental requirements of theatricality' (4). Thus, Goffman's dramaturgical model evokes Butler's (1990) theory of 'performativity' which theorizes identity, specifically gender, as discursively produced and 'performative'. Drawing on speech act theory, Butler (1993) explains that a 'performative' is a 'discursive practice that enacts or produces that which it names' (13). Local practices bring gender into being 'through the repetition or citation of a prior, authoritative set of practices' (227). Crucially, Butler point outs, 'There is no gender identity behind the expressions of gender; that gender is performatively constituted by the very "expressions" that are said to be its results' (25). In 1959, Goffman cites Simone de Beauvoir's (1953: 533) statement to much the same effect: even the 'least sophisticated of women … is, like the picture or the statue, or the actor on the stage, an agent through whom is suggested someone not there – that is, the character she represents, but is not'. As Lawler (2008) puts it, 'we are copying an imagined original' (106).

Also, like Butler, to Goffman ([1976] 1979) the gendered self is accomplished through ritualized display: exhibiting ways of talking and behaving that are conventionally associated with gender. For both Goffman and Butler, identities are always achieved; and this achievement is social and interactional; it is not entirely a matter of individual choice. The question is 'not "who we really are" but how we achieve identity, under what constraints and in what contexts' (Lawler, 2008: 104).[5] In *The Arrangement between the Sexes*, Goffman (1977) focuses on some of the institutional practices that produce structural constraints on an individual's actions.

8.4 FORMALISM: ON FACE-WORK, DEFERENCE AND DEMEANOR

In a 1980 interview, Goffman identified the primary difference between his work and symbolic interactionism as the role of structure. Scheff (2005: 148) acknowledges that 'Some of his work bears out his claim; it can be interpreted to show the powerful influence of situational and structural constraints, rather than actors' motives, as the basis for behavior'. Rock (1979: 28), suggests that 'interactionism may be usefully construed as an amalgam of Simmel's formal sociology and a pragmatist epistemology'. Certainly, this is true of Goffman's approach. Ducharme and Fine (1994) note that Goffman blended 'the individual focus' of symbolic interactionism with 'the cultural focus of Durkheim and the anthropologists, bringing together structuralism and interactionism' (90–1). Goffman applies 'macro-level analysis (focusing on institutions, social structure, and the normative order) to micro-level variables (face-to-face interactions)', illustrating 'the specific ways in which actors are routinely influenced by the powerful but unseen forces of social structure in their everyday lives' (91).

Goffman was strongly influenced by social anthropologist Radcliffe-Brown, who was at Chicago during a time when those in anthropology and sociology 'knew each other fairly well' (Verhoeven, 1993: 345). Radcliffe-Brown was influenced by Durkheim and Simmel (Stark, 1989: 85) and is considered the founder of structural functionalism. However, for Radcliffe-Brown, structure emerges through social action: 'concrete reality ... is not any sort of entity but a process, the process of social life .... The process itself consists of an immense multitude of actions and interactions of human beings, acting as individuals or in combinations or groups' ([1952] 1965: 4).

Through Durkheim and Radcliffe-Brown, Goffman was impressed by 'the impact of culture and macrostructures on even the most minute details of everyday interactions' (Ducharme and Fine, 1994: 90). Smith remarks that:

> Just as Durkheim demonstrated the social determinants of the apparently personal act of suicide,
> Goffman showed how many of our seemingly insignificant and idiosyncratic concerns (our expletives when we drop a glass, our discomfort when a stranger on a street holds a glance at us too long) are consequences of the normative ordering of interactional conduct. (2006: 32)

In fact, Goffman's very notion of the 'interaction order' is a 'continuation of the classical project instigated by Marx, Weber, and Durkheim, of defining the contours of the social domain' (Layder, 2006: 250).

The influence of Durkheim is explicit in Goffman's ritual model of interaction. In two early writings (1955 and 1956, later appearing together in 1967), he outlines the processes (face-work) and primary forms (deference and demeanor) of ceremonial behavior. Although he presents the concepts separately, they are compatible enough to fuse into a single model, as I do in my description here and in Kendall (2004). In introducing deference and demeanor, Goffman (1967) draws on Durkheim's suggestion that the 'individual's personality can be seen as one apportionment of the collective *mana*', and that 'rites performed to representations of the social collectivity will sometimes be performed to the individual'. Goffman states that he will explore 'some of the senses in which the person in our urban secular world is allotted a kind of sacredness that is displayed and confirmed by symbolic acts' (47).

According to Goffman (1967), people tend to interact as though 'the self is ... a ceremonial thing, a sacred object which must be treated with proper ritual care and in turn must be presented in a proper light to others' (91). This principle is realized in interaction by what he calls 'the traffic rules of social interaction': face (12). When interacting with others, individuals assume that each person has a 'face', a public 'image of self', which consists of 'approved social attributes' and must be continually maintained and protected (5). People maintain (or do not maintain) the faces of self and other through the 'expressive (or ceremonial)' component of language, that 'component of verbal and non-verbal acts' that 'symbolically convey[s] appraisals of the social worth' of the self and the other (5, 19, 31). Goffman identifies demeanor and deference as two basic elements of this ceremonial component. Demeanor is that element of an individual's conduct that expresses that the individual is 'a person of certain desirable or undesirable qualities'. Deference is that element of an individual's conduct that expresses 'the appreciation an individual shows of another to that other' (77). Goffman (1967) defines two types of deference based on Durkheim's (1954) classification of religious rites into 'negative' and 'positive' rites, respectively: through avoidance rituals, the individual 'keep[s] at a distance from the recipient', addressing the need for 'privacy and separateness' (62, 67). For example, speakers extend ceremonial respect and politeness, discretely avoid embarrassing facts, and employ 'careful ambiguity' when making demands on, or appraisals of, the other (11). Through presentational rituals, the individual shows that he or she approves of the recipient's private objectives or concerns, addressing the need to feel that one is someone whom 'others are, or seek to be, involved with' (73). For example, speakers give salutations, invitations, compliments, smiles, farewells, and notice changes in appearance, status or repute (71).

According to Goffman (1967: 12), the actions individuals perform or do not perform to make what they are doing 'consistent with face' is face-work, which serves to counteract 'events whose effective symbolic implications threaten face'. Goffman's conceptualization of face-work was operationalized by Brown and Levinson (1987) in *Politeness: Some Universals in Language Usage*. Building on Goffman's concept of face, they argue that some actions are intrinsically threatening to face (although which actions are 'intrinsically' threatening varies socially, culturally and situationally). They identify numerous modifications and additions participants use to mitigate these face-threatening acts to 'indicate clearly that no such face threat is intended or desired' (69–70).

In Kendall (2004), I observe that Goffman (1967) makes an additional point about the relationship between deference and demeanor: individuals create a demeanor, in part, through deference. An individual expresses deference to create and sustain the other's self, but deference is also a 'means by which [the individual] expresses the fact that he [or she] is a well or badly demeaned individual'. In other words, the individual expresses that he or she has certain qualities through actions which convey demeanor, and an important component of these qualities is the manner in which the individual extends deference to others – i.e. the individual's face-related practices. Based on this model, I demonstrate that a woman, who is a technical director of a radio news and talk show, expends linguistic effort to save the faces of her interlocutors as she speaks with two colleagues on separate occasions. I propose that some women who might appear to be speaking in a 'powerless' way by interactionally downplaying their institutional authority may, instead, be constructing a more egalitarian demeanor of authority.

Goffman's initial conceptions and Brown and Levinson's extensive elaboration have served as the basis for a vast amount of scholarship in sociolinguistics (see, for example, Bargiela-Chiappini, 2003; Hickey and Stewart, 2004; Holtgraves, 2002; Placencia and García, 2007; Watts, 2003; Watts et al., 2006). Recent scholarship employing Goffman's conception of face includes: a contrastive analysis of British English and Uruguayan Spanish (Marquez-Reiter, 2000); interactions among friends (Manusov et al., 2004); clinical interviews (Cepeda, 2006); psychotherapy (Kurri and Wahlstrom, 2007); hip-hop (Cutler, 2007); classroom language instruction (Nguyen, 2007); and workplace interaction (Stewart, 2008; Tracy, 2008).

8.5 PHENOMENOLOGY: FRAMING ANALYSIS

In *Frame Analysis*, Goffman (1974) rejects the 'W. I. Thomas dictum':[6] 'If men define situations as real, they are real in their consequences' in favor of William James' ([1890] 1950) question which, Goffman states, 'gave matters a subversive phenomenological twist': 'Under what circumstances do we think things are real?' (1–2). In this way, he enters the realm of philosophical phenomenology developed in the early twentieth century by Edmund Husserl and other German philosophers, questioning 'the nature of social action, interpretation, and meaning in everyday life' (Turner, 2000: xiv).[7] James addressed this question by positing different worlds, each of which, 'whilst it is attended to, is real after its own fashion; only the reality lapses with the attention' (293). Goffman agrees to a point; he states that 'James copped out' because he granted the 'world of the senses ... a special status, being the one we judge to be the realest reality, the one that retains our liveliest belief, the one before which the other worlds must give way' (3). Goffman then turns to Alfred Schütz 's (1945) argument about 'multiple realities', which follows James' closely but gives more attention to the 'possibility of uncovering the conditions that must be fulfilled if we are to generate one realm of "reality", one "finite province of meaning", as opposed to another' (3–4). However, Schütz concludes that each realm has a certain 'cognitive style' and is not, as Goffman puts it, 'generated in accordance with certain structural principles' (5). Thus, Goffman concludes that James and Schütz are 'quite unconvincing in providing any kind of account as to how many different "worlds" there are and whether everyday, wide-awake life can actually be seen as but one rule-produced plane of being, if so seen at all' (5).

Goffman (1974) observes that 'what is really happening' is a more complicated question than James or Schütz envisioned. Bateson ([1955] 1972) shows us that 'a bit of serious activity can be used as a model for putting together unserious versions of the same activity' and, following John Austin (1962) and Wittgenstein (1958), 'although an individual may dream unrealities, it is still proper to say of him on that occasion that he is really dreaming' (7). Thus, in *Frame Analysis*, Goffman (1974) begins with the assumption that individuals, when attending to any current situation, 'face the question' of 'What is it that's going on here?', and he offers 'a framework that could be appealed to for the answer' (8), which begins with a 'frame':

> I assume that definitions of a situation are built up in accordance with principles of organization which govern events – at least social ones – and our subjective involvement in them; frame is the word I use to refer to such of these basic elements as I am able to identify. (10–11)

Frames are both cognitive and action-based:

> Given their understanding of what it is that is going on, individuals fit their actions to this understanding and ordinarily find that the ongoing world supports this fitting. These organizational premises – sustained both in the mind and in activity – I call the 'frame' of the activity. (247)

Participants apply a frame to an 'everyday strip of activity' to render 'what would otherwise be a meaningless aspect of the scene into something that is meaningful' (83, 21).

Frames consist of a primary framework that is 'seen by those who apply it as not depending on or harking back to some prior or "original" interpretation' (21) or a transformed frame, which is either the result of keying, which is a primary framework 'transformed into something patterned on this activity but seen by the participants to be something quite else' (44), or fabrication, which is a primary framework deceptively managed by one or more individuals 'so that a party of one or more others will be induced to have a false belief about what it is that is going on' (83). For example, the primary framework 'fighting' may be keyed as 'playing' or 'contest' or it may be fabricated as a 'playful deceit' such as 'kidding'.

8.6 SOCIOLINGUISTICS: FOOTINGS AND *FORMS OF TALK*

In later years, Goffman increasingly turned his attention to language, beginning with the final chapter in *Frame Analysis* and culminating in *Forms of Talk* in 1981. As Duranti (2003) points

out, sociolinguistics had only recently been named as such in the early 1960s. Later that same decade, Goffman, William Labov and Dell Hymes converged at the University of Pennsylvania, contributing to 'an intellectual climate in which the study of language as used in social life gained momentum' (328). *Forms of Talk* reveals Goffman's involvement in this period of sociolinguistic development. The analyses presented in this volume are firmly situated within scholarship on language, culture and society.

The chapter on footings has provided the basis for most of the scholarship using a framing approach. Goffman (1981b) introduced 'footing' to explain how participants negotiate interpersonal relationships, or alignments, as they dynamically frame an interaction. Footings are 'the alignment we take up to ourselves and the others present as expressed in the way we manage the production or reception of an utterance' (128). Shifts in footing involve a shift in language use; a change in participation status (who is speaking, who is being addressed); and 'an alteration in the social capacities in which the persons present claim to be active' (126). Goffman predicts that sociolinguists 'can be looked to for help in the study of footing, including the most subtle examples' but 'presumably ... must find a structural means of doing so' (128). To begin this endeavor, he elaborates on the concept of 'participant status', introduced in *Frame Analysis* (224), by delineating the types of hearers into 'participation frameworks' and breaking down the traditional concept of the 'speaker' into 'production formats'.

The participation framework describes 'the relation of ... all the persons of a gathering' to a given utterance (1981b: 137). A 'hearer' or 'listener' may be a 'ratified participant' who is mutually acknowledged to be participating in the conversation or a 'bystander' who is minimally 'perceivable by the official participants'. The latter is either an 'eavesdropper' who purposively 'follow[s] the talk', or an 'overhearer' who does so 'unintentionally and inadvertently'. In multiparty talk, the current speaker may address all the ratified participants or single out one or more ratified participants, thus distinguishing between 'addressed' and 'unaddressed recipients'. In terms of production formats, given an utterance, the 'animator' articulates the utterance, 'the principal' is the person whose position or beliefs are represented by the utterance, and the 'author' is responsible for the selection of the words and sentiments (144–5). The 'participation status' is the relation of any member of a social gathering to an utterance and includes both the production format and participation framework (226).

Goffman's former students applied or extended his analysis of participation frameworks.

Philips (1972) used the approach to understand the scholastic performance of Warm Springs Indian children. Goodwin (1990) elaborated on participation frameworks with her notion of the 'participant framework' to include an understanding of speakers' and hearers' respective monitoring.

In the first sociolinguistic collection devoted to framing, Tannen (1993) demonstrates that framing theory is fundamental to linguistic discourse analysis and, conversely, that discourse analysis provides valuable insight into the linguistic means through which frames are actively created. For example, Ribeiro (1993, 1994) uses framing to demonstrate that a woman experiencing a 'psychotic crisis' during a psychiatric interview in a psychiatric hospital is incoherent based on the doctor's definition of the situation but coherent within the frame that she creates. Tannen and Wallat (1993) use framing and footing to account for the complexity of a medical encounter in which a pediatrician examines a cerebral-palsied child in the mother's presence at a Child Development Center. Tannen and Wallat explain how the pediatrician shifts among three frames to interact with four parties. Each frame consists of functions of talk, such as entertaining or explaining; linguistic register; and the footings the pediatrician takes up with respect to the four other parties (she addresses, ignores, or puts 'on hold' the child, the mother, the video crew and the medical residents who will view the recording at a later date) (65).

Goffman (1981b: 156), commenting on an earlier publication of Tannen and Wallat's study (1982, then forthcoming), notes 'the capacity of a dexterous speaker to jump back and forth, keeping different circles in play'. However, Tannen and Wallat (1993) suggest that, in this encounter, the pediatrician is burdened by the need to balance multiple, and often conflicting, frames; for example, answering the mother's questions in the consultation frame interrupts the examination sequence, and reporting medical information to the video audience 'may upset the mother, necessitating more explanation in the consultation frame' (67). They note that the pediatrician was aware of the difficulty she had in examining the child in the mother's presence and, upon hearing their analysis, 'was pleased to see a theoretical basis for what she had instinctively sensed' (71).[8]

Similarly, in Kendall (2008), a framing analysis of dinnertime interaction reveals that the mother bears a heavy interactional load through the number of frames she creates and sustains, and the need to juggle several frames simultaneously. I demonstrate that the mother accomplishes numerous tasks and activities by taking up multiple discursive positions (Davies and Harré, 1990) within several interactional frames, whereas the father takes up fewer positions within fewer frames. Furthermore, the positions they take up are gendered, reflecting a sex-based division of labor, even though both parents work full-time outside the home. Through these gendered patterns of participation, the parents create gendered parental identities and negotiate their parental authority with their daughter and with each other.

8.7 CURRENT RESEARCH: APPLYING GOFFMAN

Framing and footing have proved to be fruitful for the analysis of language and identity, which is not surprising since they are components of a broader framework in which the self is actively achieved through interaction. Schiffrin (2006) describes and employs a 'social constructivist perspective on identity drawn largely from the work of Erving Goffman' (105). Ribeiro (2006) uses a framing approach in her analysis of identity, incorporating footing (Goffman, 1981b), positioning (Davies and Harré, 1990; Hollway, 1984) and voice (Bakhtin, 1981) to elucidate different ways in which participants determine 'what's going on here' and 'how I mean what I say' (50). Together, these concepts provide a way of 'capturing what we mean by identity or "doing identity work" in everyday conversation' (50).

Other analyses involving framing and footing focus on: workplace discourse (Kendall, 2004); psychiatric interviews (Ribeiro and Bastos, 2005); political talk show interviews (Lauerbach, 2007); parent/child interaction (Gordon, 2002, 2006, 2008); children's free play in a therapeutic setting (Buchbinder, 2008); and irony in conversation (Clift, 1999). Keying appears in an analysis of pragmatic development in peer talk (Blum-Kulka et al., 2004) and in humorous narratives (Kotthoff, 2000). Fabricated frames are employed in the analysis of telephone conversations (Dornelles and Garcez, 2001).

The concept of participation frameworks has provided a particularly fruitful approach for analyzing language. Duranti (2003) identifies participation framework as one of three 'preferred units of analysis' in the current paradigm of the study of language and culture, along with 'language practice' and 'self/person/identity' (333). Participation frameworks have been used to examine: workplace discourse (Rae, 2001); courtroom discourse (Matoesian, 2001); discourse markers in discussion groups (Waring, 2003); fraternity talk (Kiesling, 2005); bilingual education (He, 2003); moral irony (Shoaps, 2007); speech therapy (Leahy, 2008); political interviews (Bull and Fetzer, 2006); family discourse (Kendall, 2006); interpreting

(Leung and Gibbons, 2008); online identities (Aarsand, 2008); and telephone conversations (Su, 2009).

Recent scholarship on language also addresses other areas of Goffman's (1976/1979) work: his analysis of gender advertisements has been employed in the analysis of magazine advertising (Bell and Milic, 2002; Rohlinger, 2002) and a Singaporean national advertising campaign (Lazar, 2000). Role distance (Goffman, 1961/1997) is used in the analysis of public participation broadcasting (Thornborrow 2001); the dramaturgical metaphor and 'response cries' in the analysis of online chat logs (Goddard, 2003); and 'remedial interchanges' (Goffman, 1971) in the analysis of complaint sequences (Dersley and Wootton, 2001).

8.8 CONCLUSION: GOFFMAN AND SOCIOLINGUISTICS

Goffman, some say, was a genius, displaying 'incredible perception of the microworld of social interaction' (Scheff, 2005: 52). He was a veritable 'microscope of human nuance' (Lemert, 1997: ix). Others praise him for 'push[ing] sociology much deeper into the complexities of action' (Cohen, 2000: 74). Others fault his approach as unsystematic (Psathas, 1980; Schegloff, 1988; Scheibe, 2000) or hopelessly small scale (Gouldner, 1970). Yet Goffman's influence throughout the social sciences is evident and, in sociolinguistics, has increased over the decades. Perhaps we do not need to look to Goffman for theory, method or data in the conventional sense. Goffman himself saw his work as fundamentally exploratory in character, a preliminary to 'the kind of sociological theorizing and investigation the critics faulted him for not providing, not a substitute for that serious, systematic work' (Smith, 2006: 111). As Scheff and Phillips (2006) argue, his contributions are 'necessary before conventional science can be applied' (6).

Goffman's approach most resembles that of Simmel (G. W. H. Smith, 1994; Smith, 2006), who distinguished form and content by examining a variety of social experiences to identify the underlying forms of human association: 'conflict and accommodation', 'deference and hierarchy', 'attachments and degradation' (Plummer, 2000: 199). Likewise, Goffman analyses interactions to identify the underlying order in the kinds of facework, the stages of remedial interchange, and so on. In terms of presentation, Smith (2006) explains that Goffman's work is primarily conceptual, again similar to Simmel. Goffman approached the new terrain of the interaction order by 'articulating the concepts', connecting them into 'conceptual

frameworks ... organized around an analytical theme', and illustrating these concepts with examples. Thus, developing 'richly illustrated conceptual frameworks is the analytical core' of Goffman's method (112). Nevertheless, like others in the Chicago school, Goffman adhered to the importance of naturalistic observation. His concepts were formed inductively in light of fieldwork and other kinds of data-gathering.

Perhaps the endurance of Goffman's work is best summed up by Lemert:

> The experience Goffman effects is that of colonizing a new social place into which the reader enters, from which to exit never quite the same. To have once, if only once, seen the social world from within such a place is never after to see it otherwise, ever after to read the world anew. In thus seeing differently, we are other than we were (1997: xiii).

Goffman's work continues to offer directions for the study of language in context, inspiring new ideas and illuminating everyday processes of talk.

NOTES

1   In fact, the term was not in popular use for several decades after Blumer's coinage in 1937 (Plummer, 2000). In interviews conducted in 1980 with 11 scholars who wrote theses in sociology at the University of Chicago between 1942 and 1959, only four claimed the label even though all were recognized as symbolic interactionists (Verhoeven, 1995). Goffman claims that the 'symbolic interaction' label was adopted in large measure in response to the separation of ethnomethodology from the Society for Social Problems (Verhoeven, 1993).

2   According to Goffman, his teacher, Everett Hughes was his greatest influence (Verhoeven, 1993). Hughes studied at the University of Chicago under Robert Ezra Park, Ernest W. Burgess, and other noted scholars. Hughes considered Park his primary mentor (Chapoulie, 1996). Park founded the Chicago School (Strauss and Fisher, 1978) and, according to Goffman, 'the whole Hughesian tradition' (Verhoeven, 1993: 321). Park and Charles H. Cooley were students of Dewey and Mead (Carey, 2009: 110) and Park was a student of Simmel (Plummer, 2000: 200). Goffman's other influential teacher, Lloyd Warner, became a protégé of Radcliffe-Brown (Smith, 2006), who was strongly influenced by Durkheim and Simmel (Stark, 1989: 85). Goffman notes that Radcliffe-Brown was central to his own interests and concerns and provided him with 'a model for writing papers – much more than any sociologist' (Verhoeven, 1993: 321). According to Goffman, Mead provided

him with his general approach to sociology but notes that 'it could have derived from Dewey almost as well' (Verhoeven, 1993: 318, 336).

3   Goffman is notoriously difficult to classify. See Smith (1999: 4–5) for citations defining him as symbolic interactionist, structuralist, phenomenological, existentialist, ethogenic and symbolic realist.

4   Goffman (1963a: 16–17 fn. 6) cites Park (1927: 738) to much the same effect.

5   In *Discourse and Identity*, Benwell and Stokoe (2006: 34) argue that, unlike Butler, Goffman's conceptualization of gender is 'premised on a rational, intending self'. Conversely, earlier scholars credit him with contributing to the continental structuralists' efforts to 'delete' or 'decenter' the subject (Gonos, 1977; Jameson, 1976), which is the theoretical work underlying Butler's later theory of performativity. In regards to gender, Butler's (1990: 25) statement that 'there is no gender identity behind the expressions of identity' echoes Goffman's earlier conclusion that '[o]ne might just as well say there is no gender identity. There is only a schedule for the portrayal of gender' ([1976] 1979: 8).

6   This quote, which became known in sociology as the 'W. I. Thomas dictum', actually appears in a book co-authored with Dorothy S. Thomas (Thomas and Thomas, 1928: 572).

7   According to Layder (2006), while symbolic interactionism is 'careful to address the "point of view of the actor,"' phenomenology takes this as its central concern', concentrating on 'people's consciousness and experience of the world through the use of their senses' (92).

8   This identification of an everyday problem harks back to the Chicago school. Gross (2007) comments that what the practitioners of the school 'had in common' is that they 'identified the practical problems and mundane exigencies that their informants experienced in the course of their everyday lives' (196).

REFERENCES

Aarsand, P. A. (2008) 'Frame switches and identity performances: alternating between online and offline', *Text and Talk*, 28(2): 147–65.

Atkinson, P., Delamont, S. and Housley, W. (2007) *Contours of Culture: Complex Ethnography and the Ethnography of Complexity*. New York: Alta Mira Press. pp. 179–204.

Austin, J. L. (1962) *Sense and Sensibilia*. Oxford: Oxford University Press.

Bakhtin, M. (1981) *The Dialogic Imagination: Four Essays*. M. Holquist (ed.). Tr. C. Emerson and M. Holquist. Austin, TX: University of Texas Press. (1st edn, 1935.)

Bargiela-Chiappini, F. (2003) 'Face and politeness: new (insights) for old (concepts)', *Journal of Pragmatics*, 35: 1453–69.

Bateson, G. (1955) 'A theory of play and fantasy', *Psychiatric Research Reports*, 2: 39–51. Reprinted in G. Bateson (1972), *Steps to an Ecology of Mind*. Chicago: Chicago University Press. pp. 177–93.

Becker, H. S. (1986) *Doing Things Together: Selected Papers*. Evanston, IL: Northwestern University Press.

Bell, P. and Milic, M. (2002) 'Goffman's gender advertisements revisited: combining content analysis with semiotic analysis', *Visual Communication*, 1(2): 203–22.

Benwell, B. and Stokoe, E. (2006) *Discourse and Identity*. Edinburgh: Edinburgh University Press.

Blum-Kulka, S., Huck-Taglicht, D. and Avni, H. (2004) 'The social and discursive spectrum of peer talk', *Discourse Studies*, 6: 307–28.

Blumer, H. (1937) 'Social psychology', in E. P. Schmidt (ed.), *Man and Society: A Substantive Introduction to the Social Science*. New York: Prentice-Hall. pp. 144–98.

Blumer, H. (1969) *Symbolic Interactionism: Perspective and Method*. Englewood Cliffs, NJ: Prentice-Hall.

Brown, P. and Levinson, S. (1987) *Politeness: Some Universals in Language Usage*. Cambridge: Cambridge University Press.

Buchbinder, M. H. (2008) '"You're still sick!" Framing, footing, and participation in children's medical play', *Discourse Studies*, 10(2): 139–59.

Bull, P. and Fetzer, A. (2006) 'Who are we and who are you?: the strategic use of forms of address in political interviews', *Text and Talk*, 26(1): 3–37.

Butler, J. (1990) *Gender Trouble: Feminism and the Subversion of Identity*. London: Routledge.

Butler, J. (1993) *Bodies that Matter: On the Discursive Limits of 'Sex'*. New York: Routledge.

Carey, J. W. (2009) *Communication as Culture: Essays on Media and Society*. Revised edn. New York: Routledge.

Cepeda, G. (2006) 'La voz empatica medica y las estrategias de cortesia verbal [The medical empathy voice and oral politeness strategies in a clinical interview]', *Estudios Filologicos*, 41: 55–69.

Chapoulie, J. (1996) 'Everett Hughes and the Chicago tradition', *Sociological Theory*, 14(1): 3–29.

Clift, R. (1999) 'Irony in conversation', *Language in Society*, 28(4): 523–53.

Cohen, I. J. (2000) 'Theories of action and praxis', in B. S. Turner (ed.), *The Blackwell Companion to Social Theory*. 2nd edn. Malden, MA: Blackwell. pp. 73–111.

Cooley, C. H. (1922) *Human Nature and the Social Order*. 2nd edn. New York: Charles Scribner's Sons.

Cutler, C. (2007) 'The co-construction of whiteness in an Mc battle', *Pragmatics*, 17(1): 9–22.

Davies, B. and Harré, R. (1990) 'Positioning: conversation and the production of selves', *Journal for the Theory of Social Behavior*, 20(1): 43–63.

de Beauvoir, S. (1953) *The Second Sex*. Tr. Howard Madison Parshley. New York: Alfred A. Knopf.

Delanty, G. (2000) 'The foundations of social theory: origins and trajectories', in B. S. Turner (ed.), *The Blackwell Companion to Social Theory*. 2nd edn. Malden, MA: Blackwell. pp. 21–46.

Denzin, N. K. (1992) *Symbolic Interactionism and Cultural Studies*. Cambridge, MA and Oxford: Blackwell.

Dersley, I. and Wootton, A. J. (2001) 'In the heat of the sequence: interactional features preceding walkouts from argumentative talk', *Language in Society*, 30: 611–38.

Dewey, J. (1896) 'The reflex arc concept in psychology', *Psychological Review*, 3: 357–70.

Dornelles, C. and Garcez, P. M. (2001) 'Making sense of nonsense: fabrication, ambiguity, error and clarification in the organization of experience in ordinary conversation', *Journal of Pragmatics*, 33(11): 1707–30.

Ducharme, L. J. and Fine, G. A. (1994) 'No escaping obligation: Erving Goffman on the demands and constraints of play', in R. Bogue and M. Spariosu (eds), *The Play of the Self*. Albany, NY: State University of New York Press. pp. 89–112.

Duranti, A. (2003) 'Language as culture in U.S. anthropology: three paradigms', *Current Anthropology*, 44(3): 323–35.

Durkheim, E. (1954) *The Elementary Forms of the Religious life*. Tr. J. W. Swain. Glencoe, IL: Free Press.

Friedsen, E. (1983) 'Celebrating Erving Goffman', *Contemporary Sociology*, 12(4): 259–62.

Goddard, A. (2003) '"Is there anybody out there?": creative language play and "literariness" in internet relay chat (IRC)', in A. Schorr, W. Campbell, and M. Schenk (eds), *Communication Research and Media Science in Europe*. Berlin: Mouton de Gruyter. pp. 325–43.

Goffman, E. (1955) 'On face-work: an analysis of ritual elements in social interaction', *Psychiatry: Journal of Interpersonal Relations*, 18(3): 213–31. Reprinted in Goffman, E. (1967) *Interaction Ritual*. pp. 5–46.

Goffman, E. (1956) 'The nature of deference and demeanor', *American Anthropologist*, 58: 473–502. Reprinted in Goffman, Erving (1967) *Interaction Ritual*. pp. 47–96.

Goffman, E. (1959) *The Presentation of Self in Everyday Life*. New York: Doubleday Anchor.

Goffman, E. (1961) *Asylums: Essays on the Social Situation of Mental Patients and Other Inmates*. New York: Doubleday Anchor. (1st edn, 1956.)

Goffman, E. (1963a) *Behavior in Public Places: Notes on the Social Organization of Gatherings*. New York: The Free Press.

Goffman, E. (1963b) *Stigma: Notes on the Management of Spoiled Identity*. Englewood Cliffs, NJ: Simon & Schuster.

Goffman, E. (1967) *Interaction Ritual: Essays on Face-To-Face Behavior*. New York: Doubleday Anchor.

Goffman, E. (1971) *Relations in Public: Microstudies of the Public Order*. New York: Basic Books.

Goffman, E. (1974) *Frame Analysis: An Essay on the Organization of Experience*. New York: Harper and Row.

Goffman, E. (1976) 'Gender advertisements', *Studies in the Anthropology of Visual Communication*, 3(2): 69–154. Reprinted as Goffman, E. (1979) *Gender Advertisements*. New York: Harper and Row.

Goffman, E. (1977) 'The arrangement between the sexes', *Theory and Society*, 4(3): 301–31.

Goffman, E. (1981a) *Forms of Talk*. Philadelphia: University of Pennsylvania Press.

Goffman, E. (1981b) 'Footing', in *Forms of Talk*. Philadelphia: University of Pennsylvania Press. pp. 124–59. First published (1979) *Semiotica*, 25(1–2): 1–29.

Goffman, E. (1983) 'Felicity's condition', *American Journal of Sociology*, 89(1): 1–53.

Goffman, E. (1961 [1997]) 'Role distance', in C. Lemert and A. Branaman (eds), *The Goffman Reader*. Oxford: Blackwell. pp. 35–41.

Gonos, G. (1977) '"Situation" vs. "frame": the "interactionist" and the "structuralist" analyses of everyday life', *American Sociological Review*, 4: 854–67.

Goodwin, M. H. (1990) *He-Said-She-Said: Talk as Social Organization Among Black Children*. Bloomington, IN: Indiana University Press.

Gordon, C. (2002) '"I'm Mommy and you're Natalie": role-reversal and embedded frames in mother–child discourse', *Language in Society*, 31(5): 679–720.

Gordon, C. (2006) 'Reshaping prior text, reshaping identities', *Text and Talk*, 26(4): 543–69.

Gordon, C. (2008) 'A(p)parent play: blending frames and reframing in family talk', *Language in Society*, 37(3): 319–49.

Gouldner, A. (1970) 'Other symptoms of the crisis: Goffman's dramaturgy and other new theories', in *The Coming Crisis of Western Sociology*. New York: Basic Books. pp. 378–90.

Gross, N. (2007) 'Pragmatism, phenomenology, and twentieth century American sociology', in C. J. Calhoun (ed.), *Sociology in America*. Chicago: The University of Chicago Press. pp.183–224.

He, A. W. (2003) 'Novices and their speech roles in Chinese heritage language classes', in R. Bayley and S. R. Schecter (eds), *Language Socialization in Bilingual and Multilingual Societies*. Clevedon, UK: Multilingual Matters. pp. 128–46.

Hickey, L. and Stewart, M. (eds) (2004) *Politeness in Europe*. Clevedon, UK: Multilingual Matters.

Hollway, W. (1984) 'Gender difference and the production of subjectivity', in J. Henriques, W. Hollway, C. Urwin, V. Couze and V. Walkerdine (eds), *Changing the Subject*. London: Methuen. pp. 227–63.

Holtgraves, T. (2002) *Language as Social Action: Social Psychology and Language Use*. Mahwah, NJ: Lawrence Erlbaum Associates.

James, W. (1918 [1890]) 'The consciousness of self', in *The Principles of Psychology*. Vol. 1. New York: Henry Holt and Company. pp. 291–401.

James, W. (1890 [1925]) *The philosophy of William James*. Modern Library edn. New York: Random House. pp. 128–9.

James, W. (1890 [1950]) 'The perception of reality', in *The principles of psychology*. Vol. 2. New York: Henry Holt and Company. pp. 283–324.

Jameson, F. (1976) 'On Goffman's frame analysis', *Theory and Society*, 3(1): 119–33.

Joas, H. (1987) 'Symbolic interactionism', in A. Giddens and J. Turner (eds), *Social Theory Today*. Oxford: Polity Press. pp. 82–115.

Karpf, K. B. (1932) *American Social Psychology*. New York: McGraw-Hill.

Kendall, S. (2004) 'Framing authority: gender, face, and mitigation at a radio network', *Discourse and Society*, 15: 55–79.

Kendall, S. (2006) '"Honey, I'm home!": framing in family dinnertime homecomings', *Text and Talk*, 26: 411–42.

Kendall, S. (2008) 'The balancing act: framing gendered parental identities at dinnertime', *Language in Society*, 37: 539–68.

Kiesling, S. F. (2005) 'Homosocial desire in men's talk: balancing and recreating cultural discourses of masculinity'. *Language in Society*, 34(5): 695–727.

Kim, K.-k. (2003) *Order and Agency in Modernity: Talcott Parsons, Erving Goffman, and Harold Garfinkel*. Albany, NY: State University of New York Press.

Kotthoff, H. (2000) 'Gender and joking: on the complexities of women's image politics in humorous narratives', *Journal of Pragmatics*, 32: 55–80.

Krueger, E. T. and Reckless, W. C. (1931) *Social Psychology*. New York: Longmans, Green.

Kurri, K. and Wahlstrom, J. (2007) 'Reformulations of agentless talk in psychotherapy', *Text and Talk*, 27(3): 315–38.

Lauerbach, G. (2007) 'Argumentation in political talk show interviews', *Journal of Pragmatics*, 39(8): 1388–419.

Lawler, S. (2008) *Identity: Sociological Perspectives*. Malden, MA and Cambridge, UK: Polity Press.

Layder, D. (2006) *Understanding Social Theory*. 2nd edn. Thousand Oaks, CA: Sage.

Lazar, M. M. (2000) 'Gender, discourse and semiotics: the politics of parenthood representations', *Discourse and Society*, 11(3): 373–400.

Leahy, M. M. (2008) 'Multiple voices in Charles Van Riper's desensitization therapy', *International Journal of Language and Communication Disorders*, 43(1): 69–80.

Lemert, C. (1997) 'Goffman', in C. Lemert and A. Branaman (eds), *The Goffman Reader*. Malden, MA: Blackwell. pp. ix–xliii.

Leung, E. S. M. and Gibbons, J. (2008) 'Who is responsible? Participant roles in legal interpreting cases', *Multilingua*, 27(3): 177–91.

McCall, M. M. and Becker, H. S. (1990) 'Introduction', in H. S. Becker and M. M. Hall (eds), *Symbolic Interaction and Cultural Studies*. Chicago: The University of Chicago Press. pp. 1–15.

Manning, P. (2005) Reinvigorating the tradition of symbolic interactionism', *Symbolic Interaction*, 28(2): 167–73.

Manusov, V., Koenig Kellas, J., and Trees, A. R. (2004) 'Do unto others? Conversational moves and perceptions of attentiveness toward other's face in accounting sequences between friends', *Human Communication Research*, 30(4): 514–39.

Marquez-Reiter, R. (2001) *Linguistic Politeness in Britain and Uruguay: A Contrastive Study of Requests and Apologies*. Amsterdam: John Benjamins.

Matoesian, G. M. (2001) *Law and the Language of Identity: Discourse in the William Kennedy Smith Rape trial*. New York: Oxford University Press.

Mead, G. H. (1934) *Mind, Self, and Society: From the Standpoint of a Social Behaviorist*. Chicago: The University of Chicago Press.

Mortensen, N. (2000) 'American pragmatism', in H. Andersen and L. B. Kaspersen (eds), *Classical and Modern Social Theory*. Malden, MA: Blackwell. pp.109–20.

Nguyen, H. t. (2007) 'Rapport building in language instruction: a microanalysis of the multiple resources in teacher talk', *Language and Education*, 21(4): 284–303.

Park, R. E. (1927) 'Human nature and collective behavior', *American Journal of Sociology*, 2: 733–41.

Philips, S. U. (1972) 'Participant structures and communicative competence: Warm Springs children in community and classroom', in C. B. Cazden, V. P. John, and D. Hymes (eds), *Functions of Language in the Classroom*. New York: Teachers College Press. pp. 370–94.

Placencia, M. E. and García, C. (eds) (2007) *Research on Politeness in the Spanish-Speaking World*. London: Lawrence Erlbaum Associates.

Plummer, K. (2000) 'Symbolic interactionism in the twentieth century', in B. S. Turner (ed.), *The Blackwell Companion to Social Theory*. 2nd edn. Malden, MA: Blackwell. pp. 193–222.

Psathas, G. (1980) 'Approaches to the study of the world of everyday life', *Human Studies*, 3: 3–17.

Radcliffe-Brown, A. R. (1952 [1965]) *Structure and Function in Primitive Society*. New York: The Free Press.

Rae, J. (2001) 'Organizing participation in interaction: doing participation framework', *Research on Language and Social Interaction*, 34(2): 253–78.

Ribeiro, B. T. (1993) 'Framing in psychotic discourse', in D. Tannen (ed.), *Framing in Discourse*. Oxford: Oxford University Press. pp. 77–112.

Ribeiro, B. T. (1994) *Coherence in Psychotic Discourse*. New York: Oxford University Press.

Ribeiro, B. T. (2006) 'Footing, positioning, voice: Are we talking about the same thing?', in A. DeFina and D. Schiffrin (eds), *Discourse and Identity*. Cambridge: Cambridge University Press. pp. 48–82.

Ribeiro, B. T. and Bastos, L. C. (2005) 'Telling stories in two psychiatric interviews: a discussion on frame and narrative', *AILA Review*, 18: 58–75.

Rock, P. (1979) *The Making of Symbolic Interactionism*. London: Macmillan.

Rohlinger, D. A. (2002) 'Eroticizing men: cultural influences on advertising and male objectification', *Sex Roles*, 46(3, 4): 61–74.

Scheff, T. J. (2005) 'Looking-glass self: Goffman as symbolic interactionist', *Symbolic Interaction*, 28(2): 147–66.

Scheff, T. J. and Phillips, B. (2006) *Goffman Unbound!: A New Paradigm for Social Science*. Boulder, CO: Paradigm Publishers.

Schegloff, E. A. (1988) 'Goffman and the analysis of conversation', in P. Drew and A. Wootton (eds), Erving Gofman: *Exploring the Interaction Order*. Cambridge: Polity. pp. 189–35.

Scheibe, K. E. (2000) *The Drama of Everyday Life*. Cambridge, MA: Harvard University Press.

Schiffrin, D. (1994) *Approaches to Discourse*. Cambridge, MA: Blackwell.

Schiffrin, D. (2006) 'From linguistic reference to social reality', in A. de Fina and D. Schiffrin (eds), *Discourse and Identity*. Cambridge: Cambridge University Press. pp. 103–34.

Schutz, A. (1945) 'On multiple realities', *Philosophy and Phenomenological Research*, 5: 533–76.

Shoaps, R. (2007) '"Moral irony": modal particles, moral persons and indirect stance-taking in Sakapultek discourse', *Pragmatics*, 17(2): 297–335.

Smith, G. (1999) 'Introduction: interpreting Goffman's Sociological legacy', in G. Smith (ed.), *Goffman and Social Organization: Studies in a Sociological Legacy*. New York and London: Routledge. pp. 1–18.

Smith, G. (2006) *Erving Goffman*. London and New York: Routledge.

Smith, G. W. H. (1994) 'Snapshots sub specie aeternitatis: Simmel, Goffman and formal sociology', in D. Frisby (ed.), *Georg Simmel: Critical Assessments*. London: Routledge. pp. 354–83.

Stark, R. (1989) *Sociology*. Belmont, CA: Wadsworth.

Stewart, M. (2008) 'Protecting speaker's face in impolite exchanges: the negotiation of face-wants in workplace interaction', *Journal of Politeness Research*, 4(1): 31–53.

Strauss, A. and Fisher, B. (1978) 'Interactionism', in T. Bottomore and R. Nisbet (eds), *A History of Sociological Analysis*. London: Hutchinson. pp. 457–98.

Su, H.-Y. (2009) 'Code-switching in managing a face-threatening communicative task: Footing and ambiguity in conversational interaction in Taiwan', *Journal of Pragmatics*, 41(2): 372–92.

Tannen, D. (ed.) (1993) *Framing in Discourse*. Oxford and New York: Oxford University Press.

Tannen, D. and Wallat, C. (1982) 'A sociolinguistic analysis of multiple demands on the pediatrician in doctor/mother/child interaction', in R. Di Pietro (ed.), *Linguistics and the Professions*. Norwood, NJ: Ablex. pp. 39–50.

Tannen, D. and Wallat, C. (1993) 'Interactive frames and knowledge schemas in interaction: examples from a medical examination/interview', in D. Tannen (ed.), *Framing in Discourse*. New York, Oxford: Oxford University Press. pp. 57–76.

Thomas, W. I. and Thomas, D. S. (1928) *The child in America: Behavior Problems and Programs*. New York: Knopf.

Thornborrow, J. (2001) 'Authenticating talk: building public identities in audience participation broadcasting', *Discourse Studies*, 3(4): 459–79.

Tracy, K. (2008) '"Reasonable hostility": situation-appropriate face-attack', *Journal of Politeness Research*, 4(2): 169–91.

Turner, B. S. (2000) 'Preface to the second edition', in B. S. Turner (ed.), *The Blackwell Companion to Social Theory*. 2nd edn. Malden, MA: Blackwell Publishers. pp. xiv–xviii.

Verhoeven, J. C. (1993) 'Interview with Erving Goffman, 1980', *Research on Language and Social Interaction*, 26(3): 317–48.

Verhoeven, J. C. (1995) *Methodological and Metascientific Problems in Symbolic Interactionism: A Report on the Opinions of Third Generation Symbolic Interactionists*. 2nd edn. Leuven: Département Sociologie.

Waring, H. Z. (2003) '"Also" as a discourse marker: its use in disjunctive and disaffiliative environments', *Discourse Studies*, 5(3): 415–36.

Watts, R. J. (2003) *Politeness*. Cambridge: Cambridge University Press.

Watts, R. J., Ide, S. and Ehlich, K. (2006) *Politeness in Language: Studies in its History, Theory and Practice*. 2nd edn. Berlin: Mouton de Gruyter.

Wittgenstein, L. (1958) *Philosophical Investigations*. Tr. G. E. M. Anscombe. Oxford: Basil Blackwell.

9

Ethnomethodology and Membership Categorization Analysis

Robert Garot and Tim Berard[1]

9.1 INTRODUCTION

Any distinction between ethnomethodology and membership categorization analysis would risk being misleading, in that membership categorization analysis is very much a variant of ethnomethodology, not an alternative tradition of inquiry. Even so, membership categorization has clearly established itself as a specific variant within the broader tradition of ethnomethodology, and therefore merits some specific attention in any longer survey of contemporary ethnomethodology. For this reason, ethnomethodology and membership categorization analysis are discussed under separate headings below. While there are no official criteria for identifying scholarship as membership categorization analysis, much of its specificity is due to a confluence of two factors. First, substantively, membership categorization analysis addresses social identity, understood as an accomplishment of practical action and practical reasoning. By contrast, ethnomethodology involves, very broadly, the study of practical action and practical reasoning, whether with respect to identity or to anything else. Secondly, with respect to foundational insights, membership categorization analysis draws heavily upon relevant insights from Harvey Sacks, the founder of conversation analysis, while also drawing on various themes and resources in the tradition of ethnomethodology, founded by Harold Garfinkel. By contrast, some ethnomethodology does not draw significantly

upon the work of Sacks, and when ethnomethodologists do utilize the work of Sacks, a wide range of his insights on language and communication can be used, many of which deal with other matters than membership categories.

Conversation analysis is considered by many ethnomethodologists to be an offshoot of early ethnomethodology, albeit an offshoot that has developed significantly and successfully into a largely autonomous discipline. Other, more recent variants of ethnomethodology, including studies of work, and especially membership categorization analysis, are not nearly so autonomous, but illustrate an important trend in ethnomethodology. The development of ethnomethodology can be characterized by a simultaneous expansion of the study of practical action and practical reasoning to an increasing variety of topics, and by the development of substantive specializations within this increasingly broad scope. Both its expansion and its specializations bring ethnomethodological scholarship into increasing contact with other traditions in the study of society, social institutions, professions and language.

9.2 ETHNOMETHODOLOGY

Ethnomethodology (EM), one of the primary social theories to emerge out of the second half of the twentieth century,[2] arose from contentious beginnings[3] to become one of the most remarkable and remarked upon approaches to social action and talk, recognized throughout the world (Lemert, 2002; Rawls, 2002; Clayman, 1995). Although this is an introductory essay, it is not in itself ethnomethodological; in fact, an essay such as this, tracing the philosophical roots and branching tendencies of EM, is not encouraged by Garfinkel, the founder of EM. As Lynch and Sharrock (2003: xxviii) state, 'Garfinkel actively discouraged his students from writing expositions of his ideas and of how those ideas relate to traditions of philosophical and social science scholarship. He encouraged them instead to conduct studies of particular activities and work out the meaning and implications of familiar sociological themes'.[4] Nonetheless, overviews of EM are not uncommon, and some are exemplary (Lynch and Sharrock, 2003; Rawls, 2002; Maynard and Clayman, 1991; Heritage, 1987, and above all, Heritage, 1984).

The corpus of EM consists of a wide range of studies, and, as Maynard and Clayman (1991: 386) note, 'it is more accurate to say there are several bodies of work, rather than a single enterprise', yet its core ideas may be defined in terms of radical reflexivity. According to Melvin Pollner (1991: 370), 'Radical reflexivity – the recursively comprehensive appreciation of the "accomplished" character of **all** social activity – enjoins the analyst to displace the discourse and practices that ground and constitute his/her endeavors and explore the very work of grounding and constituting'. As Zimmerman and Wieder (1971: 289) state, the task of EM is to explore 'how members of society go about the task of *seeing, describing,* and *explaining* order in the world in which they live' (Heap, 1980: 89). In other words, all the subject areas of the social sciences (that one might peruse in an introductory textbook), are important for EM not as objectively given facts of society, but as phenomena which members might make real through their mundane activities and accounts.[5] Early ethnomethodologists were radically reflexive in specifying how seemingly obdurate features of everyday life such as objective reality (Pollner, 1984), gender (Garfinkel, 1967: 116–85), bureaucracy (Bittner, 1965; Zimmerman, 1966, 1969a, 1969b, 1969c), the police (Bittner, 1967; Sacks, 1972), method and measurement (Lynch, 1991), the work of the discovering sciences (Bjelic and Lynch, 1989), and the convict code (Wieder, 1974) are ongoing, situated, accountable **accomplishments** of ordinary people around the world. In so doing, they **respecified** the work of the social sciences, and provided part of the groundwork for wide-ranging interpretive cultural and linguistic approaches which emphasize agency and meaning. This essay will briefly explore EM's history,

philosophical roots, and contributions to studies of language.

9.3 HISTORY

In working on Fred Strodtbeck's jury project in 1945, Garfinkel searched for a term in the Yale cross-cultural area files to describe the jurors' methodology (Turner, 1974; also see Dingwall, 2000; Rawls, 2002; Lynch and Sharrock, 2002). As Garfinkel stated, 'If it were "ethnobotany", then it had to do somehow or other with his [a member's] knowledge of and his grasp of what were for members adequate methods for dealing with botanical matters' (Turner, 1974: 16–17). For all practical purposes, jurors with limited legal training had to differentiate issues of fact from opinion, determining adequate grounds for evidence and demonstration, in extremely consequential matters. While 'it was not a methodology that any of my colleagues would honor if they were attempting to staff the sociology department ... the jurors' concerns for such issues seemed to be undeniable' (ibid.: 16). Rather than evaluating jurors' methods in terms of an extraneous criterion of adequacy, Garfinkel grappled to understand their ways of accomplishing their day's work. Such an appreciation of how big topics and consequential matters are artfully addressed as a mundane, everyday affair has the potential to alter fundamentally the foundations of social science. Pages 31–34 of *Studies in Ethnomethodology* (1967), in which Garfinkel lays out the 'policies' of ethnomethodology as a sort of manifesto, capture better than any other text the excitement and possibility of this early period.[6]

Until recently, *Studies in Ethnomethodology* remained Garfinkel's only book. Rather, 'to a large extent his contribution is embodied in the work of others on whom he has had profound influence' (Lynch and Sharrock, 2003: x). In his 'Acknowledgements as an Autobiographical Account', Garfinkel (2002) notes the many relationships that grew out of, and bore the fruit of, EM. Especially notable is how Garfinkel was able to leave an indelible impression, and sometimes even a school of scholars committed to his ideas everywhere he went. After receiving his PhD from the famous Harvard Department of Social Relations in 1952, Garfinkel went on to UCLA, from 1954 until his retirement in 1987, where he influenced such luminaries as Egon Bittner, Stacy Burns, Aaron Cicourel, Kenneth Lieberman, Eric Livingston, Michael Lynch, Melvin Pollner, David Sudnow, D. Lawrence Wieder, Don Zimmerman and, most prominently, Harvey Sacks, among many others.[7] Following from a brief month at the University of Manchester in 1973, and subsequent visits, a highly influential and rigorous British branch of EM arose, including Wesley Sharrock, E.C. Cuff, John Lee, Rod Watson, Max Atkinson, John Heritage and Jeff Coulter. Of the many people and places Garfinkel mentions, three other schools are worthy of mention as being strongly influenced by his work and presence: Boston University Sociology, which included George Psathas, Jeff Coulter and Michael Lynch, who launched dozens of graduate students; the Studies of Workplace and Technology at Xerox Palo Alto Research Center; and Yves LeCerf's Degree Programme in Ethnomethodology and Computing Science at the University of Paris VIII. In terms of iconic texts, the four-volume *Harold Garfinkel*, edited by Michael Lynch and Wes Sharrock, presents a nearly definitive selection of EM's primary texts,[8] and is certain to become a canonical resource. A bibliography of works in EM compiled in 1990 included over 1400 entries in six languages (Fehr and Stetson 1990: 473–560), and has since significantly expanded. Conversation analysts and ethnomethodologists meet at international conferences in the UK (Manchester, Oxford), the Netherlands (Amsterdam), the USA (Boston, Santa Barbara, Los Angeles) and Japan (Tokyo) (Psathas and Nasu, 1999: 135; Rawls, 2002), and communicate through various listservs.[9]

9.4 PHILOSOPHICAL ROOTS

As Garfinkel was a student of Talcott Parsons (1968 [1937]), some have mistakenly attributed Garfinkel's work, especially his respecification of norms (Garfinkel, 1963), as merely an elaboration of Parson's functionalist paradigm (Alexander, 1987). Lynch and Bogen (1994: 70) state that, 'Parson's aim was to reconstruct the ordinary actor's implicit knowledge into a logically coherent set of conceptual elements and empirical propositions'. Such an aim forms merely a backdrop to Garfinkel's programme, as Garfinkel was dissatisfied with Parson's 'sketchy treatment of the actor's knowledge and understanding within the voluntaristic theory' (Heritage, 1984: 9; also see Garfinkel, 2005). For many ethnomethodologists, the Parsonian actor, who merely follows the culturally-prescribed 'values' and their according 'norms', is a 'judgmental (or cultural) dope' (Garfinkel, 1967: 67–8), stripped of agency so analysts might realize their own views of social structure. In contrast, in order to build an understanding of the social system 'built solely from the analysis of experience structures' (Garfinkel, 1952: 1, in Heritage, 1984: 9), Garfinkel and his

students would draw upon, and at times creatively misread, the phenomenological writings of Alfred Schutz, Aron Gurwitsch and Maurice Merleau-Ponty, and the philosophical insights of Ludwig Wittgenstein.[10] As a short chapter such as this cannot hope to capture the depth and richness of these influences, we must be satisfied with a few delimited points of contact.

Schutz, who was at the New School for Social Research in New York at the time Garfinkel was at Harvard (Heritage, 1984: 37), was integral to Garfinkel's intellectual growth, as he 'developed a stance toward the nature of meaningful action which dealt directly with the themes of the actor's knowledge, its intersubjective character and the nature of its sociological analysis' (Heritage, 1984: 38).[11] Schutz (1962) furthered the phenomenological notion of *epoché*, or bracketing, upon which radical reflexivity utterly depends (Psathas, 2003 [1977]: 113–4; Wieder, 2003 [1977]: 131–2). Under the attitude of everyday life, individuals rely upon ad-hoc **recipe knowledge** for getting through the day: we don't understand how a phone works in greater detail than knowing to answer it when it rings, or push the buttons to call, for instance. An attitude of Cartesian doubt, whereby one questions reality and one's mode of perceiving it, is not a pragmatic, practical means to get through one's day (Heritage, 1984: 41). Hence, when ethnomethodologists advocated suspending the attitudes of everyday life to examine just what sociological topics might mean in the mundane course of human activities, their initiative was treated with scorn or rebuke by sociologists, just as one commonly responds when another breaches the attitude of everyday life (see especially Garfinkel, 1963). As Heap and Roth (2003 [1973]: 89) state, 'The domain of phenomenological inquiry ... consists solely of the recognizable structures of immediate consciousness; while the domain of EM inquiry consists solely of members' situated practices which produce for themselves and for observers the *sense* of objective social structures'.

The work of Aron Gurwitsch, a phenomenologist who knew Garfinkel personally, is vital for EM (Heritage, 1984: 37). In 'The Last Work of Edmund Husserl', Gurwitsch explores how the crisis of Western sciences is not one of technical validity, but one by which 'Western man ... has become alienated from himself ... science, it seems, has nothing to say regarding things that matter most for human existence' (Gurwitsch, 1966: 399–400). As an alternative, Gurwitsch (1966: 409) proposes that 'To obtain genuinely philosophical knowledge of the world, one has to go beyond the empty generality that all happenings are causally determined. A method must be found which permits specification of the general causality of the world and the construction of infinities of causal connections on the basis of what is accessible to actual experience, finite and fragmentary'.

Such a method must recognize how meaning is fundamentally determined in context. In his discussion of the principles of gestalt theory, Gurwitsch (1964: 115) states, 'By "Gestalt" is meant a unitary whole of varying degrees of richness of detail, which, by virtue of its intrinsic articulation and structure, possesses coherence and consolidation and, thus, detaches itself as an organized and closed unit from the surrounding field' (Gurwitsch, 1964: 115).[12] In order to develop a social science which respected such deep contours of everyday awareness, a Weberian scheme of ideal types, a Parsonian hierarchy of values and norms, or Lazarsfeld-inspired variable analysis, simply would not suffice. As Gurwitsch (1964: 121) elaborates, 'The part is what it is only as a constituent of the Gestalt-contexture and as integrated into its unity'.

While the writings of Merleau-Ponty have been cited increasingly in more recent writings in EM, the precise influence of this work is not always clear (Czyzewski, 2003 [1994]). Merleau-Ponty is a much more opaque, less didactic phenomenologist than Schutz, primarily known for upsetting Cartesian dualisms through his emphasis on the deep intertwining of body and mind, subject and object, as well as his explorations of the nature of perception.[13] The ethnomethodologist most notable for developing an EM inspired by Merleau-Ponty, by exploring embodiment in context, is David Sudnow (1978, 1979, 1984). MacBeth (1988) and Livingston (1987) apply the insights of Merleau-Ponty to understanding concerted social behaviour.

The insights of Ludwig Wittgenstein, considered by many to be the premier philosopher of the twentieth century, are also vital for understanding EM. In *Philosophical Investigations*, Wittgenstein (1951) demonstrates, 'the *insufficiency* of rules as either explanations of, or directives to, human action' (Heritage, 1984: 121). Such a position is demonstrated by showing how a student comes to follow, or fails to follow, a mathematical formula, $n + 2$ to generate a series of cardinal numbers of greater than 1000.[14] Through such an example, Wittgenstein elucidates the doctrine of finitism, pointing to the necessarily finite quality of rules, yet the potentially infinite circumstances of their invocation. Hence, 'No course of action could be determined by a rule, because every course of action can be made to accord with a rule' (para. 201) (also see Das, 1998: 175ff).

Kripke (1982) speaks of this as the 'skeptical paradox', resolved by an appeal to community. Similarly, Bloor (1992: 274) finds that 'collective

support' determines which actions will be seen as following a rule. Such a turn to 'external actors', such as socialization and culture as determinants of human conduct, is rejected by numerous ethnomethodologists. Instead, scholars such as Heritage (1984), Lynch (1992), Sharrock and Anderson (1984), Sharrock and Button (1999), and Sidnell (2003) read Wittgenstein as justifying a focus on how rules are used as constituent features of a setting, to make sense of action. The former position is commonly referred to as skepticist, while the latter, ethnomethodological position, is referred to as anti-scepticist.[15]

9.5 CONTRASTING PERSPECTIVES ON LANGUAGE

Topic and resource

Early, radically-reflexive, and foundational arguments of ethnomethodologists centre around the inadequacy of the language of the social sciences to capture social realities. One key paper in this regard is Zimmerman and Pollner's (2003 [1970]: 80), where they state that 'Sociologists have yet to treat the obvious as phenomenon'. The central inadequacy for sociologists 'is characterized by a confounding of topic and resource' (ibid.: 81). In other words, sociologists have yet to distinguish themselves from ordinary members of society, in that conventional sociologists use commonsense categories, commonsense knowledge and commonsense theories of the social world as unexamined resources for inquiry.[16] In providing for a new type of inquiry:

> One would examine not the factual properties of status hierarchies: one would ask how members provide for the *fact* that status hierarchies are factual features of the members' world. Similarly, instead of treating statistical rates as representations of trends, processes and factual states of society, one would ask how members manage and assemble those statistics, and how they use, read, and rely on those statistics as indications of the states of affairs they are taken to depict (ibid.: 83).

A primary contribution of EM with respect to language is its analysis of accounts, a term referring to a wide variety of communications which can include or overlap with reports, descriptions and explanations. Accounts are understood by EM as being reflexively related to the local context of language use, and to other constituents of local context, including situationally-relevant identities and attributes of persons. Accounts are generally understood in EM not in terms of communicating information which could serve as a resource for analysis, but in terms of how they constitute and display the meanings of social actions and interaction, for and by members. Most importantly, accounts are often analysed with respect to what they are doing in talk-in-interaction, such as accusing, justifying or excusing.

When a member's account is treated as a topic, the account is perceived within a different framework of understanding than if an account is treated as a resource. As Heritage (1984: 138) states, 'informants are routinely treated as competent and properly motivated reporters about their everyday affairs', but researchers rarely reflect on 'what actors might be accomplishing in and through their acts of reporting'. When accounts are studied as actions, one finds that an account is 'heavily dependent on the context of its production' (ibid.: 141).[17] First, spoken language is indexical, continually invoking common sense knowledge and context as a resource (ibid.: 142, and see below). Secondly, language heard is understood through the documentary method of interpretation, whereby the context of an utterance unavoidably elaborates the meaning of the utterance (ibid.: 150). Despite the infinite interpretive processes involved in communication, persons take for granted a shared agreement of meaning, and such interpretations will, in turn, maintain, transform or elaborate the context of the interaction (ibid.: 156).

D. Lawrence Wieder (1974) provides one of the most notable applications of this conception of accounts in his discussion of 'Telling the Convict Code'. While the convict code has often been used by sociologists of prison subcultures to account for the implicit rules that organize such subcultures, Wieder showed how the convict code is invoked by members of these subcultures in order to 'maintain, transform and elaborate' meanings in routine activities. Wieder found that 'the code' was used to account for the responses to his questions, as well as to constrain the types of questions he should ask. Additionally, the code was used by residents to remind each other of what sort of information should be told to the researcher, and by the staff, to account for why their efforts to rehabilitate the ex-cons might not have been successful. By focusing on how the code is 'tell-a-story-aboutable' (Garfinkel, 1967: 33), and by treating accounts as topics for analysis, Wieder delved into the uses of the code as a multifaceted resource for residents and staff, rather than using the accounts merely as a resource for his own analysis to interpret members' actions.

In 'In Search of the Action', Gilbert and Mulkay (1983) provide a strong critique of approaching accounts as resources. They state that sociologists often attempt to analyze social action based on little more than accounts of action, which is bound to lead to erroneous results since 'definitive accounts [of action] cannot be obtained' (ibid.: 14). Aside from problems of 'bias, deception, selective reporting, and so on', members' accounts often contradict themselves, forcing the analyst to 'infer what the participants "really meant" by certain statements' (ibid.: 14–15). In their study, they show how Blissett's (1972: 9) contention that 'professional actions of scientists are essentially political in character', is erroneously derived from accepting scientists' statements at face value. Gilbert and Mulkay interviewed many of the same scientists and, rather than using them as informants, they focused on the scientists' acts of accounting and the contexts of these accounts. They found a 'regularity ... in participants' method of accounting' (ibid.: 20), even if the accounts were contradictory at face value. For example, they found that if the scientist had decided another scientist was correct, it would be explained in terms of experimental evidence that preserved positivist assumptions. On the other hand, if a scientist had decided another scientist was incorrect, they would account for this on the basis of 'non-scientific factors', including political factors, as Blissett had found (ibid.: 22). Thus, by looking at accounts as action, Gilbert and Mulkay gained deeper insights than an earlier researcher who had looked at similar data as a resource which **revealed** action. They posit that their insights could begin to show how a 'traditional positivist conception of science is achieved and maintained', in that the positivist tradition is invoked when describing what the scientist believes are 'successful' theories, but not for describing unsuccessful ones (ibid.: 22).

Indexicality

Aside from critiquing how social scientists conventionally treat language, ethnomethodologists also critique linguists' understanding of language. A foundational article is 'On Formal Structures of Practical Actions', in which Garfinkel and Sacks (1970) point out the inadequacy of the sociolinguistics of the time, for failing to consider the centrality of context as determinative of the meaning of utterances. As they state, 'Features of indexical expressions have motivated among professionals endless methodological studies directed to their remedy', as they aim to provide a distinction between objective and indexical expressions, and to substitute objective for indexical expressions (ibid.: 349). Instead, Garfinkel and Sacks point out that indexical expressions are fundamentally without remedy. Hence, no law or rule of semantics or syntax can provide for talk's meaning. Rather, meaning is constituted by what individuals do with words in specific settings of talk.[18] As Heritage (1984: 139–40) states, 'descriptions are not to be regarded as disembodied commentaries on states of affairs', since 'understanding language is not, in the first instance, a matter of understanding sentences but of understanding actions ... an utterance is thus the starting point for a complicated process of interpretive inference rather than something which can be treated as self-subsistently intelligible'.

D. Lawrence Wieder (1971) explains in detail how indexicals might be overlooked in theories of anthropological or structural semantics, which construct 'theoretical puppets that do nothing other than what a specific theorist proposes' (ibid.: 108). In this article, he takes issue with 'the criteria for using names, the extent to which a definite set of criteria could be employed by name users, and the extent to which meaning is determined by criteria of proper use', for the theorists Goodenough, Lounsbury, Frake and Conklin (ibid.: 110). As many of these theorists' rules are found to be invariant to the occasion in which a sign is used, Wieder finds that their methods are inappropriate to the phenomenon, 'since criteria vary in their meaning over the occasions in which they are used' (ibid.: 134). Hence, 'structural semantic analyses appear to be idealizations of what members are actually doing when they look and describe', so instead, the analyst's task should be to understand 'the work that members do in making the *orderly* properties of the setting in which they act visible to each other' (ibid.: 135).[19]

Another ethnomethodologist who critiques the linguistic canon is Roy Turner (1970), who complexifies J. L. Austin's notions of performatives by which words are not merely **saying** something but **doing** something, a seminal insight for speech act theory.[20] Turner provides a transcript of a tale, told by a former mental patient of being snubbed in public, told at a support group. While the orderliness of the talk seems 'terribly obvious, if not trite' to societal members, the same utterances are 'forbiddingly opaque' if we must locate our analysis within the confines of theoretical concepts (Turner, 1970: 176). Turner hears the talk as constituting a 'complaint', but is utterly 'unable to locate any obvious syntactic properties that might be seen as structural correlates of complaints, nor do I have any operational means for identifying its boundaries' (ibid.:178). Throughout his analysis, Turner shows how he must have 'recourse to member's knowledge in providing the substance of my account', especially since this is a '*category-generated activity*',[21] leaving the sociolinguist with 'no choice but to reflect upon and analyze the social order to which he himself subscribes' (ibid.: 187).

An especially fruitful use of ethnomethodological insights for studying the indexical nuances of communication is to be found in the work of David A. Goode, in his studies of the communication practices of people who carry severe handicaps. In contrast to work by Wikler and Pollner (1985), which examines a family's denial of their child's retardation as *folie à famille*, Goode finds that "everything," for all practical purposes, may be communicated' between Bianca, a severely handicapped young girl, and her mother. Such an analysis involves phenomenologically bracketing the predominant discourses of scientific rationality, measurement, categorization and professional expertise by which doctors and other caregivers of Bianca characterized her as 'slug like' and 'low-functioning, multihandicapped, alingual, and non-ambulatory ... with a poor prognosis for medical, sensory, cognitive and social development' (Goode, 2003 [1990]: 331). After spending hundreds of hours with Bianca's family over a nine-month period, Goode was able to find how Bianca indicated to others how to feed her, how to follow common routines, and even how many blankets to put on her bed. These were '*essentially circumstantial forms of communication*' (ibid.: 343), fundamentally products of intimacy, which were constantly subject to ironicization by outsiders (ibid.: 353). By perceiving via the standardized, exogenous categorization schemes of the medical establishment, the 'experts' were unable to perceive Bianca's ways of relating to others. In other words, the various 'fields' (Merleau-Ponty, 1962: 10) in which different observers placed Bianca constituted her in fundamentally alternative ways, with great consequences for her well-being and life chances.

Garfinkel and Sacks' insights into the inadequacy of approaching language as simply a conduit of meaning are exemplified in a number of 'aids to the sluggish imagination' (Garfinkel, 1967: 38–46). In his tutorial project, Garfinkel asked his students to treat indexicals as if they were as problematic for themselves as they are for philosophers and linguists. For one study, Garfinkel asked his students to write on one side of a sheet what was actually said in a conversation, and write on the other side what they and their interlocutor understood that they were talking about. After enumerating a number of the features of such 'common understandings', Garfinkel (ibid.: 41) states that: 'It hardly needs to be pointed out that the sense of the expressions depended upon where the expression occurred in serial order, the expressive character of the terms that comprised it, and the importance to the conversationalists of the events depicted'. In another study, students asked, in the course of an ordinary conversation, for clarification of a common utterance. For instance, when a woman stated, 'I had a flat tire,' Garfinkel's student responded, 'What do you mean, you had a flat tire?' The challenges Garfinkel's students were met with serve as telling rejoinders to those who may wish to address 'the problem' of indexicals, as they faced such responses as outright rage, 'peevishness', and a remarkably high response rate of, 'What's wrong with you?'[22] Thus, Garfinkel demonstrated how the indexical character of language use is typically not problematic to members, thus suggesting how the indexical use of language might serve as a more apt topic of study than the 'problem' of indexicals.

9.6 MEMBERSHIP CATEGORIZATION ANALYSIS

Membership categorization analysis (MCA) is a development from within ethnomethodology (EM), focusing on the empirical, qualitative understanding of membership categories as they are used by people in talk and social interaction, and also in texts and other communication media. Membership categories refer to identities, essentially, and MCA centers around the study of identities as they are achieved or contested, organized and understood, within the practical contexts of social interaction and language use. Membership categories are extremely numerous and diverse, referring for example to categories of class, race, gender, nationality, religion, linguistic community, age and occupation, to memberships of associations, political parties or social clubs, and many other types of identity which are more obviously contextual in nature, such as driver, applicant and organ donor. The vast variety of identity categories are termed membership categories with reference to the convention within EM of referring to people (speakers, subjects, agents, actors, etc.) as 'members'. The notions of member and membership often implicitly allude to the competence in cultural and linguistic methods of practical reasoning and practical action (folk methods or **ethno**methods) which can be found in members of any culture or linguistic community. Although MCA is situated within the social sciences, the approach is often philosophically informed and humanistic, as well as empirical, illuminating and explicating not only empirical data and patterns but also the logic and the rhetoric of social identities in their relations to social practices and social organization.

MCA, following EM and conversation analysis (CA), is open-mindedly empirical in its approach, understanding issues and practices of identity without privileging certain types of identities, such as public speakers, without privileging certain types of communication, such as mass communication, and without privileging communication in institutional contexts, such as political or professional communication. MCA can and does encompass studies of specific varieties of identity, and studies of identity with reference to specific kinds of communication or specific institutional contexts, but such interests are not exclusive of or privileged with respect to the study of membership categories and membership categorization practices observable in vernacular speech, among laypeople.

Originating from the seminal scholarship of Harvey Sacks at the time he was laying the foundations of CA, MCA has generally been neglected by the subsequent trajectory of CA, which has focused on the analysis of conversational sequencing rather than questions of identity. One dimension of this divergence can be related to distinctions between different national trajectories taken by EM, in that the primary development of MCA, understood as a development within EM, has been more international than that of CA.[23] The tradition of British EM, as taught for example in Manchester, has been particularly influential for MCA, but foundational figures in MCA can be found in several countries, not just the USA and the UK. Jayyusi, whose book *Categorization and the Moral Order* (1984) was a pivotal contribution for MCA, studied in the UK before teaching in the USA, and now teaches in the United Arab Emirates. Both Hester and Eglin, who coined the term 'membership categorization analysis' in their seminal edited collection *Culture in Action* (1997), have careers associated with British and Canadian universities. None of the primary authors associated with MCA, after Harvey Sacks, have held positions in the University of California system, which has been a remarkable source of both EM and CA scholarship. The fact that after Sacks' untimely death the development of MCA became quite international may have provided additional opportunities for innovation.

The divergence between MCA and sequentially-oriented CA has been subjected to a penetrating critique by Watson (1997), who forwards a more inclusive position, but the divergence is now perhaps beyond repair. While CA has generally diverged away from MCA and much CA has diverged from EM as well, MCA has retained a more inclusive and complementary understanding of the relationship between CA and MCA, and especially between MCA and EM. Hence, MCA studies of identity can include elements of sequential analysis, and are often attentive to methods of practical reasoning and practical action, in keeping with ethnomethodological interests. To a degree that is unusual in EM, MCA continues to draw upon Sacks' work, integrating relevant insights from Sacks into ethnomethodological studies and extending them within a developing body of interdisciplinary research on identity categories. MCA is today an established international research tradition in its own right, with its own practitioners and literature, even as it continues to be identified in relation to either CA or EM, if not both.

The scope of MCA is quite broad, and the potential applications numerous. In the process of studying the deployment and understanding of membership categories in talk and other media of communication, MCA has developed a wide range of insights about how identities are organized across membership categories and how they can be related to a variety of other aspects of social interaction and social contexts.

The fact that certain membership categories can be conventionally or contextually heard to belong together, such as 'baby' and 'mommy', or 'teacher' and student', is taken up in the analysis of membership category devices, or collections of categories. While many such devices could be understood formally, as elements of a culture and a language, MCA typically analyses membership category devices empirically, with respect to particular instances of talk-in-interaction, in contrast to traditions such as structuralism and conceptual analysis. Many membership category devices, which may be operative in particular instances of talk-in-interaction, would be quite difficult to understand except by reference to features of local context and action. A collection of suspects for a store robbery, for example, including the owner's homeless sister-in-law, a disgruntled former tenant, and a neighborhood heroin addict, would in many ways defy formal analysis, as would a collection of potential interviewees for a media report on salmon fishing, including a biologist, an amateur fisherman, and a lieutenant governor. Collecting members of such disparate categories together into collections of potential suspects or interviewees could not make sense formally, as with abstract collections of identities such as types of occupation, types of family relative, types of criminal, types of political office-holder, types of hobbyist, etc. Many collections only make sense contextually, in isolated cases of talk-in-interaction, in a manner that would entirely escape broader, decontextualized analyses of cultural and linguistic classifications. In the same way that devices or collections like these can be more obviously context-dependent, other, more conventional category devices or collections such as those of family and religion can also be understood and analyzed as context-sensitive or context-dependent. Hence, in different contexts, the family might be understood in terms of household residence, in terms of financial dependents, in terms of medical history, or in terms of holiday invitations, all of which can yield different collections of family members, contrary to any formal, de-contextualized classification or enumeration of the set of membership categories constituting the collection 'family'.[24]

It is important to note, however, that MCA typically begins not by trying to find the relevance or sense of particular categories (e.g. husband and wife) or category devices (e.g. family), but by identifying **whichever** identities are achieved and understood to be contextually relevant by members, and how they are achieved and understood to be relevant by members, without prejudgment. An example is provided in Berard (2005), in which a dispute about gender discrimination between a man and a woman is found to end in such a way as to suggest the importance of differences in profession and age, neither of which refer to the category device of gender. Empirical analysis often reveals that the identities which are observably relevant in given instances are different and/ or more numerous than would be predicted by theorists, social critics and laypeople.

Similarly, the ways in which category devices may be contextually constituted and deployed can also be surprisingly organized and surprisingly methodical. One example is provided by Berard's (2002) analysis of historical arguments before the US Supreme Court on the treatment of Japanese Americans during World War II, in which opposing sides treated Japanese Americans either with respect to their nationality/national ancestry, to emphasize the perceived military threat, or with respect to their race/ethnicity, to emphasize their abuse and their constitutional rights as minorities.

A related insight refers to standardized relational pairs of categories, referring to pairs of categories which can be understood to be related, such as husband/wife and teacher/student, and which, moreover, often involve relational features such as rights and obligations, which may be either symmetric, as in the pair 'neighbour–neighbour' or asymmetric, as in the pair 'parent–child.' While these insights may be reminiscent of other, more popularized approaches to identity, such as role theory, a distinction of MCA is that the category pairings and any relational features understood to be applicable to them are typically illustrated by, or even worked up from, the closely detailed analysis of empirical data. Watson (1983), for example, builds upon a transcript of a police interrogation in his discussion of the two relational pairs 'offender' and 'victim', and 'white' and 'black', with reference to how a racial epithet used by a White suspect to describe the victim makes observable a motive for the offence, namely racial prejudice. In this manner, even topics such as race and race relations, which are widely understood as features of social structure, can be understood as local accomplishments, the products of observable social and communicative practices.

The fact that individuals can be correctly described by means of an indefinite number of membership categories gives rise to questioning and analyzing how identifications are done minimally, selectively, relevantly, contextually and intelligibly. The close attention within MCA to just those identities which become observably relevant in situated contexts of communication, with reference to participants' own displayed understandings, distinguishes MCA from many other traditions of inquiry. By contrast, a variety of other approaches, often of a theoretical or critical nature, stipulate which identities are relevant for the study of social interaction and social organization rather than treating relevant identity as an empirical question. The fact that references to persons involve pragmatic selections from among the many categories which could correctly be used to refer to them is a specific application of the general problem of multiple description, noted by Sacks (see, e.g., Sacks, 1995: 41, 326).[25] The implicit selection operative in mundane practices of description and reference illustrates again the complex, methodical and pragmatic nature of commonsense reasoning, as available through talk and texts.

MCA also investigates and analyzes the intricate and complex relationships which obtain between (1) identities, and (2) attributes or predicates of persons such as their actions, their motives, their beliefs or knowledge and (3) interactional contexts. These relationships, addressed for example in the work of Eglin and Hester (see, e.g., Eglin and Hester, 1992; Hester and Eglin, 1997) and Jayyusi (1984) allow studies of membership categorization to branch out considerably, addressing many more facets of social interaction and communication than might be immediately apparent.

MCA has also been used, most notably by Coulter (2001), to address collectivity categories (categories referring to social collectivities such as companies, churches, governments and armies) and also their features and their actions, thus respecifying many 'macro' social and institutional phenomena by reference to conventional methods of invoking and using collectivity categories in communication and interaction. A developing genre of MCA studies addresses interactions in institutional settings, especially settings associated with mass media, schooling and legal settings, suggesting at least one potential line of convergence with CA, which has developed a significant literature on studies of work.[26] Such overlaps between MCA and other traditions,

whether with sociological theory, CA, discourse analysis, discursive psychology, or other traditions, suggest some of the potential lines of development and influence for MCA in the future.

Throughout their variety, MCA studies share an empirical and analytic focus on illuminating the pragmatic and categorical logic of social identities. Central concerns include how membership categories are related to each other and, furthermore, how they are inferentially related to issues of social action, social context or social structure, by means of the cultural and linguistic competencies and methods which are the topics and the findings of MCA.

9.7 CONCLUSION

While many students directly influenced by Garfinkel tend to be purists, insisting that ethnomethodology is fundamentally incommensurable with other methods of the social sciences (what they termed formal analysis, or FA), such is not necessarily the case. One well-known ethnomethodologist who co-authored the very article on incommensurability with Garfinkel (Garfinkel and Wieder, 1992), D. Lawrence Wieder, in fact, also wrote about how EM could be incorporated with such theories and methods as conversation analysis, microanalysis (based on the work of Goffman) and the ethnography of speaking. Speaking optimistically, he notes that 'the search itself may yield the discovery of new phenomena, reclassifications, new classifications, new dimensions of taxonomies, the need for new concepts, and other comparable matters' (Wieder, 1999: 163; also see Berard, 2003). In other words, the contentions of our forebears need not be extended indefinitely.[27]

EM still holds the promise to shake up our common assumptions and categorical ways of understanding reality. What Dingwall (2000: 909) states in regards to law and society studies could just as well apply to any discipline of the social sciences:

Ethnomethodology and conversation analysis may indeed be what their founders claimed them to be: not merely new research technologies but new ways of thinking about sociology and its core intellectual project. As such, they necessarily challenge some of the currently hegemonic assumptions of law and society studies about both the positive and normative aspects of its research agenda. Are we really trying to find out how law works or to find illustrations for an a priori critique, aping the current fashion of the humanities to disdain modernism and the society which has given rise to it?

However contentiously the findings and insights of EM may have been reported or received, future generations of scholars will nonetheless continue to find amazement, bewilderment and room for growth in Garfinkel's noticing that there is order in the plenum (Garfinkel, 2002: 95).

NOTES

1   While the authors shared comments on drafts of this article, Garot drafted the section on ethnomethodology, and Berard drafted the section on membership categorization analysis.

2   As Lynch and Sharrock (2003: vii) state: 'Harold Garfinkel is one of a very few sociologists to have founded a program of sociological investigation, and is perhaps the only one to have done so in the late 20th century'.

3   See Lemert (2002), Dingwall (2000: 890).

4   As Lynch and Peyrot (1992: 120) note: 'What ethnomethodology is "about" comes less from reading the literature than from engaging in the sorts of investigations exemplified in that literature. This could perhaps be said of any organized practice, but it is an explicit – indeed obsessive – concern in ethnomethodology's pedagogy'. This explains why the substantive chapters of Garfinkel's (2002) long-awaited sequel to *Studies* consist primarily of tutorial problems for students. See Lynch (1999) for a telling, 'behind the scenes' elucidation of the indifference of the leading lights of EM in regards to matters of theory and method.

5   As Garfinkel (1996: 7) states, 'The principal formal analytic devices currently in hand, of paying careful attention to the use, the design, and administration of generic representational theorizing – models, for example, get a job done that with the same technical skills in administering them lose the very phenomenon that they profess'. Anderson and Sharrock (1983) point out how such techniques often use irony to make their case.

6   A short sample may suffice:

'No inquiries can be excluded … . Procedures and results of water witching, divination, mathematics, sociology – whether done by lay persons or professionals – are addressed according to the policy that every feature of sense, of fact, of method, for every particular case of inquiry without exception, is the managed accomplishment of organized settings of practical actions, and that particular determinations in members' practices of consistency, planfulness, relevance, or reproducibility of their practices and results – from witchcraft to topology – are acquired and assured only through particular, located organizations of artful practices … . Thus, a leading

policy is to refuse serious consideration to the prevailing proposal that efficiency, efficacy, effectiveness, intelligibility, consistency, planfulness, typicality, uniformity, reproducibility of activities – i.e., the rational properties of practical activities – be assessed, recognized, categorized, described by using a rule or a standard obtained outside actual settings within which such properties are recognized, used, produced, and talked about by settings' members. (Garfinkel, 1967: 32–3)

7   See Silverman (1998) for an account of the intellectual development of Harvey Sacks.

8   Prior indispensable volumes include Douglas (1970), Turner (1974), Coulter (1990), Button (1991), Watson and Seiler (1992), Volume 15, Numbers 2 and 3 of *Qualitative Sociology*, and Volume 22, issue 2/4, of *Human Studies*.

9   http://www.paultenhave.nl/EMCA.htm, http://www.paultenhave.nl/lists.htm, http://list.hum.aau.dk/mailman/listinfo/languse.

10   O'Neill (2003 [1980]) provides a fascinating analysis of the ways in which misreading has been purposeful and constructive within the ethnomethodological tradition.

11   See O'Neil (2003 [1980]) and Anderson, Hughes and Sharrock (2003 [1985]) for cogent discussions of the intellectual relationships of Parsons, Schutz and Garfinkel. For further reading, see Parson's and Schutz's exchange of correspondence (Grathhoff, 1978) and its reviews (Coser, 1979; Giddens, 1979; Wagner, 1979; Heritage, 1984: 7–36).

12   Maynard (1996: 1) discusses how 'social psychology might well have been ethnomethodology', had such a notion of the experientially-based gestalt phenomenon, that 'the whole is more than its parts', been accepted over the stimuli-based theories which forged the core of the discipline.

13   Aron Gurwitsch (1964: 113) highlights a point from Merleau-Ponty (1962: 10) which is central for understanding radical reflexivity: 'The figure-ground-structure belongs to the very nature of perception and is not merely a contingent perceptual fact: …that without which a phenomenon cannot be called perception. The perceptual something is always in the midst of things. It is always part of a field'. See Emerson and Messinger (1977) for an application of this insight to the definition of everyday troubles.

14   Now we get the pupil to continue a series (say +2) beyond 1000, and he writes 1000, 1004, 1008, 1012. We say to him:

'Look what you've done!' – He doesn't understand. We say: 'You were meant to add two: look how you began the series!' – He answers: 'Yes, isn't it right? I thought that was how I was meant to do it.' – Or suppose he pointed to the series and said: 'But I went on in the same way'. (para. 185)

15 See Heritage (1978 and 1984: 103–34) for a broader discussion of the importance of Wittgenstein for EM.

16 The paradigmatic example of ethnomethodological work, which treats the incorrigible **resource** of talk as a **topic**, is conversation analysis, addressed in a separate essay (also see Heritage, 1984: 135–78 and 232–92).

17 Note that, for ethnomethodologists, to treat meaning **contextually** 'means that they endeavor analytically to unpack relational configurations that enable sense to be made and understood *in situ*. 'Context' for ethnomethodologists is not a fixed set of social, cultural, environmental or cognitive 'factors' impinging on specific instances of conduct as though from outside. Instead, the term describes a 'reflexively' constituted relationship between singular actions and the relevant specifications of identity, place, time, and meaning implicated by the intelligibility of those actions' (Lynch and Peyrot, 1992: 114).

18 See Heritage's (1984: 142–50) discussion of 'that's a nice one'.

19 Cicourel (1970: 148–50) provides a list of such orderly properties as: the reciprocity of perspectives, the et cetera assumption, normal forms, retrospective-prospective sense of occurrence, talk itself as reflexive, and descriptive vocabularies as indexical expressions. Also see Coulter (1973) for a cogent critique of structural semantics, in arguing that 'human actions cannot logically be explained in terms of causal laws' (ibid.: 174), and a thorough discussion, ranging from the Greeks to Wittgenstein, of the problem of applying the formulas of logic to language (Coulter, 1991).

20 Examples provided by Turner (1970: 170–1), from Austin's (1962: 22) speech act theory, are: the words 'I do' in a marriage ceremony, 'I apologize' after stepping on your toe, 'I name this ship the Queen Elizabeth', 'I bet you sixpence it will rain tomorrow', or 'I bequeath… '.

21 See the section below on membership categorization analysis.

22 As Heap (1980: 103) notes, 'Reflexivity is a solution to indexicality.' For revealing studies of how indexicals are mundanely deproblematized, see Pollner (1984), Atkinson (1978) and Garfinkel (1967: 18–24, 186–207).

23 CA has also become very international, but has developed rather more around American figures and contributions, compared with MCA.

24 See generally Hester and Eglin (1997: 1–23, including esp. fn. 9, 165–6.) The membership category device 'family' is discussed by Hester and Eglin, following Sacks, as a primary example of a membership category device which is more conventional or 'natural' than many other devices, which are more obviously contextual or 'topic-occasioned'. But the more important point, following Hester and Eglin, is

that for EM all membership category devices can and should be studied with detailed reference to the occasions of their use.

25 The problem of multiple description, briefly, is a pragmatic problem facing speakers when they engage in description, and can also be discussed as an analytic problem with respect to how analysts handle the same issues. There are typically many correct descriptions which could be offered by way of a description: for example, a person could be described in terms of gender, profession, age, nationality, race, etc., and the problem of multiple description is the problem of selecting from among the many available category devices and categories. Much of Sacks' work on membership categories and membership category devices can be understood as illuminating the social logic displayed in the production and understanding of such selective descriptions of persons.

26 Indeed, MCA scholarship on institutional settings, EM studies of work and CA studies of talk at work already overlap significantly and often. Whereas CA generally brings more focus on such matters as conversational sequencing, the design of turns at talk and richly detailed transcripts, MCA stands to contribute to EM and CA studies of institutional settings, especially insofar as MCA can contribute uniquely to the understanding of how institutional and professional phenomena, including work activities and specialized knowledges, are related to institutional/professional identities, and can be understood better with knowledge of how institutional and professional identities are organized and accomplished.

27 The extensive bibliographies of Bob Emerson, James Holstein and Gale Miller are examples of how an EM sensitivity may be incorporated in work that is not exclusively EM.

REFERENCES

Alexander, J. (1987) *Twenty Lectures*. New York: Columbia University Press.

Anderson, D. C. and Sharrock, W. W. (1983) 'Irony as methodological theory: a sketch of four variations', *Poetics Today* 4(3): 565–79.

Anderson, R. J., Hughes, J. A. and Sharrock, W. W. (2003) 'The relationship between ethnomethodology and phenomenology', in M. Lynch and W. Sharrock (eds), *Harold Garfinkel*. London: Sage. pp. 135–50. (1st edn, 1985.)

Atkinson, J. M. (1978) *Discovering Suicide: Studies in the Social Organization of Sudden Death*. London: Macmillan.

Austin, J. (1962) *How to do Things With Words*. Cambridge, MA: Harvard University Press.

Berard, T. (2002) '"Japanese American" identity and the problem of multiple description: disjunctive versions of the Japanese exclusion order', in S. Hester and W. Housley (eds), *Language, Interaction and National Identity: Studies in the Social Organization of Talk-in-Interaction.* Burlington, VT: Ashgate. pp. 144–68.

Berard, T. (2003) 'Ethnomethodology as radical sociology: an expansive appreciation of Melvin Pollner's "constitutive and mundane versions of labeling theory"', *Human Studies*, 26(4): 431–48.

Berard, T. (2005) 'On multiple identities and educational contexts: remarks on the study of inequalities and discrimination', *Journal of Language, Identity and Education*, 4(1): 67–76.

Bittner, E. (1965) 'The concept of organization', *Social Research*, 32: 230–55.

Bittner, E. (1967) 'Police discretion in emergency apprehension of mentally ill persons', *Social Problems*, 14: 278–92.

Bjelic, D. and M. Lynch (1989) 'The work of a [scientific] demonstration: respecifying Newton's and Goethe's theories of prismatic color'. Unpublished manuscript, Boston University.

Blissett, M. (1972) *Politics in Science.* Boston: Little, Brown.

Bloor, D. (1983) *Wittgenstein: a Social Theory of Knowledge.* New York: Columbia University Press.

Button, G. (ed.) (1991) *Ethnomethodology and the Human Sciences.* New York: Cambridge University Press.

Cicourel, A. (1970) 'The acquisition of social language: toward a developmental sociology of language and meaning', in J. Douglas (ed.), *Understanding Everyday Life.* Chicago: Aldine. pp. 136–68.

Clayman, S. (1995) 'The dialectic of ethnomethodology', *Semiotica*, 107(1–2): 105–23.

Coser, L. A. (1979) 'A dialogue of the deaf', *Contemporary Sociology*, 8: 680–2.

Coulter, J. (1973) 'Language and the conceptualization of meaning', *Sociology*, 7(2): 173–89.

Coulter, J. (ed.) (1990) *Ethnomethodological Sociology.* Brookfield, VT: Edward Elgar.

Coulter, J. (1991) 'Logic: ethnomethodology and the logic of language', in G. Button (ed.), *Ethnomethodology and the Human Sciences.* New York: Cambridge University Press. pp. 20–50.

Coulter, J. (2001) 'Human practices and the observability of the "macro-social"', in T. Schatzki, K. Cetina and E. Von Savigny (eds), *The Practice Turn in Contemporary Theory.* New York: Routledge. pp. 29–41,

Czyzewski, M. (2003) 'Reflexivity of actors versus reflexivity of accounts', in M. Lynch and W. Sharrock (eds), *Harold Garfinkel.* London: Sage. pp. 227–33. (1st edn, 1994.)

Das, V. (1998) 'Wittgenstein and anthropology', *Annual Review of Anthropology*, 27: 171–95.

Dingwall, R. (2000) 'Language law and power: ethnomethodology, conversation analysis, and the politics of law and society studies', *Law and Social Inquiry*, 25(3): 885–911.

Douglas, J. (ed.) (1970) *Understanding Everyday Life.* Chicago: Aldine.

Eglin, P. and Hester, S. (1992) 'Category, predicate and task: the pragmatics of practical action', *Semiotica*, 88: 243–68.

Emerson, R. M. and Messinger, S. L. (1977) 'The micro-politics of trouble', *Social Problems*, 25: 121–34.

Fehr, B. J. and Stetson, J. with Mizukawa, Y. (1990) 'A bibliography for ethnomethodology', in J. Coulter (ed.), *Ethnomethodological Sociology.* Brookfield, VT: Edward Elgar. pp. 473–559.

Garfinkel, H. (1952) 'The perception of the other: a study in social order'. PhD dissertation, Harvard University.

Garfinkel, H. (1963) 'A conception of, and experiments with, "trust" as a condition of stable concerted actions', in O. J. Harvey (ed.), *Motivation and Social Interaction.* New York: Ronald Press.

Garfinkel, H. (1967) *Studies in Ethnomethodology.* Oxford, UK: Polity Press.

Garfinkel, H. (1996) 'Ethnomethodology's program', *Social Psychology Quarterly*, 59(1): 5–21.

Garfinkel, H. (2002) *Ethnomethodology's Program: Working Out Durkeim's Aphorism.* Lanham, MD: Rowman and Littlefield.

Garfinkel, H. (2005) *Seeing Sociologically: The Routine Grounds of Social Action.* Boulder, CO: Paradigm Publishers.

Garfinkel, H. and Sacks, H. (1970) 'On formal structures of practical actions', in J. C. McKinney and E. A. Tiryakian (eds), *Theoretical Sociology.* New York: Appleton Century Crofts.

Garfinkel, H. and Wieder, D. L. (1992) 'Evidence for locally produced ... phenomena of order* ... (IV): two incommensurable, asymmetrically alternate technologies of social analysis', in G. Watson and R. Seiler (eds), *Text in Context: Contributions to Ethnomethodology.* Newbury Park, CA: Sage. pp. 175–206.

Giddens, A. (1979) 'Schutz and Parsons: problems of meaning and subjectivity', *Contemporary Sociology*, 8: 682–5.

Gilbert, G. N. and Mulkay, M. (1983) 'In search of the action', in G. N. Gilbert and P. Abell (eds), *Accounts and Action: Survey Conferences on Sociological Theory and Method.* Aldershot: Gower. pp. 8–34.

Goode, D. A. (2003) 'On understanding without words: communication between a deaf-blind child and her parents', in M. Lynch and W. Sharrock (eds), *Harold Garfinkel.* London: Sage. pp. 327–60. (1st edn, 1990.)

Grathoff, R. (1978) *The Theory of Social Action: The Correspondence of Alfred Schutz and Talcott Parsons.* Bloomington, IN: Indiana University Press.

Gurwitsch, A. (1964) *Field of Consciousness.* Pittsburg: Duquesne University Press.

Gurwitsch, A. (1966) *Studies in Phenomenology and Psychology.* Evanston: Northwestern University Press.

Heap, J. L. (1980) 'Description in ethnomethodology', *Human Studies*, 3: 87–106.

Heap, J. L. and Roth, P. A. (2003) 'On phenomenological sociology', in M. N. Lynch and W. Sharrock (eds), *Harold Garfinkel.* London: Sage. pp. 77–95. (1st edn, 1973.)

Heritage, J. (1978) 'Aspects of the flexibilities of natural language use: a reply to Phillips', *Sociology*, 12: 79–103.

Heritage, J. (1984) *Garfinkel and Ethnomethodology.* New York: Polity Press.

Heritage, J. (1987) 'Ethnomethodology', in A. Giddens and J. H. Turner (eds), *Social Theory Today.* New York: Polity Press.

Hester, S. and Eglin, P. (eds) (1997) *Culture in Action: Studies in Membership Categorization Analysis*. Washington, DC: International Institute for Ethnomethodology and Conversation Analysis, and University Press of America.

Jayyusi, L. (1984) *Categorization and the Moral Order*. Boston: Routledge and Kegan Paul.

Kripke, S. A. (1982) *Wittgenstein on Rules and Private Language: An Elementary Exposition*. Cambridge, MA: Harvard University Press.

Lemert, C. (2002) 'The pleasure of Garfinkel's indexical ways', in *Ethnomethodology's Program: Working Out Durkheim's Aphorism*. Lanham, MD: Rowman and Littlefield. pp. ix–xiii.

Livingston, E. (1987) 'Pedestrian traffic flow', in *Making Sense of Ethnomethodology*. London: Routledge and Kegan Paul. pp. 21–7.

Lynch, M. (1991) 'Method: measurement – ordinary and scientific measurement as ethnomethodological phenomena', in G. Button (ed.), *Ethnomethodology and the Human Sciences*. Cambridge: Cambridge University Press. pp. 77–108.

Lynch, M. (1992) 'Extending Wittgenstein: the pivotal move from epistemology to the sociology of science', in A. Pickering (ed.), *Science as Practice and Culture*. Chicago: Chicago University Press. pp. 215–65.

Lynch, M. (1999) 'Silence in context: ethnomethodology and social theory', *Human Studies*, 22: 211–33.

Lynch, M. and Bogen, D. (1994) 'Harvey Sacks's primitive natural science', *Theory, Culture and Society*, 11: 65–104.

Lynch, M. and Peyrot, M. (1992) 'Introduction: a reader's guide to ethnomethodology', *Qualitative Sociology*, 15(2): 113–22.

Lynch, M. and Sharrock, W. (eds) (2003) *Harold Garfinkel*. Vols 1–4. London: Sage.

MacBeth, D. (1988) 'Basketball notes', in *Respecifying the Natural Sciences as Discovering Sciences of Practical Action*. Vols. I and II. Unpublished manuscript, UCLA. pp.73–90.

Maynard, D. W. (1996) 'Introduction of Harold Garfinkel for the Cooley-Mead award', *Social Psychology Quarterly*, 59(1): 1–4.

Maynard, D. W. and Clayman, S. E. (1991) 'The diversity of ethnomethodology', *Annual Review of Sociology*, 17: 385–418.

Merleau-Ponty, M. (1962) *The Phenomenology of Perception*. London: Routledge and Kegan Paul.

O'Neill, J. (2003) [1980] 'From phenomenology to ethnomethodology: some radical "misreadings" ', in M. Lynch and W. Sharrock (eds), *Harold Garfinkel*. London: Sage. pp. 97–110.

Parsons, T. (1968) *The Structure of Social Action*. New York: The Free Press. (1st edn, 1937.)

Pollner, M. (1984) *Mundane reason: Reality in Everyday and Sociological Discourse*. Cambridge: Cambridge University Press.

Pollner, M. (1991) 'Left of ethnomethodology: the rise and decline of radical reflexivity', *American Sociological Review*, 56(June): 370–80.

Psathas, G. (2003) 'Ethnomethodology as a phenomenological approach in the social sciences', in M. Lynch and W. Sharrock (eds), *Harold Garfinkel*. London: Sage. pp.111–28. (1st edn, 1977.)

Psathas, G. and Nasu, H. (1999) 'Introduction', *Human Studies*, 22: 135–7.

Rawls, A. (2002) 'Editor's introduction', in *Ethnomethodology's Program: Working Out Durkheim's Aphorism*. Boston: Rowman and Littlefield. pp. 1–64.

Sacks, H. (1972) 'Notes on police assessment of moral character', in D. Sudnow (ed.), *Studies in Social Interaction*. New York: Free Press. pp. 280–93.

Sacks, H. (1995) *Lectures on Conversation*, Vols 1 and 2. Cambridge, MA: Blackwell.

Sharrock, W. and Anderson, R. J. (1984) 'The Wittgenstein connection', *Human Studies*, 7: 375–86.

Sharrock, W. and Button, G. (1999) 'Do the right thing! Rule finitism, rule scepticism and rule following', *Human Studies*, 22: 193–210.

Schutz, A. (1962) 'Common-sense and scientific interpretation of human action', in A. Schutz (ed.), *Collected Papers I: The Problem of Social Reality*. The Hague: Martinus Nijhoff. pp. 3–47.

Sidnell, J. (2003) 'An ethnographic consideration of rule following', *Journal of the Royal Anthropology Institute*, 9: 429–45.

Silverman, D. (1998) *Harvey Sacks: Social Science and Conversation Analysis*. New York: Oxford University Press.

Sudnow, D. (1978) *Ways of the Hand*. Cambridge, MA: Harvard University Press.

Sudnow, D. (1979) *Talk's Body*. New York: Knopf.

Sudnow, D. (1984) *Pilgrim in the Microworld*. New York: Warner Books.

Turner, R. (1970) 'Words, utterances and activities', in J. Douglas (ed.), *Understanding Everyday Life*. Chicago: Aldine. pp. 169–87.

Turner, R. (ed.) (1974) *Ethnomethodology*. Harmondsworth, UK: Penguin.

Wagner, H. (1979) 'Theory of action and sociology of the life-world', *Contemporary Sociology*, 8: 685–7.

Watson, R. (1983) 'The presentation of victim and motive in discourse: the case of police interrogations and interviews', *Victimology*, 8(1–2): 31–52.

Watson, R. (1997) 'Some general reflections on "categorization" and "sequence" in the analysis of conversation', in S. Hester and P. Eglin (eds), *Culture in Action: Studies in Membership Categorization Analysis*. Washington, DC: International Institute for Ethnomethodology and Conversation Analysis & University Press of America. pp. 49–75.

Watson, G. and Seiler, R. M. (eds) (1992) *Talk in Context: Contributions to Ethnomethodology*. London: Sage.

Wieder, D. L. (1971) 'On meaning by rule', in J. Douglas (ed.), *Understanding Everyday Life*. London: Aldine. pp. 107–35.

Wieder, D. L. (1974) *Language and Social Reality*. The Hague: Mouton.

Wieder, D. L. (1999) 'Ethnomethodology, conversation analysis, microanalysis, and the ethnography of speaking (EM–CA–MA–ES): resonances and basic issues', *Research on Language and Social Interaction*, 32(1, 2): 163–71.

Wieder, D. L. (2003) 'When is phenomenology sociological?', in M. Lynch and W. Sharrock (eds.), *Harold Garfinkel*. London: Sage. pp. 129–33. (1st edn, 1977.)

Wikler, L. and Pollner, M. (1985) 'The social construction of unreality: a case study of a family's attribution of competence to a severely retarded child', *Family Process*, 24(2): 241–54.

Wittgenstein, L. (1951) *Philosophical Investigations*. Oxford: Basil Blackwell.

Zimmerman, D. H. (1966) 'Paper work and people work: a study of a public assistance agency'. Unpublished PhD dissertation, UCLA.

Zimmerman, D. H. (1969a) 'Facts as a practical accomplishment', in R. Turner (ed.), *Ethnomethodology*. Harmondsworth, UK: Penguin Education.

Zimmerman, D. H. (1969b) 'Record-keeping and the intake process in a public welfare agency', in S. Wheeler (ed.), *On Record: Files and Dossiers in American life*. Beverly Hills, CA: Sage.

Zimmerman, D. H. (1969c) 'Tasks and troubles: the practical bases of work activities in a public assistance agency', in D. A. Hansen (ed.), *Explorations in Sociology and Counselling*. Boston: Houghton Mifflin.

Zimmerman, D. H. and Pollner, M. (2003) 'The everyday world as phenomenon', in M. Lynch and W. Sharrock (eds), *Harold Garfinkel*. London: Sage. pp. 201–26 (1st edn, 1970.)

Zimmerman, D. H. and Wieder, D. L. (1971) 'Ethnomethodology and the problem of order: comment on Denzin', in J. Douglas (ed.), *Understanding Everyday Life*. London: Routledge and Kegan Paul. pp. 285–98.

10

The Power of Discourse and the Discourse of Power

José Antonio Flores Farfán
and Anna Holzscheiter

10.1 INTRODUCTION

Power is an omnipresent facet of discourse and beyond. That is to say that in all semiotic processes such as (less studied) non-verbal communication there are power expressions. Yet most works that have discussed the relationship of discourse and power vary not only in their (usually implicit) definitions of what these phenomena are but also seldom explicate their particular perspective on power and its relationship to discourse. Regarding the type of relationship each establishes with the other, the intimate link between power and discourse invites a number of reflections, installing a series of open questions in the social sciences (e.g. Wodak, 1989), stemming from different research traditions, including discourse analysis and critical linguistics (Fairclough, 1989), linguistic anthropology (Duranti, 2001), or sociolinguistics (Labov, 1972a). For instance, in the latter tradition, also commonly known as quantitative sociolinguistics, power and discourse are treated as contiguous and interdependent phenomena. Yet more recently their interfaces are stressed as relational, dynamic and complex interactive phenomena (e.g. van Dijk, 1993; Locher, 2004). Most scholars that have faced the question seriously would agree that power constitutes and reproduces discourse, while at the same being shaped and reshaped by discourse itself (e.g. Foucault, 1981; Bourdieu and Wacquant, 1992). In other words, power constitutes and is reproduced via

discourse, and vice versa. Therefore one interesting development regarding the theoretical question of the relationship of power and discourse is the discursive shaping and reshaping of power in discourse production. As we will see, power and discourse cannot be conceived as static phenomena, but as (hopefully!) ever changing constituents of social life in interactive, relational, contextual and constructivist ways (Gumperz, 1982; Fairclough, 1989; Wodak, 1989).

All this suggests that the ecology of power and discourse encompasses a number of complex relationships that analytically and empirically still require finer distinctions and clarifications. The core questions guiding this chapter revolve around this complex interrelation between power and discourse, the way it manifests itself, and the approaches and methods by which it can be studied empirically. We will argue that there are different conceptualizations of the interplay between power and discourse that relate to different levels of discourse and its analysis. On the one hand, discursive power is often understood as the **power of discourses**, i.e. large, historical meaning-structures that shape and 'govern' human interaction. On the other hand, many authors, e.g. those in the tradition of conversation analysis (Drew and Heritage, 1992; Linell, 1998) or discursive psychology (Potter and Wetherell, 1987; Edwards and Potter, 1992; Potter, 2003) study discursive power by looking at concrete and very limited social settings in which a small number of individuals seek to influence each other through communicative interaction (power in discourse). Considering these two perspectives, we will therefore ask:

- How does the naturalization and institutionalization of power occur through discourse?
- How are power and those who exert it legitimized in discourse?
- How does the play of power in discourse produce relationships of domination, coercion and exclusion?
- How do sociolinguistic approaches and models expose the display and workings of power of/in discourse and how do they analyse it?
- How can an analytical model of power and discourse productively incorporate other interacting phenomena such as agency, gender, identity and the like?

After a general discussion of these questions, and after an outline of some of the most influential sociolinguistic approaches to power, we will then go on to illustrate how the discipline of sociolinguistics has worked its way around a number of prominent empirical research areas in which the critical exploration of power relations has helped to uncover the exclusionary force of discourse and its, often, stigmatizing effects on human beings. Finally, we will argue that revisiting the issue of power and discourse also offers the possibility of advancing the sociolinguistic agenda in a number of ways. Academic research represents probably one of the most important forms of institutionalized power through discourse in which specific ways of perceiving, analysing and theorizing about the world and human action dominate and 'govern' disciplines. Elaborating on the critical linguistics approach by Fowler, Fairclough and van Dijk – among others – (Fowler et al., 1979; Fairclough, 1989; van Dijk, 1993) we will show how the discipline of sociolinguistics itself potentially acts as an authoritative, exclusionary ensemble of discourses and social practices that contributes to the 'silencing' of specific research objects, subjects or perspectives.

Illustrations will be presented of brief but crucial discursive instances of power disclosure in the production of research, especially in the area of field linguistics. These illustrations suggest ways to go beyond disciplinary boundaries and develop a holistic approach to the interface of power and discourse. For these purposes, we will primarily call attention to what we find most interesting in the contemporary debate about power and discourse in the social sciences: namely, the role and place of sociolinguistic research in society as a whole. We will take the example of endangered languages as being emblematic of several power differentials which have come to reconfigure the

discipline in the face of the notion of language revitalization (e.g. Tsunoda, 2002) and, more recently, developmental sociolinguistics (Djitév, 2008).

Theories on the relationship between power and discourse

Power is, perhaps, one of the most outstanding, fascinating and complex phenomena studied in the social sciences. The ways in which individual human beings aim to influence and control each other (either in subtle or more direct, offensive ways) or the ways in which social institutions, societal discourses and political authority constrain the behaviour of human beings have always attracted the attention of disciplines such as sociology, political science, psychology, linguistics, media studies or economics. Thus, it is not surprising that in sociolinguistics too, the study of power occupies a central place. Building heavily on the sociological theories of Bourdieu (1977), Habermas (1981), Foucault (1981) or Lukes (1974), this discipline has, over time, developed a whole range of different approaches that aim to translate abstract theory on the interplay between language and power into analytical frameworks for the study of the empirical manifestation of power in social life. Above all, it is the more critical branches of sociolinguistics that have emphasized the role of power in communication and discourse, and their potential exclusionary effects.

Readers of this chapter might be pleased if we formulated a concise definition of power. Alas, power qualifies like few other concepts as an essentially contested concept. There are probably as many power concepts as there are authors writing about power. In general, however, it seems at least possible to distinguish between different understandings of power that relate to differing levels of analysis chosen for the study of social life. On the one hand, power is often seen – in its simplest form – as the capacity of an individual to pursue his or her interest even against the resistance of another person (Dahl, 1957; Weber, 1978). Such a behaviouralist notion of power assumes that power is at play where one human being's interests or will prevail over another's. Related to discourse, such a perspective would, for example, look at the ways in which people seek to dominate others in language exchange and communication, the ways in which individuals attempt to silence others when talking or writing, the manifold ways in which human beings seek to gain control over discourses and to manipulate others using language, or the argumentative moves that people make to convince others that their opinion is right and the other person's wrong. On the other hand, power is also seen as a much more diffuse phenomenon that is embodied in the social structures in which human interaction is integrated. These social structures, for example, in the form of institutions, 'govern' and discipline the interaction of human beings to a certain extent and, as such, act as powerful constraining forces in social life. Put in very simplistic terms, there is a fundamental difference between concepts of power that are located at the level of subjects or agents and those that are located at the level of social structures.

In sociolinguistics, however, discourse has offered itself as an interface that allows us to understand the emergence and effects of power relations through a complex co-constitutive relationship between agents and structures. Discourse is, on the one hand, seen as the most important location for the production of asymmetric relationships of power and, on the other hand, seen as the place where individuals are in a position to renegotiate or even level out relationships of power. Discourses in themselves act as powerful structures of social conventions (meaning-conventions) by limiting the potentially indefinite ways of talking about and perceiving social and material reality. Yet, it is also linguistic interaction which is seen as constantly transforming and challenging dominant perceptions of this social and material reality. Every speech-act, thus, at the same time represents **and** transforms patterns of meaning.

Among the most influential approaches on the intimate relationship between power and discourse that have been seized in sociolinguistic works on power are, without doubt, the writings of Habermas (1981) and Foucault (1981). Their critical thinking has highlighted the linkage between discourse, power and exclusion, albeit from very different angles. The writings of these two authors also reflect the different levels of analysis that an investigation of power in discourse follows: structures of meaning (Foucault) or communicative interaction (Habermas). Foucault's (1981) perspectives on power continue to influence discourse analysis to this day – he sees discourse production as guided by large discursive formations which define what can and what cannot be uttered in a given society at a given historical point in time. Discursive formations are determined by historical formations, and such overarching determinism is of course in principle beyond the individual's conscious will, weakening subjects' possibilities of transforming society. Over time, certain ways of speaking about reality and seeing the world materialize, and slowly generate institutionalized practices that directly affect the lives of individuals in a society. Certain claims and utterances remain 'said' and valid much longer than just for the instant in which they were uttered – their lasting influence on human thought, speech and action becomes manifest in the constant repetition of similar arguments. For Foucault, discourses understood as conglomerates of larger systems of meaning are necessarily powerful in that they 'govern' the everyday lives of subjects (Foucault, 1970, 1984a, 1984b, 1992, 2003).

Yet the question of power and discourse cannot be limited to discursive formations. Individuals potentially have the possibility to interrupt such societal arrangements, basically although not exclusively via discourse (Habermas, 1981). The Habermasian understanding of discourse emphasizes the emancipatory potential of discursive interaction as a place where power relations can be challenged and renegotiated. His theory on communicative action formulates the ideal social setting for such a renegotiation in a counterfactual thought experiment – the ideal-speech situation. By measuring any process of social interaction against the democratic or deliberative standards[1] of this ideal speech-situation it is, according to Habermas, possible to observe and, potentially, rectify or at least contest the power asymmetries that characterize a specific social situation. While a Foucauldian understanding of discourse is, hence, associated with the underlying social conventions (the power **of** discourse) that give meaning to social interaction, the Habermasian concept of discourse relates to the quality of linguistic interaction, to the procedures and social settings that lead to the formulation and re-formulation of these social conventions (the power **in** discourse). Foucault's theory of discourse is often misinterpreted with regard to the possibility of agents (not only 'subjects') consciously confronting, challenging or transforming power in specific settings. Even though his thinking focuses on the powerful role of discourses and narratives in history, he does not deny the potentially transformative and emancipatory role of human beings. In other words, although the existence of discursive formations entails specific dynamics and realms of power microphysics, for Foucault power is constantly (re)defined as resistance to hegemonic forces. However, it is particularly the Habermasian notion of discourse that has become associated with the potential to confront the crude exercise of power in (quasi) argumentative terms (cf. Habermas, 1981).

In Habermas' (1981) theory of communicative action, discourse is understood as an instance that, by its very nature, installs the possibility of communicative universals, to which we all should have access. Yet there are always many ethical dilemmas posed by the exercise of power in discourse in specific fields which tend to block such open possibility. Similar *a priori* universals stem from the Gricean categorical *a priori* postulate of the cooperative principle in conversation, which encompasses maxims such as quality and quantity (Grice, 1975). These idealizations are supposed to operate independently of the power contexts in which conversation always takes place. Such speakers' idealizations are consonant with Habermas' theory of communicative action, in which the individual's intentionality and his or her right to argumentative justification plays an outstanding role in defining what can or cannot be uttered (Ducrot, 1984). In contrast, for Foucault, power depends on *régimes du savoir* as related realms of dominance in communication. In this sense, Foucault understands power as the ways in which human beings are transformed into subjects, as compartmentalized instantiations of, for example, *homo economicus*, *homo academicus* or *homo ludens*. Powerful historical narratives draw lines of differentiation that impose a socially acceptable or inacceptable identity on human beings – dividing the sane from the insane, the normal from the deviant, etc.

While Habermas (1981) and Foucault (1981) have emphasized – although from very different perspectives – the exclusionary dimensions of discourses, a range of sociological theories have highlighted the central effects of (social) institutions on the relative power of individuals in and over discourse. Most important here are Bourdieu's ideas on the linguistic market and symbolic violence, referring to the ways actors internalize and legitimize specific power arrangements (such as boss–secretary, husband–wife, colonizer–colonized, etc.). Symbolic violence is accepted as part of certain *habitus* – a set of socially determined predispositions or preferences for certain linguistic varieties considered more legitimate than others in a linguistic market. Thus, any 'discursive field' (Bourdieu, 1977, 1985) is characterized by expressions of asymmetry in which certain actors are more authoritative in the production of discourses. Of course this approach obliges understanding linguistic competence not as a limited isolated technical capacity, but rather as a highly uneven, stratified materialization of discourse practices which, in turn, pertain to, and at the same time are relatively independent of, specific power arrangements and differentials (Bourdieu and Wacquant, 1992).

Similar to Bourdieu's thinking on the ways in which power relationships are constituted through language and institutionalized in discursive fields, sociological theories on the multi-dimensional character of power have also strongly shaped current sociolinguistic studies on the interplay between power and discourse. The conceptualizations of power of Bachrach and Baratz (1970) and Lukes (1974) are most prominent in this regard.

As a consequence of their multi-dimensional nature, these conceptualizations challenge subject-focused understandings of power as simply the ability to assert one's will against another person's resistance. Even though they differ with regard to which dimensions they see as relevant, these authors point to the central role of institutions in constituting and materializing power relationships between individuals. Bachrach and Baratz (1970) still adhere to two classical presuppositions of behavioural power theory: the supremacy of material resources as power assets and the belief in actors' desire to have their interests fulfilled. However, they point to the importance of observing and analysing the role of institutional barriers or filters that make it difficult if not impossible for minority interests or the interests of the powerless (in the sense that they are 'poor', without material means) to be incorporated into collective decision-making processes. Thus, their two-dimensional understanding of power emphasizes that power analysis has to look beyond intra-personal relations of power and coercion and incorporate the norms and rules that precondition which issues and opinions can be addressed and are considered legitimate in a given social context.

The play of power thus relates not only to the potential to threaten and coerce but also to struggles over institutional design and political and social agendas (Schattschneider 1975: 69; Bachrach and Baratz, 1977: 46). Analytical interest shifts from an identification of **who** is powerful to an investigation of **why** certain actors are better positioned in an institutional framework than others. Hence, what these authors make us aware of is the strong exclusionary dimension of social and political processes and the fact that every decision-making process is based on 'non-decisions' and that no consensus would be possible without shunning those views or voices that greatly threaten this consensus.

Like Bachrach and Baratz (1970), Lukes departs from a perspective on power that focuses on how individuals realize their will against the resistance of others. He stresses the necessity to take into account the influence of 'collective forces and social arrangements' in analysing power relations (Lukes, 1974: 22). Consequently, Lukes introduces his well-known third dimension of power that stresses the critical role of institutional frameworks in determining the relative position of individuals in communicative processes, as well as the selection and exclusion of specific topics, worldviews or modes of speaking. Lukes has paved the way for a perspective on power that accommodates the constraining influence of the situational, contextual framework within which social struggles take place. Despite the fact that

Lukes stops short of addressing the actual communicative processes that take place within powerful institutional frameworks, he grants a decisive position to communicative interaction, the force of speech-acts, the legitimacy of speakers and the 'power of language' in the endeavour to develop alternative conceptualizations of power politics. Here, power is an effect of exclusionary social practices and the limited accessibility of social structures. Most importantly, what both Bachrach and Baratz (1970) and Lukes (1974) have made us aware of is that the most effective workings of power do not find their expression in situations of conflict among individuals, but become particularly obvious in situations in which **no** conflict arises (Lukes, 1974: 23). What the authors discussed here have emphasized in their study of power is the centrality of exclusion as both an effect of power relationships as well as, at times, a precondition for the unchallenged authority of individuals. It is this facet of the power–discourse nexus in particular that has become most prominent in sociolinguistic research on discourse and that constitutes the core of critical thinking in sociolinguistics.

While the authors mentioned above have inspired sociolinguistic thought on the relationship between power and discourse from a pronounced sociological standpoint, influential stimulus has also come from the field of linguistics. Bakhtin's (1981) theory on heteroglossia has also strongly influenced the conceptions of power and discourse in the literature beyond critical linguistics, as manifested for example in linguistic anthropology. This approach allows an understanding of competing voices as part of the multivocality of discourse, manifested for instance in opposing idealized conceptions of linguistic homogeneity or monoglot perspectives on language (Bauman and Briggs, 2003) that prevail in received (not only orthodox formal) linguistic theories. This model allows, and at the same time remits to at times, extremely antagonistic social positions, for instance, exemplified in precisely the existence of received approaches on language, against its everyday use in social interaction in different (e.g. multilingual) settings. Bakhtin (1981) understands language as heterogeneously linked to specific ideologies conceived in a struggle between different power and even individuals' antagonistic relationships as expressed in different voices; of course, this requires a constant reference to **utterances**, not isolated words. This necessarily makes reference to different speakers and previous (con)texts in a flow of intertextuality and interdiscourse, enacting specific social positions with respect to language in society. In this case, speakers are not *porte-paroles* but most of all agents of different conflicting voices in a given text, representing dominant or subordinated voices, linked to power differentials associated with heteroglot language(s), voices that are constantly competing and present in each and every genre (Bakhtin 1973), ranging from everyday to political and of course, as we will suggest, even 'scientific', academic discourse.

In this sense, several approaches in linguistics and its idealizations are good examples of (monolingual) prescriptive ideologies (Silverstein, 1979; Blommaert, 1999), manifested in the presumed homogeneous status of a language. This is evidenced in how several grammatical descriptions ironically resemble an 'idiolectal' or 'private' language, which Jakobson (1976) or Wittgenstein (1988) demonstrated constitute a fiction. Moreover, ideolects are possible as extreme exercises of power linked to linguistic theories in which a power relationship between an 'informant' and the linguist operates, and are expressed in imposed categorizations and methods as interviews (see below) with their communicative hegemonies (Briggs 1983). Categorizations such as 'acceptable' and 'grammatical' expressions are absent of clarification in 'homogeneous' monolingual ideologies. In field linguistics, 'acceptable', 'grammatical', 'correct' forms of a language are connected to purism, which arises as a hypocritical contempt towards the researcher from the side of the speaker. Exacerbated in its written form, the issue of possible degrees of intelligibility also arises here, in which the operation of writing is a way of erasing the oral indigenous form of the language in an enigmatic world (Duranti and Goodwin, 1992). In this connection, access is very limited if at all granted to speakers themselves, a common power operation discursively materialized in (almost) unintelligible varieties from the actors' point of view – not to speak of grammatical terminology.

In practice, similar issues stem from and frequently represent particular and absolutely decontextualized forms of social uses of a language, and are of course linked to fairly unequal power interactions. As an overall effect, linguistic descriptions tend to inhibit and at the same time materialize the variable nature of language in its relation to power and discourse, as an eloquent expression of the direct link between linguistic variability and power. As the example of (e.g. formal) linguistics suggests, selecting one variety against discarding many others constitutes an egregious manifestation of social differentiation linked to hegemonic linguistic ideologies which frequently assert the linguistic purity of an imagined 'standard' code. As we will see, the use of discourse marks a series of hierarchical power structures, materialized in such effects as those produced for instance in elicitation in the linguist 'informant' encounter, differentiated along the lines of several linguistic varieties associated with specific power differentials.

In contrast to the radical assumption of conversational analysis practitioners that society is constituted in verbal interaction itself (which obscures power relationships and treats discourse as independent with regards to more global structures), and although not necessarily using the specific terms power and discourse, several traditions, including that of linguistic anthropology (Bauman and Briggs, 2003) touch upon power and discourse at least indirectly. Linguistic anthropologists analyse cross-discourse practices, that vary cross-culturally, involving, for instance, the violation of presumed universal maxims such as those entailed in Grice's principle of cooperation (1975). Such investigations include among many others Ochs (1988) on Madagascar and Haviland (1997) on Tzotzil (Maya).

In sum, critical social theories on the link between power and discourse have made us aware of two core, underlying assumptions in particular. First, discourse and power are co-constitutive. Discourse is constitutive of power by privileging certain perceptions of (social) reality and excluding others. Societal discourses shape and sustain discriminatory and stigmatizing practices and, as such, bring about 'disorders of discourses' (Wodak, 1996) in which some human beings are muted while the speaking authority of others is naturalized. Power relationships predispose which individuals are in a position to participate in and shape discourses. Secondly, however, discourse is also seen as bearing emancipatory potential, being the place where power and authority might eventually be challenged and resisted. In general, therefore, language and communication as the primary discursive practices are perceived as playing a critical role both in the perpetuation as well as the transformation of powerful discourses. In the following, we will show how empirical sociolinguistic research has sought to exemplify these core assumptions. We have chosen some of the most prominent fields of research in contemporary sociolinguistics, i.e. studies on national identity and racism, social conventions (such as politeness), field linguistics and academic research, in order to show how the discipline of sociolinguistics has approached the interplay between power and discourse.

10.2 POWER IN THE TERRAIN: SOME PROMINENT EMPIRICAL FIELDS

The exploration of the issue of power and discourse includes a wealth of empirical studies which touch upon features such as the status,

authority and variable nature and role of discourse in multiple settings where power is disclosed and the ways in which identities are created through powerful discourses, e.g. gender discourses (see, for example, Tannen, 1990; for a brief review see Gal, 2001). Much empirical research in this field can be classified as 'political' discourse research inasmuch as it investigates how power manifests itself in the discourses sustaining particular political institutions and systems as well as in their formal and informal discursive forums (e.g. Wodak 1989). As it is impossible to fully cover the wealth of empirical investigations that in one way or another deal with the topic at hand, we will only mention some illustrative key cases, ranging from investigations on the expression of racism (cf. van Dijk, 1989, 1993, 2005; Hill, 2001) to politeness as examples of the power of social conventions and, finally, of the power of linguistic research and its methods in shaping identities and 'truths'.

Racism, identity and ideology

The exclusionary, stigmatizing and 'governing' force of discourse has perhaps been most critically and thoroughly studied with regard to racist ideologies and the construction and manipulation of national identities. For instance, van Dijk (1989), while studying the expression of racism in the British press, shows that the link between power and discourse includes a number of different types of interfaces for which consideration is required; these include representational devices that are presented as objective 'facts', as discursively constructed 'truths', which of course stem from ideological 'white' matrices (cf. Hill, 2001) that in turn surface as specific attitudinal representations of the social world. This and several other works on racism (e.g. Reisigl and Wodak, 2001) and its multiple linguistic expressions show how, through ethnic differentiation, elite ideologies pursue transmitting to public opinion, a way of perpetuating the status quo; this might include, for instance, identifying 'blacks' and 'Latinos' (e.g. migrants in the USA, especially Mexicans, Hill, 2001) as deviant, problematic and of course dangerous, violent, lazy, stupid and so on. For these groups, there are frequently specific derogatory terminologies that exist, such as 'greaser' (for more details on this see below). Other recent studies on the discursive expression of racism as social differentiation and exclusion encompass macro and micro structures and their interfaces, exploring the constitution and reproduction of diverse societal arrangements or power differentials linked to discourse and thus power naturalization (e.g. Reisigl and Wodak, 2001, and more recently, van Dijk, 2005).

A good example of how power linked to the expression of White racism against Latinos in the USA, especially Mexicans, as indexicalized in discourse, is presented in the work of Jane H. Hill (2001) on the semiotics of mock languages. Several Spanish terms in US English convey highly pejorative racist overtones, which are expressed in phrases such as *hasta la vista baby* by Schwarzenegger in *Terminator 2*, or *comprende* by Cameron Diaz in *What Happens in Vegas*? while instructing Ashton Kutchner to use the toilet cover. These are all forms of racist indexicality (Ochs, 1988) which encodes covert racist meanings, elevating Whites' superiority and reproducing stereotypical representations of Mexicans as lazy, stupid, corrupt, treacherous and the like. Given their very nature, these indexes are part of the ideologies of power that manifest themselves in everyday interactions.

Other types of studies investigate bilingual **diglossic** conflicts – power and discourse here entail an indigenous tongue shift (Zimmerman, 1992, Hamel, 1988 and Flores Farfán, 2003 on the asymmetrical relationship between Otomí and Spanish). Conflictive diglossia is outstandingly manifested in the high rates of penetration of Spanish over the indigenous tongues, in contrast to the effects of these on Spanish. The colonial language's strong impact at all levels of linguistic analysis (Dorian, 1992) often produces obsolescent forms, stylistic reduction and levelling of paradigms, among others. This is coupled with clear sequels of linguistic insecurity and stereotypes considering indigenous languages to be 'inferior', 'corrupted', etc., ideologies at times interiorized by speakers themselves, reaching the point at which Spanish is becoming the primary tongue of many of these communities, paradoxically producing pretty much stigmatized non-standard versions of the hegemonic language.

In contrast to many of these traditions which focus on the relationship of language and society, although from different perspectives, such as sociolinguistics, linguistic anthropology and discourse analysis, linguistic's conception of language as an idealized uniform system conveys also a political stance which can be systematically criticized as having a close relationship to the emergence of national states, with their monolingual ideologies, in which only one official language is coupled with national identity and state formation. This is of course a power issue that presents a linguistic expression – namely, a monoglotic (idealized) presumed standard language – whose gatekeepers are, precisely, academics. Take as an expression of this hegemony, for example, the fact that this chapter is written in English, and not say in Spanish, not to mention an indigenous tongue or other marginal varieties.

In other words, discursive social differentiation already implies (other) specific power differentials that are linguistically materialized such as the exclusion of certain social groups and their languages in favour of others. Thus, discursive ideological power stances entail a politics of exclusion as an expression of inequality as presented in terms of the space allocated and thus the visibility (or not) granted to speakers of non-standard varieties – not to speak of endangered languages (Bauman and Briggs, 2003).

Examples of how identities are constructed and institutionalized through powerful discourses abound in the literature, even where, as suggested, they are not at times explicitly stated as such. Some of the most interesting examples of the power relationships in and via analysed discourse have been developed in the field of power and gender in which speakers reach unshared perceptions of confronted identities (e.g. Tannen, 1990) and the expression of racism in, for example, mock languages (Hill, 2001) or newspaper rhetoric (Van Dijk, 1993). Let us review another aspect which has permeated the discussion of power and discourse, namely, politeness.

Social conventions, discourse and power: the example of politeness

We pointed to the centrality of institutions in sociolinguistic research on power and discourse earlier, seeing them both as concrete social venues in which power asymmetries can be studied (e.g. a school, a hospital, an office) **and as** social conventions that govern the everyday actions and interactions of individuals. Important studies have highlighted how power can be studied with regard to both of these dimensions of the notion of institution. By using the example of politeness, we will illustrate here how social conventions can be studied through discourse analysis. From a number of studies, we know that direct power confrontations are, in principle, limited by politeness. Although its displays vary across different cultures and, more importantly, its interpretation is open to a relational approach, politeness can be understood as a ritual procedure in which, in different ways, specific cultures mitigate the crude exercise of power, via its dulcification, a sort of masking strategy to keep positive face and not threaten the identity of participants in given interactions. Thus, politeness has first been studied as an index to power and solidarity. Brown and Gilman (1968) studied power differentials expressed in systems of pronouns which imply different types of treatments; the pronouns ranged from the most 'neutral' to honorific ones in specific languages. Brown and Gilman also open the study of the interactive linguistic adjustments between speakers of different dialects in what they conceive as a solidarity strategy, and develop a theory of linguistic accommodation which, nevertheless, should confront specific power arrangements. Yet the classic work on politeness is that of Brown and Levinson (1987) who examine the ways speakers construct positive and avoid negative face, limiting losing ground on imagined or imputed identities in specific settings. This work can be criticized precisely on the grounds of not taking power into consideration, and even from stemming from a Eurocentric viewpoint on discourse, which not only presumes its rational and individual performance but also tends to overstate it. Yet this is probably also its merit, since it can be thought of as an appeal to discourse, much in the way of a right that speakers can exert at any given moment, vindicating the chance of critical thinking. As we have seen, the right to discourse constitutes a strong premise when considering the nature of discourse, which it itself allows, against the crude exercise of power (Habermas, 1981).

Moreover, analogous to the discursive definition of power, another criticism of this work stems from the idea that politeness is framed within specific contexts that are relationally negotiated, and cannot simply be equated to simplistic taken-for-granted dichotomist oppositions such as positive versus negative face, directness versus indirectness, but rather on *hic et nunc* (here and now) interactive negotiations of appropriate or marked behaviour, based on the quest for balance between 'involvement and independence' of the speaker with respect to the hearer (Locher, 2004, *passim*). Such a recent approach conceives of politeness as part of a process in which participants in conversation aim at maintaining basic functions of discourse. These include the referential and the interactional levels, which in practice overlap and are subject to contextual interpretations and negotiations. Such interpretations take place within specific cultural and normative frames against which speakers judge different emergent behaviours as being appropriate or not, positive or negative, marked or unmarked.

All in all, politeness constitutes an intermediate level between communicative universals and direct strategic action or the exercise of power via discourse, inasmuch as it points to specific negotiated identities that should contextually be maintained in order to allow for the 'normal' flow of conversation and interaction.

Sociolinguistic research practice as an instantiation of discursive power

A number of recent works have endeavoured to document the emergence of different coexistent voices in the making of research. Studies have stressed the active negotiation of sociolinguistic identities in research making (Garner et al., 2006) as heteroglossic performances in the realm of social interaction (Hill and Hill, 1986 on Mexicano translinguistics; Duranti and Ochs, 1986 on literacy; Cameron, 1992 on power and method; and Flores Farfán (2005, 2006) on co-authoring as empowerment). A most interesting approach to power and discourse, which is becoming more prominent due to its ethical relevance, relates to the sociolinguistic models that investigate discourse and power trying to raise awareness for issues such as unequal social relations, linguistic discrimination or cultural 'misunderstandings' beyond the academic world (Gumperz, 1982; Philips, 1983; Scollon and Scollon, 2000). Collaborative or advocacy research in sociolinguistics (Cameron, 1992; Milroy and Gordon, 2003) are also present in public anthropology in the USA (Hill, 2001), responsible (Hale, 1992), committed or even peace linguistics (Crystal, 2004), all of which aim for the greater visibility of the agency of actors in the construction of data and their social relevance. Such a stream of sociolinguistic research was developed as early as in the 1970s in studies on the expression of power in interethnic encounters in so-called cultural crosstalk. Take for example South Asian immigrants and British nationals in the workplace or other public spheres (Jupp et al., 1982), or the vindication of non-standard varieties of Black English (Labov, 1972b), the visibility of the power-discourse-nexus in fields such as language and gender (Tannen, 1990), language and education (Crystal, 2004), or language revitalization (Fishman, 1991; Tsunoda, 2002). In all of these areas of research, levelling power relationships between actors has been an important methodological development, summarized here as research co-authoring, conceived as emergent new (power) epistemologies between actors in the social sciences (e.g. Cameron, 1992; Flores Farfán, 2005).

In fact, all contrasting antagonistic traditions in the study of language, as is made clear in, for instance, opposing systems (or structures) of discourse (or use) (e.g. Chomsky, 1957 vs Hymes, 1972), entail a struggle for imposing a (re)configuration of paradigms in the making of research, which of course depend on specific power arrangements and the possibility of interrupting received paradigms via discourse:

> ... language is not a neutral medium that passes freely and easily into the private property of speakers intentions; it is ... overpopulated with the intentions of others. Expropriating it, forcing it to submit to ones own intentions and accents, is a difficult and complicated process (Bakhtin, 1981: 299, quoted in Duranti, 2001: 23).

The power of discourse in society is recognized in a number of works. Consider Goody's discussion of literacy as a step in the development of Western civilization, shifting from oral mythical narratives to rational historical modalities of thought (Duranti, 2001: 27). Yet literacy understood as alphabetical (writing) praxis has been and is still linked to power in society, to perpetuating authority and to access and control of institutional (linguistic or not) resources.

Yet there has been a thoughtful, albeit still incomplete, revision of the ways in which power is determined via discourse and vice versa. Recall that a basic premise is the uneven treatment that different, at times antagonistic, research traditions provide to the relationship between power and discourse. As we have suggested, it is the French philosophical tradition that has inspired more theoretical and empirical studies regarding concepts such as power and discourse, particularly linked to the names of Foucault (1981) and Bourdieu (1977). This is especially reflected in a series of studies in the field of discourse analysis which concentrate on the **written** form of discourse, evoking the sociocultural membership of analysts to a given cultural matrix, a written one (e.g. Foucault, 1981). In contrast, the almost total omission of the concept or even the word power is characteristic of North American sociology, particularly linked to the ethnomethodological tradition, today represented by conversational analysis practitioners such as Sacks, Schegloff and Jefferson (1974), which has also become one nurturing contemporary analytical force at work in anthropological linguistics (Duranti, 2001). The constructive confrontation of these and other traditions seems a productive endeavour, since one probably underestimates and thus obscures what the other emphasizes (for an effort in this sense, see Flores Farfán, 2003).

Let us recover what, in 2003, Flores Farfán called the 'conversational paradox', which draws attention to two outstanding instances of contrasting viewpoints to suggest a discourse analysis model, represented by the names of, for example, Foucault (1981) on the one hand, and, for example, Habermas (1981), on the other. The study attempts to analyse prototypical market interactions in which *Mestizo* (the mainstream population in Mexico and most Latin America) brokers force their goods, verbally and non-verbally, from indigenous people, and it shows that even in these types of extreme exploitative situations, discourse is still an open resource to which, in principle, all human beings should have the right to access. This implies a communicative ethics of discourse that is always confronted by more down-to-earth approaches, or Foucault's microphysics, which is where the deployment of power actually takes place, always confronted by such presumed ontogenetic and philogenetic principles of communication which, after all, warrant or at least virtually allow the possibility of emancipation.

The examples alluded to above illustrate how issues relating to historical or cultural backgrounds, which guide and even to a certain extend determine (or at least influence) discourse production, establish certain limits on what can and cannot be said within a specific context and a specific historical discursive formation (Foucault, 1981; Bourdieu, 1977). Saville Troike (1982: 38) provides several examples, such as the fact that rural Cuban varieties acquired prestige after the revolution, together with a devaluation of the former educated standard, entailing a decline in use of former common religious terminologies and forms of address such as *Dios* or *Jesus mio* (my God), attributed to the introduction of Marxist criticism towards religion.

Another illustration of the close relationship of discourse and power is the relatively recent introduction of gender-neutral language to mark political correctness in the usage of politicians in public discourse in countries such as Mexico. Thus, expressions such as *los niños y las niñas de Mexico* 'the boys and girls of Mexico' and *los hombres y las mujeres de nuestro pais* 'the men and women of our country' have become trendy in the mouths of Mexican politicians.

However, one cannot deny the possibility that not only contingent circumstances but also conscious operations interrupt specific discourse and power arrangements, or even question specific economic, political and ideological formations as a whole. Take as an example the political action and militancy of Greenpeace against global warming, or the assertion of indigenous populations' rights against total assimilation and destruction of their intangible heritage which has produced recent legislation in favour of indigenous people. This is precisely linked not only to the universal right to gain access to discourse but also to the specific possibilities of discourse itself in specific power arrangements, such as the political scenarios of modern states' policies in the face of economic development and indigenous rights. Yet in countries such as Mexico, and even the United States, Greenpeace is weak in terms of its effective possibilities against, for example, ongoing deforestation, versus strong economic interests. This is of course also a power issue that has manifested itself in recent declarations of Greenpeace in Mexico regarding their inability to impact on environmental protection of the country.

From recent approaches to discourse and power, discourse is, and even should be thought of within the framework of critical thinking, to enable individuals to develop critical approaches to different specific contexts, such as academia and political contestation. It is within the tradition of Norman Fairclough and his associates that this endeavour has been made possible in the last couple of decades, especially with regard to the role of academia in society (Fairclough, 1989). As an example, take Labov's (1982) classic critique of a uniform (idealized) homogeneous linguistic system, together with its political consequences regarding the vindication of non-standard varieties, specifically the logic of Black vernacular English conceived of not as an impoverished, but rather as a separate legitimate variety in its own right. Or consider the recent efforts to develop the field of language revitalization linked to ideas on committed or responsible (Hale, 1992) or even preventive linguistics (Crystal, 2004), aimed at reversing language shift (Fishman, 1991), a process which most languages of the world are today experiencing (Crystal, 2000) – all this along the lines of what has been called 'advocacy research' (Cameron, 1992). Yet this is not, of course, the dominant paradigm in linguistic research. Let us take a look at the exercise of power while investigating endangered languages, as the most prominent emergent field in linguistics these days.

The ideologies of power in discourse: language and power in research methods

Another eloquent illustration of ideologies and discourses at work is the field of endangered languages, which turns out to be fairly telling of the politics of power in academia, especially, although of course not exclusively, in the field of linguistics. The very existence of the emergent field of language documentation (Gippert et al., 2006), in and by itself, pinpoints to the reconfiguration of the field of linguistics in terms of its different interests, represented in its extreme poles by the interests of descriptive linguistics, on the one hand, and the interests of the members of the community, on the other. Revisiting the field of language documentation requires a constructive critique in terms of its programme and the agenda in the field of language revitalization, an even more recent attempt to cope with the many dilemmas posed by the question of language endangerment, where other, different voices – apart from those of 'experts' – emerge, especially those of indigenous people. Language revitalization is precisely about (re)balancing power relationships between researchers and, more generally, society and speakers of endangered languages. Thus, the field of language revitalization allows an interruption, of received linguistics approaches. Raising awareness of the power entailed in the making of

research, as manifested in research protocols, observation, documentation, cataloguing, classifying and the like as ways of social control, would allow sociolinguistics to start making more sense of academic work in the face of communities' interests and expectations. In contrast, the predominant approach is still pervasive in the social sciences, as manifested in the use of received methods such as questionnaires and interviews.

The deployment of power in research methods: interviews

Historically, interviews are certainly the best-known example of the exercise of power, not only in academic praxis. In interviews, the structure of the whole interaction is defined by a hierarchical stratification in which a dominant voice, such as the researcher's, actively participates in the definition of, the situation from specific power arrangements (Kress and Fowler, 1979). In Western societies, interviews are a constitutive part of everyday discursive practices and a well-established genre. In these societies and its face-to-face encounters, such as employer–employee in the job industry or teacher–student in university settings, interviews are marked by clear asymmetries, guided by the existence of an authoritative voice which imposes a conversational lead in interaction, defining who speaks first, the interview's thematic structure, its duration, and the like. Kress and Fowler (1979) even formulate the hypothesis that all conversations are, in a way, types of interviews, inasmuch as all conversations present some type of asymmetry. Their examples even examine the reversing of roles between a young interviewer dealing with an experienced politician. Likewise, Hill and Hill (1986) show how Mexicano (Nahuatl) speakers question the dominant voice of the interview, opposing the authoritative role of a respected elder to an adolescent status: all these are power issues.

In contrast, in the case of cross-cultural research, which often involves cultures that are relatively or totally unfamiliar with interviews, the literature alerts us that the asymmetrical structure as materialized in interview practices is evidenced by the imposition of a communicative hegemony, which obscures and even exerts violence on the native meta-communicative competence; in contrast, it highlights the observer's communicative blunders or the 'incompetence of fieldworkers' (Briggs, 1983). In this sense, Briggs (op cit., 24–5) concludes that interviews are of little value in the first stages of fieldwork, and recommends that the researcher positions and presents him/herself as an apprentice of the communicative repertoire of the community in order to, at a later stage, be able to adapt the interview to the native ways of speaking that are characteristic of diverse speech communities. This is something that the agency of speakers themselves exerts, often infiltrating the logic of the interview itself as a counter-power to the imposition of foreign ways of communication, which are generally eyed with suspicion and distrust, and which can even lead to a total block on communication. Moreover, from the point of view of linguistic anthropology, interviews might even be discarded altogether, inasmuch as they distance the researcher from the ethnographic description of communicative competence or an 'emic' point of view. At best, interviews would constitute a complementary strategy for the observation and description of the 'native theory' of communication and the cosmology associated that is of such great interest to the linguistic anthropology investigative agenda.

In turn, in the sociolinguistic paradigm as launched by Labov (1972a, 1972b), interviews have been overwhelmingly used, paradoxically, to obtain samples of 'spontaneous' speech. Sociolinguistic interviews endeavour to obtain discourse not too affected by asymmetrical relationships, a difficulty formulated as the observer's paradox by Labov himself. To overcome the authoritative voice that the interview conveys, techniques include questions allowing interviewees to forget symbolic power represented by the tape recorder: the famous question related to the fear of being dead. Other recent developments productively integrate features of the ethnography of communication, conceiving interviews as speech events to recover local forms of conveying information (the network modules appropriate to speakers themselves and organized as flexible conversational networks in Labov, 1984; Milroy and Gordon, 2003). A recent critique of this paradigm attacks the classical idea that actors are monitoring their speech (represented by a tape recorder) and not so much the (power) identity attached to participants in the interview situation (the idea of audience design in Bell, 1984, 2001).

If the ethical and political dilemmas posed by interviews are indeed linked to a clear discursive deployment of power in face-to-face encounters, the need to develop more culturally-sensitive approaches to the organization of linguistic and cultural diversity entails levelling power relationships developed in the making of research. An interesting effort in this sense, which is meant to have an impact on wider society, has been developed in the work of Jupp, Roberts and Gumperz (1982) with immigrant South Asian populations in London, specifically with Punjabis. As a most revealing investigation of the construction of racism and discrimination, which is based on the interactive unconscious confrontation of different sociolinguistic competences in encounters such as job interviews, the authors describe how different ways of speaking 'crosstalk' each other and how this provides grounds for cultural misunderstanding, the reproduction of stereotypes and, of course, potential interethnic friction (the Gumperz video for the BBC, 1979, precisely entitled *Crosstalk*). For instance, in an interview for a librarian job where a South Asian applicant faces British interviewers, when asked why he had an interest in the particular college, the interviewee follows a common pattern for Punjabis which first offers generalities of his personal desperate situation to find a job (plus his academic qualifications), a reply which shows that, in his culture, honesty is highly valued, while the British expect a specific answer related to the prestige and importance of the institution, even if it is a hypocritical one. Training the actors to become aware of such cultural diverse ways of speech behaviour, including the ways that information is presented differentially in terms of specific cultural-relevant matrices, values and styles, would hopefully allow opening productive power dialogues that could enable participants to reflect positively on ongoing misunderstandings and even 'solve', or at least mitigate, deep-rooted historical interethnic conflicts.

As a representative of a dominant voice in research and its symbolic rituals, the roles and status of participants are admittedly one-sided and defined by the researcher (e.g. Hill and Hill, 1986). Several indexicals materialize authority relations as power differentials. Consider endangered languages as eloquent indexicals of such power: purist presentations of the self trigger hypercorrection and neologisms designed to please the researcher, one of two types of attitudes in interviews identified in the literature. Another interesting example is the emergence of foreign talk (the case of aboriginal Australians, Evans, 2001: 263). In contrast, in a non-cooperative attitude, speakers interrupt asymmetrical relationships imposed by interviews. Such inverse investigation or even contestation suggests interesting quests for the sociolinguistic research agenda (Flores Farfán, 2006). All this suggests that, in field linguistics, received prescriptive ideologies emerge, even creating new varieties of the language which very few people understand, which at times are even published in the form of complete grammars!

10.3 CONCLUDING REMARKS

As suggested, a number of research traditions have, in one way or another, faced the question of power and discourse, although not explicitly stated in such terms: traditions which do not normally communicate with each other, at times even ignoring parallel developments, as has, until recently, mostly been the case between sociolinguistics and linguistic anthropology (for a discussion see Duranti, 2001). This is of course an example of how epistemological rearrangements related to social facts can have an impact on the reconfiguration of the research agenda in linguistic anthropology and sociolinguistics agenda, favoring cross-fertilization (Duranti, 2001: 19–20). Parallel to these works, in the tradition of textual linguistics, discourse analysis and of course critical linguistics (Fairclough 1989; van Dijk, 1993) seek to bring together macro and micro levels in the investigation of the power-discourse-nexus. Such approaches show the ways in which power shapes and reshapes the uses of discourse as manifested in specific discourses and linguistic varieties such as hegemonic political discourse in the press.

As power is discourse and discourse is the ultimate expression of power, so discourse analysis is confronted with the multimodalities of its expression in, for example, grammatical, illocutionary and complex communicative forces and specific encounters. Yet, from our point of view, discourse analysis should really be about challenging received models and inviting a reorientation of academic practice to critical thinking, along the lines of critical linguistics (Fairclough, 1989). This can be done on the basis of recovering schemes from such scholars as Bourdieu (1977, 1985) who suggest a critique of the commodification, reification and technologization of discourse in areas such as linguistics. It can be done, as Fairclough (1989: 6) suggests, by revisiting schools as spaces for argumentation and critical thinking to invite effective ways of favouring dialogue, or through what is termed 'peace linguistics' (Crystal, 2004). This approach does not rely on the referential function of language, but rather on its communicative and affective base, onto- and philogenetically speaking, and instantiates differences as an expression of linguistic and cultural diversity and heterogeneity. Of course these cannot be reduced to simple technical skills. Discourse is not an instantiation of received models and for this reason education cannot be viewed as, exclusively, a transmission of skills. The question of what counts as knowledge is contested to produce new knowledge and this is dependent on power instantiations of science. One brief example is the practice of field linguistics. Some of the most interesting analyses which revolve around the relationship of power and discourse in the making of research stem from the development of 'advocacy' research in linguistics and anthropology which interrupts previous conceptualizations and reminds us that the workings of power in discourse are present in our own work, inviting us to rethink new power epistemologies such as critical thinking.

As suggested, it seems reasonable to plead for more integrated relational and contextual approaches to these and other theoretical issues for a better comprehension of the layers of power involved in discourse production, suggesting a dialectical focus on the complex relationship of power and discourse. Therefore, at least two levels are present in the production of discourse: the contexts of power differentials that historically define specific societal arrangements, versus the presumed ontogenetic, universal counter-facts of communication, instances which are constantly confronted in actual discourse praxis. In other words, a more realistic or ecological approach to power and discourse will not reduce the question to one of these specific aspects, but would allow a much more complex view on the issue, incorporating both perspectives on the ecology of power and its co-constitutive relationship with discourse.

NOTE

1 Bächtiger et al. (2004), for example, have developed what they call the 'discourse quality index' (DQI), which allows for quantitative assessment of the deliberative quality of political debates.

REFERENCES

Bachrach, P. and Baratz, M. S. (1970) *Power and Poverty. Theory and Practice.* New York: Oxford University Press.

Bachrach, P. and Baratz, M. S. (1977) *Macht und Armut.* Frankfurt am Main: Suhrkamp.

Bächtiger, A., Spörndli, M., Steenbergen, M. R. and Steiner, J. (2004) 'The study of deliberation in real world politics: the deliberative dimensions of legislatures and sketches of a future research agenda', paper presented at the 2004 Conference 'Empirical Approaches to Deliberative Politics', Florence, European University Institute.

Bakhtin, M. (1973) *Problems of Dostoevsky's poetics.* Ann Arbor, MI: Ardis.

Bakhtin, M. (1981) *The Dialogic Imagination.* Tr. C. Emerson and M. Holquist. Austin, TX: University of Texas Press.

Bauman, R. and Briggs, C. L. (2003) *Voices of Modernity.* Cambridge: Cambridge University Press.

Bell, A. (1984) 'Language style as audience design', *Language in Society,* 13(2): 145–204.

Bell, A. (2001) 'Back in style: reworking the audience design', in P. Eckert and J. Rickford (eds), *Style and Sociolinguistic Variation.* Cambridge: Cambridge University Press. pp. 139–69.

Blommaert, J. (1999) *Language Ideological Debates*. Berlin: Mouton de Gruyter.

Bourdieu, P. (1977) *Outline of a Theory of Practice*. Tr. R. Nice. Cambridge: Cambridge University Press.

Bourdieu, P. (1985) *Distinction*. Cambridge: Cambridge, MA: MIT Press.

Bourdieu, P. and Wacquant, L. (1992) *An Invitation to Reflexive Sociology*. Chicago: University of Chicago Press.

Briggs, C. L. (1983) 'Learning how to ask', *Language in Society*, 13(1): 1–27.

Brown, R. and Gilman, A. (1968) 'The pronouns of power and solidarity', in J. Fishman (ed.), *Readings in the Sociology of Language*. The Hague: Mouton. pp. 252–75.

Brown, P. and Levinson, S. (1987) *Politeness*. Cambridge: Cambridge University Press.

Cameron, D. (1992) *Researching Language: Issues of Power and Method*. London: Routledge.

Chomsky, N. (1957) *Syntactic Structures*. The Hague: Mouton.

Crystal, D. (2000) *Language Death*. Cambridge: Cambridge University Press.

Crystal, D. (2004) 'Creating a world of languages'. Online version: http://www.linguapax.org/congres04/pdf/crystal.pdf

Dahl, R. (1957) 'The concept of power', *Behavioural Science*, 2: 201–15.

Djitév, P. (2008) *The Sociolinguistics of Development in Africa*. London: Multilingual Matters.

Dorian, N. C. (1992) *Investigating Obsolescence: Studies in Language Contraction and Death*. Cambridge: Cambridge University Press.

Drew, P. and Heritage, J. (1992) 'Analyzing talk at work', in P. Drew and J. Heritage (eds), *Talk at Work*. Cambridge: Cambridge University Press. pp. 3–65.

Ducrot, O. (1984) *El decir y lo dicho*. Buenos Aires: Hachette.

Duranti, A. (2001) *Linguistic Anthropology*. Cambridge: Cambridge University Press.

Duranti, A. and Goodwin, C. (eds) (1992) *Rethinking Context: Language as Interactive Phenomenon*. Cambridge: Cambridge University Press.

Duranti, A. and Ochs, E. (1986) 'Literacy instruction in a Samoan village', in B. B. Schieffelin and P. Gilmore (eds), *Acquisition of Literacy: Ethnographic Perspectives*. Norwood, NJ: Ablex. pp. 213–32.

Edwards, D. and Potter, J. (1992) *Discursive Psychology*. London: Sage.

Evans, N. (2001) 'The last speaker is death: long live the last speaker!', in P. Newman and M. Ratliff (eds), *Linguistic Fieldwork*. Cambridge: Cambridge University Press. pp. 250–81.

Fairclough, N. (1989) *Language and Power*. London: Longman.

Fishman, J. (1991) *Reversing Language Shift*. Clevedon, UK: Multilingual Matters.

Flores Farfán, J. A. (2003) 'Al fin que ya los cueros no van a correr: the pragmatics of power in Hñahñu (Otomi) markets', *Language in Society*, 32: 629–58.

Flores Farfán, J. A. (2005) 'Intervention in indigenous education. Culturally-sensitive materials for bilingual Nahuatl speakers', in M. Hidalgo (ed.), *Mexican Indigenous Languages at the Dawn of the 21st Century*. Berlin: Mouton de Gruyter. pp. 301–23.

Flores Farfán, J. A. (2006) 'Who studies whom and who benefits from sociolinguistic research?', *Journal of Multilingual and Multicultural Development*, 27(1): 79–86.

Foucault, M. (1970) *The Order of Things*. London: Tavistock.

Foucault, M. (1981) *Un diálogo sobre el poder*. Madrid: Alianza Editorial.

Foucault, M. (1984a) 'Docile bodies', in P. Rabinow (ed.), *The Foucault Reader*. Harmondsworth: Penguin. pp. 179–87.

Foucault, M. (1984b) 'The repressive hypothesis', in P. Rabinow (ed.), *The Foucault Reader*. Harmondsworth: Penguin. pp. 301–29.

Foucault, M. (1992) 'Die Anreizung zu Diskursen', in M. Foucault (ed.), *Sexualität und Wahrheit. Bd. I.* Frankfurt am Main: Suhrkamp. pp. 27–49.

Foucault, M. (2003) *Die Ordnung des Diskurses*. Frankfurt am Main: Fischer.

Fowler, R., Hodge, R., Kress, G. and Trew, T. (1979) *Language and Control*. London: Routledge.

Gal, S. (2001) 'Language, gender and power', in A. Duranti (ed.), *Linguistic Anthropology*. Oxford: Blackwell. pp. 421–30.

Garner, M., Raschka, C. and Sercombe, P. (2006) 'Sociolinguistic minorities, research, and social relationships', in P. Sercombe, M. Garner and C. Raschka (eds), *Sociolinguistic Research – Who Wins? Research on, with or for Speakers of Minority Languages, Journal of Multilingual and Multicultural Development*, 27(1): 61–78.

Gippert, J., Himmelmann, N. P. and Mosel, U. (eds) (2006) *Essentials of Language Documentation*. Berlin: Mouton de Gruyter.

Grice, P. H. (1975) 'Logic and conversation', in P. Cole and J. L. Morgan (eds), *Syntax and Semantics 3, speech acts*. New York: Academic Press. pp. 41–58.

Gumperz, J. (1979) *Crosstalk*. Video for the BBC, London. London: Communication Documentary Series Broadcast on the BBC.

Gumperz, J. (1982) (ed.) *Language and Social Identity*. Cambridge: Cambridge University Press.

Habermas, J. (1981) *Theorie des Kommunikativen Handels*. Frankfurt am Main: Verlag.

Hale, K. (1992) 'Endangered languages', *Language*, 68(1): 1–3.

Hamel, R. E. (1988) *Sprachenkonflikt und Sprachverdrängung. Die zweisprachige Kommunikations-praxis der Otomí-Indianer in Mexico*. Frankfurt: Verlag Peter Lang.

Haviland, J. B. (1997) 'Shouts, shrieks, and shots: unruly political conversations in indigenous Chiapas', *Pragmatics*, 7(4): 547–73.

Hill, J. H. (2001) 'Language, race and White public space', in A. Duranti (ed.), *Linguistic Anthropology*. Oxford: Blackwell. pp. 451–64.

Hill, J. H. and Hill, K. (1986) *Speaking Mexicano. Dynamics of Syncretic Language in Central Mexico*. Tucson, AZ: The University of Arizona Press.

Hymes, D. (1972) 'On communicative competence', in J. P. Pride and J. Holmes (eds), *Sociolinguistics*. Harmondsworth: Penguin. pp. 269–85.

Jakobson, R. (1976) *Nuevos ensayos de lingüística general*. México: Siglo Veintiuno.

Jupp, T. C., Roberts, C. and Cook-Gumperz, J. (1982) 'The hidden process', in J. Gumperz (ed.), *Language and Social Identity*. Cambridge: Cambridge University Press. pp. 232–56.

Kress, G. and Fowler, R. (1979) 'Interviews', in R. Fowler et al. (eds), *Language and Control*. London: Routledge and Kegan. pp. 63–80.

Labov, W. (1972a) *Sociolinguistic Patterns*. Philadelphia: University of Pennsylvania Press.

Labov, W. (1972b) *Language in the Inner City*. Philadelphia: University of Pennsylvania Press.

Labov, W. (1982) 'Objectivity and commitment in linguistic science', *Language in Society*, 11: 165–201.

Labov, W. (1984) 'Field methods of the project on linguistic change and variation', in J. Baugh and J. Scherzer (eds), *Language in Use: Readings in Sociolinguistics*. Englewood Cliffs, NJ: Prentice Hall. pp. 28–66.

Linell, P. (1998) *Approaching Dialogue. Talk, Interaction and Contexts in Dialogical Perspectives*. Amsterdam: John Benjamins.

Locher, Miriam A. (2004) *Power and Politeness in Action. Disagreements in Oral Communication*. Berlin: Mouton de Gruyter.

Lukes, S. (1974) *Power: A Radical View*. London: MacMillan.

Milroy, L. and Gordon, M. (2003) *Sociolinguistics. Method and Interpretation*. London: Blackwell.

Ochs, E. (1988) *Culture and Language Development. Language Acquisition and Language Socialization in a Samoan Village*. Cambridge: Cambridge University Press.

Philips, S. U. (1983) *The Invisible Culture. Communication in Classroom and on the Warm Springs Indian Reservation*. New York: Longman.

Potter, J. (2003) 'Discursive psychology: between method and paradigm', *Discourse and Society*, 14(6): 783–4.

Potter, J. and Wetherell, M. (1987) *Discourse and Social Psychology. Beyond Attitudes and Behaviour*. London: Sage.

Reisigl, M. and Wodak, R. (2001) *Discourse and Discrimination: Rhetorics of Racism and Anti-Semitism*. London: Blackwell.

Sacks, H., Schegloff, E. and Jefferson, G. (1974) 'A simplest systematics for the organization of turn taking in conversation', *Language*, 50: 696–735.

Saville Troike, M. (1982) *The Ethnography of Communication*. Oxford: Basil Blackwell.

Schattschneider, E. E. (1975) *The Semisovereign People*. Hinsdale, IL: Dryden Press.

Scollon, R., and Scollon, S. B. K. (2000) *Intercultural Communication: A Discourse Approach*. 2nd edn. Oxford: Blackwell.

Silverstein, M. (1979) 'Language structure and linguistic ideology', *Proceedings of the 15th Annual Meeting of the Chicago Linguistic Society*, 2: 193–247.

Tannen, D. (1990) *You Just Don't Understand: Talk Between the Sexes*. New York: Morrow.

Tsunoda, T. (2002) *Language Revitalization and Endangerment*. Berlin: Mouton de Gruyter.

van Dijk, T. A. (1989) 'Mediating racism. The role of the media in the reproduction of racism', in R. Wodak (ed.), *Language, Power and Ideology*. Amsterdam: John Benjamins. pp. 192–226.

van Dijk, T. A. (1993) 'Principles of critical discourse analysis', *Discourse and Society*, 4(2): 249–83.

van Dijk, T. A. (2005) *Racism and Discourse in Spain and Latin America. Discourse Approaches to Politics, Society, and Culture*. Vol. 14. Amsterdam: John Benjamins.

Weber, M. (1978) *Economy and Society*. Berkeley, CA: University of California Press.

Wittgenstein, L. (1988) *Investigaciones filosóficas*. Tr. A. García Suárez, and C. U. Moulines. México: Instituto de Investigaciones Filosóficas, Universidad Autónoma de México.

Wodak, R. (ed.) (1989) *Language, Power and Ideology*. Amsterdam: John Benjamins.

Wodak, R. (1996) *Disorders of Discourse*. London: Longman.

Zimmermann, K. (1992) *Sprachkontakt, ethnische Identität und Identitätsbeschädigung. Aspekte der Assimilation der Otomí-Indianer an die hispanophone mexikanischeKultur*. Frankfurt am Main: Vervuert.

11

Globalization Theory and Migration

Stef Slembrouck

11.1 INTRODUCTION

This chapter engages with theories of globalization
and migration through the lens of sociolinguistic
inquiry. Globalization processes tend to be commonly talked about, sometimes celebrated and
often contested, in terms of accelerated geographical reorderings in the fields of economic production, in money flows and technological spread.
This chapter, however, asserts the centrality of
language and symbolic practices and it does so by
attending to one salient aspect of contemporary
globalization processes, namely migration, while
discussing implications for sociolinguistics. Two
further introductory points deserve mention and
help set the scope of discussion. Contemporary
forms of migration are nowadays understood as a
dimension of globalization processes, but it is
worth reminding ourselves that the study of
migration is in fact a much older theme, both in
social and economic studies and in sociolinguistic
enquiry. In more than one respect, the theme of
migration predates the present burgeoning of
empirical and theoretical interest in boundary-
crossing processes, which are looked at through
the lens of globalization phenomena (e.g. Thomas
and Znaniecki, 1918, a pioneering work in the
biographic approach to the sociology of migration). My second point therefore entails an historical horizon: to connect the present concern
with, for instance, heightened multilingualism,
which has resulted from an unrivalled increase in
contemporary human movement around the world,
with earlier historical linguistic and sociolinguistic understandings of migration-connected

language developments which concentrated on
the genesis of historically-recognized languages,
language families and functional varieties, often
in a context of imperialist expansion and colonial
settlement.

11.2 GLOBALIZATION AND THE LINGUISTIC CULTURAL TURN IN LATE MODERNITY

To talk and write about 'globalization' as a process
of accelerated transformation of local and regional
phenomena into 'global' ones raises both the
question of its 'naturalized' upper limit (phenomena that would truly cover the globe in its entirety)
and its lower threshold (the extent to which phenomena can no longer be exclusively understood
in 'local' terms or – perhaps more prominently –
escape the category and unit of the 'nation-state',
which for quite some time has dominated the way
in which sociopolitical and economic spaces have
been inventorized, measured and regulated). The
latter originated in the long-held assumption that
societies would be coterminous with nation-states.
Discussions about the upper limit of globalization
are mostly invested with an idealized perspective.
This is evident from the opposing teleologies of
either a completely deregulated world economy or
one driven by worldwide solidarity. Therefore, the
stricter answer to the question (when it is posed
from the 'global' end) is probably that we do not
(as yet) inhabit a globalized world and it remains
to be seen whether we ever will. As far as the

lower threshold is concerned, one can conversely state the progressive evaporation of a sense of self-sufficient bounded locality (and, with it, the unit of the nation-state) in a range of transnational processes. One must add immediately here that what marks the present era as one of globalization is more a matter of degree, intensity and acceleration in social geographic complexity than that it would be possible to clearly identify an earlier era as pre-globalization (cf. Robertson's 1990 use of the term 'glocalization' to stress the tailoring effects of local conditions which interact with global flows). Globalization has been advocated as progress and advancement; it has also been denounced for its disruptive, de-authenticating and hegemonic effects. Boundary-crossing contact is probably as old as organized humanity itself, but this does not detract from the fact that the positing of the 'transnational' of course presumes the existence of geopolitical units that can be understood as nation-states, in itself a construction of modernity. Moreover, understandings of contemporary geographical orderings in terms of a dynamics of neatly-nested spatial units prove insufficient, as the nation-state has by now been widely observed as being bypassed from two ends. This is captured in Lash and Urry's (1994: 279) two-sided formulation that 'contemporary nation states are now too small for the big problems of contemporary social life and too big for the small problems'. See also Swyngedouw (1996), and Persson and Stråth (2007), on the hollowing out of the functions of the nation-state by supranational and subnational forms of organization that compete with it, in the case of Swyngedouw (1996) with particular reference to economic collapse and industrial conflict within the European Union (EU). Bypassing the state cannot however be equated with its erasure. Especially when one turns to migration, it must be observed how the state and its typical sectoral divisions into fields (e.g. health, education, law, politics, etc.) continue to function as major channels for official policy, research funding, and publically-regulated responses to migration.

Different but related understandings of globalization phenomena have prioritized: (i) the agentive role of people in transnational 'networks of exchange'; (ii) the spread of goods, services and social categories such as labour, money, etc., via exchange relationships which are often captured conceptually as 'flows' (Appadurai, 1996); as well as (iii) resultant geographical demarcations of scope, distribution, circulation and uptake which are posited through the concept of '–scapes' (Appadurai 1990) – a metaphorical use which originates in the term *landscape*. Appadurai distinguishes five different types of 'scapes', depending on the content that has a particular

distribution (ethnoscapes, financescapes, technoscapes, mediascapes and ideoscapes; the category of ideoscapes particularly includes the international spread of an European–American master narrative of capitalist democracy around which political cultures are organized). Appadurai also notes multi-centredness and increasing disjunction between the 'scapes' of different spheres. The underlying emphasis is on constructedness, including how a 'scape' is always invested with viewpoint, and the bigger challenge here is indeed one of sustained cartographic effort. Thus, as a first example: throughout the 1990s, the US–Swedish-owned television station VT4 was cable-transmitted throughout Flanders and broadcast in Dutch only (using subtitles for imported material); its television studios were situated near Brussels; yet, as the television station's corporate seat was registered in Britain and the station was answerable to British courts of law, it succeeded in circumventing Flemish restrictions on the broadcasting of commercials during children's programmes that would 'normally' apply to it (compare with Triandafyllidou et al., 2009 on the European media space).

In facing the challenges posed by globalization, historians, geographers and linguists, etc., have mostly (some would argue: inevitably) embraced a cultural turn, as it is difficult to separate our specific understandings of the contemporary era of globalization from other significant sociocultural shifts which originate in the latter half of the twentieth century: e.g. post-Fordist information economy (Bryson et al., 2000), risk society (Beck, 1992), reflexive late modern subjectivity (Giddens, 1991), etc., to name just three of these. Thus, accounts of deterritorialized finance and economy remain partial unless one also engages with the ways in which these are premised on particular culturalized communicative practices, as indeed is captured in the title of Lash and Urry (1994), *Economies of Signs and Space*. Similarly, a discussion of 'risk society' (in short: modern society is driven by its responses to particular types of risk which are intrinsic to modernization itself) will be at the heart of any analysis of durable economic, climatological and ecological development. Compare also with Giddens (2006) who anchors a proposed redefinition of the European 'social model' of the welfare state in the recognition of key shifts in sociocultural values.

Not surprisingly then, globalization has also been understood in more processual terms. For instance, 'space/time-compression' (Harvey, 1990) is a term used to describe the condition of (near-)simultaneity despite physical distance. It refers to the diminished importance of distance during a given historical moment – both the shortening of time and the shrinking of space.

The analytical imperatives that follow from it include the manifold complexities and incongruities that follow from resultant co-temporalities. A related concept is that of 'space/time-distanciation' (Giddens, 1984, 1990), which refers to the interlacing of social relations at a distance with local contextualities. Such relations are increasingly stretched across greater distances. For Giddens, social life is ordered across space and time. The problematic of 'space/time-distanciation' denotes a historical trajectory in the evolution of societies and it is central to understanding both globalization and late modernity: the increase in opportunity for human control that comes with space/time-distanciation is matched by a corresponding increase in the relevance of larger-scale challenges (see: Callinicos, 1985; and Lash and Urry, 1994: 230ff. for a critical assessment). As Fairclough (2006: 94ff.) stresses, space-time distanciation brings out the intimate ties between mediated meaning-making and power.

Finally, globalization has also been understood in terms of determinate relationships of inequality. The categories of 'core', 'periphery' and 'semi-periphery' as developed in world-systems analysis (Wallerstein, 2004) here appear as yardstick concepts of cultural-geographic proximity and distance. Inequality through dependency has been noted in relations of a global scope (e.g. inter- and intracontinental North/South-relations, or within smaller-scale units, e.g. a sharpened contrast between urban and rural spaces). In the latter example, the set of contrasts has entailed (again quoting Lash and Urry, 1994: 28) that the urban spaces, being information-soaked, service-rich and heavily-networked, come closer to inhabiting the highly 'wired villages of non-contiguous communities' which by one definition would be called cosmopolitan and globalized. One must also immediately add here the ways in which such relations are being replayed in dislocated contrasts which involve diaspora and migration. Think for instance of the state-organized migration of the 1960s which resulted in large sections of a rural Anatolian population in Turkey ending up in the urban periphery of cities such as Essen, Ghent, Rotterdam, etc.; or consider an example at the scale of particular institutions, e.g. how doctors with Third-World degrees find themselves employed in the pharmacy of a Brussels hospital and are occasionally called into the wards to act as interpreters during medical encounters with patients who share their first language (Collins and Slembrouck, 2009: 35–6). Coe and Yeung's (2001: 368) observations in the context of economic globalization can be extended to attendant sociolinguistic processes: globalization 'is not spatially homogenizing, but instead depends upon, and contributes to uneven geographic development

at different scales'. The same is true of increases in space-time distanciation. However, at the same time, the constructedness of these processes, including their potentially being encouraged, embraced, appropriated or resisted, does not come with an immutable inevitability, as globalization entails 'a set of complex and conflicting tendencies, the outcomes of which cannot be predicted *a priori'*.

Central to sociolinguistic enquiry here are questions of the (often simultaneous but divergent) representations of (trans-)locality, as spatialized and as inserted in time, and as struggled-over realities of person, place, group, object, etc. This has been the subject of much sociological enquiry, e.g. Fenton and Bradley's (2002) study of the role of economic action in the articulation of co-occurring ethnic identities, while sociolinguistic research has focused on representations of both élite and ordinary actors, representations distributed along mass media and high-tech channels or expressed in the secluded space of face-to-face encounters (e.g. Baynham and De Fina (2005) on experiential narratives of displacement and relocation; Delanty et al. (2008) on the cultural resources, framing devices and repertoires of justification articulated in racial exclusion; Caldas-Coulthard and Iedema's (2008) on the effects of failure and uncertainty in people's constructions of identity when they face change in diverse border-crossing contexts, including migration and asylum). The study of such representations and their circulation dynamics is however best not divorced from an analysis of sociolinguistic resources, understood in the widest sense possible: languages, registers, discourse formats, interactional set-ups, etc., which, in their own right, are often subject to (trans)local processes of recontextualization – appropriation, shift and transformation. In this, purchase in mobility and articulation at a higher scale are often at stake (cf. Haarstad and Fløysand, 2007 on 'scale jumping' and empowerment). Here are two fairly rudimentary examples of 'national' articulation which attend to their reception at a higher scale and the role which sociolinguistic choices play in these: the ANC's (African National Congress) choice for an anglophone articulation of the category *Black* (rather than 'non-racial' or 'non-white', see Howarth, 2000: 106) was both a unifying factor in South Africa's struggle against apartheid and a tactical choice which facilitated uptake in news media around the world and in world political forums such as the UN. This can be contrasted in the post-apartheid era with, for instance, the reconciliatory philosophy of *Ubuntu* (a mobilizing category borrowed from Nguni) which, since 1994, has been frequently invoked as a specifically pan-African and racially-inclusive approach to defining one's humanity through that of others (cf. in Zulu, 'Umuntu Ngumuntu Ngabantu' means that 'a person is a person through other persons'). As Haarstad and Fløysand (2007: 289) point out, 'it it is necessary to probe deeper into the power relationships that are produced by the restructuring of relationships in time and space'. Let me now turn to migration.

11.3 MIGRATION, COLONIALISM AND THE FORMATION OF LINGUISTIC RESOURCES

Migration, then, specifically brings out the aspect of human movement. It is an old theme – traditionally discussed in relation to tribally-organized collectivities (e.g. Germanic migration within Europe in the first centuries; large-scale Bantu migration across Southern Africa from the fourteenth century onwards), or in terms of colonial settlement which accompanied trade missions and military campaigns (e.g. Roman settlement across Europe or successive waves of European settlement in North America). The impact of such migrations on the formation of 'languages' as durable effects of sustained language contact is one theme within historical linguistics, e.g. substratal effects (Bynon, 1997: 252ff.) of local Germanic vernaculars on the language use of the Roman colonizers which underpin the transition from Latin to French (see also: Lass, 1997; Campbell, 1998). It has also been a theme within sociolinguistics: pidginization and creolization are typically associated with the colonization of the New World by European-based powers (Thomason and Kaufman, 1998 is a key reference in this area). Specific concepts and terminology thus reflect an interest in specific periods in history, though research, even where change has been presented as 'contact-induced' (Kaufman, 2003), has not necessarily been couched in an analysis of lived experiences of migration, while the distinction between 'creoles' and 'languages' has been challenged both on theoretical and empirical grounds (e.g. Ansaldo and Matthews, 2001).

What marks the current era of globalization as different is, first of all, the unprecedented surge in human movement around the globe (refugees, displaced persons, migrants), mostly in the form of selective or collective responses to economic deprivation, war and conflict, political prosecution and genocide. This is the migration of the 'have-nots' in search of a better or safer life elsewhere, often, though not exclusively, moving from relative '(semi)-periphery' to the 'core'. Note that what counts as 'centre' and 'margin' will be highly circumstantial and invites sophisticated and

layered readings of 'difference'. Secondly, there are the increasing flows around the world of a whole range of 'haves' who, in various functional modalities, spend time away from base localities because they can afford to do so, either travelling as tourists or as members of specific professional, occupational and retirement communities. Students can be found in both categories. The theme of migration invites inquiries into the positioning of groups in transformed labour relations (e.g. Lamont, 2000) and a second important area of attention is of course that of minority rights, especially in relation to the institutional domains of the welfare state (e.g. Kymlicka, 1995, 2001). Experiences of migration are often continual or recursive processes (more than just one-way experiences), and may involve continued contact with, even physical movement between, contexts of ancestry and current residence (Basch et al., 1994; Sassen, 1999; e.g. Galasin´ski and Galasin´ska, 2007 and Galasin´ska and Koslowska, 2009 for sociolinguistic enquiries into how immigrants makes sense of evolving 'parallel' worlds; e.g. Budach, 2009 for how this may be tied up with the transnational exchange of commodities; e.g. Valentine et al., 2009 for the effects of subsequent moves in a migration trajectory on functional distribution within specific sociolinguistic repertoires).

Typically, effects on the language use of individuals (as part of collectivities) is, in this area of inquiry, talked about in terms of 'linguistic fate', one of language maintenance – e.g. through heritage language programmes, language adaptation, shift, death or loss, patterns of code selection, code-switching and style shifting as discernible processes of (emergent) language change in successive generations who are born in/outside the host country (Saville-Troike, 2003: 201ff.; see McConnell, 1997: 353ff on the structural variables of 'status', 'demography' and 'institutional support' which affect ethnolinguistic vitality). Three comments must be added here immediately:

1   The theme of language maintenance/loss brings together postcolonial contexts (in which the hegemony of the colonizer's language is asserted) with contexts of migration (in which the migrant community's language encounters a local language which is established throughout the social spheres). Language dominance is probably a common factor. Note that some national contexts have both, e.g. the USA or New Zealand.

2   Language contact must also be put in the context of 'return'. 'Return' here can mean 'in person' – when returning for a shorter or longer period of time (e.g. Zentella, 2003). This may come with a focus on 'second languages' (e.g. Taura, 2008 on the retention/loss of English by returnees in a Japanese context). Return is also to be

interpreted 'symbolically', often in processes of language learning and use which continue to assert the prestige of a collective language of ancestry (e.g. Heller (2003) on Franco-Ontarians for whom French-French plays a major role in the regulation of access to international jobs and Kirkpatrick (2007: 106ff.) who notes continued expectations of British RP for contemporary newsreaders in South Africa).

3   In addition, studies of migration have unprecedentedly resulted in the thematization of the social indexicalities and language ideological aspects of valuations which cluster around various forms of code-switching, mixings, stylizations, crossings, lingua franca uses and ethnicized accents (e.g. Rampton, 1995; Auer, 2007).

However, we still need to ask how the linguistic resources of individuals, resources we can see being used in actual interaction, can, be projected to the level of language communities, in view of pronouncements about the long-term directions in which linguistic resources develop (see below for a further discussion). In addition, we must ask what else is needed to come to terms with the complexities of language practice in contexts of contemporary migration. Set against the wider interest in globalization processes outlined in the previous section, the relationship between language and migration has, in some respects, been modelled further by drawing beneficially on the wide range of interests developed in various niches of linguistic and sociolinguistic enquiry and the specific contributions which these niches can make to studies of globalization and migration.

11.4 AN ON-THE-GROUND ANALYSIS OF MIGRANT-RELATED SOCIOLINGUISTIC DIVERSITY

Globalization and contemporary migration have pushed sociolinguistic researchers to question some of the received boundaries of their discipline, as it has become difficult to 'do' sociolinguistics without taking on board some of the key themes of, just to name four 'disciplines' here: translation studies, language learning and education, analysis of institutional and professional discourses, and literacy studies. The challenge also applies conversely.

Globalization and contemporary forms of migration have resulted in an exponential growth in translation and interpreting (Cronin, 2003) – up to a point where analyses of medical consultations or, more generally, social welfare encounters have to shrug off the boundedness of received

monolingual contours. In recent years, one has equally witnessed a number of reorientations in language education and language pedagogical efforts which invite a sociolinguistic turn sensitive to aspects of bi- and trilingualism, emergent language varieties, and the complex workings of language ideologies and sociolinguistic attitudes. For instance, national education departments have had to rethink their 'national language curriculum', so as to include also the learning of official languages as a second language (a novel experience in quite a few Western European states). Research in this area has also noted the specific challenges of curricular design. In some contexts, this has meant facing highly diversified needs for X as a second language resulting from successive waves of immigration: e.g. newcomers who have just arrived with no X at all vs users with pre-school neighbourhood experience in language X as a second language. At the same time, challenges of teacher recruitment have been posed by the organization of language courses in the immigrant languages when they are taught in the diaspora (Creese et al., 2008). These themes are not new in their own right, but they may well be unprecedented in contexts affected by recent waves of migration; the need to address them may also have come with greater urgency and increased complexity (e.g. hyperdiversity because many different language background are simultaneously at play, or the complexities of a situation in which the language learning needs of recently-arrived immigrants are being addressed through an established second language learner curriculum for indigenous minorities). Similarly, professional and institutional discourse studies were previously very much a monolingual terrain, in which attention to diversity in linguistic resources was mostly restricted to matters of 'lay speak' vs 'expert speak' with some attention paid to social-class orientations in the coding of experience and degrees of client education. It has now become a terrain which ventures into the specifics of multilingual institutional encounters in which professional–client communication is mediated through informal or professional interpretation, code-switching, or by resorting to a lingua franca with varying levels of functional proficiency brought to the encounter (e.g. Collins and Slembrouck, 2006; Gotti and Salager-Meyer, 2006; Moyer (forthcoming) on medical interaction; e.g. Benmaman, 2000; Haviland, 2003 and Trinch, 2003 on legal contexts). Following these developments, questions of literacy have been posed, too – not only the more traditional questions raised in a context where professionals and institutional agents face clients who thus far have not acquired written language or who experience difficulties in managing it but also literacy in the use of IT-driven technologies of communication, next to cross-national experiences in institutional literacy, literacy related to expert-systems as presupposed by the late modern ideal of self-governance, and literacy in response to institutional shifts in value which favour client-centredness, choice and the negotiation of institutional courses of action (see chapter by Barton and Lee in this volume). The paradigmatic shift towards 'New Literacy Studies' (e.g. Street, 1993; Collins and Blot, 2003) not only accords with these programmatic requirements but also is much necessitated by the complexities of the migrant experience. One specific theme that has often been noted in this area concerns the interactional deficits of decontextualized written solutions for the communicative gaps induced by language difference. That this is an area at the interstices of analysing institutional regimes of client-oriented communication and multilingual encounters underlines the importance stated earlier of studying the language impact of migration in relation to contemporary value orientations in institutional cultures.

In a more general vein, Coupland states (2003: 466) that 'the qualities of linguistically mediated social experience that define "local" ... all potentially carry an imprint from shifting global structures and relationships'. Echoing Comaroff and Comaroff (1992: 32ff.), macro processes always 'have their feet on the ground'. There is a need for a sociolinguistic perspective which invites equal attention to representations of difference and the situated actions of individuals, both in the micro-interactional spaces in which difference and diversity are acted out and in the mediated spaces of mass communication. In practice, it is not possible to maintain a strict distinction between the two types of context. The difference is one of scale of inquiry, not one of priority. In fact, studies of mass media representations of globalization and migration are invited to pursue also the question of how situated individuals interactionally engage with such representations (adopting an actional perspective, alongside the more commonly adopted perspective of textual constitution which is characteristic of much in media studies). Conversely, studies which prioritize the micro-sequential dynamics of face-to-face interaction are equally invited to address the larger-scale structuration effects brought about by mass media representations, as they permeate local sense-making in face-to-face interaction. Thus, representations in (inter)national media will tend to 'dawn upon' the neighbourhood experiences of migration which they cover, while neighbourhood experiences through national exposure impact upon the construction of relevant socioeconomic realities in areas unaffected by migration flows. Expressed boldly: the notion of the global itself is best

approached as articulated across interacting levels of social geographic reality. Burawoy (2001:148) adds the meta-reflection that the pulses of academic endeavour are equally implicated: inasmuch as for him the global invites ethnographic understanding, ethnography has gone global, too (anthropology in particular had for a long time already depended on a fundamental perception of border-crossing colonial relationships, whereas sociology mostly took for granted the nation-state as its natural unit of analysis).

Recent work in political, cultural and economic geography has thematized the problematic of interacting levels of analysis through the notion of 'scale' itself (see above) –, the construction of spatial and temporal units and coordinates in socioeconomic processes and, as sociolinguists will add, their articulation 'in' discourse. Scale is a very old concept in geography: in fact, it is hard to think about geographical units of analysis unless one deploys a concept of 'scale'. More recent work emphasizes how scale is socially produced. In the words of Haarstad and Fløysand (2007: 292):

> ... the 'scale question' has been addressed in recognition of the increasing interconnectivity of social relations caused by time-space compression, which necessarily problematizes the spatial parameters of those relations and the geographical context in which they occur .... Globalization does not merely detach social relations from space (deterritorializing), but also reinscribes these relations in new ways (reterritorializing).

Attention to 'scale' and processes of 'scaling' ('upscaling', 'downscaling', 'rescaling', etc.) allows us to circumvent some of the circularity that comes with received micro/macro-reasoning: communicative events are often best viewed as 'micro', 'meso' and 'macro' at the same time – and much will depend here on whose interpretative viewpoint is given priority in analysis. Thus, the child's limited Dutch displayed in a language-immersion classroom in Ghent may, at one and the same time, represent (for the teacher) a recently-arrived child who is coming to terms with a challenging new environment and who copes reasonably well given that the parents do not speak the language either, and (for the visiting school inspector) yet another instance of a failing national policy of language integration for immigrants. The construction of contextual categories is subject to the indexicalities which are presupposed, played out or interactionally worked up at the moment of speaking (and, retroactively, when interpreting discourse, as an aspect of recontextualization). Indexicalities can be viewed as 'ordered' (Silverstein, 2003). The use of 'scale' and 'scaling' can thus be extended to address a theoretical concern with the effects of de/re-territorialization and dis/re-location on the construal of place, time and situational reference as they are interpretatively and interactionally 'pinned down' or exported to a new context of expression (Baynham, 2009). The following vignette is anecdotal but illustrates well the related point of 'fractal recursivity' (Irvine and Gal, 2000). A former colleague, who grew up in Dublin but has lived in Belgium for over 20 years, during a discussion of the concept of 'scale' intimated how, when frequenting one and the same Irish pub in the centre of town, he embodied different units of reference for his interlocutors. This, he said, bore both on the topics attended to and the evaluative meanings exchanged on these: (i) 'Ireland', when he visited the pub with Flemish friends; (ii) 'Flanders', when meeting with visitors from Dublin or the Irish Republic; and (iii) the 'guys from the other side we never got to talk to', when having a drink with a colleague from the UK who grew up in Ulster. Distinctions are applied recursively to a fraction of a unit, as meaningful distinctions are played out to constitute a smaller group or individual with presupposed ancestry in the larger-scale unit.

Note, in addition, that the interest in scale takes up beyond this. As a further illustration, therefore, here is what Creese et al. (2008: 18) state about heritage language classes in the UK complementary schools they studied (complementary schools are voluntary schools which serve specific linguistic, religious or cultural communities):

> Young people in complementary schools negotiated paths for themselves which were in some ways contrary to the ideologies of the teaching materials used in complementary schools. If teachers and administrators held the view that students ought to learn a community language as an endowment of knowledge of a national history, nationalism, and identity, this was not necessarily accepted unproblematically. Rather, the young people's attitudes to their languages, and their multilingual practices, constituted an urbane response to their place in the world, as they negotiated subject positions which took them on a path through language ideological worlds constructed by others.

What is noteworthy about this instance is that the spatialization of the young learners which is presupposed in the learning materials intersects with two timescales: that of heritage and that of urban adolescence. The latter contrast is organized hierarchically in internally-conflicting directions: heritage as valuable tradition which is supported institutionally and urban adolescence as lived time valued by the adolescents. The net result is a

social dynamics which is undecided and in flux (Creese et al., 2008: 18):

> Young people found ways to parody the texts, their teachers and themselves, often questioning and sometimes ridiculing the folk stories, traditional rituals, ceremonies and festivals. At other times, young people showed a willingness and interest in the 'heritage' chosen by their teachers to focus on in class and assemblies and showed much enthusiasm in participating in community events such as Diwali festivities (Gujurati case study) and Children's Day (Turkish case study).

The further point illustrated is that of certain 'sites of engagement' (Scollon, 1997) over others being particularly amenable to articulations of scale and even scale-shifting.

One of the specific challenges posed to scalar analysis resides in the multiple uses of the term 'scale'. One can detect at least four uses:

1 Scale as a category rooted in experience and participant perception – refers to particular practices attended to by participants as reflecting and bearing upon particular time/space-scales?
2 Scale as a value-oriented gauge in the assessment of structured relationships – scale analysable as determinate relationships of inequality; as Fairclough (2006) stresses, this need not be transparent to those immediately involved.
3 Related to this, 'scaling' refers to a dynamic process which connects situated phenomena with trans-situational power, purchase and mobility (or the lack of these).
4 Finally, there is scale in the way it is more traditionally understood by geographers, as by and large a matter of drawing on a set of decontextualized units of analysis and inventory (calendar and clock time and units of square measurement, together with received geopolitical and institutional-organizational units).

One response to the challenges noted is that of multiple, interconnected readings and of adequacy in interpretation. The problem of interpretation is confounded by the inevitable dilemmas posed by Fairclough (2006: 5) when he draws attention to the paradox that, in practice, it is not possible to draw a strict separation between, on the one hand, discourses about globalization (which are often contested) and, on the other hand, globalization as real processes which are not necessarily recognized by participants for what they are. The paradox is that processes can only be talked about by resorting to representations. The resultant programme is threefold: it is one of developing an analytical-interpretative vocabulary which adequately captures process, does justice to experience and has purchase in the formulation of equitable policy and feasible intervention. In addition, what appears to be needed is not only that we dynamically conceive of a large-scale process in direct relation to detailed analysis of local symbolic processes but also that we capture the scalar complexities and contradictions that accompany the many different aspects of globalization. This way we may also succeed in capturing the unpredictable, push-pull effects of globalization which are easily missed in the sweeping manifestos. This calls for an ethnographic turn, much in the spirit of Burawoy (1991) and Gal and Kligman (2000) for whom ethnography counts as a specific engagement with 'thick' empirical detail which is oriented to the advancement of realistic social-theoretically-informed understandings.

11.5 CHALLENGES POSED TO RECEIVED SOCIOLINGUISTIC NOTIONS AND THEORIZING

The challenges posed by a sociolinguistics of globalization and migration invite multiple connections with long-standing sociolinguistic themes such as studying the effects of language contact. While stressing the continuities, there is also a need to think through the discontinuities which have been foregrounded in recent research. The shift from a sociolinguistics of 'community' to one of 'contact' is one of these (Clyne and Kipp, 2006; Collins et al., 2009; Rampton, 2009). Some definitions of speech communities have stressed commonality of language – the monolingual paradigm (e.g. Lyons, 1970) – while other definitions go by regularity of interaction (e.g. Gumperz, 1962), in this way allowing bi/multilingual speech communities. The impact of migration reaches further than the latter, as rather fundamental questions are raised about 'contexts' of interpretation, especially the temporal/spatial dimensions of language use and meaning-making (the shift towards a paradigm of spatialization and its central category of 'scale' discussed above bears testimony to this). Not surprisingly, this comes with conceptual challenges which extend to the category of 'language' itself (e.g. Blackledge and Creese, 2008). Migration has posed challenges of hybridity and the occurrence of selectively emergent varieties with limited distribution as socially identifiable registers (e.g. the adolescents of Maghreb descent in Jaspers' (2005) fieldwork who socially identify and regularly deploy stylizations of 'newcomer Flemish' and 'Turkish Flemish'). Similarly, the theme of world languages, recast more recently into a debate about

linguistic imperialism and imposition 'from above' (Mazrui, 1975; Phillipson, 1992; Canagarajah, 2002; Holliday, 2005), has been addressed as one of local and global dominance through global circulation (e.g. standard English as a colonial inheritance; standard English and its purchase in a transnational job market). At the same time, various kinds of hybridization have been described as coming 'from below' (e.g. Alim et al., 2008 on hip-hop registers; e.g. English learned and developed en route as a medium for articulating refugee experiences). With this, questions of coexistence and competition with local languages have been raised for both postcolonial and diaspora contexts (e.g. Vigouroux and Mufwene, 2008). Note that competitive coexistence is also a major aspect of language policy in supranational spaces such as the EU or globalized markets for mobile phones and software (Krzyżanowski and Wodak, 2007 on the hegemonic multilingualism of a number of 'core' working languages in the EU; e.g. Cronin, 2003 and House, 2008 on the implications of a growing distributional dynamics of 'covert translation': the need for fast global dissemination has resulted in simultaneous and automated access to a dominant anglophone source text and its translations for recipients in many different linguistic and cultural contexts.) In addition, questions such as, 'What is English?', in fact an old theme in the sociolinguistics literature, have returned, now with more stress on the face-to-face contact between non-native Englishes. For instance, Maryns (2005) gauges the impact of different 'Englishes' as a dimension of the interactional and interpretative asymmetries which bear on the contact between bureaucrat and asylum seeker in which, say, a variety of English which builds on Krio from Sierra Leona meets 'face-to-face' with the 'outer circle' secondary-school English of the Flemish institutional representative. The outcome of the contact is deeply consequential for the applicant. Attempts at formulating workable (de-ethnicized and translocal) criteria for 'international English' or 'English as a lingua franca' have given rise to intense debate. (Key tenets of this debate are captured in, for example, Rubdy and Saraceni, 2006.)

Less often dwelled upon are the challenges posed to the concept of 'genre'. Genres are traditionally thought of as contained by a societally-defined community of practice or a language community. Thus, the next step from locating discursive formats which are relatively more/less mobile across situational contexts (e.g. the in-depth interview as a trans-situational discursive format) is to talk about genres which are better understood as ordered in transnational spaces of circulation (through processes of borrowing, appropriation, imposition and translation). Genres possess or lack transnational mobility. Certain genres can be thought of as almost ontogenetically connected to global landscapes (e.g. email), whereas other genres just appear to travel very fast (e.g. hip-hop). Questions of relative homogeneity across transnational landscapes and/or relative susceptibility to local adaptation and recontextualization are very much at the forefront and undermine often-held assumptions that generic variation is mostly to be situated inside the space of a particular language or a community. (See research on the adoption of television formats worldwide: the use of a single language in the broadcasted artefact is often a mistaken indicator that the 'genre' would belong to the 'language community'; e.g. Slembrouck, 1998.)

In addition, it is also worth noting how a prevailing logic of homogeneous language communities defined by language, ethnicity and nationality (now sized down to the scale of cities, regions, neighbourhoods) in more than one respect has continued to inform both institutional-organizational responses to migration in education, health, etc., and along with this, many research initiatives. Research tends to be organized ethnolinguistically, often for heuristic reasons of uniformity of sample and focus. Also, in this area we face challenges to a paradigm in which 'the systematicity of language' is perhaps too easily taken for granted (Rampton, 2009).

Other methodological challenges to a sociolinguistics of migration and globalization pertain to the logistical difficulties involved when concentrating sociolinguistic and ethnographic effort across transnationally-constituted constituencies of text interpretation and sites of engagement. This has been noted earlier for analyses of media products which are consumed simultaneously (Hanks, 1996: 140ff. on television). Globalization has added the further challenge of transnational audiences who consume one and the same video artefact on CNN or Eurosport, a channel which provides simultaneous commentary in different languages, with advertisements during the breaks tailored to different audience segments (cf. Richardson and Meinhof, 1999). Where is the text? And, what is the best vantage point for observing interpretive practice? In a different variant, a similar set of heuristic and logistical problems presents itself when one is analysing institutional contact in a neighbourhood which is characterized by hyperdiversity, or indeed if one is to engage with linguistic ethnographies of transnational mobility which invite the researcher to take part in a journey rather than do fieldwork within a single community space. (See also Marcus's 1998 advocacy for multi-locale ethnography which seeks to overcome some of the stifling effects of a straightforward micro–macro

dichotomy; the advocacy is to be systems-directed; ethnography can become more 'flows'-sensitive by actively participating in the complex connections between places, rather than being single-place focused.)

The question of 'community' as a unit of analysis also surfaces in the need to revisit language/class-analysis in contexts of migration – especially how social class connects to particular language experiences in institutional contexts (see chapters by Mallinson and Dodsworth in this volume). Collins and La Santa (2006: 1) observe how we currently 'lack models which translate ethnicity and class, as social categories, into the processual and interactional concepts likely to generate insight into learning processes'. The concept of 'social class' has been much tied up with the sociology of the nation-state. It has tended to be absent from sociolinguistic efforts to come to terms with the sociolinguistics of the transnational, often replaced in this by 'ethnicity', 'culture' and 'ethno-national identity' as categories which would be more easily amenable to transnationally-defined populations.

Finally, the theme of the nation-state, although problematized, is far from absent in globalization and migration studies. The nation-state continues to be articulated in literature, film, discourses of government, popular events, etc. (e.g. Billig, 1995). Especially in the context of migration studies, there are various indications of a continued role for the nation-state as a significant regulating force in how sectors of society (e.g. politics, health, education, etc.) respond to waves of migration. This brings us full circle, returning to the oldest theme in sociolinguistics, that of society and language use. What might we mean then by 'society'?

REFERENCES

Alim, H., Ibrahim, A. and Pennycook, A. (2008) *Global Linguistic Flows: Hip Hop Cultures, Youth Identities, and The Politics of Language.* New York: Taylor and Francis.

Ansaldo, U. and Matthews, S. J. (2001) 'Typical creoles and simple languages. The case of Sinitic', *Linguistic Typology,* 5(2, 3): 311–26.

Appadurai, A. (1990) 'Disjuncture and difference in the global culture economy', *Theory, Culture and Society,* 7(2), 295–310.

Appadurai, A. (1996) *Modernity At Large: Cultural Dimensions of Globalization.* Minneapolis, MN: University of Minnesota Press.

Auer, P. (ed.) (2007) *Style and Social Identities. Alternative Approaches to Linguistic Heterogeneity.* Berlin: Mouton de Gruyter.

Basch, L., Schiller, N. and Blanc, C. (1994) *Nations Unbound: Transnational Projects, Postcolonial Predicaments, and Deterritorialized Nation-States*. Langhorne, PA: Gordon and Breach.

Baynham, M. (2009) '"Just one day like today": scale and the analysis of space/time orientation in narratives of displacement', in J. Collins, S. Slembrouck, and M. Baynham (eds), *Globalization and Languages in Contact: Scale, Migration, and Communicative Practices*. London: Continuum. pp. 130–47.

Baynham, M. and De Fina, A. (2005) *Dislocations/Relocations. Narratives of Displacement*. Manchester: St Jerome.

Beck, U. (1992) *Risk Society: Towards a New Modernity*. New Delhi: Sage.

Benmaman, V. (2000) 'The Spanish speaker + interpreter services = equal access to the judicial system: Is the equation accurate?', in A. Roca (ed.), *Research on Spanish in the United States: Linguistic Issues and Challenges*. Somerville, MA: Cascadilla Press. pp. 82–94.

Billig, M. (1995) *Banal Nationalism*. London: Routledge.

Blackledge, A. and Creese, A. (2008) 'Contesting 'language' as 'heritage': negotiation of identities in late modernity', *Applied Linguistics*, 29(4): 533–54.

Bryson, J., Daniels, P., Henry, N. and J. Pollard (2000) (eds) *Knowledge, Space, Economy*. London: Routledge.

Budach, G. (2009) '"Canada meets France": recasting identities of Canadienness and *Francité* through global economic exchanges', in J. Collins, S. Slembrouck and M. Baynham (eds), *Globalization and Languages in Contact: Scale, Migration, and Communicative Practices*. London: Continuum. pp. 209–32.

Burawoy, M. (1991) *Ethnography Unbound: Power and Resistance in the Modern Metropolis*. Berkeley, CA: University of California Press.

Burawoy, M. (2001) 'Manufacturing the global', *Ethnography*, 2(2): 147–59.

Bynon, T. (1997) *Historical Linguistics*. Cambridge: Cambridge University Press.

Caldas-Coulthard, C.-R. and Iedema, R. (2008) *Identity trouble. Critical Discourse and Contested Identities*. New York: Palgrave Macmillan.

Callinicos, A. (1985) 'Anthony Giddens. A contemporary critique', *Theory and Society*, 14(2): 133–66.

Campbell, L. (1998) *Historical Linguistics. An Introduction*. Durham, NC: Duke University Press.

Canagarajah, S. (2002) *A Geopolitics of Academic Writing*. Pittsburgh: University of Pittsburgh Press.

Clyne, M. and Kipp, S. (2006) *Tiles in a Multilingual Mosaic: Macedonian, Somali and Filipino in Melbourne*. Canberra: Pacific Linguistics.

Coe, N. M. and Yeung, H. W. C. (2001) 'Geographical perspectives on mapping globalization', *Journal of Economic Geography*, 1: 367–80.

Collins, J. and Blot, R. (2003) *Literacy and Literacies: Texts, Power, and Identity*. Cambridge: Cambridge University Press.

Collins, J. and La Santa, A. (2006) 'Analyzing class and ethnicity as communicative practices: a case study of migration-based multilingualism in Upstate New York'. Working

Papers in Urban Language and Literacies, 40. London: King's College. Available at http://www.kcl.ac.uk/schools/sspp/education//research/groups/llg/wpull.html.

Collins, J. and Slembrouck, S. (2006) '"You don't know what they translate": language contact, institutional procedure and literacy practice in neighbourhood health clinics in urban Flanders', *Journal of Linguistic Anthropology*, 16(2): 249–68.

Collins, J. and Slembrouck, S. (2009) 'Goffman and globalisation: frame, footing and scale in migration-connected multilingualism', in J. Collins, S. Slembrouck, and M. Baynham (eds), *Globalization and Languages in Contact: Scale, Migration, and Communicative Practices*. London: Continuum. pp. 19–41.

Collins, J., Slembrouck, S. and Baynham, M. (eds) (2009) *Globalization and Languages in Contact: Scale, Migration, and Communicative Practices*. London: Continuum.

Comaroff, J. and Comaroff, J. (1992) *Ethnography and the Historical Imagination*. Boulder, CO: Westview.

Coupland, N. (2003) 'Introduction: sociolinguistics and globalisation', *Journal of Sociolinguistics*, 7(4): 465–72.

Creese, A., Baraç, T., Bhatt, A., et al. (2008). *Multilingualism in Complementary Schools in Four Linguistic Communities*. University of Birmingham.

Cronin, M. (2003) *Translation and Globalization*. London: Routledge.

Delanty, G., Wodak, R. and Jones, P. (eds) (2008) *Identity, Belonging and Migration*. Liverpool: Liverpool University Press.

Fairclough, N. (2006) *Language and Globalization*. London: Routledge.

Fenton, S. and Bradley, H. (eds) (2002) *Ethnicity and Economy. Race and Class Revisited*. New York: Palgrave Macmillan.

Gal, S. and Kligman, G. (2000) *The Politics of Gender After Socialism: A Comparative-Historical Essay*. Princeton: Princeton University Press.

Galasiński, D and Galasińska, A. (2007) 'Lost in Communism, lost in migration: narratives of the post-1989 Polish migrant experience', *Journal of Multicultural Discourses*, 2(1): 47–62.

Galasińska, A. and Koslowska, O. (2009) '"Either" and "Both"– the changing concept of living space among Polish post-communist migrants to the UK', in J. Collins, S. Slembrouck, and M. Baynham (eds), *Globalization and Languages In Contact: Scale, Migration, and Communicative Practices*. London: Continuum. pp.170–88.

Giddens, A. (1984) *The Constitution of Society*. Cambridge: Polity Press.

Giddens, A. (1990) *The Consequences of Modernity*. Cambridge: Polity Press.

Giddens, A. (1991) *Modernity and Self-identity*. Stanford, CA: Stanford University Press.

Giddens, A. (2006) *Europe in the Global Age*. Cambridge: Polity Press.

Gotti, M. and Salager-Meyer, F. (2006) *Advances in Medical Discourse Analysis: Oral and Written Contexts*. Bern: Peter Lang.

Gumperz, J. (1962) 'Types of linguistic community', *Anthropological Linguistics*, 4: 28–40.

Haarstad, H. and Fløysand, A. (2007) 'Globalization and the power of rescaled narratives: a case of opposition to mining in Tambogrande, Peru', *Political Geography*, 26: 289–308.

Hanks, W. (1996) *Language and Communciative Practices*. Oxford: Westview Press.

Harvey, D. (1990) *The condition of Post-Modernity. An Enquiry into the Origins of Cultural Change*. Oxford: Blackwell.

Haviland, J. (2003) 'Ideologies of language: some reflections on language and U.S. Law', *American Anthropologist*, 105(4): 764–74.

Heller, M. (2003) *Crosswords. Language, Education and Ethnicity in French Ontario*. Berlin: Mouton.

Holliday, A. (2005) *The Struggle to Teach English as an International Language*. Oxford: Oxford University Press.

House, J. (2008) 'Towards a linguistic theory of translation as re-contextualization and a Third Space phenomenon', *Linguistica Antverpiensia*, 7: 149–75.

Howarth, D. (2000) *Discourse*. Buckingham: Open University Press.

Irvine, J. T. and Gal, S. (2000) 'Language ideology and linguistic differentiation', in P. Kroskrity (ed.), *Regimes of Language*. Santa Fe, NM: School of American Research Press. pp. 35–83.

Jaspers, J. (2005) 'Linguistic sabotage in a context of monolingualism and standardization', *Language and Communication*, 25: 279–97.

Kaufman, S. (2003) 'What motivates changes that occur in pidgins and creoles', *Journal of Pidgin and Creole Languages*, 18(1): 107–20.

Kirkpatrick, A. (2007) *World Englishes: Implications for International Communication and English Language Teaching*. Cambridge: Cambridge University Press.

Krzyżanowski, M. and Wodak, R. (2007) 'Multilingual European institutions and the discourse of EU enlargement in the national public spheres', a pilot study. Lancaster: Department of Linguistics and English Language, Lancaster University. Available at http://www.lancs.ac.uk/fass/doc_library/linguistics/wodakr/DYLANWP2Lancasterfinal.pdf.

Kymlicka, W. (1995) *Multicultural Citizenship: A Liberal Theory of Minority Rights*. Oxford: Oxford University Press.

Kymlikca, W. (2001) *Politics in the Vernacular: Nationalism, Multiculturalism and Citizenship*. Oxford: Oxford University Press.

Lamont, M. (2000) *The Dignity of Working Men. Morality and the Boundaries of Race, Class and Immigration*. Harvard: Harvard University Press.

Lash, S., and Urry, R. (1994) *Economies of Signs and Space*. London: Sage.

Lass, R. (1997) *Historical Linguistics*. Cambridge: Cambridge University Press.

Lyons, J. (1970) *New horizons in Linguistics*. Harmondsworth: Penguin.

McConnell, G. (1997) 'Global scale sociolinguistics', in F. Coulmas (ed.), *The Handbook of Sociolinguistics*. London: Blackwell. pp. 344–57.

Manda, D. S. (2009) Ubuntu philosophy as an African philosophy for peace. Available at http://www.africafiles.org/article.asp?ID=20359. Accessed 30 March 2009.

Marcus, G. (1998) *Ethnography Through Thick and Thin*. Princeton, NJ: Princeton University Press.

Maryns, K. (2005) 'Monolingual language ideologies and code choice in the Belgian asylum procedure', *Language and Communication*, 25: 299–314.

Mazrui, A. (1975) *The Political Sociology of the English Language: An African Perspective*. The Hague: Mouton and Co.

Moyer, M. (forthcoming) 'Language ideologies and multilingual practices in a health care clinic in Barcelona', *Journal of Pragmatics*.

Persson, H-A. and Stråth, B. (2007) 'Time and space. Introduction to reflections on Europe as a political order', in H. Persson, and B. Stråth (eds), *Reflections on Europe. Defining a Political Order in Time and Space*. Brussels: Peter Lang. pp. 11–34.

Phillipson, R. (1992) *Linguistic Imperialism*. Oxford: Oxford University Press.

Preston, P. (2008) *Making the News. Journalism and News Cultures in Europe*. London: Routledge.

Rampton, B. (1995) *Crossing. Language and Ethnicity Among Adolescents*. London: Longman.

Rampton, B. (2009) 'Speech community and beyond', in N. Coupland, and A. Jaworski (eds), *The New Sociolinguistics Readers*. Houndmills: Palgrave Macmillan. pp. 694–713.

Richardson, K. and Meinhof, U. (1999) *Worlds in Common? Television Discourse in a Changing Europe*. London: Routledge.

Robertson, R. (1990) 'Mapping the global conditions: globalization as the central concept', *Theory, Culture and Society*, 7(2, 3): 15–30.

Rubdy, R. and Saraceni, M. (2006) *English in the World: Global Rules, Global Roles*. London: Continuum.

Sassen, S. (1999) *Guests and Aliens*. New York: The New Press.

Saville-Troike, M. (2003) *The Ethnography of Communication: An Introduction*. (3 ed.) Oxford: Blackwell.

Scollon, R. (1997) 'Handbills, tissues, and condoms: a site of engagement for the construction of identity in public discourse', *Journal of Sociolinguistics*, 1(1): 39–61.

Silverstein, M. (2003) 'Indexical order and the dialectics of sociolinguistic life', *Language and Communication*, 23(3, 4): 193–229.

Slembrouck, S. (1998) '"Você decide": formatting the commodified nation', *ALW Cahiers*, 11: 11–21.

Street B. (1993) *Social literacies: Critical Approaches to Literacy in Development, Ethnography and Education*. London: Longman.

Swyngedouw, E. (1996) 'Reconstructing citizenship, the re-scaling of the State and the New Authoritarianism: closing the Belgian mines', *Urban Studies*, 33: 1499–521.

Taura, H. (2008) *Language Attrition and Retention in Japanese Return Students*. Sotokanda: Akashi Shoten.

Thomas, W. and Znaniecki, F. (1918) *The Polish Peasant in Europe and America.* New York: Alfred Knopf.

Thomason, S. and Kaufman, T. (1988) *Language Contact, Creolization and Genetic Linguistics.* Berkeley, CA: University of California Press.

Triandafyllidou, A., Wodak, R. and Krzyżanowski, M. (2009) *The European Public Sphere and the Media.* London: Palgrave Macmillan.

Trinch, S. (2003) *Latinas' Narratives of Domestic Abuse. Discrepant Versions of Violence.* Amsterdam: John Benjamins.

Valentine, G., Sporton, D. and Bang Nielsen, K. (2009) 'The spaces of language: the everyday practices of young Somali refugees and asylum seekers', in J. Collins, S. Slembrouck, and M. Baynham (eds), *Globalization and Languages in Contact: Scale, Migration, and Communicative Practices.* London: Continuum. pp. 189–206.

Vigouroux, C. and Mufwene, S. (eds) (2008) *Globalization and Language Vitality.* London: Continuum.

Wallerstein, I. (2004) *World-Systems Analysis: An Introduction.* Durham, NC: Duke University Press.

Zentella, A. (1990) 'Returned migration, language, and identity. Puerto Rico bilinguals in two worlds/dos mundos', in N. Gutmann, F. Rodríguez, L. Stephen and P. Zavella (eds), *Perspectives on Las Américas: A Reader in Culture, History, and Representation.* Malden, MA: Wiley-Blackwell. pp. 245–58.

12

Semiotics: Interpretants, Inference, and Intersubjectivity

Paul Kockelman

12.1 INTRODUCTION[1]

Charles Sanders Peirce (1839–1914) was an American philosopher, mathematician and logician. To sociolinguists, he is perhaps best known for his theory of semiotics, with its focus on logic and nature, and the ways this contrasted with Saussure's semiology, with its focus on language and convention. In particular, he foregrounded iconic and indexical relations between signs and objects, theorizing the way meaning is motivated and context-bound. And he foregrounded inferential relations between signs and interpretants, foregrounding the role of abduction (or hypothesis) over deduction, and thereby the role of context over code. He inspired Roman Jakobson's (1990) understanding of the role of shifters in language – which has provided a central insight for three decades of linguistic anthropology and discourse analysis: for example, Haliday and Hasan (1976) on cohesion, Brown and Gilman (1972 [1960]) on pronouns, and Silverstein (1995 [1976]) and Hanks (1990) on social and spatial deixis. He inspired George Herbert Mead's (1934) understanding of the relation between selves and others, as generated by the unfolding of gestures and symbols – which grounded influential ideas in philosophy and biosemiosis (Morris 1938; Sebeok and Umiker-Sebeok, 1992), conversational analysis (Sachs, Schegloff and Jefferson, 1974), sociolinguistics (Goffman, 1959; Labov, 1966), and even speech act theory (Austin, 2003 [1955]; Searle, 1969).

This chapter explicates key terms from semiotics and pragmatics, and uses these to reconceptualize the relation between mental states, social statuses and speech acts. Section 12.2 lays out the fundamental features of semiotic processes through the lens of Peirce's lexicon: sign, object, interpretant; iconic, indexical, symbolic; and so forth. It differs from the usual readings of Peirce by focusing on the interpretant (in contrast to the sign or object), and by focusing on inference (in contrast to indexicality). Section 12.3 uses these concepts to reframe the nature of social relations and cognitive representations. Starting out from the work of the Boasian, Ralph Linton, it theorizes social statuses and mental states through the lens of semiosis and intersubjectivity. Section 12.4 uses this reframing to recast performativity and agency. By reading Mead through the lens of Peirce, and reading Austin through the lens of Mead, it widens our understanding of the efficacity of speech acts to include sign events more generally.

12.2 SEMIOSIS: THE PUBLIC FACE OF COGNITIVE PROCESSES

Semiotics is the study of semiosis, or 'meaning,' a process which involves three components: 'signs' (whatever stands for something else); 'objects' (whatever a sign stands for); and 'interpretants' (whatever a sign creates insofar as it stands for an object) – see Table 12.1 (column 2).

In particular, any **semiotic process** relates these three components in the following way: a sign stands for its object on the one hand, and its interpretant on the other, in such a way as to make the interpretant stand in relation to the object corresponding to its own relation to the object

Table 12.1   Typology of distinctions (semiosis)

Categories	Semiotic process	Sign	Ground	Interpretant	Social relation	Agent	Community
Firstness	Sign	Qualisign	Iconic	Affective	Role	Control	Commonality
Secondness	Object	Sinsign (token)	Indexical	Energetic	Status	Compose	Contrast
Thirdness	Interpretant	Legisign (type)	Symbolic	Representational	Attitude	Commit	Consciousness

(see Peirce, 1931–35). What is at issue in mean-ingfulness, then, is not one relation between a sign and an object (qua 'standing for'), but rather a relation between two such relations (qua 'corre-spondence'). The logic of this **relation between relations** is shown in Figure 12.1.

For example, 'joint-attention' is a semiotic process. In particular, a child turning to observe what her father is observing, or turning to look at where her mother is pointing, involves an interpre-tant (the child's change of attention), an object (what the parent is attending to, or pointing towards) and a sign (the parent's direction of attention, or gesture that directs attention). As Mead noted (1934), any 'interaction' is a semiotic process. For example, if I pull back my fist (first phase of an action, or the sign), you duck (reaction, or the interpretant) insofar as my next move (second phase of action, or the object) would be to punch you. Generalizing interaction, the 'pair-part structures' of everyday interaction – the fact that questions are usually followed by answers, offers by acceptances, commands by undertakings, assessments by agreements, and so forth (Goffman, 1981; Sachs et al., 1974) – consist of semiotic processes in which two components

(the sign and interpretant) are foregrounded. In particular, a type of utterance (or action) gives rise to another type of utterance (or action) insofar as it is understood to express a proposition (or purpose).

Indeed, the constituents of so-called 'material culture' are semiotic processes (Kockelman, 2006a). For example, an 'affordance' is a semiotic process whose sign is a natural feature, whose object is a purchase, and whose key interpretant is an action that heeds that feature, or an instrument that incorporates that feature (so far as the feature 'provides purchase'). For example, walking care-fully over a frozen pond (as an action) is an inter-pretant of the purchase provided by ice (as an affordance), insofar as such a form of movement heeds the slipperiness of ice. An 'instrument' is a semiotic process whose sign is an artificed entity, whose object is a function, and whose key interpre-tant is an action that wields that entity, or another instrument that incorporates that instrument (so far as it 'serves a function'). For example, a knife (as an instrument) is an interpretant of the purchase provided by steel (as another instrument), insofar as such a tool incorporates the hardness and sharpness of steel.

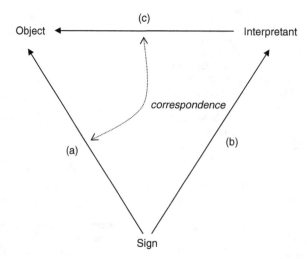

Figure 12.1   Semiosis as a Relation between Relations. A sign stands for its object on the one hand (a), and its interpretant on the other (b), in such a way as to bring the latter into a relation to the former (c), **corresponding** to its own relation to the former (a).

Notice from these examples that signs can be eye-directions, pointing gestures, utterances, controlled behaviours, environmental features and artificial entities. Objects can be the focus of attention, purposes, propositions and functions. And interpretants can be other utterances, changes in attention, reactions, instruments, and heeding and wielding actions. Notice that very few of these interpretants are 'in the minds' of the interpreters; yet all of these semiotic processes embody properties normally associated with mental entities: attention, desire, purpose, propositionality, thoughts and goals. Notice that very few of these signs are addressed to the interpreters (in the sense of purposely expressed for the sake of their interpretants) – so that most semiotic processes (such as wielding an instrument) are not intentionally communicative. And notice how the interpretant component of each of these semiotic processes is itself the sign component of an incipient semiotic process – and hence the threefold relationality continues indefinitely.

While many theorists take semiotic objects to be relatively 'objective' (things like oxen and trees), these examples show that most objects are relatively intersubjective (a shared perspective, turning on correspondence, in regard to a relatively intangible entity – such as a proposition or purpose). An object, then, is whatever a signer and interpreter can correspondingly stand in relation to – it need not be continuously present to the senses, taking up volume in space, detachable from context, or 'objective' in any other sense of the word. And while many theorists take interpretants – if they consider them at all – to be relatively 'subjective' (say, a thought in the mind of an addressee), these examples show that most interpretants are as objective as signs. Indeed, it may be argued that the typical focus on sign–object relations (or 'signifiers' and 'signifieds'), at the expense of sign–interpretant relations, and this concomitant understanding of objects as 'objective' and interpretants as 'subjective' – and hence the assimilation of meaning to mind, rather than grounding mind in meaning – is the fatal flaw of twentieth-century semiotics (Kockelman, 2005, 2006a). These claims will be further fleshed out in what follows.

Peirce theorized three kinds of signs (1955a). A 'qualisign' is a quality that could possibly be paired with an object: i.e. any quality that is accessible to the human sensorium – and hence could be used to stand for something else (to someone). A 'sinsign' is a quality that is actually paired with an object (in some event) and is sometimes referred to as a 'token'. A 'legisign' is a type of quality that must necessarily be paired with a type of object (across all events) and is sometimes referred to as a 'type' – see Table 12.1 (column 3).

For example, in the case of utterances, a qualisign is a potential cry (say, what is conceivably utterable by a human voice); a sinsign is an actual cry (say, the interjection *ouch* uttered at a particular time and place); and a legisign is a type of cry (say, the interjection *ouch* in the abstract, or what every token of *ouch* has in common as a type).

Any sinsign that is a token of a legisign as a type may be called a 'replica'. Replicas, then, are just run-of-the mill sinsigns: any utterance of the word *ouch*. And, in keeping within this Peircean framework, we might call any unreplicable or unprecedented sinsign a 'singularity' – that is, any sinsign that is not a token of a type. Singularities, then, are one-of-a-kind sinsigns: e.g., Nixon's resignation speech. One of the key design features of language may be stated as follows: given a finite number of replicas (qua individual signs as parts), speakers may create an infinite number of singularities (qua aggregates of signs as wholes).

Given the definition of semiotic process offered above, the object of a sign is really that to which all (appropriate and effective) interpretants of that sign correspondingly relate (Kockelman, 2005). Objects, then, are relatively abstract entities by definition. They should not be confused with 'objects' in the Cartesian sense of res extensa. Nor should they be confused with the 'things' that words seem to stand for. Indeed, it is best to think of the object as a 'correspondence-preserving projection' from all interpretants of a sign. It may be more or less precise, and more or less consistent, as seen by the dotted portion of Figure 12.2.

For example, if a cat's purr is a sign, the object of that sign is a correspondence-preserving projection from the set of behaviours (or interpretants) humans may or must do (within some particular community) in the context of, and because of, a cat's purr: pick it up and pet it; stroke in under the chin; exclaim, 'Oh, that's so cute!'; offer a sympathetic low guttural; stay seated, petting it even when one needs to pee; and so on. Needless to say, humans tend to objectify such objects by glossing them in terms of physiology (say, the 'purr-organ' has been activated), emotion (say, 'she must be content'), or purpose (say, 'she wants me to continue petting her').

While the abstract nature of objects is clearly true for semiotic processes like instruments and actions, it is less clearly true for words like 'cat,' or utterances such as 'the ball is on the table,' which seem to have 'objects' (in the Cartesian sense) as their objects (in the semiotic sense). In order to understand the meaning of such signs, several more distinctions need to be made. First, just as there are sin-signs (or sign tokens) and legisigns (or sign types), there are 'sin–objects' and 'legi–objects'. Thus, an assertion (or a sentence with declarative illocutionary force – say,

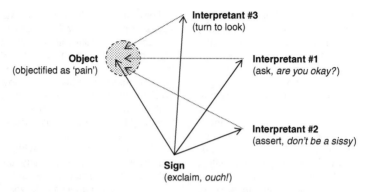

Figure 12.2 Object as Correspondence-Preserving Projection. The object of a sign is that to which all appropriate and effective interpretants of that sign correspondingly relate. It may be understood as a correspondence-preserving projection from all interpretants.

'the dog is under the table') is a sign whose object type is a **proposition**, and whose object token is a **state of affairs**. A word (or a substitutable lexical constituent of a sentence – say, 'dog' and 'table') is a sign whose object type is a **concept**, and whose object token is a **referent**. Finally, the set of all possible states of affairs of an assertion – or what the assertion could be used to represent – may be called an 'extension'. And the set of all possible referents of a word – or what the word could be used to refer to – may be called a 'category' – see Table 12.2. As is well known, many battles have been fought over the vector of mediation: words mediating concepts and categories ('nominalism'); concepts mediating words and categories ('conceptualism'); and categories mediating words and concepts ('realism'). In general, contributions come from all sides.

Unlike other object types (say, the general function of a hammer across wieldings, or the general cause of a scream across utterances), propositions (and concepts) are **inferentially articulated**. In particular, there is a key species of conditional relationality which may be called logical relationality, where the object in question relates interpretants via inferential articulation (material and formal deduction and induction). And, hand in hand with this inferential articulation, unlike other object tokens (say, the specific function of a hammer as wielded on some particu-

lar occasion, or the specific cause of a scream uttered on some particular occasion), states of affairs and referents are 'objective' – in that there seem to be actual events that an assertion 'represents,' or actual things that a word 'refers to'. In short, as will be further developed below, sentences and words have the property of **aboutness** that characterizes intentional phenomena more generally – not only speech acts like assertions and promises but also 'mental states' like beliefs and intentions. While all signs have a property of directedness by definition (i.e. they stand for objects), signs whose objects are propositions have received extensive characterization – for their objects seem to be 'of the world', and so metaphysical worries about mind-world mediation can flourish.

In Peircean semiotics, the relation between the sign and object is fundamental, and is sometimes referred to as the 'ground' (Parmentier, 1994: 4; Peirce, 1955a). Famously, in the case of **symbols**, this relation is arbitrary, and is usually thought to reside in 'convention'. Examples include words like *boy* and *run*. In the case of **indices**, this relation is based in spatiotemporal and/or causal contiguity. Examples include exclamations like 'ouch!' and symptoms like fevers. And in the case of **icons**, this relation is based in similarity of qualities (such as shape, size, colour or texture). Examples include portraits and diagrams. Notice, then, that the exact same object may be stood for by a symbol (say, the word *dogs*), an index (say, pointing to a dog), or an icon (say, a picture of a dog). When Saussure speaks of the 'arbitrary' and the 'motivated' (1983 [1916]), he is really speaking about semiotic processes whose sign–object relations are relatively symbolic vs relatively iconic–indexical – see Table 1 (column 4).

Table 12.2 The objects of inferentially articulated signs

Sign	Sentence	Word
Object (type)	Proposition	Concept
Object (token)	State of affairs	Referent
Object (set of tokens)	Extension (world)	Category

Another sense of motivated is the type of regimentation that keeps a sign–object–interpretant relation in place – be it grounded in norms, rules, laws, causes and so on. In particular, for an entity to have 'norms' requires two basic capacities: it must be able to imitate the behaviour of those around it, as they are able to imitate its behaviour; and it must be able to sanction the (non-) imitative behaviour of those around it, and be subject to their sanctions (Brandom, 1979; Haugeland, 1998; Sapir, 1985 [1927]). Norms, then, are embodied in dispositions: one behaves a certain way because one is disposed to behave that way; and one is so disposed because of imitation and sanctioning. While 'rules' presuppose a normative capacity, they also involve a linguistic ability: a rule must be formulated in some language (oral or written); and one must 'read' the rule, and do what it says because that's what it says (Haugeland, 1998: 149). Rules, then, are like recipes; following a rule is like following a recipe; and to have and follow rules requires a linguistic ability. As used here, 'laws' are rules that are promulgated and enforced by a political entity – say, following Weber (1978: 54), an organization with a monopoly on the legitimate use of force within a given territory. Laws, then, typically make reference to the threat of violence within the scope of polity. Notice, then, that laws presuppose rules, and rules presuppose norms. Sometimes when scholars speak about motivation, they mean iconic and indexical grounds rather than symbolic ones; and sometimes they mean regimentation by natural causes rather than cultural norms (rules, laws or conventions). The issues are clearly related; but they should not be conflated.

Peirce distinguished between immediate objects and dynamic objects. By the 'immediate object', he means 'the object as the sign itself represents it, and whose Being is thus dependent upon the representation of it in the Sign' (4.536, cited in Colapietro, 1989: 15). This is to be contrasted with the 'dynamic object', which Peirce takes to be 'the Reality which by some means contrives to determine the Sign to its Representation' (ibid.). In short, the dynamic object is the object that determines the existence of the sign; and the immediate object is the object represented by the sign. Immediate objects only exist by virtue of the signs that represent them, whereas dynamic objects exist independently of the signs that stand for them.

Importantly, every sign has both an immediate and a dynamic object, and hence involves both a vector of representation and a vector of determination. In certain cases, these immediate and dynamic objects can overlap – as least in lay understandings. For example, an interjection 'ouch!' or a facial expression of pain may be understood as determined by pain (as their dynamic objects) and as representing pain (as their immediate objects): one only knows about another's pain through their cry; yet their pain is what caused that cry. Indeed, a 'symptom' should really be defined as a sign whose immediate object is identical to its dynamic object. Dynamic objects, needless to say, often bear a primarily (iconic) indexical relation to their signs, whereas immediate objects often bear a primarily (indexical) symbolic relation to their signs. However, just as any semiotic process is symbolic, indexical and iconic, so any sign is partially determined (having a dynamic object) and partially representing (having an immediate object). Stereotypically, however, one takes the grounds of signs to be symbolic and representing, rather than (iconic) indexical and determining.

Reframing Grice's insights (1989; and see Strawson, 1954) in a semiotic idiom, there are at least four objects of interest in non-natural meaning:

1   My intention to direct your attention to an object (or bring an object to your attention).
2   The object that I direct your attention to (or bring to your attention).
3   My intention that you use (2), usually in conjunction with (1), to attend to another object.
4   The object that you come to attend to.

There are several ways of looking at the details of this process. Focusing on the relation between (2) and (4), there are two conjoined semiotic processes, the first as means and the second as ends. Using some kind of pointing gesture as a sign, I direct your attention to some relatively immediate object in concrete space (indexically recoverable); and this object, or any of its features, is then used as a sign to direct your attention to some relatively distal object in abstract space (inferentially recoverable). In other words, the first sign (whatever initially points) is a 'way marker' in a relatively concrete environment; and the second sign (whatever is pointed to by the first sign, and subsequently points) is a 'way marker' in a relatively abstract environment. Loosely speaking, if the first sign causes one's head to turn, the second sign, itself the object of the first sign, causes one's mind to search. Relatively speaking, the first path taken is maximally concrete-indexical; and the second path taken is maximally abstract-inferential.

Objects (2) and (4), then, are relatively foregrounded. They are immediate objects in Peirce's sense: objects which signs represent (and hence which exist because the sign brought some interpreter's attention to them). Objects (1) and (3) are, in contrast, relatively backgrounded. They are dynamic objects: objects which give rise to the existence of signs (and hence which are causes of, or reasons for, the signer having expressed them). In other words, whenever someone directs our attention there are two objects: as a foregrounded, immediate object, there is whatever they direct our attention to (2); and as a backgrounded, dynamic object, there is their intention to direct our attention (1). Grice's key insight is that, for a wide range of semiotic processes, my interpretant of your dynamic object is a condition for my interpretant of your immediate object. In other words, learning of your intention to communicate is a key resource for learning what you intend to communicate. Loosely speaking, whereas the object is revealed by what the point ostends (or by what the utterance represents), the intention is revealed by the act of pointing (or by the act of uttering).

While many linguists and anthropologists are familiar with Peirce's distinction between icons, indices and symbols, most are not familiar with his threefold typology of interpretants – and so these should be fleshed out in detail. In particular, as inspired by Peirce, there are three basic types of interpretants (1955c: 276–7; Kockelman, 2005). An 'affective interpretant' is a change in one's bodily state. It can range from an increase in metabolism to a blush, from a feeling of pain to a feeling of being off-balance, from sweating to an erection. This change in bodily state is itself a sign that is potentially perceptible to the body's owner, or others who can perceive the owner's body. And, as signs themselves, these interpretants may lead to subsequent, and perhaps more developed, interpretants. 'Energetic interpretants' involve effort, and individual causality; they do not necessarily involve purpose, intention or planning. For example, flinching at the sound of a gun is an energetic interpretant; as is craning one's neck to see what made a sound; as is saluting a superior when she walks by; as is wielding an instrument (say, pounding in a nail with a hammer); as is heeding an affordance (say, tiptoeing on a creaky floor). And 'representational interpretants' are signs with propositional content, such as an assertion (or explicit speech act more generally). Thus, to describe someone's movement as *he raised his hand*, is to offer an interpretant of such a controlled behaviour (qua sign) so far as it has a purpose (qua object). And hence while such representations are signs (that may be subsequently interpreted), they are also interpretants (of prior signs). Finally, it should be emphasized that the same sign can lead to different kinds of interpretants – sometimes simultaneously and sometimes sequentially. For example, upon being exposed to a violent image, one may blush (affective interpretant), avert one's gaze (energetic interpretant), or say 'that shocks me' (representational interpretant) – see Table 12.1 (column 5).

Finally, each of these three types of interpretants may be paired with a slightly more abstract double, known as an ultimate interpretant (cf. Peirce, 1955c: 277). In particular, an 'ultimate affective interpretant' is not a change in bodily state per se, but rather a disposition to have one's bodily state change – and hence is a disposition to express affective interpretants (of a particular type). Such an interpretant, then, is not itself a sign, but is only evinced in a pattern of behaviour (as the exercise of that disposition). Analogously, an 'ultimate energetic interpretant' is a disposition to express energetic interpretants (of a particular type). In short, it is a disposition to behave in certain ways – as evinced in purposeful and non-purposeful behaviours. And finally, an 'ultimate representational interpretant' is the propositional content of a representational interpretant, plus all the propositions that may be inferred from it, when all of these propositions are embodied in a change of habit, as evinced in behaviour that conforms to these propositional contents. For example, a **belief** is the quintessential ultimate representational interpretant: in being committed to a proposition (i.e. 'holding a belief'), one is also committed to any propositions that may be inferred from it; and one's commitment to this inferentially articulated set of propositions is evinced in one's behaviour: what one is likely or unlikely to do or say insofar as it confirms or contradicts these propositional contents. Notice that these ultimate interpretants are not signs in themselves: while they dispose one toward certain behaviours (affective, energetic, representational), they are not the behaviours per se – but rather **dispositions to behave** in certain ways. Ultimate interpretants are therefore a very precise way of accounting for a **habitus**: which, in some sense, is just an ensemble of ultimate interpretants as embodied in an individual, and as distributed among members of a community (cf. Bourdieu, 1977 [1972]).

While such a six-fold typology of interpretants may seem complicated at first, it should accord with one's intuitions. Indeed, most **emotions** really involve a complicated bundling together of all these types of interpretants (Kockelman, 2006b). For example, upon hearing a gunshot (as a sign), one may be suffused with adrenaline (affective interpretant); one might make a frightened facial expression (relatively non-purposeful energetic interpretant); one may run over to see what happened (relatively purposeful energetic interpretant); and one might say 'that scared the hell out of me' (representational interpretant). Moreover, one may forever tremble at the sight of the woods (ultimate affective interpretant); one may never go into that part of the woods again (ultimate energetic interpretant); and one might forever believe that the woods are filled with dangerous men (ultimate representational interpretant). In this way, most so-called emotions may be decomposed into a bouquet of more basic and varied interpretants. And, in this way, the seemingly most subjective forms of experience are reframed in terms of their intersubjective effects.

Putting all the foregoing ideas together, a set of three-fold distinctions may be enumerated. First, any semiotic process has three components: sign, object, interpretant. There are three kinds of signs (and objects): quali-, sin- and legi-. There are three kinds of sign–object relations, or grounds: iconicity (quality), indexicality (contiguity) and symbolism (convention). And there are three kinds of interpretants: affective, energetic and representational (along with their ultimate variants). Finally, Peirce's categories of firstness, secondness and thirdness (1955b), while notoriously difficult to define, are best understood as genus categories, which include the foregoing categories as species – see Table 12.1 (column 1). In particular, firstness is to secondness is to thirdness, as sign is to object is to interpretant, as iconic is to indexical is to symbolic, as affective is to energetic is to representational. Thus, firstness relates to sense and possibility; secondness relates to force and actuality; and thirdness relates to understanding and generality. Indeed, given that thirdness presupposes secondness, and secondness presupposes firstness, Peirce's theory assumes that human-specific modes of semiosis (thirdness per se) are grounded in modes of firstness and secondness. Peirce's pragmatism, then, is a semiotic materialism – one in which meaning is as embodied and embedded as it is 'enminded'.

12.3 SOCIAL RELATIONS AND COGNITIVE REPRESENTATIONS

Ultimate (representational) interpretants deserve further theorization. For the Boasian, Ralph Linton (1936), a 'status' (as distinct from the one who holds it) is a collection of rights and responsibilities attendant upon inhabiting a certain position in the social fabric: i.e. the rights and responsibilities that go with being a parent or child, a husband or wife, a citizen or foreigner, a patrician or plebian, and so forth. A 'role' is any enactment of one's status: i.e. the behaviour that arises when one puts one's status into effect by acting on one's rights and according to one's responsibilities. And, while untheorized by Linton, we may define an 'attitude' as another's reaction to one's status by having perceived one's role. Many attitudes, then,

are themselves statuses: upon inferring your status (by perceiving your role), I adopt a complementary status.

Roles, statuses and attitudes, then, are three components of the same semiotic process – mapping onto signs, objects and interpretants, respectively – see Table 12.1 (column 6). Indeed, one cannot perceive a status (which is just a collection of rights and responsibilities); one can only infer a status from a role (any enactment of those rights and responsibilities); and one may therefore adopt an attitude towards a status. In this way, a status may be understood in terms similar to an ultimate interpretant: a disposition or propensity to signify and interpret in certain ways. A role may be understood as any sign of one's propensity to signify and interpret in particular ways – itself often a particular mode of signifying or interpreting. And an attitude, qua complementary status, may itself just be an embodied sense of what to expect from another, itself often an ultimate interpretant, where this embodied sense is evinced by being surprised by or disposed to sanction non-expected behaviours. The basic process is therefore as follows: we perceive others' roles; from these perceived roles, we infer their statuses; and from these inferred statuses, we anticipate other roles from them which would be in keeping with those statuses. In short, a status is modality personified, a role is personhood actualized, and an attitude is another's persona internalized. Here, then, we may understand social relations, and identity more generally, in terms of semiotic processes.

With these basic definitions in hand, several finer distinctions may be introduced, and several caveats may be established. First, Linton focused on rights and responsibilities, with no indication of how these were to be regimented. For present purposes, the modes of permission and obligation that make up a status may be regimented by any number of means: while typically grounded in norms (as commitments and entitlements), they may also be grounded in rules (as articulated norms) or laws (as legally-promulgated and politically-enforced rules).

While the three classic types of status come from the **Politics** of Aristotle (husband/wife, master/slave, parent/child), statuses are really much more varied and much more basic. For example, kinship relations involve complementary statuses: aunt/niece, father-in-law/daughter-in-law, and so forth. Positions in the division of labour are statuses: spinner, guard, nurse, waiter, etc. Positions within civil and military organizations are statuses: CEO, private, sergeant, secretary. Goffman's 'participant roles' (1981) are really statuses: speaker and addressee; participant and bystander. What Marx called the 'dramatis personae' of economic processes (1967: 113) are also statuses: buyer and seller, creditor and debtor, broker and proxy. Social categories of the more colourful kind are statuses: geek, stoner, slut, bon vivant, as are social categories of the more political kind: male, black, Mexican, rich, gay. Finally, and quite crucially, any form of possession is a status: one has rights to, and responsibilities for, the possession in question: i.e. to own a home (qua use-value), or have $50.00 (qua exchange-value), is a kind of status.

Just as the notion of status can be quite complicated, so can the role that enacts it. In particular, a role can be any normative practice – and hence anything that one does or says, any sign that one purposely gives or unconsciously gives off (cf. Goffman, 1959). It may range from wearing a particular kind of hat to having a particular style of beard, from techniques of the self to regional cooking, from standing at a certain point in a soccer field to sitting at a certain place at a dinner table, from deferring judgment to a certain set of people to praying before certain icons, from having various physical traits to partying on certain dates, from expressing certain desires to espousing certain beliefs. More generally, a role can be any sign that one gives (off) for others to interpret, and any interpretant of the signs others give (off).

Just as statuses are no more mysterious than any other object, attitudes are no more mysterious than any other interpretant. Hence attitudes may be affective interpretants (blushing when you learn your date used to be a porn star), energetic interpretants (reaching for your pistol when you learn your date is a bounty hunter), or representational interpretants (saying 'you can't be serious' when your date makes his or her intentions known). In particular, attitudes may themselves be ultimate interpretants, and hence statuses: i.e. my status might be regimented by others' attitudes towards my status, which are themselves just statuses.

Given that others may use any sign or interpretant that one expresses as a means to infer one's status, and given that one inhabits a multitude of constantly changing statuses, there is much ambiguity: not only does the same person inhabit many statuses and many persons inhabit the same status but also many different roles can indicate the same status and the same role can indicate many different statuses. For these reasons, the idea of an 'emblematic role' should be introduced. For example, wearing a uniform (say, that of a sergeant in the army) is probably the exemplary emblematic role. It is minimally ambiguous and maximally public. Members of a status have it in common; it contrasts them with members of other statuses; and members of all such statuses are conscious of this contrastive commonality. It may only and must always be worn by members of a certain status. And finally, it provides necessary and sufficient criteria for inferring that the bearer has the status in question – see Table 12.3. While most statuses don't come with uniforms, they nonetheless have **relatively** emblematic roles – or roles which satisfy some, but not all, of these criteria.

In addition to emblematic roles, there are several other key means by which statuses are distinguished, perpetuated, explicated and objectified. While the emphasis so far has been on the commitments and entitlements that constitute a particular status, this is merely the substance of a status: what anyone who holds that status has in common with others who hold that status. As implicit in Linton's definition, any status is also defined by its contrast to other statuses (its commitments and entitlements in relation to their commitments and entitlements): husband versus wife, parent versus child, etc. And finally, though not remarked upon by Linton, anyone who inhabits a status usually has a second-order, or 'reflexive' understanding of this contrastive commonality – typically called self-consciousness. These are often structured as stereotypes, and they may be the crucial locus for the expectations underlying another's behaviour: he must be a waiter, because he has a stereotypic sign of being a waiter; and if he is a waiter, then he should behave in further stereotypic ways – not so much grounded in commitments and entitlements, as similar to some culturally-circulating exemplar or prototype of a waiter.

Table 12.3 The four dimensions of relatively emblematic roles

Phenomenological	A role which is **maximally public** (i.e. perceivable and interpretable); and a role which is **minimally ambiguous** (i.e. one-to-one and onto)
Relational	A role which all members of a status have in **common**; a role by which members of different statuses **contrast**, and a role of which all members are **conscious**
Normative	A role which may (only) be expressed by members of a particular status; and a role which **must (always)** be expressed by members of a particular status
Epistemic	A role which provides **necessary** and **sufficient** criteria for inferring (and/or ascribing) the status in question

In short, a status should be defined as a collection of commitments and entitlements to signify and interpret in particular ways; a role should be defined as any mode of signification or interpretation that enacts these commitments and entitlements; and an attitude should be defined as any interpretant of a status through a role – usually itself another status. Here, then, is where modality (entitlement and commitment) is most intimately tied to meaning (signification and interpretation).

It should be emphasized, then, that the definition of status being developed here should not be confused with the folk-sociological understanding of status as relative prestige, qua 'high status' and 'low status'. Moreover, the definition of role being developed here should not be confused with the folk-sociological sense of 'status symbols'.

So far the discussion has been about social statuses as particular kinds of object, or ultimate interpretants. However, the entire analysis can be extended to cover mental states – or what might best be called 'intentional statuses' – as particular kinds of ultimate (representational) interpretants. For example, believing it will rain, or intending to go to the store, or remembering that one had bacon for breakfast can each be understood as an inferentially articulated set of commitments and entitlements to signify and interpret in particular ways: normative ways of speaking and acting attendant upon being a certain sort of person – a believer that the earth is flat, or a lover of dogs. A role is just any enactment of that status: actually putting one or more of those commitments and entitlements into effect; or speaking and acting in a way that conforms with one's mental states. And an attitude is just another's interpretant of one's mental state by way of having perceived one's roles: I know you are afraid of dogs, as a mental state, insofar as I have seen you act like someone afraid of dogs; and as a function of this knowledge (of your mental state through your role), I come to expect you to act in certain ways – and perhaps sanction your behaviour as a function of those expectations (where such sanctions are often the best evidence of my attitude towards your mental state).

The real difference, then, between social statuses and mental states, is that mental states are inferentially articulated (their propositional contents stand in logical relation to other propositional contents) and indexically articulated (their propositional contents stand in causal relation to states of affairs). For example, and loosely speaking: beliefs may logically justify and be logically justified by other beliefs; perceptions may logically justify beliefs and be indexically caused by states of affairs; and intentions may be logically justified by beliefs and be indexically causal of states of affairs (Brandom, 1994; Kockelman, 2006c). Table 12.4 orders what are perhaps the five most basic mental states as a function of their prototypic inferential and indexical articulation: memory, perception, belief, intention and plan.

Finally, there are relatively emblematic roles of mental states: behaviours (such as facial expressions and speech acts) which provide relatively incontrovertible evidence of one's mental state. This means that the so-called privateness of mental states is no different from the privateness of social statuses: each is only known through the roles that enact them, and only incontrovertibly known when these roles are emblematic. Such a fact is captured in the phrase *to wear one's heart on one's sleeve*. As we will take up in detail, speech acts such as *I believe it's going to rain* are relatively emblematic signs of both the propositional mode (belief) and the propositional content (that it's going to rain). Moreover, the so-called subjectivity of mental states arises from the fact that they may fail (normatively speaking) to be logically justified (or logically justifying), and they may fail (normatively speaking) to be indexically causal (or indexically caused). There are nonsated intentions, false beliefs, invented memories, non-veridical perceptions, plans that fall through, and so forth. In short, mental states have been theorized from the standpoint of social statuses, on the one hand, and speech acts, on the other. This is the proper generalization of Peirce's

Table 12.4 Inferential and indexical articulation of intentional statuses

	Observation		Assertion	Action	
Couched as semiotic process	Observation		Assertion	Action	
Couched as mode of commitment	Empirical		Epistemic	Practical	
Couched as mental state	Memory	Perception	Belief	Intention	Plan
Stand as reason	×	×	×		
Stand in need of reason			×	×	×
Caused by state of affairs	×	×			
Causal of state of affairs				×	×
Non-displaced causality		×		×	
Displaced causality	×				×

understanding of ultimate representational inter-pretants – when grounded in a wider theory of sociality and linguistics.

Another way to characterize all these ultimate (representational) interpretants is as 'embodied signs'. In particular, ultimate (representational) interpretants, and mental states and social statuses more generally, have the basic structure of semiotic processes: they have roots leading to them (insofar as they are the proper significant effects, or interpretants, of other signs); and they have fruits following from them (insofar as they give rise to modes of signifying and interpreting, or roles, that may be interpreted by others' attitudes). The key caveat is that the mental state or social status itself is non-sensible or 'invisible': one knows it only by its roots and fruits, the sign and interpretant events that lead to it and follow from it. For example, any number of sign events may lead to the belief that it will rain tomorrow (you hear it on TV, your farmer friend tells you, the sky has a certain colour, you hear the croaking of the toads, etc.), and any number of sign events may follow from the belief it will rain tomorrow (you shut the windows, you tell your friends, you buy an umbrella, you take in the washing, etc.). Thus, intentional statuses are inferentially and indexically articulated: they may logically lead to and follow from other intentional statuses; and they may causally lead to and follow from states of affairs. In this way, so-called 'mental states' may be understood as complex kinds of embodied signs that humans are singularly adept at tracking. And so-called 'theory of mind' is really just a particular mode of the 'interpretation of signs'.

More generally, the attitudes of others towards our social statuses and mental states are evinced in their modes of interacting with us: they expect certain modes of signification and interpretation from us (as a function of what they take our social statuses and mental states to be); and they sanction certain modes of signification and interpretation from us (as a function of these expectations). Thus, we perceive others' attitudes towards our social statuses and mental states in their modes of interacting with us (just as we perceive others' social statuses and mental states by their patterns of behaviour). In this way, if one wants to know where social statuses and mental states reside, or where ultimate (representational) interpretants are embodied and embedded, the answer is as follows: in the sanctioning practices of a sign-community, as embodied in the dispositions of its members, and as regimented by reciprocal attitudes towards each others' social statuses and mental states (as evinced in each other's roles). If you think this is circular, you're right; if you think circularity is bad or somehow avoidable, you're wrong. Indeed, if there is any sense to the slogan *meaning is public*, this is it.

12.4 PERFORMATIVITY REVISITED: SEMIOTIC AGENTS AND GENERALIZED OTHERS

The 'signer' is the entity that brings a sign into being – that is, brings a sign into being (in a particular time and place) such that it can be interpreted as standing for an object, and thereby give rise to an interpretant. It is often accorded a maximum sort of agency, such that not only does it control the expression of a sign but also it composes the sign–object relation, and commits to the interpretant of that relation. As will be used here, to **control** the expression of a sign means to determine its position in space and time. Loosely speaking, one determines where and when a sign is expressed. To **compose** the relation between a sign and an object means to determine which sign stands for the object and/or which object is stood for by the sign. Loosely speaking, one determines what a sign expresses and/or how this is expressed. To **commit** to the interpretant of a sign–object relation, means to determine what its interpretant will be. This means being able to anticipate what the interpreter will do – be the interpreter the signer itself (at one degree of remove), another (say, someone other than the signer), or 'nature' (in the case of regimentation by natural causes rather than by cultural norms): see Table 12.1, column 7. Phrasing all these points about residential agency in an Aristotelian idiom, the committer determines the end, the composer determines the means, and the controller determines when and where the means will be wielded for the end. In this way, one may distinguish between 'undertaker-based agency' (control: when and where), 'means-based agency' (composition: what and how), and 'ends-based agency' (commitment: why and to what effect).

Notice, then, that there are three distinguishable components of a signer (controller, composer and committer), corresponding to three distinguishable components of a semiotic process (sign, object and interpretant). When the sign involves verbal behaviour, and the signer controls, composes and commits, the signer is usually called a 'speaker'. And when the sign involves non-verbal behaviour, and the signer controls, composes and commits, the signer is usually called an 'actor'. In both cases, responsibility for some utterance or action – some 'word' or 'deed' – is usually assigned as a function of the degree to which the signer controls, composes and commits. And, as a function of this responsibility, the signer may be rewarded or punished, praised or blamed, held accountable or excused, and so on.

One understanding of agency would locate it at the intersection of these dimensions of control, composition and commitment. In particular, it may be shown that each of these three dimensions, or statuses, is not usually simultaneously inhabited by identical, individual, human entities. For example, the signer need not an individual (nor need be any of its individual components – controller, composer, committer). It may be some less than or larger than individual entity – say, a super-individual (e.g. a nation-state) or a sub-individual (e.g. the unconscious). The signer need not be human. It may be any sapient entity (e.g. a rational adult person or an alien life form with something like natural language), sentient entity (e.g. a dog or fish), responsive entity (e.g. a thermostat or pinwheel), or even the most unsapient, unsentient and unresponsive entity imaginable (e.g. rocks and sand as responsive only to gravity and entropy). More generally, these signers may be distributed in time (now or then), space (here or there), unity (super-individual or sub-individual), individual (John or Harry), entity (human or non-human) and number (one or several). In this way, agency involves processes which are multi-dimensional, by degrees, and distributed. Accountability scales with the degree of agency one has over each of these dimensions.

For the moment, it is enough to focus on the last of these three dimensions. By 'commitment' is meant that a signer can 'internalize' another's interpretant. More carefully phrased, to commit to the interpretant of a sign means that one is able to anticipate what sign the interpreter will express, where this anticipation is evinced in being surprised by and/or disposed to sanction, non-anticipated interpretants. Mead (1934), for example, made a famous distinction between the gestural and the symbolic (and see Vygotsky, 1978). In particular, he says that

> The vocal gesture becomes a significant symbol … when it has the same effect on the individual making it that it has on the individual to whom it is addressed or who explicitly responds to it, and thus involves a reference to the self of the individual making it. (Mead, 1934: 46)

That is, for Mead, symbols are inherently self-reflexive signs: the signer can anticipate another's interpretant of a sign insofar as the signer can stand in the shoes of the other, and thereby expect and/or predict the other's reaction insofar as they know how they themself would respond in a similar situation. In this way, the symbolic for Mead is the realm of intersubjective behaviour in which one can seize control of one's appearance – and

thereby act for the sake of others' interpretants. For example, in Mead's terms, using a hammer to pound in a nail is gestural, whereas wielding a hammer to (covertly) inform another of one's purpose (rather than, or in addition to, driving a nail through a board) is symbolic.

Crucially, while Mead's distinction between the gestural and the symbolic relates to Peirce's distinction between index and symbol, they should not be confused. Moreover, Mead's terms should not be confused with the everyday meaning of gesture (say, in comparison to verbal language). Indeed, for Mead, the features of a semiotic process that really contribute to its being a symbol rather than a gesture are whether the ground (or sign–object relation) is symbolic rather than indexical, and whether the sign is symmetrically accessible to the signer's and interpreter's senses: i.e. signs with relatively conventional grounds (in Peirce's sense) are more likely to be symbols (in Mead's sense); and signs with relatively indexical grounds (in Peirce's sense) are more likely to be gestures (in Mead's sense). And by symmetric is meant that the sign appears to the signer and interpreter in a way that is sensibly identical: both perceive (hear, see, smell, touch) the sign in a relatively similar fashion. For example, spoken language is relatively symmetric and a facial expression is relatively asymmetric, with sign language being somewhere in the middle. (Mirrors are one of the ways we endeavour to make symmetric relatively asymmetric signs.) In short, taking Mead's cues, semiotic processes whose signs are relatively symmetric, and whose grounds are relatively symbolic, are easier to commit to than semiotic processes whose signs are relatively asymmetric, and whose grounds are relatively iconic-indexical. And commitment is crucial because it allows for self-reflexive semiosis, in which a signer has internalized – and hence can anticipate – the interpretants of others. Commitment, then, is fundamental to reflexivity as a defining feature of selfhood.

As used here, an **addressed** semiotic process is one whose interpretant a signer commits to, and one whose sign is expressed for the purpose of that interpretant. Address may be **overt** or **covert** depending on whether or not the interpreter is meant to (or may easily) infer the signer's commitment and purpose. These distinctions (committed and non-committed, addressed and non-addressed, overt and covert) cross-cut pre-theoretical distinctions such as Mead's distinction between 'gesture' and 'symbol' (1934), and Goffman's distinction between signs 'given' and signs 'given off' (1959). Needless to say, the ability to commit to an interpretant of a sign – and thereby address one's semiotic processes and/or dissemble with one's addressed semiotic processes – turns on relatively peculiar cognitive properties of signers, social properties of sign communities and semiotic properties of signs.

Just as one can commit to others' interpretants of one's signs, one can commit to others' attitudes towards one's roles: i.e. one can anticipate what attitude the interpreter will adopt, where this anticipation is evinced in being surprised by and/or disposed to sanction, non-anticipated attitudes. In a Meadian or Vygotskian idiom, one can 'internalize' another's attitude (towards one's status). And, in cases of self-reflexive semiosis, where this other is oneself, one can self-sanction one's own behaviour as conforming or not with one's status. This is, of course, a crucial aspect of selfhood.

For the moment, it should be noted that it is both a relatively human-specific and a relatively sign-specific capability. In particular, it seems that only humans, and only humans at a particular age, can commit to others' attitudes (i.e. affect certain roles such that others will take them to have certain statuses as evinced in these others' attitudes); and this commitment is differentially possible as a function of what kind of role, and hence sign, is being committed to (e.g. relatively symbolic semiotic processes are easier to commit to than relatively indexical semiotic processes, and emblematic roles are relatively easy to commit to almost by definition). Indeed, this relative ability to commit to others' attitudes may lead to three sorts of discrepancies:

- cases where the attitudes of others take us to have statuses our own attitudes don't;
- cases where our own attitudes take us to have statuses the attitudes of others don't;
- and cases where neither our own attitudes, nor the attitudes of others, take us to have statuses we seem to have (insofar as our behaviour evinces it as a regularity, though perhaps not a norm).

Some senses of the term 'unconscious' turn on exactly these kinds of discrepancies.

Each individual has many statuses, and each of these statuses is regimented via the attitudes of different sets of others (cf. Mead, 1934; Linton, 1936). Usually, these sets are institution-specific (indeed, this is one of the key criteria of any institution). For example, as a mother, my status is regimented by the attitudes of my children, my husband, the babysitter, several close friends, my own parents, and so forth. As a bank-teller, my status is regimented by the attitudes of my boss, my co-workers, my customers, and so forth. As a shortstop (baseball fielder), my status is regimented by the attitudes of the pitcher, the basemen, the other fielders, the batter, the fans, and so forth. As someone committed to the claim that you had ice-cream for dessert last night, my status is regimented by your attitude (insofar as you just

informed me of this), and perhaps the attitudes of any other participants in the speech event, and so forth. And, within each of these institutions, my attitudes regiment the statuses of my children and husband, my boss and customers, my basemen and batters, the participants in our speech event. In short, for each of our statuses, there is usually a set of others whose attitudes regiment it, and whose statuses our attitudes help regiment. The speech event is perhaps the minimal generalized other: a speaker and an addressee, each regimenting the social statuses and mental states of the other; what we intersubjectively know about each other given the immediate context; what we intersubjectively know about each other given the ongoing discourse; and what we intersubjectively know about each other given our shared culture.

In cases where one has committed to the regimenting attitudes of sets of others towards one's status (within some institution), the sets of committed to (or 'internalized') attitudes may be called a 'generalized other', loosely following Mead's famous definition (1936: 154). (Indeed, we can say that a status is that to which all attitudes conditionally relate.) Most of us have an infinity of generalized others, some being wide enough to encompass all of humanity (say, our status as a person – at least we hope so), some being so narrow as to encompass only our lovers (say, as holding a certain awkward desire that we have shyly informed them of). And sometimes we have statuses, as regimented by the attitudes of others, that we have not internalized. These form part of what may be called our unconscious self. These questions – of different kinds of multiply overlapping generalized others, and of conscious and unconscious selves (via committed to and uncommitted to, or internalized and uninternalized attitudes) – are crucial for understanding agency and selfhood. Here, then, the true importance of emblematic roles comes to the fore: they are our best means of securing mutual recognition, or rather intersubjective attitudes.

Putting all these ideas together we may revisit Austin's understanding of performativity. For a sign event to be felicitous it must be appropriate in context and effective on context. And sign events are only **appropriate** insofar as participants already have certain social statuses and mental states (or in which a space of intersubjectively recognized commitments and entitlements is already in place), and are only **effective** insofar as participants come to have certain social statuses and mental states (or by which a change in the space of intersubjectively recognized commitments and entitlements takes place). Thus, just as we comport within a given space of commitments and entitlements, our comportment changes the space of commitments and entitlements. Finally, Austin made a distinction between relatively explicit and relatively implicit speech acts – usually signs with propositional content and illocutionary force (e.g. *shut the door* or *sixpence it won't rain*). Indeed, his real focus is on 'explicit performatives', or verbal utterances whose illocutionary force has propositional content (e.g. *I order you to shut the door* or *I bet you sixpence that it won't rain*). In the idiom of Brandom, such primary performatives make explicit the action being performed and hence, in the idiom introduced above, count as relatively emblematic signs of already existing and subsequently existing social statuses and mental states.

But prior to Austin's understanding of performativity in terms of explicitness/implicitness and appropriateness/effectiveness, and the legions of scholars influenced by it, Mead (1934) made a distinction between the me versus the I on the one hand, and symbols versus gestures on the other. As already discussed, the symbol/gesture distinction is really a distinction between semiotic processes whose interpretants one can or cannot commit to (and hence is a question of relative degrees of self-reflexivity, emblemeticity, and/or explicitness). And, for Mead, 'The "I" is the response of the organism to the attitudes of the others; the "me" is the organized set of attitudes of others which one himself assumes' (1934: 175). That is, the me is the status of the self as regimented by the attitudes of some generalized other. And the I is the role of the self that transforms the generalized other. Or, in the idiom introduced above – a semiotic and temporal reading of Linton, Mead and Austin – the me is the self as appropriating, having taking into account others' attitudes towards its social and intentional statuses; and the I is the self as effecting, enacting social and intentional roles that change others' attitudes.

NOTE

1 This essay is a highly abridged and slightly extended version of Kockelman, P. (2005) 'The semiotic stance', which appeared in *Semiotica*, 157(1): 233–304.

REFERENCES

Austin, J. L. (2003 [1955]). *How to do Things with Words*. 2nd edn. Cambridge, MA: Harvard University Press.

Bourdieu, P. (1977 [1972]) *Outline of a Theory of Practice*. Cambridge: Cambridge University Press.

Brandom, R. (1979) 'Freedom and Constraint by Norms'. *American Philosophical Quarterly*, 16(3): 187–196.

Brandom, R. (1994) *Making it Explicit: Reasoning, Representing, and Discursive Commitment*. Cambridge, MA: Harvard University Press.

Brown, R. and Gilman, A. (1972 [1960]) 'The pronouns of power and solidarity', in P. P. Giglioli (ed.), *Language and Social Context*. New York: Penguin. pp. 252–82.

Colapietro, V. M. (1989) *Peirce's Approach to the Self: A Semiotic Perspective on Human Subjectivity*. Albany, NY: State University of New York Press.

Goffman, E. (1959) *The Presentation of Self in Everyday Life*. New York: Anchor Books, Doubleday.

Goffman, E. (1981) 'Footing', in *Forms of Talk*. Philadelphia: University of Pennsylvania Press. pp. 124–59.

Grice, P. (1989) Utterer's meaning and intentions. In *Studies in the Ways of Words*, Cambridge: Harvard University Press. pp. 86–116.

Halliday, M. A. K. and Hasan, R. (1976). *Cohesion in English*. London: Longman.

Hanks, W. F. (1990) *Referential Practice*. Chicago: University of Chicago Press.

Haugeland, J. (1998) 'The Intentionality All-Stars'. In *Having Thought: Essays in the Metaphysics of Mind*, Cambridge: Harvard University Press pp. 127–170.

Jakobson, R. (1990). 'The speech event and the functions of language'. In *On Language*, L. R. Waugh and M. Monville-Burston (eds) Cambridge: Harvard University Press. pp. 69–79.

Kockelman, P. (2005) 'The semiotic stance', *Semiotica*, 157: 233–304.

Kockelman, P. (2006a) 'Residence in the World: Affordances, instruments, actions, roles, and identities', *Semiotica*, 162(1): 19–71.

Kockelman, P. (2006b) 'Representations of the World: Memories, perceptions, beliefs, plans, and intentions', *Semiotica*, 162(1): 72–125.

Labov, W. (1966) 'Hypercorrection by the lower middle class as a factor in linguistic change'. In W. Bright (ed), *Sociolinguistics: Proceedings of the UCLA Sociolinguistics Conference, 1964*. The Hague: Mouton. pp. 84–113.

Linton, R. (1936) *The Study of Man*. Appleton, Century, and Crofts.

Marx, K. (1967) Capital, Vol. 1. New York: Free Press.

Mead, G. H. (1934) *Mind, Self, and Society From the Standpoint of a Social Behavioralist*. Edited by Charles S. Morris. Chicago: University of Chicago Press.

Morris, C. W. (1938) *Foundations of the Theory of Signs*. Chicago: University of Chicago Press.

Parmentier, R. J. (1994) 'Peirce divested for nonintimates' in *Signs in Society: Studies in Semiotic Anthropology*. Bloomington, IN: Indiana University Press. pp. 3–22.

Peirce, C. S. (1931–35) *Collected Papers of Charles Sanders Peirce*, 6 volumes. Edited by C. Hartshorne and P. Weiss. Cambridge, MA: Harvard University Press.

Peirce, C. S. (1955a) 'Logic as semiotic: the theory of signs', in Justus Buchler (ed) *Philosophical Writings of Peirce*. New York: Dover Publications. pp. 98–119.

Peirce, C. S. (1955b) 'The principles of phenomenology', in J. Buchler (ed.), *Philosophical Writings of Peirce*. New York: Dover Publications. pp. 74–97.

Peirce, C. S. (1955c) 'Pragmatism in retrospect: a last formulation', in J. Buchler (ed.), *Philosophical Writings of Peirce*. New York: Dover Publications. pp. 269–89.

Sachs, H., Schegloff, E. A. and Jefferson, G. (1974) 'A simplest systematics for the organization of turn-taking for conversation', *Language*, 50, 696–734.

Sapir, E. (1985 [1927]) 'The unconscious patterning of behavior in society', in D. G. Mandelbaum (ed.), *Selected Writings in Language, Culture, and Personality*. Berkeley, CA: University of California Press. pp. 544–59.

Saussure, F. de (1983 [1916]) *Course in general linguistics*. La Salle, IL: Open Court Press.

Searle, J. R. (1969) *Speech Acts*. Cambridge: Cambridge University Press.

Sebeok, T. A. and Umiker-Sebeok, J. (eds) (1992) *Biosemiotics. The Semiotic Web 1991*. Berlin and New York: Mouton de Gruyter.

Silverstein, M. (1995 [1976]). 'Shifters, linguistic categories, and cultural description', in B. G. Blount (ed.), *Language, Culture, and Society: A Book of Readings*. Prospect Heights, IL: Waveland Press. pp. 187–221.

Strawson, P. F. (1971 [1954]) 'Intention and Convention in Speech Acts', in J. Rosenberg and C. Travis (eds.), *Readings in the Philosophy of Language*, Englewood Cliffs, NJ: Prentice-Hall. pp. 599–614.

Vygotsky, L. S. (1978) 'Tool and symbol in child development', in M. Cole, V. John-Steiner, S. Scribner and E. Souberman (eds), *Mind and Society: The Development of Higher Psychological Processes*. Cambridge, MA: Harvard University Press. pp. 19–30.

Weber, M. (1978) *Economy and Society*, Vol. 1, G. Roth, and C. Wittich (eds). Berkeley: University of California Press.

PART 3

Language Variation
and Change

13

Individuals and Communities

Norma Mendoza-Denton

13.1 INTRODUCTION

Some of the greatest controversies taking shape today in sociolinguistics focus on the relationship between the individual and the community. How do individuals' language patterns and individuals' language ideologies fit into society-wide patterns of usage and change? The mechanisms relating individual behaviour to community-wide patterning provide the material for both enduring and new debates within our field. These debates may, for various scholars, take the form of familiar dualisms such as langue/parole, grammar/usage, structure/agency, society/praxis, macro/micro, emic/etic (defined by participants vs defined by researchers; see an especially relevant discussion in Coupland, 2001). This chapter takes as its domain some of the major areas of sociolinguistics and seeks to adumbrate the controversies surrounding the dualisms mentioned above. Despite a conciliatory desire to provide a middle way between the dualisms, I will argue that holding these dualisms in tension gives us analytical affordances that might otherwise be lost. In discussing the history of the field of sociolinguistics from what I have termed Type I, II, and III variationist analyses (Mendoza-Denton, 2002), roughly corresponding to Eckert's three waves (2005), I also aim to elucidate how studies engaging the constructs of practice, performance and identity have emerged as pivotal in modern understandings of the relationship between individuals and communities.

13.2 THE SPEECH COMMUNITY

Much of the study of quantitative sociolinguistics hinges on accounting for the coherence of individual behaviour as it is nested within larger and larger sociocultural structures. We go from individuals to small units, like families or households, to progressively larger and larger units, such as communities of practice and speech communities, all the way out to major sociopolitical aggregates such as the city or nation-state, and beyond to virtual communities that involve no face-to-face interaction across members and which must in effect be imagined (Anderson, 2006 [1983]; though Anderson makes the point that both cities and nation-states are imagined communities as well).

Carpenter and Hilliard (2005) and Meyerhoff and Walker (2007) and Bayley and Langman (2004) all follow Guy (1980) in identifying the relationship of the group to the individual as one of the central issues in the study of language variation and change. Differences in production, basic physical perception and social evaluation are the hallmarks of language in use, and the fact that these dimensions exhibit variation both across individuals in a community, as well as within single individuals, remains a challenge in modelling collectivities at various levels of abstraction.

The term 'speech community' is a hallmark of the twentieth-century innovations in the study of language by anthropologists, sociologists and linguists, and was in use well before these fields had drifted into separate academic entities in the United States (for an excellent extended review of the concept of speech community, see Patrick, 2002). This section will consider the beginnings of the concept of speech community as it arose from the joint theorizing of linguists and anthropologists in the 1960s and 1970s.

Leonard Bloomfield, considered both a linguist and an anthropologist, in 1933 offered the following definition: 'A speech community is a group of people who interact by means of speech … differences of speech within a community are due to differences in the density of communication … sub-groups are separated by lines of weakness in this net of oral communication' (1933: 153–4). Within this definition, two aspects must be noted. The first aspect is that the reference to the density of communication effectively prefigures – down to suggestions for social networking diagrams – the later developments in understanding communities of speakers as social networks (see Vetter, this volume). The second aspect is that such a definition sidesteps the sometimes politically- and historically-motivated, more general notions of 'language' and 'dialect', focusing less on the linguistic object and more on the people using it. Dell Hymes underlines this aspect of the term, going so far as to consider it a prime for analysis:

> Speech community is a necessary, primary concept in that … it postulates the unit of description as a social, rather than a linguistic, entity. One starts with a social group and considers the entire organization of linguistic means within it, rather than start with some partial, named organization of linguistic means, called a "language" (Hymes, 1974: 47).

(See also Johnstone and Marcellino, this volume.)

In privileging social collectivities over linguistic entities, Hymes erected a sustained challenge to the emerging core of the field of linguistics that focused on the abstract faculty of language rather than language in use (Chomsky, 1965), privileging Saussurean *langue* over *parole*, and taking as its domain the architecture of grammar over speakers' actual usage (see Guy, this volume). It is in the focus on speakers' usage that Hymes found commonalities with the work of another emerging figure in linguistics, William Labov.

Variationist starting points: Labov

One of the earliest and most influential statements with regard to speech communities in what was then the nascent field of quantitative sociolinguistics was made in the work of William Labov. In his groundbreaking 1972 study of social stratification in the speech of New Yorkers, he advances a definition of the speech community: 'the speech community is defined … by participation in a set of shared norms; these norms may be observed in overt types of evaluative behavior, and by the uniformity of abstract patterns of variation which are invariant with respect to particular levels of usage' (Labov, 1972: 120). The latter portion of this definition, the phrase 'particular levels of usage', can be understood as having a double

referent: on the one hand, it refers to levels within the speech of individuals (further explained below when we talk about styles) and, on the other hand, it refers to levels within the community as a whole: social stratification. For Labov, social stratification means that: 'the normal workings of society have produced systematic differences between certain institutions or people, and that these differentiated forms have been ranked in status or prestige by general agreement' (1972: 72).

In Labov's model of the speech community, members of the community share social evaluation by means of ranking performances relative to each other, despite the fact that they do not all produce the whole spectrum of styles. In Labov's framework, production differences are expected precisely because of the stratification of the population (not everyone has access to the same language resources), but the key in this framework is that members of the community judge particular performances in the same way, orienting to linguistic features as producing the same status matrix. It is precisely the uniformity of their orientation that **constitutes** the speech community. Some scholars (Rickford, 1986; Williams, 1992; Bucholtz, 1999; Dodsworth, 2005) have argued that Labov puts forth a structural-functionalist, consensus-based model of language, one that stresses underlying agreement and solidarity, privileging *structure* over *agency* (for a sociological precursor to this view, see e.g. Durkheim, 1893; Parsons, 1964). Dodsworth explains:

> Labov … notes that there is inherent individual variation which is usually too constrained to interfere with the regularity of the community pattern … [individuals] are grouped together so that generalizations can be made, and individuals who skew the generalizations are considered aberrant. Social *types*, in other words, are considered robust' (2005: 18).

An important feature of the Labovian framework for speech communities is that it allowed for the quantitative operationalization and replication of his basic findings: by relying on sociodemographic characteristics to divide the community (the social categories in the second column), and making those demographic characteristics relatively uniform (usually based on widely-used multi-index scales of social class), Labov introduced a new way of thinking about social attributes and about the place of individuals in the social matrix. Indeed, in his study of the distribution of (r) in New York City, Labov advances the following strong hypothesis: 'If any two subgroups of New York City speakers are ranked in a scale of social stratification, then they will be ranked in the same order by their differential use of (r)'

(Labov 1972: 44). It was the testability and replicability of these initial bold hypotheses that allowed the Labovian paradigm to emerge as a contender in the newly-emergent field of sociolinguistics. This etic classificatory approach, aiming for scientific objectivity, allowed for a methodological independence from the particulars of communities and led to a focus on the internal workings of social structures, yielding such concepts as *hypercorrection* (the tendency of some groups of speakers to talk above their station, as it were, using greater percentages of features ordinarily associated with a higher social class), and the *lower middle class crossover* (a related phenomenon where the lower middle class overgeneralizes the production of the linguistic features that carry prestige, effectively overshooting the most prestigious target). Broad psychological attributions and motivations such as a group's *linguistic insecurity* (the purported reason for hypercorrection) were advanced, though it was at that level that the testability of the claims ceased. The paradigm established by these studies is what I call Type I: sociodemographic variation (Mendoza-Denton, 2002), see also Eckert's first wave (2005).

Ethnography of speaking/ethnography of communication: Gumperz and Hymes

Shortly before Labov began work on developing his framework based on the linguistic analysis of urban dialects on the East Coast of the United States, anthropologists Dell Hymes and John Gumperz, working within the discipline of anthropology at Berkeley, were contributing to the development of the ethnography of speaking approach (proposed by Hymes in a 1962 essay), a new approach within linguistic anthropology that sought to go beyond traditional grammatical descriptions of 'exotic' languages to put emphasis on the uses to which language was put. (See also chapters by Johnstone and Marcellino, and by Gordon, this volume.) Ethnography of speaking was concerned with describing **speaking** in its own right, and looked to bounded events and ritual performance as descriptive starting points. Thus, instead of focusing exclusively on the rules of grammar, or the possible grammaticality of sentences, or even on the collective agreement of social evaluations of particular features (as Labov did), ethnographers of speaking sought to discover ways of speaking through in-depth investigations within the community, starting with analyst-determined **etic** approaches, but always seeking to uncover, through ethnography, participants' **emic** categories. Discovering ways of speaking might involve finding out what counts as a refusal, which situations require a greeting, how one

marks irony or politeness, what might be the appropriate length of a pause – in short, the culturally-specific ways that speech use above the level of the sentence might be organized. This allowed ethnography of speaking to conceptualize not only a *Sprachbünd* 'language area' (German: 'language bond'), where despite having different languages an area might share language features in common (the Balkan *Sprachbünd* has for instance morphosyntactic commonalities that obtain in languages from different families), but also to identify a *Sprechbünd* ('speech area': Neustupný, 1978), where ways of speaking could be shown to be commonly held, even though these crossed language boundaries and even families: in Hymes' example (1974: 49), Austria, Czechoslovakia, Southern Germany and Hungary might form a *Sprechbünd*, and a non-German speaking Czech might display some communicative competence, understanding the pragmatics and speech appropriateness of German hosts despite an inability to speak the language. A recently-emerging *Sprechbünd* would be the current popularity and spread of hip-hop musical and linguistic forms around the globe, where people from radically different languages participate in commonly-held ways of speaking and aesthetic practices. And yet, neither *Sprachbünde* nor *Sprechbünde* are speech communities: 'a speech community [is] defined through the concurrence of rules of grammar and rules of use' (Hymes 1974: 120). Note that in this conception, there is nothing preventing more than one language from applying within a speech community. Indeed, one of the hallmarks of the 1970s ethnography-of-speaking approach is that bilingual and multilingual aggregates could be conceptualized as speech communities (Gumperz, 1962: 16). Although having more than one language in a speech community is not completely inconsistent with the Labovian framework, in practice, the focus on phonological variable patterning has meant that the variants must indeed be quite close to each other so as to form part of a single phonology (see also Kerswill, 1994: 34–6).

Gumperz's (1958, 1968, 1972 [1962]) work in India, and his work in Norway with Jan Petter Blom (Blom and Gumperz, 1972), set the standard for talking about multilingual communities in which diglossia (India) and code-switching (Norway; though see Mæhlum, 1996) were present. In cases of diglossia, specifically in a community such as Khalapur in Northern India which was divided into stable caste/occupational groups, Gumperz found that it was not Bloomfield's frequency of interaction that was predictive of differences, but rather the nature of these interactions: he found more pressures toward uniformity and similarity in the speech of people who were in friendship groups than among people of the same caste or of the same status (touchable/untouchable) (1958: 681). In his later work (1996), Gumperz does take the notion of social networks as building blocks for speech communities, in which 'interpretive strategies are embedded ... and passed on as shared communicative traditions' (Gumperz 1996: 362). Similarly, Hymes observes (1974: 47) that relying solely on frequency of interaction might not be enough, since it is the 'definition of situations in which, and identities through which, interaction occurs [that] is decisive'. In practice, this would mean that a quotidian service interaction with a mere acquaintance might have less of an effect on an individual's speech, despite greater frequency, than occasional contact with an important friend.

Duranti (2003), in a sweeping essay reviewing the history of linguistic anthropology, credits the Hymes/Gumperz ethnography of communication approach for putting the speech community front and centre as a unit of analysis along with speech events and genres. Today, the basic tenets of ethnography of speaking and ethnography of communication have become part of the way that modern discourse-analytic sociolinguists and linguistic anthropologists carry out their work (regrettably, space constraints prevent me from fully covering developments in linguistic anthropology). However, now that these ideas have been incorporated into the basic assumptions of linguistic anthropology and some branches of ethnographically-oriented sociolinguistics, relatively few scholars still label their work ethnography of speaking/communication. Part of the reason is that anthropology itself (though not linguistics) has lost much of its taxonomic drive. In 1974, Bauman and Sherzer could write of ethnography of speaking as

> Consistent with the current views and purpose of ethnography, ... [EoS is research] directed toward the formulation of descriptive theories of speaking as a cultural system. In order to formulate such theories we need to describe the **range** of things that might enable us to comprehend the organization of speaking in social life ... (Bauman and Sherzer, 1974: 98; my emphasis).

Now firmly in a postcolonial, postmodern and post-positivist era, the aims of anthropology are no longer cultural taxonomy or cultural comparison (see *Epistemologies* in Herzfeld, 2001); rather, the focus has moved to analyses of circulation, power, ideologies, reflexivity and identities (for a linguistic anthropological example of this kind of analysis regarding the making of the nation-state as community, see Eisenlohr, 2007).

And yet the modern reflexes and contemporary consequences of the ethnography of speaking

approach are dramatic and perduring: a major contribution of this approach has been definitively liberating sociolinguists and linguistic anthropologists from a narrow descriptive, syntax-and-phonology-based view of language patterns and linguistic variation, and fomenting multiple new foci such as pragmatic patterns, intonational inventories, discourse structures, conversational routines and face-to-face interaction. Imagining community as taking place beyond the constructional blocks of a segmental feature (or even the productive combination of several) has allowed the investigation of:

- political oratory patterns that travel with modernist leanings in Madagascar (Keenan, 1974; Jackson, 2006);
- the diversity of oratory, puberty rites and ways of speaking among the Kuna (Sherzer, 1983);
- language socialization and its imagining of kinship structure in Papua New Guinea (Schieffelin, 1984).

Work on the ethnography of communication also laid the groundwork for the consideration of non-linguistic material (such as silences and their symbolism (Bauman, 1983)), and of the ways that discourse and other semiotic modes such as gesture and intonation work in concert to produce specific speech events (Mendoza-Denton and Jannedy, forthcoming).

Cross-cultural applications of concepts of the speech community

The generality of the initial challenge of both the Labovian and the Hymes/Gumperz notions of speech communities lent itself to cross-cultural exploration: Could this basic unit of analysis hold up cross-linguistically? As speech communities have continued to be theorized, there has emerged a general notion that 'agreement on the social meaning of various linguistic parameters' (Kerswill, 1994: 24) is important, and yet there is still no consensus on how to treat individual performances in the distribution of community norms. The Labovian speech community is nowadays defined and tested by the agreement on social meaning implicit in the patterned production of variables that is the outcome of research designs such as that outlined above.

We are still left with a thorny question originally raised by Bickerton (1971): Is it the case that what looks like community variation is the disparate idiolects of individuals, lumped together by the analysts? Gumperz (1982: 24) remarks on the flip side of this question: that patterns that seem 'irregular at the level of the individual nonetheless show systematic regularities at the level of social facts'.

Meyerhoff and Walker (2007) explicitly address some of these issues by testing different models of creole grammars in their study of the Caribbean community of Bequia, a small creole-speaking island in St. Vincent and the Grenadines that exhibits patterns of circular migration to cities in the United Kingdom and Canada. Meyerhoff and Walker conclude that, despite sometimes long absences, the urban sojourners from Bequia largely share the grammatical constraints of their specific villages of origin within the island, patterns which can be distinguished by the ordering of insertion/deletion of the copula *be*. They propose that the degree of embeddedness in strong social networks (for more on social networks, see Vetter, this volume) both before and during the sojourn will affect an individual sojourner's retention of features and constraint rankings in their specific, localized variety of Caribbean English. This hypothesis remains a challenge in quantitative studies of migrants.

Santa Ana and Parodi (1998) sought to address the evaluation aspect of the quantitative speech communities framework, and proposed some modifications to Labov's original concept, in particular questioning the notion of agreement on evaluation of forms across the speech community. They sampled a rural Mexican population in El Bajío, Michoacán, where they were unable to argue for a single **unified** speech community in the classical sense, but rather found that some community members 'demonstrated no awareness of any of the social evaluation patterns of language variation' (1998: 26). They hypothesized that it was possible for single individuals to be part of such tight-knit social networks that they would be relatively unaware of the stigma of their own speech forms, even when surrounded by community members who perceived the stigma. Santa Ana and Parodi follow Kerswill's (1994) idea of nestedness of speech communities (and propose four nested levels), focusing on defining speech communities only in reference to the linguistic variable, setting aside all considerations of the social function of language (1998: 33). This particular criterion turns out to be a major difference in the definition of the role that individuals play in linguistic communities. Is it the case that the use of linguistic variables and the presence of associated evaluative behaviours (following Labov) are the primary criteria for delimiting speech communities? As was discussed above, scholars working from an ethnographically- or historically-oriented perspective might disagree: social functions of language such as participation in speech genres, cross-cutting discourse styles, self-identification and feelings of ethnolinguistic identity would certainly be some of the criteria for community membership according to scholars conducting ethnographic work (Spitulnik, 1997; Lo, 1999; Ahlers, 2006; Hill, 2006; Levon, 2007). On the other hand, some quantitative linguists would agree with Santa Ana and Parodi, not only Guy (1980), who argued that the relationship between the group and the individual would reveal that, given enough data, individuals would mirror the rank ordering and constraints of their communities; in addition, recent developments in comparative sociolinguistics have advocated both historical and contemporary grouping and differentiation of speech communities precisely on the basis of the ranking and ordering of variable constraints (Poplack and Tagliamonte, 1991; Poplack 2001; Horvath and Horvath, 2003; for a review of method see Tagliamonte, 2002). Still other scholars, especially in historically-oriented creole studies, follow a mixed method of triangulating variable constraint analysis with historical events that refer to the social life of language in the community (Rickford, 1999). Carpenter (2005) goes so far as to divide the age groups of her speakers according to major historical events in the community that distinguished various phases of racism and contact for African-Americans. Here the epistemological status of emic vs etic classifications begins to emerge; we will return to this point in the section on communities of practice.

Kerswill (1994) tests the Labovian model of speech communities further, this time challenging the assumption that members of a speech community must share a uniform structural [language] base (Labov, 1989: 2), a criterion that would exclude persons who are not originally from the community, community members in contact with other varieties, as well as communities undergoing language shift (Romaine, 1992; Dorian, 1994; Ahlers, 2006). In his study of rural Stril migrants to the city of Bergen, Norway, Kerswill makes the argument that migrants, despite their variable realizations in the production of Bergen variables, nevertheless interpret the production of Bergen features relative to their own Strilelandet phonology, and in fact construct some of their own prestige norms. For example, the lowering of schwa, ordinarily a non-standard feature in native Bergen production, is reinterpreted by Stril migrants as a prestige feature (they use more of it in formal contexts), perhaps giving a sense of sounding more like a true Bergener (Kerswill, 1994: 144–5). Not only is this shift in production creating a sort of micro-speech community, since the Stril migrants all agree on the direction of this style-shifting, but this production norm differentiates Stril migrants from Bergeners as well as from non-migrated Strils.

Crucially, however, this interpretation would be unavailable if one studied migrated Strils separately from Bergeners: Kerswill argues for the necessity of interpreting variation in the whole community rather than restricted parts of it. We might understand these studies as a means of discovering micro-norms and emergent innovations which, if understood through the close analysis of individual speech, can shed light on the processes of *actuation* of linguistic change (Weinreich, Labov and Herzog, 1968).

13.3 THE ROLE OF INDIVIDUALS

The close, contextually-rich analysis of individuals' speech advocated by Kerswill (1994) has been a growing part of quantitative sociolinguistics (though seeded from the beginning in Labov's earliest work), with the growth attributed by some (Johnstone, 1996; Coupland, 2001; Dodsworth, 2005) to a shift from more structure-based to more agency-based theories of language, and roughly from macro-oriented to micro-oriented approaches (Mendoza-Denton, 2002). An ethnographic turn within quantitative sociolinguistics (Bayley, 2002) as well as the *rapprochement* between sociolinguistics and linguistic anthropology (Duranti, 2003) have contributed to this shift as well. One of the main features of the trend toward studying individuals has been the re-theorization of Labov's original concept of style.

Theorizing style

From the perspective of sociolinguistics, linguistic style has been largely understood in a statistical-correlational frame, and variously viewed as a class-stratified byproduct of formality and attention paid to speech (Labov, 1972) – as a phenomenon where speakers actively design their speech for a specific audience (Coupland, 1980; Bell, 1994), or as the codified reflex of repetition and habituation. A more recent line of work in this area (Eckert, 2000; Mendoza-Denton, 2002; Half Moon Bay Collective, 2007; Podesva, 2008) has sought to expand sociolinguistic understanding by viewing style as a jointly-accomplished performance between interlocutors, and by taking its study beyond social stratification to look at communities of practice and beyond single linguistic units to include discourse and interaction-level processes.

In theorizing style beyond the dualisms of formality and informality, Coupland (1980) and Bell (1984) both investigate the ways in which individuals (a travel agent and a newsreader,

respectively) deploy the linguistic resources available to them to accommodate and reflect their audience's expectations. Bell (1984) called it audience design, and took us beyond the construct of attention paid to speech, which had been used by Labov (1972) to explain the difference between formal and informal styles within a single speaker (the more attention paid to speech, the more formal the style), to new territory where one could imagine that individual speakers were actively planning and calibrating how they were going to sound to different interlocutors, whether they were addressees, auditors or overhearers. Bell assumed that 'persons respond mainly to other persons, that speakers take the most account of their hearers in designing their talk' (Bell, 1984: 159). After this point, the study of individuals and their stylistic dimensions became a productive new area that allowed varying combinations of Coupland's social-psychological approach of accommodation with the in-depth case study methods that were more reminiscent of anthropology than the sociologically-oriented random-sample urban studies that had been dominant through the 1970s and early 1980s. Johnstone (1996) effectively spearheads the call for more attention to individuals in language, while Rickford and McNair-Knox (1994) provided further confirmation of Coupland and Bell's claims by showing that a single speaker, whom they nicknamed Foxy Boston, would style-shift not only in response to different addressees, but also style-shift across different topics in an interview. Mendoza-Denton, Hay and Jannedy (2003) show that the talk show host Oprah Winfrey similarly style-shifts according to the ethnicity of referees (persons she is referring to) in her deployment of variably monophthongized /ay/, an African-American English variable.

Radical changes in how we think about individuals and communities become necessary if we are to incorporate the findings of new studies of style. Here, individuals command more than just formal and informal styles, and there is no community-wide agreement on a hierarchy of which styles are more prestigious, since even informal styles are thought to be performed and involve attention paid to speech (Schilling-Estes, 1998, 2002). A crucial point in the new studies of style is that individuals may belong to more than one subcommunity, and in many cases the subcommunities themselves will be defined in terms of networks or practices and will merge, overlap or otherwise coalesce to form even larger communities. Podesva (2008) follows Eckert (2003) and Irvine (2001) in advancing the claim that styles take meaning in relation to one another. In his study of the stylistic resources of a gay San Francisco doctor named Heath, Podesva shows how the phonetic features of stop release and falsetto differ in distribution and combine with other features to create at least two distinct styles, or personae, for Heath: *caring doctor*, while he is interacting with his patients; and *gay diva*, when he is at a barbecue with friends (2008: 4–5). Heath is thus part of two subcommunities (let's call them communities of practice): San Francisco medical professionals and San Francisco middle-class gay men. These two subcommunities would be part of the larger San Francisco Bay Area community. Hence we find that the relationships between styles, individuals and communities described by the Labovian framework are quite different from the relationships envisioned in current studies of individual styles. These differences are most apparent for the researchers known as the third wave of variation theory (Eckert, 2005), often working in the framework of communities of practice.

13.4 COMMUNITIES OF PRACTICE

In addition to speech communities and social networks, the concept of communities of practice (CofP) is one of the main analytic tools used to understand communities in sociolinguistics. Pioneered by Lave and Wenger (1991), with strong roots in the practice theory of Bourdieu (1978), the Cofp framework has been elaborated in Eckert and McConnell-Ginet (1992) and Wenger (1998) (for a review see Meyerhoff, 2001). Communities of practice can be defined via three criteria (Wenger, 1998: 73–83): (a) mutual engagement, (b) a joint enterprise and (c) a shared repertoire. Broadly speaking, CofPs are composed of individuals who routinely interact in a joint activity (a practice that structures their engagement), and it is through the routine and recurrent engagement in these practices that they develop a shared repertoire, linguistic and non-linguistic. A CofP typically describes a small, locally-relevant group such as a family, or a card-playing group, or a corporate subculture. The classic examples are the apprentice tailors studied by Lave and Wenger and the high school students studied by Eckert who labelled themselves jocks and burnouts, and had correspondingly different behaviour toward school norms and vowels to match.

Members of a CofP can name and recognize each other as being engaged in the practice, and crucially this **emic** (member-categorizing) perspective is also shared with social network theorists, and contrasts with the **etic** (researcher-categorizing) perspective adopted in most other quantitative sociolinguistic work. Both Eckert (2000) and Wagner (2008), for instance, created

elaborate social network diagrams, from participant observation and by interviewing students at high schools in Detroit and Philadelphia, respectively. It would be fair to say that, within sociolinguistics, one of the hallmarks of CofP work is an emphasis on ethnographic methods, often resulting in the combination of participant-observation methodology with quantitative linguistic work that is characteristic of variation's third wave.

Although some scholars (Bucholtz, 1999) reject speech communities as a language-based unit of analysis which is incapable of more broadly addressing social theory, in fact CofPs encompass a wider range of phenomena (including non-linguistic phenomena) than speech communities and can thus make different predictions. This creates an interesting tension that I will illustrate with reference to my own work.

The disjunct between what might be found in a CofP analysis vs a speech community framework is especially striking. At the outset I will state that I do not believe that one or other framework is 'right', or that one provides consistently better results than the other. Most of the time, there is no way to evaluate the different predictions that speech communities vs social network analyses vs CofPs might make because researchers ordinarily collect their data within a single set of assumptions. I myself have collected the data I present below ethnographically and within the CofP framework (for reasons explained in Mendoza-Denton (2008) where a full quantitative account is presented), but here I will stress some of the ethnography-language data mismatches for expository purposes.

For my analysis of two communities of practice, the Norteña and Sureña female gang members of Sor Juana High School in Northern California, I conducted in-depth ethnography over the course of more than two years on the high school campus and in the community. Through participant observation and interviews, I was able to identify CofPs corresponding to different groups of young Latinos in the high school; for the linguistic measurements I focused primarily on the girls. The most vigorously marked and defended oppositions were between the core Norteña and the core Sureña gang members, each identifying with different aspects of the Mexican-American migration experience. The Sureñas claimed a recent-immigrant, Mexico-oriented cultural identity, whereas the Norteñas saw themselves as being American minorities, but wholly American. These distinctions permeated every aspect of their recorded discourse and observable behaviour. Semiotically opposed, they claimed not only separateness but outright hostility. Norteñas and Sureñas wore colour-coded clothing (red and blue, respectively), listened to different symbolic music, had differing language ideologies and got into fights with each other. But were they really so different? Although real violence was at stake in their claims, and they protested at the suggestion of being compared to each other, the purely linguistic data on tensing and raising of /I/ > [i] told a different story: core Norteña and Sureña girls had very similar linguistic behaviour, both with high rates of /I/ raising, and the groups that exhibited differences from them were girls who did not share the gang networks, the Latina Jocks and some girls who called themselves the Disco Girls and who were participating in African-American oriented hip-hop culture. The Latina Jocks and the Disco Girls, who named each other in friendship networks, would not have shown up as different in a classic Labovian social-index scale, even if we took their parents' education and social-class background into account: too many of the Latina Jocks' parents had migratory histories indistinguishable from those of the Sureñas, earning the same amount of money and living in the same neighbourhoods (though as Kerswill (1994) points out, perhaps looking into parental social-class background – and racialized status in Mexico, I would add – prior to migration might yield some different results). The point here is that the 'social facts' gathered here were complicated by the 'sociolinguistic facts'. As I mentioned before, one is not better or worse, and with triangulation a fuller picture has emerged. It is entirely possible that the variable measured was simply not very sensitive to the Norteña/Sureña identity dimension, and that other variables still lurk in the data that would show this opposition more robustly (see an especially relevant discussion by Bayley, 2002). In any case, the CofP analytic framework uncovered rich patterning that would have been ignored in a traditional speech communities analysis. For Labov, the problem of actuation is

> ... not a search for individuals, but rather for social locations and social types. The leaders of linguistic change are not individual inventors of a certain form, but rather those who, by reason of their social histories and patterns of behavior, will advance the ongoing change most strongly (Labov, 2001: 34).

In focusing on the positioning of individuals with respect to broad sweeping changes (are they ahead of or behind the curve?), this perspective misses the importance of clustering in the construction of styles and personae.

A feature of Cofp work is that, because it can concentrate on the styles that are built up around specific features, it allows for the historical investigation of styles, something that is not currently possible in the speech communities framework.

Certainly speech-community modelling is the bedrock of the historical investigation of language change, but recognizing overtly-named, and salient, styles or personae has allowed a completely new kind of inquiry. Zhang (2005) looks historically to find that speakers draw on preexisting resources to establish the social meaning of linguistic variation, and that sociolinguistic meaning-making is a cumulative endeavour. She traces Beijing rhotacization back to Qing-dynasty literature in the construction of a specific social type, the Beijing smooth operator, who is a male, working-class, Beijing vernacular speaker with a high degree of rhotacization. Looking historically at styles and personae is a novel development within third-wave variationist sociolinguistics, one that can find productive synergy with historical linguistics and the study of language change.

13.5 PERFORMANCES: DO WE ALWAYS NEED TO PICK A VARIABLE?

One further productive point of tension in the literature arises from the classic definition of a variable, 'a construct that unites a class of fluctuating variants within a language set' (Wolfram, 1991: 23). In this conceptualization, a variable reflects a decision point at which a speaker chooses between alternative ways of saying the same thing. But what if, in performance, individuals did not always need to pick a variable? What if the variants did not have to fluctuate, but could be used simultaneously? Quantitative sociolinguistics does not have a way of modelling this kind of situation, but it is worthwhile to draw attention to the phenomenon Woolard terms *bivalency*, 'the use by a bilingual of words or segments that could "belong" equally, descriptively and even prescriptively, to both codes' (Woolard, 1999: 7). This particular strategy in bilingualism calls attention to forms that resolutely belong to both of the source languages. Woolard argues that this is an agentive, and underanalysed, strategy on the part of bilingual speakers. Woolard provides an example from a Catalan comedian whose comedy lies precisely in not resolving for the audience whether he is speaking Castilian or Catalan, creating ideological uncertainty in a sociolinguistic situation in which language choice is fraught with tension. A somewhat different example comes from Kerswill (1994: 141–2) who, in his study of rural–urban migration in Norway, identified novel pronunciations by Stril migrants of Bergen words with mid-front vowels. Thus, the word for 'freedom', /fri:hɛit/ in Stril dialects and /fri:he:t/ in Bergen, becomes /fri:hɛ:t/ in the speech of Stril migrants to Bergen, despite the existence of /e:/ in

Stril dialects. The use of /ɛ:/ can be interpreted as a strategy of neutrality, this vowel being much more frequent in Stril than /e:/ – the inverse being the case in Bergen. Together with the assignment of a new sociolinguistic function to the Bergen lowering of schwa, this 'mixed' strategy adds evidence to the argument of the creation of a new micro-community that takes elements from both its source and target linguistic varieties.

Some researchers have understood these syncretic elements as 'substratal interference', but I follow Woolard in arguing for a deeper analysis that looks at the interactional context of bivalent utterances to understand what speakers are actively constructing as they creatively and aesthetically combine linguistic elements (see also Johnstone, 1996; Schilling-Estes, 1998).

Not only do the variants not need to fluctuate but also we find that a specific variable usage could have a different social indexicality depending on the context and the time course of the event. Agha (1994), in a discussion of honorification and T/V forms, observes

> … no two tokens of T or V can necessarily be interpreted as alike. Consequently, even if an individual consistently uses T forms over an entire stretch of discourse, different tokens of T may reflect distinct configurations of situational variables at different points in the same discourse. Silverstein suggests that the data of honorific usage does not permit any kind of 'social semantic' calculus at all. Rather, the norms of usage in some particular community indexically associate linguistic categories with multiple, alternative configurations of contextual factors that become apparent only in the T or V usage responding to the one at issue, confirming, as it were, or disconfirming its invoked social dimensions 'in play' (Agha, 1994: 280).

Conceiving of styles in performance – creative, agentive, and unfolding through time, legible to addressees and still with enough room for innovation – is a hallmark of modern sociolinguistics' view of how individuals use and shape language.

13.6 CONCLUSION

This chapter has traced some of the current issues, tensions and controversies in sociolinguistics regarding the constitution of communities and the relationship of individuals to communities. We have covered the variationist beginnings of the notion of speech communities, as well as the understanding of the term in the tradition of ethnography of speaking. Putting that notion to the test, we found that various scholars working with non-homogeneous speech communities found it necessary to expand the definition, calling for attention to the individuals that make up the communities. Retheorizing style in variation theory has been a consequence of the attempt to understand how individual repertoires fit into larger social patterns, and these questions have also given rise to new frameworks such as the community of practice concept. We have noted the dearth of work that can compare predictions and findings made under the speech communities or social networks or community of practice approaches. New understandings of style and individual variation allow for the ambiguity and bivalency of some linguistic variables, and place an emphasis on clustering, historicity and the unfolding of stylistic aggregates either through time or as the accretion of stylistic moves into personae. Future directions include further exploration of the historical dimensions of styles and personae, placing those histories side by side with accounts of language variation and change.

REFERENCES

Agha, A. (1994) 'Honorification' *Annual Review of Anthropology* 3: 277–302.

Ahlers, J. (2006) 'Framing discourse: creating community through native language use', *Journal of Linguistic Anthropology*, 16(1): 58–75.

Anderson, B. (2006) *Imagined Communities*. London, New York: Verso. (1st edn, 1983.)

Bauman, R. (1983) *Let Your Words be Few: Symbolism of Speaking and Silence Among Seventeenth-Century Quakers*. New York: Cambridge University Press.

Bauman, R. and Sherzer, J. (eds) (1974) *Explorations in the ethnography of speaking*. Cambridge: Cambridge University Press.

Bayley, R. (2002) 'The quantitative paradigm', in P. Trudgill, J. Chambers and N. Schilling-Estes (eds), *Handbook of Language Variation and Change*. Oxford: Blackwell.

Bayley, R. and Langman, J. (2004) 'Variation in the group and the individual: Evidence from second language acquisition', *International Review of Applied Linguistics in Language Teaching*. Volume 42, Issue 4, Pages 303–18.

Bell, A. (1984) 'Language style as audience design', *Language in Society*, 13: 145–204.

Bickerton, D. (1971) 'Inherent variability and variable rules', *Foundations of Language*, 7: 457–92.

Blom, J. and Gumperz J. J. (1972) 'Social meaning in linguistic structure: Codeswitching in Norway'. In John Gomperz and Dell Hymes (eds.) *Directions in Sociolinguistics*. New York: Holt, Reinhart and Winston, pp. 407–34.

Bloomfield, L. (1933) *Language*. New York: Henry Holt And Company.

Bourdieu, P. (1978) *Outline of a Theory of Practice*. Cambridge: Cambridge University Press.

Bucholtz, M. (1999) 'Why be normal? Language and Identity Practices in a Community of Nerd Girls', *Language in Society*, 28: 203–23.

Carpenter, J. (2005) 'The invisible community of the lost colony: African American English on Roanoke Island', *American Speech*, 80(3): 227–55.

Carpenter, J. and Hilliard, S. (2005) 'Shifting parameters of individual and group variation: African American English on Roanoke Island', *Journal of English Linguistics*, 33: 161–84.

Chomsky, N. (1965) *Aspects of the Theory of Syntax*. Cambridge, MA: MIT Press.

Coupland, N. (1980) 'Style-shifting in a Cardiff work setting', *Language in Society*, 9(1): 1–12.

Coupland, N. (2001) 'Introduction: sociolinguistic theory and social theory', in N. Coupland, S. Sarangi and C. Candlin (eds), *Sociolinguistics and Social Theory*. London: Addison-Wesley Longman.

Dodsworth, R. (2005) 'Linguistic variation and sociological consciousness'. PhD dissertation, Ohio State University.

Dorian, N. C. (1994) 'Varieties of variation in a very small place: social homogeneity, prestige norms, and linguistic variation', *Language*, 70: 631–96.

Duranti, A. (2003) 'Language as culture in U.S. anthropology', *Current Anthropology*, 44: 323–35.

Durkheim, E. (1893) *De la division du travail social: étude de l'organisation des sociétés supérieures*. Paris: Félix Alcan.

Eckert, P. (2000) *Linguistic Variation as Social Practice*. Oxford: Blackwell.

Eckert, P. (2003) 'The meaning of style'. *Texas Linguistic Forum*, 47: 41–53.

Eckert, P. (2005) 'Variation, convention, and social meaning', plenary address delivered at the Linguistic Society of America annual meeting. Downloaded 30 May 2009 from http://www.stanford.edu/~eckert/thirdwave.html.

Eckert, P. and McConnell-Ginet, S. (1992) 'Think practically and look locally: language and gender as community-based practice', *Annual Review of Anthropology*, 21: 461–90.

Eisenlohr, P. (2007) 'Creole publics: language, cultural citizenship, and the spread of the nation in Mauritius', *Comparative Studies in Society and History*, 49(4): 968–96.

Gumperz, J. J. (1958) 'Dialect differences and social stratification in a North Indian Village', *American Anthropologist*, 60(4): 668–81.

Gumperz, J. J. (1962) 'Types of linguistic communities', *Anthropological Linguistics*, 4: 28–40. (Reprinted (1972) in J. A. Fishman (ed.), *Readings in the Sociology of Language*. The Hague: Mouton. pp. 460–72.)

Gumperz, J. J. (1996) in J. J. Gumperz and S. C. Levinson (eds), *Rethinking Linguistic Relativity* (Introduction to part IV). Cambridge: Cambridge University Press. pp. 359–73.

Gumperz, J. J. (1968) 'The speech community', in D. L. Sills (ed.), *International Encyclopedia of the Social Sciences*. New York: Macmillan. pp. 381–6.

Guy, G. R. (1980) 'Variation in the group and the individual: the case of final stop deletion', in W. Labov (ed.), *Locating Language in Time and Space*. New York: Academic Press. pp. 1–36.

Half Moon Bay Collective (2007) 'The elements of style', poster presented at New Ways of Analyzing Variation Conference, Philadelphia, PA.

Herzfeld, M. (2001) *Anthropology: Theoretical Practice in Culture and Society*. Oxford: Blackwell.

Hill, J. H. (2006) 'The ethnography of language and language documentation', in J. Gippert and N. Himmelmann (eds), *Essentials of Language Documentation*. Berlin: Walter de Gruyter.

Horvath, B. M. and Horvath, R. J. (2003) 'A closer look at the constraint hierarchy: order, contrast, and geographic scale', *Language Variation and Change*, 15(2):143–70.

Hymes, D. (1962) 'The ethnography of speaking', in T. Gladwin and W. Sturtevant (eds), *Anthropology and Human Behavior*. Washington, DC: Anthropological Society of Washington. pp. 13–53.

Hymes, D. H. (1974) *Foundations of Sociolinguistics*. Philadelphia: University of Pennsylvania Press.

Irvine, J. (2001) '"Style" as distinctiveness: the culture and ideology of linguistic differentiation', in P. Eckert and J. R. Rickford (eds), *Style and Sociolinguistic Variation*. Cambridge: Cambridge University Press. pp. 21–43.

Jackson, J. (2006) Getting an edge in wordwise: the social and productive role of political oratory and cartooning in Malagasy democratic political process. PhD Dissertation, Yale University.

Keenan, E. O. (1974) 'Norm-makers, norm-breakers: uses of speech by men and women in a Malagasy community', in R. Bauman and J. Sherzer (eds), *Explorations in the Ethnography of Speaking*. Cambridge: Cambridge University Press.

Kerswill, P. (1994) *Dialects Converging: Rural Speech in Urban Norway*. Oxford: Oxford University Press.

Johnstone, B. (1996) *The Linguistic Individual: Self-Expression in Language and Linguistics*. Oxford: Oxford University Press.

Labov, W. (1972) *Sociolinguistic Patterns*. Philadelphia: University of Pennsylvania Press.

Labov, W. (1989) 'The exact description of the speech community: short-a in Philadelphia', in R. Fasold and D. Schiffrin (eds), *Language Change and Variation*. Amsterdam: Benjamins. pp. 1–57.

Labov, W. (2001) *Principles of Linguistic Change: Social Factors*. Malden and Oxford: Blackwell.

Lave, J. and Wenger, E. (1991) *Situated Learning: Legitimate Peripheral Participation*. Cambridge: Cambridge University Press.

Levon, E. (2007) 'National discord: language, sexuality and the politics of belonging in Israel'. PhD dissertation, New York University.

Lo, A. (1999) 'Codeswitching, speech community membership, and the construction of ethnic identity', *Journal of Sociolinguistics*, 3(4): 461–79.

Mæhlum, B. (1996) 'Code-switching in Hemnesberget – myth or reality?', *Journal of Pragmatics*, 25: 749–61.

Mendoza-Denton, N. (2002) 'Language and identity', in P. Trudgill, J. Chambers and N. Schilling-Estes (eds), *Handbook of Language Variation and Change*. Oxford: Blackwell. pp. 475–99.

Mendoza-Denton, N. (2008) *Homegirls: Language and Cultural Practice Among Latina Youth Gangs*. London: Blackwell.

Mendoza-Denton, N., Hay, J. and Jannedy, S. (2003) 'Probabilistic sociolinguistcs: beyond variable rules', in R. Bod, J. Hay and S. Jannedy (eds), *Probabilistic Linguistics*. Cambridge, MA: MIT Press. pp. 98–138.

Mendoza-Denton, N. and Jannedy, S. (forthcoming) 'Semiotic layering through gesture and intonation: a case study of complementary and supplementary multimodality in political speech'.

Meyerhoff, M. (2001) 'Dynamics of differentiation: on social psychology and cases of language variation', in N. Coupland, S. Sarangi and C. N. Candlin (eds), *Sociolinguistics and Social Theory*. Harlow: Longman. pp. 61–87.

Meyerhoff, M. and Walker, J. (2007) 'The persistence of variation in individual grammars: copula absence in 'urban sojourners' and their stay-at-home peers, Bequia (St Vincent and the Grenadines)', *Journal of Sociolinguistics*, 11(3): 346–66.

Neustupný, J. V. (1978) *Post-structural Approaches to Linguistics*. Tokyo: University of Tokyo Press.

Parsons, T. (1964) *Essays in Sociological Theory*. New York: Free Press.

Patrick, P. L. (2002) 'The speech community', in J. K. Chambers, P. Trudgill and N. Schilling-Estes (eds), *The Handbook of Language Variation and Change*. Oxford: Blackwell. pp. 573–602.

Podesva, R. (2008) 'Three sources of stylistic meaning', *Texas Linguistic Forum. Proceedings of the Symposium about Language and Society – Austin*, 15(51): 1–10.

Poplack, S. (2001) *African American English in the Diaspora*. Malden, MA: Blackwell.

Poplack, S. and Tagliamonte, S. (1991) 'African American English in the diaspora: evidence from old-line Nova Scotians', *Language Variation and Change*, 3: 301–39.

Rickford, J. R. (1986) 'The need for new approaches to social class analysis in sociolinguistics', *Language and Communication*, 6(3): 215–21.

Rickford, J. R. (1999) *African American Vernacular English*. London: Blackwell.

Rickford, J. R. and McNair-Knox, F. (1994) 'Addressee- and topic-influenced style shift', in D. Biber and E. Finegan (eds), *Sociolinguistic Perspectives on Register*. Oxford: Oxford University Press. pp. 235–76.

Romaine, S. (ed.) (1992) *Sociolinguistic Variation in Speech Communities*. London: Edward Arnold.

Santa Ana, O. and Parodi, C. (1998) 'Modeling the speech community: configurations and variable types in the Mexican Spanish setting', *Language in Society*, 27: 23–51.

Schieffelin, B. (1984) 'Ade: a sociolinguistic analysis of a relationship', in J. Baugh and J. Sherzer (eds), *Language in Use: Readings in Sociolinguistics*. Englewood Cliffs, NJ: Prentice Hall. pp. 229–43.

Schilling-Estes, N. (1998) 'Investigating "self-conscious" speech: the performance register in Ocracoke English', *Language and Society*, 27: 53–83.

Schilling-Estes, N. (2002) 'Investigating stylistic variation', in J. K. Chambers, P. Trudgill and N. Schilling-Estes (eds), *The Handbook of Language Variation and Change*. Oxford: Blackwell. pp. 375–401.

Sherzer, J. (1983) *Kuna ways of speaking: An ethnographic perspective*. Austin: University of Texas Press.

Spitulnik, D. (1996) 'The social circulation of media discourse and the mediation of communities', *Journal of Linguistic Anthropology*, 6: 161–87.

Tagliamonte, S. (2002) 'Comparative sociolinguistics', in J. K. Chambers, P. Trudgill and N. Schilling-Estes (eds), *The Handbook of Language Variation and Change*. Oxford: Blackwell. pp. 729–63.

Wagner, S. (2008) *Linguistic change and stabilization in the transition from adolescence to adulthood*. PhD Dissertation, University of Pennsylvania.

Weinreich, U., Labov, W. and Herzog, M. (1968) 'Empirical foundations for a theory of language change', in W. Lehmann and Y. Malkiel (eds), *Directions for Historical Linguistics*, Austin, TX: University of Texas Press. pp. 97–195.

Wenger, E. (1998) *Communities of Practice*. Cambridge: Cambridge University Press.

Williams, G. (1992) *Sociolinguistics: a Sociological Critique*. London: Routledge.

Wolfram, W. (1991) 'The linguistic variable: fact and fantasy', *Journal of American Speech*, 66(1): 22–32.

Woolard, K. (1999) 'Simultaneity and bivalency as strategies in bilingualism', *Journal of Linguistic Anthropology*, 8(1): 3–29.

Zhang, Q. (2005) 'A Chinese yuppie in Beijing: phonological variation and the construction of a new professional identity', *Language in Society*, 34(3): 431–56.

14

Social Class

Robin Dodsworth

14.1 INTRODUCTION

The first empirical linguistic studies to consider social class sought to demonstrate that language variation is structured at the community level. Although variability in language may appear unpatterned at the level of the individual speaker, a clear picture of structured variation emerges when groups of speakers are investigated together. 'Structure' in this rubric refers, in part, to the social patterning of language variation; in the case of class, it refers to the correlation between a speaker's location in a socioeconomic system and use of standard or non-standard language features.

For the purpose of quantitative analysis, social class was originally, and generally continues to be, represented as a set of discrete locations in a socioeconomic hierarchy. Although this approach carries several methodological and theoretical disadvantages, it allowed the discovery of some patterns that persist across languages and settings. Later sociolinguistic approaches to class have produced new kinds of explanations for these patterns, also exploring non-economic components of class. Section 14.2 of this chapter describes early methods and theory, followed by critiques in Section 14.3 and emerging sociolinguistic approaches to class in Section 14.4. Future directions are considered in Section 14.5.

14.2 EARLY APPROACHES

One of the earliest discussions of the relationship between language and social class is to be found in the extensive work of Basil Bernstein (1971), who posited a broad distinction between working-class and middle-class children's discourse. Working-class children, Bernstein claimed, grow up speaking a 'restricted' or 'context-specific' code by virtue of their family and class culture, whereas middle-class children natively use an 'elaborated' or 'context-independent' code. While the concepts of restricted and elaborated codes evolved throughout Bernstein's work, partly in response to linguists' (mis-)reading of restricted as 'deficient', a basic distinction between them is that restricted codes are not used as often to express 'universal' meanings, showing a bias toward meanings that are tied to particular, immediate situations. Because an elaborated code is the norm in academic institutions, middle-class students have an inherent advantage relative to working-class students. Ivinson (Chapter 3) offers a detailed description of Bernstein's view of social class and its relationship to semantic space (see Kerswill, 2007: 58–60 for a discussion of the evidence for restricted and elaborated codes).

Within variationist sociolinguistics, William Labov largely established the early methods in the investigation of class through his quantitative studies of linguistic variation in New York City (NYC) and Philadelphia. Labov (1966a) hypothesized that the variable deletion of word-final or preconsonantal /r/ in words such as *four* and *park*, and ultimately several other linguistic variables, would exhibit the following distribution in New York City: 'given any groups of New York speakers who are ranked in a scale of social stratification, these groups will be ranked in the same order by their differential use of (r)' (38). This hypothesis offers the beginnings of the class model that dominated the early investigations of linguistic variation as a function of socioeconomic status. In particular, it implies that a 'scale of social stratification' is a useful model of the NYC social space, a perspective that led to compelling empirical results but which was later challenged.

The hypothesis was first tested through the analysis of (r) as spoken by salespeople in three NYC department stores: Saks, the most expensive and fashionable; Macy's, moderately priced; and Klein, the least expensive. Citing the sociologist C. Wright Mills' (1951) assertion that salespeople appropriate their customers' prestige, Labov took the salespeople as representatives of three broad socioeconomic groups. To elicit instances of word-final and preconsonantal /r/, Labov approached a total of 264 salespeople, posing as a customer, and asked for the location of a department located on the fourth floor. After hearing the initial response of *fourth floor*, Labov leaned forward and said, 'Excuse me?', thereby eliciting another answer of *fourth floor* spoken in 'careful style' (1966a: 46). Through this method, each speaker provided two instances of preconsonantal /r/ in *fourth* and two instances of word-final /r/ in *floor*. The results are shown in Figures 14.1 and 14.2, omitting tokens that were judged to have neither a fully constricted nor fully absent rhotic consonant.

The results confirm Labov's hypothesis insofar as the salespeople associated with the highest socioeconomic status pronounce [r] at the highest rates, and those associated with the lowest class have the highest deletion rates. In addition, there is a trend towards more frequent pronunciation of [r] in careful as opposed to casual speech.

The results of the department-store survey motivated a large-scale study of five phonological variables through sociolinguistic interviews in the Lower East Side of NYC. The class model used in this study replicates, with some revisions, the model developed in 1961 by the Mobilization for Youth project, a federally-funded programme intended to address juvenile delinquency in NYC. Class is represented as a socioeconomic scale combining the three components of education level, family income and occupational rank.[1]

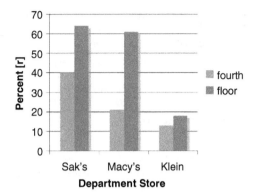

Figure 14.2   Careful Speech (Based on Labov, 1966a: 50).

Uniting three class indicators was considered advantageous, both in Labov's NYC and Philadelphia studies, on the grounds that it would achieve more consistent results than any single indicator and would simultaneously tap multiple dimensions of socioeconomic status (cf. Labov, 2001: 60). Trudgill (1974) uses a similar combined-class scale but considers occupation the most important class indicator because, although economic mobility is possible, class identity and the associated behaviours tend to remain constant: 'even the most affluent manual workers retain the values, ideas, behaviour patterns and general culture of the working class, and there has been little embourgeoisement of the British working class' (Trudgill, 1974: 4). Macaulay (1977) takes Trudgill's reliance on occupation to its extreme by constructing a class scale for Glasgow, Scotland, based **only** on occupational rank. This was done for several reasons: occupational data is relatively easy to collect and is not as sensitive a topic as income; the local schools kept records of each student's father's occupation; and there was no recent demographic survey of Glasgow that could serve as the background for constructing a combined-class index.

In fact, Labov's Philadelphia study includes a comparison of the combined-class index with the individual components of occupation, education and house value: which shows the strongest, most consistent correlations with stable sociolinguistic variables? Multiple regression analyses of three stable sociolinguistic variables, with casual and careful speech treated separately, show occupation to be a more consistent predictor of linguistic variation than education or house value. However, the combined index outperformed any of the individual class indicators. For that reason, a six-category combined-class index was used in the subsequent analysis of linguistic changes in progress (Labov, 2001: 185–6).

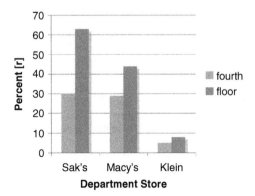

Figure 14.1   Casual Speech (Based on Labov, 1966a: 50).

Table 14.1 Occupational rankings used in the linguistic survey of the Lower East Side of New York City

Occupational rank	Description
IV	Professionals, managers, and officials (salaried and self-employed)
III	Clerks and salesmen
II	Craftsmen and foremen; self-employed white- and blue-collar workers
I	Operatives, service workers, labourers, and permanently unemployed persons

Source: Labov (1966a: 139)

The combined-class index, in various forms, has persisted in studies of sociolinguistic variation since Labov's NYC study, as have many of the methods for constructing it. The occupation component of the NYC class scale has four categories, derived from US Census categories and shown in Table 14.1.

Not directly represented in Table 14.1, but present in Labov's sample, are women who do not work outside the home, and students. To assign occupational ranks to these speakers, Labov used the following procedure:

(1) Husband's occupation was used for all married women except in cases where the wife is working and the husband is retired; (2) widows who do not work were classified by their dead husband's occupation; (3) college students were assigned the highest occupational rank to represent their probable occupational destinations (Labov, 1966a: 178, endnote 5).

The education component is also a set of four categories (Table 14.2). In this case, each individual's educational achievement was used.

The family income component of the class scale (Table 14.3) controls for number of adults and number of children.

For each speaker, occupational, educational and income rank were combined to produce a score between 0 and 9 on a linear class scale. Although this 10-point scale is divided into groups in various ways to show linguistic patterns, Labov broadly designates groups 0–2 as the 'lower class', groups 3–5 as the 'working class', groups

Table 14.2 Educational rankings used in the linguistic survey of the Lower East Side of New York City

Educational rank	Description
IV	Completed some college or more
III	Finished high school
II	Completed some high school
I	Finished grade school or less

Source: Labov (1966a: 139)

6–8 as the 'lower middle class', and group 9 as the 'upper middle class' (1966: 143).

Five primary phonological variables are examined in NYC:

1 Word-final or preconsonantal /r/ as described above.
2 The height of (eh) before voiced stops, voiceless fricatives and nasals, as in *bag, pass* and *ham.*
3 The height of (oh) as in *caught, talk* and *dog.*
4 The (th) as in *thing,* which is variably realized as a stop (*ting*) or fricative (*thing*).
5 The (dh) as in *then,* also realized as a stop (*den*) or fricative (*then*).

In addition, the alveolarization of the nasal in the (-ing) suffix (*talkin* vs *talking*), the fronting of (aw) as in *how,* and the raising and backing of (ay) as in *why* are investigated.

The results are consistent with the hypothesis that the variables would show class stratification, though several different patterns emerge. The first pattern, found for the variables (th), (dh) and (-ing), and idealized in Figure 14.3, is associated with 'stable' sociolinguistic variables,: i.e., those carrying social meaning but not undergoing change.[2] The horizontal axis shows speaking tasks in the sociolinguistic interview that were designed to elicit speech at different locations along a careful/casual continuum, style A being the most casual and D the most careful. The highest social classes show the least overall use of non-standard variants and, for all classes, rates of the non-standard variant decline at approximately the same rate as formality increases. The gradual decline in the use of the standard linguistic form across styles has been understood as evidence that all speakers view the standard form as more prestigious or proper; i.e. speakers from different class groups may show quantitative linguistic differences, but there exists a **shared sociolinguistic norm** concerning which forms are prestigious. Stable sociolinguistic variables may also pattern into two broad class groups – roughly working class and middle/upper class – as is the case for (th) and (dh) in NYC, rather than showing fine class gradations, as in Figure 14.3. Regardless of the number of discernible class groups, women

Table 14.3. Educational rankings used in the linguistic survey of the Lower East Side of NYC New York City

Income rank	Description	Adjusted weekly income per equivalent adult
IV	More than nation's median	$37.32 and above
III	More than Lower East Side median, but less than nation's median	$25.01 to $37.31
II	More than minimum wage, but less than Lower East Side median	$18.01 to $25.00
I	Less than minimum wage	$18.00 and less

Source: Labov (1966a: 140)

generally show higher rates of the standard variants relative to men.

Some stable variables show 'hypercorrection', also called 'crossover', wherein the second-highest class shows lower rates of the non-standard variant than the uppermost class in formal speech contexts. This pattern is often considered evidence of linguistic insecurity, and general social insecurity, by extension, on the part of the second-highest class. Other types of explanations are available, however. For example, Chung (2006) reports anecdotal evidence of Taiwanese Mandarin speakers' hypercorrect use of the standard Beijing Mandarin retroflex word-initial consonants *zh-*, *ch-* and *sh-* in words that normally have the vernacular dental forms *z-*, *c-* and *s-*, respectively. While the use of retroflex consonants does appear to reflect linguistic insecurity or an attempt at formality in some cases, in other cases Chung considers it an emphatic device, carrying true pragmatic meaning.

As Labov (2001: 81–2) observes, the basic pattern for stable variables has been replicated in numerous, regionally-diverse studies, with variability in the magnitude of difference between classes and in the steepness of slopes along the stylistic axis.

A second type of variable, very similar in pattern to stable sociolinguistic variables, is known as 'change from above', led by the uppermost social class and to some extent available for conscious evaluation. In NYC, (r) is a change from above; the prestige variant, [r], rises with class level, and each class also shows a roughly linear rise in percentage of [r] as speaking style becomes more careful. Because changes from above operate within public consciousness, they often show more pronounced hypercorrection relative to stable variables, particularly for women, and the female lead in the prestige form may be similarly more dramatic (Labov, 2001: 274–5).

A third pattern is found for the variable (oh) in NYC and is associated with variables undergoing change 'from below', meaning below public consciousness. Here the working class, or lower middle class, shows higher rates of the non-standard form

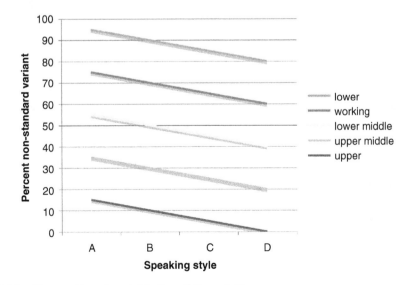

Figure 14.3 Class pattern for stable linguistic variables.

than both the lower and middle classes, except in the most careful style (Figure 14.4). Labov terms this the 'curvilinear' pattern (1966a: 147).

The Philadelphia study, in fact, sets out to test the hypothesis that changes from below show the curvilinear pattern early in their progression. This hypothesis represents a shift away from previous claims that the highest socioeconomic classes lead language change. As Labov (1980) explains, the curvilinear hypothesis was motivated by parallel findings in three independent studies: the raising of (oh), (ay) and (aw) in NYC (Labov, 1966a); the lenition of /ch/ in Panamanian Spanish (Cedergren, 1973); and the backing of (e), as in *bet*, before [l] in Norwich English (Trudgill, 1974).

The Philadelphia study class index combines occupation, education and house value; house upkeep and social mobility (i.e. head of household's occupation relative to that of his/her parents) are also examined but not included in the class index. The dependent variables include eight phonological changes in progress (Labov, 2001: 165). Two of the eight are found to be the newest and most vigorous changes: the fronting of the (aw) nucleus as in *how*, and the fronting of the preconsonantal (ey) nucleus as in *take*. The results of multiple regression, including the independent variables of gender, age and class, show the upper working class to lead both of the new variables, though the significance level is weak in both cases ($p < 0.10$). By contrast, the changes nearing completion, particularly the fronting of (ae) before voiceless fricatives, nasal consonants and voiced stops (treated as three distinct variables), show no significant differentiation across the lower, middle and upper working classes, dropping off gradually in the lower middle, upper middle and upper classes (Labov, 2001: 168, Table 5.4). In other words, the older changes in progress have reached a working-class vs. middle-class distinction, while the newer changes show an overall upper-working-class lead. These findings are consistent with the curvilinear hypothesis.

Stable sociolinguistic variables, as noted, show a monotonic (linear) class distribution rather than the curvilinear pattern. However, the distinction is reliable only for adult speakers because adolescent speakers tend to show disproportionately high rates of stigmatized variants for both stable variables and changes in progress. For that reason, Labov ultimately restates the curvilinear hypothesis (2001: 460): 'Stable sociolinguistic variables combine a flat age distribution for adults with a monotonic social class stratification; changes in progress combine a monotonic distribution in adult age groups with a curvilinear pattern in the socioeconomic hierarchy'.

Not every change in progress, from below, shows the curvilinear pattern; the social trajectory of a variable depends on several factors in addition to class, including the indexical meaning of the variable as it diffuses in time and space (e.g. Johnstone and Kiesling, 2008).

Generalizing Labovian methods and patterns

Several early large-scale urban studies both confirmed and extended Labov's methods and results.

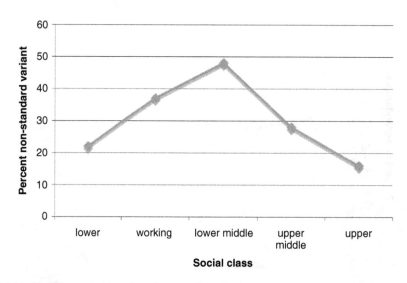

Figure 14.4   Curvilinear pattern for changes from below.

Wolfram (1969), for example, investigated 48 speakers of African-American English in Detroit, building a class model on the criteria of education, occupation, income and residency. Residency included the number of rooms in the speaker's residence, the average number of rooms per person on the block and the percentage of houses with plumbing facilities. The resulting index scores were collapsed into four class categories: upper middle, lower middle, upper working and lower working. The linguistic variable of consonant cluster reduction (CCR) – whereby words such as *most* are pronounced without the final consonant, as in *mos'* – shows a linear class pattern, with the highest classes showing the lowest CCR rates. Females show lower rates of CCR than males except in the upper working class, where the difference is reduced for monomorphemes such as *mist* and reversed for bimorphemes such as *missed*. This finding supports Labov's conclusion that women are more sensitive to socially-diagnostic linguistic processes.

A second variable, theta-stopping – the pronunciation of words like *them* as *dem* – shows a large distinction between the middle classes and working classes, a finding repeated in other work discussed below. Two further variables, the deletion or devoicing of final [d] and the deletion of final [r], show nearly linear class patterns. On the basis of these results, Wolfram concludes that class differences are generally quantitative rather than qualitative; i.e. middle-class and working-class dialects differ chiefly in their **frequencies** of non-standard linguistic forms, rather than in the presence or absence of those forms.

The findings reported in Trudgill's (1974) study of linguistic variation in Norwich, England, follow patterns similar to those of Labov and Wolfram.[3] The analysis of 60 speakers in Norwich employs a class model based on occupation, income, education, father's occupation, type of housing and neighbourhood; the occupational categories were informed by the 1966 Registrar-General occupational ranking. A total of 30 initial class categories were collapsed, based on linguistic results, resulting in five class categories: middle middle class, lower middle class, upper working class, middle working class and lower working class. Third person singular –s deletion (*she talk* vs *she talks*) and 14 phonological variables show (often fine-grained) class sensitivity, with the lower classes using higher rates of non-standard linguistic forms. In addition, some of the changes from below, including the lowering/backing of (e) and the raising and diphthongization of (ae), show evidence of an upper-working-class or middle-working-class lead, consistent with the curvilinear hypothesis.

Macaulay (1977) offers yet more evidence for the structured nature of the relationship between language and class through a sociolinguistic survey of Glasgow. Following both the Registrar-General's ranking of occupations and Kellas' (1968) class model for Scotland, Macaulay uses a four-category class scale to categorize 48 speakers. Classes I and IIa correspond to the middle class, or non-manual labourers, while classes IIb and III correspond to working class/manual labourers. The linguistic variables examined are the vowels in *hit, book, hat* and *now*, plus the glottalization of the intervocalic or coda stop in words such as *better* and *get*. All of the variables show class stratification, with the largest quantitative gap generally found between the middle and working classes. Further, the sex and age groups (men, women, girls aged 15, boys aged 15, girls aged 10, boys aged 10) show nearly perfect in-group patterning of individuals by class, with the age 10 girls showing the only notable divergence from this pattern. Macaulay's findings provide support for the use of occupation as a sole class indicator, and they are consistent with previous findings in showing a middle/working-class distinction.

Covert prestige

All of the preceding studies found higher rates of the non-standard linguistic forms produced by the lower classes, and yet both Labov and Trudgill – and many others – also found that in formal speech settings, most speakers' rates of the standard forms increased significantly. Further, Labov's speakers tended to overreport their use of standard forms. Labov takes these results as evidence of shared linguistic norms within the community: all speakers assign prestige to the standard linguistic forms. But why does the shared norm fail to result in uniform speech across socioeconomic classes? If everyone recognizes the standard forms as prestigious, why do some of them use the non-standard forms at high rates, even in formal speech settings? Labov (1966b: 108) argues that in addition to the prestige of standard linguistic forms:

> ... One can't avoid the implication that in New York City we must have an equal and opposing prestige for informal, working-class speech – a *covert prestige* enforcing this speech pattern. We must assume that people in New York City want to talk as they do, yet this fact is not at all obvious in any overt response that you can draw from interview subjects (emphasis added).

The label 'covert prestige' implies that more than one kind of status drives the distribution of linguistic variables; the mainstream value of standard linguistic forms competes with some other value which is perhaps not legitimate at the top of the economic hierarchy. Specifically, Labov hypothesizes that working-class speech carries masculine or 'tough' connotations, desirable attributes for some. Trudgill (1972) provides evidence for this position, and for covert prestige generally, through Norwich speakers' self-reports of language use. Unlike Labov, Trudgill finds that men **under**-report their use of standard forms, while women **over**-report, and men's self-reports are more accurate than women's. He concludes that 'privately and subconsciously, a large number of male speakers are more concerned with acquiring prestige of the covert sort and with signaling group solidarity than with obtaining social status, as this is more usually defined' (Trudgill, 1972: 188).

Although the overt/covert dichotomy was later refined to allow for more variegated social meaning and practice (Section 14.4), the basic insight that speakers employ linguistic variables toward multiple social ends remains a critical element in the interpretation of class-based variation.

Evidence for the productivity of the Labovian approach to class – categorical, economic, hierarchical and represented as a composite index – has been found through many studies of linguistic variation across languages and geographic regions, including: strong and weak palatalization of stops in Cairene Arabic (Haeri, 1996); the diphthongization of several vowels in Quebecois French (Santerre and Milo, 1978); the merger of unstressed mid-back vowels and the phonemic splitting of a post-alveolar fricative in a northern Russian dialect (Kochetov, 2006); and others cited in Kerswill (2007). In addition to the large-scale urban studies already cited, see those in: Ottawa (Woods, 1979); Paris (Lennig, 1978); Belo Horizonte, Brazil (de Oliveira, 1983); Amman (Abdel-Jawad, 1981); Buenos Aires (Lavandera, 1975); San Juan (Cameron, 1991); Tokyo (Hibiya, 1988); Seoul (Chae, 1995); and others cited in Labov (2001).

Nevertheless, criticisms of the assumptions underlying the Labovian class paradigm, and alternatives to it, have called into question the explanatory power of these findings.

14.3 CRITIQUES OF THE EARLY CLASS MODELS

The use of ordered-class categories to investigate patterns of linguistic variation has met with several areas of criticism. A basic shortcoming which may be seen as having particular relevance for small communities is that the class categories determined by the researcher are not recognizable social groups from the perspective(s) of community members. This criticism need not imply that the class categories have no value, but that their explanatory power is limited. Milroy (1980: 14) argues this point, observing that a composite-class scale:

> ... obviously does reflect social reality to a certain extent and is a sensible way of ordering large amounts of data such as those collected from a large sample of speakers in New York City. But we must not lose sight of the fact that the groups we end up with by segmenting our scale – such as 'lower class', 'working class', 'middle class' – do not necessarily have any kind of objective, or even intersubjective, reality. ... Membership of a group labelled 'lower middle class' does not necessarily form an important part of a person's definition of his social identity.

Rickford (1986), drawing on Macaulay's (1977) justification of occupation as a sole-class indicator, similarly argues that a composite-class scale fails on ethnographic grounds, ignoring locally meaningful distinctions in socioeconomic (or other types of) status that vary by region and community. Despite the community-external validity of composite-class scales – people do indeed have varying levels of income, occupation and education – other types of status indicators may hold greater relevance for sociolinguistic patterns. Linguistic variation within a community arises not only from differential access to the standard language but also from the symbolic marking of locally-recognized social identities.

Rickford argues further that composite-class scales place too much importance on status or prestige, thereby 'failing to take the economic relations and power asymmetries between classes into account' (1986: 216). Class scales imply consensual hierarchy: all community members recognize wealthy and educated people as having the highest status. By contrast, **conflict**-based class theories (Marx, 1906; Weber, 1947) prioritize the antipathy between classes stemming from material and ideological differences. For sociolinguistic analysis, this paradigm predicts that members of the lower classes may aspire to different linguistic standards than those in the middle and upper classes, in symbolic pursuit of in-group allegiance, rather than accommodating to upper-class prestige standards.[4] As Milroy (1980: 19) explains:

> Thus, instead of positing a sociolinguistic continuum with a local vernacular at the bottom and a

prestige dialect at the top, with linguistic movement of individuals in a generally upward direction, we may view the vernacular as a positive force: it may be in direct conflict with standardized norms, utilized as a symbol by speakers to carry powerful social meanings and so resistant to external pressures.

Here we return to the notion of 'covert prestige' but give it overt status: there are types of publicly acknowledged prestige that are not acquired through, and in fact may be compromised by, economic status. A hierarchical class model that ignores this ideological class conflict may produce valid empirical results but fail to engage the social processes that motivate them. More generally, Rickford and others (including Ash, 2002; Mallinson, 2007; Romaine (1984); Williams, 1992; Woolard, 1985) argue for more purposeful and reflective incorporation of social theory in sociolinguistic approaches to class (see also Mallinson, this volume). Milroy and Milroy, referring to the uncritical importation of the traditional consensus-driven class model from sociology, even contend that 'although many impressively consistent patterns of variation have emerged from urban sociolinguistic work, an adequate social framework within which to interpret the results is still lacking' (1992: 2).

Rickford's study of grammatical forms in Cane Walk, Guyana, illustrates the explanatory value of a conflict-based view of class, also showing that lower-class speakers may perceive that no personal gain will come from using standard linguistic forms because the class structure is too rigid. Workers in the sugar plantation fields, members of the Estate Class, use standard English forms including first person pronoun *ai* with an average frequency of 18%, preferring non-standard forms such as the basilectal *mi*. By contrast, members of the Non-Estate Class, who tend to be skilled labourers or foremen, use *ai* with an average frequency of 83%. This dramatic linguistic difference, Rickford contends, results from the rejection of standard English by the Estate Class, who have not experienced it as a means to upward mobility; they believe socioeconomic improvement will only be achieved through class struggle, rather than accommodation to the standard.

The assumption that all classes accommodate towards a single norm was motivated by the stylistic patterns cited in Section 4.2, wherein speakers of all classes show higher frequencies of standard forms in formal speech settings. But as Rickford and others observe, shared ideology – knowing which linguistic forms are prestigious – need not result in shared accommodation to the prestige variety. In addition, sociolinguistic change, particularly change from below, can be viewed as

evidence in support of a conflict model because social change generally results not from community consensus but from some sort of tension (Milroy and Milroy, 1992: 3).

Another shortcoming of early approaches to class pertains to the classification of women. Typically, women were assigned the class level of their husbands ('heads of household') without independent justification for assuming that women derive their class identity from their husbands (Nichols, 1983). Unmarried women were given either the class rank of their fathers or evaluated on the basis of their own socioeconomic information. The latter option has the disadvantage that women, to an even greater extent at the time of the early studies, tended to be excluded from prestigious and high-paying occupations. As Nichols and others observe, these methods preclude the true comparison of women's and men's language, and they call into question the validity of the aggregate results. The problem here is inherent to the structure of the early class models; with a near-exclusive focus on production (see Labov, 1966a: 138), the class index renders marginal anyone without a paid occupation.

There are several additional well-known problems with the early class indices. First, what justifies the placement of boundaries between classes on the scale that results from combining income, education, occupation, etc.? Labov essentially treats the boundaries as artificial, using multiple class groupings to show sociolinguistic patterns. We may instead look for an approach to class that does not require the analysts themselves to create class boundaries in the absence of community-internal evidence. Secondly, discrete class groupings can be seen as overly static, not allowing for individual mobility. Labov (2001) does include mobility as a function of current occupation and father's occupation, but in general an individual's class position is treated as fixed rather than dynamic. Finally, the early class models defined class in isolation from other dimensions of social identity such as gender, ethnicity, age and geographic location. This practice is a particular problem in non-Western and Third-World societies, which have been the subject of relatively little quantitative investigation.

14.4 ALTERNATIVES TO THE EARLY CLASS MODELS

In response to the weaknesses of the early approaches to class, some alternative methods and perspectives emerged, though none has yet led to a full framework for analysing class-based linguistic variation that has definitively replaced Labov's paradigm.

The linguistic market(s)

Sankoff and Laberge (1978) contend that grouping speakers according to their positions in a purely economic hierarchy neglects the fact that economic positions carry varying linguistic demands. For example, although a secretary in a high-profile firm may not occupy the upper middle class in terms of income, education or residence, the secretary must consistently use standard language as a representative of the firm when talking to clients (cf. Macaulay, 1977: 115 for comments to this effect from a Glasgow personnel manager). A speaker's use of standard language forms, Sankoff and Laberge argue, should be measured directly against the speaker's **need** for the standard. Drawing from contemporary social/cultural theorists, they devised a 'class' index to serve this goal:

> Adapting the notion of linguistic market developed by Bourdieu and Boltanski (1975), we undertook to construct an index which measures specifically how speakers' economic activity, taken in its widest sense, requires or is necessarily associated with, competence in the legitimized language (or standard, elite, educated, etc., language) (Sankoff and Laberge, 1978: 239).

For 120 Montreal French speakers, eight judges were asked to rate 'the relative importance of the legitimized language in the socioeconomic life of the speaker' (Sankoff and Laberge, 1978: 241) on the basis of life histories and the judges' familiarity with Montreal's socioeconomic space. On this basis, each speaker was assigned a score on the 'linguistic market' index. Three grammatical variables were examined: the indefinite plural subject pronoun *ils/on*, the auxiliary verb *avoir/être*, and *qu'est-ce que/ce que* as the syntactic head for dependent clauses and other embedded phrases. The speakers who were judged to occupy low positions on the linguistic market index, and thus to have little need for standard language forms, also used lower rates of the standard forms. These results (see also Sankoff et al., 1989) support the use of a linguistic market index as a substitute for the traditional economic class index.

In highlighting the varying economic relevance of standard language forms across positions in the socioeconomic system, the linguistic market index allows for a conflict-based approach to class, as championed by Rickford (1986). It also takes as given that the value of standard language is determined by the community's socioeconomic system, thereby centralizing local social facts rather than imposing an externally constructed 'class' dimension. Woolard (1985) contends that the value of linguistic forms across mutually antipathetic

social classes requires the assumption of 'alternative linguistic markets'. In this view, instead of a single prestige-based market, the linguistic space consists of multiple markets associated with different social groups and thus attaching different values to the various available linguistic forms. The multiple values of a given linguistic variant therefore directly spring from class conflict and the local social space.

Eckert and McConnell-Ginet (1999) use a linguistic market perspective to account for Labov's (1990) findings in Philadelphia that among unskilled workers, women use higher rates of the non-standard (fronter) forms of (ae) and (aw) than men, but among professionals, women use **lower** rates of the non-standard variables. The same basic pattern emerges in Eckert's (1989, 2000) data from Detroit-area high school speakers' (uh) backing and (ay) raising: middle-class 'jock' girls show lower rates of the new, stigmatized variants than boys, while the working class 'burnout' girls use higher rates than the burnout boys. They conclude, 'Such data suggest an extension of the generalization that women have to do much more than men simply to maintain their place in the standard language market. ... women may have to use linguistic extremes in order to solidify their place, wherever it may be' (Eckert and McConnell-Ginet 1999: 195–196).

The linguistic market is also central to Eckert's explanation of the curvilinear pattern. She observes that 'there is an interpretation of [the curvilinear] pattern that suggests that the lower middle class constitutes the buffer between the opposed linguistic markets, demonstrating a tension between participation in the standard and the vernacular markets' (Eckert, 2000: 26). Conscious of this 'buffer' status and also their (often) working-class roots, members of the lower middle class are linguistically insecure.

Life-modes, networks and communities of practice

The role of local social realities in defining class, and evidence for the relevance of class conflict/ tension for sociolinguistics, are even more prominent in subsequent approaches. Milroy and Milroy (1992) argue that an adequate model of sociolinguistic variation will link social class with information about the density and multiplexity of social networks (for an overview of language and social networks, see Vetter, this volume). For example, they contend that the curvilinear pattern cited above, in which the middle socioeconomic groups lead linguistic changes from below, is explicable in terms of network structure. Both the lower and upper classes tend to have the most dense and multiplex social networks, which stifle linguistic change among their members. (But see Kerswill and Williams' 2005 study of working-class residents of a newly-formed town for an example of the co-occurrence of uniplex network ties and low socioeconomic status.) The relatively weak and uniplex ties that characterize middle-class networks enact no such conservative force, and so the middle classes are able to lead linguistic changes.

More generally, Milroy and Milroy argue that the demonstrated correlations between network type and social class 'suggest a route for constructing a two-level sociolinguistic theory, linking small-scale structures such as networks, in which individuals are embedded and act purposively in their daily lives, with larger scale and more abstract social structures (classes) that determine relationships of power at the institutional level' (1992: 16).

In view of the links between network and class, and the demonstrated importance of both for patterns of linguistic variation, Milroy and Milroy posit the anthropologist Thomas Højrup's (1983) concept of 'life-mode' as a useful integrated tool. Højrup recognized three life-modes in Western Europe, each resulting from the macroeconomic structure and defined partly in opposition to the others:

- Life-mode 1 describes those who are self-employed in family businesses, where strong and multiplex network ties are essential to economic success.
- Life-mode 2 is that of unskilled or low-skilled wage earners – the working or lower middle class, using traditional terms. As long as these workers experience some economic insecurity, their class solidarity will ensure dense, multiplex networks.
- People with life-mode 3 are highly skilled wage earners, likely to have some managerial functions and possess considerable career ambition. Because those in life-mode 3 are likely to be individually competitive and geographically mobile and to separate work and family life, they are more likely to have loose-knit networks of the sort that do not impede linguistic change.

The concept of life-mode, Milroy and Milroy argue, represents the organic linking of network and class while also engaging class conflict, particularly in the distinction between life-modes 2 and 3. The difference between strong and weak ties, they contend, and the economic determination of network features, 'will further enable us to specify the conditions in which the linguistic norms of the groups are likely to be focused or diffuse, and the conditions in which they are open to, or resistant to, change' Milroy and Milroy, 1992: 241. With the notable exception of Lane (1998, 2000), subsequent research has not employed the life-mode approach to class.

Many of the insights derived from social network studies are combined with the notion of linguistic markets in the **community of practice** approach formulated by Eckert (2000).[5] In this perspective, communities of practice are linked to class structures inasmuch as 'people's access and exposure to, need for, and interest in different communities of practice are related to where they find themselves in the world, as embodied in such things as class, age, ethnicity, and gender' (Eckert, 2000: 39). Stated differently, class and other macro-social structures are viewed as being instantiated by daily practices: 'Ultimately, categories such as age, class, ethnicity, and gender are produced and reproduced in their differential forms of participation in communities of practice. And these categories are not produced separately, but co-produced' (Eckert, 2000: 40). Therefore, class-related linguistic practices must be analysed in the context of locally meaningful social groups that are small enough for interactions – 'the process of making meaning' – to be observed (Eckert, 2000: 42). In this approach, the relationship between linguistic variables and economic status, as measured by traditional indicators, is still worthy of evaluation to the extent that it provides a foundation for the analysis of social meanings produced when linguistic forms are used in the contexts of communities of practice. However, economic status as such is considered secondary to class **identity**, which is the primary motivator of linguistic patterns.

Eckert demonstrates the value of this paradigm with an investigation of vowels produced by the members of two communities of practice in a Detroit high school, jocks and burnouts: jocks affiliate with school culture and activities, valuing academic achievement; burnouts, by contrast, affiliate with an urban culture, which stands in opposition to school-based institutional activities and achievements. Although there is a correlation between jock/burnout identity and parents' socioeconomic status, particularly father's occupation and father's socioeconomic index (a composite of education, occupation and home value), there is considerable mobility in jock/burnout membership. Examining five Northern Cities vowels – (oh), (o), (ae), (e) and (uh) – as well as (ay) and negative concord, Eckert finds that only negative concord and the raising of the nucleus of (ay) correlate at $p < 0.05$ with any of the parents' socioeconomic indicators. The older Northern Cities variables, (ae) raising and (o) fronting, are correlated only with gender (girls leading), and not with jock/burnout identity. However, the newer

Northern Cities variables, (e) and (uh) backing, correlate **only** with jock/burnout identity, not with gender and not with parents' socioeconomic status. The burnouts, who show higher rates of (e) and (uh) backing than the jocks, embrace and reinforce the backed variants' urban, working-class meaning. In doing so, they symbolically reproduce the supralocal category of 'working class'.

The relevance of this picture of variation for sociolinguists' approach to class is that the newest and perhaps most symbolically potent variables only indirectly index class as it has been traditionally conceived. The jock and burnout communities of practice spring from and reproduce middle-class and working-class identities in Eckert's argument, but the pattern of linguistic variation is tied to the local high school identities, not macro-social class categories. This finding reinforces claims the early class studies found valid statistical patterns but not adequate explanations; linguistic variation is an element in the symbolic construction of class-sensitive local identities.

In an original approach that follows Eckert in foregrounding locally meaningful practices, Mallinson (2007) adopts a broadly **relational** view of class, wherein 'class is defined by people's relationships to various income-generating resources or assets' (Mallinson, 2007: 153). This approach differs from the use of a gradational class scale insofar as it focuses not on locations of economic production within a class system but rather on access to resources – in short, a consumption- rather than production-based view. This is in contrast with Labov (1966a: 138), who explicitly chooses a production-centred class model. Specifically, Mallinson follows the sociologist Joan Acker's (2006a) class framework, in which an analysis of class entails:

> ... first, thinking about social relations and structures as active practices, occurring in specific historical and geographic places; second, beginning the exploration of class from the standpoints of women and men located differently from white male class actors; third, clarifying the meaning of gendering and racializing; and fourth, broadening the understanding of the economic relations that constitute class and extending the analysis of gendering and racializing processes beyond production (Acker, 2006a: 45–46, cited in Mallinson, 2007: 154).

A significant implication of this perspective is that class as a concept and analytical tool cannot be confined to economic status, in two respects. First, class is viewed as inextricable from gender and race.[6] Secondly, economic status is distinct from the processes that lead to status, and these processes, or class mechanisms, lend greater insight as

to the nature of the class system. Mallinson (2007) adapts Acker's framework for empirical investigation by:

> ... paying attention to class-related social divisions, which are constituted by norms, lifestyle, status displays, and consumption habits. Second, we can observe and measure how images and symbols (language is included here) also constitute and reinforce these class-related social divisions. Third, we can focus on how these class-related social divisions are created, are gendered and raced (etc.), and change over time. Finally, we can interpret how these class-related divisions connect to what Acker calls 'regimes of inequality', or extralocal relations that shape social practice and that are constituted with different bases of inequality, degrees of visibility, legitimacy, hierarchy, participation, and ideology (Mallinson, 2007: 154).

In Mallinson's (2007; see also Mallinson, 2006; Mallinson and Childs, 2008) investigation of African American English (AAE) in the small rural community of Texana, North Carolina, this approach to class leads to a greater explanatory role for class than traditional sociolinguistic inquiry would have found. The study focuses on two communities of practice, both consisting entirely of African-American women: the upright, proper 'church ladies' and the more laid-back 'porch sitters'. The two groups are nearly identical in terms of educational achievement and neighbourhood of residence. However, they have markedly different lifestyle habits, including hair and dressing styles, religious observance (or lack thereof), attitudes toward smoking and parenting styles. Furthermore, the two groups favour different types of occupation: the church ladies tend to hold 'pink collar' service-sector jobs, typically occupied by women, while the porch sitters work in more industrial jobs such as tool-making. Employing Acker's terminology, Mallinson concludes that the porch sitters' jobs 'afford them less access to economic, cultural and social capital, and they communicate little concern about adhering to institutional expectations or norms' (Mallinson 2007: 158).

The linguistic differences between the two groups are consistent with their lifestyle differences. The church ladies show significantly lower rates of five grammatical features associated with AAE: third person singular –s absence, as in *she walk*; singular copula absence, as in *she hungry*; plural copula absence, as in *they hungry*; and levelling of *were* and *weren't* to *was* and *wasn't*, as in *we was/wasn't home*. The porch sitters also use more expletives than the church ladies. The church ladies therefore use standard (non-AAE) linguistic features consistent with their institutional legitimacy as churchgoers and non-manual labourers, while the porch sitters' use of AAE features constructs a class/gender identity not dependent on institutional power. Furthermore, gendered practices such as hairstyle choices are bound to class identities; the church ladies' 'feminine' style is a component of their class identity as 'pink collar' workers and church leaders. In Acker's framework, Mallinson argues, all of the social – including linguistic – practices that distinguish the two groups are components of their class identities, ' … we thus see language use as one of multivariate, intersecting symbols and practices that construct class-related social divisions within the stratification system' (Mallinson, 2007: 161).

Following Acker's rejection of class **positions** in favour of class **processes** and relations to the distribution of resources, Mallinson does not attempt to delineate Labov-style class categories. The statistical analysis is shaped by the community of practice boundaries, and those boundaries, in turn, are determined in part by differential access to material resources. Class identities are understood as being constructed by a range of processes, including linguistic practices, as in Eckert's analysis.

These post-Labovian, identity-based approaches to class may be viewed as problematic in two ways. First, they do not seem to be about class anymore, if we understand class as an **economic** phenomenon. If 'class' refers not just to one's relationship to the means of production and/or consumption but also to the use of locally and globally meaningful linguistic and non-linguistic symbols, membership in local social groups and the possession of ideologies, then does it truly address the intuitively clear (if nebulous) social fact of material inequality? Secondly, and related to the first point, is that identity-based approaches appear to ignore the fine-grained stratificational patterns that Labov (1966a, 1966b, 1972a, 1972b, 2001) finds for variables such as (r) and (-ing), yet surely those patterns must be accounted for by any sociolinguistic class model.

The rejoinder to both concerns is that 'class' as an economic position/set of relations remains, but with an interactional layer. Sociolinguistic variables do not simply reflect economic stratification; they are symbols representing social meanings, and manipulated actively by speakers from one setting to the next. For that reason, sociolinguists pursuing the socioeconomic dimensions of variation are most directly interested not in economic inequality but rather in the social divisions that stem from it. Identity-driven approaches thus recognize social patterns as mediating between linguistic variation and economic reality. Labov-style patterns are understood as reflecting very potent social meanings associated with linguistic variables, rather than directly indexing economic inequality.

Recent approaches to class in discourse analysis

Whereas studies of linguistic variation have consistently uncovered and sometimes explained quantitative relationships between language and class, the quantitative paradigm alone has limited power to explore issues such as class consciousness, the representation and construction of class in discourse and the intersection of class with other aspects of social identity. Recent qualitative inquiry has begun to fill these gaps. Whereas some discourse studies elucidate class ideologies and identities, focusing chiefly on the **content** of talk, others ask what the linguistic **forms** present in situated discourse contribute to the performance and construction of class.[7]

Bucholtz (2007) is of the former type, investigating class ideologies through a discourse analysis of talk about clothing consumption among middle-class and upper-middle-class American teenagers. Like Mallinson, Bucholtz approaches class from a consumption rather than production standpoint. However, Bucholtz takes the additional position that an adequate analysis of consumption patterns requires both a top-down (position within the economic structure) and a bottom-up perspective. The latter perspective is available through ethnographic observation of interaction related to consumption, in this case, discourse about consumption. On the basis of interviews with the teenagers and observed conversations among them, Bucholtz concludes that discourse about clothing consumption is a strategy for constructing class, gender and race identity. On the one hand, the teenagers consciously avoid ostentatious symbols of wealth, but on the other hand, they want to be perceived as having a certain level of access to material resources. Thus, the class conflict/consensus dichotomy emerges in discourse. Bucholtz also finds that the teenagers, and people generally, show greater willingness to talk explicitly about the association of clothing styles with ethnic/racial identities than with class positions; therefore, class identities are often racialized in discourse.

Messing (2007) similarly reveals the racialization of class and of socioeconomic change in discourse about socioeconomic and technological improvement in indigenous communities in the Mexican state of Tlaxcala. Two distinct ideological stances emerge from discourse concerning both material improvement and language shift from Mexicano to Spanish. One type of discourse denigrates indigenous culture and people, setting up indigenous ways of life as being in opposition to economic improvement. This theme 'is particularly vocalized by the upper classes, or by anyone who has internalized racist attitudes, reproduced from outside their community' (Messing, 2007: 561). The competing 'pro-indigenous' discourse questions the negative attitudes toward indigenous culture and values the Mexicano language. In practice, the two discourses are mingled in the community, creating a complex, class- and race-based ideological space that, Messing argues, is critical to an understanding of the ongoing language shift toward Spanish.

The interplay of class with race, gender, sexuality and other dimensions of identity is central to other recent qualitative studies that examine the construction of these aspects of identity through discourse. For example, Hall (2005) investigates the discursive **construction** of marginal sexual identities in India. *Kotis*, cross-dressing males who have wives and children but who also engage in sexual relations with men, distinguish themselves from *hijras*, eunuchs (by birth or castration) who occupy the quasi-legitimate (and paid) role of bestowing blessings at ritual events such as weddings. Kotis are often scorned as fake hijras, but they discursively carve out their own identity as distinct from both hijras and gay men. Broadly speaking, kotis' use of Hindi places them in opposition to gay men in terms of both sexual and class identity:

... an educated English-speaking gay identity has developed in Indian urban centers that rejects the transgendered stance associated with its hijra predecessors, perceiving their forays into femininity as a marker of lower-class sexuality. Hindi and English, as languages infused with class associations, have accordingly become symbolic of these identity distinctions, with the use of English indexing a cosmopolitan gay sexuality and the use of Hindi a more traditional transgender sexuality. But whereas gay men view the use of Hindi as sexually backward, kotis view the use of English as overly modest (Hall, 2005: 127).

Whereas kotis' choice of language marks them as distinct from urban, higher-class gay men, they discursively construct hijras as **below** them in the socioeconomic system. This is accomplished in part during public imitations of hijras, when kotis use discourse features including high pitch and volume, nasalization, elongated and high-pitched vowels at the end of intonational units, intimate pronouns and address terms, sexual innuendo, and vocabulary associated with uneducated, rural speakers (Hall, 2005: 133–4). By rejecting the English of upper-class gay men and portraying hijras as lower class, 'the kotis

establish a fissure between lower-class and upper-class sexualities, thereby suggesting themselves as the desirable alternative to two extremes of undesirability' (135).

As exemplified by Hall's study of kotis, a chief insight emerging from sociolinguistic discourse studies is that social identities, while linked to macro-social structures such as class, gender and ethnicity, are partly (some would say wholly) constructed in interaction. The situated, strategic choices of even solitary but meaningful linguistic forms can create a complex array of class-related meanings that would not be accessible to purely quantitative analysis. Rampton (2001; see also 1995) takes this perspective in examining the discursive construction of class through 'speech stylization', 'the intensification or exaggeration of a particular way of speaking for symbolic and rhetorical effect' (cf. Bakhtin, 1981) (Rampton, 2001: 85). In an analysis of working-class London adolescent boys' interaction at school, Rampton finds several stylized uses of Cockney features that stand in contrast to the standard speech setting of the classroom. In one case, a 14-year-old boy uses Cockney phonology when greeting a friend. In another, he uses a 'hyper-Cockney' pronunciation of *okay* to call his friends' attention to schoolwork:

Here it contributed to a more collectively oriented effort to get his peers to focus on school-related activities, and rather than apologetic self-mitigation, switches like these looked more like attempts at the *vernacularization* of school knowledge itself.

Small acts of stylization like these can be seen as part of a low-level but insistent struggle against the dominant meanings of sociolinguistic stratification, an effort to *extract* school and education from the complex of social factors which created the differences between 'Cockney' and 'posh' (Rampton, 2001: 90).

Rampton concludes that 'while quantitative analysis usefully points to the reproduction of sociolinguistic class structure in relatively routine speech, stylization can display a range of more heterodox perspectives on what it might mean to be a young lower-class Londoner' (Rampton, 2001: 94–5). In fact, Rampton's study demonstrates the complementary relationship between quantitative and qualitative approaches: preceding the discourse analysis is a set of quantitative results showing that the speaker uses vernacular features chiefly during informal talk among friends, style-shifting almost entirely to standard features during an academic assessment activity (Rampton, 2001: 86–7). These results lay the foundation for the later interpretation of Cockney features as contributing to a 'struggle against the dominant meanings of sociolinguistic stratification' (Rampton, 2001: 90).

If quantitative sociolinguistic studies involving class ask in what ways class identities both determine and are constituted by linguistic variation, then discourse studies ask what class identities **mean** and how they are negotiated in talk. As Rampton and others (cf. Mendoza-Denton, 2002) demonstrate, combining variationist and discourse-analytic methods, though still rare, promises insights into the relationship between language and social class.

14.5 FUTURE DIRECTIONS

In the germinal investigations of language and class by Labov and others, the essential goal was to uncover the structured nature of linguistic variation at the community level. More recent work has fleshed out the goal to include questions of social motivation; to some extent, theory and methods have evolved accordingly. However, the sociolinguistic study of class is perhaps still awaiting its revolution.

Significant progress can be made from two complementary directions. First, some basic but critical empirical questions posed in the early work can be revisited. For example, Labov, Trudgill and Macaulay all contend that occupation is the best single-class indicator, though Labov and Trudgill opt for combined-class scales as described in Section 14.2. Most subsequent class studies in linguistics have followed their lead in amalgamating class indicators, with the result that very few outside of Labov's work have directly compared one single indicator with another. The primary benefit of systematic comparison would not be the conclusion that occupation (for example) tends to correlate more closely with linguistic variation than other indicators; in any case, the results would likely differ from one community to another and one variable to another. Instead, the main benefit would be the individual patterns themselves: precisely because the different indicators measure distinct aspects of class identity, as Labov observed, they each have something different to teach us about linguistic variation. Close attention to the results for each separate indicator, for a single set of linguistic data, could promote a more nuanced definition of class for sociolinguistics.

Another long-standing but somewhat forgotten empirical question is the relationship between socioeconomic indicators and network structures. At present, the majority of network and community of practice studies in sociolinguistics treat

class as a related but separate phenomenon, hence statements like 'the working class is characterized by dense, multiplex networks'. While it does not seem necessary or advisable to merge network and class as concepts, the empirical relations between them, where linguistic variation is concerned, must be more complex than currently understood. More advanced quantitative network techniques offer one avenue for pursuing this link, particularly for the analysis of observable interaction in local settings.

The second and complementary direction involves, and transcends, more aggressive questions concerning the ways in which class, defined as relational and intersectional, is manifest in local and regional identities. Several researchers cited in this chapter take significant steps along these lines. Although the combined top-down (aggregate) and bottom-up (grounded) nature of this type of approach is often cited as its chief advantage, it is also applauded for allowing considerable variation in how class is defined. Characteristics without direct economic import, such as hairstyle and swearing, can be class indicators. But another perspective is also possible for a specifically **sociolinguistic** approach to class: the intricate and often noisy linguistic patterns resulting from the construction of these hybrid economic/non-economic class categories point to the need for a **more** intersectional, relational view of social space altogether. Few current sociolinguists would deny that the separate but interacting independent variables of class, gender, age, ethnicity, etc., are a collective, statistically-convenient approximation of a more complex social space. Emerging and future approaches to class are likely to reject this approximation by not looking for 'class' per se but rather for the nebulous identities, such as 'porch sitter', that provide both robust empirical linguistic patterns and satisfying sociocultural explanations. Under an extreme – but perhaps productive – version of this approach, identifying social-class boundaries would no longer be a goal independent of identifying other types of social boundaries.

This holistic approach would not devalue the kinds of more traditional empirical questions that began this section. With the two agendas combined, and assisted by the continued incorporation of cross-disciplinary theory and methods, the sociolinguistic study of class may yet encounter new questions altogether.

NOTES

1 Notably, the scale includes only **production** variables, purposely excluding **consumption** variables

such as clothing choices. We return to this issue in Section 14.4.

2 For a fuller description of stable sociolinguistic variables, see Labov, 2001: 80–1.

3 Trudgill (1974) also discusses the complications confronting any attempt at defining and operationalizing class in Western industrialized settings. Notably, contemporary sociological work, including Mayer (1955) and Goldthorpe and Lockwood (1963), is cited throughout this discussion. Macaulay (1977: 55) also cites sociological literature to the effect that occupation is considered the best single class indicator.

4 However, as Eckert (2000: 32) observes, ' ... the consensual and conflict models of social class are not entirely incompatible – upward economic mobility and class loyalty frequently go together as well – and the tension between the two may be an important source of complex social meaning'.

5 For discussion of communities of practice, see Chapter 13 of this volume.

6 Ethnicity is, both ideologically and observably, a stronger correlate of linguistic variation in US English than in British English or other Western European languages (Milroy, 2001a,b).

7 Socioeconomic facts have even been claimed to have impact on the types of parent–child discourse that occur day to day. Heath (2006) reports that middle-class, dual-income families facing limited time with their children talk to them with a narrow range of discourse patterns, largely confined to directives, present-tense observations about the immediate surroundings and gratification of children's desires. Discussion of past events, and longer narratives, are relatively rare. This truncated linguistic interaction occurs not only because both parents work outside the home, as is the case for many working-class families, but also by virtue of a particularly middle-class ambition for children to be heavily involved in extracurricular activities that stand in place of family dinnertime and evenings at home.

REFERENCES

Abdel-Jawad, H. (1981) 'Phonological and social variation in Arabic in Amman'. University of Pennsylvania dissertation.

Acker, J. (2006a) *Class Questions: Feminist Answers.* New York: Rowman and Littlefield.

Acker, J. (2006b) 'Inequality regimes: gender, class, and race in organizations', *Gender and Society,* 20: 441–64.

Ash, S. (2002) 'Social class', in J. K. Chambers, P. Trudgill, and N. Schilling-Estes (eds), *The Handbook of Language Variation and Change.* Malden, MA: Blackwell. pp. 402–22.

Bakhtin, M. (1981) *The Dialogic Imagination.* Austin, TX: University of Texas Press.

Bernstein, B. (1971) *Class, Codes and Control 1, Theoretical Studies Towards a Sociology of Language.* London: Routledge.

Bourdieu, P. and Boltanski, L. (1975) 'Le fétichisme de la langue', *Actes de la Recherche en Sciences Sociales,* 4: 2–32.

Bucholtz, M. (2007) 'Shop talk: branding, consumption, and gender in American middle-class youth interaction', in B. McElhinny (ed.), *Words, Worlds, and Material Girls: Language, Gender, and Globalized Economy.* Mouton de Gruyter. pp. 371–402.

Cameron, R. (1991) Pronominal and null subject variation in Spanish: constraints, dialects and functional compensation. University of Pennsylvania dissertation.

Cedergren, H. (1973) 'The interplay of social and linguistic factors in Panama'. Cornell University dissertation.

Chae, S. (1995) 'External constraints on sound change: the raising of /o/ in Seoul Korean'. University of Pennsylvania dissertation.

Chung, K. S. (2006) 'Hypercorrection in Taiwan Mandarin', *Journal of Asian Pacific Communication,* 16(2): 197–214.

Eckert, P. (1989) 'The whole woman: sex and gender differences in variation', *Language Variation and Change,* 1: 245–67.

Eckert, P. (2000) *Linguistic Variation as Social Practice.* Malden, MA: Blackwell.

Eckert, P. and McConnell-Ginet, S. (1999) 'New generalizations and explanations in language and gender research', *Language in Society,* 2: 185–201.

Goldthorpe, J. H. and Lockwood, D. (1963) 'Affluence and the British class structure', *Sociological Review,* 11(2): 133–63.

Haeri, N. (1996) *The Sociolinguistic Market of Cairo: Gender, Class, and Education.* London: Kegan Paul International.

Hall, K. (2005) 'Intertextual sexuality: parodies of class, identity, and desire in liminal Delhi', *Journal of Linguistic Anthropology,* 15: 125–44.

Heath, S. B. (2006) 'Building the micros toward seeing the macro', *Text and Talk,* 26(4–5): 627–34.

Hibiya, J. (1988) Social stratification of Tokyo Japanese. University of Pennsylvania dissertation.

Højrup, T. (1983) 'The concept of life-mode: a form-specifying mode of analysis applied to contemporary Europe', *Ethnologia Scandinavica,* 1–50.

Johnstone, B. and Kiesling, S. F. (2008) 'Indexicality and experience: exploring the meanings of /aw/-monophthongization in Pittsburgh', *Journal of Sociolinguistics,* 12(1): 5–33.

Kellas, J. G. (1968) *Modern Scotland.* New York: Praeger.

Kerswill, P. (2007) 'Social class', in C. Llamas, L. Mullany and P. Stockwell (eds), *The Routledge Companion to Sociolinguistics.* New York: Routledge. pp. 51–61.

Kerswill, P. and Williams, A. (2005) 'New towns and koineization: linguistic and social correlates', *Linguistics,* 43(5): 1023–48.

Kochetov, A. (2006) 'The role of social factors in the dynamics of sound change: a case study of a Russian dialect', *Language Variation and Change,* 18(1): 99–119.

Labov, W. (1966a) *The Social Stratification of English in New York City*. Washington, DC: Center for Applied Linguistics.

Labov, W. (1966b) 'Hypercorrection by the lower middle class as a factor in linguistic change', in W. Bright (ed.), *Sociolinguistics*. The Hague: Mouton. pp. 84–113.

Labov, W. (1972a) *Language in the Inner City: Studies in the Black English vernacular*. Philadelphia: University of Pennsylvania Press.

Labov, W. (1972b) *Sociolinguistic Patterns*. Philadelphia: University of Pennsylvania Press.

Labov, W. (1980) 'The social origins of sound change', in W. Labov (ed.), *Locating Language in Time and Space*. New York: Academic Press. pp. 251–65.

Labov, W. (2001) *Principles of Linguistic Change: Social Factors*. Malden, MA: Blackwell.

Lane, L. A. (1998) 'Emergence and transformation of a dialect: Thyboronsk (Danish)'. University of Chicago dissertation.

Lane, L. A. (2000) 'Trajectories of linguistic variation: emergence of a dialect', *Language Variation and Change*, 12(3): 267–94.

Lavandera, B. (1975) 'Linguistic structure and sociolinguistic conditioning in the use of verbal endings in 'SI' clauses'. University of Pennsylvania dissertation.

Lennig, M. (1978) 'Acoustic measurement of linguistic change: the modern Paris vowel system'. University of Pennsylvania dissertation.

Macaulay, R. K. S. (1977) *Language, Social Class, and Education: A Glasgow Study*. Edinburgh: Edinburgh University Press.

Mallinson, C. (2006) 'The dynamic construction of race, class, and gender through linguistic practice among women in a Black Appalachian community'. North Carolina State University dissertation.

Mallinson, C. (2007) *Social Class, Social Status, and Stratification: Revisiting Familiar Concepts in Sociolinguistics*. Penn Working Papers in Linguistics, 13 (2): 149–163.

Mallinson, C. and Childs, B. (2008) 'Communities of practice in sociolinguistic description: analyzing language and identity practices among Black women in Appalachia', *Gender and Language*, 1: 173–206.

Marx, K. (1906) *Capital*. Chicago: Kerr.

Mayer, K. (1955) *Class and Society*. New York: Doubleday & Co.

Mendoza-Denton, N. (2002) 'Language and identity', in J. K. Chambers, P. Trudgill, and N. Schilling-Estes (eds), *The Handbook of Language Variation and Change*. Malden, MA: Blackwell. pp. 475–99.

Messing, J. (2007) 'Multiple ideologies and competing discourses: language shift in Tlaxcala, Mexico', *Language in Society*, 36: 555–77.

Mills, C. W. (1951) *White Collar: the American Middle Classes*. New York: Oxford University Press.

Milroy, L. (1980) *Language and Social Networks*. Oxford: Blackwell.

Milroy, L. (2001a) 'The social categories of race and class: language ideology and sociolinguistics', in N. Coupland,

S. Sarangi and C. N. Candlin (eds), *Sociolinguistics and Social Theory*. Harlow: Pearson. pp. 235–60.

Milroy, L. (2001b) 'Britain and the United States: two nations divided by the same language (and different language ideologies)', *Journal of Linguistic Anthropology*, 10: 56–89.

Milroy, L. and Milroy, J. (1992) 'Social network and social class: toward an integrated sociolinguistic model', *Language in Society*, 21(1): 1–26.

Nichols, P. (1983) 'Linguistic options and choices for Black women in the rural South', in B. Thorne, C. Kramerae, and N. Henley (eds), *Language, Gender, and Society*. Boston: Heinle and Heinle. pp. 54–68.

Oliveira, M. de (1983) 'Phonological variation in Brazilian Portuguese'. University of Pennsylvania dissertation.

Rampton, B. (1995) *Crossing: Language and Ethnicity Among Adolescents*. London: Longman.

Rampton, B. (2001) Critique in internation. Critique of Anthropology 21: 83–107.

Rickford, J. R. (1986) 'The need for new approaches to social class analysis in sociolinguistics', *Journal of Communication*, 6: 215–21.

Romaine, S. (1984) 'The status of sociological models and categories in explaining linguistic variation', *Linguistische Berichte*, 90: 25–38.

Sankoff, D. and Laberge, S. (1978) 'The linguistic market and the statistical explanation of variability', in D. Sankoff (ed.), *Linguistic Variation: Models and Methods*. New York: Academic Press. pp. 239–50.

Sankoff, D., Cedergren, H. J., Kemp, W., Thibault, P. and Vincent, D. (1989) 'Montreal French: language, class, and ideology', in R. Fasold and D. Schiffrin (eds), *Language Change and Variation*. Amsterdam: John Benjamins. pp. 107–18.

Santerre, L. and Millo, J. (1978) 'Diphthongization in Montreal French', in D. Sankoff (ed.), *Linguistic Variation: Models and Methods*. New York: Academic Press. pp. 173–84.

Trudgill, P. (1972) 'Sex, covert prestige and linguistic change in urban British English', *Language in Society*, 1: 179–95.

Trudgill, P. (1974) *The Social Differentiation of English in Norwich*. Cambridge: Cambridge University Press.

Weber, M. (1947) *The Theory of Social and Economic Organization*. Tr. A. M. Henderson and T. Parsons. New York: The Free Press.

Williams, G. (1992) *Sociolinguistics: a Sociological Critique*. London: Routledge.

Wolfram, W. (1969) *A Sociolinguistic Description of Detroit Negro Speech*. Washington, DC: Center for Applied Linguistics.

Woolard, K. (1985) 'Language variation and cultural hegemony', *American Ethnologist*, 12: 738–48.

Woods, H. (1979) 'A socio-dialectology survey of the English spoken in Ottawa: a study of sociological and stylistic variation in Canadian English'. University of British Columbia dissertation.

15

Social Network

Eva Vetter

15.1 THE DEVELOPMENT OF SOCIAL NETWORKS PERSPECTIVES IN THE SOCIAL SCIENCES

Social network analysis is concerned with understanding the relationships between social entities such as individual actors, sets of individuals, groups or organizations, and the patterns and implications of these relationships. The network approach postulates that social entities create ties which provide a meaningful framework for problem-solving (Mitchell, 1986: 74). Its fundamental assumption is that the patterning of the social ties in which these social entities are embedded 'has important consequences' for them (Freeman, 2004: 2). From this it follows that a wide range of empirical phenomena can be explored from social networks perspectives.

Although the social network approach received its initial impetus from sociology and anthropology (e.g. Simmel, 1908; Radcliffe-Brown, 1940; Bott, 1957; Mitchell, 1973) as well as sociometry (Moreno, 1934), its applications and methodological refinements have always transcended disciplinary boundaries. Very different disciplines such as economics, marketing, industrial engineering or geography have adopted a network approach and have contributed to its characteristic profiles (in the respective disciplines) or sometimes even built up schools of network research.

In the 1950s, the Manchester School of anthropologists (John A. Barnes, Elizabeth Bott, J. Clyde Mitchell) began to introduce the network as a systematic (and non-metaphorical) concept into the social sciences. These anthropologists contributed to the description of networks by elaborating on network features such as density, clusterability or connexity. It was, however, at Harvard that the

'crucial breakthrough' (Scott, 2000: 33) occurred: with the development of algebraic models of groups and of multidimensional scaling, the Harvard group (Harrison White and his disciples Stephen Berkowitz, Mark Granovetter, Ronald Breiger, Francois Lorrain and Barry Wellman) established social network analysis as a method of structural analysis from the 1960s onwards (White et al., 1976; White, 1992). Further work in the area (Lorrain and White, 1971; Boorman and White, 1976; White et al., 1976) built on Simmel and Durkheim and established social network analysis as a theoretical paradigm distinct from both positivistic survey-based research and the structural functionalism of Talcott Parsons.

The success of the social network is strongly linked to the so-called 'structural analysis' of Harrison White and his group. However, it cannot be reduced to the developments initiated by the Harvard group for at least three reasons. First, influential network analysts, such as e.g. Ronald Burt and Linton Freeman, were not based in Harvard. Secondly, network analysis has been spread over a large geographic area through its own scientific networks: In 1979 Barry Wellman founded the International Network of Social Network Analysts (INSNA, http://www.insna.org/), which, alongside its other responsibilities, is in charge of the organization of an annual conference, the International Sunbelt Social Network Conference.

The network community has also produced scholarly journals, such as *Connections* (founded by Barry Wellman), *Social Networks* (founded by Lin Freeman) and *Social Structure* (founded by David Krackhardt). Network analysis is thus influenced by different research clusters, which becomes evident through the growing interest in social networks since 1990 (Wasserman et al.,

2005: 1) and the considerable technical and formal sophistication associated with this growth (Wasserman and Faust, 1994; Scott, 2000; Freeman, 2004; Carrington et al., 2005; Marsden, 2005; Jansen, 2006).

Thirdly and most important, although structural analysis probably constitutes the most prominent branch of the networks perspective, it cannot cover the heterogeneity of this scientific area. An example for this dilemma is network research outside the English-speaking world, in particular the research conducted by Michel Forsé and his peers in France (Degenne and Forsé, 1994 [2004]; Forsé and Langlois, 1997; Forsé 2002; Mercklé, 2004; Forsé, 2008). These researchers in their structural interactionism the network approach combines with the theory of rational choice in the broader sense. Concurrently, German-language network researchers are trying to sound out the potential of qualitative data collection and analysis of networks in different research areas, for example biographical research, literature and politics (see e.g. Hollstein and Straus, 2006). However, the connections between the different research clusters are not always bidirectional: comparing the reference lists for the work done in France and Germany with the work being done in and around Harvard, there is – unsurprisingly – a strong asymmetry.

Despite this heterogeneity of the networks approach and theoretical as well as methodological differences between the various schools of thought, some central principles of the network perspective can be derived, to which a large part of the researchers subscribe:

1   Actors and their actions are viewed as interdependent (and not independent).
2   Linkages between actors are channels for resource transfer (material and non-material).
3   The network structure provides opportunities for or constraints on individual action.
4   Network models conceptualize structure (social, economic, political…) as lasting patterns of relations among actors (Wasserman/Faust, 1994: 4).

These principles appear to constitute the common ground of the modern social networks perspective and to indicate that a social network is far more than a metaphor for relationships among individuals – but less than a unified research paradigm.

15.2 NETWORKS IN SOCIOLINGUISTICS

Main research areas

In sociolinguistics, the network approach is most commonly applied in order to explain linguistic variation or language choice from a diachronic as well as synchronic perspective. Sociolinguistic network research is based on the assumption that the traditional macro-scale categories such as social class or gender cannot explain linguistic features in an adequate or sufficient way and that networks may constitute supplementary explanatory devices. In their overview of sociolinguistic network research, Schenk and Bergs (2004) identify four core areas in which sociolinguistic networks are applied: synchronic variationist sociolinguistics (urban dialectology and research into vernaculars), diachronic sociolinguistics (language change and maintenance), code-switching and language acquisition/loss. In other words, linguistic variation and language choice come out as the main areas of investigation – from a snapshot, as well as from a change-in-time perspective. Sociolinguistic network research approaches this rather ambitious research agenda from synchronic and diachronic perspectives, whether the object of investigation is historical or present-day language use.

A brief history of the interest in networks in sociolinguistics would normally begin in the 1960s or 1970s, although some authors go as far back as the turn of the previous century (Gauchat, 1905; cited in Milroy, 2002: 553). Variationist research, in particular Labov's study of Martha's Vineyard (1963) and on 'being a lame' (Labov, 1972), and Blom and Gumperz's (1972) Hemnesberget study are generally considered as early and rather intuitive sociolinguistic applications of the network approach. With Lesley Milroy's (1980) Belfast study, the first systematic account of the relationship between social network and language variation, the social network ultimately found its way into sociolinguistics and has been used extensively since then (for an overview see Milroy, 2002; Wiklund, 2002; Marshall, 2004; Schenk and Bergs, 2004; Schlobinski, 2005).

Areas of application include linguistic variation within a language (e.g. Milroy, 1980; Bortoni-Ricardo, 1985; Marshall, 2004), and also language choice in multilingual contexts with regional minorities (e.g. Gal, 1979; Rindler-Schjerve, 1987; Vetter, 1997) and migrants (e.g. Labrie, 1988; Dabène and Moore, 1995; de Bot and Stoessel, 2002; Hulsen et al., 2002). More recently, in addition to these areas, the impact of networks on language proficiency has become an important topic (e.g. Zentella, 1997; Raschka et al., 2002; Wiklund, 2002). While studies to date have mainly investigated face-to-face interaction, the increase in virtual communication networks has expanded the potential scope of sociolinguistic network research to new contexts (e.g. Paolillo, 1999, 2001; Bergs, 2006) and has opened a large new area for future investigation.

Like virtual communication networks, historical sociolinguistic research lacks data from face-to-face interactions. As a number of studies have shown, however, historical sociolinguistics presents interesting research perspectives and thus provides a burgeoning research agenda for networks (Tieken-Boon van Ostade et al., 2001; Bergs, 2005).

Theoretical background

Despite the popularity of network research, a number of studies, particularly comparative studies, point to the notable lack of theoretical work in the area (e.g. Salancik, 1995; Schlobinski, 2005). These studies show that different and not always compatible theoretical foundations are pursued within sociolinguistics. In particular, establishing a firm connection between using the network as an analytical tool and embedding it in a broader theoretical framework represents a major challenge.

Network researchers often draw on the work of the sociologist Georg Simmel. Some go further, and see Durkheim, Tarde or Weber as the vanguard of the network approach. These attempts focus particularly on Durkheim's category of egoistic suicide (in 'Le suicide'), which is interpreted as a forerunner of social network theory since it shows the influence of structural properties of social groups on individual behavior (Degenne and Forsé, 1994; Forsé and Langlois, 1997). Nevertheless, it is far more common for researchers to look back to Georg Simmel, explicitly or otherwise (e.g. Moreno, 1960; Burt, 1982, 1992; Forsé, 2002; Bergs, 2005: 24), despite the fact that Simmel himself never used the term 'network'. To be precise, the connection to networks was first made explicit by Simmel's student Von Wiese (1932). Simmel provides a theory for a taxonomy of social structures that are based on relationships between individuals. It is these relationships and not individuals or their characteristics that are the objects of sociological investigation for Simmel. Thus, Simmel's concepts of 'door' and 'bridge' intuitively preempt the assumptions that underlie network research (Javeau, 1986) and his concept of the stranger is seen as an impetus for the development of geometric methods for calculating social distance (Raphael, 1986). The obvious compatibility with the basic assumptions underlying contemporary network research is the reason why theoretical links to Simmel are so frequently (re)constructed.

A further, albeit rather peripheral, theoretical strand is symbolic interactionism. This is linked to Gumperz's conception of the network as an interactive concept, itself a reaction to perceived shortcomings in Labovian variationist linguistics (Gumperz, 1994). For Gumperz, linguistic differences reflect differences in networks of human relations. Individuals who are bound up in long-term and goal-oriented networked relationships share a common background and have similar communicative experiences. Gumperz argues that in workplaces, families, and voluntary clubs or associations, which are typical examples of networks, particular linguistic conventions with specific meanings develop (Gumperz, 1994: 624). However, the links to symbolic interactionism are not followed through in much network research (see also critiques by Rindler-Schjerve, 1991: 225 and Vetter, 1997, which may be seen as attempts to ground the network as an interactive category in symbolic interactionism and apply it to a minority group situation). Within sociolinguistics, this theoretical approach is yet peripheral and has not been systematically developed.

The breakthrough of the network approach in sociolinguistics is usually seen as Lesley Milroy's Belfast study (1980, 2001), which enjoys wide acceptance, is usually seen as the breakthrough in drawing on the use of networks as analytical concepts in anthropological and sociological research (Barnes, 1954; Mitchell, 1969; Boissevain and Mitchell, 1973; Boissevain, 1974), on exchange theory (Homans, 1958) and on the theory of tie strength (Granovetter, 1973).

From the perspective of exchange theory, social networks emerge from repeated exchanges between individuals. Individuals who interact frequently thereby develop positive feelings of mutual reciprocity. Their relationship can be seen as a kind of resource that may be useful to them. In Homans's exchange theory, individuals tend to repeat behaviours that provide the best overall reward/cost outcomes. Within social networks, costs and rewards flow through specific channels and individuals repeat satisfying exchange transactions over and over again. These repetitive exchanges reflect habits and routines that people develop in order to avoid the costs (time, emotional energy and other resources) of exploring other alternatives and the risk that new choices may be less rewarding than the old ones. Therefore, network structures are often characterized by a general stability. The opportunity for and quality of interaction within networks depends upon the exchange patterns: social exchanges between close friends are based on more intense emotional bonds than more casual network exchanges, for example. Despite the general stability of networks, relationships are at the same time open to changes over time, as a result of changes in people's social locations and because individuals reassess the costs and benefits periodically (Johnson, 2008: 201).

In his theory of strong and weak ties, Granovetter (1973) postulates that weak ties, i.e. those with low-frequency, low-transactional content and a low degree of reciprocity, are important channels for the flow of information between dense networks. This assumption is particularly prevalent within sociolinguistics in connection with language change and linguistic innovation (e.g. Milroy and Milroy, 1985; Bergs, 2005).

To sum up, sociolinguistic network research tends to see networks as analytical categories. This differs from other disciplines, in which networks tend to be seen as models or theoretical constructs, and in which human behaviour is explained in terms of the characteristics of networks (e.g. Wasserman and Faust, 1994). The question concerning the theoretical foundations of social networks in sociolinguistics can give rise to several different answers. Even if this question is not at the heart of most sociolinguistic research, its methodological implications can be far-reaching. Based on their underlying theoretical framework, interactionist network studies can be differentiated from variationist ones. While the former tend to use qualitative data, the latter rather opt for standardized and quantifiable data. Thus, it is important to note that the different theoretical assumptions underlying sociolinguistic network research may have far-reaching implications.

15.3 NETWORK PROPERTIES

Networks are generally described on the basis of specific characteristics which refer on the one hand to the researchers' perspective (see the distinction between personal and total networks) and to the network properties (emerging/latent, lose/open and a catalogue of structural and interactional characteristics commonly used within sociolinguistic research).

Scholarly perspectives on networks can be divided into two groups: egocentric personal networks starting with individual actors and their relations, and total networks involving an attempt to capture all the connections within a networked system, for example the relationships between all the pupils in a particular class. Both perspectives are represented in sociolinguistic research.

Personal egocentric networks start from the 'anchor' of the network, 'ego', and those with whom ego directly interacts. To capture the constituents and structure of the entire personal network, information about these first-order ties is supplemented by further information on second-order ties, i.e. about relationships between the people with whom ego interacts, but is not directly involved with, for example, friends of a friend.

Sociolinguistic interest generally focuses on the first-order network ties and less on the ties of the second order. The precise description of relationships depends on data that give information about their structural and interactional properties, allowing researchers to differentiate between different types and strengths of ties. Sociolinguistic studies in the variationist tradition usually elicit information about a certain amount of personal networks and give their members different scores depending on the properties and structures of their respective networks. These network scores are then correlated with data on language use (such as phonological variables). Many classic sociolinguistic studies, and in particular the most-cited ones in both present-day and historical linguistic variation (e.g. Milroy, 1980; Bortoni-Ricardo, 1985; Lippi-Green, 1989; Bergs, 2005) are based on the analysis of personal networks.

Unlike personal egocentric networks, total networks can only be analysed as part of a specific, clearly defined system. Only once all the members involved in the system (e.g. an organization or school class) are identified can the total network, i.e. all the existing relationships in the network, be accounted for. Once again, the structural and interactional properties of ties can be used to describe the network. Those members with similar patterns of social relationships can be compared even if they are not directly connected to each other. Sociolinguistic analyses of total networks have been conducted in primary school classes (e.g. Berthele, 2000) and in Internet chat-rooms (e.g. Paolillo, 2001).

In differentiating between emerging and latent networks, what is important is not so much the researcher's perspective but rather the properties of the networks themselves. The emerging/latent distinction was first described by Watts (1991) and later taken up by Bergs (2005) and by Schenk and Bergs (2004). Latent networks are potentially available and have yet to be activated, while emergent networks result from a concrete communicative event and are discursively negotiated by actors with particular social roles.

A further distinction, which was adopted from early sociolinguistic research, is that between open and closed networks. In the Hemnesberget study, it is postulated that members of open networks have had more varied experiences because they meet each other as members of different categories such as students and members of the élite, or as friends. These additional relationships are manifested as style shifts (Gumperz, 1975: 162), whereas closed networks are characterized by more homogeneous linguistic practices. Lippi-Green (1989) supports this view and distinguishes between open personal networks, which extend outside the established networks in the community, and closed networks.

A basic model of a social network is easy to visualize. It consists of points (dots, nodes, vertices) and links (lines, connections, edges, arcs) to indicate the relationships between individual entities. Further characteristics of relationships such as those mentioned above (and others) can then be added to the model. Sociolinguistic studies usually follow Boissevain's (1987: 164–9) suggestion to distinguish between structural components (size, density, centrality and cluster-formation) and interactional components (multiplexity, transactional content, direction, frequency and duration).

The density of a network is the number of actual links divided by the number of potential links. A density of 1 would indicate that everyone knows everyone else in the network. Centrality describes the degree of social integration or isolation of individuals within a network: the more first- and second-order contacts an individual has (in comparison to other individuals within that network), the more central this person is. Clusters or cliques are defined as subgroups with high partial density. Individuals who link one network or subgroup with another are frequently called bridges or structural holes (Burt, 1992). These structural components are essentially based on graph theory (relational approach), whereas the interactional (content) criteria relate back to exchange theory (positional approach).

Multiplexity, transactional content, reciprocity and symmetry, duration, frequency and intensity are the most commonly mentioned interactional criteria. Multiplexity indicates the number of social functions or roles that two individuals fulfil in their relationship. If they know each other only as friends, their link is uniplex. But as friends, neighbours and members of the same sports club, they would have a multiplex relationship. The transactional content of the exchange between network members can be of a material (money transfer) or a non-material (emotional backup, gossip,...) nature. Milroy draws on Milardo (1988: 26–36) in this respect, who distinguishes between exchange and interactive networks: personal exchange networks consist of persons with whom ego exchanges direct aid, advice, criticism and support. Interactive networks, on the other hand, are only based on (frequent) interaction and not on the exchange of material or symbolic resources, e.g. the relationship between a store owner and a customer. Milroy and Li (1995) and Li (1994) find this distinction useful, while others (e.g. Lanza and Svendson, 2007) find it hard to operationalize. The strength of network relationships is also connected to their quality, which is usually described in terms of duration, frequency and intensity (in combination with multiplexity). Frequent and intensive exchanges are typical of multiplex relationships and indicate strong ties. The interactional criterion of reciprocity is also relevant here, i.e. the question of whether an exchange is uni- or bidirectional. Strong ties are often bidirectional, whereas unidirectional asymmetric ties normally relate to social inequality.

Figure 15.1 illustrates the most important characteristics of networks. The first-order personal network of anchor X is a dense and multiplex network with strong network ties, while the second-order network is more open and uniplex.

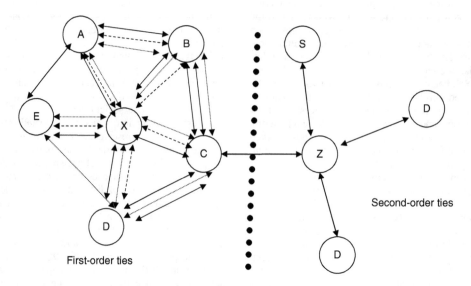

Figure 15.1   First- and second-order network.

15.4 COLLECTING NETWORK DATA

Sociolinguistic network studies deal with three different kinds of data: attribute, linguistic and relational. Attribute data comprise the attributes of people and the individuals with whom they interact. Usually demographic information about individuals such as age, sex and place of residence is collected and it is assumed that these have some influence on personal networks. Precisely what information is collected depends on research questions and on the context in which the research is carried out. Thus, Gal (1979), for example, determined the relative 'peasantness' of the network members. More recent studies use diverse and extensive attribute data: e.g. in the work of Marshall (2004), who collected data on mental urbanization, attitude to dialect and national pride.

In his historical study of language variation in the Late Middle English Paston letters, Bergs (2005) establishes a tentative network checklist for Late Medieval England, based upon categories such as gender, education, literacy, marital status, place of living, reference group or travel activities. The manner in which these attributes affect personal networks in England in the Late Middle Ages are illustrated by Bergs through two fictitious, extreme positions: a well-educated bachelor, member of several committees, groups and organizations, who holds important political positions and travels frequently throughout the whole country can be expected to have a rather loose-knit network with many uniplex ties; an uneducated peasant, married with children, who has never left his village and who is not involved in politics, would have a very close-knit network with few, but multiplex ties. Bergs concludes that marriage would decrease the number of ties an individual has and increase the multiplexity of the ties because married actors supposedly assume more roles. Education and gender would similarly correlate with network size: males and more-educated individuals would have more ties than females and less-educated individuals and their networks are at the same time presumed to be more multiplex because they assume more social roles (Bergs, 2005: 57ff.).

The second kind of network data, linguistic data, also hold information about the properties of individuals, and can thus be seen as a type of attribute data. In sociolinguistic research, they are compared with other attribute data and with relational data, and are thus given particular emphasis as a dependent variable. Generally, linguistic data investigated in these studies relate to a wide range of phenomena related to language. For example, Milroy's Belfast study (1980) concentrates on eight phonological variables that are clearly indexical of the Belfast urban speech community. In his Huntly study, Marshall identifies phonological, morphological and lexical variables that have two variants: the north-eastern Scots variant and the Scottish Standard English one (Marshall, 2004: 102). In Bergs's (2005) historical study, in this case, the linguistic data thus comprise personal pronouns, relativizers and light verb constructions.

Relational data refer to the links between the members of a network and may stem from observing or questioning the actor(s) under investigation. Researchers can note who interacts with whom, how, and for what purpose. These observations will provide for a 'slice-of-life picture' (Meyerhoff, 2009: 186) of the community or ego-network at the time of research. Another way of gaining relational data is to ask the actors about their networks. 'Who are your best friends?' or 'Name all the people that you had a conversation with yesterday' may constitute a good starting point. Fischer's instrument can be used as a standardized method of establishing relational data based on 10 network stimuli. It contains questions such as 'With whom do you discuss personal affairs and worries?' or 'Who looks after your house or apartment when you are away?' (Fischer, 1982). Reciprocity of namings might constitute an issue and researchers have to decide if they will only count reciprocal namings (e.g. Eckert, 2000; Meyerhoff, 2009) or build up the social networks based on responses regardless of whether the naming is reciprocal.

Precisely which methods of data collection are used in a given study depends largely on the context and the research design. In sociolinguistic network research, different kinds of questionnaires, informants' self-reports, ethnographic methods or triangulation of various methods (e.g. Lanza and Svendsen, 2007) are all used. Researchers agree that a thorough knowledge of the networks under investigation is required, which suggests that at least some ethnographic observation is required.

Often, and particularly in the tradition of Milroy's network approach (Milroy, 1980), network strength scales are used to evaluate data. These are based on a range of questions used to assess network characteristics. Individuals are assigned scores that can be compared to linguistic data. As in other fields, sociolinguistic studies often use statistical methods to assess network strength.

The social sciences as a whole have developed various criteria and extensively described methods for the description, visualization and analysis of network relations (Wasserman and Faust, 1994; Scott, 2000; Carrington et al., 2005, see also the latest issues of network journals such as

Social Networks). Clear definitions of network properties are given in order to develop and test (formal) models. However, this potential is not (yet) exploited in sociolinguistic research.

15.5 BASIC ASSUMPTIONS IN SOCIOLINGUISTIC NETWORK ANALYSES

Milroy's (1980) Belfast study makes plain the basic assumptions in sociolinguistic network analysis that have, since then, been the focus of discussions in this area. Milroy uses the social network as an analytical tool to account for systematic differences in language use between individuals and between subgroups within the community under investigation. In her study, a social network is seen as a mechanism for exchanging goods and services, as well as for imposing obligations and conferring privileges. Individuals who want to maintain their network relations have to account for the network's system of rights and obligations from which the network's norm-enforcement mechanism can be derived. Milroy's network strength scale, which she allocates to each of the 46 speakers from three low-status urban working-class communities, is based upon five indicators relating to two properties of networks (see below), multiplexity and density. A person with a high score (1) is a member of a high-density, territorially-based group (e.g. a bingo or card-playing group); (2) has substantial ties of kinship with more than two households in the neighbourhood; (3) works at the same place as at least two others from the same neighbourhood; and (4) works at the same place as at least two others of the same gender from the same neighbourhood; (5) associates voluntarily with work mates in leisure hours (Milroy, 1980: 54). As a result of the statistical correlation between the network scores and the eight phonological variables, Milroy claims to find strong evidence that a dense and multiplex social network closely relates to the maintenance of vernacular norms.

More generally, sociolinguistic network research assumes a strong correlation between the properties of social networks and language variation and choice. Strong network relationships lead to strong normative pressure, whereas weak relationships facilitate language change (Granovetter, 1973). If the structure of the whole network changes, this has linguistic consequences. For example, if networks become more open, this reduces the pressure on networks. This pressure is seen as responsible for the maintenance of vernacular and minority varieties, and any reduction thus leads to a shift away from these varieties,

e.g. language shift. This basic assumption – that normative pressures result from strong network relationships – has been confirmed in different areas of application within sociolinguistic network research, albeit not without intensive debate (e.g. Rindler-Schjerve, 1987; Vetter, 1997; Meyerhoff, 2009: 184–200). This has ultimately contributed to further developments in the field.

15.6 DISCUSSION

To sum up, the far-reaching discussions and further applications of the network perspective within sociolinguistics have challenged the explanatory power of social networks and have led to a different understanding of the relationship between networks and linguistic behaviour. The most important changes can be seen as associated with three broad themes. First, the focus on the explicit application of networks in macro-social contexts enhances the importance of categories like gender, age, social class and the question of agency for social networks. Secondly, the paradigm shift in identity research has led to different understandings of the link between networks and language. Thirdly, there has been an increased interest in investigating the influence of networks on language proficiency.

Within sociolinguistic network research it has never been claimed that networks should replace the analysis of the social, economic or political frameworks constraining individual behaviour. The network has never been interpreted as being in conflict with social categories such as social class (Milroy, 2002: 500). Thus, Gumperz (1982), for example, connects changes in networks with the shift from subsistence farming to a primarily service economy. Social network analysis may be seen as an attempt to examine more closely individuals' language behaviour and social interaction without ignoring the broader context. In this sense, social networks can be regarded as a buffer between macro-sociolinguistic concepts and micro-sociolinguistic interaction.

This leads to the paradox that network studies are often chosen because of the shortcomings of traditional social categories (e.g. Bortoni-Ricardo, 1985; Lippi-Green 1989), although they cannot be seen as independent of these macro-social categories. Often the efficacy of networks is only shown when they are combined with macro-scale categories. This means that the work of networks is hard to disentangle from other categories, particularly gender (Marshall, 2004: 28) It has become clear that networks are only a part of what makes people behave linguistically the way they do and that networks generally have to be interpreted against the background of the wider social context. The establishment of explicit links between networks and macro-structural contexts can be seen as a product of the past three decades of sociolinguistic network research.

The influence of gender was established by Cheshire (1982) on the basis of heterogeneous results for individual linguistic variables. She ascribes this to their differing and strongly gender-related functions: some features of non-standard English function as markers of vernacular loyalty for girls, boys, or both, while others function as sex markers and some function as markers of both loyalty and sex. Docherty et al. (1997) and Milroy (1999) also point to gender-specific differences.

Similarly, Kerswill und Williams (1999) also draw attention to the importance of the category of social class. They too confirm the basic assumption of normative pressure in social networks, although somewhat differently from others: mobile low-status groups and mobile high-status groups are both characterized by weak networks, but differ in terms of linguistic behaviours, ascribable in this case to differing orientations to the prevailing language ideologies of the UK. Studies of virtual networks also give a very differentiated picture that cannot be explained by the network alone. The function of linguistic variables as markers of social position is seen as particularly important (Paolillo 1999, 2001).

In a later study, Milroy and Milroy (1993) further tease out this micro–macro link and relate networks to wider social contexts via Højrup's (1983) life-mode concept. This suggests that macro-level factors are responsible for assigning individuals to particular modes of production, which then leads to differing strengths of network ties.

Bergs' analysis of historical networks also comes to different conclusions. Following the observation that individual linguistic variables behave very differently, he finds that linguistic variation is a much more conscious and goal-oriented process than is commonly assumed (Bergs, 2005: 264). He does not call into question the heuristic value of networks, but suggests that the questions of when, how and for which purposes particular linguistic forms are employed should also be given due importance. Marshall even goes one step further since he generally calls into question the validity of social networks as an analytical tool. In his study in a rural community, attitudinal factors turn out to be more significant factors in the use of phonological and morphological variables than a network integration index. He concludes that the presence of network norms may serve as a stimulus, but that the response of the individual is mediated by other factors such as attitudes (Marshall, 2004: 231).

To sum up, sociolinguistic network research since 1980 has clearly shown that network indices alone cannot account for linguistic variation and language choice. A comprehensive framework that both integrates networks into wider social contexts and also accounts for the agency of speakers has not yet been developed, and may be seen as a challenge for future research.

A second contentious area results from the paradigm shift in identity research, which has not yet been adequately transferred to network research. Sociolinguistic network research faces criticism because it assumes a 'natural' or iconic link between language and ethnic identity (Lanza and Svendsen, 2007). It is particularly recent research in multilingualism that rejects this essentialization of identity and argues that fluidity of identities is more applicable: multilinguals have multiple identities, not just ethnic but also other identities, which are negotiated in contact situations. A sense of belonging need not be achieved through language, but can also be achieved through other means. A multiplicity of identities can be at play in specific interactions, for example with children, as Lanza and Svendsen (2007) have shown for Filipinos in Oslo. Govindasamy and Nambiar (2003) arrived at similar results in their study of the Malayalees, an Asian community coming from Kerala (India) to Malaysia.

That identity plays a central role in linguistic behaviour is shown in a study that has been highly acclaimed by sociolinguistic network researchers: Eckert's (2000) long-term study of the speech of teenagers in Belten High School. She conceives of style as an individual and communal endeavour and as a means of negotiating meanings in the world. Moreover, she argues that variationist studies should focus on the relation between variation and identity. Eckert prefers the notion of a community of practice to that of a network. Communities of practice are a smaller unit than networks and can be characterized by mutual engagement, a jointly negotiated enterprise and a shared repertoire. In this sense, they can be considered as a specific kind of highly local networks (Meyerhoff, 2009: 289) which constitute a good framework for negotiating identity.

The third area of contention relates to the expansion of the explanatory power of networks for language proficiency. Networks have tended to be seen as a key to understanding the linguistic behaviour of individuals. In their study of three generations of Dutch migrants in New Zealand, however, Madeleine Hulsen, Kees de Bot and Bert Welten (2002) argue that limited contact with the first language leads to changes in the way lexical items are retrieved from the mental lexicon. Zentella (1997) drew similar conclusions in her study of 'the Puerto Rico language learning connection', which is based on continuing net-work ties. She sees these as an important reason for the strong position of Spanish in New York City. The limited language proficiency in the com-munity language of the younger generation thus leads to code-mixing and code-switching. A rela-tionship between the nature and orientation of social networks and competence in the target lan-guage is established in Wiklund's (2002) study of children from various migration contexts attend-ing a secondary school in Sweden. Language proficiency and processing are research areas that will be further explored in the future; it goes with-out saying that network data cannot be the only explanation for observed phenomena in these areas either.

To sum up the discussions in the field, simple correlations between a single independent social variable and dependent linguistic variables are always problematic – the network approach does not provide a remedy. The rich tradition of socio-linguistic research has shed light on concepts that are closely related to networks, in particular macro-social contexts, agency and questions of identity. This sets the scene for further discussions that may lead to advances in the application of networks to areas like language processing and competence.

15.7 OPEN QUESTIONS

The discussion so far was intended to show that social networks constitute neither a stable concept nor a coherent research paradigm in sociolinguistics. There are many open questions and future research promises to give rise to interesting discussions. Three lines of inquiry are immediately apparent: definitions of terminology and theoretical concepts; theoretical influences on the field; and the relation-ship between sociolinguistics and sociology.

The clarity of the network concept can only be enhanced by critical comparison with concepts like speech community and community of prac-tice. The first questions that must be asked relate to how the differences between the concepts can be identified and what gives each concept its explanatory power. These questions cannot be discussed without reference to underlying theo-ries. The interactionist approach pioneered by Gumperz may well turn out to be compatible with the concept of the community of practice, and this may lead to a research perspective which succeeds both concepts. But even in the correlational para-digm the theory of networks is vague. Most socio-linguists seem to agree that the network is not a theory. However, the theoretical foundations which gave rise to the concept should be discussed

above and beyond the limits set by the pioneers in the field. This will also lead to further methodo-logical developments.

It seems that the problematization of these issues is a prerequisite for engaging in discussion with those disciplines with a long history of network research. This is not to suggest a simple applica-tion of the rich inventory of formal research meth-ods from these disciplines. Rather, based on a theoretically-grounded and differentiated concept of a social network in sociolinguistics, a critical comparison with sociological network research could enrich the sociolinguistic methodological inventory. Nevertheless, the concept of the net-work may eventually be clearly differentiated from concepts in other disciplines. Without enlarg-ing the horizon of network research beyond socio-linguistics, however, it is most difficult to seriously confront the critisism that there are discrepancies in the quality of network studies between sociol-ogy and sociolinguistics (Schlobinski, 2005).

REFERENCES

Barnes, J. A. (1954) 'Class and committees in a Norwegian Island parish', *Human Relations*, 7: 39–58.
Bergs, A. (2005) *Social Networks and Historical Sociolinguistics: Studies in Morphosyntactic Variation in the Paston Letters, 1421–1503*. Berlin: De Gruyter.
Bergs, A. (2006) 'Analyzing online communication from a social network point of view: questions, problems, perspec-tives', *Language @ Internet*. Available at: http://www.languageatinternet.de/articles/2006/371/index_html.
Berthele, R. (2002) *Sprache in der Klasse: eine dialektologisch-soziolinguistische Untersuchung von Primarschulkindern in multilingualem Umfeld*. Tübingen: Niemeyer.
Blom, J.-P. and Gumperz, J. J. (1972) 'Social meaning in linguistic structures: code-switching in Norway', in J. J. Gumperz, and D. Hymes (eds), *Directions in Sociolinguistics. The Ethnography of Communication*. New York: Holt-Rinehart-Winston. pp. 407–34.
Boissevain, J. (1974) *Friends of Friends: Networks, Manipulators and Coalitions*. Oxford: Basil Blackwell.
Boissevain, J. (1987) 'Social networks', in U. Ammon, N. Dittmar and K. J. Mattheier (eds), *An International Handbook of the Science of Language and Society*. Vol. 1. 1st edn. Berlin: de Gruyter. pp. 164–9.
Boissevain, J. and J. C. Mitchell (eds) (1973) *Network Analysis: Studies in Human Interaction*. The Hague: Mouton.
Boorman, S. A. and White, H. C. (1976) 'Social structure from multiple networks. II. Role structures', *American Journal of Sociology*, 81(6): 1384–1446.
Bortoni-Ricardo, S. M. (1985) *The Urbanisation of Rural Dialect Speakers: a Sociolinguistic Study in Brazil*. Cambridge: Cambridge University Press.
Bott, E. (1957) *Family and Social Network*. London: Tavistock.

Burt, R. S. (1982) *Toward a Structural Theory of Action. Networks Models of Social Structure, Perception and Action.* New York: Academic Press.

Burt, R. S. (1992) *Structural Holes. The Social Structure of Competition.* Cambridge, CA: Harvard University Press.

Carrington, P. J., Scott, J. and Wasserman, S. (eds) (2005) *Models and Methods in Social Network Analysis.* Cambridge, Cambridge University Press.

Cheshire, J. (1982) *Variation in an English Dialect: a Sociolinguistic Study.* Cambridge: Cambridge University Press.

Dabène, L. and Moore, D. (1995) 'Bilingual speech of migrant people', in L. Milroy, and P. Muysken (eds), *One speaker, two languages.* Cambridge: Cambridge University Press. pp. 17–44.

de Bot, K. and Stoessel, S. (2002) 'Introduction', *International Journal of the Sociology of Language*, 153: 1–7.

Degenne A. and Forsé, M. (eds) (2004) *Les réseaux sociaux.* 2nd edn. Paris: Armand Colin. (1st edn, 1994).

Docherty, G., Foulkes, P., Milroy, J., Milroy, L. and Walshaw, D. (1997) 'Descriptive adequacy in phonology: a variationist perspective', *Journal of Linguistics*, 33: 1–36.

Eckert, P. (2000) *Linguistic Variation as Social Practice.* Oxford: Blackwell.

Fischer, C. (1982) *To Dwell Among Friends. Personal Networks in Town and City.* Chicago: University Press of Chicago.

Forsé, M. (2002) 'Les réseaux sociaux chez Simmel: les fondements d'un modèle individualiste et structural', in L. Deroche-Gurcel and P. Watier (eds), *La sociologie de Georg Simmel.* Paris: Presses Universitaires de France. pp. 63–107.

Forsé, M. (2008) 'Définir et analyser les réseaux sociaux. Les enjeux de l'analyse structurale', CAIRN 147 (2008/3). Available at: http://www.cairn.info/revue-informations-sociales-2008-3-page-10.htmn.

Forsé, M. and Langlois, S. (1997) 'Réseaux, structures et rationalités', *L'Année sociologique* 47(1), 27–35.

Freeman, L. C. (2004) *The Development of Social Network Analysis: A study in the Sociology of Science.* Vancouver, BC: Empirical Press.

Gal, S. (1979) *Language Shift. Social Determinants of Linguistic Change in Bilingual Austria.* New York: Academic Press.

Gauchat, L. (1905) 'L'unité phonétique dans le patois d'une commune', in *Aus Romanischen Sprachen und Literaturen.* Festschrift Heinrich. Morf:. Halle: Niemeyer. pp. 175–232.

Govindasamy, S. and Nambiar, M. (2003) 'Social networks: applicability to minority communities in multilingual settings', *IJSL*, 161: 25–45.

Granovetter, M. (1973) 'The strength of weak ties', *American Journal of Sociology*, 78: 1360–80.

Gumperz, J. J. (1975) *Sprache, lokale Kultur und soziale Identität.* Düsseldorf: Schwann.

Gumperz, J. J. (1982) 'Social network and language shift', in J. J. Gumperz (ed.), *Discourse Strategies.* Cambridge: Cambridge University Press. pp. 38–58.

Gumperz, J. J. (1994) 'Sprachliche Variabilität in interaktionsanalytischer Perspektive', in W. Kallmeyer (ed.), *Kommunikation in der Stadt. Teil 1. Exemplarische Analysen des Sprachverhaltens in Mannheim.* Berlin: de Gruyter. pp. 611–39.

Højrup, T. (1983) 'The concept of lifemode: a form-specifying mode of analysis applied to contemporary western Europe', *Ethnologia Scandinavica*, 1–50.

Hollstein, B. and Straus, F. (eds) (2006) *Qualitative Netzwerkanalyse. Konzepte, Methoden, Anwendungen.* Wiesbaden: VS-Verlag.

Homans, G. C. (1958) 'Social behavior as exchange', *American Journal of Sociology*, 63(6): 597–606.

Hulsen, M., de Bot, K. and Welten, B. (2002) 'Between two worlds. Social networks, language shift, and language processing in three generations of Dutch migrants in New Zealand', *International Journal of the Sociology of Language*, 153: 27–52.

Jansen, D. (2006) *Einführung in die Netzwerkanalyse.* 3rd edn. Wiesbaden: VS Verlag für Sozialwissenschaften. (1st edn, 1999.)

Javeau, C. (1986) 'Georg Simmel et la vie quotidienne: *Tür* et *Brücke* et socialité', in P. Watier (ed.), *Georg Simmel, la sociologie et l'expérience du monde moderne.* Paris: Méridiens Klincksieck. pp. 177–88.

Johnson, D. P. (2008): *Contemporary Sociological Theory. An Integrated Multi-Level Approach.* New York: Springer.

Kerswill, P. and Williams, A. (1999) 'Mobility versus social class in dialect levelling: evidence from new and old towns in England', *Cuadernos de Filologia Inglesa*, 8: 47–57.

Labov, W. (1963) 'The social motivation of a sound change' Word, 19: 273–309.

Labov, W. (1972) 'The linguistic consequences of being a lame', in W. Labov (ed.), Language in the inner city. Philadelphia: University of pennsylvania Press. pp. 255–92.

Labrie, N. (1988) 'Social networks and code-switching: a sociolinguistic investigation of Italians in Montreal', in N. Dittmar and P. Schlobinski (eds) *The Sociolinguistics of Urban Vernaculars.* Berlin: de Gruyter. pp. 217–32.

Lanza, E. and Svendsen, B. A. (2007) 'Tell me who your friends are and I might be able to tell you what language(s) you speak: social network analysis, multilingualism, and identity', *International Journal of Bilingualism*, 11(3): 275–300.

Li, W. (1994) *Three Generations, Two Languages, One Family. Language Choice and Language Shift in a Chinese Community in Britain.* Clevedon, UK: Multilingual Matters.

Lippi-Green, R. (1989) 'Social network integration and language change in progress in an alpine rural village', *Language in Society*, 18: 213–34.

Lorrain, F. and White, H. C. (1971) 'The structural equivalence of individuals in social networks', *Journal of Mathematical Sociology*, 1: 49–80.

Marsden, P. V. (2005) 'Recent developments in network measurement', in P. J. Carrington, J. Scott and S. Wasserman (eds), *Models and Methods in Social Network Analysis.* Cambridge: Cambridge University Press. pp. 8–30.

Marshall, J. (2004) *Language Change and Sociolinguistics. Rethinking Social Networks.* New York: Palgrave Macmillan.

Mercklé P. (2004) *Sociologie des réseaux sociaux.* Paris: La Découverte.

Meyerhoff, M. (2009) *Introducing Sociolinguistics*. New York: Routledge.

Milardo, R. M. (1988) 'Families and social networks: an overview of theory and methodology', in R. M. Milardo (ed.), *Families and Social Networks*. Newbury Park, CA: Sage. pp. 13–47.

Milroy, L. (1980) *Language and Social Networks*. Blackwell: Oxford.

Milroy, L. (1999) 'Women as innovators and norm-creators: the sociolinguistics of dialect leveling in a northern English city', in S. Wertheim, A. C. Bailey and M. Corston-Oliver (eds), *Engendering Communication, Proceedings of the Fifth Berkeley Women and Language Conference*. Berkeley: Berkeley Women and Language Group. pp. 361–76.

Milroy, L. (2001) 'Bridging the micro–macro gap: social change, social network and bilingual repertoires', in J. Klatter-Folmer and P. van Avermaet (eds), *Theories on Maintenance and Loss of Minority Languages: Towards a More Integrated Explanatory Framework*. Munich: Waxmann. pp. 39–64.

Milroy, L. (2002) '22. Social networks', in J. Chambers, and N. Schilling-Estes (eds), *Handbook of Language Variation and Change*. Oxford: Blackwell. pp. 549–73.

Milroy, L. and Li, W. (1995) 'A social network approach to codeswitching', in L. Milroy and P. Muysken (eds), *One speaker, two languages*. Cambridge: Cambridge University Press. pp. 136–57.

Milroy, J. and Milroy, L. (1985) 'Linguistic change, social network and speaker innovation', *Journal of Linguistics*, 21: 339–84.

Milroy, J. and Milroy, L. (1993) 'Mechanisms of change in urban dialects: the role of class, social network and gender', *International Journal of Applied Linguistics*, 3(1): 57–78.

Mitchell, J. C. (ed.) (1969) *Social Networks in Urban Situations*. Manchester: Manchester University Press.

Mitchell, J. C. (1973) 'Networks, norms and institutions', in J. Boissevain and J. C. Mitchell (eds), *Network Analysis; Studies in Human Interaction*. The Hague: Mouton. pp. 2–35.

Mitchell, J. C. (1986) 'Network procedures', in D. Frick, H. W. Hoefert, H. Legewie, R. Mackensen and R. K. Silbereisen (eds), *The Quality of Urban life*. Berlin: de Gruyter. pp. 73–92.

Moreno, J. L. (1934) *Who Shall Survive? A New Approach to the Problem of Human Interrelations*. Washington, DC: Nervous and Mental Disease Publishing.

Moreno, J. L. (1960) 'Political prospects of sociometry', *International Journal of Sociometry and Society*, 2: 3–6.

Paolillo, J. (1999) 'The virtual speech community: social network and language variation on IRC', *Journal of Computer-Mediated Communication*, 4(4). Available at: http://jcmc. indiana.edu/vol4/issue4/paolillo.html.

Paolillo, J. (2001) 'Language variation on Internet Relay Chat: a social network approach', *Journal of Sociolinguistics*, 5(2): 180–213.

Radcliffe-Brown, A. R. (1940) 'On social structure', *Journal of the Royal Anthropological Society of Great Britain and Ireland*, 70: 1–12.

Raphael, F. (1986): '"L'etranger" de Georg Simmel', in P. Watier (ed.), *Georg Simmel, la sociologie et l'expérience du monde moderne*. Paris: Méridiens Klincksieck. pp. 257–78.

Raschka, C., Li, W. and Sherman, L. (2002) 'Bilingual development and social networks of British-born Chinese children', *International Journal of the Sociology of Language*, 153: 9–25.

Rindler-Schjerve, R. (1987) *Sprachkontakt auf Sardinien. Soziolinguistische Untersuchung des Sprachenwechsels im ländlichen Bereich*. Tübingen: Niemeyer.

Rindler-Schjerve, R. (1991) 'Ethnolinguistic and interpretative concepts in explaining language shift', in J. Verschueren (ed.), *Levels of Linguistic Adaptation. Selected Papers of the International Pragmatics Conference, Antwerp 1987*. Philadelphia: Benjamins. pp. 223–33.

Salancik, G. R. (1995) 'Wanted: a good network theory of organization', *Administrative Science Quarterly*, 40: 345–9.

Schenk, M. and Bergs, A. (2004) '55. Netzwerk/Network', in U. Ammon, N. Dittmar and K. J. Mattheier (eds) *An International Handbook of the Science of Language and Society*. 2nd edn. Berlin: de Gruyter. pp. 438–43. (1st edn, 1987.)

Schlobinski, P. (2005) '143. Netzwerk-Untersuchungen. Research on networks', in U. Ammon, N. Dittmar and K. J. Mattheier (eds), *An International Handbook of the Science of Language and Society*. 2nd edn. Berlin: de Gruyter. pp. 1459–69. (1st edn, 1987.)

Scott, J. (2000) *Social Network Analysis: A Handbook*. 2nd edn. London: Sage. (1st edn, 1991.)

Simmel, G. (1908) *Soziologie. Untersuchungen über die Formen der Vergesellschaftung*. 1992 edited by Otthein Rammstedt. Vol. 11. Frankfurt am Main: Suhrkamp.

Tieken-Boon van Ostade, I., Nevalainen, T. and Caon, L. (eds) (2001) *Social network theory and the history of english* (special issue of the *European Journal of English Studies*).

Vetter, E. (1997) *Nicht mehr Bretonisch? Sprachkonflikt in der ländlichen Bretagne*. Frankfurt: Peter Lang.

Von Wiese, L. (1932) 'Sociologie relationnelle', *Revue internationale de sociologie*, I-II: 23–56.

Wasserman, S. and Faust, K. (1994) *Social Network Analysis: Methods and Applications*. Cambridge: Cambridge University Press.

Wasserman, S., Scott, J. and Carrington, P. (2005) 'Introduction', in P. J. Carrington, J. Scott and S. Wasserman (eds), *Models and Methods in Social Network Analysis*. Cambridge: Cambridge University Press. pp. 1–7.

Watts, R. (1991) *Power in Family Discourse*. New York: Mouton de Gruyter.

White, H. C. (1992) *Identity and Control: A Structural Theory of Social Action*. Princeton, NJ: Princeton University Press.

White, H. C., Boorman, S. A. and Breiger, R. R. (1976) 'Social structure from multiple networks: I. blockmodels of roles and positions', *American Journal of Sociology*, 81: 730–80.

Wiklund, I. (2002) 'Social networks from a sociolinguistic perspective', *IJSL*, 153: 53–92.

Zentella, A. C. (1997) *Growing up Bilingual*. Oxford: Blackwell.

16

Sociolinguistic Approaches to Language Change: Phonology

Paul Kerswill

16.1 SOCIAL APPROACHES TO LANGUAGE CHANGE

Taking a sociolinguistic approach to the explanation of language change has two consequences. The first is that, with the exception of a growing body of work in historical sociolinguistics (see Nevalainen, this volume), the subject matter is restricted in time to the rather brief period, leading up to the present, during which extensive and reliable records of natural speech have been available – or sociolinguistically valid simulations of such speech. The second is that sociolinguistics is a young discipline, and in its 'variationist' guise is mainly the brainchild of a single scholar, William Labov. Particularly in its approach to language change (mainly on the phonological level), variationist sociolinguistics has been dominated by Labov. The by now 'classical' variationist approach to change, as set out in Weinreich, Labov and Herzog (1968) and encapsulated in Labov's New York City (NYC) study (1966), sits alongside his own development of that paradigm (Labov, 1994; 2001; Labov, Ash and Boberg, 2006) as well as other distinct research enterprises which are mostly post-Labovian, though some (in cognitive linguistics and experimental phonetics) are not specifically informed by his work. The development of Labov's ideas is discussed in detail in Hazen (this volume). Here, I focus on the way his work sheds light on the central subject matter of historical linguistics, namely change in the linguistic system (the transition from state A to state B in the same language across a given period of time). But in their wider concern for patterning in naturally-occurring speech, sociolinguists

interested in change tend to debate the locus of that change. This discussion can be seen as involving two independent dichotomies: the individual vs the group, and system vs use. In the course of this chapter, we will touch upon these concerns, too.

Labov (1994: 19) traces the origin of his approach to Gauchat (1905), who conducted a study of a Swiss village using what is now known as the 'apparent-time' method, i.e. inferring change from differences between the speech of older and younger people (see Romaine, 1988). Despite the interest in variation and change in both urban and rural dialects in Scandinavia in the early twentieth century (e.g. Larsen and Stoltz, 1911–12; Skautrup, 1921), Gauchat's study was unique in combining empiricism with an explicit theoretical language-change agenda, in this case attempting to refute the Neogrammarians' regularity hypothesis. It is only with Labov's Martha's Vineyard study (1963; see Hazen, this volume) that a closely-related data/theory combination reappears. As for datasets gathered according to sociolinguistic principles, it is obvious that as time goes on there will be increasing scope for studies of real-time change (revisiting a community, say, a generation later in order to gauge change). Notable studies are by Cedergren (1987; Panama) and Sundgren (2009; Eskilstuna). Nevertheless, pessimism about the time depth of variationist sociolinguistics is very much tempered by the routine use of older data collected by other means and for other purposes, notably by Labov himself who used data from the *Linguistic Atlas of New England*, collected in 1933 in locations including Martha's Vineyard. The series of studies of New Zealand English by Gordon, Trudgill and others are based on recordings of elderly speakers made in the 1940s, as well as of more recent data (Gordon et al., 2004; Trudgill, 2004). In both the Martha's Vineyard and New Zealand cases, we see a combination of apparent- and real-time methods which, after some triangulation, provide a reliable picture of change over some 150 years – at least at the micro-level of individual phonetic features. Ongoing large-scale projects making extensive use of both old and new material in Germany (Schwartz and Streck, 2009) and Denmark (Gregersen, Maegaard and Pharao, 2009) are promising. An interesting perspective is afforded by so-called 'language islands', where populations are isolated from their linguistic homelands and so do not take part in mainstream changes (Rosenberg, 2005: 222; Loudon, 2006). We return to the issue of time and the transmission of dialect in the final section.

Historical linguistics is a much older discipline and has the advantage of being able to take a long view of change, over several centuries, and with outcomes clearly visible. The age of the discipline brings with it huge changes in perspective, however. In the late eighteenth to early twentieth centuries, 'outcomes' were often identified with the endpoint of a teleological process which had striven for, and achieved, perfection. Thus, the early nineteenth-century German linguist Jakob Grimm, following Herder, saw the High German Consonant Shift as 'an early assertion of independence on the part of the ancestors of the German peoples' (Robins, 1990: 190). Much later, H. C. Wyld was of the opinion that English dialects could be ignored except insofar as they 'throw light on those forms of our language which are the main objects of our solicitude, namely the language of literature and Received Standard Spoken English'(1927: 16; cited in Crystal, 2004: 5). Nowadays, these opinions are seen by historians of linguistics in a critical light, as embedded in their time and place. Sociolinguists, however, recognize that similar views remain firmly entrenched today as everyday ideologies. The manifestation of this, particularly in developed countries, is a so-called 'standard ideology' (J. Milroy, 2000): a common-sense view of the essential, even moral, rightness of the standard language. This sociolinguistic insight is actually one component of the explanation of a particular type of linguistic change – standardization and dedialectalization – to which we will return.

However dispassionate sociolinguists would like to be, as observers of linguistic behaviour, a lesson from these earlier scholars' work is that objectivity remains mediated by the observer's stance. Among variationist sociolinguists, there is now an acceptance that language change can be

'observed', replacing earlier linguists' pessimism on this point (Labov, 1994: 44). Labov's speech community model (2006a [1966]) shows that, even if it is difficult to observe change directly across a speaker's lifetime, the social stratification of linguistic features, coupled with age differentiation in the same features, gives us a way of understanding how change can proceed in a manner that is indirectly observable. (See Wolfram, this volume, for a discussion of the speech community concept.) The discovery of socially-patterned variation and, crucially, the inference of a mechanism of change underlying this patterning have been fundamental to thinking about language change since the early 1960s. Because of this patterning, which is quantitative in nature (i.e. it is rarely a question of categorical presence vs absence of a feature, but differing frequencies or differing positions on a continuous phonetic scale), Labov believes that systematicity is greater at the group level than at the individual level: 'We find that in New York City, most idiolects do not form a simple, coherent system: on the contrary, they are studded with oscillations and contradictions ... ' (2006a [1966]: 5). Later, he refines this position as follows:

> Many writers on sociolinguistic themes ... have argued that the major focus of sociolinguistic analysis should be placed on the individual speaker rather than the group ... . If the net result of such a policy is to plunge more deeply into the internal workings of the group, then it is likely to be productive. (2001: 33) ... . [T]his unique object, the individual speaker, can only be understood as the product of a unique social history, and **the intersection of the linguistic patterns of all the social groups and categories that define that individual** [my emphasis – PK] (Labov, 2001: 34).

The uniqueness of an idiolect is not random, but is the product of the speaker's various group affiliations and exposure, over a lifetime, to those groups' distinctive ways of speaking. This is relatively uncontroversial. What may be considered problematic is the positivism implied by Labov's work. First, he uses a hierarchical social model, strongly influenced by the functionalism of Parsons (Kerswill, 2007a: 52). Secondly, this model is composed of predetermined categories, especially social class. The quotation above can, then, easily lead to the view that speakers respond to their socioeconomic position as if they were automata. Whatever the criticisms, Labov presents a broad-brush picture of language variation at the speech community level. As we shall see below, the model's great benefit is that it allows for intricate social patterns to be uncovered in the mechanism of language change; the implication is that if language is the property of the group, then change should be explained at the level of the group.

Labov's work is often referred to as representative of 'first-wave' variation studies, giving us the backdrop to variation. (Eckert (2005) gives an excellent overview of the 'waves' of language variation studies.) 'Second-wave' studies are concerned with explaining the link between social categories – which this time need not be imposed by the researcher, but may be allowed to emerge from the local context – and people's linguistic behaviour; in other words, the research investigates 'how ways of speaking are imbued with local meaning' (Eckert, 2005: 5). The focus is very much on the individual speaker, and ethnographic rather than survey methods are preferred. A prime exemplar is the Milroys' research on Belfast English (L. Milroy 1980 (2nd edition, 1987); J. Milroy 1992). Here, the researchers quickly realized that social class could not account for variation in inner-city lower-working-class neighbourhoods – the speakers were all objectively in the same bracket. Instead, they found that variation seemed related to differences in the way individuals were connected socially with their own local community and extended families. The mechanism involved is the **social network**: 'the aggregate of relationships contracted with others, a boundless web of ties which reaches out through social and geographical space linking many individuals, sometimes remotely' (Milroy and Gordon, 2003: 117; see also Vetter, this volume). We will turn later to the way in which a network analysis contributes to the explanation of language change. For now, we can note that a close-knit network serves as a powerful norm-enforcement mechanism, inhibiting change, while a looser-knit one allows, or even promotes, change.

Despite its focus on individual behaviour, the social network concept, too, has been considered overly deterministic, even as early as Romaine (1982: 269–70). 'Third-wave' variation studies compensate for this by focusing firmly on the social meaning of variant forms, showing how they are combined by speakers into 'styles' indexing identities and personae (see Eckert, 2005 for discussion). Interest in language change varies strongly across third-wave studies: Eckert (2000) deals with vocalic variables in a Detroit suburban high school, investigating how they are manipulated to index identities within the school population, while relating this indexation to the progress of a vowel shift known as the Northern Cities Shift (Labov, Yaeger and Steiner, 1972; Labov, 1994; and below). For some other broadly third-wave studies, language change is not a central concern. Focusing on the vocalic variable (aw), as in *mouth* in Pittsburgh, Johnstone and Kiesling (2008) use a series of interviews with Pittsburghers

to explore differences in the way the local, monophthongal realization of this vowel indexes a local Pittsburgh identity, in the process becoming stereotyped. By contrast, Moore (2003, 2006), who explored adolescent peer groups in a Bolton secondary school, did not relate the use of variables to ongoing change.

At this point in the history of variationist sociolinguistics, we can detect an incipient bifurcation. Although some third-wave studies do relate their findings to language structure and change, probably a larger number are more closely allied to interpretive, interactional and constructivist sociolinguistic approaches represented by Gumperz, Scollon and Kotthoff (see Kotthoff, this volume]). However, first- and second-wave studies of change continue unabated (e.g., Baranowski, 2007; Kerswill, Torgersen and Fox, 2008), but in the early twenty-first century their central focus on language change has been extended, not by the next 'wave', but by usage-based and cognitive models of language acquisition and language change. Some of these are firmly within the Labovian tradition (Clark, 2008; Docherty, 2008; Hay, 2008), while others do not use his methods or frameworks at all (Bybee, 2000, 2002; Pierrehumbert, 2003; Hollmann and Siewierska, 2008). Although integration between the variationist and cognitive/usage-based research traditions has yet to be achieved, the synergy between them is likely to be fruitful. I briefly discuss the work of Clark and Bybee in section 16.4, below.

16.2 SOUND CHANGE

Much variationist work has been on sound change, and this work has become field-defining. Perhaps not surprisingly, most of the social (as opposed to linguistic) mechanisms of change apply equally to change in other linguistic components. The central concept of the 'linguistic variable' is well suited to phonology because variation in the realization of a variable is meaning-preserving – cf. the variable '(t)' in British English, which usually refers to the use of the glottal stop as a *variant*, alongside alveolar [t], of intervocalic /t/. This concept can be applied to other types of structural linguistic change as well, particularly in morphosyntax. (Kerswill (2004: 24–7) contains a discussion of the variable and the limits of its meaning-preserving properties; Cheshire (2007) presents a variationist analysis of discourse markers, where the strict delimitation of the variants of the variables is not possible and the preservation of meaning must be interpreted, using pragmatic analyses, as rough functional equivalence.) We will return to the variable in the Neogrammarian context at the end of this section.

Sound change was central to nineteenth-century linguistic thinking, and was an important motivation for the new discipline of dialectology in the last quarter of that century. Methodologically, variationist sociolinguistics shares much with dialectology, non-standardized speech being placed centre-stage. In both, strict criteria for speaker selection are set, with some notion of 'nativeness' being significant; for dialectology, speakers must be as local as possible with a low level of education in order for the 'true' dialect to emerge (see Chambers and Trudgill, 1998: 29 for discussion); for variationists, speakers should have spent most of their years, especially the early ones, in the location (though practice varies). They differ in that dialectology considers only geographical space, in order to examine better the spread of a feature, while variationism operates at the community level – social space, in other words. In many respects, the two disciplines can now be seen as modelling complementary sides of the same reality (Trudgill, 1992; Britain, 2004), and their combination increases the explanatory power of each.

We begin with the motivation of sound change. The comparative method (Hock, 1991: 556–80) relies heavily on the notion of 'regular' sound change in its reconstruction of hypothetical past states of language, establishing 'genetic' relationships between 'daughter' languages. Thus, the following set of phonetically and semantically related words (which can be greatly multiplied) suggests such a relationship between Norwegian and English:

is [iːs]	*ice* [aɪs]
smile [smiːlə]	*smile* [smaɪl]
mil [miːl]	*mile* [maɪl]

Other evidence tells us that the vowel [aɪ] in English was formerly pronounced [iː], and that this change took place in Late Middle/Early Modern English – many centuries after the ancestor languages of Norwegian and English split off from each other. This is an example of a *regular* (or *Neogrammarian*) sound change. The dictum is that 'phonemes change' (Bloomfield 1933: 353–4): every instance of phoneme A is affected in the same way in the same period of time in the same geographical area (see Hock, 1991: 34–91). There appear to be exceptions, however. In French, Proto-Romance /k/ before /a/ was shifted to [ʃ], yielding modern French *champ* 'field', *chat* 'cat', *chandelle* 'candle', *chanson* 'song', etc. (Bynon 1977: 181). In Normandy French dialects, /k/ was preserved. However, dialectology showed that standard French /ʃ/ has encroached on the /k/ region in certain words more than others, namely *chandelle*, *chanson* and *chaîne* 'chain'

(Bynon 1977: 182). Such findings as these led to the alternative slogan: 'each word has its own history'.

There are several issues surrounding sound change which need to be resolved in the face of this contradictory evidence. Two issues that have exercised scholars since the late nineteenth century are (1) whether sound change is phonetically gradual or abrupt and (2) whether it is lexically abrupt (covering all lexical items, and hence regular), or gradual (proceeding by **lexical diffusion**, as, apparently, in the French k→ʃ shift). As I noted earlier, in more recent times, scholars have asked (3) whether such change is 'observable' and (4) whether change is a property of the individual or of the community. Finally (5): Is sound change internally motivated (as a consequence of structural properties of the language), or is it the consequence of external motivation (i.e. contact-induced)? Following Farrar and Jones (2002: 1), one should additionally ask if 'extra-linguistic (i.e. sociopolitical and economic)' factors bear on change – though we will not be concerned with these factors here.

Sound changes appear to be divided into those which have a clear phonetic, i.e. articulatory, basis, and those for which there is no such clear motivation available. An example comes from the development of Spanish, where Latin /p/, /t/ and /k/ when they occurred between vowels were lenited (weakened). An example is Latin *pacatum*, in which we assume /k/ and /t/ first changed to [g] and [d] and then to [ɣ] and [ð], with the additional possibility of deletion. This gives the presumed chronological sequence:

[pakatum] → *[pagado] → [paɣaðo] (→ dialectal [paɣao], with deletion of /ð/) 'pleased' ('*' stands for 'unattested'; adapted from Hock, 1991: 81)

where the two medial consonants gradually take on phonological features from the surrounding vowels, viz. +voice and then +continuant, before (in some varieties) being deleted, i.e. fully assimilated to the vowels, leaving no trace. The initial /p/, being word initial, was not affected. The change of intervocalic plosives to voiced fricatives is regular in Spanish, in that all cases have shifted. A well-documented lenition in present-day Spanish is that of the affricate /tʃ/ to [ʃ] in Panama (Cedergren, 1987; Tagliamonte and D'Arcy, 2009: 60). Another example, this time involving vowels and the process of assimilation, is the fronting of back vowels /u/, /o/ and /a/ in Germanic to [y], [ø] and [ɛ], respectively, before a syllable containing the high front vowel /i/ (the vowels assimilate the front property of /i/): reflexes of this ancient change ('*Umlaut*'; Hock, 1991: 66–8) still appear in German morphology in, e.g. *Buch – Bücher* ('book' – 'books'). The question which arises, of course, is why the lenition of /p/, /t/ and /k/ didn't happen in the other daughter languages of Latin, and why *Umlaut* happened in the other Germanic languages but not in Gothic; and we must ask why the changes happened just **when** they did and not at some other time, given that they were phonetically motivated and hence 'natural', and so should apply whenever the phonological conditions were right.

To try to gain an understanding of how lenitions and assimilations become fully-fledged changes in the language, we need to know how they reached this state, from having been 'connected speech processes' (CSPs). CSPs are the range of reductions affecting phonological segments in normal, fluent speech (Nolan and Kerswill, 1990). They result from conflicts between different articulatory gestures for adjacent sounds and (related to this) the failure of articulators to reach targets, such as that of forming a stop closure. As such, CSPs occur in all speech most of the time, depending on speech style – whether slow, careful, or fast, casual. They are phonetically **gradual**. Dressler and Wodak (1982) offer one approach to the transition to 'sound change', at the same time offering a model of dialect switching (between dialect and standard) to account for the linguistic behaviour of speakers of Viennese German. Each variety (dialect or standard) is associated with a set of reduction rules (lenitions), as well as fortitions (clarification processes characteristic of slow, careful speech). Dressler and Wodak conceptualize phonological change as 'the spread of optional PRs [phonological rules – PK] from casual speech to more formal phonological styles until they become obligatory for all styles' (1982: 350). In other words, CSPs, which are characteristic of everyday speech, begin to be used in more formal speech, and then become fossilized as permanent features of the phonology. However, Spanish lenition and German *Umlaut* are today not gradual and variable, but discrete and obligatory. Experimental methods can be applied in order to see how gradualness gives way to discreteness. An indication of this is given by Wright (1989) and by Kerswill and Wright (1990). Using electropalatography to record tongue contact with the palate, they discovered that a typical CSP, regressive place assimilation affecting final /d/ before velars, giving [bæggaɪ] for *bad guy*, was phonetically gradual in local Cambridge English, with many intermediate articulations between [d] and [g]. It was susceptible to speaking rate, but not socially evaluated. On the other hand, another CSP, the vocalization of syllable-coda /l/ as in *bell* or *milk*, was applied almost categorically and was only weakly affected

by speaking rate, but was socially (negatively) evaluated. The assumption is that regressive assimilation is not (yet) a sound change in English (though it might be), while l-vocalization, a common CSP, is a sound change nearing completion in south-east England (Johnson and Britain 2007).

I mentioned social evaluation in relation to a CSP becoming an established change. This turns out to be of central importance to more mainstream variationist treatments of sound change (and language change generally). Variationist studies of vowels deal with the various shifts, diphthongizations and monophthongizations which take place in all languages. They are generally unconditioned: i.e. they occur in all instances of the particular vowel and not in restricted phonological environments – the diphthongization of Middle English /iː/ is a case in point. Perhaps because of the absence of an obvious phonetic motivation, these became the focus of much variationist work, starting in particular with Labov's NYC study (2006a [1966]). Figure 16.1 shows data for the fronting of the vowel (aw), as in *mouth*, in Philadelphia, from Labov's later, 1970s project. As explained by Guy (2003: 366), the y-axis is a coefficient relating to the second formant of the vowel, measured in Hertz; the higher the value, the greater the fronting. The x-axis represents five socioeconomic classes, from lowest to highest. The fact that there is,

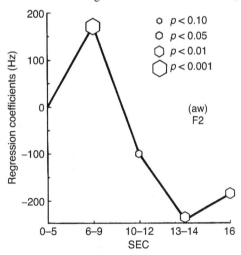

Figure 16.1   The variable (aw), referring to the fronting of /aʊ/ (as in *mouth*) in Philadelphia: regression coefficients for socioeconomic classes (adapted from Labov, 1980: 261; reproduced from Guy, 2003: 387).

additionally, a strong negative correlation between age and the value of the second formant (younger people front the vowel more) shows that the feature is increasing with time (Labov, 2001: 165). It is one of the internal classes, in this case the upper working class, which uses the feature the most. These facts taken together lead Labov to conclude that this social class is leading in this change. He calls this the 'curvilinear pattern', and it is typical of 'change from below' – i.e. the introduction of a feature which is not standard or overtly valued, but is non-standard and potentially stigmatized.

There is no natural connection between this fronted vowel and the social group which uses it the most (compare the 'natural' lenitions and assimilations noted earlier); social evaluation is, therefore, arbitrary. This begs the causal question: 'why does sound (or, more widely, feature) X have social connotation Y?', and this remains unanswerable. There is, however, some headway to be made through an exploration of a feature's 'salience' – the property of being noticeable to the extent that it can be socially evaluated. Trudgill (1986) sets out the following predictors of salience:

1 The variable (i.e. variable feature) has at least one variant (realization) which is overtly stigmatized.
2 The variable has a high-status variant reflected in the orthography.
3 The variable is undergoing linguistic change.
4 Variants are phonetically radically different.
5 Variants are involved in the maintenance of phonological contrasts in the accommodating speaker's variety (in the case of a speaker attempting to acquire another variety).
(adapted from Trudgill, 1986: 11)

The salience concept is potentially valuable because it could bring together factors which make a feature available for social marking. Ultimately, as an explanatory concept in change it is unhelpful because of the circularity of the first two predictors, because it cannot predict the polarity of social evaluation (either negative or positive) (Kerswill, 2002; Kerswill and Williams, 2002), and because it does not deal with the initial phase of a change – how a sporadic innovation is communally selected as a change.

Returning to the lenition of /tʃ/ in Panamanian Spanish, which we assume is phonetically motivated but on the way to becoming a fully-established change, we find the same negative correlation with age and the same curvilinear social distribution as with Philadelphia (aw) (Cedergren, 1987: 52). This strongly suggests that factors other than phonetic ones drive **all** sound

changes, phonetically motivated or not. That said, the directionality of phonetically-motivated changes is not random, unlike the case, apparently, for unconditioned change. Even here, however, there are very strong tendencies for vowels to move in some directions, and not others, and for vowels to shift as whole systems. Variationist work demonstrates this. Based on an inspection of cases in a number of languages, Labov established three Principles of Vowel Shifting, related to the important phenomenon of the **chain shift**, by which two or more vowels change in lockstep over time, always maintaining the same or a similar phonetic distance from each other. The Principles are as follows (Labov, 1994: 116):

Principle I
In chain shifts, long vowels rise

Principle II
In chain shifts, short vowels fall

Principle IIA
In chain shifts, the nuclei of upgliding diphthongs fall

Principle III
In chain shifts, back vowels move to the front

Figure 16.2 shows a partial chain shift involving three short vowels of London English: /ʊ/ as in FOOT, /æ/ as in TRAP and /ʌ/ as in STRUT, plus the long vowel /uː/ as in GOOSE (keywords in small capitals relate to the lexical sets of English as outlined by Wells, 1982).

The basic shift is very much in line with Labov's Principles II and III (indeed, he established these before he was aware of this London shift). The arrows show the movement of the vowels in 'apparent time' (see Section 16.6, below), the circles representing the mean normalized formant 1/formant 2 values for 8 working-class lifelong residents (4 female, 4 male) aged over 70, the diamonds representing working-class residents aged 17/18. (See Cheshire et al., 2008 for details.) This is a bald summary diagram: change is clearly mapped out, but there is no sociolinguistic detail. This is provided in Table 16.1.

The Age column of the table simply confirms that the age-related shifts shown by the arrows in Figure 16.2 are statistically significant. The Ethnicity column refers to the young speakers only, and shows that GOOSE is more fronted and more raised for speakers of 'non-Anglo' origin – these are Londoners with origins outside the British Isles, mainly in developing countries. Likewise, the STRUT vowel is more raised among this group. The Network column refers to the ethnic make-up of the Anglo young people's friendship networks. Those with strongly non-Anglo networks follow the non-Anglo speakers'

Table 16.1 Statistical effects on monophthongs in the inner-city London borough of Hackney

Vowel	Age	Ethnicity	Network
FOOT	$p<0.05$ (F2)	ns	ns
GOOSE	$p<0.001$ (F2)	$p<0.005$ (F1) $p<0.05$ (F2)	$p<0.05$ (F1) $p<0.05$ (F2)
TRAP	$p<0.001$ (F1) $p<0.001$ (F2)	ns	ns
STRUT	$p<0.001$ (F1) $p<0.001$ (F2)	$p<0.05$ (F1)	$p<0.05$ (F2)

Source: from Cheshire et al. (2008)

GOOSE vowel in being more fronted and raised than that of Anglos with mainly Anglo networks. Similarly, there is a significant effect of network for STRUT, in a direction which brings the pronunciation close to that of the non-Anglos. In terms of change, it appears to be the non-Anglos, particularly in fact the males, who are in the lead. This seems to be true at least in inner-city multiethnic districts of London. This pattern is unusual, since changes 'from below' are almost always female-led (Tagliamonte and D'Arcy, 2009). Notably, the fronting of the GOOSE vowel is led by young **females** outside London (Kerswill and Williams, 2005), leading to speculations as to why two very different social groups should be in the lead in the same change in different parts of the south-east of England (Kerswill et al., 2008); we will examine

this data in the final section. The tentative conclusion is that patterns of innovation are very different in metropolises with heavy concentrations of people with non host-language backgrounds.

The use of ethnicity and network represents the first two 'waves' mentioned above. Ethnicity, being a fixed speaker-variable used to sample the population and to aggregate data across speakers, very much fits into a first-wave approach, in that a broad picture is given. Network information was obtained through careful interviewing, and each individual allocated a score of 1–5 depending on the proportion of non-Anglos in her or his network. These individual scores were placed into 'low' vs 'high' scoring groups. Thus, the network variable combines a first-wave method (speakers being aggregated) with a second-wave approach (data being qualitative in origin but 'reduced' to a quantitative measure). The 1970s participant-observation study by the Milroys in Belfast likewise produced a five-point network measure, based in their case on indicators of integration into neighbourhood networks (L. Milroy, 1980).

Eckert (1989, 2000) investigated sociolinguistic factors in another vowel shift, the Northern Cities Shift (Labov, 1994: 177–201), illustrated in Figure 16.3. Using ethnographic methods in a Detroit high school, Eckert was able to establish that the interaction of gender and distinct cultures based on orientation towards or away from organized school-based activities patterned with whether or not young people were advanced in

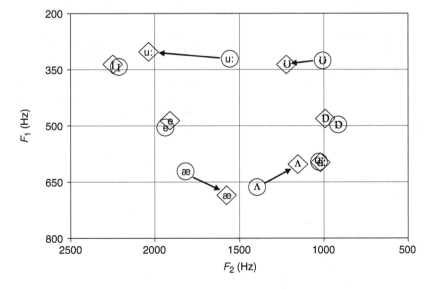

Figure 16.2 Anti-clockwise monophthong shift in inner-city working-class London speech, late twentieth century (see text for explanation) (from Cheshire et al., 2008).

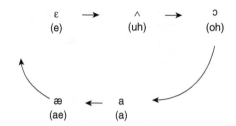

Figure 16.3 The Northern Cities Shift
(Labov, 1994: 177–201; diagram from Eckert, 1989: 260).

their use of the new, shifted vowels. For Eckert, the 'community of practice' is where cultural and linguistic styles emerge (see Vetter, this volume). Her study is representative of the 'third-wave' approach to language variation.

16.3 VARIATIONIST SOCIOLINGUISTICS AND THE LOCUS OF NEOGRAMMARIAN CHANGE

Variationist conceptualizations reveal a particular stance towards the organization of variation – and this is especially clear in the context of phonology. The notion of the variable seems to be closely tied in with the Neogrammarian notion of a 'sound', which is subject to 'laws'. Variants of the variable (aw) in Philadelphia are not conditioned *prima facie* by linguistic environment, provided the variable is properly phonologically delimited: pre-variationist work would have referred to them as 'free variants'. The theoretical implication that linguistic units may vary in form further implies the presence of 'inherent variation', as opposed to the alternation between invariant and discrete linguistic systems (Labov, 1969; see discussion in Fasold and Preston, 2007). The idea of variability being immanent was anathema to phonologists (and grammarians), for whom the main concern was the theoretical possibility of a form being produced, not its frequency in actual use or its range on a continuous phonetic scale (see discussion in Guy, this volume). The corollary is that, for phonological features, there is a concept of a Neogrammarian 'sound', which, while having a range of actual realizations, is an abstract unit which maintains its identity across time, space, community and the individual. The range of variation only becomes comprehensible, and the continuity of the unit visible, when data in a community is aggregated, as illustrated in Figure 16.1. It is in this sense that Labov believes

that systematicity is greater at the group level than within or between individuals. Even so, in a speech community, unique idiolects rarely contain random or inexplicable features. This is equally true of 'anomalous' speakers, or outliers, who despite being 'native' have unusual accent and dialect features, typically mixed or from somewhere else: these turn out to be perfectly understandable in the light of the speakers' life histories (Newbrook, 1982; Britain, 2003). Other speakers are firmly embedded in the 'community grammar' both with respect to their phonology and grammar and in their social evaluation of features (see Kristiansen, this volume, for an extended discussion of social evaluation and language change). Everyone's linguistic behaviour is socially meaningful in relation to it (see Labov, 1989 and critique in Downes, 1998: 121–6). Second- and third-wave variationist studies both recognize and, crucially, depend on this insight.

The Dressler and Wodak dialect-switching model is at odds with Labov, being closer to the 'alternating systems' model. In speech communities where there is a large linguistic distance between vernacular and standard, code-switching behaviour can be observed (Berruto, 2005). While acknowledging such differences, we should note there is still usually a linguistic continuum **between** the two alternating codes.

16.4 NEOGRAMMARIAN CHANGE AND LEXICAL DIFFUSION

Not all phonological change is exceptionless, as we saw in the case of the French k→ʃ shift. A contemporary example concerns the tensing/raising of /æ/ in the northern United States, typically to [eːə] or [ɪːə]. This change is exceptionless (i.e. Neogrammarian) in varieties affected by the Northern Cities Shift, for example Detroit and Chicago (see Figure 16.3). However, in New York and Philadelphia, raising only takes place before particular, and different, consonants, as shown in Figure 16.4.

In both cities, the pattern could also be seen as the result of a Neogrammarian change, were it not for the several lexical exceptions to the tensing/raising process.[1] Thus, in New York City, *avenue* is normally tense, while (in conformity with the general pattern) *average*, *savage* and *gavel* are lax, i.e. pronounced [æ] (Labov, 2007: 355). In Philadelphia, /æ/ before /d/ is generally lax, as in *sad* and *dad*, while in just three words, *mad*, *bad* and *glad* (indicated by the dotted line in Figure 16.4), /æ/ is tense (Payne, 1980; Labov, 1994: 341). In both cities, there is a clear phonetic

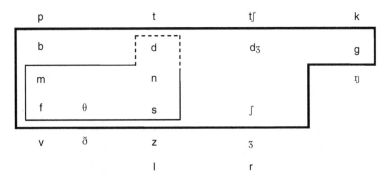

Figure 16.4 Consonants following /æ/ that condition tensing and raising in Philadelphia (inner line) and New York City (outer line) (from Labov, 1994: 430).

gap between the tense and lax variants of the variable, while the tense variant itself exists on a continuous scale of raising akin to that of the Northern Cities Shift. Labov concludes from this that 'It is clear that the NYC short-*a* system is very far from whatever beginnings it had as a simple, phonetically determined sound change. It has developed the lexical and morphological irregularities characteristic of many late stages of change (Janda and Joseph, 2001)' (Labov, 2007: 356). Thus, its present state is the outcome of lexical diffusion, characterized thus: 'Words change their pronunciations by discrete, perceptible increments (i.e. phonetically abrupt), but severally at a time (i.e. lexically gradual)' (Wang and Cheng, 1977: 150, cited in Labov, 1981: 270).

Labov (2007) is concerned with the later transmission of both the Neogrammarian Northern Cities Shift and the New York City lexical diffusion pattern to other regions of the USA. It is possible, however, to get a window on the transition from Neogrammarian change to lexical diffusion by looking at the historical and geographical record of a known change. Labov (1992; 1994) discusses the diphthongization of Middle English /uː/ as in *mouth, town, house, mouse* in England as part of the Great Vowel Shift. Labov (1992; 1994: 486) maps the diphthongization of this vowel in *mouse* and *house* in the material collected by the *Survey of English Dialects* (Orton et al., 1962–71).

Labov's map (Figure 16.5) shows that the monophthong is best preserved in the north. At least along the east coast, the transition appears to be quite gradual, starting with a shift to [ʊu], then via [aʊ] and [æʊ] to [ɛʊ] in the south-east. Given that the transcribers did not use a particularly narrow phonetic transcription, it is reasonable

to suppose that, across much of the country, this represents a phonetic continuum. In order to adjudicate between a diffusionist or a Neogrammarian interpretation of the change, Labov considers whether *mouse* and *house* have the same distribution: in almost all cases, they do. He concludes that almost all the data support a Neogrammarian interpretation. This is evidence that the change was gradual, both phonetically and geographically – though, of course, our evidence for this claim is indirect. What we see represented is the result of a vigorous sound change which proceeded incrementally (each generation slightly exaggerating the previous generation's production – we return to this mechanism in Section 16.6), and the change being slowly diffused and picked up by new speakers further from the point of origin. This happened centuries ago; Figure 16.5 represents the residue of a long-since 'spent' sound change, which has left its imprint on the speech of twentieth-century conservative, non-mobile rural speakers.

The Great Vowel Shift was a series of vowel changes, originating in southern England, affecting all the long vowels and stretching over a period of some 300 years up to some time in the early eighteenth century (McMahon, 2006). There is some debate as to where in the vowel system the shift started, but it is clear that the high vowels of Middle English, /iː/ (as in *ice*) and /uː/ (as in *house*) shifted together **except** in the far north of England and in Scotland (McMahon, 2006: 166). Here, /uː/ failed to diphthongize altogether until the twentieth century; Figure 16.5 shows the **pre**-shifted state in the North. Table 16.2 shows twentieth-century real-time incidence of the vowels /uː/, /aʊ/ and /ɔː/ in County Durham in the north-east of England. In lexical set 2, there has

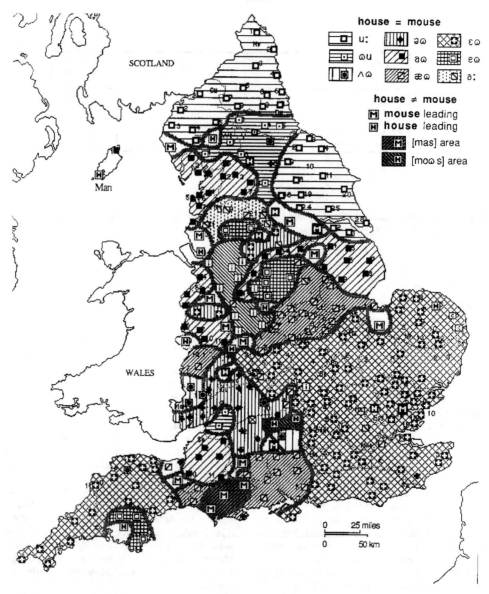

Figure 16.5 Development of Middle English /uː/ in *house* and *mouse* in 311 localities in England (Labov, 1994: 486, based on the *Survey of English Dialects*).

been an almost total change, over two generations, from the use of a near-monophthong [ʊu] to [aʊ]. This has happened not by a phonetically gradual shift, but by the substitution of /aʊ/ for /uː/. Older people today alternate between [hʊus] and [haʊs], etc., while the youngsters on the whole do not, with the result that *out* now contains /aʊ/ and has become homophonous with *owt* ('anything').

This pattern is characteristic of lexical diffusion, with an alternation between phones which are phonologically distinct in the dialect. The data

is not sufficient to tell us anything about the lexical diffusion of the diphthong in lexical set 2, however. A study of working-class teenagers by Clark (2008) in Fife, Scotland, gives an indication of how such diffusion might take place. A similar variable, (au), shows that high-frequency items such as *about*, *down*, *round* and *our* are pronounced with the original monophthong some 90–100 per cent of the time, while less frequent items, including *sound*, *our*, *house* and *allowed*, are pronounced with the incoming diphthong around 50 per cent of the time (Clark 2008: 262).

Table 16.2 /uː/ and /aʊ/ in central County Durham

Lexical set	Examples	Village/year of birth		
		Byers Green 1880 (Orton, 1933)	Ushaw Moor 1940 (Kerswill, 1987)	Ushaw Moor 1987 (recordings by Kreswill, 2002)
1	food, choose, move, prove ...	/uː/	/uː/	/uː/
2	out, house, mouse, town, cow, down ...		/uː/~/aʊ/	/aʊ/
3	owt ('anything'), nowt ('nothing')	/aʊ/	/aʊ/	
4	four, daughter, thought, bought ...		/aʊ/~/ɔː/	/ɔː/

She argues for a cognitive linguistic model to explain this difference.

Similar frequency effects doubtless partly account for the lexically gradual nature of the French k→ʃ shift, too, where low-frequency items (often belonging to a formal register) shift first. However, the reverse pattern is also found. It is the 'natural' reductions of connected speech which shift first in high-frequency words. This is thought to be because such words are more automated in production, and because of their predictability in discourse they allow for greater redundancy in the speech signal. (See Bybee, 2002: 268–71 for discussion.) There is, thus, a difference between conditioned sound change representing reductions and assimilations and lexical diffusion in this respect. As for unconditioned sound change, the picture is, again, different. Labov (2006b) finds no frequency effects, only phonetic effects, while Dinkin (2008) finds small frequency effects but only when a regular sound change represents a potential lenition, or reduction in articulatory effort.

16.5 GENERALIZATIONS AND EXPLANATIONS

The changes seen in Table 16.2 are the result of two sociolinguistic processes affecting British English dialects, 'regional dialect levelling' (or 'supralocalization': L. Milroy, 2002; Kerswill, 2003; Hickey, 2009) and 'dedialectalization' (Trudgill and Foxcroft, 1978; Trudgill, 1999). Regional dialect levelling/supralocalization leads to a reduction in the **amount** of regional variation across a given area; it is characterized by the adoption of new forms, or an increase in existing forms, which thereby gain currency across a wider area than before. Seen from the perspective of neighbouring dialects, convergence is observed. It is usually the consequence of intensive face-

to-face contacts within a relatively mobile area. These contacts also facilitate the geographical diffusion of new features, replacing existing ones and leading to further homogenization. (See Britain, 2002, pp 142–163; Hinskens, Auer and Kerswill, 2005; Kerswill, 2006.) Dedialectalization is not principally a contact phenomenon, however. More often than not, it is coextensive with standardization, by which forms are adopted which correspond closely to the standard variety (the 'roof' – Kloss, 1967) in their lexical incidence of phonemes (Kerswill, 2007b). This process has all but gone to completion, at least in England. Table 16.2 clearly shows its effects, though in many cases the adoption of the more standard variants is also the adoption of supralocal forms.

Variationists have generally not attempted to explain dedialectalization and standardization, though the 'linguistic market' is doubtless highly relevant (Sankoff and Laberge, 1978; cf. Bourdieu, 1991). Regional dialect levelling, on the other hand, has been associated with the loosening of network ties (L. Milroy, 2002; Stuart-Smith, Timmins and Tweedie, 2007), greater mobility (Williams and Kerswill, 1999; Kerswill, 2006) and a desire to gain a regional, rather than local identity (Watt, 2002).

16.6 TIME AND TRANSMISSION

One of the major challenges is to find optimal ways of mapping language change in a community onto the time dimension. First, we need to consider what constitutes change, and this brings us again to a consideration of individual vs group behaviour. Change in language structure implies a permanent, categorical modification. As we have seen, both speakers and speech communities are variable. In some cases, what we observe is a change in the frequency of some feature, such as the glottal stop for intervocalic /t/ in British

English; children increase their use of it as they reach adolescence, only to reduce it again by adulthood (Kerswill and Williams, 2000: 105; cf. Sankoff, 2006 on change across the life span). This does not amount to a change in the phonology of the individual speaker: 'change', in this case, implies the learning, or loss, of a phonological contrast, or in the case of a (gradual) Neogrammarian change, a quasi-permanent modification of the sound, such as the fronting of a vowel.

Yet frequency changes and gradual phonetic changes are part and parcel of long-term communal linguistic change – language change 'proper'. Tagliamonte and D'Arcy (2009) deal not with phonology, but with morphosyntax. They show that frequency changes can be mapped onto the so-called S-curve of change: from the point of view of the community, changes start by small steps, then in the middle stage the increase in frequency is rapid, and finally the last few speakers adopt the change before it becomes categorical. The authors show that late adolescent cohorts use the incoming feature with the highest frequency, more than either children or adults. This implies, of course, that children actually change their speech as they grow older, peaking in late adolescence, after which, for reasons of both social and cognitive maturation, there is little or no change. Not only do they increase their use of the feature during these years but also the feature is exaggerated in relation to the immediately preceding generation's use – a process referred to as 'incrementation' (Labov, 2007: 346). For phonological features, Tagliamonte and D'Arcy point out that females are almost always in the lead, while they find that this is not the case for morphosyntax.

This model only works if it can be shown that children do indeed change their speech, and that the change is in the direction of communal change. There is ample evidence that both are true. Figures 16.6 and 16.7 show the fronting in real time of the vowel of GOOSE in the speech of a girl and boy from Milton Keynes in the south-east of England. These informants were interviewed twice, first aged 12 and then 18 months later aged 13 or 14. As can be seen, their GOOSE vowels were considerably fronter in the second recording than in the first. This can be seen in relation to three reference vowels, which proved stable across this period. These are two of eight young people in the study, and all eight showed significant fronting between the first and second recordings, with average fronting being in the region of 10 per cent in relation to the distance between GHOUL and FLEECE. In other studies, adults have also been shown to change frequencies and to participate in vowels shifts, at least to some extent (Sankoff, 2006; Sankoff and Blondeau, 2007).

As mentioned earlier, apparent-time studies compare older and younger speakers. If it is the case that children, and adults, modify their speech in the direction of the change, then an apparent-time study will significantly underestimate the amount of change in real time. It may also be the case that age-grading is present, i.e. changes which occur across the life span in the same way in every generation, but without leading to language change. To get round this, a combination of a trend study and a panel study is valuable. Trend studies sample the community at different times, but using the same age and social groups. Panel studies record the same people at least twice. This provides evidence of how speakers change, but without an accompanying trend study little can be said about communal change.

The LANCHART project has set out to replicate a number of sociolinguistic studies originally carried out in the 1970s and 1980s in Denmark (Gregersen, 2009; Gregersen et al., 2009). Working on LANCHART data, Schøning (2008) investigated a number of variables in the Jutland town of Odder. She analysed two cohorts, the first born in 1971/2 and recorded in 1986/7 and again in 2005/6, the second born in 1989/90 and recorded in 2006. This allowed a direct comparison of the apparent-time method (cohorts 1 and 2 recorded in 2005/6), a trend study (cohort 1 recorded in 1989/90 and cohort 2 recorded in 2005/6) and a panel study (the two recordings of cohort 1). For the most part, the results showed that the apparent-time method indeed underestimated change. An example is the variable HUSET, which refers to the pronunciation of the neuter suffixed definite article –et. The standard form is [əð], the local dialect form [ət]. Tables 16.3–16.5 show the distributions.

Table 16.3 shows an apparent-time change from 19 per cent to 63 per cent standard, suggesting rapid change. The panel study (Table 16.4) shows that cohort 1 have to a small, but significant extent, participated in this change. The communal change is shown in Table 16.5, and, as expected, this shows a greater change than the apparent-time method.

Individual and group change are linked in specific, statable ways. The study of dialect transmission holds the key to the mechanism of change: it is adolescents, who do the 'work' (Eckert, 2000), not, as historical linguists have supposed, young children who fail to learn their parents' language properly (Aitchison, 1981: 180).

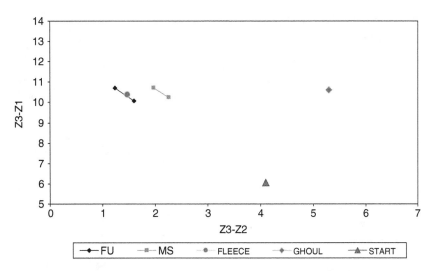

Figure 16.6   The fronting of /uː/ as in GOOSE, girl born 1979, Milton Keynes, recorded in 1991 and in 1993 (from Kassab, 2008).

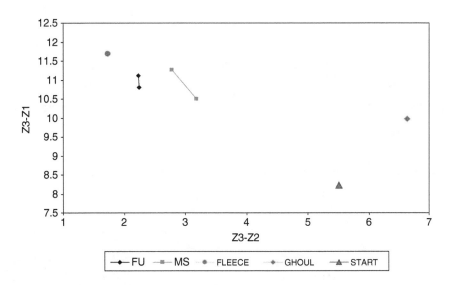

Figure 16.7   The fronting of /uː/ as in GOOSE, boy born 1979, Milton Keynes, recorded in 1991 and in 1993 (from Kassab 2008).

Key to Figures 16.6 and 16.7:
MS = average formant 1/formant 2 of GOOSE, first recording ('main study').
FU = average formant 1/formant 2 of GOOSE, second recording 18 months later ('follow-up').
FLEECE, GHOUL, START: average formants for /iː/, /uː/ before /l/, and /ɑː/, acting as stable reference vowels.
Note   Formants 1 and 2 are here shown as normalized scores, Z1 and Z2, and are subtracted from Z3, the normalized formant 3.

Table 16.3 Apparent time 2005–6, adult and young speakers

Speakers	Standard observed frequency	Per cent	Local observed frequency	Per cent	Total
Adult	26	19	111	81	137
Young	46	63	27	37	73
Total	72		138		210
chi-square	39.05702636				
p	<0.01				

Table 16.4 Real-time, panel study, cohort 1 1986–87 and 2005–6

Speakers	Standard observed frequency	Per cent	Local observed frequency	Per cent	Total
1986–7	8	8	91	92	99
2005–6	26	19	111	81	137
Total	34		202		236
chi-square	4.686016047				
p	0.030409078				

Table 16.5 Real-time, trend study, cohort 1 (1986–7) and cohort 2 (2006)

Speakers	Standard observed frequency	Per cent	Local observed frequency	Per cent	Total
Cohort 1	8	8	91	92	99
Cohort 2	46	63	27	37	73
Total	54		118		172
chi-square	56.34469956				
p	<0.01				

NOTE

1 Tensing and raising are conceived of by Labov as different processes; here, the best measure is vowel height.

ACKNOWLEDGEMENT

Labov 2001 quote: This article was published in *Principles of Linguistics Change*, Vol. 2: *External Factors*, p. 34, Copyright Elseiver.

Tables 16.3, 16.4 and 16.5 Reprinted with permission.

Gregersen, Frans. 2009. The data and design of the LANCHART study, Acta Linguistica Hafniensia 41, 3–29, Routledge.

Gregersen, Frans, Maegaard, Marie and Pharao, Nicolai. 2009. The long and short of (ae)-variation in Danish –a panel study of short (ae)-variation in Danish real time, Acta Linguistica Hafniensia 41, 64–82, Routledge.

REFERENCES

Aitchison, J. (1981) *Language Change: Progress or Decay?* London: Fontana.

Baranowski, M. (2007) *Phonological Variation and Change in the Dialect of Charleston, South Carolina.* Publication of the American Dialect Society, No. 92. Durham, NC: Duke University Press.

Berruto, G. (2005) 'Dialect/standard convergence, mixing, and models of language contact: the case of Italy', in P. Auer,

F. Hinskens and P. Kerswill (eds), *Dialect Change: Convergence and Divergence in European Languages*. Cambridge: Cambridge University Press. pp. 81–95.

Bloomfield, L. (1933) *Language*. New York: Holt, Rinehart and Winston.

Bourdieu, P. (1991) *Language and Symbolic Power*. Cambridge, MA: Harvard University Press.

Britain, D. (2002) 'Space and spatial diffusion', in J. K. Chambers P. Trudgill and N. Schilling-Estes (eds) *The Handbook of Language Variation and Change*. Oxford: Blackwell. pp. 603–37.

Britain, D. (2003) 'Exploring the importance of the outlier in sociolinguistic dialectology', in D. Britain and J. Cheshire (eds), *Social Dialectology: In Honour of Peter Trudgill*. Amsterdam: Benjamins. pp. 191–208.

Britain, D. (2004) 'Geolinguistics – diffusion of language', in U. Ammon, N. Dittmar, K. Mattheier and P. Trudgill (eds), *Sociolinguistics: International Handbook of the Science of Language and Society*. Berlin: Mouton De Gruyter. pp. 34–48.

Britain, D. (in press) 'Language and space: the variationist approach', in P. Auer and J. E. Schmidt (eds), *Language and Space: An International Handbook of Linguistic Variation*. Berlin: Mouton de Gruyter.

Bybee, J. (2000) 'Lexicalization of sound change and alternating environments', in M. B. Broe and J. Pierrehumbert (eds), *Papers in Laboratory Phonology V*. Cambridge: Cambridge University Press. pp. 20–68.

Bybee, J. (2002) 'Word frequency and context of use in the lexical diffusion of phonetically conditioned sound change', *Language Variation and Change*, 14: 261–90.

Bynon, T. (1977) *Historical Linguistics*. Cambridge: Cambridge University Press.

Cedergren, H. (1987) 'The spread of language change. Verifying inferences of linguistic diffusion', in P. H. Lowenberg (ed.), *Language Spread and Language Policy. Issues, Implications and Case Studies*. Washington, DC: Georgetown University Press. pp. 45–60.

Chambers, J. K. and Trudgill, P. (1998) *Dialectology*. 2nd edn. Cambridge: Cambridge University Press.

Cheshire, J. (2007) 'Discourse variation, grammaticalisation and stuff like that', *Journal of Sociolinguistics*, 11(2): 155–93.

Cheshire, J., Fox, S., Kerswill, P. and Eivind, T. (2008) *Linguistic Innovators: the English of Adolescents in London*. Final report submitted to the Economic and Social Research Council of Great Britain, ref. RES 000 23 0680.

Clark, L. (2008) 'Re-examining vocalic *variation* in Scottish English: a cognitive grammar approach', *Language Variation and Change*, 20(2): 255–73.

Crystal, D. (2004) *The Stories of English*. London: Penguin.

Dinkin, A. J. (2008) 'The real effect of word frequency on phonetic variation', *University of Pennsylvania Working Papers in Linguistics*, 14: 97–106.

Docherty, G. (2008) 'An evaluation of usage-based approaches to the modelling of sociophonetic variability'. Paper given at Sociolinguistics Symposium 17, Amsterdam, April.

Downes, W. (1998) *Language in Society*. 2nd edn. Cambridge: Cambridge University Press.

Dressler, W. U. and Wodak, R. (1982) 'Sociophonological methods in the study of sociolinguistic variation in Viennese German'. *Language in Society*, 11: 339–70.

Eckert, P. (1989) 'The whole woman: sex and gender differences in variation', *Language Variation and Change*, 1: 245–67.

Eckert, P. (2000) *Linguistic Variation as Social Practice*. Oxford: Blackwell.

Eckert, P. (2005) 'Variation, convention, and social meaning'. Paper presented at the annual meeting of the Linguistic Society of America, Oakland, California. Accessed 22 April 2009 at: http://www.stanford.edu/~eckert/EckertLSA2005.pdf.

Farrar, K. and Jones, M. C. (2002) 'Introduction', in K. Farrar and M. C. Jones (eds), *Language Change: the Interplay of Internal, External and Extra-Linguistic Factors*. Berlin: Mouton de Gruyter. pp. 1–16.

Fasold, R. W. and Preston, D. R. (2007) 'The psycholinguistics unity of inherent variability: old Occam whips out his razor', in R. Bayley and C. Lucas (eds), *Sociolinguistic Variation: Theories, Methods, and Applications*. Cambridge: Cambridge University Press. pp. 45–69.

Gauchat, L. (1905) 'L'unité phonétique dans le patois d'une commune', in *Romanische Sprachen und Literaturen: Festschrift Heinrich Mort*. pp. 175–232.

Gordon, E., Campbell, L., Hay, J., et al. (2004) *New Zealand English: Its Origins and Evolution*. Cambridge: Cambridge University Press.

Gregersen, F. (2009). 'The data and design of the LANCHART study', *Acta Linguistica Hafniensia*, 41, 3–29.

Gregersen, F., Maegaard, M. and Pharao, N. (2009). 'The long and short of (æ)-variation in Danish – a panel study of short (æ)-variation in Danish in real time', *Acta Linguistica Hafniensia*, 41, 64–82.

Guy, G. (2003) 'Variationist approaches to phonological change', in B. Joseph and R. Janda (eds), *The Handbook of Historical Linguistics*. Oxford: Blackwell. pp. 369–400.

Hay, J. (2008) 'Coronal stop deletion revisited'. Paper given to the Language Variation and Change Research Group, Department of Linguistics and English Language, Lancaster University, 12 December 2008.

Hickey, R. (2009) 'Supraregionalisation', in L. Brinton and A. Bergs (eds), *Historical linguistics of English*. HSK series. Berlin: de Gruyter.

Hinskens, F., Auer, P. and Kerswill, P. (2005) 'The study of dialect convergence and divergence: conceptual and methodological considerations', in P. Auer, F. Hinskens and P. Kerswill (eds), *Dialect Change: Convergence and Divergence in European Languages*. Cambridge: Cambridge University Press. pp. 1–48.

Hock, H. H. (1991) *Principles of Historical Linguistics*. Berlin: Mouton de Gruyter.

Hollmann, W. and Siewierska, A. (2008) 'Definite article reduction in Lancashire dialect: constructions in a sociolinguistic context'. First Triennial Conference of the International Society for the Linguistics of English, University of Freiburg.

Janda, R. D. and Joseph, B. D. (2001) 'Reconsidering the canons of sound-change: towards a 'Big Bang' theory', in

B. J. Blake, J. Barry and K. Burridge (eds.), *Selected Papers from the 15th International Conference on Historical Linguistics*. Amsterdam: John Benjamins. pp. 205–19.

Johnson, W. and Britain, D. (2007) 'L-vocalisation as a natural phenomenon: explorations in sociophonology', *Language Sciences*, 29: 294–315.

Johnstone, B. and Kiesling, S. F. (2008) 'Indexicality and experience: variation and identity in Pittsburgh', *Journal of Sociolinguistics*, 12(1): 5–33.

Kassab, W. (2008) 'A linguistic change in a newly-formed town'. Unpublished MA dissertation, Department of Linguistics and English Language, Lancaster University.

Kerswill, P. (1987) 'Levels of linguistic variation in Durham', *Journal of Linguistics*, 23: 25–49.

Kerswill, P. (2002) 'Koineization and accommodation', in J. K. Chambers, P. Trudgill and N. Schilling-Estes (eds), *The Handbook of Language Variation and Change*. Oxford: Blackwell. pp. 669–702.

Kerswill, P. (2003) 'Dialect levelling and geographical diffusion in British English'. In D. Britain and J. Cheshire (eds.) Social dialectology. In honour of Peter Trudgill. Amsterdam: Benjamins. 223–43.

Kerswill, P. (2004) 'Social dialectology/Sozialdialektologie', in K. Mattheier, U. Ammon and P. Trudgill (eds), *Sociolinguistics/Soziolinguistik. An International Handbook of the Science of Language and Society*. 2nd edn. Vol. 1. Berlin: De Gruyter. pp. 22–33.

Kerswill, P. (2006) 'Migration and language', in K. Mattheier, U. Ammon and P. Trudgill (eds), *Sociolinguistics/ Soziolinguistik. An International Handbook of the Science of language and society*. 2nd edn. Vol. 3. Berlin: De Gruyter. pp. 2271–85.

Kerswill, P. (2007a) 'Social class', in C. Llamas and P. Stockwell (eds), *The Routledge Companion to Sociolinguistics*. London: Routledge. pp. 51–61.

Kerswill, P. (2007b) 'Standard and non-standard English', in D. Britain (ed.), *Language in the British Isles*. Cambridge: Cambridge University Press. pp. 34–51.

Kerswill, P. and Williams, A. (2000) 'Creating a new town koine: children and language change in Milton Keynes', *Language in Society*, 29: 65–115.

Kerswill, P. and Williams, A. (2002) '"Salience" as an explanatory factor in language change: evidence from dialect levelling in urban England', in M. C. Jones and E. Esch (eds), *Language change. The Interplay of Internal, External and Extra-Linguistic Factors*. Berlin: Mouton de Gruyter. pp. 81–110.

Kerswill, P. and Williams, A. (2005) 'New towns and koineisation: linguistic and social correlates', *Linguistics*, 43(5): 1023–48.

Kerswill, P. and Wright, S. (1990) 'The validity of phonetic transcription: limitations of a sociolinguistic research tool', *Language Variation and Change*, 2: 255–75.

Kerswill, P., Torgersen, E. and Fox, S. (2008) 'Reversing 'drift': innovation and diffusion in the London diphthong system', *Language Variation and Change*, 20: 451–91.

Kloss, H. (1967) '"Abstand languages" and "Ausbau languages"', *Anthropological Linguistics*, 9(7): 29–41.

Labov, W. (1963) 'The Social motivation of language change', *Word*, 19: 273–309.

Labov, W. (1966) *The Social Stratification of English in New York City*. Washington, DC: Center for Applied Linguistics.

Labov, W. (1969) 'Contraction, deletion, and inherent variability of the English copula', *Language*, 45(4): 715–62.

Labov, W. (1980) 'The social origin of sound change', in Labov, W. (ed.), *Locating language in Time and Space*. New York: Academic Press. pp. 251–66.

Labov, W. (1981) 'Resolving the Neogrammarian controversy', *Language*, 57: 267–309.

Labov, W. (1989) 'Exact description of the speech community: short *a* in Philadelphia', in: R. W. Fasold and D. Schiffrin (eds), *Language Change and Variation*. Amsterdam: Benjamins. pp. 1–57.

Labov, W. (1992) 'Evidence for regular sound change in English dialect geography', in M. Rissanen, O. Ihalainen, T. Nevalainen and I. Taavitsainen (eds), *History of Englishes: New Methods and Interpretations in Historical Linguistics*. Berlin: Mouton de Gruyter. pp. 42–71.

Labov, W. (1994) *Principles of Linguistic Change*. Vol. 1: *Internal factors*. Oxford: Blackwell.

Labov, W. (2001) *Principles of Linguistic Change*. Vol. 2: *External factors*. Oxford: Blackwell.

Labov, W. (2006a) *The Social Stratification of English in New York City*. 2nd edn. New York: Cambridge University Press.

Labov, W. (2006b) 'A sociolinguistic perspective on sociophonetic research', *Journal of Phonetics*, 34: 500–15.

Labov, W. (2007) 'Transmission and diffusion', *Language*, 83(2): 344–87.

Labov, W., Ash, S. and Boberg, C. (2006) *The atlas of North American English: Phonetics, Phonology, and Sound Change*. New York: Mouton de Gruyter.

Labov, W., Yaeger, M. and Steiner, R. (1972) *A Quantitative Study of Sound Change in Progress*. Philadelphia: US Regional Survey.

Larsen, A. B. and Stoltz, G. (1911–12) *Bergens bymål*. Kristiania/Oslo: Aschehoug.

Louden, M. (2006) 'Pennsylvania German in the 21st century', in N. Berend and E. Knipf-Komlosi (eds), *Sprachinselwelten – The World of Language Islands. Entwicklung und Beschreibung der deutschen Sprachinseln am Anfang des 21. Jahrhunderts. [The developmental Stages and the Description of German Language Islands at the Beginning of the 21st Century.]* Frankfurt/Main: Peter Lang. pp. 89–107.

McMahon, A. (2006) 'Restructuring Renaissance English', in L. Mugglestone (ed.), *The Oxford History of English*. Oxford: Oxford University Press. pp. 148–77.

Milroy, J. (1992) *Linguistic Variation and Change: on the Historical Sociolinguistics of English*. Oxford: Blackwell.

Milroy, J. (2000) 'The ideology of the standard language', in L. Wright (ed.), *The Development of Standard English, 1300–1800*. Cambridge: Cambridge University Press. pp. 11–128.

Milroy, L. (1980) *Language and Social Networks*. Oxford: Blackwell. (2nd edn, 1987).

Milroy, L. (2002) 'Introduction: mobility, contact and language change – working with contemporary speech communities', *Journal of Sociolinguistics*, 6(1): 3–15.

Milroy, L. and Gordon, M. (2003) *Sociolinguistics: Method and Interpretation*. Oxford: Blackwell.

Moore, E. (2003) *'Learning Style and Identity: A Sociolinguistic analysis of a Bolton High School*. Unpublished PhD dissertation, University of Manchester.

Moore, E. (2006) '"You tell all the stories": using narrative to understand hierarchy in a Community of Practice', *Journal of Sociolinguistics*, 10: 611–40.

Newbrook, M. (1982) 'Scot or scouser? An anomalous informant in outer Merseyside', *English World-Wide*, 3: 77–86.

Nolan, F. and Kerswill, P. (1990) 'The description of connected speech processes', in S. Ramsaran (ed.), *Essays in Honour of A. C. Gimson*. London: Routledge. pp. 295–316.

Orton, H. (1933) *The Phonology of a South Durham dialect*. London: Kegan Paul, Trench and Co.

Orton, H. et al. (1962–71) *Survey of English Dialects: Basic Material*. Four volumes in 12 parts. Leeds: E. J. Arnold.

Payne, A. (1980) 'Factors controlling the acquisition of the Philadelphia dialect by out-of-state children', in W. Labov (ed.), *Locating Language in Time and Space*. New York: Academic Press. pp. 143–78.

Pierrehumbert, J. (2003) 'Phonetic diversity, statistical learning, and acquisition of phonology', *Language and Speech*, 46(2, 3): 115–54.

Robins, R. H. (1990) *A Short History of Linguistics*. 3rd edn. London: Longman.

Romaine, S. (1982) *Socio-Historical Linguistics: Its Status and Methodology*. Cambridge: Cambridge University Press.

Romaine, S. (1988) 'The role of Children in linguistic change', in L. E. Breivik and E. H. Jahr (eds), *Language Change: Contributions to the Study of its Causes*. Berlin: Mouton de Gruyter. pp. 195–225.

Rosenberg, P. (2005) 'Dialect convergence in the German language islands (*Sprachinseln*)', in P. Auer, F. Hinskens and P. Kerswill (eds), *Dialect Change: Convergence and Divergence in European Languages*. Cambridge: Cambridge University Press. pp. 221–35.

Sankoff, G. (2006) 'Age: apparent time and real time', in K. Brown (ed.), *Encyclopedia of Language and Linguistics*, 2nd edn. Oxford: Elsevier. pp. 110–16.

Sankoff, G. and Blondeau, H. (2007) 'Language change across the lifespan: /r/ in Montreal French', *Language*, 83(3): 560–88.

Sankoff, D. and Laberge, S. (1978) 'The linguistic market and the statistical explanation of variability', in D. Sankoff (ed.), *Linguistic Variation: Models and Methods*. New York: Academic Press. pp. 239–50.

Schøning, S. (2009) 'Investigating the apparent time method: the example of Odder'. Unpublished MA dissertation, Department of Linguistics and English Language, Lancaster University.

Schwarz, C. and Streck, T. (2009) 'New approaches to describing phonological change: the realisation of Middle High German *î* in the Alemannic dialects of Southwest Germany',

in S. Tsiplakou, M. Karyolemou and P. Pavlou (eds), *Language Variation — European Perspectives II. Selected Papers from the 4th International Conference on Language Variation in Europe (ICLaVE 4), Nicosia, June 2007*. Amsterdam: Benjamins. pp. 205–214.

Skautrup, P. (1921) 'Om Folke- og Sprogblanding i et vestjysk Sogn', reprinted in P. Skautrup (1976) *Dansk sprog og kultur. Udvalgte afhandlinger og artikler 1921–1971*. Copenhagen: Gyldendal. pp. 9–21.

Stuart-Smith, J., Timmins, C. and Tweedie, F. (2007) ''Talkin' jockney'? Variation and change in Glaswegian accent', *Journal of Sociolinguistics*, 11: 221–60.

Sundgren, E. (2009) 'The varying influence of social and linguistic factors on language stability and change: the case of Eskilstuna', *Language Variation and Change*, 21: 97–113.

Tagliamonte, S. and D'Arcy, A. (2009) 'Peaks beyond phonology: adolescence, incrementation and language change', *Language*, 85(1): 58–108.

Trudgill, P. (1986) *Dialects in Contact*. Oxford: Blackwell.

Trudgill, P. (1992) 'Dialect contact, dialectology and sociolinguistics', in K. Bolton and H. Kwok (eds), *Sociolinguistics Today: International Perspectives*. London: Routledge. pp. 71–9.

Trudgill, P. (1999) 'Norwich: endogenous and exogenous linguistic changes', in P. Foulkes and G. Docherty (eds), *Urban Voices: Accent Studies in the British Isles*. London: Arnold. pp. 124–40.

Trudgill, P. (2004) *New-Dialect Formation: the Inevitability of Colonial Englishes*. Edinburgh: Edinburgh University Press.

Trudgill, P. and Foxcroft, T. (1978) 'On the sociolinguistics of vocalic mergers: transfer and approximation in East Anglia', in P. Trudgill (ed.), *Sociolinguistic Patterns in British English*. London: Edward Arnold. pp. 69–79.

Wells, J. (1982) *Accents of English*. 3 vols. Cambridge: Cambridge University Press.

Wang, W. S.-Y. and Cheng, C.-C. (1977) 'Implementation of phonological change: the Shuang-Feng Chinese case', in W. S.-Y. Wang (ed.), *The Lexicon in Phonological Change*. The Hague: Mouton. pp. 148–58.

Watt, D. J. L. (2002) ''I don't speak with a Geordie accent, I speak, like, the Northern accent': contact induced levelling in the Tyneside vowel system', *Journal of Sociolinguistics*, 6: 44–63.

Weinreich, U., Labov, W. and Herzog, M. (1968) 'Empirical foundations for a theory of language change', in W. Lehmann and Y. Malkiel (eds), *Directions for Historical Linguistics*. Austin, TX: University of Texas Press. pp. 97–195.

Williams, A. and Kerswill, P. (1999) 'Dialect levelling: change and continuity in Milton Keynes, Reading and Hull', in P. Foulkes and G. Docherty (eds), *Urban Voices: Accent Studies in the British Isles*. London: Arnold. pp. 141–62.

Wright, S. (1989) 'The effects of style and speaking rate on /l/-vocalization in local Cambridge English', *York Papers in Linguistics*, 13: 355–65. York: Department of Language and Linguistic Science, University of York.

Wyld, H. C. (1927) *A Short History of English*. 3rd edn. London: John Murray.

17

Social Structure, Language Contact and Language Change

Peter Trudgill

17.1 INTRODUCTION

This chapter explores aspects of the hypothesis that the distribution of linguistic structures and features over languages is sociolinguistically not entirely random.[1] The suggestion is that there may be a tendency for different types of social environment and social structure to give rise to, or at least be accompanied by, different types of linguistic structure (Trudgill, forthcoming). In this chapter, I will outline facets of this sociolinguistic take on linguistic typology with respect to linguistic change, with a particular focus on changes that might be labelled 'simplification' and 'complexification'. I suggest that linguistic simplification is most likely to occur in social environments of certain types, and that linguistic complexification is most likely to occur against social backgrounds of other, different types.

The relevant key parameters which go into the composition of these different types of society would appear to include the following:

(a) Contact vs isolation: the degree of contact that a linguistic community has with other communities speaking other language varieties.
(b) Dense vs loose social networks: the key factor here as adumbrated, on the basis of sociological research, by James Milroy and Lesley Milroy (1985; and see also Milroy, 1992), is a distinction between communities with relatively dense, multiplex social networks, which is to say communities where it is common for everybody to know everybody else, and where, for example, your neighbour and your second cousin and your workmate may be one and the same person, and

on the other hand communities with relatively loose networks, where the reverse is the case.
(c) Social stability vs instability (cf. Dixon, 1997): the degree to which communities have relatively well-established, long-term, continuing social structures and patterns.
(d) Relatively small vs relatively large community size (cf. Haudricourt, 1961).

While these parameters are in principle independent of one another, they are in practice of course by no means totally so: small, stable communities with relatively few outside contacts are more likely to demonstrate relatively dense social networks. In the rest of this paper, I will focus on communities with this particular cluster of features, which I will for convenience refer to as 'high-contact societies', as well as on communities of the polar opposite type: large, fluid, high-contact societies characterized by relatively loose networks, which I will term 'low-contact' societies.

To begin our discussion with high-contact societies, there is considerable agreement in the literature about the relationship between high contact and one type of language change: language contact, it is widely believed, leads to simplification. This is the view which is quite naturally taken by linguists in pidgin and creole studies: koines, pidgins, creoles and creoloids (Trudgill, 1996) are all widely and uncontroversially agreed to owe their relative structural simplicity to language contact. But agreement about the role of contact in producing simplification generally, in languages other than pidgins, creoles and creoloids, is also widespread in sociolinguistics and dialectology. For example, Milroy (1992: 203) suggests that the trend towards simplification in late Old English/ early Middle English is clearly 'at least to some extent associated with *language contact*'. Vogt (1948: 39) says that *'on observe souvent qu'une langue ... perd des distinctions formelles, dans des circonstances qui rendent l'hypothese d'influence étrangère assez naturelle'.*[2] Sankoff (2002: 657) notes that, according to Bokamba (1993), multi-lingual language contact situations 'may result in morphological simplification' where a language is used as a lingua franca. And Kusters (2003) has demonstrated the link between contact and simpli-fication quantitatively in connection with inflec-tional morphology. Jahr (2001) has argued for the role of language contact with Low German in producing the relative simplification of Danish, Swedish and Norwegian (as compared to Icelandic and Faroese), a view which has been shared by others, including Pedersen (1999) and Askedal (2005). And many more examples could be given.

On the other hand, the linguistic-typological literature is notable for the widespread acceptance of the diametrically opposed point of view. For example, Nichols (1992: 192) says that 'contact among languages fosters complexity, or, put dif-ferently, diversity among neighbouring languages fosters complexity in each of the languages'. Aikhenvald (2002) cites numerous examples of contact-induced complexification in Amazonia, and Aikenvald (2008) describes contact-induced elaboration of an unusually complex 11-imperative system in Tariana. Vanhove (2001) discusses lan-guage contact, with its resultant complexification, in the history of Maltese. And once again many other examples could be cited.

It is a nice illustration of these two different perspectives that in a paper where he asks 'What happens to inflectional morphology in cases of language contact?', Comrie (2008) does not even mention a development which sociolinguists have routinely pointed to as being particularly likely to occur in such situations, namely a reduction in or total loss of inflectional morphology.

The conflict between these two opposing posi-tions has been noted by historical linguists, who have contented themselves with observations such as 'all the examples that support the claim that interference leads to simplification are of course counterexamples to the opposite claim' (Thomason, 2001: 65). Harris and Campbell, too, mention the claim that contact leads to 'structural simplifica-tion', but they also point out that 'there are clear counterexamples' (1995: 133).

In Trudgill (2009), I have suggested that a socio-linguistic typological approach can help to shed light on this apparent contradiction. Language con-tact can indeed have two totally opposed types of outcome, but a sociolinguistically-informed perspective suggests that this is likely to be due to the fact that the different outcomes involve two typologically different forms of contact, in terms of the sociolinguistic matrices in which they occur.

In Trudgill (2009), I make the not very startling suggestion that in fact simplification is most likely to occur in situations involving language learning by adults, who are typically poor second-language learners as compared to small children, particu-larly insofar as informal acquisition in short-term contact situations is concerned. In such situations, features which are 'outsider difficult? (Kusters, 2003: 6) or 'L2 difficult' (Dahl, 2004: 294), are likely to disappear. The most extreme of these situations are of course those which lead to the emergence of pidgins.

Correspondingly, complexification is most likely to occur in long-term co-territorial contact situations involving children and therefore profi-cient bilingualism. The most extreme of these situ-ations are probably those involving *Sprachbünde/* linguistic areas. For example, Dixon and Aikhenvald (1999) discuss the linguistic area formed by the languages of Amazonia, specifically the Amazon and Orinoco basins, which has at least 10 major language families and many more smaller ones. Here, the vast majority of the languages, regard-less of language family membership, have come over the centuries to share a large number of fea-tures. Dixon and Aikhenvald (1999: 8–9) give a non-exhaustive list of 15 features which are common to most or all of the languages of this vast region, including the expression of verbal categories through optional suffixes, and the formation of subordinate clauses through verb nominalization.

The contrast between the two different types of contact becomes particularly clear if we compare Comrie (2008) with Kusters (2003); it is clear that they are looking at two very different types of social situation. Comrie discusses the way in which contact led to the growth of mixed lan-guages such as Michif, which is a French–Cree mixed or intertwined language with considerable morphological complexity (Bakker, 1997), and says that it is clear that the generation which devel-oped this language must have had a high degree of fluency in both French and Cree or some other form of Algonquian. Kusters, on the other hand, relates simplification in, e.g., Arabic, to the acqui-sition of Arabic, by adult non-native speakers.

17.2 SIMPLIFICATION AND COMPLEXIFICATION

Further light can be shed on this issue if we now further explore what is meant in the context of this chapter by the terms 'simplification' and 'complexification'. I readily acknowledge that there are other, perhaps many other, facets of linguistic simplicity and complexity which I am not addressing here. And I intend to illustrate my usage of the terms in this chapter rather than define them in any detail.

Following Mühlhäusler (1977), I suggest that consideration of the growth of pidgins leads to the understanding that simplification, as discussed by Milroy, Vogt and Kusters, consists of the following subprocesses:

- the regularization of irregularities
- an increase in lexical/ morphological transparency
- a reduction in syntagmatic redundancy, e.g. grammatical agreement
- the loss of morphological categories.

It therefore follows that complexification, as discussed by Nichols, consists of the reverse processes:

- irregularization
- increase in opacity
- increase in syntagmatic redundancy
- acquisition of morphological categories.

We can now note, however, that the complexification discussed by Nichols consists of only one of these processes. In her data, there are no irregularizations, no increases in opacity, and no increases in syntagmatic redundancy. The complexification described by typologists such as Nichols consists solely of **the addition of morphological categories** – indeed, Nichols computes complexity in terms of numbers of morphological markers – and, moreover, it is a very particular type of addition. The cases studied by Aikhenvald (2002), which are quite typical, are all instances of morphological categories being acquired by one language from another language with which it is in contact – and, crucially, being acquired in addition to categories which it already has. That is, we are dealing with **additive borrowing** as opposed to **replacive borrowing**.

The interesting question therefore arises as to the origins of the other forms of complexity – of complexification, which is the precise antithesis to the simplification which leads to pidgins. If simplification occurs in short-term, adult contact situations, and additive complexification in long-term child contact situations, then what exactly are the sociolinguistic conditions which give rise to irregularization, increase in opacity and increase in syntagmatic redundancy, and to the **spontaneous** addition of morphological categories, i.e. categories which are not borrowed from other languages? As Thurston (1994: 603) says, what

we need to do be able to do is 'to explain how complexity arose in languages in the first place'. In the rest of this chapter I attempt a preliminary investigation of this issue.

17.3 LANGUAGE IN ISOLATION

It is clear that we cannot look for the development of this type of complexification in any type of **contact** situation. If short-term adult (post-critical threshold) contact tends to favour simplification, and if long-term co-territorial pre-threshold contact tends to favour additive complexification only, as illustrated in Trudgill (2009), then we must surely seek the locus of non-additive complexification in languages which experience low levels of language contact.

It does seem to be very clearly the case that, in general, languages spoken in low-contact societies tend to demonstrate the preservation of existing complexity. This is one of the major points made by the authors quoted above who have dealt with simplification in the Nordic languages: not only is it the case that the continental languages have undergone simplification, it is also true that the insular languages Icelandic and Faroese have preserved a very great deal of the complexity that was present in Old Norse.

In the rest of this chapter, I hypothesize that it is in low-contact communities that we are most likely to find not only the preservation of complexity but also an **increase** in irregularity, opacity, syntagmatic redundancy and non-borrowed morphological categories. In other words, we should look for the growth of complexity in situations which are the opposite in every respect, including degree of contact, to those in which pidgins develop.

In this chapter, I look for this phenomenon in the Germanic languages. All the major standard language varieties in Europe today are now relatively high-contact koinés and creoloids which are the result in part of simplification resulting from dialect contact. The precursor to modern Standard English referred to by Hope (2000: 50) as 'a Londonish–East Midlandish–Northernish–Southernish' mixture is very typical. The hypothesis therefore suggests that cases of spontaneous, non-additive complexification should be looked for in relatively isolated low-contact non-standardized varieties of modern European languages in comparison with their respective standards. We can also look at those languages which are spoken by small groups of speakers in tightly-knit communities and compare them to related languages. For English, we can look at the traditional dialects (Wells, 1982), and for

German at the *Mundarten*, for instance. And we can also look at 'small' languages like Frisian and Faroese.

It is important that this work be carried out comparatively, by ranging English Traditional-Dialects against General English (Wells, 1982), *Mundart* against *Umgangssprache*, Faroese against Swedish, and so on. And we must necessarily be concerned with diachronically demonstrable complexification, because different levels of complexity between high-contact and low-contact varieties will be due just as often to simplification in the high-contact varieties as to complexification in low-contact varieties. By doing this work comparatively, and feature-by-feature, we will also be able to avoid the pitfalls associated with attempting to develop some kind of measure for the calculation of complexity.

There is no claim here, of course, that complexification occurs only in low-contact varieties, merely that there is a tendency for this to be more common – perhaps a good deal more common – in low-contact than in high-contact varieties. I simply suggest that if the most common pattern is one of complexification events in traditional dialects and 'small languages' which are not paralleled by similar developments in high-contact urban, colonial or standard varieties, then the thesis that the growth of complexity does tend to depend for its genesis largely on low-contact linguistic environments will be strengthened.

I now go on to produce evidence in favour of the hypothesis by describing linguistic changes which are of the complexification type and which have occurred in varieties of the Germanic languages spoken in communities that most closely meet the category of **low contact** – and changes which, crucially, have no counterpart in related high-contact urban dialects or standard varieties. I will do so by examining, in turn, apparent cases of the four different subtypes of complexification as listed above (although close examination of the actual examples will show that the distinction between the four categories is not a clear-cut one).

Complexification 1: growth of morphological categories

Under this heading are examples of the historical development of new morphological categories which are not paralleled in other related varieties, and where there is no evidence of the new category having been acquired as a result of additive borrowing.

1. A few Traditional-Dialects in a small area of the southwest of England developed a new and fascinating marking of the difference between transitive and intransitive infinitives. Intransitive infinitives in these dialects are (or at least were – the distinction appears no longer to be current) marked by the word-final morpheme *-y*, while transitive infinitives were unmarked. So in Dorset we find (Trudgill 1999: 103):

   Can you zew up thease zeam? 'Can you sew up this seam?'
   vs
   The cat vell zick an' woulden mousy. 'The cat fell sick and wouldn't catch mice'.

The important point is that this is unparalleled anywhere else in the English-speaking world, and is quite possibly unparalleled anywhere else at all. My inquiry on the Linguistic Typology List asking for examples of other languages which have morphological marking for intransitive but not transitive infinitives received three answers, none of them producing a precise parallel.

2. A number of traditional dialects in the southwest of England developed an interesting phenomenon described by Ihalainen (1976), in which there is a category distinction between habitual and punctual verb forms such as (note that the forms *do, did* are unemphatic):

   I do go there every day.
   I did go there every day.
   vs
   I goes tomorrow.
   I went last week.

This of course is a distinction between two categories which is common enough in the languages of the world. In English, however, it represents an innovation, and one which is unknown in any of the General English varieties.

3. Certain North Frisian dialects have developed a distinction between two different definite articles (Ebert, 1971; Ebert and Keenan, 1973; Walker, 1990: 14–15). In the Mooring dialect of the Bökingharde area the two sets of forms are:

Masc.	*di*	e
Fem.	*jü*	e
Neut.	*dåt*	et
Pl.	*da*	et

The usage of the two forms is grammatically and semantically complex (see Markey, 1981: 228), but typically the *-e/-et* forms are proximal and/or refer to a unique referent, as in *e moune* 'the moon', *e wjaard* 'the truth', whereas the *di/jü/dåt/*

da forms are distal and/or are context-bound and apply to definite but non-unique referents. For example, 'I have spoken to the village-mayor' can be rendered in two ways:

a) *ik hääw ma e bürgermäister snaaked*
b) *ik hääw ma di bürgermäister snaaked*
 'I have with the mayor spoken'

In (a) the reference is to the mayor of one's own village, whereas in (b) it is to the mayor of some other village. Equally, in the Fering dialect, as Ebert (1984) points out, a question posed by some non-native-speaking outsider in a particular village along the lines of:

Huar wenet di bürgermäister　　'Where does
　　　　　　　　　　　　　　　the mayor live?'

Would solicit the answer:

Hün bürgermäister manst du?　　'Which mayor do
　　　　　　　　　　　　　　you mean?'

This distinction is clearly an innovation and, to say the least, has no parallel in any of the standard forms of other Germanic languages.

4. In the Toten dialect of Norwegian (Faarlund, 2000), complexification has occurred in the demonstrative system. A system of demonstrative pronouns and adjectives has developed which is not found in either of the standard forms of Norwegian, nor in most other Norwegian dialects. A three-way distinction has evolved, as follows:

(a) There is, first, a group of proximal demonstratives corresponding to *this* in English and to *denne/dette/desse* (masc.-fem. sing./neut. sing./plur.) in Nynorsk and *denne/dette/disse* in Bokmål. In Toten these are:

　　denni/detti/dessi.

(b) Then we find the second Toten group:

　　danna/datta/dassa.

These distal demonstratives refer 'to something which is visible in the conversational situation, and which the speaker ... can point to' (Faarlund, 2000: 54, my translation):

　　Danna boka (somm ligg dær) har je itte lesi
　　'That book (which is-lying there) have I not read'
　　Veit du åkke somm bor i datta husi dær?

'Know you who that lives in that house there?'
Dassa såkka (somm ligg bortpå stola) er reine
'Those socks (which are-lying over-there-on) the chair are clean'

(c) The third series 'is used for something which is not visible to the interlocutors, but has recently been mentioned in the conversation' (Faarlund, 2000: 54, my translation):

　　Denn boka (somm du næmnde) har je itte lesi
　　'That book (which you mentioned) have I not read'
　　Veit du åkke somm bor i dæ huse (somm vi nettopp tala om)?
　　'Know you who lives in that house (which we just were-speaking about)?'
　　Dei såkka (somm du spør ætter) ær møkkete
　　'Those socks (which you are-asking about) are dirty'

5. The rural English dialect of Norfolk has developed a new verbal category which is not found in Standard English. The non-negative present tense of the verb *to be* is identical to the Standard English paradigm: *I am, he/she/it is, we/you/they are*. However, there is also a distinct presentative form of the verb which has *be* for all persons (Trudgill, 2003):

　　Here I be!
　　Ah, here you be!
　　Where's Bill – ah, there he be.

Complexification 2: increase in syntagmatic redundancy

It is interesting to note that the examples I have located under this heading are of two different types. Example 6 is a case of a particular discourse strategy whereby speakers choose optionally to repeat information more frequently in some dialects than others. Examples 8 to 11, on the other hand, represent examples of grammatical agreement. It is possible that the latter type derive diachronically from earlier stages which resembled the former type – and this may in fact be what we are seeing in Example 7.

6. The empirical and theoretical work of Berthele (2006), which is based on field recordings of discourse in dialects of Swiss German (as well as French and Romansch), is especially helpful on this topic because it provides some quantitative data. One of the phenomena which Berthele has focused on is the use of complex, redundant pleonastic constructions involving prepositions

and adverbials with motion and posture verbs, in which information appears to be given twice. Swiss German examples from his recordings (Berthele, 2006) include:

und iez tuet er ufe baumstamm uufchläddere (p. 183)
and now does he up-a tree-trunk up-climb
'and now he climbs up a tree trunk'

de hirsch hed ne da übernes bord abbegrüärt ine täich ine (p. 184)
the stag has him then over-a bank down-thrown into-a pond into
'the stag then threw him over a bank down into a pond'

ischer dri usse gsprunge übernes nesseli usse (p. 184)
is-he in-there out jumped over-a nettle out
'he jumped out into there over a nettle'

Of particular value is Berthele's discussion of the data from the Swiss German dialect of Muotathal. The Muotathal 'is a place with a high degree of linguistic and cultural idiosyncrasy. The population is characterized by relatively dense, close-knit and multiplex social networks, which can easily be inferred from the small set of last names borne by a large portion of the native population' (Berthele, 2006: 101). And it has 'relatively traditional language-ecology conditions' with 'low levels of migration, higher education, and valley-external ties' (ibid.: 102).

According to Berthele, Swiss German dialects as a whole tend to show greater syntagmatic redundancy in both stative and dynamic spatial expressions than Standard German, which is of course interesting for our thesis. But it is clear from Berthele's data that this is much truer of Muotathal than of the other dialects he investigated: the rural dialect of the Wallis/Valais, the rural Sensler dialect of Canton Freiburg, the urban dialect of Berne, and Standard German. The percentage of verb phrases with redundant direction marking in the different Swiss dialects is as follows:

Wallis	12%
Berne	15%
Sensler	17%
Muotathal	23%

Speakers of the high-contact Standard German in Berthele's sample, on the other hand, use less than half the number of redundant expressions as those used by Muotathal speakers: 11% (Berthele, 2006: 188). This is consistent with the suggestion that it is in small, dense, close-knit societies that redundancy is most likely to increase.

7. In the English traditional dialect of Norfolk, a form of double tense marking or 'past-tense infinitives' can be found which is absent from Standard English. For example:

Have the fox left?
No that ain't, do Bailey would've let them went.
'No it hasn't, or Bailey would've let them [the hounds] go.' (Trudgill, 1995)

8. According to Van der Auwera and Neuckermans (2004: 455), some dialects of East Flemish have developed considerable redundancy of the repetition-of-information type in the form of triple negation, as in:

'k en ben niemand ni tegengekomen
I not am nobody not met
'I haven't met anybody'

Crucially, triple negation in this dialect is clearly an innovation out of earlier double negation: as Van der Auwera and Neuckermans say, while *en* is an 'old negative marker', *ni* is a 'relatively new marker' (idem. 455).

Even more remarkably the peripheral West Flemish dialects, as described by Haegeman (1995: 132), have gone even further down this path of growth of syntagmatic redundancy, with the development of no less than quadruple negation, as in:

da Valère nooit an geen mens niets gezeid en-oat
that Valère never to no person nothing said not-had
'that Valère had never told anyone anything'

Standardized Dutch, in contrast, has single negation only:

dat Valeer aan niemand ooit iets gezegd had
that Valère to nobody ever anything said had

9. De Vogelaer (2004: 190) notes that subject doubling occurs in a number of Belgian Dutch dialects. For example,

Ze hebbe-en zieder drie kinderen
they have they three kids
'They have three kids'

contains three person markers: the *-en* third-person plural marker on the verb, the clitic pronominal form *ze*, and the pronoun *zieder.*
More remarkably, in East Flemish dialects (de Vogelaer, 2004: 191), subject tripling actually occurs, in the first-person plural. A verb can take a preverbal pronoun and two postverbal pronouns.

The three pronominal forms are *wij* 'we', *we* 'we' [weak form], and *me* 'we' [clitic form]. De Vogelaer cites as an example:

> *We zulle-me wij dat doen*
> we shall-we we that do
> 'We shall do that'

10. According to De Vogelaer (2005: 35), certain Flemish dialects have developed a system of obligatory person agreement on the words corresponding to English yes and no, referred to by him as 'answer particles'.

> *Zullen we gaan? Jom.* 'Shall we go? Yes [1pl]'.
> *Heb je dat gedaan? Jok.* 'Have you done it? Yes [1sg]'
> *Is het warm vandaag? Jot.* Is it warm today? Yes [3sg]'

11. Dialects of Bavarian German (Bayer, 1984) have developed person agreement marking on complementizers. For example, second-person singular marking occurs on ob 'whether' in agreement together with the pronoun du 'you-sg.' and kumm-st 'come-2nd sg.' in:

> ... *obst du noch Minga kummst*
> whether you (sg) to Munich come
> '... whether you are coming to Munich'

Second-person plural marking occurs on ob, with the suffix -ts being repeated, in:

> ... *obts ihr noch Minga kummts*
> ... whether you (pl) to Munich come
> '... whether you are coming to Munich'

The same phenomenon occurs in certain dialects of Dutch/Flemish (Van Haeringen, 1939).

Complexification 3: increase in morphological opacity

The most relevant aspect of opacity for the current discussion is one which has been treated by a number of authors and is referred to by Kusters (2003: 21) in his 'transparency principle' as a demand 'that the relation between form and meaning is as transparent as possible'. The highest level of transparency or analyticity is when 'every single meaning is expressed in a separate form'. Kusters cites the loss of allomorphy in Arabic as an obvious simplification under this heading. Growth in allomorphy, obviously, correspondingly represents a clear case of loss of morphological transparency, and thus an increase in complexity. The examples in this section are all cases of increases in allomorphy.

12. The first example of increase in allomorphy comes from an English dialect and, crucially, has not been paralleled in high-contact varieties of English. This concerns the third-person singular neuter pronoun. In nearly all English dialects, including Standard English, *it* is both the subjective and the objective form. In the dialect of Norfolk, however, a complication has developed. In preverbal position, the neuter singular pronoun is not *it* but *that*. This is particularly clear in the case of the 'weather pronoun' where no possibility exists that we are dealing with the homophonous demonstrative:

> *That's raining.*
> *That's cold in here.*

But there is no doubt that it also operates in genuine pronominalization:

> *I see the cat – that was on the wall.*

However, in postverbal position the pronoun takes the form *it*:

> *Oh, that's raining, is it?*
> *That's cold in here, in't it?*
> *The cat? – I just see it on the wall*

13. In the traditional dialect of East Somerset (Ihalainen, 1991), a pronominal allomorphy more complex than that found in other dialects has developed, notably in the third-person singular masculine. The subject form of the pronoun is the expected *he*:

> *He's older than what I be.*

The object form is '*n* /ən ~ n ɳ/:

> *I looked up to un and said 'What's say?'*

However, there is an additional form of the subject pronoun which Ihalainen refers to as a question clitic, and which occurs obligatorily in tag questions. This Ihalainen writes as *her* or *er*, but it is phonologically phonologically / ər ~ ɽ/:

> *He do live in Latcham, don' er?*

14. Most varieties of Frisian have two forms of the infinitive, but the Bökingharde dialect of North Frisian (Walker and Wilts, 2001: 295–6) has developed an even richer allomorphy, with three different infinitival forms.

    (a) Forms with the suffix -e occur after modal and auxiliary verbs: *hi wal bål kaame* 'he will soon come'. In some cases, this form of the infinitive shows even greater opacity by being irregular and having palatalization in place of the *-e* suffix: *düünj* cf. *douen* 'to do, give', *schiinj* cf. *schaien* 'to happen'.

(b) Forms ending in *-en* occur when the infinitive stands alone, after the preposition *tu* 'to', and after certain verbs such as *bliwe* 'to stay', *hiire* 'to hear': *douen än fouen hiire tuhuupe* 'giving and receiving belong together'.

(c) Forms with a zero ending occur after the conjunction *än* 'and': *dåt as ai lacht än snååk tjüsch* 'it is not easy to speak German'. The corresponding form of the verb 'to do' is *dou*.

Complexification 4: irregularization

Here I discuss two cases of irregularization. The first is quite clearly due to sound changes which, as is usually the case, were themselves quite regular. The second is rather different. Some of the irregularizations are examples of regular verbs fitting into established strong verb patterns, but others are somewhat mysterious.

15. Older Faroese had a complex system of noun declension, including numerous irregular paradigms such as that for *dagur* 'day':

	singular	plural
nom.	[dagur]	[dagar]
acc.	[dag]	[dagar]
gen.	[dags]	[daga]
dat.	[degi]	[døgum]

This was a system which was relatively complex in post-threshold learnability terms. There were seven different forms to learn, and there was a low level of morphological transparency.

However, crucially for our hypothesis, the complexity of the nominal system of modern Faroese is now even greater than that of the earlier language. The contemporary declension for this same noun is (Braunmüller, 2001: 73):

	singular	plural
nom.	[dɛavʊr]	[dɛːar]
acc.	[dɛa]	[dɛːar]
gen.	[daǥs]	[dɛːa]
dat.	[deːji]	[døːvʊn]

The complexity – the irregularity – of this paradigm is colossal. As Braunmüller says, only the consonantal onset remains constant throughout

the paradigm. Braunmüller cites similar cases in a number of other modern noun subclasses also.

High-contact continental Scandinavian, on the other hand, has lost complexity rather than adding it. The corresponding noun *dag* in Standard Norwegian Bokmål, for instance, has only two forms: *dag* (sing.), *dager* (pl.).

16. In the English traditional dialect of Norfolk, for example, we find a number of irregular preterites which occur in cases where Standard English has regular forms. These include (Forby, 1830; Trudgill, 2003):

hoe	hew
mow	*mew*
owe	ewe
row	rew
save	seft
sew /soʊ/	*sew* /sʉː/ (as of stitches)
show	shew
snow	snew
sow	*sew* /sʉː/ (as of seed)
thow (thaw)	*thew*
shriek	shruck
wave	weft
wrap	wrop

In fact, a few of these verbs did have strong or irregular preterites on their first attested appearance in Old English or Middle English. This is true of *mow* and *row*, while *sew* had both strong and weak forms in Old English. In these cases, then, regularization has taken place in Standard English and in the General English nonstandard dialects, while the traditional Norfolk dialect has preserved the original irregularity. The other irregular forms, however, are not historical. *Show,* for example, was a weak verb in Old English, with the preterite *sceawed*, as was *thaw;* and the other verbs were also regular from their earliest appearance. The only exception is *owe*, which goes back to Old English again, with the early Old English preterite *ahte*, which later of course gave rise to *ought*, and was superseded as preterite by regular *awede > owed.* So the Norfolk forms *ewe, hew, sew* (of sew), *shew, snew, thew, shruck, seft, weft, wrop* are all innovations which involved irregularization. The changes to *ewe, hew, sew, shew, sew, thew* are obviously the result of analogy with the *blow* class, but the origins of *shruck, seft, weft* and *wrop* are less clear.

17.4 SPECULATIVE CONCLUSION

I have attempted to demonstrate that there is a good case to be made for the role of societal type in language change by examining briefly the social contexts in which simplification occurs, and then by producing comparative evidence in favour of the argument that complexification, in the sense in which the term has been used in this chapter, is most likely to develop in low-contact communities. I have argued for the legitimacy of this sociolinguistic typological insight with examples from morphological data, but there is some indication that it may well be valid for phonology as well (see Trudgill, 2004). The argumentation, moreover, has relied on material from Germanic languages only. These languages do lend themselves particularly well to this discussion, because in the Germanic languages we can find striking contrasts, within a limited geographical area, between communities speaking related dialects and languages in which we can deduce with some accuracy which complex features are retentions, corresponding to simplification in other varieties, and which are the result of actual complexification. But comparisons within other language families would obviously be desirable.

Of course, it is one thing to demonstrate that there may be a link between community type and simplification/complexification, but it is another matter to explain why there should be such a link. What exactly can the connection be between social structure and linguistic features of this type? I now attempt some elucidation of this point by discussing further the relevance of the sociolinguistic parameters outlined at the beginning of this chapter: networks, size and stability.

As far as social network structure is concerned, we can follow the lead of the Milroys who argue, on the basis especially of their work in Belfast, that dense networks lead to strong social ties, and that strong social ties lead to closer maintenance of community norms, in language as in other forms of behaviour. On the other hand, loose networks lead to weaker social ties and so to a relative lack of maintenance of community norms. The Milroys argue that the consequence is that 'linguistic change is slow to the extent that the relevant populations are well established and bound by strong ties whereas it is rapid to the extent that weak ties exist in populations' (see also L. Milroy, 2000). Dense social networks, as we noted earlier, are most likely to be found in small, stable communities with few external contacts and a high degree of social cohesion. Loose social networks are more liable to develop in larger, unstable communities which have relatively many external contacts and a relative lack of social cohesion. Linguistic change is therefore liable, other things being equal, to be faster in larger than in smaller communities (see Trudgill, in preparation).

This insight about speed of change can also be extended to differences of the sort we have been discussing here, between types of change. Given that there is a strong tendency for relative density of social networks to correlate with community size, we can note the comment made by Grace (1990: 126), who writes:

> A language exists in the people who speak it, but people do not live very long, and the language goes on much longer. This continuity is achieved by the recruitment of new speakers, but it is not a perfect continuity. Children (or adults) learning a language learn it from people who already speak it, but these teachers exercise considerably less than total control over the learning process.

We must accept that no teachers exercise total control, but this perspective does also suggest that, because of network structure, there is a possibility that in smaller, more stable communities the 'teachers' have more control than in larger societies. Because of this, small tightly-knit communities are better able to encourage the preservation of norms and the continued adherence to norms from one generation to another, **however complex they may be**, and the absence of external contacts and social instability will also strengthen a community's ability to maintain linguistic complexity.

If this is so, then it is not unreasonable to suppose that these same societal factors may also assist in the **production** of complexification. In small isolated communities, linguistic change will be slower. But when it **does** occur, there is a greater chance that it will be of the complexification type – the other side of the coin from high contact and loose networks, leading to rapid change and simplification. Small isolated communities are more able, because of their network structures, to push through, enforce and sustain linguistic innovations which would have a much smaller chance of success in larger, more fluid communities – namely, changes of a relatively complex type. So not only is there less simplification in low-contact situations, there is indeed also more complexification, because innovations which complexify the system have a greater chance of succeeding than they would in other types of community. That is, it may well be that innovations of a complexification type occur with roughly equal frequency in all types of community, but that it is simply the case that these innovations are likely, perhaps much more likely, to succeed and become established linguistic changes in small isolated communities. If we can agree that irregularity is more complex than regularity, then we can see why it is in larger language communities that irregular verbs are more likely to become regular, while the reverse may occur in smaller communities – irregularization is just less likely to succeed in larger societies.

The same point can be made from the point of view of opacity. In an important paper, Braunmüller (1985) has argued that *Undurchsichtigkeit* (itself a more transparent form than English **opacity**) is a typical characteristic of small languages. We can now see why this would be. Innovations which render forms less transparent – these are typically phonological innovations – may well develop in all types of community, but they are much more likely to be successful ultimately in communities with tight social networks.

On the other hand, the tendency we have seen for syntagmatic redundancy – repetition of information – to become more common in smaller communities is less obviously explicable. Indeed, it would have seemed more logical if it were the other way round. In small tightly-knit communities where there is a higher degree of shared knowledge and information, one would have thought that less repetition would be necessary, not more. The clue, however, may lie in the word 'necessary'. Linguistic change is not teleological (Lass, 1990, 1997: 340ff): changes are never 'necessary'; they just happen. And the development of agreement does seem to be an extraordinarily common process in linguistic change, since agreement is a very common phenomenon in the world's languages; it is 'a widespread and varied phenomenon' (Corbett, 2006: 1). That is, if linguistic change proceeds without the involvement of non-native speakers, agreement is rather likely to develop even in constructions where there was none before. We can suppose that this type of development is less common in large fluid high-contact communities because, as we said above, repetition of information means that there is more for non-native speakers to learn – it makes for L2 difficulty/outsider complexity. Moreover, as Corbett says, the functions of agreement are by no means totally clear, and 'agreement often appears to involve a lot of effort for a questionable payoff' (2006: 274). It is therefore hardly surprising that pidgins, creoles and other high-contact varieties tend to manage without it. As to why it is typical for linguistic changes to occur in which agreement develops out of situations in which there was originally none – this seems not yet to be fully understood: Corbett's book (2006) on *Agreement* consists of 284 pages of text, only five of which are actually devoted to origins. As Corbett says, 'agreement remains deeply puzzling' (2006: 1). Perhaps we can content ourselves for the time being with noting that human languages are 'like that' in situations where no significant intervention of non-native speakers occurs. It is the type of change, in other words, that is referred to be Bailey (1982) as 'connatural' – the sort of change which naturally takes place when a language is not in contact with other languages.

Finally, the greater likelihood of the development of morphological categories in smaller communities is also a puzzling phenomenon. Here the social factor of community size may be relevant, however. Linguists are naturally sceptical about relating linguistic and cultural complexity. As Bickerton (1996) says, 'if there were any link between cultural complexity and linguistic complexity, we would expect to find that the most complex societies had the most complex languages while simpler societies had simpler languages ... . We do not find any such thing'. Interestingly, though, I would like to point out that, in this chapter, we have presented some data which could be interpreted as suggesting that there **is** a relationship but that it is the other way round: some aspects of linguistic complexity may be more evident in simpler societies than in more complex societies.

Some suggestive work which bears on this point has been carried out by Perkins (1980, 1995). He investigates certain aspects of linguistic complexity, concentrating on morphological categories in deixis. He takes as the starting point for his research a suggestion by Keenan (1976) that deictic systems are better developed in non-literate communities with fewer than 4000 speakers. Kay (1976: 18), for instance, says that

> in small, homogeneous speech communities there is a maximum of shared background between speakers, which is the stuff on which deixis depends. As society evolves toward complexity and the speech community becomes less homogeneous, speakers share less background information, and so one would need to build more of the message into what was actually said.

Givón (1979), too, observes that people in more complex cultures are more frequently required to interact with other people who they do not know.

Perkins' argument is that deictics identify referents by connecting them to the spatial–temporal axis of speech events. Deictics in his terms include persons, tenses, demonstratives, directionals (*here, there*), inclusive vs exclusive etc. The point about deictics, he argues, is that they involve the requirement that the spatio-temporal context of their use be available for the interpretation of the intended referents. Sacha Aikhenvald (pers.comm,) also points out that large complex systems of evidentiality – with four, five or six specifications – are found only in small communities. She suggests that this may be because in such communities there is much pressure for everyone to be fully explicit about their source of information.

Perkins thus conjectures that deictics will be more salient in less complex than in more complex cultures, and are therefore more likely to appear in the central inflectional systems of the languages concerned than more peripherally in the lexis or periphrastically. This is, in turn, because the more frequently free deictic morphemes occur, the more likely they are to be subject to grammaticalization processes, which turn them into bound morphemes through coalescence and morphologization.

Perkins investigated 50 languages and their usage of seven deictic affixes: tense; person on verb; person on nouns; spatial demonstratives on verbs; spatial demonstratives on nouns; inclusive vs exclusive on person markers; and dual in person markers. Communities are ranged for cultural complexity from 1 (e.g. Andamanese) to 5 (e.g. Vietnamese). The measurement of cultural complexity that Perkins uses is based on the work of anthropologists such as Carneiro (1973) and computed in terms of factors such as type of agriculture, settlement size in terms of population, craft specialization, and numbers of levels in political and social hierarchies.

Perkins shows statistically that there is a correlation between complexity and the presence of deictic affixes. For example, languages associated with the most complex cultures – those scoring 5 – have on average 1.22 deictic affixes, while those scoring 1, the lowest, have on average 3.28. Perkins concludes that deictic affixes are lost as cultures become complex.

Most linguists are likely to feel a little uncomfortable about the notion of cultural complexity. I am therefore happy, at least for the time being, to leave this issue to the anthropologists, and to point out that we probably do not need to look any further, for our own linguistic purposes, than actual community size. What is probably crucial here is simply how many individuals are involved in a particular speech community, and how much shared information is available. It is possible that the same or similar factors are associated with the development of other morphological factors; and in any case we can note that a number of the developments outlined above under 1–5 do indeed involve some kind of deixis.

We may speculate, then, that the crucial factors stemming from social structure which help to determine aspects of language structure, of the type discussed in this chapter, are social network structure and degree of shared information, both of which of course also relate to community size and degree of contact and social stability.

NOTES

1   I am very grateful for information, discussions, help and advice in connection with the subject matter of this paper to: Raphael Berthele, Kurt Braunmüller, Gunther De Vogelaer, Jan Terje Faarlund, Liliane Haegeman, Jean Hannah, Lukas Pietsch, Jacques Van Keymeulen, Wim Vandenbussche, Alastair Walker, and especially Peter Siemund, as well as to members of audiences in different parts of the world who have heard presentations of this material, and responded with helpful questions and vital information.

2   'It can often be observed that a language loses formal distinctions in circumstances in which the hypothesis of a foreign influence is very natural'.

REFERENCES

Aikhenvald, A. (2002) *Language Contact in Amazonia.* Oxford: Oxford University Press.

Aikhenvald, A. (2008) 'Multilingual imperatives: the elaboration of a category in northwest Amazonia', *International Journal of American Linguistics,* 74: 189–225.

Askedal, J. O. (2005) 'The typological development of the Nordic languages I: morphology and syntax', in O. Bandle (ed.), *The Nordic Languages: an International Handbook of the History of the North Germanic Languages II.* Berlin: de Gruyter. pp. 1872–86.

Bailey, C.-J. (1982) *On the Yin and yang Nature of Language.* Ann Arbor, MI: Karoma.

Bakker, P. (1997) *A Language of our Own: the Genesis of Michif, the Mixed Cree–French Language of the Canadian Métis.* Oxford: Oxford University Press.

Bayer, J. (1984) 'COMP in Bavarian syntax', *Linguistic Review,* 3: 209–74.

Berthele, R. (2006) *Ort und Weg: die sprachliche Raumreferenz in Varietäten des Deutschen, Rätoromanischen und Französischen.* Berlin: de Gruyter.

Bickerton, D. (1996) *Language and Human Behaviour.* London: UCL Press.

Bokamba, E. (1993) 'Language variation and change in pervasively multilingual societies: Bantu languages', in S. Mufwene and L. Moshi (eds), *Topics in African Linguistics.* Amsterdam: Benjamins. pp. 207–52.

Braunmüller, K. (1985) 'Morphologische Undurchsichtigkeit – ein Charakteristikum kleiner Sprachen', *Kopenhagener Beiträge zur germanistischen Linguistik,* 22: 48–68.

Braunmüller, K. (2001) 'Morfologisk typologi og færøsk', in K. Braunmüller and J. L. Jacobsen (eds), *Moderne lingvistiske teorier og færøsk.* Oslo: Novus. pp. 67–88.

Carneiro, R. (1973) 'Scale analysis, evolutionary sequences, and the range of cultures', in: R. Naroll and R. Cohen (eds), *A Handbook of Method in Cultural Anthropology.* New York: Columbia University Press. pp. 834–71.

Comrie, B. (2008) 'Inflectional morphology and language contact, with special reference to mixed languages', in P. Siemund, and N. Kintana (eds), *Language Contact and Contact Languages.* Amsterdam: Benjamins.

Corbett, G. (2006) *Agreement.* Cambridge: Cambridge University Press.

Dahl, Ö. (2004) *The Growth and Maintenance of Linguistic Complexity.* Amsterdam: Benjamins.

De Vogelaer, G. (2004) 'Person marking in Dutch dialects', in B. Kortmann (ed.), *Dialectology Meets Typology: Dialect Grammar from a Cross-Linguistic Perspective.* Berlin: Mouton de Gruyter. pp. 181–10.

De Vogelaer, G. (2005) *Persoonsmarkering in de dialecten in het nederlandse taalgebied.* Ghent: Universiteit Gent.

Dixon, R. M. W. (1997) *The Rise and Fall of Languages,* Cambridge: Cambridge University Press.

Dixon, R. M. W. and Aikhenvald, A. (eds) (1999) *The Amazonian Languages.* Cambridge: Cambridge University Press.

Ebert, K. H. (1971) *Referenz, Sprechsituation und die bestimmten Artikel in einem nordfriesischen Dialekt (Fering).* Bredstedt: Nordfriisk Instituut.

Ebert, K. H. (1984) 'Zur grammatischen Differenziertheit des Dialektes (am Beispiel Fering)', *Nordfriesisches Jahrbuch,* 20: 227–38.

Ebert, K. and Keenan, E. (1973) 'A note on marking transparency and opacity', *Linguistic Inquiry,* 4: 421–4

Faarlund, J. T. (2000) *Totenmålet.* Lena: Østre Toten Kommune.

Forby, R. [1830] (1970) *The Vocabulary of East Anglia.* New York: Augustus Kelley.

Givón, T. (1979) *On Understanding Grammar.* New York: Academic Press.

Grace, G. (1990) 'The 'aberrant' (vs. 'exemplary') Melanesian languages', in: P. Baldi (ed.), *Linguistic Change and Reconstruction Methodology.* Berlin: Mouton de Gruyter. pp. 155–73.

Haegeman, L. (1995) *The Syntax of Negation.* Cambridge: Cambridge University Press.

Harnard, S. R., Steklis, H. D. and Lancaster, J. (eds) 1976 *Origins and Evolution of Language and Speech.* New York: New York Academy of Sciences.

Harris, A. and Campbell, L. (1995) *Historical Syntax in Cross-Linguistic Perspective.* Cambridge: Cambridge University Press.

Haudricourt, A. (1961) 'Richesse en phonèmes et richesse en locateurs', *L'Homme,* 1: 5–10.

Hope, J. (2000) 'Rats, bats, sparrows and dogs: biology, linguistics and the nature of Standard English', in L. Wright (ed.) *The Development of Standard English 1300–1800,* Cambridge: Cambridge University Press.

Ihalainen, O. (1976) 'Periphrastic *do* in affirmative sentences in the dialect of East Somerset', *Neuphilologische Mitteilungen,* 77: 608–22.

Ihalainen, Ossi (1991) 'On grammatical diffusion in Somerset folk speech', in P. Trudgill and J. K. Chambers (eds), *Dialects of English: Studies in Grammatical Variation.* London: Longman. pp. 148–60.

Jahr, E. H. (2001) 'Historical sociolinguistics: the role of Low German language contact in the Scandinavian typological split of the late Middle Ages', *Lingua Posnaniensis,* 43: 95–104.

Kay, P. (1976) 'Discussion of papers by Kiparsky and Wescott', in S. R. Harnard, Steklis, H. D. and Lancaster, J.

(eds), *Origin and Evolution of Language and Speech.* New York Academy of Sciences. pp. 17–19.

Keenan, E. (1976) 'Discussion', in S. R. Harnard, Steklis, H. D. and Lancaster, (eds). *Origins and Evolution of Language and Speech.* New York: New York, Academy of Sciences. pp. 92–6.

Kusters, W. (2003) *Linguistic Complexity: The Influence of Social Change on Verbal Inflection.* Leiden: Leiden University.

Lass, R. (1990) 'How to do things with junk: exaptation in language evolution', *Journal of Linguistics,* 26: 79–102.

Lass, R. (1997) *Historical Linguistics and Language Change.* Cambridge: Cambridge University Press.

Markey, T. (1981) *Frisian.* The Hague: Mouton.

Milroy, J. (1992) 'Middle English dialectology', in N. Blake (ed.), *The History of the English Language II: 1066–1476.* Cambridge: Cambridge University Press. pp. 156–206.

Milroy, J. and Milroy, L. (1985) 'Linguistic change, social network and speaker innovation', *Journal of Linguistics,* 21: 339–84.

Milroy, L. (2000) 'Social network analysis and language change', *European Journal of English Studies,* 4: 217–24.

Mühlhäusler, P. (1977) *Pidginisation and Simplification of Language.* Canberra: Pacific Linguistics.

Nichols, J. (1992) *Linguistic Diversity in Space and Time.* Chicago: Chicago University Press.

Pedersen, K. M. (1999) 'Genusforenkling i Københavnsk', *Danske Folkemål,* 41: 79–106.

Perkins, R. (1980) 'The covariation of culture and grammar'. PhD thesis, University of Michigan, Ann Arbor.

Perkins, R. (1995) *Deixis, Grammar, and Culture.* Amsterdam: Benjamins.

Sankoff, G. (2002) 'Linguistic outcomes of language contact', in J. K. Chambers, P. Trudgill and N. Schilling-Estes (eds), *The Handbook of Language Variation and Change.* Oxford: Blackwell.

Thomason, S. G. (2001) *Language Contact: an Introduction.* Edinburgh: Edinburgh University Press.

Thurston, W. (1994) 'Renovation and innovation in the languages of north-western New Britain', in T. Dutton and D. Tryon (eds), *Language Contact and Change in the Austronesian World.* Berlin: Mouton de Gruyter. pp. 573–609.

Trudgill, P. (1995) 'Grammaticalisation and social structure: nonstandard conjunction-formation in East Anglian English', in F. R. Palmer (ed.), *Grammar and Semantics: Papers in Honour of John Lyons.* Cambridge: Cambridge University Press. pp. 136–47.

Trudgill, P. (1996) 'Dual-source pidgins and reverse creoloids: northern perspectives on language contact', in E. H. Jahr and I. Broch (eds), *Language Contact in the Arctic: Northern Pidgins and Contact Languages.* Berlin: Mouton de Gruyter. pp. 5–14.

Trudgill, P. (1999) *The Dialects of England.* 2nd edition. Oxford: Blackwell.

Trudgill, P. (2003) *The Norfolk Dialect.* Cromer: Poppyland.

Trudgill, P. (2004) 'Linguistic and social typology: the Austronesian migrations and phoneme inventories', *Linguistic Typology*, 8: 305–20.

Trudgill, P. (2009) 'Contact and sociolinguistic typology', in R. Hickey (ed.), *Handbook of Language Contact*. Oxford: Blackwell.

Trudgill, P. (forthcoming) *Language in Contact and Isolation: Social Determinants of Linguistic Structure.*

Van der Auwera, J. and Neuckermans, A. (2004) 'On the interaction of predicate and quantifier negation in Flemish', in B. Kortmann (ed.), *Dialectology Meets Typology: Dialect Grammar from a Cross-Linguistic Perspective*. Berlin: Mouton de Gruyter. pp. 453–78.

Van Haeringen, C. B. (1939) 'Congruerende voegwoorden', *Tijdschrift voor Nederlandse Taal- en Letterkunde*, 60: 126–7.

Vanhove, M. (2001) 'Contacts de langues et complexification des systèmes: le cas du maltais', *Faits de Langues*, 18: 65–74.

Vogt, H. (1948) 'Dans quelles conditions et dans quelles limites peut s'exercer sur le système morphologique d'une langue l'action du système morphologique d'une autre langue?', in M. Lejeune (ed.), *Actes du Sixième Congrès International des Linguistes*. Paris: Klincksieck. pp. 31–45.

Walker, A. (1990) 'Frisian', in C. Russ (ed.), *The Dialects of Modern German: A Linguistic Survey*. London: Routledge. pp. 1–30.

Walker, A. and Wilts, O. (2001) 'Die nordfriesichen Mundarten', in H.H. Munske et al. (eds), *Handbuch des friesischen/Handbook of Frisian Studies*. Tübingen: Niemeyer. pp. 284–305.

Wells, J. C. (1982) *Accents of English*. Cambridge: Cambridge University Press.

18

Sociolinguistics and Formal Linguistics

Gregory R. Guy

18.1 INTRODUCTION

Sociolinguistics is often seen as having little relevance to formal linguistic theory. Indeed, a formal linguist once told the present author that sociolinguistics 'is not linguistics'. While such a comment reveals a narrow and sectarian view of linguistics, it also shows that the relationship between social aspects of language and formal models of language structure is not self-evident – at least, given prevailing theoretical frameworks in the field. So why does this volume have a chapter addressing this relationship?

The most obvious connection lies in the fundamental scientific concern with theoretical adequacy. Chomsky (1964: 29) identifies the lowest level of adequacy as 'observational' – providing a faithful representation of the data. Formal linguistic theories that ignore social diversity – a demonstrable characteristic of all languages – do not meet this most elementary criterion, let alone the highly valued descriptive or explanatory adequacy they aspire to. Formalists have glossed over this glaring lacuna by addressing their models to ever-narrower social universes, ultimately the 'idiolect' – the grammar of a hypothetical monostylistic invariant individual. But observation denies even this refuge, demonstrating that such an object does not exist in the world. And even if it did, a formal model that accounted for only this would be limited to production, leaving the other two pillars of the language tripod – perception and acquisition – unaddressed, since human beings encounter sociolinguistic diversity in the speech of others, and must be able to learn language and understand others even when they speak differently. Hence the obvious conclusion is that the human language faculty acquires, generates, recognizes and interprets variability, and that formal theories of this faculty are inadequate unless they account for this.

One contribution of sociolinguistics to formal linguistics is therefore observational and descriptive – it turns up facts that theory must account for. Formal models sometimes flee from the seemingly disorganized multitude of such facts and declare themselves not responsible for the mess. This is an appropriate initial scientific response to complexity – focusing on a subset of facts, idealizing them and ignoring interactions with other facts. But when disciplines mature to the point of achieving some mastery over their subject matter, the gains from idealization are outweighed by the concomitant limits on the theory's capacity to achieve a more accurate account of reality. At this point a serious science is obliged to engage with what was previously ignored. Linguistics has now reached this phase, and formal linguistics has begun to recognize the need for a sounder empirical basis, and to seek broader empirical testing of theory, which can only be achieved in the messy world of language use. Sociolinguistic studies thus provide a proving ground for theory that is unavailable in the introspective, intuitive paradigm of theoretical research.

Sociolinguistic research also points towards what is needed in linguistic theory to achieve higher levels of adequacy. Adequate formal models must eventually account for variability – an individual's capacity for stylistic variation, for accommodation, for performing acts of identity by linguistic means – But what are the limits and the landscape of that variability? An adequate formal theory must incorporate social information – social interpretations of variables and ways of speaking; But what kinds of social information are linguistically relevant? Sociolinguistic work is developing the outlines of the necessary elements of an adequate theory of language – one that accounts not only for narrow Chomskyan competence but also, following Hymes (1972; see Johnstone and Marcellino, this volume), for speakers' sociolinguistic or communicative competence, their capacity to speak and understand in a diverse and varying linguistic world. Encouragingly, this work is meeting complementary developments from the formal side, in theoretical frameworks such as Optimality Theory (OT) and usage-based phonology.

The other side of this relationship is the importance of formal linguistics to sociolinguistics. Sociolinguists have, unfortunately, sometimes adopted a reciprocally sceptical view of the relevance of formal theory to their subdiscipline. Ironically, their reasons for doing so are similar to formalists' reasons for neglecting sociolinguistic results: the models of formalists are diverse, messy and constantly in flux. The impression that outsiders sometimes have of formal linguistics is reminiscent of T. S. Eliot's famous poem, *Prufrock*: 'In the field, the theories come and go, talking of Michelangelo; there is time for a hundred visions and revisions before the taking of the toast and tea'. If theories are ephemeral, focus on irrelevancies, and change a hundred times before tea, an empirical researcher might be wise to avoid making them a central concern of a study that might take years to complete.

Despite sometimes holding such attitudes, sociolinguists cannot avoid theory when they analyse data. Whenever they formulate a hypothesis, or even identify a variable, they are relying on some model of events, some 'theory' (perhaps implicit) of the structure of language. When Labov famously studied coda /r/ in New York City (1966), he made a formal claim to the effect that /r/-less and /r/-ful pronunciations of words like *source*, *car*, *beer* alternated in the speech of New Yorkers, and that the alternants counted as lexically equivalent even though they were phonologically and socially differentiated. This analysis rested on theoretical constructs such as phoneme, word, equivalence, difference and phonological alternation. In general, theoretical models suggest to the sociolinguist what things might be interesting to investigate. A great deal of sociolinguistic research has been devoted to investigating and testing hypotheses derived from theoretical models.

And much sociolinguistic work seriously engages with the construction of formal models. Bailey (1973) proposed a contextually-driven theory of variation and change, in which change is hypothesized to begin earliest and proceed fastest in maximally favourable contexts. Kroch (1989b) tested this model against data on syntactic change and disproved it, proposing instead an alternative

theory – the Constant Rate Hypothesis – that states that changes move at the same rate in all contexts, and are therefore not driven by contextual effects. Guy (1991, 1992) applied the Lexical Phonology model of Kiparsky (1982a) to variable coronal stop deletion (CSD) in English, deriving predictions of an exponential relationship among retention and deletion rates in three different morphological categories, which has been confirmed in studies of several English dialects (cf. Santa Ana, 1992; Bayley, 1994).

Some of the formal models in sociolinguistic work have pioneered in areas where other formal theories have feared to tread. Sociolinguists have been at the forefront of work on interlingual issues, notably the formal models of code-switching proposed by scholars such as Poplack (1980), Myers-Scotton (1993) and Nishimura (1997). Formalists have done little work on linguistic structure above the level of the sentence, but sociolinguists have proposed formal models of discourse level phenomena such as narrative structure (Labov and Waletzky, 1967), conversational turn-taking (Sacks et al., 1974) and therapeutic discourse (Labov and Fanshel, 1977). Thus the relationship of sociolinguistics to formal theory comes full circle, with sociolinguists not only following up the analyses suggested by formal models but also testing and revising them, and proposing new ones.

Of course, as this volume makes clear, sociolinguistics has become a very broad discipline that encompasses a considerable variety of interests and approaches, and not all of these will have the same level of engagement with formal linguistics. Studies of language policy and planning, or language endangerment, are marginal to the construction of formal models of language, whereas sociolinguistic research that examines detailed contextual constraints on phonological or syntactic variation is intimately involved with analysing linguistic structure. But subdividing sociolinguistic interests into those that engage with formal theory and those that do not is not necessarily simple or clear. Consider work on language contact. The Franco-Norman conquest of England in 1066 is a sociohistorical fact with no direct connection to linguistic theory. But the massive borrowing of French and Latinate words into English that ensued has complicated English phonology in ways of considerable interest to formal linguists. Much theoretical work in phonology addresses problems of this sort, such as how to associate certain phonological patterns with specific subsets of the lexicon. Similarly, code-switching was first studied by sociolinguists interested in the social phenomenon of alternating languages in bilingual communities. But it has attracted much formal theoretical attention, due to the insights it offers into questions of syntactic structure and linguistic cognition.

Therefore we cannot, a priori, partition socio-linguistics into theoretically relevant and theoreti-cally uninteresting components. All its subdivisions have the two connections to linguistic theory we have identified: all have the descriptive connec-tion, revealing facts that theories may eventually seek to explain, and all rely on hypotheses about language structure that are ultimately derived from theoretical models. Since we assume, in principle, that language cannot be adequately understood in isolation from its social embedding, we assume a general relevance of sociolinguistics to formal theory.

In what follows, this chapter considers the fol-lowing topics: how theory informs sociolinguis-tics, how sociolinguistic studies address formal issues, and current developments in formal theory that constitute progress towards an adequate model of language – one that has some possibility of accounting for the sociolinguistic facts. But before addressing these topics, we begin with a brief survey of the history of linguistic theory insofar as it has spoken to, or ignored, sociolin-guistic questions.

18.2 PAROLE, PERFORMANCE, PERIPHERY: THE MARGINALIZATION OF SOCIOLINGUISTICS IN FORMAL THEORY

Ever since the Neogrammarian movement revolu-tionized linguistic theory in the late nineteenth century, the mainstream of formal thinking about language has pushed sociolinguistic questions either to the margins of the discipline, or beyond the pale. The Neogrammarians provided a key idealizing assumption that justified this marginali-zation: the concept of invariance in linguistic proc-esses. The dominant focus of linguistics in the nineteenth century was historical and comparative, leading to the discovery of numerous phonological correspondences between related languages, such as the 'Grimm's Law' relationship between Germanic and Proto-Indo-European (roughly speaking, Germanic underwent a chain shift of the form: /bh, dh, gh/ > /b, d, g/ > /p, t, k/ > /f, θ, h/). Many exceptions to such correspondences were well known, and an emergent dialectological tradi-tion was documenting extensive variability in lexi-cal development. But despite the empirical evidence of variability, the Neogrammarians argued that correspondences arose from EXCEPTIONLESS sound change. The hypothesis of 'exceptionlessness' was

justified by a formal model in which words were composed of phoneme-like units on which sound change operated (Paul, 1978 [1886]). When such a unit changed, all words containing it changed simultaneously. Apparent 'exceptions' to these cor-respondences were postulated to result from proc-esses like borrowing and analogical change that operated after the categorical change occurred. Sociolinguistic and dialectological observations of variability were relegated to the periphery of this research paradigm, by definition; they were noise obscuring the systematic big picture. (See also discussion in Kerswill, this volume.)

The Neogrammarian worldview was motivated in part by the discovery of phonological condi-tioning. For example, Verner (1978 [1877]) famously discovered a prosodic constraint on Grimm's Law: voiceless stops following an unstressed vowel in Proto-Indo-European are voiced in Germanic, instead of becoming voice-less fricatives. Such discoveries provided a para-digm for formal analysis in linguistics that persists in some measure to the present day: search for invariant generalizations, ignoring variability present in usage; where persistent exceptions to those generalizations are encountered, search for other invariant sub-generalizations delimited by formally definable contexts. This has been a productive heuristic for linguists, but it has also provided formal linguistics with an oubliette for disposing of inconvenient facts: one postulates that any exceptions will be accounted for in the future by some more refined statement of the context. At worst, this is unfalsifiable: all formal processes are exceptionless, and any observable exceptions will be explained by future Verners. For linguists who take a Popperian view of their science, such a hypothesis need not be taken seriously.

The invariant view of linguistic process was adapted to synchronic theory by Saussure, the founder of modern formal linguistics. Saussure (1916) elevated the separation of social and formal elements of language to a theoretical prin-ciple via his dichotomy between *langue* and *parole*. For Saussure, *langue* is the abstract, sys-tematic aspect of language, while the social diver-sity of language use is assigned to *parole*. These have unequal status in linguistic science: Saussure privileges *langue* as the object of study of serious linguistics. Sociolinguistic concerns are consigned to the periphery of Saussurean thought, as the study of *parole*.

Saussure's dichotomy is recast by Chomsky as **competence** and **performance**, and later, I-language (internalized) and E-language (exter-nalized). Competence/I-language is the mental linguistic system governing production – the mental grammar. It is assumed to follow invariant principles in the Neogrammarian 'exceptionless' tradition. Performance is the product of the system – actual speech, or any other externalized linguistic output (hence E-language). Mediating between the mental grammar and its products are psychological and physiological factors that do not share the property of invariance; hence, they introduce variability into performance. Chomsky cites factors such as slips of the tongue, memory lapses and performance errors as common flaws in everyday language use, and argues that such flaws are not the product of the mental grammar and do not provide useful evidence about its nature (1965).

The competence/performance distinction has logical elegance, opposing a mental machine to its products. But in the give-and-take of linguistic argumentation, it becomes the neutron bomb of generative theory, removing humans from the battlefield, leaving only naked linguistic structures behind. Sociolinguistics is collateral damage in this battle; it provides no data relevant to the construction of formal theory, because it looks only at performance. Chomsky specifically argues that 'observed use of language … surely cannot constitute the actual subject matter of linguistics, if this is to be a serious discipline' (1965: 4). Performance is thus an even deeper oubliette for the disposal of empirical counter-examples: data from usage bears unknown deviances from the mental grammar, and therefore cannot contradict theories about that grammar.

Chomskyan thought and its theoretical successors thus continue the century-old tradition of consigning sociolinguistic concerns to the periphery. Linguists interested in the topics addressed in this volume therefore find themselves with just two options for relating to linguistic theory. They can accept that their work addresses 'mere' performance, and is consequently irrelevant to formal theory, or they can problematize the assumptions that lead to this conclusion, most importantly the assumption of invariance and the postulated opposition between competence and performance. One encounters, in sociolinguistics, work that follows both of these paths. One trend eschews attention to theoretical issues – a position consistent with the Chomskyan view that evidence from language use is not, in principle, relevant to formal theory.

Another, perhaps dominant, trend in sociolinguistic research has been to reject the sectarian definition that excludes sociolinguistic concerns and denies their relevance to formal models of competence, and instead proposes alternatives that embrace variability and social diversity. This approach found an influential formulation in the work of Weinreich, Labov and Herzog (1968, henceforth WLH), which enunciates two principles that contradict the assumption of invariance. First is 'inherent variability': since language use is

full of variety, it is reasonable to postulate that linguistic systems – mental grammars – generate, perceive and interpret variability. Since no Chomskyan invariant 'ideal speaker-listener' exists, why postulate such a person as the object that our theories seek to explain? Indeed, WLH go further; they argue that if such invariant speakers did exist, they would be social monsters, unable to adapt to changing circumstances, or accommodate to different interlocutors, or to use language to communicate all the social messages performed by variant means.

The second WLH principle is 'orderly heterogeneity': linguistic variability is not random and unstructured, the product of errors. Rather, it is deeply structured by social and linguistic contexts. Essentially, this counterposes a probabilistic interpretation of orderliness to the categorical interpretation prevailing in formal theory. If system and order are equated to exceptionlessness, all valid generalizations must be categorically true; in quantitative terms, they must apply to 100% of cases. But a probabilistic model allows valid generalizations about values below 100%. Social groups are rarely distinguished by the categorical presence or absence of a particular form, but they are often characterized by particular rates of use; thus, in New York City, middle-class speakers use more coda [r] than working-class speakers. And orderly heterogeneity is also evident in linguistic structure: many sociolinguistic variables show strong probabilistic – but not categorical – conditioning by linguistic contexts. Thus, English final CSD is much more likely preconsonantally (eas' side) than in prevocalic position (eas' end). Nobody does this categorically, with 100% deletion before consonants and 0% before vowels, but every speaker's usage shows probabilistic favouring of preconsonantal contexts. This process always has 'exceptions', but it is still systematic and orderly.

The challenge to formal linguistics that WLH present, therefore, is to design theoretical models that accommodate variability and probabilistic orderliness. Formal models that continue to adhere to the assumption of invariance and the marginalization of *parole*/performance cannot account for the results emerging from sociolinguistic research, and run the risk of ultimate irrelevance. But many models are emerging that take up this challenge; some of these are discussed in subsequent sections.

18.3 FORMAL THEORY INFORMS SOCIOLINGUISTICS

The fundamental finding of sociolinguistic research is that variation and diversity permeate language. Individual speakers vary their usage constantly and adaptively, to construct social identities, demonstrate attitudes and manage social relationships. Collectively, speakers are differentiated by geography and time, and by social dimensions of class, sex, ethnicity, age and linguistic experience. Therefore, the fundamental questions in sociolinguistic research are: What is it about language that varies, and why?

Because of the nature of the field, some answers to the 'Why?' questions will be linguistic, and some social and historical. Formal linguistics has great relevance to the former, providing potential explanations of constraints on variation. It will not necessarily contribute to understanding the latter: nothing about the structure of language accounts for the social dominance of Spanish over Mayan in Guatemala, or for the spread of Northern Cities dialect features in American English from larger to smaller urban areas (Callary, 1975). But it is often difficult to distinguish one line of explanation from another, and they may interact (if, for example, the linguistic markedness of forms limits borrowability). Therefore, sociolinguistics must allow the possibility of formal linguistic accounts of any patterns of variation it encounters.

The most important contribution of formal theory may lie in answering the 'What?' questions. To make progress in appreciating the workings of sociolinguistic diversity, we require concepts and hypotheses about the structure of language – a 'theory' that suggests what things are worth studying and where to look for them. Clearly, our investigations are best served by bringing the best theories available to bear on the issues. If we want to know how speakers differ, or what linguistic items they respond to in formulating social evaluations, we would do well to turn to formal theories to delineate the elements and processes that may be relevant.

As an example of the theoretical contributions to sociolinguistic research, consider the variable process of final coronal stop deletion (CSD) in English, a coda-simplification process with parallels in many other languages. It shows classic traits of a linguistic variable: it is conditioned by linguistic contexts, stylistically constrained (speakers delete less in more careful styles) and socially stratified (higher-status speakers delete less). But the linguistic constraints affecting it have a curious interaction with the social constraints: some constraints are constant for all speakers of English, while others vary from dialect to dialect. Why is this so?

Let us consider two constraints affecting this process. First, as noted above, CSD is markedly affected by following phonological context, with significantly more deletion in preconsonantal than prevocalic position. Also, the process is sensitive to morphology: stops representing the -ed suffix in regular verbs are deleted less often than those that are part of the root morpheme. Relevant values from several studies are found in Table 18.1.

The effect of following vowel (V) and consonant (C) is, as the table indicates, systematic across all dialects. But, strikingly, the effect of following pause (P) varies considerably from group to group. For some speech communities, pause is the most conservative environment, disfavouring deletion even more than vowels, while for others it is associated with high deletion rates. The first discovery of this dialect-specific effect of pause was made by Guy (1980), who found that New Yorkers favoured deletion before pause, while Philadelphians disfavoured it. The effect was systematic within each speech community, as Table 18.2 illustrates. Everybody in both communities (except two Philadelphians with small ns) has more deletion before C than V, but 18 of 19 Philadelphians show pause as the least favourable environment for deletion (P deletion rates below V), while no New Yorkers have this ranking of vowel and pause.

A similar issue arises with respect to morphology. Most speakers in most dialects systematically show higher deletion rates in monomorphemic (M) words like *mist*, *pact*, *bold*, vs reduced rates in regular past tense verbs (R) like *missed*, *packed*, *bowled*. But speakers vary considerably in their

Table 18.1 Effects of morphological class and following segment on English coronal stop deletion

	Morphological				Following segment			
	M		I	R	C	V		P
Bayley	.53	<	.62	.36	.73	.27	<	.46
Santa Ana	.55	>	.43	.28	.62	.33	>	.32
Lim and Guy	.60	<	.65	.26	.61	.37	<	.48
Guy	.64	>	.55	.32	.66	.19	<	.37

M, monomorphemic words; I, irregular past tense verbs; R, regular past tense verbs; V, vowel; C, consonant; P, pause.

Source: (from Bayley (1994), Guy (1991) Lim and Guy (2003) and Santa Ana (1992))

Table 18.2   Comparing constraint effects in two speech communities: following context constraint orderings for coronal stop deletion in New York and Philadelphia

| | Following context | | | |
| | Number of speakers showing the order: | | | |
	C>V	V>C	V>Pause	Pause>V
Philadelphians	16	2	18	1
New Yorkers	4	0	0	4

C, consonant; V, vowel.

treatment of the irregular past tense verbs (I) that take both a root vowel change and a coronal stop affix in the past, such as *lost, kept, told*. Guy and Boyd (1990) found that the treatment of this morphological class varied with age: older speakers treat irregular verbs conservatively, with lower deletion rates, while younger speakers are more likely to delete them (Figure 18.1).

Such findings provoke an obvious question: Why are some constraints constant across speakers and dialects, while others are inconstant, either dialect-specific or age-graded? Since sociolinguistics is simultaneously concerned with linguistic structure and social context, we might entertain both social and linguistic explanations of these facts. On the social side, a possible hypothesis is that speakers arbitrarily select linguistic items for social-indexical purposes. This is akin to the arbitrariness of the linguistic sign: just as a book does not intrinsically demand the label *book*, since it is labelled *hon* in Japanese and *kitab* in Arabic, so there is no intrinsic reason that pronouncing coda /r/ is socially favoured in New York. Therefore, we might suppose that the prepausal deletion rate for coronal stops is arbitrarily selected as a dialect marker, and the deletion rate in irregular verbs has been arbitrarily associated with particular age cohorts.

Pending a more comprehensive analysis of what variables and constraints have what social interpretations and associations, we cannot rule out this account on purely social grounds. But the fact that numerous studies of CSD show the same effects for many other constraints, leaving just these two contexts to vary greatly across speakers, should give us pause. Perhaps some linguistic property makes these constraints more amenable to social differentiation.

This is where formal theory comes to our aid. Many strands of phonological theory agree that there is a universal hierarchy of syllable types, with CV being the most basic, found in all languages, while other structures, including complex codas, complex onsets and zero onsets, are more marked and typologically less common. These principles are explicitly incorporated in CV

phonology (Clements and Keyser, 1983), and in postulated OT constraints such as NoCoda, *CxCoda, Onset, etc. Hence, these theories suggest a prediction, to the effect that ... VCCCV... sequences, in phrases like east side, are universally more marked than ... VCCV ... sequences, like *east end*. This being the case, a process that simplified the coda sequence should always be more strongly motivated in the former than the latter. If these are linguistic universals, we should not expect to find any dialect or speaker that contradicts them, which, essentially, is what the data show – everybody deletes more before consonants than before vowels.

But what do formal models say about following pause? Eligible words for English CSD have the form ...VCC, so when no other subsequent segments are considered, they will violate NoCoda and *CxCoda constraints just like eligible words occurring in other contexts, but are they more or less marked than prevocalic or preconsonantal contexts? Formal theories are largely silent on this point; an answer would depend on a formal analysis of non-speech (What are the distinctive features of silence?), or on an additional set of hypotheses about syllabification, stop release, etc., which would not be universal in nature. Therefore, it is a fair conclusion from phonological theory that the effects of prevocalic and preconsonantal contexts are determined by linguistic universals, but the effect of following pause is not universally defined, and hence is available for dialect-specific, dialectally arbitrary treatments.

Formal theory suggests a similarly ambiguous status for the treatment of CSD in irregular verbs. The difference between monomorphemic and regular past tense forms is modelled in several ways in different theories: by functional constraints against loss of information; by a historical constraint against loss of morphological distinctions (Kiparsky, 1982b, the 'distinctness condition'); and by the different derivational histories of the two classes (underived vs derived, cf. Guy, 1991). But all models assign a distinct status to the morphological marker in *missed, bowled* that is absent in *mist, bold*, with a consistent prediction that deletion of the past tense forms is disfavoured.

But what about irregular past forms? There is no obvious universal explanation for how they should be treated by a deletion process. The final stops in *left, told* mark tense redundantly, so they have no greater functional load than those in monomorphemes. Their derivational histories depend on specific hypotheses about what form classes exist and how they are stored and generated, on which there is little theoretical consensus. Therefore, we can again entertain a reasonable hypothesis that while the difference between monomorphemes and regular past tense forms is subject to universal conditions, the status of the irregular forms is precisely irregular, subject to different analyses and different treatments by the deletion process.

This is what Guy and Boyd (1990) argue. They see the age-grading in Figure 18.1 as a product of successive reanalyses of these words by English speakers as they develop linguistically. The youngest (pre-teen) speakers classify them as strong verbs, lacking a suffix (thus keep~kep, analogous with feed~fed); hence, final stops are almost completely absent. By adolescence, most speakers construct a special morphological class for such words, combining traits of the strong and weak classes, but without any internal morphological analysis (thus keep~kept). Hence, they show the

same deletion rates as monomorphemes, which also lack internal morphology. Finally, in adult life, many speakers proceed to a complex analysis in which the final coronal stop acquires a separate morphemic analysis, no doubt by analogy with the regular affix in *missed, bowled* (thus keep~kep#t); hence they begin to partake of the morphological resistance to deletion that regular past forms exhibit.

In both of these examples we find that theoretical analysis supplies a principled basis for distinguishing the constant constraints from those that vary dialectally or generationally; some elements of linguistic structure are universal, and cannot vary between speakers, dialects or languages, while others are not universally specified, and hence are available for social differentiation.

This conclusion is supported by other studies of sociolinguistic variation, beyond phonology and beyond English. A case in point is Cameron's (1993) study of subject pronoun expression in Spanish. Spanish is a PRO-drop language – subject pronouns are optional. In the meaning 'I want', a Spanish speaker can say either *Yo quiero* or *Quiero* with the pronoun *Yo* 'I' expressed or omitted. Cameron reports a major dialect difference between Puerto Rico and Spain: Puerto Ricans use many more overt pronouns than their Spanish counterparts. He also identifies linguistic constraints on this process, including switch reference: speakers are more likely to use an overt

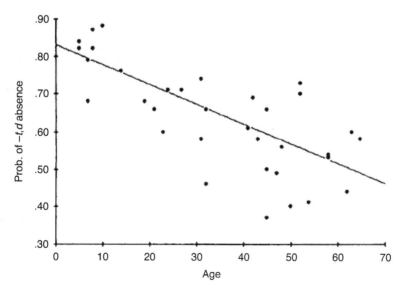

Figure 18.1   Probability of −*t,d* absence in irregular past-tense verbs, by age (from Guy and Boyd, 1990: 8.)

pronoun to mark a change in subject between the previous clause and the current clause. Most linguistic constraints are common across the two dialects, but one is treated differently: specificity of reference (the difference between references to specific individuals and generic references meaning 'somebody, one, people in general'). For the second-person singular (2sg) pronoun *tú*, this constraint is significant in both countries, but with opposite effect. Puerto Ricans use overt *tú* more often when making a generic reference, while Madrileños favour overt *tú* for specific reference (Table 18.3).

What does linguistic theory say about these constraints? The switch-reference effect has a clear functional motivation: the low information alternative (with no overt pronoun) serves as a gap onto which earlier references are projected. But the higher information form, with an overt pronoun, is used to signal a new subject. English uses contrastive stress in much the same way. In a sentence like 'Billy talked to Paul about it, and HE said ... ' the stressed 'HE' refers to Paul, as a new subject, whereas an unstressed alternative '... and he said ... ', would ordinarily indicate a continuation of the same subject, i.e., Billy. In each case, greater emphasis on the subject (via an overt pronoun or contrastive stress) signals a switched reference. This is a possible universal. But the specificity constraint has no such universal association with overt or zero pronouns. English, which only allows overt pronouns, uses the 2sg pronoun for both meanings. A sentence like 'You know what it means' can mean either specifically 'you (the hearer) know ... ', or generically 'one knows ... '. This suggests no intrinsic association of overt pronouns with either meaning; rather, such an association is arbitrary, and two Spanish dialects have made different selections for indicating genericity and specificity.

18.4 SOCIOLINGUISTIC CONTRIBUTIONS TO FORMAL THEORY

In formal linguistics one encounters many examples of principles that are originally proposed as categorical – unsurprising, given the categorical bias of linguistic theory. A case in point is the Obligatory Contour Principle (OCP), a generalization in phonology to the effect that languages prefer alternations (or 'contours') over repetition of identical elements. Thus the preferred structure for syllables and words involves alternating consonants and vowels, not strings of one or the other: CVCV over CCC or VVV. Similarly, tone languages prefer alternating tones, not strings of identical tones: HLHL, not HHH or LLL. Indeed, the OCP was first proposed by Leben (1973) to account for categorical tonal alternations in African tone languages.

A common finding of sociolinguistic research, and of other quantitative studies of language, however, is that essentially the same principles are observed in linguistic variation, but in a probabilistic, rather than categorical form. This discovery has been termed the 'stochastic generalization' (Bresnan et al., 2001; Clark, 2005): generalizations that may be categorically true in one language exist as quantitative constraints on variation in another language or social variety.

This is the result Guy and Boberg (1997) find for the OCP in their research on English CSD. The segment preceding a deletable final stop has a proven constraining effect on the likelihood of deletion; roughly speaking, obstruents promote deletion more than sonorants. Guy and Boberg accounted for this effect in terms of the similarity between the preceding context and the deletion target (the final coronal stop): greater similarity (measured in terms of shared distinctive features) favours deletion. The values appear in Table 18.4.

The results show that segments that share two of the defining features with [t, d] all promote deletion more than those that share only one feature, while preceding vowels, which are completely dissimilar, almost never trigger deletion. Note further that adjacent identical stops are categorically prohibited in English (*tt, *dd) – itself an OCP effect. Thus the results demonstrate a continuum: the phonology of English disfavours sequences of segments to the extent that those segments are similar; sequences of partially similar segments are partially suppressed by means of CSD, and sequences of completely similar

Table 18.3 Subject pronoun expression in Spanish: dialect differences in the effect of specificity of reference with second-person singular pronoun *tú*

	San Juan, Puerto Rico			Madrid, Spain		
	Per cent overt pronouns	Factor weight	n	Per cent overt pronouns	Factor weight	n
[+specific]	48%	.51	145	40%	.72	58
[–specific]	69%	.72	188	19%	.50	150

Source: Cameron (1993: 325)

Table 18.4   Preceding segment effect: an OCP analysis

Preceding segment		Deletion		
		N	Per cent	Factor weight
/t,d/	[+cor, −son, −cont]	−	(categorical absence, i.e. 1.00)	
/s,z,ʃ,ž/	[+cor, −son]	276	49	.69
/p,b,k,g/	[−son, −cont]	136	37	.69
/n/	[+cor, −cont]	337	46	.73
/f,v/	[−son]	45	29	.55
/l/	[+cor]	182	32	.45
/m,ŋ/	[−cont]	9	11	.33
vowels	−	−	(nearly categorical retention, i.e. 0.00)	

Source: Guy and Boberg (1997: 3 Philadelphians)

(i.e. identical) segments are completely suppressed, banned in underlying forms, and avoided in derived forms by epenthesis (thus, bisyllabic *raided* vs monosyllabic *rained*).

Results of this sort have two-fold implications. First, they confirm the theory; here they show that OCP is an active principle in English. But, secondly, they show the principle to have graded, probabilistic effects, not only categorical ones. In the Guy and Boberg data we see not an 'obligatory' principle, but rather a contour preference whose force is inversely proportionate to the slope of the contour: flat contours are prohibited, gentle slopes are disfavoured and steep slopes are promoted. This preference operates gradiently in sociolinguistic variation, not as a 'knockout' effect. Words with disfavoured consonant sequences like *act* are not categorically deleted in some social dialects or styles and retained in others; rather, they are variable in all dialects, but always show higher rates of deletion than those with more favourable contours, like *old*. The sociolinguistic findings thus test the formal model – the OCP – and in this case confirm it, but recast it as a stochastic generalization.

The OCP example shows a formal principle, conceived in the Neogrammarian tradition as discrete and invariant, being reformulated in the light of sociolinguistic evidence as a probabilistic generalization. What might the impact of sociolinguistic evidence be on larger elements of formal theory, such as an entire grammar? Formal linguistics since Chomsky attributes a speaker's capacity to use language to a mental grammar that codifies and encompasses linguistic knowledge. This is constructed by speakers in the course of language acquisition, based on input from the language they hear spoken around them (along with, presumably, some universal elements).

This model presupposes that the speaker is embedded in a social universe, with other speakers from whom the individual hears evidence needed for language acquisition, and with whom the individual communicates using his or her mental grammar. So an obvious question is, how similar or different are the mental grammars of individuals who speak what we informally call 'the same language'? Given the diversity that sociolinguistic research documents, even among members of the same speech community, what elements of their mental grammars are diverse, allowing differentiation, and what are the same, allowing them to communicate in a language that they believe they share?

In the mainstream tradition the mental grammar is an apparatus with categorical, invariant properties. Hence even a small alteration to its internal structure, if it produces any difference in output, would count as a discretely different grammar. Linguistic diversity, therefore, would imply that speakers have grammars that differ in some component or set of components (features, rules, constraints, constraint rankings, etc.). Different speech styles would be handled the same way: to shift among different speech styles or registers, speakers would have to switch between discretely different grammars. By implication, styles and speakers would exhibit categorical differences: speaker A would use some form in some context that speaker B did not or could not use.

In the social world, it is clear that diversity is orderly: socially proximal individuals are linguistically proximal as well; family members speak more alike than those who are unrelated; people in the same community or dialect region are more alike than those who live farther away; and people of the same ethnicity, class or age group also tend to be more similar than those of other groups. What does this scale of sociolinguistic similarity correlate with in the mental grammar? Is the scale a gradient continuum, or is it composed of discrete steps, so speakers who are more dissimilar simply have a larger number of quantum differences in their grammars?

Sociolinguistic research suggests nuanced answers to such questions. We encounter both discrete and continuous differences between varieties, and we encounter different orders of quantitative diversity. First, much sociolinguistic variability is indeed continuous. One finding, by now classic, is that speech communities are replete with variables showing social stratification: higher-status speakers use more and lower-status speakers use less of a given variant and, simultaneously, all speakers use more of that variant in more careful styles. Labov's (1966) findings on the use of coda /r/ in New York City cogently illustrate this pattern.

The data in Figure 18.2 clearly suggest a continuum of usage; New Yorkers make finely graded quantitative adjustments in their individual production, and are collectively finely graded in /r/ usage by socioeconomic status. It is implausible to perceive in these data a series of discretely different grammars, each associated with a particular speaker in a particular speech style, each displaying some quantum difference from socially or stylistically adjacent grammars. Instead, it suggests a quantitative component of the mental linguistic capacity that controls the frequency of coda /r/ – in other words, a probability. Each speaker has a characteristic value for this probability, but they can adjust it continuously for stylistic purposes, to accommodate the social

demands of a situation, or for expressive value. Social proximity between individuals is reflected in their settings of this probability: one's experiences in language acquisition, daily interaction and accommodation, and attitudinal factors such as solidarity, all combine to make it likely that speakers who belong to common networks and who share social characteristics such as class, ethnicity, etc., will have common values for these probabilities. And what the speech community as a whole shares, including New Yorkers of different social classes and ethnicities, is a common social evaluation of the use of the /r/ variant: they all understand it is associated with higher-status speakers and more formal styles, and reflect this shared evaluation in their own usage.

However, beyond these scalar patterns of variation associated with style, class, age, etc., we also encounter discrete differences. The data presented above in Tables 18.2 and 18.3 demonstrate this, showing discrete differences between speech communities. Notice, however, that those examples involved the effects of context on linguistic variation: the effect of a following pause on English CSD, and the effect of specificity of reference on pronoun expression in Spanish. Notice further that

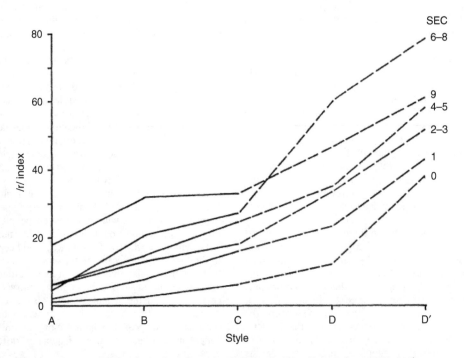

Figure 18.2   Class stratification of coda /r/ in New York City. (from Labov, 1972: 114). Socioeconomic class (SEC) scale: 0–1, lower class; 2–5, working class; 6–8, lower middle class; 9, upper middle class. Style scale: A, casual speech: B, careful speech: C, reading style: D, word lists: D', minimal pairs. Reprinted with permission.

these discrete differences lay between different speech communities – Philadelphia vs New York, San Juan vs Madrid – whereas the continuously varying data of Figure 18.2 come from speakers in the same community, in fact the same neighbourhood (the Lower East Side of New York).

This suggests a basic distinction between two dimensions of quantitative variability. We distinguish overall rates of use of a variant (a context-free statement of the alternation) from differential rates of use by linguistic context (context-sensitivity). Quantitative variation in the overall rate of use of social variables, differentiating classes, speech styles, etc., is in principle continuous, and speakers within a given community are accustomed to, and accomplished at, varying freely in this dimension. But the contextual effects, although they may also be probabilistic, do not vary freely within the grammar of an individual, or within a community. Thus there is no social class of speakers in Philadelphia, for example, for whom pause is a more favourable context for deletion, and no speech style in which Philadelphians use pause as a favourable context. Hence we advance a hypothesis: the rankings, and quite possibly the specific probabilities, associated with constraints on linguistic processes are a fixed feature of the grammar of a speaker, and are one of the shared linguistic characteristics common to all members of a speech community.

This distinction is given formal representation in the 'variable rule' model (Labov, 1969; Cedergren and Sankoff, 1974; Sankoff, 1978). This model associates an 'input' probability (p_0) with every option or rule in the grammar; in addition, context-sensitive processes may have probabilistic weights associated with relevant contexts (contexts i, j, k, etc., are associated with weights p_i, p_j, p_k). In this model, the value of p_0 is what varies within a community, whether stylistically or socially, while the values of specific constraints p_i, p_j, p_k are fixed. This is an original contribution of sociolinguistic research to the theory of grammars, specifically to the question of grammatical similarity and difference.

18.5 TOWARDS AN ADEQUATE FORMAL LINGUISTICS

What does an adequate theory of language need – one that accounts for speakers' capacity to produce and deal with diversity? The first requirement is that it must accommodate variation. The Neogrammarian-inspired model of exceptionless linguistic processes has been mistaken in much of formal linguistics for a design principle of language; in fact it is a hypothesis, which has been tested against reality and found wanting. Language is neither Platonic nor digital; it is a neurological, physiological and social system, an analog device that doesn't always do the same thing in exactly the same way. An adequate formal theory must recognize inherent variability, and generate it.

Secondly, the sociolinguistic evidence suggests that an adequate model must incorporate quantification. This point is still the subject of some debate, as some scholars propose to leave the grammar unquantified and derive quantitative regularities observed in language use by other means, as an epiphenomenal consequence of the range of possibilities (cf. Anttila's OT analyses of variation – see below), or by some mechanism external to the grammar proper that selects among different grammars. We shall argue, however, that these alternatives are not adequate to account for the full range of quantitatively orderly heterogeneity.

Thirdly, an adequate model must accommodate social information. Linguistic representations must be capable of modeling the capacity of speakers to speak in socially adaptive ways, and to perceive the social significance of the usage of others. Since individuals smoothly vary their usage both expressively and responsively, thereby communicating social meanings and adapting to social expectations, an adequate formal model of this capacity must incorporate a social semantics not only of words but also of linguistic forms and processes. The formal account must also be capable of representing diversity at the community level, differences in the usage of others that speech community members can passively recognize the social significance of, even if their own grammars do not productively generate them.

The sociolinguistic adequacy of a formal model can therefore be evaluated on the basis of these three criteria: accounting for variation, quantification and social information. Let us consider some formal models that have been proposed to address sociolinguistic issues, and how they fare by these criteria.

The first issue, of modelling variation, has been widely addressed, by a variety of formal approaches. The variable rule (VR) model, mentioned above, uses a generative framework in which probabilities are attached to operations; conventional obligatory processes have a probability of 1, but probabilities of less than 1 indicate variable outcomes. This is the model most widely used in sociolinguistic research on variation. In OT, several proposals have been made to generate variability using variable or underspecified constraint rankings (Anttila, 1997, 2002; Nagy and Reynolds, 1997): instead of a fixed constraint hierarchy that always gives the same outcome, speakers are hypothesized to vary among several rankings of the relevant constraints which select different variants. In treatments of historical change, diachronic variability has been modelled by means of alternation between grammars that generate old and new variants (Kroch, 1989b, 2000; Yang, 2000). All of these models are adequate for generating variable outcomes.

Greater differences between approaches are found when we consider the second criterion, quantification: How should a formal model account for the probabilistic patterns of natural language? Do they result from one grammar or from alternation between grammars? Should they be generated directly, by quantification within the linguistic system, or derivatively, as a secondary consequence of the way a grammar operates to generate a range of options, or the diversity of representations or inputs?

The quantificational strategy that involves the smallest departure from the theoretical tradition of invariance is grammar competition. In this approach, traditional invariant grammar is preserved, and variation and change are taken as evidence that speakers command multiple grammars, each one discretely generating one observed variant. These alternative grammars are selected with different probabilities to produce the quantitative patterns that are found in language use. This approach is exemplified in work on diachronic change by Kroch (1989b), Yang (2000) and others. Kroch (1989a), for example, takes this approach to model the development of periphrastic *do* in English. In early Middle English (ME), before AD 1300, negative constructions inserted *not* after a verb or auxiliary (e.g., *They know not what they do*), and questions were formed by inverting subject and verb (e.g. *Slept you well?*). In late ME and early Modern English, modern equivalents with auxiliary *do* began to appear (*They don't know what they're doing*; *Did you sleep well?*); for the next 400 years, usage varied between the two forms, with the modern constructions steadily increasing in frequency.

Kroch accounts for these facts in terms of a parametric shift. The grammar of early ME permitted the main verb to raise to an auxiliary position (or an INFL, a functional head containing auxiliaries and/or tense or agreement features), so that it could do whatever auxiliary verbs do (in Modern English other auxiliaries also occur before *not* and invert with subjects to form questions: e.g. *They must not know*; *Have you slept well?*). But in late ME an alternative grammar emerged that did not permit verb-to-INFL raising, so that when the auxiliary position was separated from the verb by another element, such as an inverted subject or a negative, *do* was inserted as an empty auxiliary to carry tense and agreement. In Kroch's analysis, during the four or five centuries when this variation was evident, speakers entertained two mental

grammars, one with and one without V-to-INFL raising, and their variation consisted of choosing one grammar or the other for each relevant sentence they uttered. What changed across time was the probability of speakers selecting one or the other grammar, while within each grammar, there was no variation.

While providing an elegant treatment of historical change, this strategy does not offer a general quantitative model for sociolinguistic variation. First, it does not, strictly speaking, solve the problem of variation; rather, it relocates it from inside the grammar to outside. To account for the quantitative facts of orderly heterogeneity – all the subtle probabilistic variation evident in sociolinguistic usage – this approach requires an additional theory of grammar selection. Secondly, it runs afoul of Occam's razor – the elementary scientific principle of economy, that proliferation of explanatory elements should be avoided. For the English *do* case, Kroch requires two grammars that are identical in every respect except for the V-to-INFL parameter setting. But at any given moment, languages typically have not one but many variables – thus ME also has variable deletion of *that* complementizers (*I thought THAT he knew* vs *I thought he knew*), among other variables. If each alternant of each variable requires a separate grammar, and these variables intersect, so that a speaker may in one utterance use periphrastic *do* and complementizer deletion and, in the next, periphrastic *do* but complementizer retention, and so on, then a language with n binary variables would require speakers to maintain 2^n mental grammars, each trivially different from the next. Besides constituting a massive violation of Occam's razor, this would rapidly exhaust the storage capacity of the brain, if the language had as few as a score of variables.

The alternative to grammar competition is to step off the Neogrammarian path and locate variation inside the grammar. But there are still competing strategies on how to formalize this so as to achieve quantitative adequacy. The VR model uses explicit quantification; in principle, it permits the probabilistic quantification of all grammatical operations and contextual conditions. This allows it to achieve excellent accuracy in accounting for the quantitative patterns observed in sociolinguistic variation. However, some scholars have argued that incorporating a probabilistic component in the grammar gives an overly powerful formal model, capable of generating patterns that do not occur. A notable alternative is found in versions of OT using variably ordered constraints (VOC), which treat quantitative patterns as, in a sense, epiphenomena – statistical reflections of the range of possibilities permitted by grammatical options, rather than the product of a specific probabilistic element. This approach is exemplified by Anttila's treatment of phonological variables in several languages (Anttila, 1997; Anttila et al., 2008).

As a simplified example, consider a VOC treatment of English CSD. Suppose there were only three relevant constraints: one disfavouring syllabic codas (NoCoda), one disfavouring complex codas (*CxCoda), and one favouring the faithful articulation of underlying consonants (FAITH). If the ranking of these constraints was unspecified in the grammar, and randomly varied whenever speakers articulated a relevant word, they could occur in any of six possible orders (NoCoda highest, followed by the other two in either order; *CxCoda highest, followed by either order of the other two, and FAITH highest, with either order of the other two). Following standard OT conventions, we assume the grammar selects outputs consistent with (i.e. incurring the fewest violations of) the highest ranked constraints. Therefore, when FAITH is highest-ranked, words like *act, mist* are pronounced with final /t/, but when either of the other constraints outrank FAITH, a pronunciation with a deleted /t/ results, because NoCoda and *CxCoda are both violated by candidates preserving the final stop. Since two of the six possible orders generate retention of /t/, and the other four generate deletion, this model predicts deletion should occur in two-thirds of occurrences.

Using the VOC strategy, Anttila has achieved impressively accurate quantitative models of several cases of linguistic variation. He also argues that VOC explains dialect patterning – why certain combinations of variants are dialectally attested, while other patterns we might imagine, but which are not generated by any possible order of constraints, do not occur. These results present a serious challenge to other formal models addressing these questions. However, the approach is inadequate as a general model of sociolinguistic variation. As we have noted, quantitative variation has two aspects: differences in overall rates, which vary between speakers and across speech styles, and differences in constraint rankings and contextual effects. VOC can model the latter, but lacks any formal treatment of the former. The only way predicted probabilities can differ in VOC, among styles, speakers or dialects, is by varying the number of constraints that are variably ranked. In the simplified example above, three constraints have 3! = 6 possible rankings; if four constraints were involved, they would have 4!, or 24 possible rankings. So adding more constraints to the set that are variably ranked gives more possible rankings, and therefore different possible proportions among the selected variants, but it also means the variation will now occur or fail to occur at different rates in whatever contexts are affected by the constraints that have been added to the mix.

To illustrate this point, we can extend the previous example. Suppose, in another speech style, or a different group of speakers, a fourth constraint is added to the variably ranked group, an OCP constraint prohibiting sequences of overly-similar consonants, ruling out cases like *act, mist*, but permitting *left, old*. When this constraint outranks FAITH, deletion is selected in words like *act*. Hence when OCP is variably ranked with respect to the other three, undeleted forms of *act* are selected only one-quarter of the time (the possible orders in which FAITH is highest ranked), rather than one-third, raising the expected deletion rate from 67 per cent to 75 per cent. But this constraint has no effect on deletion of words like *old*, which will continue to show deletion in 67 per cent of all cases. Hence the consequence of involving an additional variably-ranked constraint is to introduce a new difference between contexts, not to change deletion rates across the board. As we have noted, this is not how sociolinguistic variation actually works; styles and social groups in the same speech community differ in overall rates of use of variables, not in contextual constraints.

Finally, consider the third criterion, the formal modelling of social information. The above example shows the difficulties OT encounters in this respect; it could incorporate social information by associating styles or social indexicality with certain constraint rankings, but this incorrectly predicts regular differences between speakers or styles in contextual constraints on variables. VR models treat social information as probabilistic constraints on production; thus stylistic constraints fit into the model in the same way as linguistic constraints. In speech community studies using VR, it is routine practice to treat social groups in the same way; so age or gender groups, for example, are treated as if they were contexts for usage associated with probabilities that increase or decrease the use of a variable. However, this practice has a hazy theoretical status. It may more or less accurately model the collective behaviour of a community, but it is not clear what it means for the grammar or usage of an individual.

An important lacuna in all of these theoretical approaches to sociolinguistic variation is that, since they focus on variable production, they have little to say about the perception and mental representation of diversity, so that speakers' passive knowledge of the social significance of the usage of others is not explicitly accounted for. It is a central argument of sociolinguistics that speakers understand the social significance of the linguistic behaviour of other members of their speech communities, even when these others are doing things with their language that the speaker does not personally do. This understanding is reflected in shared evaluations of variables, and it influences production in such ways as the shared directions of style shifting. But how is this knowledge represented in the mind? Should it have formal representation in the mental grammar? To conclude our consideration of formal models, we turn now to a theory that puts such representations at the centre of linguistic structure.

18.6　NEW DIRECTIONS: USAGE-BASED GRAMMAR

An important theoretical development that explicitly seeks to offer a formal account of usage, variation and change, and to provide a model of speakers' knowledge that incorporates social and stylistic information, is the emergence of usage-based approaches to grammar, notably Exemplar Theory (Bybee, 2001; Pierrehumbert, 2001). This theory is a radical departure from mainstream formal linguistics; it embraces variability and rejects categorical, exceptionless processes. Indeed, it denies the existence of general abstract processes, along with abstract representations of words and segments. Instead, Exemplar Theory (ET) begins by postulating that speakers remember, in rich phonetic detail, the tokens of words they hear pronounced, or produce themselves. Therefore, speakers have stored in memory the full range of variation they have encountered, and use these memories (the 'exemplar cloud') as targets for their own productions, which necessarily also vary. Words are not decomposed into strings of phonemes, but remembered holistically; hence each word can behave distinctly, showing idiosyncratic patterns of variation and change that diverge from other words containing the same phonemes. The substance of other approaches to phonology, such as segments, morphemes and phonological processes, are, in ET, all secondary generalizations and analogic operations, rather than primary components of representation and grammar.

Exemplar theory thus incorporates a comprehensive rejection of Neogrammarian exceptionlessness, phonemic representation, categorical and invariant grammar, and the *langue/parole* and competence/performance distinctions. It puts variation and diversity at the centre of the theory. It is inherently quantified: frequencies, proportions and contextual effects can be deduced from the distribution of variants in the exemplar cloud. But perhaps its clearest advantage for sociolinguistics is that, with modest elaboration, it can be extended to incorporate a formal representation of speakers' knowledge of the social significance of linguistic variables, including their passive knowledge of the use of others. Thus Foulkes and Docherty (2006) suggest that the memories of exemplars

also incorporate memories of who uttered them and what the social circumstances of usage were. In this way, a speaker can deduce from memory what variants are more often associated with what social context or identity. This allows them to interpret the usage of others, and to adapt their own usage accordingly. An indexical association between linguistic characteristic and social characteristic emerges statistically from the distribution of exemplars in the cloud.

Such a model addresses all the shortcomings of conventional formalisms, providing a framework for explicitly modelling inherent variability, orderly heterogeneity and social embedding. This is an attractive framework for sociolinguistics. But there are open questions about the theory concerning its capacity to explain the things that the theoretical mainstream was designed for and does well, such as categorical processes and abstract operations. Many linguistic generalizations are indeed categorical: articles precede nouns in English, without exception; many sound changes show Neogrammarian regularity: Germanic languages have no residual voiced aspirates (/bh, dh, gh/) left over from Proto-Indo-European in lexically-diffused defiance of Grimm's Law. Speakers use language in ways that go beyond the evidence, for which they have no exemplars.

For example, how does a child language learner do something new, which he or she has not encountered in the input? Consider the case of Jesse, an American-English (AmEng)-speaking child, observed by the author, who was moved to Australia at the age of 1 year, 11 months. After two months of exposure to Australian English, he abruptly reformulated his pronunciation of posttonic intervocalic obstruents: he made them all voiceless. The only exemplars in his Australian English (AusEng) input relevant to this change were AusEng pronunciations of [t] in words like *water, little*, which contrasted with the voiced flap in his native AmEng phonology. But rather than changing just the words for which he had such exemplars, Jesse repronounced his entire vocabulary, affecting other medial flaps, other voiced stops and even voiced fricatives: thus daddy>datty, table>tapu, doggy>dockie, fuzzy>fussy. During this period he acquired, from his AmEng-speaking parents, the words *driver* and *driving*, and duly pronounced them *drifer* and *drifing*. Aside from the intervocalic /t/ cases, he had no exemplars whatsoever for any of these new pronunciations; in fact, the input from American parents, Australian peers and childcare workers offered massive counter-examples. Jesse's behaviour suggests not a probabilistic exemplar-driven adjustment to his lexicon, but rather, an abstract reanalysis, a generalization of the form [+obs] → [-voice]/´V___V.

ET addresses such issues by recognizing processes of generalization and analogy, but these are vaguely defined and formalized. It is not clear how the generalizations across exemplars and experience that ET permits are substantively distinct from the abstract grammar it rejects. Notably, recent work in this framework takes steps to address such issues by formally recognizing abstract operations (cf. Pierrehumbert, 2006).

There are also empirical challenges to certain predictions of ET. For example, it is a central claim of the model that production is strongly influenced by such statistical properties of the input as lexical frequency. This hypothesis is in the process of being empirically tested, with mixed results to date – some studies confirm significant frequency effects on variation, while others are more equivocal. Guy et al. (2008), for example, found a frequency effect on CSD in early New Zealand English – final coronal stops in words that are more common in everyday usage were more likely to be deleted, but this result depended on using frequency counts from the corpus under study. Standard frequency counts from a large corpus of contemporary English (the CELEX corpus) did not have a significant effect.

18.7 CONCLUSION

For over a century the dominant formal theories in linguistics have paid little attention to the findings or concerns of sociolinguistics, because they treated the USE of language as fundamentally different from, and not particularly relevant to, the mental linguistic capacity of human speakers, which was the declared concern of theoretical linguistics. In place of natural language, they studied an idealization. But the limits of this strategy are now becoming clear: the idealization cannot explain the real world. If anything unifies the field of sociolinguistics, it is a shared concern with the real world, in the form of language in use. By conjoining the findings and interests of sociolinguistics with the best products of formal linguistic thinking, we can illuminate a path towards a genuine science of language.

REFERENCES

Anttila, A. (1997) 'Deriving variation from grammar', in F. Hinskens, R. van Hout and L. Wetzels (eds), *Variation, Change and Phonological Theory*. Amsterdam: John Benjamins. pp. 35–68.

Anttila, A. (2002) 'Morphologically conditioned phonological alternations', *Natural Language and Linguistic Theory*, 20: 1–42.

Anttila, A., Fong, V., Benus, S. and Nycz, J. (2008) 'Variation and opacity in Singapore English consonant clusters', *Phonology*, 25: 81–216.

Bailey, C.-J. N. (1973) *Variation and Linguistic Theory*. Arlington, VA: Center for Applied Linguistics.

Bayley, R. (1994) 'Consonant cluster reduction in Tejano English', *Language Variation and Change*, 6(3): 303–26.

Bresnan, J., Dingare, S. and Manning, C. (2001) *'Soft Constraints Mirror Hard Constraints:* voice and person in English and Lummi', in M. Butt and T. H. King (eds), Proceedings of the LFG 01 Conference, University of Hong Kong, online proceedings. Stanford, CSLI Publications: http://csli-publications. stanford.edu.

Bybee, J. (2001) *Phonology and Language Use*. Cambridge: Cambridge University Press.

Callary, R. E. (1975) 'Phonological change and the development of an urban dialect in Illinois', *Language in Society*, 4(2): 155–69.

Cameron, R. (1993) 'Agreement, functional compensation, and nonspecific tu in the Spanish of San Juan, Puerto Rico, and Madrid, Spain', *Language Variation and Change*, 5(3): 305–34.

Cedergren, H. J. and Sankoff, D. (1974) 'Variable rules: performance as a statistical reflection of competence', *Language*, 50(2): 333–55.

Chomsky, N. (1964) *Current Issues in Linguistic Theory*. The Hague: Mouton.

Chomsky, N. (1965) *Aspects of the Theory of Syntax*. Cambridge, MA: MIT Press.

Clark, B. (2005) 'On stochastic grammar', *Language*, 81(1): 207–17.

Clements, G. N. and Keyser, S. J. (1983) *CV Phonology: a Generative Theory of the Syllable*. Cambridge, MA: MIT Press.

Foulkes, P. and Docherty, G. (2006) 'The social life of phonetics and phonology', *Journal of Phonetics*, 34: 409–38.

Guy, G. R. (1980) 'Variation in the group and the individual: the case of final stop deletion', in W. Labov (ed.), *Locating Language in Time and Space*. New York: Academic Press. pp. 251–65.

Guy, G. R. (1991) 'Explanation in variable phonology: an exponential model of morphological constraints', *Language Variation and Change*, 3(1): 1–22.

Guy, G. R. (1992) 'Contextual conditioning in variable lexical phonology', *Language Variation and Change*, 3(2): 223–39.

Guy, G. R. and Boberg, C. (1997) 'Inherent variability and the obligatory contour principle', *Language Variation and Change*, 9(2): 149–64.

Guy, G. R. and Boyd, Sally (1990) 'The development of a morphological class', *Language Variation and Change*, 2(1): 1–18.

Guy, G. R., Hay, J. and Walker, A. (2008) 'Phonological, lexical and frequency factors in coronal stop deletion in early New Zealand English', poster presented at Laboratory Phonology 11, Wellington, New Zealand.

Hymes, D. H. (1972) 'On communicative competence', in J. B. Pride and J. Holmes (eds), *Sociolinguistics*. Harmondsworth: Penguin.

Kiparsky, P. (1982a) *Explanation in Phonology*. Dordrecht: Foris.

Kiparsky, P. (1982b) 'Lexical phonology and morphology', in S. Yang (ed.), *Linguistics in the Morning Calm*. Seoul: Hanshin. pp. 3–91.

Kroch, A. (1989a) 'Function and grammar in the history of English: periphrastic "do"', in R. Fasold and D. Schiffrin (eds), *Language Change and Variation*. Amsterdam: Benjamins. pp. 133–72.

Kroch, A. (1989b) 'Reflexes of grammar in patterns of language change', *Language Variation and Change*, 1(3): 199–244.

Kroch, A. (2000) 'Syntactic change', in M. Baltin and C. Collins (eds), *The Handbook of Contemporary Syntactic Theory*. Malden, MA: Blackwell. pp. 629–739.

Labov, W. (1966) *The Social Stratification of English in New York City*. Washington, DC: Center for Applied Linguistics.

Labov, W. (1969) 'Contraction, deletion, and inherent variability of the English copula', *Language*, 4: 715–62.

Labov, W. (1972) *Sociolinguistic Patterns*. Philadelphia: University of Pennsylvania Press.

Labov, W. and Fanshel, D. (1977) *Therapeutic Discourse: Psychotherapy as Conversation*. New York: Academic Press.

Labov, W. and Waletzky, J. (1967) 'Narrative analysis', in J. Helm (ed.), *Essays on the Verbal and Visual Arts*. Seattle: University of Washington Press. pp. 12–44.

Leben, W. (1973) 'Suprasegmental phonology'. PhD dissertation, Massachusetts Institute of Technology.

Lim, L. T. and Guy, G. R. (2003) 'The limits of linguistic community: speech styles and variable constraint effects', *Penn Working Papers in Linguistics: Selected Papers from NWAVE 32*, 10(2): 157–70.

Myers-Scotton, C. (1993) *Social Motivation for Codeswitching: Evidence from Africa*. Oxford: Clarendon Press.

Nagy, N. and Reynolds, B. (1997) 'Optimality Theory and variable word-final deletion in Faetar', *Language Variation and Change*, 9(1): 37–55.

Nishimura, M. (1997) *Japanese–English Code-Switching: Syntax and Pragmatics*. New York: Peter Lang.

Paul, H. (1978 [1886]) 'On sound change', in P. Baldi and R. N. Werth (eds), *Readings in Historical Phonology: Chapters in the Theory of Sound Change*. Tr. by H. A. Strong from *Prinzipien der Sprachgeschichte*. University Park: the Pennsylvania State University Press. pp. 3–22.

Pierrehumbert, J. (2001) 'Exemplar dynamics: word frequency, lenition and contrast', in J. Bybee and P. Hopper (eds), *Frequency and the Emergence of Linguistic Structure*. Amsterdam: Benjamins. pp. 137–58.

Pierrehumbert, J. (2006) 'The next toolkit', *Journal of Phonetics*, 34(6): 516–30.

Poplack, S. (1980) 'Sometimes I'll start a sentence in Spanish y termino en español: toward a typology of code-switching', *Linguistics*, 18(7, 8): 581–618.

Sacks, H., Schegloff, E. A. and Jefferson, G. (1974) 'A simplest systematics for the organization of turn-taking for conversation', *Language*, 50: 696–735.

Sankoff, D. (1978) 'Probability and linguistic variation', *Synthese*, 37: 217–38.

Santa Ana, O. (1992) 'Chicano evidence for the exponential hypothesis: a variable rule pervades lexical phonology', *Language Variation and Change*, 4(3): 275–88.

Saussure, F. de (1916) *Cours de linguistique générale*. Published by C. Bally, E. Sechehaye, and A. Reidlinger. Paris, Geneva: Payot.

Verner, K. (1978 [1877]) 'An exception to Grimm's law', in P. Baldi and R. N. Werth (eds), *Readings in Historical Phonology: Chapters in the Theory of Sound Change*. Tr. by R. Stanley, from *Eine Aushnahme der ersten Lautverschiebung*. University Park: the Pennsylvania State University Press. pp. 3–22.

Weinreich, U., Labov, W. and Herzog, M. (1968) 'Empirical foundations for a theory of language change', in W. P. Lehmann and Y. Malkiel (eds), *Directions for Historical Linguistics*. Austin, TX: University of Texas Press. pp. 95–195.

Yang, C. (2000) 'Internal and external forces in language change', *Language Variation and Change*, 12(3), 231–50.

19

Attitudes, Ideology and Awareness

Tore Kristiansen

19.1 SOCIAL EVALUATION OF VARIATION IN A *CHANGE* PERSPECTIVE

Text genres that introduce or provide overviews of sociolinguistics as a discipline (historical accounts, introductory books, handbooks), normally group attitudes and ideology with the **applications** (language planning, politics, education, etc.), or with the types of topics (language contact, choice, multilingualism, etc.) that characterize the **sociology of language**. Against this backdrop, the present handbook's inclusion of a language attitudes chapter in its Part III (Language Variation and Change) is noteworthy.

Theories that aim to explain language change processes operate with a number of 'factors' that make up these processes. There is little disagreement about what to put in the total pool of factors, but views differ as to how the different factors interrelate and function. The fundamental question is which factor(s) we should conceive of as the **driving force**, and which ones we should consider as **conditions**. The factors may be differently grouped in theoretical frameworks but, in general, such different groupings do not reflect the theory's answer to the driving-force versus conditions question. If a theory operates with the common distinction between internal and external factors, **internal factors** will typically refer to possibilities and constraints in terms of fundamental speaker-/hearer-based processing capacities (articulation and perception) interacting with a concrete language system, while **external factors** will cover possibilities and constraints in terms of

the material and ideological aspects of social structure. The distinction itself does not imply any commitment as to where the driving force is to be found. The same can be said of William Labov's division of his monumental work on *Principles of Linguistic Change* into three volumes, subtitled *Internal Factors* (1994), *Social Factors* (2001), and *Cognitive Factors* (forthcoming).

However if, in this chapter, I operate with a distinction between **subjective** factors (social values and evaluations) and **objective** factors (all the others), then this is not only because it gives me a cover term for 'attitudes, ideology and awareness' but also mainly because it reflects the theoretical position I want to advocate – namely, that language change is driven by what I prefer to call 'subconscious attitudes'. This position is derived from our research in Denmark, which I shall return to at the end (Section 19.3). But the bulk of the chapter is a presentation and discussion of Labov's work – simply because this is where we find the most explicit attempt within variationism to theorize the role of subjective factors on the basis of **independent** empirical data (i.e. data other than language-use data).

19.2 THE THEORETICAL AND EMPIRICAL STATUS OF SUBJECTIVE FACTORS IN LABOVIAN VARIATIONISM

From the beginning of variationist sociolinguistics, as developed in the work of Labov, the social unit of research was **the speech community**. This entity was defined at the level of subjective, not objective, facts about language use (see also Mendoza-Denton, this volume).

(1)
The speech community is not defined by any marked agreement in the use of language elements, so much as by participation in a set of shared norms. ... In fact, it seems plausible to define a speech community as a group of speakers who share a set of social attitudes towards language (1972: 120ff., 248).

In their agenda-setting paper, 'Empirical foundations for a theory of language change', Weinreich, Labov and Herzog (1968) listed *evaluation* among the five problems that had to be solved by the theory: namely, the problems of transmission, embedding (linguistic and social), evaluation, actuation and constraints. The first three of these problems in particular had been addressed empirically in Labov's research during the first half of the 1960s on Martha's Vineyard (1963) and in New York City (1966), and were thoroughly discussed in his seminal book *Sociolinguistic Patterns* (1972). The evaluation problem was defined as follows:

(2)
The evaluation problem is to find the subjective (or latent) correlates of the objective (or manifest) changes which have been observed. The indirect approach to this problem correlates the general attitudes and aspirations of the informants with their linguistic behaviour. The more direct approach is to measure the unconscious subjective reactions of the informants to values of the linguistic variable itself (1972: 162).

This definition allows for three observations that relate to the issues we need to address: the independent-evidence issue (Section 19.2.1), the consciousness issue (Section 19.2.2) and the driving-force issue (Section 19.2.3).

19.2.1 The 'independent-evidence' issue

Labov's solution to the problem of defining the speech community was derived from the discovery that people differ far more in their use of language than in their evaluations of different uses. It goes without saying that the collection and analysis of independent subjective data were a prerequisite for that discovery. Also, though not explicitly formulated, it is clearly an implicit statement of Labov's definition of the evaluation problem that it cannot be solved on the basis of facts about language use ('the objective (or manifest)

changes'); its solution requires a search for independent evidence ('the subjective (or latent) correlates'). Such evidence has been obtained and analysed in all of Labov's projects. The data are obtained in sociolinguistic interviews or group conversations and may be of two types: discursive (Section 19.2.1.1), and experimental (Section 19.2.1.2).

The insistence on the need for independent evidence is important, in order to avoid circular argumentation on the driving-force issue. To the extent that the subjectivities involved in language variation and change are not studied using independent data, it is hard to see how, in a principled way, we can constrain our ingenuity in pointing out ideologies that would appear as 'good fits' and explanations for established patterns of use. An example would be the different explanations that have been offered for the well-documented finding that women generally speak more 'correctly' than men.

19.2.1.1 Discursive data
The discursive data consist of responses to, or comments about, questions that in one way or another relate to language. Such questions and responses may address the issue of language-related values and evaluations either directly (i), or indirectly (ii).

(i) Evaluative responses with direct language-related relevance   When language-related questions are posed directly, informants' answers or comments will typically draw on well-known public discourses and appear very much the same, in one and the same speech community. Labov repeatedly refers to 'the fundamental sociolinguistic question posed to me in 1967 by a woman from New York: '"Why do I say [waɪ] when I don't *want* to?"' (2001: 215 (italics in original); see also 1972: 308). He found that 'New Yorkers show a general hostility towards New York City speech which emerges in countless ways. The term "linguistic self-hatred" is not too extreme to apply to the situation which emerges from the interviews' (1966: 344). Thus, analyses of 'what they say' may shed light on the significance of social values and evaluation for language use.

(ii) Evaluative responses with indirect language-related relevance   Answers to questions about something other than language may allow researchers to characterize and group informants according to attitudes and values that can be assumed to be language-related in an indirect way. For instance, freely expressed statements about life on Martha's Vineyard were used by Labov to

group the informants into three categories according to whether their expressed feelings were positive, neutral or negative towards the island. Patterns emerging from such data and analyses may be of relevance for the study of language-related values and their role in language variation and change.

19.2.1.2 Experimental data

A second type of evaluative interview data results from elicitations that are more or less experimental in character. These evaluations may be divided according to whether they concern the informants' own language (i), or the language of others (ii). In both respects, a further distinction is possible according to whether the evaluations concern specific variants (most often variant pronunciations of words), or whole varieties (languages or dialects). As it is the specific-variant approach that characterizes Labov's work, I focus on that approach here (and return to the 'holistic' approach in Section 19.3).

(i) Evaluations of own language As developed in the classic variationist projects in New York (Labov, 1966) and Norwich (Trudgill, 1974), *self-evaluation tests* (also referred to as *self-report tests*) aim to tap into informants' representations (perceptions and evaluations) of their own speech and are designed to 'measure' these representations in terms of some sort of comparison, with the possibility of detecting interesting 'discrepancies' in the way informants relate to variant pronunciations of words.

In one design, the task of the informants is to select which one of two variant pronunciations of a word they think is correct, and then indicate which variant they usually use themselves (e.g. 'aunt' pronounced as either [aːnt] or [æːnt]; see Labov, 1966: Appendix A, 1972: 117). If what an informant claims to be 'correct' and their self-reported forms are not the same, the discrepancy can be made the object of interpretation; it might for instance be thought to signal a lack of confidence that one's own language is 'good enough'. Data from a series of such choices (18 in all) allowed Labov to assign scores to his New York informants on an *index of linguistic insecurity*, and thus to characterize and compare individuals and social groups in terms of linguistic insecurity. One might argue that the discrepancy indicates a lack of confidence in one's own language, resulting from the general ideological 'climate' which monitors the uses of language in the community.

(ii) Evaluations of language spoken by others
Around 1960, the Canadian social psychologist

Wallace Lambert and his colleagues developed an experimental technique, known as the *matched guise technique*, which was designed to elicit language attitudes at the level of varieties, e.g. English and French in Quebec (Lambert et al., 1960; Lambert, 1967). The idea of the approach was to collect evaluations controlling for the effects of voice quality and linguistic content. The basic procedure is to tape-record one and the same bilingual, or bidialectal, person reading the same text in the two (or more) varieties under study, and then have listeners assess the readings (the 'matched guises'). In order to prevent listener-judges from realizing that the same person appears twice (or several times), the guises are separated on the tape by filler voices. Assessments are made on some kind of evaluative scale(s).

In Labov's projects (1966: Ch.11, 2001: Section 6.3), the so-called *subjective reaction test* uses the matched guise technique in an adaptation which aims to elicit evaluations at the level of linguistic variants. The stimulus speakers appear several times on the tape, in random order, each time reading a sentence which concentrates examples of one of the variables investigated. In addition, each speaker reads a 'zero sentence' with no variables of interest. The judges' evaluations of readings with a high concentration of examples of the variables investigated may then be analysed as either upgrading or downgrading the speaker in comparison with evaluation of the zero sentence. Evaluations have been made on scales of 'job suitability' and 'friendliness' – which may be said to represent a more fundamental value distinction, treated by social psychologists in terms of **competence** versus **sociability**, or **status** versus **solidarity** (Ryan, Giles and Sebastian, 1982: 8). The possible relevance of such value distinctions for the theory of language change – and the role of subjective factors in change processes – seems quite obvious. Labov estimates that '[t]he most fruitful experimental measures of subjective reactions to linguistic variation have been through *matched guise* tests … ' (2001: 194 (italics in original)).

19.2.2 The consciousness issue

Why does the matched guise technique produce the more fruitful data? The quote above continues by qualifying the matched guise tests as tests '…which tap subjects' unconscious attitudes towards languages and dialects'. The important word here appears to be the word *unconscious*.

We recall that Labov's definition of the evaluation problem operates with two methodological approaches to its solution (see quote (2), above).

The 'indirect approach' involves gathering data that shed light on 'general attitudes and aspirations'. The reference here, to judge from Labov's empirical research as outlined above, is to data from discourse and self-reporting. The more 'direct approach' involves gathering of 'unconscious subjective reactions', and is instantiated by matched guise testing.

In brief, the 'subjective correlates' may be either conscious or unconscious. And so we may reformulate our question: Why is it that **unconscious** attitudes are the more useful data? We cannot answer that question without considering the place and role of **consciousness** within Labov's theoretical framework in general (19.2.2.1). Having done that, we shall return to considering in what sense Labov's use of the matched guise technique taps into unconscious attitudes (19.2.2.2).

19.2.2.1 The ubiquity of un-/consciousness in Labov's framework

In fact, the notion of consciousness is of crucial importance not only when the search is on for 'subjective correlates'. This holds true for Labov's entire approach to the study of language variation and change. To start with, the consciousness dimension is (described and understood as) crucial to the phenomenon of linguistic change as such – changes are classified according to whether they come from **above** or **below** consciousness (i). Furthermore, reference to the consciousness dimension constitutes the fundamental basis for the classification of linguistic variables into *stereotypes*, *markers*, and *indicators* (ii), for the style analyses in terms of **careful** versus **casual** speech (iii), and, more implicitly, for the discussion of language ideology in terms of **overt** versus **covert** norms and values (iv).

(i) Change from above and change from below It is commonplace in sociolinguistics to link the distinction between change from above and change from below to the dimension of consciousness. For instance, *A Dictionary of Sociolinguistics* (Swann, Deumert, Lillis and Mesthrie, 2004: 35ff.) explicates the notions as follows:

(3)
change from above ... linguistic changes of which speakers are consciously aware (the linguistic forms involved in the change are said to be 'above' the level of social awareness)

change from below Linguistic changes of which speakers are not consciously aware (the linguistic forms involved are said to be 'below' the level of social awareness).

The focus on consciousness reflects similar explications in Labov's own writings, e.g. 'change from below, that is, below the level of social awareness' (1972: 178; 2001: 279). Recently, Labov again noted, regarding the above/below distinction, that '[t]his terminology does not imply higher or lower on the socioeconomic scale' (2007: 346 (footnote 2)), even though elsewhere we can also read that '"Above" and "below" refer here simultaneously to levels of social awareness and positions in the socioeconomic hierarchy' (Labov, 1994: 78).

One-half of the claimed parallelism between social awareness and the socioeconomic hierarchy is easy to grasp and accept, in so far as '*Changes from above* are introduced by the dominant social class, often with full public awareness. Normally, they represent borrowings from other speech communities that have higher prestige in the view of the dominant class' (ibid.: 78 (italics in original)). The other half of the claimed parallelism is harder to follow, partly because '[c]hanges from below may be introduced by any social class' (1994: 78), but mainly because the claims about (the absence of) consciousness in changes from below seem more problematic. I shall return to this problem in connection with the driving-force issue (Section 19.2.3), but first we need to touch on the importance of un-/consciousness to other fundamental distinctions in the Labovian framework.

(ii) Stereotypes, markers and indicators Three types of linguistic variables are differentiated, essentially in terms of social awareness, additionally in terms of patterns of use.

(4)
Some variables are the overt topics of social comment and show both correction and hypercorrection (*stereotypes*); others are not at the same high level of social awareness, but show consistent stylistic and social stratification (*markers*); still others are never commented on or even recognized by native speakers, but are differentiated only in their relative degrees of advancement among the initiating social groups (*indicators*) (Labov, 1994: 78 (italics in original)).

A change from below appears in the vernacular. At first, there is no social awareness of the variation, and the use of the variable by community members produces a systematic pattern only in terms of social group membership; the variants used are *indicators* of social affiliation. As the social awareness surrounding the variable rises, the variants become *markers* of social affiliation, and the pattern of use no longer shows only systematic social-group-related variation but also systematic stylistic (i.e. social-context-related) variation. Whether the change comes from above or below, the variation may become the object of high-level social awareness and strong evaluations, mostly in terms of negative comments concerning one of the variants; the variable has become a *stereotype*, and its use shows correctional behaviour of a more irregular kind (see e.g. Labov, 2001: 196).

(iii) Careful and casual speech
As raised social awareness is accompanied by style shifting, we are not surprised to learn that Labov's analysis of stylistic variation is founded on the notion of *attention*, i.e. a notion with clear links to *consciousness* and *awareness*.

(5)
There are a great many styles and stylistic dimensions that can be isolated by an analyst. But we find that *styles can be ranged along a single dimension, measured by the amount of attention paid to speech* (1972: 208 (italics in original)).

[Subjective reaction tests] must be considered as sensitive measures of the place of a given variable on a scale of social awareness. As a rule, social awareness of a given variable corresponds to the slope of style shifting (2001: 196).

In terms of social embedding, stylistic variation is analysed along a single contextual dimension. The speech situation is manipulated in the sociolinguistic interview and is characterized as more or less formal. The basic idea is that a more formal context triggers more attention to speech, which in turn triggers more careful speech. Inversely, a less formal context triggers less attention to speech, which in turn triggers less careful, more casual, speech. This conception of stylistic variation has been much criticized, but what we need to notice is again the decisive importance accorded to unconsciously produced (unmonitored) speech. '[T]he vernacular [is] the style in which the minimum attention is given to the monitoring of speech' (Labov, 1972: 208). Monitoring yields irregular patterns of use (cf. stereotypes above), whereas the less monitored – casual, vernacular – styles yield 'more systematic speech, where the fundamental relations which determine the course of linguistic evolution can be seen most clearly' (1972: 208).

(iv) Overt and covert values
Any study of 'attitudes' and 'ideology' needs to start by somehow explicating these entities in terms of social meanings, norms or values. Ever since the New York study, Labov's basic distinction in the realm of language ideology has been between *overt* and *covert* social values. This distinction, however, has never been based, like the speech-related distinctions in (ii) and (iii) above, on explicit reference to awareness or attention.

The connection between the dimensions of social values (in terms of overt vs covert) and consciousness (in terms of above vs below, or conscious vs unconscious) is clear so far as the 'overt–conscious' connection is concerned. 'The process [of 'overt social pressures applied from above' (TK)] is out in the open for us to observe, in public performances, in the attitudes of teachers in the schools, and in the conscious reactions of some middle class persons' (Labov, 1966: 224). In contrast, the 'covert–unconscious' connection is harder to establish with reference to explicit claims in Labov's writings. Consider, however, the following statements:

(6)
For change from below, there is no important distinction between stigmatized and prestige forms: the speech form assumed by each group may be taken as an unconscious mark of self-identification (1966: 225ff.).

(7)
There are surely other values [than the overt values (TK)], at a deeper level of consciousness, which reinforce the vernacular speech forms of New York City ... recent studies of the black English vernacular in New York City have demonstrated the existence of such covert norms... (1972: 177).

By contrast with change from above, which we know to be accompanied by overt, conscious, social valuations (stigma or prestige), change from below is said, in (6), to be accompanied by social valuations to do with group- and self-identification – which are **unconscious**. I take it that an alleged unconscious act of social identification will have to be classified, in terms of the overt–covert distinction, as a manifestation of **covert** values. If so, establishment of a 'covert–unconscious' connection appears the natural inference from quote (6). Quote (7), on the other hand, links **covert** norms or values, not to the unconscious, but to a **deeper level of consciousness**.

To judge from Labov's work in general, no important theoretical distinction is implied by glosses like 'a deeper level of consciousness' on the one hand, and 'unconscious' or 'below consciousness' on the other. For me, this is an important issue, which I shall return to. Here I just want to suggest that the parallelisms in the theoretical framework favour an understanding which connects 'covert' with 'unconscious' – the point being that Labov's claims about the absence of consciousness in social valuations (no matter how 'covert' they might be) are akin to his claims about the absence of consciousness in changes from below, and just as problematic.

19.2.2.2 Consciousness, values and the matched guise technique

We set out in Section 19.2.2 to shed light on the claim that 'unconscious attitudes', obtained by using the matched guise technique, are more valuable as data for students of language change than are conscious attitudes. We have seen (in Section 19.2.2.1) that the notion of consciousness (awareness, attention) is of paramount importance to Labov's understanding and analysis of how language in use varies and changes and, furthermore, that the interesting (systematic) facts of change take place 'below consciousness', when minimal or no awareness is involved in the use of language. In brief, the priorities of the Labovian framework lie with unconscious linguistic variation and change. We can conclude that the conception of unconscious attitudes as the more valuable data type in the evaluative dimension appears natural, even mandatory, within the framework as a whole.

However, the notion of *unconscious attitudes*, as used by Labov, needs further clarification. We have argued above (in Section 19.2.2.1) that the parallelisms between the analytical dimensions (consciousness, class, context and values) invite us to infer that *covert values* are 'below consciousness'. It seems then that what Labov's matched guise tests are said to be doing, as they tap into 'unconscious attitudes', is to uncover 'covert values', the social motivations from below. Accordingly, sociolinguists tend to discuss the aim and potentiality of matched guise testing in terms of attitudes that are 'covert' (e.g. Fasold, 1984: 164) or 'private' (e.g. Garrett, Coupland and Williams, 2003: 57). There is nothing surprising in this when seen against the parallelisms in Labov's theoretical framework.

Nevertheless, there are good reasons to believe that we would be mistaken if we take *unconscious attitudes*, as obtained in Labov's matched guise tests, to mean 'covert values'. The main reason, of course, is that the test's measuring instruments – the *job suitability* and *friendship* scales – are simply Labov's operationalization of the distinction between overt and covert values. Hence, the 'unconscious attitudes' obtained in the New York project, where only a *job suitability* scale was included in the test, were never meant (nor considered) to be reflections of covert values (1966: 284; 1972: 177). In Philadelphia, the *friendship* scale was added in the hope of producing evidence for covert subjective reactions. But as the 'unconscious attitudes' obtained on the *friendship* scale

by and large replicated the results of the *job suitability* scale, Labov concludes by pointing to a lack of success in establishing the existence of covert values (more about this in Section 19.2.3.2 below).

In the perspective of our discussion here, it is interesting to note that Labov argues that the difficulties experienced in establishing independent evidence for covert values should be ascribed to the conditions of data collection. The argument goes something like this: in our attempts to elicit covert values, we have only come 'as far as one can in a field experiment' (2001: 216), which is not very far, because covert values 'do not readily emerge in formal situations' (2001: 24). Yes, but we have seen how the contextual-formality dimension is linked to, in fact based on, the dimension of consciousness/awareness/attention; what emerges at a certain level of formality is a function of the level of consciousness involved. Thus, it seems to me that what the argument really says is something like: no evidence of covert values is found because the attitudes expressed in the matched guise experiment are 'conscious'.

Indeed, 'conscious attitudes' make much more sense than 'unconscious attitudes'. Consider the following conditions of data collection: the Philadelphia matched guise was carried out 'in course of the second interviews .... The 'second' interview was in many cases a third, fourth, or even tenth recording made by the field workers' (Labov, 2001: 207, 334). The *job suitability* question was phrased: 'What is the highest job this person could hold, speaking as she does?' (2001: 207). There can be little doubt that the Philadelphia informants evaluated the matched guise speakers in full awareness of giving away attitudes towards dialect differences.

In fact, there is no indication that Labov ever aimed at obtaining conditions which might produce 'unconscious attitudes' in the sense of **attitudes offered by respondents who are unaware of offering attitudes towards dialect differences** (which is what we aim at in our Danish studies: Section 19.3 below). On the contrary, about the matched guise test in the New York project, he says that: 'The respondents were told that this test was the most important part of the interview: since we had already learned how they themselves used the English language, we then wanted to know how they felt about the way other New Yorkers used it' (Labov, 1966: 281ff.). Respondents were actually controlled for whether they could hear dialect differences between the speakers (or sentences) on the test tape: three respondents were described as 'dialect deaf', whereas 'the great majority heard clear-cut differences between the test sentences' (ibid.: 284).

What does Labov mean then by labelling his matched guise data 'unconscious' (attitudes, evaluations, reactions)? As it turns out, Labov's real reason for prioritizing the matched guise data is that these data are systematic:

(8)

The type of evaluative behavior that I would like to measure here is more systematic, more completely internalized than any reply to overt questions about speech. We are searching for the evaluative norms which reflect the complex and regular structures in [the social differentiation of language use] (1966: 280).

...attitudes do not emerge in a systematic form if the subject is questioned directly about dialects; but if he makes two sets of personality judgements about the same speaker using two different forms of language, and does not realize that it is the same speaker, his subjective evaluations of language will emerge as the differences in the two ratings (1972: 146 (italics in original)).

It seems clear that Labov's 'unconscious attitudes' refers more to an aspect of the data-collection technique than to the nature of the data. His respondents are not unconscious of offering attitudes towards language; they are unconscious of offering attitudes towards the same speaker several times or, in case they realize this, unable to let it influence their ratings. ('As the listener reacted to a particular sentence, he would not be able to know exactly how he had rated the same speaker in a previous utterance' (1966: 281).). Thus, what Labov's matched guise experiments collect is not 'unconscious' language attitudes, but evaluative reactions towards language of a more 'systematic' kind than obtained in interview answers.

19.2.3 The driving-force issue

Put simply, the driving-force issue (see Section 19.1) boils down to the question of 'What comes first': does change in use result from change in attitudes, or does change in attitudes result from change in use? As correlation does not imply a cause–effect relationship, stating that 'the evaluation problem is to find the subjective (or latent) correlates of the objective (or manifest) changes which have been observed' (see quote (2)) does not in itself commit Labov to a particular position on the driving-force issue. Actually, Labov's position on the issue has never appeared particularly clear-cut to me, but I think it is right to point out a repositioning on his part from **before Philadelphia** (19.2.3.1) to **after Philadelphia** (19.2.3.2).

19.2.3.1 Before Philadelphia

Independently of how we should understand the relationship between *covert values* and *unconscious attitudes* (as obtained in the matched guise test; see Section 19.2.2.2 above), it may be firmly established that Labov, throughout all of his work, operates with social values, pressures and motivations that people are unaware of.

(9)

Social forces exerted upon linguistic forms are of two distinct types, which we may call *pressures from above*, and *pressures from below*. By *below* is meant "below the level of conscious awareness". Pressures from below operate upon entire linguistic systems, in response to social motivations which are relatively obscure and yet have the greatest signification for the general evolution of language ... social pressures from above ... represent the overt process of social correction applied to individual linguistic forms (1972: 123 (italics in original)).

My difficulties with understanding Labov's position on the driving-force issue may largely be due to quite different conceptions of the relationship between the notions of *value* and *consciousness*. I have no problems with *changes from above*. These are driven by social evaluations that function as pressures by virtue of people's awareness of the social significance involved, often referred to in terms of *correctness* and *prestige*. The problem arises with *changes from below*. How are we to understand that social motivations and pressures with the greatest significance for language use in the speech community operate below conscious awareness (while also being relatively obscure to Labov as a student of the speech community)?

In the mechanism-of-linguistic-change paragraph that concludes Labov 1966 (398–400), it is stressed that '... linguistic behavior is highly normative, or goal-directed. The need for a target, a set of norms, is evident in the casual speech of our informants as well as in their formal styles', and it is suggested that:

(10)

Hypercorrection can operate in a more general sense [i.e. can override not only upper middle class norms as in the New York study, but also target norms in general (TK)] as the mechanism of change in response to pressures from below.
[...]

Driven by the fear of not conforming, and the need to establish oneself as an authentic member of one's immediate group, the members of the speech community can gradually push these labile norms further and further in the direction that they first began to move.

[...]

the unconscious tendency of speakers to increase the measure of their identification with their immediate group may be stated as the probable mechanism of these changes.

We recall that the first stage of change from below is characterized by the absence of consciousness (see Section 19.2.2.1 above). At this stage, the established variation functions as an *indicator*, 'defined as a function of group membership' (Labov, 1972: 178). That is, even though people are not aware of the change, it is thought of as driven by the kind of evaluations that delimit and define social groups. Such evaluations were also pointed out as the driving force as Labov (1972: 178ff.) summarized his experiences with the subsequent stages of 'the mechanism of sound change':

(11)
[the sound change spread] to the extent that the values of the original subgroup were adopted by other groups in the speech community .... As the sound change with its associated values reached the limits of its expansion, the linguistic variable became one of the norms which defined the speech community, and all members of the speech community reacted in a uniform manner to its use (without necessarily being aware of it). The variable is now a *marker*, and begins to show stylistic variation.

As it develops and spreads, a linguistic variable first **indicates** social group membership, then **marks** both group and style categories. The development and spread of the variable is driven by social evaluations (attitudes come first) – which the speakers themselves are unaware of (possibly so, even at the **marker** stage). As I have indicated, I am not sure how to understand this. I see two possible readings, which to my mind entail very different theoretical assumptions and methodological implications.

One possibility is that the notion of values (social pressures and motivations) operating from below the level of conscious awareness refers to a situation in which people **pay no conscious attention to** some of the linguistic variables which constitute their speech community, in the sense that they **do not (seem able to) comment upon** the use and social signification of the variants involved. Some of Labov's formulations point in that direction, e.g.: 'To sum up, incoming linguistic changes rarely rise to the level of social comment in their initial stages, and not all changes become the focus of conscious attention even in

their advanced stages' (1972: 309). 'Though (aw) is not at a high level of conscious social awareness, and is rarely a subject of social comment ...' (2001: 187). If the absence of conscious awareness (or conscious attention) results from an absence of 'social comment', we may say that **below conscious awareness** means 'no available discourse', and such a reading may be taken – depending on the theoretical conceptions of 'the self and its values' – to allow for the existence of an **unconscious awareness** of uses and values. There is awareness, certainly, but it is implicit, linguistically inexpressible. If this is the situation, it might be better conceived of in terms of different levels or layers of consciousness/awareness.

The other possibility is that we would be mistaken in establishing and foregrounding such a distinction between **conscious** and **unconscious awareness**, or between layers of awareness. I know of no explicit attempt in Labov's work to theorize levels of consciousness/awareness. It is true that the 'either-or' treatment of this dimension (above/below, conscious/unconscious, aware/unaware) is sometimes replaced by a 'more-or-less' treatment (see quote (5)). The important point to notice, however, is that **values are talked about as decisive for variation and change, quite independently of whether consciousness/awareness is said to be involved or not.** Labov seems to operate with a driving-force role for social evaluations that are conceived of as **unconscious** in the sense of being 'beyond consciousness'.

Apparently, Labov sees no problem here. Or rather saw no problem. In a more recent statement, which is remarkable for its explicit comment on the issue that occupies us here, Labov argues that an explanation based on social symbolism (the case in question concerns gender differentiation in use) is problematic because 'it assigns social sensitivity to early stages of change that are remote from levels of social awareness' (2001: 291).

As we would expect in the work of a devoted empiricist, the continued failure to establish firm, independent evidence for the kind of social sensitivity – covert values – that was assumed to drive the more general and interesting changes in use, had to become a problem. Our discussion above suggests two possible approaches to the lack-of-evidence problem. On the one hand, if the distinction between **conscious** and **unconscious**, between **overt** and **covert**, is a question of layers of consciousness and discursive availability, the natural implication for the student of language change would be to concentrate on developing methods for tapping into the deeper layers that people lack a language to express. On the other hand, if we operate with a binary 'either-or' conception and end up with no evidence for covert values in spite of supposedly valid and reliable endeavours to establish such evidence, the result might be an instigation to rethink the driving-force issue. As we shall see, it is probably right to say that Labov has opted for the latter approach.

19.2.3.2 After Philadelphia

The matched guise test of the Philadelphia project was designed to detect indications of covert values in terms of a reversed response pattern for *friendliness* in comparison with *job suitability* (see Section 19.2.1.2 (ii) above). The result was, however, that '[n]o such tendency emerged. In general, the friendship question replicated the results of the job suitability question ... evidence for covert norms failed to appear' (Labov, 2001: 216ff.). Arguably, as a consequence of the fact that 'Philadelphians have shown a strong pattern of negative evaluation of changes in progress, and no clear evidence of covert, positive evaluation of their own behaviour' (2001: 220), a growing tendency to reduce or even refute the driving-force role attributed to subjective factors is clearly discernible in Labov's more recent work.

(12)
...Changes from below are systematic changes that appear first in the vernacular, and represent the operation of internal, linguistic factors. At the outset, and through most of their development, they are completely below the level of social awareness. No one notices them or talks about them, and even phonetically trained observers may be unconscious of them for many years. It is only when the changes are nearing completion that members of the community become aware of them (1994: 78 (italics in original)).

This description recapitulates earlier formulations as far as the role of consciousness/awareness is concerned, but **there is no mention of values**. Changes from below are not assumed to be driven by social valuations (pressures and motivations) in the same way as before (as in quote (9)), but are instead said to 'represent the operation of internal, linguistic factors'.

The importance of solving the evaluation problem by searching for the subjective correlates, including the covert values in particular, is now clearly downplayed in Labov's approach and argumentation, while the pertinence of 'interactional frequency' to the driving-force issue is upgraded in the discussion – with reference to Bloomfield's *principle of density*, the implications of which, with regard to the evaluation problem, is spelled out: 'The principle of density implicitly asserts that we do not have to search for a motivating force behind the diffusion of linguistic change.

The effect is a mechanical and inevitable one; the implicit assumption is that social evaluation and attitudes play a minor role' (Labov, 2001: 20).

In discussing other researchers' claims about the role of attitudes in terms of 'group membership' or 'acts of identity' (exemplified by Sturtevant (1947) and Le Page and Tabouret-Keller (1985)) – Labov argues that '[i]f such attitudes are to be used to account for linguistic diffusion, it is necessary to posit a covert belief structure', and goes on cautiously to admit that 'such covert attitudes and beliefs may actually be involved in linguistic change', but stresses that 'they are not usually supported by material evidence' (2001: 191). Even the few cases, where attitudinal evidence for an effect from 'local-identification' processes on sound change in progress have been considered fairly secure (as in the Martha's Vineyard study), are reopened for a possible interpretation in line with the density principle: 'The question remains as to whether the same conclusions could be drawn from frequencies of interaction with speakers with different systems, following Bloomfield's principle of density. In other words, language change may simply reflect changes in interlocutor frequencies which are in turn the result of changes in social preferences and attitudes' (ibid.: 191). In another version of his argument with the acts-of-identity position, Labov finds the group-distinguishing function of linguistic differences to be 'very likely', but, because of the lack of independent evidence for covert values, 'there is always the possibility that the effect is due to Bloomfield's principle of density: that the more often people talk to each other, the more similar their speech will be' (ibid.: 228). The consequences for the research strategy in general, and the possible consequences for the status of the evaluation problem in particular, are radical:

(13)
The strategy of this inquiry [into whether language change is driven by changes in either 'interactional frequency' or 'social identifications'] is to draw as much as possible on concrete evidence of actual behaviour as evidence for such questions. To the extent that social differences in language behaviour can be mapped onto the matrix of communicative interaction, we must give priority to this pattern of interaction in accounting for the linguistic facts .... The account based on covert attitudes is redundant to the extent that the network of daily interaction brings people into contact with the new form in proportion to their distance from the originating group (Labov, 2001: 191–2).

Thus, the Philadelphia study puts a focus on the communicative interaction of individual people in their social networks, and 'transform[s] the traditional question "Why does language change?" into a different form: "Who are the leaders of linguistic change?" ' (Labov, 2001: 29). The characteristics of these leaders are determined by studying 'their personal statements, their social histories, and their philosophies of life' (2001: 33). The study concludes that '[t]he history of our leaders of linguistic change is a history of nonconformity, and their sociolinguistic position is a display of nonconformity' (2001: 410). Celeste S. is presented as the prototypical influential person: 'She did not hesitate to use violence when it was called for. But her primary weapons were linguistic: negotiation, persuasion, and denunciation, all enlisted under a profound intolerance for cupidity, hypocrisy, and injustice. These are the qualities that make a great leader of linguistic change' (2001: 410). The Nonconformity Principle, presented as the major conclusion of the 2001 volume, says that: 'Ongoing linguistic changes are emblematic of nonconformity to established social norms of appropriate behavior, … are generated in the social milieu that most consistently defies these norms, [and] are generalized to the wider community by those who display the symbols of nonconformity in a larger pattern of upward mobility' (2001: 516).

One might argue here that the qualities given as characteristic of the leaders of change might just as well be referred to as values and, furthermore, that the Nonconformity Principle might perfectly well be read as a statement to the effect that covert values are the driving force of change. Such a reading would be tantamount to saying that the neighbourhood-based Philadelphia study does indeed offer a partly-new methodological approach to the task of establishing independent evidence for covert values.

Labov, however, reasons otherwise. The leaders of change are 'people taking deliberate and conscious actions that identify their social position and define their relations with the community', but:

(14)
[t]heir linguistic choices cannot be described as actions in the same sense. The level or rate of use of a stochastic variable is at the level of consciousness comparable to walking and breathing. There is no evidence that attitudes, ideologies, and opinions that people express in so many words will bear directly upon linguistic changes from below. These attitudes may influence who a person talks to and how often they talk, and so affect the flow of linguistic influence and the diffusion of sound changes within and across local social networks. (2001: 409)

Labov does in fact say that the notion of nonconformity 'deals with norms that are covert in some situations, but emerge more freely in others' (2001: 512). However, his theoretical point is that there is no evidence of direct influence from such norms on linguistic changes from below. Whatever their mode of existence or appearance might be, attitudes, ideologies and opinions may influence patterns of interaction, but the change-producing forces at work in interaction are 'internal, linguistic factors' – factors of a mechanical kind which should be compared to the forces behind walking and breathing rather than social identifications and evaluations.

Labov's position now seems to be that a driving-force role for social values becomes a pertinent issue only if changes cannot be accounted for in terms of 'mechanical' or 'structural' forces (see e.g. 2001: 463, 500). In discussing the acts-of-identity type of explanation, Labov explicitly refutes a more constructivist view in stressing that he does not see the leaders of change (like Celeste S.) 'as creating a system of verbal behaviour so much as responding to ambient pressures to shift their habitual range of values of Philadelphia variables', and stresses that '[a]s always, it is good practice to consider first the simpler and more mechanical view that social structure affects linguistic output through changes in the frequency of interaction' (2001: 505ff.).

The continued reduction of a role for social evaluation in language change reaches its end point in the recent article on 'Transmission and diffusion' (Labov, 2007), in which these two change processes are explained in terms of different learning strategies in children and adults, without any reference to norms or values at all.

19.3 THE DRIVING-FORCE ROLE OF COVERT ATTITUDES: THE DANISH EVIDENCE

Are subjective factors to be seen as essential to language change processes – i.e. as their driving force – or as a contingent concomitant of usage differences that emerge in virtue of other, objective factors? This issue became central to Danish sociolinguistics from its very beginning in the 1970s, as it began where Labov seems to have ended.

When Brink and Lund argue and, to some extent, document that Copenhagen speech (including its HIGH/LOW variation) is spreading to the rest of Denmark, they rely on the density principle as their main explanation, presented in a textbook for university students (Brink and Lund, 1974) as the 'Napoleon principle': always make sure you outnumber the enemy where you attack him. In other words, wherever variants compete, the victory will go to the most frequently heard variant. Brink and Lund admit that prestige may influence the battle and speed up the advance of the new variant but, in general, they treat, and condemn, attribution of social values to linguistic variants as a category mistake, in speakers and researchers alike.

The view that attitudes are alien to language use and change (and should be fought and eliminated as mistakes) appeared to accord with the facts of the Danish speech community as it developed between 1960 and 1980. The traditional dialects stopped being transferred to, or acquired by, the younger generations, and were replaced by Copenhagen speech, which spread to the whole country, most vitally in its LOW variety among young people. In contrast, Danish élite discourse (as represented for instance in official teaching guidelines) began extolling the value of local dialects, while increasingly complaining (e.g. through letters to the editor) about particular features of LOW Copenhagen speech as these became increasingly salient on national television. So, what happened at the level of use was the opposite of what happened at the level of attitudes. Language ideology did indeed seem to be of little relevance to attempts at explaining language change.

This picture has been strongly supported by the many empirical studies of language attitudes that have been conducted in Denmark from the beginning of the 1980s onwards: outside Copenhagen, young people are always, on average, found to express more positive attitudes towards LOCAL varieties of language than towards LOW Copenhagen speech. This holds true whether the data are of a discursive or an experimental kind (see Section 19.2.1) – also subjective reaction tests confirm this picture – **but with the proviso that the elicited attitudes are consciously offered.**

The ideological climate surrounding Danish varieties appears quite different whenever the subjective reaction test is constructed and conducted in such a way that **subjects do not become aware of reacting to language varieties** (see the discussion in Section 19.2.2.2). In this case, we talk of the obtained data as *subconscious attitudes*. Rather, the point is that the attitudes are **subconsciously offered** in the test situation. Besides exploiting natural situations, which is difficult (for an example, see Kristiansen, 1997), we have succeeded in collecting subconscious attitudes in experimental situations (classroom settings) from around 1000 young Danes over a period of 20 years. The same basic design has been used in more than 10 Danish localities, including all parts of the country and a wide range of community types. As our claims to a decisive role for covert values in language change are based on the results from these experiments, I shall go into some detail with the design (as it materialized in the LANCHART project; for further descriptions, see Kristiansen, 2009, a, b).

Having been based on the so-called verbal guise technique, the experiments in question have requested ninth-graders (15–16 years old, in their last year of compulsory schooling and representing the whole social gamut) to evaluate clips of about 30 seconds taken from different speakers talking about the same subject: 'What is a good teacher?'. As this design represents a relaxation of the control for voice and content effects obtained in a matched guise design, we have used four speakers for each of the accents under study in each community, and have said that conclusions, as to a decisive effect of accent differences on evaluations, are acceptable if, and only if, the assumed accents emerge as clear similarities and differences in how the speakers are evaluated. This has always turned out to be the case: the accents we have assumed to be relevant in processes of social identifications among today's adolescents (two in Copenhagen, three in all other communities) have always emerged from the evaluative patterns. As the high/low social contrast seems to have lost much of its significance at the levels of both use and attitudes in later decades, we label the three accents MODERN (characterized by previous 'low' features and recently developed 'new' features), CONSERVATIVE (with no or fewer 'low' and 'new' features) and LOCAL (i.e. Copenhagen speech with traces of local prosody). The stimulus speakers are adolescents of the same age as the subjects. The same four MODERN and the same four CONSERVATIVE speakers have been used in all communities (all of them are Copenhageners), while the four LOCAL speakers, it goes without saying, have been recorded in each of the local communities under study.

Three methodological points have been essential to the successful elicitation of subconsciously-offered attitudes. First, prior to their participation, no information was given to the informants about the purpose of the experiment, and data collection followed a strict procedure in order to avoid questions and comments that might arouse informants' awareness of the purpose. Secondly, the accent variation represented in the stimulus tape was 'natural' – i.e. a part of everyday speech in the local community under study and therefore not salient in any way that might make the informants reflect on the purpose of the evaluation as having to do with dialectal differences. Thus, the stimulus speakers represented the three accents that are naturally present as young speech in any Danish locality today. Thirdly, the measurement instrument – i.e. the scales used for evaluations – was constructed in such a way that informants' attention was not directed to the idea that the evaluations were towards dialect. Hence, evaluative items focusing on speech (correct? good? dialect?) had to be left out, of course, in favour of items addressing speaker characteristics, e.g. in terms of personality traits (intelligent? trustworthy? cool?).

After completion, informants were always asked what they thought the experiment was about. No one has ever suggested anything that could be taken to mean attitudes towards 'dialects'. When they are told, and listen to the speakers again, informants are always amazed how easy it is to hear, now that they know, that the speakers have different accents – which is informative on the nature of our 'subconscious attitudes': if 'naturally occurring' accent differences are so easily made recognizable, they are also likely to be included in listeners' reactions when they are not salient in the evaluative situation. In this sense, I find it evident that people will always have to be aware of the value issues involved in the use of language, if values have a role to play in the battle between variants. These values are **covert** in the sense that they differ radically from the **overt** attitudes expressed in general (common as well as élite) public discourse.

Now, the point is that the **covert** evaluations – in sharp contrast with the **overt** ideology of Danish society – show a pattern which is not in contradiction to, but is in accordance with, what happens at the level of use. In comparison to 'pure' Copenhagen speech (whether in CONSERVATIVE or MODERN version), young Danes everywhere strongly downgrade the 'locally coloured' speech (LOCAL) – which in most cases is their own speech. As to the variation within Copenhagen speech, the evaluative pattern is again consistently the same all over the country, including the city of Copenhagen itself: MODERN is everywhere strongly upgraded on **dynamism** traits (such as self-assured, fascinating, cool), whereas CONSERVATIVE does as well or better on **superiority** traits (such as intelligent, conscientious, trustworthy).

Thus, subconsciously-offered attitudes show no trace of positive values attached to locally coloured speech; there is no trace of the distinction often found between **status** values accorded to standard varieties and **solidarity** values accorded to non-standard varieties. In terms of covert values – i.e. at the subconscious level of social evaluation – the battle for the position as 'best language' in late-modern Danish society includes only Copenhagen speech and is a matter of **dynamism** versus **superiority**.

This evaluative pattern is reproduced in a remarkably uniform and consistent fashion by young people across the whole of Denmark. At least as far as the younger people are concerned, Denmark is a *speech community* in the Labovian sense, not only by virtue of shared **overt** values but also, and in particular, by virtue of shared **covert** values.

One might accept, I think, that our studies have established firm evidence for covert values, yet at the same time refuse to accept that we have proven a driving-force role for these values in the changes of language use. We have established 'subjective correlates' – subconsciously offered – that are in accordance with and not in contradiction to the changes in use, but can we say for sure what comes first for today's young speakers: the advance of Copenhagen speech, or its evaluative upgrading? Can we decide for sure whether the essential factor in change (the driving force) is to be found in the facts of use (the density of interaction) or in the facts of ideology (the non-cognitive functions, i.e. the connotational meanings, of variation)? Maybe not.

It seems to me, however, that the spread of Copenhagen speech is far easier to understand as an effect of the covert values we have established than as an effect of the density principle. The limited size of Denmark notwithstanding, I find it hard to see how the 'Napoleon strategy' (always make sure you outnumber the enemy where you attack him) could possibly bring Copenhagen speech to all corners of the country. I find it more natural to reason like Labov did, on Martha's Vineyard, when he found that the facts of use (centralization of the diphthongs /ay/ and /aw/) was more sharply stratified by the facts of ideology (orientation towards the island) than by any other background factor: '[this] indicates that we have come reasonably close to a valid explanation' (Labov, 1972: 39), or stated even more strongly: 'It seems plain that the noncognitive functions which are carried by these phonological elements are the essential factors in the mechanism of the change. This conclusion can be generalized to many other instances of more complex changes … ' (1972: 170).

As to the development of the nationwide uniformity of covert representations (perceptions and evaluations), it can only be understood as an effect of identical experiences with language varieties in the national public sphere. The general upgrading of Copenhagen speech and the downgrading of local speech reflect how these two types of language are treated by the most important institutions in young people's public lives: Copenhagen speech is the only 'appropriate' language in the schools and the spoken media; local speech is 'not good enough'. Also, the split between MODERN and CONSERVATIVE Copenhagen speech, and their battle for 'best language' position in terms of **dynamism** versus **superiority**, is likely to be a reflection of what young people experience as 'excellence' in language in the modern media on the one hand, and the more traditional institutions of education and business on the other (Kristiansen, 2001).[1]

19.4 CONCLUDING REMARKS

Most sociolinguists, I would imagine, will judge social values and evaluations to be of relevance to the study of language use in very many of its aspects, maybe even in all of its aspects. Quite a few feel that we learned this from Labov, and therefore find reasons to ponder when Labov (2001) begins the *Social Factors* volume by stressing the narrowness of the interface between language and society. Having pointed out that '[a]t one point in the development of sociolinguistics, it was not uncommon for scholars to suggest that the social and linguistic aspects of language were coextensive in the sense that each linguistic element had a social aspect or evaluation', Labov continues: 'Yet the actual situation seems to be quite the reverse. For the most part, linguistic structure and social structure are isolated domains, which do not bear upon each other .... The force of social evaluation, positive or negative, is generally brought to bear only upon superficial aspects of language: the lexicon and phonetics' (2001: 28).

On the face of it, this just reiterates what Labov has always said: namely, that '[i]n speaking of the role of social factors influencing linguistic evolution, it is important not to overestimate the amount of contact or overlap between social values and the structure of language' (1972: 251). In reality, however, the significance of this claim about the relationship between social values and language is different 'after Philadelphia' from what it was 'before Philadelphia', because of the general change in theoretical perspective. The claim now reads, and serves, as an argument for omitting the evaluation problem from the privileged position it once was accorded among the theoretical and methodological problems that had to be solved by the theory of language change.

In my reading, Labov's own failure to establish firm independent evidence of covert values appears the decisive reason why he changes position on the driving-force role of social values. However, one might suggest that this change has been radicalized as a reaction to how social-value explanations have proliferated, in terms of 'identity' and 'prestige', mostly without any other evidence than the patterns of use themselves: 'It is

not uncommon to speak of linguistic changes as the result of speakers' desires to assume a certain social identity. But, for most linguistic changes from below, operating well below the level of social awareness, the only evidence for such acts of identity is simply the fact that successive generations change their ways of speaking' (Labov, 2001: xv). 'In recent years, a great deal of attention has been given to the association of linguistic variables with local identity .... As with the covert values ... the evidence for the association of such values is largely the linguistic distributions themselves' (Labov, 2001: 228).

It is interesting to note also that that other important scholar in Labovian sociolinguistics, Peter Trudgill, has, in recent years, addressed the driving-force issue by stressing the role of mechanistic factors at the expense of social evaluations, while expressing similar reservations with regard to the omnipresence of identity as an explanatory notion (Trudgill, 2004; see the discussion in *Language in Society* 37(2), 2008).

The issue of whether and how different aspects of language may be differently available to awareness and/or social evaluation is certainly of importance to our understanding of language variation and change, but a discussion of this issue has not been my aim in this chapter (for such discussions, see Labov, 2001: 25–8; Preston, 1996, forthcoming; discussions of 'salience' as a central notion in this regard may be found in Auer et al., 1998; Kerswill and Williams, 2002). My aim has been of a more foundational kind: while wholly sharing the scepticism towards social-identity explanations which are inferred solely from patterns of use, my intention has been to defend the driving-force view of social values which Labov and Trudgill seem to have abandoned, and hence to defend a privileged position for the evaluation problem in the study of language change – in accordance with Labov's first assumptions and guidelines, which I find fundamentally sound: (i) the role of ideology should be studied and established using independent evidence, i.e. in data other than the established patterns of use, and (ii) the study of ideological data should focus on social motivations 'from below', in particular, because (iii) these motivations, appearing in subconsciously-offered attitudes as covert values, are important to language change in a way that overt values are not. These fundamentals of the original Labovian framework are sustained by the Danish evidence. My moral goes as follows: the failure to establish independent evidence for covert values should stimulate us, as students of language change, to develop our methods (allowing for elicitations of subconsciously-offered attitudes) rather than lead us to abandon the driving-force view of social evaluation.

NOTE

1   We hope to be able to shed further light on the driving-force issue in future studies within the LANCHART project (www.lanchart.dk); the design of such a study is outlined in Kristiansen and Jørgensen, 2005; for fuller descriptions of the Danish speech community, see Kristiansen and Jørgensen (eds), 2003; Gregersen (ed.), 2009.

REFERENCES

Auer, P., Barden, B. and Grosskopf, B. (1998) 'Subjective and objective parameters determining "salience" in long-term dialect accommodation', *Journal of Sociolinguistics*, 2(2): 163–87.

Brink, L. and Lund, J. (1974) *Udtaleforskelle i Danmark. Aldersbestemte – geografiske – sociale*. København: Gjellerup.

Fasold, R. (1984) *The Sociolinguistics of Society*. Oxford: Blackwell.

Garrett, P., Coupland, N. and Williams, A. (2003) *Investigating Language Attitudes. Social Meanings of Dialect, Ethnicity and Performance*. Cardiff: University of Wales Press.

Gregersen, F. (ed.) (2009) *Acta Linguistica Hafniensia*, 41.

Kerswill, P. and Williams, A. (2002) '"Salience" as an explanatory factor in language change: evidence from dialect levelling in urban England', in M. C. Jones and E. Esch (eds), *Contact-Induced Language Change. An Examination of Internal, External and Non-Linguistic Factors*. Berlin: Mouton de Gruyter. pp. 81–110.

Kristiansen, T. (1997) 'Language attitudes in a Danish cinema', in N. Coupland and A. Jaworski (eds), *Sociolinguistics. A Reader and Coursebook*. London: Macmillan Press. pp. 291–305.

Kristiansen, T. (2001) 'Two standards: one for the media and one for the school', *Language Awareness*, 10(1): 9–24.

Kristiansen, T. (2009a) 'Investigating language in space: experimental techniques', in P. Auer and J. E. Schmidt (eds), *Language and Space: Theories and Methods*. HSK. An International Handbook of Linguistic Variation. Berlin, Walter de Gruyter. pp. 528–49.

Kristiansen, T. (2009b) 'The macro-level social meanings of late-modern Danish accents', *Acta Linguistica Hafniensia*, 41: 167–192.

Kristiansen, T. and Jørgensen, J. N. (eds) (2003) 'The sociolinguistics of Danish', *International Journal of the Sociology of Language*, 159.

Kristiansen, T. and Jørgensen, J. N. (2005) 'Subjective factors in dialect convergence and divergence', in P. Auer,

F. Hinskens and P. Kerswill (eds), *Dialect Change. Convergence and Divergence in European Languages*. Cambridge: Cambridge University Press. pp. 287–302.

Labov, W. (1963) 'The social motivation of a sound change', *Word*, 19: 273–309.

Labov, W. (1966) *The Social Stratification of English in New York City*. Washington, DC: Center for Applied Linguistics.

Labov, W. (1972) *Sociolinguistic Patterns*. Philadelphia: University of Pennsylvania Press.

Labov, W. (1994) *Principles of Linguistic Change*. Vol. 1, *Internal factors*. Oxford: Blackwell.

Labov, W. (2001) *Principles of Linguistic Change*. Vol. 2, *Social factors*. Oxford: Blackwell.

Labov, W. (2007) 'Transmission and diffusion', *Language*, 83(2): 344–87.

Labov, W. (forthcoming) *Principles of Linguistic Change*. Vol. 3, *Cognitive factors*. Oxford: Blackwell.

Lambert, W., Hodgson, R., Gardner, R. and Fillenbaum, S. (1960) 'Evaluational reactions to spoken languages', *Journal of Abnormal and Social Psychology*, 60: 44–51.

Lambert, W. E. (1967) 'A social psychology of bilingualism', *Journal of Social Issues*, 23: 91–108.

Le Page, R. B. and Tabouret-Keller, A. (1985) *Acts of Identity: Creole-Based Approaches to Language and Ethnicity*. Cambridge: Cambridge University Press.

Preston, D. (1996) 'Whaddayaknow? The modes of folklinguistic awareness', *Language Awareness*, 5(1): 40–74.

Preston, D. (forthcoming) 'Variation in language regard', in E. Ziegler, J. Scharloth and P. Gilles (eds), *Empirische Evidenzen und theoretische Passungen sprachlicher Variation*. P. Lang-Verlag. Variolingua. Nonstandard–Standard–Substandard Vol. 37.

Ryan, E. B., Giles, H. and Sebastian, R. (1982) 'An integrative perspective for the study of attitudes towards language variation', in E. B. Ryan and H. Giles (eds), *Attitudes Towards Language Variation: Social and Applied Contexts*. London: Edward Arnold. pp. 1–19.

Sturtevant, E. (1947) *An Introduction to Linguistic Science*. New Haven, CT: Yale University Press.

Swann, J., Deumert, A., Lillis, T. and Mesthrie, R. (2004) *A Dictionary of Sociolinguistics*. Tuscaloosa, AL: The University of Alabama Press.

Trudgill, P. (1974) *The Social Differentiation of English in Norwich*. Cambridge: Cambridge University Press.

Trudgill, P. (2004) *New Dialect Formation: The Inevitability of Colonial Englishes*. Edinburgh: Edinburgh University Press.

Weinreich, U., Labov, W. and Herzog, M. (1968) 'Empirical foundations for a theory of language change', in W. P. Lehmann and Y. Malkiel (eds), *Directions for Historical Linguistics*. Austin, TX: University of Texas Press. pp. 95–189.

20

Historical Sociolinguistics

Terttu Nevalainen

20.1 NEW SUBDISCIPLINE

Over the last three decades, historical sociolinguistics has emerged as a subdiscipline at the
interface of sociolinguistics and historical
linguistics. It appears in the titles of Romaine
(1988), Milroy (1992), Machan and Scott (1992),
Ammon, Mattheier and Nelde (1999), Jahr (1999),
Nevalainen and Raumolin-Brunberg (2003) and
Bergs (2005), as well as in the forthcoming
Handbook of Historical Sociolinguistics edited by
Hernández-Campoy and *Historical Sociolinguistics and Sociohistorical Linguistics*, an e-journal
launched by Tieken-Boon van Ostade in 2000.[1] To
get an idea of the scope of historical sociolinguistics, let us begin by considering how its two parent
disciplines, sociolinguistics and historical linguistics, perceive each other.

In contradistinction to their own field, sociolinguists working with present-day spoken language
often regard historical linguistics as 'the art of
making the best use of bad data' (Labov, 1994: 11).
This characterization derives from what are seen
as the historical linguists' impoverished and
incomplete data sources, lack of controlled experiments and absence of native speakers. Taking a
global view of the scope of historical linguistics,
this is of course true: few of the world's languages
have a spoken record of their past of any considerable time depth, and the vast majority have no
written records. Not all languages have a written
form even today. This is also the case with many
social and regional varieties of languages that
have a standard written form. Even languages that
have written documentation of the past lack
a written record representative of the language

community as a whole. Wide-ranging illiteracy
lies at the root of this historical 'bad-data problem'. This is not only the case of the distant past
but would also apply to modern sociolinguistics if
it were to rely on written material as its data
source. According to the statistics published by
UNESCO, 774 million people, about one-fifth of
the world's adult population, could not read or
write in 2008.

Historical linguistics, in turn, has a long tradition
of defining its objectives in rather abstract terms.
This is justified, as noted above, because all the
prehistory and most of the history of human languages even since the advent of writing have gone
unrecorded. What can be reconstructed is based on
comparisons of the information available on the
sound systems, morpheme inventories and vocabulary of genetically related languages. The comparative method relies on the basic hypothesis that
language change, and sound change in particular, is
regular. The application of this method requires that
the object of investigation is limited to one system
at a time. A typical view of a historical linguist is
expressed by André Martinet, who specifies the
object of historical linguistics as the study of a
perfectly homogeneous community. He writes:

> To simplify our analysis, we shall assume that the
> language in process of evolution is that of a strictly
> monoglot community, perfectly homogeneous in
> the sense that observable differences represent
> successive stages of the same usage and not con-
> current usages (Martinet, 1964: 164).

However, aware of linguistic variation, Martinet
refers to central concepts used by sociolinguists,

such as the speech community. Twenty years on, in his *Historical and Comparative Linguistics*, Raimo Anttila (1989: 47–54) has an extended discussion of linguistic variation as the precondition for language change. By the latter half of the twentieth century, sociolinguistic thinking has impacted on historical linguistics to the extent that 'social variation must be included in the background as a necessary prerequisite for understanding change' (Anttila, 1989: 47; see also Janda and Joseph, 2003).

While discussing work that applies sociolinguistic insights to the study of the past, this chapter stresses the commonalities between historical linguistics and sociolinguistics. I will begin by introducing some assumptions, shared by both disciplines, about the nature of human language and its use (Section 20.2). The sections that follow are devoted to discussions of language contact (Section 20.3), the diffusion of linguistic changes (Section 20.4), their connections with 'central places' (Section 20.5) and processes of standardization in relation to vernaculars (Section 20.6). In one form or another, these topic areas are addressed by sociolinguists and historical linguists alike, and they occupy the centre stage in historical sociolinguistics. The prerequisites for doing historical sociolinguistics empirically are discussed in Section 20.7, where I illustrate the extent to which variation studies, a distinct growth area in the new subdiscipline, can make use of sociolinguistic models and methods.

20.2 THE UNIFORMITARIAN PRINCIPLE

One of the key topics of research shared by sociolinguists and historical linguists is language change. Sociolinguists typically analyse language change in progress, whereas traditional historical linguists work with the results of these processes. However, it is a sign of the rapprochement of the two fields that the sociolinguist William Labov and his co-workers have set out to find empirical evidence for the Neogrammarian hypothesis on the regularity of sound change. Similarly, aware of sociolinguistic thinking, those working with the historical comparative method have advanced alternative speaker-based hypotheses concerning the diffusion of sound changes (Durie and Ross (eds), 1996).

The theoretical justification of this hypothesis testing, and of the historical sociolinguistic enterprise more generally, derives from the uniformitarian hypothesis. Historical linguists should not expect that human languages in the past were in any principled way different from those spoken today, or as Lass (1997: 25) puts it, '[w]hat we can say about any aspect of the past in any domain

has to be constrained by the (known or hypothesized) properties of its present-day analogues'. In his *Sociolinguistic Patterns*, Labov (1985 [1972]: 275) views the uniformitarian principle in terms of extralinguistic conditioning of language variation:

> If there are relatively constant, day-to-day effects of social interaction upon grammar and phonology, the uniformitarian principle asserts that these influences continue to operate today the same way that they have in the past.

Romaine (1988: 1454) similarly promotes uniformitarianism to an axiom of sociolinguistic reconstruction:

> The linguistic forces which operate today and are observable around us are not unlike those which have operated in the past. This principle is of course basic to purely linguistic reconstruction as well, but sociolinguistically speaking, it means that there is no reason for believing that language did not vary in the same patterned ways in the past as it has been observed to do today.

While Labov and Romaine stress the impact of social interaction on language use across time, it is clear that the uniformitarian notion should not be interpreted naively or anachronistically on the basis of present-day findings. Rather, it should be tested, wherever possible, with empirical data. This is of course only possible in the historical period, and to the extent that records of varied situated language use have been preserved from the language community.

Due to differences in data sources, sociolinguistic enquiries are bound to have different foci depending on whether they are dealing with the present or the past. Table 20.1 outlines some of these differences based on the empirical sociolinguistic work Helena Raumolin-Brunberg and I have carried out on Late Middle and Early Modern English (Nevalainen and Raumolin-Brunberg, 1996, 2003). By the sixteenth and seventeenth centuries, the regularization of English spelling had reached a stage when even texts such as personal letters had become difficult to localize on the basis of spelling. This state of affairs to a large extent rules out the study of phonological variation, which is the primary focus of present-day research. However, as normative grammar does not have a role to play in the English language in this period, prescriptivism does not impact on syntactic and morphological variation and change. Grammatical variation therefore presents a good target for the study of English in this period.

Focusing on grammar does not mean that written evidence could not be used to reconstruct

Table 20.1 Dimensions of sociolinguistic research

	Present	Past
Object of investigation	Phonological variation and change	Grammatical and lexical variation and change
Research material	Spoken language	Written language
	All people	Only literate people
	Authentic speech; observation, elicitation	Randomly preserved texts, commentary
Social context	Society familiar; rich context available	Society unfamiliar; amount of contextual information varies
Standardization	Significant element	Significance varies
Associated discipline	Sociology	Social history
Duration and outcome of a process of change	Unknown	Known

Source: Modified from Raumolin-Brunberg (1996: 18)

variation in speech in the past. In the Middle English period, for instance, a good deal of phonological variation was recorded in writing, and verse form preserved information on rhyming sounds. Moreover, metalinguistic material of different kinds is plentiful from later periods, ranging from the work of sixteenth-century spelling reformers to the publications of eighteenth-century grammarians and elocutionists (Wyld, 1936; Nevalainen, 2006: 12–26, 118–120; Nevalainen and Tieken-Boon van Ostade, 2006). These sources provide information on the salient speech patterns of various social groups, discussed, for example, in Mugglestone (2003). The particularly rich tradition of literary parody offers a good source for the study of a number of stigmatized variants in French in the early modern period (Lodge, 2003).

However, looking for authentic material produced by individuals, the historical sociolinguist is faced with the fact that it is only available from the literate section of the population. This represents the tip of the iceberg at a time when the vast majority of the population was illiterate. As the social structures of an earlier era are not familiar to the researcher, they have to be reconstructed on the basis of social, demographic and economic history. Placing historical linguistic findings in their social contexts thus requires more background information than those present-day studies in which the researchers are familiar with the communities they investigate. Nevertheless, the outcome of linguistic processes of change will usually be known to the researcher working with real-time diachronic materials. This is where historical sociolinguists come into their own and may have an advantage over their colleagues working with synchronic, present-day data.

20.3 LANGUAGE AND DIALECT CONTACT

As noted above, the historical comparative method starts with the basic assumption that language change is regular and language-internal. If two languages share a common feature it need not, however, be a sign of their common genetic origins but it may reflect their geographic proximity and thus be the result of borrowing.[2] Since language and dialect contact is ubiquitous in the world, it is a prototypical source of language variation and linguistic change. Linguistic pluralism was also commoner than monolingualism in the past, before the close association of language and nation, and the standardization and codification of languages that we often take for granted today (Burke, 2004: 63–4; see also Section 20.6).

At the macro-sociolinguistic level, the effects of language contact can vary a great deal, depending on the type and duration of the contact situation. These effects range from typical contact-induced changes, such as lexical and morphological borrowing, to extreme language mixtures, which result in new languages, pidgins and creoles. The ultimate result of a contact situation is language death, which is being witnessed on a large scale in the languages of the world today.[3] Nevertheless, contact can give rise to linguistic areas where genetically unrelated languages come to share a varying number of linguistic features over time. As Thomason (2001: 101–2) points out, these areas typically have fuzzy boundaries:

... since the way a linguistic area arises is through contact-induced changes that occur over a long period of time and spread widely through the region – but always from language to language in a series of events, not in some single mystical area-wide process that affects many languages at once.

In individual languages, contact can often provide an explanation for certain linguistic developments such as morphological simplification. McWhorter (2007) goes so far as to claim that in languages that appear to have been simplified beyond what can be expected on the basis of regular linguistic change, this simplification must be due to extensive contact with non-native learners. Simplification contrasts with complexity, which is described in terms of semantic overspecification, structural elaboration and irregularity. The languages McWhorter considers to be simplified compared with their cognate languages include, among others, English (contact with Scandinavian invaders and settlers in the Old English period before AD 1000), Mandarin Chinese (contact with Tibetan and Altaic populations during the Tang dynasty), Persian (possibly through the acquisition of Persian as a foreign language by large populations between the Old and Middle Persian periods), Colloquial Arabic (various historical language and dialect contacts) and Malay (various contacts). (See Trudgill, this volume.)

Contact may also alter the typological make-up of a linguistic area. Jahr (2001) suggests that the typological shift from a synthetic to an analytic language type, which occurred in the Mainland Scandinavian languages, Danish, Swedish and Norwegian, in the late Middle Ages, was due to their close contact with Low German. Low German was the language used by the Hanseatic League, an alliance of trading centres, which was a strong influence in Northern Europe from the thirteenth to the seventeenth centuries. Significantly, a similar change failed to occur in Icelandic, whose contact with Low German was much less intense.

The historical circumstances in which radical linguistic changes have taken place have often gone unrecorded. However, in some well-documented cases, basic contact models may be enriched by considering social networks. Networks can serve as a norm-enforcement mechanism, and their breakdown can accelerate language change through a decline in norm enforcement. James and Lesley Milroy (1985: 377–9) contrast the two Germanic languages, Icelandic and English, whose recorded histories display vastly different rates of language change. Icelandic has to a large extent retained its morphological and phonological structures, while the much faster rate of change in English has resulted in a phonologically quite different, minimally-inflected language.

The Milroys suggest that, in Iceland, the slow rate of linguistic change could be correlated with strong social network ties based on kinship and friendship networks which were established over long distances and through many generations. These network links ensured practical support in time of need but also acted as a norm-enforcement mechanism in various domains of human activity, including language use. By contrast, a combination of external factors such as the Scandinavian invasions and the Norman Conquest contributed to the breakdown of pre-existing strong ties in Anglo-Saxon England. This process, the Milroys argue, created social distance between sectors of the population and paved the way for an institutional system of social stratification. The rise of London as the seat of government and the national centre of commerce further reinforced weak ties and accelerated language change in the late Middle Ages and the Renaissance.

20.4 MODELLING PROCESSES OF LINGUISTIC CHANGE

Another focus of interest for historical linguists and sociolinguists alike concerns the ways in which language changes spread over time. The traditional *tree* and *wave models* represent complementary aspects of the issue at different levels of abstraction. The tree model describes the outcome of the divergence of genetically related languages: the speakers of Proto-Indo-European, for example, are assumed to have spread out to distinctive communities, and during this process become linguistically more dissimilar over time. The traditional wave model, by contrast, accounts for the diffusion of ongoing linguistic changes. As changes spread gradually outwards from a centre, neighbouring dialects become increasingly more similar linguistically. Dialects constitute continua, 'a series of systems where those nearest and most in contact show only slight differences' (Samuels, 1972: 90).

Could the tree model be used to account for more recent historical changes such as the divergence of the Romance languages from Latin? This is a complex issue in that the spoken and written Latin varieties diverged to the extent of becoming mutually unintelligible in the course of the Middle Ages. The archaic written variety that was promoted and standardized by the Carolingian Reforms around AD 800 became the language of education and the Church in Western Europe. This reform was politically motivated, to quote Pulgram (1950: 461), 'to enforce the revival, at least for formal use, of "good" Roman speech (which was dead) in the new Roman Empire (which was the Frankish state) under the new Roman Emperor (who was a German)'. This archaic written variety was diffused not only in southern and south-western Europe, where Latin had been a spoken language during the Roman Empire (roughly, modern Italy, Spain, Portugal, France and Romania), but also in central and northern Europe. At the same time, the spoken forms of Latin continued to diverge and fragment. The two modes of communication, written and spoken, thus operated with different varieties.

The national languages that are today known as Italian, Spanish, Portuguese, French, Romanian and the other Romance varieties spoken in southern Europe are direct continuations of spoken Latin – in the same way as historical linguists identify contemporary Greek and English as the descendents of Ancient Greek and Old English, respectively. Wright (2004: 5) points out that, while English and Greek have not changed their names in the course of time, for political reasons the spoken Latin varieties have, and are identified as separate languages. The processes that led to these national varieties were neither simultaneous nor straightforward. Just as in the case of Latin itself, the use of which had expanded with the Roman Empire, political power promoted certain regional forms of speech over others. In the thirteenth century, Parisian French started to gain prestige and with time surpassed Provençal, a widely recognized literary language. Castilian Spanish, associated with Madrid, similarly displaced Catalan, spoken in the Barcelona region. However, as Italy's political unification only took place in the nineteenth century, the Tuscan prestige variety of Florence, the model for modern standard Italian, was not supplanted by the speech of Rome (McColl Millar, 2007: 220–3).

However, identifying the modern spoken varieties of Latin as separate languages, Wright (1999: 179) argues, also has to do with the comparative method, which stresses the evolution of separate languages from a common source. The family-tree model presents fragmentation as geographically discrete and historically linear. This abstract model is not applicable, he suggests, to language divergence with a relatively shallow time depth. Proto-Indo-European speakers spread out to distinctive communities with no unifying standards, but this did not happen with Romance speakers, who had access to written standard Latin. Moreover, the regional variation and fragmentation attested in Romance is not easily reducible to neatly separated languages. This divergence can best be understood with a knowledge of history combined with a knowledge of what is plausible sociolinguistically (Wright, 1999: 184).

It is obvious that historical developments can be described at various levels of delicacy. Consider the rise of Castilian Spanish referred to above. Penny (2000) and Tuten (2003) suggest that it was due to its recurrent contacts with other Hispano-Romance varieties in the Iberian Peninsula in the Middle Ages, reinforced by internal migration to Madrid after it had been made the capital in 1561, that Castilian Spanish became more levelled and structurally less irregular than the other varieties in the northern Hispano-Romance dialect continuum, notably Catalan, Galician and Portuguese. Castilian was, for instance, the first Hispano-Romance variety to show a reduction of the Romance seven-vowel system to five vowels, but this reduced pattern also spread to the other varieties. It therefore becomes difficult, if not impossible, to determine clear-cut boundaries between the different regional varieties, especially as these processes continued in the New World.

Penny (2000) argues that the result of successive migrations was the formation of new speech communities where speakers from different regions came together but were connected by weak rather than strong ties, which speeded up language change. This is notably the case with the American varieties of Spanish, which arose as a consequence of the Spanish colonization of Latin America, beginning in the fifteenth century. They are largely based on western Andalusian varieties, and show, for example, the weakening of the syllable-final /s/ and the merger of /l/ and /r/. In some other respects they resemble varieties of central and northern Spain, and the coming together of the Sevillan and Madrilenian norms of Castilian (Penny, 2000: 145–6, Conde Silvestre, 2007: 296–306).

However, moving from linguistic varieties to individual processes of change, the family-tree metaphor has been re-evoked in accounts of ongoing changes under stable conditions. Labov (2007: 346–7) makes a distinction between linguistic 'transmission', by which he understands a regular unbroken sequence of native-language acquisition by children, and 'diffusion', which he defines as transfer across language communities, i.e. across the branches of the family tree. He bases this distinction on the notion of a well-defined speech community with clear boundaries. Although adults can participate in ongoing changes, they are expected to do it more sporadically and at a slower rate than children.[4]

Sociolinguists naturally recognize that the transfer of language change is by no means automatic but subject to various psychological and social factors. These are related to the social evaluation of the features undergoing change and speakers' perceptions of them, as well as the general tendency of speakers to modify their language in the presence of others (Trudgill, 1986; Eckert, 2000; Kerswill and Williams, 2000; Milroy and Gordon, 2003: 116–35; Sankoff, 2004; Raumolin-Brunberg, 2005).

Labov's empirical evidence for diffusion comes from studies on the geographical distribution of certain ongoing North American sound changes. His studies show, first, that structural constraints are lost in the diffusion of the New York City pattern of tensing short -*a* to other speech communities. Secondly, they show that the spread of a chain shift of six vowels, known as the Northern Cities Shift from the Chicago area across a dialect boundary to St. Louis, only represents the borrowing of certain individual sound changes rather than the adoption of the whole system. Labov (2007: 383) argues that the results of dialect contact can be expected to be slower, less regular and less governed by structural constraints than the internal developments based on parent-to-child transmission.

Unlike the borrowing of individual sound changes across a major dialect boundary, the Northern Cities Shift progresses quite regularly in all the major cities within the Inland North dialect region. Although parts of the shift were first recorded only 50 years ago, Labov (2007: 373) assumes that the conditions for it go back 100 years earlier, and were transmitted across the Inland North with the westward migration of entire communities.

20.5 THE GRAVITY OF CENTRAL PLACES

Migration holds the key to understanding many developments connected with the diffusion of language change. In the case of Romance languages, for instance, demographic growth was propelled by internal migration, which led to dialect mixing and levelling in large cities, as happened, for example, in Madrid. Medieval Paris is another case in point. Lodge (2003, 2004) shows that by the thirteenth century, Paris had became the largest city in Western Europe. Due to internal migration and dialect contact, extensive dialect mixing and levelling took place in this pre-industrial city, which had become what dialectologists identify as a 'central place' for a large hinterland. Features of the Parisian urban dialect, Parisian spoken koiné, such as the fricative pronunciation of the initial consonant in words like *chat* (< Latin *cattus*), began to make their way to varieties of northern Gallo-Romance in the late Middle Ages. However, by the time of the Renaissance, social stratification had taken place in the capital to the extent that the élites sought to distinguish their language from that of the lower ranks (Lodge, 2003).

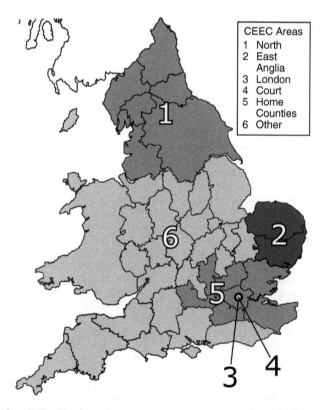

Figure 20.1   Regional distribution of the data in *The Corpus of Early English Correspondence* (© Terttu Nevalainen and the CEEC Team).

Most morphological changes that diffused in England between the fifteenth and eighteenth centuries, and that have been studied empirically, were promoted by the capital region or gathered momentum in the capital. It is obvious that London English reflects the various waves of migration to the capital and the dialect mixing that took place there. The features of northern origin, for instance, that diffused throughout the country include the third-person present-tense indicative ending -(e)s (sings) as opposed to the southern -(e)th (singeth) and the use of are instead of be in the present indicative plural of the verb be.

If these features had followed the wave model of diffusion in a regular manner, they would have spread southwards from the North of England covering all the intervening regions. Are followed the pattern (Nevalainen, 2000), but this did not happen with -(e)s. Nevalainen and Raumolin-Brunberg (2003) studied its diffusion in The Corpus of Early English Correspondence (CEEC), which indicated that this suffix was, as expected, the preferred form in the North in the latter half of the fifteenth century. It was also used in about one-third of the cases in the City of London but not at all in East Anglia, which represents the East Midland region (for the areas studied, see Figure 20.1).

This state of affairs was also observed by H. C. Wyld (1936), the eminent philologist, who analysed the diffusion of linguistic changes in this period. He writes:

We are placed in this dilemma, that the only apparent possible intermediary between the North and London and the South, by which a dialectal peculiarity could pass, is the E. Midland area, whereas this peculiar characteristic does not appear to be especially widespread in the E. Midland dialects, or among such writers as might be expected to show direct influence from these dialects in the fifteenth and sixteenth centuries (Wyld 1936: 336).

A plausible answer to Wyld's dilemma is supplied by the central places theory and London demographics: a steady flow of migrants, especially from the northern regions, to the capital in the fifteenth and early sixteenth centuries. Throughout the early modern period the growth of the capital entirely depended on internal migration. East Anglia, by contrast, was quite self-contained and Norwich, its capital, was the largest provincial town in England at that time. It is therefore probable that the northern suffix reached London by means of 'dialect hopping' rather than as a result of steady dialect diffusion (Nevalainen, 2000; Nevalainen and Raumolin-Brunberg, 2000; see also Section 20.7).

Similar demographic and linguistic developments can be found in many other cities in Early Modern Europe. Howell (2006) argues that the rapid growth of urban centres in Holland, especially that of Amsterdam, is entirely attributable to immigration. The urban population more than tripled in the northern Netherlands between 1550 and 1650, and marriage records show that dialect contact must have been common, even within nuclear families. Linguistically, the situation led to dialect levelling and koinéization, i.e. favouring majority forms and disfavouring marked regional forms in the post-contact variety. Phonologically, grammatically and lexically simpler elements also came to be preferred to more complex ones (Howell, 2006: 216–17; cf. Kerswill and Williams, 2000).

While acknowledging the roles of both adults and children in the rise of new urban koinés, Howell (2006) stresses the importance of second-generation immigrants to the koinéization process in his material. He analyses the personal correspondence of an immigrant family in The Hague, and demonstrates how the daughters' usages closely reflect those of urban centres in the northern Netherlands at large. These include the adoption of the new reflexive pronouns sich and of the prefix ge- in past participles. The uninflected form sich represents a simplifying innovation that replaced the inflected object pronouns hem and haer of the native Holland dialects, while the prefix ge- replaced the reduced e-, which was a salient feature of the Holland dialects at the time (but is today only found in rural dialects). It is noteworthy that the various innovations that Howell (2006) studied do not all come from the same immigrant dialects; neither are they necessarily present in the native Holland varieties, but represent new dialect formation taking place in the urban centres.

The history of Japanese demonstrates how the linguistic influence of the capital city can be transferred from one locality to another. When the dominant centre of political and cultural influence shifted from the Kyoto region in the west to Edo (present-day Tokyo) in the east in the seventeenth century, the focus of linguistic prestige shifted accordingly. However, Inoue (1983, 1986) finds that not only do new standard and dialect forms spread from modern Tokyo to the rest of country but also that new dialect lexis also spreads to Tokyo from other localities.

Although historical linguistics is, as Campbell (2007: 21) points out, by definition a retrospective science, the gravity model, coupled with knowledge about past developments, may be used to make predictions about the future. Trudgill (1999) bases his future dialect map of England on urban dialects. Over the past couple of centuries, large cities have been instrumental in the formation of modern dialects, which Trudgill contrasts with traditional dialects. He predicts the survival of areas such as those focused on Newcastle, Liverpool, Birmingham and Manchester, and the growth of a new region focused on Bristol. In this scenario, East Anglia is expected to contract, and the South Midlands to disappear in the face of the expansion of the Home Counties area based on London (Trudgill, 1999: 83–4; cf. Figure 20.1).

20.6 LINGUISTIC STANDARDIZATION

Selection of standards

The rise of standard languages is of interest to both modern sociologists of language and historical sociolinguists.[5] One of the influential models analysing the process was proposed by Einar Haugen (1997 [1966]). He traces the phases of standardization, from the selection of a language variety as the basis of the standard and its acceptance by the language community via its elaboration (*Ausbau*), to its codification in grammars and dictionaries. More detailed models have also been proposed on the basis of Haugen's, adding to the process the diffusion, maintenance and prescription of the standard (Milroy and Milroy, 1999: 22–3).

As suggested by Table 20.1, above, the role played by standardization on language variation and change does not remain constant over time. The standardization of European languages shows that even the selection processes that lead to the adoption of a vernacular norm can be expected to vary greatly from one language community to another (Deumert and Vandenbussche (eds), 2003). Good candidates to be selected are those varieties that are spoken in the political, economic and cultural capitals of their respective areas. As shown above, they often represent levelled varieties which are comprehensible outside the region, and ones to which a large number of people have been exposed. In the case of London, it has been argued that one English adult in eight in 1550–1650 and one in six in 1650–1750 had some experience of life in London regardless of their social status (Nevalainen and Raumolin-Brunberg, 2003: 39).

One step further from urban dialects, but often including them, are deregionalized varieties used in supraregional communication. These *koinés* are good candidates for a standard in that they are characterized by levelling, the process which reduces those features that show the most regional variation among the dialects or languages involved (Trudgill, 1986). A case in point is the Hellenistic Koiné, which was the 'common language' of the Greece of Alexander the Great. It was based on the dialect of Athens, perhaps the most important city-state in Greece in this and subsequent periods. It was 'de-Atticized' when the extensive trade, cultural and political contacts that the inhabitants of Athens had with the other city-states exposed them to their local dialects. Other illustrations of more recent koiné-based standard languages are Swahili and Lingala (Hock, 1986: 485–91).

The selection of a future standard language can also be the product of language planning. This was how, for example, the Norwegian and Finnish literary languages were created in the nineteenth century. In the case of Norwegian, the result was two standard written varieties, *nynorsk* and *bokmål*, which became native alternatives to written Danish. Nynorsk was created by Ivar Aasen on the basis of different regional varieties in the mid-nineteenth century, while bokmål developed from an existing koiné, the Norwegianized spoken variety of Danish that was associated with the urban élite, especially that of the capital. Although nynorsk and bokmål both continue to have the status of official written standards, the vast majority of the Norwegian population use bokmål in their written communication today (Kerswill, 1994: 32–7).

The conscious planning of the Finnish literary language in the nineteenth century resulted in a single norm that combined elements from various regional dialects. The dialect to form the basis of the standard was subject to a prolonged debate among language professionals. The (south)western dialects had the prestige of a long literary history, which could be traced back to the first religious texts printed in Finnish in the 1540s. The eastern varieties were, in turn, associated with a rich folklore tradition, which was captured in the *Kalevala*, first published by Elias Lönnrot in 1835, and soon hailed as the national epic of Finland. The written norm came to be based on western structures, with considerable lexical enrichment from eastern dialects (Huumo, Laitinen and Paloposki (eds), 2004).

Standards and vernaculars

Since standardization is a process, the relations between standard and vernacular varieties in a language community are liable to change over time. In multilingual communities, standard norms can arise both from within the language community ('endoglossic' norms) and from outside it ('exoglossic' norms). In Medieval Europe, endoglossic standards were typically preceded by exoglossic ones, such as Latin in western and central Europe, Arabic in Spain, and Old Church Slavonic in Russia and Romania (Auer, 2005: 9–12).

However, it is worth bearing in mind that linguistic pluralism was commonplace both in Medieval and Early Modern Europe, and different languages could be used for different functions at the same time. Even with Latin as an exoglossic standard, Burke (2004: 63) points out the 'literary' uses of varieties of French, Anglo-Saxon and Irish in the ninth century, of Spanish and Slovene in the tenth century, Italian at the turn of the millennium, Provençal around AD 1100, Dutch and Icelandic in the twelfth century, Hungarian and Danish in the thirteenth, and Catalan and Polish in the fourteenth. In early fifteenth-century England, Latin continued as the language of learning and the Catholic Church, and the Anglo-Norman variety of French was used as the language of the law. The earlier widespread use of French as the language of the administration had considerably declined by this time and English had begun to be employed in government documents emanating from the King's writing offices at Westminster. English also continued in literary use (Nevalainen and Tieken-Boon van Ostade, 2006).

Vernacularization, the shift from an exoglossic to an endoglossic standard, can be a prolonged process, with exoglossic and endoglossic norms coexisting side by side. It could take a vernacular variety a long time to become the standard, according to the definition offered by Haugen (1997: 348), with 'minimal variation in form' and 'maximal variation in function'. In this process, a distinction can be made between a mainly written endoglossic standard and spoken local dialects. As shown above, however, written endoglossic supraregional varieties can also be attested before the rise of a focused vernacular standard. In general, as Auer (2005: 10) points out, interdialectal levelling can serve as a useful step paving the way for a national standard variety. The previous sections have shown that levelling commonly takes place in dialect contact situations as a result of speakers accommodating to each other in social interaction.

Such levelled varieties also arose in Late Medieval England, which was triglossic between Latin, French and English. They include some more distinct regiolects, such as the Central Midland variety, which is attested in a large number of texts, including religious and medical writings. Another local norm is found in mid-fourteenth-century official documents in the London area, and a later type of London writing appears in texts copied in the late fourteenth century, which contain, for instance, Chaucer's *Canterbury Tales*. Late Middle English non-literary texts were in general characterized by 'colourless' mixtures of regional dialects. They were unstable and showed local register variation, but as they displayed the more widespread features of their respective varieties to the exclusion of those that were more distinctly local, these usages are often referred to as 'colourless regional standard' (Samuels, 1963; Benskin, 1992: 82–5; Smith, 1996: 73–7).

The variety to undergo standardization is connected with political and economic power, but its acceptance as a shared norm is a matter of focusing and speakers' awareness of a common norm. This awareness is raised by education and the mass media, such as the advent of printing in the late fifteenth and early sixteenth centuries. In some communities, the process of focusing on a given norm is more diffuse and unmonitored than in others. However, as many parallel processes of vernacularization took place in Europe in the sixteenth century, the praise of the vernacular became something of a Renaissance genre. Burke (2004: 65–70) provides a long list of such publications, apparently sparked off by Dante's 1529 Latin treatise on the eloquence of the Italian vernacular. The list given below could be supplemented with a number of similar treatises on these and other European languages, among them Czech, Hungarian, Icelandic, Russian and Swedish. As Burke (2004: 66) points out, orations were also dedicated to languages that may now be considered dialects, including Bolognese, Milanese and Neapolitan.

Italian:	1529 Dante, *De vulgari eloquentia*
	1542 S. Speroni, *Dialogo delle lingue*
Portuguese:	1540 J. de Barros, *Louvor da nossa linguagem*
French:	1549 J. Du Bellai, *Deffense et illustration de la langue françoise*
	1579 H. Estienne, *Precellance du language françois*
Spanish:	1574 M. Viziana, *Alabanças de las lenguas … castellana y valenciana*
Dutch:	1586 S. Stevin, *Weerdigheyt der duytsche tael*
German:	1617 M. Opitz, *De contemptu linguae teutonicae*
	1642 J. Rist, *Rettung der edlen teutschen Hauptsprache*
Polish:	1589 J. Rybinski, *De lingua polonica praestantia*
English:	1615 R. Carew, *On the Excellency of the English Tongue*

One of the concerns typically raised by the functional elaboration of vernaculars was their adequacy as a literary medium in comparison with Latin. English is here a case in point. To meet the needs of creating new vocabulary for new concepts and registers, a large number of words were borrowed into the vernacular from the classical languages directly or via French. As these words presented problems for those without a classical education, their use created linguistic insecurity among the less educated – and a flourishing market for publishers. The first monolingual English dictionaries, which started to appear from the beginning of the seventeenth century onwards, focused on definitions of 'hard vsuall English wordes'. They were intended for the uneducated, women in particular, and contributed to the codification of the borrowed lexical element in English (Nevalainen, 2003).

However, the processes of standardization need not stop with the fixing of an endoglossic norm, for de- and restandardization can also take place for demographic, political and ideological reasons (Auer, 2005: 24–6). Even spelling norms are not immutably fixed by the codification of an endoglossic norm in the print medium. A written standard can break up, yielding new codified regional norms, as to some extent happened with British and American English in the nineteenth century. This is not uncommon in postcolonial orthography in general. Scripts and spelling conventions can be rejected if they are closely identified with the former dominant or colonial power. As Sebba (2007: 81–101) shows in detail, numerous orthographic upheavals have taken place after the break-up of former world powers such as the Ottoman and Tsarist Russian empires and the Soviet Union, and in newly-independent Third World countries.

Even attempts at reforming established spelling norms can cause far-reaching debates, which reveal that spelling standardization is not simply a matter of common conventions but also of language ideology. Linguistic standardization creates identities in that it forms what Anderson (1991) calls 'imagined communities', and a reform proposal can hence be seen as an identity-threatening act. A case in point is the introduction of the reform of German orthography in the 1990s, which only concerned about 0.5 per cent of the lexicon but caused a huge public outcry and even escalated into a constitutional crisis (Johnson, 2005; Sebba, 2007).

20.7 VARIATIONIST HISTORICAL SOCIOLINGUISTICS

Register variation

The historical study of standard languages is intimately connected with that of vernaculars. As modern sociolinguistics generally prioritizes speech, the concentration of historical sociolinguists on written materials may appear problematic (cf. Section 20.2). However, historical linguists have long recognized the need not only to relate the two modes of communication to each other but also to treat, as emphasized by Romaine

(1988), the written language in its own right. One common way to depict the relation between the two is by polarizing them into two contrasting modes of communication, which, rather than remaining equidistant, may either diverge or converge over time.

Linguistic differences between the written and spoken medium may be discussed at various levels of delicacy. Sloping lines connecting the two media have been diagrammed for languages with considerable time depth, such as the six classical or written languages of Egyptian from c. 4000 BC down to AD 1000. While the spoken vernacular is assumed to continue to change throughout the history of Egyptian, the six classical languages are traditionally each assumed to represent steps that adhere to a standard without any major changes as long as the society that uses it remains stable (Pulgram, 1950). The written language is realigned with the vernacular only after the breakdown of a culture, as the new culture succeeding it creates its own literary language. As already noted, similar abstract models based on the written and spoken media have been proposed for Latin and the Romance languages.

At a more delicate level of description, written language can be found to move either away from informal speech or closer to it over time. However, no strict dichotomy between the two can be proposed – at any one time, language variation remains situation-dependent. Research into this variability requires data sources that represent a range of *genres* or *registers,* i.e. situationally defined varieties (Biber, 1995: 7–10). The register comparisons that Biber and Finegan have carried out are based on well over 60 linguistic features. Their multivariate analysis produces textual dimensions that can be used to describe linguistic variation in different communicative situations today, as well as in the past. Three dimensions emerge as salient in present-day English: (D1) involved vs informational production, (D2) situation-dependent vs elaborated reference, and (D3) non-impersonal vs impersonal style (Biber, 1995; Biber and Finegan, 1997).

Face-to-face conversations and personal letters, for example, show high frequencies of features that express personal involvement, including first- and second-person pronouns, private verbs (e.g. *think, know*), *that*-deletion, present tense verbs, contractions (*it's, won't*), hedges (*maybe, sort of*) and emphatics and amplifiers (*really, totally*). By contrast, academic texts, such as scientific research articles, exhibit few such involvement markers. Focusing on information, they show high frequencies of nouns, prepositions, attributive adjectives, long words and varied lexis, as well as both agentless and *by*-passives.

These dimensions can distinguish typically oral (conversational) genres or registers from typically literate (written expository) ones. The studies carried out on historical corpora using the same methodology also reveal trends of diachronic register evolution along these dimensions. Biber (1995: 283–300) and Biber and Finegan (1997) analyse how such popular written registers, in essays and fiction for instance, develop in a more oral direction or 'colloquialize' along these dimensions between 1650 and 1990 in British and American English alike, becoming more involved, situation-dependent and less impersonal. However, they also detect simultaneous generic drifts towards more formal expression as such specialist expository registers as legal, medical and other scientific writings reveal a consistent trend towards the more literate end of these three dimensions, and show increasing tendencies towards informational production, elaborated reference and impersonal style.[6]

Reconstructing real-time processes of change

Having access to a systematic diachronic corpus makes it possible for a historical sociolinguist to study linguistic changes over extended periods of time. Significantly, however, reconstructing language use in its social context is a question of time depth: even late medieval sources may prove too scarce to provide a sufficient basis for sociolinguistic investigations of many European vernaculars. For English, the situation improves from the fifteenth century onwards when full vernacular literacy – the ability not only to read but also to write – begins to spread outside professional circles, thus providing access to a wider section of the population.[7]

According to David Cressy's 1980 study based on people's ability to sign their names ('signature literacy'), an average of 10 per cent of men and 1 per cent of women could both read and write in England in 1500. By 1700, the corresponding figure had risen to 40 per cent for men and 25 per cent for women. Literacy studies give us an idea of the kind of people whose language has been recorded in writing. The social circumstances of the past are brought to life by research into social, economic, cultural and demographic history. Indeed, information provided by historians is vital for an adequate sociohistorical reconstruction of the social conditions, categories and hierarchies of the past.

Personal letters offer certain advantages as source material for historical variation studies: (1) work carried out by, among others, Biber and Finegan, indicates that letters share a number of genre characteristics with face-to-face conversations, and (2) they can provide authentic data produced by known individuals, similar to interview data used in present-day sociolinguistic research.[8] The generic differences between personal letters and face-to-face conversations as data sources are also obvious, and need not be elaborated upon here. However, as many processes of language change proceed below the level of conscious awareness, they may not be regulated by generic constraints to the same extent as more conscious processes. This becomes obvious when analysing linguistic changes in progress, an extended example of which is given below.

As shown by the case of 'dialect hopping' discussed in Section 20.6, correspondence can be used to trace real-time processes of language change in their social context. Much of the variationist sociolinguistic research that has been carried out using *The Corpus of Early English Correspondence* has concentrated on morphosyntactic processes between the fifteenth and seventeenth centuries. The 14 changes reported in Nevalainen and Raumolin-Brunberg (2003) range from pronominal and verbal changes to abstract structural patterns, such as the disappearance of multiple negation. They are all instances of supralocalization (and all but two are successful) in that they spread from their region of origin to the rest of the country. They hence contribute to the rise of what Trudgill (1999: 6) refers to as Mainstream Modern Dialects of English.

The case of verbal -(e)s

In the fifteenth and sixteenth centuries, English did not have a codified standard language, and the education system, centred on Latin, had little impact on linguistic changes in progress. The rivalry between the third-person singular indicative suffixes -(e)s and -(e)th serves as an illustrative case study on this issue. When it first appeared in the City of London in the fifteenth century, the verbal -(e)s probably counted as a northernism and failed to diffuse further to the south, while the southern -(e)th continued to spread across the country (Moore, 2002). However, the trend was reversed in the course of the sixteenth century. Figure 20.2 shows the S-shaped curve of the diffusion of -(e)s in the aggregate data provided by the CEEC. It suggests that the southern -(e)th continued to dominate until the 1580s.[9] Letter-writers coming from different parts of the country used both forms from the latter half of the century onwards, as in excerpt (1), and some well into the seventeenth century, as in excerpt (2).

(1) … that a question may, upon allegeance, be demanded by yourselfe of the mastar Gray,

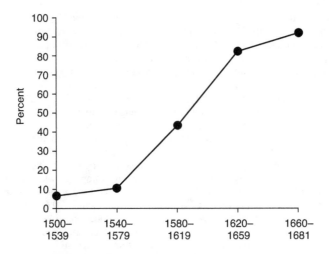

**Figure 20.2   Replacement of the third-person indicative singular suffix -(e)th by -(e)s.
Relative frequencies of -(e)s in verbs other than *have* and *do* (based on Nevalainen and Raumolin-
Brunberg, 2003: 178).**

whether he **knoweth** not the prise of my bloude, wiche shuld be spild by bloudy hande of a murtherar, wiche some of your nere-a-kin did graunt. A sore question, you may suppose, but no other act than suche as I am assured he **knowes**, and therfor I hope he wyl not dare deny you a truthe; (CEEC, Queen Elizabeth I, 1585; ROYAL 2, 11)

(2) ... thy father **remembers** his loue to the and **take** thy wrightinge to him very kindly: thy brother **remember** his louingest loue to the [...] I had thought to haue written to mr Roberts this time. but this sudene lornye of this mesinger **affordethe**

me not so much time, (CEEC, Lady Katherine Paston, 1626?; PASTONK, 90)

Excerpt (1) comes from a letter that Queen Elizabeth I wrote to King James VI of Scotland (and her successor on the throne of England) in 1585. The letter excerpted in (2) was written by Lady Katherine Paston, a Norfolk gentlewoman, to her son, who was a student at Cambridge in the mid-1620s. Both show variation in the third-person singular endings, Lady Paston also exhibiting the suffixless alternative (*take*, *remember*). The situation is not atypical when a change has reached mid-range: many letter-writers use

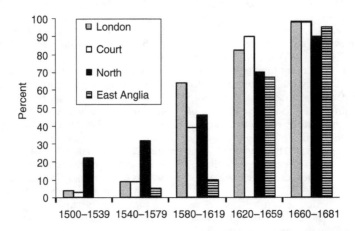

**Figure 20.3   Replacement of -(e)th by -(e)s in verbs other than *have* and *do*. Regional distri-
bution of -(e)s (based on Nevalainen and Raumolin-Brunberg, 2003: 178).**

both the old and the new form. However, some more general tendencies can also be detected. Figure 20.3 presents the patterns that emerge when the data are broken down into four of the regions shown in Figure 20.1 in Section 20.5.

Two things appear from Figure 20.3. First, although -(e)s was of northern origin and was common there in the early part of the sixteenth century, the southern -(e)th was the dominant form in all the four areas studied. However, once -(e)s begins to spread, the City of London leads the process. At this stage, the Royal Court at Westminster was much slower in adopting the incoming form, which suggests that the change spread from the lower social ranks to the higher. This impression is confirmed by a social rank analysis of the aggregate data, which divides the sixteenth-century social hierarchy into upper (gentry, clergy), middle (professionals, merchants)

and lower ranks: the lower ranks are in the vanguard of the process from the 1540s onwards (Nevalainen and Raumolin-Brunberg, 2003: 144–5).

However, Figure 20.3 indicates that the process was slowest not at Court but in East Anglia, where the traditional southern form dominated well into the early decades of the seventeenth century. Besides the gravity model discussed in Section 20.5, the reasons why this should have been the case range from the relative isolation and self-sufficiency of East Anglia at the time to a three-competing-forms hypothesis (the third being the suffixless form; Nevalainen, Raumolin-Brunberg and Trudgill, 2001). All three occur in Lady Katherine Paston's letter excerpt in (2). Whatever the retarding factors, -(e)th was replaced by -(e)s in the East Anglian data in the seventeenth century. As a result of the successful supralocalization of

Table 20.2 Three VARBRUL analyses of the verbal -(e)s variable: period means show the relative frequency of -(e)s

Period/mean (%)	Factor group	Weight	Range	Total N
1540–79	**Region**		0.478	**741**
	North	**0.788**		22
8%	London	0.451		217
	Court	0.421		212
	East Anglia	0.310		290
	Gender		0.232	**741**
	Women	0.616		39
	Men	0.384		702
	Register		0.054	**741**
	Intimate	0.473		316
	Distant	0.527		425
1580–1619	**Region**		0.612	**952**
	North	0.616		83
42%	London	**0.767**		303
	Court	0.509		375
	East Anglia	0.155		191
	Gender		0.216	**952**
	Women	0.608		170
	Men	0.392		782
	Register		0.068	952
	Intimate	0.534		490
	Distant	0.466		462
1620–59	**Region**		0.314	**904**
	North	0.405		288
74%	London	0.576		218
	Court	**0.688**		102
	East Anglia	0.329		296
	Gender		0.062	**904**
	Women	0.531		157
	Men	0.469		747
	Register		0.094	**904**
	Intimate	0.547		693
	Distant	0.453		211

the originally northern ending, a reallocation of the regional and stylistic features of the suffixes took place: *-(e)s* became the regionally unmarked form, whereas the southern variant *-(e)th* came to be relegated to literary and religious registers.[10]

Multivariate analysis

As to the use of quantitative methods, historical sociolinguistic work need not differ from that carried out on present-day sociolinguistic data. Let us finish by considering the situational factors that correlate with the diffusion of *-(e)s* in Early Modern English. The tool I have used is the VARBRUL application GoldVarb2 (Rand and Sankoff, 1990).

The results of this multivariate analysis, shown in Table 20.2, confirm the fact that *region* has a key role to play throughout the diffusion of the third-person suffix *-(e)s*. Compared to *gender* and *register*, the top factor weights for region are higher (closer to 1) and their variation range is consistently wider. In the incipient phase of the process, from 1540 to 1579, *-(e)s* is favoured by northern writers (0.788), which is suggestive of its origins. In mid-range (42%), the process continues to be promoted by the North (0.616), but especially by the City of London (0.767). When it is nearing completion, at 74%, the Royal Court catches up and takes the lead. The multivariate analysis confirms the information in Figure 20.3 that, in comparison with the other areas, East Anglia disfavours the incoming form until the mid-seventeenth century.

As with most of the changes studied, women favour the incoming form. This gender difference is statistically significant in the first two periods, but neutralizes when the process approaches completion in the third. Finally, the narrow range of the factor weights suggests that register differences, accounted for in terms of the writer–recipient relationship (intimate or distant), play only a minor role compared with region and gender.[11]

Concluding remarks

Going back to the uniformitarian principle discussed in Section 20.2, the broadest historical generalization that can be made, based on modern sociolinguistic research, is that links between linguistic variables and other variables correlating with them are probabilistic (more or less) rather than categorical. Being probabilistic, a linguistic variable may be sensitive to a whole range of other variables, linguistic and social, each exerting a different degree of influence on how it is realized. The gender of the speaker or writer may

account for linguistic variation better than social status. In the CEEC studies, women proved to be the leaders of 11 out of the 14 changes investigated. The historical role of cities as centres of linguistic innovation and dialect levelling was also well documented. The majority of the changes studied, which diffused throughout England between the fifteenth and eighteenth centuries, were promoted either by the City of London, the Royal Court, or by both, or were given new impetus for their supralocalization by the capital.

ACKNOWLEDGEMENT

The research for this article was supported by the funding awarded by the Academy of Finland and the University of Helsinki to the Research Unit for Variation, Contacts and Change in English (2006–11). I would like to thank Paul Kerswill, Mark Shackleton and Ruth Wodak for their comments on the prefinal version of this chapter, Tanja Säily for help with the references and Simo Ahava and Tanja Säily for the print version of Figure 20.1.

NOTES

1 See: http://www.let.leidenuniv.nl/hsl_shl/. Ammon et al. (1999) list the German and French equivalents of the term, *Historische Soziolinguistik* and *la sociolinguistique historique*. Similarly, the Spanish term used in Conde Silvestre (2007) is *sociolingüística histórica*. Romaine's earlier term (1982), *socio-historical linguistics*, occurs in the titles of Tieken-Boon van Ostade (1987) and Kielkiewicz-Janowiak (1992). Nevalainen and Raumolin-Brunberg (1996) refer to both.

2 Language change is characterized by both regularity and contact-induced variability. Language contact and borrowing were of course also recognized by nineteenth-century Neogrammarians and have preoccupied linguists ever since (cf. Haugen, 1950). James and Lesley Milroy (1985: 339) strive for 'a theory which is sensible both to the constrained and regular nature of change and to its relationship with social structure'. Campbell (2007: 19) similarly points out that we need both models, those based on common ancestors and those considering contact and borrowing, to account for the 'whole history' of a language or a group of languages. A third source of shared features between languages, which does not go back to a historical relationship, is related to language universals (Thomason, 2001: 100).

3 Language attrition has been an active concern of sociolinguists since the 1970s. A special issue edited by Dressler and Wodak-Leodolter was devoted to this topic by the *International Journal of the Sociology of Language* (IJSL) in 1977, and Dorian's 1981 seminal work on Scottish Gaelic was followed by global discussions such as Crystal (2000) and Nettle and Romaine (2000). A special issue on regional dialect attrition appeared in the 2009 volume of IJSL edited by Vandekerckhove and Britain with the title 'Dialects in western Europe: a balanced picture of language death, innovation, and change'.

4 A similar account of the regularity of linguistic change was given by Hockett (1950), who contrasted the roles of children and adults in the transmission of language change (I owe this classic reference to Peter Mühlhäusler).

5 I use the term 'rise' for want of a better one, although, as Burke (2004: 64) rightly points out, it is ambiguous in that it may refer to an increase in prestige, in the number of speakers, or the number of functions. Moreover, the trend is not irresistible, although the term may imply that.

6 For reasons of space, a number of issues to do with sociohistorical pragmatics have to be omitted here. One of them is forms of address, which have been extensively studied in a number of periods, languages and language communities. Another area is historical dialogue analysis: for English, see e.g. Kytö and Culpeper 2010.

7 For a range of English historical corpora, see Beal, Corrigan and Moisl (eds) (2007). Personal letters as data sources are discussed by Fitzmaurice, Meurman-Solin, Raumolin-Brunberg and Nevalainen, and van Bergen and Denison.

8 Access to authentic materials can provide striking new information about the linguistic system of social groups. Van Herk (2008) found wide-ranging use of the present perfect in nineteenth-century letters written by semi-literate African-American settlers in Liberia. His data provide new light on the core grammar of these writers, and suggest that the verb form was far from marginal, as previously suggested on the basis of narratives elicited in sociolinguistic interviews.

9 The 'second coming' of -(e)s may also have involved reduction of the unstressed vowel in the suffix (Nevalainen and Raumolin-Brunberg, 2003: 67). *Have* and *do* are excluded from the analysis, because they both retained their southern forms (*hath*, *doeth*) much longer than other verbs, in some traditional dialects until the twentieth century, which suggests a degree of lexical diffusion in this process. The extent to which -(e)s was adopted in regional and social varieties of English is witnessed, for example, by its use in early African-American English, where it was most common in the third-person singular, but also found in the third-person plural and first-person singular (Poplack, 2006).

10 Echoing the King James Bible, the archaic suffix continues to be used by the press for humorous effect, as in 'But what the tabloids *giveth* they may also *taketh* away, and Charles must watch his step' (*Time*, June 19, 2000; 33), where the suffix appears in the plural, and '*Cometh* the hour, *cometh* the man with the cheeky grin' (*The Times*, Oct. 29, 2007; 4).

11 The much lower overall number of instances produced by women than men is a direct reflection of women's much lower rate of full literacy at the time. However, the significance of the gender difference persists with other statistical measures as well – for instance, in randomization tests.

REFERENCES

Ammon, U., Mattheier, K. J. and Nelde, P. H. (eds) (1999) *Historische Soziolinguistik = Historical Sociolinguistics = La sociolinguistique historique* (*Sociolinguistica* 13). Tübingen: Niemeyer.

Anderson, B. (1991) *Imagined Communities: Reflections on the Origin and Spread of Nationalism*. London: Verso.

Anttila, R. (1989) *Historical and Comparative Linguistics* (Current Issues in Linguistic Theory 6). 2nd rev. edn. Amsterdam: Benjamins. (1st edn, 1972.)

Auer, P. (2005) 'Europe's sociolinguistic unity, or: A typology of European dialect/standard constellations', in N. Delbecque, J. van der Auwera and D. Geeraerts (eds), *Perspectives on Variation: Sociolinguistic, Historical, Comparative* (Trends in Linguistics 163). Berlin: Mouton de Gruyter. pp. 7–42.

Beal, J. C., Corrigan, K. P. and Moisl, H. L. (eds) (2007) *Creating and Digitizing Language Corpora.* Vol. 2, *Diachronic Databases.* Houndsmills: Palgrave-Macmillan.

Benskin, M. (1992) 'Some new perspectives on the origins of standard written English', in J. A. van Leuvensteijn and J. B. Berns (eds), *Dialect and Standard Language in the English, Dutch, German and Norwegian Language Areas.* Amsterdam: North Holland. pp. 71–105.

Bergs, A. (2005) *Social Networks and Historical Sociolinguistics: Studies in Morphosyntactic Variation in the Paston Letters (1421–1503)* (Topics in English Linguistics 51). Berlin and New York: Mouton de Gruyter.

Biber, D. (1995) *Dimensions of Register Variation: a Cross-Linguistic Comparison.* Cambridge: Cambridge University Press.

Biber, D. and Finegan, E. (1997) 'Diachronic relations among speech-based and written registers in English', in T. Nevalainen and L. Kahlas-Tarkka (eds), *To Explain the Present: Studies in the Changing English Language in Honour of Matti Rissanen.* Helsinki: Société Néophilologique. pp. 253–75.

Burke, P. (2004) *Languages and Communities in Early Modern Europe.* Cambridge: Cambridge University Press.

Campbell, L. (2007) 'Areal linguistics: a closer scrutiny', in Y. Matras, A. McMahon and N. Vincent (eds), *Linguistic*

Areas: Convergence in Historical and Typological Perspective. Houndmills: Palgrave Macmillan. pp. 1–31.

CEEC = Nevalainen, T., Raumolin-Brunberg, H., Keränen, J., Nevala, M., Nurmi, A. and Palander-Collin, M. (eds) (1998) *The Corpus of Early English Correspondence.* Helsinki: University of Helsinki.

Conde Silvestre, J.C. (2007) *Sociolingüística histórica.* Madrid: Gredos.

Cressy, D. (1980) *Literacy and Social Order: Reading and Writing in Tudor and Stuart England.* Cambridge: Cambridge University Press.

Crystal, D. (2000) *Language Death.* Cambridge: Cambridge University Press.

Deumert, A. and Vandenbussche, W. (eds) (2003) *Germanic Standardizations: Past to Present* (Impact: Studies in Language and Society 18). Amsterdam: Benjamins.

Dorian, N. C. (1981) *Language Death: the Life Cycle of a Scottish Gaelic dialect.* Philadelphia: University of Pennsylvania Press.

Durie, M. and Ross, M. (eds) (1996) *The Comparative Method Reviewed: Regularity and Irregularity in Language Change.* Oxford: Oxford University Press.

Eckert, P. (2000) *Linguistic Variation as Social Practice.* Malden, MA: Blackwell.

Haugen, E. (1950) 'The analysis of linguistic borrowing', *Language*, 26 (2): 210–31.

Haugen, E. (1997) 'Language standardization', in N. Coupland and A. Jaworski (eds), *Sociolinguistics.* London: Macmillan. (1st published 1966). pp. 341–52.

Hernández-Campoy, J. M. (ed.) (forthcoming) *The Handbook of Historical Sociolinguistics.* Malden, MA: Wiley-Blackwell.

Hock, H. H. (1986) *Principles of Historical Linguistics.* Berlin: Mouton de Gruyter.

Hockett, C. (1950) 'Age-grading and linguistic continuity', *Language*, 26(4): 449–57.

Howell, R. B. (2006) 'Immigration and koineisation: the formation of early modern Dutch urban vernaculars', *Transactions of the Philological Society*, 104(2): 207–27.

Huumo, K., Laitinen, L. and Paloposki, O. (eds) (2004) *Yhteistä kieltä tekemässä. Näkökulmia suomen kirjakielen kehitykseen 1800-luvulla.* Helsinki: Suomalaisen Kirjallisuuden Seura.

Inoue, F. (1983) 'A note on recent changes of dialect near Tokyo', *Area and Culture Studies*, 33: 363–7.

Inoue, F. (1986) 'Sociolinguistic aspects of new dialect forms: language change in progress in Tokyo', *International Journal of the Sociology of Language*, 58: 73–89.

Jahr, E. H. (ed.) (1999) *Language Change: Advances in Historical Sociolinguistics.* Berlin: Mouton de Gruyter.

Jahr, E. H. (2001) 'Historical sociolinguistics: the role of Low German language contact in the Scandinavian typological shift of the Late Middle Ages', *Lingua Posnaniensis*, 43: 95–104.

Janda, R. D. and Joseph, B. D. (2003) 'On language, change, and language change – or of history, linguistics, and historical linguistics', in B. D. Joseph and R. D. Janda (eds), *The Handbook of Historical Linguistics.* Malden, MA: Blackwell. pp. 3–180.

Johnson, S. A. (2005) *Spelling Trouble: Language, Ideology and the Reform of German Orthography.* Clevedon, UK: Multilingual Matters.

Kerswill, P. (1994) *Dialects Converging: Rural Speech in Urban Norway.* Oxford: Oxford University Press.

Kerswill, P. and Williams, A. (2000) 'Creating a new town koiné: children and language change in Milton Keynes', *Language in Society*, 29: 65–115.

Kielkiewicz-Janowiak, A. (1992) *A Socio-Historical Study in Address: Polish and English* (Bamberger Beiträge zur englischen Sprachwissenschaft 30). Frankfurt am Main: Peter Lang.

Kytö, M. and Culpeper, J. (2010) *Speech in Writing: Explorations in Early Modern English Dialogues.* Cambridge: Cambridge University Press.

Labov, W. (1985) *Sociolinguistic Patterns.* Oxford: Blackwell. (1st edn, 1972.)

Labov, W. (1994) *Principles of Linguistic Change.* Vol. 1, *Internal Factors.* Oxford: Blackwell.

Labov, W. (2007) 'Transmission and diffusion', *Language*, 83(2): 344–87.

Lass, R. (1997) *Historical Linguistics and Language Change.* Cambridge: Cambridge University Press.

Lodge, R. A. (2003) 'Reallocation between standard and vernacular in early modern Paris', *Sociolinguistica*, 17: 88–107.

Lodge, R. A. (2004) *A Sociolinguistic History of Parisian French.* Cambridge: Cambridge University Press.

Machan, T. W. and Scott, C. T. (eds) (1992) *English in Its Social Contexts: Essays in Historical Sociolinguistics.* Oxford: Oxford University Press.

McColl Millar, R. (rev.) (2007) *Trask's Historical Linguistics.* 2nd edn. London: Hodder Arnold.

McWhorter, J. (2007) *Language Interrupted: Signs of Non-Native Acquisition in Standard Language Grammars.* Oxford: Oxford University Press.

Martinet, A. (1964) *Elements of General Linguistics.* London: Faber.

Milroy, J. (1992) *Linguistic Variation and Change: on the Historical Sociolinguistics of English.* Oxford: Blackwell.

Milroy, J. and Milroy, L. (1985) 'Linguistic change, social network and speaker innovation', *Journal of Linguistics*, 21: 339–84.

Milroy, J. and Milroy, L. (1999) *Authority in Language: Investigating Standard English.* 3rd edn. New York: Routledge.

Milroy, L. and Gordon, M. (2003) *Sociolinguistics: Method and Interpretation.* Malden, MA: Blackwell.

Moore, C. (2002) 'Writing good Southerne: local and supralocal norms in the Plumpton letter collection', *Language Variation and Change*, 14 (1): 1–17.

Mugglestone, L. (2003) *Talking Proper: The Rise and Fall of the English Accent as a Social Symbol.* 2nd edn. Oxford: Clarendon Press. (1st edn, 1995.)

Nettle, D. and Romaine, S. (2000) *Vanishing Voices: the Extinction of the World's Languages.* Oxford: Oxford University Press.

Nevalainen, T. (2000) 'Processes of supralocalisation and the rise of Standard English in the Early Modern period', in R. Bermúdez-Otero, D. Denison, R. M. Hogg, and C. B. McCully (eds), *Generative Theory and Corpus Studies: a Dialogue from 10 ICEHL*. Berlin: Mouton de Gruyter. pp. 329–71.

Nevalainen, T. (2003) 'English', in A. Deumert and W. Vandenbussche (eds), *Germanic Standardizations: Past to Present* (Impact: Studies in Language and Society 18). Amsterdam: Benjamins. pp. 127–56.

Nevalainen, T. (2006) *An Introduction to Early Modern English*. Edinburgh: Edinburgh University Press.

Nevalainen, T. and Raumolin-Brunberg, H. (eds) (1996) *Sociolinguistics and Language History: Studies Based on the Corpus of Early English Correspondence*. Amsterdam: Rodopi.

Nevalainen, T. and Raumolin-Brunberg, H. (2000) 'The changing role of London on the linguistic map of Tudor and Stuart England', in D. Kastovsky and A. Mettinger (eds), *The History of English in a Social Context: a Contribution to Historical Socio-Linguistics*. Berlin: Mouton de Gruyter. pp. 279–337.

Nevalainen, T. and Raumolin-Brunberg, H. (2003) *Historical Sociolinguistics: Linguistic Change in Tudor and Stuart England*. London: Pearson Education.

Nevalainen, T. and Tieken-Boon van Ostade, I. (2006) 'Standardisation', in R. Hogg and D. Denison (eds), *A History of the English Language*. Cambridge: Cambridge University Press. pp. 271–311.

Nevalainen, T., Raumolin-Brunberg, H. and Trudgill, P. (2001) 'Chapters in the social history of East Anglian English: the case of third person singular', in J. Fisiak and P. Trudgill (eds), *East Anglian English*. Cambridge: D. S. Brewer. pp. 187–204.

Penny, R. (2000) *Variation and Change in Spanish*. Cambridge: Cambridge University Press.

Poplack, S. (2006) 'How English became African American English', in A. van Kemenade and B. Los (eds), *The Handbook of the History of English*. Malden, MA: Blackwell. pp. 452–76.

Pulgram, E. (1950) 'Spoken and written Latin', *Language*, 26(4): 458–66.

Raumolin-Brunberg, H. (1996) 'Historical sociolinguistics', in T. Nevalainen and H. Raumolin-Brunberg (eds), *Sociolinguistics and Language History: Studies Based on the Corpus of Early English Correspondence*. Amsterdam: Rodopi. pp. 11–37.

Raumolin-Brunberg, H. (2005) 'Language change in adulthood: historical letters as evidence', *European Journal of English Studies*, 9(1): 37–51.

Rand, D. and Sankoff, D. (1990) *GoldVarb Version 2: A Variable Rule Application for the Macintosh*. Montréal: Centre de recherches mathématiques, Université de Montréal.

Romaine, S. (1982) *Socio-Historical Linguistics: Its Status and Methodology*. Cambridge: Cambridge University Press.

Romaine, S. (1988) 'Historical sociolinguistics: problems and methodology', in U. Ammon, N. Dittmar and K. J. Mattheier (eds), *Sociolinguistics: an International handbook of the Science of Language and Society*. Berlin: Walter de Gruyter. pp. 1452–69.

Samuels, M. L. (1963) 'Some applications of Middle English dialectology', *English Studies*, 44: 81–94.

Samuels, M. L. (1972) *Linguistic Evolution, with Special Reference to English*. Cambridge: Cambridge University Press.

Sankoff, G. (2004) 'Adolescents, young adults and the critical period: two case studies from 'Seven Up'', in C. Fought (ed.), *Sociolinguistic Variation: Critical Reflections*. Oxford: Oxford University Press. pp. 121–39.

Sebba, M. (2007) *Spelling and Society: the Culture and Politics of Orthography Around the World*. Cambridge: Cambridge University Press.

Smith, J. (1996) *An Historical Study of English*. London: Routledge.

Thomason, S. G. (2001) *Language Contact: an Introduction*. Edinburgh: Edinburgh University Press.

Tieken-Boon van Ostade, I. (1987) *The Auxiliary Do in Eighteenth-Century English: A Sociohistorical-Linguistic Approach*. Dordrecht: Foris Publications.

Tieken-Boon van Ostade, I. (ed.) (2000–) *Historical Sociolinguistics and Sociohistorical Linguistics*. http://www.let.leidenuniv.nl/hsl_shl/ Accessed 4 November 2008.

Trudgill, P. (1986) *Dialects in Contact*. Oxford: Basil Blackwell.

Trudgill, P. (1999) *The Dialects of England*. 2nd edn. Oxford: Blackwell.

Tuten, D. N. (2003) *Koineization in Medieval Spanish* (Contributions to the Sociology of Language 88). Berlin: Mouton de Gruyter.

UNESCO-UIS (2008) *International Literacy Statistics: A Review of Concepts, Methodology and Current Data*. Montreal: UNESCO Institute for Statistics. http://www.uis.unesco.org/template/pdf/Literacy/ LiteracyReport2008.pdf. Accessed 2 November 2008.

Van Herk, G. (2008) 'Letter perfect: the present perfect in early African American correspondence', *English World-Wide*, 29(1): 45–69.

Wright, R. (1999) 'Comparative, structural and sociolinguistic analyses of the history of the Romance languages', in S. Embleton, J. E. Joseph and H.-J. Niederehe (eds), *The Emergence of the Modern Language Sciences*. Amsterdam: John Benjamins. pp. 175–88.

Wright, R. (2004) 'Latin and English as world languages', *English Today*, 20(4): 3–13.

Wyld, H. C. (1936) *A History of Modern Colloquial English*. 3rd edn. Oxford: Blackwell.

21

Fieldwork Methods in Language Variation

Walt Wolfram

21.1 DEFINING SOCIOLINGUISTIC FIELDWORK

The label 'sociolinguistic fieldwork' has been assigned to cover a wide variety of activities and procedures for collecting speech data, extending from the incidental observation of language use in the course of everyday interaction to the systematic elicitation of structural responses conducted within an experimental study. In this context, the role of the fieldworker can be as diverse as the types of studies conducted on the social life of language. The relatively loose, operational definition of fieldwork that prevails in sociolinguistics is, of course, a far cry from the model of participant observation set forth by Bronislaw Malinowski (1915, 1922) when he argued that cultural anthropologists needed to have daily contact with their subjects for an extended period of time if they were to record the 'imponderabilia of everyday life'.

In the cultural anthropological tradition, we think of social scientists who enter a completely different, preferably non-Western culture, for extended periods of time in order to observe and understand behaviours quite different from their own from the standpoint of the indigenous culture. Such is hardly the case in sociolinguistic fieldwork, although there are many instances in which researchers travel to distant community sites for extended periods of time in order to profile sociolinguistic variation in a culture different from their own (e.g. Nagy, 2000; Meyerhoff, 2001; Schreier, 2003). More frequently, however, sociolinguistic researchers are likely to work with communities in their country of residency, and may even focus on communities of which they are a part.

The range of community involvement may further extend from one-time interaction with subjects through a rapid, anonymous interview in the context of a department store (Labov, 1966) to the video recording of a politician on the political trail to examine variation that includes linguistic and paralinguistic behaviour (Mendoza-Denton and Mjahed, 2002). Or, it may involve a professional community (Holmes and Stubbe, 2003; Holmes, 2006), a prescribed professional interaction (e.g. Hagstrom, 2004), a subcultural community (e.g. Alim, 2004), or any other specialized setting or interaction. It may even involve living in a community context for years without relying on audio- or video-recording in order to observe language use in its natural context (Dayton, 1996). Sociolinguistic fieldwork is much more fluid and open in its definition than in some other fields of social science inquiry. At the same time, it is often a neglected dimension of discussion within the sociolinguistic enterprise, and most sociolinguistic studies simply offer a limited description of their fieldwork, in some cases consigning it to a footnote. But a footnote of sociolinguistic study may alter the narrative text of the sociolinguistic description in ways that greatly affect our description and interpretation of data – and it can never be marginalized.

In this survey, we consider a variety of topics that have fallen under the rubric of fieldwork methods, from the selection of a community of study to the discussion of specific methods for collecting data from the community. On one level, sociolinguistic fieldwork may be viewed in terms of a set of questions about choosing a community of study, working with the community and gathering appropriate data to answer research questions posed in a study of sociolinguistic differences. Schilling-Estes (2008: 165) identifies the challenges of fieldwork as:

1 How do I decide who to get data from?
2 How do I get people to talk to me?
3 How do I explain to people why I'm recording them?
4 How do I make good quality recordings in the field?
5 How should I be involved with my research participants?

We address some of these questions as well as some additional considerations as we examine some of the traditions that have developed during the last half-century of sociolinguistic field methods.

21.2 IDENTIFYING THE COMMUNITY

It is hard to imagine any social group or community from which an attendant set of research issues related to the life of language does not emerge, thus making just about any community eligible for sociolinguistic study. By the same token, the type of community selected for study depends, to a large extent, on the researcher's interests and questions. While sociolinguists conveniently refer to 'speech community' as a primitive sociolinguistic notion, defining the speech community can be theoretically elusive and communities can be quite fluid. William Labov, a pioneer in the development of fieldwork methods as well as other areas in sociolinguistics, defined the speech community as a group of people with shared norms, or common evaluations of linguistic variables (1966, 1972b). Though this may seem like a reasonable working definition, it is important to understand the difficulties involved with such a seemingly straightforward definition of a speech community (Patrick, 2002). 'Shared language norms' does not mean that everyone in a speech community speaks exactly the same way, or even similarly, only that they orient toward the same language norms. But language norms can also be elusive and negotiated rather than proscribed.

A number of issues arise when attempting to delimit a community in order to conduct a sociolinguistic study. For example, should researchers apply external, predetermined 'objective' criteria in delimiting a community, or allow the definition of the community to emerge as particular populations are studied so that researchers realize how participants themselves demarcate their communities? Should the researcher start by identifying a particular social unit and seeing how people within the group use language, or start with the particular language variety, an ideal construct in its own right, and then see who uses it and how they are tied together socially? Further, there are questions of size and uniformity. Can we really talk about a very large social aggregate like the Lower East Side of New York City (Labov, 1966) or perhaps a region like the Fens of Eastern England (Britain, 2001) as a single unified community with a shared set of norms, or is it more likely that different subpopulations have different norms for language use and other social behaviours? It may, in fact, be best to view the 'speech community' as more of a multilayered construct, since people have affiliations at different levels, ranging from various communities of practice, neighbourhood communities, migrant communities (Kerswill, 1993), larger politically-defined groups (e.g. a city or state) and broadly-based regional groups (e.g. US Southerners). A resident of Charleston, South Carolina, for example, may be affiliated with an individualized set of communities of practice, some of which extend beyond Charleston or South Carolina, at the same time that he or she is affiliated with a particular neighbourhood group that may be based on ethnic and family ties as well as geographic proximity and the broader-based notion of the American South.

In considering the various intersecting communities of which all speakers are necessarily a part, we need to consider whether we should take a 'top-down' approach, in which we begin by focusing on large social aggregates such as cities or regions, or a 'bottom-up' approach, in which we begin by studying individuals and their various interconnections. Better yet, it may be best to work 'back and forth' between the individual and the community, and between the social and the linguistic, as we study the interrelation of language and community. For example, Labov began his study of New York City by first applying social criteria to the identification of a particular group as a 'community'. He then narrowed this group down through linguistic criteria, selecting only native speakers of the New York City English varieties he was particularly interested in studying. Though his focus was on community patterns of language variation and change, he did not neglect individuals and included in his studies investigations of individual speech patterns in different stylistic contexts, as well as individual speakers' comments about stigmatized vs prestigious language features. In more recent work (Labov, 2001), Labov relies even more heavily on detailed studies of individuals, including individual personality traits and social networks, in seeking to understand the large-scale patterns of variation and change that reflect their multilayered and overlapping interactions, affiliations and orientations, and in addition use features with a variety of social associations to help shape social groups and social meanings in their daily conversational interactions.

Early fieldwork techniques in sociolinguistics tended to start with predetermined populations, defined by language, political or social boundaries. Pioneering studies in the USA, for example, focused on politically-based metropolitan areas such as New York City (Labov, 1966) and Detroit (Shuy, Wolfram and Riley, 1967), whereas Trudgill's (1974) early sociolinguistic analysis in England focused on Norwich. As studies of speech communities progressed, however, enquiry turned towards social groups within large-scale communities – in particular, interaction within social groups. In the 1970s, following Leslie Milroy's (1987) innovative studies of Belfast English, focus shifted to social networks and the kinds of people the residents of a given community tended to interact with most often on a daily basis. In examining social networks, the concern is on the DENSITY, the extent to which members of a social network all interact with one another, and MULTIPLEXITY, the extent to which people interact with the same people in different spheres of activity, for example, in work, in leisure activities and in the neighbourhood. Researchers have shown that social network density and multiplexity can have a significant impact on dialect maintenance and change. In particular, speakers in high-density, multiplex networks tend to maintain localized, vernacular language varieties far more tenaciously than speakers in uniplex, low-density networks, who are quicker to adopt language features from outside their local communities. In more recent work, Dodsworth (2005) extends network analysis to a model related to social perceptions in attributes.

In addition to looking at people's patterns of interaction, focus has extended to the investigation of why people come together as they do – i.e. what sorts of activities people join together to participate in, and what these social practices reveal about people's values, as well as the role of language in shaping and projecting these values. Accordingly, the COMMUNITY OF PRACTICE (Eckert and McConnell-Ginet, 1992) approach has become a central community-based social group for sociolinguistic inquiry. Community of practice is defined as 'an aggregate of people who come together around some enterprise' and which is 'simultaneously defined by its membership and the shared practices in which that membership engages' (Eckert, 2000: 35). In other words, when considering people's communities of practice, the focus shifts from pre-established **structures**,

whether the small-scale structures of localized social networks or large-scale structures like social class groups, to the ongoing social **practices** through which social structures are sustained and changed. In addition, communities of practice are defined in terms of people's subjective experiences and sense of belonging rather than the external criteria often used to delimit social group memberships (e.g. type of residence, income level) or determine the strength of an individual's social network ties (e.g. number of workmates who live in one's neighbourhood). Communities of practice are also viewed as dynamic and fluid rather than as static entities, and individuals are seen as active agents in the construction of individual and group identity, rather than simply as passive respondents to the social situations in which they find themselves (e.g. the social class group to which they belong).

In examining individualized, localized practices rather than social structures, we begin to understand not only what sorts of language patterns correlate with which groups but also **why** people use the language features they do. For example, in conducting a study of a small African-American community in the Smoky Mountain region of Appalachia, Christine Mallinson and Becky Childs (Childs and Mallinson, 2004; Mallinson, 2006) found that the linguistic practices of some adult women in the community could only be explained in terms of the different communities of practice in which the women participated. One group, the 'church ladies' engaged in practices such as church-going and other activities associated with cultural conservatism and propriety. The other primary group, the 'porch sitters' engaged in regular socializing on one group member's porch, where they would listen to music and engage in other activities indicative of affiliation with more widespread African-American culture, especially youth culture. Such patterns of practice help explain why the 'porch sitters' showed high usage levels for features of African-American English, while the 'church ladies' showed low usage levels for these features and instead used features associated with the local European-American variety, as well as more features of standard American English.

To carry the permeable, fluid definition of a community to its logical extension, sociolinguistic analysis may even focus on a single speaker as a representative of a community type. Thus, focus on the speech of a political figure (Mendoza Denton, 1995; Mendoza-Denton and Mjahed, 2002; Podesva et al., 2008) or a linguistic isolate might provide critical sociolinguistic insight into a community. One instructive study on the ethnolinguistic development of African-American English is limited to the last surviving member of the only

African-American family to have lived on the island of Ocracoke since the 1860s (Wolfram et al. 1999). This study of a single African-American speaker born in 1904, who was part of an ethnically-isolated family on a geographically-isolated island, demonstrated how one family and one speaker could indeed constitute a type of community.

In the final analysis, communities come in many sizes and shapes, and they are usually quite dynamic. They range from predetermined, bound-aried political populations to shared-experience communities of different types. On a practical level, they are operationally limited to our sample of participants, though inferences about their representativeness of population beyond the sample are inevitable and appropriate.

21.3 SELECTING PARTICIPANTS

Like other aspects of fieldwork, the selection of participants in a sociolinguistic study is constrained by the goals of the study. Validity, the extent to which a procedure measures what it is supposed to measure, and reliability, the degree to which an item is consistently measured by the same or another analyst, are the cornerstones of sociolinguistic research, as they are in any type of social science research. However, the assumptions of and the operationalization of these constructs in sociolinguistics may differ somewhat from other fields of social science inquiry. Early in the regional survey game, Pickford (1956) criticized linguistic atlas surveys in terms of sociological sampling theory, noting that they suffered from significant deficiencies of validity and reliability.

Though some of these criticisms are indeed valid – for example, to this day, sociolinguists do not seem sufficiently concerned about issues of intra- and inter-judge reliability in data extraction and measurement (e.g. Kerswill and Wright, 1990; Thomas, 2002; Kendall, 2009) – it also needs to be recognized that the assumptions and goals of sociolinguistics are also quite different from those in other social science disciplines. Accordingly, a survey focusing on the historical linguistic development of a region might legitimately be restricted to older, lifetime local residents rather than a random sample of the entire population. Furthermore, there are assumptions of representativeness and homogeneity that set linguistic behaviour apart from some other types of social behaviour. Thus, it is not uncommon in linguistic description to use a single speaker as a representative for an entire language, and millions of speakers of the language due to the shared features among its speakers. Given the breadth of diversity in American English or British English,

we can still safely assume that the vast majority of structures are shared by all varieties. This kind of homogeneity reduces the need for extensive sampling to make generalizations from the perspective of social science sampling (Neuman, 2002). For sociolinguistics, of course, the relevant question is how much and what type of sampling is needed in order to investigate the differences and generalize about them. Ultimately, it is not how many subjects are included in a sample, but how many speakers are needed to adequately represent a **cell** in a study, i.e. a particular demographic or social attribute category that is being examined as a variable in the analysis (e.g. older, Latino, male, length of residency 10–15 years). The number of cells is the number of factors in each variable multiplied by each other. Thus, a study that considers three age categories, two ethnicities, and two gender groups (3 x 2 x 2) would involve 12 cells. With just five speakers in each cell, we would then have a sample of 60 speakers.

Logistically, large-scale sampling of in-person interviews in sociolinguistics is simply not practical given the microscopic attention to linguistic detail characteristic of most sociolinguistic analyses. In one of the largest urban sociolinguistic surveys ever conducted, the Detroit Dialect Study (Shuy, Wolfram and Riley, 1967, 1968), more than 700 speakers were interviewed in the Detroit metropolitan area based on a quasi-random sampling of school children, but less than 100 of the interviews were ever subjected to detailed sociolinguistic analysis of any type (e.g. Shuy, Wolfram and Riley, 1968; Wolfram, 1969). In Labov, Ash, and Boberg (2006), arguably the most influential survey in the history of North American dialect geography, only two native speakers were selected for phone interviews from each US city with a population of more than 50,000; 772 speakers in all were included. On the basis of this sample, major vowel patterns and shifts in North American English were plotted, based on the assumption that a couple of native speakers is adequate to make generalizations about major dialect patterning. Other studies have operated with a threshold of five speakers per cell for quantitative analysis (Guy, 1980), but of course this is sensitive to the type of linguistic phenomenon being investigated and the assumptions of representativeness of the speakers in the cell. It should be noted that small cell sizes may work fine for variationist studies but not for opinion polls, because linguistic variation is often much more constrained and less amenable to conscious reflection.

As might be predicted, one of the emerging trends in the examination of sociolinguistic surveys is the use of online surveys, with all of the advantages and limitations of self-selected participants and self-reported data. The personal and social attributes of such participants are worthy of careful study since the respondents from such studies typically show a distinctive set of social, educational and ethnic attributes, in addition to the personal traits that make them respond. Surveys such as the Cambridge Online Survey of World Englishes (http://www.ling.cam.ac.uk/survey/) and the Harvard Survey of English dialects (http://www4.uwm.edu/FLL/linguistics/dialect/index.html) provide important data that appear to match some of the data elicited by fieldworkers conducting linguistic field surveys. For example, general surveys of particular lexical items (*pop* vs *soda* http://popvssoda.com:2998), and regionalized online surveys for lexical items in Canada by Boberg (2005), tend to confirm data from linguistic atlas surveys, at least for lexical data.

Another type of sociolinguistic participant to emerge from online communication comes from those who participate in computed-mediated communication, including instant messaging, blogs and other types of online postings (Johnstone and Baumgardt, 2004; Tagliamonte and Denis, 2008). Such studies are clearly expanding the profile of the participant and community in sociolinguistic studies, and virtual communities can no longer be dismissed as extraneous to the collection of data in sociolinguistics.

21.4 THE SOCIOLINGUISTIC FIELDWORKER

In Labov's (1972: 99) pioneering article on linguistic methodology, he notes that the methods used in linguistics can be captured by looking at where linguists might be found, noting that 'In this search, we would find linguists working in the *library*, the *bush*, the *closet*, the *laboratory*, and the *street*'. In sociolinguistics, the *bush* and the *street* are prime locations for sociolinguists in the traditional focus of sociolinguistic inquiry, and *online* would certainly be added now to the list of places linguists might be found. As the field of sociolinguistics has developed, the role of the sociolinguistic fieldworker has become more closely scrutinized, with growing sensitivity to the affect of the fieldworker in the collection of data (Cameron et al., 1992; Hazen, 2000; Nagy, 2000; Schilling-Estes, 2000, 2008). Though some researchers study communities of which they are already a part, the majority of sociolinguists venture into new communities as strangers. Accordingly, they are assigned a social role within the community that may range from a proscribed role as an external social science researcher to a negotiated status as participant observer in the life of the community. In between, there is a range of roles and relationships that fieldworkers may assume, and the process is a dynamic, evolving one. Over the past 15 years and more than 50 trips to the island, our fieldwork team (Wolfram, Hazen and Schilling-Estes, 1999) has gone from our initial role in Ocracoke as academic sociolinguists to partners in a variety of community activities that extend from collaborative projects documenting and celebrating local language history and other cultural traditions within the community, to friends who celebrate special occasions with families, including birthdays, graduations and funerals (Wolfram, Reaser and Vaughn, 2008).

In earlier (and current) sociolinguistic surveys such as Labov (1966) and Shuy, Wolfram and Riley (1967), which relied on stratified and quasi-random sampling, the sociolinguistic fieldworker assumed the status of an outside social scientist who had a single encounter with subjects during the interview. As sociolinguists migrated away from the sociologically-based survey model for selecting a sample (Wolfram and Fasold, 1974) towards convenience or judgment samples (Milroy, 1987; Milroy and Gordon, 2003), they have typically spent more time getting to know the community and people within the community, resorting to the so-called 'friend of a friend' method (Milroy, 1987) for establishing a common acquaintance within the community. Such a method often has a 'snowballing' effect (Milroy and Gordon, 2003: 23) in that it can lead to a natural network of friends and a role that somewhat mitigates the status of the social science researcher. Though there are obvious advantages in securing participants through this method, there are also disadvantages associated with the friend-of-a-friend technique (Schilling-Estes, 2008). It limits representativeness in terms of the broader population and applying parametric statistical testing. Furthermore, the fieldworker's association with one group may inhibit access to other groups. By the same token, the advantages of working with a group over time may help ease some of the awkwardness and social obstacles associated with an outside fieldworker and lead to more natural interaction.

While audio-recording is standard procedure for the collection of sociolinguistic data, there are some occasions where data may be collected and even quantified from unrecorded natural conversation. Hazen (2002), for example, shows how the use of a generalized form of the past tense form of *be, wont* (e.g. *I/you/(s)he/we/you/they wont there*) showed significant differentiation when family members were and were not being recorded, and Wolfram and Smith (2008) showed how meaningful stylistic variation took place in the use of the generalized negative past tense form of *be* (e.g. *She weren't nice*) when three friends were not being recorded. There are only a few instances, however, where sociolinguistic data have been collected completely from participant observation without the aid of any audio or video recording. Dayton (1996) is an exceptional case; she spent almost a decade in an African-American community in Philadelphia as a participant observer, collecting examples of different uses of verb structures in African-American English exclusively on note cards. In part, her motivation was to escape the limitations of the sociolinguistic interview as a specialized speech event (Wolfson, 1976) and to observe the use of grammatical forms only in their natural setting of conversation through the course of everyday life. Dayton's study is an admirable but painstaking exception to the usual method for gathering data.

In working with communities, there are a number of relationships and roles that sociolinguists can assume. Cameron, Frazer, Harvey, Rampton and Richardson (1992) define several different kinds of research based on relationships between researchers and those they are researching, including ETHICAL RESEARCH, ADVOCACY RESEARCH and EMPOWERING RESEARCH. Ethical research assumes that there is minimal inconvenience to participants and that the subjects are adequately acknowledged for their contributions. Advocacy-based research is characterized by a 'commitment on the part of the researcher not just to do research on subjects but research *on* and *for* subjects' (Cameron et al., 1992: 14), whereas empowering research is research **on**, **for**, and **with** the community in light of the fact that 'subjects have their own agendas and research should try to address them'. As Cameron et al. noted (1992: 24), 'if knowledge is worth having, it is worth sharing'. In the current sociolinguistic context, a number of sociolinguists have proactively sought to share their insights with community members and to 'give back' to the community, with the goal of empowering the community in some way. As John Rickford (1999: 315) puts it:

The fundamental rationale for getting involved in application, advocacy, and empowerment is that we owe it to the people whose data fuel our theories and descriptions; but these are good things to do even if we don't deal directly with native speakers and communities, and enacting them may help us to respond to the interests of our students and to the needs of our field.

Sociolinguists can work with community members to ensure that language variation is documented and described to raise the level of consciousness within and outside the community about the past, current and future state of the language variation, and to engage representative community agents and agencies in an effort to understand and explicate the role of language in community life.

There are a variety of stances, positions and roles that sociolinguistic researchers might assume in the field, but one of the most essential aspects of current fieldwork is the increasing self-awareness of the role of the fieldworker in the fieldwork process. As Schilling-Estes (2000: 84) observes:

More and more, we are coming to realize that genuine detachment is impossible and that there indeed exists a reality outside our individual and societal interpretations of it, it is virtually impossible to access it (Cameron et al., 1992). This inability to separate ourselves and our biases from that which we are studying is especially acute for those of us whose object of study is our fellow humans … .Thus, it is imperative that we consider exactly how what we as researchers bring to the field with us impacts on the observations and analysis we take home.

If nothing else, fieldworkers are becoming increasingly reflexive about their role in the gathering, shaping and interpreting of data in the field (Hazen, 2000; Mendoza-Denton, 2008; Wolfram et al., 2008).

Many surveys of vernacular dialects now employ fieldworkers from the community itself, and some of the richest sources of data we have collected over the years come from interviews conducted by indigenous fieldworkers, but this condition in itself is also no guarantee of a more useful interview for analysis. Outsiders also possess the personal characteristics that make for an effective fieldworker, and sometimes the 'intimate stranger' who has outsider status (Briggs, 1986) will be offered information not shared with community members. People with empathetic, non-threatening conversational styles often end up getting more useful interviews than fieldworkers who are carefully selected to match the status, age and gender characteristics of the interviewee (Cukor-Avila and Bailey, 2001). In the final analysis, the role of rapport and empathy in promoting an effective conversational interview may be discussed at length, but ultimately those qualities are difficult to programme.

21.5 COLLECTING DATA

As noted previously, the collection of data in sociolinguistics is related to the research questions that underlie the study (Milroy and Gordon, 2003). At the same time, the articulation of research questions is not a predetermined, static process; instead, there is a synergy that binds together methods, description and theory. I personally cannot identify one project in which the predetermined research questions remained unaltered throughout the course of the research project – in more than four decades of field-initiated research that has included dozens of different projects. Notwithstanding our best attempts to identify our primary research issues before beginning a study, research questions continue to be formulated and reformulated during the course of the study, invariably linking methods, description and theory. In such a context, complementary methods of data collection are often included in sociolinguistic fieldwork. In the following sections, we consider some of the traditional and developing trends for collecting data in field-initiated sociolinguistic research.

21.6 THE SOCIOLINGUISTIC INTERVIEW

The methodological heart of the sociolinguistic movement over the past half-century, particularly in the variationist paradigm pioneered by William Labov (1963, 1966, 1972a, 1984; Wolfram and Fasold, 1974), is the so-called 'sociolinguistic interview', a conversational interview intended to elicit conversation comparable to everyday, ordinary speech. The underlying goal of most conversational interviews is quite straightforward: to get as much natural conversational speech as possible from the interviewee, i.e. speech that represents how the interviewee speaks in everyday conversation when language is not directly under examination. Even in a conversational interview focused on relatively neutral topics of discussion, the fact that a person is being interviewed and tape-recorded is a formidable obstacle to obtaining ordinary speech – the kind of speech that is so central to most studies of dialect variation. This problem has become known in sociolinguistics as the OBSERVER'S PARADOX, which Labov formulated thus: 'To obtain the data most important for linguistic theory, we have to observe how people speak when they are not being observed' (Labov, 1972b: 113). A lot of attention has been given to developing strategies for overcoming the inherent constraints of a tape-recorded interview with a relative stranger, ranging from concern with the personal characteristics of interviewers (Edwards, 1986; Rickford and McNair-Knox, 1994; Cukor Avila and Bailey, 1995, 2001) to the best physical locations for conducting these interviews and the kinds of questions to be asked in the interview (Cukor-Avila and Bailey, 2001; Kendall, 2009).

Topics of conversation in the sociolinguistic interview are centred on themes of common interest, eliciting discussions that might be of most natural interest to community participants and which minimize the attention paid to speech. Open-ended questions are grouped into common areas or 'modules' and most are open-ended to maximize conversation by the participants. One set of questions might, for example, focus on childhood games, another on friends, another on community concerns, and so forth. The key element of these questionnaires is the elicitation of spontaneous conversation that taps into personal and community interests and is non-threatening to the participant.

There are important theoretical reasons for targeting the most casual and ordinary conversations as the basis for analysing sociolinguistic data. It was originally based on the assumption of Labov's vernacular principle (1972a: 112, 113), which maintained that most important speech for linguistic theory came from relatively unmonitored, natural conversation. The more participants focused on the topic of conversation vis-à-vis the speech per se, the better the data would be for analysing authentic linguistic patterning. Operationally, the sociolinguistic interview was also considered essential in order to examine the orderly nature of language variation, since it was the basis for examining the fluctuating patterns of socially-diagnostic variants. The careful examination of dialect forms (Fischer, 1958; Labov, 1966; Wolfram, 1969) showed that dialects sometimes were differentiated on the basis of how frequently particular forms are used rather than whether or not a given variant is used. Individual speakers may fluctuate in their use of variants, sometimes using one form and sometimes using an alternate form, and the relative frequencies of usage helped differentiate varieties of a language and correlated with various linguistic and social traits. For example, the production of unstressed -ing as -in' in words like *swimming* or *taking* might fluctuate within the speech of a single speaker during a single speech event, referred to as INHERENT VARIABILITY. At the same time, the relative frequency of different variants correlates significantly with various linguistic factors, for example, – ing is more likely to become – in' when it functions as a verb vs a noun (e.g. She was swimmin' > He likes swimmin'), and by various social attributes: for example, as a group, lower working-class speakers use more – in' than middle-class speakers, men more than women, and so forth. But in order to tap into such systematic variability, sociolinguists need sufficient amounts of natural conversation to produce enough cases for meaningful quantitative study of orderly variation (Tagliamonte, 2006).

Although a fieldworker cannot control the elicitation of particular diagnostic forms when the focus of the interview is simply upon obtaining reasonable amounts of conversation, it is possible to include certain kinds of questions that raise the likelihood for targeted structures to occur. Thus, interview questions may be designed to yield narratives of past experiences or of movie plots in order to obtain significant numbers of past tense verb forms. Similarly, descriptions of different attributes (e.g. 'What does he look like?') may raise the potential for predicate adjective constructions to occur (e.g. *He's tall and he's kinda thin ...*).

The kinds of questions that promote the potential for certain structures are, of course, determined only after pilot trials with various formats and, in some cases, after some of the analysis has already begun. In our early studies of Detroit speech (Wolfram, 1969), we found that many of the occurrences of habitual *be* (e.g. *They be tagging somebody when they catch them*) among children occurred during their descriptions of traditional game activities, since such speech events call for the description of regularly-occurring, or habitual activities. Such information not only aided in the analysis of the invariant form of *be* (Fasold, 1969) but also helped researchers studying this form to devise questions that might bring out the use of *be* (Bailey and Maynor, 1987). Care may therefore be given in a conversational interview to the kinds of questions that might elicit sufficient data for analysis, the kinds of linguistic structures that certain questions are likely to call forth and the cultural topics that are relevant to the community. When these considerations are taken into account, the demands of the conversational interview may present a significant challenge. These concerns also point to the need for extensive pilot testing before large-scale series of sociolinguistic interviews are undertaken. The success of particular topics in eliciting conversation varies considerably from community to community and from subject to subject, and the actual interview sometimes strays far from the structured topics as the fieldworker follows the interviewee's interests.

Notwithstanding the important data that can be obtained from the sociolinguistic interview, there are a number of concerns about the focus on data derived from this primary method (Schilling-Estes, 2008). Wolfson (1976), for example, has criticized the sociolinguistic interview as being a specialized speech event and less, rather than more, like typical kinds of interviews; furthermore, she notes that it excludes certain types of narrative styles that are important for the analysis of conversational speech. It has also been noted that some of the questions are not typical of everyday speech and could be considered impolite or inappropriate for different cultural groups

(Schilling-Estes, 2008). Another concern with the sociolinguistic interview emerges from the focus on the most vernacular, unconscious speech style. For non-mainstream varieties of speech, this obsession has led to a focus on vernacular structures and basilectal versions of speech, resulting in a kind of sociolinguistic nostalgia for the authentic vernacular speaker and reification of non-mainstream vernacular speech and speakers (Bucholtz, 2003).

Schilling-Estes observes that the focus in the Labovian interview on vernacular, unselfconscious speech lapses into unjustified assumptions about a monolithic vernacular. Schilling-Estes notes (2008: 173):

> ... it is by no means certain that each speaker can be said to have a single, "genuine" vernacular style unaffected by situational and speaker-internal factors such as who they're talking to and how much attention they're paying to their speech. Instead, people may have a range of quite casual, unselfconscious styles they use with various people in different circumstances.

The focus on unselfconscious styles ignores the sociolinguistic insights provided by examining more self-conscious styles of speech. Studies of performative styles within and outside of interviews (Preston, 1992, 1996; Schilling-Estes, 1998) provide insight into the significant distribution of socially diagnostic forms. For example, these forms may be prone to linguistic overproduction when speakers are conscious about their speech so that it signifies ironic roles in the symbolic representation and language change. Notwithstanding some major and minor concerns about the role of the sociolinguistic interview in fieldwork, the data provided by such interviews have been indispensable in the growth of sociolinguistic methodology, description and theory.

21.7 BEYOND THE SOCIOLINGUISTIC INTERVIEW

While the sociolinguistic interview has been a staple method for gathering data in sociolinguistics for a half-century now, it has often been augmented by other techniques to gather a full range of sociolinguistic information and behaviour. Even within the sociolinguistic interview, there is a tradition of supplementing conversational speech with other types of tasks such as reading passages, word lists and minimal word pair lists to collect complementary data or simulate different levels of formality (Labov, 1966; Shuy, Wolfram and Riley, 1968). And, of course, there is a tradition of collecting data from groups of participants in naturally occurring speech events that characterized the earliest sociolinguistic studies. Labov's early study of African-American English in the mid-1960s relied on interviews with peer groups of African-American teenagers (Labov et al., 1968) to access the more vernacular style of speech as well as to compare group speech with the speech style used during individual interviews. Controlling for different permutations of interview participants, interviewers and speech events is fairly common in sociolinguistic fieldwork now (e.g. Edwards, 1986; Renn, 2007; Van Hofwegen and Wolfram, forthcoming) in order to examine systematically the effects of various participant attributes and speech conditions on language variation. Thus, in one current study of the longitudinal development of African-American English over a 17-year span (Burchinal, Roberts, Zeisel and Rowley, 2008), participants are examined speaking with their mothers, with peers at different age levels and with adults. Furthermore, there are different conditions for each of these participant sets, including formal speech (such as constructing a formal speech for parents with a peer), and informal speech events (such as eating a snack or planning a MySpace page with a peer) for each combination of participants. Such proscribed designs for data collection allow researchers to maintain experimental control in their examination of systematic language variation while maintaining relatively spontaneous speech as the basis for the systematic investigation of language variation.

As creative and innovative as sociolinguistic interviews have become over the past decades, there are still inherent limitations to the types of data collected from these interviews for both linguistic and sociolinguistic analysis. Theoretically, sociolinguistic data are not conducive to tapping linguistic intuitions of speakers, one of the mainstays of 'descriptive adequacy' in formulating a linguistic description. The goal of a grammar of a socially subordinate language variety is no different from that of a standard variety in this respect. The basic problem is simple: we want to obtain the most complete data possible in order to arrive at an adequate, representative, descriptive account. The fieldwork situation for the collection of data is, at best, not conducive to the probing of linguistic intuitions, and, at worst, actively resistant to such probing. In reality, there are some occasions in linguistic description when particular hypotheses about vernacular structures need to go beyond the simple observation of language in a naturalistic context.

On one occasion, for example, preliminary observations about *a*-prefixing in constructions

such as *She was a-huntin'* and *They came a-runnin'* led to hypotheses about its linguistic boundaries as well as a set of hypotheses about cross-dialectal knowledge of this form (Wolfram, 1982, 1988). Direct intuition questions about the grammaticality of vernacular structures, however, are confounded by prevailing attitudes about social acceptability, so it is impossible to obtain reliable data from straightforward questions about intuitions (Labov, 1972a; Wolfram, 1986). To counter this tendency, we devised a forced-choice test of sentence pairs in which we simply asked speakers to choose which sentence sounded better; for example, does the speaker prefer adding the prefix *a*- to *He likes working* vs *He was working*. We found that speakers given a forced choice task would, in fact, resort to their native speaker intuitions (viz., *He was a-workin'* vs *He likes a-workin'*) and overcome the social acceptability judgments that lead them to reject as 'ungrammatical' any structure that was not associated with the mainstream standard variety. In a similar forced choice test with habitual *be* (*They always be going to school* vs *They be going to school today*) administered to native speakers of African-American English and middle-class speakers of Standard American English, we found important contrasts between these two groups that led to significant hypotheses about cross-dialectal grammaticality (Wolfram 1982, 1988) and the grammaticalization of habitual *be* in African-American English (Fasold, 1969; Green, 2002).

The indirect probing of linguistic intuitions is not the only method that can be used to confirm or reject various hypotheses about the structures of non-mainstream language varieties. There is a tradition of structural elicitation tasks in sociolinguistic studies that ranges from simple repetition tasks to the elicitation of sentence fragments or cloze techniques of various types that expose underlying forms and patterns. In one early task to test out a hypothesis about different underlying forms for invariant *be* in African-American English, Fasold (1969, 1972) devised a task to elicit an elliptical form that would force the choice of an underlying modal. Fasold hypothesized that there were three underlying forms from which invariant *be* in an African-American sentence might be derived, which were indicated by the co-occurring auxiliary with the verb. The habitual derivation of *He be there*, occurs with *do* support (e.g. *He don't be there all the time*), the future co-occurs with *will* (e.g. *He won't be there tomorrow*), and past requires *would* (e.g. *He wouldn't be there if he had a choice*). To examine his hypothesis, Fasold devised sentence-stimulus frames that would require the subject to respond with an elliptical form that required a full auxiliary.

After training the subject to a response pattern on non-diagnostic sentences, the subject would then provide responses such as the following:

Tape stimulus: *He be in in a few minutes*
Subject response: *I know he will*
Fieldworker response: *Will what?*
Subject response: *Be in in a few minutes*

The elicitation frame offered strong support for Fasold's (1969, 1972) claim that invariant *be* in African-American English is derived from at least several different sources, a couple of which parallel its uses in the standard variety and one (habitual *be*) that was unique to this variety.[1] A variety of structural elicitation frames have been used to supplement the data from natural conversation in testing hypotheses for formulating grammars of vernacular varieties (e.g. Schilling-Estes and Wolfram, 1994; Wolfram, 1996; Rickford, 1999).

It is also possible to extend elicitations in sociolinguistic fieldwork to pragmatics and language use, though this type of elicitation is considerably less frequent than the elicitation of structural linguistic forms. In one sociolinguistic study of assumed information and felicitous questioning, my son, who was seven years old at the time, and I collaborated to ask a series of 'How come?' questions to people of different ages (Wolfram and Wolfram, 1977). We approached acquaintances of different ages and asked them how old they were, then followed it up with a 'How come?' question, as in the following sample:

Fieldworker: How old are you?
Subject: Twenty-four.
Fieldworker: How come?
Subject: How come [laughter] How come, what do you mean how come?
Fieldworker: How come?
Subject: Because 24 years ago my parents worked something out.

Responses were not recorded, but each was written down on a file card after the interaction was observed by the senior fieldworker. The responses of subjects showed important differences based on the age of the subject and the age of the fieldworker. For the adult fieldworker with an adult subject, the subject typically assumed that it was a behaviour that plays on the known-information joking genre (e.g. *Why did the chicken cross the road? To get to the other side*). However, when asked by the seven-year-old fieldworker, adults assumed it was a sincere question and responded accordingly (e.g. 'The years have been hard on me', 'The years just fly by'). By the same token,

younger children assumed it was a sincere question that required a criterion-based response, as in the following example:

Fieldworker: How old are you?
Subject: Six.
Fieldworker: How come?
Subject: Because I'm in kindergarten.

Slightly older adolescents (9–13) interpreted it as a literal question related to a simple mathematical calculation (e.g. I'm 8 years old because I was born in 1966). Most importantly, the data indicated the developmental trajectory of assumed information in questions and the developmental acquisition of productive and receptive pragmatic competence. While such deliberate conversational manipulation admittedly extends the boundaries of data collection, it demonstrates that the collection of data is only limited by the willingness of fieldworkers to take conversational risks and think creatively about eliciting relevant data to address issues of linguistic form and use.

21.8 PERCEPTUAL STUDIES

The consideration of speakers' subjective viewpoints on language differences adds an important dimension to understanding and interpreting sociolinguistic differences (Preston, 1989, 1992, 1993). In recent years, fuelled by advances in technology and the accessibility of software programs, a proliferation of perceptual studies have taken place in the field, led by a variety of sociophonetic experiments (Thomas, 2002). Many current perceptual studies show the influence of experimental psychology in terms of their design, their controlled manipulation of variables and their associated statistical analyses. At the same time, some of these perceptual research studies have shifted research samples from the indigenous research community to convenient, generic populations of middle-class university students. Indeed, there is a trade-off in terms of rigorous experimental design and field-initiated, community-based research that typifies current perceptual studies.

Thomas (2002) has identified a number of different issues that frame the tradition of socio-perceptual approaches to sociolinguistics. One is the ability of listeners to identify regional varieties, ethnicity or socioeconomic levels of speakers. There is a well-established tradition of compiling a stimulus tape of different speakers representing dissimilar groups and then having listeners identify the language variety, socioeconomic status or ethnicity of the speaker. Earlier studies, for example, had listeners identify whether speakers on a tape recording were using American, British or Indian English (Bush, 1967), or identify the social-class and ethnicity of speakers from Detroit or Michigan based on tape recordings extracted from natural conversation (Shuy, Baratz and Wolfram, 1969). In the latter study, different social-class groups and ethnicities from Detroit were included as listener groups to match the social attributes of speakers in the stimulus recording, leading to important conclusions about social class and ethnic identification. For example, middle-class speakers and working-class speakers were not significantly differentiated in identifying speakers from different social classes; at the same time, Black listeners of different social classes were better able to identify middle-class Black speakers than their cohort white groups. Such results are not only significant for sociolinguistic description but also they underscore the value of including different social groups of listeners from the study population as a methodological procedure. In a recent study, Wolfram, Dannenberg, Knick and Oxendine (2002) examined listener accuracy in identifying Native-American Lumbees, African Americans, and European Americans in a tri-ethnic community in North Carolina (NC). By comparing reactions of listeners from within the community with listeners from Raleigh, NC, a metropolitan area located about 100 miles away, it was shown that tri-ethnic identity in Robeson County was a highly localized phenomenon, endemic to the community where the Lumbee reside. While listeners from both communities reliably identified African Americans and European Americans at the same level of accuracy, only local community members could reliably identify Lumbee Indians. The enlistment of the local community in the experiment thus proved to be critical for understanding dimensions of local and broad-based notions of ethnic identity in the American South.

Analyses of listeners' reactions to different productions can become quite sophisticated, thanks to computer software that allows for various kinds of experimental manipulations of speech, including speech synthesis. For example, it is possible to alter just the production of a particular vowel or consonant while keeping the rest of the utterance constant so that the specific contribution of the manipulated production to listeners' reaction can be teased out (Graff, Labov and Harris, 1986; Grimes, 2005; Campbell-Kibler, 2007). Experimentation of this type has advanced our understanding of the role of vowel and consonant production in listeners' judgments of regionality as well as the interaction of regionality with social factors such as ethnicity, social status and gender. For example, perception tests indicate that the fronting of the vowel in *boat* so that it sounds

more like *bewt* is strongly associated with European-American speech in the American South and that African Americans who use this feature are regularly identified as being European American rather than African American (Torbert, 2004). In contrast, the fronting of the vowel in *boot*, so that it sounds more like *biwt* is not as strongly associated with European-American ethnicity, and African Americans with this feature tend to be identified correctly as African Americans. This indicates that the fronted productions of these two vowels, both common in many Southern-based speech varieties, have quite different ethnic associations. Careful perceptual studies of this type help sort out the effects of subtle nuances of vowel production on listeners, and may help determine the relative perceptual saliency of different phonetic factors in marking regional and ethnic identity.

Another area of study relates to the relationship of stereotypes and speech perception, ranging from the association of personal and social attributes ascribed to different voices (e.g. Labov, 1966; Shuy et al., 1969) to the effect of social stereotypes on speech perception (Niedzielski, 1999; Strand, 1999). Studies now abound in which researchers manipulate the stimulus to determine the effect of various phonetic traits on personal and social attribution (see Thomas, 2002 for a review). For example, van Bezooiyen (1988) investigated how listeners judge speakers' personalities in the Netherlands based on speech samples from speakers of various socioeconomic statuses in the city of Nijmegen. The speech was presented in four ways: (1) as excerpts of the unaltered recording; (2) lowpass filtered at 300 Hz in order to focus listeners' attention on prosody; (3) with the recordings cut and respliced digitally to focus listeners' attention on voice quality; and (4) as written text. The listeners rated the speech in the different conditions on various personality scales (e.g. 'educated', 'strong-willed', 'fair'), resulting in an analysis that concluded that strong personality was inferred from prosody but intellectual and socioeconomic status were inferred from the segmental aspects of speech.

One of the long-standing methods used in sociolinguistic research to elicit subjective reactions to speech is the MATCHED GUISE TECHNIQUE, developed by Wallace Lambert and colleagues in the 1960s to evaluate the reactions of Montreal residents towards both French speakers and English speakers. In this technique a bilingual or bidialectal speaker renders the same passage in the two varieties, thus controlling for individual speaker traits. The results of the initial investigation by Lambert and his colleagues (Lambert, 1967) showed that the Canadian English speakers evaluated the Canadian French guises less favourably, as predicted, but that the Canadian French speakers also attributed the Canadian French guises with less positive characteristics, a surprising conclusion.

A more recent use of the matched guise technique by Baugh (2003) applied it to linguistic profiling and housing discrimination. In response to advertisements for vacant apartments in the newspaper, Baugh telephoned using three different guises – African American, Chicano American and European American – and found that the proportion of vacant apartments reported was significantly differentiated based on the three guises and the location of the apartments. To a large extent, the use of speech synthesis has now replaced the matched guise technique in sociolinguistic experimentation type since it is easier to manipulate variables in a speech sample more precisely while strictly controlling other speaker variables.

The previous studies relate to the social evaluations and stereotypes evoked from speech. A different tack is taken by Strand (1999), who examined how stereotypes may alter a subject's perception of speech. Strand's study, based on part of the 'McGurk effect' (McGurk and MacDonald, 1976), showed an interaction between hearing and vision in speech perception as speakers hearing one sound, while watching a video with another sound, tended to perceive the sound they lip-read from the video. Her study showed that subjects altered their perception of the sound based on the sex of the speaker, concluding that perception was influenced by gender stereotypes.

The development of experimental methods in perceptual studies is one of the fastest growing areas of sociolinguistics, and there are many experiments related to vowel mergers, vowel splits and comprehension across different dialects (see Labov, 1994; Thomas, 2002) that have advanced our understanding of the role between perception and production in sociolinguistic description. However, these studies take us beyond our focus on field methods here and are best treated as a burgeoning subfield of sociolinguistics in its own right (Thomas, 2002).

Not all studies of subjective viewpoints of speakers are dependent on tape-recorded stimuli of various types. The research of Dennis Preston and his colleagues (Preston, 1986, 1989, 1991, 1999) focuses on people's 'commonsense' beliefs and subjective mental categories rather than spoken language data. Such beliefs and mental representations are important to sociolinguists, since they may play an important role in shaping language variation and change across regional and social space. In the most straightforward procedure for determining people's 'mental dialect maps', study participants are simply asked to draw, on a blank or minimally detailed map, lines around regional speech zones. Instructions that guide such drawings involve eliciting people's perceptions of the boundaries of Southern and Northern speech areas. These lines can then be traced onto digitized pads and software can then be used to generate composite maps of various types based on drawings from a large number of respondents. Differences in mental maps may correlate with a range of respondent attributes such as region, age, social class, ethnicity and gender – the same kinds of social factors shown to be relevant in the patterning of variable dialect productions. For example, respondents from Southeastern Michigan and Southern Indiana in the USA draw very similar Southern dialect regions. However, there seems to be a 'home region effect' that influences how each group draws their Northern and Southern Midland boundaries, with each group drawing a larger dialect area around their home region.

These maps are supplemented by people's evaluative judgments of different regional dialects, elicited through instructions such as 'Rank the states on a scale of 1 to 10 showing where the most correct and the most incorrect English are spoken' 'Rank the states showing where the most pleasant and unpleasant English are spoken' and 'Rank the states showing where English is most and least like your own variety'. For example, New York City and the South tend to be ranked as 'most different' by respondents from Michigan and Indiana. New York City and the South were also ranked as 'most incorrect' by these same respondents. At the same time, Southern dialect is rated high on a scale of pleasantness, showing people's complicated and sometimes somewhat contradictory reactions to regional speech varieties.

21.9 ETHNOGRAPHIC DESCRIPTION

Over the past couple of decades, the role of ethnographic description has taken on increased significance in sociolinguistic field methods. Most ethnographic description is based on some level of participant observation and long-term involvement in a community, whether it be through extended residency in the community or regular visits and participation in the life of the community. The benefits of an ethnographic approach include the quality and amount of data and the familiarity with community practices that allow researchers to uncover the essential social and cultural factors that may affect language variation and change from the standpoint of the community itself (Johnstone, 2000; Milroy and Gordon, 2003). Most sociolinguistic analyses that use social network or community-of-practice approaches to sociolinguistic description rely on ethnographic approaches to some extent, and there are several paradigm examples of the benefits of long-term involvement in an observation of a community. Eckert (2000), in her study of high-school students in a Detroit suburb, spent two years at the school, regularly attending the school in the first year and occasionally attending it in the second year. Her years at the school helped her make sense of the linguistic and behavioural patterns of the school, particularly as they related to different social groups of students (viz. 'jocks' and 'burnouts'). In a similar vein, Mendoza-Denton's (2008) description of language and cultural practices among Latina youth gangs was based on several years of participation in the lives of high school girls in California. In the process, she recorded them on different occasions, she copied their drawings, and she took notes and video-taped them when they went on trips to the beauty salon or to the amusement park. This regular engagement over time led Mendoza-Denton not only to a description of their speech but also to a description of their bodily practices and symbolic exchanges that signal gang affiliations, cultural practices and ideologies.

The richness of accounts based on extensive ethnographic involvement speak for themselves, but they also suggest that greater explanatory power in sociolinguistic description is dependent on understanding the local social categories and ideologies that emerge from long-term participation. Ethnographic approaches are by their very nature more interdisciplinary and involve the observation and description of a wide range of behaviours. For example, Mallinson's (2008) description of two communities of practice in a small African-American community in the Smoky Mountains in western North Carolina, the 'church ladies' and 'the porch ladies', includes a description of physical details such as the layout and decoration of their homes, their style of dress and their physical complexion, as well as their attitudes about religion, family, race and social mores. The ethnographic description thus frames the social groups that constitute the communities of practice and the language differences that distinguish them. As Milroy and Gordon (2003: 70) note, participant observation tends to work well in small, well-delineated communities if the community is responsive to the fieldworkers on a personal basis.

The model of participant observation used by fieldworkers from the North Carolina Language and Life Project in Ocracoke (Wolfram, Hazen and Schilling-Estes, 1999; Wolfram, 2008) has lasted more than 15 years with numerous trips to the island for up to a week at a time. Furthermore, it has involved multiple teams of student fieldworkers over the years with one of two constant faculty members of the team involved in each trip. Without our extended participation, we would not have been able to identify some of the social groups and personal attributes critical to our description of language change. For example, the so-called 'Poker Game Network' is a male-exclusive group that values traditional island themes, which in turn correlates with their maintenance of several iconic dialect features (Wolfram and Schilling-Estes, 1995). Our long-term participation in the life of the community has now led to real-time studies that combine panel studies with trend studies at different periods, including a comparison of a current analogue of the 'Poker Game Network' (Wolfram and Smith, 2008). While this extended participation has resulted in some unique insights into the relation between real-time and apparent-time studies, it has also uncovered some methodological cautions for real-life studies of language change. Keeping data points in time equal in terms of social conditions, interaction and even acoustic conditions for recording also need to be considered in order to conduct systematic comparative studies of the same community and speakers at different points in time. And, of course, in the current vein of sociolinguistic studies, both groups and individuals need to be considered in real-time language change – just as they are in apparent-time studies. Indeed, qualitatively-based fieldwork is necessary to complement and inform our quantitative analyses in sociolinguistics. The balance between the qualitative perspective provided through ethnographic study and the quantitative analysis of variable speech data is one of the challenges for sociolinguistics in the future development of field methods that are rooted in both humanities and social science traditions.

ACKNOWLEDGEMENT

Support from NSF grants BCS-0542139 and BCS-0542139 for research and writing is gratefully acknowledged.

NOTE

1 Dayton (1996) and Labov (1998) have since rejected Fasold's hypotheses about the different underlying structures for invariant *be* in African-American English based solely on naturalistically-acquired data, but it remains an issue in dispute (Green, 2002).

REFERENCES

Alim, H. S. (2004) *You Know My Steez: An Ethnographic and Sociolinguistic Study of Style Shifting in a Black American speech community*. Publication of the American Dialect Society 89. Durham, NC: Duke University Press.

Bailey, G. and Maynor, N. (1987) 'Decreolization', *Language in Society*, 16: 449–74.

Baugh, J. (2003) 'Linguistic profiling', in M. Cinfree, G. Smitherman, A. F. Ball and A. K. Spears (eds), *Black Linguistics: Language, Society, and Politics in Africa and the Americas*. New York: Routledge. pp. 155–68.

Boberg, C. (2005) 'The North American Regional Vocabulary Survey: renewing the study of lexical variation in North American English', *American Speech*, 80: 22–60.

Briggs, C. (1986) *Learning How to Ask: A Sociolinguistic Appraisal of the Role of the Interview in Social Science Research*. Cambridge: Cambridge University Press.

Britain, D. (2001) 'Welcome to East Anglia!: two major dialect 'boundaries' in the Fens', in P. Trudgill and J. Fisiak (eds), *East Anglian English*. Woodbridge: Boydell and Brewer. pp. 217–42.

Bucholtz, M. (2003) 'Sociolinguistic nostalgia and the authentication of identity', *Journal of Sociolinguistics*, 7: 398–416.

Burchinal, M., Roberts, J. E., Zeisel, S. A. and Rowley, S. (2008) 'Social risk and protective factors for African American children's academic achievement and adjustment during the transition to middle school', *Developmental Psychology*, 44: 286–92.

Bush, C. N. (1967) 'Some acoustic parameters of speech and their relationships to the perception of dialect differences', *TESOL Quarterly*, 1(3): 20-30.

Cameron, D., Fraser, E., Harvey, P., Rampton, M. B. H. and Richardson, K. (1992) *Researching Language: Issues of Power and Method*. New York: Routledge.

Campbell-Kibler, K. (2007) 'Accent, (ING) and the social logic of listener perceptions', *American Speech*, 82: 32–64.

Childs, B. and Mallinson C. (2004) 'African American English in Appalachia: Dialect accommodation and substrate influence'. *English World-Wide*, 25: 25–50.

Cukor-Avila, P. and Bailey, G. (1995) 'An approach to sociolinguistic fieldwork: A site study of rural AAVE in a Texas community', *English World-Wide*, 16: 21–59.

Cukor-Avila, P. and Bailey, G. (2001) 'The effects of the race of the interviewer on sociolinguistic fieldwork', *Journal of Sociolinguistics*, 5: 254–70.

Dayton, E. (1996) 'Grammatical categories of the verb in African American Vernacular English'. University of Pennsylvania dissertation.

Dodsworth, R. (2005) 'Attribute networking: a technique for modeling social perceptions', *Journal of Sociolinguistics*, 9: 225–53.

Eckert, P. (2000) *Linguistic Variation as Social Practice*. Malden, MA: Blackwell.

Eckert, P. and McConnell-Ginet, S. (1992) 'Think practically and look locally: language and gender as community-based practice', *Annual Review of Anthropology*, 21: 461–90.

Edwards, V. (1986) *Language in a Black Community*. Clevedon, UK: Multilingual Matters.

Fasold, R. W. (1969) 'Tense and the form *be* in Black English', *Language*, 45: 763–76.

Fasold, R. W. (1972) *Tense Marking in Black English: A Linguistic and Social Analysis*. Arlington: Center for Applied Linguistics.

Fischer, J. N. L. (1958) 'Social influences on the choice of a linguistic variant', *Word*, 14: 47–56.

Graff, D., Labov, W. and Harris, W. A. (1986) 'Testing listeners's reactions to phonological markers of ethnic identity: a new method for sociolinguistic research', in D. Sankoff (ed.), *Diversity and Diachrony*. Amsterdam: John Benjamins. pp. 45–58.

Green, L. J. (2002) *African American English: A Linguistic Introduction*. New York: Cambridge University Press.

Grimes, A. (2005) 'In search of ethnic cues: the status of /æ/ and /ɪ/ and their implications for linguistic profiling'. MA thesis, North Carolina State University.

Guy, G. (1980) 'Variation in the group and the individual: the case of final stop deletion', in W. Labov (ed.), *Locating Language in Time and Space*. New York: Academic Press. pp. 1–36.

Hagstrom, C. (2004) 'The language of doctors and patients', in E. Finegan and J. R. Rickford (eds), *Language in the USA: Themes for the Twenty-First Century*. Cambridge: Cambridge University Press. pp. 445–62.

Hazen, K. (2000) 'The role of researcher identity in conducting sociolinguistic research: a reflective case study', *Southern Journal of Linguistics*, 24: 103–20.

Hazen, K. (2002) 'Identity and language variation in a rural community', *Language*, 78: 240–57.

Holmes, J. (2006) *Gendered Talk at Work: Constructing Gender Identity Through Workplace Discourse*. Malden, MA: Blackwell.

Holmes, J. and Stubbe, M. (2003) *Power and Politeness in the Workplace: A Sociolinguistic Analysis of Talk at Work*. London: Pearson.

Johnstone, B. (2000) *Qualitative Methods in Sociolinguistics*. Oxford: Oxford University Press.

Johnstone, B. and Baumgardt, D. (2004) 'Pittsburghese online: vernacular norming in conversation', *American Speech*, 79: 115–45.

Kendall, T. (2009) 'Speech rate, pause, and linguistic variation: an examination through the sociolinguistic archive and analysis project'. Duke University dissertation.

Kerswill, P. (1993) 'Rural dialect speakers in an urban speech community: the role of dialect contact in defining a sociolinguistic concept', *International Journal of Applied Linguistics*, 3: 33–56.

Kerswill, P. and Wright, S. (1990) 'The validity of phonetic transcription: limitations of a sociolinguistic research tool', *Language Variation and Change*, 2: 255–75.

Labov, W. (1963) 'The social motivation of a sound change', *Word*, 19: 273–307.

Labov, W. (1966) *The Social Stratification of English in New York City*. Washington, DC: Center for Applied Linguistics.

Labov, W. (1972a) 'Some principles of linguistic methodology', *Language in Society*, 1: 97–120.

Labov, W. (1972b) *Sociolinguistic Patterns.* Philadelphia: University of Pennsylvania Press.

Labov, W. (1984) 'Field methods of the project on language change and variation', in J. Baugh and J. Sherzer (eds), *Language in Use: Readings in Sociolinguistics.* Englewood Cliffs, NJ: Prentice Hall. pp. 28–53.

Labov, W. (1994) *Principles of Language Change.* Vol. 1, *Internal Factors.* Oxford: Blackwell.

Labov, W. (1998) 'Coexistent systems in African-American vernacular English', in S. Mufwene, J. R. Rickford, G. Bailey and J. Baugh (eds), *African American Vernacular English.* New York: Routledge. pp. 110–53.

Labov, W. (2001) *Principles of Linguistic Change.* Vol. 2, *Social Factors.* Malden, MA: Blackwell.

Labov, W., Cohen, P., Robins, C. and Lewis, J. (1968) *A Study of the Non-Standard English of Negro and Puerto Rican Speakers in New York City.* United States Office of Education Final Report, Research Project 3288.

Labov, W., Ash, S. and Boberg, C. (2006) *The atlas of North American English: Phonetics, Phonology, and Sound Change.* Berlin: Mouton de Gruyter.

Lambert, W. E. (1967) 'A social psychology of bilingualism', *Journal of Social Issues,* 23: 91–108.

McGurk, H. and MacDonald, J. (1976) 'Hearing lips and seeing voices', *Nature,* 264: 385–403.

Malinowski, B. (1915) 'The natives of Mailu: preliminary results of the Robert Mond research work in British New Guinea', *Transactions and Proceedings of the Royal Society of South Australia,* 39: 494–706.

Malinowski, B. (1922) *Argonauts of the Western Pacific: An Account of the Native Enterprise and Adventure in the Archipelagoes of Melanesian New Guinea.* Studies in Economics and Political Science, No. 65. London: Routledge and Kegan Paul.

Mallinson, C. (2006) 'The dynamic construction of race, class, and gender through linguistic practice among women in a Black Appalachian community'. Raleigh, NC: North Carolina State University dissertation,

Mendoza-Denton, N. (1995) 'Pregnant pauses: silence and authority in the Hill-Thomas hearings', in M. Bucholtz and K. Hall (eds), *Gender Articulated: Language and the Culturally Constructed Self.* Routledge: New York. pp. 51–66.

Mendoza-Denton, N. (2008) *Homegirls: Language and Cultural Practice among Latina Youth Gangs.* London: Wiley/Blackwell.

Mendoza-Denton, N. and Mjahed, M. (2002) *A Congressman's Response to Face-Threatening Acts in Town Hall Meetings: Implications for Habermas' Public Sphere.* American Anthropological Association, New Orleans, LA.

Meyerhoff, M. (2001) 'Formal and cultural constraints on optional objects in Bislama', *Language Variation and Change,* 13: 323–46.

Milory, L. (1987) 'Language and Social Networks', 2nd ed. Oxford: Blackwell.

Milroy, L. and Gordon, M. (2003) *Sociolinguistics: Method and Interpretation.* Malden, MA: Blackwell.

Nagy, N. (2000) 'Fieldwork in the new century: working, in facto, an endangered language community', *Southern Journal of Linguistics,* 24: 121–36.

Neuman, W. L. (2002) *Social Research Methods: Qualitative and Quantitative Approaches.* 5th edn. Boston: Allyn and Bacon.

Niedzielski, N. (1999) 'The effect of social information on the perception of sociolinguistic variables', *Journal of Language and Social Psychology,* 18: 62–85.

Patrick, P. L. (2002) 'The speech community', in J. K. Chambers, P. Trudgill and N. Schilling-Estes (eds), *Handbook of Language Variation and Change.* Malden, MA: Blackwell. pp. 573–97.

Pickford, G. R. (1956) 'American linguistic geography: a sociological appraisal', *Word,* 11: 211–33.

Podesva, R. J., Jamsu, J., Calllier, P. and Heitman, J. (2008) 'The social meaning of released /t/ among US polititicians: insights from production and perceptions'. Paper given at New Ways of Analyzing Variation, Houston, TX, November 2008.

Preston, D. (1986) 'Five visions of America', *Language in Society,* 15: 221–40.

Preston, D. R. (1989) *Perceptual Dialectology: Nonlinguists' Views of Areal Linguistics.* Dordrecht: Foris.

Preston, D. R. (1991) 'Sorting out the variables in sociolinguistic theory', *American Speech.* 66: 33–56.

Preston, D. R. (1992) 'Talking black and talking white: a study in variety imitation', in J. J. Hall, N. Doanne and D. Ringler (eds), *Old English and New: Studies in Language and Linguistics in Honor of Frederic G. Cassidy.* New York: Garland. pp. 327–55.

Preston, D. R. (1993) 'Folk dialectology', in D. R. Preston (ed.), *American Dialect Research.* Amsterdam: John Benjamins. pp. 333–77.

Preston, D. R. (1996) '*Whaddayaknow?* The modes of folk linguistic awareness', *Language Awareness,* 5: 40–77.

Renn, J. (2007) 'Measuring style shift: a quantitative analysis of African American English'. University of North Carolina at Chapel Hill thesis.

Rickford, J. R. (1999) *African American English: Features, Evolution, and Educational Implications.* Malden, MA: Blackwell.

Rickford, J. R. and McNair-Knox, F. (1994) 'Addressee- and topic-influenced style shift', in D. Biber and E. Finegan (eds), *Sociolinguistic Perspectives on Register.* New York: Oxford University Press. pp. 235–76.

Schilling-Estes, N. (1998) 'Investigating "self-conscious" speech: the performance register in Ocracoke English', *Language in Society,* 27: 53–83.

Schilling-Estes, N. (2000) 'Fieldwork for the new century', *Southern Journal of Linguistics,* 24: 83–90.

Schilling-Estes, N. (2008) 'Sociolinguistic fieldwork', in R. Bayley and C. Lucas (eds), *Sociolinguistic Variation: Theories, Methods, and Applications.* Cambridge: Cambridge University Press. pp.165–89.

Schilling-Estes, N. and Wolfram, W. (1994) 'Convergent explanation and alternative regularization patterns: *were/weren't* leveling in a vernacular English variety', *Language Variation and Change,* 6: 273–302.

Schreier, D. (2003) *Isolation and Language Change: Contemporary and Sociohistorical Evidence from Tristan da Cunha English.* New York: Palgrave Macmillan.

Shuy, R., Wolfram, W. and Riley, W. K. (1967) *Linguistic Correlates of Social Stratification in Detroit Speech*. USOE Final Report No. 6-1347. Washington, DC: Center for Applied Linguistics.

Shuy, R. W., Wolfram, W. and Riley, W. K (1968) *Field Techniques in an Urban Language Study*. Washington, DC: Center for Applied Linguistics.

Shuy, R., Baratz, J. C. and Wolfram, W. (1969) *Sociolinguistic Factors in Speech Identification*. NIMH Research Project No. MH 15048-01. Washington, DC: Center for Applied Linguistics.

Strand, E. (1999) 'Understanding the role of gender stereotypes in speech perception', *Journal of Language and Social Psychology*, 18: 86–100.

Tagliamonte, S. (2006) *Analyzing Sociolinguistic Variation*. Cambridge: Cambridge University Press.

Tagliamonte, S. and Denis, D. (2008) 'Linguistic ruin? LOL! Instant messaging and teen language', *American Speech*, 83: 3–34

Thomas, E. R. (2002) 'Sociophonetic applications of speech perception experiments', *American Speech*, 77: 115–47.

Torbert, B. (2004) 'Southern vowels and the social construction of salience'. Duke University dissertation.

Trudgill, P. (1974) *The Social Differentiation of English in Norwich*. Cambridge: Cambridge University Press.

Van Bezooijen, R. (1988) 'The relative importance of pronunciation, prosody, and voice quality for the attribution of social status and personality characteristics', in R. van Hout and U. Knops (eds), *Language Attitudes in the Dutch Language Area*. Dordrecht: Foris. pp. 85–103.

Van Hofwegen, J. and Wolfram, W. (forthcoming) *Coming of Age in African American English: A Longitudinal Study*, Journal of Sociolinguistics.

Wolfram, W. (1969) *A Sociolinguistic Description of Detroit Negro Speech*. Washington, DC: Center for Applied Linguistics.

Wolfram, W. (1982) 'Language knowledge and other dialects', *American Speech*, 57: 3–18.

Wolfram, W. (1986) 'Good data in a bad situation: eliciting vernacular structures', in J. Fishman, A. Tabouret-Keller, M. Cline, B. Khrishnamurti and M. Abdulziz (eds), *The Fergusonian Impact*. Vol. 2. The Hague: Mouton. pp. 3–33.

Wolfram, W. (1988) 'Reconsidering the semantics of *a*-prefixing', *American Speech*, 63: 247–54.

Wolfram, W. (1996) 'Delineation and description in dialectology: the case of perfective *I'm* in Lumbee English', *American Speech*, 71: 5–26.

Wolfram, W. (2008) 'When islands lose dialects: the case of the Ocracoke Brogue', *Shima: The International Journal for Research on Island Cultures*, 2: 1–13.

Wolfram, W. and Fasold, R. (1974) *The Study of Social Dialects in the United States*. Englewood Cliffs, NJ: Prentice Hall.

Wolfram, W. and Schilling-Estes, N. (1995) 'Moribund dialects and the endangerment canon: the case of the Ocracoke brogue', *Language*, 71: 696–71.

Wolfram, W. and Smith, A. (2008) Re-examining dialect recession: integrating real and apparent time. Houston, TX. NWAV 37. November 2008.

Wolfram, W. and Wolfram, T. D. (1977) 'How come you asked how come?', in R. W. Fasold and R. W. Shuy (eds), *Studies in Language Variation*. Washington, DC: Georgetown University Press. pp. 33–41.

Wolfram, W., Hazen, K., and Schilling-Estes, N. (1999) *Dialect Maintenance and Change on the Outer Banks*. Publications of the American Dialect Society 81. Tuscaloosa, AL: University of Alabama Press.

Wolfram, W., Dannenberg, C., Knick, S. and Oxendine, L. (2002) *Fine in the World: Lumbee Language in Time and Place*. Raleigh: NC State Humanity Extension Program/Publications.

Wolfram, W., Reaser, J. and Vaughn, C. (2008). 'Operationalizing linguistic gratuity: from principle to practice', *Linguistic and Language Compass*, 2(6): 1109–34.

Wolfson, N. (1976) 'Speech events and natural speech: some implications for sociolinguistic methodology', *Language in Society*, 5: 168–82.

PART 4

Interaction

Sociolinguistic Potentials of Face-to-Face Interaction

Helga Kotthoff

22.1 INTRODUCTION

Class, race and gender divisions continue to be among the central forces shaping how we live. Social theorists, particularly sociologists, try to understand how societies are structured and how 'power', 'class' or 'gender' are distributed, organized and indexed. It is a major concern of sociolinguistics to examine the possible relationships between language, on the one hand, and concepts such as those mentioned above, on the other (Wardhaugh, 2002: 9). Through the introduction of a systematic methodology for investigating social dialects, Labov (1972) was able to show that variations in features such as the postvocalic (r) in words such as *car* were not a matter of free choice, but rather were conditioned in predictable ways by social factors such as social class, age, sex and style (Romaine, 1995: 494). Since then, this approach has been refined and broadened by linguists from various different traditions, many of whom believe that the relationship between language and the social structure is complex and multifaceted. The analysis of face-to-face interaction contributes to this enterprise in important ways.

In this chapter, I aim to summarize and discuss sociolinguistic dimensions of interactional features. Most sociologists regard structural categories such as 'class' or 'gender' as macro issues. The micro/macro distinction is a great source of confusion in thinking about the causes of inequality. Social scientists sometimes blur the distinction between the individual and societal causes of certain phenomena. What causes a single person to be poor is not always what causes high societal rates of poverty. Sociolinguists distinguish a macro level of society and a micro level of discourse phenomena. There are different ways to connect these levels and different views as to what kinds of evidence are appropriate for what kinds of question. Boxer (2002: 19ff.) points out that many researchers who combine sociolinguistics and the study of face-to-face interaction successfully triangulate their methods (see also Wodak and Krzyzanowski, 2008):

> The manner in which research is carried out constrains findings. This fact has long been known to researchers of social sciences. Sociolinguistics is particularly vulnerable to differential interpretation of research results that have used different methods of data collection and analysis. How one studies a particular issue both determines and is determined by the research question(s). Thus, if we want to study the realization of a particular speech act in a particular speech community, we will choose to collect the data in face-to-face interaction. If the speech behaviour is rare, employing a method other than that which relies on naturally occurring data may be in order. Having said this, one must understand the limitations of any approach and proceed with caution, hedging on claims that may be beyond the possibility of analysis when using any one particular method. A combination of approaches is always recommended, and triangulating data sheds light on how and why people said what they did.

Interaction studies can shed light on the complexity of social life beyond reifying static stratified groups, and they are particularly concerned with the intersection between class, gender and other kinds of identity.

Various schools have contributed to the emergence of interaction analysis as a discipline bridging anthropology, linguistics, communication science and sociology. In this chapter, I deal with the following:

- ethnography of communication and interactional sociolinguistics
- ethnomethodology and conversation analysis
- (critical) discourse analysis
- gender studies.

The focus will be on the findings and approaches these schools have contributed to the sociolinguistics of face-to-face interaction. In the last 30 years a lot of research has been done on gender in communication (see, e.g., the handbook by Holmes and Meyerhoff, 2003) and also on ethnic discrimination (see, e.g., Kotthoff and Spencer-Oatey, 2007). But to write about stratification according to class was seen as 'proof you belonged to the past age – an age where old-fashioned macho and egotistical union leaders endangered the national good' (Machin and Richardson, 2008: 282; see Hellinger in this volume).

Not only is there a gap as far as class and class experience are concerned but also a theoretical gap in our understanding of both individual experience and structurally stratified inequalities because, as well, in discourse studies idealistic philosophical approaches dominated, according to which discourse 'creates' social positions and social realities (Machin and Richardson, 2008: 283).

22.2 ETHNOGRAPHY OF COMMUNICATION AND INTERACTIONAL SOCIOLINGUISTICS

The American linguists and anthropologists Dell H. Hymes and John Gumperz were among the first to study 'ways of speaking' as they differ from culture to culture, from speech community to speech community (Hymes, 1972, reprinted 2001; Gumperz, 1968, reprinted 2001).

The studies concentrated on rigidly stratified communities where roles were strictly compartmentalized and associated varieties of language clearly differentiated (Saville-Troike, 1982: 87). In many societies roles are marked by different pronouns or terms of address and may require different levels of formality, corresponding to the different levels of prestige or deference assigned to them.

Speakers possess 'communicative competence', i.e. knowledge of appropriate ways of speaking within their culture. An important unit of analysis is the communicative event, a single verbal interaction (e.g. 'nagging' in a family context; Boxer, 2002) within a specific communicative situation as recognized by the culture (e.g. an evening meal or an examination). The object of study in this tradition is situated discourse. 'Ethnography' refers to fieldwork, supplemented by techniques developed in other areas of study such as pragmatics, anthropology and conversation analysis (Fitch and Philipsen, 1995). Since the appearance of a special issue of *American Anthropologist* compiled by John Gumperz and Dell Hymes in 1964, the ethnography of speaking, as both a methodology and as a model of how human beings construct shared meaning from social experience, has studied diverse questions. It often analyses social issues reflected in language use, including discrimination and stigma and their effects. Societies differ in the communicative resources available for their members. The relative status of speakers and their role relationship may be marked in a variety of ways. Role relationships may also be marked by the order in which participants speak, eye contact or avoidance and body position, as Saville-Troike (1982: 88) points out. In a cyclical or interactional event with several people speaking in sequence, such as greetings, introductions, or expressing thanks, the order of address may mark relative deference or closeness (Saville-Troike, 1982: 91).

Let us look at ethnographic studies of communication that examine the world of schooling and education, where sociolinguistic interference is frequently found (see also Rojo in this volume). School-induced socialization has enormous sociopolitical significance, and as a result the forms and content of schooling are an enduring source of social conflict.

Susan U. Philips (1970, reprinted 2001) studied 'Participant Structures and Communicative Competence' and showed that Native American children failed to participate in classroom interaction because the social conditions for participation to which they become accustomed in their Indian community differ from those they encounter in school. Philips spent sufficient time on the Warm Springs Reservation in Oregon to observe classroom and reservation communicative situations and pinpoint sources of potential conflict for Warm Springs Native American children. The teachers repeatedly stated that Native American (Indian) children show a great deal of reluctance to speak in class. Philips writes (2001: 305) that the most immediate concern of the teachers is to teach children the basic rules of classroom behaviour necessary to maintain continuous and ordered activity.

The teacher controls all the activities taking place in the classroom; in particular, she determines who can speak and when they can speak. The teacher often relates to the class as an undifferentiated mass (one type of participation structure), much like a performer before an audience, or she relates to only some of the students (another type of participation structure). In comparing Indian and non-Indian first-graders, Philips noticed that the Indian first-graders are consistently slower in beginning to act in accordance with many basic class arrangements. They do not raise their hands before speaking, wander around the room and talk to other students. They show a great deal more interest in what other students are doing than in what the teacher is doing. A third participation structure consists in all students working independently. A fourth consists of group projects with student chairpersons. In the first two settings, Native American children speak rarely or so softly that only their neighbours can understand them. In the other two participation frameworks, they are much more successful. Philips compares participation in the classroom to Indian children's participation in other contexts. For a Native American child it is very unusual that a person places herself outside the interaction and activity of the students (as the teachers do in the first two frameworks). In the Indians' social experience, one is either part of a group or outside it. The notion of a single individual such as the teacher being structurally set apart from all the others, and yet still part of the group organization, is one that these children encounter for the first time in school and continue to experience only in non-Indian derived activities. It is not the case that all the students in the classroom may participate in any given activity, as in Indian community activities. Nor are they given the opportunity to choose the degree of participation, which in Native American contexts would be based on the individual having already ascertained in private that he or she was capable of successful communication of competence. Educators, Philips concludes, cannot assume that because Indian children (or any children from cultural backgrounds other than European American) speak English, they have assimilated all the sociolinguistic rules underlying classroom interaction. Her work aims at sensitizing teachers to cultural differences.

Whereas Philips shows a classroom situation in which children of more than one cultural background come together, and those who do not meet the dominant standards do not get equal opportunities within the system, Paul Willis' *Learning to Labour* (1977)[1] focuses on class distinctions in the British school system. He points to the resistance of working-class 'lads' to the oppression of a British school which attempts to mould them into compliant workers who will fill jobs in degrading occupations. Willis details creative ways in which working-class boys retain a sense of importance and identity at school in the face of an oppressive system which treats them as 'deviant'. He points out that the sector of the educational system he studied was intended to reproduce a class structure marked by inequality resting on the backs of labourers.

School is not just a place where the dominant culture's hegemony is expressed and reproduced, it is also the site of daily conflicts over legitimate vs illegitimate behaviours and languages, as well as over the recognition of the social relevance of hegemonic values, norms and knowledge. Jünger (2008) shows for contemporary Switzerland that school success depends decisively on what framework conditions affect children and how school-compatible their habitus is (in Bourdieu's sense). Underprivileged and privileged primary school children have their own resource-specific school logic and experience and use the school in different ways. As a result, in regard to the acquisition of competency, disadvantages arise for the one and, to the contrary, advantages for the other.

Recent studies of multicultural education have also shown that in the interaction between teachers and pupils, popular ethnic, religious and cultural stereotypes shape teachers' expectations about the pupils' abilities. In language education, for example, a recent German study shows that teachers tend to attribute linguistic deficits to children with immigrant backgrounds and to over look those of the native children (Weber, 2003). This phenomenon perpetuates the judgment that immigrant children have low linguistic and cultural competence. Hugh Mehan et al. (2001) cite various studies demonstrating that in US schools as well, minority pupils' deficiencies are attributed to cultural factors. Instead of an increased sensitivity to cultural differences, we often face a sort of ethnicization of social conflict. Conflicts among social groups can be projected onto immigrants or minorities, while other potentially meaningful differences, like those between middle-class and working-class cultures or between various political milieux, are neglected (Scherr, 2007).

Recently, Monica Heller and Marilyn Martin-Jones (2001) edited a volume of studies whose authors analyse school interactions as a window to the contradictions between educational policy *idealism* and classroom *reality*. All their authors aim at combining an analysis of structure with one of agency. In Part 1, discourse analysts from Hong Kong, England and Burundi show how even after the curriculum is opened up to marginalized languages, domination may still be re-established through unequal patterns of turn-taking and code-switching. Others analyse routinized talk sequences characterized by heavy repetition, which prevents meaningful pupil engagement with the curriculum. Parts 2 and 3 explore responses by planners and students to dominant social categories and educational discourses. Here there is some optimism, as students exuberantly code switch, call attention to classroom rules, parody one another and reject unstated norms. The studies discuss students' resistance strategies, situated in institutional interactions such as, for example, choices of indigenous languages against the school norm.

The ethnography of communication is an integrative approach which embraces various practices. Its approach to discourse in general often combines context description, speech events and interactional approaches within a larger framework of inquiry. It views all phases and aspects of interaction (from the cognitive to the political) as relevant to cultural meanings (Schiffrin, 1994: 144). Gumperz (1982: 12) later turned his attention to modern urban societies and their social and cultural heterogeneity. His studies of both inter-racial and inter-ethnic settings show that, in particular, differences in the marginal features of language that can cause misunderstandings lead to the formation of racial and ethnic stereotypes and contribute to inequalities in power and status. He called these signalling mechanisms 'contextualization cues'. When speakers share contextualization cues, interactions proceed smoothly.

Researchers who regard themselves as interactional or interpretive sociolinguists work with interactional data recorded in natural situations. They do not take isolated sequences, but rather situated interactions as their starting point, because context extends beyond the immediate context of the discourse sequence (local context). They integrate ethnography, sociocultural structures, ideologies and power relations as resources for interpreting communication (Auer and di Luzio, 1992; Kotthoff, 1996a). Since language and speech are viewed in their function for the (re)construction of social reality, analyses of conversations should permit inferences beyond structural patterns about:

- how social relationships and social identities are created, affirmed and changed
- how the cultural norms of life worlds are formed and
- how societies generate evaluations of speech and thereby create political orders (Gal and Woolard, 1995).

Qualitative approaches to data are regarded as important, since researchers reconstruct how speakers acquire social meaning through the simultaneous processing of verbal sequences and ethnographic surroundings. But quantification is often relevant, too.

Neither institutional nor other types of discourse are regarded as automatically obeying normative sociolinguistic appropriateness constraints. Everywhere, interpretive processes are responsible for the specific scope of action and the definition of social relationships that speakers negotiate within sociohistorically transmitted power structures. Parameters such as gender, class, group or ethnicity – structural dimensions of most societies – can be contextualized as more or less relevant categories in situated practice (Cook-Gumperz and Gumperz, 2007). Their influence is historically strong, but not set completely extra-situationally. Social stylistics is a further important domain of interactional sociolinguistics (Sandig and Selting, 1997; Eckert, 2000); different ways of speaking are not merely attributed to speakers' social conditions (to extra-situational factors), but rather the conversational dynamics are analysed from the complexity of the power distribution to style repertoires on up to the social distinction interests of the participants. The two summaries presented below demonstrate how interactional sociolinguists combine micro analysis with reflections on power structures.

Cook-Gumperz and Gumperz (1996) focus on the hidden role that gender plays in a dissertation defence. They demonstrate how a turn-by-turn analysis can be connected with broader problems of gender ideology that affect many aspects of the proceedings. The authors demonstrate, contrary to official ideologies according to which academic assessments are solely based on personal achievement, that subtextual scientific ideologies play a role that, in the given defence, leads to a subtle devaluation of the student's high involvement with her subject ('lack of academic distance'). A sequential contextualization of the event is combined with a concentration on the sociohistorical roots of ideologies about professional judgment and gender. The authors show how contextualization choices constitute the event as a ritual. The article goes beyond microanalysis to deal with matters of broader context, such as the authority relations of traditional male dominance in academia (see also chapters by Pavlidou and Hellinger in this volume).

Marco Jacquemet's book *Credibility in Court* (1996) analyses trials of members of the Nuova Camorra Organizzata (NCO) in Naples, Italy, a criminal organization which in the 1980s controlled as much as a third of the economic activity in that region. In winter 1982, the NCO suffered a fatal blow: the desertion of some of its key men who, when arrested, broke the code of silence and provided evidence to incriminate their former associates. His study focuses on the relationship between the judges in charge of the court proceedings and a new kind of witness: the so-called *pentiti* (repentants), who cooperated with the Justice Department in exchange for reduced sentences. The mass trials lasted three years. The recordings stem from trials that took place in various political atmospheres. The construction of legal evidence was in each case a negotiated process carried out mainly through communicative performance. Jacquemet does not deny the existence and importance of institutional authority, but points out that an ongoing, communicative negotiation characterizes the regulation of conflicts in institutional settings. The unstable situation of the Italian legal system and its structural transformations examined in the book constitute a clear example of the dynamic nature of the relationship between social structures and communicative practices, showing the dynamic tension between so-called micro and macro dimensions. The social structure of the courtroom environment provided the initial 'rules of the game', as well as the necessary resources for acting in the 1983 trial. These rules and resources both constrained and facilitated participants' communicative behaviour. However, as soon as the trial started, the focus shifted to the manoeuvres, strategies and alliances of the courtroom participants, who used the given rules and resources to try to obtain a favourable outcome. Jacquemet documented the shifting relationship between the *pentiti* and the Justice Department – especially the trial judges. The confessions the *pentiti* made to law-enforcement agents had to be re-enacted in the courtroom in order to be accepted as judicial evidence for the prosecution's case. In the courtroom, the *pentiti* had to produce a 'true' discourse, i.e. a discourse accepted as truthful by its recipients. In this quest for credibility, they drew on the communicative strategies available to them – ones acquired over the years in everyday interactions within their local networks, which were mainly made up of people engaged in 'state-disapproved' (i.e. illegal) activities. In an unfamiliar role and under stress caused by the close scrutiny, they based their performance in the witness stand on their local communal values – above all their code of honour (Jacquemet, 1996: 5). Coming from a moral universe which recognizes credibility on the basis of social reputation rather than on propositional accuracy, they presented themselves as 'men of honour' in order to get the Justice Department to acknowledge their credibility, not through an examination of the referential content of their testimony, but rather through the recognition of their high social standing. The judge–*pentito* rapport became the determining axis in the construction of judicial evidence.

Anthropological studies of the legal process, sociocultural studies of Southern Italy, and communicative studies of courtroom interaction and conflict talk are blended into a single paradigm to explore the role of power, truth and credibility in courtroom communication. Jacquemet shows how social systems operate through dynamic feedback, become legitimized and eventually evolve (see also Ehrlich in this volume). By suggesting that truth is a field of communicative practice, he sheds light on the dynamic tension between communicative practices and social structures. The discourse practices of judicial ritual provide the foundation upon which the apparent contradiction between rational truth and effective communication is resolved. Public speakers – lawyers, orators, mediators, disputants and so on – employ such practices, recognizing that courtroom questioning techniques are primarily used to win cases, not to help the court discover the facts.

In order not to create a misleading image of strong lines of separation between the various sociolinguistic approaches to interaction, it should be noted that many analysts of talk-in-interaction combine ethnography and detailed conversation analyses (Deppermann, 2000). This 'provides a way of understanding the meaning of particular forms of action within the larger repertoires of possible actions important to the ongoing social projects' (Goodwin, 2008: 9). In her work on various groups of children (mostly girls) from different ethnic and class backgrounds, Goodwin describes the ways in which class- and gender-based forms of inequality coexist, setting forth the idea that social differences arise in the course of the various activities. She uses traditional conversation analyses of numerous detailed transcripts, besides describing the girls' use of semiotic resources (not neglecting the differing income levels). The girls also perform victimization using the tactics of social exclusion and ridicule. Access to certain forms of cultural capital in the sense of Bourdieu (consumer products, sports) identifies who is included in an activity and who is not. Material resources thus play a role.

22.3 ETHNOMETHODOLOGY AND CONVERSATION ANALYSIS

Harvey Sacks (Sacks, 1992) is generally considered the great inspiration for conversation analysis, a sociological approach that is chiefly interested in the interactional organization of social activities (Hutchby and Woofitt, 1998: 14). Sacks himself was influenced by Harold Garfinkel, who wanted to explain the 'ethnomethods' (ethnos = folk) of sense-making by social actors. Garfinkel (1967) assumed that the members of a society behave in ways that can be interpreted by others in their society. Laypersons orient themselves to each other with their 'ethnomethods', without being able to specify this in detail (p. 42). The term 'ethno-' refers, by analogy with ethno-medicine or ethno-botany, to people's everyday systems of knowledge and action, beyond scientific theories. Garfinkel wanted to uncover such normative practices of seamless understanding upon which getting-along is based. For the purposes of conducting their everyday affairs, it is not necessary to understand 'what people are really talking about'. The anticipation that persons will understand, the occasionality of expressions, the specific vagueness of references, the retrospective–prospective sense of a present occurrence, waiting for something later in order to see what was meant before, are sanctioned characteristics of common discourse. They furnish a background of seen but unnoticed features of common discourse, whereby actual utterances are recognized as events of common, reasonable, understandable, plain talk. Conventional theories, by contrast, treated social orders as resulting from individual interests, external constraint and/or some conjunction between the two. For Garfinkel, however, individual motivation, power and constraint must be managed by communicators in and through the details of communication. He insists that the need of participants to mutually orient their ways of producing order on each subsequent occasion adequately explains the details of order and sense-making.

Derived from the principles and beliefs of ethnomethodology (Garfinkel, 1967), conversation analysis is a significant domain that interprets the patterns through which people handle conversations. Conversation analysis (CA) generally attempts to describe the orderliness, structure and sequential patterns of interaction, whether institutional (in school, in the courtroom or elsewhere) or in casual conversation. Research in conversation analysis over the past 30 years has shown that the technical aspects of talk-in-interaction are structured, socially organized resources – or methods – whereby participants perform and coordinate their activities through talking together. Conversational interaction is the primordial site of human sociality. Thus, these methods are the technical bedrock upon which people build their social lives and construct their social relations with one another. In the light of this, one of CA's principal practitioners, Emanuel Schegloff, has more recently identified 'talk-in-interaction' as CA's central subject. Perhaps for the same reason, some scholars, who do not limit themselves to using CA methods, call themselves discourse analysts (DAs), although that term was first used to identify researchers using methods different from CA (e.g. Levinson, 1983) and still identifies a group of scholars larger than the group that uses only CA methods.

Conversation analysts (as pragmaticists) assume that potentially ambiguous utterances are disambiguated in the specific context. Since the procedures are recursive, the members of a culture can coordinate their actions. Their largely consistent 'ethnomethods' are shown in the 'display' of utterances. 'Stick to your data' is Schegloff's instruction whenever anyone claims that an external category, such as, for example, power could have played a role in a conversation. The relevance of a certain identity category needs to be recognized as an orientation to this in the details of the interaction. In 1987 he stated in 'Between micro and macro: context and other connections' that macro categories are only relevant if they have direct effects on the micro level of behaviour. We should even assume that the entire social structure is created in interaction. Levinson (2005: 431ff.) criticizes this as 'interactional reductionism'. Schegloff opposes the importation of the *macro* (sociological/sociolinguistic) into the *micro* (interaction analysis), suggesting innocently that one might *reverse* the strategy instead (as Levinson points out). Schegloff suggests we should think of interaction patterns as engendering social institutions.

Before getting back to Levinson's article, I recall the critique of CA by Hymes (1974: 81):

> Some sociologists become so absorbed in words as to fail to renew their relation to actual contexts. Admittedly, it is fascinating to discover the richness of speech, coming from a disciplinary background that has neglected it; but it is a bit absurd to treat transcribed tapes of interaction as if they were the Dead Sea Scrolls. When a society is gone, we must glean all we can from texts that remain, and contrary to some opinion, such work is arduous, disciplined, and often revealing. But again, it is a bit absurd to invent an amateur philology to deal with the life outside one's door. I have read elaborate analysis of verbal interaction that failed to consider the other aspects of the parties' presence to each other, attributing to complexities of words what may have depended on eye-contact; and imputations of intention and construal that neglected intonation [like many grammarians, to be sure] and that failed to consult or consider the interpretations of the participants themselves.

For a field researcher like Hymes, it was simply incomprehensible that, in interaction analysis, he should proceed as though he were deciphering hieroglyphics instead of exploring the broader context, which he as an ethnographer of communication regarded as self-evident. In the meantime we have many studies of gaze direction (Kendon, 1990) and prosody in interaction (Couper-Kuhlen and Selting, 1996), but the question remains of whether social order is the product of local interaction.

Goffman (1981: 14–15) referred to conversation analysts as 'communication engineers', because he saw them as only capturing 'the sheer physical constraints of any communication system'. According to him, they are interested in 'culture-free formulations'. Above all, the omnipresent plea of conversation analysis to limit itself to the analysis of local contexts provoked Goffman's critique that historicity was being screened out. I would add that historicity starts where we take into account the shared history of the interactants.

Again and again there were reactions by leading conversation analysts to this sort of critique. Schegloff (1997: 166) writes:

> ... we need first to understand the object – the conversational episode in its endogenous constitution, what it was for the parties involved in it, in its course, as embodied and displayed in the very details of its realization. Only then can we even begin to explore what forms of critical approach it might take, and what political issue ...

According to Levinson (2005: 432), there are two ways to read the CA literature with regard to the linkage of micro and macro. The one (the variant which some other discourse analysts would share) gives the interaction structure a certain autonomy, its own system with its own mechanisms; the other sees the overall social structure as interactionally generated (in his view the 'dangerous variant' – as in mine):

> The kernel idea – the dangerous idea of my title – is that social order is the local product of interaction. Stated thus, it seems innocuous enough. But suppose we read it as all social order, everything – from institutions to economics, from kinship to politics, from etiquette to grammar. Now it is no longer innocent.

Above all, in the debate carried on in *Discourse & Society*, 5(6) (2002) on gender in CA, it became clear that Schegloff, for example, limits the relevance of the social category of gender to an orientation to this in the current context. In his examples this sometimes corresponds to a thematization, for example, of the 'Ladies first' type. It can be objected that ordinarily many identity categories remain in the background of interaction, and yet they can still be made quite relevant at a later point in time, e.g. in another conversation, e.g. the stylization of clothing is often done in a gendered way, but it is seldom explicitly thematized. Can we really assume that biographical, historical, institutional and socio-structural givens are always only relevant when they are on 'display' in the local interactional context, thus when they become visible in the details of speech? For gender studies,

the limitation to 'display in context' has often led writers down the garden path.

Mey (1993: 271–2) formulates the following points of criticism:

> However, restricting oneself to the problems of description that one encounters during the analysis of actual conversation puts a severe limitation on the explanatory potential of one's analysis. A satisfactory account of the realities of conversation relies heavily on the wider context of the conversational interaction, and will not limit itself to strictly linguistic, or strictly CA-relevant factors. A pragmatic analysis cannot remain on the object language level, describing 'the facts, all the facts, and nothing but the facts', as the conversational analysts (often implicitly) seem to advocate. A pragmatic explanation requires a meta-level, where the facts and factors of the analysis are placed in an overall explanatory framework, and where the analyst him-/herself is engaged beyond the immediate context. This higher level of analysis (often called 'critical') is where societal critique and social action have their places – topics which in the eyes of many scientists, including linguists, are as much anathema to their profession as the introduction of meaning into linguistic description used to be for the strict structuralists of the thirties and forties.

I will take the activity type of teasing as an example to show that in order to interpret conversational data we have to draw on a lot of background knowledge.

With Drew (1987) we define 'teasing'[2] as a speech activity in which the actions or attitudes of another person who is present are taken as an occasion for amusement. Since as a rule this includes critical components, usually serious and humorous dimensions are combined in teasing. Also with Drew we assert that teasing episodes have a distinctive structure that is known. Even with a serious reaction to teasing, there are signs that it is still regarded by the participants as an amusing activity.

Drew discusses many examples: among others, is one found on a videotape of family interactions that he obtained from anthropologist Charles Goodwin. I present the example using Drew's notation:

Example 1

Dot:	Do we have two forks cause we're on television?
Mother:	No we-
Angie:	huh huh huh hh h ( )
Father:	Yeah h hah [hh =
Mother:	[uh [huh huh huh

Angie   [heh heh heh
Father: = Right yeah probably the answer right
         (the re)
Angie: eh hah hah
Mother: .hhh You have pie,
Mother: You have pie tonight.
(Goodwin according to Drew, 1987: 223)

A daughter teases her mother about the two forks that she has set at each place on the table. The mother at first dismisses the daughter's interpretation, which imputes that she is displaying refinement in order to impress the researchers. Then, first the other daughter laughs; after that the father, and finally the mother herself. However, the mother afterwards reacts seriously to the teaser's supposition that she wanted to make a good impression on the researchers. With their laughter, everyone signals that they have understood the humorous dimension of the question. The mother, however, defends herself at first quite seriously, which Drew calls 'po-faced' (pokerfaced). Sometimes the person who was teased does not laugh at all and only reacts seriously. Drew is of the opinion that the teasing activity is nevertheless immediately understood as humorous, since it contains strong indicators for this – e.g. the exaggerated and extreme formulations, reformulations of something that the recipient has said or done (1987: 231). They resemble other forms of humorous discourse, because they also contain a sudden frame change from a serious to a humorous keying (Kotthoff, 1998). The recipients of teasing in Drew's study usually react seriously at first; some also laugh additionally, others do not. No one in his data immediately teases back (in my data there are some cases of teasing back; Kotthoff, 1998). The connection of the teasing to elements of reality is quite clear, although fictional dimensions also play a role.

Teasing activities usually represent a sort of sociability that integrates disagreement and social difference into relationships of friendship or intimacy. Depending on the state of the relationship, face-threatening humorous utterances are received quite differently, be they teasing, ironic or even sarcastic. Tannen (1994) and Boxer (2002) have pointed to the dynamics of the communication of power and solidarity. For example, blunt expressions of volition can point to a difference in power in some contexts, in others to social relationships of equality and solidarity. This makes it clear that speech activity alone tells us little. The dynamics of power and solidarity, of symmetry and asymmetry, and of formality/informality are significant in humorous communication, but not just there. In familiar symmetrical relationships, stepping outside of conventional politeness patterns communicates on a meta-level that the relationship does not

depend on conventional safeguards and can also integrate differences (Kotthoff, 1996a).

Now an example of a humorous attack game whose harmlessness is not immediately apparent: The following interaction[3] took place at a barbecue while the speakers were trying to start a fire together. Donald and Manni compete with Holger and Ivo for the role of expert on starting a fire.

Example 2 (young men; Kotthoff, 2009b)

Ivo (I), Thomas (T), Manni (M), Holger (H), Donald (D), all (a)

1 D: slEhsch wie=s gut brennt.
2 H: °hei meier. (-) du bist=n Echtes genie.°
3 D: ich weiß. (-) du musst halt nur=s richtige holz reinschmeißen,
4 du wurscht.
5 (1.0)
6 H: danke. (-) vergiss es.
7 D: darfsch halt keine buche anschmeißen und dann anzünden wollen.
8 M: hehehehe
9 I: da spricht der b(h)auer. hehehe
10 D: ha jA. bitte (-) was isch=n des?
11 M: buche macht man drauf wenn's brennt mann.
12 D: ha ja.
13 (1.0)
14 D: hasch wohl noch nie e feuerle gemacht, oder?
15 I: doch schon.
16 D: ja isch klar.
17 (1.0)
18 H: in kroatien.
19 D: du hasch aufgelegt höchstens.
20 T: der Ivo hat=s haus seiner nachbarn verbrannt. mann.
21 scheissserben mann.
22 a: hahahahahahahahaha

1 D: see how good it burns.
2 H: °hey meier. (-) you are a real genius.°
3 D: I know. (-) you just have to throw in the right wood,
4 you wiener.
5 (1.0)
6 H: thanks. (-) forget it.
7 D: you can't just throw on some beech-wood and set it on fire.
8 M: hehehehe
9 I: there speaks the peasant. hehehe
10 D: ha yeah. please (-) what is that?
11 M: you put on beech-wood when it is burning man.
12 D: ha yeah.
13 (1.0)

14 D: you've probably never started a fire, have you?
15 I: of course I have.
16 D: yeah it's obvious.
17 (1.0)
18 H: in Croatia.
19 D: at most you put something on it.
20 T: Ivo burned down his neighbor's house, man.
21 shit Serbs, man.
22 a: hahahahahahahahahaha

Donald's first comment refers ironically to Holger's fire-making skills. Holger parries the irony. He judges Donald's attempts to ignite the stack of wood as unconvincing. In line 3 Donald gives further instructions, and with 'du wurscht' (you wiener) he underlines his opponent's incompetence. Holger thanks him ironically and explicitly rejects the instructions with 'vergiss es' (forget it). Nevertheless, Donald continues to instruct him and presents himself as an expert. He insinuates that Holger has made the beginner's mistake of trying to start a fire with beech-wood (7). This is especially amusing, because they had no beech-wood at all. Thereby Holger's competency is further challenged before the public. Manni laughs. Accusing him of trying to use beech-wood is a fiction.

Ivo razzes Donald as a 'Bauernsohn' peasant's son (country bumpkin). The formulation 'da spricht der Bauer' (there speaks the peasant) is clearly oriented to a public. The laughter modalizes the utterance. Ivo attacks Donald, who also promptly reacts. As well, Manni chips in with expert knowledge (line 11).

Donald insinuates that Ivo, who is pottering around, has never started a fire before. Ivo defends himself (15). Holger then points out that in Croatia, his country of origin, he could already have started one. Daniel objects that as well there he could, at best, have helped. Finally, Thomas chimes in by insinuating that in Croatia Ivo had burnt down his neighbour's house. He alleges that out of envy he had set the house of some Serbian neighbours on fire. He comments: 'scheissserben mann' (shit Serbs, man) with a Slavic accent that Ivo in reality does not have. Despite this, it is meant as a quotation. Playfully he implies feelings of hatred and vengefulness that were reported in the press in connection with the armed conflict in the former Yugoslavia. Ivo was in Germany throughout the conflict and is not known for harbouring hatred of Serbs. The teasing insinuation that he could have learned to make a fire while taking part in the war is fictitious, but not harmless. In the context everybody laughs, including Ivo. In many groups of youths we find forms of disparagement humour, sometimes including ethnic or religious allusions. When I interviewed the young men taking part in the fire-starting episode, they told

me that they all know how to take such a joke, that nobody in this group of friends would feel offended and that their principle is to joke about everyone in equal measure. They would, however, not allow outsiders to make jests like those in Example 2. Aggressive teasing could serve as an index of belonging together. My point here is simply that we cannot decide what is going on in the young men's circle just by looking at only one conversation in a certain context. We would need more data from that group and also comparative data to answer questions about the social order of the group, about ritualization and possible ideals of 'playing cool' in some subcultures. We need to take a look at other texts and contexts (e.g., mass media products) to see whether such humour has to do with a display of masculinity or just of camaraderie or other identity categories. We accept the claim that teasing and all sorts of risky humour demand a long-term balance within a group. Negotiations of social relationships accordingly require going beyond local contexts – both from an emic and an etic perspective.

Let us now look at another variant that Levinson finds 'dangerous'. West and Fenstermaker (1995: 9) see 'difference' as an ongoing interactional accomplishment. Gender, race and class are regarded as 'doings' that consist in the 'local management of conduct in relation to normative conceptions of appropriate attitudes and activities' (West and Fenstermaker, 2002: 541). Is only local management relevant? How does it become global? Scharff (2008: 334) summarizes the approach as follows:

> West and Fenstermaker (1995: 508) are critical of distinctions between 'face-to-face interaction 'versus' 'structural discrimination', arguing that the impact of social structure and history is realized in variously situated social relationships as the sites for doing difference. While West and Fenstermaker's ethnomethodological approach to difference has been challenged for obfuscating power relations and neglecting the influence of macro-societal structures (Collins, 1995: 494; Weber, 1995: 500), their view of the interactional and structural levels as closely intertwined means that interaction is 'integral' (West and Fenstermaker, 1995: 508) to the production of class divisions. The focus on social inequality as situated and dynamic does not erase the existence of broader unequal power structures, but offers insights into how they are produced.

It remains unclear whether and how the production of power structures rests on specific resources and how it is embedded in political and institutional structures that also regulate access to the levels of power. Scharff claims that West and

Fenstermaker do not erase the existence of unequal power structures, but she leaves out that they do not give us much of an idea about how the interplay between sociocultural systems and interaction systems works.

To CA we surely owe the most careful analysis of the organization of conversational interaction. In fact, it is the most appropriate method for studying the manner in which talk in interaction unfolds. But, 'for CA what is found in the transcript is the only legitimate source of knowledge for inferring participants' concern' (Duranti, 1988: 223). As always, the methods of inquiry chosen depend on the questions asked. There is certainly more to the reproduction of class, race, age or gender divisions.

22.4 (CRITICAL) DISCOURSE ANALYSIS

Östman and Virtanen (1995: 240) treat discourse analysis as an umbrella term for all the issues that have been dealt with in the linguistic study of texts and discourses. They have in some respects accepted Levinson's (1983) controversial distinction between discourse analysis (including text linguistics) and approaches such as conversation analysis and dialogical analysis, which are closely related to ethnomethodology and attempt as much as possible to avoid a priori theorizing. While many of the interests of discourse analysis, such as those in the information structure of a text, in cohesion and coherence, do not necessarily have to do with social stratification, studies of intertextuality and the management of point of view surely do. Discourse analysts who focus on face-to-face interaction with a sociolinguistic perspective have shown that in institutional communication chances very often have to do with educational backgrounds (which in turn reflect the class structure in many societies).

A lot can be found out indirectly about the social structure of a group or an institution by studying its humorous interactions (Kotthoff, 1996b; Holmes, 2006) or its politeness standards (see Kotthoff, 2009a).

Holmes (1998) also focuses on the social functions of humour, exploring first the ways in which humour serves to express politeness, and, secondly, the ways in which humour may express or construct different types of power relations. Humorous utterances are typically multifunctional, conveying many types of meaning simultaneously. Hence, any instance of humour serves several functions at once. The examples below inevitably focus on and highlight particular aspects of the many potential meanings of a humorous utterance.

Humour in the workplace can have an aggressive side (www.victoria.ac.nz/lals/lwp/research/humour.aspx), although it is often used as a social lubricant. It can be used as a repressive discourse device: e.g. managers often use humour to soften directives or criticisms, making it harder for subordinates to contest them, as data on Holmes' webpage show: Neil, a manager, has come to remind his administrative assistant, Ken, that he is late for a meeting. Ken is working at his computer:

Example 3

Neil: hate to drag you away when you're obviously having so much fun but it IS after ten
Ken: [laughs] some fun

In asymmetrical interactions, humour is often used to emphasize power relationships or to subtly steer the behaviour of others. Pizzini (1996: 205), for example, describes how gynaecologists used humour to 'move interview talk along' and 'stop patients rambling on [sic]'. When humour is used downwards in this way, it can be analysed as evidence of 'repressive discourse'. It takes the sting out of a less than agreeable message.

In Example 4 (Holmes, 1998: Example 5), Sheila is advising her colleagues on how to extricate themselves from a situation she deplores. She has been diplomatic and kept the tone light throughout a protracted session of implicit criticism of their behaviour. Suddenly she uses blunt language, which has a shock effect, causing laughter because of its incongruity.

Example 4

She: how are we gonna get this thing resolved if she's saying no and we're saying no we might as well say no forever
Val: so shall we just
She: pay the bloody money
[All laugh]

The humorous tone masks her impatience with her subordinates' handling of the situation, an excellent example of repressive discourse. She sugarcoats the pill, but still intends them to take it.

Humour may also be used by subordinates to challenge the power relations in the institutional structures in their workplace. Here it functions as a critical discourse device, a contestive strategy, and one of the few acceptable means available to subordinates who wish to contest, even if only momentarily, the existing authority structures.

In Example 5, during a planning meeting, May uses humour to suggest that Jenny, her superior, should make the next presentation.

Example 5

May: I'm sure you would just love to show off your new whizz-bang computer with all its special effects wouldn't you Jenny.
[General laughter]

May is not in a position to give Jenny instructions. The humour serves as an expedient disguise for what could be regarded as an implicit challenge to the superior's authority.

Humour is also used contestively in the workplace data in cases where a subordinate expresses opinions that are 'socially risky' or where it serves to disguise criticism of a superior.

An analysis which considers the possibility that humour may function as repressive discourse thus involves a thorough examination of the underlying power relationships and the explicitness with which they are performed (Holmes, 2006).

Critical discourse analysis (CDA) would require a theorization and description of both the social processes and structures that give rise to the production of an oral or written text and also of those within which individuals or groups, as sociohistorical subjects, create meanings in their interactions with texts (Wodak, 1995: 204; van Dijk, 2008). Consequently, three concepts are indispensable in all CDA: the concept of power, the concept of history and the concept of ideology.

Van Dijk (2003: 353) points out that CDA is not so much a direction, school, or specialization alongside many other 'approaches' in discourse studies, but rather it offers a perspective of analysis and may well integrate pragmatics, conversation analysis, stylistics and many other methods. Common to them is a tradition of rejecting 'value free' science. CDA addresses social problems, power relations and links between texts and society by integrating discourse data with political theory (such as, for example, with Habermas) (see Wodak and Meyer (2009) for an overview of the most recent developments in CDA).

Let us turn again to studies from the educational world. Wodak and Andraschko (1994) examined the relationship between power and interaction in schools: to be exact, in an Austrian 'school partnership' project. This concerned the participation of teachers, parents and pupils in school affairs and was meant to prescribe equal opportunity within what was formerly described as a rigidly hierarchical school system. Wodak (1996) combined fieldwork and the interaction analysis of many committee meetings with interviews with teachers, directors, parents and students to show that, even after the reform, Austrian teachers were still being superintended by principals. Principals made decisions inside the school and had to defend these decisions to the Department of Education. Parents remained outside the power structure. They were needed in several ways, as fund-raisers and also as scapegoats (Wodak, 1996: 173), 'because problem pupils were always consigned to their mothers [sic!] (the school rarely sees itself as a cause of the problems)'. The team working with Wodak demonstrated that the implementation of the new law had not actually altered the previous hierarchy and dependencies in the schools. Even tenured teachers did not dare, or did not want, to participate in many discussions. When interviewed, they said that decisions were still being taken elsewhere.

What is methodically interesting is that a system of dependencies within an institutional setting becomes apparent. We learn that there is more than a 'local logic' in a current situation, but also societal structures of inequality that cause conflicts and disorder (van Dijk, 2008).

22.5 GENDER STUDIES

For more than 30 years, interactional gender studies have shown how societal power asymmetries between the sexes, a gender-oriented division of labour and differences in socialization, result in subcultural interaction strategies. In the field of gender and interaction, there is no approach that, for example, assumes that sex/gender identity is first given, and, depending on this identity, people choose a gender-conditioned speech style. Discourse studies has never put it as simply as that. Early feminist linguistics enlightened women about being too modest in their positioning. In the first phase of linguistic gender studies, it was assumed that male dominance was always communicatively expressed in a similar way, regardless of context. This is not the case, however. Today, we see that there are very few conversational behaviours that are performed differently by men and women independently of the context. Many scholars have in the meantime showed the complex ways in which people practice turn-taking and how little evidence there is that men generally interrupt more than women (James and Clarke, 1993; Kotthoff, 1993). Each sex commands an entire spectrum of styles that, however, manifest themselves differently depending on context and also co-produce the context as such.

Asking many questions, using the subjunctive, modality markers and hedges were, at the time, mono-functionally interpreted as expressing insecurity and subordination. However, thanks to linguists like Robin Lakoff (1973), we came to see the connections between gender and men's and women's positions in society. Since the 1980s, intensive research has been carried out on the forms and functions of modality strategies. We now know that there is no overall gender difference in the use of these strategies (Günthner and Kotthoff, 1991).

Many studies on gender and communication have been strongly influenced by ethnomethodology and other schools of social constructivism. The field has borrowed ideas from ethnomethodological conversation analysis, and many gender researchers adopted, among others, its methodological approaches. From the very start, scholars drew on the works of Harold Garfinkel (1967) and Erving Goffman (1977, 1981), even if often not very consistently (as Günthner (2001) and Kotthoff (2002) point out).

With Connell (1987), most gender scholars stress the historicity of 'gender' and reject biologistic approaches. Gender 'is nothing but historicity', and doing gender is regarded as a practice that shapes and transforms bodies as well as relationships and cognitive categorizations. The self actively positions itself in regard to gender ideologies, mass media images, etc. – be it affirmatively or oppositionally (Kotthoff and Wodak, 1997).

Tannen and others, in a number of books (e.g. Tannen, 1990), promoted the thesis that women practice a more cooperative speech style, whereas men practice a more competitive style. Other authors see a certain mirror effect of preformed perception in some of Tannen's findings (1990). Goodwin's (2008) and Kyratzis's (2001) studies of children's speech behaviour show many gender tendencies and, at the same time, that these are not acted out in every context. They stress the importance of looking at communication in context, as do the studies published in Baron and Kotthoff (2002).

Gender studies bring together a variety of studies of parent–child interaction that have shown that the differences in the ways a father talks to a son as opposed to a daughter are much greater than the differences in the ways a mother interacts with a son as opposed to a daughter. Fathers are more direct with their sons than with their daughters. Eckert and McConnell-Ginet discuss in detail (2003; 41 ff.) how influential ideologies are in our everyday interactions. The norms of heterosexual relationship formation become more and more relevant in later childhood. Success in teenage romantic efforts is highly respected by peer groups. Gender patterns are not simply copied, but vary in accord with differing environmental and personal conditions. In the USA, for example, studies by Carol Gilligan et al. (1990) show that

unlike White middle-class girls, who suffer from a considerable loss of self-esteem during adolescence, at this age lower-class Black girls show a strong tendency toward self-assertive and aggressive behaviour. Ironically, many teachers regard this as antisocial. Not only was feminist linguistics quite middle-class centred, so was research on schools, as mentioned above.

Although, fundamentally, it has been clear that gender research in discourse analysis has to deal with the communicative construction of both femininity and masculinity, for many years scholars analysed only women's speech. According to Johnson and Meinhof (1997), this phenomenon has to be interpreted as a remnant of a traditional ideology: female speech as a deviation from the (male) norm that has to be closely examined in its peculiarity. Coates (2003) pointed out how masculinity is constructed in the types of stories that men tell each other in contexts such as the pub. She shows that they avoid self-disclosure and prefer to talk about impersonal topics such as current affairs, travel or sport. Nowadays we start from the assumption of diverse 'masculinities' and 'femininities' which, phenomenologically viewed, may differ considerably from person to person and situation to situation. However, there is also stability in performing and perceiving gendered styles of behaviour.

Eckert (2000: 56ff.) shows for Detroit adolescents a gendered semiotics that also holds true for other heterosexual orders. For the girls a supportive role is formalized in many high school activities. There is a gender-based division of labour in many activities which is supported by a certain speech style. Violence, urban toughness and know-how are prominent among lower-class boys. The girls from this milieu do not enjoy the same claim to physical prowess and autonomy, and they do not have the same admiration for a good fight (not even a verbal fight). Girls from the middle class try to avoid a 'slut' image, including styles of hair, makeup and demeanour. Middle-class boys show technical competence and demonstrate their independence from adults (as do working-class boys).

Eckert (2000: 34ff.) focuses on Lave and Wenger's 'community of practice' construct to show that identity, social participation and speech styles develop in a mutual continuing engagement in practice. Class, ethnicity and gender gain significance via 'native' categories such as being a certain type of adolescent ('jock' or 'burnout' in her case). Such categories emerge around aspects of social practice that are sufficiently salient in the community to warrant a differentiation and separation between people on the basis of their participation in these practices (p. 3). Her theory of variation as social practice sees speakers as constituting, rather than representing, broad social categories.

The linguistic market is part of a broader symbolic market. Vernacular speech, for example, has a positive value in local communities. Standard language, in contrast, gains its power by virtue of its association with the institutions of societal hierarchy and cosmopolitan networks. It has to do with socioeconomic status, occupation and education, with whether an individual orients him- or herself either to local or to non-local marketplaces.

22.6 CONCLUSIONS

Speech styles and interaction patterns reflect, support, (re)create or sometimes undermine macro-categories. The approaches discussed in this chapter vary in how they analyse verbal interaction and in how they tie it to culture and social institutions. Some try to place the interaction system so centrally that they threaten to reduce all other systems to outcomes of the workings of interaction. Some accept interaction as a system among interrelated systems. How much a certain study of face-to-face interaction integrates other theories or how deeply it goes into the details of talk may be what differentiates critical discourse studies from interactional sociolinguistics. With Levinson (2005), we call for linking sociocultural, linguistic and interactional systems together in a Durkheimian manner – being aware that the last word on the intermediate variables of interaction and society has not yet been spoken.

ACKNOWLEDGEMENT

I am grateful to Ruth Wodak for her valuable comments.

NOTES

1 I base this discussion on the summary of the book presented in Fitch and Philipsen (1995: 267).

2 The English word 'teasing' can be translated into German as Necken, Sticheln, Pflaumen, Foppen or Frotzeln. All these concepts refer to playful provocations. Necken is more friendly than Frotzeln, Foppen or Pflaumen. On the ethnocategories and their equivalences cf. Günhner (1996).

3 I am indebted to Henrik Hügin for the recording of the group of five young men, friends who finished their high school degree (German: Abitur) together.

REFERENCES

Auer, P. and di Luzio, A. (eds) (1992) *Interpretive Sociolinguistics*. Tübingen: Narr. pp. 87–113.

Baron, B. and Kotthoff, H. (eds) (2002) *Gender in Interaction. Perspectives on Femininity and Masculinity in Ethnography and Discourse*. Amsterdam: Benjamins.

Boxer, D. (2002) *Applying Sociolinguistics. Domains of Face-To-Face Interaction*. Amsterdam: Benjamins.

Coates, J. (2003) *Men Talk*. London: Blackwell.

Collins, P. H. (1995) Symposium: On West and Fenstermarker's 'doing differences.' *Gender and Society*, 9(4): 491–594.

Connell, R. W. (1987) *Gender and Power. Society, the Person and Sexual Politics*. Cambridge: Polity Press.

Cook-Gumperz, J. and Gumperz, J. (1996) *Treacherous Words: Gender and Power in Academic Assessment. Folia Linguistica*, XXX(3, 4): 167–89. (Special issue on Interactional Sociolinguistics.)

Cook-Gumperz, J. and Gumperz, J. (2007) 'Discourse, cultural diversity and communication: a linguistic anthropological perspective', in H. Kotthoff and H. Spencer-Oatey (eds), *Handbook of Intercultural Communication*. Berlin: Mouton de Gruyter. pp. 13–31.

Couper-Kuhlen, E. and Selting, M. (1996) *Prosody in Conversation. Interactional Studies*. Cambridge: Cambridge University Press.

Deppermann, A. (2000) 'Ethnografische Gesprächsanalyse: Zu Nutzen und Notwendigkeit von Ethnografie für die Konversationsanalyse', *Gesprächsforschung – Online-Zeitschrift zur verbalen Interaktion*, 1: 96–124.

Discourse & Society (2002) 13(6). (Special issue on gender, language, conversation analysis and feminism. Edited by E. A. Stokoe and A. Weatherall.)

Drew, P. (1987) 'Po-faced receipts of teases', *Linguistics* 25: 219–53.

Duranti, A. (1988) 'Ethnography of speaking: toward a linguistics of praxis', in F. J. Newmeyer (ed.), *Linguistics: The Cambridge Survey*. Cambridge: Cambridge University Press. pp. 210–29.

Eckert, P. (2000) *Linguistic Variation as Social Practice*. Oxford: Blackwell.

Eckert, P. and McConnell-Ginet, S. (2003) *Language and Gender*. Cambridge: Cambridge University Press.

Fitch, K. L. and Philipsen, G. (1995) 'Ethnography of speaking', in J. Verschueren, J.-O. Östman, J. Blommaert and C. Bulcaen (eds), *Handbook of Pragmatics. Manual*. Amsterdam: Benjamins. pp. 263–9.

Gal, S. and Woolard, C. (1995) 'Constructing languages and publics: authority and representation', *Pragmatics*, 5(2): 129–38.

Garfinkel, H. (1967) *Studies in Ethnomethodolgy*. Englewood Cliffs, NJ: Prentice Hall.

Gilligan, C., Lyons, N. P. and Hanmer, T. (eds) (1990) *Making Connections: The Relational Worlds of Adolescent Girls at Emma Willard School*. Cambridge, MA: Harvard University Press.

Goffman, E. (1977) 'The arrangement between the sexes', *Theory and Society*, 4: 301–31.

Goffman, Er. (1981) *Forms of Talk*. Philadelphia: University of Pennsylvania Press.

Goodwin, M. (1990) *He Said & She Said*. Philadelphia: University of Pennsylvania Press.

Goodwin, M. (2008) *The Hidden Life of Girls*. London: Blackwell.

Gumperz, J. (1982) *Discourse Strategies*. Cambridge: Cambridge University Press.

Gumperz, J. (2001) 'The speech community', in A. Duranti (ed.), *Linguistic Anthropology. A Reader*. London: Blackwell. pp. 43–53. (1st edn, 1968.)

Günthner, S. (1996) 'Zwischen Scherz und Schmerz. Frotzelaktivitäten im Alltag', in H. Kotthoff (ed.), *Scherzkommunikation. Beiträge aus der empirischen Gesprächsforschung*. Opladen: Westdeutscher Verlag. pp. 81–109.

Günthner, S. (2001) 'Die kommunikative Konstruktion der Geschlechterdifferenz: Sprach- und kulturvergleichende Perspektiven', *Muttersprache*, 3: 205–19.

Günthner, S. and Kotthoff, H. (1991) 'Vorwort,' in Günthner, S. and Kotthoff, H. (eds), *Von fremden Stimmen. Weibliches und männliches Sprechen im Kulturvergleich*. Frankfurt: Suhrkamp.

Heller, M. and Martin-Jones, M. (eds) (2001) *Voices of Authority: Education and Linguistic Difference*. Westport, CT: Ablex.

Holmes, J. (1998) 'No joking matter', *Australian Linguistic Papers*, 98.

Holmes, J. (2006) 'Sharing a laugh: pragmatic aspects of humour and gender in the workplace', *Journal of Pragmatics*, 38(1): 26–50.

Holmes, J. and Meyerhoff, M. (eds) (2003) *The Handbook of Language and Gender*. Oxford: Blackwell.

Hutchby, I. and Woofitt, R. (1998) *Conversation analysis*. Cambridge: Polity Press.

Hymes, D. (1974): *Foundations of Sociolinguistics*. Philadelphia: University of Pennsylvania Press.

Hymes, D. (2001) 'On communicative competence', in A. Duranti (ed.), *Linguistic Anthropology. A reader*. London: Blackwell. pp. 53–74. (1st edn, 1972.)

Jacquemet, M. (1996) *Credibility in Court*. Cambridge: Cambridge University Press.

James, D. and Clarke, S. (1993) 'Women, men, and interruptions: a critical review', in D. Tannen (ed.), *Gender and Conversational Interaction*. Oxford: Oxford University Press.

Johnson, S. and Meinhof, H. (eds) (1997) *Language and Masculinity*. Oxford: Blackwell.

Jünger, R. (2008) *Bildung für alle? Die schulischen Logiken von ressourcenprivilegierten undnichtprivilegierten kindern als Ursache der bestehenden Bildungsungleichheit*. Wiesbaden: VS Verlag für Sozialwissenschaften.

Kendon, A. (1990) *Conducting Interaction. Patterns of Behavior in Focused Encounters*. Cambridge: Cambridge University Press.

Kotthoff, H. (1993) 'Unterbrechungen, Überlappungen und andere Interventionen', *Deutsche Sprache*, 2: 162–85.

Kotthoff, H. (ed.) (1996a) *Interactional Sociolinguistics*. Special issue. *Folia Linguistica* XXX(3, 4).

Kotthoff, H. (1996b) 'Impoliteness and conversational joking: on relational politics', *Folia Linguistica* XXX(3, 4): 299–327.

Kotthoff, H. (2008) *Spass Verstehen. Zur Pragmatik von konversationellem Humor*. Tuebingen: Niemeyer.

Kotthoff, H. (2002) 'Was heißt eigentlich 'doing gender?'', *Wiener Linguistischer Almanach. Sonderband*, 55: 1–29.

Kotthoff, H. (2009a) 'Politeness/Linguistik der Höflichkeit', in B. Kortmann (ed.), *WSK Dictionary on "Theories and Methods in Linguistics"*. Freiburg: University of Freiburg. (http://www.anglistik.unifreiburg.de/seminar/abteilungen/ sprachwissenschaft/ ls_kortmann/WSK

Kotthoff, H. (2009b) 'Humor mit Biss zwischen sozialer Konjunktion und Disjunktion', in E. Koch and S. Krämer (eds), *Gewalt in der Sprache*. Munich: Fink.

Kotthoff, H. and Spencer-Oatey, H. (eds) (2007) *Handbook of Intercultural Communication*. Berlin: Mouton de Gruyter.

Kotthoff, H. and Wodak, R. (eds) (1997) *Communicating Gender in Context*. Amsterdam: Benjamins.

Kyratzis, A. (2001) 'Constituting the emotions: a longitudinal study of emotion talk in a preschool friendship group of boys', in B. Baron and H. Kotthoff (eds), *Gender in Interaction. Perspectives on Femininity and Masculinity in Ethnography and Discourse*. Amsterdam: Benjamins.

Labov, W. (1972) *Sociolinguistic Patterns*. Philadelphia: University of Pennsylvania Press.

Lakoff, R. (1973) 'Language and women's place', *Language in Society*, 2: 45–79.

Levinson, S. (1983) *Pragmatics*. Cambridge: Cambridge University Press.

Levinson, S. C. (2005) 'Living with Manny's dangerous idea', *Discourse Studies*, 7(4, 5) 431–53.

Machin, D. and Richardson, J. E. (2008) 'Renewing an academic interest in structural inequalities', *Critical Discourse Studies*, 5(4): 281–7.

Mehan, H., Lintz, A., Okamoto, D. and Wills, J. S. (2001) 'Ethnographic studies of multicultural education in classrooms and schools', in J. A. Banks and C. A. M. Banks (eds), *Handbook of Research on Multicultural Education*. San Francisco: Jossey-Bass. pp. 129–44.

Mey, J. (1993) *Pragmatics*. Oxford: Blackwell.

Östman, J.-O. and Virtanen, T. (1995) 'Discourse analysis', in J. Verschueren, J.-O. Östman, J. Blommaert and C. Bulcaen (eds), *Handbook of Pragmatics. Manual*. Amsterdam: Benjamins. pp. 239–53.

Philips, S. U. (1970, reprinted, 2001) 'Participant structures and communicative competence: Warm Springs children in community and classroom', in A. Duranti (ed.), *Linguistic Anthropology. A Reader*. London: Blackwell. pp. 302–17.

Pizzini, F. (1996) 'Hierarchie in der Scherzkommunikation. Kommunikation im gynäkologischen und geburtshilflichen Bereich', in H. Kotthoff (ed.), *Das Gelächter der Geschlechter*. Konstanz: Universitätsverlag. pp. 201–17.

Romaine, S. (1995) 'Sociolinguistics', in J. Verschueren, J.-O. Östman, J. Blommaert and C. Bulcaen (eds), *Handbook of Pragmatics. Manual*. Amsterdam: Benjamins. pp. 489–95.

Sacks, H. (1992) *Lectures on Conversation*. 2 volumes. Edited by G. Jefferson. Oxford: Blackwell.

Sandig, B. and Selting, M. (1997) 'Discourse styles', in T. van Dijk (ed.), *Discourse as Structure and Process: A Multidisciplinary Introduction*. London: Sage. pp. 138–56.

Saville-Troike, M. (1982) *The Ethnography of Communication*. Oxford: Oxford University Press.

Scharff, C. M. (2008) 'Doing class: a discursive and ethnomethodological approach', *Critical Discourse Studies*, 5(4), 331–45.

Schegloff, E. A. (1987) 'Between micro and macro: contexts and other connections', in J. C. Alexander, B. Giesen, R. Munch and N. J. Smelser (eds), *The Micro–Macro Link*. Los Angeles: University of California Press. pp. 207–34.

Schegloff, E. A. (1997) 'Whose text? Whose context?', *Discourse and Society*, 8: 165–87.

Scherr, A. (2007) 'Schools and cultural difference', in H. Kotthoff and H. Spencer-Oatey (eds), *Handbook of Intercultural Communication*. Berlin: Mouton de Gruyter. pp. 303–23.

Schiffrin, D. (1994) *Approaches to Discourse*. London: Blackwell.

Tannen, D. (1990) *You Just Don't Understand. Women and Men in Conversation*. New York: William Morrow.

Tannen, D. (1994) 'The relativity of linguistic strategies', in D. Tannen (ed.), *Discourse and Gender*. Oxford: Oxford University Press. pp. 19–52.

van Dijk, T. (2008) *Discourse and Power*. Houndsmill: Macmillan.

Wardhaugh, R. (2002) *Sociolinguistics*. London: Blackwell.

Weber, L. (1995) Symposium: On West and Fenstermarker's 'doing differences'. *Gender and Society*, 9(4): 499–503.

Weber, M. (2003) *Heterogenität im Schulalltag*. Wiesbaden: Westdeutscher Verlag.

West, C. and Fenstermaker, S. (1995) 'Doing difference', *Gender and Society*, 9: 8–37.

West, C. and Fenstermaker, S. (2002) 'Accountability in action: the accomplishment of gender, race and class in a University of California Board of Regents', *Discourse and Society*, 13: 537–63.

Willis, P. (1977) *Learning to Labour: How Working-Class Kids Get Working-Class Jobs*. Farnborough: Saxon House.

Wodak, R. (1995) 'Critical linguistics and critical discourse analysis', in J. Verschueren, J.-O. Östman, J. Blommaert and C. Bulcaen (eds), *Handbook of Pragmatics. Manual*. Amsterdam: Benjamins. pp. 204–10.

Wodak, R. (1996) *Disorders of Discourse*. London: Longman.

Wodak, R. and Andraschko, E. (1994) 'Frauen führen anders? Eine diskurssoziolinguistische Untersuchung, Teil 1', *Erziehung heute*, 1: 41–9.

Wodak, R. and Krzyzanowski, M. (eds) (2008) *Qualitative Discourse Analysis for the Social Sciences*. Basingstoke: Palgrave.

Wodak, R. and Meyer, M. (eds) (2nd rev. edn, 2009) *Methods of Critical Discourse Analysis*. London: Sage. (1st edn, 2001.)

Doctor–Patient Communication

Florian Menz

23.1 INTRODUCTION: SELECTION OF RESEARCH AREAS

Since the 1970s, doctor–patient communication has become increasingly well established as an area of inquiry within sociolinguistics and discourse analysis, initially focusing, in particular, on the institutional frames of communication (Becker-Mrotzek, 1992; Drew and Heritage, 1992; Hein et al., 1985; Lalouschek et al., 1990; Menz, 1991; Sarangi and Roberts, 1999). At the time of writing this chapter, in 2008, a quick search in the bibliographical database 'medonline' using the keywords 'doctor patient communication' yielded over 7500 publication entries, while the keyword 'communication' alone results in an astounding 360,000 hits. The scope of the present chapter is therefore necessarily limited.

The area of patient–care communication (interaction between patients and nursing staff, which includes non-medical aspects; see e.g. Candlin, 2006; Walther, 1997; see also Weinhold, 1997 for medical patient care and Sachweh, 2005, 2006 for care of the elderly) must be excluded here, as must be studies that focus on peer interaction among doctors (De Valck and Van den Wostijne, 1996; Herb and Streeck 1995; Lackner et al., 1996; Ploeger, 2005). Furthermore, the vast field of communication in psychotherapeutic and psychiatric contexts (Buchholz, 1998; Fritzsche and Wirsching, 2005; Kütemeyer, 2003; Morris and Chenail, 1995; Peräkylä, 2004; Schöndienst, 2002) as well as in medical consulting (see e.g. Sarangi and Brookes-Howell, 2006) cannot be treated here, nor can studies using experimental settings which thus analyse non-naturally occurring communication between doctors and patients (e.g. Li, 1999; Watson and Gallois, 1999). Lastly, neither the interface of transformation from oral to written discourse and vice versa can be taken into consideration here (but see Iedema, 2003, 2006), nor can research concerned with the specifics of professional medical literature (Gotti and Salager-Meyer, 2006; Pahta, 2006) be included. Rather, this chapter will be restricted to a discussion of the most recent investigations, referring the reader to existing anthologies (Atkinson and Heath, 1981; Ehlich et al., 1990; Fisher and Todd, 1983; Heritage and Maynard, 2006b; Köhle and Raspe, 1982; Löning and Rehbein, 1993; Morris and Chenail, 1995; Neises et al., 2005; Redder and Wiese, 1994; Sarangi and Roberts, 1999; Tanner, 1976), and Hydén and Mishler's (1999) review article for in-depth coverage of past research and the status quo of linguistic inquiry into these subject matters.

Recent research on doctor–patient communication (DPC) from a linguistic perspective can be categorized under three broad headings: (1) microstructure-oriented analyses of both conversational organization and interaction dynamics at a syntactic and semantic level; (2) investigations into the influence of macrostructural social dimensions; and, increasingly, (3) practically-oriented studies of the interest of social applicability. Conversation-analytic research on DPC is particularly concerned with the different phases of doctor–patient talk and the interactional tasks it fulfils. Such research is therefore oriented towards formal and structural processes, increasingly taking an interest in settings that include more than two participants ('triadic and multiparty interaction' – see Section 23.2.1). Furthermore, actual language usage and different forms of representation of symptoms, disorders and the subjective experience of illness are of special interest for sociolinguistic analysis (see Section 23.2.3).

Because the issue of the representation of pain also has great significance from a medical perspective, it is discussed in more detail in Section 23.2.3.

In contrast, the studies presented in Section 23.3 also take macrosocial dimensions beyond the local conversation into consideration in their analyses. Issues of multilingualism and migration (see Section 23.3.1) and of gender (see Section 23.3.2) constitute major areas of inquiry here, to which sociolinguistic research contributes notable insights. Questions regarding the practical applicability and social relevance of scientific research play an increasingly central role in a knowledge society. This is reflected in linguistic inquiry as well. Thus, Section 23.4 summarizes those studies that concern themselves with issues of applicability and are aimed at the (re-) integration of linguistic findings into medical practice. The concluding Section 23.5 represents an attempt to assess future research questions and trends that will play a role within sociolinguistic and interactional linguistic approaches to medical communication in the years to come. Content-based aspects will be discussed alongside those of methodological and interdisciplinary concern.

23.2 MICROSTRUCTURAL ASPECTS OF DOCTOR–PATIENT COMMUNICATION

23.2.1 Phases of doctor–patient talk/ interaction dynamics

Starting with a first broad field study by Byrne and Long (1976), discourse analytic and sociolinguistic investigation has repeatedly pointed out a systematic overall structure in doctor–patient talk. With only slight variations, the following phases recur in the context of acute primary care visits: greetings and openings; presentation of the complaint, exploration; examination; diagnosis; establishment of a therapeutic plan; closing of the talk; and leave-taking (Heritage and Maynard, 2006a; Nowak, 2009; Spranz-Fogasy, 2005). This overall structure can be further subdivided and differentiated. Thus, Nowak (2009), in a broad-range empirical meta-study, identifies and categorizes 48 activity types and over 100 activities within doctor–patient talk. Some special cases and recent findings will be discussed in the following.

At the **opening of a conversation**, doctors and patients must carry out a number of cooperative activities (greetings, offering a seat), as well as non-cooperative ones (patients closing the door, doctors reading the record, consulting the computer, etc.), to achieve mutual orientation and in order to establish their readiness to address the chief complaint, the reason for the patient's visit.

Communicating engagement or disengagement happens mainly via gaze and body orientation, whereby lower-body segments are used to determine the frame in which long-term action (communicating with patient vs studying records for example) is to be situated (Robinson, 1998: 114). Thus, multimodal resources are systematically employed to fulfil complex communication and orientation tasks here.

Subsequent medical **exchange of information** between doctors and patients is mainly carried out through question–response sequences, which have been discussed extensively in the linguistic literature. Different types of opening moves (Nowak, 2009) define and delimit a frame for patient responses which may restrict their 'room for maneuvering' (Spranz-Fogasy, 2005). The extent to which minimal variations in wording may trigger different responses was attested to in an experimental setting in a study by Heritage et al. (2007). The question 'Is there something else you want to address in the visit today?' elicited significantly more hitherto unmet concerns than the same question using the word 'anything' instead of 'something'. However, the length of the interaction did not increase.

Multi-topic presentations and so-called 'door handle' remarks (introduction of a new problem upon leaving a room), dreaded by many doctors, have in fact turned out not to present any real problems: such presentations and remarks have been shown to be the rule rather than the exception in medical consultations; and yet, because patients tend to announce them in the opening phase of presenting the complaint, doctors are able to process them successfully at the communicative level (Campion and Langdon, 2004).

Even potential information discrepancies between doctors and patients can usually be processed and cleared up by doctors without difficulty: for example by integrating divergences in patients' knowledge into their own knowledge and information system, or by offering additional information for support (Lehtinen, 2007).

Furthermore, Collins (2005) shows how doctoral explanations may in some cases be usefully supplemented with explanations by nursing staff. While doctors adopted the viewpoint of a biomedical intervention in their explanations, the latter, i.e. the nursing staff, incorporated the viewpoint of patient responsibility and oriented their interactional moves towards patient contributions. Thus, clashes of the voice of medicine with the voice of the 'life-world', as attested to by Mishler (1984) and confirmed by Lalouschek (2002), could be attenuated or altogether circumvented.

Yet, doctors may comply only in a limited way with interactive pressures to provide answers to or explanations for questions. Thus, doctors were shown to invoke clinical agendas to postpone certain types of patient questions if they did not want to reply, and once postponing has taken place, patients do not tend to pursue their questions further, so that they often remain unanswered (Roberts, 2000). The exchange of information is driven by institutional agendas, and certain standard phrases and expressions in the initiation phase of medical diagnosis and treatment additionally inhibit patient participation (Diaz, 2000: 386) and reinforce the asymmetry in much doctor–patient talk. Also, the gate-keeping function that doctors have, by virtue of their power to make decisions about access to medical treatment, medication and other services, is also processed and reenacted via certain forms and content of questions. (Speer and Parsons, 2006). The situation increases in complexity in the case of multiparty encounters, for example in paediatrician consultations. Here, a number of factors naturally play a role in next speaker selection – both concerning the paediatrician's selection of addressee as well as in the parent–child negotiation of who will present the problem (Stivers, 2001). Factors that increase the likelihood that a child will be the presenter of the problem, and which thus deserve attention in view of promoting active involvement of the patient, are the child's age, preceding speaker selection/address (e.g. during the greeting phase) and direct addressing by the doctor. Adolescents, by contrast, may explicitly disallow the addressing of a parent, usually a mother, as a stand-in informant for the medical problem (Mondada, 2002).

23.2.2 Forms of representation of illness and its subjective experience

In addition to an interest in the interactive processes of doctor–patient talk, some sociolinguistic and discourse analytic studies have also concerned themselves with content/semantic representations of illness and ailments. The use of professional jargon in particular is frequently cited as a problem area. But it has also been shown that the use of (English) medical vocabulary can have a practical function in rural African contexts (Odebunmi, 2006) – to avoid giving disturbing information as long as the diagnosis is not yet confirmed, and to avoid stigmatizing the patient in the presence of relatives. Mastery of code-switching is therefore a basic qualification for practitioners there.

Investigations of metaphorical language used in representations of illness constitute another important area of inquiry, although here data are not always drawn from natural contexts (Rees et al., 2007; Semino et al., 2004).

Metaphors and other forms of illustration are used as resources for a variety of purposes in the process of knowledge transfer between experts and laypersons (Brünner and Gülich, 2002: 77). Experts may use such resources to explain and break down complex facts, while patients may employ them to grasp and illustrate sensations and experiences that are otherwise difficult to describe, such as experiences of pain, or of auras preceding epileptic seizures. Metaphors and similes are commonly used in these contexts, while exemplification and expositions of scenarios are more frequent when the intention is to draw parallels to day-to-day life.

It is to be noted that such illustration processes are of course co-constructed, and that experts and laypersons do not necessarily employ different resources, but rather may employ the same ones in differentiated ways and for different purposes (Brünner and Gülich, 2002: 82ff.).

Divergences in usage preferences can also be analysed for the purposes of differential diagnostics. For example, epilepsy patients tend to employ metaphor more frequently in their description of seizure attacks than patients with dissociative disorders (Surmann, 2005). The ways in which either group tends to reconstruct the gap in consciousness during attacks show significant differences as well (Furchner, 2002). Analyses of divergences in linguistic strategies therefore lend themselves readily to support differential diagnosis, which in traditional terms and methods is complex, costly and prone to error.

23.2.3 Pain representation

The representation of pain, which is pivotal in medical communication, is typically rather problematic, because here, everyday language provides only a limited repertoire of expression, in contrast to, for example, the repertoires for the description of visual or acoustic phenomena, which are typologically highly developed in most languages. Category sets for the representation of pain have indeed been established from a medical perspective (see Reisigl, 2006 for systematic description and critique). These sets list dimensions such as temporal occurrence ('When?'), localization ('Where?'), intensity ('How severe?'), quality (e.g. 'stinging', 'piercing'), side symptoms (e.g. nausea), conditions of occurrence (e.g. when walking, when lying down), and pain management ('What eases or increases the pain?'). One problem of such classifications is that it may not always be easy for patients to assign their subjective experience of pain to any particular medical category listed. For this reason, representations of pain typically also employ non-verbal, gestural resources, which nowadays can be easily captured with recording technology and have therefore become a strong focus in DPC research.

Non-verbal resources are mainly used to accentuate dimensions of the **intensity** and quality of pain. Such 'demonstrative suffering' (Heath, 2002) emphasizes the unique and particular qualities of pain.[1] By expressing the severity of the illness, it also serves to gain access to the 'sick role' in the first place, thus legitimizing medical consultation (Heritage and Robinson, 2006).

Non-verbal activity is well integrated into the frame of medical consultation: the turn-by-turn structure is maintained, and gesture is usually accompanied by talk, in accordance with the sequential requirements of interaction (Heath, 2002).

Non-verbal activity also plays a role in connection with the **localization** of pain. Resources like gaze, pointing gestures and body movement are typically combined with verbal deictic expressions (e.g. 'here'), as in fact two interactional tasks have to be fulfilled: defining the locus of the pain and maintaining the interactive frame established with the doctor. In this context, differences in the expression of visible versus invisible targets have been confirmed (Stukenbrock, 2008). With visible targets (e.g. pain in the knee), the domain of scrutiny for the verbal deictic is pre-established via a partly simultaneous employment of gaze and gesture. The gaze moves from the addressee to the pointing hand and from there to the target (the knee). The co-orientation is therefore multimodal, being gradually intensified through gaze, gesture and talk (in this order). In the case of an invisible target however (e.g. pain in the back), the patient's gaze remains on the addressee, in order to maintain the interactional frame.

The expression of the **quality** of pain then falls back, to a large degree, on verbal resources. A lack of 'basic pain terms' forces patients to use indirect means of description such as metaphor or visualization, as evidenced in a recent study on written and oral German data (Overlach, 2008). Within the oral context, lexical and syntactic variation was more strongly focused on basic metaphors of possession ('to have a pain') and copula construction ('the pain is …').

In addition, not all resources that L1 speakers have at their disposal for the expression of pain are actually employed (Blasch et al., 2010). Thus, whenever patients are asked about their pain in **non-medical** contexts, they mainly talk about:

- subjective theories about the illness and possible sources of the pain
- various impairments they are subjected to due to the pain
- pain management in general – how they (successfully) try to avoid pain, or measures taken to attain relief.

Thus, the dimensions of **conditions of occurrence** and **pain management** are foregrounded.

By contrast, in **medical contexts**, the following themes dominate:

- talk about medication
- talk about side symptoms of the pain that occasioned the medical consultation
- differentiated specification of the pain and its occurrence (quality of the pain, local and temporal dimensions, intensity).

The points of discrepancy here can be subsumed under the headings of **contextualizing** vs **symptom-oriented** expressions of pain (see Figure 23.1). In informal, non-medical talk, patients put their expressions of pain into a broader context, and relate them to everyday experience, and in particular to personal experience and impairment. Thus, pain is not so much characterized in terms of its sensations and symptoms, but rather in terms of its suspected sources, its effects, and possibilities for avoidance or relief (Blasch et al., 2010).

Such divergences in strategies and foci in the representation of pain can lead to interactive difficulties. Thus, divergent **concepts of 'pain'** may result in communication problems: for example, when doctors explore pain as a measure of mental sensation that is to be isolated, while patients describe it in practical terms as a phenomenon that is relative to context and has observable consequences (Deppermann, 2003). This manifests itself, for example, in divergences in the dimensions of expressions of pain, which can again be subsumed under the headings 'contextualizing' and 'symptom-oriented' (Blasch et al., 2010; Menz and Lalouschek, 2006). Pain consultations that are adapted to the patient's perception of priorities and allow for narrative structuring may, instead of applying pre-established sets of categorization, succeed in eliciting new facts and information from patients with multiple complaints that other forms of anamnesis may be unable to reach. Thus, discourse analytic and/or conversation analytic preoccupation with forms of expression rather than content can contribute to the establishment and enhancement of medical diagnoses (Gülich et al., 2003).

Gender-based variation in the representation of pain is discussed in Section 23.3.2.

23.3 MACROSTRUCTURAL ASPECTS

23.3.1 Migration: multilingualism in doctor–patient interactions

Despite the fact that, because of mass globalization, multilingualism due to migration has become the norm in large urban areas, the issue has not yet been sufficiently addressed in research on medical

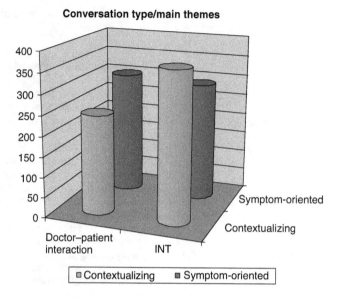

Figure 23.1   Different topics according to conversation type (medical consultation vs interview). Reprinted with permission from Universitätsverlag Rhein-Ruhr OHG.

communication. There are indeed indications that doctors' role expectations and communicative tasks change in interactions with non-native speakers, for example towards an increase in non-medical questioning and a higher percentage of bureaucratic negotiation (Valero-Garcés, 2002). In addition, however, specific types of misunderstandings occur, at all levels of the linguistic system and social interaction, such as (a) pronunciation and word stress, (b) intonation and speech delivery, (c) grammar, vocabulary, and lack of contextual information, and, especially, (d) style of presentation (Roberts et al., 2005). The latter, in particular, typically plays a decisive role in misunderstandings, suggesting that differences in the styles of self-presentation may have more bearing on communication problems than, for example, culturally-specific health beliefs.

Of similar importance are structural discrepancies that can be traced back to the bureaucratic (administrative) organization of the respective health systems (Roberts, 2006), such as, for example, an increasing demand for documentation and the concomitantly required use of electronic forms and processes. These are geared towards monolingual English speakers and put patients with limited English knowledge, who have yet to familiarize themselves with the 'rules', at a disadvantage. Moreover, the exigencies of a health bureaucracy concerning parameters such as length of consultation, active monitoring of cholesterol levels, addressing drug use, etc., which in part form the basis of calculation for a family doctor's salary, may cause problems when patients do not

adhere to unfamiliar structures and, for example, raise multiple topics in the course of one consultation, which in turn cannot easily be processed by computerized systems (Roberts, 2006).

Most importantly, however, patient-centred conversational strategies, which are increasingly in demand in Western society, may stand in direct contradiction to the expectations regarding the doctor–patient interaction sought by patients with a different cultural background. In such situations, an increase in metatalk (Roberts, 2006: 190) tends to complicate communication rather than facilitate it. Thus, increasing sensitivity and raising awareness of different presentation strategies are important measures for improvement of the status quo. Conventional communication coaching on the basis of monolingual native speaker contexts is obsolete here, as it fails to address discrepancies in self-presentation, expectations and assumptions regarding consultations.

One frequently-employed remedy to address potential interactivity problems in multilingual and multicultural encounters is to enlist the help of **interpreters**. Due to the extensive literature in this area, the present discussion will limit itself to discourse-based approaches, which have recently gained importance and increasing attention as a research strand within interpreting studies, to the point that some scholars have begun to speak of 'dialogic discourse in triadic interaction' as a new research paradigm in its own right (Pöchhacker and Shlesinger, 2005: 157; see also Bolden, 2000; Bührig, 2001; Meyer et al., 2003; Bührig and Meyer, 2004b; Pöchhacker and Shlesinger, 2007).

In the literature on community interpreting, two broad areas can be distinguished: professional interpreting and un-trained (ad-hoc) interpreting. Those two areas represent two fundamentally different settings within multiparty communication. In addition, discourse analytic studies of professional interpreting are located on the interface between the classic research area of interpreting and translation, which to this day is strongly influenced by the traditional norms applying within the interpreting profession, and the applied linguistic research paradigm that foregrounds the interactive functions of interpreting activity. Contradictions growing out of the tensions between role-specific postulations and the ethic rules of associations of interpreters, on the one hand, and interactive situations and activities, on the ground on the other, may result in veritable interactional dilemmas (Angelelli, 2004). For example, institutions for interpreter education frequently still insist on the notion that interpreters should not intervene as individual 'entities' in interpreting situations but rather should take care to remain 'invisible'. Yet, Angelelli's analysis of almost 400 communicative events involving interpretation (of which the majority occurred in the context of telephone conversations) evidences a number of linguistic activities that point to the 'visibility' of the interpreter. These activities notably include the following: interpreters introducing themselves as participants in the interpreted event; verbalizing of interactional rules (e.g. for turn transition); paraphrasing of professional jargon and terminology; register changes (e.g. rendering translation more informal than the original statement); filtering of information; and taking up the perspective of one of the parties.

In addition, the interactional participation of interpreters in itself is largely determined by their conception of the purpose of the interaction, not only by the immediate goal of interpreting (Bolden, 2000). Interpreters are not merely passive participants in interactional activity: rather, their interpretations are substantially shaped by a medical/doctoral perspective. They share the doctors' normative bias for objective, biomedically-relevant information. Such an orientation is not only manifest in an amplification of the kinds of information that are deemed relevant in the above sense (e.g. an exhaustive listing of symptoms the interpreter holds to be relevant) but also in the suppression of more subjectively-oriented patient information concerning socio-psychological aspects.

While Bolden's study thus attests to an amplification of the 'voice of medicine' in Mishler's (1984) sense, others have shown different results. In their analysis of (only three) interpreted conversations, Merlini and Favaron (2005) found that interpreters develop an individual, third 'interpreter's voice' in order to mediate between the voice of medicine and a patient's 'voice of lifeworld'. The investigation of a list of linguistic features (turn-taking, topic development, the interpreter's choice of footing, departures from the primary speakers' utterances, prosodic resources) led the authors to regard strong interactional involvement on the interpreter's part as characteristic of the voice of interpreting, though only as an amplification of the voice of lifeworld, and hence in concomitance with strong involvement of the patient.

Multiparty conversations with **ad hoc interpreters** face a different set of clear communicative challenges. Such conversations appear to occur much more frequently in practice than is commonly assumed (see Pöchhacker and Kadric, 1999). In the course of knowledge transfer during briefings for informed consent, the translation of professional terminology is a particularly salient source of trouble here; it is often negotiated using procedures such as repetition of the word in the source language ('insertional code switching') or replacement with non-terminological wordings (Meyer, 2004). Further support measures include pointing gestures indicating the afflicted body part on the body itself or on illustrations in information leaflets, as well as morpheme-by-morpheme translations into the target language. The latter, however, may be prone to causing comprehension problems, so that the quality of interpreted briefings for informed consent can suffer and information is less exact and complete than in monolingual situations (Bührig and Meyer, 2004a; Meyer, 2002, 2004).

Additional differences in multilingual interactions without interpreting, with professional interpreting, or with ad hoc interpreting have been noted in the literature. For example, Valero Garcés (2002; 2005) finds that professional interpreters translate all doctoral questions and rarely add new ones, while ad hoc interpreters only translate about 14% of questions, answering an average of 50% of questions themselves, and raise a considerable number of new questions (with the interpreter and patient in this case being a spouse). More notable, however, are qualitative differences and commonalities in the different scenarios. Thus, the ad hoc interpreted conversations frequently exhibit shifts in the assignment of participant roles, in interaction order and in contribution type, whilst demonstrating a relatively low linguistic competence of the ad hoc interpreter. Similar to non-interpreted conversations, ad hoc interpreted interactions typically feature strategies meant to ensure comprehension, such as frequent questions, repetitions and recasts. In contrast to professionally interpreted conversations, situations of ad hoc interpretation are additionally characterized by the interpreter's changing of roles, in the sense that s/he may take over questioning from the doctor, or give answers directly without translation. When the interpreter talks directly to one of the parties, those passages usually remain untranslated for the other, which is never the case in professionally interpreted settings. Thus, according to Valero Garcés, ad hoc interpretations carry a high risk of misunderstanding. Professional interpreters, furthermore, frequently use the first person in their translation, while ad hoc interpreters often use the third person in the context of reporting verbs ('she says').

Bot (2007) reports similar findings with regards to therapy sessions. However, Bot does not consider the shift in perspective from first to third person to be as problematic as commonly described in the literature; rather, she casts it as a necessary adaptation to interactive reality. These findings are, however, relativized by the small size of the corpora used, and thus must be regarded as tentative.

23.3.2 Gender

The fact that gender plays a role in institutional communication, including medical consultation, has been well established in past research, both with regards to the patient's as well as the doctor's gender (West, 1990). In particular, research has investigated interruptions as indices of status and power (Holmes, 1992; West, 1984), though with discrepant results that were later traced back to shortcomings in the methodology, such as the fact that interruptions were technically defined on the basis of overlaps, with no allowance for the fact that overlaps are not necessarily disruptive but can also be communicatively supportive.

Controlling for and taking into account these methodological issues gives rise to more differentiated results (Menz and Al-Roubaie, 2008: 657ff.). Thus, non-supportive interruptions (meaning those that involve a change of topic or addressee) seem to grow out of status rather than gender differences: doctors of either sex interrupt more often than male or female patients (Li et al., 2004). Furthermore, interruption attempts by patients are increasingly less successful as the status of the doctor becomes higher. In all, this points to the fact that with regards to dominant linguistic behaviour, position and (social) status play a more important role than gender, as illustrated in Figure 23.2.

The situation is different in the case of supportive interruptions. Here, the numbers are significantly higher for both female patients and female doctors, in comparison with male doctors and patients, as illustrated in Figure 23.3.

This appears to be evidence for the fact that in the institutional setting of medical communication, women are more strongly consensus-oriented and cooperative than men, just as they are in other settings (Menz and Al-Roubaie, 2008: 659).

In addition to showing differences regarding interactional dynamics, the variable of gender also correlates with differences of linguistic realizations in, for example, representations of pain

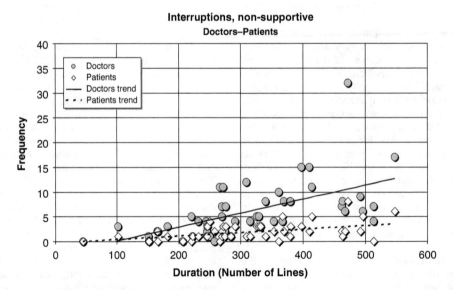

Figure 23.2 Distribution of non-supportive interruptions by doctors and patients over the course of an anamnesis (p = 0.000) (Menz and Al-Roubaie, 2008: 657).

Interactive Support

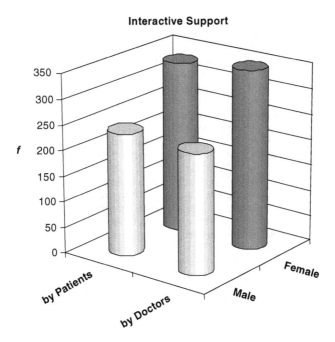

Figure 23.3 Cross-tabulation of the distribution of supportive interruptions for doctors vs patients, male vs female (*p*=0.013) (Menz and Al-Roubaie, 2008: 659).

(Blasch et al., 2010). Thus, in the context of medical consultations:

- Women, on referring to pain, use semantically-rich concepts and fewer 'empty subject' constructions ('it', 'this') than men.
- Women use significantly more 'marked' (non-formulaic) processes to represent pain than men. While men more frequently fall back on ready-made formulations ('to have a pain', 'to hurt'), women's expressions show more diversity and variation.
- Women produce a higher number of relativizing temporal qualifiers (often, sometimes ...) than men, who more frequently use the absolute qualifier 'always'. This can also be interpreted in the sense that female patients appear to produce more differentiated representations.

Overall then, representations of pain appear to exhibit more variation and diversity when produced by women than by men. However, some medical studies (Penque et al., 1998; Shaw et al., 1994) have pointed out that it may in fact be due to these divergences in strategies for the representation of pain that certain syndromes like coronary heart disorders are more frequently overlooked in female patients than in males, which in turn increases women's mortality rate. Because the description of pain is a central diagnostic tool

used to distinguish severe from less harmful complaints and thus to assess the necessity of (life-saving) measures, verbal representation plays a central role that is not to be underestimated. Differences in verbal expression occur notably in the following four areas (Menz and Lalouschek, 2006; Vodopiutz et al., 2002):

1 Women tend to downplay their pain (making light of it or focusing more on the psychological and social context); men, by contrast, tend to overstate their pain (taking it seriously, showing they are interested and well informed).

2 From an interactional perspective, women are more likely to view themselves as being able to endure the pain (passively, and ready to delegate and entrust the treatment to the medical institution), while men tend to present themselves interactively as mastering the pain (actively, and to undertake therapy).

3 Men tend to show a stronger wish to know the cause of pain than women.

4 Men tend to describe pain in (very) concrete terms, by providing ample descriptions of symptoms, while women's descriptions of pain tend to be more contextualizing, showing little focus on symptomatic aspects and frequently using markers of diffusion as well as metacommunicative remarks that topicalize the impossibility of providing an exact description of the pain.

The reason why such divergences are important issues for study within doctor–patient communication is that the linguistic enactments typically found with men correspond more closely to doctors' expectations with regards to providing the desired information than do women's enactments. Doctors require and demand symptomatic descriptions of pain, which means as exact an indication of the locality, intensity, duration and frequency of (e.g. chest) pain as possible. Thus, patients who themselves prefer and pursue a diagnostic path of investigating causes and producing symptomatic descriptions of pain are more readily regarded as precise, informative and cooperative by doctors. This mainly applies to male patients. Furthermore, due to the fact that the majority of cardiologists to this day are male and that, historically, descriptions of symptoms and clinical differential diagnoses in the realm of coronary heart disorders were developed mainly with male patients, the bias may actually be immanent in the system (Menz and Lalouschek, 2006; Vodopiutz et al., 2002).

23.4 APPLICATIONS: TEACHING/EDUCATION

In recent years, an increasing number of linguistic findings in the area of DPC have given rise to considerations of transference to and practical applicability within medical practice. Here, different theoretical models lead to preferences for different propositions. From a conversation analytic perspective, sequential turn-by-turn analyses lend themselves readily to the comparative study of, and ultimately to the differentiation between, successful and less-than-successful interactions, underlining the notion that both (all) conversational parties share equal responsibility in the co-construction of a setting. Thus, conversation analysis (CA) is particularly conducive to findings in the context of patient-centred and biopsychosocial approaches (Maynard and Heritage, 2005). Discourse analytic approaches take up another focus, integrating more strongly theme-oriented aspects such as frames, footing and face-work, but also content-related aspects such as shared decision-making into their propositions (Roberts and Sarangi, 2005). Considerations of grammar, intonation, vocabulary, as well as of rhetorical processes of facework, are all integral parts of discourse analytic models.

Proposals growing out of the 'Vienna School' (see e.g. Lalouschek, 2004; Menz and Nowak, 1992; Wodak, 1996) are more strongly oriented towards practice and the development of specific training programmes.

Furthermore, Menz et al. (2008a), using an innovative two-phase study design, report validated results for a set of communication characteristics that proved to be salient. Data from a first series of recordings formed the basis for a short (and thus easily implemented) one-hour training programme focusing on two areas that analysis had shown to be significant: **orientation** with regards to the local interactional process as well as the global context of the treatment and also transparency with regards to laying out the conversation. A second set of recordings served to test the effectiveness of the training programme. Compared to the first data-set, the second set attested to clear modifications in the participating doctors' conversation design: doctors provided more orientation for the patients regarding the course of the conversation that was to be expected; there were fewer topic jumps, and doctors reacted more sensitively towards indications of patients' concerns, while nevertheless adhering more closely to their original mapping of the conversation. Thus, even short-term didactic intervention was shown to have noticeable ramifications for conversational conduct. It would be desirable for similar programmes, addressing further linguistic processes such as the use of relevance markers (Sator et al., 2008: 169), to be introduced into the medical curriculum.

Also of great importance is the work on seizure disorders (epilepsy, dissociative disorders, etc.) conducted by a research group around Elisabeth Gülich and Martin Schöndienst. Their work is not only relevant to focusing and improving doctors' communicative competence but also on a more immediate level for the development of diagnoses. Thus, Gülich and her collaborators, in a series of conversation analytic studies (Furchner, 2002; Furchner and Gülich, 2001; Gülich and Furchner, 2002; Gülich and Schöndienst, 1998, 1999) have provided evidence for the fact that different subtypes of epilepsy can be distinguished on the basis of the forms of representations of seizure attacks and so-called auras. Hesitation phenomena, reformulations, elaborations on the description of auras, as well as the use of adversative structures and of ready-made phrases, were all shown to be discriminatory features of certain types of epilepsy and dissociative attacks. Thus, the generation of findings, which in traditional medicine would have taken up long periods of observation during hospitalization or even invasive measures such as surgery, can now be elicited in more straightforward and comparatively easy ways in the course of careful anamnesis, due to the parameters established. (For similar results in the context of chest pain, see Vodopiutz et al., 2002.) The work of Sator (e.g. 2009) promises to yield results of comparable significance with regards to the differentiation of headaches, the classification of which has, until now, proved impossible using medical testing and machinery. Here too, careful and precise anamnesis is of vital importance.

Differently cast, but also of increasing significance, are discussions following Roberts and Sarangi's (2003) treatise that problematizes attempts to disseminate discourse analytic findings among medical practitioners in the form of academic publications. In particular, potential clashes of inherently different methodological paradigms (quantitative vs qualitative), the presentation of qualitative conversational data, as well as issues of academic writing style warrant reflection in view of a dissemination via out-of-discipline (i.e. medical) scientific journals. Such discussions vividly illustrate both the opportunities afforded by and the limits imposed on inter-/trans-disciplinary research (see also Menz et al., 2008b; Nowak, 2009).

23.5 TRENDS AND FUTURE RESEARCH: INTERDISCIPLINARITY, CONSOLIDATION, GENERALIZATION

Research on doctor–patient interaction is an area of analysis approached from the perspectives of a variety of disciplines (medical psychology, medical sociology, medical science per se, sociolinguistics) using a variety of methods and research questions. As the analysis of medical communication is, by definition, located on the interface of two fields, the interdisciplinary approach will continue to gain importance. This is likely to have direct bearings on methodological and topical issues and concerns, which shall be briefly considered in the following.

From a methodological perspective, medical and sociolinguistic research on doctor–patient communication developed out of two very different scientific paradigms. In sociolinguistics/conversation analysis (CA)/discourse analysis (DA), the qualitative approach dominates, which treats comparatively small corpora of data in depth and great detail. By contrast, medical research, including research on communication and interaction, is traditionally rooted in, and thus held accountable to, the standards of evidence-based medicine, whose findings primarily grow out of statistical calculations of probabilities and significances. Thus, detailed analyses that do not lend themselves easily to broad generalization are not necessarily considered reliable from this perspective.

Overall, three approaches can be discerned that attempt to bridge or at least narrow this perceived gap and prepare the ground for sociolinguistic research to be more readily integrated into medical and medico-social work. First, within discourse analysis, there appears to be a noticeable trend towards combining genuinely qualitative analysis with quantification of observations (see, for example, a recent collection by Heritage and Maynard, 2006b; see also, for example, Haakana, 2002; Menz and Al-Roubaie, 2008; Stivers, 2001). Such combinations of different empirical methods (Wodak, 1997) is conducive to giving sociolinguistic studies more prominence within the field of medical science and to bringing it in closer contact with well-established medical research.

Secondly, modern approaches to the aggregation and dissemination of scientific data and findings are continually gaining importance in general. A first step here is the compilation of a database registering all linguistic studies on the topic of German-based doctor–patient communication that have been published (see Menz et al., 2008b). It is hoped this database will contribute to the internal consolidation and theoretical development of the research area and, ideally, constitute a pivotal point of reference for future sociolinguistic studies. To this end, the primary studies captured in the database, along with the concomitant systematized metadata and individual analyses, were made publicly and freely accessible to the scientific community in an open-access-database format. At the same time, all interested researchers and scholars are invited to become involved in the critical assessment of the database as well as its development and expansion. In that sense, the database partakes in an international trend towards open access to scientific data and findings generated on the basis of public funding. Through systematic, comprehensive presentation and electronic accessibility, such findings are henceforth available for research and discussion far beyond the linguistic discipline and tradition. This is in line with a strong desire within sociolinguistic and discourse analytic research to establish close linkages with other scientific discourse communities in the realm of medical and health communications. As a third point, so-called **metastudies** must be mentioned as a further method of generalizing and systematizing research findings, along with comprehensive bibliographies (see, for example, Nowak and Spranz-Fogasy, 2007). The purpose of metastudies is to collect and evaluate individual studies systematically. This method of generating scientific insight is well established within quantitatively-oriented disciplines such as psychology or medical science, and plays an important role with regards to the generalization and validation of results there. In a more recent development, the methodology of metastudies has been adapted for qualitatively-oriented disciplines as well. Here, Nowak's (2009) work is pioneering in the context of DPC, showing how systematic metastudy of comprehensive analyses of conversational components of DCP can supplement or even replace entire collections of individual studies.

Beyond methodological innovations and trends, it can be predicted that, from a content-oriented perspective, attention will increasingly focus on multilingual, inter- and transcultural settings and issues (see Section 23.3.2 above). It is in this area in particular that doctors face special challenges, and here interactional sociolinguistics has much insight to offer by virtue of its long-standing and rich tradition (see also the chapters on multilingualism in this handbook).

Last but not least, a notable trend within the development of medical science itself should be mentioned. The traditional paradigm of Western medicine is gradually being supplemented with, or partially even replaced by, alternative, more holistic conceptions of illness and health, which may to some extent be due to the fact that within alternative forms of medicine such as homeopathy (Konitzer et al., 2002; Ruusuvuori, 2005), psychosomatic approaches, bio-psychosocial medicine (Lalouschek, 2005), or Traditional Chinese Medicine (TCM), different, and unconventional, forms of communication pertain that may be more conducive to patient satisfaction. The global development in the direction of post-bureaucratic forms of organization (Iedema, 2003), in the course of which communication and negotiation are increasingly gaining in importance, is another factor contributing to the high significance accorded to communicative needs and demands today. This situation will continue to call for and challenge sociolinguistic research on doctor–patient communication in the years to come.

NOTE

1 By contrast, Heath (1989) shows that forms of expressions of pain such as groaning, whimpering, or interjections can actually be inhibiting in the medical setting. Doctoral diagnosis relies on an exact description of pain, while the acute expression of pain is diagnostically not helpful or even a hindrance in the sense that other witnesses have to be consulted for the description of pain in cases where patients are themselves unable to provide an 'objective' assessment (Heath 1989: 114).

REFERENCES

Angelelli, C. V. (2004) *Medical Interpreting and Cross-Cultural Communication*. Cambridge: Cambridge University Press.

Atkinson, P. and Heath, C. (eds) (1981) *Medical Work: Realities and Routines*. Farnborough: Gower.

Becker-Mrotzek, M. (1992) *Diskursforschung und Kommunikation in Institutionen*. Heidelberg: Groos.

Blasch, L., Menz, F., and Wetschanow, K. (2010) 'Texttypspezifische und gendertypische Unterschiede in der Darstellung von Kopfschmerzen', in F. Menz J. Lalouschek, M. Sator and K. Wetschanow (eds), *Sprechen über Schmerzen*. Duisburg: Universitätsverlag Rhein-Ruhr (UVRR). pp. 225–94.

Bolden, G. B. (2000) 'Toward understanding practices of medical interpreting: interpreters' involvement in history taking', *Discourse Studies: An Interdisciplinary Journal for the Study of Text and Talk*, 2: 387–419.

Bot, H. (2007) 'Dialogue interpreting as a specific case of reported speech', in F. Pöchhacker and M. Shlesinger (eds), *Healthcare Interpreting: Discourse and Interaction*. Amsterdam: Jon Benjamins. pp. 77–99.

Brünner, G. and Gülich, E. (2002) 'Verfahren der Veranschaulichung in der Experten-Laien-Kommunikation', in G.Brünner and E. Gülich (eds), *Krankheit verstehen. Interdisziplinäre Beiträge zur Sprache in Krankheitsdarstellungen*. Bielefeld: Aisthesis Verlag. pp. 17–94.

Buchholz, M. B. (1998) 'Die Metapher im psychoanalytischen Dialog', *Psyche*, 545–71.

Bührig, K. (2001) 'Interpreting in hospitals', in S. Cigada, S. Gilardoni and M. Matey (eds), *Communicare in Ambiente Professionale Plurilingue*. Lugano: Universitá della Svizzera italiana. pp. 107–9.

Bührig, K. and Meyer, B. (2004a) *Ad Hoc-Interpreting and the Achievement of Communicative in Specific Kinds of Doctor-Patient Discourse*. (Rep. No. 57). Hamburg: Universität Hamburg: Sonderforschungsbereich Mehrsprachigkeit.

Bührig, K. and Meyer, B. (2004b) 'Ad-hoc-interpreting and the Achievement of Communicative Purposes in Doctor-Patient-Communication', in J. House and J. Rehbein (eds), *Multilingual Communication*. Amsterdam: Benjamins. pp. 43–62.

Byrne, P. S. and Long, B. E. L. (1976) *Doctors Talking to Patients: A Study of the Verbal Behaviour of General Practitioners Consulting in their Surgeries*. London: HSMO, Royal College of General Practitioners.

Campion, P. and Langdon, M. (2004) 'Achieving multiple topic shifts in primary care medical consultations: a conversation analysis study in UK general practice', *Sociology of Health and Illness*, 26: 81–101.

Candlin, S. (2006) 'Constructing knowledge, understanding and meaning between patients and nurses', in M. Gotti and F. Salager-Meyer (eds), *Advances in Medical Discourse Analysis: Oral and Written Contexts*. Berne: Peter Lang. pp. 65–86.

Collins, S. (2005) 'Explanations in consultations: the combined effectiveness of doctors' and nurses' communication with patients', *Medical Education*, 39: 785–96.

Deppermann, A. (2003) 'Wenn Semantik zum praktischen Problem wird: Divergierende Schmerzkonzepte von Ärztin und Patientin in der psychosomatischen Exploration', *Psychotherapie und Sozialwissenschaft. Zeitschrift für qualitative Forschung*, 5: 165–81.

de Valck, C. and Van den Wostijne, K. P. (1996) 'Communication problems on an oncology ward', *Patient Education and Counseling*, 29: 131–6.

Diaz, F. (2000) 'The social organisation of chemotherapy treatment consultations', *Sociology of Health and Illness,* 22: 364–89.

Drew, P. and Heritage, J. C. (eds) (1992) *Talk at Work. Interaction in Institutional Settings.* Cambridge: Cambridge University Press.

Ehlich, K, Koerfer, A., Redder, A. and Weingarten, R. (eds) (1990) *Medizinische und therapeutische Kommunikation. Diskursanalytische Untersuchungen.* Opladen: Westdeutscher Verlag.

Fisher, S. and Todd, A. D. (eds) (1983) *The Social Organization of Doctor Patient Communication.* Washington, DC: Center for Applied Linguistics.

Fritzsche, K. and Wirsching, M. (2005) *Psychosomatische Medizin und Psychotherapie.* Berlin: Springer.

Furchner, I. (2002) ' "Keine absence gleicht der anderen." Die Darstellung von Bewusstseinslücken in "Anfallsbeschreibungen"', in G. Brünner and E. Gülich (eds), *Krankheit verstehen. Interdisziplinäre Beiträge zur Sprache in Krankheitsdarstellungen.* Bielefeld: Aisthesis Verlag. pp. 121–42.

Furchner, I. and Gülich, E. (2001) 'L'expertise des patients dans l'établissment d'un diagnostic médical', *Bulletin VALS-ASLA,* 74: 83–107.

Gotti, M. and Salager-Meyer, F. (eds) (2006) *Advances in Medical Discourse Analysis: Oral and Written Contexts.* Berne: Peter Lang. p. 148.

Gülich, E. and Furchner, I. (2002) 'Die Beschreibung von Unbeschreibbarem. Eine konversationsanalytische Annäherung an Gespräche mit Anfallskranken', in I. Keim and W. Schütte (eds), *Soziale Welten und kommunikative Stile. Festschrift für Werner Kallmeyer zum 60. Geburtstag.* Tübingen: Narr. pp. 161–86.

Gülich, E. and Schöndienst, M. (1998) Anfallsbeschreibung von PatientInnen mit epileptischen oder pseudoepileptischen Anfällen: Differentialdiagnostische Aspekte und interventionstechnische Implikationen. Bielefeld. 21-2-2007. Unpublished work.

Gülich, E. and Schöndienst, M. (1999) ' "Das ist unheimlich schwer zu beschreiben" '. Formulierungsmuster in Krankheitsbeschreibungen anfallskranker Patienten: differentialdiagnostische und therapeutische Aspekte', *Psychotherapie und Sozialwissenschaft, Zeitschrift für Qualitative Forschung,* 199–227.

Gülich, E., Schöndienst, M. and Surmann, V. (2003) 'Schmerzen erzählen Geschichten – Geschichten erzählen Schmerzen', *Psychotherapie und Sozialwissenschaft. Zeitschrift für qualitative Forschung,* 5: 220–49.

Haakana, M. (2002) 'Laughter in medical interaction: from quantification to analysis, and back', *Journal of Sociolinguistics,* 6: 207–35.

Heath, C. (1989) 'Pain talk. The expression of suffering in the medical consultation', *Social Psychology Quarterly,* 52: 113–25.

Heath, C. (2002) 'Demonstrative suffering: the gestural (re)embodiment of symptoms', *Journal of Communication,* 52: 597–616.

Hein, N., Hoffmann-Richter, U., Lalouschek, J., Nowak, P. and Wodak, R. (1985) 'Kommunikation zwischen Arzt und Patient', *Wiener Linguistische Gazette,* 1–87.

Herb, G. and Streeck, S. (1995) 'Der Diagnoseprozess bei Spina bifida: Elterliche Wahrnehmung und Sicht des klinischen Fachpersonals', *Praxis der Kinderpsychologie und Kinderpsychiatrie,* 44: 150–8.

Heritage, J. C. and Maynard, D. W. (2006a) 'Introduction: analyzing interaction between doctors and patients in primary care encounters', in J. C. Heritage and D. W. Maynard (eds), *Communication in Medical Care: Interaction between Primary Care Physicians and Patients.* Cambridge: Cambridge University Press. pp. 1–21.

Heritage, J. C. and Maynard, D. W. (eds) (2006b) *Communication in medical care: interaction between primary care physicians and patients.* Cambridge: Cambridge University Press.

Heritage, J. C. and Robinson, J. D. (2006) 'Accounting for the visit: giving reasons for seeking medical care', in J. C. Heritage and D. W. Maynard (eds), *Communication in medical care: interaction between primary care physicians and patients.* Cambridge: Cambridge University Press. pp. 48–85.

Heritage, J. C., Robinson, J. D., Elliott, M. N., Beckett, M. and Wilkes, M. (2007) 'Reducing patients' unmet concerns in primary care: the difference one word can make', *Journal of General Internal Medicine,* 22: 1429–33.

Holmes, J. (1992) 'Women's talk in public contexts', *Discourse and Society,* 3: 131–50.

Hydén, L.-C. and Mishler, E. G. (1999) 'Language and medicine', *Annual Review of Applied Linguistics,* 19: 174–92.

Iedema, R. (2003) *Discourses of Post-Bureaucratic Organization.* Amsterdam: John Benjamins.

Iedema, Ri. (2006) '(Post-)bureaucratizing medicine: health reform and the reconfiguration of contemporary clinical work', in M. Gotti and F. Salager-Meyer (eds), *Advances in Medical Discourse Analysis: Oral and Written Contexts.* Berne: Peter Lang. pp.111–31.

Köhle, K. and Raspe, H.-H. (eds) (1982) *Das Gespräch während der ärztlichen Visite. Empirische Untersuchungen.* Wien: Urban and Schwarzenberg.

Konitzer, M., Schemm, W., Freudenberg, N. and Fischer, G. C. (2002) 'Therapeutic interaction through metaphor: a textual approach to homeopathy', *Semiotica,* 141: 1–27.

Kütemeyer, M. (2003) 'Psychogener Schmerz als Dissoziation', *Psychotherapie und Sozialwissenschaft. Zeitschrift für qualitative Forschung,* 3: 203–20.

Lackner, M., Jager, B. and Kunsbeck, H. W. (1996) ' Patient – medical staff – consultant triad: Conditions for satisfaction in psychosomatic consultation service (translation)', *Psychother Psychosom Med. Psychol.,* 333–9.

Lalouschek, J. (2002) *Ärztliche Gesprächsausbildung. Eine diskursanalytische Studie zu Formen des ärztlichen Gesprächs.* Radolfzell: Verlag für Gesprächsforschung.

Lalouschek, J. (2004) 'Kommunikatives Selbst-Coaching im beruflichen Alltag. Ein sprachwissenschaftliches Trainingskonzept am Beispiel der klinischen Gesprächsführung', in M. Becker-Mrotzek and G. Brünner (eds), *Analyse und Vermittlung von Gesprächskompetenz.* Radolfzell: Verlag für Gesprächsforschung. pp.137–58.

Lalouschek, J. (2005) 'Medizinische Konzepte und ärztliche Gesprächsführung – am Beispiel der psychosomatischen Anamnese', in M. Neises, S. Ditz and T. Spranz-Fogasy (eds), *Psychosomatische Gesprächsführung in der Frauenheilkunde. Ein interdisziplinärer Ansatz zur verbalen*

Intervention. Stuttgart: Wissenschaftliche Verlagsgesellschaft. pp. 48–72.

Lalouschek, J., Menz, F. and Wodak, R. (1990) *Alltag in der Ambulanz. Gespräche zwischen Ärzten, Schwestern und Patienten*. Tübingen: Gunter Narr Verlag.

Lehtinen, E. (2007) 'Merging doctor and client knowledge: on doctors' ways of dealing with clients' potentially discrepant information in genetic counseling', *Journal of Pragmatics: an Interdisciplinary Journal of Language Studies*, 39: 389–427.

Li, H. Z. (1999) 'Grounding and information communication in intercultural and intracultural dyadic discourse', *Discourse Processes: a Multidisciplinary Journal*, 28: 195–215.

Li, H. Z., Krysko, M., Desroches, N. G. and Deagle, G. (2004) 'Reconceptualizing interruptions in physician – patient interviews: cooperative and intrusive', *Communication and Medicine: An Interdisciplinary Journal of Healthcare, Ethics and Society*, 1: 145–57.

Löning, P. and Rehbein, J. (eds) (1993) *Arzt-Patienten-Kommunikation. Analysen zu interdisziplinären Problemen des medizinischen Diskurses*. Berlin: de Gruyter.

Maynard, D. W. and Heritage, J. C. (2005) 'Conversation analysis, doctor – patient interaction and medical communication', *Medical Education*, 39: 428–35.

Menz, F. (1991) *Der geheime Dialog. Medizinische Ausbildung und institutionalisierte Verschleierungen in der Arzt-Patient-Kommunikation*. Frankfurt am Main: Peter Lang.

Menz, F. and Al-Roubaie, A. (2008) 'Interruptions, status and gender in medical interviews: the harder you brake, the longer it takes', *Discourse and Society*, 19: 645–66.

Menz, F. and Lalouschek, J. (2006) ' "I just can't tell you how much it hurts." Gender-relevant differences in the description of chest pain', in M. Gotti and F. Salager-Meyer (eds), *Advances in Medical Discourse Analysis: Oral and Written Contexts*. Berne: Peter Lang.

Menz, F. and Nowak, P. (1992) 'Kommunikationstraining für Ärzte und Ärztinnen in Österreich. Eine Anamnese', in R. Fiehler and W. Sucharowski (eds), *Kommunikationsberatung und -ausbildung. Anwendungsfelder der Diskursforschung*. Opladen: Westdeutscher Verlag. pp. 79–86.

Menz, F., Lalouschek, J. and Gstettner, A. (2008a) *Effiziente ärztliche Gesprächsführung. Optimierung kommunikativer Kompetenz in der ambulanten medizinischen Versorgung. Ein gesprächsanalytisches Trainingskonzept*. Münster: LIT-Verlag.

Menz, F., Nowak, P., Rappl, A. and Nezhiba, S. (2008b) 'Arzt-Patient-Interaktion im deutschsprachigen Raum – eine Online-Forschungsdatenbank (API-on) als Basis für Metaanalysen', *Gesprächsforschung – Online-Zeitschrift zur verbalen Interaktion*, 9: 129–63.

Merlini, R. and Favaron, R. (2005) 'Examining the "voice of interpreting" in speech pathology', *Interpreting: International Journal of Research and Practice in Interpreting*, 7: 263–302.

Meyer, B. (2002) 'Medical interpreting: some salient features', in G. Garzone, M. Viezzi, D. C. Snelling, A. Amato, and P. Mead (eds), *Interpreting in the 21st Century: Challenges and Opportunities*. Amsterdam: Benjamins. pp. 159–69.

Meyer, B. (2004) *Dolmetschen im medizinischen Aufklärungsgespräch. Eine diskursanalytische Untersuchung zur Wissensvermittlung im mehrsprachigen Krankenhaus*. Münster: Waxmann.

Meyer, B., Apfelbaum, B., Pöchhacker, F. and Bischoff, A. (2003) 'Analysing interpreted doctor-patient communication from the perspectives of linguistics, interpreting studies and health sciences', in L. Brunette, G. Bastin, I. Hemlin and H. Clarke (eds), *The Critical Link 3: Interpreters in the Community*. Amsterdam: Benjamins. pp. 67–79.

Mishler, E. G. (1984) *The Discourse of Medicine. Dialectics of Medical Interviews*. Norwood, NJ: Ablex.

Mondada, L. (2002) 'Die interaktive Formulierung der medizinischen Beschreibung', *Psychotherapie und Sozialwissenschaft. Zeitschrift für qualitative Forschung*, 5: 341–53.

Morris, G. H. and Chenail, R. J. (eds) (1995) *The Talk of the Clinic. Explorations in the Analysis of Medical and Therapeutic Discourse*. Hillsdale, NJ: Erlbaum.

Neises, M., Ditz, S. and Spranz-Fogasy, T. (eds) (2005) *Psychosomatische Gesprächsführung in der Frauenheilkunde. Ein interdisziplinärer Ansatz zur verbalen Intervention*. Stuttgart: Wissenschaftliche Verlagsgesellschaft.

Nowak, P. (2009) *Eine Systematik sprachlichen Handelns von Ärzt/inn/en. Metastudie über Diskursforschungen zu deutschsprachigen Arzt-Patient-Interaktionen*. Frankfurt/am Main: Peter Lang.

Nowak, P. and Spranz-Fogasy, T. (2007) *Literatur zur Arzt-Patient-Kommunikation*. Mannheim: Institut für Deutsche Sprache.

Odebunmi, A. (2006) 'Locutions in medical discourse in Southwestern Nigeria', *Pragmatics: Quarterly Publication of the International Pragmatics Association*, 16: 25–41.

Overlach, F. (2008) *Sprache des Schmerzes – Sprechen über Schmerzen. Eine grammatisch-semantische und gesprächsanalytische Untersuchung von Schmerzausdrücken im Deutschen*. Berlin: de Gruyter.

Pahta, P. (2006) '"This is very important": a corpus study of amplifiers in medical writing', in M. Gotti and F. Salager-Meyer (eds), *Advances in Medical Discourse Analysis: Oral and Written Contexts*. Berne: Peter Lang. pp. 357–81.

Penque, S., Halm, M., Smith, M., et al. (1998) 'Women and coronary disease: relationship between descriptors of signs and symptoms and diagnostic and treatment course', *American Journal of Critical Care*, 175–82.

Peräkylä, A. (2004) 'Making links in psychoanalytic interpretations: a conversation analytical perspective', *Psychotherapy Research*, 289–307.

Ploeger, A. (2005) 'Verbale Interaktion im Kollektiv', in M. Neises, S. Ditz and T. Spranz-Fogasy (eds), *Psychosomatische Gesprächsführung in der Frauenheilkunde. Ein interdisziplinärer Ansatz zur verbalen Intervention*. Stuttgart: Wissenschaftliche Verlagsgesellschaft. pp. 285–98.

Pöchhacker, F. and Kadric, M. (1999) 'The hospital cleaner as healthcare interpreter. A case study', *The Interpreter*, 5: 161–78.

Pöchhacker, F. and Shlesinger, M. (2005) 'Introduction. Discourse-based research on healthcare interpreting',

Interpreting: International Journal of Research and Practice in Interpreting, 7: 157–67.

Pöchhacker, F. and Shlesinger, M. (eds) (2007) *Healthcare Interpreting: Discourse and Interaction.* Amsterdam: Benjamins.

Redder, A. and Wiese, I. (eds) (1994) *Medizinische Kommunikation. Diskurspraxis, Diskursethik, Diskursanalyse.* Opladen: Westdeutscher Verlag.

Rees, C. E., Knight, L. V. and Wilkinson, C. E. (2007) 'Doctors being up there and we being down here: a metaphorical analysis of talk about student/doctor – patient relationships', *Social Science and Medicine,* 65: 725–37.

Reisigl, M. (2006). *Semiotik des Schmerzes – das medizinsemiotische Framework der Untersuchung.* Wien: Institut für Sprachwissenschaft.

Roberts, C. (2006) 'Continuities and discontinuities in doctor – patient consultations in a multilingual society', in M. Gotti and F. Salager-Meyer (eds), *Advances in Medical Discourse Analysis: Oral and Written Contexts.* Berne: Peter Lang. pp. 177–95.

Roberts, C. and Sarangi, S. (2003) 'Uptake of discourse research in interprofessional settings: reporting from medical consultancy', *Applied Linguistics,* 24: 338–59.

Roberts, C. and Sarangi, S. (2005) 'Theme-oriented discourse analysis of medical encounters', *Medical Education,* 39: 632–40.

Roberts, C., Moss, B., Wass, V., Sarangi, S. and Jones, R. (2005) 'Misunderstandings: a qualitative study of primary care consultations in multilingual settings, and educational implications', *Medical Education:* 465–75.

Roberts, F. D. (2000) 'The interactional construction of asymmetry: the medical agenda as a resource for delaying response to patient questions', *The Sociological Quarterly:* 151–70.

Robinson, J. D. (1998) 'Getting down to business. Talk, gaze and body orientation during openings of doctor – patient consultations', *Human Communication Research,* 25: 97–123.

Ruusuvuori, J. (2005) 'Comparing homeopathic and general practice consultations: the case of problem presentation', *Communication and Medicine,* 2: 123–35.

Sachweh, S. (2005) '"Gut Herrr Doktor!" Gespräche mit alten Patientinnen', in M. Neises, S. Ditz and T. Spranz-Fogasy (eds), *Psychosomatische Gesprächsführung in der Frauenheilkunde. Ein interdisziplinärer Ansatz zur verbalen Intervention.* Stuttgart: Wissenschaftliche Verlagsgesellschaft. pp. 339–51.

Sachweh, S. (2006) '"Noch ein Löffelchen?" Effektive Kommunikation in der Altenpflege',* (2., vollst. überarb. und erw. Aufl. ed.) Hans Huber.

Sarangi, S. and Brookes-Howell, L. (2006) 'Recontextualising the familial lifeworld in genetic counseling: case notes', in M. Gotti and F. Salager-Meyer (eds), *Advances in Medical Discourse Analysis: Oral and Written Contexts.* Berne: Peter Lang. pp. 197–225.

Sarangi, S. and Roberts, C. (eds) (1999) *Talk, Work and Institutional Order: Discourse in Medical, Mediation and Management Settings.* Berlin: Mouton de Gruyter.

Sator, M. (2009) ' "Irgendwie schwierig zu differenzieren!" " Schmerzdifferenzierung in ärztlichen Erstgesprächen an der Kopfschmerzambulanz. Eine gesprächsanalytische Untersuchung'. Unpublished work.

Sator, M., Gstettner, A. and Hladschik-Kermer, B. (2008) 'Seitdem mir der Arzt gesagt hat "Tumor" – Das war's', *Wiener Klinische Wochenschrift,* 120: 158–70.

Schöndienst, M. (2002) 'The Role of psychotherapy in the treatment of epilepsies', in M. R. Trimble and B. Schmitz (eds), *The Neuropsychiatry of Epilepsy.* Cambridge: Cambridge University Press. pp. 313–23.

Semino, E., Heywood, J. and Short, M. (2004) 'Methodological problems in the analysis of metaphors in a corpus of conversations about cancer', *Journal of Pragmatics: an Interdisciplinary Journal of Language Studies,* 36: 1271–94.

Shaw, L. J., Miller, D. D., Romeis, J. C., et al. (1994) 'Gender differences in the noninvasive evaluation and management of patients with suspected coronary disease', *Annals of Internal Medicine:* 559–66.

Speer, S. A. and Parsons, C. (2006) 'Gatekeeping gender: some features of the use of hypothetical questions in the psychiatric assessment of transsexual patients', *Discourse and Society: An International Journal for the Study of Discourse and Communication in Their Social, Political and Cultural Contexts,* 17: 785–812.

Spranz-Fogasy, T. (2005) 'Kommunikatives Handeln in ärztlichen Gesprächen – Gesprächseröffnung und Beschwerdenexploration', in M. Neises, S. Ditz and T. Spranz-Fogasy (eds), *Psychosomatische Gesprächsführung in der Frauenheilkunde. Ein interdisziplinärer Ansatz zur verbalen Intervention.* Stuttgart: Wissenschaftliche Verlagsgesellschaft. pp. 17–47.

Stivers, T. (2001) 'Negotiating who presents the problem: next speaker selection in pediatric encounters', *Journal of Communication,* 51: 1–31.

Stukenbrock, A. (2008) '"Wo ist der Hauptschmerz?" – Zeigen am menschlichen Körper', *Gesprächsforschung – Online-Zeitschrift zur verbalen Interaktion,* 9: 1–33.

Surmann, V. (2005) *Anfallsbilder. Metaphorische Konzepte im Sprechen anfallskranker Menschen.* Würzburg: Königshausen u. Neumann.

Tanner, B. A. (eds) (1976) *Language and Communication in General Practice.* London: Hodder and Stoughton.

Valero-Garcés, C. (2002) 'Interaction and conversational constructions in the relationships between suppliers of services and immigrant users', *Pragmatics: Quarterly Publication of the International Pragmatics Association,* 12: 469–95.

Valero Garcés, C. (2005) 'Doctor–patient consultations in dyadic and triadic exchanges', *Interpreting: International Journal of Research and Practice in Interpreting,* 7: 193–210.

Vodopiutz, J., Poller, S., Schneider, B., et al. (2002) 'Chest pain in hospitalized patient: cause-specific and gender-specific differences', *Journal of Women's Health and Gender-Based Medicine,* 11: 1–9.

Walther, S. (1997) *Im Mittelpunkt der Patient? Übergabegespräche im Krankenhaus.* Stuttgart: Thieme.

Walther, S. (2005). *Erstgespräch zwischen Pflegepersonal und Patienten im Krankenhausalltag. Ein Transkriptband.* Radolfzell: Verlag für Gesprächsforschung.

Watson, B. M. and Gallois, C. (1999) 'Communication accommodation between patients and health professionals: themes and strategies in satisfying and unsatisfying encounters', *International Journal of Applied Linguistics,* 9: 167–83.

Weinhold, C. (1997) *Kommunikation zwischen Patienten und Pflegepersonal.* Berne: Verlag Hans Huber.

West, C. (1984) *Routine Complications. Troubles with Talk Between Doctors and Patients.* Bloomington; IN: Indiana University Press.

West, C. (1990) 'Not just "doctors' orders": directive-response sequences in patients' visits to women and men physicians', *Discourse and Society,* 1: 85–112.

Wodak, R. (1996) *Disorders of Discourse.* London: Longman.

Wodak, R. (1997) 'Critical discourse analysis and the study of doctor – patient interaction', in B.-L. Gunnarsson, P. Linell, B. Nordberg and C. N. Candlin (eds), *The Construction of Professional Discourse* London: Longman. pp. 173–200.

24

Discourse and Schools

Luisa Martín Rojo

24.1 INTRODUCTION

In this chapter, I present an overview of the broad field of discourse and schools, focusing mainly on its key topics, the evolution of this field of study, the questions which remain open and foreseeable future developments. On occasion, I present texts and examples from my own research in order to illustrate particular points and approaches.[1] Nevertheless, given the scope of the field and the amount of research that has been conducted, throughout the world, in countries with dissimilar educative and linguistic situations, this chapter cannot cover all the contributions made, nor even all the topics addressed. Therefore, I shall focus this review from the standpoint of a particular research question, one shared by many sociolinguists and discourse analysts: namely, that of the role played by **linguistic practices in constructing inequalities in schools** – and in this respect, the use made by the speakers of linguistic resources in this construction.

The fact that this question has become a mainstream focus of research in sociolinguistics is justified by the assumption that school plays a key role not only in capacity building and social development but also in normalization and social mobility. This significant role played by schools, as social institutions, is rooted in the production and distribution of knowledge and other forms of symbolic capital, which take place through educational practices. By analysing the production and distribution of these resources, we can explore the processes of social stratification, as Heller notes. Furthermore, in schools this distribution often contradicts the principles of democracy and equity that schools are committed to (Heller, 2007: 634–6).

Sociolinguists, linguistic anthropologists and discourse analysts have a common interest in this research question because of the key role played by discursive practices in the field of education. Everyday life in schools and classroom activities is organized and takes place through linguistic practices (this view of institutions and the role of communicative practices refers to Ervin Goffman; see, for example, Goffman (1961) and Gumperz (1989)). Organizing a school, applying its rules, teaching and learning, assessing and studying, legitimating particular languages and knowledge, and accepting or rejecting authority, among other actions, always involve discourse production and textual and conversational practices. In these daily practices, teacher–student and student–student relations are reproduced and recreated, as are the school rules, the syllabus asserted to be necessary and legitimate, the essential demands made of students and the characteristics of that which is considered to be adequate, good or useful, and of those who are attentive or disciplined, as well as the characteristics of items and people not meeting these criteria. These are routines, but not mechanical actions. Neither are they anonymous: on the contrary, they are produced by real social agents (Giddens, 1984: 3). The members of the school community are familiar with them and even seek to influence them, as is revealed in the discourses they produce, in which they build up a representation of their tasks and behaviour patterns and those of the community.

These communicative exchanges are triggered, guided and constrained by organizational policies (often implicit or tacit) and routine work practices (Cicourel, 2002: 3–4). Thus, interaction within the classroom is influenced by the institutional order (for example, how the school is organized, what principles and rules are applied, what values and ideologies underpin its existence, what programmes are applied, etc.). This institutional order, in turn, is part of the social order that governs it and assigns it a function in society (for example, that of education, or of integration) to be implemented in the context of differences in wealth, class, gender or other factors. Simultaneously, both of these orders may be modified through local linguistic practices. As Fairclough and Wodak remark, the understanding of discourse as 'social practice', 'implies a dialectical relationship between a particular discursive event and the situation(s), institution(s) and social structure(s) which frame it. As a dialectical relationship, it is a two-way relationship: the discursive event is shaped by situations, institutions and social structures, but it also shapes them' (1997: 258).

24.2 LINGUISTIC PRACTICES IN THE CONSTRUCTION OF INEQUALITY IN SCHOOLS

From the outset, sociolinguistics has sought to clarify the role played by linguistic processes in the construction of inequality in schools. This debate has evolved over time from a standpoint of evaluating and defending 'difference' to a more critical one in which it is observed that linguistic discrimination 'intersects' with many other forms of *discrimination*, such as those based on *race/ethnicity*, social class, *gender, religion, nationality* or *sexual orientation* (for the concept of 'intersectionality', see McCall 2007: 1786–8). These forms of oppression interrelate, and the dissimilar evaluation of linguistic differences intervenes in their production, naturalization and legitimation. The debate, too, has evolved, reflecting the fact that multilingualism has emerged as a major concern, focusing on the progressive commodification of languages in the new economy.

The dissimilar social valuation of linguistic varieties

One of the processes revealed by the research on discourse and education is the dissimilar social **valuation** of linguistic varieties. Some speakers, from the outset, possess the linguistic varieties valued and demanded in significant social contexts, such as schools, while others have to acquire them. Furthermore, the vernacular forms used by the latter speakers were rejected. For linguists, differences in valuation are only explained by the **unequal** status of individuals and groups, and have, in turn, a profound impact on the image of those who are 'different' as not-competent, and in predicting their potential success or failure (Labov, 1972; Bernstein, 1975). Following these views, the Linguistics Society of America (see Kroch and Labov, 1972: 17–18; Baugh, 1988: 65–8) refuted the linguistic arguments (judgements on the primitivism and the non-grammaticality of certain linguistic varieties) of 'deficit theorists' (Jensen, 1969), and showed that one of the causes of educational failure is, rather than any 'deficit', the unequal social evaluation of linguistic differences. Since then, reactions against this notion have multiplied among linguistics theorists in several countries. Instead of enrichment, difference is seen as a 'disadvantage' that needs to be compensated for. Frequently, these children are separated in order to receive the compensatory 'injection' that will bring them up to speed, and they receive the same kind of guidance as do students lagging behind their peers for other, non-language-related, reasons.

Current sociolinguistic research has shown that linguistic and cultural differences have a negative effect on minorities when they have a weak position in the social structure and have to overcome structural obstacles for their social and economic success (see Ogbu, 1993; see also Heller, 2004, for a review of the deficit vs difference debate). It is precisely through the unequal valuation of the languages spoken by students in multilingual and multicultural schools that the construction of the 'other' as deficient, as part of a domination process, takes place (Heller and Martin-Jones, 2001; Heller, 2007; Rassool, Canvin, Heugh and Mansoor, 2007). Monolingualism at school limits the possibilities of academic success of the neediest social classes in most of the world (the bibliography on this question is very extensive: for example, García and Baker, 2007; Rassool, 2007; Cummins and Hornberger, 2008; May and Hornberger, 2007; Skutnabb-Kangas, 2007; Skutnabb-Kangas, 2008). Educational actions and resources are directed preferentially to ensuring the teaching of the language of instruction, and the substitution of other student languages.

Furthermore, English is becoming a language of instructions in many countries, on occasion even displacing homegrown languages – in particular, minority and regional languages within states (Watts, 2008). The influence of English in education extends in parallel to processes of globalization, and is linked to current forms of postcolonial re-colonialization (e.g. Cooke, 1988; Pennycook, 1999; Phillipson and Skutnabb-Kangas, 1992, 1999; Canagarajah, 1999, 2002; Negri and Hardt, 2000; Macedo, Gounari and Dendrinos, 2003). The emergence of a deregulated, hypercompetitive, post-industrial, globalized economy during the 1980s and 1990s, accompanied the rapid growth of the tertiary sector and the increased importance of information activities in the provision of, and as part of, services, and produced important shifts both in the valuation of languages (Heller, 2003), and in the conceptualization and the experience of work. As Heller and Duchene point out, in such tertiary sector sites, language is the primary working tool, the primary materiality of work and often its principal product (see Cameron, 2000; Duchêne, 2009; and Duchene and Heller, forthcoming).

Thus, globalization has increased the importance of English as a dominant language and/or medium of instruction in the education system. As Pennycook (2000) observes, this process cannot be seen simply as 'the Empire strikes back', because currently the 'Empire' is taking the form of various (sometimes conflictual) forces of globalization, and is not necessarily one-sidedly against national and local community interests. Appropriated by local agents, English can serve diverse sets of intentions and purposes in their respective local contexts (Lin and Martin, 2005: 4–5). Furthermore, the resulting 'new work order' makes new demands on workers, and puts more pressure on literacy and interpersonal communication skills (Cameron, 1992: 72). Key actors in the new economy – including neoliberal governments – invest in training a new task force, in the use of a global language, as a way to ensure their participation in the new economy.

The example of European policies on languages is paradigmatic of this dissimilar valuation of linguistic resources (see also chapter by Berthoud and Lüdi, this volume). European laws reveal the different values attributed to languages, and they also illustrate how language programmes and policies are traversed by nationalist ideologies, both within the nation-states that constitute the European Union (EU), and in the migrants' countries of origin. While languages from EU nation-states such as English or German are highly valued and introduced into the curricula, resources are not provided, nor are steps taken to promote the learning and development

of 'migrant languages'.[2] Migration flux in Europe is producing challenges to the monolingual model of 'one state – one language', and in this context some languages are seen as a resource while others as a threat (see Extra and Verhoeven, 1993). In fact, as Mijares notes (2006: 59–65), the ELCO programme (the Teaching of the Language and Culture of Origin programme) is developed through bilateral agreements between European States and the non-EU countries which finance them (see the 1987: *European Parliament Resolution on the languages and cultures of regional and ethnic minorities in the European Community*). It was not until the late 1990s that the teaching of 'migrant languages' started to be seen as a bridge between cultures, i.e. an essential part of intercultural education within European countries, rather than ways to keep open the possibilities of return. However, this new orientation does not enjoy any financing (Bekemans and Ortiz de Urbina, 1997), nor, indeed, any official recognition from the EU (EURYDICE, 2004: 71).

In European policies, no emphasis is placed on the integrating effect of this kind of programme, although it formally seeks to ensure that everyone can become proficient in several languages in Europe, in which mobility and cooperation are intensifying. Against this background, CLIL (content and language integrated learning) programmes began to be adopted in Europe as an integral part of foreign language teaching in the 1990s. Although the stated aim of CLIL is to promote language learning and linguistic diversity, close examination of CLIL target languages reveals that English, followed by French and German, are the most widespread foreign target languages in the 30 countries in which these programmes have been implemented (EURYDICE, 2006: 18).

In spite of a critical shift, from research into students' competences and the acquisition processes in linguistic programmes to concern about the effects of the social distribution of linguistic resources, the ideology of monolingualism has yet to be rejected. Similarly, despite the reaction of linguistic research against the 'deficit theory', the core assumptions of this theory are still to be encountered quite frequently in schools in many parts of the world. Deficit arguments are evoked to explain and justify the educational failure of minorities (poor command of the language of instruction, poverty of expression, weak speaking skills, etc.), which in turn is considered to be the consequence of educational, cultural and economic shortcomings (poor school attendance record, dysfunctional families, rural background, etc.). The arguments of the deficit theory persist, and they are especially prevalent in sociocultural and linguistic terms. Thus, for example, in Spain, it is relatively frequent to hear teachers and tutors referring to the previous 'poor schooling' of these students, to 'cultural distance', to the 'dysfunctional families' or to the 'lack of fluency in the teaching language'. Whichever of these judgements is applied, the result is the same: an inadequate evaluation of the student body in question, and an attitude tending to favour segregation (see, for a detailed analysis, Martín Rojo, 2010). Consequently, many linguists feel the need to intervene. The fact that compensatory education programmes are still aimed at the descendants of immigrant workers in several European countries is further evidence of the continuing acceptance of these propositions in European countries (see Luciak's report (2004), for the European Monitoring Centre on Racism and Xenophobia).

Differences in the sociocultural regulation of communicative practices

The second process singled out in sociolinguistic and linguistic anthropologist research is the different sociocultural regulation of communicative practices. This regulation varies from one community to another; accordingly, it is not uncommon to find ways and means of communication that are clearly differentiated (Gumperz and Roberts, 1979; Gumperz, 1982). Misunderstandings emerge when people from different speech communities interact. Diverse values may be attributed to a given linguistic resource (for example, the use of an imperative, or a certain tone of voice, or a closer or more distant interpersonal distance) by speakers from different linguistic communities.

Research into intercultural communication, building upon the interactional sociolinguistic tradition and on equally interactional pragmatic developments, has contributed to the analysis of this type of interactions (Scollon and Scollon, 1981, 2001; Wiercbicka, 1991; Kasper and Blum-Kulka, 1993; Singy and Trudgill, 1997). Scollon and Scollon, in their early research, claim that 'much of the miscommunication between members of different ethnic groups occurs because of fundamental differences in the values placed on communication itself, and because of differences in interpretation caused by differences in the values placed on interpersonal face relations' (1981: 4). Recent studies in this field have highlighted the effects resulting from misunderstandings during interactional encounters when differences in conversational attitudes among communities are underestimated; at the same time, it is often assumed that one's own behaviour is the 'normal, logical' one. In fact, speakers often

seem unaware that these differences reflect different cultural values or, at least, different scales of values (for example, individualism versus collectivism). Thus, intercultural misunderstandings are interpreted as failures of communicative competence by the other party (in general, those who belong to the cultural minority), and these are then brandished as 'evidence' to reinforce negative stereotypes or to justify social exclusion.

In my research conducted in multilingual classrooms in Madrid, I found many examples of cross-cultural differences in interactions. The local teachers and even the students choose forms of address that are fairly symmetrical (through the mutual choice of the pronominal form *tú*, 'you'), and that illustrate a well-established trend in Spanish classrooms. However, this style of address conflicts with that normally encountered in the classrooms of Colombia, Ecuador and the Dominican Republic, which is where a significant number of the students are from. They remark that, in their countries, a politeness of deference and an asymmetric relation (marking social differences between participants, with some speakers in a superordinate position and others in a subordinate one) are prevalent in classrooms (Scollon and Scollon, 2001). In Spanish classrooms, though, teachers often resort to forms that are typical of the linguistic style of carers (see Wodak, 1986), such as '¿*Nos callamos?*' ('Can we have some quiet?'). The choice of this inclusive form makes the action of silencing the conversation seem to be a collective one, including the teacher in its scope. Newcomers might assign an incorrect value to this form of address, taking it as a contextual cue, which indexes a moment of relaxation or for play within the lesson. However, for the teacher, the expression 'Can we have some quiet?' is an order that must be obeyed. The same is true when s/he demands not to be 'cheeked' by choosing a colloquial register. Moreover, the value of these politeness resources changes, when the conflict develops. In all these cases, what the teacher is doing is giving orders. Certainly, the teacher's colloquial register may induce the students to say what they otherwise wouldn't dare, if asymmetries had been emphasized, with answers such as 'not now, teacher, this is important'. But, on the other hand, the students are well aware that, irrespective of the speech style employed, it is the teacher who has the authority; they realize that s/he is telling them to be quiet, even when the inclusive 'us' is chosen. In addition, they know the value of their replies, and they understand that their replies could heighten or resolve the conflict. It would be naive to believe these replies to be the product of a misunderstanding arising from cultural differences, and simplistic to deny the repercussions of these differences.

A careful analysis of speakers' choices and their interpretations reveals the risk of adopting an approach which contributes to an essentialist re-conceptualization of diversity. First, communicative styles and linguistic choices are presented as essential traits in the construction of cultural groups as homogeneous entities, suppressing differences among group members. Secondly, broad categories emerge from approaches like this, such as Asian or Southern European communicative styles, which are defined by a selection of what is considered to be 'essential' to the group and what is not. This view of diversity presents itself as a given entity, and ignores the fact that it is the product of power relations among individuals and groups, embedded in a particular context.

Thus, the issue is not merely the existence of cultural differences, but the fact that these are viewed and valued differently in asymmetric interactions. In the above examples, if the students, who are not native speakers of 'Castilian' Spanish, do not adapt to dominant systems of politeness within this institutional context, they risk reinforcing their image as being 'undisciplined' students, who are not legitimate participants in the class, with the subsequent impact on the teacher's expectations regarding these students and their academic results. Thus, focusing intercultural communication on purely linguistic elements is a reductionist attitude. Cross-cultural communication occurs, precisely, in spheres in which there are profound social differences and where the members of the host community are in a position of control (education, social services, health clinics), which is a factor that clearly restrains conversational dynamics (Ogbu, 1987; Singh, Lele and Martohardjono, 1988).

This role of members of the host society as gatekeepers in service encounters, in multilingual and multicultural settings, has received a great deal of attention in recent years. As Erickson (1975) found, discrimination in these encounters has a linguistic basis: members of a minority community require the approval of majority-community members to advance professionally. Various studies have investigated the impact of current social and cultural changes on the valuation and legitimizing of linguistic resources and practices (Heller, 2004, 2007; Blommaert, Collins and Slembrouck, 2005), in the same area as that of Sarangi and Roberts (1999), or more recently: Maryns (2006); Moyer and Martín Rojo, 2007; Codó (2008); and Valero Garcés and Martin (2008). However, few of these studies focused on the context of schools, apart from Pérez-Milans and Martín Rojo (2007), who showed that in the classroom, peers may assume the role of gatekeepers, obliging their classmates to speak standard Spanish, and that this communicative behaviour is linked to the perception of nationality.

Thus, there has occurred a critical shift in the field, one highlighting the role of communicative styles as a gatekeeper to education, and the role of larger social and economic differences in it: the styles demanded and imposed constrain the possibilities of success of those who are not familiar with them. In consequence, what is at stake is the production and distribution of linguistic resources in schooling. This shift reveals the complexity and significance of the role of linguistic practices as part of the stratification processes taking place in schools as well as the fact that, in order to understand this role, it is necessary to examine the process by which value is assigned to linguistic varieties and communicative practices. The analysis of linguistic practices reveals the active involvement of social agents (students and teachers, in this case) in the production and reproduction of (but also in challenging) the sociolinguistic order.

The impact of Bourdieu's work has been crucial in this change of viewpoint. Bourdieu explained just how schools perform the gatekeeping role, through processes that 'convert' economic relations into symbolic capital (Bourdieu 1977: 195). By means of this 'conversion', relations of dependence are presented as the consequence of inequalities of talent or educational ability. This is what happens in remedial and compensatory programmes, and others supposedly justified by the existence of 'different levels' or by a 'lack of knowledge'. The concepts of 'conversion' and 'capital' immediately bring to mind others proposed by Bourdieu: namely, those of 'value' and 'measure'. This value-giving process is inextricably bound to the representation of students as legitimate or non-legitimate participants in the classroom. Furthermore, social and cultural conditions are changing and there is currently a great deal of tension and contradiction in the valuation and legitimization of knowledge-capital, including languages. As Heller (1992, 1995) has shown, dominant groups rely on norms of linguistic resources and practices to maintain symbolic domination, while subordinate groups may use linguistic resources and practices, such as code-switching, to resist or redefine the value of symbolic resources in the linguistic marketplace.

The construction of social inequality within discursive practices

The third process remarked upon by discourse researchers is the construction of social inequality within discursive practices. Interactions may constitute, at given times, resources 'for constructing, levelling, contesting, and blurring boundaries in order to attempt to maintain, contest and modify relations of power' (Heller and Martín-Jones, 2001: 4). The analysis of local discursive practices shows how they are embedded and shape the social order (Martin-Jones, 2007:171 and ff.; for a review of current trends in discourse studies, see Martín Rojo, 2001). From this perspective, the analysis should go beyond the fine-grained scrutiny of language practices in educational settings in multilingual contexts, and thus distance itself from research into the characteristics of classroom interaction. This change in perspective entails a parallel change in the aim of research: not just to reveal interactional patterns or to investigate the acquisition process that takes place in the classroom (e.g. Sinclair and Coulthard, 1975; Gajo and Mondada, 2000; Nussbaum and Unamuno, 2006). According to this critical shift, the aim is rather to discover how linguistic resources are allocated and how this allocation affects the construction of inequalities. In fact, the relations constructed in the classroom cannot be understood in ignorance of the context of colonial processes, globalization and national and supranational ideologies and projects (Ramptom, 1995; Heller, 2006).

The guiding question in this overview, namely the extent to which the unequal yardstick applied to students' linguistic and cultural resources contributes to the construction of inequality, preceded a second one. The question, in this case, is to what extent are the cultural forms underlying this valuation of linguistic and cultural resources presented in schools as natural or given? Students' failures would thus be understood as the effect of their 'cultural' or 'linguistic' deficit instead of as the result of an unequal distribution of capital among different social classes and groups, established as the norm. From this point of view, education not only plays an essential part in the reproduction of social inequalities but also naturalizes and legitimates them (Bourdieu and Passeron, 1977). The reproduction of structures of domination in society therefore depends on the imposition of cultural values which are presented as universal but whose content and context are politically and historically determined – and therefore arbitrary. This process was termed 'symbolic violence' by Bourdieu, a form of domination that masks its concrete sources. The decision to tackle this second question had significant repercussions on research, because social agents' discourse representations and social practices were also to be analysed.

In fact, studies of naturalization and legitimization have led to the identification of a fourth process in the construction of inequality mediated by linguistic practices. Critical discourse analysis (CDA) has focused on the social construction of

the learner, particularly in textbooks in education (e.g. Peled-Elhanan, 2008), and in teachers' discourse and practices (e.g. Martín Rojo, 2008a, 2008 b). Similarly, contradictions in policies have been highlighted in the discourses of education planning and language pedagogy (e.g. Dendrinos, 1992, 2000).[3] 'Critical linguistic awareness' needs to be taken into the classroom (Fairclough, 1992), in order to integrate the characteristics of language in use in society, and to reveal the ways language works in relation to social mobility and other social processes. (For an overview of the contributions of this approach, see Rogers, 2004).

It should be taken into account, nonetheless, that it is also important to consider how social agents represent their role within schools. In fact, the very process of assigning value can only be understood in relation to a shared body of social representations. Thus, the view of students as being poorly educated and lacking competence, interest and motivation results in little effort being made to integrate their knowledge. These representations are presented as true – entering into the 'game of truth and falsehood', in Foucault's terms (see Foucault, 1994, Vol. 4: 670). Thus, discursive representations play a decisive role in the naturalization and legitimization of education policies and in the distribution of capital which takes place through their implementation. Analysis of these representations also highlights teachers' contradictions and unresolved dilemmas, together with students' search to discover just why they are where they are in the school. For an analysis of discursive representations, Foucault's concept of 'conditions of possibilities' has to be considered: What enables a particular understanding and representation of 'language', 'diversity as deficit' or 'education', at a particular time and in a particular place? Key issues are the conditions explaining how social change, like the increasing linguistic diversity in schools, has given rise to particular discourses and social representations. Specifically, we explore the sociocultural conditions that explain the emergence of discourses representing diversity as a deficit or as richness, and particular languages and knowledge as legitimate, and particular students as competent or skilful.

Thus, in our research conducted in Madrid schools (from 2000 to 2003), we found a distinction between 'our students' and 'immigrant students'. This category did not have clear boundaries and sometimes included naturalized citizens, second-generation students, while at other times it included only newcomers (see Luciak, 2004, for the use of this category in education in several European countries). The macro category 'immigrant students' seems to share some significant traits that specifically challenge the education system, if not actually representing a problem for it. However, over time, this single category no longer appears to be perceived as homogeneous, and some national and gender differences are established ('Moroccan students are the worst', 'Students from Ecuador have a very low level', 'Students from Eastern Europe are really, really good') (Martín Rojo et al., 2010). While fuzzy boundaries still exist, distinctions are made according to national or cultural origins, including differences in religion and language. These categories seem to present an explanatory power of students' school performance and skills as a process of ethnicization. Ethnicization is produced in discourse and generates knowledge about students, their capacities and communities. It has a crucial role in the legitimation of the implementation of some educational programmes and linguistic policies. This process also impacts not only on teachers' but also on students' expectations.

However, discourses and representations are not solely linked to domination, but also to 'colonization', i.e. what Goffman (1961) sees as the construction of a tolerable world within the interstices of managed time and space, and a 'situational withdrawal', refusing to behave as a capable agent is expected to do, and, moreover, with resistance. As observed by Scott (1990: xvi), this includes 'foot dragging, dissimulations, desertion, false compliance, pilfering, feigned ignorance, slander, arson, sabotage'. Examples can be found in interactions among peers, or when students respond to a teacher's indirect directive acts as if they were requests for information: 'What are you doing?' or 'Why don't you shut up?'. In these cases, the students may produce replies such as 'Looking for a pen' or 'Because it's important'. Thus, as Scott suggests, sometimes a direct symbolic confrontation with authority is avoided, and sometimes students do not fear confrontation. Covert resistance involves playing with the norm in order to mask resistance, creating ambiguity, and feigning enthusiasm to cooperate and participate in activities. D'Amato (1993: 187) labelled this attitude 'playful mischievous challenges' involving playing with legitimate performance parameters so as to produce actions which are legal in form but subversive in intent. Among these challenges, linguistic transgressions play a significant role, as the 'playful linguistic sabotage' studied by Jaspers (2005: 285), which involves exaggerated performances by Moroccan students of varieties of Dutch and was explicitly related to non-authenticity and juxtaposed ('*doing ridiculous*' vs '*talking serious*', in his terms), or language 'crossing', when speakers use a linguistic variety s/he is not expected to use (Rampton 1995: 299).

Both the 'conversion' of economic relations into symbolic capital and the production and legitimization of social representation are related to the social order they stem from and impact upon, and also to their inherent conflicts and inequalities. Both are core issues in the research of discourse and education, shaping the two processes I consider paramount to my interpretation of the data collected: namely, the 'decapitalization' and the 'hierarchization' of students. At the same time, the devaluation of other languages, knowledge and national/ethnic groups is also neutralized, resisted and even contested in classrooms.

24.3 LOCAL PRACTICES AND SOCIAL PROCESSES: THE DECAPITALIZATION OF STUDENTS

In this section, I focus on the process of students' decapitalization, through classroom interaction and discursive representations, as a key process in building inequality. The examples examined in this section illustrate how the dissimilar evaluation of languages and knowledge leads to students becoming decapitalized, such that their symbolic capital is considered inadequate in the construction of knowledge. I use the term 'decapitalization' to refer to acts by which capital is taken away and capital formation discouraged. This approach enables us to study how the valuation and distribution of capital take place within interactions, and the role of social agents in not just reproducing, but also challenging and resisting the value of symbolic resources in the linguistic marketplace. The term should be considered within the context of Bourdieu's theory of symbolic capital: on the one hand, so that we may further develop his metaphor of the market of symbolic resources; but on the other, in order to avoid his unified and static viewpoint. The concept of decapitalization also focuses on the practices through which the distribution of capital takes place and, in consequence, on processes of deprivation and constraints to capital formation.

I refer to the data compiled in the research projects conducted by the MIRCO team in Madrid.[4] We studied two educational linguistics programmes implemented in the Madrid region: the Spanish as a Second Language programme for newcomers, called Bridging Classes, and the English–Spanish bilingual programmes currently being implemented in public secondary schools, and particularly the programme run jointly by the Spanish Ministry of Education and Science and the British Council. This is a programme designed for compulsory education students (3–16 years old) where students learn curricular contents through two languages, English and Spanish.[5] Our main research goal was to explore how these two programmes are managed by the 'actors' involved: first, by the regional administration (concerning issues such as funding, training, planning, teacher training and other resources); secondly, by the schools (their involvement, and how the programmes stand in relation to all other activities at the school); thirdly, by the teachers (methods of language teaching, the integration of content and language learning, teachers' aims and expectations). Finally, we studied the students' progress, in order to discover which programmes, methods, practices and integration strategies are used to favour academic success and to integrate student diversity.

My analysis illustrates that linguistic order in the classroom is shaped by the distribution of capital, with power relations within the classroom setting, and within the social order itself.

In the first example (Example 1), I study what happens when Latin-American varieties of Spanish are located at the front-stage area in a History lesson at a Madrid secondary school.[6] (The code (*number*) refers to the discourse text following the "(letter a, b, c, ...)" in the excerpt).

(1)
1 *Profesor Genaro: ¿un producto que gracias a consumirle / que era barato / que dabas muchas energías y permitía que la gente no pasase hambre y por tanto no cogiera pestes y en-/ enfermedades y virus de todo tipo? / ¿eh? / a partir del siglo dieciocho / un producto que se con- / que se consigue en América y se establece en Europa / permite que todo el mundo pueda comer lo mínimo y tener las calorías suficientes como para poder resistir //*
2 *Jose: ¡pan! / no*
 (...)
3 *Brian: ¡patata!*
4 *Alumnos: ¡patata!*
5 *Profesor Genaro: PATATA! O BANANA *1* / ¿eh? / [risas]*
6 *Jorge: banana [risa]*
7 *Profesor Genaro: ¡no la *2* banana es el plátano! / *3* perdón! / ¡la PATATA! / ¿otro nombre de patata que *4* tenéis en América? /*
8 *Paola: ¡papa!*
9 *Estudiantes: ¡las papas! /*
10 *Jorge: papa [risas]*
11 *Profesor Genaro: las papas*
 (...)
12 *Michael: ¡ las patatas no son papas!*

(1)
Teacher Genaro: something that when it was eaten / it was cheap / and gave you lots of energy and meant people didn't go hungry and so didn't catch germs and ill-/ illnesses and viruses of all kinds? / eh?

/ from the eighteenth century / something that you f-/ that you find in America and that was brought to Europe / it allows everyone to eat just a little and have enough calories so they can keep going //
 2 Jose: bread! / no
 (...)
 3 Brian: potatoes!
 4 Students: potatoes!
 5 Teacher Genaro: POTATOES! OR PLANTAIN PLANTAIN / eh? /
 [laughter]
 6 Jorge: plantain [laughter]
 7 Teacher Genaro: no a plantain is a banana! / sorry! / a POTATO! / another name for potato that you have in America? /
 8 Paola: spud!
 9 Students: spuds! /
 10 Jorge: spud [laughter]
 11 Teacher Genaro: spuds
 (...)
 12 Michael: potatoes aren't spuds![7]

In this example, the teacher uses a Latin American expression *'banana'* instead of *'plátano'*, the normal term in the Madrid region. In *1* in turn 5, he makes a mistake, and the students laugh, *'banana'* is not a synonym of *'patata'* (potato). In line 13, the teacher corrects himself, evoking the local norm: 'a plantain is a banana'. In *2* in 7, he then seeks to incorporate other lexical variants. The pronominal choice shows that this strategy is only apparently inclusive: 'another name for potato that *you* have in America'. As a result, he divides the class between himself, the (Spanish) teacher, and the (Latin American) students, and national identities are highlighted. In line 17, we see that the teacher's inclusion of linguistic differences is considered by the students as something exceptional, and they greet this with laughter. In line 12, a student corrects the teacher: 'potatoes aren't spuds!'. We can see, then, to what extent this inclusion challenge the traditional teacher-centred order in the class, given that when these non-standard forms are included, the student can correct the teacher, and thus the asymmetry between the two is reduced. We can also see how knowledge asymmetries are levelled. The teacher cannot continue to present himself as the only source of knowledge. Students' voices have a place in the front stage.

In Example 2, we see how, when migrant languages appear in the lesson, something similar is happening. Here, migrant languages are located in the back stage area, and are exchanged among students quickly, in low voices. In this case, the use of Arabic marks a distinction between the organization of an activity (the instructions, the tools), and the task (answers to the questions and exercises) (for similar uses of code-switching among peers, see Nussbaum and Unamuno, 2006; Unamuno, 2008). This use also illustrates how students seek cooperation, and often a guide (interaction between an expert and a learner), that they do not find in front-stage activities in the classroom, and which the teacher does not provide.

(2)

1 Aisha: {to Amina}! أشنو هي؟
{transliteration: ashnu hiya?}
translation: what is it?

2 Amina: {to Aisha} قالت ليك تكتب بروفيسيونس
{transliteration n: qaleṭ lik ṭekṭeb profesiones}
translation:: she told you to write down the jobs}

3 Aisha: {to Amina} !!!!!!! أشنو؟ ما فهمتش هنا. شنو نكتب؟
{transliteration: Ashenu? Ma-fehemeṭ-sh hena. Shenu nekṭeb? Ahhhh.}
{translation: what? I didn't understand that. what do I write? Ahhhhh.}

4 Amina: {to Aisha} ما مفهومش
{transliteration:}
{translation: incomprehensible}[8]

In example 2, students use migrant languages as a strategy to improve their performance in the classroom and to gain capital. This linguistic choice shows how they seek to cooperate with the teacher and are open to learning. However, as in Example 1, the inclusion of these languages challenges the traditional teacher-centred order in the class. When they are included, the student gets help from her peers and thus the teacher–student asymmetry is reduced, as are knowledge asymmetries. When students' voices have a place in the front-stage area, (monolingual) teachers cannot continue to present themselves as the only source of knowledge.

However, the monolingual norm imposed in Madrid classrooms neutralizes these challenges, relegating migrant varieties to the back stage. This imposition is naturalized and legitimized through the lower evaluation granted to migrant languages as an instrument of communication, but also as a learning tool. In this case, a decapitalization process took place through the imposition of a monolingual norm: competence in the language of instruction is required and is a key factor in achieving integration within the school and in society in general. Indeed, speaking Spanish is one of the most important membership criteria to be considered a Spaniard. However, the access to this capital is restricted. And, as the linguistic choice in Example 2 shows, subordinate groups may use linguistic resources and practices, such as code-switching, to gain capital, or even to resist or redefine the value of symbolic resources in the linguistic marketplace.

In contrast to the increasing multilingual order, a monodialectal and monolingual norm was built up through interaction. I observed three interactional patterns. The first, and often the most common, pattern is the explicit or implicit rejection or negative evaluation of the use of other languages, by means of directive acts, such as 'not Chinese / eh ?/, only in Spanish /'. The second pattern is the teachers' lack of response (indifference), as in Example 2, in which the students' languages are not integrated into the class but retain a position of non-focal side-play. Rarely did I find inclusive responses such as those reported by Mondada and Gajo (2001: 250) in the *classes d'accueil* in Switzerland, where together with the rule 'say it in French', the teachers allow the use of migrant languages in eliciting exchanges in order to facilitate the task or to reduce tension in students with interventions like: 'say it in your language' or 'try … it doesn't matter', 'say it, even though it's wrong'. As a result, 'migrant' languages are made invisible and minorized.

The sociolinguistic order which emerges from the English–Spanish bilingual instruction programmes in Madrid illustrates to what extent this monolingual norm depends on the evaluation of languages.

(3)

1 **Teacher**: ok can-can we can we read it aloud and … . So / let me

2 (18)

3 **Teacher**: ok? Right?

4 **Female Student**: empiezo

5 Translation.: Shall I start?

6 **Teacher**: You want to begin? Ok perfect

7 **Female Student**: {she starts to read} Drake wasn't just an explorer[9]

If we compare Examples 2 and 3, extracted from a different language educational programme, a similar interactional pattern appears, with code-switching taking place in events programmed by the teacher. Students resort then to patrimonial migrant languages, migrant languages in Example 2 and to the national and official language in Example 3, particularly when the teacher explains the day's agenda, an exercise, the meaning of a term, or transition points between tasks. In both cases, code-switching is a strategy for self-facilitation, in order to follow the activities. However, a significant difference is apparent: while in Example 2, these sequences occur in parallel conversations between peers; in Example 3, the teacher can be addressed in a language different from that of the language of instruction (line 4), but which, as the patrimonial and national language, is shared by all the participants.

The third pattern I detected was the teacher's exceptional suspension of the monolingual norm. In this case, the dissimilar valuation of languages also contributes to explaining these transgressions. In Example 4, Mandarin Chinese is allowed in the front-stage area.

(4)

1 ShiQing: and 差多少毛？/ 我不知道路差多少毛
{trasliteración: cha duoshao mao? and / wo bu zhidao lu cha duoshao mao}
{traducción: ¿más o menos a cuánto está de distancia? / yo no sé a cuánto está}
2 Investigador Miguel: 啊！/ 我不知道 我也不知道
{trasliteración: ah! / wo bu zhidao wo ye bu zhidao}
{traducción: ¡ah! / no lo sé / yo tampoco lo sé}
3 Amina: *1* ¡español / chino no!
4 Investigador Miguel: [(())]
5 Profesora Vistoria: *2* {a Fátima} [aquí se permite]
6 Investigador Miguel: {a la profesora} [está cerca de shanghai]
7 Amina: *3* [¡aquí no se permite!]
8 Profesora Victoria: está cerca de Shanghai

1 ShiQing: and 差多少毛？/ 我不知道路差多少毛
{transliteration: cha duoshao mao? and / wo bu zhidao lu cha duoshao mao}
{translation: roughly how far is it? / I don't know how far}
2 Researcher Miguel: 啊！/ 我不知道 我也不知道
{transliteration: ah! / wo bu zhidao wo ye bu zhidao}
{translation: ah! / I don't know / I don't know either}
3 Amina: *1* Spanish! / not Chinese!
4 Researcher Miguel: [(())]
5 Teacher Victoria: *2* {to Amina} [here it's allowed]
6 Researcher Miguel: {to the teacher} [it's near Shanghai]
7 Amina: *3* [it's not allowed here]
8 Teacher Victoria: it's near Shanghai.[10]

The researcher's competence in Mandarin and his status as a legitimate member of the class modified the value assigned to the migrant language and challenged the monolingual norm. Mandarin appears in the front stage, but not to help the students follow the activity (with translations of the topics and of the instructions given), but to establish closer interpersonal relations. In *1* in line 3, the student demands the use of the monolingual norm, as the teacher does when other languages are involved. Amina chooses a chain of directive speech acts: 'Spanish; not in Chinese'. In *2* in line 5, the teacher takes the floor to re-establish her authority to implement the

norm: 'Here, it's allowed'. Amina's response, in line 9, appears to stem from the arbitrary way the norm is applied, since the use of a particular migrant language and the exclusion of others causes ill-feeling amongst the students. This example shows to what extent the inclusion or exclusion of migrant languages from the front stage is related to the status of the speaker and the valuation of the language(s) in question.

The same may be observed with respect to the Spanish language in the bilingual programme. In this case, as in other bilingual programmes (Lin, 2008), the patrimonial language is introduced by the teachers themselves in disciplinary or procedural sequences. In the data we compiled, it is apparent that the monolingual norm can be suspended by the teacher when so required for the purposes of the language programme.

(5)

1 **Teacher:** what about modern times let me think What did you understand tell me that in Spanish // what did you understand by modern times
2 **David:** Now
3 **Students:** now
4 **Teacher:** now ok that's the problem because this part of history we are studying is called Modern history.[11]

The sociolinguistic order in the Spanish as a Second Language programme is different from that found in the English–Spanish bilingual programme. In the former, the prevalent interactional patterns, disapproval and indifference, relegate other languages to the back stage of the class, delegitimizing them, and contribute to reinforcing asymmetries in the classroom. The imposition of a monolingual norm not only reflects the adoption of an asymmetrical and traditional educational model but also constitutes resistance to changes in the social, linguistic and cultural make-up of the student body. In the English–Spanish bilingual programme, however, Spanish is omnipresent in the lessons taught in English, as usually happens when the aim of such a programme is to teach a language different from that of the community (see Lin, 2008: 274, for similar examples). Both languages are legitimized as a language of instruction. Spanish is legitimate for explaining procedures, for negotiating relationships and for ensuring understanding; i.e. it functions as a community language.

The previous examples highlight that the 'valuation' of the different linguistic varieties plays a key role in explaining the sociolinguistic order within classrooms. Only linguistic varieties which are highly valued – being 'well-mannered', 'appropriate' and 'useful' – as a tool for integration, are allowed on front stage in the lessons.

In Example 6, this hierarchization of language is linked to a ranking of students, as more or less competent.

(6)

1 **Teacher Elena**: [they're very good at-] you know/
they're very good
at the- I'm a language teacher / right?// well they're really (*1*) very good at spoken language
// you've heard all the // Bolivians and- or- they speak [fantastic/ (*2*) better than our students]

2 **Chairperson Cristina**: [the Colombians do speak so well / don't they? / (())]

3 **Teacher Elena**: =but nevertheless then / when it comes to writing //skills and such /
terrible/ I mean/ terrible// starting with the *3*problems of **seseo** or not / well our students from here / even the ones from Andalusia / myself, I'm from Andalusia they don't have it // from a very young age it's corrected / they don't / don't- don't manage to -> //
they're in the fourth grade and they still have this problem // I mean // *4* it's really hard
for them / to express ideas / eh and- well/ our Spanish students do too / but really //.[12]

The teacher's line of argument begins with superlative and comparative (*1*, *2*) structures (very ... better than), which explicitly affirm the superiority of the Latin American students' oral skills and the superiority of American varieties of Spanish. Such superlatives and comparisons implicitly presuppose the existence of an 'us' ('our students') and a 'them', created, among other elements, on the basis of linguistic differences – 'they' speak better than 'our students'. In this excerpt, however, a counter-argument is begun, from the use of the **discursive marker** 'but'; superlative and comparative structures remain, but they are now used to point out the lack of competence of these same students in writing skills.

'Problems' arise from the *seseo* (i.e. the lack of distinction between /θ/ and /s/) that the teachers cannot manage to 'correct' (*3*). This linguistic difference presents consequences for the school: as many studies have revealed, the written language is considered the model of legitimate language.

In the arguments deployed, two generalizing moves are present. First, with respect to the student body: the teacher extends her judgements, relating these particular students to the entirety of Latin American students. And secondly, that of skills – from excellence in oral skills, the focus switches to the lack of ability at writing. Subsequently, what seems to be a spelling problem becomes an inability to express oneself (*4*). In this final equivalence, established through the

connector 'I mean', we again encounter some of the traits, attributed to Latin American students, related to two features of colonial narrative (Mignolo, 1998; Castro-Gómez, 2002). The colonization of geographic space is maintained, thus pointing to the notion of European centrality. As observed by Moreno Cabrera, colonialism remains in the area of language which is no longer possible in a political context (Moreno and Carlos, 2008: 133).

Migrant linguistic varieties are kept off-stage. Thus, the representation of students as being poorly educated and lacking competence, interest and motivation results in little effort being made to integrate their knowledge and languages. Social representations of this kind are widespread in society, and are also shared by some teachers. It should be noted, however, that in interactions it is difficult to ascertain just what exactly the students' representations are, as shared by teachers. However, interviews and focus group discussions, where speakers are confronted with their representations and the ideologies shaping them, reveal more elaborate representations. Moderators and interviewers have also attempted to arrive at the reasoning underlying the legitimization of the answers given. Thus, argumentation schemes have emerged to explain, question and legitimize everyday classroom practices and representations, regarding the academic integration of students from migrant backgrounds.

In analysing these code-switching instances, as a contextualization cue (Gumperz, 1982: 131), it is revealed that the interpretation of this linguistic element is not necessarily shared by all the participants in the class (Martín Rojo, 2009). In relation to the use of migrant languages in the Spanish short-term immersion programme, for students, migrant languages are a tool to follow that activity, and to carry out tasks more efficiently. In this way, code-switching shows students' interest and involvement. When migrant languages are evoked in peer interactions, this means that the student needs help or is trying to be more efficient. Thus, other students must be ready to provide assistance. For teachers, it apparently indexes just the opposite, being considered a side-play event, one showing that students are not following the activity, and that they are trying to subvert the class. Although code-switching sequences among peers would seem to indicate that something had not been understood or that instructions have to be clarified in order to carry out tasks, teachers in these classes do not perform clarification or comprehension checks ('Have you got any questions? Haven't you understood?'), or reformulations (such as the use of synonyms or paraphrasing to illustrate terms or uses that might not have been understood).

The lack of adaptation to linguistic diversity revealed by our analysis of interactional local practices not only reflects the existence of a monolingual order despite the emergence of multilingual practices in classrooms. What seems to be significant is that the inclusion of some linguistic varieties, and the exclusion of those other than the local language of instruction, produces a decapitalization of students. Their participation in classroom activities is limited, their competences in other languages are ignored, and the access to learning tools is restricted. Thus, the building of a monolingual norm points to a monolingual understanding of linguistic competence by means of which languages are not seen as tools for learning other languages or for improving performance in class. This is possible in the context of very traditional educational models, characterized as being teacher-centred, highly asymmetrical, non-cooperational, and so forth.

24.4 SCHOOL AND SOCIAL MOBILITY

The panorama presented above shows that it is not sufficient to demonstrate the existence of an unequal valuation of linguistic varieties; we must also attempt to understand why it occurs. This question immediately takes us away from a culturalist-oriented approach, by which educational success and failure are related to cultural and linguistic differences, to consider instead how the latter diverge from what is viewed as 'normal' at school. On asking why this unequal yardstick is applied, it is necessary to adopt a sociohistoric standpoint, examining migratory flows, the creation of minority populations and the process(es) by which a population evolves. Moreover, it involves taking a socio-institutional standpoint, focusing on the functioning of the school system itself and on the possibilities offered to students. An approach like this avoids the dangers of 'tunnel vision', in Erickson's terms, which focuses so closely on specific features of talking that the global aspects of talk's ecologies are overlooked (2004: 108). Such an approach builds upon prior work aimed at connecting linguistic variability with the ways in which schools act as institutions of social selection (e.g. Erickson, 1998, 2004; Erickson and Shultz, 1982; Gumperz, 1982, 1986; Hymes, 1974; and Duff, 2002[13]).

In this chapter, I discuss how the distribution of symbolic resources accounts for those who are integrated into school but at the same time marginalized, in the context of late modernity and the increasing flow of population from Third-World countries towards the ever more fortified promised lands of Europe and North America. The role of the school is analysed in a socio-demographic context that threatens the previous cultural dominance and homogeneity. In the case of Spain there seems to be occurring, moreover, a progressive ethnic stratification of the job market and of society as a whole (Cachón, 2002). Schools seem to be influencing this stratification, given the rising dropout rate of the immigrant population at the conclusion of compulsory education, and of their premature entry into the job market as unskilled labour (Serra, 2007). Following Rampton (1995), the present overview tells us a great deal about contemporary society. Social class identities do not seem to have lost their significance, and remain intertwined with ethnic and national identities. Thus, by focusing on language-in-education practices, a window is opened onto wider social, political and ideological processes (Martin-Jones, 2007: 174–8).

An analysis focusing on the distribution of symbolic capital through classroom interaction also points to a dominant, although not completely closed, homogeneous market. The linguistic, cultural and curricular order is not only reproduced but also contested (Woolard, 1985; Martin-Jones, 2007: 173). Finally, symbolic domination, exercised through the devaluation of other languages, can also be neutralized, resisted and even contested in classrooms (see, Heller, 2006; Martín Rojo, 2009).[14]

ACKNOWLEDGEMENT

The author wishes to acknowledge the suppport received from the Ministerio de Ciencia e Innovación, Plan Nacional de la Ciencia I+D+I through project HUM2007-64694/FILO, 'School and multilingualism: a critical sociolinguistic study on educational linguistic programmes set in the Madrid Region'.

NOTES

1 The R and D research project, 'School and multilingualism: a critical sociolinguistic study on educational linguistic programmes set in the Madrid Region (HUM2007-64694/FILO)'.

2 The designation of these varieties as 'migrant varieties' or 'migrant languages' is preferable to more traditional ones such as 'home languages', or more recently coined ones like 'community languages', which are increasingly used within the EU (McPake et al., 2006). The latter term refers to all languages used in EU countries that do not possess an officially recognized status (see Baker and Jones, 1998; Corson, 1999; Wiley 2001, 2005).

3 For a review of the findings of CDA in educational research, see Rogers et al., 2005.

4 The group I lead, MIRCO (Multilingualism, Social identities, Intercultural communication and Relationships), has conducted several studies since 1990. The data used in this paper come mainly from the two latest research projects, 'Socio-pragmatic analysis of intercultural communication in educational practices: toward integration in the classroom' (BFF 2003-04830), and 'School and multilingualism: a critical sociolinguistic study on educational linguistic programmes set in the Madrid Region' (HUM2007-64694/FILO).

5 The Bilingual Schools Project is the Ministry of Education (MEC) and the British Council joint programme which aims to 'provide students from the age of three to sixteen with a bilingual, bi-cultural education through an integrated Spanish/English curriculum', according to the guidelines for the development of the integrated curriculum in secondary education. (MEC/ British Council)

6 Transcription conventions are:

7 *Ethnographic observation and recording by Patiño Santos [1d_E220104S1].*

8 *Ethnographic observation and recording by*

{}	Comments made by the transcriber
and	Turn latched to previous turn
=	Maintaining of a participant's turn in an overlap
[]	Turn overlapping with similarly-marked turn
-	Re-starts and self-interruptions without any pause
/	Short pause (0.5 seconds)
//	Long pause (0.5–1.5 seconds)
(5")	Silence (lapse or interval) of 5 seconds. When it is particularly meaningful, the number of seconds is indicated in pauses longer than 1 second
RIGHT	Loud talking
(())	Non-understandable fragment
pa'l	Syntactical phonetic phenomena between words
()°	Quiet talking

Pérez-Milans [3v_V200404A-C].

9 Corpus MIRCO 2-bilingual programme.

10 *Ethnographic observation and recording by Pérez-Milans [3d_V090605DS].*

11 Corpus MIRCO-2, bilingual programme.

12 *Focus group of school Principals [1a_080606GD].*

13 In particular, Duff's research shows that the ethnography of communication is a viable, context- and culture-sensitive method for recognizing the role of participation in language-mediated activities in students' development as fully competent members of mainstream classes, in which for them the language of instruction is a second language (Duff, 2002).

14 The analysis of contestation also puts into question a reading of Bourdieu's analysis of the education field, by which he is purported to be a structuralist, allowing no room for other factors or any individual agency. This theoretical point neutralizes the potentially deterministic nature of Bourdieu's work.

REFERENCES

Baker, C. and Jones, S. P. (1998) *Encyclopedia of Bilingual Education and Bilingualism*. Clevedon, UK: Multilingual Matters.

Baugh, J. (1988) 'Language and race: some implications for linguistics science', in F. Newmeyer (ed.), *Linguistics: The Cambridge Survey*. Vol. 4, *Language. The Socio-Cultural Context*. Cambridge: Cambridge University Press. pp. 64–74.

Bekemans, L. and Ortiz de Urbina, J. (1997) *The Teaching of Immigrants in the European Union. Working Document*. Luxembourg: European Parliament. Education and Culture Series. EDUC 100 EN.

Bernstein, B. (1975) *Class, Codes and Control: Towards a Theory of Educational Transmission*. London: Routledge and Kegan Paul.

Blommaert, J., Collins, J. and Slembrouck, S. (2005) 'Spaces of multilingualism', *Language and Communication*, 25(3): 197–216.

Bourdieu, P. (1977) *Outline of a Theory of Practice*. Cambridge: Cambridge University Press.

Bourdieu, P. and Passeron, J.-C. (1977) *Reproduction in Education, Society and Culture*. Tr. Richard Nice. London: Sage.

Cachón, L. (2002) 'La formación de la 'España inmigrante': mercado y ciudadanía', *Revista Española de Investigaciones Sociológica*, 97: 95–126 (en www.cis.es).

Cameron, D. (1992) 'Globalization and the teaching of "communication skills"', in D. Block and D. Cameron (eds), *Globalization and Language Teaching*. New York: Routledge. pp. 67–82.

Cameron, D. (2000) *Good to Talk? Living and Working in a Communication Culture*. London: Sage.

Canagarajah, A. S. (1999) *Resisting Linguistic Imperialism in English Teaching*. Oxford: Oxford University Press.

Canagarajah, A. S. (2002) Globalization, methods, and practice in periphery classrooms. In Block, D. and Cameron, D. (eds) (2002) *Globalisation and Language Teaching*. London: Routledge.

Castro-Gómez, S. (2002) '*Latinoamericanismo, modernidad, globalización: prolegómenos a una crítica postcolonial de la razón*' [Latin-Americanism, Modernity, Globalization: *Introduction to a Post Colonial Critique of Reason.*] (http:www.ensayo.rom.uga.edu/teoria/castro/castroG.htm)

Cicourel, A. (2002) 'Organisation et communication en régime de surcharge cognitive' [Discourse and organizational practices in the workplace: coping with 'normal' task interruptions and 'cognitive overload'], *Actes de la Recherche en Sciences Sociales*, 143: 3–17.

Codó, E. (2008) *Immigration and Bureaucratic Control. Language Practices in the Public Administration.* Berlin: Mouton de Gruyter.

Corson, D. (1999) 'Community-based education for indigenous cultures', in S. May, (ed.), *Indigenous Community-Based Education.* Clevedon, UK: Multilingual Matters. pp. 8–19.

Cummins, J. and Hornberger, N. H. (eds) (2008) *Encyclopedia of Language and Education.* Vol. 5, *Bilingual Education.* 2nd edn. New York: Springer.

d'Amato, J. (1993) 'Resistance and compliance in minority classrooms', in E. Jacob and J. Cathie (eds), *Minority Education. Anthropological Perspectives.* London: Ablex. pp. 181–207.

Dendrinos, B. (1992) *The EFL Textbook and Ideology.* Athens: Griva.

Dendrinos, B. (2001) Linguoracism in European foreign language education discourse. In M. Riesigl and R. Wodak (eds), *The Semiotics of Racism: Approaches in Critical Discourse Analysis,* 177–198. Vienna: Passagen Verlag.

Dendrinos, B. (2005) *Conflicting Ideologies in Discourses of Resistance to the Hegemony of English.* São Paulo: Parábola Editorial.

Duchêne, A. (2009) 'Marketing, management and performance: multilingualism as commodity in a tourism call centre', *Language Policy,* 8: 27–50.

Duchêne, A. and Heller, M. (forthcoming) *Language, Ideologies and the New Economy.*

Duchêne, A. and Heller, M. (in progress) *Pride and Profit. Language in Late Capitalism.*

Duff, P. (2002) 'The discursive co-construction of knowledge, identity, and difference: an ethnography of communication in the high school mainstream', *Applied Linguistics,* 23(3): 289–322.

Erickson, F. (1975) Gatekeeping and the melting pot: interaction in counseling encounters. *Harvard Educational Review,* 45(1): 44–70.

Erickson, F. (2004 [1998]) *Talk and Social Theory.* Cambridge: Polity Press. (1st edn, 1998.)

Erickson, F. and Shultz , J. (1982) *The Counsellor as Gatekeeper: Social Interaction in Interviews.* New York: Academic Press.

European Parliament Resolution (1987) 'On the languages and cultures of regional and ethnic minorities in the European Community', *Official Journal of the European Communities,* No C 318, 30.11.1987. pp. 160–4.

EURYDICE (2004) *The Academic Integration of the Immigrant Student Body in Europe.* Brussels: Bruselas Eurydice. European Commission: http://eurydice.org.

EURYDICE (2006) *Content and Language Integrated Learning (CLIL) at School in Europe.* European Commission: http://www.eurydice.org/ressources/eurydice/pdf/0_integral/071EN.pdf

Extra, G. and Verhoeven, L. (eds) (1993) *Immigrant Languages in Europe.* Bristol: Multilingual Matters.

Fairclough, N. (1992) *Discourse and Social Change.* Cambridge: Polity Press.

Fairclough, N. and Wodak, R. (1997) 'Critical discourse analysis', in T. van Dijk (ed.), *Discourse as Social Interaction.* London: Sage. pp. 258–84.

Foucault, M. (1994) 'Le souci de la verité' [The concern for truth], in D. Defert, and F. Ewald (eds), *Dits et Écrits.* Vol. 4. Paris: Gallimard. pp. 668–78.

Gajo, L. and Mondada, L. (2000) *Interactions et Acquisitions en Contexte. Modes d'appropiation de Compétences Discursives Plurilingues par des Jeunes.* [*Interactions and Acquisitions in Context. How Young People Acquire Plurilingual Discourse Competence.*] Fribourg: Editions Universitaires.

García, O. and Baker, C. (eds) (2007) *Bilingual Education. An Introductory Reader.* Clevedon, Buffalo and Toronto: Multilingual Matters. pp. 137–44.

Giddens, A. (1984) *The Constitution of Society: Outline of the Theory of Structuration.* Cambridge: Polity Press.

Goffman, E. (1961) *Asylums: Essays on the Social Situation of Mental Patients and other inmates.* New York: Doubleday.

Gumperz, J. (1982) *Discourse Strategies.* Cambridge: Cambridge University Press.

Gumperz, J. (1986) 'Interactional sociolinguistics in the study of schooling', in J. Cook-Gumperz (ed.), *The Social Construction of Literacy.* New York: Cambridge University Press. pp. 45–68.

Gumperz, J. (1989) *Engager la Conversation.* [*Engaging in Conversation.*] Paris: Les Editions de Minuit. Collection 'Le Sens Commun'.

Gumperz, J. and Roberts, C. (1979) *Crosstalk. A Study of Cross-Cultural Communication.* The National Centre for Industrial Training by BBC Continuing Education Department.

Heller, M. (1992) 'The politics of codeswitching and language choice', in C. Eastman (ed.), *Codeswitching.* Clevedon, UK: Multilingual Matters. pp. 123–42.

Heller, M. (1995) 'Language choice, social institutions and symbolic domination', *Language and Society,* 24(3): 373–405.

Heller, M. (2003) 'Globalization, the new economy, and the *commodification* of language and identity', *Journal of Sociolinguistics,* 7(4): 473–92.

Heller, M. (2004) 'Pratiques et structuration à l'école en milieu multilingue' [School practices and structuration in a multilingual context]', *Sociolinguistica,* 18: 73–85.

Heller, M. (2006) *Linguistic Minorities and Modernity: a Sociolinguistic Ethnography.* London: Longman. 2nd. edn. London: Continuum. (1st edn, 1999.)

Heller, M. (2007) 'Distributed knowledge, distributed power: a sociolinguistics of structuration', *Text and Talk,* 27(5, 6): 633–53.

Heller, M. and Martin-Jones, M. (eds) (2001) *Voices of Authority: Education and Linguistic Difference.* Westport, CT: Ablex.

Hymes, D. (1974) *Foundations in Sociolinguistics: An Ethnographic Approach.* Philadelphia: University of Pennsylvania Press.

Jaspers, J. (2005) 'Linguistic sabotage in a context of monolingualism and standardization', *Language and Communication,* 25(3): 279–97.

Jensen, A. (1969) 'How much can we boost IQ and scholastic achievement?', *Harvard Educational Review,* 39: 1–123.

Kasper, G. and Blum-Kulka, S. (eds) (1993) *Interlanguage Pragmatics*. Oxford: Oxford University Press.

Kroch, A. and Labov, W. (1972) 'Linguistic Society of America: resolution in response to Arthur Jensen (1969)', *Linguistic Society of American Bulletin*. March. Washington, DC: Linguistic Society of America.

Labov, W. (1972) 'The logic of nonstandard English', in W. Labov (ed.), *Language in the Inner City: Studies in the Black English Vernacular*. Philadelphia: University of Pennsylvania Press. pp. 200–40.

Lin, A. M. Y. (2008) 'Code-switching in the classroom: research paradigms and approaches', in A. Creese, P. Martin and N. H. Hornberger (eds), *Encyclopedia of Language and Education*. Vol. 9. 2nd edn. New York: Springer Science. pp. 3–14.

Lin, A. and Martin, P. (2005) 'From a critical deconstruction paradigm to a critical construction paradigm: an introduction to decolonisation, globalisation and language-in-education policy and practice', in A. Lin and P. Martin (eds), *Decolonisation, Globalisation. Language-In-Education Policy and Practice*. Clevedon, UK: Multilingual Matters.

Luciak, M. (2004) 'Migrants, minorities and education. Documenting: discrimination and integration in 15 member states of the E.U.', report submitted by European Monitoring Centre on Racism and Xenophobia (EUMC). Luxembourg: Office for official publications of the European Communities.

McCall, L. (2007) 'The complexity of intersectionality', *Journal of Women in Culture and Society*, 30.02005 1771–1800. 26 Nov 2007. Available at: http://www.journals.uchicago.edu/doi/pdf/10.1086/426800?cookieSet=1.

Macedo, D., Gounari, P. and Dendrinos, B. (2003) The hegemony of English. Boulder, CO: Paradigm.

McPake, J., Waldemar M., Aarts, R., et al., (2006) *Community Languages in Europe: Challenges and Opportunities*. Manuscript.

Martin-Jones, M. (2007) 'Bilingualism, education, and the regulation of access to language resources', in M. Heller (ed.), *Bilingualism: A Social Approach*. New York: Palgrave. pp.161–82.

Martín Rojo, L. (2001) New developments in discourse analysis: Discourse as social practice. *Folia Linguistica* 35(1 & 2), 41–78.

Martín Rojo, L. (2008a) 'Imposing and resisting ethnic categorization in multicultural classrooms', in R. Dolón and J. Todolí (eds), *Analysing Identities in Discourse*. Amsterdam: John Benjamins.

Martín Rojo, L. (2008b) 'Competent vs. incompetent students: polarization and social closure in Madrid schools', in G. Delanty, P. Jones, and R. Wodak (eds), *Identity, Belonging, and Migration*. Liverpool: Liverpool University Press.

Martin Rojo, L. (2009) *Constructing Inequality in Multilingual Classrooms*. Berlin: Mouton de Gruyter.

Martín Rojo, L., A. M. Relaño and I. Rasskin (2009) 'Who is a "legitimate participant" in multilingual classrooms? Essentializing and naturalizing culture', in L. Martin Rojo (ed.), *Constructing Inequality in Multilingual Classrooms*. Berlin: Mouton de Gruyter.

Maryns, K. (2006) *The Asylum Speaker. Language in the Belgian Asylum Procedure*. Manchester: St. Jerome.

May, S. and Hornberger, N. H. (2007) *Encyclopedia of Language and Education*. Vol. 1. *Language Policy and Political Issues in Education*. 2nd edn. New York: Springer.

McPake, J., Waldemar M., Aarts, R., et al., (2007) *Valuing all languages in Europe*. Strasbourg: Council of Europe/ Graz: European Centre for Modern Languages.

Mignolo, W. (1998) 'Globalization, civilization process, and the relocation of languages and cultures', in F. Jameson and M. Miyoshi (eds), *The Cultures of Globalization*. Durham, NC: Duke University Press.

Mijares, L. (2006) *Aprendiendo a ser marroquíes. Inmigración, diversidad lingüística y escuela*. [*Learning to be Moroccan. Immigration, Lnguistic Diversity and Schools*.] Madrid: Ediciones del Oriente y del Mediterráneo.

Mondada, L. and Laurent, G. (2001) Bilingual resources of migrant students and their role in classroom interactions. In Monica Heller and Marilyn Martin-Jones (eds), *Voices of Authority: Education and Linguistic Difference*, 235–69. Westport: Ablex.

Moreno C. and Carlos, J. (2008) *El nacionalismo Lingüístico. Análisis crítico*. [*Linguistic Nationalism. A Critical Analysis*.] Barcelona: Península.

Moyer, M. G. and Martín Rojo, L. (2007) 'Language, migration and citizenship: new challenges in the regulation of bilingualism', in M. Heller (ed.), *Bilingualism: A Social Approach*. Palgrave: Macmillan. pp. 137–60.

Negri, A. and Hardt, M. (2000) *Empire*. Cambridge, MA: Harvard University Press.

Nussbaum, L. and Unamuno, V. (2006) 'Les compétences comunicatives multilingues' [Multilingual communicative competence], in L. Nussbaum, and V. Unamuno (eds), *Usos i competències multilingües entre escolars d'origen immigrants*. [*Multilanguage Uses and Competences among Students of Immigrant Origin*.] Barcelona: Universitat Autònoma de Barcelona.

Ogbu, J. U. (1987) 'Variability in minority school performance: a problem in search of an explanation', *Anthropology and Education Quarterly*, 12(1): 2–29.

Ogbu, J. U. (1993) 'Variability in minority school performance: a problem in search of an explanation', in E. Jacob and C. Jordan (eds), *Minority Education: Anthropological Perspectives*. Norwood, NJ: Ablex. pp. 83–111.

Peled-Elhanan, N. (2008) 'The denial of Palestinian national and territorial identity in Israeli schoolbooks of history and geography 1996–2003', in R. Dolón and J. Todolí (eds), *Analysing Identities in Discourse*. Amsterdam: John Benjamins.

Pennycook, A. (1999) *English and the Discourses of Colonialism*. New York: Routledge.

Pennycook, A. (2000) 'English, politics, ideology: from colonial celebration to postcolonial performativity', in T. Ricento (ed.), *Ideology, Politics and Language Policies: Focus on English*. Amsterdam: John Benjamins. pp. 107–19.

Pérez Milans, M. and Martín Rojo, L. (2007) 'Barreras interaccionales en aulas multilingües: una aproximación crítica a la comunicación intercultural', [*Interactional Barriers in*

Multilingual Classes: A Critical Approach to Intercultural Communication] *Revista Cultura, Lenguaje y Representación*, 4: 203–26.

Phillipson, R. (1992) *Linguistic Imperialism*. Oxford: Oxford University Press.

Phillipson, R. and Skutnabb-Kangas, T. (1999) 'Englishisation: one dimension of globalisation, English in a changing world', in D. Graddol and U. H. Meinhof (eds), *English in a Changing World*. AILA Review. Oxford: Catchline/AILA. pp. 19–36.

Rampton, B. (1995) *Crossing: Language and Ethnicity among Adolescents*. London: Longman.

Rassool, N., Canvin, M., Heugh, M., and Mansoor, S., (2007) *Global Issues in Language, Education and Development. Perspectives from Post-Colonial Countries*. Clevedon: Multilingual Matters.

Rogers, R. (2004) (ed.), An introduction to *critical discourse analysis* in education. Mahwah, NJ: Lawrence Erlbaum.

Sarangi, S. and Roberts, C. (1999) (eds) *Talk, Work and Institutional Order. Discourse in Medical, Mediation and Management Settings*. Berlin: Mouton de Gruyter.

Scollon, R. and Scollon, S. (1981) *Narrative, Literacy and Face in Interethnic Communication*. Norwood, NJ: Ablex.

Scollon, R. and Scollon, S. W. (2001) *Intercultural Communication: A Discourse Approach*. 2nd edn. London: Blackwell. (1st edn, 1995.)

Scott, J. (1990) *Domination and the Arts of Resistance: Hidden Transcripts*. New Haven, CT: Yale University Press.

Serra, C. and Palaudàrias, J. M. (2007) L'alumnat de nacionalitat estrangera en els estudis postobligtoris [Students with a foreign background in secondary education]. In Jesús Larios and Monica Nadal (dirs.), *L'estat de la immigració a Catalunya. Anuari* 2006 [The state of education in Catalonia. 2006 survey], 301–334. Barcelona: Mediterrània.

Sinclair, J. and Coulthard, M. (1975) *Towards an Analysis of Discourse*. Oxford: Oxford University Press.

Singh, R., Lele, J. and Martohardjono, G. (1988) 'Communication in a multilingual society: some missed opportunities', *Language in Society*, 17: 43–59.

Singy, P. and Trudgill, P. (1997) 'Communication et pragmatique interculturelles', *Journal de l'Association Suisse de Linguistique Appliquée*, 65: 9–24. Neuchâtel: Institut de Linguistique de l'Université de Neuchâtel.

Skutnabb-Kangas, T. (2007) 'Linguistic human rights in education?', in O. García and C. Baker (eds), *Bilingual Education. An Introductory Reader*. Clevedon, Buffalo and Toronto: Multilingual Matters. pp. 137–44.

Skutnabb-Kangas, T. (2008) *Linguistic Genocide in Education–or Worldwide Diversity and Human Rights?* New Delhi: Orient Longman. http://www.orientlongman. com/search.asp?txt1=Tove&list1=2&B1=SEARCH

Unamuno, V. (2008) 'Multilingual switch in peer classroom interaction', *Linguistics and Education*, 19(1): 1–19.

Valero Garcés, C. and Martin, A. (2008) (eds) *Crossing Borders in Community Interpreting: Definitions and Dilemmas*. Amsterdam: John Benjamins.

Watts, R. (2008) 'The price of English in Switzerland: deconstructing language ideologies'. *Farewell Lecture University of Berne*. May 2008.

Wierzbicka, A. (1991) *Cross-Cultural Pragmatics: the Semantics of Human Interaction*. Berlin: Mouton de Gruyter.

Wiley, T, G., (2001) On defining heritage languages and their speakers. In J. Kreeft, D. A. Ranard and S. McGinnis (eds), *Preserving a National Resource*, 29–36. Washington, DC and McHenry, IL: Center for Applied Linguistics and Delta Systems.

Wodak, R. and Muriel S., (1986) *The Language of Love and Guilt. Mother-Daughter Relationships from a Cross-Cultural Perspective*. Amsterdam: John Benjamins Publishing.

Woolard, K. (1985) 'Language variation and cultural hegemony', *American Ethnologist*, 12: 738–48.

25

Courtroom Discourse

Susan Ehrlich

25.1 INTRODUCTION

A recurring theme in the study of courtroom discourse has been the role of language and linguistic practices in the creation and maintenance of social power in the courtroom. For example, early research in the area, conducted by O'Barr (and others) in the United States (e.g. Conley, O'Barr and Lind, 1978; O'Barr and Atkins, 1980; O'Barr, 1982) and by Wodak in Austria (e.g. Wodak, 1981, 1985), found that linguistic variation in witness testimony was socially-conditioned and that this socially-conditioned variation influenced the decision-making of judges and juries. In particular, witnesses who produced linguistic variables that correlated with social powerlessness (e.g. the working class), as opposed to social power, were generally found to be less credible in the eyes of the law.[1] Among the methodologies adopted by O'Barr and Wodak in their investigations of courtroom discourse was variationist analysis, i.e. correlating linguistic variables found in witness testimony with social factors such as class, educational background or sex. Indeed, Conley and O'Barr (1998: 63) remark that when they first began their collaborative research on courtroom discourse, they were very much influenced 'by sociolinguistics' then-current focus on the social conditioning of language variation'. While subsequent work by Conley and O'Barr – and by other investigators of courtroom discourse – has not generally adopted a variationist approach to sociolinguistics, Conley and O'Barr's research

in the 1980s continued to examine the social consequences of witnesses' linguistic practices, taking larger linguistic units (i.e. narratives) into consideration. Their 1990 book (Conley and O'Barr, 1990), for example, demonstrated that litigants in small claims court who structured their legal problems according to the logic of the law ('rule-oriented' accounts) – as opposed to the logic of morality ('relational' accounts) – were more comprehensible to judges and thus more likely to receive rulings in their favour. And, according to Conley and O'Barr (1998: 73), the ability to recount legal problems according to the logic of the law is intimately connected to social power: 'the crucial factor associated with this skill is exposure to the culture of business and law'.

Research in the 1980s not only investigated the talk of courtroom witnesses, as Wodak's and Conley's and O'Barr's did, but also examined talk that was **co-constructed** by lawyers and witnesses. In particular, this research developed typologies of question types used by lawyers in both direct- and cross-examination (e.g. Danet, Hoffman, Kermish, Rafn and Stayman, 1980; Harris, 1984; Philips, 1987; Walker, 1987; Woodbury, 1984), with the aim of determining the extent to which lawyers' questions could constrain or control witnesses' answers and, by extension, impose lawyers' interpretations or words on witness testimony (Woodbury, 1984: 199). Since the vast majority of research in courtroom discourse has, since the 1980s, focused on the

interaction between lawyers and witnesses as well as how this interaction **constructs** the various versions of events that emerge in trial contexts, the remainder of this chapter will also focus on these two dimensions of courtroom discourse.[2] The research that I report on draws from a range of methodologies. For example, much of the literature describing the interaction between lawyers and witnesses employs methods from conversation analysis (CA), given CA's concern with the sequential aspects of interaction (see Schegloff, 2007), and from pragmatics, given pragmatics' concern with meaning in context (see Levinson, 1983). And, much of the literature describing the way courtroom language constructs 'facts' in the courtroom employs methods from critical discourse analysis (CDA), given CDA's emphasis on the constitutive nature of discursive practices (see Fairclough and Wodak, 1997). I close the chapter by returning to the issue of language and social power in the courtroom.

25.2 QUESTIONS AND ANSWERS IN COURTROOM DISCOURSE

Like much work on institutional discourse, investigations of courtroom discourse have devoted a great deal of attention to the study of questions and answers. This is perhaps not surprising given that the primary discursive activity within trials is the examination of witnesses – direct examination or examination-in-chief, cross-examination and re-examination. Adversarial dispute resolution, of which trials (in the Anglo-American common law system) are a notable example, requires that two parties come together formally, typically with representation (e.g. lawyers), to present their (probably different) versions of the dispute to a third party (e.g. judge, jury, tribunal) who hears the evidence, applies the appropriate laws or regulations, and determines the guilt or innocence of the parties. Lawyers have as their task, then, that of convincing the adjudicating body that their (i.e. their client's) version of events is the most credible. Apart from making opening and closing arguments, however, lawyers do not themselves testify. Rather, it is through the posing of questions that lawyers must elicit, from witnesses, testimony that will build a credible version of events in support of their own clients' interests in addition to testimony that will challenge, weaken and/or cast doubt on the opposing parties' version of events.[3] Atkinson and Drew (1979: 70) note that while trial discourse is conducted predominantly through a series of question–answer sequences, other actions are accomplished in the form of such questions and answers. For example, in cross-examination, questions may be

designed to accuse witnesses or to challenge or undermine the truth of what they are saying. To the extent that witnesses recognize these actions are being performed in questions, they may design their answers as rebuttals, denials, justifications, etc.[4]

Atkinson and Drew (1979) have called the question–answer turn-taking system characteristic of the courtroom 'turn-type pre-allocation', indicating that the types of turns participants can take are predetermined by their institutional roles. Indeed, for many scholars in CA, what distinguishes ordinary conversation from institutional discourse is this 'direct relationship between status and role, on the one hand, and discursive rights and obligations, on the other' (Drew and Heritage, 1992: 49). In courtrooms, for example, lawyers have the right to initiate and allocate turns by asking questions of witnesses but the reverse is not true; witnesses are obligated to answer questions or run the risk of being sanctioned by the court. An important dimension of this kind of turn-type pre-allocation, according to Drew and Heritage (1992: 49), is the interactional control it bestows upon questioners: answerers, typically laypeople, have little opportunity to initiate talk, while questioners, typically institutional representatives, are able 'to gain a measure of control over the introduction of topics and hence of the "agenda" for the occasion'. Discussing doctor–patient interactions, Drew and Heritage note that the question–answer sequences that characterize most such interactions not only allow doctors to gather information from patients but can also result in doctors' directing and controlling the talk: introducing topics, changing topics, and selectively formulating and reformulating the terms in which patients' problems are expressed.

Within the context of the courtroom, the discursive power afforded to questioners (i.e. lawyers) is most extreme, many researchers (e.g. Conley and O'Barr, 1998) have argued, in cross-examination. While direct examination is typically characterized by relatively open-ended questions (Barry, 1991; Maley, 1994; Woodbury, 1984) that ostensibly encourage and facilitate witness testimony, the closed-question forms of cross-examination have been said to control witnesses in at least two ways: (1) they impose lawyers' own (i.e. their clients') version of events on evidence and (2) they restrict the types of answers witnesses can logically provide. Not surprisingly, these features of cross-examining questions correspond to what Gibbons (2003: 97) has said are the two goals of cross-examining lawyers: (1) constructing a particular version of events (i.e. that of their own clients) for the benefit of judges and juries[5] and (2) committing an opposing witness to this particular version of events.

Syntactic form of questions

Given that the **form** of questions is closely related to the issue of interactional control, a number of researchers (e.g. Danet et al., 1980; Harris, 1984; Philips, 1987; Walker, 1987), as noted above, have developed taxonomies of questions used in the courtroom based on the extent to which a question's syntactic form logically constrains or limits a witness's response – this is associated with the second of Gibbons' functions identified above. For example, in Danet et al.'s (1980) taxonomy, the most 'coercive' of question types is the declarative question (e.g. 'As a matter of fact, you signed that letter, didn't you?') because its form functions to severely restrict the expected response. First, it is a question that expects a 'yes' or 'no' answer, what Raymond (2003) calls a 'type-conforming response'; secondly, its declarative form and negative tag (i.e., its 'preference' organization in the terms of conversation analysis) favours a 'yes' (as opposed to a 'no') response. By contrast, what Danet et al. call the imperative question (e.g. 'Tell us what took place at the meeting with the patient') is the least 'coercive' of question types within their taxonomy because it imposes few constraints on the form of the expected response. While Danet et al. (1980) found 'coercive' questions to be more frequent in cross-examination than in direct examination, the effectiveness of coercive questions in influencing the responses of witnesses varied. That is, although coercive questions were found to restrict the **form** of responses (i.e. they elicited shorter responses, for example, 'yes' or 'no'), they did not necessarily elicit the response that was 'preferred' by the design of the questions. For example, a declarative question with a negative tag (e.g. 'As a matter of fact, you signed that letter, didn't you?') was just as likely to receive a 'no' response (i.e. a dispreferred response) as it was to receive a 'yes' response (i.e. a preferred response).

The use of 'coercive' questions in the courtroom has also been connected to lawyers' ability to impose their (i.e. their clients') interpretation of events on evidence for the benefit of judges and juries – this is associated with the first of Gibbons' functions identified above. As Gibbons (2003: 98) says, 'one way of constructing a particular version of events during questioning is to include elements of this desired version of the events in the questions'. Indeed, Woodbury (1984) developed a taxonomy of question types that classifies questions according to questioners' ability to 'control' information. 'Control', according to Woodbury (1984: 199), refers 'to the degree to which the questioner can impose his [sic] own interpretations on evidence'. (Note that while Woodbury's principle of categorization differs from the one used by Danet et al., which categorizes question types according to their expected responses, the two taxonomies essentially categorize questions in the same way in the sense that the most 'coercive' of question types are also the most 'controlling' of question types, etc.) Within Woodbury's continuum of 'control', a broad *wh*-question such as 'And, then what happened?' displays little control because it functions to impose little of the questioner's interpretation or words on the testimony: there is no proposition contained within the *wh*-question other than the notion that 'something happened'. (Notice that this *wh*-question would also not be 'coercive' within Danet et al.'s taxonomy.) By contrast, a question such as 'You were attracted to Brian, weren't you?' (which Woodbury calls a prosodic yes–no question and Danet et al. call a declarative question) displays more control (and is more coercive) than a *wh*-question because it contains a more substantive proposition – that the addressee was attracted to Brian. It is in this respect that prosodic yes–no questions (or declarative questions in Danet et al.'s taxonomy) are more 'controlling' than broad *wh*-questions or imperative questions: they make available to third-party recipients (i.e. judges and/or juries) the questioner's interpretation of events, irrespective of the addressee's answer. Indeed, for Conley and O'Barr (1998: 26), 'controlling' questions are instrumental in transforming cross-examination 'from dialogue into self-serving monologue'.

The following two examples from a Canadian sexual assault trial (Ehrlich, 2001) show a cross-examining lawyer asking the complainant 'controlling' questions in Woodbury's sense. As Woodbury suggests, these types of questions have the function of imposing a particular interpretation on the events in question: in this case, that the events in question were not sexual assault but rather were consensual sex. (SC is the cross-examining lawyer and CD is the complainant.)

1. SC: And all of this happened fairly quickly. Again, I realize it's ridiculous to suggest that you are looking at a watch, but I take it that we've got this ongoing behaviour, that it's so physical that you are in no position to leave or do anything?
   CD: That's right. I mean, before I could be in a position to pick up a phone to, to leave, I had to be in a position to move and I wasn't. So before thinking of I have to pick up the phone and I have to walk out the door, I had to think of how am I going to get out from underneath this man.
   SC: Right. Did you try to push him off?
   CD: Yes, I did.
   SC: You weren't able to?
   CD: No, I wasn't.
   SC: Is that because you weren't able to get your arms free or because he was on top of you?

CD: I couldn't get my arms free and I couldn't push him off.
SC: At one point you were naked?
CD: Yes.
SC: At what point was that?
CD: I can't even pinpoint a specific time.
SC: *Well, your shirt came off first as a result of the fondling of your breasts, right?*
CD: Yes.

2. SC: And there was no response to that because he just kept going as if he never even heard it?
CD: That's right.
SC: So did you realize that it was so futile at that point that you wouldn't try and do anything at this point?
CD: At that point is when he grabbed my hair and wrapped it around his hands and pushed my face down between his legs and gave me an ultimatum. At that point that became the more pressing matter to get out of that situation more than to get him out of my room.
SC: *So in fact was the fellatio, was that the last act of sex that was between the two of you before everything died down and before Mr. A. went to sleep and you went into the chair?*
CD: Yes.

In both of these examples, CD is describing sexual acts of aggression committed by the accused: in Example 1, the situation CD describes is one in which the accused is on top of her as she attempts (unsuccessfully) to push him off; in Example 2, the situation CD describes is one in which the accused forces her to perform oral sex on him. By contrast, the italicized questions in Examples 1 and 2 ('controlling' questions in Woodbury's sense) show the cross-examining lawyer reformulating the complainant's version of events so that the accused's responsibility for these acts of sexual aggression is obscured and/or so that the events in question are represented as consensual sex. For example, the italicized question of Example 1, *Well, your shirt came off first as a result of the fondling of your breasts, right?*, contains both an unaccusative construction,[6] *your shirt came off*, and a nominalization, *fondling*. Both of these constructions allow the accused's agency vis-à-vis these acts to be obscured; moreover, the word, *fondling*, represents the acts as affectionate and consensual sex. In a similar way, the italicized question of Example 2, *So in fact was the fellatio, was that the last act of sex that was between the two of you before everything died down and before Mr. A. went to sleep and you went into the chair?* transforms CD's representations of the accused's violent acts (i.e. *At that point is when he grabbed my hair and wrapped it*

around his hands and pushed my face down between his legs and gave me an ultimatum) into a scene of non-violent and consensual sex. That is, what CD describes in the language of coercion and force is characterized by SC as *the last act of sex*. Atkinson and Drew (1979: 180) have argued that cross-examining lawyers will design their questions so as to repeat some aspects of the cross-examined witnesses' version of events, while 'retaining the crucial features' of their clients' own version of events. This is precisely what we see in the italic questions of Examples 1 and 2. The cross-examining lawyer designs his utterances so as to represent the events described in the complainant's prior talk, but obscures/discards crucial aspects of her rendition of events – specifically, that the accused was the agent of sexually violent and aggressive acts. Moreover, the cross-examining lawyer is successful in committing CD to these reformulations even though they are more compatible with the accused's defence strategy than they are with the complainant's charges of sexual assault.

While the examples above show the complainant **assenting** to the version of events put forward by the cross-examining lawyer, Danet et al.'s (1980) study, as noted above, demonstrates that coercive or controlling questions do not necessarily produce the responses that are favoured by their preference design. For example, in excerpt Example 3 below, CD denies the damaging characterization of her behaviour – that she did little to resist the accused's sexual aggression – contained within SC's controlling question (what Woodbury calls a prosodic yes–no question).

3. SC: So do I take it then – correct me if I am wrong – that the only effort that you would have made to try and jolly him out of this or have him leave was to say that 'I have a class in the morning so you'll have to leave' or words to that effect?
CD: No. That was not the only effort I made with regards to making him stop doing what he was doing. It may have been the only time that I outright said, "Now you have to leave," but I certainly did make it clear beforehand.

Given the possibility that witnesses may deny these kinds of damaging formulations (contained within controlling questions), Gibbons (2003: 101) has commented that a 'particularly clever … technique for controlling information' is the use of questions with presuppositions because the information content of presuppositions is 'difficult to challenge'. Presupposition is a term used by linguists 'to refer to propositions whose truth is taken for granted in the utterance of a linguistic expression' (Green, 1996: 72). For example, the sentence 'John realizes that Mary is seriously ill' presupposes the truth of the proposition 'Mary is seriously ill'. That is, in uttering such a sentence, the speaker takes for granted that the proposition 'Mary is seriously ill' is assumed knowledge between speaker and addressee, forming the background for the assertion 'John realizes X'. By contrast, the sentence 'John thinks that Mary is seriously ill' does not presuppose the truth of the proposition 'Mary is seriously ill'. The speaker who utters such a sentence does not take for granted or assume that 'Mary is seriously ill'; in fact, the sentence could be appropriately produced by a speaker who knows the embedded proposition to be false. What these two examples demonstrate is that certain linguistic constructions (e.g. the predicate 'realize' in 'John realizes that Mary is seriously ill') act to trigger presuppositions whereas others do not (e.g. the predicate 'think' in 'John thinks that Mary is seriously ill'). Indeed, a variety of linguistic forms (e.g. words, phrases, syntactic constructions) have been isolated as sources of presuppositions and thus designated as 'presupposition-triggers' (Levinson, 1983).

One of the defining features of presupposition is its ability to remain constant or true under negation and interrogation. Thus, like the sentence 'John realizes that Mary is seriously ill', both its negative – 'John doesn't realize that Mary is seriously ill' – and interrogative – 'Does John realize that Mary is seriously ill?' – versions presuppose the proposition 'Mary is seriously ill'. This ability to survive negation and interrogation has consequences for the way presuppositions 'control' information in the courtroom. While controlling questions make available to third-party recipients certain propositions, they do not presuppose or even assert these propositions. That is, by definition, a question always contains a variable or unknown quantity, which the addressee of a question is being asked to supply (Lyons, 1977). And, as we have seen, the damaging information contained within cross-examining lawyers' controlling questions can be denied. By contrast, propositions that are **presupposed** by linguistic expressions cannot be denied (easily) and thus are made available to judges and juries, even if the primary proposition of a question is denied.

Consider the following example from Eades' (2008) analysis of a preliminary hearing in the Pinkenba case, an Australian case in which six police officers faced criminal charges for allegedly abducting three young Australian Aboriginal boys. (The police officers were charged with 'unlawful deprivation of liberty'.) According to Eades, even though the three Aboriginal boys were not themselves on trial (but rather served as prosecution witnesses in the state's case against the six police officers), their evidence was so undermined by the defence that 'the magistrate not only dropped the charges against the police officers, but also devoted a considerable part of his decision to delivering a negative evaluation of the character of the boys' (Eades, 2008: 3). As the following example demonstrates, representing the boys as criminals was one of the strategies employed by the defence in its attempt to discredit the boys' testimony.

> 4. DC1: What sort of things did you steal – when you were wan-prowling around the streets?
>   Barry: (3.5) Just purses.

Significant about Example 4 for the current discussion is the fact that the *wh*-question presupposes that Barry *prowled around the streets*, even though in previous testimony Barry had rejected the verb, *prowl*, as a way of describing what he and his friends used to do. And, because Barry answers the question in a direct way, the presupposition that Barry *prowled around* is confirmed. What we see here, then, is the cross-examining lawyer communicating damaging evidence in the form of a presupposition and, given that presuppositions, by definition, are never the primary focus of questioning, Barry has difficulty denying this particular piece of evidence. In the words of Luchjenbroers and Aldridge (2007), the lawyer has managed to 'smuggle' information into the context of the court proceedings.

The power of answers to 'control' information

The claim that 'asking questions amounts to interactional control' (Eades, 2008) is a pervasive one in the literature courtroom discourse, but it is not a claim that has gone unchallenged. Eades (2000), for example, questions the idea that the syntactic form of questions has any predictable effect on the form of responses. Based on a study of Aboriginal witnesses in Australian courts, Eades (2000: 171) determined that coercive or controlling questions were often interpreted by witnesses as 'an invitation to explain some situation or present a narrative account'. Ultimately, Eades (2000: 189) concludes that 'witnesses are not necessarily constrained or controlled by question-type'. In a similar way, Matoesian (2005: 621) challenges the assumption that 'questions … are more powerful than answers', arguing that such an assumption 'risks the problem of reifying structure'.

> Just as we assume questions do more than merely question (for instance in court they may work as accusations, etc.), why presume any less of answers (which may recalibrate the question, produce

a new question and so on)? A more detailed consideration of answers and how they function in detail may demonstrate just how powerful they are (Matoesian, 2005: 621).

Drew (1992) provides precisely this kind of 'detailed consideration of answers' in his analysis of a rape victim's cross-examination. In particular, Drew shows how the complainant (i.e. the rape victim) in this particular trial often produced 'alternative descriptions' in her answers – descriptions that contested the cross-examining lawyer's version of events. That is, rather than providing 'yes' or 'no' answers to the cross-examining lawyer's yes–no questions (i.e. type-conforming answers to questions), the complainant provided competing descriptions that transformed the lawyer's damaging characterizations into more benign ones. In Example 5 below, for example, the cross-examining lawyer, through the use of 'controlling' questions, attempts to represent the events that preceded the alleged rape as precursors to a consensual sexual relationship.

5. 16 A: Well yuh had some uh (p) (.) uh fairly
        lengthy conversations with the defen-
   17   dant uh: did'n you?
   18   (0.7)
   19 A: On that evening uv February fourteenth?
   20   (1.0)
   21 W: We:ll we were all talkin.
   22   (0.8)
   23 A: Well you kne:w, at that ti:me. that the
   24   defendant was. in:terested (.) in you (.)
   25   did'n you?
   26   (1.3)
   27 W: He: asked me how I'(d) bin: en
   28   (1.1)
   29 W: J- just stuff like that

While the lawyer's questions in lines 16–17 and 23–25 suggest that there was a closeness or intimacy developing between the defendant and the complainant, Drew argues that the complainant's answers, although not containing any 'overt correction markers' (Drew, 1992: 487), do not support this version of events. Rather, the complainant provides answers that depict a lack of intimacy between the complainant and the defendant: i.e. a scene in which there were a number of people who *were all talkin* and in which the defendant issued a greeting that was more friendly than intimate. What is significant about Drew's analysis for the present discussion is the fact that the answerer is shown to 'control' evidence (in Woodbury's sense) by resisting and transforming the (pseudo)assertions contained in the lawyer's questions. In fact, Drew comments explicitly on the need to be attentive to the way that competing descriptions from witnesses may influence

third-party recipients, in this case, juries: 'the complainant's attempts to counter the lawyer's descriptive strategies, and hence herself control the information which is available to the jury, should not be overlooked' (Drew, 1992: 517).

A similar finding is reported by Galatolo and Drew (2006) in the context of a 1998 Italian criminal trial. They found that expanded answers to yes–no questions (i.e. answers that 'control' evidence to some extent) were in fact more frequent than 'yes' or 'no' responses in this particular trial and that when the expanded answers were preceded by the expected 'yes' or 'no' response they rarely received negative sanctions. By contrast, if witnesses produced expanded answers without first answering 'yes' or 'no' they were more likely to be sanctioned. For Galatolo and Drew (2006: 688), then, expanded answers preceded by yes/no responses represent a valuable conversational resource for witnesses to resist the interactional control of questioners: expanded answers permit 'witnesses to respect the constraints imposed by the form of … questions and, at the same time, to gain a conversational space in which *they can exert a partial control over … information*' (emphasis added).

A more dramatic example of an answerer's interactional resistance can be seen in Ehrlich and Sidnell's (2006) study of a 2001 Canadian public inquiry where a prominent politician consistently challenged the damaging presuppositions encoded in cross-examining lawyers' questions. Because the politician was **not** compelled to produce type-conforming responses to yes–no questions (i.e. 'yes' or 'no'), Ehrlich and Sidnell (2006: 674) argue that he was able to address the presuppositions of questions directly, 'either challenging their status as appropriately presupposed or denying the presuppositions themselves'. For example, in the following excerpt (Example 6), the ex-premier of Ontario, Michael Harris, is asked a question that presupposes that he did not intervene in the business plan process for the Ministry of Environment. Notice that the question (in lines 49–52) contains the predicate, 'have regret', which like the predicate, 'realize' (discussed above), presupposes the truth of its complement clause.

6. 49 M: knowing what you know no:w (.)
   50   do you have any **regret** in not
             interve:ning in the business plan
   51   p-process and saying: you're
             go:ing:
   52   too fa:r.
   53 Harris: Well:you assumed that I didn't
             intervene
   54   in the business process and I think
   55   that's-that's not an assumption you
             ought

56	to make.=I have <u>no</u> concern ah: that- that everybody involved in the
57	business planning process didn't take
58	their job seriously,
59	an didn't do ah-an honest, conscientious <u>job</u>. of assessing
60	potential risks,
61	identifying them, and assessing them.

3 (1.6)
4 AM: I was not uhfraid of him (.) no (.) I was not uhfraid of (him)
5 RB: That's not my question Miss Mercer, you understand my question?
6 (.) my question is did you meet this man (.) who your friend says
7 is the alleged rapist?
8 (0.6)
9 AM: Yes.

If Harris had answered (or had been forced to answer) the question in lines 49–52 with a 'yes' or 'no' response (i.e. with a type-conforming response), the presupposition – that he had not intervened in the business plan – would have remained intact. This presupposition, in turn, would have implicated Harris in the water contamination scandal that the public inquiry was set up to investigate. Recognizing the potential damage of the lawyer's presupposition, Harris withholds a type-conforming response to the question and instead explicitly challenges the presupposition, characterizing it as an 'assumption' that the lawyer ought not to make (lines 55–56). On the basis of these kinds of examples, Ehrlich and Sidnell (2006: 655) argue that Harris managed to 'usurp control over the topical agenda of the proceedings'.

There are two points that are important to make about this particular study and its finding that answerers are able to assume the interactional control normally associated with questioners in institutional discourse. First, as Eades (2008: 154) points out, this particular witness may be somewhat unique in the sense that he had 'remarkable astuteness and ability to challenge presuppositions', an ability that may be connected to 'his experience as a leading politician'. By contrast, witnesses without comparable experience may not be able to resist presuppositions in the same way.[7] Secondly, while Ehrlich and Sidnell conclude that Harris's ability to control 'the topical agenda of the proceedings' was a function of his not being compelled to produce type-conforming responses to questions, in many trials witnesses **are** compelled to produce type-conforming responses. Indeed, the Italian study by Galatolo and Drew (2006), as noted above, found that witnesses who provided expanded answers to yes–no questions that were **not** preceded by a type-conforming response were negatively sanctioned. The example below, from Matoesian's (2001) analysis of the William Kennedy Smith rape trial, provides an illustration of such a negative sanction: the witness initially produces an expanded answer to the cross-examining lawyer's yes–no question but is subsequently forced to produce a type-conforming response.

7. 1 RB: You meet up with this man who your
2 friend says is a rapist isn't that correct.

According to Matoesian's analysis, in this example the cross-examining lawyer, Roy Black, is attempting to create an inconsistency between the fact that Ann Mercer (a witness for the rape victim, Patricia Bowman) was told that William Kennedy Smith had raped her friend yet, at the same time, was willing to enlist his help in order to find Patricia Bowman's shoes. The establishment of such inconsistencies was a recurring theme in Roy Black's questioning of both Patricia Bowman and Ann Mercer and was meant to undermine the claim that William Kennedy Smith had raped Patricia Bowman. By answering Roy Black's first question above (in lines 1–2) with a non type-conforming response, Ann Mercer (in line 4) fails to confirm the presupposition contained within Black's question – that Bowman had told Mercer that Smith was a rapist. Since this presupposition is crucial to Black's establishment of the inconsistent nature of Mercer's behaviour (and, more generally, to Black's strategy of calling into question Bowman's accusation of rape), he forces Mercer to answer the question directly, that is, to produce a type-conforming response that leaves the presupposition of his question intact. On the basis of examples such as this one (in contrast to those like Example 6 above where a witness is **not** forced to produce type-conforming responses), Ehrlich and Sidnell (2006: 655) conclude that the power of cross-examining lawyers does not derive solely from their ability to ask controlling and restrictive questions of witnesses, 'but rather is crucially dependent on their ability to compel witnesses to produce type-conforming answers to these controlling and restrictive questions'.

25.3 CONSTRUCTING AND CONSTITUTING 'FACTS' IN THE COURTROOM

As noted above, the adversarial nature of the Anglo-American legal system means that various versions of events will emerge within the context of a trial as the prosecution and the defence each attempt to put forward an account of the events that will support their own clients' interests. The trial, therefore, provides a good illustration of the role of language in constructing and constituting different kinds of social realities. Put somewhat differently, lawyers, through their questions, and witnesses, through their answers, do not simply describe events in a transparent and straightforward way: they are actively involved in shaping and 'building the character' of those events (Hutchby and Wooffitt 1998: 228). Duranti (1994: 4–5) elaborates on this view of language as constitutive of social realities:

> Reality is routinely negotiated by participants in an interaction and "facts" are constituted differently according to the points of view of the actors involved, the norms evoked, and the processes activated within specific institutional settings (e.g. legal, medical, educational). This view does not imply that there is no reality outside of talk or that all interpretations are equally acceptable, but rather it holds that in institutional as well as in mundane settings various versions of reality are proposed, sustained or challenged precisely by the language that describes or sustains them and that such negotiations are not irrelevant linguistic games but potentially important social acts.

While the previous section of this chapter discussed the ways that both lawyers and witnesses can potentially control evidence through their questions and answers respectively, this section considers the ways that linguistic features of such questions and answers help to build the 'facts' of legal cases for the benefit of judges and juries. And, given the **adversarial** nature of courtroom discourse, it is perhaps not surprising that these 'facts' come to be built differently depending on the interests and points of view of the parties involved. In Examples 1 and 2 above, for instance, the lexical and syntactic features of the cross-examining lawyer's questions function to construct the events as consensual sex, whereas those of the complainant construct these same events as coerced sex. (e.g. *So in fact was the fellatio, was that the last act of sex that was between the two of you before everything died down.* versus *At that point is when he grabbed my hair and wrapped it around his hands and pushed my face down between his legs and gave me an ultimatum.*)

Lexical items and the construction of 'facts'

That lexical items designating objects and events in a trial can constitute the 'facts' of cases differently is convincingly demonstrated by Danet (1980) in her analysis of a Massachusetts trial in which a Boston obstetrician–gynecologist was charged with manslaughter for performing a late abortion. Focusing on the ways that the prosecution and the defence named and categorized the aborted entity, Danet illuminates the strategic significance of such choices. Because a conviction of manslaughter was dependent on proving that the doctor had 'killed' the foetus, the prosecution consistently used terms that presupposed the foetus to be a 'living' entity, terms such as *baby*, *child* and *little baby boy*. By contrast, the defence used terms such as *foetus* and *product of conception* as a way of communicating that the aborted entity had no independent life and therefore could not be 'killed'.

Cotterill (2003) also examines the strategic use of lexical items within trial contexts; in particular, she analyses the 'connotational and collocational properties of the lexical items selected' by the prosecution and the defence in the opening statements of the O. J. Simpson trial. Cotterill argues that lawyers exploit these features of lexical items in order to create for the jury 'a particular conceptualization of the trial events and personalities' (Cotterill, 2003: 67). Indeed, the prosecution in the O. J. Simpson case 'conceptualized' O. J. Simpson as a violent and aggressive husband, whose long history of abuse of Nicole Brown Simpson 'culminated in the double murder of Nicole Brown and Ron Goldman in a jealous rage killing' (Cotterill, 2003: 68). According to Cotterill, this particular portrayal of O. J. Simpson resulted from a series of 'significant lexical choices' in the prosecution's opening statement. First, the word *control* was used 66 times in the opening statement, with O. J. Simpson as its agent and Nicole Brown Smith as its recipient. An examination of the collocational profile of the word *control* (i.e. a profile of words that typically co-occur with *control*) showed that the sorts of people who are typically agents of the verb are those with some official authority to do so. And, the kinds of entities that are typically the recipients of the verb are 'things that represent a danger or a negative influence of some kind' (Cotterill, 2003: 72). Because O. J. Simpson was not in an official position to control Nicole Brown Simpson (i.e. husbands are no longer thought to be the masters of their household) and because Nicole Brown Simpson did not 'represent a danger' to Simpson, Cotterill argues that the prosecution used *control* in an *atypical* way (i.e. its collocations were atypical) and that this atypical use represented Simpson's controlling behaviour as 'unjustified and unreasonable' (p. 73). In keeping with this kind of representation of Simpson was a second term used by the prosecution – the violence perpetrated by Simpson was characterized as *a cycle of violence*. Cotterill's examination of the collocational profile of *cycle of violence* showed that it is typically associated with violence that 'increase[s] in severity over a long period of time' (p. 77). Thus, by representing the events that led up to Nicole Brown Simpson's murder as a long series of increasingly brutal acts of violence perpetrated by an over-controlling husband, the prosecution was able to construct the murder as the logical outcome of an escalating cycle of violence.

In response to the prosecution's representation of O. J. Simpson, the defence, according to Cotterill, used lexical items that challenged both the systematic and the physical nature of Simpson's violence. For example, the lexical item *incident* was used throughout the defence's opening argument to refer to acts of violence committed by Simpson against Nicole Brown Simpson. Cotterill shows that a collocational profile of the word *incident* reveals its association with random and unrelated events. Unlike the prosecution, then, the defence represented Simpson's acts of violence as sporadic events that were unconnected to one another as opposed to repeated events that constituted a pattern of abuse. In addition, 'the theme of verbal debate rather than physical violence ... was developed by [Johnny] Cochran through the use of verbal process nominalizations – *dispute, discussion* and *conversation*' (Cotterill, 2003: 83). A striking example of this kind of lexical strategy was evident when Cochran employed the lexical item *discussion* to refer to Simpson's shouting of expletives during one of Nicole Brown Simpson's 911 calls. As Cotterill points out, terms such as *discussion* and *conversation* do not 'involve any degree of violence or aggression' (p. 87), and thereby contributed to the defence's construction of the Simpson marriage as fundamentally non-violent.

Eades' (2008) analysis of the Pinkenba case, discussed above, also involves a discussion of lexical items; indeed, Eades argues that there was a significant lexical struggle between the two defence lawyers and the three Aboriginal boys over how to label the central issue in the case, i.e. whether the boys were coerced by the police officers to enter the police cars or whether they did so voluntarily. (Recall that the police officers were charged with 'unlawful deprivation of liberty' for allegedly abducting the three Australian Aboriginal boys.) For example, the boys used the verb *told* in describing the central speech act of the police officers (e.g. *They told us to jump in the car*), whereas the defence lawyers consistently substituted *asked* for *told* in their questions to the boys (e.g. *Did you say you were asked to jump in the car – and you jumped in the car?*). In a similar way, while the boys said that the police officers *forced* them to enter the police car, we see in the following example one of the defence lawyers

downplaying the coercive nature of this characterization:

8. DC2: When you say <u>forced</u> – all <u>you</u> mean is – the police <u>said</u> so?
   David: Yeh.

And, in line with what we have seen in Examples 1 and 2 above, the cross-examining lawyer here (DC2) is successful in committing David (one of the boys) to this lexical reformulation. Eades labels these kinds of corrections and substitutions, 'lexical perversions', as a way of capturing 'the manipulative and sinister ways' in which the defence lawyers performed such operations on the witnesses' answers (Eades, 2008: 126). Indeed, Eades' more general argument about this case is that the court legitimized the police officers' actions, i.e. their abduction of the boys, and, in so doing, upheld and reinforced the control that the Australian state has exercised over Aboriginal peoples for more than 200 years (Eades, 2008: 3).

Syntactic choices and the construction of 'facts'

Just as lexical items can help to build the 'facts' of legal cases, so can the syntactic features of lawyers' questions and witnesses' answers. Cotterill (2003), for example, notes that the defence in the O. J. Simpson case reinforced the idea that Simpson's violence towards his wife consisted of a few unrelated *incidents* by using syntactic structures, such as agentless passives, that minimized Simpson's responsibility for the violence (e.g. *He and his wife got into an altercation and she **was struck** on January 1st 1989*). Ehrlich's (2001) work on the language of a sexual assault case documents a similar phenomenon: the defendant in the case, charged with sexual assault within the context of a university tribunal and a criminal trial, used a variety of syntactic constructions that obscured his agency vis-à-vis the acts of violence he allegedly committed against the two complainants. These included agentless passives (e.g. *all our clothes at one point were taken off*) and unaccusative constructions (e.g. *the sexual activity started escalating even further*). The defendant's representatives also employed structures in their questions that de-emphasized and obscured the defendant's agency, as can be seen in Example 1 above (*your shirt came off* and *fondling*), and in the following question: *So you do admit that you said nothing to him at that point about **the insertion of his finger in the vagina**?* The nominalization *insertion* allows for the deletion of the defendant as the agent of this action.

Coherence and the construction of 'facts'

Because the examples of lexical and syntactic features discussed above are necessarily decontextualized for the purposes of presentation, it may be difficult to perceive the **cumulative** effect of a series of lexical items and/or a series of syntactic structures in conveying a certain version of events. Matoesian's (2001) work on the William Kennedy Smith trial is useful in this respect as he specifically analyses what happens when a series of similar syntactic structures are repeated over an extended piece of talk.

William Kennedy Smith, the nephew of the late President John Kennedy, the late Senator Robert Kennedy and Senator Edward Kennedy, was charged with, and subsequently acquitted of, simple battery (unwanted touching) and second-degree sexual battery (rape without the use of a weapon) in the state of Florida in 1991. A striking feature of this case was the jury's unanimous acquittal of Kennedy Smith (on both counts) within the first five minutes of its deliberations. As noted above, a major theme in Matoesian's analysis of this trial involves the inconsistencies in 'logic' created by the defence attorney, Roy Black, in his cross-examination of the complainant, Patricia Bowman, and her primary witness, Ann Mercer. While Matoesian notes that the exposing of inconsistencies in witness testimony is a **generic** trial practice designed to undermine the credibility of witnesses, in this particular case he argues that the 'logical' standard against which the two women's testimonies were measured – and rendered inconsistent – was not a gender-neutral standard, but rather a male standard of sexuality: what he terms 'the patriarchal logic of sexual rationality'. In Example 9 below, Matoesian (2001: 46) argues that Roy Black's (RB) questions to Patricia Bowman (PB) functioned to create an inconsistency 'between the victim's claim of having been raped and her actions with the defendant before the alleged incident' and thereby helped to undermine the charges that Kennedy Smith had raped Patricia Bowman.

9.   1 RB: And you were interested in *him* as a
        person.
     (0.9)
     2 PB: He seemed like a nice *person*.
     (0.5)
     3 RB: Interested enough that tuh- (0.5) to
        give him a ride home.
     (0.9)
     4 PB: I saw no-(.) no *problem* with giving him
        a ride *home* as I stated because it was
     5   up the street it wasn't out of my *way* (.) he
        hadn't *tou::ched* me (.) I felt no *threats*

6   from him and I assumed that there
     would be *security* at the *home*.
(0.5)
7 RB: You were interested *enough* (.) that
     you were ho:::ping that he would ask
     for
8   your pho::ne *number*.
(0.7)
9 PB: That was *later*.
(0.7)
10 RB: Interested enough (.) tha:t when he
     said to come into the *hou::se* you
     went
11   into the *hou::se* with him.
(1.6)
12 PB: I (woul-) it wasn't necessarily an inter-
     est with *William* (.) it was an interest
     in
13   the *house*. (0.6)
14 RB: Interested enough that uh:: at some-
     time during that period of time *you took*
15   *off your panty hose?*
(1.2)
16 PB: I still don't *know* how my panty hose
     came off.

In this excerpt, Roy Black puts forward a number of propositions in his questions that are confirmed by Patricia Bowman: that she gave the defendant a ride home, that she went into the house with him, that she took off her panty hose and that she hoped he would ask for her telephone number. And, as Matoesian (2001: 47) points out, when these propositions were brought together, Patricia Bowman's actions began to look more like precursors to a consensual sexual relationship than to the crime of rape. For Matoesian, however, it was not just the propositional content of a series of questions like the ones above that functioned to construct Patricia Bowman's testimony as inconsistent, it was also the **coherence** created by their juxtaposition.

The defence attorney, Roy Black, had impressive oratorical skills and, according to Matoesian, employed these skills to amplify and intensify the 'inconsistencies' in the complainant's testimony. More specifically, Black foregrounded the referential content of his questions (and his talk, more generally) by using 'creative and improvisational poetic structures' (Matoesian 2001: 33), such as structural repetition and parallelism. In Example 9, for example, an element of the main clause of line 1 – *interested* – is incorporated into the syntactic frame, *interested enough* plus complementizer, and then this syntactic frame is repeated four times (in lines 3, 7–8, 10–11 and 14–15), each time with a different complement clause. In this way, a semantic link is created between the referential content of the complement clauses that are embedded within the syntactic frame, *interested enough* plus complementizer. As Matoesian says, 'incremental repetition ... unifies and organizes otherwise disparate particulars of evidence into a coherent, gestalt-like pattern of persuasive parallelism' (Matoesian 2001: 57). That is, the syntactic repetition in Example 9 functions to create a link among a series of 'facts' that might not otherwise appear connected; and, once this link is created, the **linked** 'facts' of the case seem more compatible with consensual sex than with the crime of rape. For Matoesian, then, this particular construction of events is not just the result of lexical and syntactic features of Roy Black's questions, but also a result of the coherence created when certain of these features are repeated over extended sequences of talk.

25.4 DETERMINING THE 'OFFICIAL' STORY: POWER AND IDEOLOGY

Given the presence of competing and contradictory 'facts' within the courtroom, Cotterill (2003: 25) has argued that 'the name often given to the jury in adversarial trial procedure, that of the "factfinder", is actually something of a misnomer'. For Cotterill, juries do not determine the facts, rather they 'adjudicate between more and less plausible narrative accounts'. Capps and Ochs (1995: 21) make similar observations about adjudicators in trials:

> On the basis of divergent versions of events, jury members construct a narrative that is plausible and coherent in their eyes, but the truth is beyond their reach. In this sense, rendering a verdict is analogous not to ascertaining the facts but to determining an official story.

So, if the truth and the facts are 'beyond the reach' of juries, and adjudicators more generally, what kind of criteria are used in determining 'official stories'? Capps and Ochs (1995: 20) suggest that, while the internal consistency and external corroboration of stories told in the courtroom are important to their believability,[8] of equal importance is the 'rhetorical prowess' of the witnesses and lawyers who tell the stories. Matoesian's (2001) analysis of Roy Black's 'rhetorical prowess' in the William Kennedy Smith trial certainly supports this idea. According to Matoesian (2001: 31), the testimonies of Patricia Bowman and Ann Mercer were not 'that inconsistent'; rather, 'Black knew how to *create* inconsistency through powerful and affective forms of language, much more so than prosecutor Lasch' (emphasis in original).

But, Black's success was not solely the result of his impressive oratorical skills. According to Matoesian (2001: 31), 'persuasive forms of language' and ideology worked together to create an interpretive lens 'through which jurors evaluate[d] legal issues such as consent, coercion, and violence'. In particular, when Black successfully created inconsistencies in the testimony of Bowman and Mercer, he did so by measuring their behaviour against 'the expectations of patriarchal ideology governing victim identity'. For example, through the lens of 'patriarchal ideology', the actions of Patricia Bowman, as represented in Example 9, were inconsistent with her claim that she was a victim of rape.

The idea that power and ideology are at play when adjudicators decide between conflicting stories in the courtroom is also evident in the work of Ehrlich (2001) and Eades (2008). Ehrlich (2001) notes that the judge in the Canadian sexual assault case described above seemed to authorize and legitimize the representations of the defendant (put forward by the defendant and his representatives) as a non-agent of sexual aggression. Specifically, the judge invoked the 'male sexual drive' discourse[9] (Hollway, 1989) in acquitting the defendant on one count of sexual assault, citing hormones as responsible for men's sexual aggression. While Ehrlich does not make the strong claim that the defendant's representation of himself as a non-agent of a sexual aggression 'caused' the judge to rule in the way that he did, she does claim that the defendant and his defence put forward a version of events that was consistent with dominant understandings of male sexuality and violence against women and thus seemed to resonate with the adjudicator.

In the same way that Matoesian's and Ehrlich's analyses elucidate the workings of **gendered** ideologies in the courtroom, Eades' analysis of the Pinkenba case shows how ideologies of race and ethnicity can be strategically invoked by lawyers. The lawyers defending the police officers constructed the Aboriginal boys, not as victims of police abuse who were coerced into entering police cars, but as lying criminals who were 'the legitimate subject of removal by police, even when they [had] not committed any offence' (Eades, 2008: 24). And, given the long history of racism against Aboriginal peoples in Australia, it is fair to say that these ideas resonated in a powerful way with those adjudicating the case.

25.5 CONCLUSION

I began this chapter by reporting on early research in the area of courtroom discourse that investigated (1) the relationship between social power and the linguistic variables used by courtroom witnesses and (2) the effect of such variables on witnesses' ability to access justice. In closing this chapter, I have returned to a similar theme – how power and ideology influence the way that juries and judges adjudicate among conflicting narratives that emerge within the courtroom. One of the accomplishments of this chapter, then, has been to demonstrate the continuities between early work in the field and more recent work, in spite of the difference in sociolinguistic methods. As we have seen, early work (e.g. O'Barr, 1982; Wodak, 1985) was influenced by variationist sociolinguistics and thus focused on the standard or non-standard nature of witnesses' linguistic variables, whereas more recent work (e.g. Eades, 2008; Ehrlich, 2001; Matoesian, 2001) has been influenced by critical approaches to discourse analysis and thus has focused on the ideological nature of narratives produced in the courtroom. What unifies this work is the concern with variation in courtroom linguistic practices and the effect of such variation on the decision-making of judges and juries. Conley and O'Barr (1998) have argued that language and the law scholars need to move beyond the mere description of linguistic variation in the legal system in order to understand how language and discourse is **consequential** for the law. This chapter has attempted to show the range of linguistic phenomena that can have social consequences within the legal system.

ACKNOWLEDGEMENT

I thank Ruth Wodak for her very helpful comments on an earlier version of this chapter. This research was supported, in part, by a Standard Research Grant from the Social Sciences and Humanities Research Council of Canada, Grant #410-2006-0647.

NOTES

1 The most highly-publicized finding of the Duke University's Law and Language Project, led by William O'Barr, concerned the use of 'powerful' and 'powerless' speech styles: speech styles associated with social power were judged by mock jurors to be more believable, more credible, and more intelligent than speech styles associated with social powerlessness.

2 While investigations of courtroom discourse have generally acknowledged that the trial is a 'complex genre' (Heffer, 2005), consisting of a number of 'trial phases', this chapter, like the majority of studies of courtroom discourse, will focus on the *evidential* phase of the trial (Cotterill, 2003: 93), i.e. the examination and the cross-examination of witnesses, and the opening and closing arguments that frame the examination of witnesses. Cotterill (2003: 93) identifies the three major stages of the trial as:

> the *preliminary* phase, involving jury selection questionnaires and *voir dire* interviews; the *evidential* phase, consisting of the examination and cross-examination of witnesses, framed by the opening and closing arguments; and finally the *judicial* phase, where the judge and jury take centre stage, in the adjudicatory portion of the trial, including the delivery of jury instructions and the deliberation process, followed by the verdict and the sentencing or release of the defendant.

For examples of work that deals with the *judicial* phase of the trial, specifically, judicial rulings, see Solan (1993) and Philips (1998).

3 Technically, only witness testimony (as opposed to the talk of lawyers) constitutes evidence in a trial. However, as this chapter demonstrates, lawyers' questions can function to shape and control the way this evidence comes to be expressed.

4 Atkinson and Drew (1979: 136) note that witnesses often display their recognition that a series of questions is leading to a 'blame allocation' by producing 'justification/excuse components in answers' prematurely, i.e. before 'blame allocations' are actually produced by lawyers.

5 On a very superficial level, trials involve dialogue, the examination and cross-examination of witnesses by lawyers, and monologue, the opening and closing arguments of lawyers. However, given that these modes of speech are produced for the benefit of adjudicators – judges and/or juries – trial talk is more accurately characterized as multiparty in its structure (Cotterill, 2003).

6 Unaccusative constructions are intransitive verbs that take as their grammatical subjects non-agents (i.e. non-causers) of the actions or processes designated by the intransitive verbs.

7 Cotterill (2003) has argued that it is problematic to treat witnesses as a homogeneous group in relation to claims about the interactional asymmetry between witnesses and lawyers. Indeed, a number of researchers have shown that the interaction between expert witnesses and lawyers is not as asymmetrical as has been claimed for the interaction between lay witnesses and lawyers (e.g. Cotterill, 2003; Matoesian, 2001; Stygall, 2001).

8 Early work on this issue (i.e. Bennett and Feldman, 1981) concluded that a well-constructed

story may be more important to jurors' assessments of plausibility than the existence of evidence.

9 This discourse constructs male sexuality as driven by a powerful biological imperative such that women become responsible for controlling men's 'uncontrollable' sexual urges.

REFERENCES

Atkinson, J. M. and Drew, P. (1979) *Order in Court*. Atlantic Highlands, NJ: Highlands Humanities Press.

Barry, A. (1991) 'Narrative style and witness testimony', *Journal of Narrative and Life History*, 1: 281–93.

Bennett, L. and Feldman, M.S. (1981) *Reconstructing Reality in the Courtroom*. London: Tavistock.

Capps, L. and Ochs, E. (1995) *Constructing Panic: The Discourse of Agoraphobia*. Cambridge, MA: Harvard University Press.

Conley, J. M. and O'Barr, W. M. (1990) *Rules versus relationships*. Chicago: University of Chicago Press.

Conley, J. M. and O'Barr, W. M. (1998) *Just Words: Law, Language and Power*. Chicago: University of Chicago Press.

Conley, J. M., O'Barr, W. M. and Lind, E. A. (1978) 'The power of language: presentational styles in the courtroom', *Duke Law Journal*, 78: 1375–99.

Cotterill, J. (2003) *Language and Power in Court: A Linguistic Analysis of the O. J. Simpson trial*. Basingstoke: Palgrave Macmillan.

Danet, B. (1980) '"Baby" or "fetus"?: language and the construction of reality in a manslaughter trial', *Semiotica*, 32: 187–219.

Danet, B., Hoffman, K., Kermish, N., Rafn, H. and Stayman, D. (1980) 'An ethnography of questioning', in R. Shuy and A. Shnukal (eds), *Language Use and the Uses of Language*. Washington, DC: Georgetown University Press. pp. 222–34.

Drew, P. (1992) 'Contested evidence in courtroom examination: the case of a trial for rape', in P. Drew and J. Heritage (eds), *Talk at Work: Interaction in Institutional Settings*. Cambridge: Cambridge University Press. pp. 470–520.

Drew, P. and Heritage, J. (eds) (1992) 'Analyzing talk at work: an introduction', in *Talk at work: interaction in institutional settings*. Cambridge: Cambridge University Press. pp. 3–65.

Duranti, A. (1994) *From Grammar to Politics: Linguistic Anthropology in a Western Samoan Village*. Berkeley, CA: University of California Press.

Eades, D. (2000) 'I don't think it's an answer to the question: silencing Aboriginal witnesses in court', *Language in Society*, 29: 161–95.

Eades, D. (2008) *Courtroom Talk and Neocolonial Control*. Berlin: Mouton de Gruyter.

Ehrlich, S. (2001) *Representing Rape: Language and Sexual Consent*. London: Routledge.

Ehrlich, S. and Sidnell, J. (2006) '"I think that's not an assumption you ought to make": challenging presuppositions in inquiry testimony', *Language in Society*, 2006: 655–76.

Fairclough, N. and Wodak, R. (1997) 'Critical discourse analysis', in T. A. van Dijk (ed.), *Discourse as Social Interaction*. London: Sage. pp. 258–84.

Galatolo, R. and Drew, P. (2006) 'Narrative expansions as defensive practices in courtroom testimony', *Text and Talk*, 26: 661–98.

Gibbons, J. (2003) *Forensic Linguistics: An Introduction to Language in the Justice System*. Oxford: Blackwell.

Green, G. (1996) *Pragmatics and Natural Language Understanding*. 2nd edn. Mahwah, NJ: Lawrence Erlbaum.

Harris, S. (1984) 'Questions as a mode of control in magistrates' courts', *International Journal of Sociology of Language*, 49: 5–28.

Heffer, C. (2005) *The Language of Jury Trial: A Corpus-Aided Analysis of Legal-Lay Discourse*. Basingstoke: Palgrave Macmillan.

Hollway, W. (1989) *Subjectivity and Method in Psychology: Gender, Meaning and Science*. London: Sage.

Hutchby, I. and Wooffitt, R. (1998) *Conversation Analysis*. Oxford: Polity Press.

Levinson, S. (1983) *Pragmatics*. Cambridge: Cambridge University Press.

Luchjenbroers, J. and Aldridge, M. (2007) 'Conceptual manipulation by metaphors and frames: dealing with rape victims in legal discourse', *Text and Talk*, 27: 339–59.

Lyons, J. (1977) *Semantics*. Cambridge: Cambridge University Press.

Maley, Y. (1994) 'The language of the law', in J. Gibbons (ed.), *Language and the Law*. London: Longman. pp. 11–50.

Matoesian, G. (2001) *Law and the Language of Identity: Discourse in the William Kennedy Rape Trial*. New York: Oxford University Press.

Matoesian, G. (2005) 'Review of J. Cotterill, Language and Power in Court: A Linguistic Analysis of the O. J. Simpson Trial', *Journal of Sociolinguistics*, 9: 619–22.

O'Barr, W. M. and Atkins, B. K. (1980) '"Women's language" or "powerless language"?' in S. McConnell-Ginet, R. Borker, and N. Furman (eds), *Women in Language and Society*. New York: Praeger. pp. 193–210.

O'Barr, W. M. (1982) *Linguistic Evidence: Language, Power and Strategy in the Courtroom*. New York: Academic Press.

Philips, S. (1987) 'The social organization of questions and answers in courtroom discourse', in L. Kedar (ed.), *Power Through Discourse*. Norwood, NJ: Ablex. pp. 83–113.

Philips, S. (1998) *Ideology in the Language of Judges*. New York: Oxford University Press.

Raymond, G. (2003) 'Grammar and social organization: yes/no type interrogatives and the structure of responding', *American Sociological Review*, 68: 939–66.

Schegloff, E. A. (2007) *Sequence Organization in Interaction*. Cambridge: Cambridge University Press.

Solan, L. M. (1993) *The Language of Judges*. Chicago: Chicago University Press.

Stygall, G. (2001) 'A different class of witnesses: experts in the courtroom', *Discourse Studies*, 3: 327–49.

Walker, A. G. (1987) 'Linguistic manipulation, power and the legal setting', in L. Kedar (ed.), *Power Through Discourse*. Norwood, NJ: Ablex. pp. 57–80.

Wodak, R. (1981) 'Discourse analysis and courtroom interaction', *Discourse Processes*, 3: 369–80.

Wodak, R. (1985) 'The interaction between judge and defendant', in T. A. van Dijk (ed.), *Handbook of Discourse Analysis*, Vol. 4. New York: Academic Press. pp. 181–91.

Woodbury, H. (1984) 'The strategic use of questions in court', *Semiotica*, 48: 197–228.

Analysing Conversation

Christian M.I.M. Matthiessen
and Diana Slade

> The magical power of talk derives from the fact that it is, in every instance, the manifestation of a systematic resource, a resource which has been built up through acts of conversation in the first place, and which goes on being modified in each of us as we talk our way through life.
>
> Halliday (1984: 32)

26.1 INTRODUCTION

Conversation is an all-pervasive phenomenon found in all societies. It must have emerged early in human history as an important mode of interaction, creating and sustaining interpersonal relations in social groups and societies (see e.g. Dunbar, 1996) and giving our ancestors the advantage of a 'collective' brain and collective learning (cf. Christian, 2004: 146).

Conversation is a critical site for the maintenance and modification of our social identities: it both creates and reflects our social worlds. It plays a key role in many of the key institutions of any society, including the core institutions of family, friendship, recreation and mateship in workplaces. Since conversation is so central to the operations of any society, the analysis of conversation is central to sociolinguistics. The study of conversation is our most important window on the relationship between language (and other accompanying

semiotic systems) and the social system of any society.

In conversation, the interactants taking part construe their experiences, unselfconsciously constructing commonsense understandings of the world around them and inside them, often reaching consensus and sometimes identifying areas of conflict but always negotiating their understandings. Interpersonally, conversation is the primary site where people take on roles as interactants to enact their social values and relationships. Textually, it is where interactants collaborate in constructing a shareable and shared semiotic reality. And as Berger and Luckman (1966: 172–3) pointed out many years ago, it is precisely because of the essential spontaneity and informality of conversation that it can do the work it does.

In the life of an individual, conversation emerges very early as a child learns how to mean (see Halliday, 1975, 1984, 2004); researchers have even identified very early exchanges of attention between mother and child (e.g. Trevarthen, 1979, 1987) – what Bateson (e.g. 1979) has called 'proto-conversation'. The steps leading from early interaction to the exchange of meaning in true dialogue have been documented, described and theorized by Halliday (1984).

Thus the role conversation plays in our formation as social beings starts from when we are very young. It is the form of language to which we are all first exposed – it is the prototypical kind of language use and so it provides a gateway into language. But how do we characterize conversation and how do we study it? The general answer is that conversation is a very complex phenomenon involving many strands of patterned activity, within different orders of system (see. Figure 26.3). Consequently, conversation can – and must – be investigated from different angles if we are to arrive at a well-rounded understanding of what it is like.

In this chapter we will first describe what we mean by conversation, and then turn to an outline of the different approaches to the analysis of conversation. The final section will demonstrate some analytical tools for describing conversation.

26.2 TYPES OF CONVERSATION

While technical uses of the term 'conversation' are related to the everyday sense of conversation, they differ in where they draw the boundaries and how they relate 'conversation' to other kinds of text. To avoid confusion and to emphasize the scope of the phenomenon they study, researchers within the originally sociological framework for the analysis of conversation known as conversation analysis have used the term 'talk-in-interaction' (see e.g. Schegloff, 1988; Psathas, 1995; Hutchby and Wooffitt, 1998). For the purposes of our discussion of approaches to the analysis of conversation, we will use the term 'conversation' to denote dialogic text where the control of turn-taking is relatively low, thus contrasting it with more formal dialogues where turn-taking is more controlled or pre-allocated (see e.g. Halliday and Plum 1983). Figure 26.1 below locates conversation as a type of dialogic text, where the there is little or no formal turn assignment.

Using turn control as one of the criteria, we can describe conversation as follows (cf. Thornbury and Slade, 2006: 25):

> ... dialogue (i.e. interactive text) between two or more people with a high degree of freedom in turn allocation – spontaneous (rather than pre-planned), unfolding in real time, typically with an orientation towards interpersonal meaning and often involving interactants with symmetrical rights.

As outlined in Figure 26.1, the continuum of conversations ranges from the most casual of spoken interactions – chatting with a friend at coffee time at work, gossiping at a dinner party or telling anecdotes at a family gathering – to what we have

called task conversations and chatting during a service encounter.[1] These are all conversations that are informal, dialogic and where turn-taking is not pre-allocated (as opposed to for example, a job interview, a lecture, a debate). Conversations then are primarily concerned with the interpersonal – the creation and maintenance of social relationships. Conversations can operate in many institutional settings: before, after and in the middle of lectures at university; during informal meetings at work; an informal chat with the doctor that is interspersed with medical and pragmatic interaction. Task (-oriented) conversations are those which enable two or more people to undertake some joint activity such as moving a heavy piece of furniture or cooking a meal. Conversation is primarily spoken (or signed in the case of sign language of deaf communities) but also, increasingly, in forms of written discourse, such as online chat:

> 1 It includes conversation carried out in any medium – spoken, written or signed, or some mixture of these, and through any channel – face-to-face, telephonic, online chat and so on. There are tendencies for preferred combinations, but it is important to recognize that medium and channel are, in principle, independently-variable parameters. With respect to channel, there has been a recent dramatic expansion of the range of conversation – technology has paved the way for new modes of conversation such as email exchanges, electronic chat (written, audio, or audio and video), and text messages by mobile phones. These developments are interesting from a social point of view since they have fairly far-reaching implications for the formation and maintenance of social groups and communities.
> 2 It Does not restrict the nature or the number of the interactants involved in a conversation. There can be anywhere from two interactants to a large group of interactants. (Sometimes the term 'multilogue' is used to designate dialogues, including conversations, involving more than two interactants.)
> 3 It is not restricted in terms of the field of discourse; we include different kinds of activity such as sharing, joint doing, recommending, and we have not imposed any restrictions in terms of the topic or subject matter of conversation. (Some scholars would restrict conversation in terms of field, e.g. excluding task-oriented dialogue; cf. e.g. Ruhlemann, 2007.)

In the Section 26.3 we outline the different approaches to the analysis of conversation, and in Section 26.4 we demonstrate a range of analytical tools for describing and focusing on different aspects of conversation.

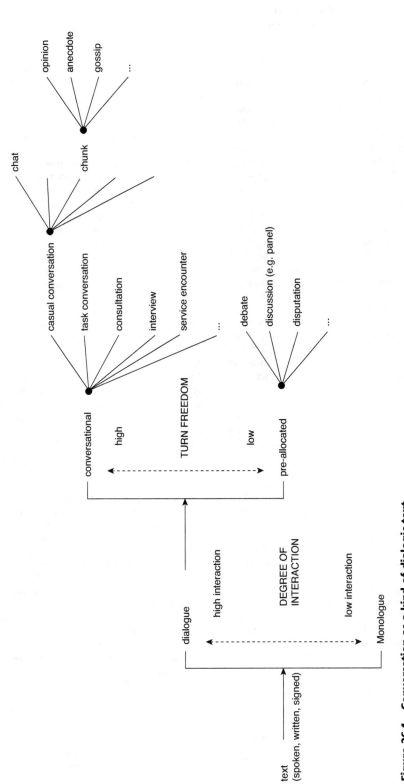

Figure 26.1   Conversation as a kind of dialogic text.

26.3 DIFFERENT APPROACHES TO ANALYSING CONVERSATION

Ways of characterizing approaches

There are many ways of characterizing approaches to the analysis of conversation. For example, it is possible to survey such approaches in disciplinary terms, taking note of work in linguistics, anthropology, sociology and social psychology, philosophy and artificial intelligence (AI), human-computer interaction (HCI) and natural language processing (NLP). This can be helpful in identifying relevant work that might otherwise be overlooked simply because of the boundaries between disciplines. For example, while speech act theory was first proposed and developed in philosophy, it has now been incorporated in work in linguistics and also in AI/HCI/NLP, and most of the work involving the theory that is relevant to sociolinguistics is arguably done within this cluster of related disciplines. Similarly, while conversation analysis was pioneered in sociology, it has been taken up in linguistics. Therefore it is more helpful to develop a map of approaches to the analysis of discourse based on the orientation towards phenomena in discourse, regardless of the discipline in which these phenomena are investigated.

For present purposes, we have selected two factors, shown in Figure 26.2: on the one hand, approaches to the analysis of conversation may focus on individuals or on persons (social agents) operating in groups; (ii) on the other hand, approaches to the analysis of conversation may interpret conversation in social terms – conversation as a form of interpersonal behaviour – in the first instance, or in semiotic terms – conversation as exchange of meaning (or of knowledge, in a more cognitive frame of interpretation).

Taking these two factors into consideration, we can locate major approaches to conversation, as shown in Figure 26.2. A number of approaches focus on the investigation of conversation in terms of individuals and what they intend and know – speech act theory and various types of dialogue modelling in AI/HCI/NLP. Other approaches focus on persons in social groups, interpreting conversation as an ongoing exchange of meaning – systemic functional linguistics (SFL), the Birmingham school, critical discourse Analysis. Yet other approaches also focus on persons in social groups, but tend to interpret conversation as interpersonal behaviour rather than as exchange of meaning – conversation analysis, interactive sociolinguistics.

Some of the approaches shown in Figure 26.2 have developed as frameworks dedicated to the study of conversation, e.g. speech act theory and conversation analysis. In contrast, other approaches have developed as part of a general theory of language, e.g. systemic functional linguistics and the closely related Birmingham school. Not surprisingly, these other approaches tend to come from linguistics, and include a technical account of intonation in conversation.

In addition to the two factors we have just mentioned, there are other factors that are important in a comprehensive account of approaches to the study of conversation. We will mention just one of them. This is the question of how conversation is approached, in terms of system and text. Like any other linguistic phenomenon, conversation can be observed as instance – as spoken, written or signed texts unfolding in particular contexts; and conversation can be described and theorized as potential – as the system that lies behind such discursive instances. Here classical speech act theory and conversation analysis represent a sharp contrast. speech act theory focused on the system, and researchers probed it by constructing examples. In contrast, CA focused on the instance, and researchers worked with corpora of situated discourse, basing their generalizations on examples found in these corpora. In this respect, both differ from SFL, which has been concerned with the relationship between system and text. Here system and text are modelled as the outer poles of a cline – the cline of instantiation – and researchers have shunted between these two poles in their account of conversation and also identified intermediate patterns associated with particular institutional settings (e.g. conversation during tea breaks in the workplace, conversation during dinners among close friends).

In this chapter we will review two approaches, CA and SFL, to the analysis of conversation that can be seen as complementary in a socially-oriented analysis of conversation. These two approaches are both concerned specifically with the social nature of conversation, analysing the relationship between language and its context of use; and each has engaged in the analysis of naturally-occurring data. Coming from sociology and linguistics, respectively, they both went through formative stages in the 1960s and 1970s and have continued to flourish since then. During the formative period, the Atlantic still constituted a considerable divide between American (CA) and British (SFL) efforts. Thus, when Coulthard and Sinclair worked out the framework reported on in Sinclair and Coulthard (1975), the early CA work was still not known,[2] so what we have are two fairly independent lines of development. It is therefore important that both these approaches focus on text as well as lexical and grammatical features of language, and share a concern with

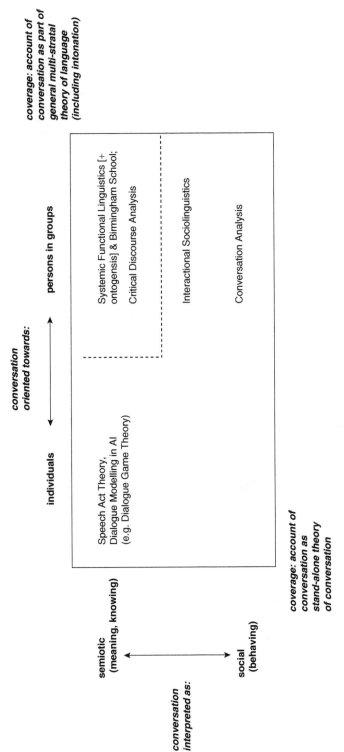

Figure 26.2 Approaches to the study of conversation differentiated in terms of (i) orientation and (ii) level of interpretation.

describing interaction and the dynamic unfolding of talk. It is also interesting to note that both these approaches developed during a time when they had to struggle on the margins of the disciplines that they emerged from, and both have to a certain extent been more warmly welcomed in other disciplines. Unlike CA, SFL has had the added challenge of developing outside the USA during a period when US scholarship has tended to dominate the world.

In Section 26.4 we outline some analytical techniques for describing conversation, drawn from aspects of these three different approaches.

Conversation analysis: a sociological approach to the analysis of conversation

Background to development of conversation analysis

Conversational analysis was stimulated by the sociological initiatives of Garfinkel (1967)[3] and Goffman (e.g. 1981), and developed into a distinctive field of enquiry by Sacks (e.g. Sacks, 1972a, 1972b, 1974, 1978, 1992). Like Garfinkel's ethnomethodology, it was developed partly as reaction against the mainstream macro sociology that was current at the time; and CA researchers have been very careful to work only with categories that emerge from the study of conversation and which interactants can be shown to orient towards. Sacks also worked in collaboration with Schegloff and Jefferson to develop this field of sociological enquiry further (Schegloff and Sacks, 1973, Jefferson, Sacks and Schegloff, 1987; Schegloff, 2006; Sacks, Schegloff and Jefferson, 1974). More recently, there has been a good deal of work devoted to linking CA to features of grammar as interpreted by West-Coast Functionalists (see e.g. Ochs, Schegloff and Thompson, 1996), and on applications involving CA work (see e.g. Hutchby and Wooffitt, 1998: Part III; McHoul and Rapley, 2001).

CA is a distinctive research paradigm located within the wider field of enquiry of ethnomethodology, the focus of which, according to Heritage (1989: 21), is:

> ...the study of the common-sense reasoning skills and abilities through which the ordinary members of a culture produce and recognise intelligible courses of action.

CA is based on the insight that it is in and through conversation that most of our routine everyday activities are accomplished. It also argues that it is through more formal or 'institutional talk in interaction' (e.g. Schegloff, 1987) that the institutional world is constructed and significant decisions are made. In either case, naturally-occurring texts constitute the only real form of data.

A primary concern is to explain how it is that everyday talk makes sense: how it is for example that, normally, only one person speaks at a time, and that speakers know when to change turns, when to initiate new topics, when it is appropriate to interrupt or to complete another's utterance, and recognize the signals that speakers use to indicate they want to close the conversation.

CA research has focused, therefore, on the micro-interactional features of conversation:[4] the turn-taking mechanisms we use in conversation; how speakers initiate, shift and close topics (referred to as topic management); and how it is that conversations can keep going indefinitely and continue to make sense.[5] We will look briefly at each of these areas in turn.

Turn-taking

Sacks (1974) describes how turn-taking works in English. The current speaker can either select the next speaker by, for example, naming them, looking at them, directing a question to them – or the next speaker can self-select, with many possible strategies, such as 'that reminds me of' or 'have you heard what Bron did yesterday'.

In trying to explain how it is that speakers keep taking turns, Sacks (1974) argued that it is because interactants in the conversation recognize points of potential speaker change, these being indicated by linguistic units which he calls turn constructional units (TCUs). A TCU is the minimal unit that can constitute one complete turn of talk. For example:[6]

+A: Let's go to the cinema tonight?
+B: No, I have to finish my assignment

In this invented example, each of these turns is a TCU. However, in the following example, there are two TCU within one speaker turn:

+ A: Let's go to the cinema tonight? We could have dinner beforehand

Here each utterance could constitute a complete turn in its own right so there are two TCUs.

The turn-constructional unit is a central concept in the CA explanation of how it is that in conversation:

(i) only one speaker speaks at a time
(ii) speaker change recurs (Sacks, Schegloff and Jefferson, 1974: 700)

It is at the end of the TCU that interactants in conversation recognize points of potential speaker change. One of the problems with using the TCU as the basic descriptive unit of conversational interaction is that it is not clear how to identify the boundaries of a TCU, and there have been various proposals put forward (cf. Ford and Thompson, 1996).

CA researchers are also interested in how, at the end of the TCU, interactants determine who the next speaker will be. There are two possibilities: the first is that the current speaker selects the person who is to be the next speaker, and the second possibility is that the next speaker self-selects. Sacks, Schegloff and Jefferson (1974) argue that this needs to be negotiated at every turn and, in fact, in conversation, interactants avoid the possibility of a lapse – the possibility of no-one speaking. Thus, central to CA's modelling of conversation, is the existence of a turn-taking mechanism, having the function of assigning turns to interactants in conversation.

Adjacency pairs

Another significant contribution of CA is the concept of the adjacency pair (cf. Taylor and Cameron, 1987). An adjacency pair is composed of two turns produced by different speakers which are placed adjacently. Schegloff and Sacks (1973: 239) defined the rules of adjacency pair production as:

> Given the recognisable production of a first pair part, at its first possible completion, its speaker should stop, a next speaker should start, and should produce a second pair part of the same pair type.

Adjacency pairs are (in our terms) sequences of moves in an exchange with paired speech functions such as: question/answer; complaint/denial; compliment/rejection; request/grant; and offer/accept. As Heritage (1984: 247) points out, an adjacency pair is a structural organization to which speakers orient, expecting an appropriate second pair part to follow the first pair part.

A sequence is an adjacency pair and any expansions of that adjacency. There are three types of expansions – pre-sequences, insertion sequences and post-sequences – where the sequence is the base adjacency (Adj.) pair and its expansions. For example:

1 Pre-sequence First Pair Part: A: *What are you doing now?*
2 Pre-sequence Second Pair Part B: *Not sure, maybe I will grab a cup of tea.*

3 Base Adj. Pair First Pair Part A: *Do you want to come and get a real coffee?*
4 Insertion seq. First Pair Part B: *Where?*
5 Insertion seq. Second Pair Part A: *We could go to that restaurant across the road.*
6 Base Adj. Pair Second Pair Part B: *That sounds great.*

In this example, taken from recorded conversational data, each turn is a TCU. Turns 3 and 6 constitute a question/answer pair; however, turns 1–6 are all related semantically – there is a sense of these belonging together. It is instances such as these that CA refers to as sequences.

The significance of the adjacency pair and sequence is twofold. First, it provides an environment in which the conversational principle of sequential relevance can be assigned across utterances (cf. Grice, 1967/75), and secondly it provides a way of capturing the local organization of talk.

CA researchers have also described the different feedback mechanisms used in conversation, as well as ways in which interactants open and close conversations, the ways interactants repair and clarify, etc.

Like leading text-oriented linguists active in the first half of the twentieth century, such as C. C. Fries and J. R. Firth, and the linguists who pioneered the compilation of corpora of spoken language in the late 1950s and early 1960s, CA researchers, coming initially from sociology, have emphasized the importance of the analysis of authentic data collected in naturally-occurring interactions. Their research has confirmed the pervasiveness of local organization in talk and the need to account for this organization. It has offered a powerful way of thinking about the dynamic unfolding of conversation, as well as ways of modelling the procedures and expectations employed by interactants in producing and understanding conversation. In addition, its insistence that categories should only be postulated when interactants can be shown to orient towards them has been methodologically very important, and has resonated with approaches such as SFL that are also grounded in authentic textual data.

Systemic functional linguistics

Background

Systemic functional linguistics (SFL) is largely derived from the work of M. A. K. Halliday (see Halliday, 1961, 1978, 1985a/1994; Halliday and Matthiessen, 2004; Hasan, Matthiessen and

Webster, 2005, 2007; Matthiessen, Teruya and Lam, forthcoming), and it was originally grounded in his own experience of doing fieldwork in China in the late 1940s, in his work on Chinese text and, towards the end of the 1950s, his work on spoken English text. As Halliday's teacher, Firth (e.g. 1957) was an important influence, including his emphasis on the importance of conversation. Throughout its history, SFL has been inter-disciplinary – or rather trans-disciplinary – in orientation; and in the area of the study of social systems, two key influences have been the anthropology of Bronislaw Malinowski and the sociology of Basil Bernstein.

A central concern of SFL is to relate language to its social context, by linking the functions of language to the organization of the context it operates in. SFL stresses the centrality of the study of conversation to the study of language, both because conversation is the most important vehicle by means of which social reality is represented and enacted in language, and because conversation is, as it were, the frontier in the evolution of language. Moreover, 'to understand the nature of text as social action we are led naturally to consider spontaneous conversation, as being the most accessible to interpretation' (Halliday, 1978: 140).

In SFL, the focus on conversation is on the way that language is organized to enable conversation to work and to have the power it does. By contrast, in CA, the focus is on social life and conversation is seen as a key to that. However, the two approaches are similar in that they are both concerned with describing the dialectic between language and its social context; both are concerned with describing ways in which conversation socializes individuals and regulates the social order.

Overview (1): systemic orders and instantiation

SFL has made many contributions to the study of conversation since around 1960, including the study of intonation (Halliday, 1963a, 1963b, 1967, 1970a), the study of mood (Halliday, 1970b), the study of speech function and exchange (Halliday, 1984) and the study of tenor relations (Halliday, 1978); but the most important contribution it has made, and can make, is arguably that it provides us with a comprehensive account of language in context that we can use as a resource in investigating conversation.[7]

We can locate conversation on a schematic map representing (1) systems of different orders (2) extended along the cline of instantiation, from instance to potential, as shown in Figure 26.3.

(1) Hierarchy of systemic orders. A conversation is simultaneously (i) physical activity, (ii) biological activity, (iii) social activity and (iv) semiotic activity (see Halliday and Matthiessen, 1999; Halliday, 2006; Matthiessen, 2007). (i) In terms of orders of systems, we can observe and analyse a given conversation as sound waves, in its physical order of manifestation, as we do in acoustic phonetics, e.g. with the help of speech analysis software such as Praat (see e.g. Halliday and Greaves, 2008: Ch. 2). (ii) Taking one step up the ordered typology of systems, we can also observe and analyse a given conversation as bodily activity, in its biological order of manifestation, e.g. as articulatory/auditory activity or as neural activity. (iii) Taking one more step up the ordered typology of systems, we can observe and analyse a given conversation as interactive behaviour – as social interaction, in its social order of manifestation, as people in different roles taking turns. This is of course the 'level' of analysis where conversation analysis has made a significant contribution, deriving originally from sociology. As Hutchby and Wooffitt (1998: 14) put it, 'CA is only marginally interested in language as such; its actual object of study is the interactional organization of social activities' (italics in original). To treat language as the object of study, we need to move from the order of social systems to that of semiotic systems. (iv) Thus, taking a final step up the ordered typology of systems, we can observe and analyse a given conversation as exchanges of meanings, in its semiotic order of manifestation. All these orders of analyses are relevant to our understanding of conversation, but in the context of 'sociolinguistics', we are likely to focus on the relationship between the two 'immaterial' orders of system – the social and semiotic orders.

(2) Cline of instantiation. In terms of the cline of instantiation, a given conversation in its context of situation unfolds as an instance. We may investigate this conversation purely as an instance, without trying to relate it to any more general patterns further towards the potential pole of the cline of instantiation. This would be a kind of commentary on the conversation – a kind of explication de texte – without the benefit of a description of the systemic potential that lies behind the conversation and without any attempt to make any generalizations beyond the particular conversation being investigated. However, for most purposes in sociolinguistics, we would analyse the conversation by relating it to a description of the system that lies behind it.[8] This is the standard practice in the analysis of any text, as text analysis has developed in the last few decades under the headings of

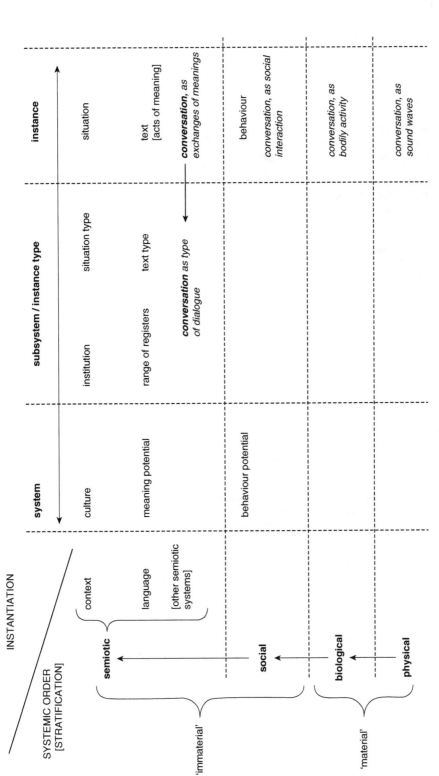

Figure 26.3 Location of 'conversation' in terms of orders of system and in terms of the cline of instantiation.

'text linguistics' and 'discourse analysis' – with the analysis of conversation as a special case, as illustrated by Halliday (1985c). At the same time, every text that is analysed will provide material for the description of the general system that lies behind the text: the analysis of texts and the description of the system are always dialectically related.

As just noted, a given conversation unfolds in its context of situation at the instance pole of the cline of instantiation (as discussed in the next section and illustrated there in Figure 26.3). But this instance is an instance of some more general instance type; for example, in the conversation presented in Text 26.1, 'Joanne' is an instance of a recurrent type of conversation – a type of conversation that has been called 'gossip'. More generally, we can interpret conversation as a kind of dialogic text (see the typology presented in Figure 26.1), locating it mid-region along the cline of instantiation between the potential pole and the instance pole. Conversation operates in a range of different institutions, such as those of family and of friendship; and particular types of conversation operate in different situation types, such as those of a dinner among close friends (e.g. Eggins, 1990) and a tea break in a workplace (e.g. Slade, 1996).

Overview (2): stratification and metafunction
In text analysis in general, and in conversation analysis in particular, we thus carry out the analysis by relating the text we are concerned with to a description of the system that lies behind it (always allowing for the possibility that this description will need to be revised in the light of the analysis of each new text). We can provide an overview of the system of language in context by intersecting two 'semiotic dimensions', the hierarchy of stratification and the spectrum of metafunctions, as shown in Table 26.1. This overview identifies systems such as SPEECH FUNCTION that are likely to be important in the analysis of conversation.

(1) Hierarchy of stratification. In terms of the hierarchy of stratification, conversation unfolds in context as patterns of meaning (semantics), wordings (lexicogrammar) and sounding (phonology).[9] A stratally-comprehensive analysis of conversation thus involves contextual, semantic, lexicogrammatical and phonological analysis (cf. Halliday, 1984; Matthiessen et al., 2005):

- **Context**: Contextual analysis of conversation involves characterizing the context in which the conversation unfolds in terms of three parameters (see e.g. Halliday, 1978; Martin, 1992; Ghadessy, 1999): what's going on (field), who's taking part (tenor) and what role the context is playing in the context (mode) – and in terms of the structure of the context as reflection of these parameters (see e.g. Hasan, 1984; Eggins and Slade, 1997: Ch. 6). This is done by relating the context of the conversation to the situation type, or genre, that it instantiates.
- **Semantics**: Semantic analysis of conversation involves tracking the meanings that are made in the course of the unfolding of the conversation, relating them to the meaning potential of

Table 26.1   Function-stratification matrix showing key systems of context and language of importance in the analysis of conversation

	Ideational: logical	Ideational: experiential	*Interpersonal*	*Textual*
Context	Field		Tenor	Mode
	SOCIO-SEMIOTIC PROCESS		INSTITUTIONAL ROLES	MEDIUM
	EXPERIENTIAL DOMAIN		POWER ROLES	CHANNEL
			SOCIOMETRIC ROLES	DIVISION OF LABOUR
			FAMILIARITY	
	Situation types (genres) [as combinations of field, tenor and mode values, with distinctive contextual (generic) structures]			
Semantics	RHETORICAL COMPLEXING	EPISODE	TRANSACTION	PROGRESSION [macro to
[above 'move']	[macro to micro]		EXCHANGE	micro]
[move]		FIGURATION	SPEECH FUNCTION	
Lexicogrammar	TAXIS and LOGICO-SEMANTIC	TRANSITIVITY	MOOD (including MODALITY,	THEME; CONJUNCTION
[clause]	TYPE		MODAL ASSESSMENT, POLARITY)	
[information unit]				INFORMATION
Phonology [tone group]			TONE	TONICITY

the language (see e.g. Eggins and Slade, 1997; Halliday and Matthiessen, 2006: Hasan et al., 2007; Chs 4 and 5). Semantic analysis ranges in scale from whole conversations to local elements of meaning. The nature and number of units along this scale will depend on the nature of the context. For example, dialogic texts in a formal institutional setting, such as a classroom, will have more intermediate units, as Sinclair and Coulthard's (1975) classic study showed, but dialogic texts of a more conversational kind tend to be organized and managed mainly locally.

- **Lexicogrammar**: Lexicogrammatical analysis of conversation involves tracking the wordings that realize the meanings made in the course of the unfolding of the conversation, relating them to the wording potential of the language (see e.g. Halliday, 1985c; Eggins and Slade, 1997; Halliday and Matthiessen, 2004: Ch. 3). Lexicogrammatical analysis ranges in scale from clauses (and clause complexes) to morphemes; and through the analysis of cohesion (see Halliday and Hasan, 1976), we can also detect patterns beyond the domain of grammatical units.
- **Phonology**: Phonological analysis of conversation involves tracking the soundings that realize the wordings made in the course of the unfolding of the conversation, relating them to the sounding potential of the language. Phonological analysis ranges in scale from tone groups (and tone-group sequences) to phonemes. While all aspects of sounding are in principle relevant, in the context of research in sociolinguistics, higher-ranking aspects are likely to be of greater interest – those of the tone group (intonation) and of the foot (rhythm) (see Halliday, 1967; Halliday and Greaves, 2008).

(2) Spectrum of metafunction. The spectrum of metafunction is the organization of language, according to the functions it has evolved to serve, into three simultaneous strands of meaning (see e.g. Halliday, 1978):

- **ideational metafunction** – construing our experience of the world as meaning
- **interpersonal metafunction** – enacting our roles and relationships as meaning
- **textual metafunction** – constructing ideational and interpersonal meanings as discourse.

As these different strands of meaning operate simultaneously in text, conversations can be analysed ideationally, interpersonally and textually.

(i) We can focus on the **ideational meanings** (e.g. Halliday and Matthiessen, 2006). This involves looking at what activities and what topics get talked about, when, by whom, and how topic transition and closure are achieved, etc. Here we may be concerned with what kind of 'world view' the interactants in conversation construe together. These patterns can be seen in the analysis of TRANSITIVITY.

(ii) We can focus on the **interpersonal meanings** (e.g. Eggins and Slade, 1997: Chs 4 and 5). This involves looking at what kinds of role relations are established through talk, what attitudes interactants express to and about each other, what kinds of things they find funny, and how they negotiate taking turns, etc. These patterns can be seen from the analysis of MOOD at the grammatical level, or at the semantic level by the analysis of SPEECH FUNCTION (move analysis) and of EXCHANGE, and by the analysis of APPRAISAL – evaluative meanings (see Martin, 2000; Martin and White, 2005).

(iii) We can focus on the **textual meanings**. This involves looking at different types of COHESION used to tie chunks of the talk together (e.g. Halliday and Hasan, 1976), different patterns of salience and foregrounding, etc. Here a key concern is how interactants manage the flow of information in such a way that they can guide each other's processes of analysis and interpretation.

In summary, in our analysis of conversation, we can focus on contextual or linguistic systems. In the linguistic analysis of conversation, we can focus on any of the units of semantics, lexicogrammar and phonology, undertaking the analysis in terms of their ideational (logical, experiential), interpersonal and textual systems: see Figure 26.4.

26.4 ANALYTICAL TOOLS

In this section we draw on a range of analytical techniques discussed above to describe different aspects of conversation. Using the stratal organization of language in context set out in Table 26.1 above as a guide, we start with context, focusing on the concept of genre, to describe the macro-structure of conversation; we then move down to semantics to examine the discourse structure; and, finally, we move further down to the micro-patterns of the grammar and phonology of conversation. We will only be focusing on some selected analytical techniques at each level, so these are intended to be illustrative only and by no means comprehensive.

Context: genre (situation type)

Any conversation operates in a context of communication – a context of situation; thus, we can

Semantics

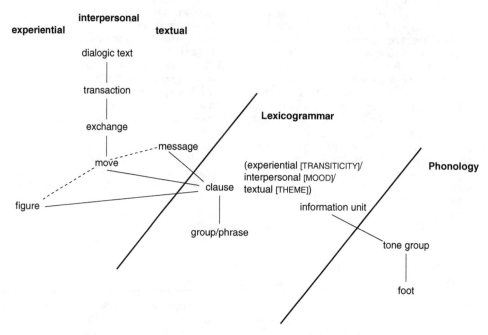

Figure 26.4   Metafunction and stratification, with indication of some compositional hierarchies.

analyse the conversation 'from above', exploring it in terms of the contextual parameters of field, tenor and mode and in terms of the contextual structure they jointly determine[10] (see Table 26.1). It is, of course, possible to treat each conversation as if it was unique – the first of its kind; however, a given conversation is typically an instance of a recurrent type of conversation and the situation that it operates in is similarly an instance of a recurrent type of situation. In other words, in our analysis of a given conversation in its context of situation, we can relate these to patterns that are intermediate between the instance pole and the potential pole of the cline of instantiation – the mid-region of the cline shown in Figure 26.3 above.

Thus, the excerpt from the conversation set out in Text 26.1 ('Joanne') is an instance of a gossip text (shown here together with some types of analysis to be discussed below), and when we look at it 'from above', from the point of view of its context of situation, we can see that this situation instantiates a recurrent situation type, or genre. This situation type is one that is likely to occur during tea breaks in workplace institutions: it is a situation type in which interactants who are workmates share personal experiences and values – more specifically, they set out to judge the behaviour of a colleague who is not part of the

in-group, in casual face-to-face interaction. We can also recognize the stages that are characteristic of such situation type: the bid to put a colleague on trial for behaviour that is judged to be unacceptable to the members of the in-group (Third Person Focus), the negative judgement of this colleague (Pejorative Evaluation), and the evidence cited to support this judgement (Substantiating Behaviour).

The excerpt in Text 26.1 is taken from our corpus of spoken conversational Australian English, OzTalk. The most commonly occurring texts types in the OzTalk corpus are story-telling (narratives, anecdotes, exempla and recounts), observation/comment, opinion texts, gossip and joke-telling. These **chunks** of talk (see Eggins and Slade, 1997: Ch. 6) are those sections of talk where interactants get to hold the floor for extended turns. However, there are large sections of the conversational data that cannot be characterized in terms of generic structure. These sections we have labelled **chat**. Conversation, we argue, therefore consists of different types of talk: the 'chunks' and the 'chat'. The chunks are those types of talk that have an identifiable generic structure. The 'chat' sections are those that do not display such structure. For these 'chat' sections, a dynamic approach to conversational analysis is

Text 26.1 'Joanne' (from OzTalk), with examples of contextual, semantic and lexicogrammatical analyses.

Context	Semantics		Lexicogrammar		Speaker	Clause
Generic stage	Exchange: move (SPEECH FUNCTION)		Clause (MOOD)	Clause (TRANSITIVITY)		
Third Person Focus	initiating and statement		declarative	material	Bron:	I'm about to throw Joanne out the window.
	→	initiating and question	interrogative: wh-	material	Pat:	Joanne who?
		responding and answer	declarative	material	Bron:	Blackwell.
	initiating and question		interrogative: wh-	material	Pat:	Why?
Pejorative Evaluation	responding and answer		declarative	relational	Bron:	She gets really pushy.
Substantiating Behaviour	initiating and statement		declarative	behavioural		I'm looking for a file for Gary;
			declarative	material		Kerry gave me three others
			declarative	relational		and I was in the middle of finding the third one for her.
	initiating and question		declarative: tagged	material	Gary:	Kerry gave you three, did she?
	responding and answer		declarative	mental: cognitive	Bron:	Yeah, you know
			bound	material		they have to be done
			declarative	material		and Joanne came up
			declarative	verbal		and she said
			interrogative: yes/no	material		"oh, can you do this?"
			declarative	verbal		and I said
						[...]
			declarative	verbal		and she went
			declarative	relational		"oh it's just that they can wait until after this one
			bound	relational		'cause they're needed today."
			declarative	material		Oh I was about ready to strangle her =
						she gets
	responding and acknowledge		declarative	relational	Gary:	Joanne's too busy.
	responding and acknowledge		declarative	mental: cognitive	Bron:	I know
			declarative	mental: cognitive		and I appreciate
			bound	relational		that she's busy
Pejorative Evaluation			declarative	relational		but she gets really pushy.
	responding and acknowledge		declarative	mental: emotive	Pat:	Yeah, I don't like pushy people either.

needed, which focuses on the processes by which moves succeed other moves.

Genres that occur in spontaneous, informal conversation are analysed in detail by Eggins and Slade (1997). (For purposes of comparison, it is also helpful to refer to spoken texts in other contexts such as those of service encounters (e.g. Ventola, 1987), the analysis of spoken, pedagogic discourse (e.g. and narratives elicited by means of sociolinguistic interviews (Plum, 1988).)

To illustrate the contextual, generic analysis of conversation, let us now return to Text 26.1 ('Joanne'). It takes place in the coffee room of a hospital at morning break time. There are four interactants: Gary, Pauline, Bron and Pat. They are all clerical staff in the hospital, and have worked together for over two years. They are in their mid- to late twenties.

This conversation instantiates the conversation type we have labelled gossip (see Eggins and Slade, 1997; Thornbury and Slade, 2006). This means that it operates in a context of situation with certain field, tenor and mode values:

- Field: Socio-semiotic process – sharing personal values and experiences – judging negatively (condemning) a colleague who's not a member of the in-group; experiential domain – the behaviour and properties of the person being judged.
- Tenor: Institutional roles – workmates (members of in-group); status and power roles – equal; familiarity daily – contact as workmates; socio-metric roles – supportive alignment (but antagonistic towards person being judged); valuation – condemnation of the behaviour of the person being judged.
- Mode: Mode – spoken; channel – face-to-face; orientation – oriented towards tenor, with field being concerned with tenor relations; division of semiotic labour – semiotic activity constitutive (rather than ancillary) of the context, with language as primary semiotic but accompanied by selections from other semiotic systems.

These field, tenor and mode values together determine the contextual or generic structure of the text. The obligatory elements of this structure occur in a specified sequence and are defining of this genre. These elements are (see Eggins and Slade, 1997, and Thornbury and Slade, 2006, for a characterization of these elements):

Third Person Focus ^ Substantiating Behaviour ^ Pejorative Evaluation ^ Wrap-up

As the characterization of field, tenor and mode suggests, the key element here is Pejorative Evaluation.

In a similar way, any conversation can be analysed in contextual terms – in terms of their field, tenor and mode values and the generic structure determined by these values (unless we are concerned with a 'chat' phase of a conversation). In the case of our gossip texts, all the elements of the gossip situation are realized by passages of conversation; however, such contextual elements may be realized non-verbally, either by contributions from semiotic systems other than language or by non-semiotic, social acts (cf. Steiner, 1991).

Semantics: moves and exchanges

Semantics is the highest stratum of language; it is the interface between language and context, and between language and other semiotic system. It covers the three modes of meaning outlined above – ideational, interpersonal and textual meanings[11] (see Table 26.1 above). These different strands of meaning are thus covered in the semantic analysis of conversation, bringing out how the interactants jointly construe their experience of the world (ideational) enact their roles and relations (interpersonal), and manage the flow of information (textual).

It is the interpersonal metafunction that provides interactants in conversation with the resources for creating conversation through the exchange of meaning, and in this section we will focus on interpersonal meaning. We will build on the contextual description of Text 26.1 ('Joanne') by exploring the unfolding of conversational exchanges, describing how one speaker's move leads to another, and then to another. The concern in this interpersonal analysis is to account for the interactivity of the conversation – how the conversation unfolds.

In the interactive development of conversation, each utterance serves as a **move** (described in CA as one pair part of an adjacency pair); it is the basic interpersonal semantic unit in conversation and other types dialogue. It indicates a point of possible turn-transfer, and therefore carries with it the idea of 'it could stop here'. (This is what the CA researchers call a TCU.) In a move, by selecting a speech function from the system of SPEECH FUNCTION, the speaker takes on a speech role (e.g. questioner), and assigns a complementary speech role to the addressee (e.g. answerer).[12] The primary initiating speech functions are **command**, **statement**, **offer** and **question**, set out in Table 26.2 together with typical grammatical realizations (see Halliday, 1984; Halliday and Matthiessen, 2004: Ch. 4). They embody two crucial variables in an exchange: the nature of the commodity being exchanged (information [a knowledge exchange] vs goods-and-services [an action exchange]) and the orientation of the exchange (giving vs demanding).

For each initiating speech function, there is an expected response and a discretionary alternative (see Halliday, 1984; Halliday and Matthiessen, 2004: Ch. 4): see Table 26.3.

Both expected and discretionary responses engage with the initiating move. However, the difference is that the expected responses tend to finish the exchange as there has been a resolution (e.g. an offer followed by an acceptance; or a question followed by an answer). Discretionary responses, on the other hand, tend to open out the

Table 26.2   The basic system of SPEECH FUNCTION (semantics) as the intersection of orientation (giving/demanding) and commodity (information/goods-and-services), with grammatical realization (MOOD, indicative by ↘)

	Information	Goods-and-services
giving	statement ↘ declarative *he gave her a cup of tea*	offer ↘ various *have a cup of tea!; would you like a cup of tea?*
demanding	question ↘ interrogative *did he give her a cup of tea?*	command ↘ imperative *give me a cup of tea!*

Table 26.3   Initiating and responding speech functions

Initiating speech function	Expected response	Discretionary alternative
offer [O] *Do you want to get married?*	acceptance [R/O]* *Absolutely!*	rejection *Certainly not!*
command [I/C] *Get married first!*	compliance [R/C]* *Okay.*	refusal *I won't!*
statement [I/S] *Sally is getting married.*	acknowledgment [R/K] *Is she?*	contradiction *No, she isn't.*
question [I/Q] *Is Sally getting married?*	answer [R/A] *Yes.*	disclaimer *I don't know.*

*These responses are frequently non-verbal.

exchange because, for example, if an offer is rejected or a statement contradicted, further negotiation is needed – such as a reason, an excuse or an apology. Expected responses (preferred second pair parts in CA terms) support the proposition or proposal of the speaker and thereby serve to create alignment and solidarity. By contrast, the discretionary responses (dispreferred second pair parts) are either disengaging and non-committal or openly confronting.

When we focus on the interactional structuring of exchanges, we find that a single move will often make a distinct contribution to the development of the exchange. However, at other times, these functions in an exchange will be achieved not by a single move but by a group of moves. We will refer to this as a **move complex** (cf. Ventola, 1988). Such move complexes can be modelled as rhetorical complexes, using rhetorical structure theory (RST; see e.g. Mann, Matthiessen and Thompson, 1992), which may – but need not – be realized grammatically by clause complexes (see Matthiessen, 2002). For example, in Text 26.1: *Joanne* below Bron's response to Gary's question is not a single move but three rhetorically-related moves that form her answer to the question; this rhetorical move complex is realized grammatically as a clause complex. This then is followed by a new exchange, initiated by Jessie asking another question. For this reason, functional linguists refer to this basic interactive pattern as an

exchange (e.g. Coulthard and Brazil, 1979; Halliday, 1984), which is similar to the concept of an adjacency pair in CA. An exchange then can be defined as (adapted from Eggins and Slade, 1997: 222):

...the sequence of moves concerned with negotiating a proposition or proposal presented in an initiating move. An exchange can be identified as beginning with an initiating move, and continuing until another initiating move occurs.

We will now analyse 'Joanne' in terms of its exchange structure made up of moves selecting in the system of SPEECH FUNCTION: see Text 26.1 ('Joanne') above. Bron's first initiating statement, *I'm about to throw **Joanne** out the window*, immediately establishes Joanne as the Focus of New information. Since there is presumably more than one person called *Joanne* at the hospital, Pat initiates another exchange by demanding a clarification, *Joanne who?* After Bron responds, Pat asks Bron why she is annoyed with Joanne and Bron provides a detailed response, clearly stating her negative evaluation. Bron then initiates another statement, providing evidence or justification for her negative evaluation of Joanne. In the rest of the text, Bron develops the 'case' that Joanne is really pushy. Gary and Pat contribute to the construction of the gossip sequence by means of a few simple moves where they ask for further information from Bron. She then responds, in turn, using a series of move complexes in each case. Initially, Pat and Gary are reluctant to gossip about Joanne, but Pat's final 'response: acknowledgement' provides tacit approval of the gossip, with her comment: *I don't like pushy people either.*

The exchange structure analysis has demonstrated that the gossip text is jointly constructed by the two roles of gossip provider and gossip seeker/participant, where the gossip provider then launches into longer move complexes in order to build up a case against 'the absent other'. The analysis has also demonstrated whom the dominant and incidental interactants are, which interactants produced the most moves and move complexes, and the kind of speech functional selections the speakers made. In this way, we can create **interactant profiles** to show, for each interactant, what his or her preferred selections are (cf. Matthiessen, 1995; Lam and Webster, 2009).

Lexicogrammar

Lexicogrammar consists of both grammar (grammatical items and structures, including both 'syntax' and 'morphology') and lexis (lexical items, or 'vocabulary'). It stands in a natural relationship to semantics: wordings are semantically transparent as patterns of meaning, although this natural relationship is more complex and less direct in the case of lexical and grammatical metaphor.

Like semantics, lexicogrammar is organized metafunctionally into resources concerned with different modes of meaning – ideational (experiential and logical), interpersonal and textual. Moves and exchanges are part of the interpersonal organization of semantics, and moves are realized by clauses in the lexicogrammar. At the same time, clauses also realize messages: quanta of information in the flow of information (textual) and figures (process configuration); quanta of change in the flow of events (experiential). Clauses consist of groups and phrases, and these consist of words, which in turn consist of morphemes.

All these grammatical units contribute to the construction of conversation and are consequently relevant to comprehensive lexicogrammatical analysis of conversation. However, the clause – with its potential to form clause complexes – is the 'gateway' into lexicogrammar from semantics; it constitutes the window on patterns of meaning in conversation. Therefore, lexicogrammatical analysts of conversation have tended to start with the clause, as shown and modelled by, for example, Halliday (1985c, 1994), and Eggins and Slade (1997).

The major systems of the clause are set out in Table 26.1 above. We have tracked the selection in two of them in Text 26.1 ('Joanne'), the interpersonal system of MOOD and the experiential system of TRANSITIVITY. Let us just illustrate these two systems, together with the textual system of THEME for a couple of key clauses in our conversation: see Figure 26.5.

We'll comment only on the first clause, *I'm about to throw Joanne out of the window.* This clause realizes the move that serves as Third Person Focus in the structure of the context in which the text unfolds.

(i) THEME. Textually, it gives the speaker (*I*) the status of Theme – the point of departure of the clause as a message. In other words, Bron is setting herself up as the orientation for what's to follow – her angle as the context in which the remainder of the clause is to be interpreted. She also chose *throw Joanne out of the window* as New Information and *out of the window* as the Focus of New information; in other words, the person who is to be judged in the gossip is presented as newsworthy and her destiny as the focus of this news.

(ii) MOOD. Interpersonally, the clause realizes the statement selected by this initiating move of the gossip; its mood is 'declarative', with the speaker as the element upon which the validity of the statement rests. In the groups realizing the Finite/ Predicator and the Adjunct, the speaker has chosen lexical items with negative connotation (*throw out of the window*). Such interpersonal lexical resources have been described under the heading of APPRAISAL in SFL (see Martin and White, 2005), and this description has been applied in the study of conversation (see Eggins and Slade, 1997).

(iii) TRANSITIVITY. Experientially, the clause realizes a figure of 'doing', one in which the speaker is construed as the Actor bringing about the act of throwing and Joanne as the one impacted, the Goal. This is of course figurative, representing the speaker's extreme frustration with Joanne; but it is interesting that she has construed herself as the aggressor in an act of punishing Joanne for her transgression. This motif is in fact picked up later in the conversation: [Actor:] *I* [Process:] *was about ready to strangle* [Goal:] *her.*

The discussion of *I'm about to throw Joanne out of the window* gives a hint of the contribution that the lexicogrammatical analysis of conversation can make to an understanding of how the selections made by the speakers create the patterns of meaning that make up the conversation. For more detailed illustrations see, for example, Halliday (1985c, 1994).

	I	*'m*	*about to throw*	*Joanne*	*out the* ***window***
THEME	Theme	Rheme			
MOOD	Subject	Finite	Predicator	Complement	Adjunct
	Mood		Residue		
TRANSITIVITY	Actor	Process		Goal	Place
	nom. gp.	verbal group [lexis: negative]		nominal group	prepositional phrase [lexis: negative]

	she	*gets*		***really pushy***
THEME	Theme	Rheme		
MOOD	Subject	Finite	Predicator	Complement
	Mood		Residue	
TRANSITIVITY	Carrier	Process		Attribute
	nom. gp.	verbal group		nominal group [lexis: negative]

Figure 26.5 Analysis of two key clauses from Text 26.1 ('Joanne').

Phonology

In addition to analysing conversation at the levels of context, semantics and lexicogrammar, we can also analyse the 'expression' of conversation. Prototypically, conversation is spoken – although, as we have noted, new technology has opened up new channels for written conversation, and conversations are signed in sign languages in deaf communities. Spoken conversation can also be analysed phonologically and phonetically; and a well-rounded comprehensive analysis of conversation needs to take these levels of expression into account. In phonological and phonetic analysis, conversation is interpreted in terms of patterns of sounding. In phonological analysis, patterns of sounding are analysed in abstract terms, with an orientation towards patterns of wording: phonology is, as it were, an interface between linguistic content and the material manifestation of language as sound. The material manifestation of language in sound is the responsibility of phonetic analysis.

Phonetic analysis of conversation will clearly be important in a range of contexts of research and application such as clinical contexts (e.g. in speech therapy), forensic contexts (e.g. speaker identification) and speech processing contexts (e.g. in the development of dialogue systems). All these have – or should have – a prominent social component (see chapter by Coulthard et al., this volume).

Phonological analysis of conversation is important in all the contexts where phonetic analysis may be considered; but it is also important more generally whenever analysis of conversation is undertaken. Phonological analysis includes both prosody and articulation. Prosodic analysis involves tone groups (intonation units) and feet (rhythm units), whereas articulatory analysis involves syllables and phonemes. In most analysis of conversation, it is prosodic analysis that is particularly critical to an understanding of conversational patterns. Therefore, the inclusion of annotation of intonation (tone groups) and rhythm (feet) in transcripts of conversation is a valuable step in the analysis of conversation. Here are some examples from 'Joanne':

//1 ^ I'm a/bout to /throw Jo/anne out the /window //
// 1 Kerry gave you / **three** // 2 **did** she? //
// 2 ^ Did Kerry / give you those / **files** / there? //
// 1 Why / couldn't she / grab / someone / **else**? //
// 1 ^ I was a/bout /ready to /**strangle** her //
//3 **yeah** I don't // 1 like /pushy /people /**ei**ther //

(Here double slashes mark boundaries between tone groups, single slashes boundaries between feet; Arabic numeral at the beginning of tone groups indicate the tone selected, and bold indicates the location of the Tonic. The caret indicates a silent beat in the rhythmic pattern.)

Both intonation and rhythm play a significant role in the construction of conversation. But while rhythm is largely internal to the level of phonology, intonation is directly related to grammatical systems, so we will say a few more words about it. Various descriptions of intonation in English have been put forward: the more widely used ones include Halliday's account (e.g. Halliday, 1967, 1970a; Tench, 1996; Halliday and Greaves, 2008); Brazil's account, which is similar to Halliday's (e.g. Brazil, 1985); Crystal's account (e.g., Crystal, 1969; used in the London-Lund corpus of spoken English); and the ToBI framework developed by Janet Pierrehumbert and Mary Beckman. Halliday's account of intonation is part of a holistic account of language in context and his analysis of intonation in conversation complements and extends the semantic and lexicogrammatical analyses. With the help of Halliday and Greaves (2008), the analysis of conversation in terms of intonation is now very accessible.

Language and other semiotic systems

In this section, we have looked at some analytical tools for describing the generic, discourse, lexicogrammatical and phonological structure of conversation. We have analysed the same authentic extract of casual conversation from different perspectives. Other semiotic systems may also play an important role in accompanying language. The range of other semiotic systems will depend not only on the mode variable within context – whether the channel is graphic or aural – but also on more delicate differentiations such as the distinction within aural between face-to-face and other channels such as over the telephone

(cf. Matthiessen, 2009, pp. 11–38). Conversation must have evolved as face-to-face conversation, and conversational language must therefore have evolved together with paralanguage, gestures and other forms of 'body language' (cf. Thibault's (2004) notion of the signifying body). These other semiotic systems accompanying language in conversation have been studied by a growing number of researchers; see for example, McNeill (2000) for recent contributions to the study of gesture.

26.5 CONCLUSION

In this chapter, after describing conversation, we briefly reviewed key ideas from the approaches we consider most relevant to the analysis of conversation, suggesting that an eclectic approach to analysing conversation is not only richer but also essential when dealing with the complexities of spoken language. We then outlined a range of analytical techniques for describing the different levels of conversational structure–from genre, to discourse, to lexicogrammar to phonology. What we hope to have demonstrated is that, to analyse conversation, multidimensional interpretations are needed and that these different analyses provide complementary perspectives on the nature and description of conversation in English. By analysing the same text ('Joanne') from different perspectives, we can build up a picture of how conversation functions to achieve 'social work' at both the micro (interaction) and macro (cultural) levels.

In presenting this text and the descriptions used in the analysis of conversation, we have drawn on English. We have done this purely for practical reasons, not for theoretical ones. From a theoretical point of view, any general account of conversation must take a wide range of languages into account. This is certainly a real challenge – there are just over 6900 languages spoken today (according to the best source, the Ethnologue[13]), although many, perhaps even most, will have disappeared in another century or so. Only a few languages have been described in rich comprehensive ways that would give us sufficient information about the nature of conversation in these languages and a true basis for robust generalizations across languages. There are of course valuable contributions to the description of conversation in a range of languages, particularly in anthropologically-oriented linguistics such as the Ethnography of Speaking framework and Tagmemics; and there are investigations in cross-cultural pragmatics that will give us some important indications of the degree of variation we can expect to find. For a

typological perspective on the interpersonal
resources of languages, see Teruya et al. (2007)
and Matthiessen, Teruya and Wu (2008); and for
sketches of the interpersonal resources of the
grammars of eight different languages, see
Caffarel, Martin and Matthiessen (2004).

NOTES

1   There are obviously many ways of classifying
conversation. In the field of human–computer
interaction, a well-known contribution is Winograd's
(1987: Section 5) taxonomy: 'conversation for clarification, conversation for possibilities, and conversation for orientation'.

2   Malcolm Coulthard (pers comm 2006).

3   Psathas (1995: 2) suggests that the concerns
of conversation analysis would be reflected by the
name 'ethnomethodological interaction analysis'.

4   For transcription method and conventions,
see e.g. http://www.sscnet.ucla.edu/soc/faculty/
schegloff/TranscriptionProject/index.html

5   For research on turn-taking, see Sacks,
Schegloff and Jefferson 1974; on topic manage-
ment, see Sacks, 1992; and on adjacency pairs, see
Sacks 1992.

6   + indicates a constructed example.

7   In addition to the work we will deal with
here, there have also been SFL contributions made
in the context of computational modelling, e.g.
Bateman (1985) and O'Donnell and Sefton (1995).

8   The system that lies behind it is of course a
collective resource; the cline of instantiation is an
important dimension in linking the 'micro-patterns'
of a particular conversation to the 'macro-patterns'
of the system of language in the context of
culture.

9   This is the prototypical expression of conversation, as in spoken face-to-face conversation; but
conversation may also be signed, in the case of sign
languages of deaf communities, or written, as on
online chat.

10   The focus on context is due to the anthropologist Bronislaw Malinowski. Other schemes for
describing context include those proposed in linguistics by J. R. Firth, Dell Hymes (as part of the
Ethnography of Communication), in AI by Roger
Schank (frames and scripts), and in sociology (e.g.
Argyle, Furnham and Graham, 1981).

11   In certain other approaches, the realm of
meaning is divided into 'semantics' and 'pragmatics';
but in SFL, they are treated as a unified system of
meaning, differentiated in metafunctional terms.

12   Speech functions have also been interpreted
in philosophical terms in the different versions of
speech act theory, covered in an extensive literature.
Here the emphasis tends to be on individual action

rather than on interaction between persons,
but speech acts have been used quite widely in the
analysis of dialogic texts.

13   See http://www.ethnologue.com/

REFERENCES

Argyle, M., Furnham, A. and Graham, J. A. (1981) *Social Situations*. Cambridge: Cambridge University Press.

Bateman, J. A. (1985) 'Utterances in context: towards a systemic theory of the intersubjective achievement of discourse'. PhD thesis, Department of Artificial Intelligence / School of Epistemics, University of Edinburgh.

Bateson, M. C. (1979) '"The epigenesis of conversational interaction": a personal account of research development', in Bullowa M. (ed.). *Before Speech the Beginnings of Interpersonal Communication*. Cambridge: Cambridge University Press pp. 63–77.

Berger, P. L. and Luckmann, T. (1966) *The Social Construction of Reality*. Garden City, NY: Doubleday.

Brazil, D. (1985) 'Phonology: intonation in discourse', in T. A. van Dijk (ed.), *Handbook of Discourse Analysis*. New York: Academic Press. pp. 57–75.

Bullowa, M. (ed.) (1979) *Before Speech: The Beginnings of Interpersonal Communication*. Cambridge: Cambridge University Press.

Caffarel, A., Martin, J. R. and Matthiessen, C. M. I. M. (eds) (2004) *Language Typology: A Functional Perspective*. (Current Issues in Linguistic Theory 253.) Amsterdam: Benjamins. xiii, p. 692, index.

Christian, D. (2004) *Maps of Time: An Introduction to Big History*. Berkeley, CA: University of California Press.

Coulthard, M. and Brazil, D. (1979) *Exchange Structure*. Discourse analysis Monograph No. 5. English Language Research, University of Birmingham, Birmingham. (Abridged version appears in M. Coulthard and M. Montgomery (eds) *Studies in Discourse Analysis*. London: Routledge and Kegan Paul: pp. 82–106.)

Crystal, D. (1969) *Prosodic Systems and Intonation in English*. Cambridge: Cambridge University Press.

Dunbar, R. (1996) *Grooming, Gossip and the Evolution of Language*. London: Faber and Faber.

Eggins, S. (1990) 'Conversational structure: a systemic-functional analysis of interpersonal and logical meaning in multiparty sustained talk'. PhD thesis, Department of Linguistics, University of Sydney.

Eggins, S. and Slade, D. (1997) *Analysing Casual Conversation*. London: Equinox. (Previously published by Continuum.)

Firth, J. R. (1957) *Papers in Linguistics 1934–51*. London: Oxford University Press.

Ford, C. and Thompson, S. A. (1996) 'Interactional units in conversation: syntactic, intonational, and pragmatic resources for turn management', in E. Ochs, E. Schegloff and S. A. Thompson, (eds), *Interaction and Grammar* Cambridge: Cambridge University Press. pp. 134–84.

Garfinkel, H. (1967) *Studies in Ethnomethodology*. Englewood Cliffs; NJ: Prentice Hall.

Ghadessy, M. (ed.) (1999) *Text and Context in Functional Linguistics*. Amsterdam: Benjamins.

Goffman, E. (1981) *Forms of Talk*. Philadelphia: University of Pennsylvania Press.

Grice, P. (1967/75) 'Logic and conversation', William James Lectures, Harvard University. Reprinted in Cole, P. and Morgan, J. (eds) (1975) *Syntax and Semantics*. Vol. 3: Speech Acts. New York: Academic Press. pp. 43–58.

Halliday, M. A. K. (1961) 'Categories of the theory of grammar', *Word*, 17(3): 242–92.

Halliday, M. A. K. (1963a) 'The tones of English', *Archivum Linguisticum*, 15(1): 1–28.

Halliday, M. A. K. (1963b) 'Intonation in English grammar', *Transactions of the Philological Society*. pp. 143–69.

Halliday, M. A. K. (1967) *Intonation and Grammar in British English*. The Hague: Mouton. (Janua Linguarum Series Practica 48.)

Halliday, M. A. K. (1970a) *A Course in Spoken English: Intonation*. London: Oxford University Press.

Halliday, M. A. K. (1970b) 'Functional diversity in language, as seen from a consideration of modality and mood in English', *Foundations of Language*, 6: 322–61. Reprinted in Halliday, M. A. K. (2005) *Studies in English Language*. Volume 7 in the Collected Works of M. A. K. Halliday, edited by J. Webster. London: Continuum. Chapter 5: 164–204.

Halliday, M. A. K. (1975) *Learning How to Mean: Explorations in the Development of Language*. London: Edward Arnold.

Halliday, M. A. K. (1978) *Language as Social Semiotic: The Social Interpretation of Language and Meaning*. London: Edward Arnold.

Halliday, M. A. K. (1984) 'Language as code and language as behaviour: a systemic-functional interpretation of the nature and ontogenesis of dialogue', in M. A. K. Halliday, R. P. Fawcett, S. Lamb and A. Makkai (eds), *The Semiotics of Language and Culture*. London: Frances Pinter. Volume 1. pp. 3–35. Reprinted in Halliday, M. A. K. (2003) *On Language and Linguistics*. Volume 3 of Collected Works of M. A. K. Halliday. Edited by J. Webster. London: Continuum. Chapter 10: 226–50.

Halliday, M.A.K. (1994) 'So you say "pass" ... thank you three muchly'. A.D. Grimshaw (ed.), *What's going on here: complementary studies of professional talk*. Norwood, N.J.: Ablex. 175–229.

Halliday, M. A. K. (1985a/1994) *An Introduction to Functional Grammar*. 2nd edn. London: Edward Arnold.

Halliday, M. A. K. (1985c) 'Dimensions of discourse analysis: grammar', in T. A. van Dijk (ed.), *Handbook of Discourse Analysis*. New York: Academic Press. pp. 29–56.

Halliday, M. A. K. & C. M. I. M Matthiessen (2004) *An introduction to functional grammar*. 3rd Edn. London: Edward Arnold.

Halliday, M. A. K. (2004) *The Language of Early Childhood*. Volume 4 of Collected Works of M.A.K. Halliday. Edited by Jonathan Webster. London & New York: Continuum.

Halliday, M. A. K. (2005) 'On matter and meaning: the two realms of human experience', *Linguistics and the Human Sciences*, 1(1): 59–82.

Halliday, M. A. K. and Greaves, W. S. (2008) *Intonation in the Grammar of English*. London: Equinox.

Halliday, M. A. K. and Hasan, R. (1976) *Cohesion in English*. London: Longman.

Halliday, M. A. K. and Matthiessen, C. M. I. M. (2006) *Construing Experience through Meaning: A Language-Based Approach to Cognition*. (Study Edition.) London: Continuum.

Halliday, M. A. K. and Plum, G. (1983) 'On casual conversation', in R. Hasan (ed.), *Discourse on Discourse*. Occasional Papers No. 7, 1983. Macquarie University.

Hasan, R. (1984) 'The nursery tale as a genre', *Nottingham Linguistic Circular*, 13: 71–102.

Hasan, R., Matthiessen, C. M. I. M. and Webster, J. (eds) (2005) *Continuing Discourse on Language*. Volume 1. London: Equinox.

Hasan, R., Cloran, C. Williams, G. and Lukin, A. (2007) 'Semantic networks: the description of linguistic meaning in SFL', in R. Hasan, C. M. I. M. Matthiessen and J. Webster (eds), *Continuing Discourse on Language*. Volume 2. London: Equinox. pp. 697–738.

Hasan, R., Matthiessen, C. M. I. M. and Webster, J. (eds) (2007) *Continuing Discourse on Language*. Volume 2. London: Equinox.

Heritage, J. 1989. 'Current developments in conversation analysis.' In D. Roger and P. Bull (eds.), *Conversation*. Clevedon: Multilingual Matters. pp. 21–47.

Heritage, J. (1984) *Garfinkel and Ethnomethodology*. Cambridge: Polity Press.

Hutchby, I. and Wooffitt, R. (1998) *Conversation Analysis: Principles, Practices and Applications*. Cambridge: Polity Press.

Jefferson, G., Sacks, H. and Schegloff, E. (1987) 'Notes on laughter in the pursuit of intimacy', in G. Button and J. Lee (eds), *Talk and Social Organisation*. London: Multilingual Matters.

Lam, M. and Webster, J. (2009) 'The lexicogrammatical reflection of interpersonal relationship in conversation', *Discourse Studies*, 11(1): 37–57.

McHoul, A. and Rapley, M. (eds) (2001) *How to Analyse Talk in Institutional Settings: a casebook of methods*. London: Continuum.

McNeill, D. (ed.) (2000) *Language and Gesture*. Cambridge: Cambridge University Press.

Mann, W. C., Matthiessen, C. M. I. M. and Thompson, S. A. (1992) 'Rhetorical structure theory and text analysis', in W. C. Mann and S. A. Thompson (eds), *Discourse Description: Diverse Linguistic Analyses of a Fund Raising Text*. Amsterdam: Benjamins. pp. 39–78.

Martin, J.R. (1992) *English Text: System and Structure*. Amsterdam: Benjamins.

Martin, J. R. (2000) 'Beyond exchange: appraisal systems in English', in S. Hunston and G. Thompson (eds), *Evaluation in Text: Authorial Stance and the Construction of Discourse*. Oxford: Oxford University Press pp. 142–175.

Martin, J. R. and White, P. R. R. (2005) *The Language of Evaluation: Appraisal in English*. London: Palgrave Macmillan.

Matthiessen, C. M. I. M. (1995) *Lexicogrammatical Cartography: English Systems*. Tokyo: International Language Sciences Publishers.

Matthiessen, C. M. I. M. (2002) 'Combining clauses into clause complexes: a multi-faceted view', in J. Bybee and

M. Noonan (eds), *Complex Sentences in Grammar and Discourse: Essays in Honor of Sandra A. Thompson.* Amsterdam: Benjamins. pp. 237–322.

Matthiessen, C. M. I. M. (2007) 'The "architecture" of language according to systemic functional theory: developments since the 1970', in R. Hasan, C. M. I. M. Matthiessen and J. Webster (eds), *Continuing Discourse on Language.* Volume 2. London: Equinox. pp. 505–61.

Matthiessen, C. M. I. M. (forthcoming) 'Multisemiotic and context-based register typology: registerial variation in the complementarity of semiotic systems', in E. Ventola, and A. J. M. Guijarro (eds), *The World Shown and the World Told.* Basingstoke, UK: Palgrave Macmillan.

Matthiessen, C. M. I. M., Lukin, A. Butt, D. G. Cleirigh, C. and Nesbitt, C. (2005) 'Welcome to Pizza Hut: a case study of multistratal analysis', *Australian Review of Applied Linguistics,* 19: 123–50.

Matthiessen, C. M. I. M., Teruya, K. and WU, C. (2008) 'Multilingual studies as a multi-dimensional space of interconnected language studies', in J. Webster (ed.), *Meaning in Context.* London: Continuum. pp. 146–221.

Matthiessen, C. M. I. M., Teruya, K. and Lam, M. (in press) *Key Terms in Systemic Functional Linguistics.* London: Continuum.

Matthiessen, C. M. I. M., Teruya, K. and Lam, M. (forthcoming) *Key Terms in Systemic Functional Linguistics.* London: Continuum.

Ochs, E., Schegloff, E. A. and Thompson, S. A. (eds) (1996) *Interaction and Grammar.* (Studies in Interactional Sociolinguistics 13.) Cambridge: Cambridge University Press.

O'Donnell, M. and Sefton, P. (1995) 'Modelling telephonic interaction: a dynamic approach', *Journal of Applied Linguistics,* 10(1): 63–78.

Psathas, G. (1995) *Conversation Analysis: The Study of Talk-In-Interaction.* (Qualitative Research Methods.) London: Sage.

Plum, G.A. (1988) Textual and contextual conditioning in spoken English: a genre-based approach. University of Sydney: Ph.D. Dissertation.

Ruhlemann, C. (2007) *Conversation in Context: A Corpus-Driven Approach.* London: Continuum.

Sacks, H. (1972a) 'An initial investigation of the usability of conversational data for doing sociology', in D. Sudnow (ed.), *Studies in Social Interaction.* New York: Free Press. pp. 31–74.

Sacks, H. (1972b) 'On the analysability of stories by children', in J. H. Gumperz and Hymes, D. (eds), *Directions in Sociolinguistics.* New York: Holt, Rinehart and Winston.

Sacks, H. (1974) 'An analysis of the course of a joke's telling in conversation', in R. Bauman and J. Sherzer (eds), *Explorations in the Ethnography of Speaking.* Cambridge: Cambridge University Press.

Sacks, H. (1978) 'Some technical considerations of a dirty joke', in J. Schenkein (ed.). *Studies in the Organization at Conversational Interaction.* New York: Academic Press pp. 249–69.

Sacks, H. (1992) *Lectures on Conversation.* Volumes I and II. Edited by G. Jefferson with Introduction by E.A. Schegloff. Oxford: Blackwell.

Sacks, H., Schegloff, E. A. and Jefferson, G. (1974) 'A simplest systematics for the organisation of turn-taking for conversation', *Language,* 50: 696–735.

Schegloff, E. A. (1986) 'The routine as achievement', *Human Studies,* 9: 111–51.

Schegloff, E.A. (1987) 'Some Sources of Misunderstanding in Talk-in-Interaction.' *Linguistics* 25: 201–218.

Schegloff, E. A. (1988) 'Description in the social sciences I: talk-in-interaction', *Papers in Pragmatics,* 2: 1–24.

Schegloff, E. A. (2006) *Sequence Organization in Interaction.* Vol. 1, *A Primer in Conversation Analysis.* Cambridge: Cambridge University Press,

Schegloff, E. A. and Sacks, H. (1973) 'Opening up closings', *Semiotica,* 7(3, 4): 289–327.

Schenkein, J. (ed.) (1978) *Studies in the Organization of Conversational Interaction.* New York: Academic Press.

Sinclair, J. and Coulthard, M. (1975) *Towards an Analysis of Discourse.* London: Oxford University Press.

Slade, D. M. (1996) 'The texture of casual conversation in English'. PhD thesis, University of Sydney.

Steiner, E. (1991) *A Functional Perspective on Language, Action and Interpretation.* Berlin: Mouton de Gruyter.

Taylor, T. J. and Cameron, D. (1987) *Analysing Conversation: Rules and Units in the Structure of Talk.* Oxford: Pergamon Press.

Tench, P. (1996) *The Intonation Systems of English.* London: Cassell.

Teruya, K., Akerejola, E. Andersen, T. H. et al., (2007) 'Typology of MOOD: a text-based and system-based functional view', in R. Hasan, C. M. I. M. Matthiessen and J. J. Webster (eds), *Continuing Discourse on Language: A Functional Perspective.* Volume 2. London: Equinox. pp. 859–920.

Thibault, P. J. (2004) *Brain, Mind and the Signifying Body: An Ecosocial Semiotic Theory.* London, New York: Continuum.

Thornbury, S. and Slade, D. (2006) *Conversation: From Description to Pedagogy.* Cambridge: Cambridge University Press.

Trevarthen, C. (1979) 'Communication and cooperation in early infancy: a description of primary intersubjectivity', in Bullowa (ed.), *Before Speech: The Beginnings of Interpersonal Communication.* Cambridge: Cambridge University Press. pp. 321–47.

Trevarthen, C. (1987) 'Sharing making sense: intersubjectivity and the making of an infant's meaning', in R. Steele and T. Threadgold (eds), *Language Topics: Essays in Honour of Michael Halliday.* Volume 1. Amsterdam: Benjamins.

Ventola, E. (1987) The structure of social interaction: a systemic approach to the semiotics of service encounters. London: Frances Pinter.

Ventola, E. (1988) 'The logical relations in exchange', in J. D. Benson and W. S. Greaves (eds), *Systemic Functional Approaches to Discourse.* Norwood, NJ: Ablex. pp. 51–72.

Winograd, T. (1987) 'A language/action perspective on the design of cooperative work', *Human–Computer Interaction,* 3(1): 3–30.

27

Narrative Analysis

Alexandra Georgakopoulou

27.1 INTRODUCTION

The current fascination with oral (cf. vernacular, non-literary) narrative spans a wide range of social science disciplines, e.g. sociology, psychology, social anthropology, etc., and is frequently referred to as the 'narrative turn' (see papers in Bamberg, 2006; Brockmeier and Carbaugh, 2001; Daiute and Lightfoot, 2004; and De Fina, Schiffrin and Bamberg, 2006). In these disciplines, narrative is seen as an archetypal, fundamental mode for making sense of the world and, as such, as a privileged structure, system, or mode for tapping into the teller's social identities and sense of self. The significance of narrative for identity analysis does not however mean that there is consensus on the definitions and views of narrative as an object of inquiry. In fact, narrative remains a particularly elusive, contested and indeterminate in meaning concept. It is variously used not only as an epistemology, a quintessentially qualitative method, but also as a fundamental communication mode, an archetypal or supra-genre. It is also sometimes used as an all-encompassing term – in a sort of 'everything is narrative' way – defined so broadly as to be equated with experience, time, history and life itself. On the other hand, it is also viewed more specifically as a kind of discourse or text-type with conventionalized textual features (see Georgakopoulou and Goutsos, 2000: 64–8).[1] The downsides to this diversity have been frequently noted (e.g. Josselson, 2006) and there is concern that it often breeds an interpretative vacuum, thus leaving the area exposed to impressionistic work that does not contribute to the creation of a critical mass. A related issue is the narrative turn which has celebrated narrative as a way of doing research that privileges the experiential, and as a welcome antidote to the traditional

positivist-based science that was dominant for a long time, well into the 1970s and 1980s (cf. Bruner, 1997: 62). This has often resulted in the idealization and essentialization of narrative. In turn, as we will see below, it has hampered empirical research on the numerous genres and situated micro instances of stories (cf. Georgakopoulou and Goutsos, 2000).

In the light of the above, to talk about well-defined and delimited schools of narrative analysis necessitates a crude process of abstraction which does not do justice to the many different strands of existing work. Bearing this in mind, I will propose here that within sociolinguistic research on narrative, we can talk about two distinct ways of doing narrative analysis: one inspired by a conventional and largely canonical paradigm; the other based on a social interactional view of narrative (for a detailed discussion see De Fina and Georgakopoulou, 2008a). The former is traceable to Labov and Waletzky's (1967) foundational model of narrative analysis, but is also informed by the narrative turn in the social sciences. Social interactional approaches on the other hand stress variously the role of context in the shaping of narrative tellings and see them as being intimately linked with the production of social life.

In this chapter, I focus more on the social interactional approaches and register their latest advances. This is, in part, a conscious attempt to redress the balance. Until recently, ample time and space have been devoted to the 'Labovian' model and its importance has been duly acknowledged (not least in my own work; for example, see Georgakopoulou, 1997; Georgakopoulou and Goutsos, 2004; see also Toolan, 1988). As of late, however, sociolinguistic approaches to narrative have been making a decisive shift towards social interactional approaches, which we have described as the shift from narrative as text to narrative as social practices (De Fina and Georgakopoulou, 2008a, 2008b).

27.2 THE LABOVIAN MODEL AS THE CONVENTIONAL PARADIGM

In 1997, the then *Journal of Narrative and Life History* (now *Narrative Inquiry*) produced a substantial Special Issue (also published as a book) entitled 'Oral versions of personal experience: three decades of narrative analysis' (ed. by Michael Bamberg). The dozens of contributions by a galaxy of names in the area confirmed two things: first, the undeniably profound – and for some, surprising[2] – influence that Labov's model has had within sociolinguistics to the point that narrative analysis has, until recently, been synonymous with it. In addition, those contributions registered the fierce critique that the model has been on the receiving end of, sometimes from allies' sources: i.e. from scholars who had more or less taken the model on board and who showed in their empirical studies that it did not quite work or that it needed further systematization. As already suggested, a full account of the model is beyond the scope of this chapter. Instead, I will single out what I see as its key elements. By examining oral narratives of personal, past experience in interview settings, Labov and Waletzky (1967), and later Labov working alone (1972), showed that there is structure and systematicity in the storytelling of ordinary people of a kind that was expected to be found in artful forms of narrative. They defined narrative in functional terms as 'one verbal technique for recapitulating past experience, in particular a technique of constructing narrative units which match the temporal sequence of that experience' (Labov and Waletzky, 1967: 13). Their analysis resulted in the description of a fully-formed (or classic) narrative which 'begins with an orientation, proceeds to the complicating action, is suspended at the focus of evaluation before the resolution, concludes with the resolution and returns the listener to the present time with the coda' (p. 369).[3]

Of these structural components, evaluation (i.e. the expression of the narrator's point of view of the events) has been the most influential and at the same time controversial one. With its addition, the model was instrumental in incorporating into narrative structure what least lent itself to that: namely, the affective, emotive, subjective and experiential aspects of narrative. This was done by means of postulating evaluation both as a separate structural unit and as a micro-level mechanism

that can apply to the entire narrative. In later writings, and in response to critics, Labov rephrased his definition of narrative in the following terms: 'A narrative of personal experience is a report of a sequence of events that have entered into the biography of the speaker by a sequence of clauses that correspond to the original events' (1997: 393). Labov's revisions did no more than emphasize and reinforce some of the most heavily-contested aspects of his model: for instance, the fact that it privileges stories of past, personal experience events, at the expense of a wide range of different types of stories that abound in conversational settings, also, that the credibility of a story, i.e. the way a teller shields their telling against accusations of lying, is presented as a 'universal' need and value. The role of credibility is intimately linked with Labov subscribing to what is often referred to as the minimal definitional criterion of narrative – namely, that of the temporal ordering of events.[4] In addition, credibility goes hand in hand with a referential and realist view of the relationship between a story's events and real-world events. In contrast, constructionist views of this relationship, which are nowadays in wide currency, stress that there is no such thing as a one-to-one mapping between what really happened and what is recounted as having happened. Instead, what is presented and how it is presented in a telling are ultimately shaped by the here and now of the story's telling and the teller's current perspective on the past.[5]

As sustained critique of Labov's model has shown (e.g. see contributions in Bamberg 1997a), one of the model's main problems is that it sees narrative as a detached, autonomous and self-contained unit with clearly identifiable parts. Many scholars have pointed out that, as stories in Labov's data occurred in research interviews and as responses to an interviewer's questions, they tended to be well-organized, with a beginning, middle and an end, and largely monological. In this respect, the teller appeared to be the main producer of meaning. Since then, conversational stories in ordinary environments have been found to be highly collaborative (e.g. Goodwin 1990). More generally, the context-sensitivity of the forms that the telling of a story can take has, by now, been amply demonstrated by, amongst others, studies that were inspired in the first place by Labov's model. This substantial line of inquiry consists of numerous empirically-based projects[6] in a wide range of settings that have documented: the culturally-based expectations about what stories are about and how they are told (e.g. Chafe, 1980; Polanyi, 1985; Tannen, 1978); the sociocultural and situational variability of narrative structure, in particular evaluation (e.g. Linde, 1993); the dispensability of certain structural components (particularly the abstract and the coda) and the infrequent occurrence of other factors (e.g. evaluation as a separate component); and the context-specific degrees of audience participation during the telling of a story (e.g. Cedeborg and Aronsson, 1994; Goodwin, 1984). Labov's model coincided with and surely benefited from the insights of the narrative turn in the social sciences. As we will discuss below, these two influential trends have, together, based their insights on the study of narratives about the teller's past experiences that are told in research interviews.

27.3 THE SOCIAL INTERACTIONAL APPROACHES

Narrative as talk-in-interaction

Some of the biggest challenges to Labov have originated in research on conversational storytelling, much of which broadly aligns itself with the sociologically-informed school of analysing conversational data called conversation analysis (henceforth CA). CA advocates attention to the details of the sequential management of any interaction and, in the case of narrative, this means that where a story occurs, the 'how and why' and what local actions it performs would be of paramount importance for the analysis. Narrative in any context is therefore seen as talk-in-interaction, as an embedded unit, enmeshed in local business, not free-standing or detached. From the CA point of view, viewing narratives as more or less self-contained texts that can be abstracted from their original context of occurrence misses out on the fact that both the telling of a story and the ways in which it is told are shaped by previous talk and action. Stories occur in some kind of discourse environment, before and after other discourse activities, and are thus enmeshed in its local surroundings. Stories are also sequentially managed; their tellings unfold online, moment by moment in the here and now of interactions. As such, they can be expected to raise different types of action and tasks for different interlocutors (Goodwin, 1984). In his critique of Labov's model, one of the most influential CA proponents, Emmanuel Schegloff, argues that it is to this view of narrative as a sequence, in itself part of a sequentially-ordered event, that subsequent work on narrative 'should be redirected' in order for us to get 'toward a differently targeted and more compelling grasp of vernacular storytelling' (1997: 101).

A view of narrative as unfolding sequentially, as outlined above, goes hand in hand with a view of it as *emergent*. In this sense, its tellings emerge in specific interactional contexts as a joint venture and as the outcome of negotiation by interlocutors. Put differently, we cannot talk about a universal narrative structure, as Labov did, a priori of specific contexts of storytelling where the analysis of narrative 'opens up rather than closes off the investigation of talk's business' (Edwards, 1997: 142). Narrative tellings are thus seen as irreducibly situational and locally occasioned: 'a good part of [their] meaning is to be found in the occasion of their production, in the local state of affairs that was operative at that exact moment of interactional time' (Antaki and Widdicombe, 1998: 4). CA advocates attention to the details of their sequential management in specific kinds of interaction: where they occur, how and why; what local actions they perform.

The CA view of narrative as talk-in-interaction presents important implications not only for the analysis of narrative but also for the processes and methods of data collection and transcription. In contrast to the conventional paradigm, the narrative data that form the mainstay of research arise naturally in conversations (be they in everyday, informal or institutional contexts). There is thus a clear privileging of conversational sites as the main event under scrutiny and in that respect narrative is not seen a priori as a special or unique mode of communication but simply as 'another format of telling' (Edwards, 1997) within that event. By extension, it is recognized that narrative interviews are ultimately interactional data in which the researcher is very much part of the narrative telling, and that their role should be recorded as faithfully as possible in the transcription process. This means that any verbal or non-verbal contributions on the researcher's part should be included in the transcript. As Potter and Hepburn have argued in relation to interview data in general, 'they should be transcribed to a level that allows interactional features to be appreciated even if interactional features are not the topic of study' (2005: 295).

Conversation analysts have been successful and influential in documenting stories as sequentially-ordered activities (e.g. see Sacks, Schegloff and Jefferson 1974) by paying attention to the ways in which they are introduced into the local context of a conversation and subsequently exited from (e.g. Jefferson 1978, Sacks 1974). However, as I have argued elsewhere (Georgakopoulou, 2007: 61–87), there is still much scope for study of the part that comes between a story's opening and a story's ending. In this respect, whether structural components of a Labovian kind, e.g. complicating action or evaluation, are generally accepted (even if redefined) by CA is not altogether clear, nor is what would replace them if they were dismissed.[7] Furthermore, the stories analysed within CA are by and large of the 'prototypical' kind – i.e. involving personal experience past events – and, in that respect, not too dissimilar to Labov's data, even if the approach has been different. As we will see in Section 27.4, narrative analysis is currently moving away from this long-standing emphasis towards the study of more atypical stories.

Generally speaking, CA as its name suggests, privileges conversation as the main unit of social order from the outset and, in that respect, neither historically nor epistemologically does it share with narrative analysis the commitment to studying narrative in its own right. This fundamental difference in outlook has perhaps hampered cross-fertilization between the two. More than that, within socially-minded linguistics, CA has become implicated in a larger debate about the role of context in the analysis of interaction in general (e.g. see the dialogue between Wetherell, 1998, and Schegloff, 1998). This debate is beyond the scope of this chapter, but it is worth noting that CA has generally come under fire as being a too nose-to-data approach that does not easily abstract itself from local contexts, and that does not provide a way for forging links between local instances of interactions and larger contexts and processes pertaining above and beyond single communicative events.[8]

Narrative in context

As I argued above, a view of narrative as talk-in-interaction allows us to explore narrative as a socially-meaningful and orderly activity. It affords an intimate view of what is going on in the here and now of any narrative interaction, firmly locating us in the flow of everyday lived experience. It does, however, diverge from the tradition of contextualized approaches to language that set out to navigate between the here and now of interactions and the discourses impacting on them, recognizing that any strip of activity is configured on momentary-quotidian-biographical-historical frames and across socio-spatial arenas. In the case of narrative, this forging of relationships between local and global contexts has been attempted by, broadly speaking, post-Labovian work on the one hand and the ethnography of communication studies on the other.

To take each separately, in post-Labovian work, evaluation appeared to be the most appealing of the structural components: not only did the model allow for different positions and different types of evaluation but also evaluation was the component that rested on the intersection between narrative organization and narrative affectivity. Evaluation did not just bind a story together, it also showed what the story's point or moral was. Consequently, it is

no accident that there have been various attempts to expand on the scope of evaluation and further systematize it on the one hand (e.g. see Polanyi, 1985)[9] and, on the other hand, to develop concepts that present various degrees of more or less explicitly acknowledged affiliation with evaluation, such as that of involvement (Tannen, 1989).[10] As suggested above, there is indeed a volume of work which has documented the culture-specificity of evaluation, particularly in relation to the following questions:

- Who is entitled to tell whose stories?
- What is the attitude of audiences to telling, tales and tellers?
- How do cultures vary in the relative support granted by recipients to tellers, tellings and tales? (Blum-Kulka, 1997)
- What is the role of fact and fiction in storytelling?
- What culture-specific values are attached to each?
- How do stories invoke and re-inscribe the physical and social space familiar to the tellers and audience?

A case in point is Johnstone's study of storytelling in a Middle American community, Fort Wayne (1990). The study brought to the fore largely monologic and teller-led tellings that placed emphasis on situating the stories locally, mainly by means of the (over)use of details about place. In the same spirit as Tannen, Johnstone viewed details as involvement strategies that invite audience participation in meaning-making. She also attributed their use to the prevailing cultural attitudes to factuality.

Specifically, as Johnstone stated, 'for Fort Wayners, personal experience stories are taken to be iconic representations of events, as the events were experienced by the teller. They cannot appear to be fictions. Or else they will count as lies' (1990: 101). Fort Wayners thus valued good stories as opposed to good storytellers. Within this cultural bias towards factually-verifiable events, details in stories acted as a conventional mechanism for enhancing the 'reality' and 'actuality' of stories, by precisely locating them in time and space.

Post-Labovian work on the context-sensitivity of storytelling has contributed rich insights into, to borrow Schiffrin's terms, how stories are situated locally, in the here and now of their tellings, but also globally too, in their sociocultural contexts, by means of invoking cultural knowledge and norms (1996: 168). Nonetheless, at the time that these studies were conducted, there was still a strong lingering of social, psychological and anthropological approaches that defined culture as a unifying, homogeneous, static and a priori defined set of values, beliefs and behaviours that are invoked in communication (e.g. Markus and Kitayama, 1991; Triandis, 1989). It is fair to say that many of the sociolinguistic studies of storytelling in context were thus informed by these views and invoked them as their interpretative framework. This is evident in the fact that there was a preoccupation with uncovering certain communication styles in storytelling that, in turn, provided evidence for or were interpreted in the light of 'core' cultural values (e.g. sociability, solidarity). In some cases, these values were more or less directly traceable to the distinction between individualist and interdependent cultures (e.g. Polanyi, 1985). Since then, views of culture that prioritize fluidity and heterogeneity have become increasingly accepted and there has been a decisive shift away from earlier normative accounts of culture. At the linguistic level, there is also nowadays a reluctance to form one-to-one conceptual links between linguistic forms and social meanings. Similarly, attributing singular functions to linguistic devices is widely recognized as a complex enterprise.[11]

In parallel with what I have broadly called here post-Labovian studies, another tradition of studying language in general and storytelling in particular in context was developing in the 1970s and 1980s that has set beacons for the current study of narrative in social life. This tradition can be broadly classified as being linguistic-anthropological in nature, but some of its main proponents are, more specifically, ethnographers of communication, as we will see below. The main foci of inquiry in this research are: the linguistic means by which cultural meanings are encoded in narrative; the social situations in which narratives occur and how these shape narrative tellings; and the culturally-shaped communicative functions fulfilled by narratives and their role in socialization within communities. The data that have mainly been studied in this respect come from traditional storytelling in non-Western communities. However, as we will see below, more recent work, inspired by earlier studies, has turned attention to narratives in institutional contexts and has examined their role in the formation and transmission of institutional values and norms as well as in the exclusion of certain social groups (e.g. see Jacquemet, 2005, and chapters in Briggs, 1996, and in Mumby, 1993).

What brings together work with this focus is the recognition that narrative tellings are shaped by, as well as being instrumental in, shaping the macro processes that constitute them. There is constant navigation between the fine-grained analysis of narrative data and the study of sociocultural processes. This rests on the notions of social practice, genre and performance as being central to the understanding of narrative. These ideas have been instrumental in precipitating a shift in the study of narratives from types of texts to types of events, with an emphasis on the social spaces, in which stories occur and are habitually associated with, their local functions in those spaces and the participants' roles and relations. Increasingly then, as we will see below, this line of inquiry has moved from earlier views of context as a surrounding frame, a list of situational and cultural elements that determine narrative tellings, to a dynamic notion of *contextualization*. This captures both the irreducible contingency of narrative tellings and their active role in (re) shaping their contexts. In a similar vein, viewing narratives as practices and not just as texts has meant that there is an emphasis on both the habituality and regularity of tellings (in the sense of recurrent evolving responses to given situations) and their emergence and situational contingency. This is in tune with the recent re-theorizing of genres away from formal classifications as the basis for text-distinctions, and with an emphasis on members' conventionalized expectations about the activities they are engaged in, the roles and relationships typically involved and the organizational systems of those activities. In this way, more than a 'constellation of systematically related, co-occurring formal features' (Bauman, 2004: 3), genre becomes a 'primary means for dealing with recurrent social exigencies ... a routinized vehicle for encoding and expressing particular orders of knowledge and experience' (p. 6). As orienting frameworks of conventionalized expectations, genres force the analytical attention to routine and socioculturally shaped 'ways of telling' (Hymes, 1996) in specific settings and for specific purposes.

What this means for the study of narrative is that instead of treating it as a macro genre with fixed structural characteristics (i.e. invariant and inflexible structural units), emphasis is placed on narrative forms as dynamic and evolving responses to recurring rhetorical situations and as resources more or less strategically drawn upon, negotiated and reconstructed anew in local contexts. As I have argued in detail elsewhere (Georgakopoulou, 2007: 12–29), the move to such a practice-oriented view of narrative genres also requires that we firmly locate them in place and time and scrutinize the social and discourse activities they are habitually associated with. In particular, it focuses our attention on the 'social values of space as inscribed upon the practices' (Hanks, 1996: 246) that take place within narrative tellings.

Many of the above recent advances in the study of narrative are traceable to insights gained from the influential work of Dell Hymes (e.g. 1981) who studied narrative organization in Native American communities. To capture the ways in which narrative forms are both shaped by and (re) create cultural knowledge and norms, Hymes developed *ethnopoetics*, a painstaking and fairly technical modus operandi involving intense and repeated listening of recorded data. Its basic units of analysis (e.g. line, verse, stanzas, scenes and acts) were identified with a combination of intonational, thematic, lexical and syntactic criteria. Despite the lack of convergence on the number and definition of such units in subsequent studies (e.g. see Gee, 1986), what is important to note is how, with their introduction to the study of narrative, the poetic organization of oral narratives was recognized, visually displayed (in the form of stanza-like segments) and respected in the transcripts. Furthermore, it was shown that this organization embodied a 'rhetoric of action, that is, an implicit schema for the organization of experience' (Hymes, 1996: 121) that was culturally-specific and revolved around numbers of cultural importance. For instance, Chinookan narratives were found to be organized in patterns of two and four.[12] This organization was reflected in the stories' units (i.e. lines, verses, stanzas, scenes). In other words, Chinookan stories routinely presented two-line verses, stanzas made up of two or four verses, and so on.

Ethnopoetic analysis has had little application to narratives that are produced outside oral cultures.[13] Gee (1986) further documented its value as a tool for uncovering oral culture influences in narrative form with his analysis of the stories told by a black girl during sharing-time at a school that had been previously studied by Michaels (1981).[14] Gee uncovered a host of rhythmical patterns characteristic of oral cultures. In his study, as in more recent work (e.g. Blommaert and Maryns, 2001), the visually-poetic display of narrative organization becomes an epistemological statement on how narrative units more or less subtly point to sociocultural forces at work. In this way, a model of narrative structure becomes something more than a sophisticated apparatus for segmenting text: it actually serves to document social inequalities and differential access to differentially-valued storytelling styles.

Another strand of inquiry within linguistic anthropology, espousing comparable ideas about the pairing of text-context but without employing ethnopoetics, is that of *performance studies of narrative*. As the name suggests, the central concept here is that of performance, defined within Bauman's influential study of tales of dog-trading in Texas (1986) as an assumption of responsibility on the part of the performer for the display of communicative skill and competence and an acceptance that such a display is going to be evaluated by the audience (cf. Goffman, 1981). In this sense, exactly like narrative organization in Hymes, performance is a culturally-shaped way of speaking, and 'just as speaking itself as a cultural system (or as part of cultural systems defined in other terms) will vary from speech community to speech community, so too will the nature and extent of performance and verbal art' (Bauman, 1969: 13). As Bauman has repeatedly stressed, the devices that mark narrative tellings as performances are expected to vary cross-culturally and need to be discovered empirically.

In contrast to earlier anthropological studies of verbal art, Bauman saw performance as a site where tradition (in the sense of adherence to performance norms) and innovation (in the sense of individual improvisation and situational contingency) are interwoven. Narrative performance is thus the complex outcome of the interrelationships between the narrative event (i.e. the here and now of a narrative telling), the narrated event (the reported world of events and characters), and the text (the actual language and stylistic choices for telling the story).

Insights from the ethnography of communication and performance studies of narrative have found their way into a critical analysis of stories as a vehicle for power and ideologies in various institutions ranging from interviews to assess asylum-seeking applications (Maryns and Blommaert, 2001) to courtroom cases (Trinch and Berk-Selingson).[15] Such studies have seriously problematized the earlier optimism about narrative as an empowering mode of lay experience and voices. Instead, they have shown that there are serious issues of narrative inequality to be found in, among others, the tellers' access to ownership and control of the resources required for shaping their stories so as to be tellable and acceptable in the contexts in which they occur. They have also documented the ways in which institutionally powerful social actors can control storytelling by, for example, interrupting, reformulating it or pushing it in certain directions.

Let us look at one particular study that illustrates some of the above foci more closely. Ehrlich (2001) has shown in her study of sexual assault trials in Canada how the version of events that may emerge in a trial can be determined by the type of questions the lawyers ask of witnesses; also, how these questions control the topic or selectively reformulate witnesses' responses. Ehrlich's study has thus provided further evidence for the ways in which 'the institutionally sanctioned, pre-allocated role of lawyer as questioner and witness as answerer has significant implications for the co-constructed nature of courtroom narratives' (2007: 455). In her analysis of three trials on the same sexual assault case (2007),[16]

Ehrlich showed how the norms of cultural intelligibility about gender in operation in each case were instrumental in the co-construction of versions of events between the complainant and the Crown Attorney. Specifically, in the trials that acquitted the accused, the complainant and the Crown Attorney co-constructed a narrative in which the sexual activity was presented as consensual. In contrast, as Ehrlich shows, the same events and facts of the case 'were interpreted by the Supreme Court in a way which was compatible with the complainant's version of events' (2007: 472) and thus presented the sexual activity as coerced and not as consensual. A widespread strategy used to negotiate the interpretation of a narrative or parts of it was that of *re-contextualization* (cf. Bernstein, 1996), i.e. the creation of a new context of interpretation of aspects of the story that was being told.

In sum, the study of narrative in social practice has increasingly moved to densely contextualized approaches that call for attention to the particularities and exigencies of specific data in specific contexts at the same time as shedding light on how wider social relations of power and control shape narrative tellings. Such situated analyses look at sociocultural phenomena close up, i.e. in the moment-to-moment unfolding of communication. As such, their analytic point of entry is specific interactional events in which stories occur. The focus has thus shifted from asking what is culture-specific about narrative tellings to how cultural resources may be drawn upon and reconciled but also contested in the contingencies of situated activity. In addition, with the latest turn of narrative analysis to identities within sociolinguistics, which we will discuss below, culture is no longer examined in isolation and as a distinguishable attribute that can be singled out and kept apart from other identity aspects, but in its interaction with other aspects of identity (e.g. gender, age, social class). Finally, the ethnographic perspective that these studies normally take currently presents a dramatic difference in scale: the exploration of the sociocultural roles of narrative in whole communities has gradually given way to the study of shrunk-down and much more manageable groups of people and their micro cultures.[17]

27.4 NARRATIVE AND IDENTITIES

As already suggested, outside sociolinguistics, narrative has served as a major methodological tool for researching people's identities. It is important, however, to emphasize that only a particular type of narrative has mainly served as the object of this inquiry, namely that of a life story, and less frequently the so-called short-range stories of landmark events (e.g. stories of pregnancy, marriage, divorce, illness, etc.). The latter are reminiscent of Labov's stories which were collected as a response to the question, 'Were you ever in danger of dying?'. Common to both types of stories is that they are routinely elicited in research interviews. Also, both involve personal experience past events that the teller has sufficient distance from, and thus is able to reflect on. Such stories have been employed as heuristics for the inquiry into tellers' representations of past events, and how the tellers make sense of themselves in the light of these past events. The guiding assumption here is that the telling of stories allows the teller to bring the coordinates of time, space and personhood into a unitary frame so that the sources 'behind' these representations can be made empirically visible for further analytical scrutiny in the form of 'identity analysis'.

In tune with this approach, there has been a long-standing tradition of investigating how pre-existent, socioculturally available, capital D-discourses (variously called 'meta-narratives', 'master-narratives', 'scenarios', etc.) are drawn upon by tellers in order to make sense of themselves over time and of the defining events that happened to them (e.g. see Kerby, 1991). What these discourses are is decided by the analysts, sometimes before the actual data collection and analysis. Selves and identities are thus viewed as the product of such prevailing discourses. A concept that has informed numerous studies of narrative and identity with this focus is that of positioning. In Davies and Harré's (1990) seminal paper, positioning was defined as 'the discursive process whereby selves are located in conversations as observably and subjectively coherent participants in jointly produced story lines' (p. 48). Following on from that study, which tellingly employed made-up examples of narratives, work on positioning tends to postulate culturally-available subject positions a priori of specific data and subsequently 'look' for how they impact on specific narratives. This kind of work does not seem to be tuned into the emergence of positioning processes through details intrinsic to an interaction. and has shied away from an exploration of the fleetingness and contingency of positionings in local contexts (for a critique see Bamberg, 1997b: 335–42; Lucius-Hoene and Depperman, 2000; Wortham, 2000: 164–166). Bamberg's (1997b) attempt to re-define positioning so as to be suited to an interactional approach to narrative resulted in the postulation of three levels of analysis, which have often been employed by analysts as heuristics for the ways in which tellers 'do' self in narrative tellings.[18]

It is fair to say that research on narrative and identity within biographical studies has privileged both a certain kind of subjectivity and certain kinds of identities. More specifically, there has been a focus on the project of 'storying' oneself as intrinsically-oriented towards coherence and authenticity. In this respect, the volume of studies has focused on how, even through a dynamic process, tellers gradually move to a unified and rather stable account of self that is interwoven into their life story (e.g. Brockmeier and Carbaugh, 2001; Daiute and Lightfoot, 2004). Self and narrative[19] are thus typically brought together in ways that emphasize the ideas of autonomy, integration and coherence over those of a fragmented, relational self. Fragmented in this case would refer to being self-discursively constructed as different things on different occasions that can neither be automatically reduced to a singular and coherent entity, nor easily abstracted from local contexts. A relational self on the other hand would derive its capacity for self-perception and self-definition through relations with others and in interactional negotiations with others.

Both these ideas have met with resistance within biographical narrative analysis. In Roberts' terms, there is a danger in the area that 'narrative is used too restrictively to refer to a version of life given at a particular moment as expressing the given story as consistent and sequencing experience as lived, and even, if only momentarily either the self as a consistent surface expression or an inner constant entity' (2004: 270). In this way, Roberts continues, linearity remains dominant even if implicit in the use of story and in turn 'life as stories' becomes itself a restrictive metaphor emphasizing consistency while overlooking the deficiencies and inconsistencies of speech (idem). In similar vein, Parker alerts us to the risk of prescribing a certain kind of subjectivity through the analysis of narrative. He notes that personal narrative seems to be presented as a model of how we should configure ourselves as selves striving for a purposeful and convincing whole (Parker, 2003: 314). To many, this is a Western type of ideal encompassing neo-Cartesian individualist views of personhood and privileging unity and the integration of a singular and 'authentic' self through the piecing together of a well-structured and orderly life story (e.g. see De Peuter, 1998: 32–4).

To sum up, narrative identity in the sense of the 'storied self' is a well-established paradigm across a wide array of disciplines. This emphasis on the construction of self has meant that relational and dialogical processes of making sense of self have

been under-represented.[20] Furthermore, narrative and identity analysis in the social sciences has mainly relied on a specific type of narrative elicited in interviews. It has also been slow to move away from representational accounts of the self (i.e. accounts of the type of person that a life story presents its teller to be) that treat stories as more or less authentic, transparent and unmediated records (for a discussion see Atkinson and Delamore, 2006) to interactional views of identity construction and the ways in which narrators perform and locally occasion themselves through their stories.

In contrast, such interactional approaches to identities have become increasingly mainstream within sociolinguistics. Research on the communicative how of identities in talk has been flourishing and recently there has been a proliferation of sociolinguistic studies of narrative and identities (e.g. De Fina, 2003; chapters in De Fina, Schiffrin and Bamberg, 2006; Georgakopoulou, 2007).[21] Before this systematic turn to identities, one of the first domains to capture the sociolinguists' attention was the ways in which tellers presented aspects of their self by making the most of the possibilities that the separation between the here and now of narrative telling and the there and then of the taleworld (cf. told, narrated events) afforded them. As Schiffrin's oft-quoted study showed (1990), this separation allows tellers to manipulate different aspects of 'self', as defined by Goffman (1974). For example, tellers can appear both as narrators and as characters in the taleworld. Or, they can appear to be the animator (the aspect of self that physically produces the story) but not the author (i.e. the aspect of self responsible for the content of talk). They can do this with the use of various devices, such as quoting what characters in the taleworld said or thought. This play with who tells, who is responsible for the content of talk and who is committed to what is being said allows storytellers to control their self-presentation. They may diffuse their agency or responsibility in the social field, create a widened base of support for their views and beliefs, cast positive light on them, increase the validity of their claims and so on (cf. Hill, 1995).

More recently, however, there has been a shift towards exploring ways of connecting narrative tellings with larger social identities (e.g. see Wagner and Wodak, 2006; Wodak and De Cillia, 2007). This inquiry involves scrutinizing the genres that narrative tellings present, and their specific language and interactional choices for how they more or less subtly and indirectly point to (cf. index) aspects of the teller's identities, such as ethnicity, gender, age, etc. For example, in De Fina's study of the personal experience narratives of border crossings of Mexican immigrants in the USA, identity construction in narrative is related to three levels (2003: 19):

1　The tellers' adherence to cultural ways of telling (e.g. involving specific linguistic and rhetorical resources) that identify them as members of specific communities.
2　The 'enactment, reflection or negation' (idem) of personal social roles and relationships in the actual story world.
3　The 'expression, discussion and negotiation of membership into communities' (idem) normally realized in the categorization of self and others (cf. Georgakopoulou, 2008).

This line of inquiry has come a long way in forging links that are by no means presented as deterministic between narrative and identities through a focus on the action properties of language in narrative and away from the representational accounts of narrative studies in the social sciences. However, as I have argued elsewhere (Georgakopoulou, 2006a), there is much scope here for cross-fertilization with CA, and I have pointed to one strand that merits systematic attention – namely, the sequential management of stories as a point of entry into the teller's as well as the other storytelling participant's local roles. More specifically, I have drawn on Zimmerman's (1998) study of how local participation roles or *discourse identities,* tied with the sequence of adjacency pairs such as questioner–answerer and speaker–recipient, provide a platform for larger, i.e. extra–situational or 'portable', social identities (e.g. spouse, parent, layperson, expert, etc.).[22]

One question that tantalizes current sociolinguistic work on narrative and identities is how we can move from the locally-performed and on-the-spot constructed identities that are marked by irreducible contingency, to being able to show some kind of continuity in these identities, i.e. aspects that would seem to hold above and beyond local contexts as part of a 'rehearsed' self. This question is, however, being posed in different methodological ways and with different data to those of biographical approaches. It is out of this problem space within narrative and identities-interaction work that the *small stories paradigm* has grown, as I will explain below.

The turn to small stories

In recent work, we have proposed small stories (Bamberg, 2004; Georgakopoulou, 2006b, 2006c; 2007; 2008; Bamberg and Georgakopoulou, 2008) as an alternative to canonical narrative studies, a 'new' narrative turn that sets out to include certain under-represented activities in the focal concerns of narrative and identity analysis. The initial motivation came from seeing how the assumptions of the biographical approaches to the analysis of narratives in combination with Labov's model have filtered down to analytic work on conversational (cf. non-elicited) narratives. As a result, they have informed analysts' definitions of what constitutes a tellable story and/or a story that can be used as a point of entry into identity analysis. Despite numerous studies of conversational storytelling that have, over the years, brought to the fore stories that depart from personal, past experience stories, as Ochs and Capps have rightly pointed out (2001), stories that depart from this narrative canon remain under-explored. Thus, our aims were: to document the forms and contexts of these atypical stories which we have collectively called 'small stories'; to put forth analytical tools that are appropriate for them; and last but not least, to argue for their importance in narrative and identity research.

'Small stories' is thus an umbrella term that captures a gamut of frequent and salient narrative activities in conversational contexts, such as tellings of ongoing events, future or hypothetical events, shared or known events, also allusions to previous tellings, deferrals of tellings, and refusals to tell. These tellings are typically small when compared to the pages and pages of transcripts of interview narratives. On a metaphorical level, the term locates a level and even an aesthetic for the identification and analysis of narrative: the smallness of talk, where fleeting moments of narrative orientation to the world (Hymes, 1996) can be easily missed out on by an analytical lens which only takes fully-fledged stories as the prototype from where the analytic vocabulary is supposed to emerge. Small stories can be about very recent (e.g. yesterday, this morning) or still unfolding events, thus immediately reworking slices of experience and arising out of a need to share what has just happened. For instance, as I have shown elsewhere (Georgakopoulou, 2007), it is common in email correspondence between friends for an event that has just happened to be communicated straight away (normally in the subject heading of the message) with a brief telling and the promise of a further update by email or for a fuller telling in a near-future face-to-face meeting between the friends. I have tried to capture the topicality of such stories' events and the urgency with which they are communicated with the term 'breaking news'.

Small stories can also be quickly and elliptically told to back up or elaborate on an argumentative point occurring in an ongoing conversation. Certain small stories may fulfil prototypical definitional criteria such as the temporal ordering of events but others do not (for a detailed discussion of the definition of small stories see Georgakopoulou, 2007: 31–40). In all cases, the identification of small stories does not rest exclusively on prototypical textual criteria.[23] Instead, small stories are seen as discourse engagements that integrally connect with what gets done on particular occasions and in particular settings. The claim is that recognizing 'narrativity' or a 'narrative orientation' in certain activities shows regard for situated understandings.[24]

Small stories research has begun to document how attention to everyday instances of storytelling, however incomplete, can serve as a window into the micro-genetic processes of identities as 'in-the-making' or 'coming-into-being'. By conceptualizing small stories as the *sites of engagement* where identities are continuously practised and tested out, we have begun to show how these practices 'compare to the tellers' engagement in reflexive positions in life stories. that are typically elicited in clinical or research settings (Bamberg and Georgakopoulou, 2008). Such a line of inquiry into everyday, interactional stories shows that it is in the everyday narrative practices that identity work is primarily being conducted. Habitual engagement with certain identity positions articulated through stories over time ends up becoming the source for a continuous sense of who we are – a sense of us as 'same' in spite of continuous change. Put differently, the actual identity work that is being conducted by individuals in interactive engagement with stories so to speak, feeds into a sense of self – in the form of a continuous process within which this sense comes into existence (emerges).

Exactly as in other current social interactional work on narrative and identities, small stories approach the topic of identity construction in narratives in a way that is crucially different to that of biographical approaches. They accept that 'doing self' is not all that storytellers do. They also do rhetorical work through storytelling: they put forth arguments, challenge their interlocutors' views and generally attune their stories to various local, interpersonal purposes, sequentially orienting them to prior and upcoming talk. It is in and through this type of relational activity that any representations in the form of content, i.e. what the story is about, should be seen. This suggests that the emphasis within narrative interview research on the representational aspects of stories (cf. Atkinson and Delamont, 2006) may be overstating their role in identity work as well as skewing the ways in which they are intimately linked with the interview as talk-in-interaction. This sort of analysis takes us away from documenting self as a finished and static product. Instead, it urges us to scrutinize the inconsistencies, contradictions,

moments of trouble and tension, and the tellers' constant navigation and finessing between different versions of selfhood in local contexts.

Small stories research has also shown that identity work in stories among intimates draws irrevocably on the participants' lived and shared experience (Georgakopoulou, 2007). This has been obscured in interview narratives, where primacy is given to the single event and where the researcher tends to be a 'stranger'.[25]

27.5 CONCLUSIONS

This chapter has selectively charted advances in the socially-minded linguistic analysis of narrative by focusing on social interactional approaches that have precipitated a shift from narrative as text to narrative as social practice. We have seen that some of the hallmarks of this line of inquiry involve fine-grained analysis of narrative data, emphasis on the communicative how, and on both the local context of a story and the larger sociocultural processes that shape and are shaped by it. Similarly, narrative tellings are examined for the ways in which they function as social practices and within other social practices. This necessitates a move from narrative as one undifferentiated and homogeneous mode towards the careful documentation of *narrative genres*, viewed as interconnections between social expectations about narrative form and emergence of meanings in concrete events. This opening up to variability in narrative has brought to the fore non-canonical narratives and narrative formats and genres that had traditionally been neglected in conventional narrative analysis. It has also advanced our understanding of the interactional features of such narratives and the contexts which engender or prohibit their telling. We have seen that small stories research is an important step in this direction: one of its primary aims has been to work through the implications for identity research of including non-canonical stories in the focal concerns of narrative analysis. This sociolinguistic turn to narrative and identities is the single latest advance within social interactional approaches and it has been made with a view of identities as performed and discursively emergent.

Without wishing to box in social interactional work on narrative, we could nonetheless attempt an abstraction and summarize its main foci of interest in terms of three interrelated levels of analysis, which of course different analysts may prioritize differently. 'As I have explained elsewhere (Georgakopoulou, 2007: 20–23), these three levels of analysis illustrate the constant navigation and multi-layered work involved in this kind of work. They show how the analysts' main effort is to capture the moment of synthesis of a single communicative event while at the same time not divorcing that moment from sociocultural histories and operative timescales. In this way, narratives are studied not only in the here and now but also as texts that get transposed in time and space and that establish intertextual ties with other narratives and other genres.

The analytical levels in question can thus be described as follows: *ways of (story)telling* capture socioculturally-shaped and conventionalized themes and styles of telling that are, in turn, seen as modes of acting, interacting, producing and dynamically receiving text, the revealing of a rhetorical stance and orientation to the world. *Sites* involve sociocultural spheres and spaces for semiotic activity in real time (cf. site of engagement, Scollon and Scollon, 2004) that may be conventionally associated with specific kinds of storytelling, shaping their ways of telling, as well as becoming an integral part of the stories' plot. Finally, *tellers* is a dynamically-conceived adaptation of the lay term employed for social actors within storytelling activities seen as having a complex make-up: personal–autobiographical, social–relational and partaking in both a taleworld (as character with other characters) and in the here and now (as interlocutor). This level includes the interactional history of participants, where applicable, the participant roles and relationships, and entitlement issues as well as systems of norms and expectations.

As already suggested, social interactional approaches to narrative tend to employ ethnographic methods that allow for local, reflexive and situated understandings of narratives as more or less partial and valid accounts within systems of production and articulation. This results in an increased reflexivity on the researcher–researched relationships and a scepticism concerning the dominant view (within the narrative turn) of narrative as a primary and unique mode for making sense of self and the world. It is, instead, more interesting for social interactional approaches to explore how different situational and sociocultural contexts interrelate with narrative genres, and also to employ narrative analysis as part of a multi-method, in which a particular problem-space for the sociolinguist is explored with various kinds of data and various multi-layered analyses.

NOTES

1   In some cases, the two terms 'narrative' and 'story' are not used interchangeably but, rather,

'narrative' is seen as a super-ordinate term and 'story' as an instance. It is also common that a piece of data may be characterized as a story but not as a narrative. In Kohler Riessman study of divorce narratives for example, accounts of events that happened repeatedly in the past, and not once, were classified as habitual stories but not narratives. Within 'narratology' (literary approaches to narrative), a lot of ink has been spent on what is to be included in the category of narrative and what is to be excluded, resulting in, for example, the exclusion of 'reports' and 'chronicles' (for details, see Fludernik, 1996). In this chapter, the two terms are used interchangeably. Furthermore, we will see how, in sociolinguistics, there has been a gradual opening up of narrative analysis to data that depart from the narrative canon of stories of personal, past experience and events.

2   As Schegloff has noted, 'It is striking to what degree features of the 1967 paper have remained characteristic of treatments of narrative' (1997: 101). In a similar vein, Holmes has talked about not being able to move away from Labov's model: 'As I proceeded I found that in whichever direction I attempted to develop the analysis, I kept inescapably returning to the need to first establish the basic structure of narratives' (1997: 95).

3   Very briefly described, the abstract is a brief summary statement that encapsulates the point of the story; orientation identifies the time, place, situations and characters; the complicating action answers the repeated question, 'Then what happened?'; resolution marks the end of the events of the complicating action; evaluation comprises the devices by which the narrator indicates the point of a narrative, i.e. why it is worth telling; finally, the coda closes a narrative off, normally by bringing it back to the moment of telling.

4   The quest for textually-defined and universally-applied criteria for defining narrative and narrative structure is part of a long-standing line of inquiry that predates Labov. Propp's (1968) study of folktales and Lévi-Strauss' (1955, 1966) study of myths are notable examples of such attempts. For alternative studies of (narrative) structure within linguistics, see Quasthoff (1980) and van Dijk (1980). A detailed discussion of this structuralist line of work is beyond the scope of this chapter (for details, see Johnstone, 2001).

5   While discussing Labov's (2001) quest for truth in relation to stories told as part of the work of the South-African Truth and Reconciliation Commission (TRC), Slembrouck (2003) claims that the kind of 'forensic' approach represented in his work is mainly aimed at inferring 'responsibility claims' and 'what really happened' from the study of 'linguistic structure' (p. 467). He goes on to contrast this approach to the 'strand of narrative inquiry … in which subjective orientations yield an experiential

truth-fragmented, identity-enabling, narrative, invested with point of view, subjectifying' (idem). See also Anthonissen and Blommaert (2007) for analyses of the TRC; see also Verdoolaege (2008).

6   As already suggested, the *Journal of Narrative and Life History* (1997), a retrospective of Labov and Waletzky 1967, makes reference to several of those. Polanyi (1985) is a notable case, inasmuch as it was one of the earlier studies to bring into sharp focus the context-specificity of the model, evaluation in particular.

7   For example, C. Goodwin (1984) takes on board the categories of complicating action and evaluation, but shows their negotiability and joint fashioning in conversational stories (see also M. H. Goodwin, 1997).

8   This is an ongoing debate with more or less moderate positions as well as attempts to reconcile these concerns (e.g. see Myers, 2008) to which I cannot do justice here.

9   Polanyi first broke down Labov's evaluative devices into a more detailed and elaborate list. She also addressed the question of how exactly we can identify a device as evaluative by claiming that we cannot do so a priori of the analysis. Instead, evaluation is a scalar rather than a binary category that assigns various degrees of prominence and different weights to various textual elements (1985: 22), and so we can only identify something as evaluative within the environment of specific storytelling and on the basis of how salient it is in that environment. Finally, Polanyi abstracted from what was frequently evaluated in the stories that she analysed certain core cultural values which she identified as typical of 'American' culture.

10   In Tannen's terms, involvement strategies comprise stylistic devices (e.g. repetition, sound patterns, constructed dialogue, details, etc.) which convey the teller's attitudes and feelings towards the events narrated and which shape the audience's engagement in them. Tannen has explored the culture-sensitivity of involvement strategies (1989), claiming for instance that Greek storytelling is based on a high involvement style with the recurrent use of certain involvement strategies.

11   In an earlier study of mine (Georgakopoulou, 1997), I showed how it was not straightforward to attribute 'functions' to the two salient and sustained linguistic devices in Greek conversational storytelling – namely, narrative present and instances of direct speech. Both had been classified as involvement strategies by Tannen (1989) but their use in my data presented clear organizational purposes too: they demarcated narrative parts. At the same time, I did not have to look far to find these devices receding and other choices taking their place – namely, in stories addressed to children by adults and used for pragmatic socialization purposes. Context-specificity in this case involved what style of narration was deemed appropriate for which context and which purpose, and it thus militated against drawing sweeping generalizations about how 'Greeks tell stories'.

12   A similar perspective on narrative as embodying modes of social knowledge and social organization is an underlying theme in Scollon and Scollon's (1981) ethnography of Athabaskan narrative. For these authors, Athabaskan narrative reflects its fundamental role as the main tool for the acquisition of knowledge in its poetic organization and interactional structure. Scollon and Scollon argue that the presentation of action and commentary in narrative discourse also follows patterns characteristic of the culture.

13   The analysis is of a highly technical nature requiring skills in phonetics, grammar, syntax and discourse and has put off certain analysts (Blommaert 2006: 3ff). In addition, ethnopoetics has often been criticized for the high level of subjectivity and potential circularity involved in the actual identification of narrative units.

14   In Michaels' terms, this narrative style was described as topic-associating: it involved frequent shifts in spatio-temporal focus across segments to mark them out, and it valued implicitness in structuring. By contrast, the topic-centred style, characteristic of literate cultures and more specifically of middle-class children in the school that Michaels studied, worked with lexically- and grammatically-explicit connections and a clear thematic and temporal progression. These contrastive styles were differentially valued at schools. Specifically, the oral-based or topic-associating style was not favoured by the literate schooled models, with the result of disadvantaging children from ethnic and socioeconomic backgrounds that came to school with this culturally shaped 'way of speaking'.

15   There is a volume of studies here that cannot be done justice to (for a detailed review, see De Fina and Georgakopoulou forthcoming, Ch. 5). The overall emphasis is on oral stories but there is also work on written stories, particularly in the media (e.g. see chapters in Mumby, 1993). Researchers operating within this tradition have done well to document storytelling in public discourse, and in the media as a crucial site for the construction of cultural hegemony and therefore also as a crucial area of investigation into power and inequality. Studies are somewhat polarized between those that opt for macro accounts and are lacking in close textual analysis, and those that focus on the textual organization of stories but fail to pay attention to local practices of meaning-making.

16   The second trial by a Court of Appeal upheld the acquittal of the accused by the first trial, while the third trial at the Supreme Court of Canada dramatically overturned the acquittal and convicted the accused.

17 We can see early and defining examples of this in the influential studies of the storytelling practices of female peer groups at school and in the playground, respectively, by Shuman (1986) and Goodwin (1990).

18 The first level explores positioning in the taleworld: how the narrator as character is positioned vis-à-vis other characters. The second level looks at positioning as an interactional process, emerging from the ways in which the narrator as teller in the here and now positions himself vis-à-vis his interlocutors. Finally, the third level seeks to provide an answer to the question of 'Who am I?' – the teller's self as a more or less stable entity holding above and beyond the current storytelling situation.

19 The issue of how storied self is partly personal/autobiographical and partly shaped by collective and culturally–shaped plots (variously called story-lines, master plots, master narratives, etc.) or equally resistant to them (as in counter-narratives) also forms a well-researched focus of inquiry (e.g. chapters in Brockmeier and Carbaugh, 2001) with still many unanswered and contentious questions: e.g. How do we know that something is a 'master plot' (see Kölbl, 2002)? That said, the interplay between the individual and the social in narrative meaning-making cannot be possibly negated and its exploration remains high on the agenda of narrative and identities research.

20   As De Peuter puts it,

By reconceiving narratives as active dialogues, relationship is privileged over authorship; the multiple centres of organization of the self and their relations, pursuing on the boundaries of self and other, identity and difference, may be celebrated rather than silenced thus ensuring the dynamic tensions among opposing forces which in turn enable the dialogical self to be unfinalizable, emergent and ongoing. (1998: 40)

21 This turn to identities has been slow and the focal concerns of the area looked very different in 1996, when Schiffrin made a plea for sociolinguistic studies of narrative and identities (in her terms, narratives act 'self-portraits').

22 The study of discourse identities in the conversational stories of a group of female adolescents showed that the participants differed in how (much) they contributed to different story components, particularly plotline and evaluation, and in what ways. Furthermore, the participants differed in the degree to which their contributions were ratified and taken on board by others or, equally, challenged and delegitimated. I showed that such local telling roles made visible and were based on the participants' gendered identities and their relational identities as close friends who shared an interactional history.

23 In this respect, we are in tune with Ochs and Capps (2001), who, rather than identifying a set of distinctive features that always characterize narrative, stipulate dimensions (e.g. tellability, tellership, linearity, moral stance, etc.) that are relevant to a narrative, even if not elaborately manifest. These pertain both to narrating as an activity and to narrative as text. The point about these narrative dimensions is that they make the definition of narrative not an all-or-nothing matter but a more-or-less matter. To be specific, each dimension establishes a range of possibilities which may or may not be realized in a particular narrative. For example, tellership allows for one main teller but also multiple co-tellers. Similarly, a story's tellability may be high or low.

24 For example, Bamberg and Georgakopoulou's (2008) analysis of a moderated discussion of 10-year-old boys about girls follows closely one boy's offer to tell a story which is immediately taken back, setting in motion a variety of interactional moves that result in the boy whispering the story to one of his friends and asking him to be the 'animator'.

25 One-to-one interviews undoubtedly form the main pool of narrative (autobiographical) data in the social sciences, leaving focus groups lagging behind in that respect. Perhaps, as a result, the otherwise illuminating studies of focus group interviews (e.g. see Myers, 2004) as a communicative event have hardly touched upon storytelling and what the differences may be between stories elicited in interviews and stories told in focus groups.

REFERENCES

Antaki, C. and Widdicombe, S. (1998) 'Identity as an achievement and as a tool', in C. Antaki, and S. Widdicombe, (eds), *Identities in Talk*. London: Sage.

Anthonissen, C. and Blommaert, J. (eds) (2007) Discourse and Human Rights Violations. Amsterdam: John Benjamins.

Atkinson, P. and Delamont, S. (2006) Rescuing narrative from qualitative research. *Narrative Inquiry*, 16: 173–81.

Bamberg, M. (1997b) 'Positioning between structure and performance', in M. Bamberg, (ed.), 'Oral versions of personal experience: three decades of narrative analysis', *Journal of Narrative and Life History* 7: 335–42.

Bamberg, M. (ed.) (1997a) 'Oral versions of personal experience: three decades of narrative analysis', *Journal of Narrative and Life History*, 7(1–4).

Bamberg, M. (2004) 'Talk, small stories, and adolescent identities', *Human Development*, 47: 331–53.

Bamberg, M. and Georgakopoulou, A. (2008) 'Small stories as a new perspective in narrative and identity analysis', in A. De Fina and A. Georgakopoulou (eds), *Text and Talk*, 28. Special Issue. *Narrative Analysis in the Shift from Texts to Practices*. pp. 377–96.

Bauman, R. (1969) *Verbal Art as Performance*. Rowley, MA: Newbury House.

Bauman, R. (1986) *Story, Performance and Event: Contextual Studies of Oral Narrative.* Cambridge: Cambridge University Press.

Bauman, R. (2004) *A World of Others' Words. Cross-Cultural Perspectives on Intertextuality.* Oxford: Blackwell.

Bernstein, B. (1996) *Pedagogy, Symbolic Control and Identity.* London: Taylor & Francis.

Blommaert, J. (2006) 'Ethnopoetics as functional reconstruction: Dell Hymes' narrative view of the world', *Working Papers in Urban Language and Literacies,* 32. Available at: www.kcl.ac.uk/schools/sspp/education/research/groups/llg/wpu

Blommaert, J. and Maryns, K. (2001) Stylistic and thematic shifting as a narrative resource: assessing asylum seekers' repertoires. *Multilingua,* 20: 161–184.

Blum-Kulka, S. (1997) *Dinner Talk: Cultural Patterns of Sociability and Socialization in Family Discourse.* Hillsdale, NJ: Lawrence Erlbaum.

Briggs, C. (1996) (ed.) *Disorderly Discourse. Narrative, Conflict and Inequality.* New York, Oxford: Oxford University Press.

Brockmeier, J. and Carbaugh, D. (2001) (eds) *Narrative and Identity Studies: Autobiography, Self and Culture.* Amsterdam,: Benjamins.

Bruner, J. (1997) 'Labov and Waletzky thirty years on', in M. Bamberg, (ed.), 'Oral versions of personal experience: three decades of narrative analysis', *Journal of Narrative and Life History,* 7(1–4): 61–8.

Cedeborg, A. C. and Aronsson, K. (1994) 'Co-narration and voice in family therapy: voicing, devoicing and orchestration', *Text,* 14: 345–70.

Chafe, W. (1980) (ed.) *The Pear Stories.* Norwood, NJ: Ablex.

Davies, Bronwyn, and Rom Harre (1990) 'Positioning': The social construction of selves', *Journal for the Theory of Social Behaviour,* 20, 43–63.

Daiute, C. and Lightfoot, C. (2004) (eds), *Narrative Analysis: Studying the Development of Individuals in Society.* London: Sage.

De Fina, A. (2003) *Identity in Narrative: A Study of Immigrant Discourse.* Amsterdam: John Benjamins.

De Fina, A. and Georgakopoulou, A. (2008a) 'Analysing narratives as practices', Special Issue, *Narrative methods. Journal of Qualitative Research,* 8: 379–87.

De Fina, A. and Georgakopoulou, A. (2008b) (eds), 'Narrative analysis in the shift from texts to practices', Special Issue. *Text and Talk,* 28.

De Fina, A. and Georgakopoulou, A. (forthcoming) *Analysing Narrative: Sociolinguistic Approaches.* Cambridge: Cambridge University Press.

De Fina, A. Schiffrin, D. and Bamberg, M. (2006) (eds), *Discourse and Identity.* Cambridge: Cambridge University Press.

De Peuter, J. (1998) 'The dialogics of narrative identity', in M. M. Bell, and M. Gardiner, (eds), *Bakhtin and the Human Sciences: No Last Words.* London: Sage. pp. 30–48.

Edwards, D. (1997) 'Structure and function in the analysis of everyday', *Journal of Narrative and Life History,* 7: 139–46.

Ehrlich, S. (2001) *Representing Rape. Language and Sexual Consent.* London: Routledge.

Ehrlich, S. (2007) 'Legal discourse and the cultural intelligibility of gendered meanings', *Journal of Sociolinguistics,* 11: 452–77.

Fludernik, M. (1996) *Towards a Natural Narratology.* New York: Routledge.

Gee, J. P. (1986) 'Units in the production of narrative discourse', *Discourse Processes,* 9: 391–422.

Georgakopoulou, A. (1997) *Narrative Performances. A study of Modern Greek Storytelling.* Amsterdam: John Benjamins.

Georgakopoulou, A. (2006a) 'Small and large identities in narrative (inter)-action', in A. De Fina, D. Schiffrin, and M. Bamberg (eds), *Discourse and Identity.* Cambridge: Cambridge University Press. pp. 83–102.

Georgakopoulou, A. (2006b) 'Thinking big with small stories in narrative and identity analysis', Special Issue. *Narrative – State of the Art. Narrative Inquiry,* 16: 129–37.

Georgakopoulou, A. (2006c) 'The other side of the story: towards a narrative analysis of narratives-in-interaction', *Discourse Studies,* 8: 265–87.

Georgakopoulou, A. (2007) *Small Stories, Interaction and Identities.* Amsterdam: John Benjamins.

Georgakopoulou, A. (2008) 'On MSN with buff boys': Self- and other-identity claims in the context of small stories. *Journal of Sociolinguistics,* 12: 597–626.

Georgakopoulou, A. and Goutsos, D. (2000) 'Revisiting discourse boundaries: The narrative and non-narrative modes', *Text,* 20: 63–82.

Georgakopoulou, A. and Goutsos, D. (2004) *Discourse Analysis. An Introduction.* 2nd edn. Edinburgh: Edinburgh University Press.

Goffman, E. (1974). *Frame Analysis: An Essay on the Organization of Experience.* New York: Harper and Row.

Goffman, E. (1981) *Forms of talk.* Philadelphia: University of Pennsylvania Press.

Goodwin, C. (1984). 'Notes on story structure and the organization of participation', in J. M. Atkinson, and J. Heritage, (eds), *Structures of Social Action.* Cambridge: Cambridge University Press. pp. 225–46.

Goodwin, M.H. (1990) *He-said-She-Said: Talk as Social Organization among Black Children.* Bloomington: IN: Indiana University Press.

Goodwin, M. H. (1997) 'By-play: negotiating evaluation in story-telling', in G. R. Guy, C. Feagin, D. Schiffrin, and J. Baugh, (eds), *Towards a Social Science of Language: Papers in Honor of William Labov.* Vol. 2, *Social Interaction and Discourse Structures.* Amsterdam: Benjamins. pp. 77–102.

Hanks, W. F. (1996) *Language and Communicative Practices.* Boulder, CO: Westview Press.

Hill, J. (1995) The Voices of Don Gabriel: Responsibility and Self in a Modern Mexicano Narrative. In D. Tedlock and B. Mannheim (eds), *The Dialogic Emergence of Culture.* Urbana: University of Illinois Press. 97–147.

Holmes, J. (1997) 'Struggling beyond Labov and Waletzky', in M. Bamberg, (ed.), 'Oral versions of personal experience: three decades of narrative analysis', *Journal of Narrative and Life History,* 7(1–4): 91–6.

Hymes, D. (1981) *'In vain I tried to tell You': Essays in Native American Ethnopoetics*. Philadelphia: University of Pennsylvania Press.

Hymes, D. (1996) *Ethnography, Linguistics, Narrative Inequality. Toward an Understanding of Voice*. London: Taylor & Francis.

Jacquemet, M. (2005) 'The registration interview. Restricting refugees' narrative Performances', in M. Baynham, and A. De Fina, (eds), *Dislocations/Relocations. Narratives of Displacement*. Manchester: St. Jerome. pp. 194–216.

Jefferson, G. (1978) 'Sequential aspects of storytelling in conversation', in J. Schenkein (ed.), *Studies in the Organisation of Conversational Interaction*. New York: Academic Press. pp. 219–49.

Johnstone, B. (1990) *Stories, Community, and Place*. Bloomington: IN: Indiana University Press.

Johnstone, R. (2001) 'Discourse analysis and narrative', in D. Schiffrin, D. Tannen, and H.E. Hamilton, (eds), *The Handbook of Discourse Analysis*. Malden, MA: Blackwell. pp. 635–49.

Josselson, R. (2006) 'Narrative research and the challenge of accumulating knowledge', *Narrative Inquiry*, 16: 3–10.

Kerby, A. (1991) *Narrative and the Self*. Bloomington: IN: Indiana University Press.

Kölbl, C. (2002) 'Blame it on psychology!?', *Narrative Inquiry*, 12: 29–35.

Labov, W. (1972) *Language in the Inner City*. Philadelphia: University of Pennsylvania Press.

Labov, W. (1997) 'Some further steps in narrative analysis', in M. Bamberg, (ed.), Oral versions of personal experience: three decades of narrative analysis, Special Issue. *Journal of Narrative and Life History*, 7(1–4): 395–415.

Labov, W. (2001) 'Uncovering the event structure of narrative', in D. Tannen and J. Alatis (eds), *Georgetown University Round Table on Languages and Linguistics 2001*. Washington, DC: Georgetown University Press. pp. 63–83.

Labov, W. and Waletzky, J. (1967) 'Narrative analysis: Oral versions of personal Experience', in J. Helm, (ed.), *Essays on the Verbal and Visual Arts*. Seattle; WA: University of Washington Press.

Lévi-Strauss, C. (1955) 'The structural study of myth', *Journal of American Folklore*, 68: 428–44.

Lévi-Strauss, C. (1964) *Mythologiques: le cru et le cuit*. Paris: Plon.

Linde, C. (1993) *Life Stories: The Creation of Coherence*. Oxford: Oxford University Press.

Lucius-Hoene, G. and Deppermann, A. (2000) 'Narrative identity empiricized: a dialogical and positioning approach to autobiographical research interviews', Special Issue: *Narrative Identity. Narrative Inquiry*, 10: 199–222.

Markus, H. R. and Kitayama, S. (1991) 'Culture and the self: implications for cognition, emotion and motivation', *Psychological Review*, 98: 224–53.

Maryns, K. and Blommaert, J. (2001) 'Stylistic and thematic shifting as a narrative resource: assessing asylum speakers' repertoires', *Multilingua*, 20: 61–84.

Michaels, S. (1981) '"Sharing time": children's narrative styles and differential access to literacy', *Language in Society*, 10(4): 423–42.

Mumby, D. (1993) (ed.) *Narrative and Social Control*. Newbury Park; CA: Sage.

Myers, G. (2004) *Matters of Opinion: Talking about Public Issues*. Cambridge: Cambridge University Press.

Myers, G. (2008) 'Analyzing interaction in broadcast debates', in R. Wodak, and M. Krzyzanowski, (eds), *Qualitative Discourse Analysis in the Social Sciences*. Basingstoke, UK: Palgrave Macmillan.

Ochs, E. and Capps, L. (2001) *Living Narrative*. Cambridge, MA: Harvard University Press.

Parker, I. (2003) 'Psychoanalytic narratives: writing the self into contemporary cultural phenomena', *Narrative Inquiry*, 13: 301–15.

Polanyi, L. 1985, *Telling the American Story: A Structural and Cultural Analysis of Conversational Storytelling*. Norwood, NJ: Ablex.

Potter, J. and Hepburn, A. (2005) 'Qualitative interviews in psychology', *Qualitative Research in Psychology*, 2: 281–307.

Propp, V. (1968) *Morphology of the Folktale*. Tr. L. Scott. Austin; TX: University of Texas Press.

Quasthoff, U. (1980) *Erzählen in Gesprächen*. Tübingen: Narr.

Riessman Kohler, C. (2002) 'Doing justice: positioning the interpreter in narrative work', in W. Patterson (ed.), *Strategic Narrative*. New York: Lexington Books.

Roberts, B. (2004) 'Poetics and the composition of life', *Narrative Inquiry*, 14: 261–73.

Sacks, H. (1974) 'An analysis of the course of a joke's telling in conversation', in R. Bauman, and J. F. Sherzer, (eds), *Explorations in the Ethnography of Speaking*. Cambridge: Cambridge University Press. pp. 337–53.

Sacks, H., Schegloff, E. A. and Jefferson, G. (1974) 'A simplest systematics for the organization of turn-taking for conversation', *Language*, 50: 696–735.

Schegloff, E. (1997) 'Narrative analysis: thirty years later', in M. Bamberg (ed.), 'Oral versions of personal experience: three decades of narrative analysis'. Special Issue. *Journal of Narrative and Life History*, 7(1–4): 97–105.

Schegloff, E. (1998) 'Reply to Wetherell', *Discourse and Society*, 9: 413–16.

Schiffrin, D. (1990) 'The management of a co-operative self during argument: the role of opinions and stories', in A. D. Grimshaw, (ed.), *Conflict Talk: Sociolinguistic Investigations of Arguments in Conversations*. Cambridge: Cambridge University Press. pp. 241–59.

Schiffrin, D. (1996) 'Language as self-portrait: sociolinguistic constructions of identity', *Language in Society*, 25: 167–203.

Scollon, Ron, and Suzanne Scollon. 1981. Narrative, literacy and face in interethnic communication. Norwood, NJ: Ablex.

Scollon, R. & Scollon, S.W. (2004) Nexus analysis: Discourse and the emerging internet. London: Routledge.

Shuman, A. (1986) *Storytelling Rights. The Uses of Oral and Written Texts by Urban Adolescents*. Cambridge: Cambridge University Press.

Slembrouck, S. (2003) 'What the map cuts up, the story cuts across', *Narrative Inquiry*, 13: 459–67.

Tannen, D. (1978) 'The effect of expectations on conversation', *Discourse Processes*, 1: 203–9.

Tannen, D. (1989) *Talking Voices: Repetition, Dialogue and Images in Conversational Discourse*. Cambridge: Cambridge University Press.

Toolan, M. (1988) *Narrative: A Critical Linguistic Introduction*. New York: Routledge.

Triandis, H. C. (1989) 'The self and social behaviour in differing cultural contexts', *Psychological Review*, 96: 506–20.

Trinch, S. and Berk-Seligson, S. (2002) 'Narrating in protective order interviews: a source of interactional trouble', *Language in Society*, 31: 383–418.

van Dijk, T. (1980) *Macrostructures: An Interdisciplinary Study of Global Structures in Discourse, Interaction and Cognition*. Hillsdale, NJ: Erlbaum.

Verdoolaege, A. (2008) *Reconciliation Discourse*. Amsterdam: John Benjamins.

Wagner, I. and Wodak, R. (2006) 'Performing success: identifying strategies of self-presentation in women's biographical narratives', *Discourse and Society*, 17: 385–411.

Wetherell, M. (1998) 'Positioning and interpretative repertoires: conversation analysis and post-structuralism in dialogue', *Discourse and Society*, 9: 387–412.

Wodak, R. and De Cillia (2007) 'Commemorating the past: the discursive construction of official narratives about the 'Rebirth of the Second Austrian Republic', *Discourse and Communication*, 1: 315–41.

Wortham, S. (2000) 'Interactional positioning and narrative self-construction', *Narrative Inquiry*, 10: 157–84.

Zimmerman, D. (1998) Identity, context and interaction. In C. Antaki & S. Widdicombe (eds) *Identities in Talk*. London: Sage. 87–106.

28

Gender and Interaction

Theodossia-Soula Pavlidou

28.1 INTRODUCTION

Research on language and gender has now been carried out for almost 40 years, and has produced a huge body of literature, including some outstanding introductions to the subject (e.g. Eckert and McConnell-Ginet, 2003), a handbook on this topic (Holmes and Meyerhoff, 2003) and even a journal (*Gender and Language*), launched in 2007. Over time, several changes have taken place in the kinds of questions that have been raised, the methods that have been employed and the types of explanations that have been sought. Such a development is not unique to this particular field of inquiry; rather, it goes hand in hand with and reflects shifts in paradigms within linguistics and women's/gender studies, as well as in the ways in which 'gender' and 'interaction' are conceptualized.

'Gender' has been a familiar notion in the study of language – in contrast to other scientific fields – albeit with varying senses. Dating back to the fifth century BC, 'grammatical gender' in Indo-European languages has been associated with 'natural gender', i.e. the sex of animate beings denoted by those words. The contact of Europeans with languages and cultures in colonized countries, from the seventeenth century onwards, as well as later ethnographic work, gave rise to reports about 'women's languages': language varieties that diverged from the 'norm' (i.e. men's speech) and which were used exclusively or preferentially by women (see, for example, Bodine, 1975; Glück, 1979). In modern linguistics, it was sociolinguistics – in its variationist version (e.g. Labov, 1972) – that introduced 'sex' as an independent variable which, along with class, age and style, is correlated with the manifestation of specific linguistic variables to describe

variation and explain change in language (see, for example, Wodak and Benke, 1997).

However, it was not until the emergence of the women's movement in the late 1960s that the notion of gender entered the field of linguistics from the point of view of sexism against women. At that time, the interest in gender was not confined to academic contingencies, but was clearly motivated by the dissatisfaction with the social order and the need to explore how the study of language could contribute to social change. The linguistic publication that marked this transition, in an emblematic way, was Robin Lakoff's article 'Language and Woman's Place' (1973). This article – and a couple of years later, the homonymous booklet (1975) – made the subject of linguistic sexism visible, and paved the way for the immense amount of research on language and gender. Since then, a central question – though at times downplayed or forgotten – has been how language and/or linguistic interaction helps produce, consolidate and reproduce unequal power relationships between women and men. Yet the balance gradually shifted from the more system-oriented studies[1] to empirical research on how gender relates to interaction, discourse, or communication.[2] This is not to say that there have not been cross-overs all along, but it was around 1990 that a major change in perspective took place, motivated by, among other things, an 'interactional turn' in sociolinguistics and the performative turn in feminist theory.

The phenomenon of interaction, though hardly irrelevant for language and linguistics at any time, has not always been called by that name: 'language use', 'interpersonal communication', 'conversation', 'discourse', etc., are some of the designations that have been deployed, without necessarily providing explications on the delineation of these terms. For example, as long as the use of linguistic signs was equated to the Saussurian 'parole' or the Chomskyan 'performance' (i.e. as lacking systematicity), there was no danger of confusing 'language use' with interaction (as understood in, for example, ethnomethodology). However, once the dimension of regularity in language use was established through sociolinguistic work, the two terms were no longer that distinct. The boundaries became even more blurred when, through speech act theory and the rise of linguistic pragmatics, language use (or, more generally, linguistic communication) was conceptualized as activity, thus encompassing intentionality and agency. The term 'interaction' itself became more visible in linguistics, when social linguistic approaches other than the variationist paradigm – for example, the ethnography of communication, interactional sociolinguistics and conversation analysis – gained prominence in the field. Such approaches were informed by linguistic anthropology and/or ethnomethodology and, while retaining a view of interaction as an activity, they advanced the dyad as its minimal unit. They proposed kinds of analyses that were grounded in naturalistic data and intended to be compatible with the participants' own views of what is going on in their interaction, thus underscoring interaction as the locus of the production of social meaning and emphasizing its constitutive character. However, it would be impossible to offer a formal definition of 'interaction' (or 'conversation', 'talk-in-interaction', 'communication', 'discourse', for that matter) that would do justice to the analytic aims and epistemological commitments of all these approaches at the same time.[3] To give an example, context is a crucial notion in any analysis of interaction, but 'context' can be understood in very different ways, ranging from the most immediate sequential surroundings of an utterance, in conversation analysis, to the broadest institutional, societal, cultural environment in interactional sociolinguistics.

So talking about gender and interaction is weaving narrative threads relating to each of these topics as well as the broader areas they arose in, and telling a story that can be told in different ways, even if the same constituents are used and the same goals are pursued. My aim in this chapter is not to present an exhaustive account of the research on gender and interaction, but to highlight some of the work done against the background of tensions and debates that have shaped the field. Since the present volume includes separate chapters on sociolinguistic paradigms, I will not examine here the different approaches to interaction. Instead, I will start with a presentation of some major issues in feminist approaches to gender (Section 28.2); in particular, I will focus on

those approaches which consider gender as an activity (practice, accomplishment, performance), because these mark a turning point also in language and gender research. I will then discuss findings on gender and interaction under three different headings that reflect different stances on how gender relates to interaction. Section 28.3 (*Gendering interaction*) looks into constraints, linguistic as well as more broadly social, that gender the interactional scene before interactants even make their entrance. Section 28.4 (*Gendered interaction*) focuses on research which associates certain interactional features with specific genders. Section 28.5 (*Constructing gender in interaction*) turns to the making of gendered selves and gendered others in interaction – in other words, on how gender is actually 'done'. Finally, Section 28.6 discusses perspectives and challenges for the future.

28.2 FEMINIST APPROACHES TO GENDER

In many academic fields, the transition from a non-feminist perspective on gender to a feminist approach is echoed in the tension between the concepts of *sex* and *gender*. While the former is usually associated with the reproductive function and divides human beings into men and women, the latter – deriving from ideas articulated for the first time by Simone de Beauvoir (1949) – is regarded as the product of social and cultural factors. Although the focus of 'gender' changed considerably over time, the underlying assumption has been that 'gender' encompasses two genders – men and women – which are built upon or presuppose the two sex categories. And, although the historicity of gender was indisputable, the two gender categories were treated as homogeneous and stable. As a consequence, the idea that the distinction between women and men is not biologically but socially and culturally motivated often degenerated into a simple change of jargon, i.e. substituting the word *sex* with the word *gender*.

The above-mentioned assumptions were contested from at least two perspectives (not always distinct in more recent years). The first is associated with the idea that gender cannot or should not be isolated from other aspects of one's identity. 'Intersectionality' was the term employed for conceptualizing ways in which 'sociocultural hierarchies, power differentials and in/exclusions around discursively and institutionally constructed categories such as gender, ethnicity, race, class, sexuality, age/generation, nationality, etc. mutually co-construct each other' (Lykke, 2006: 151).

Although it was first used in the context of Black feminist theory, intersectionality, according to Lykke, has always been at the heart of feminist theorizing. The second perspective comprises standpoints which oppose the very idea of gender as an attribute, a property of individuals, a stable and static aspect of identity. Two independently originating approaches in the late 1980s have been very influential in this context. The first, known as 'doing gender', was proposed by West and Zimmerman and is, sociologically, more specifically ethnomethodologically informed.[4] The second, labelled as 'gender performativity', is associated with the poststructuralist philosopher Judith Butler and draws on theatrical, anthropological and philosophical analyses.[5]

The notion of 'doing' was not a novel concept in ethnomethodology, but the term 'doing gender' was coined by West and Zimmerman in a talk, in 1977, that was published in 1987 (see West and Zimmerman, 2002). Their proposal was to understand gender as the product of social doings, more specifically 'as a routine, methodical, and recurring accomplishment' (West and Zimmerman, 2002: 4) rather than as a set of traits, a variable, or a role (i.e. situated identity), as was the case up to that point. In particular, to do gender is to achieve being categorized as a member of the female or male sex and *preserving* that categorization. Based on Garfinkel, Kessler and McKenna, and also Sacks,[6] West and Zimmerman argue that it is this categorization that counts and not the fulfillment of some 'essential' criteria for 'maleness' or 'femaleness', because in everyday life, congruence between the sex category a person is put into and this person's sex is taken for granted. This is quite evident in cases where the 'essential' (biological, hormonal, chromosomal) criteria accepted by a social/cultural group at a given time are not fulfilled, as for example with the transsexual 'Agnes' studied by Garfinkel. As West and Zimmerman emphasize, Agnes' problem was exactly how to preserve her categorization as female, which goes far beyond applying blindly ready-made recipes for normative feminine bundles of behaviour: it entails managing any occasion in such a way that 'whatever the particulars, the outcome is seen and is seeable in context as gender appropriate or, as the case may be, gender inappropriate – that is, *accountable*' (West and Zimmerman, 2002: 12).

Only shortly after West and Zimmerman's 1987 publication, Butler's proposal on gender as performance was articulated in a paper (1988), and further elaborated in the book that she became famous with, *Gender Trouble* (1990). In the 1988 paper, Butler set out to examine the ways in which gender is constructed through specific corporeal acts and the possibilities that exist for its cultural

transformation through such acts. She argued that gender identity is 'instituted through a stylized repetition of acts' and through 'the stylization of the body' (1988: 519). Butler considered such acts to be performative both in the sense of 'dramatic' and of 'non-referential'. The dramaturgical aspect involves two key elements: (a) repetition (incorporating both re-enactment and re-experience at the same time) of a set of meanings that are already socially established; (b) the public nature of the act, which entails that gender cannot be a matter of merely individual choice, especially when this runs counter to the established binary and heterosexual gender frame, but is subjected to social sanctions and taboos. Non-referentiality, on the other hand, relates directly, though without explicit reference at that time, to Austin's (1962) original idea of performative utterances, i.e. utterances that do not describe or represent the world as opposed to constatives and, therefore, cannot be said to be true or false. Instead, performative utterances *do* something – e.g. *marrying, promising, baptizing*, etc. – and in this sense they constitute a 'reality'. Analogously, gender attributes are not referential: they do not express or reveal an identity 'behind' the act itself, but *constitute* that very identity.

Despite their different disciplinary backgrounds (and the different aims originating from these, i.e. Butler's interest in deconstructing gender, West and Zimmerman's emphasis on 'doing' gender), the two approaches address basically the same issues in ways that are not incompatible.[7] Both argue against a pre-existing, essential nature of gender and conceptualize it as an activity, thus making the aspects of agency and intentionality salient, while stressing the non-voluntaristic dimension of gender. At the same time, both West and Zimmerman, and Butler, integrate in their framework the possibility of resistance and, hence, of change of the social order. Neither approach, however, explicates what is actually involved in constructing gender: what tools are employed, how this process of doing/performing gender is actually enacted and what kind of empirical data would be needed, in order to detect resistance to and change of the social order. It is exactly at this point that the study of language and gender, and in particular of interaction and gender, can make an important contribution to the analysis of gender construction.

However, where Butler goes further[8] than West and Zimmerman is the idea that not only gender but also sex itself is a construction, i.e. that bodies are cultivated, through a series of acts which are reiterated, revised and consolidated over time into discrete sexes 'with "natural" appearances and "natural" heterosexual dispositions' (Butler, 1988: 524). This is not to deny the materiality of bodies, as is explicated in her later work, but to argue that corporeality has been framed and formed through normative conditions.[9] In other words, there is no clear-cut way of 'extracting' sex from gender, because, as stressed by Fausto-Sterling (2000: 5), 'choosing which criteria to use in determining sex, and choosing to make the determination at all, are social decisions for which scientists can offer no absolute guidelines'. Consequently, the differentiation between sex and gender (and the relationship between the two) is not as evident as assumed in the first two decades of feminist discussions.[10]

In the same direction, though based on different grounds, another critique has been recently articulated. Literature on gender has taken for granted that the distinction between 'sex' and 'gender' made in English is transferable also to other languages. This was a consequence not only of the hegemony of the English language in academic discourse, in general, but also of the formation and early institutionalization of women's/gender studies in the Anglo-Saxon countries. It was not until the late 1990s that the issue of the transferability of key feminist terms and concepts was explicitly taken up within the European context,[11] leading to a series of publications in which the sex–gender terminology is examined in several languages.[12] It was shown that some European languages do not provide different words for 'sex' and 'gender' (in the non-grammatical sense), for example, or that the semantic fields around those words are not equivalent to the English ones, and that all this is quite consequential for the ideological debates, including the naming of the field as women's/gender, etc.[13]

In what follows, I will continue to employ the term 'gender' since no discussion of these matters, either synchronically or diachronically, is possible in English without employing it, but we do have to keep in mind the different contextualizations of the term in the discussions and critiques of feminist theorizing after the performative turn.

28.3 GENDERING INTERACTION

By 'gendering interaction' I mean the linguistic and sociocultural constraints that inform interaction and which are invested with dominant gender ideologies[14] i.e. representations of reality that are the product of asymmetrical power relations between the genders and in which gender differences and heteronormativity are taken for granted.[15] Some of the constraints gendering interaction are structural: they result from broader social and institutional arrangements that create, maintain and reinforce gender differences.[16] Structural constraints entail, among other things, differential access for men and women to positions, activities,

spaces, etc., in society, and to the kind of discourses associated with them, including talk and silence, speech genres/events/acts (see Eckert and McConnell-Ginet, 2003: 92ff). Moreover, the linguistic tools that we have at our disposal encode gender stereotypes and ideologies, and restrict accordingly the choices in communication. At the same time, the groups we operate in have certain stereotypical conceptions about how men, women, gays, lesbians, etc., communicate and normative expectations about how they should communicate. In the following, I will look briefly at some linguistic constraints and stereotypes/norms that set up the interactional game in a gendered way.

28.3.1 Constraints of the linguistic system

Engaging in linguistic interaction involves the use of at least one language, and languages have various ways for dividing humans into two mutually exclusive categories according to sex. The most common means for establishing such a dichotomy are *lexical* and *grammatical gender*. Since the present handbook contains a chapter on these topics (Hellinger, in this volume),[17] I will confine myself to some interesting intertwinings of grammatical/lexical gender and sex of the person denoted, with consequences for interaction, using Modern Greek as an example.

A recent study[18] of all nouns (about 28,000) in a contemporary Modern Greek dictionary indicated that there are almost twice as many feminine nouns as masculine ones (45.0% vs 23.8%). However, analysis of the literal meaning of these nouns showed that this ratio is reversed when they denote human beings; in other words, in Modern Greek there are almost twice as many masculine nouns denoting humans as feminine ones. Moreover, on the level of literal meaning, grammatical gender fits almost perfectly with lexical gender.[19] The masculine gender is predominant also when denoting humans metaphorically. In addition, metaphors for men have as source OTHER HUMANS to a much greater extent (74.7%) than do metaphors for women (46.6%). This means that the extensive presence of feminine gender does not ensure female visibility or imply female agency; rather, as has been argued (Pavlidou, 2006b), it enables a 'feminization' of the world in a not so innocent way – for example, by projecting stereotypical representations of women onto the inanimate world which, in turn, consolidate gender norms.

If, as McConnell-Ginet (2003: 91) observes, it is difficult for English speakers 'to talk about a third person without attributing sex to them – and virtually impossible to do so over an extended period', because of the gendered third-person pronouns in English, one can imagine the impact of a gendered language like Greek on speakers' choices. In this respect, Ochs' statement (1992) that only a few items in a language are directly related to gender and that indexing of gender is accomplished indirectly, although accurate, fails to capture the extent to which languages with grammatical gender impose a gendered stance on their users. Even if one contests the view that such a dichotomy of humans into men and women is 'natural', one is forced to invoke a categorization since the words used, carry a 'presumption of sex attribution' (McConnell-Ginet, 2003: 91).[20] Sexually-liminal communities (e.g. transsexuals or hermaphrodites) use, as research on language and sexuality has shown, 'linguistic gender in ways both paradoxical and ironic, for the very system whose simple binary excludes them, is called into play to generate their own meanings and construct the communities' own network of alliances' (Livia, 1997: 365). However, practices like, for example, alternating between the masculine and the feminine gender, while indeed expressing gender fluidity, also show the grammatical impasse in which one is entrapped (and which as a matter of fact would not be overcome by simply adding more 'genders').

The systemic constraints relating to gender (and the male bias of languages) may prove to have even further-reaching consequences, if thought is influenced by the way in which a language is structured (the linguistic relativity hypothesis). Recent experimental work[21] by Boroditsky, Schmidt and Phillips (2003) suggests that grammatical gender has effects on people's descriptions of objects, their assessments of picture similarities, etc. Therefore, the authors conclude: 'it is striking that even a fluke of grammar (the arbitrary designation of a noun as masculine or feminine) can have an effect on how people think about things in the world' (2003: 77).

28.3.2 Sociocultural constraints on interaction: gender stereotypes and norms

Being categorized through lexical and/or grammatical gender as a 'woman' or a 'man' brings with it a whole range of stereotypical attributions that stem from dominant gender ideologies. Stereotyping can be seen as a particular kind of categorizing; i.e. a cognitive process through which schemata of classification are imposed on events, states of affairs, objects, people and so on, by 'putting together diverse particulars into a single category – and relating the categories they create' (Eckert and McConnell-Ginet, 2003: 228).

In particular, according to Talbot (2003: 470), 'stereotyping involves simplification, reduction, and naturalization' of some real or imagined differences among social groups; these differences are taken as fixed and essential, dividing people into 'normal'/'acceptable'/'Us' and 'abnormal'/'unacceptable'/'Them', depending on the constellations of power in a society. In reproducing naturalized gender differences, gender stereotypes function 'to sustain hegemonic male dominance and female subordination' (Talbot, 2003: 472). Some gender stereotypes refer explicitly to the linguistic behaviour of women and men; the extent to which they correspond to real behaviour has become the object of several studies in research on gender and interaction.

Despite the cultural diversity in the representation and evaluation of the speech attributed to different genders, there is a recurring stereotype across languages and cultures as reflected in proverbs, 'great men's' sayings jokes, shows, etc., concerning women's volubility. Yet, experimental findings on the amount of speech produced by adults – also before the topic gained the attention of feminist linguists – did not provide evidence to support it;[22] on the contrary, it indicated that the opposite was sometimes the case. Other studies on mixed-sex interactions between adult middle-class English-speaking Americans, drawing on both experimental and naturalistic data, converge on the whole in a direction that does not align with the stereotypical representation of women as verbose.[23]

Another popular stereotype that concerns the linguistic behaviour of men and women elaborates on the non-significance (and unreliability) of women's speech: women are claimed to 'gossip', i.e. to engage in casual and superficial talk, including talking negatively about non-present parties, particularly when among themselves; they 'chit-chat', 'chatter', 'jabber', and so on, while a 'man' seems to be almost semantically incompatible with this type of talk. As Johnson and Finlay (1997: 131) argue, gossip is not sex-exclusive; yet, when men engage in it, it is not named as such. Their analysis of a TV programme on football indicates that men 'gossip in order to create solidarity within their own gender group', using discursive strategies that are very similar to those of women, when they do 'identity work' (p. 142). Similarly, Cameron (1997) shows that the men, in an all-male informal conversation she analysed, engage in talk that bears all the features of 'gossip'; the 'identity work' these men do, consists in the display of a masculinity that is based on heterosexual orientation.

Along with the 'de-gendering' of gossip, research has elaborated on its positive functions – for example, establishing and maintaining social relationships, reaffirming and strengthening of friendship (Coates, 1988: 98) – thus changing the grounds for its assessment.[24] This re-evaluation of features held typical of 'women's language' seems to have taken place, also on a societal level, in the course of the last 30 years, as Cameron (2003) argues, due to the changing nature both of work in the global economy and of personal life in late modern societies: women have been upgraded from inadequate language users to models for communication skills. However, this does not entail that the stereotypes themselves have changed; despite the fact that linguistic research has produced evidence to the contrary, and that more and more people challenge such stereotypes both individually and collectively, the dominant stereotypical beliefs about men's/women's linguistic behaviour have proved to be very persistent.

The durability of certain stereotypes is undoubtedly related to the prescriptive power they exercise on the members of a community, both with respect to the way linguistic behaviour is shaped and the way it is perceived. People talk like 'women' or 'men' because they comply with a model of feminine or masculine speech prescribed by a stereotype (thus rendering stereotypical expectations self-fulfilling prophecies). For example, the fact that a pre-pubertal child's voice is recognizable as 'female' or 'male', before anatomical differentiation of the vocal tract has taken place (Sachs, 1975), indicates that children have adjusted their speech production to a gendered model.[25] On the other hand, linguists themselves are held responsible for the vitality of certain stereotypes. Freed (2003), for example, argues that linguists have not paid enough attention to public stereotypical views on women's and men's talk.[26] In particular, they have neglected to communicate to a broader public how the results of their research run counter to the stereotypical beliefs of society or to address the discrepancy between actual language use and perceptions of it, as well as expectations about language use, as an object of research. Moreover, it has been claimed that even when they intend to refute such stereotypes, linguists sometimes contribute to their reproduction.[27] The very approach to gender and interaction that looks for differences in the linguistic behaviour of men and women (see next section) is held to be reinforcing the stereotype that men and women are different.

28.4 GENDERED INTERACTION

Research on gendered interaction was a direct follow-up to Lakoff's (1975) observations on the characteristics of women's linguistic behaviour, as contrasted to men's, and culminated in Tannen's (1990) publication on the roots of miscommunication between women and men. An impressive number of studies, mainly with respect to the English language and Anglo-Saxon society, have been carried out with considerable diversity in the kind of linguistic items investigated, the contexts and settings in which the use of these items is examined, the types of speech events and/or genres that have been analysed, and sometimes even in the findings. Some of these studies are quantitative, others qualitative, or employ combined methods; on the whole, however, there is over time a recess of experimental (and/or quantitative) methodology and a growing preference for naturalistic data and qualitative approaches.

Given this diversity, in presenting some of the research I will orient myself towards what Janet Holmes' (1998: 462) suggests as possible 'sociolinguistic universal tendencies'. Holmes' exploratory, as she emphasizes, generalizations are formulated along four dimensions of analysis, regarding the (primary) function of interaction and the indexing of solidarity, power and status through speech. The first generalization that Holmes draws from the available empirical research is that women tend 'to focus on the affective functions of interaction' (1998: 463), i.e. that women are more strongly orientated towards establishing connections, negotiating relationships, etc., in interaction, rather than to reporting facts, imparting information, and so on. Tannen (1990: 74–85) coined the terms 'rapport-talk' and 'report-talk' for this difference in orientation and associated it with 'private speaking' and 'public speaking', respectively – an association that also underscores the differences in the kinds of topics raised in each type of talk. Besides conversations among friends or partners, findings from a number of settings and genres provide supporting evidence. For example, Wodak (1981) in her study of a therapeutic group of potential suicide candidates found that women and men employ different types of text to talk about their problems (women relate, men report). Further, with respect to storytelling, Johnstone (1993) argued that in women's narratives the protagonists manage disturbing events 'in concert with others' (1993: 76), while in men's it is through the individual characteristics of the protagonist that disturbances in the usual flow of events are overcome; also Georgakopoulou (2006) observed differences in the kinds of events that women and men tell stories about: men's stories revolve around activities, while those of women are about events that caused negative feelings. Finally, in classroom interaction, girls' 'non-compliant turns' to the teacher (disagreeing, arguing, complaining, etc.) were found to be mainly about the management of classroom matters, turn-taking, etc., while boys' turns of the same type focused on the content of the lesson (e.g. Pavlidou, 2003).

The most prominent instantiation of the first generalization, however, is to be found in 'the work women do' to keep interaction going (Fishman, 1983): asking questions, employing devices to attract the attention of other interactants, using minimal responses to encourage a speaker to continue. It is this strategy that spans over to the second generalization: namely, that women tend 'to use linguistic devices that stress solidarity' more often than men do (Holmes, 1998: 468). Along with supportive feedback and facilitative tags, i.e. tags that invite the addressee to contribute to the conversation (see Holmes, 1995: 55–59 and 79–86), women have been found to employ further linguistic items that signal closeness and solidarity. Compliments, for example, are a case in point: across a range of cultures women tend to pay (but also to receive) more compliments than men (see Holmes, 1995: 115–38, for New Zealand English and for further references; Sifianou, 2001, for Modern Greek). In a broader framework, all these features in women's behaviour are considered to be tokens of positive politeness, and make up the conversational style, variously described as 'cooperative' or 'affiliative' (see, for example, Makri-Tsilipakou, 1991; Coates, 1996), that has been attributed to women.

Men, on the other hand, 'tend to interact in ways which will maintain and increase their power and status', especially in formal contexts, (Holmes, 1998: 472). This generalization is based on evidence from research on two phenomena that have been mainly associated with dominance in interaction – namely, the amount of talk, discussed in Section 28.3.2, and interruptions. In contrast to the amount of talk, which is relatively straightforward to define, the definition of 'interruption' (*emic* vs *etic* criteria) and its functions (supportive/cooperative vs disruptive/competitive) have been much debated (see, for example, James and Drakich, 1993; Tannen, 1994). As Holmes (1998: 469) emphasizes, it is important to distinguish 'a mistimed unintended overlap, or an overenthusiastic supportive comment with no 'take-over-the floor' intention [...] from a deliberative disruptive interruption'. It is the latter kind that men have been found to exercise more frequently than women (who in turn are more frequently disruptively interrupted by men than vice versa).

Tying in closely to the sociolinguistic tradition in the Labovian paradigm is Holmes' generalization with respect to the indexing of status: 'women use more standard forms than men from the same social group in the same social context'

(Holmes, 1998: 473). Supporting evidence is provided not only by classical social dialect research studying language variation across different social groups in a given society (e.g. Labov, 1972) but also by subsequent approaches focusing on variation within one social group.[28] Holmes explains the apparent contradiction between the third generalization (i.e. that men interact in such ways that their status is maintained and increased) and the fourth with the additional generalization that women are 'stylistically more flexible than men' (1998: 475).

The presentation above has deliberately glossed over a number of complexities,[29] because what is at issue here is less the observational adequacy of such generalizations and more the kinds of explanations that have been invoked to account for the findings. In other words, assuming that these generalizations are adequate on a descriptive level, how are the observed differences to be explained? Until the early 1990s, two kinds of explanations, known as the *dominance* and the *difference* models, prevailed.

The first concerns differences in the linguistic behaviour of men and women as a consequence of their differential power in society: the dominance–subordination relation between men and women in society is carried over to interaction (see, for example, Thorne and Henley, 1975). Men develop interactional patterns, like interrupting others or unduly holding the floor, congruent with their dominant position in society; women, on the other hand, as the subordinate group, cannot afford to be inconsiderate about, for instance, their interlocutors' feelings and needs. Moreover, as is the case with the social division of labour between men and women, 'there is an unequal distribution of work in conversation' (Fishman, 1983: 98), with women doing routinely interactional work without, however, profiting themselves (e.g. being successful in having discussed the topics they raise). While there have been many studies aligning with this type of explanation of gender differences in interaction, the 'dominance' approach has never been spelled out in a systematic way, so that it could explain coherently all observed differences in the linguistic behaviour of men and women.

In contrast to the dominance model that sees difference as an outcome of social inequality between men and women, in the second type of explanation interactional differences are associated – on a meta-linguistic level – with equality: men and women have different, but equally good, conversational styles. In the language and gender research, the second model was originally put forward by Maltz and Borker (1982) but gained prominence (and popularity) through Tannen's (1990) elaboration. Maltz and Borker, in attempting to explain how miscommunication between the genders arises, suggested that the same linguistic features may carry different meanings for men and women – this being a result of their socialization in same-sex groups during critical stages in the acquisition of communication skills. This difference in 'subcultures' may lead to different interpretations, for example, concerning the appearance and placing of minimal responses, and hence to misunderstandings in communication, as is the case when people from different ethnic backgrounds communicate with each other. While these approaches take context more seriously into account, talking of difference, without considering explicitly the power matrix that nurtures it, has severe implications, not only for the resolution of 'misunderstandings' but also for social change. The fact that linguists (or sociologists, anthropologists, etc.) recognize the two different styles or linguistic behaviours as equal does not in itself grant them equal currency in the interactional market, and may disguise social conflicts as 'misunderstandings', as Cameron (1998) argues.

Although the two models have often been discussed in a polarized manner (the first as being political, the second as apolitical), it would not in principle be difficult to reconcile them. This, however, would not resolve a major weakness inherent in both: namely, accounting for *similarities* between women and men. In other words, how would the 'dominance' model explain those cases in interaction in which women and men behave in the same ways? Alternatively, how would the 'difference' model interpret 'smooth' communication: i.e. when no 'misunderstandings' between men and women take place? Neither model can provide an answer because underlying both there seems to lurk a fundamental assumption – namely, that men and women *are* different. This assumption, however, is problematical in several respects. For one, it does not acknowledge the fact that differentiation in the linguistic behaviour of men and women is enmeshed with a whole range of similarities. For another, it fails to recognize how difference has been historically invoked to justify dominance. Finally, it bears upon an implicit understanding of gender as a stable social binary that presupposes a biological binary, thus, essentializing 'woman' and 'man' and homogenizing 'all women' (and 'all men'); but as we saw in Section 28.2, it is exactly this relationship that has been called into question by Butler. So, looking for differences without articulating explicitly and/or critiquing related assumptions and implications and implications may be a trap into which researchers themselves may fall, serving the enhancement of stereotypes rather than social change in a feminist understanding.

28.5 CONSTRUCTING GENDER IN INTERACTION

In the previous section, it was indicated that research on gendered interaction reached a deadlock partly because of the research question itself (looking for differences between women and men) and its presumptions (taking 'gender' for granted). However, with the performative turn in feminist theorizing (see Section 28.2), older notions of gender as a kind of superstructure on sex eventually came under scrutiny, while 'gender' as doing or performance pointed to interaction as the crucial locus for the conceptualization of gender. Within research on language and gender itself, the spotlight on interaction was necessitated also by quandaries about diverging or conflicting findings. To overcome such problems, functional and strategic considerations had increasingly to be taken into account.[30] Acknowledging, however, the different functions of tag questions or interruptions, for example, and accounting for choices among different options called for detailed examination of the interactional conditions under which the linguistic behaviour of women and men comes about. This development allowed anthropologically and sociologically informed approaches, for which interaction was of primordial importance, to move from the periphery of language and gender research (and, more generally, of mainstream sociolinguistics) to its centre and paved the way for a paradigm shift in the early 1990s that entailed:

- a social constructionist view of gender (or other aspects of identity) whereby gender is not a constant, a pre-given to interaction, but a product of it in which language plays a constitutive role
- a pragmatic (or non-deterministic) perspective on language use – speakers are rational beings that make strategic use of language in order to achieve certain goals
- explicit delineations of context, ranging from the very practical activity in which utterances are embedded up to broader cultural and social formations.

This change of paradigm was anticipated in Goodwin and Goodwin's (1987: 241) conclusion of their paper on children's arguing:

If we are to describe accurately the organization of male and female language, we shall have to go beyond global generalizations that contrast all men with all women in all situations and instead describe in detail the organization of talk within specific activity systems. Such an approach permits study of the similarities as well as differences in female and male language usage and relates specific utterance forms to both ongoing practical activities and the cultures that underlie them'.

Moreover, Goodwin's (1990) examination of how aspects of gender are manifested in a range of speech activities showed that articulation of gender and talk by the same individual will vary across different activities so that 'social personae appropriate to the events of the moment' can be constructed (1990: 9). The ethnographic study of activity, as the basic unit of analysis, has been undertaken in social formations like the peer group (Goodwin, 1990), the dyad of caregiving mother and infant (Ochs, 1992), the family at the dinner table (Ochs and Taylor, 1995), etc. Such groupings of people are not only much smaller and more local than 'social class' in the Labovian paradigm, but also they make visible the iterative and ritual character of particular activities that turns them into *practices*.

The notion of practice as a collaborative and socially regulated achievement comes into full play in the ground-breaking paper by Eckert and McConnell-Ginet (1992), in which much of the methodological and epistemological differentiation – entailed in the research just cited – from classical sociolinguistic work is articulated explicitly, and an alternative approach based on the concept of a community of practice is proposed. 'Community of practice', a notion stemming from Lave and Wenger's (1991) social theory of learning, was introduced by Eckert and McConnell-Ginet (1992: 464) as 'an aggregate of people who come together around mutual engagement in an endeavor. Ways of doing things, ways of talking, beliefs, values, power relations – in short, practices – emerge in the course of this mutual endeavor'. Obviously, this construct offers a more general and abstract conceptualization of particular groupings of people (peer group, family, etc.) than previously examined;[31] but at the same time it goes further, as it aims to articulate local social practice with individual place and 'with larger social configurations' (Eckert and McConnell-Ginet, 2007: 28), thus building an intermediate link between a single interaction and social structures. Gender as well as other aspects of identity, all intertwined, are seen as part of a meaning-making process (producing, reproducing, negotiating meaning) which is a function of one's participation in different communities of practice and of the differential modes of participation in those communities. This leads, inevitably, to a diversity of gender categories whose homogeneity (or heterogeneity, for that matter) cannot be a priori postulated but has to be proven through

detailed analyses of the 'local' practices and their relationship to the 'global' contexts in which they are embedded.

Language – more accurately, language use – features in this context in two important ways. The first has to do with the question of how language can signify gender. As mentioned in Section 28.3.1, all languages provide in their system for *lexical gender*, and many, additionally, for *grammatical gender*. Ochs (1992), drawing on Silverstein,[32] argues that this 'direct' or 'referential' indexing of gender and, more generally, of social meaning (i.e. social conditions, social context, social identities), is only part of the story, because gender is also indexed 'non-referentially': namely, by means of two mediating components between linguistic forms and gender. The first component consists of social constructs which are interactant-related (for example, stances, speech activities, etc.) and which are *directly* signified by particular linguistic forms; the second comprises society-related constructs (e.g. norms, preferences, and expectations with respect to social identities, including gender) which are operant in a particular community and which relate particular distributions of stances, activities, etc., with preferred images of men and women, (in other words, they count as gendered). Thus, 'the relation of language to gender is constituted and mediated by the relation of language to stances, social acts, social activities, and other social constructs' (Ochs, 1992: 337). A second way in which language use is involved in producing 'gender' is stylistic differentiation. According to Eckert (2008), following Irvine and Gal,[33] style involves distinguishing oneself through clothing, articulation, ways of speaking, etc., from a given social landscape. Eckert understands a stylistic move as a kind of bricolage whereby 'linguistic resources come to be associated with particular salient social meanings, to be combined with other meanings – or exaggerated and tweaked to slightly modify these meanings' (2008: 15), leading to social reproduction or social change. Consequently, it is through such practices that gender hierarchies develop in interaction and through which the gender order is maintained or challenged.

Clearly, these approaches to gender and interaction open arrays of research questions that move away from the search for differences between women and men on the presumption of disjunctiveness of these two genders/sexes. For example, Eckert and McConnell-Ginet (1995), using data from Eckert's ethnographic study of a Detroit high school, showed how gender, class and power relations are mutually constructed within a particular institution and, more specifically, how the social categories 'jocks' and 'burnouts' are established in communities of practice, whereby the central practices for claiming membership in these categories are different for girls and boys (popularity vs coolness for jocks and burnout girls, respectively; sports vs toughness for jocks and burnout boys, respectively). Furthermore, they showed how labelling and pronunciation of certain vowels – two different aspects of language use – are involved in constructing selves in class–gender–power constellations. Social labelling, in the form of gendered 'person formulation' or 'membership categorization' terms like 'girl' and 'boy', is also investigated by Goodwin (forthcoming) in three pre-adolescent peer groups. More specifically, Goodwin indicates various ways in which children in these peer groups orient themselves to gender in their spontaneous talk, and what they accomplish by invoking gendered identity categories (e.g. 'girl' functions as carrier of stance, displaying heightened affiliation or derision).

Since the late 1990s, there has been growing interest in communities of practice that develop in institutional and workplace settings,[34] because in such settings both the discrepancy between lipservice to equality and the gendered distribution of positions of power as well as the double-bind of women in positions of power are evident in most acute forms (see Holmes, 2007). The work of Holmes and her collaborators has shown that in order to 'do leadership' effectively, women leaders exploit various kinds of strategies (which comply to varying degrees with normative expectations of 'feminine' or 'masculine' behaviour), depending on the situational and workplace context (type of workplace and workplace culture). Some women managers also 'effectively switch between normatively gendered styles of discourse, or strategically integrate aspects of normatively feminine discourse styles into their workplace talk, skillfully meshing transactional and relational discourse features' (Holmes, 2007: 58). Similarly, Wodak (2003), in her investigation of a very particular elite workplace, has argued that female EU parliamentarians, in order to be successful in 'doing politics', develop practices that construct them as 'assertive activists', 'experts', 'being different in a positive way (special bird)', or combinations of these habitus, and that these types of female gender role constructions of successful women are quite different from those found in other institutional or workplace settings.

Along with the study of diverse 'femininities' (and 'masculinities') in relation to interaction, increasing attention has been paid, since the late 1990s, to gender as dissociated from sex, and to sexuality (see, for example, Livia and Hall, 1997; McIlvenny, 2002; Cameron and Kulick, 2003).

This turn to sexual orientation, rather than 'sex', and to the construction of sexual identitities in interaction is another consequence of the feminist theorists' contesting of the body as the anchor point of gender and their disclosing of heterosexuality as the normative condition for sexing the body (see Section 28.2). For example, Livia argues, based on work on the gender performances of sexually-liminal communities, that 'gender is not an essential identity derived from the body of the speaker but constructed from codifiable rules recognized by society as a whole' (1997: 363). However, according to Kulick (2003), sexuality is not tantamount to sexual identity, and a theory of language and sexuality cannot do without central aspects of sexuality, like desire and fantasy, which are essentially not intentional.

Since the community of practice approach does not only offer a social constructionist perspective on gender and language but also encapsulates important insights of feminist theorizing that make it congruent with a post-structuralist view of gender, it can well accommodate all these strands of inquiry. However, as already mentioned in Section 28.2, the specific contribution that linguistics can make to the study of gender 'doing' or 'performing' is through the analysis of language use. Such an analysis has to be warranted by methodological principles that make it intersubjectively reliable – both with respect to the participants' own interpretations and to those of other analysts. The most explicit and elegant proposal in this respect comes from conversation analysis (CA). See, for example, Schegloff (2007). Despite heated debates on the efficacy and legitimacy of applying CA to feminist work on gender and language, an increasing number of scholars, especially from discursive psychology, have employed conversation analytic perspectives in their study of gender and interaction (see, for example, McIlvenny, 2002; Speer, 2005). In particular, Kitzinger (2002) has made an excellent case for CA, arguing that it is not only compatible with social constructionist, postmodern and queer theories (though not with essentialist feminism) but also offers to these theories a method for studying gender and sexuality as accomplishments. In a series of publications, Kitzinger (for example, 2002; 2006) has illustrated how CA can be deployed to uncover conversationalists' resources for sustaining or resisting the taken-for-granted world of 'women' and 'men', 'heterosexuals' and 'homosexuals', etc; she has also demonstrated (Kitzinger, 2007) that the use of terms like 'woman', 'man', etc., in conversation is neither a necessary nor a sufficient condition for establishing that conversationalists are relevantly oriented to gender.

28.6 CONCLUSION: PERSPECTIVES AND CHALLENGES

This chapter was aimed at highlighting work on gender and interaction from a perspective that both reflects the historicity of the research agendas and points to three interrelated dimensions that have to be taken into account: gendering interaction gendered interaction and constructing gender in interaction.

The first dimension implies that we have to scrutinize the language(s) used in interaction in order to be aware of the limits and possibilities available for talking of (referring to, signifying, indexing, etc.) gender and categorizing people into gendered classes – both as analysts and as participants in an interaction. Such limits are not rigid, as has been variously shown, and can be successfully contested, but changing the available possibilities in language is usually a long-term process contingent on the power distribution in interaction and society. Moreover, shifting the boundaries between categories or changing the categories does not affect categorization itself as a necessary process for the organization of people's lives; in other words, even if the number of gender categories for humans were to be substantially increased in a language, that would not principally alter the gendering of interaction, unless we, as analysts, would do away with 'gender' itself, although that would hardly make gender disappear from language and society. As many have argued, from Butler (1988) to Holmes (2007), for example, it is one enterprise to deconstruct a gendered term like 'woman' and quite another to use it strategically in order to change the gender order. On the other hand, the extent to which gender or gendered terms are significant for participants in interaction has to be warranted, not presumed, by the analysis we provide. So one challenge is the meta-language used for describing gendered languages and societies, and its relation to the people who use those languages and inhabit those societies.

Gendering interaction also necessitates an analysis of normative expectations and stereotypical beliefs related to gendered categories. Such analyses usually rely on etiquette manuals for appropriate behaviour, proverbs, 'great men's' sayings, literary works, etc. However, to my knowledge, there is no systematic reflection on how we establish the existence of stereotypes for gendered behaviour in a certain community and how these stereotypes relate to the beliefs and stances of those people whose behaviour is actually analysed. This is particularly important in connection to the 'non-referential' indexing of gender (see Section 28.5). The route from linguistic forms to stances, activities, etc., and then to gendered behaviour (via norms and expectations that relate stances, activities, etc., to preferred images of men and women), as suggested by Ochs (1992), rests on the tacit assumption that the latter link involves no language. In addition to being hardly self-evident, this assumption would make the question of accessing such norms and expectations even more pertinent.

Gendered interaction, the second dimension, is a direct consequence of complying with or orienting oneself to norms and expectations concerning preferred gender behaviour, and of course of accepting being categorized in a certain gender class in the first place on the basis of opposition to and exclusion of the other gender classes. The issue here is how we ensure that our research on linguistic behaviour, on divergences and convergences (among men and women, homosexual and heterosexual women, etc.), exclusions and inclusions, and so forth, does not fall victim to the same gender stereotypes that our everyday sociolinguistic lives are susceptible to. Awareness and reflexivity on the part of language and gender scholars 'about the cultural resources that have shaped their own understandings, as well the understandings of the people whose language use they study' (Cameron, 2003: 465) is certainly well-advised, but better than good intentions is an analytical method that justifies our talk of 'women', 'men', 'gays', 'lesbians', etc., and warrants the 'discovery' of gendered interaction (differences and similarities).

Constructing gender in interaction, the third dimension, involves the strategic employment of language (and other semiotic means) by participants in interaction in order to position themselves in relation to available gender categories and to do or perform gender – exclusively, fluidly, crossing-over, 'with anxiety and pleasure' (Butler, 1988: 531), and so on. The issue here is how this positioning (and, doing gender accordingly) relates to and informs those categories themselves: in other words, how we move from the here–and–now of a single interaction to social categories ('woman', 'gender', etc.) and social structures (e.g. the gender order) – and this theoretical link is currently missing.[35] Eckert and McConnell-Ginet have variously underlined that analysis of interactional practices within one community of practice has to be augmented with: (1) analyses of interactions within similar communities of practice in order to allow for generalizations of, for example, how gender is constructed in this kind of community of practice, and (2) analyses of the interactions through which the members of the original community of practice participate in other communities and relate to broader social formatives and orders (Eckert and

McConnell-Ginet, 2007). As already emphasized, a fundamental prerequisite for attaining empirically sound generalizations, both within one community of practice as well as over similar communities (Eckert and McConnell-Ginet's 'comparative direction'), is the quality of the analysis of *one single interaction*, in the first place. CA was mentioned in this respect as offering a most promising perspective. A prerequisite for the second (Eckert and McConnell-Ginet's 'relational direction') would be an explicit theory about the societal and institutional context in which a community of practice is situated, as for example critical discourse analysis (CDA; see, for example, Fairclough 1989: 1992).[36] After all, CDA did set out to investigate the dialectics between discourse, i.e. the use of language as a *social practice*, and social structures, and the mechanisms that sustain or resist the social order. Moreover, the two theories, being both 'social', would have to be compatible with one another, and while CDA can readily encompass CA, the opposite would run counter to CA's principles.

In conclusion, then, four decades of research on gender and language have led to significant insights for gender and interaction, though not to a coherent theory or to clear evidence for the impossibility of such an enterprise. The most important gain has probably been the process of learning to ask better questions, whereas the greatest challenge remains the theoretical articulation and analytic implementation of the link between the 'here and now' of a single interaction to social categories ('woman', 'gender', etc.) and social structures (e.g. the gender order).

NOTES

1 For relevant references, see for example, the annotated bibliography in Thorne and Henley (1975a). By the end of the 1970s the topic of sexism in language enters non-Anglo-Saxon academic communities as well, and languages other than English start to get analysed from this point of view; see, for example, Ryen's (1978) overview of the research in Scandinavian countries, Yaguello (1978) for French, Brouwer et al. (1979) for Dutch and Pusch and Trömel-Plötz (1980) for German, Pavlidou (1984) for Greek.

2 See, for example, Baron and Kotthoff (2001), Kotthoff and Wodak (1997a), Wodak (1997a), and Speer (2005).

3 For an overview of the different traditions in the study of discourse and interaction and the embedding of linguistic research on gender in those paradigms see Bucholtz (2003). See also Kotthoff and Wodak (1997).

4 For a discussion of the ethnomethodological approach to doing gender, see also, for example, Kotthoff (2002).

5 For a discussion of gender performativity, see for example, Livia and Hall (1997).

6 See references in West and Zimmerman (2002).

7 This is why I deliberately referred to the early publications of West and Zimmerman, and also Butler (and not to the much more familiar book where her 1988 paper is basically included). For a further elaboration of convergences and divergences between the two approaches, based also on their later work, see Maloney and Fenstermaker (2002). Given the chronological proximity of the two publications (with West and Zimmerman's article preceding Butler's publication) and the affinity of their views, it is quite remarkable that they do not appear to take notice of each other, even in later publications. This lack of dialogue may seem normal in the usual academic praxis of monodisciplinary institutional traditions; it is, however, a paradox in the context of women/gender studies, since interdisciplinarity has been one of the cornerstones of this field right from the beginning.

8 Don Kulick emphasizes that 'performativity theory, as Butler has elaborated it, is inseparable from psychoanalytic assumptions about the relationship between desire, sexuality, and sex' and that if psychoanalysis is removed 'what remains is simply a kind of performance theory *à la* Goffman –the kind of theory that inattentive readers mistakenly accused Butler of promoting in *Gender Trouble*' (Kulick, 2003: 127).

9 See, for example, Butler (1993: 17).

10 See also for example, Cameron (1997a); and Wodak (1997).

11 In particular, it was within ATHENA, the Advanced Thematic Network in European Women's Studies, that efforts have been made 'to investigate critically the uses and abuses of cultural dominant terminologies' and to approach translation as an epistemological stance (Braidotti, 2002: 301, 302).

12 For an overview of the problem, see Braidotti (2002a).

13 See also Hellinger, in this volume.

14 Ideologies are understood here as representations of reality which are culturally-informed and which are the product of asymmetrical power relations in that culture. For the main definitional features of ideologies as well as the complexities involved in defining the term, see Eagleton (1991), Fairclough (1992); and van Dijk (1998).

15 Gender differences are regarded as natural, i.e. deriving directly from biology (see, for example, Andermahr et al., 2000: 127). Dominant gender ideologies reproduce naturalized gender differences and sustain hegemonic male dominance and female subordination (Talbot, 2003: 472).

16   See Goffman's (1977) 'institutional reflexivity' and Connell's (2002: 53–66) 'four structures of gender relations' (power, production, emotional and symbolic relations).

17   See also Hellinger and Bussmann (2001–03).

18   See Pavlidou et al., (2004); and Pavlidou (2006b).

19   The exceptions are of the order of 0.1% for masculine nouns and 0.2% for the feminine ones. Conversely, male and female human beings are denoted by the masculine or feminine gender respectively; only a very small number of nouns denoting humans are of neuter gender.

20   Resisting or subverting the dichotomy imposed by grammatical gender is not as simple as some measures against linguistic sexism seem to suggest (for a discussion of this point, see Pavlidou 2006a).

21   Research on the influence of grammatical gender on perception and other cognitive processes goes back to the 1980s (see Mills, 1986; see also Topsakal, 1995, who partly reproduced Mills' experiments for Modern Greek), but is still quite scarce.

22   See the annotated bibliography in Thorne and Henley (1975a: 257–263).

23   See James and Drakich's (1993a) critical review of the research.

24   However, as Aebischer (1979) has argued, in her analysis of interviews with 60 women, gossip or chit-chat is perceived differently – be it positively or negatively – according to those women's representation of what it meant for them to be a 'woman'.

25   But it is also the case that linguistic behaviour may be perceived differently depending on whether it is attributed to 'men' or 'women' as, for example, Cutler and Scott's study (1990) on the perceived apportionment of talk demonstrates.

26   In a similar vein, Cameron (2007) warns against the danger of re-marginalization of feminist linguistic scholarship if people working on language and gender refrain from engaging in discourses on this topic produced in academic fields other than linguistics.

27   The much discussed notion of women's language, as attributed to Lakoff (1975), has been held to be one such stereotype (Cameron, 1985: 34). However, as later acknowledged (see for example, Cameron, 1997a: 28; Talbot, 2003: 474), even by some of her critics, Lakoff's interest did not lie in giving an empirical account of what was going on in reality, but in describing the symbolic ideal which shapes the cultural expectations about appropriate linguistic behaviour of women/men, thus influencing, in extension, the way they actually talk in particular situations.

28   For useful summaries and discussion see, for example, Meyerhoff (2006: 200–222); and Wodak and Benke (1997).

29   Among other things, I did not consider research on the linguistic behaviour within same-sex groups; see, for example, Coates (1996); Wodak and Schulz (1986).

30   See, for example, Holmes (1995) on the multifunctionality of linguistic items and Tannen (1994) on the relativity of linguistic strategies.

31   On the issue of what differentiates a community of practice from any grouping of people, see Eckert and McConnell-Ginet (1995: 504, 2007: 28).

32   Reference in Ochs (1992).

33   Reference in Eckert (2008).

34   See for example, Holmes (2006); and Lazar (2005, (Part I)).

35   See, however, Pavlidou (2008) for an attempt to conceptualize such a link, exploiting the specificities of a particular language.

36   See also Fairclough (2003); van Dijk (2008); Wodak and Meyer (2009).

REFERENCES

Aebischer, V. (1979) 'Chit-chat: women in interaction', *Osnabrücker Beiträge zur Sprachtheorie*, 9: 96–108.

Andermahr, S., Lovell, T. and Wolkowitz, C. (2000) *A Glossary of Feminist Theory*. London: Arnold.

—— (1962) *How to Do Things with Words*. Ed. J. O. Urmson. New York: Oxford University Press.

Baron, B. and Kotthoff, H. (eds) (2001) *Gender in Interaction: Perspectives on Femininity and Masculinity in Ethnography and Discourse*. Amsterdam: John Benjamins.

Bodine, A. (1975) 'Sex differentiation in language', in B. Thorne and N. Henley (eds), *Language and Sex: Difference and Dominance*. Rowley, MA: Newbury House. pp. 130–51.

Boroditsky, L., Schmidt, L. A. and Phillips, W. (2003) 'Sex, syntax, and semantics', in D. Gentner, S. Goldin-Meadow and S. Goldin (eds), *Language in Mind: Advances in the Study of Language and Thought*. Cambridge, MA: MIT Press. pp. 61–79.

Braidotti, R. (2002) 'The uses and abuses of the sex/gender distinction in European feminist practices', in G. Griffin and R. Braidotti (eds), *Thinking Differently: A Reader in European Women's Studies*. London: Zed Books. pp. 285–307.

Brouwer, D., Gerritsen, M., de Haan, D. and van der Post, A. (1979) 'Eine Übersicht zum Thema 'Sprache und Geschlecht' in den Niederlanden', *Osnabrücker Beiträge zur Sprachtheorie* 9 (Sprache und Geschlecht II): 150–62.

Bucholtz, M. (2003) 'Theories of discourse as theories of gender', in J. Holmes and M. Meyerhof (eds), *The Handbook of Language and Gender*. Oxford: Blackwell. pp. 43–68.

Butler, J. (1988) 'Performative acts and gender constitution: an essay in phenomenology and feminist theory', *Theatre Journal*, 40(4): 519–31.

Butler, J. (1990) *Gender Trouble: Feminism and the Subversion of Identity*. London: Routledge.

Butler, J. (1993) *Bodies that Matter: On the Discursive Limits of 'Sex'*. London: Routledge.

Cameron, D. (1985) *Feminism and Linguistic Theory*. Basingstoke: Macmillan.

Cameron, D. (1997) 'Performing gender identity: young men's talk and the construction of heterosexual masculinity', in S. Johnson and U. H. Meinhof (eds), *Language and Masculinity*. Oxford: Blackwell. pp. 47–64.

Cameron, D. (1997a) 'Theoretical debates in feminist linguistics: questions of sex and gender', in R. Wodak (ed.), *Discourse and Gender*. Thousand Oaks, CA: Sage. pp. 21–36.

Cameron, D. (1998) 'Is there any ketchup, Vera?' *Discourse and Society*, 9(4): 437–55.

Cameron, D. (2003) 'Gender and language ideologies', in J. Holmes and M. Meyerhof (eds), *The Handbook of Language and Gender*. Oxford: Blackwell. pp. 447–67.

Cameron, D. and Kulick, D. (2003) *Language and Sexuality*. Cambridge: Cambridge University Press.

Coates, J. (1988) 'Gossip revisited: language in all-female groups', in J. Coates and D. Cameron (eds), *Women in their Speech Communities: New Perspectives on Language and Sex*. London: Longman. pp. 94–122.

Coates, J. (1996) *Women Talk: Conversation between Women Friends*. Oxford: Blackwell.

Connell, R. W. (2002) *Gender*. Cambridge: Polity Press.

Cutler, A. and Scott, D. R. (1990) 'Speaker sex and perceived apportionment of talk', *Applied Psycholinguistics*, 11: 253–72.

De Beauvoir, S. (1949) *Le deuxième sexe*. Paris: Gallimard.

Eagleton, T. (1991) *Ideology: An Introduction*. London: Verso.

Eckert, P. (2008) 'Style matters', *Studies in Greek Linguistics*, 28: 13–29.

Eckert, P. and McConnell-Ginet, S. (1992) 'Think practically and look locally: language and gender as community-based practice', *Annual Review of Anthropology*, 21: 461–90.

Eckert, P. and McConnell-Ginet, S. (1995) 'Constructing meaning, constructing selves: snapshots of language, gender, and class from Belten High', in K. Hall and M. Bucholtz (eds), *Gender Articulated: Language and the Constructed Self*. New York: Routledge. pp. 469–507.

Eckert, P. and McConnell-Ginet, S. (2003) *Language and gender*. Cambridge: Cambridge University Press.

Eckert, P. and McConnell-Ginet, S. (2007) 'Putting communities of practice in their place', *Gender and Language*, 1(1): 27–37.

Fairclough, N. (1989) *Language and Power*. London: Longman.

Fairclough, N. (1992) *Discourse and Social Change*. Cambridge: Polity Press.

Fairclough, N. (2003) *Analysing Discourse: Textual Analysis for Social Research*. London: Routledge.

Fausto-Sterling, A. (2000) *Sexing the Body: Gender Politics and the Construction of Sexuality*. New York: Basic Books.

Fishman, P. (1983) 'Interaction: the work women do', in B. Thorne, C. Kramarae and N. Henley (eds), *Language, Gender and Society*. Rowley, MA: Newbury House. pp. 89–102.

Freed, A. F. (2003) 'Epilogue: reflections on language and gender research', in J. Holmes and M. Meyerhof (eds), *The Handbook of Language and Gender*. Oxford: Blackwell. pp. 697–721.

Georgakopoulou, A. (2006) 'Conversational storytelling with (and about) gender' [in Greek: Συνομιλιακές αφηγήσεις με (και για) φύλο'], in T.-S. Pavlidou (ed.), *Γλώσσα-Γένος-Φύλο* [Language – (grammatical) gender – (social) gender]. 2nd edn. Thessaloniki: Institute of Modern Greek Studies. pp. 65–80. (1st edn, 2002.)

Glück, H. (1979) 'Der Mythos von den Frauensprachen' *Osnabrücker Beiträge zur Sprachtheorie*, 9: 60–95.

Goffman, E. (1977) 'The arrangement between the sexes', *Theory and Society*, 4(3): 301–31.

Goodwin, M. H. (1990) *He-Said-She-Said: Talk as Social Organization Among Black Children*. Bloomington, IN: Indiana University Press.

Goodwin, M. H. (forthcoming) 'Engendering children's play: person reference in children's conflictual interaction', in S. S. Speer and E. H. Stokoe (eds), *Conversation and Gender*. Cambridge: Cambridge University Press.

Goodwin, M. H. and Goodwin, C. (1987) 'Children's arguing', in S. U. Philips, S. Steele and C. Tanz (eds), *Language, Gender and Sex in Comparative Perspective*. Cambridge: Cambridge University Press. pp. 200–48.

Hellinger, M. and Bussmann, H. (eds) (2001–03) *Gender Across Languages: The Linguistic Representation of Women and Men*. 3 volumes. Amsterdam: John Benjamins.

Holmes, J. (1995) *Women, Men and Politeness*. London: Longman.

Holmes, J. (1998) 'Women's talk: the question of sociolinguistic universals', in J. Coates (ed.), *Language and Gender: A Reader*. Oxford: Blackwell. pp. 461–83. (1st edn, 1993.)

Holmes, J. (2006) *Gendered Talk at Work*. Oxford: Blackwell.

Holmes, J. (2007) 'Social constructionism, postmodernism and feminist linguistics', *Gender and Language*, 1(1): 51–65.

Holmes, J. and Meyerhoff, M. (eds) (2003) *The Handbook of Language and Gender*. Oxford: Blackwell.

James, D. and Drakich, J. (1993) 'Women, men, and interruptions: a critical review', in D. Tannen (ed.), *Gender and Conversational Interaction*. Oxford: Oxford University Press. pp. 231–80.

James, D. and Drakich, J. (1993a) 'Understanding gender differences in amount of talk: a critical review of research', in D. Tannen (ed.), *Gender and Conversational Interaction*. Oxford: Oxford University Press. pp. 281–312.

Johnson, S. and Finlay, F. (1997) 'Do men gossip? An analysis of football talk on television', in S. Johnson and U. H. Meinhof (eds), *Language and Masculinity*. Oxford: Blackwell. pp. 130–43.

Johnstone, B. (1993) 'Community and contest: Midwestern men and women creating their worlds in conversational storytelling', in D. Tannen (ed.), *Gender and Conversational Interaction*. Oxford: Oxford University Press. pp. 62–80.

Kitzinger, C. (2002) 'Doing feminist Conversation Analysis' in P. Mcilvenny (ed.), *Talking Gender and Sexuality*. Amsterdam: John Benjamins. pp. 49–77. (1st edn, 2000.)

Kitzinger, C. (2006) '"Speaking as a heterosexual": (how) does sexuality matter for talk-in-interaction?', in D. Cameron and D. Kulick (eds), *The Language and Sexuality Reader*. London: Routledge. pp. 169–88. (1st edn, 2005.)

Kitzinger, C. (2007) 'Is "woman" always relevantly gendered?', *Gender and Language*, 1(1): 39–49.

Kotthoff, H. (2002) 'Was heisst eigentlich *doing gender?*' *Wiener Slawistischer Almanach*, Sonderband 55: 1–29.

Kotthoff, H. and Wodak, R. (1997) 'Preface', in H. Kotthoff and R. Wodak (eds), *Communicating Gender in Context*. Amsterdam: John Benjamins. pp. vii–xxv.

Kotthoff, H. and Wodak, R. (eds) (1997a) *Communicating Gender in Context*. Amsterdam: John Benjamins.

Kulick, D. (2003) 'Language and desire', in J. Holmes and M. Meyerhof (eds), *The Handbook of Language and Gender*. Oxford: Blackwell. pp. 119–41.

Labov, W. (1972) *Sociolinguistic Patterns*. Philadelphia: University of Pennsylvania Press.

Lakoff, R. (1973) 'Language and woman's place', *Language in Society*, 2: 45–80.

Lakoff, R. (1975) *Language and Woman's Place*. New York: Harper and Row.

Lave, J. and Wenger, E. (1991) *Situated Learning: Legitimate Peripheral Participation*. Cambridge: Cambridge University Press.

Lazar, M. M. (ed.) (2005) *Feminist Critical Discourse Analysis: Gender, Power and Ideology in Discourse*. New York: Palgrave Macmillan.

Livia, A. (1997) 'Disloyal to masculinity: linguistic gender and liminal identity in French', in A. Livia and K. Hall (eds), *Queerly Phrased: Language, Gender, and Sexuality*. Oxford: Oxford University Press. pp. 349–68.

Livia, A. and Hall, K. (1997) '*It's a girl!*: bringing performativity back to linguistics', in A. Livia and K. Hall (eds), *Queerly Phrased Language, Gender, and Sexuality*. Oxford: Oxford University Press. pp. 3–18.

Lykke, N. (2006) 'Intersectionality – a useful concept?', in T.-S. Pavlidou (ed.), *Gender Studies: Trends/Tensions in Greece and other European Countries*. Thessaloniki: Zitis. pp. 151–60.

McConnell-Ginet, S. (2003) '"What's in a name?" Social labeling and gender practices', in J. Holmes and M. Meyerhof (eds), *The Handbook of Language and Gender*. Oxford: Blackwell. pp. 69–97.

McIlvenny, P. (ed.) (2002) *Talking Gender and Sexuality*. Amsterdam: John Benjamins.

Makri-Tsilipakou, M. (1991) 'Agreement/disagreement: affiliative vs. disaffiliative display in cross-sex conversations'. PhD thesis, Aristotle University of Thessaloniki.

Maloney, M. and Fenstermaker, S. (2002) 'Performance as an accomplishment: reconciling feminist conceptions of gender', in S. Fenstermaker and C. West (eds), *Doing Gender, Doing Difference: Inequality, Power, and Institutional Change*. London: Routledge. pp. 189–204.

Maltz, D. N. and Borker, R. A. (1982) 'A cultural approach to male–female miscommunication', in J. J. Gumperz (ed.), *Language and Social Identity*. Cambridge: Cambridge University Press. pp. 196–216.

Meyerhof, M. (2006) *Introducing Sociolinguistics*. London: Routledge.

Mills, A. E. (1986) *The Acquisition of Gender: A Study of English and German*. Berlin: Springer Verlag.

Ochs, E. (1992) 'Indexing gender', in A. Duranti and C. Goodwin (eds), *Rethinking Context: Language as an Interactive Phenomenon*. Cambridge: Cambridge University Press. pp. 335–58.

Ochs, E. and Taylor, C. (1995) 'The "father knows best" dynamic in dinnertime narratives', in K. Hall and M. Bucholtz (eds), *Gender Articulated: Language and the Socially Constructed Self*. New York: Routledge. pp. 97–120.

Pavlidou, T.-S. (1984) 'Language-linguistics-sexism' [in Greek: 'Γλώσσα-γλωσσολογία–σεξισμός'], *Synchrona Themata*, 21: 69–79.

Pavlidou, T.-S. (2003) 'Patterns of participation in classroom interaction: girls' and boys' non-compliance in a Greek high school', *Linguistics and Education*, 14(1): 123–41.

Pavlidou, T.-S. (2006a) 'Language-(grammatical) gender-(social) gender: problems, inquiries/queries, and the Greek language' [in Greek: 'Γλώσσα-γένος-φύλο: προβλήματα, αναζητήσεις και ελληνική γλώσσα'], in T.-S. Pavlidou (ed.), *Γλώσσα-Γένος-Φύλο* [Language – (grammatical) gender – (social) gender]. 2nd edn. Thessaloniki: Institute of Modern Greek Studies. pp. 15–64. (1st edn, 2002.)

Pavlidou, T.-S. (2006b) 'On the lexical representation of women and men in Modern Greek', talk presented at the 4th International Gender and Language Conference (igala4), Valencia.

Pavlidou, T.-S. (2008) '*We* and the construction of (gendered) collectivities' [in Greek: 'Εμείς και η συγκρότηση (έμφυλων) συλλογικοτήτων'], in M. Theodoropoulou (ed.), *Light and Warmth: In Memory of A.-Ph. Christidis*. Thessaloniki: Center for the Greek Language. pp. 437–53.

Pavlidou, T.-S., Alavanoudi, A. and Karafoti, E. (2004), 'Grammatical gender and semantic content: preliminary remarks on the lexical representation of social gender' [in Greek: 'Γραμματικό γένος και σημασιακό περιεχόμενο: προκαταρκτικές παρατηρήσεις για τη λεξιλογική αναπαράσταση των φύλων'], *Studies in Greek Linguistics*, 24: 543–53.

Pusch, L. and Trömel-Plötz, S. (eds) (1980) *Sprache, Geschlecht und Macht I* (Special issue of *Linguistische Berichte* 69).

Ryen, E. (1978) 'Über Forschung und Diskussion zum Thema 'Sprache und Geschlecht' in Skandinavien'. *Osnabrücker Beiträge zur Sprachtheorie* 8 (*Sprache und Geschlecht I*). pp. 105–18.

Sachs, J. (1975) 'Cues to the identification of sex in children's speech', in B. Thorne and N. Henley (eds), *Language and Sex: Difference and Dominance*. Rowley, MA: Newburg House. pp. 152–71.

Schegloff, E. A. (2007) *Sequence Organization in Interaction: A Primer in Conversation Analysis*. Cambridge: Cambridge University Press.

Sifianou, M. (2001) '"Oh! How appropriate!" Compliments and politeness', in A. Bayraktarglou and M. Sifianou (eds), *Linguistic Politeness: The Case of Greece and Turkey*. Amsterdam: John Benjamins. pp. 391–430.

Speer, S. (2005) *Gender Talk: Feminism, Discourse, and Conversation Analysis*. London: Routledge.

Talbot, M. (2003) 'Gender stereotypes: reproduction and challenge', in J. Holmes and M. Meyerhof (eds), *The Handbook of Language and Gender*. Oxford: Blackwell. pp. 468–86.

Tannen, D. (1990) *You Just Don't Understand: Women and Men in Conversation*. New York: William Morrow.

Tannen, D. (ed.) (1994) *Gender and Discourse*. Oxford: Oxford University Press.

Thorne, B. and Henley, N. (1975) 'Difference and dominance: an overview of language, gender, and society', in B. Thorne and N. Henley (eds), *Language and Sex: Difference and Dominance*. Rowley, MA: Newburg House. pp. 5–42.

Thorne, B. and Henley, N. (eds) (1975a) *Language and Sex: Difference and Dominance*. Rowley, MA: Newburg House.

Topsakal, M. (1995) 'The influence of grammatical gender on the perception of sex in Modern Greek'. MA thesis, Aristotle University of Thessaloniki.

van Dijk, T. A. (1998) *Ideology: A Multidisciplinary Approach*. London: Sage.

van Dijk, T. A. (2008) *Discourse and Power*. Houndsmills: Palgrave MacMillan.

West, C. and Zimmerman, D. (2002) 'Doing gender', in S. Fenstermaker and C. West (eds), *Doing Gender, Doing Difference: Inequality, Power, and Institutional Change*. London: Routledge. pp. 3–23.

Wodak, R. (1981) 'Women relate, men report: sex differences in language behaviour in a therapeutic group', *Journal of Pragmatics*, 5: 261–85.

Wodak, R. (1997) 'Introduction: some important issues in the research of gender and discourse', in R. Wodak (ed.), *Gender and Discourse*. London: Sage. pp. 1–20.

Wodak, R. (ed.) (1997a) *Gender and Discourse*. London: Sage.

Wodak, R. (2003) 'Multiple identities: the roles of female parliamentarians in the EU parliament', in J. Holmes and M. Meyerhof (eds), *The Handbook of Language and Gender*. Oxford: Blackwell. pp. 671–98.

Wodak, R. and Benke, G. (1997) 'Gender as a sociolinguistic variable', in F. Coulmas (ed.), *The Handbook of Sociolinguistics*. Oxford: Blackwell. pp. 127–50.

Wodak, R. and Meyer, M. (2009) 'Critical Discourse Analysis: history, agenda, theory, and methodology', in R. Wodak and M. Meyer (eds), *Methods of Critical Discourse Analysis*. 2nd rev. edn. London: Sage. pp. 1–33.

Wodak, R. and Schulz, M. (1986) *The Language of Love and Guilt: Mother–Daughter Relationships from a Cross-Cultural Perspective*. Amsterdam: Benjamins.

Yaguello, M. (1978) *Les mots et les femmes: essay d' approche socio-linguistique de la condition féminine*. Paris: Payot.

Interaction and the Media

Brigitta Busch and Petra Pfisterer

29.1 INTRODUCTION

Present media developments are described as rapid and fundamental changes with deep impacts on our daily lives. Topics raised in media discourse and political discourse about the media concern issues related to media production as well as to individual media habits in everyday life. The categorization of media into distinct sectors such as print, film, radio and television becomes increasingly blurred as media companies adopt a multimedia orientation, and a multiplicity of new receiving devices (computers, mobile phones) allow access to a wide range of media products almost everywhere and at any time. The traditional distinction between different genres such as news, entertainment, documentary, fiction, etc., cannot be maintained. New – often interactive and hybrid – formats emerge regularly with constantly changing labels and definitions such as infotainment, reality soaps, private news blogs, etc. These formats make the identification of sources, the differentiation between fact and fiction, and the awareness of transitions between real and virtual worlds increasingly difficult (Busch, 2004: 29ff). Equally, the distinction between (public) mass media communication, characterized as a one-to-many process, and (private) interpersonal mediated communication, characterized as a one-to-one process, is being called into question, for instance by new forms of Internet communication, characterized as network communication. The notion of a dominant national public sphere which was conceived – through multiple exclusions on the basis of gender, race, class and language – as homogeneous and monolingual is being challenged by a fragmentation[1] into a complex configuration of

sometimes overlapping and sometimes mutually exclusive spaces of communication with their particular policies of representation (Wodak and Koller, 2008). The dominance of media industries in a globalized market and the commodification of media communication create new exclusions in terms of access and representations which are subsumed under the notion of the 'digital divide'. Such developments also represent a challenge for research into the interconnections between linguistic practices and the media. This chapter gives, in its first part (Section 29.2), an overview of approaches to media communication, media texts and the connection between language and the media within linguistics. In its second part (Section 29.3) it introduces the reader to a framework for the analysis of media communication that combines elements from sociolinguistics, discourse analysis and media studies.

29.2 APPROACHES TO THE MEDIA IN LINGUISTICS

Within media studies, linguistics, and more particularly sociolinguistics, there has been a variety of scientific approaches to the interconnections between language and the media.

Language policy, language planning and the media

In language policy and language planning research, the media were for a long time neglected as a factor. Joshua Fishman even warned in his early sociolinguistic work against overemphasis on the media in the context of language policy and language planning, and against media fetishism in language policy (Fishman, 1991: 374). Under the more traditional paradigm in the field, which saw language policy mainly as a top-down strategy, the potential role of the media was by definition limited as they had been, to a large extent, exempted from direct state control ever since the Declaration of Human Rights in the course of the French Revolution. Nevertheless, state authorities have always exercised a certain amount of control and intervention in this domain via media laws, licensing procedures, frequency and paper allocations, subsidies, etc. (Busch, 2006). Also, after World War II, in most Western European countries, public service audio and audio-visual media – for which direct regulating measures are possible – were protected by state monopolies that persisted for almost 50 years. National laws and regulations outline the confines of media production and also intervene on the level of language use in the media. An example of this kind of intervention is the French legislation on the limitation of anglicisms in the public domain, which was copied by a number of Eastern European countries in the 1990s (Busch, 2004: 151). The role of the media in the formation and implementation of standard and national languages has been a concern of substantial research (Anderson, 1983; Innis, 1951, 1997).

Since the beginning of the twenty-first century a new interest in language policy can be noted. In these approaches, language policy is seen rather as a process of negotiation between top-down measures enacted by macro-level institutional agents and bottom-up initiatives and practices by communities and speakers (Ricento, 2006; Shohamy, 2006). The focus on social, economic and political effects of language contact which sees linguistic practices as social practices allows a new take on the media in the field. Under the condition of present media developments, language policy is challenged from a double perspective: from the macro perspective of globalized markets and supranational regulatory bodies as well as from the micro perspective of changing individual *Lebenswelten* (lifeworlds) in which multilingualism has become a salient feature of everyday life. On the macro level the debate about the influence of the media on the spread of languages and especially on the dominance of English has been a concern (Crystal, 2001). It has been observed that language plays an important part in the process of reconfiguration of media spaces, in regrouping larger regional areas beyond nation-state boundaries as well as in linking dispersed diasporas (Robins, 1997). Thussu (2000: 197 ff.) explains

the example of a TV channel that picked up the urban jargon Hinglish[2] for news programmes to develop markets beyond the Hindi-speaking area on the Indian subcontinent and in the British diaspora.

In the debate on minority media three main approaches can be distinguished (Busch, 1999):

- a minority or human rights approach in which the question of access and participation of linguistic/ ethnic minorities (in a national public sphere) dominates;
- an approach that is more oriented towards questions of language loss and language revitalization;
- and finally a more recent paradigm that takes a speaker-centred approach and focuses on questions of constructions of (multiple, hybrid) identities.

Early research in the field was often initiated and commissioned by international and European institutions to inform their language policies (Franchon and Vargaftig, 1995; Husband, 1994; the publications of the European Bureau for Lesser Used Languages in the Mercator Media series). The European instruments to implement linguistic rights in the media field also to some extent mirror this change of paradigms: whereas the European Charter for Regional or Minority Languages (1992) (Article 11) is still mainly concerned with access of (autochthonous) minorities to the media and to information, the Framework Convention for the Protection of National Minorities (1995) refrains from a definition of minorities and declares an obligation to foster intercultural dialogue in the media (Articles 6 and 19). The European Union (EU) increasingly includes questions of language and the media in its language policy action plans (European Commission, 2005).

Multilingualism and the media

There is also an extensive literature mapping the multiple intersections of **minority media** and their impact upon ethnic identities. In complementarity to literature on the representation of minorities in majority news media and the misrepresentation of minorities in majority entertainment (for an overview of research in the EU member states see ter Wal, 2002), a body of works exists that combines media studies and linguistics and addresses the significance of minority control and ownership of the media to guarantee self-representation and participation in a heterogeneous and diverse public sphere (see, for example, Busch, 1999, 2004; Cormack, 1998, 2004;

Husband, 2000). Cormack (2004: 4) suggests five types of minority media impact: (1) a symbolic role (signalling the full functionality of the community/language and referring to its connectedness to modernity); (2) an economic role (job creation, career prospects); (3) developing a public sphere within a community that can carry a distinct news agenda; (4) allowing the community to be represented within and towards the outside; and (5) acting as a key conveyor of culture and as a producer of cultural products. Moring and Husband (2007: 78) add two other aspects: the media's role in providing an opportunity for (minority) language use (as a reader or listener), and the role of the media in the reconstruction of language as well as in the development and diffusion of language innovation and of new vocabulary. The issue of ethnolinguistic vitality remains a topic in research on minority and indigenous media (Moring and Husband, 2007), mainly taking an approach based on the concept developed by Giles (1977) which offers a conceptual tool to analyse sociostructural variables that shape the strength of an ethnocultural community for language retention.

Beginning with the 1980s and 1990s, research into **media and migration** became a central issue on the research agenda. Studies examining media policies and language policies directed at migrant communities found a striking correlation between media and migration policies. Whereas in the early days of labour migration into Western Europe, when a rapid rotation principle was the norm, media products for migrants (especially programmes in public service radio and TV) were predominantly in the language of migrant communities, when policy orientations shifted towards assimilation or integration, media products directed at migrant communities tended to be in the dominant languages of the respective countries (Busch, 2004; Cottle, 2000; Franchon and Vargaftig, 1995; Kosnick, 2007). The refocusing of national language policies in some Western European countries on state languages opened the way for arguing that diaspora media, broadcast via satellite in the languages of migration, were a hindrance on the way to successful integration in the so-called host countries. Extensive reception studies, as in the work by Hargreaves (2001), showed that media habits among migrants in Western Europe were far more diversified and satellite programmes from the so-called countries of origin were usually only one element among others. Under the current diversity policy paradigm that is being implemented to some extent in North American and European metropolises, differences and diversity are seen as a possible asset, and languages of migration are (at least theoretically) seen as a potential resource. In migration

research, diasporas are no longer primarily seen as homogeneous groups depending on a motherland but as a socially-differentiated nexus of persons living in a variety of complex lifeworlds. Recent approaches to the media and migration are more concerned with questions of construction of identities and with modes of representation (see Style and stylization subsection in this chapter) and tend to focus on media texts rather than on modes of production and reception. In media studies the concept of media reception as a distinct activity is being gradually replaced by an approach that foregrounds everyday practices in which media are present.

Concern with the effects of **globalization** on bilingual or multilingual communities and with the commodification and referential use of language is found in the work of Monica Heller (e.g. 2000). Together with Normand Labrie (2003: 16), Heller describes three types of discourses of affirmative heteroglossia linked to particular imaginations of society that are simultaneously present: the traditionalist, the modernizing and the globalizing. Homogenization in language use is much more difficult to implement today under the condition of globalized communication and media flows. Using regional vernaculars or local dialects is no longer necessarily indexical of a traditionalist orientation, but can also represent a rejection of national categorizations, especially when communication flows develop a translocal dimension that transgresses state borders. This change in connotation is linked to the fact that language has become a tradable commodity, on the local level in the form of commercialization of authenticity (Heller, 2003). Languages are used strategically in order to reference identities and attract audiences. This is valid for mass media and advertising as well as for minority media. Kelly-Holmes (2005) speaks moreover of minimal or token bilingualism in advertising that assumes limited competence of the audience and exploits the symbolic rather than the referential function of communication/language.

In media studies the concept of the reconfiguration of media spaces has been influential throughout the past two decades (Appadurai, 1998; Morley and Robins, 1996). **Spatial approaches** in linguistics and cultural studies also foreground a topological perspective which has mainly been applied in research on multilingualism in urban contexts. Referring to Goffman's (1974) interaction analysis and Halliday's (1978) social semiotic approach to language, Scollon and Scollon (2003) drafted an instrument based on multimodality and discourse analysis to examine the way in which language is located in physical space. Blommaert, Collins and Slembrouck (2005) draw on a spatial analysis for the understanding of multilingual interactions, power relations and hierarchizations between languages. Based on research in a multilingual neighbourhood, they examine how different localities (shops, healthcare institutions, schools, cafés, etc.) develop specific language regimes. Languages in the public space and in the media are part of such language regimes. Scollon and Scollon (2004) conceive those intersections of different interaction practices as a 'nexus of practice', in which a multitude of discursive strands and semiotic reference systems create meaning. Jacquemet (2005: 265) coins the term 'transidiomatic practices' for the overlapping multilingual interaction regimes that crystallize in particular localities when multilingual talk (exercised by de/reterritorialized speakers) and electronic media are co-present. In the past few years a small body of research literature has been published under the label of 'linguistic landscape' (Shohamy and Gorter (eds), 2009), examining manifestations of multilingualism – mainly of signage – in public spaces.

According to the regular Eurobarometer surveys (European Commission, 2006), listening to the radio, watching films or TV, reading books and newspapers or browsing the Internet account for the most important occasions in which European citizens use their foreign languages. The media, other than educational media, seem to play an important role in lifelong learning and the maintenance of competences in foreign languages. Only a few studies have dealt so far with this aspect of **multilingualism, media and language learning** (Meinhof, 1998). Dubbing and subtitling in television are a topic connected with language learning (Koolstra and Beentjes, 1999), especially as a study commissioned by the European Commission (2002) revealed that in countries with subtitling practice citizens estimated that their language competences in foreign languages were better.

A growing body of research inspired by sociolinguistics and discourse analysis aims at exploring the social and contextual diversity of language use in **computer-mediated communication** (CMC). There has been a shift of focus from medium- to user-related patterns of language use, and an increasing emphasis on the varying instantiations of online genres in their particular social contexts (see Androutsopoulos, 2007b: 281; Danet and Herring, 2007; Wright, 2006). Androutsopoulos sees the Web as a social space in which like-minded individuals use the resources of the medium, such as interactivity, multimodality and easy access to media production, to construct identity and community (2007b: 282). He follows Castells in the definition of virtual community: a virtual community 'is generally understood as a

self-defined electronic network of interactive communication organized around a shared interest or purpose, although sometimes communication becomes a goal in itself' (Castells, 2000: 386).

A focus on the media text

In recent approaches to media texts, the 'text' as such has been somewhat 'decentralized' and the focus of interest has shifted to the (social, cultural, political) context and to the 'localization' of meaning. A similar change of paradigm in approaches to texts has been occurring in linguistics. The present trend in approaches to media texts can be characterized by turning away from 'text-internal readings, where readers are theorized as decoders of fixed meanings, to more dynamic models, where meanings are negotiated by actively participating readers' (Meinhof, 1994: 212). Some of the works that have influenced the change of paradigms in media studies have been equally influential in critical linguistic approaches, such as aspects of the work of the Bakhtin Circle by the early twentieth-century Russian semioticians, Halliday's (1978) work on social semiotics and pragmatics, Hall's (2000) model of encoding/decoding, the Foucauldian notion of discourse, argumentation theories and van Dijk's sociocognitive approach (1988, 1991). All these approaches endorse an interactive model of communication which is far more complex than the traditional linear sender–receiver models in mass communication. Media texts are perceived as dialogic (Bakhtin, 1981), and the readings depend on the receivers and on the settings. Researchers presume, therefore, that readers/listeners or viewers interact with media (not only by writing letters to the editor but also by interpreting and understanding media in specific subjective ways). Media texts also depend on intertextual relations with many other genres, diachronically or synchronically. Texts relate to other texts through quotes or indirect references, thus already adding particular meanings or decontextualizing and recontextualizing meanings. Media thus produce and reproduce social meanings.

Also, Barthes (1994/1966) focuses on the aspect of negotiation and, in his essay *Introduction to the structural analysis of narrative*, differentiates between the work and the text. **Work** refers to the artefact, to the fixed pattern of signifiers on pages, whereas **text** refers to the process of meaning-making, of reading. Fiske takes up Barthes's differentiation to distinguish between a programme (on television) and a text:

> Programmes are produced, distributed, and defined by the industry: texts are the product of

their readers. So a programme becomes a text at the moment of reading, that is, when its interaction with one of its many audiences activates some of the meanings/pleasures that it is capable of provoking. (1989: 14)

Adopting this stance means to conceive media communication as a process of textual transformations in which the analysis of reception and production requires specific attention because the text as an artefact constitutes only a moment within a chain of recontextualizations (see also Section 29.3 of this chapter).

Media linguistics

At the intersection of communication studies and linguistics, media linguistics (Burger, 2005; Perrin, 2006; Schmitz, 2004) deals with language in the media mainly from the angles of text linguistics, discourse analysis or conversation analysis. In a synchronic, often comparative perspective as well as in a diachronic perspective it focuses on language use in specific media; among others, the language of news media (Bell, 1991), the language of advertising, the language of computer-mediated communication or particular forms of communication such as Internet chats, talk shows, news interviews (Clayman and Heritage, 2002) are studied. Burger (2005: 64) summarizes under the term '*Medienlinguistik*' the analysis of all texts proposed by mass media. From the diachronic perspective, language variation (standard, vernacular, dialect) is a main field of interest. Burger for instance refers to a whole range of studies on language change in German language media in Austria, Germany and Switzerland. For the whole German-speaking area he summarizes that tolerance for 'regional coloring' is increasingly replacing the former ideal of '*Bühnendeutsch*' (received pronunciation) (2005: 365). Whereas text categories and genres in media practices used to be relatively stable and coherent, the current rapid media developments render classification increasingly difficult; new genre classifications, like infotainment, edutainment, reality soap, introduced by the media industries, illustrate the dilemma (Burger, 2000: 614). At present the main corpus of works in media linguistics concentrates on language in new media whereby the relationship between written and oral language is a focus.

Critical linguistics

Particularly productive in the analysis of media texts was work that can be subsumed under the label of critical linguistics, as developed in the 1970s and 1980s. Drawing mainly on functional linguistics (Halliday, 1978) and social semiotics (Hodge and Kress, 1988), critical linguistics focused on media texts with the aim of isolating the production of ideology and of showing the intimate link between detailed linguistic choices and the production of ideologies. Thereby a dialectical relationship is assumed: words function as a kind of mental grid through which we perceive reality and they in turn influence/construct social realities. The linguistic and discursive choices are not made at will but are dependent on power dimensions. Analytical tools from critical linguistics aim to identify and interpret lexical choices such as transitivity, nominalization, passivization, lexical structure, syntactic forms of clauses, modality and speech acts to make ideological positions visible. There was a clear focus on news (as in Fowler, 1991). The Glasgow University Media Group (1976, 1980) and the Birmingham Centre for Contemporary Cultural Studies elaborated an alternative picture of news, viewing it as socially constructed; news is conceived of as a social practice, a discourse.

Critical discourse analysis (CDA)

Critical discourse analysis (CDA) represents a methodological advance towards an interdisciplinary study of the media (among others, Fairclough, 1995; van Dijk, 1988, 1991; Wodak and Meyer, 2009). The roots of CDA lie in classical rhetoric, text linguistics and sociolinguistics as well as in applied linguistics and pragmatics. The notions of ideology, power, hierarchy and gender, together with sociological variables, are all seen as relevant for an interpretation or explanation of text. The term 'CDA' is used nowadays to refer more specifically to the critical linguistic approach of scholars who find the larger discursive unit of text to be the basic unit of communication. CDA is concerned with 'language as social practice' and considers the context of language use to be crucial (Fairclough and Wodak, 1997: 258):

CDA sees discourse – language use in speech and writing – as a form of social practice. Describing discourse as social practice implies a dialectical relationship between a particular discursive event and the situation(s), institution(s) and social structure(s), which frame it: the discursive event is shaped by them, but it also shapes them.

In CDA, **discourse** is seen as a form of knowledge and memory, whereas **text** illustrates concrete oral utterances or written documents (Reisigl and Wodak, 2001). The aim is to illuminate the way texts represent social reality and discursive constructions of identities. A key concept in CDA is intertextuality – the ways in which a particular text draws on different texts and is situated with respect to the 'order of discourse' (Fairclough, 1998: 45). Fairclough, referring to Foucault, understands orders of discourse as 'a structured configuration of genres and discourses ... associated with a given social domain'. Dealing with media texts, discourse scholars underline the importance of analysing not only the text but also practices of production, distribution and reception (Fairclough, 1995; Scollon, 1998). However, Fairclough acknowledges that he has virtually excluded reception and to some extent also production from his own analyses, but focused on the artefact text (1995: 62). The analysis of media texts has been a central focus within CDA; research agendas focus on such diverse issues as racism and xenophobia, social exclusion, hate speech and war, and the constructedness of gender roles and of ethnic or national identities (van Dijk, 2009; Wodak, 2009 ; Wodak and Busch, 2004).

Conversation analysis

Conversation analysis (CA) emerged in the 1960s (Drew and Heritage, 2006). It is based on ethnomethodology (Garfinkel, 1967; Sacks, Schegloff and Jefferson, 1974) as an interpretative approach to sociology, which focuses mainly on the organization of everyday life and represents a generic approach to the study of social interaction. CA describes the formal structure of conversations (openings, turn-takings, closings, topic control, interruptions, etc.) and analyses how they operate under the institutional constraints of the media. The strength of CA is based in detailed linguistic description, focusing on the organization of interaction, without considering the context. Context is defined within the text, dependent on the explicit mentioning of relevant factors by the speakers.

Much of the media text research in this field focuses on relevant aspects of broadcast news interviews (Clayman and Heritage, 2002; Greatbach, 1986), talk radio (Hutchby, 1991) and talk shows (Drew and Heritage (eds), 2006; Kotthoff, 2004). Thornborrow (2006) gives an overview of current foci in media research within CA. At the core were, among others, issues of agenda setting, agenda shifting and neutrality in news interviews; as interview styles have been changing, also other kinds of interviews are being analysed, such as adversarial interviewing and debate interviews. Another focus are phone-in programmes (Hutchby, 2006) in which listeners have to be maintained as ratified participants in the talk event, for instance by moving from the particular to the general. The design of talk for the overhearing audience has been one of the central concepts in CA. Scholars who see themselves as conversation analysts work on media discourse from a situational perspective (Greatbach, 1998; Scannel, 1991). Media talk is considered as institutional talk. CA shows that there are specific constraints and options that determine, for example, the situation of the production of interviews in public service broadcasting. Heritage (1985) shows that the usual pattern of question–answer–receipt feedback is replaced by a question–answer–question pattern as the broadcasts are produced for an overhearing audience and as the journalist seeks to demonstrate neutrality by avoiding the evaluation of the answer with a receipt. Attention is focused on the dynamics of interviews, comparing turn-taking practices in the media to turn-taking in 'ordinary' conversations.

Style and stylization

In sociolinguistics the question of how linguistic practices in the media relate to everyday linguistic practices is a matter of concern. At present there seems to be a large consensus among different approaches in linguistics that media texts cannot be assumed to reflect the language regimes of linguistic reality. The question is not only how the distribution and configuration of variation in broadcasting reflects the parameters of linguistic everyday reality but also whether it impacts on this linguistic reality (Burger, 2005: 369).

Citing the work of Labov, who claimed that language change is not systematically affected by mass media but primarily by face-to-face interaction with peers, Coupland (2007b: 184) observes that variationist sociolinguistics has been consistently hostile to the idea that mass media are a regular or important factor in triggering linguistic change. He challenges this stance, concluding his study on style in which he draws on numerous examples from media texts that 'mass media do generate some new sociolinguistic resources and these are sometimes used and developed in everyday practice, however short-lived the phenomena might be'. Recent research into interaction among adolescents (Rampton, 2006) has shown how media-derived expressions, such as radio jingles or lines from popular music, enter into everyday sociolinguistic practices. Similarly, Deppermann in his analysis of interactional practices in a group of young males identified how stylized *Kanak Sprak*, as produced on comedy programmes on German TV, impacts on their interactions. His study shows how linguistic resources distributed by the media are integrated into everyday experience:

Media sources provide speakers with linguistic blueprints they can use for interactional work on social categorization, stereotyping and coping with real-world experiences as well as a resource for interactional self-positioning, display of fandom and self-entertainment as the business of conversation. (2007: 351)

The relationship between linguistic practices in the media and everyday linguistic practices can also be approached by referring to Bourdieu's concept of field. In this sense, by using language as one of the semiotic modes in media communication, the media contribute to shape language practices as they provide linguistic resources. Or, as Bourdieu develops, speaking more generally about the literary field, they 'produce means of production', 'word and thought associations' and, moreover, all of the forms of discourse that are seen as 'authoritative', and that can be cited as examples of 'correct language use' (1982: 35). Also the media are engaged in metalinguistic discourses and in contributing to shape language ideologies (often even in specific language programmes and columns). Language criticism in the media can, for instance, contribute to the creation of an environment for policing language use and for the spread of language purism, through coining what 'correct' language is and stigmatizing 'wrong' language use as deviant.

In communication studies, Goffman's work on 'forms of talk' (1981) and on 'frame analysis' (1974) has been very influential in developing a differentiated approach to analysing media communication, challenging the speaker–hearer model of communication, and in understanding media talk as institutional talk. Goffman coined the term of 'mutually ratified participants' in a communicative interaction and also analysed the role of the speaker, which can be decomposed to reveal a range of participating frameworks: the role of the author (the agent who puts together, composes and scripts the lines uttered), the role of the animator (the sounding box from which the announcement comes) and the role of the principal (the party to whose position, stand and belief the utterance attests). These three possibilities constitute the participation framework. Fresh talk normally presents congruence between the three; this is less the case in institutional talk and, consequently, also in media talk. The analysis of participant roles and turn-taking position allows identifying, for example, the influence of an institutional context on a communicative event in the media (such as talk shows, interviews, etc.). Goffman's notion of 'footing' describes the notion of the speaker to his utterance. In this sense radio and TV talk are not addressed to 'a massed but visible grouping off the stage, but to imagined recipients; in fact broadcasters are under pressure to style their talk as though it were addressed to a single listener' (Goffman, 1981: 138).

Dealing with the question of authenticity in broadcasting talk, Montgomery (2001) – following Goffman (1981: 401) – argues that a conversational tone, sometimes adopted in broadcasting, may be more scripted than it seems, and may be simulated, although it is currently designed to approximate as much as possible to 'naturally occurring' talk. Although broadcasting means communication to many, broadcasters have evolved or borrowed techniques associated with small-scale interaction. Montgomery distinguishes between three different (overlapping) types of authenticity: '(1) talk that projects itself as nothing more or less than talk itself; (2) talk that is true to the event/experience; (3) talk that is true to the self/person' (2001: 404). In post-variationist approaches there is a shift from authenticity to processes of authentication and from linguistic features representing social stratifications to the impact of style and stylized features on the negotiation of social positions (Coupland, 2001).

In connection with media communication, research that engages with the concept of style and stylization is presently very influential. Variationist linguistics treated style as an interesting but relatively marginal dimension of language variation. Coupland (2007b) distinguishes between three waves of style research. The idea of stylistic variation was first used in sociolinguistics by Labov (1972) to refer to intra-individual speech variation, variation within the speech of a single person (Coupland, 2007b: 7). Other parts of sociolinguistics, in particular the ethnography of speaking (Gumperz and Hymes, 1972; Hymes, 1962) were already, from the very beginning, interested in contextualization processes and social styles. Coupland (2007a: 219) identifies a second wave in style research which was concerned with the search for patterns of style shift (for example the shift of pronunciation towards prestige variants in more formal situations such as interviews). Influential with regards to media communication are Giles' accommodation theory (1973) and Bell's audience design (1999) – the idea of converging to non-present audiences in initiative style shift. Both approaches posit a more social basis of style shift (accommodating a listener, designing one's speech for an audience). A move away from Labov's linear concept of contextual style, from styles as objects, represents also the conceptualization of social styles and stylization as processes (Hinnenkamp and Selting, 1989).

Whereas, according to Coupland (2007b), in the first and second wave of sociolinguistic research into style the emphasis was on style shift, studying linguistic deviation from a presumed norm, the focus is now on how style creates meaning in discursive operations. Stylistic operations are possible because of the socially-structured indexicalities that link ways of speaking to social groups or specific situations, and to ideological conditions that define these at particular times and places. Style becomes similar to lifestyle, described by Bourdieu (1979) as the surface correlate of habitus. Style is more than saying the same things in other ways; what can be said and what cannot be said is an integral part of communicative style (Auer, 2007: 12). 'The basic unit of analysis for a sociolinguistics of style is a single semiotic unit, and the analytical demand is to explain how its activation contributes to speakers' negotiation of social meaning in a discourse' (Coupland, 2007a: 220). According to Coupland, style is also social practice as its meaning potential is realized in the construction of social identities and relations:

> Styling is part of the construction and deployment of a speaker's and others' social identities, which might be to invoke and to consolidate the values and attributes associated with a 'speech community'. ... On the other hand it might involve establishing a particular stance vis-à-vis those community norms, where ownership becomes more or less clear – e.g. a class position one wants to subvert. (2007a: 221)

The concept of style was applied in a productive way in connection with media, among others by Bell's relationally-oriented audience design framework and, recently, Ben Rampton's work on sociolinguistic crossing and stylistic creativity in relation to ethnicity and social class, followed by other works usually linked theoretically to the work of Mikhail Bakhtin and Erving Goffman. Recent media-related research that draws on concepts of style and stylization focuses on a variety of topics such as youth culture and the media (e.g. Deppermann, 2007), media and migration (e.g. Böse and Busch, 2007; Morley, 2000), advertising (e.g. Kelly-Holmes, 2005), computer mediated communication (e.g. Androutsopoulos, 2007a, 2007b; Sebba, 2007), presentation of self in diaspora media (e.g. Coupland, 2007a), and gender (Cameron, 2006).

29.3 A FRAMEWORK FOR THE ANALYSIS OF MEDIA COMMUNICATION

When analysing language in media interaction it is necessary to take into consideration the specific conditions under which media communication takes place. As in any other type of communicative interaction, media communication has a dialogic nature and cannot be conceived simply within a sender–receiver model. Furthermore, again as in any other type of communication, media communication is multimodal and multifunctional, i.e. every act of media communication encompasses a propositional, a social and a personal dimension: drawing on several semiotic modes it provides content and is involved in processes of meaning-making, it structures social relationships and it results in the production and reproduction of subject positions. Media communication mediates between the public and the private sphere: it can be seen as a form of organizational communication framed by institutional contexts. Media products are publicly available and media are, in their self-understanding, constitutive elements of the public sphere(s). Whereas their distribution is public, their reception takes mostly place in private surroundings. As discussed earlier in this chapter, present developments in media make traditional categorizations according to sectors, genres, etc., increasingly difficult. The following subsections of this contribution presents elements for an open and flexible framework for the analysis of language and the media. The framework shown in Figure 29.1 was first developed for and applied to the analysis of language policies in the context of media in multilingual environments (Busch, 2004).

Recontextualization and intertextuality

Media communication can be understood and analysed as a chain of recontextualizations. These transformations occur at any stage of the communication process, linking the sphere of production to the situations of everyday practices in which media are present. From the perspective of media studies, linear models of communication that dissociate meaning from its contextualization during production and reception were replaced by models that see communication as a circular process, comprising the totality of the means employed to collect, exploit, store, transmit and impart information (Mattelart, 2003: 51 referring to Wiener's cybernetics approach). From the perspective of linguistics the process of media communication can best be captured by the notion of intertextuality, as developed by Julia Kristeva (1980), drawing on Mikhail Bakthin's concepts. In this concept every text is part of a tissue of texts and intertextual relationships; it is (not necessarily consciously) linked to previous texts to which it refers and becomes, in turn, a resource for future texts. Intertextuality becomes apparent on the level of the meaning potential as well as on the level of the linguistic practices visible in the text.

Media production encompasses the collection and selection of 'raw material'. At each stage in

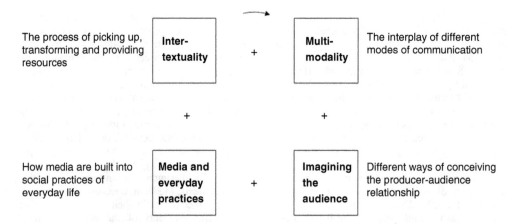

Figure 29.1   Analytical layers for the study of media communication with respect to language.

media production, earlier versions of the text are transformed and recontextualized in ways that correspond to the priorities and goals of the current stage. Recontextualization can involve suppression and filtering of meaning potentials, but it can also result in expanding meaning potentials by adding or elaborating upon an earlier version of the text (Chouliaraki and Fairclough, 1999). Media production is regulated by institutional routines, media reception by everyday practices and arrangements, both depending on available resources. Journalists can revert to different kinds of source material: such as speeches, interviews, press releases, photos and graphs provided by news agencies, archive material, other media texts, personal communications, amateur videos, rumours and assumptions. Current transformations in media production can be characterized on the one hand by an increasing specialization of journalists on narrower fields of reporting, and on the other hand by a decreasing division of labour between technical and journalistic parts of production. In print for instance, the journalist is not only responsible for the text but also for the layout and the selection of images, and thereby becomes the designer of a multimodal text. At the same time, due to the economic imperative of reducing the fixed costs in media enterprises, the amount of genuine journalistic investigation decreases in favour of 'ready made products' such as news agency material, pre-produced elements and formats. This process is encouraged by an oligopolistic owner structure and practices of cross-referencing between different media.

On the level of discourse and linguistic practices, van Leeuwen and Wodak (1999: 96) suggest that transformations due to recontextualization can include deletion, rearrangement (e.g. changing the order of propositions, altering of emphasis),

substitution (through linguistic means such as nominalization, metaphor, metonymy, synecdoche, personalization) and addition (adding new elements to the representation of social practices). Kress and van Leeuwen mention, in the context of transformations, the 'import' of signs from other contexts (another era, another social group or cultural environment) 'to signify ideas and values which are associated with that other context from which we import the sign' (2001: 10). Bell (1997: 248) subsumes a similar idea under the notion of 'referee design'. Referees are, for Bell, third persons or groups 'who are so salient for a speaker that they influence style even in their absence'.

Media are linked to processes of mediation and to mediators that control the process of transmission, obeying to institutional hierarchies and power relations, depending on and creating rules of belonging and ways of doing (Debray, 2004). In this sense, social power relations, institutional hierarchies and economic constraints impact on how transformation within the intertextual chain takes place – on the discursive level as well as on the level of the linguistic (and other semiotic) means employed. On a macro-sociolinguistic level, media contributed under the nation-state paradigm to linguistic homogenization and to the rise of standard languages; under the present conditions of globalization they can equally contribute to the de-centring of unified standards and to reconfiguring linguistic spaces and language regimes (Busch, 2004).

Modalities and meanings

Media communication is inherently multimodal communication: this means that language in written and spoken form is only one of several modes available for expressing a potential of meanings. For instance, in print media, layout and image are available in addition to the written word; in radio, language is present in its spoken form, alongside music and various sounds; in television, all the aforementioned modes can be drawn upon in a context in which the moving image holds a central position. Similarly, in CMC a wide range of modes is available. Kress states:

A multimodal approach assumes that the message is 'spread across' all the modes of communication. If this is so, then each mode is a partial bearer of the overall meaning of the message. All modes, speech and writing included, are then seen as always partial bearers of meaning only. This is a fundamental challenge to hitherto current notions of 'language' as a full means of making meaning (2002: 6)

Walter Benjamin's writings, especially on 'The Work of Art in the Age of Mechanical Reproduction' (Benjamin, 1938), were extremely influential in media studies. Taking the example of a painting being transformed into a photograph, he shows that the media content of the original work is still present, but is structured in a new way that reflects interdependency between the medium and new meanings. Harold Innis underlined in the 1950s (1997) the importance of technical developments in communication, of ways of transmission of information and of means of transport for cultural developments. Marshall McLuhan (1964) developed this idea further by coining the aphorism 'the medium is the message'. Cultural studies caution against a technical determinism that postulates a simple causal relationship between the technical and the social (Mattelart, 2003). How different modes interact in the communication process is, from this point of view, not only a question of technical availability but also a question of social appropriation and convention, as Kress and van Leeuwen (2001) point out in their multimodal social semiotic theory.

The interplay between the different modes has undergone substantial changes in media history. Writing was considered in many cultural environments as the central mode for the transfer of canonical knowledge and authoritative discourse. This practice, of the predominance of the written text, influenced radio production so that practically all radio texts in the early days of the medium were produced first in written form and then read in the radio broadcast. Even in television for some time news broadcasts were read without a transmission of the image of the speaker as it was considered that the moving image could distract attention. Gradually the image has moved into a central position. The 'conversationalization'

of (political) discourse in the media gained in momentum with the image and with television (Fairclough, 1995: 9ff.). The so-called new media can contribute through their interactive practices to a further de-centring of standard languages and favour practices that draw on multiple stylistic and linguistic resources. Such practices in turn are taken up by traditional mass media and incorporated into their journalistic routines.

Imagining the audience

Present approaches exploring the relationship between language and the media generally draw on Mikhail Bakhtin's dialogic principle (1981) which assumes that in any utterance an interlocutor is present. Unlike in direct communication, in media communication, due to its specific spatially and temporally shifted conditions of reception, the interlocutor becomes an imagined, ideal counterpart. Bakhtin's work inspired Bell to develop his model of audience design. Observing a radio speaker who read the news bulletin on different radio stations, he noticed a style shift on the micro level of pronunciation and concluded: 'style shift occurs primarily in response to the speaker's audience' (Bell, 1997: 242). The audience design model differentiates between the 'addressees' who are directly addressed, the 'auditors' who are assumed to be the target audience of a particular media, the 'overhearers' who might be present but do not form part of the target audience, and the 'eavesdroppers' who the speaker does not think of (1997: 241ff.). Bell's model, initially conceived for radio broadcasting, can be applied to other forms of media communication.

The notion of the target audience, which encompasses a spatial (local, regional, national, global) and/or a social (social status, income, age, gender) dimension is based on rigid and reified audience categories. Research on media coverage and definitions of target audiences are instruments of marketing research and correspond to criteria established by the advertising industry. Ang (1991) demonstrates that this approach is based on a discursive construct of audience that is unable to grasp the actual relationship between media and audiences or to conceive communication processes. She distinguishes between two main orientations: audience-as-public and audience-as-market. The first configuration of audience is generally associated with the public service media sector in which the addressee is seen as a citizen (of a state), and the relationship with the audience is paternal and aims at transmitting values, habits and tastes. It is linked to the so-called transmission model of communication, in which the transmission of a message and the ordered transfer of meaning is the intended consequence of the communication process.

The second configuration of audience is associated with the private commercial media sector. Audiences are addressed as consumers in a double sense: as consumers of the media product and as potential consumers of the products advertised in the programmes. In the attention model of communication (McQuail, 1987), communication is considered successful as soon as attention is actually raised in audiences. The transfer of meaning plays a secondary role. The scoop, the extraordinary and the scandal gain in importance as means of awakening attention.

In the alternative media sector the conception of the audience is determined by the idea of an active public that participates in social action and media production. The aim is to overcome the division between producers and audiences, and to move closer to a situation in which 'the Other' is able to represent itself, and in which the heterogeneity of 'authentic informants' is not reduced. Alternative or third-sector media are consequently closer to the ideal of representing the multivoicedness of society in all three dimensions which Bakhtin described: heterology (*raznorečie*), i.e. the diversity of discourses; heteroglossia (*raznojazyčnie*), i.e. the diversity of language(s); and heterophony (*raznoglossie*), i.e. the diversity of individual voices (Todorov, 1984: 56).

These different basic orientations in conceiving the producer–audience relationship result in preferences for particular media formats (e.g. authoritative information-centred programmes, infotainment programmes, dialogic forms as phone-in programmes), and in a choice of particular linguistic practices. They also determine the way in which discourses are being shaped, reproduced and transformed.

Media and everyday practices

The question of how language and discourse in media communication relate to everyday linguistic and discursive practices is a matter of concern in the exploration of sociolinguistic interactions. As discussed above, recent work in style and stylization shows that the traditional scepticism concerning the impact of media on individual linguistic practices and on language shift is being challenged by empirical work investigating communication in style communities.

Reception studies within the traditional quantitative media studies approaches, often setting out from a sender-receiver model of communication without taking into account the actual environment and conditions of media reception, are not suitable for a processual analysis of media and

their role in everyday life. Whereas within the traditional paradigm it was somehow possible to differentiate between different media sectors (as print, TV, radio) and to measure their impact in individual reception habits in terms of time and intensity of contact, with present media developments and the diversification of receiving devices this seems virtually impossible. Under the conditions of a changing media landscape, the categories of producers and audiences blur as well as the demarcations between private mediated communication and public media communication. There is a claim for a new approach to the notion of audiences and everyday media practices which rejects models of passive media consumption (Gauntlett, 2007).

The multiplication of the possibilities of media contact and of media–recipient interfaces has increased with recent technical developments. Print media such as daily newspapers can for instance not only be read in their paper version but also in a modified form as (interactive) online versions or adapted for mobile phones. This means that the ways in which media are being appropriated in daily life are subjected to permanent change. New time–space articulations become salient. Whereas some two decades ago relatively stable reception habits could be assumed as bringing together audiences into national, ethnic or other social communities (Morley and Robins, 1996), present media reception is more characterized by individual practices, which become more ephemeral and deterritorialized. As in linguistics, in media studies and in media anthropology, everyday media practices, style and style communities have become an important focus (Kosnick, 2007). Such practices can also be understood as technologies of the self in a Foucauldian sense, as spaces for the production and reproduction of situated subject positions (Reckwitz, 2006).

In everyday life people participate in a range of different media spaces: besides the traditional national sphere, globalized spaces as well as localized media gain in importance, regional spaces beyond state borders emerge as broadcasting spaces, and transnational and translocal media link geographically-dispersed groups. Within these spaces, particular language regimes and linguistic practices develop. The development of such regimes and practices as well as the way in which they are related to other everyday language practices opens up a vast field of research.

NOTES

1 For the question of public sphere and its fragmentations see the discussions of Habermas' model

which was developed in the 1960s and which was based on the assumption of a single unified (national) public sphere (Habermas, 1990). Critiques of Habermas' model were formulated by feminist studies (e.g. Benhabib, 1992; Fraser, 1992) and also later by scholars accenting questions of ethnicity, race and language as factors of exclusion (e.g. Husband, 2000; Morley, 2000). Habermas concedes, in a revision of his model, that he neglected the existence of counter publics and counter discourses (Habermas, 1990).

2 Hinglish (a combination of the words Hindi and English) designates a blend of Hindi and English vernaculars in the urban areas of the states of India where Hindi is spoken.

REFERENCES

Anderson, B. (1983) *Imagined Communities: Reflections on the Origins and Spread of Nationalism*. London: Verso.

Androutsopoulos, J. (2007a) 'Bilingualism in the mass media and on the Internet', in M. Heller (ed.), *Bilingualism: a Social Approach*. Basingstoke: Palgrave Macmillan. pp. 207–30

Androutsopoulos, J. (2007b) 'Style online: doing hip-hop on the German speaking web', in P. Auer (ed.), *Style and Social Identities. Alternative Approaches to Linguistic Heterogeneity*. Berlin: Mouton de Gruyter. pp. 279–321.

Ang, I. (1991) *Desperately Seeking the Audience*. London: Routledge.

Appadurai, A. (1998) 'Globale ethnische Räume. Bemerkungen und Fragen zur Entwicklung einer transnationalen Anthropologie', in U. Beck (ed.), *Perspektiven der Weltgesellschaft*. Frankfurt am Main: Suhrkamp. pp. 11–41.

Auer, P. (2007) 'Introduction', in P. Auer (ed.), *Style and Social Identities. Alternative Approaches to Linguistic Heterogeneity*. Berlin: Mouton de Gruyter. pp. 1–21.

Bakhtin, M. (1981) *The Dialogic Imagination*. Ed. M. Holquist. Austin, TX: University of Texas Press.

Barthes, R. (1994/1966) 'Introduction à l'analyse structurale des récits' ['Introduction to the structural analysis of narrative'], in E. Marty (ed.), *Roland Barthes. Oeuvres complètes. Tome II. 1966–1973. Édition établie et présentée par Éric Marty*. Paris: Éditions du Seuil.

Bell, A. (1991) *The Language of News Media*. London: Blackwell.

Bell, A. (1997) 'Language style as audience design', in N. Coupland and A. Jaworski (eds), *Sociolinguistics. A Reader and Coursebook*. New York: St. Martin's Press. pp. 240–50.

Bell, A. (1999) 'Styling the other to define the self: a study in New Zealand identity making', *Journal of Sociolinguistics*, 3(4): 523–41.

Benhabib, S. (1992) 'Models of public space: Hannah Arendt, the Liberal tradition, and Jürgen Habermas' in C. Calhoun (ed.), *Habermas and the Public Sphere*. Cambridge, MA: MIT Press. pp. 73–99.

Benjamin, W. (1938) 'Das Kunstwerk im Zeitalter seiner technischen Reproduzierbarkeit' ['The Work of art in the age of mechanical reproduction'], in R. Tiedermann and H. Schweppenhäuser (eds) (1980), *Walter Benjamin: Gesammelte Schriften I, 2*. (Werkausgabe Band 2). Frankfurt am Main: Suhrkamp. pp. 471–508.

Blommaert, J., Collins, J. and Slembrouck, S. (2005) 'Spaces of multilingualism', *Language and Communication*, 25(3): 197–216.

Böse, M. and Busch, B. (2007) 'The political potential of multi-accentuality in the exhibition title "gastarbajteri"', *Journal of Language and Politics*, 6(3): 437–57.

Bourdieu, P. (1979) *La distinction: critique sociale du jugement*. Paris: Les Éditions de Minuit.

Bourdieu, P. (1982) *Ce que parler veut dire. L'économie des échanges linguistiques*. Paris: Fayard.

Burger, H. (2000) 'Textsorten in Massenmedien', in K. Brinker, G. Antos, W. Heinemann and S. Sager (eds), *Text-und Gesprächslinguistik. Ein internationales Handbuch zeitgenössischer Forschung. 1. Halbband*. Berlin: de Gruyter. pp. 614–28.

Burger, H. (2005) *Mediensprache*. 3rd edn. Berlin: de Gruyter.

Busch, B. (1999) *Der virtuelle Dorfplatz. Minderheitenmedien, Globalisierung und kulturelle Identität*. Klagenfurt, Celovec: Drava.

Busch, B. (2004) *Sprachen im Disput. Medien und Öffentlichkeit in multilingualen Gesellschaften*. Klagenfurt: Drava.

Busch, B. (2006) 'Media, politics and discourse: interactions' in K. Brown (ed.), *Encyclopedia of Language and Linguistics*. 2nd edn. Oxford: Elsevier. pp. 609–16.

Cameron, D. (2006) 'Theorizing the female voice in public contexts', in J. Baxter (ed.), *Speaking Out: The Female Voice in Public Contexts*. Houndmills: Palgrave. pp. 3–20.

Castells, M. (2000) *The Rise of the Network Society*. 2nd edn. Oxford: Blackwell.

Chouliaraki, L. and Fairclough, N. (1999) *Discourse in Late Modernity: Rethinking Critical Discourse Analysis*. Edinburgh: Edinburgh University Press.

Clayman, S. and Heritage, J. (2002) *The News Interview: Journalists and Public Figures on the Air*. Cambridge: Cambridge University Press.

Cormack, M. (1998) 'Minority language media in Western Europe. Preliminary considerations', *European Journal of Communication*, 13(1): 33–52.

Cormack, M. (2004) 'Developing minority media studies', *Mercator Media Forum*, 7(1): 3–12.

Cottle, S. (ed.) (2000) *Ethnic Minorities and the Media*. Buckingham, Open University Press.

Coupland, N. (2001) 'Dialect stylization in radio talk', *Language in Society*, 30: 345–75.

Coupland, N. (2007a) 'Aneurin Bevan, class wars and the styling of political antagonism', in P. Auer (ed.), *Style and Social Identities. Alternative Approaches to Linguistic Heterogeneity*. Berlin: Mouton de Gruyter. pp. 213–47.

Coupland, N. (2007b) *Style*. Cambridge: Cambridge University Press.

Crystal, D. (2001) *Language and the Internet*. Cambridge: Cambridge University Press.

Danet, B. and Herring, S. C. (eds) (2007) *The Multilingual Internet*. Oxford: Oxford University Press.

Debray, R. (2004) *Transmitting Culture*. New York: Columbia University Press.

Deppermann, A. (2007) 'Playing with the voice of the other: stylized Kanaksprak in conversations', in P. Auer (ed.), *Style and Social Identities. Alternative Approaches to Linguistic Heterogeneity*. Berlin: Mouton de Gruyter. pp. 325–61.

Drew, P. and Heritage, J. (eds) (2006) *Conversation Analysis*. 4 vols. London: Sage.

European Charter for Regional or Minority Languages (1992). *European Treaty Series*, 148. Strasbourg: Council of Europe Publishing.

European Commission (2002) 'Dubbed or subtitles? Le cinéma européen vu comme une opportunité de pratiquer les langues étrangères dans le cadre de l'AEL 2001', *Note de la Commission*. Bruxelles: Directorate General for Education and Culture.

European Commission (2005) A New Framework Strategy for Multilingualism. http://ec.europa.eu/education/languages/archive/doc/com596_en.pdf (COM (2005) 596 final).

European Commission (2006) *Special Eurobarometer. Europeans and their Languages*. Bruxelles: European Commission.

Fairclough, N. (1995) *Media Discourse*. London: Arnold.

Fairclough, N. (1998) 'Political discourse in the media: an analytical framework', in A. Bell and P. Garrett (eds), *Approaches to Media Discourse*. Oxford: Blackwell. pp. 142–62.

Fairclough, N. and Wodak, R. (1997) 'Critical discourse analysis', in T. van Dijk (ed.), *Introduction to Discourse Analysis*. London: Sage. pp. 258–84.

Fishman, J. (1991) *Reversing Language Shift*. Clevedon, UK: Multilingual Matters.

Fiske, J. (1987, 1989) *Television Culture*. London: Routledge.

Fowler, R. (1991) *Language in the News: Discourse and Ideology in the Press*. London: Routledge.

Framework Convention for the Protection of National Minorities (1995). *European Treaty Series*, 157. Strasbourg: Council of Europe.

Franchon, C. and Vargaftig, M. (eds) (1995) *European Television: Immigration and Ethnic Minorities*. London: Libbey.

Fraser, N. (1992) 'Rethinking the public sphere: a contribution to the critique of actually existing democracy' in C. Calhoun (ed.), *Habermas and the Public Sphere*. Cambridge, MA: MIT Press. pp. 109–142.

Garfinkel, H. (1967) *Studies in Ethnomethodology*. Englewood Cliffs, NJ: Prentice Hall.

Gauntlett, D. (2007) *Creative Explorations: New Approaches to Identities and Audiences*. London: Routledge.

Giles, H. (1973) 'Accent mobility: a model and some data', *Anthropological Linguistics*, 15: 87–105.

Giles, H. (ed.) (1977) *Language, Ethnicity and Intergroup Relations*. London: Academic Press.

Glasgow University Media Group (1976) *Bad News*. London: Routledge.

Glasgow University Media Group (1980) *More Bad News*. London: Routledge.

Goffman, E. (1974) *Frame Analysis*. New York: Harper and Row.

Goffman, E. (1981) *Forms of Talk*. Philadelphia: University of Pennsylvania Press.

Greatbach, D. (1986) 'Aspects of topical organisation in news interviews: the use of agenda-shifting procedures by news interviewees', *Media, Culture and Society*, 8(4): 441–55.

Greatbach, D. (1998) 'Conversation analysis', in A. Bell and P. Garrett (eds), *Approaches to Media Discourse*. Oxford: Blackwell. pp. 163–85.

Gumperz, J. and Hymes, D. (eds) (1972) *Directions in Sociolinguistics: The Ethnography of Communication*. New York: Holt, Rinehart and Winston.

Habermas, J. (1990) *Strukturwandel der Öffentlichkeit*. Frankfurt am Main: Suhrkamp. (1st edn, 1962.) (English translation (1989): *Structural Transformation of the Public Sphere*. Cambridge: Polity Press.)

Hall, S. (2000) 'Encoding/decoding', in P. Marris and S. Thornham (eds), *Media Studies*. New York: New York University Press. pp. 51–61.

Halliday, M. A. K. (1978) *Language as Social Semiotics. The Social Interpretation of Language and Meaning*. London: Edward Arnold.

Hargreaves, A. (2001) 'Kein monokulturelles Menü: Medienrezeption in Frankreich und Deutschland', in B. Busch, B. Hipfl and K. Robins (eds), *Bewegte Identitäten. Medien in transkulturellen Kontexten*. Klagenfurt: Drava. pp. 128–45.

Heller, M. (2000) 'Bilingualism and identity in the post-modern world', *Estudios de Sociolingüística*, 1(2): 9–24.

Heller, M. (2003) 'Globalization, the new economy, and the commodification of language and identity', *Journal of Sociolinguistics*, 7(4): 473–92.

Heller, M. and Labrie, N. (2003) 'Langage, pouvoir et identité: une étude de cas, une approche théorique, une méthodologie', in M. Heller and N. Labrie (eds), *Discours et identité. La francité canadienne entre modernité et mondialisation*. Cortil-Wodon: Editions Modulaires Européennes (E. M. E.). pp. 9–41.

Heritage, J. (1985) 'Analysing news interviews: aspects of the production of talk for an «overhearing» audience', in T. van Dijk (ed.), *Handbook of Discourse Analysis. Discourse and Dialogue*. Vol. 3. London: Academic Press. pp. 95–117.

Hinnenkamp, V. and Selting, M. (eds) (1989) *Stil und Stilisierung. Arbeiten zur interpretativen Soziolinguistik*. Tübingen: Niemeyer.

Hodge, R. and Kress, G. (1988) *Social Semiotics*. Cambridge: Polity Press.

Husband, C. (1994) *A Richer Vision: The Development of Ethnic Minority Media in Western Europe*. London: Libbey.

Husband, C. (2000) 'Media and the public sphere in multiethnic societies', in S. Cottle (ed.), *Ethnic Minorities and the Media*. Buckingham: Open University Press. pp. 199–214.

Hutchby, I. (1991) The organisation of Talk on radio, in P. Scannell (ed.), *Broadcast Talk*. London, Sage. pp. 119–37.

Hutchby, I. (2006) *Media Talk: Conversation Analysis and the Study of Broadcasting*. Maidenhead: Open University Press.

Hymes, D. (1962) 'The ethnography of speaking', in T. Gladwin and W. Sturtevant (eds), *Anthropology and Human Behavior*. Washington, DC: Anthropological Society of Washington. pp. 13–53.

Innis, H. A. (1951) The bias of communication. Toronto: University of Toronto Press.

Innis, H. A. (1997) *Kreuzwege der Kommunikation. Ausgewählte Texte*. Ed. K. Back. New York: Springer.

Jacquemet, M. (2005) 'Transidiomatic practices: language and power in the age of globalization', *Language and Communication*, 25: 257–77.

Kelly-Holmes, H. (2005) *Advertising as Multilingual Communication*. Basingstoke: Palgrave Macmillan.

Koolstra, C. M. and Beentjes, J. W. J. (1999) 'Children's vocabulary acquisition in a foreign language through watching subtitled TV programmes at home', *Educational Technology Research and Development*, 47: 51–60.

Kosnick, K. (2007) *Migrant Media: Turkish Broadcasting and Multicultural Politics in Berlin*. Bloomington, IN: Indiana University Press.

Kotthoff, H. (2004) 'Overdoing culture? Sketch-Komik, Typenstilisierung und Identitätskonstruktion bei Kaya Yanar', in J. Reuter (ed.), *Doing Culture*. Bielefeld: Transcript Verlag. pp. 184–201.

Kress, G. (2002) 'The multimodal landscape of communication', in *Medien Journal*, 4(2002): 4–19.

Kress, G. and van Leeuwen, T. (2001) *Multimodal Discourse. The Modes and Media of Contemporary Communication*. London: Arnold.

Kristeva, J. (1980) *Desire in Language. A Semiotic Approach to Literature and Art*. New York: Columbia University Press.

Labov, W. (1972) *Sociolinguistic Patterns*. Oxford: Blackwell.

McLuhan, M. (1964) *Understanding Media: The Extensions of Man*. New York: McGraw-Hill.

McQuail, D. (1987) *Mass Communication Theory: An Introduction*. London: Sage.

Mattelart, A. (2003) *The Information Society: An Introduction*. Tr. S. G. Taponier. London: Sage.

Meinhof, U. (1994) 'Double talk in news broadcasts', in D. Graddol and O. Boyd-Barrett (eds), *Media Texts: Authors and Readers*. Clevedon, UK: Multilingual Matters. pp. 212–23.

Meinhof, U. (1998) *Language Learning in the Age of Satellite Television*. Oxford: Oxford University Press.

Mercator Media (ed.) (2000) *Proceedings of the Mercator Conference on Audiovisual Translation and Minority Languages. Aberystwyth, University of Wales. (3–4 April 2000)*. Aberystwyth: Mercator Media.

Montgomery, M. (2001) 'Defining "authenticity talk"', *Discourse Studies*, 3(4): 397–405.

Moring, T. and Husband, C. (2007) 'The contribution of Swedish language media in Finland to linguistic vitality', *International Journal of the Sociology of Language*, 187/188: 75–101.

Morley, D. (2000) *Home Territories: Media, Mobility and Identity*. London: Routledge.

Morley, D. and Robins, K. (1996) *Spaces of Identity. Global Media, Electronic Landscapes and Cultural boundaries*. London: Routledge.

Perrin, D. (2006) *Medienlinguistik*. Konstanz: utb.

Rampton, B. (2006) *Language in Late Modernity: Interaction in an Urban School*. Cambridge: Cambridge University Press.

Reckwitz, A. (2006) *Das hybride Subjekt. Eine Theorie der Subjektkulturen von der bürgerlichen Moderne zur Postmoderne*. Weilerswist: Velbrück Wissenschaft.

Reisigl, M. and Wodak, R. (2001) *Discourse and Discrimination*. London: Routledge.

Ricento, T. (2006) 'Theoretical perspectives in language policy: an overview', in T. Ricento (ed.), *Language Policy: Theory and Practice – an Introduction*. London: Blackwell. pp. 10–24.

Robins, K. (1997) *Programming for People. From Cultural Rights to Cultural Responsibilities*. New York: United Nations World Television Forum.

Sacks, H., Schegloff, E. and Jefferson, G. (1974) 'A simplest systematics for the organisation of turn-taking in conversation', *Language*, 50: 696–735.

Scannel, P. (ed.) (1991) *Broadcast Talk*. London: Sage.

Schmitz, U. (2004) *Sprache in modernen Medien. Einführung in Tatsachen und Theorien, Themen und Thesen*. Berlin: Schmidt Erich Verlag.

Scollon, R. (1998) *Mediated Discourse as Social Interaction: An Ethnographic Study of News Discourse*. London: Longman.

Scollon, R. and Scollon, S. W. (2003) *Discourses in Place. Language in the Material World*. London: Routledge.

Scollon, R. and Scollon, W. S. (2004) *Nexus Analysis. Discourse and the Emerging Internet*. London: Routledge.

Sebba, M. (2007) 'Identity and language construction in an on-line community: the case of "Ali G."', in P. Auer (ed.), *Style and Social Identities. Alternative Approaches to Linguistic Heterogeneity*. Berlin: Mouton de Gruyter. pp. 361–93.

Shohamy, E. (2006) *Language Policy. Hidden Agendas and New Approaches*. London: Routledge.

Shohamy, E. and Gorter, D. (eds) (2009) *Linguistic Landscape. Expanding the Scenery*. New York: Routledge.

ter Wal, J. (ed.) (2002) *Racism and Cultural Diversity in the Mass Media. An Overview of Research and Examples of Good Practice in the EU Member States, 1995–2002*. Vienna: ERCOMER.

Thornborrow, J. (2006) 'Media: analysis and methods', in K. Brown, (ed.), *Elsevier Encyclopedia of Language and Linguistics*. 2nd edn. Oxford: Elsevier.

Thussu, D. K. (2000) *International Communication. Continuity and Change*. London: Arnold.

Todorov, T. (1984) *Mikhail Bakhtin. The Dialogic Principle*. Manchester: Manchester University Press.

van Dijk, T. (1988) *News as Discourse*. London: Routledge.

van Dijk, T. (1991) *Racism and the Press*. London: Routledge.

van Dijk, T. (2009) *Society and Discourse: How Social Contexts Influence Text and Talk*. Cambridge: Cambridge University Press.

van Leeuwen, T. and Wodak, R. (1999) 'Legitimizing immigration control: a discourse-historical analysis', *Discourse Studies*, 1(1): 83-118.

Wodak, R. (2009) *The Discourse of Politics in Action: Politics as Usual*. Basingstoke: Palgrave.

Wodak, R. and Busch, B. (2004) 'Approaches to media texts', in J. Dowing, D. McQuail, P. Schlesinger and E. Wartella (eds), *The Handbook of Media Studies*. Thousand Oaks, CA: Sage. pp. 105–22.

Wodak, R. and Koller, V. (eds) (2008) *Handbook of Communication in the Public Sphere. Handbooks of Applied Linguistics 4*. Berlin: Mouton de Gruyter.

Wodak, R. and Meyer, M. (eds) (2009) *Methods of Critical Discourse Analysis. Introducing Qualitative Methods*. 2nd edn. Los Angeles: Sage.

Wright, S. (ed.) (2006) 'Languages of the internet', *Special Issue of the Journal of Language and Politics*, 5: 2. Amsterdam: John Benjamins.

PART 5

Multilingualism and Contact

Societal Bilingualism

Mark Sebba

30.1 INTRODUCTION

'Societal bilingualism' is a broad term used to refer to any kind of bilingualism or multilingualism at a level of social organization beyond the individual or nuclear family. By this definition, almost every country and region of the world has some degree of 'societal bilingualism'. Societal bilingualism by no means implies that every individual in the society in question is bilingual, or even that a majority are. Rather, there are many different ways in which social groupings, from extended families all the way up to federal nation-states, can be said to have the property of 'societal bilingualism'. As Romaine points out (2005: 385), 'bilingual individuals may belong to communities of various sizes and types, and they interact in many kinds of networks within communities, not all of which may function bilingually'.

One way of studying societal bilingualism would be to recognize two broad categories: 'state' and 'community'. The study of societal bilingualism at the state level would focus on officially bilingual states and substates (regions, provinces, municipalities, etc.), the precise nature of their bilingualism, and the institutions and legal frameworks which exist to regulate and reproduce it. The study of societal bilingualism at the community level would focus on those groups (of whatever size) which practiced bilingualism among themselves, and would concern itself with their bilingual practices, including trends over time such as language shift (see below). Cutting across this division is the study of bilingual education, the provision of education in a bilingual medium and/or for a community of bilingual

speakers, which is a major topic in its own right (see Cummins and Hornberger, 2008; Helot and De Mejia, 2008 for overviews and recent research). At both the state and community levels, as Romaine has indicated, monolingualism may actually be the norm to varying degrees. Thus officially bilingual states may be collections of largely monolingual units, whereas bilingual communities may be made up of a mixture of monolingual and bilingual individuals. A community considered as a whole may be 'bilingual', but individuals within the community may range from completely monolingual to fully fluent in, and using, both languages, with the possibility of having different levels of active (productive) and passive (receptive) knowledge of the same language. Within individual households, different generations may have different language preferences and patterns of language use.

By way of illustration, let us look at some examples of bilingualism at the state and community levels from around the world.

1   *Belgium* as a nation has French and Dutch as official languages (with German also official in one region), but is in effect two largely autonomous, largely monolingual entities, Flanders (Flemish/Dutch) and Wallonia (French) together with the capital, Brussels, under a federal government. Only in Brussels are both languages official side by side (in other regions public signage, for example, is monolingual). Individual bilingualism in the two official languages is surprisingly uncommon. Each region has its own minority linguistic groups: Dutch in Wallonia, French in Flanders, but also speakers of other languages

(such as Arabic or Kinyarwanda (Gafaranga, 2007)) many of whom would know one or both of the official languages as well.

2 *Luxemburg*, Belgium's neighbour, is officially trilingual at the national level, but in a very different way. The first language and vernacular of the majority of the population is Lëtzebuergesch, a Germanic dialect, which is now one of the three official languages. Although Lëtzebuergesch is used as a written language, High German is used for most written publications, while French is the language of administration and government. All locally-educated adult Luxemburgers know all three of these languages and the appropriate contexts for their use. Unlike Belgium, where a majority of people can live their lives monolingually, in Luxemburg it would be difficult to participate fully without knowing how to speak the vernacular, Lëtzebuergesch, and read both German and French. The picture is even more complex, however, for Luxemburg has a high proportion of immigrants from Southern Europe, and around 16% of the population are of Portuguese nationality (Statec, 2008). Thus, Portuguese is a significant minority language in Luxemburg, and spoken by a local community most of whom also know at least one of the official languages.

3 *Canada* is officially bilingual at the federal level, in English and French. Services offered by the Federal government have to be available in both these languages, and Canadians can expect to receive communications and services from the government in whichever of these languages they prefer. But immediately below the federal level, we find that, of the 10 provinces and three territories, nearly all are monolingual in practice, though under the Canadian constitution they are required to provide some services for speakers of the other official language. New Brunswick is the only officially bilingual province, while Quebec is officially French only, and the rest English. The extent of individual bilingualism in the two official languages varies from region to region, with some areas, for example parts of Ontario and the Maritime Provinces, having a high percentage of individuals who are bilingual in English and French. Although paradoxically composed largely of officially monolingual political units, Canada is actually rich in bilingualism – involving not just the main official languages but many others – at the community level. There are minority aboriginal communities, mostly in rural areas, who use their traditional languages as well as English or French, while in the cities – whether English or French predominates – there are numerous immigrant communities from Europe, Asia and elsewhere who use, to varying extents, their heritage languages alongside the official language(s) of the place where they live.

4 *Finland* is officially a bilingual country, with both Finnish and Swedish as official languages. However, in practice, bilingualism is geographically limited: though Finnish-speaking and Swedish-speaking Finns study each other's languages as school subjects, those who use both languages regularly in everyday life would mainly be found in certain areas of the country, in the west and south. Swedish speakers make up about 5 per cent of the total population. Municipalities are monolingual Swedish, monolingual Finnish, or officially bilingual, depending on the proportions of speakers of the two languages. At a community level, we find bilingualism in Finnish and other minority languages apart from Swedish: for example, the indigenous Sami languages of the north, and immigrant languages such as Somali in the urban areas.

5 *Singapore* is a unitary city-state with an ethnically-diverse population. Four languages are recognized officially: English, Chinese (which for official purposes means Mandarin Chinese), Malay and Tamil. English (known as the 'first language') is regarded as the ethnically-neutral language of the nation as a whole, and is a compulsory school subject and the language of administration. However, the other languages also receive official support – they are compulsory school subjects for children from the ethnic groups which speak them. Thus, in theory all Singaporeans know English and one other language, the language of what is deemed to be their own ethnic group. In practice, things are much more complicated. Singaporeans from the main ethnic groups may learn ethnic languages other than their own, and may in any case not have their designated ethnic 'mother tongue' as a home language. Thus for school purposes, the only recognized form of Chinese is Mandarin, but Singaporean Chinese actually use some other forms of Chinese – Teochew, Hakka Hokkien or Cantonese for example – at home. This means that ethnic Chinese Singaporeans may well be trilingual. Apart from Standard English, which for most Singaporeans is not a home language, a local vernacular variety of English, *Singlish*, is widely spoken, although stigmatized.

The multilingual complexity demonstrated by the examples above can be accounted for by a number of factors – federation, colonization, urbanization, transnational migration, marriage – some of which can equally well be found in some officially 'monolingual' states, whether geographically large (like the USA or Brazil) or small (like England or New Zealand). A framework for studying societal bilingualism therefore needs to be able to keep in focus both large-scale issues (for example, which languages are official and have power and authority at national or regional level) and fine details (the nuances of language choice in an encounter between family members of different generations).

Martin-Jones (1992: 15) points out that research into bilingual societies has been dominated by three major research paradigms: the *structural-functional*, the *micro-interactionist* and the *critical linguistic*. The earliest of the these approaches, the structural-functional, was developed by scholars like Weinreich (1953), Ferguson (1959) and Fishman (1967, 1972), who were preoccupied with accounting for the functional division between language varieties in bilingual communities and making comparisons, with a view to achieving a general understanding of the patterns of language use among bilinguals. The key concept within this approach to bilingualism is the notion of 'diglossia', which is discussed in detail below. The structural-functional perspective tended to be deterministic, to look at large social groupings such as whole nation-states, and to view bilingual societies as relatively static and homogeneous. In contrast to this, the interactionist perspective developed by Gumperz and others (e.g. Gumperz, 1982) focused on communication between individuals as the key to understanding societal bilingualism. It was within their day-to-day interactions that individual speakers would define and reproduce the symbolic values of the language within the community's own repertoire of languages (Martin-Jones, 1992: 16). Studies within this framework therefore generally focused on communicative events like interviews (Gumperz, 1982), service encounters, classroom talk, or everyday conversation (Auer, 1984), using detailed analysis of the interaction to reveal the actual practices, choices and patterns of language use within a bilingual community.

Neither of these research paradigms was particularly concerned with power relations, economics or the historical origins of the contemporary situations they studied, leading to criticisms that important aspects of the emergence and maintenance of bilingual communities were being overlooked. At this stage, a more critical paradigm, which treats power relations and history as central to understanding language behaviour, began to emerge within sociolinguistics, and a number of studies within the area of bilingualism exemplify this approach: for example, the work of Heller (e.g. 1999, 2002), Blommaert (e.g. 2005), Rampton (2004) and Jaffe (1999). Many of these studies drew of course on concepts and methodologies developed in the other research paradigms. Some recent studies (e.g. Codò, 2008) have combined interactionist methods with critical discourse analysis to provide critiques of public policy. Research on societal bilingualism can thus be said to have developed from the mainly descriptive (though by no means apolitical) to the critical and socially/politically engaged; however it would be true to say that at the present time, studies within all three paradigms (as well as combinations of these, and no doubt others not covered by this typology) are being carried out in different bilingual societies.

30.2 BILINGUALISM, BILITERACY AND MULTILINGUAL LITERACIES

Research into societal bilingualism has tended to focus on spoken language rather than written language, leading to an imbalance in the amount of attention paid to the spoken and literate modes in studies of societal bilingualism. Although literate practices are clearly of importance within many bilingual communities, early studies of bilingual literacy tended to treat it from a language acquisition or educational perspective, often in relation to learning a majority or official language. There were few studies of bilingual societies where literacy and literate practices were treated on a par with spoken bilingualism, for example, by exploring the role of literacies in different languages within the daily life of a community. The advent of the New Literacy Studies (Street, 1984; Barton, 2007) brought a new understanding of the role of literacies in everyday life, coupled with new qualitative research methods, such as ethnography, for studying them. Within this framework, there have been more studies of societal bilingualism which have either foregrounded literacy or have treated it as being on an equal footing with spoken language: see, for example, the studies in Martin-Jones and Jones (2000) and Hornberger (2003).

30.3 ORIGINS OF SOCIETAL BILINGUALISM

Contemporary societal bilingualism has complex and multiple origins. Frequently, one of two kinds of movement is involved – movement of people, or movement of national boundaries. These are discussed in more detail below. However, these certainly do not account for the origins of all bilingual societies. For example, Sorenson (1967) describes a large region in the Northwest Amazon where almost every individual is polylingual, knowing 'three, four, or more languages well'. The area is 'culturally homogeneous' but linguistically diverse, for a very specific reason – exogamous marriage is the norm in the region, and a 'tribe' is defined linguistically: thus, no one may marry an individual who has the same mother tongue as him/herself.

While this situation is certainly interesting, societal bilingualism, in most societies where it is currently found, has come about in some other way. Many of today's bilingual societies have come about through expansion or conquest, which has resulted in an indigenous population having to add a new language to their repertoire – frequently, though not always, through imposition from a more powerful group. Thus, for example, in the British Isles, speakers of Welsh, Scottish Gaelic, Irish Gaelic, Manx and Cornish have at different times become bilingual under pressure from English, as the speakers of English have expanded into and/or taken political power over their territories. Similar things have happened with indigenous minorities all over the world: they have been incorporated into centralized states and left with no option but to learn the national language. So, in many countries, we find bilingual linguistic minorities who have moved little or not at all from their traditional homelands. In other cases, territorial expansion has involved colonization, often resulting in the existence of a bilingual élite in the (former) colony who speak both the colonizer's language and their own indigenous language. Less frequently, colonization results in widespread bilingualism at all levels of society (Malta and Gibraltar provide examples of this).

A different kind of movement – the movement of national boundaries – may also produce bilingual linguistic minorities. This does not necessarily involve national expansion, but sometimes simply a division of territories, which may result in some people who are members of a linguistic majority on one side of the border becoming a minority on the other side of the border. This is a common situation in Europe, where political boundaries have often been redrawn following wars. Thus, for example, Alsace is a part of France where the vernacular language is a Germanic dialect (Alsatian). The boundary between 'French' and 'German' territories in this region has been redrawn many times over the last few centuries. Currently the people of Alsace find themselves within the French state and subject to the French education system, where French predominates, so those for whom Alsatian German is a home language are necessarily bilingual (Gardner-Chloros, 1991). Similarly the people of Corsica (Jaffe, 1999), whose ancestral language (Corsu) is closer to Italian than to French, live within the French state (which incorporated Corsica in the 18th century). While some minorities are able to maintain their community languages under such circumstances, 'language shift' (see below) is a very common consequence of the minoritization of the incorporated language, as it is in the cases just mentioned.

Movement of people is the other main source of societal bilingualism, but it can take many different forms. Some bilingual communities have resulted from forced displacement due to war, political instability or slavery, but most minority language communities today are probably the result of migration for economic reasons – whether this can be called 'voluntary' or not is a matter of interpretation. This migration may be internal – for example, from rural to urban areas – or across national boundaries. It may be on a very small scale, at least at first, but may gather momentum as time goes on, resulting in local linguistic minority communities which are sufficiently large to be self-sustaining and self-perpetuating. However, what happens in any specific case is dependent on complex sociohistorical factors that are subject to change, sometimes quite sudden change. For example, in the period from 2004, after Poland entered the European Union, there was a large influx of Polish speakers into both the United Kingdom and Ireland. In some parts of Britain there already existed Polish minority communities which had been established for some generations, although the individuals born in the last few decades were less likely to speak Polish, and might well be English-speaking monolinguals. The arrival of new Polish-speaking migrants has raised the profile of Polish culture in parts of Britain, bringing specialized Polish shops and even English–Polish bilingual road signs in some places. Meanwhile, although there is an increase in the number of Polish speakers, these new arrivals have mostly learnt some English at school in Poland and are likely to face fewer language barriers than the previous 'first generation'. What this illustrates is that in Britain, as in many countries, there is a constantly changing constellation of minority groups with differing linguistic repertoires and needs, which impact in various ways on the existing balance of languages within a multilingual state.

30.4 MEASURING SOCIETAL BILINGUALISM

It is important to consider how information about societal bilingualism is collected and documented, whether through official censuses and surveys or academic research. While pure intellectual curiosity and the desire to explain or predict patterns of change may be good enough reasons for studying bilingual communities, much of the information which is gathered is actually linked to the planning and allocation of resources in services such as education, health and welfare. Necessarily, there is an ideological aspect to all such information gathering. Decisions about what information to collect are rarely neutral. According to Haug (2003), there is a 'close relationship between a country's policy on ethnic, religious and language minorities and the availability of official statistical data, especially census data'.

In trying to judge the extent and nature of bilingualism within any one society, therefore, it is necessary to tread warily. Problems are typically of two kinds: (i) those related to the complexity of language itself, and (ii) those related to the attitudes of speakers and other social actors such as governments.

In the first category, we find issues such as a lack of clarity over language names and boundaries. Is 'Scots' just a dialect of English? Are people from Sylhet in Bengal speakers of Sylheti (a low-status variety of language) or Bengali (a relatively high-status language)? What of people who do not habitually speak one named codified language, but use several on a daily basis in a code-switching or language-mixing mode? Are creolized language varieties like Jamaican Creole or Mauritian Creole to be treated as distinct from their lexifier languages (English and French, respectively)? How 'well' must one speak a language to be able to claim to speak it? How much must one use it for it to be considered one's main language of communication?

Issues in the second category are often bound up with the first. Will speakers of Scots or Sylheti be disinclined to call themselves thus (because of the low status of these languages), and if they do so, will the collectors of language statistics account for them under those headings or simply put them down as speakers of English or Bengali? Authorities may find it convenient to overlook some languages, to 'pretend they do not exist' (an example of what Irvine and Gal (2000) call 'erasure') and to enhance others.

Allocation of resources in practice often means competition for resources. Under these circumstances, lack of information may be an advantage for some. In Belgium, which was constituted as a state in 1830, language information was collected in censuses from 1846 to 1947. After this, 'Belgium suppressed questions on language in the census in 1961/62 after the territorial boundaries of the language communities were defined' (Haug, 2003). It is now possible to know how many people **live** in the Walloon (French) and Flemish regions, but not what languages they speak. Thus the administrative status quo can be maintained, even if population movements change the

majority language in a particular locality. In England, there are no language questions on the national census at all, but in Wales a question is asked about knowledge of Welsh. In the United States, the census asks whether the respondent speaks a language other than English at home, and only in the case that the answer is 'yes', does it ask how well they speak English (US Census 2000 questionnaire long form, Question 11). The implication is that proficiency in the home language is not of interest, but proficiency in English is.

In Canada, despite the sensitivity of language issues, the census collects a lot of information about language. According to Statistics Canada, 'the long questionnaire contains questions on the first language learned in childhood, languages understood and spoken at home, as well as knowledge of official and non-official languages in the various regions of Canada' which will be 'used to establish programs to protect the rights of Canadians under the Canadian Charter of Rights and Freedoms' (Statistics Canada, 2001).

From the above selection of examples, it can be seen that official language surveys can serve a variety of purposes, some but not all of them benevolent. Surveys carried out by the academic research community, for example community and school-based surveys of linguistic minorities (e.g. Linguistic Minorities Project, 1985), are equally subject to practical, theoretical and methodological problems (see, for example, the critical account of the work of the Linguistic Minorities Project in Britain by Marilyn Martin-Jones (1991)). A potential problem with all types of survey is a tendency to essentialism (for example, treating ethnicity as a fixed, inherited attribute which also largely determines language) and reification of languages, i.e. starting from the viewpoint that languages are objects with relatively clear boundaries, which individuals select and use. In a critique of this view, Le Page (1994: 111) argues that it is more productive to 'start instead from the individual and examine in detail the linguistic behaviour of individuals toward each other in networks of relationship'. The outcome of this may be an understanding of a bi- or multilingual society which is at odds with any attempt to classify individuals as speakers of prespecified languages or members of particular 'speech communities'. As Freeland (2003: 243) puts it in her study of one 'plurilingual and interethnic' region, the Caribbean Coast of Nicaragua, individuals in this kind of complex situation are best described in terms of 'hybrid, dynamic identities, expressed multilingually'. This is just the sort of complicated relationship between language and individuals which is difficult to translate into statistics.

30.5 DIGLOSSIA

One of the key theoretical concepts in the study of societal bilingualism is 'diglossia'. This term was introduced into linguistics by Charles Ferguson (1959). Ferguson's original description of diglossia referred to a very specific type of bilingualism or bidialectalism, where a particular speech community used two related language varieties for different purposes. One variety would be used for formal and prestigious language activities, while the other would be associated with informal, everyday and low-prestige ones. Thus while the speakers would regard both varieties as in some sense 'the same language', the two would in practice be sharply differentiated in terms of their prestige and their functions.

Ferguson described four languages as what he called 'defining cases' of diglossia: Arabic (Classical Arabic and vernacular Arabic); French in Haiti (Standard French and Haitian Creole); Greek (Katharevousa and Dimotiki)[1] and German in Switzerland (High German and Swiss German). In each of these cases, there is a prestigious variety (which Ferguson called H, for 'high') which is associated with education, administration, literary works and formal speech situations. Equally, there is an L ('low') variety which is used in informal everyday speech and possibly a small number of other contexts. H and L have disjoint functions: where H is appropriate, L is inappropriate and vice versa. Furthermore, in a speech community where there is substantial social stratification, not everyone would necessarily have equal knowledge of both varieties. In particular, those with least opportunity for formal education would be likely to have little or no command of H, which would further disadvantage them and limit the activities in which they could engage.

Beyond this important similarity, all four speech communities have significant differences in the historical relationship between H and L, the contexts where they are used and the extent to which L is codified, standardized, appreciated or even acknowledged to exist. So, for example, whereas in Haiti Haitian Creole might, at least at one time, have been seen as stigmatized and a source of shame for its speakers, Swiss German has never been viewed as shameful, merely as a localized form which strongly symbolizes local identity but which is inappropriate for formal functions. Likewise, while L varieties are typically regarded as 'spoken' languages which are unsuited to writing, there is always the potential to develop an orthography for L, and this has in fact happened, to varying extents, in all four of Ferguson's defining cases. This has happened informally and unofficially in the case of some vernacular forms of Arabic, such as Egyptian, which have entered the written domain through the Internet and some printed media (Warschauer, El-Said and Zohry, 2002). It has happened formally and officially in the case of Haitian Creole, which, although still less prestigious than French, has been provided with an official orthography which has enabled it to encroach on French in written and public domains (Schieffelin and Doucet, 1994). The situation with Greek has changed radically alongside political changes in Greece (Horrocks, 1997), while Swiss German has also found a space on the Internet (Siebenhaar, 2006).

30.6 FISHMAN'S EXTENDED CONCEPT OF DIGLOSSIA

The essential characteristic of a diglossic relationship in Ferguson's terms is the existence of a clear distinction between H and L as regards the functions which they serve. Building on this, Joshua Fishman (1967) introduced an extended notion of diglossia, one where H and L need not be related varieties of one language but could be two dissimilar languages, as long as they were used for non-overlapping sets of functions. In fact, Fishman considered any community diglossic if there existed at least two functionally-differentiated stylistic registers, dialects, or languages (1972: 92). Many more speech communities could be described as 'diglossic' according to this model, including many former colonies of European countries where the former colonizer's language remained official and the indigenous languages were relatively underdeveloped for educational and administrative purposes.

Fishman also introduced the concept of **diglossia with or without bilingualism**, and **bilingualism with or without diglossia**. Some societies, such as Paraguay, could be said to be bilingual at all levels of society (in the case of Paraguay, in Spanish (H) and Guaraní (L)), but the languages are still kept apart in terms of prestige and function. This would be a case of **bilingualism with diglossia** (see Choi, 2005 for a more recent overview of bilingualism in Paraguay). Other diglossic communities might, nevertheless, have relatively little individual bilingualism, on the basis of 'one language for the rich, another for the poor'. In a true case of diglossia **without** bilingualism, the H variety would be mainly restricted to the élite, who would be the only ones with access to education. They would have to communicate with the rest of the population through intermediaries (such as semi-educated clerks or junior officials). While examples were common in the period of conquest and colonialism up to the mid-twentieth century, they are less common today. A more common situation – often a legacy of colonial language and education policies – is one where bilingualism is restricted to the élite (see, e.g. Pennycook, 1998; Blommaert, 1999). Though some members of the élite might not even be familiar with L, the majority would have some knowledge of L, which they would use in informal situations and to communicate with people from lower social classes. The bilinguals in this situation would therefore be the upper social classes, with the monolinguals being the most disadvantaged group in the society. The former Belgian central African colony of Rwanda, where the élite are bilingual in French and Kinyarwanda, and the rest of the population monolingual in Kinyarwanda, would be an example (Gafaranga, 2007). For further discussion of élite bilingualism, see De Mejía (2002) and also contributions to Ricento (2000).

A rather small number of speech communities could be said to be neither bilingual nor diglossic by Fishman's definition: the implication of this is that there is only one language in use, and that it has no differentiation between varieties in terms of prestige. There are currently very few if any independent nation-states that fulfil these criteria, although within individual speech communities, it may be true of those which have only one language and where there is little social stratification. The case of **bilingualism without diglossia** is also relatively rare: it implies a society where two languages are in regular use but without significant status differences between them. In practice, this means two high-status or prestige languages (since a community with a low-status language invariably has an H superimposed upon it even though few people have access to it). For examples, we need to look to societies where two developed and standardized languages are widely used in all areas of everyday life, with neither being considered superior overall to the other (it is possible of course, that one is considered more suitable than the other for some purposes). Canada as a federal state recognizing French and English as co-official languages is an example.

Fishman's model of diglossia can be applied not just at the level of nation-states but also at other levels of social and political organization. For example, within the Spanish state, historically diglossic relationships exist in several autonomous regions between Castilian (Spanish) and a regional language: Basque, Catalan and Galician. Language planning over the last three decades has been aimed at changing the diglossic relationship into one of equal status where either language can be used for any function: bilingualism without diglossia. Similarly, language planning in Wales, now a semi-autonomous region of the United Kingdom, has sought to raise the status of Welsh

so that it can coexist on a basis of equality with the former H language, English. Equally, in indigenous and migrant minority communities there may be a diglossic relationship between the community language (low status, used in the home/ informal situations) and the majority language (high status, used for prestigious functions). In fact the situation of Welsh could also have been described in this way, as Welsh is an indigenous minority language, spoken by about 20 per cent of the population of Wales, virtually all of whom also speak English. In migrant minority communities, especially in the second and subsequent generation, the community language (or 'heritage language') may become restricted to informal and in-group interactions, with the majority language taking on the role of H. Whether the community language in such circumstances could truly be said to lack prestige (i.e. to be a 'low' language) would be a matter for exploration in each individual case: for example, in some Welsh-medium secondary schools in Wales, Welsh has the traditional 'high' role (language of the classroom) while English is the language of the playground, the L language (Khleif, 1976).

30.7 DIGLOSSIA AND DOMAINS

The concept of 'domain' is central to the diglossic view of bilingualism. Each language is associated with characteristic (and non-overlapping) settings, known as domains, in which it is used either exclusively or predominantly: for example, the home, the school, religious institutions, media, etc. In this respect, diglossia theory can be seen as quite deterministic, with individual behaviour being determined by community norms for language use in each domain. This emphasis on domains as a key explanatory category led historically to research focusing on Fishman's question: 'Who speaks what language to Whom and when?' (1965). Early studies of societal bilingualism often tried to model language choice by means of decision trees, where the language used would be determined by such factors as domain, interlocutor, generation and formality. However, as Martin-Jones puts it (1991: 50), 'as the empirical work in bilingual communities has developed, it has become clear that the languages within the communicative repertoire of bilingual minority groups do not necessarily fall into a neat pattern of complementary distribution across domains'. In some bilingual societies, more than one language might typically be used in a particular domain, either for distinct functions or in a **code-switching** (q.v. Chapter 31) mode. Different generations of speakers may have different language competences and therefore behave differently in the same domain. Phenomena such as 'crossing' (using a language normally considered to 'belong' to a different ethnic group from that of the speaker) may occur in certain contexts, especially among adolescents (Rampton, 2004). Furthermore, domains themselves may be inventions of the researcher; members of the language community may not feel that their lives are neatly divided up in this way, and may behave accordingly, making an analysis in terms of domains very difficult. Nevertheless, the concept of domain has remained an important one in the study of societal bilingualism, and particularly in the understanding of **language shift and maintenance** (see Section 30.12).

30.8 THE STABILITY OF DIGLOSSIA

The concepts of bilingualism and diglossia together can be used to describe a wide range of types of monolingual and bilingual communities. But how stable are the situations that these labels apply to?

According to Ferguson (1959: 338), diglossia is a stable condition which may last for hundreds of years, although it may die out as a result of certain social changes over a long period, in particular an increase in literacy, better communications and social mobility and the emergence of a nationalistic movement with the vernacular as a unifying symbol. Yet within a decade of the publication of Ferguson's paper, the diglossic situation in Greece had altered, as Demotic (Dimotiki), the L language in terms of Ferguson's classic description, was made official and thus became acceptable in formal and prestigious functions. Katharevousa, the H, began to be restricted to a smaller and smaller range of domains. To understand how this came about it is necessary to understand the long history of the language question in Greece and the ideology and politics associated with the two varieties of Greek (see Horrocks, 1997 for an account of this). The important point is that diglossic relationships between languages or language varieties are indeed subject to change, possibly even rapid change when this is driven by historical forces. Fishman (1972: 105) regards communities which have bilingualism without diglossia as extremely unstable or transitional, the result of 'leaky' diglossia where one language 'leaks' into the functions associated with the other. Such situations can be taken as further evidence that any model of diglossic relationships between languages must be dynamic, allowing for changes in the nature of bilingualism in the community and the status of the language varieties concerned. In the particular case of bilingualism without diglossia, a stable state of bilingualism with two high-status languages is the desired outcome of language policy in a number of places around the world where there has previously been a diglossic relationship between the languages in question (see above).

30.9 FURTHER ELABORATIONS OF THE DIGLOSSIA CONCEPT

With an extended model of diglossia where diglossic relationships between languages can hold not only at a national but also at a regional and community level, it is possible to identify a number of elaborations and variations of Fishman's original model. For example, in Tanzania, Abdulaziz Mkilifi (1978) identified a form of 'triglossia'. At a national level, two languages, English and Kiswahili, had official status and were fairly widely spoken. However, of these two, English – the former language of colonial administration – was used for more prestigious functions and was associated with higher levels of education. Kiswahili, an indigenous lingua franca, had, in practice, lower status. However, at a local level, Kiswahili is the language of administration and first schooling and fulfils the functions of H with respect to the many indigenous vernacular languages, all of which are more localized, less developed and less prestigious than Kiswahili. According to Abdulaziz Mkilifi (1978: 134), the situation is the product of an 'intersection between two developing diglossic situations, one involving Swahili and some vernacular and the other involving Swahili and English', thus pointing again to the need for a dynamic model which takes into account the possibility of change.

Fasold (1984: 45) describes the Tanzanian situation as 'double-overlapping diglossia' and goes on to provide two further examples of elaborated forms of diglossia. The first of these he calls 'double-nested diglossia' and is exemplified by Khalapur, a rural village in India described by Gumperz (1964). In Khalapur, the H language is Hindi (one of the national languages of India), and the L is the local Khalapur vernacular, which is in fact a dialect of Hindi. The situation gains added complexity through the fact that both Hindi and the local Khalapur dialect themselves have 'high' and 'low' varieties distinguished on the usual criteria of prestige and suitability for formal or informal encounters. Thus the overall H–L distinction between Hindi and Khalapur dialect provides a matrix within which there is a continuum from the 'high high' of refined Hindi to the 'low low' of the informal variety of Khalapur dialect. An even more complex situation is the 'linear polyglossia' of English-educated Chinese communities in Malaysia, described by Fasold (1984: 48), on the basis of a description by Platt (1977). This may best be described as a language hierarchy in which formal Malaysian English lies at the top, followed by the standard form of the national language, Bahasa Malaysia (Malay), and then Mandarin Chinese. Below this comes the colloquial form of Malaysian English and other forms of Chinese. Lowest of all is Bazaar Malay, a lingua franca. Unlike the case of Khalapur, where there are 'nested' H and L versions of the same language, in the Malaysian case the formal or standard varieties of the languages, although ranked among themselves, are all at the top of the hierarchy, with the informal or low-prestige varieties of the same languages near the bottom.

30.10 BEYOND DIGLOSSIA: CRITIQUES OF DIGLOSSIA THEORY

Ferguson's initial description of diglossia, which limits it to situations where two varieties of a single language (as defined by the speech community) function as H and L, can be seen as applying to a specific, identifiable set of languages where the L but not the H is used as a home language, while the H language is acquired outside the home, through a process such as secular or religious education or enrolment in a priestly class. In most of Ferguson's classic cases, H and L are not sociolects differentiated by class; rather, as in German-speaking Switzerland, both H and L are used throughout the society, but in different situations. Although some people may not acquire H, due to lack of access to education, everyone who knows H will also know L, and when to use each variety. H and L are variant **registers**, not dialects (Hudson, 2002: 3, citing Ferguson, 1991: 222). By this account, diglossia is a sociolinguistic phenomenon which is not directly related to bilingualism at all, but it may be a **unitary** phenomenon with similar origins in different societies (Hudson, 2002: 15).

Fishman's extended model of diglossia is substantially different, as it allows for a wide range of bilingual situations to be called 'diglossic'. In doing so it proposes that the crucial distinction is essentially binary, and that practices (uses and values) are homogeneous throughout the society in question. Furthermore, it allows stylistic registers and dialects as well as languages to play a role in diglossia, suggesting that the functional differences between H and L may be a form of sociolectal variation. At this point, it could be argued, diglossia becomes a proxy for phenomena of social stratification and categorization which might be more insightfully accounted for by a less deterministic and more flexible framework, which takes into consideration, *inter alia*, the economic

status of different groups, power relations within the society, access to literacy and education, as well as communicative practices generally.

The lack of an account of power in either Ferguson's or Fishman's versions of the diglossia theory has been a major point of criticism. Early critiques came from a group of linguists working on minority languages within Europe. They developed what became known as the 'conflict tradition' in diglossia studies as a response to the way that the original definition of diglossia failed to take into account the 'origins of diglossia in social relations of inequality' (Martin-Jones, 1992: 15). These researchers were concerned with 'the ways in which divisions between linguistic groups are related to class divisions and to political and economic relations within the framework of the state', 'the processes involved in the imposition of power and the reproduction of power relations' and 'the nature of conflicts and social struggles generated by relations of power' (Martin-Jones, 1989: 118). Initially, this approach was applied to Catalan and Occitan (e.g. Aracil, 1965; Eckert, 1980; Woolard, 1989); later it was taken up by scholars working on Celtic languages (e.g. Williams, 1987 for Welsh; MacKinnon, 1984 for Scottish Gaelic). A characteristic of the conflict tradition is that it adopts the perspective of the dominated language; the researchers themselves are frequently native speakers of the languages concerned and involved in language campaigning at a grassroots level (Martin-Jones, 1989: 119). Linguists in this tradition coined the term 'normalization' for the reversal of the historic power imbalances (Aracil, 1965). The conflict tradition can be said to have had considerable influence on subsequent research, providing a basis for the emergence of a critical paradigm in research on societal bilingualism and informing debates surrounding minority and endangered languages (see, for example, many of the contributions to Duchêne and Heller, 2008).

Other elaborations of the diglossia concept have also tried to redress the omission of power relations: for example, Devonish's (2003) notion of 'Conquest Diglossia' – the type of diglossia found in former colonies of European countries (for example, in Jamaica) – where diglossia was a direct result of conquest by an external power rather than the result of differences in prestige among indigenous language varieties.

30.11 SOCIETAL BILINGUALISM AND THE ECONOMIC METAPHOR

By contrast, power relations are at the heart of the theories of language developed by the French anthropologist/sociologist Pierre Bourdieu.

Bourdieu refers to language as 'symbolic capital' which is unequally distributed among language users. Individuals can, and must, spend their linguistic capital in the symbolic marketplace, where 'the value of an utterance depends on the capacity of the various agents involved in the exchange to impose the criteria of appreciation most favourable to their own products' (1991: 67). Thus, the value of a particular language or language variety in a linguistic market depends on legitimation by the dominant group and dominant institutions, which can exercise 'symbolic domination' over the rest by means of language. In each linguistic market, a particular symbolic order is imposed, with certain varieties of language being delegitimized and others valorized: this is understood by all participants. As Bourdieu puts it, 'the whole social structure is present in each interaction' (1991: 67). Through institutions such as education and the mass media, the dominant group will reproduce the symbolic order. Heller (2005: 6) describes symbolic domination as 'masking and legitimizing relations of power': a symbolically dominated group will accept the marginalization of its own language and the valorization of that of the dominant group – the group which has power to 'impose the criteria of appreciation'.

Bourdieu's treatment of language as symbolic capital permits a nuanced view of bilingualism, with the value of language varieties depending on the symbolic order of the specific marketplace. For example, Heller's study (1999) of a French-language high school in the predominantly English Canadian province of Ontario showed that, in spite of French being the official language of the school, Canadian bilingual students massively flouted the French-only rule, preferring to use English outside class. Immigrant Francophones from former colonies tended to share the linguistic ideologies of the school and spoke the variety of French legitimated by the school – Standard French – but were marginalized among the student body because of their lack of English. At the same time, bilinguals who were speakers of English and French Canadian Vernacular were marginalized, because their French was of a stigmatized variety (1999: 27).

The economic metaphor helps to explain how, as the monetary economy globalizes, language, and bilingualism in particular, can become 'commodified', i.e. treated as tradable goods undifferentiated by quality. Sometimes this commodified bilingualism can offer unexpected opportunities. Thus, women migrants from countries with strong traditions of English as a second language, such as the Philippines and some African countries like Kenya (see Verra, 2008), may find themselves with language skills which are in demand from European families who want English-speaking carers for their children. The commodification of French–English bilingual language skills in Canada has been studied by Heller and associates (Heller, 2002), who found that the existence of large numbers of French–English bilinguals in particular areas was attractive to businesses, in particular call centres which needed bilingual operators. However, bilingualism was now less likely to be valued as a skill to be paid for and instead treated as a 'talent to be prized (as one might prize punctuality and neatness) but not to be recognized or remunerated' (Heller 2005: 6).

30.12 LANGUAGE SHIFT AND LANGUAGE MAINTENANCE

Language shift and maintenance have been a major focus of research in the area of societal bilingualism. Where language shift affects the **entire** community of speakers of a language, it becomes a case of language endangerment or language death (as documented, for example, in Dorian's study of language attrition in a Scottish Gaelic-speaking area in Scotland (1981). However, language shift may also affect only some speakers of a language, in particular those who form a minority within a larger entity where another language is dominant: typically, migrant minority communities. Thus, while a language like Cantonese, with around 55 million speakers according to *Ethnologue* (Lewis 2009), cannot reasonably be described as 'endangered' even if there are some pressures on it, it is quite possible that Cantonese will cease to be used in some countries where it is a minority language (for example, Britain) as its speakers shift to the majority language.

An early important study of language shift was Gal's (1979) study of Oberwart, a German/Hungarian-speaking town in Austria. From being predominantly Hungarian-speaking at the time of the breakup of the Austro-Hungarian empire, Oberwart had become predominantly German-speaking 50 years later. Gal approached the question of language shift in Oberwart through an ethnographic study, observing the language in which actual interactions took place and collecting information about the social networks of her participants. Her research showed that there was some predictability regarding which language a bilingual would use in a given interaction: the main determinant was the social identity of the interlocutor. Older interlocutors, and those who were regarded as more 'peasant' and less 'urbanized', were more likely to be addressed in Hungarian. The more peasants in a person's social network, the more they were likely to use Hungarian.

Thus, Gal established that social networks had an important role in determining language shift and maintenance.

Li Wei's (1994) study of the Chinese community of Newcastle-upon-Tyne, England, also showed the importance of social networks in language shift. Li Wei's study was based on research carried out within family homes. Older women, who were recent immigrants, were most likely to use Chinese, while the youngest generation of British-born children were most likely to be dominant in, and have a preference for, English. Beyond this broad generalization about language shift in progress, however, a more detailed picture could be discerned by looking at social networks. Individuals who had most interaction with English speakers were those who developed most proficiency in English, which enabled them to interact better with English speakers. Individuals who interacted least with the majority community had least opportunity to learn English, which in turn prevented them from becoming more proficient. Furthermore, the strength of Chinese-based networks had an important effect on the extent of maintenance of Chinese; for example, one network within the community had ties to the same place of origin and attended the same church and used Chinese more and with a wider range of interlocutors.

Language shift invariably involves an intermediate stage of bilingualism, which may be relatively short – a generation or two for some migrant communities – or endure for centuries. Even in the latter case, the decisive change, from a bilingual majority to a monolingual majority, may happen rapidly (as in the case of Irish Gaelic, supplanted by English), in the course of one or two generations. It is tempting to treat the economic metaphor of Bourdieu rather literally and say that the major cause of language shift is the overwhelming marketplace value of certain languages when compared with others, but the truth is that it is not **necessary** to give up a language in order to acquire a new one, a fact demonstrated clearly by the existence of societies which remain stably bilingual over long periods. Therefore, while there is no doubt that economic factors are very important in language shift, any approach to this topic needs to be more nuanced, taking into account the exact mechanisms whereby communities, families and individuals gradually become first bilingual and then monolingual. So, for example, Gal found that the preference for German in Oberwart was connected with an increasingly positive view of the social identity of 'industrial worker', associated with German, as opposed to the identity of 'peasant farmer', associated with Hungarian. But this preference translated itself into language shift in very specific ways; for example, as male Hungarian-speaking peasant farmers could not find wives in their own community they were forced to marry German-speaking women from the surrounding area, because women from Hungarian-speaking peasant backgrounds preferred a German-speaking, urbanized lifestyle. With German established as the 'mother tongue' of the peasant family, it was less likely that Hungarian would be passed on to the next generation (Gal, 1978).

In a very different setting, Kulick (1992) studied language shift in Gapun, a village in Papua New Guinea. The traditional language of the village, Taiap, had largely been abandoned by its speakers in favour of Tok Pisin (New Guinea Pidgin, an official language and nationwide lingua franca). Although the village had grown, the number of Taiap speakers had dwindled, with boys being least competent in Taiap. Kulick found that each language had been associated with a different set of attributes within the traditional culture of the village: Taiap with *hed*, the individualistic, selfish, irascible and proud aspect of personality; and Tok Pisin with *save*, 'knowledge', the sociable, cooperative side of a person. Whereas once these traditional concepts had been articulated through the medium of Taiap, now

> ' ... what was once a dual concept of personhood subsumed under one language has become a duality split along linguistic lines. *Hed* has become linked to the vernacular, which in turn has associations with women, the ancestors, and the past. *Save*, on the other hand, has come to be expressed through and by Tok Pisin, which in turn is strongly associated with men, the Catholic church, and modernity'
>
> (Kulick, 1992: 20).

Since *hed* is regarded as childish, maturation is seen as involving a movement from *hed* to *save*; hence Tok Pisin is strongly foregrounded in speech directed at children, particularly boys. This preference for using Tok Pisin, the vehicle of *save*, in interaction with children was the key to understanding language shift in Gapun.

From the perspective of social psychology, Giles, Bourhis and Taylor (1977) developed the concept of 'ethnolinguistic vitality', which can be applied to situations of language maintenance and shift. Three sets of factors are involved in determining the ethnolinguistic vitality of a language community:

- **status** (including access to political power, social status, history and status of the community language)
- **demography** (size of the group, how densely or sparsely its members are distributed over the

area where they live, birth rate and patterns of migration, etc.)

- **institutional support** (support within mass media, education and other social institutions).

All of these factors, according to Giles et al., could be hypothesized to impact on the vitality of the group and hence on its language. 'Ethnolinguistic vitality' attempts to provide a framework for using external, and relatively measurable, factors, to assess the likelihood of language maintenance or shift. Bourhis et al. (1981) further introduced the idea of subjective ethnolinguistic vitality, reflecting the fact that group members' perceptions of their own ethnolinguistic vitality are often very different from an assessment based on the 'objective' factors set out by Giles et al. The concept of ethnolinguistic vitality has been further developed and widely applied to different situations, but also criticized: for example, for failing to take into account the issues of power and ideology which underlie notions like 'status' (Williams, 1992, Chapter 8) and for its oversimplification of complex and problematic concepts like 'identity' (Atkinson, 2000) and 'ethnicity', and the relations between these (see Pavlenko and Blackledge, 2004: 4–8 for a more detailed critique). A new research approach, 'Multilingual Landscapes', has developed since 1997 from within this framework (see Section 30.13). (A range of other frameworks for language vitality is discussed by Sallabank (in this volume.)

To conclude, research indicates that social networks are important for understanding language shift and maintenance. However, they do not necessarily provide the whole story; language ideologies and 'the relationship between language and identity' are also potentially important as 'complementary sources of explanation for language choice and language maintenance' (Lanza and Svendsen, 2007) among multilingual communities, and any research approach to language shift needs to be sufficiently nuanced to capture this complexity.

30.13 NEW DIRECTIONS IN BILINGUALISM RESEARCH

In this section I will look at some recent developments in the research on societal bilingualism.

Linguistic ethnography

The emerging mainly British research approach of 'linguistic ethnography' holds that 'language and social life are mutually shaping, and that close analysis of situated language use can provide both fundamental and distinctive insights into the mechanisms and dynamics of social and cultural production in everyday activity' (Rampton et al., 2004: 2). Linguistic ethnography is described by Rampton (2007: 585) not as a paradigm, but 'a site of encounter where a number of established lines of research interact' under an 'overarching intellectual warrant'. It owes much to an earlier American tradition of linguistic anthropology, which has no British counterpart. The lines of research mentioned by Rampton include several which have already contributed significantly to research in the field of societal bilingualism: interactional sociolinguistics (Gumperz, 1982), the new literacy studies, and critical discourse analysis (the others mentioned are neo-Vygotskian research on language and cognitive development, and interpretive applied linguistics for language teaching). A number of the studies mentioned above might be said to be either within this framework or in sympathy with it (e.g. Heller, 1999; Jaffe, 1999; Rampton, 2004; Codò, 2008;) and it is likely to continue to make important contributions to research in societal bilingualism.

Bilingualism on the Internet and in other digital media

The growth of communication via new media has enabled not only more multilingual communication but also new types of multilingualism, of which research has only scratched the surface. Web pages, newsgroups, chat rooms, instant messaging, text messaging, blogs and social networking sites are all potential sites for bilingual interactions; in some cases this is because of the involvement of global languages like English and French as Internet lingua francas, but often the participants concerned are reflecting local (or diasporic) practices of societal bilingualism (see Lam and Rosario-Ramos, 2009). Whether these multilingual Internet communications should be described as 'societal bilingualism' is a moot point; certainly, multilingual 'communities of practice' are quite common on the Internet, though there is relatively little research to date: see Barton and Lee, (this volume); Androutsopoulos (2007) and Danet and Herring (2007) for overviews.

Urban bilingualism studies

In the early period of research into societal bilingualism, attention tended to focus either on entire states or regions (a 'macro' approach), or on individual communities (a 'micro' approach). The latter were typically indigenous or migrant ethnic minority communities and would be investigated in detail, but without much reference to other minorities who might live alongside them. More recently, there has been a move towards focusing on urban communities in a different sense – the sense of 'neighbourhoods' – and the histories, narratives, practices and networks which construct them as distinctive multilingual linguistic spaces. Examples of this approach are McCormick (2002) and Blommaert et al. (2005). A different approach, which follows young multilinguals through their different activities in a city, capturing their language practices in different sites, is taken by Patricia Lamarre's project (2006–10) *Montréal multilingue: an ethnographic study of the language practices of young multilinguals in a city redefined* (see Lamarre and Lamarre 2009). This interest in the multilingual city is also reflected in the Linguistic Landscapes approach (see below).

Linguistic landscapes

Further evidence of the interest in cities as multilingual spaces is the development of a new research tradition exploring multilingual linguistic landscapes. According to Landry and Bourhis (1997: 25), the linguistic landscape consists of 'the language of public road signs, advertising billboards, street names, place names, commercial shop signs, and public signs on government buildings'. The significance of the landscape is that 'the presence or absence of the in-group language in the linguistic landscape is related to how much speakers use their in-group language with family members, friends, neighbors and store clerks; in social gatherings; in cultural activities; and as consumers of in-group language [...] media' (Landry and Bourhis, 1997: 45). This approach developed originally within the framework of 'ethnolinguistic vitality', but has its limitations: in spite of what Landry and Bourhis say in the quote above, it is clear that the extent of use of languages **in general** cannot be directly related to the presence of those languages in fixed signage, partly because not all written languages have equal access to written spaces, and partly because some languages are not written at all. Furthermore, the visual impact of languages in the environment is not limited to fixed signage (Stroud 2009, Sebba 2010) and is subject to manipulation and management to meet ideological and policy objectives (Leeman and Modan 2009). However, the idea of 'multilingual landscapes' could also be taken as an invitation to carry out visual ethnographies of textually mediated cityscapes, using

photography as a principal fieldwork method, and to recognise these visual environments as linguistic resources for identity construction (Curtin 2009). A number of studies have been published so far, including two collections (Gorter 2006, Shohamy and Gorter 2008) and a book (Backhaus 2007), with a third to appear (Jaworski and Thurlow, 2010).

NOTE

1 It is important to realize that Ferguson was discussing the situation of Greece at the time he was writing. Since the 1970s, Dimotiki has become the official as well as the everyday form of Greek, with Katharevousa being restricted increasingly to a narrow range of contexts.

REFERENCES

Abdulaziz Mkilifi, M. H. (1978) 'Triglossia and Swahili–English bilingualism in Tanzania', in J. Fishman. (ed.), *Advances in the Study of Societal Multilingualism*, The Hague: Mouton. pp. 129–52.

Androutsopoulos, J. (2007) 'Bilingualism in the mass media and on the Internet', in M. Heller, (ed.), *Bilingualism: a Social Approach*. London: Palgrave Macmillan. pp. 207–30.

Aracil, L.V. (1965) *Conflit linguistique et normalisation linguistique dans l'Europe nouvelle*. Nancy: Centre Européen Universitaire.

Atkinson, D. (2000) 'Minoritisation, identity and ethnolinguistic Vitality in Catalonia', *Journal of Multilingual and Multicultural Development* 21(3): 185–97.

Auer, J. C. P. (1984) *Bilingual Conversation*. Amsterdam: John Benjamins.

Backhaus, P. (2007) *Linguistic Landscapes: A Comparative Study of Urban Multilingualism in Tokyo*. Clevedon, UK: Multilingual Matters.

Barton, D. (2007) *Literacy: An Introduction to the Ecology of Written Language*. 2nd edn. Oxford: Blackwell.

Blommaert, J. (1999) *State Ideology and Language in Tanzania*. Cologne: Rudiger Koeppe.

Blommaert, J. (2005) 'Situating linguistic rights: English and Swahili in Tanzania revisited', *Journal of Sociolinguistics*, 9(3): 390–417.

Blommaert, J., Collins, J. and Slembrouck, S. (2005) 'Polycentricity and interactional regimes in "global neighborhoods"', *Ethnography*, 6(2): 205–35.

Bourdieu, P. (1991) *Language and Symbolic Power*. Cambridge: Polity Press.

Bourhis, R., Giles, H. and Rosenthal, D. (1981) 'Notes on the construction of a "subjective vitality questionnaire" for ethnolinguistic groups', *Journal of Multilingual and Multicultural Development*, 2(2): 145–55.

Choi, J. K. (2005) 'Bilingualism in Paraguay: forty years after Rubin's study', *Journal of Multilingual and Multicultural Development*, 26(3): 233–48.

Codò, Eva (2008) *Immigration and Bureaucratic Control: Language Practices in Public Administration*. Berlin: Mouton de Gruyter.

Cummins, J. and Hornberger, N. H. (eds) (2008) *Encyclopedia of Language and Education*. 2nd edn. Vol. 5, Bilingual education. New York: Springer.

Curtin, Melissa L. (2008) ''Languages on display: indexical signs, identities, and the linguistic landscape of Taipei''. In Shohamy and Gorter, 221–237.

Danet, B. and Herring, S. C. (eds) (2007) *The Multilingual Internet: Language, Culture and Communication Online*. Oxford: Oxford University Press.

De Mejia, A.-M. (2002) *Power, Prestige and Bilingualism: International Perspectives on Elite Bilingual Education*. Clevedon, UK: Multilingual Matters.

Devonish, H. (2003) 'Language advocacy and ''conquest'' diglossia in the ''Anglophone'' Caribbean, in C. Mair, (ed.), *The Politics of English as a World Language: New Horizons in Postcolonial Cultural Studies*. New York: Rodopi. pp. 257–77.

Dorian, N. (1981) *Language Death: The Life Cycle of a Scottish Gaelic Dialect*. Philadelphia: University of Pennsylvania Press.

Duchêne, A. and Heller, M. (eds) (2008) *Discourses of Endangerment: Ideology and Interest in the Defence of Languages*. London: Continuum.

Eckert, P. (1980) 'Diglossia: separate and unequal', *Linguistics*, 18: 1053–64.

Fasold, R. (1984) *The Sociolinguistics of Society*. Oxford: Blackwell.

Ferguson, C. (1959) 'Diglossia', *Word*, 15: 325–340.

Ferguson, C. (1991) 'Diglossia revisited', *Southwest Journal of Linguistics*, 10(1): 214–234.

Fishman, J. (1965) '''Who speaks what language to whom and when?''', *La Linguistique*, 2: 67–88. Reprinted in Li Wei (ed.) (2006) *The Bilingualism Reader*. London: Routledge. pp. 55–74.

Fishman, J. (1967) 'Bilingualism with and without diglossia; diglossia with and without bilingualism', *Journal of Social Issues*, 32(2): 29–38.

Fishman, J. (1972) 'Societal bilingualism: stable and transitional', in A. S. Dil (ed.), *Language in Sociocultural Change*. Stanford, CA: Stanford University Press. pp. 135–52.

Freeland, J. (2003) 'Intercultural-bilingual education for an interethnic-plurilingual society? The case of Nicaragua', *Comparative Education*, 39(2): 239–60.

Gafaranga, J. (2007) *Talk in Two Languages*. Basingstoke: Palgrave Macmillan.

Gal, S. (1978) 'Peasant men can't get wives: language change and sex roles in a bilingual community', *Language in Society*, 7: 1–16.

Gal, S. (1979) *Language Shift: Social Determinants of Linguistic Change in Bilingual Austria*. New York: Academic Press.

Gardner-Chloros, P. (1991) *Language Selection and Switching in Strasbourg*. Oxford: Clarendon Press.

Giles, H., Bourhis, R. Y. and Taylor, D. M. (1977) 'Towards a theory of language in ethnic group relations', in H. Giles (ed.), *Language, Ethnicity, and Intergroup Relations*. New York: Academic Press. pp. 307–48.

Gorter, D. (ed.) (2006) *Linguistic Landscape: A New Approach to Multilingualism*. Clevedon, UK: Multilingual Matters.

Gumperz, J. J. (1964), 'Linguistic and social interaction in two communities', *American Antropologist*, 66:2, 137–53.

Gumperz, J. (1982) *Discourse Strategies*. Cambridge: Cambridge University Press.

Haug, W. (2003) 'Ethnic, religious and language groups: towards a set of rules for data collection and statistical analysis', *Eumap Online Journal*. Accessed 9 December 2008 at: http://www.eumap.org/journal/features/2003/april/ethrellangroups.

Heller, M. (1999) *Linguistic Minorities and Modernity: A Sociolinguistic Ethnography*. London: Longman.

Heller, M. (2002) 'Globalization and the commodification of bilingualism in Canada', in D. Block and D. Cameron (eds), *Globalization and Language Teaching*. London: Routledge. pp. 47–64.

Heller, M. (2005) 'Language, skill and authenticity in the globalized new economy', *Noves SL. Revista de Sociolingüística*, Winter 2005. Accessed 18 December 2008 at: http://www.gencat.cat/llengua/noves.

Helot, C. and De Mejia, A.-M. (eds) (2008). *Forging Multilingual Spaces Integrating Perspectives on Majority and Minority Bilingual Education*. Bristol: Multilingual Matters.

Hornberger, N. H. (ed.) (2003) *Continua of Biliteracy: An Ecological Framework for Educational Policy, Research, and Practice in Multilingual Settings*. Clevedon, UK: Multilingual Matters.

Horrocks, G. C. (1997) *Greek: A History of the Language and its Speakers*. London: Longman.

Hudson, A. (2002) '''Outline of a theory of diglossia''', *International Journal of the Sociology of Language*, 157: 1–48.

Hvenekilde, A. and Nortier, J. (eds) (2001) *Meetings at the Crossroads. Studies of Multilingualism and Multiculturalism in Oslo and Utrecht*. Oslo: Novus.

Irvine, J. T. and Gal, S. (2000) 'Language ideology and linguistic differentiation', in P. V. Kroskrity (ed.), *Regimes of Language: Ideologies, Polities and Identities*. Oxford, James Currey. pp. 35–83.

Jaffe, A. (1999) *Ideologies in Action: Language Politics on Corsica*. Berlin: Mouton de Gruyter.

Jaworski, A. and C. Thurlow (eds.) (forthcoming) *Semiotic Landscapes: Text, Space, Globalization*. London: Continuum.

Khleif, B. B. (1976) 'Cultural regeneration and the school: an anthropological study of Welsh-medium schools in Wales, *International Review of Education*, 22(2): 177–92.

Kulick, D. (1992) *Language Shift and Cultural Reproduction: Socialization, Self, and Syncretism in a Papua New Guinean Village*. Cambridge: Cambridge University Press.

Lamarre, P. and Lamarre, S. (2009): Montréal ''on the move'': pour une approche ethnographique non-statique de l'étude des pratiques langagières de jeunes multilingue. In T. Bulot (dir.) with collaboration of A. Lounici, *Formes & normes* sociolinguistiques (Ségrégations et discriminations urbaines). Paris, L'Harmattan.

Leeman, J. and Modan, G. (2009) 'Commodified language in Chinatown: a contextualized approach to linguistic landscape'. Journal of Sociolinguistics, 13/3, 2009: 332–362.

Lewis, M. P. (ed.), (2009) Ethnologue: Languages of the World, Sixteenth edition. Dallas, Tex.: SIL International. Online version: www.ethnologue.com/.

Lam, W. S. E. and Rosario-Ramos, E. (2009) 'Multilingual literacies in transnational digitally-mediated contexts: an exploratory study of immigrant teens in the U.S.', Language and Education, 23(2): 171–190.

Landry, R. and Bourhis, R. Y. (1997) 'Linguistic landscape and ethnolinguistic vitality: an empirical study', Journal of Language and Social Psychology, 16: 23–49.

Lanza, E. and Svendsen, B. A. (2007) 'Tell me who your friends are and I might be able to tell you what language(s) you speak: Social network analysis and multilingualism', International Journal of Bilingualism, 11(3): 275–300.

Le Page, R. B. (1994) 'The notion of "linguistic system" revisited', International Journal of the Sociology of Language, 109: 109–120.

Li, W. (1994) Three Generations, Two Languages, One Family: Language Choice and Shift in a Chinese Community in Britain. Clevedon, UK: Multilingual Matters.

Linguistic Minorities Project (1985) 'Adult language use: preparing a survey', in The Other Languages of England. London: Routledge. pp. 134–79.

McCormick, K. (2002) Language in Cape Town's District Six. Oxford: Oxford University Press.

MacKinnon, K. (1984) 'Power at the periphery: the language dimension and the case of Gaelic Scotland', Journal of Multilingual and Multicultural Development, 5(6): 491–511.

Martin-Jones, M. (1989) 'Language, power and linguistic minorities; the need for an alternative approach to bilingualism, language maintenance and shift', in R. Grillo, (ed.), Social Anthropology and the Politics of Language. London: Routledge. pp. 106–25.

Martin-Jones M. (1991) 'Sociolinguistic surveys as a source of evidence in the study of bilingualism: a critical assessment of survey work conducted among linguistic minorities in three British cities', in K. de Bot and W. Fase (eds), Migrant languages in Western Europe. International Journal of the Sociology of Language. Vol. 90.

Martin-Jones, M. (1992) 'Minorities and Sociolinguistics', in W. Bright, (ed.), International Encyclopedia of Linguistics 4. Oxford: Oxford University Press. pp. 15–18.

Martin-Jones, M. and Jones K. (eds) (2000) Multilingual Literacies: Reading and Writing Different Worlds. Amsterdam: John Benjamins.

Pavlenko, A. and Blackledge, A. (eds) (2004) Negotiation of Identities in Multilingual Contexts. Clevedon, UK: Multilingual Matters.

Pennycook, A. (1998) English and the Discourses of Colonialism. London: Routledge.

Platt, J. T. (1977) 'A model for Polyglossia and Multilingualism' (with Special Reference to Singapore and Malaysia), Language in Society, 6, 3, 361–78.

Rampton, B. (2004) Crossing: Language and Ethnicity Among Adolescents. 2nd edn. Manchester: St. Jerome Publishing.

Rampton, B. (2007) 'Neo-Hymesian linguistic ethnography in the United Kingdom', Journal of Sociolinguistics, 11(5) 2007: 584–607.

Rampton, B., Tusting, K., Maybin, J. et al. (2004) UK linguistic ethnography: a discussion paper. Unpublished discussion paper. Accessed 23 December 08 at: http://www.ling-ethnog.org.uk/documents/discussion_paper_jan_05.pdf.

Ricento, T. (ed.) (2000) Ideology, Politics and Language Policies: Focus on English. Amsterdam: John Benjamins.

Romaine, S. (2005) 'The bilingual and multilingual community', in T. K. Bhatia and W.C. Ritchie (eds), Handbook of Bilingualism. Oxford: Blackwell. pp. 385–405.

Schieffelin, B. B. and Doucet, R. C. (1994) 'The "real" Haitian Creole: ideology, metalingusitics and orthographic choice', American Ethnologist, 21: 176–200.

Sebba, M. (2010) 'Discourses in Transit', in Jaworski and Thurlow (eds).

Shohamy, E. and Gorter, D. (eds) (2008). Linguistic Landscape: Expanding the Scenery. London: Routledge.

Siebenhaar, B. (2006) 'Code choice and code-switching in Swiss–German Internet Relay Chat rooms', Journal of Sociolinguistics, 10(4): 481–506.

Sorenson, A.P., Jr. (1967) 'Multilingualism in the Northwest Amazon', American Anthropologist, 69: 670–84.

Statec (Statistical portal of Luxemburg) (2008): Etat de la population. Accessed 9 December 2008 at: http://www.statistiques.public.lu/stat/TableViewer/tableViewHTML.aspx?ReportId=463&IF_Language=fra&MainTheme=2&FldrName=1.

Statistics Canada/Statistique Canada (2001) Content of the 2001 Census questionnaires. Accessed 9 December 2008 at: http://www12.statcan.ca/english/census01/Info/content.cfm#questions .

Street, B. (1984) Literacy in Theory and Practice. Cambridge: Cambridge University Press.

US Census 2000 questionnaire, long form. Accessed 9 December 2008 at: http://www.census.gov/dmd/www/pdf/d02p.pdf .

Verra, M. (2008) 'One community, two countries, many languages: the Kenyan community in Greece'. Unpublished PhD thesis, Lancaster University.

Warschauer, M., El-Said, G. and Zohry, A. (2002) 'Language choice online: globalization and identity in Egypt', Journal of Computer-Mediated Communication, 7(4).

Weinreich, U. (1953) Languages in Contact: Findings and Problems. The Hague: Mouton.

Williams, G. (1987) 'Bilingualism, class dialect and social reproduction', International Journal of Sociology of Language, 66: 85–98.

Williams, G. (1992) Sociolinguistics: a Sociological Critique. London: Routledge.

Woolard, K. (1989) Double Talk: Bilingualism and the Politics of Ethnicity in Catalonia. Stanford, CA: Stanford University Press.

Code-switching/mixing

Peter Auer

31.1 TERMINOLOGICAL AND OTHER PRELIMINARIES

Whereas humans have doubtlessly been switching codes for as long as there have been bilinguals, the phenomenon of code-switching has only received attention in linguistics, from the mid-1950s onwards – Alvarez Cáccamo (1998) traces the first mention of the term back to Vogt (1954) – and large-scale research on code-switching did not start before the late 1970s. Of course it had not escaped previous research on language contact that speakers switch between languages (cf. Paul's chapter on 'language mixture', 1898: 365–77); however, this was considered an externally-induced mishap due entirely to psychological or social factors (incompetence, laziness, lack of education) which did not merit linguistic investigation and was, in any case, temporary ('man wird von der Zweisprachigkeit wieder zur Einsprachigkeit gelangen' [one will arrive at monolingualism from bilingualism in the end], Paul, 1898: 366). In the light of this neglect, we can doubtlessly discover a monolingual bias which was characteristic of linguistics for a long time: the beginnings of the discipline (in the early nineteenth century) coincided – not by chance – with the triumph of the nation-state with its ideology of 'one nation–one language'. In this ideology, multilingual language use had no place (Auer, 2007a; Heller, 2007; Pujolar, 2007), even though forms of language contact (borrowing in particular, but also pidgin and creole formation) did. The enormous interest code-switching and related practices have found in linguistics over the last three decades is at least in part (i.e. in addition to internal developments in linguistics) due to the demise of the monolingual national language ideologies which have become more and more unrealistic in the age of globalization, transnationalism and migration. Today, multilingual practices are an undisputed everyday phenomenon, even in the European nation-states which hitherto considered themselves to be monolingual (see Stroud, 2007 for a view beyond Europe).

Despite three decades of intensive research, the field is still lacking an accepted terminology, and there are serious disputes about issues that are partly terminological in nature. It is therefore necessary to start by clarifying the terminology used here before discussing the subject matter itself.

There is general agreement that a distinction needs to be made between bilingualism as the mental ability to speak two languages, and the practice of doing so. Even though it is rare (and usually the result of an oppressive, nationalistic language policy), it can happen that a bilingual speaker exclusively performs (and passes) as a monolingual. Far more common is 'bilingual talk', particularly when two or more participants are bilingual in the same languages. In bilingual talk, the two languages in the speaker's mind are put to use in such a way that his or her bilingualism becomes a visible interactional and social fact. In the concatenation of linguistic elements for a larger unit, if elements of both language A and language B occur in juxtaposition, we speak of 'code-switching/mixing' (see Section 31.3, for a definition of these two terms). 'Concatenation' can refer to any syntagmatic combination, such as the sequencing of conversational turns within an interactional episode, the sequencing of turn constructional units within a turn at talk, or the linking of words within an independent syntactic unit ('sentence') or morphemes within a word. There are other features of bilingual talk which are usually not included under the heading code-switching/mixing, such as interferences; for instance, a phonetic or a prosodic feature of language B may be used in a word from language A, or in a sequence of words from language A. In sum, code-switching/mixing implies the use of elements from more than one language in the formulation process, where these elements are at the level of the morpheme or higher (lower threshold), and occur within a unit that must not be larger than the interactional episode (upper threshold).

Obviously, both the upper and the lower thresholds are somewhat fuzzy. Restricting code-switching/mixing to practices **within** an interactional episode excludes language choice **for** an episode (in the sense of an 'encounter'; see Goffmann, 1963 for the complexities involved in determining the boundaries of such units). The lower level is debatable, too. For instance, some researchers have argued that – contrary to borrowing – code-switching/mixing is not possible word-internally (Poplack's free morpheme constraint (1980); see also the discussion below), while others have argued against this restriction (e.g. Berruto, 2005). On the other hand, there are cases where one might argue that a shift of prosody or the ad hoc use of a foreign sound (such as a 'French' uvular fricative /R/ in the coda by a speaker of Italian which usually has apical /r/) may indeed show all the functional qualities of code-switching (Alvarez Cáccamo, 1998). However, such a wide notion of code-switching has not seen general use in linguistics.

Another problem is the meaning of 'code' in code-switching. In the preceding paragraph, we started from the presupposition that the codes of code-switching/mixing are what are usually called languages ('English', 'Swahili', 'Basque', ...). Given the notorious difficulties in distinguishing languages from other varieties, such as dialects, and the danger of equating languages with standard languages, it is more fitting to think of codes in terms of varieties. (In Section 31.3 it is argued that this definition is not entirely adequate either.) There is no a priori linguistic reason to treat code-switching/mixing between, say, Catalan and Castilian (generally considered to be languages) differently from code-switching/mixing between Bavarian (generally considered to be a dialect of German) and Standard German – the structural difference is roughly the same, and comparatively small. However, different forms of switching/mixing may occur between closely-related varieties. They are linked to another problem that to be kept in mind: the orthodox way of dealing with code-switching/mixing implies that the transition from language A into language B is abrupt. There is a precisely defined point in speech at which a set of co-occurring linguistic features (variety A) is exchanged for another set of features (variety B).

Orthodox switching/mixing:

Time   ---------------------------→

Variety A   ─────────┐
               │
Variety B   └────────

In reality, this often doesn't hold. First of all, it may be the case that while speaking one variety (A), a speaker may happen to use (or strategically employ) linguistic structures of A that are similar to/or the same as those in B (such as cognates or homophones). Clyne (1980, 2003: 162ff.) discusses many examples of this phenomenon under the heading of 'triggering' (1980) or 'facilitation' (2003). For instance, a Dutch/English bilingual speaker may say:

(1) (Clyne 200 3: 171; second-generation immigrant in Australia)
Ik   hebt een *kop* of tea or *something*
I   have-1SG a cup of tea or something
'I'll have a cup of tea or something'

Dutch *kop* is a (near) homophone of English *cup*. Having produced *kop* brings the two languages closer to each other and may facilitate transition into English. In contrast to the figure above for orthodox code-switching/mixing, the transition is not abrupt but goes through an ambiguous zone:

Facilitated code-switching/mixing:

Time   ---------------------------→

Variety A   ──────

Variety B   ──────

The problem of deciding where variety B starts may be aggravated when the facilitating structure is a loanword from variety B. In dialect/standard contact, there are even cases of gradual 'code-gliding', in which it is impossible to identify when the transition into the other code starts and when the new variety is reached (an example is given in Auer, 1986).

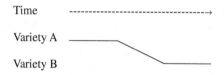

The point is that the more closely varieties are related structurally, the more the speakers' repertoires may be organized in a non-dichotomic way, allowing for numerous compromise forms in which ambiguous elements of A and B combine.

A ubiquitous instance of convergence, which is particularly hard to distinguish from code-switching/mixing, is **borrowing**. There can be no doubt that established borrowings (often called loanwords) – those which can be found in dictionaries and are used and/or known by monolingual speakers as well – do not constitute switching/mixing. However, there is considerable disagreement whether single, ad hoc insertions of lexical material from language B into a language A frame should be considered so (for a summary of arguments against this, see Poplack, 2004). It is obvious that ad hoc (or nonce) borrowings may become established borrowings in the long run if they are used repeatedly and eventually passed on from the bilinguals to A-monolinguals. Since this process can only be gradual, it is impossible to decide whether each individual borrowed token is ad hoc or established. Semantic criteria – above all the question of whether there is a corresponding non-borrowed word with approximately the same meaning available in variety A, or whether the borrowing fills a lexical gap – may influence whether a word becomes an established loan, but they cannot indicate on which point of the integration scale the word is at a given moment. Structural integration of the borrowed element into the matrix language seems like a good criterion, but upon closer examination it leads to inclusive results as well. Phonetic integration is in itself gradual, and morphological integration is often absent since ad hoc borrowings into morphologically-rich varieties often do not receive morphological marking (*bare forms*; cf. Budhzak-Jones and Poplack, 1997). It is therefore difficult/impossible to define an exact break-off point between loanwords and borrowed words. The only way out of this dilemma is definitional, not empirical. To give an example: Adalar and Tagliamonte (1998) found in a corpus of Turkish/English data, collected among ex-London migrants in Cyprus, that most English words inserted into Turkish utterances received the morphological marking required by Turkish morphology. For instance:

(2)   from Adalar and Tagliamonte (1998: 152)[1]
Ehh   ingiltere+nin   SHOP+lar+ı+nı   özle+r
Ehh   England-GEN   shop-PL-POSS-AKK   miss-3SG.AOR
'ehh she misses England's shops'

The authors argue that since *shop* is fully integrated morphologically and syntactically, it should be considered a borrowing, not a code-switch, while the (unlikely, and non-attested) version:

(2)' [fabricated]
Ehh   ingiltere'nin   SHOPS   özler

would be considered a case of switching/mixing. The counter-argument is that in **both** versions the grammatical systems of Turkish and English are activated and therefore no categorical distinction is necessary, but both alternatives can be handled within one model (Myers-Scotton 2002: 154–7). In the end, the controversy amounts to a terminological decision.

A final question to be dealt with in this introductory section may come as a surprise: Do code-switchers have to be bilinguals? The answer obviously depends on what is meant by bilingualism. But it is clear that code-switching is still possible with very little bilingual ability. Speakers can signal affiliation with a bilingual group by using token elements from a language of which they have only minimal proficiency (Reershemius, 2001, etc.), and in certain forms of 'crossing' speakers may mimic or imitate bilingual speakers by using what they think is typical of them (see Auer, 2006 for further references), without being bilingual themselves. These forms of code-switching have only moved into the focus of sociolinguistic research quite recently, but they are powerful interactional strategies.

In all these cases, the switching speakers are not usually called bilinguals, even in a very liberal sense of the word, and, surely in the case of crossing, they would not even consider themselves to be bilingual.

The upshot of this preliminary section is that even to say what code-switching is **not** a difficult task. In Sections 31.3 and 31.4, we will try to identify certain forms of switching and mixing which can be given a more precise structural and functional analysis. However, it is not only the linguistic side of switching/mixing which is hard to define but also the social side is complex. Before we move into more detailed accounts of how switching and mixing can occur, in Section 31.2 we look into the social structures which it indexes and in which it is embedded.

31.2 THE SOCIAL MEANING OF CODE-SWITCHING/MIXING

Although forms of bilingual talk such as code-switching and mixing are widespread, they do not occur in all bilingual speakers or communities. For instance, although almost all Luxemburgers with *Lëtzebuergesch* as their first language are also fluent in French, (frequent) code-switching between these varieties is rare. Using *Lëtzebuergesch* is the unmarked way of signalling one's belonging to the non-immigrant part of Luxemburg society, and French is used in public and in many institutions; the alternating use of these languages, however, would constitute a marked occurrence. Quite in contrast, code-switching/ mixing is the unmarked way of speaking among many second- and third-generation Turkish/German bilinguals among themselves, while speaking monolingual Turkish is marked. Different language ideologies are involved here, which regiment the ways in which linguistic behaviour becomes meaningful and even normative in the constitution of social groups and their boundaries. This also applies to the evaluation of bilingual talk. While it is true that in many contexts bilingual talk is evaluated negatively against the background of a monolingual language ideology, it is easy to find counter-examples as soon as one looks outside the modern European nation-states. Both in societies predating these nation-states, and in those outside the reach of the Herderian idea of (monolingual standard) language reflecting and justifying nationhood, code-switching may be typical for the social and educational élites. For instance, code-switching between Latin and a vernacular language was widespread among intellectuals in the fifteenth and sixteenth centuries (cf. Stolt, 1965; McLelland, 2004), code-switching between Russian and French was held in high esteem in the nineteenth century Russian upper classes (Timm, 1978) and English/Kiswahili switching is evaluated positively by the East African élites (cf. Blommaert, 1992 on Tanzania). In these cases of **élite code-switching**, it is doubtlessly the prestige of the bilingual talkers which lends prestige to their language; in all cases, certain linguistic resources (such as knowledge of 'good' Latin, French and English) are scarce and access to them is restricted by the educational system. A local élite in these cases combines an internationally prestigious variety with a local vernacular, thereby excluding both those who have no access to the international prestige variety and those who are not familiar with the local vernacular (Myers-Scotton, 1993b). By contrast, code-switching in the lower classes (e.g. immigrant labour) and at the peripheries of society is lacking in prestige because their speakers lack prestige (and their 'other' language has no value on the linguistic market).

Code-swiching/mixing receives its social function and meaning from a complex of interacting dimensions, among them the prestige and value of the varieties involved on the linguistic market, the social powers that regulate this market, the specific constellations of majority/ minorities (or centre/periphery) within a society that relate to these forms of power, the accessibility of language resources, and the ideologies around the languages and their (bilingual or monolingual) use. The evaluation and social interpretation of code-switching/mixing is thus dependent on a specific 'political economy of code choice' (Gal, 1988; Heller, 1992). Three examples illustrate this point.

The first case (Example 3) takes place in a small shop for household articles in Chişinău, the capital of Moldova (the former Moldovan Republic of the Soviet Union). Since 1991, the official language of the Republic of Moldova has been Moldovan-Romanian. (This variety was closely related to Romanian, the state language of the neighbouring Republic of Romania, but diverged from it while the area was under Russian control in the nineteenth and twentieth centuries; the exact nature and degree of divergence and the influence of Russian is disputed.) Despite the official status of Romanian, a large group of the population of Moldova mainly or exclusively speaks Russian, particularly Russians who immigrated to the area during the Soviet period. In Chişinău, the position of Moldovan-Romanian is strong when compared to the countryside and smaller towns, due to the support it receives from the state institutions which require all officials to be fluent in the official language. However, public life is still largely dominated by Russian.

In Example 3, a salesperson (B) and a client in the shop (A) are talking in Romanian, when another client (C) enters:

(3) (from Cechirlan, 2008) (A, C = clients, B = salesperson)

A: *bunăziua,*
    hello
B: *spuneţi vă rog, aveţi pampersuri numă raul cinci?*
    do you have pampers number five?
A: *da (-)*
    yes
B: *în mare packet*
    in large packages
A: *da (-)*
B: *daţi-mi, unul mare;*
    give them to me, a large one;
A: *unul mare?*
    a large one?
B: *mare da (-)*
    a large one yes
→C: *женщина, у вас случайно лампочек нет?*
    listen, do you happen to have bulbs?
→B: *<<laughing> есть случайно;>*
    we happen to have them;
C: *<<happily> да: :>*
    yeah::!
B: *три лея (--) вам на что,*
    three Lei (--) what do you need them for
C: *мне на сто ватт;*
    I need 100W
→A: *da în ce prêţ îs ele,*
    how much are they? (referring to the pampers)
→B: *două sute patruzecişipatru nouăzeci;*
    two hundred forty four and ninety.

The three participants do not know each other. The salesperson, obviously a Russian/Moldovan bilingual, speaks Romanian with the first client but easily switches to Russian in the first arrowed line, after the second client has asked her a question in that language. The reason is not simple accommodation to the language of the customer. Rather, there is a general rule of preference according to which language choice is organized in Moldova. This rule of preference implies that Russian is spoken as soon as one participant wishes to do so. This means that in public, and particularly among strangers, the use of Russian is still more frequent than the use of Romanian. The pattern reflects the pre-1989 dominance of Russian, and of course the power and prestige of the Russian part of the population. It has survived the collapse of the Soviet Union due in part to the monolingualism of the Russian part of the population which is only slowly giving way to Russian/Romanian bilingualism in the younger generations. More importantly, it is also the result of the continuing differences in the evaluation of these languages on the linguistic market where (Moldovan) Romanian only starts to supplant the prestige of Russian. The customer's use of Russian and the salesperson's switch into this language choice are not necessarily motivated politically, nor do they necessarily index the customer's Russian monolingualism. They just comply with the general preference for Russian in public.

Compare to this the following example (Example 4) from Estonia. Russian is in contact with the national language of Estonia, i.e. Estonian. The following utterance is from a Russian-dominant (Russian) saleswoman who offers cranberries at a market in which many customers are ethnically Estonian, and linguistically bilingual in Russian and Estonian:

(4) (from Verschik (2005), Estonian underlined)

Очень хорошие,   <u>värske</u>   u   väg   <u>magus</u>
Very good-NOM.PL fresh-NOM.SG. and very   sweet-NOM.SG

The speaker uses a Russian grammatical pattern (set by the initial-turn constructional unit, *очень хорошие,* a modified adjective with the appropriate plural nominative ending, referring to the cranberries). Into this pattern, she inserts Estonian words in the second turn constructional unit of her utterance: namely, the adjective *värske* 'fresh' and the modified adjective *väg magus* 'very sweet', conjoined by the Russian conjunction *u* 'and'. These Estonian adjectives receive no morphological marking for plural, although Russian and Estonian both require case **and** number marking in adjectives; they are inserted as bare forms into Russian. Verschik (2005) argues that mixtures of Russian and uninflected Estonian, as in Example 4, are systematically used by Russian-dominant speakers in order to accommodate linguistically the potential Estonian buyers. This is a compromise strategy used by Russians who know little Estonian. As in the first case, the salesperson converges towards the language preferences of her costumers, but the structure in which the two languages are juxtaposed is different (sentence-internal mixture). Even more important, the social interpretation the mixing receives reflects different ways in which the two languages are evaluated on the linguistic market, and they therefore index a different constellation of power. Pre-1989, the social value of Estonian and Russian was similar to that of Moldavian-Romanian and Russian in Moldavia. But due to the political, social and economic developments in Estonia, the 'Moldavian' rule of preference – switch to Russian as soon as your co-participant wishes to – no longer holds; Estonian as the national language is in a more powerful position than Moldavian-Romanian today, and although a large part of the Russian population in Estonia still knows very little Estonian, the pressure to acquire this language is high. The market woman in the example is likely to have lived most of her life in an environment in which knowledge of Estonian was not necessary at all, and she will have had few opportunities offered by the institutions to learn Estonian after 1989. But she has had to change her old patterns of monolingual Russian language behaviour. Note that most of the potential buyers know Russian, i.e. mixing is not a matter of how to transmit information efficiently here; monolingual Russian just does not 'sell' any longer. And since the market woman's knowledge of Estonian is not sufficient to switch into this language altogether, she resorts to a compromise strategy which makes her mixing of Estonian and Russian acceptable to Estonians as a sign of good will and of her submission to the new norms and ideologies of public language use.

The third example (Example 5) is again from a different context. Three adolescent girls are gossiping during group work time in the Danish/German school (*Dyborg skolen*) in Flensburg, Germany (where Danish is an official minority language). We find a mixture of these two languages, which neither formally nor functionally equals either of the previous examples.

(5) (from: Kühl, 2008: 202, Danish/German in South Schleswig, Germany, German underlined):
L: *vi skal arbejde nu*
      we have to work now
A: ((laughs)) *halløjsa*
              hallo hallo
→L: *gleich kommt lonepigebarn.*
      soon comes lone-girl
→   *så er det slut med lustig.*
      then it's done-with-fun
      æh vi skal nu lige arbejde lidt ((…))
      uhm we have to work now a bit

The interaction starts in Danish, but L switches into German in the first arrowed line. *Lonepigebarn* is an ad hoc compound made up of a proper name (*Lone*, the name of the girls' teacher) and the Danish compound *pigebarn* ('girl+child', which is unusual, as the usual word for 'girl' is *pige*). It is used as a nickname for the teacher here (presumably because she calls the girls *pigebarn* in class). More interesting is the following line (second arrow), where *slut med lustig* is modelled word for word on the German idiom *schluss mit lustig* which does not exist in Danish. The last word (the adjective *lustig* in the slot of a noun after the preposition *med*) is German, which turns the formulation into a double interfered calque. This calque doesn't just happen – it is produced on the spot for interactional purposes. The speaker plays with the two languages and intermediate forms in an act of performance (see the discussion of similar cases in Fabian, 1990; Woolard, 1989; Hinnenkamp, 2005). What is the social meaning of this artificially (and artfully) produced hybrid? First, we need to take into consideration that the interaction takes place in a school which is dominated by a 'speak Danish' ideology. The Danish minority in the north of Germany (*Südschleswig*) is not based on descent or linguistic knowledge but on membership by self-declaration. Most of its members grow up with German and only learn Danish in kindergarten or later. In everyday life, German is by far dominant. Danish is considered a symbol (and proof) of belonging to the Danish minority, but it is legitimate to acquire (instead of possess) Danish competence. The Danish traditionally spoken in the area diverges in many aspects from the old Copenhagen-based standard language which is taught at the Danish school in Flensburg (a standard not even popular among Copenhagen adolescents today). School Danish (the variety of Danish enforced by the institution) therefore offers little in terms of identity and affiliation. The adolescent girls in the example interact in the context of an institution which explicitly fosters the use of standard Danish and in which monolingual German, 'bad' Danish and bilingual talk are all disfavoured.[2] Playing around with the languages (instead of trying to speak 'good Danish') is for them an act of rebellion against, and subversion of, the linguistic norms of the school.[3]

In all three examples (Examples 3–5), two languages are combined in some way or other, but in each case, code-switching/mixing has very different social meanings. There have been attempts to develop an overarching theory of language and society which claim to predict the meaningfulness of code-switches and mixings across social embeddings, and we can now try to apply them to the three examples in order to find out how useful they are. The first influential theory is based on John Gumperz' distinction between we-code and they-code (Blom and Gumperz, 1972). The simple but persuasive idea is that in a bilingual group of speakers, one of the codes is associated with the larger, monolingual society and the other is associated with the minority to which the speakers themselves belong. By choosing the latter, the speaker positions him- or herself as being part of the 'local team'. Of course, this model is only applicable in sociolinguistic contexts in which there is a clear difference between a majority and a minority group, and a corresponding majority and minority language.

It is crucial to develop a methodology by which the we-code and they-code can be identified. Researchers usually refer to domains of usage in this context. In other words, one often finds that code A is used in more formal situations in which co-participants do not know each other, and in certain institutional settings, particularly those which imply an asymmetrical relationship, while code B is used in informal situations among equals such as friends, family members and the like. However, in the three examples (Examples 3–5) discussed, it is difficult to identify these domains, just as it is difficult to say who the 'local team' is and how this relates to the 'minority language'. For instance, in Example 5, German seems to be the students' 'we-code', but Danish, if anything, is the minority language in Flensburg (or Germany).

Elsewhere (Auer, 1984a), I have called approaches like the we/they-code model **semantic** because they build on the presupposition that the codes have a meaning which is independent of the local context in which they are used. This meaning is then channelled into the interaction and becomes relevant in it. In the unmarked case, i.e. where the situation 'fits' the language, no further inference is required. In the marked case, i.e. when language choice and the type of situation diverge, meanings are created on the basis of situation-specific inferencing (Blom and Gumperz, 1972 speak of 'metaphorical' code-switching here). The same idea underlies Myers-Scotton's model of rational choice, in which the semantics of the codes are called 'rights-and-obligation sets' (e.g. 1988, 1993a). The theory is more flexible than a simple we/they-code model, but faces the same problem: in many cases of code-switching/mixing, the rights and obligations of the two codes are not easy to establish, since they are not trans-situationally stable and the association of languages and their situational usage domains is ambiguous and open to negotiation (see Meeuwis and Blommaert, 1994 for a critique). As in Gumperz' model, in which the situationally unexpected use of another language is said to receive a metaphorical meaning (the speaker behaves as if the situation was such as to require the use of the new language), the interpretation and social meaning of 'marked code-switching' in Myers-Scotton's model is calculated against the background of a markedness matrix ('the speaker is attempting to treat the rights and obligations in effect in the current exchange as if they were the same as in an exchange where the marked choice is unmarked' Myers-Scotton 1998 [2000: 1267]). Such an approach is of some value for the interpretation of our Moldovan/Russian example (an unmarked switch into Russian), but of no help in the interpretation of the Estonian/Russian and the Danish/German examples. This is not only because the rights-and-obligation sets attached to the codes in play are not uncontested in the community, and in constant flux. The main reason is that although the code-switching/mixing speakers make rational (intentional, though not necessarily conscious) choices, and although these choices are reflexively related to the values attached to them, their interactional effect depends essentially on their situational and sequential embedding.

Mixed and hybrid utterances (such as those in Examples 4 and 5 above) are sometimes explained by a model of code-switching which starts from the assumption that, in bilingual talk, speakers wish to co-activate two identities at the same time, or remain ambiguous between the two (see, for instance, Myers-Scotton, 1988 or Pfaff, 2003). Although it is true that code-switching can be used to display identities (cf. Bailey, 2007; de Fina, 2007), and that it can create ambiguity (of language choice and of the definition of the situation, cf. Heller, 1988b), it does not in and of itself index ambiguous identities. Code-switchers do not have their souls torn in two parts; they are what they are (Moldavians, Estonians of Russian ethnicity, Germans who self-select to be part of the Danish minority), and this may in some contexts be best and most naturally expressed by bilingual talk.

I have chosen three examples in which it is difficult to identify one bilingual speech community to which all co-participants belong. For instance, it may be asked whether there is one Moldavian/Estonian speech community (or do the Estonians/Moldavians belong to one community, and the Russians to another?). Most research on code-switching presupposes a bilingual speech community, which is located in one territory; typically, this is the case of an old (autochthonous) linguistic minority (even though this may downplay internal differences). It is increasingly understood, however, that the bilingual speech community is at best a working construct for starting field work, but that its boundaries are constructed, and that membership is gradual (Rampton, 2000).

31.3 CODE-SWITCHING AS A CONVERSATIONAL ACTIVITY

So far I have used the terms code-switching and mixing without defining them. In the literature, the latter term is often used to refer to sentence-internal switching, while code-switching is reserved for cases of language alternation between independent syntactic units. I have proposed (e.g. in Auer, 1999) a different definition which captures a more fundamental and less superficial distinction. The term code-switching will be reserved for cases in which the juxtaposition of two codes (languages) is perceived and interpreted as a locally meaningful event by participants. The term mixing, on the other hand, will be used for those cases of language juxtaposition in which the use of two languages is only meaningful (to participants) as a recurrent pattern, but not in each individual case. The fact that code-switching is more common between full syntactic units falls out naturally in this approach (see below, (e)). Frequent code-switching may be the first step towards a mixed speaking style (as argued by Myers-Scotton, 1988/2000 and Auer, 1999). Under this approach, code-switching may be described as follows:

(a) It occurs in a sociolinguistic context in which speakers orient towards a preference for one language at a time; i.e. it is usually possible to identify the language-of-interaction which is valid at a given moment, and when the switch itself occurs.
(b) By departing from this established language-of-interaction, code-switching signals 'otherness' of the upcoming contextual frame and thereby achieves a change of 'footing'. The precise interpretation of this new footing needs to be 'filled in' in each individual case, a process in which previous experiences may be brought to bear on the interpretation of the case at hand.
(c) Nonetheless, the mechanisms by which code-switching generates meaning can be described in a general way. Contexts are innumerable, as are the interactional meanings of code-switching; however, the ways in which these meanings are constructed remain constant from one community to the next.
(d) Code-switching may be a personal or group style. As a group style, its use may be subject to normative constraints valid within a speech community; however, it is not a variety in its own right.
(e) Most code-switches occur at major syntactic and prosodic boundaries (at the clause or sentence level).[4] Since switching is activity-related, the utterance units affected by the switch must be large enough to constitute such an activity. For this reason, code-switching provides little interesting data for syntactic research.
(f) Although code-switching bilinguals may be highly proficient in both languages, balanced proficiency is by no means a prerequisite. Indeed, code-switching is possible with a very limited knowledge of the 'other' language.

Before looking into some forms and functions of code-switching, we have to return to the notion of a 'code'. Code-switching means that a set of co-occurring linguistic features is exchanged for another set of co-occurring features more or less at the same point in time, **which is perceived as such by the co-participants**. The co-occurring features may be those of a language or a dialect, but it is obvious that the definition is wide enough to include many other sets of features as well. Apart from instances that are not usually thought to belong to the field of bilingualism (such as the code-switch between two different sets of prosodic features), the most noteworthy type of code-switching in bilingual talk apart from code-switching between varieties is code-switching between a monolingual and a mixed style, or between two mixed styles[5] (for examples, see Meeuwis and Blommaert, 1998; Gafaranga, 2000). Meeuwis and Blommaert speak of 'layered code-switching', because code-switching seems to occur within code-switching. In the terminology proposed here, it is language mixing that occurs within code-switching. Frequently, this kind of second-order bilingual talk occurs in migration contexts among speakers who at home used to mix a colonial and a local language. In Example 6, the participants are exiled speakers from Zaire (now the Democratic Republic of Congo) recorded in the 1990s in Belgium. One of the speakers (A) usually speaks a French/Lingala mixed style, others (B, C) a mixed style of French and Swahili.

All are proficient in both mixed codes. In Belgian exile, Lingala/French is unmarked with respect to Swahili/French.

(6) (from Meeuwis and Blommaert, 1998: 89–90)
(simple italics = Lingala, underlined = French, small capitals = Swahili)

A: *ezalaki mokolo ya <u>bonne année</u> tokutan-aki na Matonge.*
       it was on New Year's day, we met in Matonge [a Zairian neighbourhood in Brussels]

B: *na ndako?*
       at home?

A: *na <u>Namur</u> wana*
       at Namur [=Porte de Namur, a well-known traffic junction in Brussels]

B: *awa na <u>Bruxelles</u>?*
       here in Brussels?

A: *ee*
       Yes

→ B→C: NIKUPATIE coca?
       shall I get you a Coke?

C: HAPANA SAA HII.
       not now

B: NANI- ILE SOKO IKO <u>fatigue</u>.
       what- that market is exhausting.

→A: *hein?*[6]
       sorry?

B: *zando wana eza <u>fatigue</u>.*
       that market is exhausting.

A: *ah. <u>Heureusement qu'okei lelo dimanche</u>! Mm!*
       you're lucky you went on Sunday. I say!
       ((walks into the kitchen))

→B: UKO UNASEMA MUTU ATEMBEE APITE, UKO UNAONA (SAA) VILE BIKO BINARUDISHA =TU NYUMA=.
       you say someone is walking and moving forward, but you have the impression as if they're just moving back

→A: ((returns into the living room)) =<u>dimanche</u> bato-=
                                            on Sundays people-

C: <u>dimanche</u> bato bazalaka mingi hein?
       on Sundays it's always crowded, isn't it?

The two codes juxtaposed in the beginning of this interactional exchange between three participants are Lingala/French mixing and Swahili/French mixing, which B switches into in the first arrowed line when he addresses C (the unmarked code between the two of them). The switch organizes the conversation: it marks a change of participant constellation, which is narrowed down from A/B/C to B/C for a side-sequence, in which B asks C whether he wants a drink. Accordingly, C's answer, still within the side-sequence and therefore the narrower constellation, is also in Swahili.[7] The next utterance is revealing. B returns to the larger constellation and to the topic preceding the side-sequence (the market at the Porte de Namur). But unexpectedly, she still uses the language of the side-sequence, i.e. Swahili with inserted French. To this, A responds with a repair marker (second arrow): he does not accept the previous utterance as it stands and invites its revision. B immediately corrects her language choice and makes the same statement again in Lingala/French (the inserted French noun *fatigue* remains the same). We therefore have clear evidence that B's original language choice is **seen by participants** as having departed from an established and 'morally' sanctioned language-of-interaction. (In contrast, the insertion of French into either Lingala or Swahili sentences would never be subject to other-initiated repair.) After this 'mistake' has been remedied, the interaction continues in the agreed-upon language of the A/B/C-constellation until A, the Lingala speaker, leaves the room for a minute, which immediately engenders B's switching into the Swahili/French mixed code (third arrow), which is again given up upon A's return (fourth arrow). In sum, the example includes a high number of concatenations of elements from two languages within one stretch of talk (i.e. it is highly multilingual), but the juxtapositions are clearly different in the case of Lingala/French and Swahili/French mixing (in these cases, the individual juxtapositions have no discourse-related function or meaning), and in the case of the second-order juxtaposition of a Lingala/French mixed code and a Swahili/French mixed code (here, the individual cases are meaningful, and we speak of switching). As shown, the conversational effect of switching here is to mark different interactional frames/

footings, such as main sequence/topic vs aside, or varying constellations of participants. The participants jointly re-contextualize the interaction (if only temporarily). In one case, the switch signals a temporary lack of congruence between the interactional frame/footing at hand and language choice, i.e. a repair of an 'inadequate' language choice is triggered.

Conversational code-switching serving this or similar functions (discourse-related code-switching in Auer, 1995) has been attested widely in many bilingual groups of speakers. The data all show that code-switching is a cue by which speakers contextualize their utterances, rendering them meaningful in their conversational context (cf., among many; Alfonzetti, 1998; Auer, 1984b; Bani-Shoraka, 2005: Chs. 8 and 9; Gafaranga, 2007; Guerini, 2006; Gumperz, 1982; Jonsson, 2005: Ch. 6; Li Wei, 1994, 2002; Sebba and Wootton, 1998;). Several sub-types suggest themselves, such as:

- The distinction between switches that are closely linked to the 'machinery' of conversational exchanges, such as turn-taking, repair work, sequence organization, preference organization or participant constellation, beginning or ending a story, and switches that may be called stylistic, such as the contextualization of a different modality (joking/serious, fake/true, fantasy/reality) and of interpersonal intimacy vs distance, expressivity vs neutrality, etc.
- The distinction between turn-external and turn-internal switching. Turns may be composed of various units which represent different (minor or major) linguistic acts. Speakers may use code-switching to create turn-internal structure, for instance to set off reported speech from their own voice, statements from evaluations/assessments, topic from comment, turn-initial responsive elements (see Karrebaek, 2003: 431–3 for examples), etc.
- The distinction between alternational and insertional code-switching. Alternational switching (as in Example 6) always questions the established language of interaction, if only for a temporary side-activity. It seems to be much more frequent than insertional code-switching of single or complex units of B talk into undisputed A talk; still, the latter also occurs and can serve discourse-related functions, such as establishing coherence across utterances or turns (Angermeyer, 2002; Guerini, 2006: 203–16; also cf. Example (8) below).
- The distinction between structural contrast and interpersonal divergence. Code-switching capitalizes on the contrast between A talk and B talk. This contrast may be of a purely structural nature, or it may express a divergence between the speakers involved, i.e. their opinions, stances, or attitudes. This may happen, for instance, when a speaker diverges from an established language-of-interaction in order to express disagreement. Example 7 – a recording of members of the Chinese population in the UK – is a case in point:

(7) (from Li Wei, 1994: 166) (Cantonese in simple italics, English underlined)
(Two young women are looking at new dresses.)

A: *nau, ni goh.*
    this one.
B: *ho leng a.*
    very pretty
A: *leng me?* (1.5)
    pretty?
    →<u>very expensive</u>.
B: *guai m gaui a?*
    expensive or not?
A: *hao guai.*
    very expensive.

The only departure from the established language-of-interaction (Cantonese) is A's English evaluative term *very expensive* in the arrowed line.B does not pick up on it; she continues to speak Cantonese. The language-of-interaction seems for a short moment to be in danger of dissolving. It is easy to see why this is so – and what conversational effect is achieved by it – if the sequential context is taken into consideration. Just prior to the switch, B had given an assessment of a dress identified by A in her first utterance. The assessment is positive. A first replies by a question repetition, which functions as an other-repair initiator. B, however, does not step back from her opinion (cf. the pause of 1.5 sec); at this point, A explicitly disagrees with B, at the same time abandoning the language-of-interaction. The disagreeing, negative assessment is given in the other language.

A comprehensive analysis of 'what people do by code-switching' has yet to be written. At this point, it should be noted that the conversational analysis of code-switching cannot be reduced to a semantic analysis of codes in question, but needs to take into account the conversational embedding of the switch.

While discourse-related code-switching has received a lot of attention, and many conversational functions have been described, it must not be overlooked that there are other forms of bilingual talk that qualify as code-switching according to the definition given above. Often, they tell us less about the structure of the interaction than about the identities of the participants; in this sense, they are participant-related. Nevertheless, their sequential position is decisive for their interpretation. An important part of such participant-related code-switching is part of language negotiation sequences in which co-participants negotiate the language for the conversation which is just about to begin, or renegotiate this language after situational shifts (see the examples in Guerini, 2006: 106–20). Such preference-related switches can, additionally, have a discourse-related meaning. As argued above in the discussion of Example 7, every code-switch can endanger the established language-of-interaction; initiating and maintaining a language negotiation sequence can therefore be disaffiliative, while 'giving in' in such a sequence can also be affiliative (see the example discussed in Auer, 2007b). Code-switching may also display a speaker's (relative and temporary) incompetence in one language over the other or ascribe such (relative and temporary) incompetence to the conversational partner (competence-related code-switching). It is often forgotten that bilingual participants in interaction are seldom bilingual to the same degree; rather, they constantly display to each other their relative competence in one code vis-à-vis the other and thereby turn bilingual competence into a visible matter. This is partly done through code-switching, which is then strongly linked to face-work: it can be either condescending or helpful to switch into the stronger language of one's partner. On the part of the speaker, a switch into one's stronger language can simply be a request for help from the co-participant or a way of gaining time to look for the right word, as in the following example:

(8) (from Auer and Rönfeldt, 2002)
(F, a second-generation Italian/German bilingual immigrant girl in Germany; B, a bilingual, non-immigrant, German-dominant adult woman; German underlined. Topic: the visit of a TV team in the family's home. Capitals represent stress.)

F: *siamo: andati n cuGIna,=*
        we went into the kitchen
B: *nhn,=*
F: *=volvavano (loro) vedere: äh:: i MMUri; (-)*
        they wanted to see the walls;
→   *perche sono tutti NE:ri e un po <u>FEUCHT</u>,*
        because they are all black and a little humid
B: *ahha,=*
F: *=un po UMmido:, (-)*
        a little humid
B: *hn[hn,*
B: *[e: hanne intervissatto, oppure le dovevo: (.) stare in cuCIna: a fare qualcossa.*
        and they interviewed (us), or I had to stay in the kitchen and do something

The speaker F inserts a German word (*feucht*) into the arrowed utterance without any hedging (often, competence-related insertional switches as in this example are introduced by hesitation markers). However, and despite the fact that her recipient B signals understanding, she retrospectively self-repairs *feucht* and replaces it with the Italian counterpart *umido*. The self-repair first of all displays competence in the **two** languages, but at the same time German is displayed as the language which comes to her mind first and is therefore dominant (cf. Auer, 1997). By self-repairing the German word in an Italian utterance, the speaker makes it clear that she orients her linguistic behaviour towards a rule of 'one language at a time', in this case Italian (a language she clearly struggles with, cf. the numerous dialectal interferences as well as the derailment in *volvavano* for standard Italian *volevano*). This also makes it possible to see the insertion of *feucht* as a competence-related switch, not as an unmarked case of mixing.

31.4 BILINGUAL MIXING

Both mixing and switching are part of what can be called bilingual styles, but while switching is primarily a stylistic-rhetorical practice to be analysed in pragmatic and, above all, conversation analytic terms, the analysis of mixing usually requires grammatical investigation since mixing tends to occur within self-contained syntactic units. Contrary to switching, it requires an advanced bilingual competence and is not frequent in bilinguals with very imbalanced competences (apart from some types of single word insertions). As in the case of code-switching, it is necessary to distinguish between *alternational and insertional mixing* (Stolt, 1965 speaks of *Umschaltung* vs *Einschaltung*).[8] The first is clearly a matter of language production, while insertional mixing occurs at a deeper level of linguistic processing.

Alternational mixing (Muysken, 2000: 96–121) in its most prototypical sense means that a sentence begins in one language and ends in another, without a clear sense of whether the entire sentence is in language A or B. Both parts of the sentence are of some complexity. (The following examples are from Luther's Dinner Conversations, i.e. Latin/Early New High German [ENHG] mixing; Latin underlined; cf. Stolt, 1965.)

(9) (Stolt, 1965: 83)

Sicut statim	*post*	*nostrum*	*saeculum*	*wirds*	*anderst*	*werden*
Thus immediately	after	our	age	will-it	different	become

'so it will immediately become different after our time'

(10) (Stolt, 1965: 91)

Unser	*Herr*	*Gott*	*ist*	*mirabiliter*	*negligens*	*in*	*descriptione*	*suarum*	*rerum*
Our	Lord	God	is	admirably	negligent	in	description	his-GEN.PL	things-GEN.PL

'God our Lord is admirably negligent in the description of his affairs'

In the Example 9, the alternation occurs after three adverbials in Latin; in Example 10, after the subject and the copula in ENHG.[9] Note that the chunks in both languages are grammatical according to the grammar of the respective languages. There seem to be restrictions which dictate this: i.e. alternational mixing occurs preferentially at points where the two grammars produce a homologous structure (equivalence constraint: Poplack, 1980; Sankoff, 1998; Sankoff and Poplack, 1981). At points in the production of a sentence in which the rules of word order and constituency of one language differ from those of the other, transition from one language into the other is less likely. For instance, if language A is strictly post-modifying and language B strictly pre-modifying, mixing is predicted to be blocked between a noun and its attributes.

Often, the two chunks of talk are relatively self-contained, i.e. there is a major syntactic boundary between the two parts, as in the following examples:

(11) (Stolt. 1965: 109)

prima tabula	*decalogi,*		*die ist*	*gar*	*des*	*Teuffels*
first	table	decalogue-GEN.SG	it is	PART	the-GEN.SG	devil-GEN.SG

'The first table of the Decalogue, this is surely the devil's'

(12) (Stolt 1965: 194)

si ego	*omnia*	*crederem,*	*wollt*	*ich*	*kein*	*pfarrherr*	*ansehen*
if I	all-ACC.PL.	believe-COND2.1SG	can-COND2.1SG	I	no	priest	look-at

'If I believed everything, I would not be able to look any priest in the eye'

In Example 11, the Latin part of the sentence is a left-dislocated noun phrase; in Example 12, the Latin part is a subordinated conditional sentence. Both are followed by an ENHG main clause.

Of course, mixing also frequently occurs between self-contained units which make up one larger speaking turn. They may be semantically coherent, and may contain cohesion markers such as adverbials or ellipses, but are both independent sentences:

(13) (Stolt, 1965: 219)
Die hat Ökolampadius nit konnen ertragen, er hatts mussen sterben, Zinglius quoque non.
'Okolampadius wasn't able to endure them, he had to die of it, Zinglius not either.'

(14) (Stolt, 1965: 236)
Haustus aquae et cervisiae est remedium sitis, ein stuckh prott vertreibt den hunger, *Christus est remedium mortis.*
'A drink of water and beer is a remedy of thirst, a piece of bread drives away hunger, Christ is the remedy of death.'

In Example 13, the Latin part is elliptical, with a strong grammatical link to the first sentence in the German part of the utterance (ENHG: ... *nit konnen ertragen*). The latter makes use of the previous German structure and could be reconstructed as *Zinglius quoque non hat konnen ertragen*. In Example 14, the three-part list with its grammatical parallelism renders the three components, two of which are in Latin, one in German, cohesive. Here, of course, transition into turn-internal code-switching for rhetorical purposes is fluid.[10]

As Muysken (2000) argues, there are good reasons to include further mixing structure under the heading of alternation, although the term may be less obvious in these cases. For instance, longer stretches of language A talk may occur in a relatively self-contained, grammatically independent way within language B talk (nested code-mixing), as in:

(15) (Stolt, 1965: 183)
Ist denn das war, so lass uns dran sezen, quidquid habemus, und druber leyden, quidquid possumus
'If this is true, then let us bet on it <u>whatever we have</u>, and suffer from <u>whatever we can</u>.'

The important criterion for distinguishing this type of nested alternation from insertions is the structural independence of the A parts to the left and right of the B section. (In the example, ... *so lass uns dran sezen* is syntactically linked to its complement, *quidquid habemus*, but *so lass uns dran sezen* is relatively independent from *und druber leyden*, which is an elliptical continuation of the *lass* clause, similar to the one in Example 13.) Equally, Muysken (2000: 97–9) suggests that peripheral elements of the sentence which are only weakly integrated should be considered alternational mixing. This applies to discourse markers, particles, certain adverbials (such as sentence adverbials) and conjunctions, such as *et tamen* and *quia* in the following example:

(16) (Stolt, 1965: 151)
<u>*Et tamen*</u> *haben wir ein forteyl fur der welt, <u>quia</u> das ampt ist unser.*
<u>And still</u> do we have an advantage over the world, <u>because</u> the office is ours.

Note that single word mixing is usually considered to be insertional (see below). Muysken's (2000) approach is more fine-grained here and distinguishes between the insertion of an A-language noun or verb into a B-language matrix, and alternational mixing on discourse markers, etc. Some evidence for this distinction may be found in the fact that sentence-initial conjunctions often go with the language of the preceding superordinated clause, a frequent pattern in Luther's code-mixing:

(17) (Stolt, 1965: 222)
<u>*Ora pro me,* **quia**</u> *du bist seer fromm*
<u>Pray for me, **because**</u> you are very pious

While alternational mixing is frequent in some data sets (such as Luther's dinner table conversations, where it occurs side by side with insertional mixing), other data sets are dominated by the *insertional type*. The most elaborate theory of this type of mixing was developed by Myers-Scotton (e.g. 2002) on the basis of East African data, and has subsequently been applied to many other bilingual situations as well (cf. Amuzu, 2005; Finlayson et al., 1998; Owens, 2005; Türker, 2000; on a more critical note; Boumans, 1998; Muhamedowa, 2006; Ziamari, 2003). In insertional mixing, the largest syntactic units (complementizer phrases in Myers-Scotton's model) are always dominated by one and only one language: the matrix language. Into this matrix, elements of the embedded language can be inserted. In this process, the rules of the matrix language must be obeyed, i.e.:

- the morpheme order must be that of the matrix language
- certain system morphemes must come from the matrix language.

In the most recent version of the model (Myers-Satton, 2002: 73–6), these morphemes are so-called late system morphemes whose selection depends on information from outside their immediate maximal projection (such as agreement markers or case). The embedded language may provide content morphemes, so-called early system morphemes (such as plural markers or determiners) whose form depends on the heads of their maximal projection but need no information from outside it, and so-called bridge system morphemes (morphemes linking content morphemes without needing information from their head; examples are genitive morphemes and suppletive morphemes). The most straightforward examples of insertional mixing are single content morpheme insertions such as the following:

(18) (Türker, 2000: 70, Turkish/Norwegian in Oslo, Turkish underlined)
geç-en sene   *serie-de-ydi-k*
past   year   league-LOC-PAST-1PL
'last year we were in the league'

(19) (Myers-Scotton, 2002: 89, Swahili/English in Nairobi, English underlined)
ile   m-geni   hata   si-ku-*comment*
DEM/CL9   CH/S-visitor   even   1SG.NEG.-PST.NEG-comment
'that visitor, I did not even comment'

In the Example 18, it is the Norwegian word *serie* which is embedded into a Turkish frame, while in the Example 19, it is the English verb (stem) *comment*. Both are treated as if they were words of the matrix language.[11] An example of a bridge morpheme which is inserted into a Turkish matrix is the German preposition *mit* in the N *mit* N-construction:

(20) (Treffers-Daller, 1995: 254, German/Turkish, German underlined)
Pilav   *mit*   piriç   yap-ıl-ır
boiled-rice   with   unboiled-rice make-PASS-AOR.
'Boiled rice is made with unboiled rice'

The special status of early system morphemes is responsible for the double marking of the same grammatical category both with the morphemes of the embedded and the matrix language, as in:

(21) (Backus, 1992: 90, Turkish/Dutch in the Netherlands, Dutch underlined)
Pol-en-lar-a   *Holanda-ca*   *ders ver-di*
pole-PL-PL-DAT   Dutch-SUFF   ders give-PASS
'he taught Dutch to Poles'

In Example 21, the plural is marked both by the Dutch suffix *–en* and the Turkish suffix *–lar* (the matrix language suffix must be more peripheral than the embedded language suffix). The opposite also occurs, however, i.e. inserted words may appear as bare forms, with no morphological/grammatical marking at all. In Example 22, the inserted Dutch noun *bibliotheek* in a Moroccan Arabic matrix clause should receive both a prepositional clitic /l/ and a definite prefix /l-/; however, it is inserted with neither of them. Note that the Dutch preposition is also lacking. According to Boumans (1998: 218), omission is particularly frequent after verbs of motion, where the role of the object can easily be reconstructed from the semantics of the verb and the object noun:

(22) (Boumans, 1998: 218; Moroccan Arabic in the Netherlands)
gadi-n   ne-mši-w   [] [] *bibliotheek*
FUT-PL   I-go-PL   library
'We'll go to the library'

Argues that bare forms are used when the structures of the two languages are not compatible (2002: 119–27; also cf. Nortier, 1990; Muysken, 2000: 83). In the same way, Myers-Scotton accounts for another way in which the dominance of the matrix language over the embedded language can be avoided, i.e. the insertion of internally complex 'islands' which follow the grammar of the embedded language instead of the matrix language. These islands may be inflected words in the embedded language, as in:

(23) (Stolt, 1964: 69; Latin/Early New High German)
omnes gentes, quae non habent religionem,   mussen   ***superstitio-nem***   haben (371)
                                            must-3PL   superstition-ACC.SG.   have-INF
'all people who don't have a religion, must have a superstition'

Islands can also be larger units, such as a noun phrase in the following example:

(24) (Stolt, 1964:81; Latin/Early New High German)
human-um   *cor*   kann   es   nicht   fassen
human-NEUTR.NOM.SG   heart-NEUTR.NOM.SG   can-3SG it   not   seize-INF
'the human heart cannot grasp it'

The model is able to deal with a large amount of insertional mixing data. However, there are also numerous cases in which the neat division between matrix and embedded language is not maintained. The deviations may go into either direction. For instance, it is possible that the embedded language influences the structure of the matrix language. In the following example, this is the case: Early New High German, the matrix language, converges toward the embedded language – Latin (more examples in Auer and Muhamedova 2005):

(25) (Stolt 1964: 71 Latin/ENHG)

obschon []	*peccator-es*	*izt*	*sind...*
although	sinner-PL	now	be-PRES.3PL

'although they are now sinners...'

ENHG, like modern German, needs an overt subject and is therefore not a pro-drop language. In Latin, information about the subject is fully encoded in the finite verb, and no overt subject pronoun is necessary.

German:	*obschon **sie** Sünder sind*
Latin:	*quamquam [] peccatores sunt*

In the Example 25, the transference of the embedded language structure to the matrix language leads to the omission of the subject pronoun.

More frequently, we find cases in which the structure of a complex embedded language island does not follow the grammar of the embedded language completely but converges towards the matrix language (Myers-Scotton, 2002: 102–5). For instance, there is strong evidence that in Kazakh/Russian code-mixing in Almaty (Muhamedowa, 2006; Muhamedova and Auer, 2005), Russian loses the gender category (as well as number), although this grammatical category is preserved in monolingual Russian discourse produced by the same speakers. The loss of gender in code-mixing is without doubt a consequence of the lack of this grammatical category in the matrix language Kazakh:

(26) (Muhamedova and Auer, 2005, Russian/Kazahk in Almaty)

Уже	*анау*	*стар-ый площадь-ті*		*не-лер-ді*	*зönde-di*
already	this	old-?	square-?-ACC	thing-PL-ACC	renovate-PAST

'there the old square and so on were alreadyrenovated'

Apart from the initial particle, the sentence is Kazakh, which is clearly the matrix language. The crucial issue is the inserted Russian island which fails to comply with the grammar of monolingual Russian since there is no gender agreement: *площадь* is a feminine noun, and the adjective modifying it should agree with it:*старая*. The use of the masculine form regardless of the gender of the nominal head in a large number of cases suggests that on the basis of Kazakh (which has no gender), the Russian used as an embedded language structurally converges towards the matrix language.[12]

Examples of mutual convergence in Hungarian/German code-mixing in the German minorities in Hungary are discussed in Szabó (2008). In this old bilingual community, we find utterances such as the following:

(27) (Szabó, 2007–8: 313, Hungarian/German dialect; Hungarian underlined)

do	*de*	*ötlet war gut*		*de mama ihre.*
PART	DET	idea was good		DET mum hers

'mum's idea was good'

den		*fogad*	*immer*	*el*
that-ACC.MASC		take-?	always	PARTICLE

'they always accept it.'

The second line is remarkable for various reasons. First, German dialect seems to underlie the sentence, since the use of a separable verb prefix (*fogad ... el* from the verb *el-fogad* 'to accept') does not conform to Hungarian grammar.[13] Rather, it seems to be modelled after the German pattern of separable verb particles (as in *nehmen ... an* from the verb *an-nehmen*). It is difficult, however, to call *fogad ... el* an island, since its two elements are discontinuous and do not follow Hungarian morphology: the verb *fogad* receives no person and number marking as would be required in Hungarian (and German), i.e. it is a bare form. On the other hand, Hungarian has an impact on the sentence beyond that of providing lexical material which is inserted into a German sentence pattern. As in Example 25, the subject pronoun is deleted, which is possible in Hungarian but not in German. Both languages seem to have converged and neither of them is used in a monolingual way, but it is difficult to say which one is the matrix language and which one the embedded language.

In sum, there is ample evidence that code-mixing creates specific forms of convergence which may not be present in the monolingual speech of the same speakers. These cases do not seem to be restricted to sociolinguistic situations of language attrition and shift, as Myers-Scotton (2002: 105) claims for 'composite codeswitching', in which 'the abstract morphosyntactic frame derive[s] from more than one source language' and in which it is therefore impossible to identify a single matrix language.

34.5 OPEN QUESTIONS

There are still considerable lacunae in research on bilingual talk. One is the question of whether and how mixing can sediment into grammatical patterns which are of mixed language origin but no longer offer a choice to their speakers and have therefore become part of the grammatical system (fused lects, see Auer, 1999). Another is psycholinguistic and neurolinguistic research on the real-time processing of bilingual talk (for recent overviews, see Basnight-Brown and Altarriba, 2007; and Gullberg, Indefrey and Muysken, 2009).

NOTES

1   Morphological gloss adapted.

2   See Musk (2006) for Welsh schools in Wales as another example.

3   Many examples of this are given by Kühl (2008, Ch. 8); see Jaspers (2005) for a similar example.

4   Exceptions are insertional code-switches (misleadingly called transfers in Auer, 1984b) in which a single word is inserted into an other-language frame to achieve a conversational effect; see Auer (1998a: 6–7) for the discussion of an example.

5   Gafaranga and Torras (2001) use the term 'medium switch' to refer to this aspect of code-switching.

6   *Hein?* is a neutral repair initiator which has been borrowed from French both into Lingala and (Congo) Swahili.

7   This shows that there is no emic difference between Swahili/French and Swahili (or for that matter, between Lingala/French and Lingala). Mixing is a form of speaking Swahili or Lingala. In contrast, the opposition between Swahili(/French) and Lingala (/French) is emic (as would the switch of either of them and French).

8   See the elaborate discussion of this distinction in Muysken (2000). In his model, there is a third type of mixing which he calls 'congruent lexicalization'; in this case, the grammatical structure of the two languages in contact is partly or completely identical (through convergence or genetic closeness), and mixing only refers to the filling in of lexical nodes in one language or the other.

9   Of course it is possible to posit theories which assign the total sentence in Examples 9 and 10 to one language. For instance, one could argue that by definition, the finite verb determines the language of the whole sentence. Then Examples 9 and 10 would be ENHG sentences with inserted material from Latin. See Auer (2000) for further discussion.

10   For instance, in list-like utterances such as Example 14, Luther always uses Latin in the third and most important list-element. This points to a rhetorical usage of the transition into Latin, which brings these examples close to code-switching.

11   This is the reason some researchers do not speak of insertional mixing, but of borrowing here.

12   A similar case of gender neutralization is reported for Malinche Mexicano/Spanish mixing by Hill and Hill (1986: 266ff.).

13   While the separation of particle and verb in German is exclusively determined by the syntactic pattern of the sentence (in which the verb provides the left bracket, i.e. second position, the particle the right bracket, i.e. final position), Hungarian separable verb prefixes are used to mark focus. In the present context, no separation is possible.

REFERENCES

Adalar, N. and Tagliamonte, S. (1998) 'Borrowed nouns – bilingual people: the case of 'Londralı' in North Cyprus', *International Journal of Bilingualism*, 2: 139–59.

Alfonzetti, G. (1998) 'The conversational dimension in code-switching between Italian and dialect in Sicily', in P. Auer, (ed.), *Code-Switching in Conversation. Language, Interaction and Identity*. London/New York: Routledge. pp. 180–214.

Alvarez Cáccamo, C. (1998) 'From 'switching code' to 'code-switching': towards a reconceptualisation of communicative codes', in P. Auer, (ed.), *Code-Switching in Conversation. Language, Interaction and Identity*. London/New York: Routledge. pp. 29–50.

Amuzu, E. K. (2005) 'Revisiting the classic codeswitching and composite codeswitching distinction: a case study of nonverbal codeswitching', *Australian Journal of Linguistics*, 25(1): 127–51.

Angermeyer, P. (2002) 'Lexical cohesion in multilingual conversation', *International Journal of Bilingualism*,6(4): 361–93.

Auer, P. (1984a) 'On the meaning of conversational code-switching', in P. Auer and di Lucio, Aldo (eds), *Interpretive Sociolinguistics: Migrants – Children – Migrant Children*.Tübingen. pp. 87–112.

Auer, P. (1984b) *Bilingual Conversation*. Vol. 8, *Pragmatics and Beyond*. Amsterdam: Benjamins.

Auer, P. (1986) 'Konversationelle Standard / Dialekt-Kontinua (Code-Shifting)', *Deutsche Sprache*, 2: 97–124.

Auer, P. (1995) 'The pragmatics of code-switching:A sequential approach', in L. Milroy and P. Muysken (eds), *One Speaker, Two Languages*. Cambridge: University Press. pp.115–35. Reprinted in W. Li (ed.) (2007) *The Bilingualism Reader*. 2nd edn. Milton Park: Routledge. pp.123–38.

Auer, P. (1997) 'Members' assessments and ascriptions of (in-)competence in bilingual conversation', in J. R. Dow and M. Wolff (eds), Languages and lives. Festschrift for W. Enninger. New York: Peter Lang. pp. 121–36.

Auer, P. (1998a) ''Bilingual conversation'' revisited', in P. Auer (ed.), *Code-Switching in Conversation. Language, Interaction and Identity*. London/New York: Routledge. pp.1–24.

Auer, P. (ed) (1998b) *Code-Switching in Conversation. Language, Interaction and Identity*. London/New York: Routledge.

Auer, P. (1999) 'From code-switching via language mixing to fused lects: toward a dynamic typology of bilingual speech', *International Journal of Bilingualism*, 3(4): 309–32.

Auer, P. (2000) 'Why should we and how can we determine the 'base language' of a bilingual conversation?', *Estudios de Sociolingüística*, 1(1): 129–44.

Auer, P. (2006) 'Sociolinguistic crossing', in: K. Brown (ed.) *Encyclopedia of Language and Linguistics*, *11*. 2nd edn. Oxford: Elsevier. pp. 40–2.

Auer, P. (2007a) 'The monolingual bias in bilingualism research or: shy bilingual talk is (still) a challenge for linguistics', in M. Heller (ed.), *Bilingualism – A Social Approach*. Houndmills: Palgrave. pp. 319–39.

Auer, P. (2007b) 'Code-switching in conversation', in N. Coupland and A. Jaworski (eds), *The New Sociolinguistics Reader*. Houndmills: Palgrave Macmillan. pp. 490–511.

Auer, P. and Rönfeldt, B. (2002) 'Erinnern und Vergessen. Erschwerte Wortfindung als soziales und interaktives Problem', in M. Schecker (ed.), *Wortfindung und Wortfindungsstörungen*. Tübingen: Narr. pp. 77–108.

Backus Ad (1992) Patterns of language mixing. A study in Turkish-Dutch bilingualism. Wiesbaden: Harrassowitz

Bailey, B. (2007) 'Language alternation as a resource for identity negotiations among Dominican American bilinguals', in P. Auer (ed.), *Style and Social Identities*. Berlin: Mouton. pp. 29–56.

Bani-Shoraka, H. (2005) 'Language choice and code-switching in the Azerbaijani community in Teheran', *Acta Universitatis Upsaliensis/ Studia Iranica*, No. 9.

Berruto, G. (2005) 'Dialect/standard convergence, mixing, and models of language contact: the case of Italy', in P. Auer, F. Hinskens and P. Kerswill (eds), *Dialect Change: Convergence and Divergence in European Languages*. Cambridge: Cambridge University Press. pp. 81–95.

Basnight-Brown, D. M. and Altarriba, J. (2007) 'Code-switching and code-mixing in bilinguals: cognitive, developmental and empirical approaches', in A. Ardila and E. Ramos (eds), *Speech and Language Discorders in Bilinguals*. Hauppauge, NY: Nova Science. pp. 69–89.

Blom, J. P. and Gumperz, J. (1972) 'Social meaning in linguistic structures: code-switching in Norway', in J. Gumperz and D. Hymes (eds), *Directions in Sociolinguistics*. New York: Holt, Rinehart and Winston. pp. 407–34.

Blommaert, J. (1992) 'Codeswitching and the exclusivity of social identities: some data from Campus Kiswahili', *Journal of Multilingual and Multicultural Development*, 13: 57–70.

Boumans, L. (1998) 'The syntax of codeswitching. Analysing Moroccan Arabic/Dutch conversation', *Studies in Multilingualism*. Vol. 12. Tilburg University Press.

Budzhak-Jones, S. and Poplack, S. (1997) 'Two generations, two strategies: the fate of bare English-origin nouns in Ukrainian', *Journal of Sociolinguistics*, 1: 225–58.

Cechirlan, N. (2008) 'Code-switching zwischen Rumänisch und Russisch in Moldawien – eine pragmatische Analyse'. Master thesis, University of Freiburg.

Clyne, M. (1980) 'Triggering and language processing', *Canadian Journal of Psychology*, 34: 400–6.

Clyne, M. (2003) *Dynamics of Language Contact*. Cambridge: Cambridge University Press.

de Fina, A. (2007) 'Style and stylization in the construction of identities in a card-playing club', in P. Auer (ed.), *Style and Social Identities*. Berlin: Mouton. pp. 57–84.

Fabian, J. (1990) *Power and Performance. Ethnographic Explorations through Proverbial Wisdom and Theater in Shaba, Zaire*. Madison: University of Wisconsin Press.

Finlayson, R., Calteaux, K. and Myers-Scotton, C. (1998) 'Orderly mixing and accommodation in South African codeswitching', *Journal of Sociolinguistics*, 2(3): 395–420.

Gafaranga, J. (2000) 'Language separateness: a normative framework in studies of language alternation', *Estudios de Sociolingüística*, 1: 65–84.

Gafaranga J. (2007) 'Code-switching as conversational strategy', in P. Auer, and W. Li (eds), *Handbook of Multilingualism and Multilingual Communication*. Berlin: de Gruyter. pp. 279–313.

Gafaranga J. and Torras, M.-C. (2001) 'Language vs. medium in the study of bilingual conversation', *International Journal of Bilingualism*, 5: 195–219.

Gal, S. (1988) 'The political economy of code choice', in M. Heller, (ed.), *Codeswitching. Anthropological and sociolinguistic Perspectives*. Berlin: Mouton de Gruyter. pp. 245–64.

Goffman, E. (1963) *Behavior in Public Places*. Toronto: The Free Press of Glencoe.

Guerini, F. (2006) *Language Alternation Strategies in Multilingual Settings*. Bern: Lang.

Gullberg, M., Indefrey, P. and Muysken, P. (2009) 'Research techniques for the study of code-switching', in B. E. Bullock and A. J. Toribio (eds), *The Cambridge Handbook on Linguistic Code-Switching*, (pp. 21–39). Cambridge: Cambridge University Press.

Gumperz, John (1982) *Discourse Strategies*. Cambridge: Cambridge University Press.

Heller, M. (ed.) (1988a) *Codeswitching. Anthropological and Sociolinguistic Perspectives*. Berlin: Mouton de Gruyter.

Heller, M. (1988b) 'Strategic ambiguity: code-switching in the management of conflict', in M. Heller (ed.), *Codeswitching. Athropological and Sociolinguistic Perspectives*. Berlin: Mouton de Grayter. pp. 77–96.

Heller, M. (1992) 'The politics of codeswitching and language choice', *Journal of Multilingual and Multicultural Development*, 13(1, 2): 123–42.

Heller, M. (2007) 'Bilingualism as ideology and practice', in M. Heller (ed.), *Bilingualism – A Social Approach*. Houndmills: Palgrave. pp. 1–22.

Hill, J. and Hill, K. (1986) *Speaking Mexicano*. Tucson, AZ: University of Arizona Press.

Hinnenkamp, V. (2005) '"Zwei zu *bir miydi?*" – Mischsprachliche Varietäten von Migrantenjugendlichen im Hybriditätsdiskurs', in V. Hinnekamp and K. Meng (eds), *Sprachgrenzen überspringen. Sprachliche Hybridität und polykulturelles Selbstverständnis*. Tübingen: Narr. pp. 51–103.

Jaspers, J. (2005) 'Linguistic sabotage in a context of monolingualism and standardization', in 'Multilingualism and diasporic populations: spatializing practices, institutional processes, and social hierarchies', *Journal of Language and Communication* (Special Issue), 25(3): 279–97.

Jonsson, C. (2005) *Code-Switching in Chicano Theater*. University of Umeå, Institutionen för moderna språk, *Skrifter* No. 17.

Karrebaek, M. S. (2003) 'Iconicity and structure in codeswitching', *International Journal of Bilingualism*,7(4): 407–41.

Kühl, K. H. (2008) 'Bilingualer Sprachgebrauch von Jugendlichen im deutsch-dänischen Grenzgebiet – eine strukturelle und pragmatische Analyse'. PhD thesis, University of Flensburg.

Li, W. (1994) *Three Generations, Two Languages, One Family. Language Choice and Language Shift in a Chinese Community in Britain*. Clevedon, UK: Multilingual Matters.

Li, W. (2002) ''What do you want me to say?'' On the conversation analysis approach to bilingual interaction', *Language and Society*, 31: 159–80.

McLelland, N. (2004) 'A historical study of codeswitching in writing: "German and Latin in Schottelius" "Ausführliche Arbeit von der Teutschen HaubtSprache" (1663)', *International Journal of Bilingualism*, 8(4): 499–523.

Meeuwis, M. and Blommaert, J. (1994) 'The "Markedness Model" and the absence of society: remarks on codeswitching', *Multilingua*, 14(4): 387–423.

Meeuwis, M. and Blommaert, J. (1998) 'A monolectal view of code-switching: layered code-switching among Zairians in Belgium', in P. Auer, (ed.), *Code-Switching in Conversation. Language, Interaction and Identity*. London/New York: Routledge. pp. 76–100.

Muhamedowa, R. (2006)*Untersuchungen zum kasachisch-russischen Code-mixing (mit Ausblicken auf den uigurisch-russischen Sprachkontakt)*. München: Lincom.

Muhamedova, R. and Auer, P. (2005) '"Embedded language" and "Matrix language" in insertional language mixing: some problematic cases', *Italian Journal of Linguistics / Rivista di linguistica*, 17(1) (Special Issue 'Commutazione di codice e teoria linguistica', edited by Gaetano Berruto): 35–54.

Musk, N. (2006) 'Performing bilingualism in Wales with the spotlight on Welsh'. *Linköping Studies in Arts and Science*, 375.

Muysken, P. (2000) *Bilingual Speech: A Typology of Code-Mixing*. Cambridge: Cambridge University Press.

Myers-Scotton, C. (1988) 'Code switching as indexical of social negotiations', in M. Heller, (ed.), *Codeswitching. Antropological and sociological perspectives*. pp. 151–86. (Reprinted in Li, W. (ed.) (2000) *The Bilingualism Reader*. London, UK: Routledge. pp. 137–165, and in Li, W. (ed.) (2007) *The Bilingualism Reader*. 2nd edn. Milton Park, UK: Routledge. pp. 97–122.)

Myers-Scotton, C. (1993a) *Social Motivations for Codeswitching*. Oxford: Oxford University Press.

Myers-Scotton, C. (1993b) 'Elite closure as a powerful language strategy: the African case', *International Journal of Sociology and Language*, 103: 149–63.

Myers-Scotton, C. (2002) *Contact Linguistics. Bilingual Encounters and Grammatical Outcomes*. Oxford: Oxford University Press.

Nortier, Jacomine (1990) *Dutch-Moroccan Arabic Code Switching Among Moroccans in the Netherlands*. Dordrecht, Holland: Foris Publications.

Owens, J. (2005) 'Hierachicalized matrices: codeswitching among urban Nigerian Arabs', *Linguistics*, 43(5): 957–93.

Paul, H. (1898) *Prinzipien der Sprachgeschichte*. Halle: Niemeyer.

Pfaff, C. (2003) 'Ideological and political framing of bilingual development: reflections on studies of Turkish/German in Berlin', in K. Fraurud and K. Hyltenstam (eds), *Multilingualism in Global and Local Perspectives*. Stockholm: Center for Research on Bilingualism. pp. 191–220.

Poplack, S. (1980) '"Sometimes I'll start a sentence in Spanish Y TERMINO EN ESPAÑOL": toward a typology of code-switching', *Linguistics*, 18: 581–618.

Poplack, S. (2004) 'Code-switching', in U. Ammon, N. Dittmar, K. J. Mattheier and P. Trudgill (eds), *Soziolinguistik, An International Handbook*. 2nd edn. Berlin: de Gruyter. pp. 589–96.

Pujolar, J. (2007) 'Bilingualism and the nation-state in the post-national era', in M. Heller (ed.), *Bilingualism – A Social Approach*. Houndmills: Palgrave. pp. 71–110.

Rampton, B. (2000) 'Speech community', in J. Verschueren, J. -O., Östman, J. Blommaert and C. Bulcaen (eds), *Handbook of Pragmatics*. Amsterdam: John Benjamins. pp. 1–34.

Reershemius, G. (2001) '"Token codeswitching" and language alternation in narrative discourse: a functional-pragmatic approach', *International Journal of Bilingualism*, 5(2): 175–94.

Sankoff, D. (1998) 'A formal production-based explanation of the facts of code-switching', *Bilingualism – Language and Cognition*, 1: 39–50.

Sankoff, D. and Poplack, S. (1981) 'A formal grammar for code-switching', *Papers in Linguistics*, 14: 3–45.

Sebba, M. and Wootton, T. (1998) 'We, they and identity: sequential versus identity-related explanation in code-switching', in P. Auer, (ed.), *Code-Switching in Conversation. Language, Interaction and Identity*. London/New York: Routledge. pp. 262–89.

Stolt, B. (1964) *Die Sprachmischung in Luthers Tischreden. Studien zum Problem der Zweisprachigkeit*. Stockholm: Almqvist and Wiksell.

Stroud, C. (2007) 'Multilingualism in ex-colonial countries', in P. Auer and W. Li, (eds), *Handbook of Multilingualism and Multilingual Communication*. Berlin: Mouton de Gruyter. pp. 509–38.

Szabó, C. (2007–08) 'Language shift und code-mixing: Deutsch-ungarisch-rumänische Mehrsprachigkeit in einer dörflichen Gemeinde in Nordwestrumänien'. PhD thesis, University of Freiburg.

Timm, L. A. (1978) 'Code-switching in "War and Peace"', in M. Paradis, (ed.), *Aspects of Bilingualism*. Columbia, SC: Hornbeam Press. pp. 236–49.

Türker, E. (2000) *Turkish–Norwegian Codeswitching*. University of Oslo, Faculty of Arts, Dissertation Series No. 83.

Verschik, A. (2005) 'Russian–Estonian contacts, linguistic creativity, and convergence: new rules in the making', *Multilingua*, 24(4): 413–29.

Vogt, H. (1954) 'Language contact', *Word*, 10(2, 3): 365–74.

Woolard, K. A. (1989) *Double Talk*. Stanford, CA: Stanford University Press.

Ziamari, K. (2003)'Le Code switching intra-phrastique dans les conversations des étudiants marocains de l'ENSAM: approche linguistique du duel entre l'árabe marocain et le français'. Thèse de doctorat, INALCO-Fès.

Language Policy and Planning

Anne-Claude Berthoud
and Georges Lüdi

32.1 INTRODUCTION

The notion of 'language policy' is vast. It includes any form of intervention (and indeed non-intervention – i.e. *laissez-faire*) by a political authority to direct and regulate the use, by the administration and/or the population, of one or more languages in a given political area. Language policy comprises, and rests on, ideological choices and their underlying principles determining the selection of various goals. These may concern the status, use, domains of use and geographical range of a language or of multiple linguistic varieties that are in competition. Thus, the linguistic framework put in place in Switzerland during the nineteenth and twentieth centuries notably focused on the introduction of a principle of territoriality and the regulation of the proportionality of linguistic groups at the heart of the federal administration (Widmer et al., 2004).

Language policies can be direct and open. In these cases, the political authority intervenes openly, for example by modifying the direction of social forces in favour of one language or another, often (but certainly not always) by repressive measures, the key to this being 'language legislation' – i.e. the culmination of juridical norms (laws,[1] regulations, decrees) which state the linguistic rights and obligations regarding the use of languages in diverse areas of social life at the heart of the political unit. However, we should not confuse the notions of language policy and language legislation, as is often the case in modern usage. If we do not make the distinction, we should restrict our understanding of 'language policy' to cases of **explicit** language policy, concerning the promotion of languages (in, for

example, their roles as 'national' languages, as is the case in the Swiss linguistic framework) or the tolerance of languages (as with minority and regional languages according to the terms of the *European Charter for Regional or Minority Languages*). And yet, language policy can also be indirect or covert. As such, enacting (or not enacting) economic development measures in favour of regions in which linguistic minorities live constitutes an indirect political measure, as does leaving social forces to develop 'freely' – for example, when an authority does not impose the language of power on a certain people, but instead offers it as a tool for social betterment, to access cultural materials, education, knowledge and political power (Mackey, 1976). Put differently, all political entities endorse linguistic policy, even in the absence of official intervention in the use of a language or of languages within the relevant geopolitical space.

The notion of language policy incorporates 'language planning'. When this term appeared, in a seminal text by Einar Haugen in 1959, it denoted 'the activity of preparing a normative orthography, grammar, and dictionary for the guidance of writers and speakers in a non-homogeneous speech community', citing the Norwegian example. Since the end of the 1960s, this notion has been widened to include any type of intervention which addresses sociolinguistic problems.[2] Since then, language planning has been considered as the enactment of (explicit) linguistic policy by way of a 'road map'. Planning implies not only decisions at the political level but also all choices relative to the domains and modes of intervention. These choices presuppose sociolinguistic knowledge of both the situation on the ground and the desired situation, as well as the enactment of a strategy (certain choices lead to a specific law; others will be simply formulated in a rather ad hoc manner, within various legal acts or regulations which themselves do not address linguistic usage, but which will indeed have repercussions in this area) and the evaluation of a strategy's impact. Such interventions may seek to influence the direction and the manner in which languages compete, or else to shape the language itself (see Maurais et al., 1987). Haugen's model (1983: 275), which has been revised by Kaplan and Baldauf (1997: 29), outlines the domains of language planning as in Table 32.1

However, useful as this Table 32.1 may be, it explains only part of the language planning process in context. Thus, we would list the principal factors which language planning must account for as follows:

- **Who** (which agents, e.g. formal élites, influentials, counter-elites, non-elite policy implementers)[5]
- **plans what** (which behaviours are to be influenced, e.g. structural (linguistic) properties of planned behaviour[6] [= corpus planning]; purposes/functions for which planned behaviour is to be used; desired level of adoption, e.g. awareness, evaluation, proficiency, usage [= status planning])
- **for whom** (type of target, e.g. individuals vs. organizations; opportunity of target to learn planned behaviour; incentives of target to learn/use or reject planned behaviour)
- **for what ends** (overt, e.g. language-related behaviours or latent – that is, non-language-related – behaviours)
- **for the benefit of whom** (reproduction of the power of a dominant group, promotion of language minorities, satisfaction of commercial interests, symbolic benefits)
- **under what conditions**[7] (in what context, e.g. types of communicative events, transient or permanent conditions; structural-political, economic, or social/demographic/ecological;[8]

cultural; environmental, e.g. influences from outside the system; informational, e.g. data required to make good decisions)
- **how** (by what means, e.g. authority, force, promotion, persuasion; through what decision-making process, e.g. by what kind of legislation; and with what effect).

As has been shown, one of the principal goals of linguistic management policies and plans concerns the selection and the development of one – and only one – 'national' language. The ideological background to this process goes back a long way. It is founded on the received wisdom that monolingualism represents an original state, intended by God and/or politically legitimized by human beings. To an extent, this stereotype can be seen in the Bible – that is to say, in the belief that multilingualism, resulting from 'confusion', has encumbered people like a divine curse ever since the construction of the Tower of Babel (Genesis 11, 6–7). It is again found in Greek philosophy, starting with Aristotle; the Renaissance, in turn, acquired it from medieval scholasticism. Between the French Revolution (Barère, 1794; Grégoire, 1794) and World War I, nationalist sentiments began to be linked with religious belief, as well as coming under the influence of Romantic ideas (Herder, 1794; Fichte, 1808; etc.); they are discussed with metaphors borrowed from religious history, and build up the myth of the 'nation' as reflected in a common language.

Within this framework, individual bilingualism is perceived as dangerous, in many ways. It is seen as a threat to people's command of the language of the nation, as well as a menace to the unitary culture attached to that language. In summary, bilinguals, particularly childhood bilinguals, will have their cognitive and social identity threatened. Similarly, language contact is mistrusted, particularly in regions known for their bilingualism. Languages spoken by non-dominant groups of the population are either ignored or even repressed. Modern examples of this philosophy can be found in many countries.[9]

Table 32.1 Language planning

	Form (policy planning)	Function (language cultivation)
Society (status planning)	1. Selection[3] (decision procedures) (a) problem identification (b) allocation of norms	3. Implementation[4] (educational spread) (a) corrective procedures (b) evaluation
Language (corpus planning)	2. Codification (standardization procedures) (a) graphization (b) grammatiction (c) lexication	4. Elaboration (functional development) (a) terminological modernization (b) stylistic development (c) internationalization

And yet, this attitude is changing, within the framework of transnational political connections and under the impact of globalization. For instance, specialists (e.g. Tutzinger Thesen, 1999; Beacco, 2004) and decision-makers are beginning to argue that Europe's identity is fundamentally linked to linguistic diversity. As the European Commissioner responsible for multilingualism formulated it in October 2008:

'Europe today is a bastion of diversity. And language is a fundamental part of this. Through it, we construct our identity. Diversity has sometimes been seen as an obstacle to European unity. Today, on the contrary, it seems a beneficial right. It is one of the ties that bind our union' (Orban, 2008).

Other continents such as Africa are following this path (cf. for example the *Accra Declaration* of 1996 (Alexander, 2006), or priority area four in the 'Plan of action' discussed at the *Second Extraordinary Meeting of the Conference of Ministers of Education of the African Union, 4–7 September 2006*). International conventions insist upon the rights of linguistic minorities (cf. Duchêne, 2008) and often impact upon national planning frameworks.

However, diversity management is not limited to geopolitical territories. More and more often, institutions (such as the European Commission or higher education institutions) or businesses (in particular, those which operate according to an 'international framework') have cause to regulate the use of the languages which they use. In order to distinguish these developmental endeavours from those which are political, the term 'linguistic strategies' (or, better, 'language management') can be introduced. This term refers to all forms of intervention of an institution or company or its agents, respectively, in its members' and/or employees' linguistic repertoires, their representations of language and multilingualism, and their language behaviour in internal and external communication. Forms of interventions could be, for example, a company's linguistic landscaping,[10] its recruitment policy, guidelines for on-the-job training, choice of language for the internal magazine, policies for oral exchanges between apprentices and employees from different language regions, choice of languages for vertical communication between management and employees (contracts, general information, salary sheets, etc.), choice of language for job adverts, and so on. Some of these interventions are overt, i.e. explicitly communicated in official documents (e.g. on a company's webpage).[11] However, these sets of interventions – which are far from monolithic – are frequently covert and must be deduced from traces in the data, as we will see later on.

It can be added that language policies, planning and strategies have always existed. And yet, the growth of population mobility, the reorganization of political frontiers and the creation of new transnational political spaces (such as the European Union) have increased the respective challenges for decision-makers at all levels. Increasingly, new situations and dynamics regarding multilingualism and languages in contact require interventions which guarantee the coexistence of languages which are, at the same time, effective and fair, with respect to different speaker groups within a given geopolitical space (or one to be created), in order to prevent one linguistic group dominating the socio-economic landscape, or to maintain that which is often termed linguistic peace or social cohesion (Lüdi et al., 2008). It is true that *laissez-faire* policies, for example regarding the increasing importance of English, can also be frequently observed.

32.2 BETWEEN ANALYSIS AND INTERVENTION: THE DYLAN PROJECT

Linguists and other social scientists can be employed with a variety of briefs in the processes of language policies and planning or linguistic strategy-making, be it in preparing the ground with sociolinguistic studies, in intervening in these processes in their capacity as experts, or in describing and explaining the processes. We shall illustrate this in the following with the example of the European DYLAN Research Project.[12] The aim was to track 'language dynamics' in order to contribute in an innovative way to the discovery of optimal manners in which to develop diversity management: the challenge being to formulate research questions which were likely to be relevant both to the immediate demands of practitioners as well as to the researchers' interests. This implies the reconciliation of two 'cultures' which are generally unaccustomed to negotiation – the culture of the researcher and the culture of those in whom political power is vested.

The overarching thrust was to show the conditions under which the linguistic diversity prevalent in Europe is potentially an asset rather than an obstacle. Against this background, three main objectives were formulated (summarized here from Berthoud, 2008a):

(a) to develop a fine-grained understanding of the ways in which multilingual repertoires are developed and used in various situations;
(b) to identify the conditions that need to be met in order for the development and use of multilingual repertoires, which are part of the

European heritage and ethos, to be prioritized so that they might contribute to the development of a knowledge-based society, and lead to broader conceptual, argumentative and strategic opportunities;

(c) to help formulate policy recommendations for the effective, cost-effective and democratic management of linguistic diversity in Europe by investigating the ways in which different modes of thinking and different forms of behaviour, carried by different languages, can promote the creation, transfer and application of knowledge, and contribute a genuinely valuable input in the sharing and transfer of information, problem solving, and operations control (strategic asset).

This is done by assessing and comparing competing communication scenarios in various professional and institutional settings, in order to identify their respective advantages and drawbacks, as well as their relative efficiency and fairness. Advantages and drawbacks should be understood in a broad sense, including social and cultural dimensions as well as financial ones. Research results intend to serve as a benchmark for a better understanding of complex processes in which key aspects of language learning and communicational practices are combined.

Four dimensions constitute the project's conceptual cornerstones: (1) actual language practices; (2) representations ('images') of multilingualism and linguistic diversity, which will be captured through discourse; (3) the language policies of states or other public bodies (local, regional or national authorities, as well as supranational organizations) and the language strategies of management of private-sector companies; and (4) the linguistic context, or 'language environment' in which agents operate. These four dimensions are related in a number of ways, and these interrelationships were to be studied in three settings: namely, private-sector companies, EU institutions and institutions of higher education.

In this chapter, the idea is not to present the project's results as a whole. Instead, we will go into more depth within two subprojects particularly related to language policy and planning. The first one deals with the analysis of the manner in which companies form linguistic strategies, and includes the measurement of the impact of these strategies; it confronts these with actual practices within these same companies. The second one deals with the question of how deep changes in the context can bring institutions of higher education to reconsider their policies and strategies related to languages, by observing multilingual learning practices in universities.

32.3 THE MANAGEMENT OF MULTILINGUALISM BY COMPANIES AND COMPANIES' IMPACT ON LINGUISTIC PRACTICE

In the following section, we will attempt to show that there is an area of tension between the declared and implicit language policies and management measures of companies on the one hand, and recurrent behavioural patterns emerging in linguistic practices on the other. We will do so, at first, by way of examples from the business world.

An example of a transactional interaction

Example 1

Employee	Gueten obe (2)((the client hands over the ticket)) merci. Was hän si für e Wunsch ? *Good evening … what can I do for you?*
Customer	ehm if you mind if I speak English ?
Employee	No problem.
Customer	Thank you. I am wondering if there's any specials available yet on the TGV from Lausanne to Paris
Employee	Mhm. When do you travel?
Customer	The 30th of (2) december.
Employee	Oh that's too early.
Customer	Too early, [okey]
Employee	[You can book it], you can book it eh (..) three months in advance.

Example 1 was recorded at the ticket booths at Basel station in 2007 (Barth, 2008). As is the case in Basel, within the diglossic framework involving Standard German (distance language, predominant in writing) and Swiss German (proximity language, predominant in speaking), the employee addresses the new customer in Swiss German. The customer asks if she may speak English. The employee consents, the customer formulates her question in English and the employee follows her choice in the response to the question. The remainder of the conversation takes place in English.

In Example 1, the employee approaches the customer according to a social rule (in German-speaking Switzerland, the reference language is Swiss German) and changes languages according to an incongruence of repertoires (the customer prefers to speak or can only speak English). Lukas Barth (2008), who has analysed some 60 hours of interactions at these booths, with different employees and numerous customers, has shown that these two choice phenomena are recurrent in his corpus and so correspond well to a fixed **schema** in this type of script (buying/selling interactions and/or advice at a booth). However, it is a form of behaviour which can be found in a variety of other contexts of workplace communication. Thus, questions arise concerning whether – and if yes, to what extent – these behavioural patterns are freely chosen by interlocutors, whether the social rules correspond to collective and non-codified knowledge, or whether these behavioural patterns are founded on recommendations/prescriptions/laws formulated by state authorities and/or the relevant company, which may in turn be influenced by observed behaviours.

Language management in Public Service B

These recordings are part of the fieldwork undertaken as part of the DYLAN Project. The University of Basel team's research task was to analyse the ways in which companies draw up their language management plans, to measure the impact of the latter, and to compare them with actual practices in these companies.[13] These measures, of which we have seen a hint at the end of Section 32.1, are to be distinguished from the 'linguistic policies' of the state or region in which the company is based, which are part of the context which will determine the manner in which it deals with languages.[14]

Let us present here some preliminary findings:

1   Ethnographic inquiry has revealed an important stratification of language management in numerous companies, with rules being established at very different hierarchical levels. A company is thus not a unique social agent, as handbooks dealing with integrated business communication suggest (see, for example, Bruhn, 2003). These rules are quite consistent when a common strategic vision is implemented by the lower echelons ('A business such as ours is, at its core, multilingual', explains the head of Diversity Management of Public Service B (the company discussed here) when responding to the question of multilingualism in that company, and continues: 'Customers as well as colleagues expect us to be able to communicate perfectly in the most important languages' [quotations of the *Werkzeugkasten zur Förderung der Sprachenvielfalt im Unternehmen*']).[15] However, significant fractures may appear where language management is influenced by contradictory factors: corporate identity vs local legislation (as in the GEMS case); the tendency to choose a single language of business vs the diversity of the employees' repertoires (as is true in the case of

Pharmaceutical Company A which recommends English as the business language, but where one employee told us 'ich habe schon x-Mal Englischkurs angefangen, und nachher jedes Mal habe ich ein Wutanfall gekriegt, muss ich diese Scheisse lernen, ich will das nicht und so, und dann früher oder später brech ich ab [Mara S.]');[16] upward accommodation ('we speak the boss's language') vs downward accommodation (the boss speaks the employees' language)[17], and so forth.

2   The distinction between 'management measures' and 'practices' becomes less distinct if one understands by 'linguistic practices' not only multilevel oral interaction and all forms of written usage but also publicity, language selection in Internet pages and the company's semiotic landscape, linguistic competence verification practices at the hiring stage, and so on. As such, Public Service B's administrative committee's strategy ('Our business is multilingual') leads, as we will see below, to a series of operational-level practices regarding company management (such as the elaboration of a 'linguistic guide' and of instructions pertaining to the drafting of publicity within an integrated communication plan framework); but these 'practices' in turn represent a new – more direct – form of intervention in employees' behaviour. Personnel management measures, in recruitment or higher-level training, as well as publicity campaigns, can be considered as practical output of a company's linguistic strategy, and at the same time perceived by the individuals concerned as new forms of intervention, and so on. A multimethodological approach guaranteed the coherence of our case study – in particular when it comes to different forms of interventions and practices at different levels – and allowed for comparisons between different companies.

What are the impacts of different forms of intervention and how can they be measured?

In Public Service B, a company from which a sample of interactions at the ticket booth has been recorded, corporate identity, such as can be observed from analyses of official texts, Internet pages and discussions with directors, can be summarized as 'we are a multilingual company'. Unlike other companies, which seek to impose a single language of work on their employees, Public Service B draws its language management ethos according to the template of a multilingual Switzerland. National languages are prioritized in internal communications;[18] to these, English must be added when considering external communication with foreign customers. This strategic vision has led to a series of language management measures. In the following, we concentrate on the potential 'impact' of some of these measures.[19] Initially, this term designates concrete results, quantifiable outputs which implement the respective 'philosophies' of companies. In the case of Public Service B, these are: allocation of necessary resources for the translation of different texts and web pages (including an internal translation service); specification of required multilingual skills in job advertisements; language classes offered as part of advanced training programmes; creation of exchange programmes between different linguistic regions; creation of 'mixed groups'; distribution of languages on the site map; and so on.

Amongst these outputs is a document of particular importance. A communications firm was commissioned to produce a 'linguistic guide' for the employees, which contains numerous recommendations regarding oral and written usage, with, amongst other things, directives concerning choice of language at ticket booths, on the telephone, and so forth. This guide is consistent with the corporate identity in that it insists on two forms of multilingualism.

(a) The **institutional multilingualism** of the company:
   - <Le Service public B> communique en trois langues. [<Public Service B> communicates in three languages]
   - Nous communiquons par écrit en français, en allemand, en italien et en anglais. [Our written communication is in French, German, Italian and English]

Ethnographic analysis confirms this: the logo is trilingual; the Intranet is trilingual German–French–Italian; employees are free to choose which of the three national languages they prefer to use to communicate with the management; as such, they receive all internal documents in the selected language, from contracts to regulations to the internal magazine; most brochures exist in three languages, with those written for tourists additionally printed in English; and most parts of the Internet site are available in German, French, Italian and English (Beydoun, 2008).

(b) On individual multilingualism required for the accommodation, so far as possible, of the customer:
   - On the telephone: 'Beim ersten Zeichen, dass uns jemand nicht versteht, wechseln wir in die Sprache des Anrufenden. Wenn das nicht möglich ist, sprechen wir Hochdeutsch'. [At the first indication of a lack of understanding, we switch into the language of the caller. If this is not possible, we speak Standard German.]

This need is reiterated through a whole series of measures concerning employees' multilingual skills during hiring and training of personnel. An initial analysis of online job offers (24 April 2008) confirms that Public Service B explicitly demands, for a variety of contexts, good linguistic skills, particularly when it comes to national languages:

- Sie sind deutscher oder französischer Muttersprache und haben ausgezeichnete Kenntnisse der jeweils anderen Sprache. [French or German mother-tongue, with excellent knowledge of the other language.]
- Vous maîtrisez la langue française et avez de bonnes connaissances d'allemand (écrit et parlé). [You have a solid command of French, with good knowledge of German (written and spoken).]

Elsewhere, Public Service B has developed linguistic profiles for its personnel:

- Kommunikation und somit auch Fremdsprachen gehören zu den Kernkompetenzen des Verkaufs- und Zugpersonals. [Communication and thus foreign languages are within the basic skills of sales and train staff.]
- Dieses Sprachprofil ist Teil des Anforderungsprofils der beiden Berufsbilder 'Zugbegleitung' und 'Verkauf' der <Public Service B>. [This linguistic profile is part of the job specifications for train and sales staff in Public Service B.]

The practice of linguistic accommodation of the customer, seen above, is thus written into the philosophy of the company. As a result, one can observe an important, visible, measurable and consistent 'impact' of the management of multilingualism in Public Service B.

However, does the behaviour illustrated at the outset truly represent the impact of the multilingual philosophy of the company? This can still be doubted to some extent. To begin with, this behaviour may not be so much part of the **output** as defined above, but part of the real effects (**outcomes**) of measures taken by the company in the field of behavioural planning and/or the representations of the relevant agents. If it is relatively easy to find indicators by which to measure **output**, it is by no means equally straightforward to do so in relation to **effects** as exemplified by the indicators mentioned below. A combination of methods – analysis of semi-directed interviews and different types of discourse (brochures, websites) for representations, participatory observation, recording and analysis of oral interaction corpora, etc., – for various practices, must be grappled with. These indicators are very diverse, such as the circulation of different versions of brochures and their availability at points of sale, the number of readers per Internet-site version, employees' real-time usage in the situations outlined in the guide, the actual linguistic competence of the employees and its outcome in salary terms, the dominance of German, the reduction of French and, particularly, Italian to minority status within mixed groups, and so forth. In this case, one would have to demonstrate that the cause–effect link between these behavioural patterns and the 'Linguistic Guide' is at least plausible. This is the case in call centres where the employees' linguistic behaviour is monitored continuously, thus raising their awareness of the rules and regulations imposed by the company (Duchêne, pers comm). As far as we could observe, no such monitoring of the application of the guidelines takes place in Public Service B.

The 'bottom-up' perspective

Having said the above, it should be noted that company interventions are far from always being transparent. Often, they seem to reveal a tacit shared knowledge; everyone 'knows' that a rule

exists, even if it is not written. Frequently, decision-making processes are opaque – in that they obfuscate responsibilities – or are simply unknown. This shows that not all of the recurrent practices which can be observed within companies can be attributed to interventions 'from upstairs'. Often, they represent social behaviour patterns co-constructed by the agents, reacting in a way which eludes managerial interventions. The relation between possible interventions and recurrent practices must be tackled 'the other way up', as it were, by describing regularities in practices before asking whether these are themselves generated by the internalization of 'hidden' interventions or by the 'free' movement of extant social forces **even if these seem to conform to the company's philosophy**.

To illustrate this, in Example 2 we analyse a second oral interaction at a ticket booth between an employee, who will here be named Studer, and a Brazilian customer:

In an extreme exolinguistic situation (where there is no common variety), the buyer and the seller negotiate the choice of language at the beginning of the interaction by laying out the possible resources

Example 2

Studer	guete tag
	good day
Customer	pardon
Studer	pardon ? Oui oui ?
	pardon ? yes yes
Customer	je parle português
	I speak Portuguese
Studer	oh je parle pas português ((final s pronounced))
	oh, I don't speak Portuguese
Customer	Brasilia
Studer	okey. italien ou français oui oui ?=
	ok, Italian or French
Customer	=<duos passagem para Freiburg deutsch>.
	Two tickets to Freiburg german
Studer	Freiburg Deutschland jä okey. (22) voilà, si vous, faire la carte à la machine? oui. (3) va bene. (5) c'est sans une code. vous fais ((sic)) la signature après. (2) non non il va revenir. ((client holds credit card instead of letting it go)) Si vous fais votre signature pour cinquante huit ?
	Freiburg Germany yeah ok … here, could you put the credit card into the machine? yes … that's good … it is without code … you sign afterwards … no no, it will get back … can you sign for fifty eight?
Customer	((signs)) (13)
	(....)
Studer	voilà. il prossimo treno (.) binario cinco hm? Dodici diciotto.
	That's good … the next train … track five yes? at eighteen past twelve
Customer	(3) merci. [obrigado].
	Thank you (in French) thank you (in Portuguese)

Studer	[bitteschön]. Service
	you're welcome (German) you're welcome (French)
Customer	obrigado (h)
	thank you (in Portuguese)
Studer	molto grazio. ((sic))
	thank you (in Italian)
Studer	((to the researcher)) es goht mit händ und füess aber
	es goht
	it works, with hands and feet, but it works

(Portuguese, Italian, French, German), but with no choice being made. Effectively, Studer at first ascertains the impossibility of choosing the customer's language; however, rather than following the 'guide' ('if you cannot speak the customer's language, choose Standard German'), he proposes two Romance languages between which a choice can be made. The customer responds with a mix of simplified Portuguese and German. This multilingual communication strategy succeeds; Studer confirms the destination in German and prints the ticket. Then, he asks the client to place his credit card into the machine in highly approximated French, confirms the action, this time in Italian ('va bene'), continues the explanation in simplified French and then oversees the act of signing. Later on, Studer gives further information on the next train in a mix of French ('voilà'), Italian ('il prossimo treno/binario/dodici diciotto') and Spanish ('cinco'). At the point of acknowledgement, the customer combines French and Portuguese, and Studer reacts with a juxtaposition of German and French ('bitteschön, service') and concludes the interaction with approximated Italian ('molto grazio).

How is this interaction to be interpreted? One of the first things that must be said is that it is a successful interaction, as Studer himself confirms; the customer buys the desired ticket. This success is clearly due, at least in part, to mutual knowledge of a simple and recurrent script (mention of the destination, payment by credit card), but also to the optimal employment of a package of verbal and non-verbal means which the agents have at their disposal. The mention of a given language does not lead to its exclusive usage, but serves as a contextualization cue to flag its pertinence. In fact, the mutually accepted solution is the multilingual mode. Furthermore, as Studer mobilizes his resources, he does so according to a subjacent representation that Romance languages are intercomprehensible; at the same time, he glosses over the boundaries between the languages by speaking – consciously or otherwise – some kind of 'pan-Romance'. Studer's behaviour and representations do not correspond to one

another entirely, but their self-clarification is mutual.

The discussion with Studer reveals a high degree of metalinguistic consciousness. He is clearly proud of his multilingualism, which represents, in a workplace context which he describes as characterized by extreme linguistic diversity, a tool indispensable for his work. Thanks to his large repertoire, he is also able to help others. Going beyond the company's basic instructions, he has developed a package of strategies used to communicate successfully. Amongst these strategies, one can note not only the use of English as a 'default' language but also recourse to the intercomprehensibility of Romance languages. His responses regarding 'language mixes' are for the most part ambivalent; he recognizes his alternation between French and the Alemannic dialect with Alsatians, and uses lexical code-switching and translinguistic wordings when he speaks Dutch.[20] However, what is most striking about Studer's representations is a perspective which is far more differentiated from the employment of multilingual repertoires than that which is found in the company's documentation, which limits agents to the choice of one language or another. Comparing what is said with what is done, it can be stated that Studer is far more 'multilingual' in his behaviour, in the sense that he mixes more languages with ease, than he is conscious of himself – and that he goes far beyond the guidelines of the company contained in its official documents.

One of the things we were interested in knowing was whether or not the recurrent behaviour patterns observed during the sales interactions at the Basel ticket booth represent the impact of the company's language management, or a social practice freely developed by the agents in question. In order to answer this question, we had to consider the significance of the company's language management and its impact. We can return to this question by making the following statement: the recurrently observable patterns in our ticket booth interaction corpus are very likely a reflection, or a manifestation, of a 'multilingual philosophy' on the part of the company, which is laid out in a 'linguistic guide' recommending certain forms of behaviour and, doubtless, training courses which seek to disseminate these forms of behaviour to newly-recruited ticketing staff. Moreover, the regular behaviour of employees, on both individual and collective bases, can be explained by the internalization and transformation of these instructions within forms of representation and lines of argument which are shared between station colleagues. The importance of recruitment and internal linguistic training policies indicates that they explicitly take into account the key role which employees' individual multilingualism plays in the enactment of a multilingual philosophy, which is, for the most part, territorial in the sense of the Swiss territoriality principle of languages.

From a conceptual point of view, this reinforces the position of those who suggest that the classical notion of competence be replaced by that of linguistic repertoire, or even verbal resources (for references, see Moore et. al., 2007). The term 'resources' designates an indefinite and open package of grammatical and syntactic (and, of course, paralinguistic) microsystems, partially stabilized and available to both speaker and interlocutor. These microsystems can stem from different varieties of one language or from different languages, as well as diverse discursive experiences. They are shaped like semi-organized sets of often heterogeneous means, similar to a handyman's toolbox. Some are prefabricated and memorized, whilse others are innovated utterance-creation procedures, amongst which can be found heuristic means designed either to reinforce already available communicative resources or to develop hypotheses pertaining to the interpretation of other languages. In other words, they allow the speaker to create and play around – to conduct a verbal activity in a particular context, and thus to take risks (Lüdi and Py, 2009), a wonderful example of which we have seen in Example 2.

32.4 THE MANAGEMENT OF MULTILINGUALISM IN AND BY HIGHER EDUCATION INSTITUTIONS

To show the indirect relations between linguistic strategies and practices, the need to introduce stratification between the different levels implied, and the need to distinguish between overt policies and covert policies, we will here cite an example of research conducted in Lausanne, taken from the DYLAN subproject on institutions of higher education. This aims to analyse the effects of multilingualism on the processes of constructing and transmitting knowledge, the comparison of these multilingual practices in the representations of the different agents implied, and the alignment of these practices and representations with linguistic strategies put in place by higher education institutions.

Language strategies and planning at university and faculty levels

The example to be analysed is taken from a marketing course given at the Faculty of Commercial Higher Education at the University of Lausanne. The University of Lausanne has recently prescribed a number of precise rules pertaining to teaching languages at all levels of the syllabus; the university's official language is French. Tuition can be given entirely in other languages, but this is restricted to teaching and examinations conducted by language departments at the Faculty of Arts and language tuition in other faculties, aside from French.

The linguistic policy of the University of Lausanne can be summarized as follows:

- *Bachelor's degree level:* first year Bachelor's teaching is obligatorily in French. If the teaching language is, in theory, French, courses can be given in other languages on a one-off basis from the second year onwards, insofar as the study path of the preceding year (or years) ensures that the student can acquire the necessary linguistic skills, according to the required level. Exam papers can be submitted, at the student's discretion, either in French or in the teaching language (with some exceptions).
- *Master's degree level:* faculties can choose the teaching and examination language and must clearly communicate their choice to the students of each subject. However, in the spirit of encouraging multilingualism, it is advised that all programmes of study include multiple teaching languages, or 'language modules' for which the language is different to the teaching language.
- At faculty level, similar regulations apply.

As such, through the prism of the Bologna system, the University of Lausanne gives clear instructions, most notably in relation to the Master's degree, which is of particular interest to us here; all Master's degrees from Lausanne must have a multilingual component, reflecting the value-added status that such a component affords to candidates in the job market and aiming to imbue the Lausanne Master's degree with a unique value when compared with the monolingual default. The university sees this as a mark of quality to be promoted alongside its faculties.

Discrepancy between declared strategies and implicit strategies

However, despite these directives, certain Master's degrees are entirely in English (finance, political economics), with others partially in English (management), and thus show the linguistic strategy's areas of inefficacy – the pockets of resistance which elude intervention, responding to different rationales which are difficult to tame. In this sense, one can describe the result (output) of these directives as partial. Beyond the output/results of the recommendations made at the institutional level, of which direct traces can be seen in the documentation produced by the faculties (teachers' and students' linguistic requirements, multilingual courses, student information, etc.), it is the real consequences/outcomes which are of more interest to us. When considering the offerings ('outputs') available, we can ask ourselves to what extent agents benefit from them, how they work, what is their quality, etc., by employing qualitative (discourse analysis, conversational analysis, etc.) and quantitative (number of courses offered in other languages, number of students enrolled in each course, etc.) methods. We should therefore question the extent to which language policies give rise to practical consequences, since their role largely seems to be the provision of a symbolic discourse, and some effects for which they are credited may be due to other causes.

Amongst the other Master's degree courses described as multilingual in the Faculty of Commercial Higher Education's documentation, certain courses are nevertheless exclusively monolingual (i.e. English) in terms of practice, and show a clear discrepancy between the Faculty's declared linguistic policy and the implicit policy, according to the effective consequences of the declared policies in their practical applications. As such, it is important to consider each level of the stratification outlined above.

Individual representations

Explicit language policies can give rise to varied language use and individual representations, more or less in accordance with these policies, and many unique language strategies and reflections on language use can be found. We will here cite the case put forward by one of the teachers. Aware of the different levels of linguistic policy on the one hand and of effective policies and practices on the other, he has constructed his own language policy which he has developed further in a reference book. In its own way, this constitutes a theorization of the impact of linguistic policies on linguistic practices in the field of management

and marketing. In particular, he has investigated the question of the influence of different languages on policies and strategies within this field, and has notably published a series of reference books which integrate the comparative dimension. Additionally, he is directing a thesis which concerns the influence of Chinese on management styles such as hierarchy, etc., and on certain aspects of marketing. He cites a particular example which has led him to acknowledge the existence of a conceptual-level difference resulting from the language factor, with the vocabulary being heterogeneous and translations being only partially possible. He gives the example of an accounting concept which he presented in French, in an introductory course, and which he thought he knew the meaning of until the day that a German-speaking student questioned his explanation, according to the translation of this concept into German. He realized that the interpretation of this concept diverged significantly according to the language into which the concept was translated. More generally, languages exercise, according to him, an influence over each discipline, and in particular his discipline of marketing. He also maintains that in his L2 English courses, marketing work prompts him to focus even more on the question of linguistic and cultural diversity, and he describes multilingualism as an 'unexploited resource', most notably in the institutional context within which he works, where knowledge of conceptual differences is only considered to be a 'soft skill', and therefore peripheral. In acknowledging this impact of language and culture on knowledge, he identifies at the same time the limits of this impact, especially in his field, management. He considered that management is **relatively neutral** when it comes to language differences, compared, for instance, to law or accounting.[21] This is due, according to him, to its essentially monolingual and monocultural character. The knowledge and know-how pertaining to management were essentially developed in the USA, with other languages adapting concepts without changing them at the most basic level. Languages would be of issue in the application of these terms, but not in their conceptual contents. Moreover, he asserts that he does not have to resort to a specific way of thinking to be able to present his material in one language or another, as his own teaching practices have always been truly bilingual – in that he has always taught the material in English and French. He has produced a 'theory', which is not short of contradictions, but which nevertheless has the merit of thematizing the question of languages in given disciplines.

What is of even greater interest to us is the way in which he thematizes the paradox arising from the double requirement of responding to the challenges of globalization (posed by English) and diversification (posed by multilingualism), and his attempt to respond to this with a solution which he terms 'thick standardization' (an expression he himself derived from the anthropologist Clifford Geertz's 'thick description')[22] – a way of articulating both unity and diversity. For him, singing the praises of radical differences and denying the advantages of standardization is an undesirable path, the danger being that one can fall into a 'retro' or *passé* defence of diversity which may often be construed as pure nostalgia. On the contrary, 'thick standardization' focuses on the complex dynamic between diversity and standardization and on the conception of the different within the homogeneous, the diversity within uniqueness. From the outset, the link between the standard and the desire to reach a minimal threshold of mutual comprehensibility must be made according to the detection of deceptive standardization – the failure to comprehend even when you think you do. As such, English as 'the only language' leads to the false impression of a shared meaning. Nevertheless, beyond a negation of the standard, which always seems to assert itself in a globalized world, a new form of standardization must be sought out, a 'thick standardization' which contains traces of multilingual comparisons. It consists more precisely of the examination of a subject in a multilingual context in order to increase its common identification (i.e. the sense truly shared, or not shared, by speakers of different languages), to find sense configurations produced by particular languages and their influence on different aspects of the research process. As such, one can glean from 'thick standardization' a better comprehension of the subjects of discourse and, at the same time, the phenomena which embed themselves within them, as the description is richer in meaning and the shared and non-shared aspects of this meaning are clearly stated and understood.

Finally, we attempt to see how the 'statements' from these discussions come into play in his teaching.

An example of a multilingual course

The example which we take relates to teaching conducted in English, the L2 of both teacher and students. The example comes from a lecture given to an audience of around 80 students of the Faculty of Commercial Higher Education enrolled in the Master of Science in Management degree, entitled 'International Marketing'. This degree lasts two years and is bilingual to the extent that the obligatory teaching takes place in English and elective modules are taught partly in English and partly in French. The aim of the course is

to familiarise students with the principal situations and the principal choices of international operations and marketing policy which companies are faced with in a global environment, to provide basic knowledge regarding the influence of culture and language on different aspects of marketing and to develop precise perspectives on selected themes within the field of international marketing management (Müller et al., 2008).

This objective makes reference to a particularity of international marketing, as the teacher interprets it, in that linguistic and cultural diversity are part of the material under consideration. In particular, the aim is to understand the influence of different languages on the marketing policy to be adopted, in order to sell a given product anywhere in the world. In this sense, the question of linguistic diversity is a disciplinary issue within the course.

Throughout this extract (Table 32.2) the central purpose of the teacher's presentation is to explain the influence of local taste on consumption patterns in different regions/cultures. In order to achieve this, he initiates a presentation which can be sliced into three parts: in the first (1–16), (the teacher US introduces the new topic (local taste for similar items) and goes on to ask if an explanation has already been given (no response from the students), alluding to the subject of *süss* vs *sucré*. In the second part (17–40), US presents two examples (one linguistic, one cultural) linked to the topic by again taking the terms *süss* and *sucré*, and adding to them *sweet*, and then develops the opposition between *sweet* and *salty*. He then details how these examples are to be dealt with and concludes in the third part (41). Our interest in this sequence is to observe how US develops his topic, which subjects he chooses as examples and what they are like, as well as to gauge the different types of strategies he uses in order to understand if – and how – multilingualism is exploited as a resource. In order to do this, we return to the second part of his presentation.

In 17–18, US introduces the lexemes *süss, sucré* and *sweet*; the example he chooses to illustrate his topic 'local taste for similar items' is thus multilingual and thematizes a possible difference between these lexemes in each language (modalizing *pure lexical equivalents* by recategorizing with *more or less*). Having introduced the idea of 'positive or negative judgment' regarding *sweet* and *süss* (19), he again introduces the notions of 'figurative sense' and 'proper sense', which he applies to the English lexeme (*my sweet darling*) (20) to demonstrate the fact that the figurative sense of *sweet* within the given expression is not translatable as *sucré* in French. This is clearly a metalinguistic treatment of a multilingual example.

Table 32.2 Course sequence

Line	Speaker	Sequence
1	US	local taste/ . for similar items:\ ok\
2		...
3	US	we all know that products can be: . made with: . a little a content of sugar/
4		...
5		...
6	US	maybe I (already) explained this about süß:/ .. ((French pronunciation)) <versus> sucré
7	US	did I:/
8		...
9	US	no/
10		(1.1)
11	US	or you do not remember/
12		(0.8)
13	US	or I really did not do it/
14		...
15	US	((quick and low)) <ok>
16		(0.8)
17	US	so ((laughter)) let me/ .. if-&if you take/ .. what are/ pure . lexical equivalents\ . more or less\ (1.2) sucré:/ sü:ß/ (2.0) and sweet\ . ((lower)) <ok\>
18		(2.1)
19	US	so there is a POsitive .. value judgement . ON .. sweet/ . and süß\ &in german/ . and in english you have a positive value judgement/ aspiration?)) which is indicated by the FIGUrative sense\
20	US	((quick and low)) <ok>&you have the proper sense/ . and you have the figurative-&figurative is/ ((aspiration)) when you say for instance/ .((slower)) <my sweet darling>\ . ((quieter)) <ok\>
21		...
22	US	and I say it in french/ . you-&you can not say/ . ((slower)) <mon chéri sucré>\ (1.0) ou ma ((pronunciation of the fem. ending)) s<chérie:>\ ((aspiration?)) you can say/ . ((slower)) <ma DOUC:E . chérie>\ ((lowering of voice)) <for instance>
23		...
24	US	looks a little bit nineteenth century\
25	S	((students laugh))
26	US	borderline\ ok/
27	US	(aspiration)) but typically/ (1.4) you have a taste/ (0.9) ok/ .. you have two sort of taste (so) very basic/
28	US	(1.0) ((writes on board))
29	US	you have salty/ (1.3) and you have sweet\
30	US	(0.5) ((writes on board))
31	US	ok\
32	US	(0.5) ((writes on board))
33	US	and in in many countries/ (0.8) there can be some overlap\
34		(0.5)
35	US	so you can A:DD/ (0.5) to . a salty . dish (0.7) some sweet ingredients\
36		(0.8)
37	US	and in SOME other countries the two universes ... ARE .. fully separated\
38		(0.5)
39	US	so people DO not tend/ ... to mix/ (0.6) sweet . and salty/ .. euh:: items\ food items\ . ok\
40		(0.25)
41	US	((clicks tongue)) ((aspiration)) and the la-&the- ... the next you know\ . its local taste for similar items/ O:R/ . different use\ [...]

Sequence: US, teacher; S; students.

However, one should note that, until this point, the multilingual dimension is only mentioned in citation, and that, where it is used as an example, it is not used as a means.[23] After a joke (24–26), US creates a topical break by introducing two sorts of taste (*sweet* and *salty*, 29); *sweet* is no longer considered in opposition to its French and German counterparts, but in opposition to *salty*; the treatment method is no longer metalinguistic. In the final part of the presentation, US presents a final eventuality (the overlaps which can exist between *sweet* and *salty* (33–35), then the opposition of the two tastes (37–39)). Without transition – and without leaving room for questions – US closes the topic and passes quickly onto the next.

Code-switching as an object vs code-switching as a resource

The degree of multilingualism in this example is fairly low and declines in two ways – in terms of translinguistic marks (all forms of traces of L1 in L2 utterances, see Lüdi, 2006) and in the subject matter considered. In this episode, there are traces of the teacher's L1 (French) in his teaching in L2. But they belong mainly to the exolinguistic-monolingual type (Lüdi and Py, 2003), i.e. they consist of an involuntary incomplete inhibition of his L1 when using L2 in a monolingual mode (Grosjean, 2001). Nevertheless, US's discourse seems to exhibit a number of translinguistic marks which suggest a degree of multilingualism in the classroom session, and that this impacts upon the manner in which knowledge is imparted and developed – even if we find no example of code-switching in the actual organization of the discourse. First, some of the explanations provided by the teacher make use of simple grammatical structures and a basic lexicon. As such, wordings and rewordings (see, for instance, 39) are characterized by a certain simplification of relatively complex content which might be beneficial for the mediation of, and access to, the latter. Secondly, there seem to be L1 calque phenomena on L2 in the syntax and general organization of the discourse (such as the introduction of the topics), according to the information provided by some L1 English teachers. This could also have an impact at the level of intercomprehension, insomuch as this calque could facilitate the transmission of information and the francophone students' comprehension.[24]

The next step in our research regarding this practice will compare the explanations provided in this class delivered in the L2 and those provided by the same teacher in the L1 equivalent ('control course'), as well as a more in-depth study on possible calques using anglophone informants' information.

Beyond the occurrence of transfers from the L1 to the L2 and vice versa, this extract – as well as the practice from which it is taken – is characterized by a relatively low degree of multilingualism. For instance, Code-switching, seen as a practice exploiting two (or more) languages to communicate and functioning in a multilingual mode as a bi-/multi-lingual repertoire resource (see: Auer, 2000; Grosjean, 2001; Lüdi and Py, 2003), is not used in the course in question. Other languages intervene, but principally in the form of what we called lexical code-switches and translinguistic wordings in Section 32-3 and which Auer (2000) calls transfers – i.e isolated units inserted into the English discourse and taken as exemplifications or explanations. In this case, these other languages are not used as means of communication, instead remaining at the level of citation.

At first blush, then, there is no exploitation of multilingual strategies as didactic interaction resources insofar as the interlocutors do not explicitly make use of bi-/multi-lingual resources such as Code-Switching. Multilingualism is not so much exploited as a (communicative) strategy, but the (didactic) strategy makes use of multilingualism as a subject.

However, in the discussion, whereas multilingualism is stated to be an 'unexploited resource', there is a very narrow notion of 'resource'. The focus is put primarily on languages as subjects of study which serve to facilitate marketing (concrete policies), and less so on the role of languages/language in the conceptual construction and knowledge-transmission within the discipline (Berthoud 2008b, Berthoud 2008c). This could be directly linked to some observations made about the recorded sequences, notably the disconnect between the linguistic (and cultural) dimension and the disciplinary dimension. The teacher himself picks up on this disconnect regarding the students' acquisition. According to him (and the exam results), students do not manage to integrate the interlinguistic and intercultural dimension within their marketing knowledge and know-how. The students do not just appear to be unsettled by the polysemy which multilingualism creates (where they would prefer a 'univocal truth'), but also seem to not to be developed or 'sophisticated' enough (or **aware** enough) of multilingual practice. One of the conditions under which multilingualism could succeed is therefore, according to the teacher, a more rigorous selection of students. The poverty of code-switches observed in his practice and, hence, the lack of full exploitation of multilingualism as a resource or a communicative strategy could be explained by his statements.

And in this sense, his teaching method appears to be the direct application of his stated linguistic policy. This is a remarkable fact if one considers the number of other instances in the DYLAN project in which effective practice largely goes beyond its potential for clarification, in which agents exploit the multilingual factor in ways far more varied than they think and say that they do, and in doing so shows considerable discrepancies between practices and representations. Here, the exploitation of the multilingual dimension – that which is theorized by the teacher for his subject – is seriously limited in the construction of didactic discourse and, evidently, in students' knowledge construction. This is as though, in some way, its explicit and controlled representations trap it within a highly rigid **schema** and prevent it from resorting to other, more spontaneous and varied strategies in which multilingualism would be exploited as a means and not just as a subject under consideration.

From this we can see the importance of achieving practices in which multilingualism is effectively exploited as a resource in a multilingual mode, capable of a richer theorization and leaving room for creativity. 'Emergent' rules guide these practices while at the same time emerging **from** these practices. And it is in this sense that we speak about a new 'bottom-up' type of linguistic policy, directly inspired by observed practices, avoiding the imposition of simplified **schemata** and instead fuelled by the complexity of practices, in order to be able, in turn, to impact upon them. This is what we converge upon as one of the principal conditions of an impact which is both possible and pertinent to linguistic policies regarding practice.

32.5 CONCLUSIONS

This Chapter was not intended to give a comprehensive overview of language policies and strategies, but rather to illustrate one possible approach to the field by way of a recent research project dealing with some key questions in the context of the management of linguistic diversity in companies and institutions of higher education.

It has become evident that the management of multilingualism has many different forms in the business and higher education worlds. And it is only partially the result of explicit management measures. These, and more implicit regulations – such as the decision of a leader of a laboratory, which can only just be considered as principally German-speaking, to privilege the use of that language, so requiring the whole team to 'juggle with languages', in the name of efficiency and the quality of the work – are essentially based on the representations of the agents. First, the advantages and disadvantages of the exploitation of multilingual repertoires, conceived of as shared resources, in the same agents' discourses can as a result be gauged. However, the work of the linguist need not stop there. The linguist cannot limit him- or herself to finding statements made by the agents which the latter more or less already know. It is often only the detailed analysis of these agents' practices which reveal the **schemas** and methods of which they make use (but of which they are not conscious) and which uncover the cognitive and strategic advantages of these multilingual practices which may result.

Indeed, our first analyses allowed us to begin to understand the great richness contained in the self-regulation of the culture of multilingual communication, provided that this is preferred or at least tolerated by those in charge. It not only became clear that a 'multilingual philosophy' contributes greatly to the emergence of such practices but also that it cannot be imposed in a 'top-down' fashion, instead needing to develop from the 'bottom up'. Institutions and businesses can significantly contribute to the creation of a framework that favours the creation of a multilingual microclimate: for example, by demanding multilingual skills, forming linguistically-mixed groups, not to mention convincing those in charge that their commercial and research success will see sustainable benefit from it.

NOTES

1 *Québec: Loi sur la langue officielle* [Official Language Law] (Bill 22, adopted in 1974 by the National Assembly of Quebec, making French the official language of the province).

Canada: Official Languages Law (1969, enacted 15 September 1988, with the objective of consolidating the equality of French and English within the federal institutions).

France: Toubon Law (adopted 23 February 1994 by the Council of Ministers, modified 27 July 1994 – it intervenes in five domains–namely, the workplace, consumption (the displaying of goods), teaching, audiovisual media (programming and advertisements), and conferences and the like (Calvet, 1996: 70).

2 Fishman (1974): 'The term language planning refers to the organized pursuit of solutions to language problems, typically at the national level'. Cooper (1989): 'The deliberate efforts to influence the behavior of others with respect to the acquisition, structure, or functional allocation of their language codes'. Schiffman (1996): 'Language planning involves formal and informal activities to change

the way people use language'. Eastman (1983): language planning refers to 'decision-making that goes into determining what language use is appropriate in particular speech communities'; it 'looks at the choices available to a speech community and at possible recommendations of language policy for adoption by that community' and 'has to do with the way people's ideas about language are coordinated'.

3   For instance, resurrection of a dead language (Hebrew), dialect selection (Francien –> French) or dialect mixing (Rumantch Grischun) [the examples are not part of the quoted table AB/GL].

4   Abandonment of Latin in favour of European languages at the beginning of the Modern Era; prescription of French as the language of jurisdiction by François I; choice of High German for the Bible translations of Luther and Zwingli; assertion of local languages in the Baltic countries since the achievement of autonomy; selection of a variety as a national language ('language of a political, social, cultural entity'), official language ('what governments use to do their business') as compared to vernacular languages ('first languages of people socially or politically dominated by a group with a different language') (UNESCO, 1951: 689–90).

5   Academies have been instituted to guard the avenues of their languages, to retain fugitives, and repulse invaders; but their vigilance and activity have hitherto been vain; sounds are too volatile and subtle for legal restraints; to enchain syllables, and to lash the wind, are equally the undertakings of pride, unwilling to measure its desires by its strength. (Samuel Johnson, Preface to the Dictionary)

6   For example, 'Whenever possible, use plurals (people, they) and feminine pronouns, rather than only masculine pronouns and 'pseudo-generics' such as man, unless referring specifically to males' (Linguistic Society of America, *Guidelines for nonsexist language*).

7   Fishman (1969) discusses the relation between the linguistic background of a country and the type of language planning in place when selecting 'national' or 'official' languages

8   For example, linguistic unity based on a foreign language has been described as 'cultural abortion' (Diop, 1974).

9   For example, in January/February 1997, the US Congress discussed the *Bill Emerson English Language Empowerment Act* containing the proposition that 'English must become our official language' [Congressional Record: 7 January and 5 February 1997 (Extensions)]. Note that the US Constitution does not specify any official language.

10   In a frequently quoted paper, Landry and Bourhis (1997: 25) proposed a new approach for the study of multilingual and polyglossic societies: the analysis of the linguistic landscape: "The landscape of public road signs, advertising billboards, street names, place names, commercial shop signs, and public signs on government buildings combines to form the linguistic landscape of a given territory, region or urban agglomeration." (cf. Gorter 2006; Backhaus, 2007; Shohamy and Gorter 2008 for bibliographical overviews).

11   'Public Service A is a multilingual company and encourages multilingualism in the workplace. In its internal linguistic provisions, it offers internal language courses as well as the possibility to work in other linguistic regions'.

12   The DYLAN Project is an integrated project from the Sixth Framework Programme, Priority 7, 'Citizens and governance in a knowledge based society', with 19 partners, from 12 countries. It addresses the core issue underlying topic 3.3.1 – whether and, if so, how a European knowledge-based society designed to ensure economic competitiveness and social cohesion can be created despite the fact that, following enlargement, the European Union is linguistically more diverse than ever before.

Table 32.3 Types of selection of official languages in developing nations

Type of language situation	A-modal	Uni-modal	Multi-modal
Examples	Indonesia	Israel	Indonesia
	Cameroon	Thailand	Pakistan
	Philippines	Somalia	Sri Lanka
	Tanzania	Ethiopia	Malaysia
Perceived sociocultural integration	No integrating great tradition at the national level	One great tradition at the national level	Several great traditions seeking separate socio political recognition
Selection of national language	Governed by considerations of political integration: nationism	Governed by considerations of authenticity: nationalism	Governed by need to compromise between political integration and separate authenticities
Language planning concerns	Minor: exonormative standardization of LWC	Modernization of traditional language	Modernization of several traditional languages

13　The 'terrains' of enquiry are international companies based in Switzerland (*Pharmaceutical Company A, Pharmaceutical Company B, Bank A*), Swiss outlets of international companies based overseas (*Financial Services A, Insurance A*), companies working in all of the linguistic regions of Switzerland (*Public Service A, Public Service B, Department Store A*) as well as companies operating in the metropolitan region of Basel (*Hospital A, Factory A, Bank B*). The example here is from Public Service B.

14　As such, CGT activists from the GEMS (General Electric Medical Systems) Society, Yvelines, France, won a legal victory – according to the Toubon Law of 1994 – against the company, which ultimately had to accept that technical documents composed overseas must be systematically translated into French. The same complaint would doubtless not be heard within a different legislative framework, such as that of the Netherlands.

15　The 'Toolbox for the promotion of linguistic diversity in the company' is a nationwide online platform initiated by ch Stiftung, a Swiss foundation which has the aim of helping companies to foster multilingualism. (http://werkzeugkasten.chstiftung. ch/Werkzeugkasten/tabid/341/Default.aspx)

16　'I have already started English courses umpteen times, and every time I've had a fit of rage, do I have to learn this shit, I don't want to etc., so in the end I give up sooner or later." For details, see Lüdi, Höchle and Yanaprasart (in press).

17　This is what is stipulated, in a slightly different context, by the *Swiss Army Service Regulations* of 22 June 1994: 'The superior expresses himself so far as possible in the language of the subordinate'.

18　German, French and Italian only; Public Service B does not operate in the Romansch-speaking region.

19　This is adapted from a study at a workshop running parallel to the DYLAN Lyon Consortium Meeting, 2008.

20　We define 'translinguistic wording' as a communicative strategy for getting oneself out of a predicament caused by limited lexical resources in L2; it consists of the conscious use of single words or longer sequences of L1 (or in any other language likely to be understood by the native speaker of L2) as a form of rescue (see Lüdi, 2003, 2006: 33).

21　A citation taken from the semi-directed discussion: *I reckon, when a concept has been stated in English from the word go, why translate it, eh?*

22　In anthropology and other fields, a 'thick description' of a human behaviour is one that explains not just the behaviour, but its context as well, such that the behaviour becomes meaningful to an outsider.

The term was used by the anthropologist Clifford Geertz in his *The Interpretation of Cultures* (1973) to describe his own method of doing ethnography (Geertz, 1973: 5–6, 9–10). Since then, the term and the methodology it represents have gained currency in the social sciences and beyond. Today, 'thick description' is used in a variety of fields, including the type of literary criticism known as New Historicism.

23　Here, we observe transfers, but not codeswitching, according to the typology of Auer (2000).

24　On the other hand, the same phenomenon could prove to be an obstacle for non-francophone students.

REFERENCES

Alexander, N. (2006) *Language Education Policy, National and Sub-National Identities in South Africa*. Strasbourg: Council of Europe.

Auer, P. (2000) 'A conversation analytic approach to codeswitching and transfer', in W. Li (ed.), *The Bilingualism Reader*. London: Routledge. pp.166–187.

Backhaus, P. (2007) *Linguistic Landscapes. A Comparative Study of Urban Multilingualism in Tokyo*. Clevedon, UK: Multilingual Matters.

Barère, B. (1794) *Rapport du Comité de salut public sur les idiomes du 8 pluviôse an II*. [Report of the Public Safety Committee on languages, 8th day of Pluviôse, Year II.]

Barth, L. A. (2008) Gestion des compétences linguistiques asymétriques dans l'interaction. L'exemple d'une gare internationale. Bâle, Institut d'études françaises et francophones. Mémoire de licence.

Beacco, J.-C. (2004) *Agir pour le plurilinguisme en Europe : Les profils nationaux des politiques linguistiques éducatives*. [Acting for multilingualism in Europe: national profiles of educational linguistic politics'] http://www.ciep.fr/courrieleuro/2004/0204_beacco.htm.

Berthoud, A.-C. (2008a) 'Le projet DYLAN 'Dynamiques des langues et gestion de la diversité.' Un aperçu', *Sociolinguistica*, 22: 171–185.

Berthoud, A.-C. (2008b) 'Regards croisés sur un plurilinguisme à inventer', in *Cahiers de l'ILSL 23*. Université de Lausanne.

Berthoud, A.-C. (2008c): 'Mehrsprachigkeit als Kaleidoskop des Wissens', in G.Lüdi, K. Seelmann, and B. Sitter-Liver, (eds), *Sprachenvieltalt and Kulturfrieden. Sprachminderheit – Einsprachigkeit – Mehrsprachigkeit: Probleme und Chancen sprachlicher Vielfalt*. Fribourg: Academic Press; Stuttgart: Kohlhammer Verlag.

Beydoun, S. (2008) *Der Webauftritt der SBB CFF FFS: eine mehrsprachige Webseite?* Bâle: Institut d'études françaises et francophones.

Bruhn, M. (2003) *Integrierte Unternehmens – und Markenkommunikation. Strategische Planung und operative Umsetzung*. Stuttgart: Schäffer-Poeschel Verlag.

Calvet, L.-J. (1996) *Les politiques linguistiques*. Paris, PUF.

Cooper, R. L. (1989) *Language Planning and Social Change*. New York: Cambridge University Press.

Diop, C. A. (1974) *The Cultural Unity of Black Africa* [Translation of L'*Unité culturelle de l'Afrique noire*.] Chicago: Third World Press.

Duchêne, A. (2008) *Ideologies Across Nations. The Construction of Linguistic Minorities at the United Nations.* Berlin: Mouton de Gruyter.

Eastman, C. M. (1983) *Language Planning: An Introduction.* San Francisco: Chandler and Sharp.

Fichte, J. G. (1808) *Reden an die Deutsche Nation [Speeches to the German Nation].* Berlin: In der Realschulbuchhandlung.

Fishman, J. A. (1969) 'National languages and languages of wider communication in the developing nations', *Anthropological Linguistics*, 11(4): 111–35.

Fishman, J. (1974) *Advances in Language Planning.* The Hague: Mouton.

Geertz, C. (1973) 'Thick description: toward an interpretive theory of culture', in *The Interpretation of Cultures: Selected Essays.* New York: Basic Books. pp. 3–30.

Gorter, D. (ed.) (2006), 'Linguistic landscape: a new approach to multilingualism', *International Journal of Multilingualism*, 3(1).

Grégoire, H. (1794) *Rapport sur la Nécessité et les Moyens d'anéantir les Patois et d'universaliser l'Usage de la Langue française du 16 prairial an II.* [Report on the necessity and means of defeating patois and universalising the use of the French language, 16th day of Prairial, Year II.]

Grosjean, F. (2001) 'The bilingual's language modes', in J. L. Nicol (ed.), *Language Processing in the Bilingual.* Oxford : Blackwell. pp. 1–25.

Haugen, E. (1959) 'Planning for a standard language in modern Norway', *Anthropological Linguistics*, 1(3): 8–21.

Haugen, E. (1983) 'The implementation of corpus planning: theory and practice', in J. Fishman, and J. Covarrubias, (eds), *Progress in Language Planning: International Perspectives.* Berlin: Mouton. pp. 269–89.

Herder, J. G. von (1794) 'Briefe zur Beförderung der Humanität [Letters for the advancement of humanitarianism]', in J. G. V. Heder: *Sämtliche werke.* Ed. B. Suphan, Vol. XVII. Berlin (1881).

Kaplan, R. and Baldauf, R. (1997) *Language Planning from Practice to Theory.* Clevedon, UK: Multilingual Matters.

Landry, R. and Bourhis, R. Y. (1997) Linguistic landscape and ethnolinguistic vitality. An empirical study, in: *Journal of Language and Social Psychology* 16/1 (1997), S. 23–49.

Lüdi, G. (2003) 'Code-switching and unbalanced bilingualism', in: J. -M. Dewaele, A. Housen, A. and W. Li (eds), *Bilingualism: Beyond Basic Principles. Festschrift in Honour of Hugo Baetens Beardsmore.* Clevedon: Multilingual Matters. pp. 174–88.

Lüdi, G. (2006) 'Multilingual repertoires and the consequences for linguistic theory', in K. Bührig and J. D. ten Thije, (eds), *Beyond Misunderstanding. Linguistic Analyses of Intercultural Communication.* Amsterdam: John Benjamins. pp. 11–42.

Lüdi G. and Py, B. (2003) *Etre bilingue.* [Being bilingual.] 3rd edn. review. New York: Lang.

Lüdi, G. and Py, B. (2009) 'To be or not to be … a multilingual speaker', *International Journal of Multilingualism and Multiculturalism*, 6(2): 154–67.

Lüdi, G., Seelmann, K. and Sitter-Liver, B. (eds), (2008) *Sprachenvielfalt und Kulturfrieden. Sprachminderheit – Einsprachigkeit – Mehrsprachigkeit: Probleme und Chancen sprachlicher Vielfalt.* Fribourg: Academic Press; Stuttgart: Kohlhammer.

Lüdi, G., Höchle, K. and Yanaprasart, P. (forthcoming) 'Dynamiques langagières et gestion de la diversité: l'exemple d'une grande entreprise pharmaceutique internationale basée en Suisse', in P. Danler et al. (eds), *Actes du XXV Congrès International de Linguistique et Philologie Romanes.*

Mackey, W. F. (1976) *Bilinguisme et contact des langues.* Paris: Klincksieck.

Maurais, J. et al. (1987) *Politique et aménagement linguistique.* Québec: Conseil de la langue française, 1987.

Moore, D. and Castellotti, V. (eds.) (2007): La compétence plurilingue: regards francophones. Bern: Peter Lang.

Müller, G., Gajo, L, Berthoud, A.C., Steffen, G., Pantet, J., Jacquin, J., (2008) *Working Paper 2.* Research team UNIL: Université de Lausanne.

Orban, L. (2008) *A New Strategy for Multilingualism: A Strategy for all EU Citizens.* Presentation of the Communication on Multilingualism to the European Parliament's Committee on Culture on 6 October 2008 in Brussels. (http://www.lanqua.eu/files/L%20Orban_EN_New_Strategy.pdf)

Schiffman, H. F. (1996) *Linguistic Culture and Language Policy.* New York: Routledge.

Shohamy, E. and Gorter, D. (eds) (2008) *Linguistic Landscape. Expanding the Scenery.* London: Routledge.

Tutzinger, T. (1999) Tutzinger Thesen zur Sprachenpolitik in Europa. Erarbeitet auf der Tagung "Euro-Deutsch" des Deutschen Germanistenverbandes in und mit der Evangelischen Akademie Tutzing am 3./4.6.1999, in: Der Sprachienst Heft 6/99, 220–222. (auch: http //www. Germanistenverband.de/akitv/tutzing.html)

UNESCO (1951): The use of vernacular languages in education. Paris, Unesco.

Widmer, J., Coray, R., Acklin M. D. and Godel, E. (2004) *Die Schweizer Sprachenvielfalt im öffentlichen Diskurs – La diversité des langues en Suisse dans le débat public.* Bern et al.: Peter Lang.

33

Language Endangerment

Julia Sallabank

33.1 INTRODUCTION

Language variation is at the heart of sociolinguistics; it is therefore to be expected that sociolinguists might take an interest in linguistic diversity, and that they might be concerned about its loss. But the nature of linguistic diversity, how to measure it, and reactions to its decline, are the subject of considerable debate.

Both sociolinguistic research and language documentation share values such as the primacy of authentic recording of natural speech, diversity, and the notion that language is/does more than just the transfer of referential information. In terms of methodology, both use audio and video recordings to produce language corpora. Both are also concerned with the effects of language contact: for example, how a language loses functionality in the face of one or more powerful language(s) of wider communication, and its impact on the structure and vocabulary of the smaller language (Muysken, 2008). Endangered language documentation goes further in that it is concerned directly with recording and maintaining linguistic diversity.

Overviews of the study of language endangerment usually start with a list of statistics about the number of languages in the world, the proportion considered endangered, etc. The validity of such an approach is questionable, as the basis of the estimates is by no means clear. The usual source of statistics concerning the number of languages and their speakers is the *Ethnologue*', subtitled 'An encyclopedic reference work cataloging all of the world's 6912 known living languages' (Gordon, 2005). Its Introduction recognizes that its headline exact figure is problematic:

Complete information on all of the world's languages is not available; thus the total number of living languages in the world cannot be known precisely. Because languages are dynamic and undergo constant change, there will never be a stable number of the living languages of the world (ibid.).

More and more sociolinguists are challenging the notion that language boundaries can be defined, seeing them as constructs established for linguists' convenience (for example, Irvine and Gal, 2000; Ricento, 2005; Makoni and Pennycook, 2006). The *Ethnologue* acknowledges such concerns, defending its approach as follows:

The Ethnologue approach to listing and counting languages as though they were discrete, countable units, does not preclude a more dynamic understanding of the linguistic makeup of the countries and regions in which clearly distinct varieties can be distinguished... . Every language is characterized by variation within the speech community that uses it (Gordon, 2005).

The usual distinction between languages and dialects is that dialects are mutually comprehensible varieties of languages, which are distinct and mutually unintelligible. Some linguists conduct experiments to measure degrees of mutual comprehensibility (e.g. Cheng, 1996; Hammarstrom, 2008; Komarova and Niyogi, 2004; Tang and van Heuven, 2009). However, mutual intelligibility is to a certain extent a function of language attitudes and ideologies – whether people **want** to understand each other. Paradoxes such as the mutual incomprehensibility of Chinese 'dialects' compared to the mutual comprehensibility of Scandinavian languages are clearly motivated by political and nationalistic considerations.

Ahmad (2008) points out that most overviews of language endangerment omit mention of sign languages (an exception is Harrison, 2007). Sign languages face similar problems to other minority languages, as well as prejudice from those who do not recognize them as full languages. Local 'village' sign languages may be threatened by contact with larger, national or international sign languages. Factors endangering sign languages include deaf education, where policies fluctuate between using sign language and speech-based strategies such as lip-reading. In richer communities, sign languages are endangered due to the increased use of cochlear implants to 'cure' deafness (Crasborn and Zwitserlood, 2008).

Language communities around the world, especially linguistic minorities, are becoming more aware of the symbolic value of their speech varieties, partly as a reaction to globalization (Trudgill, 2004; see also Section 33.6 below, and Slembrouck, this volume). This has led to an increasing demand for local varieties to be recognized as languages in their own right; to reflect this the number in *Ethnologue* has increased.

Although the number of languages counted is increasing, it is generally recognized that linguistic diversity is decreasing. Throughout history, languages have died out and been replaced by others formed through language contact, or through divergence due to lack of communication over distances (Dalby, 2002). Until recently this was seen as a natural cycle. What worries an increasing number of linguists is the growing number of linguistic varieties no longer being learnt by children, coupled with a tendency for speakers to shift to languages of wider communication, especially varieties of English. Linguistic typologists are concerned that linguistic constructions might disappear without the field even becoming aware that it might be possible to say things in a certain way. For example, there are only a few languages known to have object–verb–subject word order, which before the 1960s was thought to be non-existent.

33.2 REACTIONS TO ENDANGERMENT: FROM LINGUISTS AND FROM SPEECH COMMUNITIES

The impending loss of linguistic diversity led some linguists to issue a 'wake-up call' to the profession. A special issue of the journal *Language* (Hale et al., 1992), based on a colloquium held at the annual meeting of the Linguistic Society of America, drew attention to the scale of language endangerment. Krauss (1992: 10) estimated that the majority of the world's languages would be severely endangered by 2100 and called for 'some

rethinking of our priorities, lest linguistics go down in history as the only science that has presided obliviously over the disappearance of 90% of the very field to which it is dedicated'. Since then a number of initiatives have been launched, such as:

- The Hans Rausing Endangered Language Project,[1] which funds documentation projects, maintains an archive of recordings, transcriptions and metadata, and runs an academic programme.
- The Volkswagen Foundation's sponsorship of the DoBeS (Dokumentation Bedrohter Sprachen)[2] project.
- In the USA, The National Endowment for the Humanities (NEH) and National Science Foundation (NSF) Documenting Endangered Languages initiative (DEL): 'a new, multi-year effort to preserve records of key languages before they become extinct'.[3]
- The European Science Foundation Better Analyses Based on Endangered Languages programme (EuroBABEL) whose main purpose is 'to promote empirical research on underdescribed endangered languages, both spoken and signed'.[4]
- Smaller non-profit initiatives, notably the Foundation for Endangered Languages[5] and the Endangered Languages Fund.[6]

Apart from the Foundation for Endangered Languages (as from 2008), all of these fund only documentation, not programmes primarily aimed at language revitalization. The response of the academic community has thus been overwhelmingly to 'preserve key records' of rare language typologies before they disappear rather than to try to maintain modes of expression in active use. In contrast, if and when speaker communities become concerned about language loss, they tend to focus on language revitalization.

There has been a certain amount of tension between these two aims. A statement by two Alaskan linguists, Dora Marks Dauenhauer and Richard Dauenhauer, sums up the dichotomy neatly: 'Preservation … is what we do to berries in jam jars and salmon in cans … . Books and recordings can preserve languages, but only people and communities can keep them alive' (quoted in Lord, 1996; Maffi, 2003; Walsh, 2005).[7] Some linguists understandably feel that their strengths lie in language description, while some activists are impatient to start revitalizing and teaching their language without waiting for a corpus or description on which to base dictionaries, grammars and classroom materials.

Of course, efforts have been made to reconcile the different priorities. The longer a language can be kept in use, the more material there is to document. It is understandable that communities should prefer to focus on maintaining the living language, but documentation can also play a more active role by providing valuable data for teaching materials based on fluent usage (for example, accurate reflections of pronunciation and usage, traditional stories, songs and rhymes for use in school lessons). Some revitalization activities can of course be performed without documentation, especially those which do not rely on formal teaching. However, dictionary production, an important step for a language whose speakers wish to raise its prestige and establish it as a 'proper language' (*Ausbau*, in the terms of Kloss, 1967), is difficult without collecting a corpus of the language through documentation.

It is common for a language community not to realize, or value, what they are losing before it is gone (or almost), in which case properly archived language documentation can prove invaluable in providing future generations with an idea of how their ancestral language was used in practice and, in several instances, in piecing back together a language which is no longer used actively. The examples of Cornish, Manx, Miami and Kaurna (see below) have demonstrated that it is never too late to save at least some elements of a language. Communities are often unaware of the decline of their language, or may be in denial about it. I am not the only researcher to have noticed that speakers do not always associate lack of language use with cessation of language transmission; by the time they realize that their children cannot speak the ancestral language, it is too late to teach them (Dauenhauer and Dauenhauer, 1998; Sallabank, 2007). The arrival of an external linguist signals external interest in the language, which can have an important influence on a speech community's attitudes towards their language(s) and general self-confidence.

Field linguists in the twenty-first century are acutely aware of problems associated with earlier anthropological approaches and the assumption of intellectual property rights by external researchers, and now place great importance on collaboration with language communities. In the USA and Australia, indigenous communities are increasingly insisting on control over their linguistic resources, following numerous instances where linguists and publishers have benefited from linguistic material without even informing communities, who understandably feel aggrieved at what they perceive as the theft of their cultural heritage. Don Thornton, a member of the Cherokee Nation of Oklahoma, relates how he bought a Cherokee–English Dictionary written by a professor from Northeastern University and took it to his grandmother.

[S]he replied with her frailed but angry voice: 'That man used to come to my house for three years asking how to say words in Cherokee. Pretty soon it would be lists of phrases. I fixed his lists for three years and all I wanted was a copy of the finished work but never received one.' (Thornton Media, 2008)

Grinevald (2003) applied the sociolinguistic framework of Cameron et al. (1992, 1993) to language documentation, distinguishing:

(a) fieldwork simply conceived of as ON a language
(b) fieldwork with the added dimension of doing it FOR a language community
(c) fieldwork WITH the speakers of the language community rather than FOR them
(d) the possibility and ideally ultimate goal of fieldwork done BY speakers of the language community themselves. (Grinevald, 2003: 58)

The focus in language documentation training[8] is now strongly on a collaborative, empowerment approach. As well as being involved in project decisions, speakers acting as informants for funded projects are called 'consultants' and are usually paid for their work.

There are numerous examples of positive relations between communities and external linguists being crucial to the success of projects. For example, Amery's research on Kaurna, a 'sleeping' language (that is, with no native speakers) of the Adelaide plains, Australia, acted as a catalyst for community interest in the language (Amery, 2000). Kaurna had not been spoken since the nineteenth century, and there were no sound recordings. The only surviving elements were a few place names and a small number of words shared by nearby languages, plus some teaching materials published by two German priests in 1840. Grenoble and Whaley (2006: 66–7) describe the project as a 'remarkable success': the language has developed from no use at all to limited active use – for example, in formal greetings, public speeches and rituals – although it is seldom used in everyday conversation.

Products of linguistic documentation are usually archived at the linguist's university or at one of the documentation centres mentioned earlier, and copies are deposited with local archives where available. Audio and video recordings are made available to the community, as well as any dictionaries or literacy materials produced, and community members control the extent of wider access to the materials (David Nathan, HRELP archivist, personal comm). This is essential in cases where recordings include private or culturally-sensitive material, or where for political reasons speakers do not want to be identified but still wish to preserve their language.

Language change and attrition

Language change is universal, and a language that does not change is no longer a living tongue; it may therefore seem paradoxical that the rate and amount of language change tends to be much higher in an endangered language (Dorian, 1981: 154). Endangered languages may lack, or lose, particular registers (such as those used with officialdom), and functional reduction leads to stylistic and vocabulary shrinkage, so that the language may not have terms for all situations (Dorian, 1977). From here it is but a short step to a language being seen as inadequate and 'not a proper language', and to a downward spiral of loss of status and of speakers.

Language shift often accompanies a shift away from traditional close-knit social networks where people all know each other (see Vetter, this volume). In endangered language situations, the average age of speakers is rising, and friends and relatives from speakers' social networks are passing away: one of my consultants stated, 'I've had nobody to speak it to since my mother died in 1995'. Speakers are also increasingly infirm and immobile, and so less able to interact socially. The longer they are isolated from fellow speakers, the more of the language they forget, and consequently they feel less confident when an opportunity to speak it does arise (e.g. to a linguist).

Language revitalization measures can help maintain social networks, for example the Master–Apprentice schemes pioneered with Native American languages in California (Hinton, 1997), where fluent speakers (usually older) are paired with learners. As well as providing practice for learners or latent speakers, who may have had little passive exposure to a language but have little productive competence, such schemes give isolated older speakers opportunities to speak their native language.

Common linguistic consequences of endangerment include:

- Reduction or impoverishment: the loss of grammatical components without elaboration of another component to make up for this loss.
- Simplification or regularization: structures increase in regularity; for example, irregular verbs become more regular and marked structures give way to unmarked ones. Elaborate syntactic structures may become simplified or disappear completely, and analytic structures (made up of several words, in a particular order)

may replace synthetic ones (where inflections and morphology convey much of the meaning).

For example, in the following example from Dyirbal, a language of North Queensland, Australia, the younger speaker does not use the ergative case (which marks the subject of a transitive verb), and replaces traditional word order with English-influenced word order:

Traditional Dyirbal	'Young Dyirbal'
girimu-gu jugumbil bajan	gugar bajan ban jugumbil
snake-ERG woman bite	*goanna bite woman*
'The snake bit the woman.'	'The goanna bit the woman.'

(adapted from Schmidt, 1985)

At the same time, through language contact, a language may gain new structures (Denison, 1977). The following example is from my research on Guernesiais, spoken in the Channel Islands, between England and France:

i fao gardaï hao lé guernésiais
we must keep up Guernesiais

Some campaigners regret and resist such changes, but it is a truism that older people always complain about young people's usage, even in non-endangered languages. Some language planners wish to purify their language of contact features (for example, see Rice and Saxon, 2002). The question then arises, at what stage in its development should a language be maintained? Which form(s) should be documented? Such dilemmas illustrate the problems associated with drawing linguistic boundaries.

Attempts to expand a language into new domains are not always welcomed by traditionalists, nor by those who do not want to 'buy into' a standardizing and hegemonic ideology. An endangered language may not have terms for technological innovations, or a standard or agreed written form: How, and by whom, should decisions on such issues be made?

It should not be assumed that all linguistic change in endangered languages implies decay. In some cases an increase in grammatical complexity has been observed (Aikhenvald, 2002), and it is now clear that loss and simplification are just one aspect of a more elaborate picture (Dorian, 1999). In Guatemala, Barrett (2008) found that younger speakers of Sipakapense, a Mayan language, code-switch less with Spanish compared to the oldest generation, which contradicts trends seen elsewhere. Barrett suggests that this is due to increased confidence in the language and highlights the important role of language ideologies in cases of language contact and shift.

33.3 FACTORS IN LANGUAGE ENDANGERMENT

Assessing language vitality

Assessing levels of language knowledge and use is an important element of language planning. The best-known framework is Fishman's (1991) 'Graded Intergenerational Disruption Scale' (GIDS), which describes eight stages of community language loss and suggests revitalization measures to counter each stage. The scale runs from 8 (worst case) to 1 (fairly safe).

> 8: Reassembling the language from isolated older speakers and teaching it to adults
> 7: Most users are socially integrated and ethnolinguistically active, but they are beyond child-bearing age
> 6: Informal intergenerational oracy and its demographic concentration and institutional reinforcement
> 5: Literacy in the minority language in the home, school and community, but without extra-communal support
> 4: Use of the minority language in lower education that meets the requirements of compulsory education laws
> 3: Use of the language in the work sphere, outside the immediate community, by speakers of both the minority and the dominant language
> 2: Use of the language in local/regional mass media and governmental services
> 1: Education, work sphere, mass media and governmental operations at higher and nationwide levels
>
> (Adapted from Fishman, 1991)

The GIDS is often used to plot the status of languages. However, it has been criticized for focusing on literacy and for having a Western bias, criticisms which are not necessarily justified. According to the GIDS, intergenerational transmission in the family is the 'gold standard' of language vitality and the most important factor in language survival; education and literacy can wait. This emphasis is taken further by Krauss (1997), who analyses levels of transmission using a 10-way distinction. However, the focus on intergenerational transmission has been challenged by Romaine (2006), who points out that few, if any, language movements have actually followed Fishman's advice; most focus on school-based language teaching (see below).

Another frequently cited framework used to measure the health of a language is ethnolinguistic vitality (Giles, Bourhis and Taylor, 1977). This taxonomy utilizes a social psychological approach to measure three structural variables: status,

demographics and institutional support. It was extended in the 1980s to include 'subjective ethnolinguistic vitality', recognizing that objective assessments and comparisons are less likely to be significant in language survival than the subjective perceptions of community members (both those who do and do not speak the language). However, it focuses on economic rather than the social value of languages, and on institutional rather than community support.

A framework which takes many of these criticisms into account is that produced by a group of eminent linguists for UNESCO, which identifies nine factors in language vitality, each of which is graded on a 0–5 scale:

1   Intergenerational language transmission
2   Absolute number of speakers
3   Proportion of speakers within the local population
4   Trends in existing language domains
5   Response to new domains and media
6   Materials for language education and literacy
7   Governmental and institutional language policies, including official status and use
8   Community members' attitudes toward their own language
9   Amount and quality of documentation

(UNESCO, 2003a; Grenoble and Whaley, 2006: 4)

This framework recognizes that factors cannot easily be separated: for example, domains a language is used in relate to attitudes. It also includes the amount and quality of documentation, which can be a direct consequence of low status: minority language varieties may not have been deemed worthy of description or documentation. However, although the preamble to the framework stresses the importance of language revitalization, it is not included in the framework itself. The latest edition of the *UNESCO Atlas of Languages in Danger of Disappearing* (Moseley, 2009), which used this framework, was criticized by many communities for focusing on endangerment rather than measures being undertaken to revitalize or revive languages.

Another criticism of the UNESCO framework is that it focuses on factors relevant to developed, Western contexts, notably 5, 'Response to new domains and media'. At the same time, it omits the degree of sedentism of the population (which also reflects economic sustainability). Migration, especially to urban centres, is a major factor in language shift (Friederike Lüpke, personal comm).

Husband and Saifullah-Khan's criticism of ethnolinguistic vitality as 'an uncritical naming of parts' (1982: 195) can be aimed at most typologies. They can be useful to compare situations, but nearly all provide descriptions rather than analysis or explanation. Indeed, Schiffman (2002: 141) claims that typologies are now seen as theoretically 'passé' and 'guilty of the latter-day sin of essentialism'. Dobrin, Austin and Nathan (2007) stress that each situation is unique, and that 'documentary work derives its quality from its appropriateness to the particularities of that situation'; attempts to create one framework to fit all circumstances are not particularly useful.

Dobrin et al. (ibid.: 61–3) observe a tendency towards 'reduction of languages to common exchange values' in which languages are prioritized by 'degree of endangerment' using 'official' metrics and scales such as the 'deceptively precise' numbers published in the *Ethnologue*, or by (misuse of) the 'endangerment index' in UNESCO (2003a). They emphasize that there is a lack of an agreed framework for assessing quality, progress and value in the documentation of endangered languages (ibid.: 64); as noted in Section 33.4 below, this is also the case with revitalization.

A key feature of language endangerment is that there is frequently little data available on the kinds of questions asked in these frameworks. Rather than comparative frameworks, context-specific information on language attitudes and patterns of use can be very useful: 'Who speaks what language when, and where?' (Fishman, 1965). Such questions can only be answered after prolonged contact with a community, using ethnographic research methods: expanding 'Who, when and where?' to **'Why?'**. It is also wise to take into account the relationship of the language under study (and its speakers) to others (Calvet, 2006); speakers of endangered languages are usually multilingual. The attitudes of those who do not speak the language are also relevant, as they may influence opinions and control funding.

What causes language endangerment?

Causes of language endangerment can be divided into four main categories.

1. *Natural catastrophes, famine, disease*: for example, Native American languages (disease) and Malol, Papua New Guinea (earthquake).
2. *War and genocide*: for example, Tasmania (genocide by colonists), Brazilian indigenous peoples (land disputes) and El Salvador (civil war).
3. *Overt repression*: for example, Kurdish, Welsh and Gikuyu.
4. *Cultural/political/economic dominance*: for example, Ainu, Manx, Sorbian, Quichua and many others. (synthesized from Nettle and Romaine, 2000; Crystal, 2000)

The dividing lines between these categories can sometimes be difficult to distinguish: for example,

in the Americas, disease and suppression of native cultures spread with colonization. Overt repression can include violence and genocide, and the line between overt and covert suppression can blur. Although some linguists prefer to steer clear of 'political' issues, language endangerment is inevitably entwined with political factors (Dorian, 1993).

The fourth category, which is the most common, can be further subdivided into five common factors:

- Economic: for example, rural poverty leads to migration; if the economy improves, tourism may bring speakers of majority languages.
- Cultural dominance: for example, education and literature through the majority or state language only.
- Political: for example, education policies which ignore or exclude local languages, lack of recognition or political representation.
- Historical: for example, colonization, boundary disputes, the rise of one group and their language.
- Attitudinal: for example, minority languages become associated with poverty, illiteracy and hardship.

The first four of these all feed into the last: a strong local culture or political support can help maintain a language, but many people identify a dominant language, or a language of wider communication, with economic advancement, and a small language as 'useless'. Such views are influenced by value systems which treat multilingualism as divisive, inefficient, useless and expensive – 'language as a problem' (in the terms of Ruíz, 1984) – rather than as a resource which fosters local economies and cultures.

Languages are often associated with ethnic, regional or national identity, a tradition going back to the Romantic movement; and political autonomy or self-determination is often viewed as one of the keys to safeguarding a language's vitality (Fishman, 1991). This is not always seen in a positive light, since there is also a tendency to assume that linguistic diversity contributes to inter-ethnic conflict (Brewer, 2001; Cameron, 2007: 284). However, several studies have found recognition of linguistic rights and ethnic identity necessary for conflict resolution (e.g. Daftary, 2000; Ashmore et al., 2001).

Even where there is no overt repression of a minority or its language, there is often little active political support. Wright (2004: 187) comments that 'Laissez-faire policies mean that the languages of power and prestige will eventually take over in all situations of contact. Benign neglect … [is] always de facto support for the language of the group that is already dominant'. Inaction or 'benign neglect' on the part of authorities therefore implies collusion in language death.

Such factors have led many communities to campaign for official support for language maintenance and revitalization. An official reversal of attitudes can counteract hostility towards a minority culture (Keskitalo, 1981; Dorian, 1987: 63–4). However, Williamson (1991) and Fennell (1981) warn that official support cannot save a language without community commitment. Fennell points out that despite government support, Irish continues to decline. Dorian (1987: 66) notes that 'compulsory Irish' lessons in schools created aversion towards the language in the early days of maintenance efforts; there was little consultation with local people or representation of their views in decision-making, and no attempt to foster positive attitudes towards the language.

Negative attitudes are not only held by dominant language speakers but also are internalized by speakers of minority languages (Bourdieu, 1977: 164; Kroskrity, 2000: 13). They are thus both outcome and cause of shift to the dominant language. Denison (1977) speaks of 'language suicide', and Ladefoged (1992) asserts that many minority language speakers consciously trade their traditional language for economic gain. Language shift is often presented as language choice, but Dorian (1994) notes that people are often faced with a lack of freedom in language choice and identity formation, resulting from economic necessity and internalized ideologies of inferiority.

33.4 LANGUAGE REVITALIZATION IN PRACTICE

Numerous language communities have overcome economic disadvantage, discrimination and ideologies of deficit to support and increase the use of their languages. Negative attitudes dominate the literature; the revitalization phase of language endangerment is a more recent development which is less well documented and inadequately theorized.

Fishman's (1991) GIDS is predicated on an important prerequisite: 'assuming prior ideological clarification' – i.e. that language planners have agreed policies on fundamentals such as what exactly they are trying to preserve, and why it is desirable. In his revisiting of the framework 10 years later, Fishman (2001: 541) admitted that it is quite common for enthusiasts to embark on language planning and revitalization activities without such clarification, and without convincing arguments with which to counter critics. Revitalization movements are characterized by enthusiasm rather than by planning and evaluation

and, as noted by Romaine (2006), there is still relatively little 'prior ideological clarification'. Endangered language communities may well not be aware of revitalization measures tried elsewhere, or of choices available, and may need to develop such clarification through a process of trial and error.

It is noticeable that the vast majority of language revitalization efforts reported in academic literature take place in Westernized countries, often among 'Fourth World' indigenous peoples. The number of revitalization projects in Asia and Africa found in a recent literature search can be counted on one hand for each of these continents, although the vast majority of the world's endangered languages are to be found there. Asian and African languages feature prominently in language documentation, but as yet these rarely seem to progress to revitalization. It is unclear whether this is because of a lack of interest among speakers, funding restrictions, lack of resources, or a lack of reporting in mainstream publications.[9] But the fact that most reported revitalization takes place in economically prosperous countries with good communications and education infrastructure (albeit geared to the dominant community's needs) suggests that a certain level of resourcing is advantageous. Grenoble and Whaley (1998: 52) describe economics as 'the single strongest force influencing the fate of endangered languages'.

An increasing number of publications provide principled guidance to practitioners: e.g. Bradley and Bradley (2002); Hinton and Hale (2002); and Grenoble and Whaley (2006). Most focus on measures in a particular context, and stress that it is impossible to guarantee that they will work if transplanted elsewhere, even if the causes of language endangerment are similar. Overviews often list measures geographically rather than thematically (e.g. Hinton and Hale, 2002). An exception is Lee and McLaughlin (2001: 38–9), who list 24 suggestions under the headings 'What pairs of persons can do', 'What families can do' and 'What communities can do'. The following is an attempt to group practices according to premise.

Community-based language learning

Community-based language learning programmes are complementary or alternative to formal education (which will be discussed below). 'Master–Apprentice' schemes, mentioned earlier, are easy to implement, requiring little funding or bureaucracy (although materials and coordination are of course useful). Where funding is available, participants may be expected to spend considerable time together and be compensated for loss of earnings (Hinton, 1997).

Intensive and residential courses were used in Israel during the revival of Hebrew, and the idea has been copied elsewhere – for example, in New Zealand (Nicholson, 1990), Ireland and Wales (Baker, 1999) and in Lithuania (Csató and Nathan, 2007). In smaller communities such schemes may not be feasible, but enthusiasts may organize social gatherings where those attending are encouraged to speak the language, sometimes involving traditional games or sports, or semi-formal language teaching activities. Such gatherings are valuable in providing exposure when a language is no longer used in traditional domestic domains.

A related type of measure suggested by Lee and McLaughlin is 'fine-arts and dramatic productions that utilize and promote the native language'. Similar activities include cultural or storytelling festivals, or individuals or groups who sing in an endangered language – either traditional songs or modern ones which might attract younger learners.

Language in the environment

Increasing the visibility of a language is a key method of raising its status and increasing its domains of use. As Kallen (2005) points out, the choice of language in signage is not neutral, and reflects language policy, history, community language use and identity. Gorter (2006) notes that 'the visibility or non-visibility of a language in public is a message in and of itself'. A note of caution was sounded by Gunther (1989), however: 'It seems that bilingual road-signs and some schooling in the minority language are seen as substitutes for parental or other early-childhood language learning'.

Endangered-language media

Mass media have a considerable influence on language choice, often bringing the dominant language into the home for the first time. The provision of minority-language radio, television, websites, CD-ROMs and print media can be seen as redressing a historical wrong as well as providing motivation for increased use. They also provide useful exposure for learners, especially if a language is extremely endangered.

Radio services run by indigenous peoples can also contribute to political, cultural, educational and linguistic awareness. Since the 1960s, a radio station which broadcasts in Shuar, a Jivaroan language in Ecuador, has played an important role in enabling speakers to undertake effective community action by facilitating communication over long distances and promoting cultural traditions (Gnerre, 2008).

Like linguistic landscape, the media are a prime target area for campaigners wishing to increase the status and prestige of a language (Cotter, 1999; Kelly-Holmes, 2000; Moseley et al., 2001). Language in the media is almost always seen in this light, while the value of providing a service for what is often a dwindling, ageing base of native speakers can be overlooked. This affects the type of programming provided, as elderly speakers are likely to have tastes which differ considerably from those of younger viewers, which in turn may influence elders' confidence in their language.

In places where the technology is available, initiatives have been launched to establish a virtual presence for endangered languages on the Internet (Bauman, 2003; Bennett, 2003). Increasingly, endangered languages can be found on social networking sites and in Internet chat rooms, which can provide input and practice for learners (especially those of computer-literate age).

Organizations such as OpenOffice.org[10] and Rosetta Stone[11] cater for increasing demand for software and platforms that can accommodate many languages, though usually this is only provided for those with sufficient speakers and institutional support for software companies to take notice, such as Irish and Māori.

Not all communities welcome either new media or literacy in their languages (see below), especially if these are not developed by the community itself (or in consultation with them). As noted earlier, with regard to Kaurna, some communities are protective of their languages. The Mapuche tribe of Chile tried to sue Microsoft when the software company produced a version of Windows in their language without consultation.[12]

Once again, a note of caution has been sounded: Dauenhauer and Dauenhauer (1998) criticize 'technical fixes' which may be promoted instead of changing personal behaviour and simply speaking a language more.

Education and endangered languages

There is debate in language movements worldwide about the role of schools (for example, Hornberger and King, 1996; Romaine, 2006). Having an endangered language taught in schools is seen as 'a crucial domain for language usage .... . When mandatory schooling occurs exclusively in a national language, the use of local languages almost inevitably declines' (Grenoble and Whaley, 2006: 10), especially when speakers remember humiliating experiences such as the residential schools that indigenous children were sent to in

North America and Australia in order to 'civilize' them. Gaining acceptance in schools therefore plays a key symbolic role in many endangered language revitalization campaigns. It is also perceived as a means of increasing status, prestige and perceived utility, as well as of improving educational outcomes among indigenous peoples (Hornberger, 2008).

Language provision in schools can range from very small amounts of extra-curricular teaching to bilingual/immersion and minority-language-medium education. Grenoble and Whaley (ibid.) maintain that including the minority language as a secondary subject is not an adequate response, citing UNESCO (2003b): 'Education in the language is *essential* for language vitality' (emphasis in original). However, experiences such as that of the Isle of Man show that starting on a small scale can be necessary to gain the acceptance of the majority population: optional extra-curricular classes led eventually to a full Manx-medium school.

The Breton *Diwan* and Māori *kōhanga reo* started as community-run playschemes with native-speaker helpers, to enable transmission to skip a generation. According to census figures, this has led to a dramatic increase in the number of children in New Zealand able to speak Māori (Benton and Benton, 2001: 425). These 'language nests' are seen as a particularly successful area of language revitalization, and have led to provision growing with the children.

A major practical problem with revitalizing highly-endangered languages through schools is the lack of suitably proficient and trained teachers. Hinton (2003) provides guidance for such circumstances, stressing the need for teachers to have mentors (usually a fluent older speaker,[13] as in a Master–Apprentice programme) and to use as much of the language as possible in the classroom, for example, in ritual exchanges and class management.

There are also more fundamental issues. Educationalists and linguists now agree that mother-tongue education provides the best start for children (Baker, 1999; 2001); however, Mühlhäusler (1990) warns that this should not be simply a stepping-stone to literacy in the dominant language, as is common in Africa and in 'transitional' classes in the USA. This recommendation also raises awkward questions regarding education through an endangered language that is no longer the children's mother tongue.

Maffi (2003) quotes a comment from Nancy Dorian: 'The introduction of a heritage language into the school curriculum has been known to seduce communities whose language is at risk into believing that interrupted family transmission is no longer a problem since the schools are dealing

with transmission'. Research in Wales has found that although bilingual education had successfully increased the number of young people who could speak Welsh, it did not lead to renewal of intergenerational transmission: young people stopped speaking Welsh once they left school (Edwards and Newcombe, 2005: 137). In places where endangered languages are promoted through education, traditional domains may be reversed: as official endorsement increases, use in informal contexts decreases.

Re-establishing intergenerational transmission

Although 'informal intergenerational oracy' is a stated aim of most revitalization movements, it is the most difficult to regain once interrupted. The Irish government even tried offering payments to parents for raising children to speak Irish to a recognized standard, though without the desired success (Hindley, 1990; Ó Riagáin, 1997). A more recent programme in Wales, *Twf* ('growth'), encourages families to bring children up bilingually, and is promoted by midwives and health workers (Edwards and Newcombe, 2005). Bilingual education had produced a generation with proficiency in academic Welsh, but without the type of language (and the motivation) needed for childrearing. Project workers contribute to childbirth preparation classes, which are seen as a critical time to persuade parents of the benefits of bilingualism. Another key aim is social inclusion, as a social divide is seen in take-up of bilingual education (ibid.: 143).

33.5 LITERACY AND STANDARDIZATION

In revitalization movements, schooling and standardization often go hand in hand. Written languages are held in higher esteem than non-written vernaculars, and endangered languages are often associated with illiteracy. Many activists therefore believe that establishing a standardized written form is essential for raising the status of their language, expanding its uses and having it accepted as a 'proper language'.

As with schooling, however, these assumptions are problematic. Schieffelin, Woolard and Kroskrity (1998: 17) observe that

> Movements to save minority languages are often structured, willy-nilly, around the same received notions of language that have led to their oppression ... language activists find themselves imposing standards, elevating literate forms and uses,

and negatively sanctioning variability in order to demonstrate the reality, validity, and integrity of their languages.

A high level of local variation is common in endangered languages, which typically have no prestige or urban variant; standardization may therefore entail the loss of dialect diversity. Where endangered languages have been accepted in schools, it is common for a 'unified' standard to be developed: for example, Basque (Urtéaga, 2005) and Gaelic (Dorian, 1981: 88). Divergence may develop between younger speakers who have learnt the unified version through education, and older native speakers of 'authentic' varieties (Grenoble and Whaley, 2006). In Lagunas, Ecuador, 'the introduction of Unified Quichua into the community has created (or perhaps only accentuated) generational and educational differences within the community' (Hornberger and King, 1996: 422). However, unlike cases in Europe, the school version avoids contact influences:

> The Quichua of the older members of the community, commonly referred to as 'authentic Quichua', while reflecting the phonological system of the region, contains many Spanish loan words and has lost some elements of its morphological structure. The Quichua which is being learned and on occasion spoken by the younger, better educated, and more politicized of Lagunas is the relatively 'pure' standardized variety, known as Unified Quichua (Hornberger and King, 1996: 421).

However, Mühlhäusler (2000: 328) argues that 'the preservation of conservative constructions is far less important than the promotion of conditions in which a new generation of users can revive and adapt older forms of speech', which is both a justification for 'modernizing' languages and a challenge to linguistic purism.

The choice of terminology or orthography for a language does not simply involve choosing value-free signs or words; it can also imply 'buying in' to prescriptivism. Jaffe (1999: 28) comments that 'distinguishing good from bad usage', as is common in schools, reproduces the structures of domination. My research into the indigenous language of Guernsey suggests that writers of an endangered language may relish the freedom offered by lack of standardization by using a wide variety of non-standard spellings, although this may be due as much to lack of literacy training as to resistance to standardization. However, unpredictable spellings increase the problems of second-language learners.

The French sociolinguist Marcellesi (1986, 2003) suggested the solution of a 'polynomic' language, in which respect for variation is combined with a strong perception by speakers of a distinct, distinguishable language.[14] This concept proposes an alternative model to prescriptivism, and anticipates the postmodern challenging of languages as 'defined and static systems' (Wright, 2007). However, it may not be practicable to implement in schools. Jaffe (2005) describes lessons in Corsican which attempt to follow this model and cater for regional variation, but in practice it seems that students are simply offered a choice between two approved spellings, rather than free variation in spelling such as I found among native speakers of Guernesiais.

33.6 LANGUAGE AND IDENTITY

Many supporters of endangered languages claim that when a language dies out, a unique way of looking at the world also disappears (for example, Fishman, 1989; Nettle and Romaine, 2000; Dalby, 2002). Grimes (2001) asserts that the disappearance of a language means the extinction of a 'unique creation of human beings that houses a treasure of information and preserves a people's identity'. Major funders of language documentation take similar views: the Hans Rausing Endangered Languages Project[15] has as its motto 'because every last word means another lost world', and the US National Endowment for the Humanities Documenting Endangered Languages program website[16] cites its Chairman, Bruce Cole, as saying 'Language is the DNA of a culture, and it is the vehicle for the traditions, customs, stories, history, and beliefs of a people. A lost language is a lost culture'. This view is related to notions that a language is tied to particular local conditions (Mühlhäusler, 2000: 335), territory (Laponce, 1987) and culture. A link between language and identity is often treated as a given, with little discussion of its nature.

Much of the discourse on endangered languages thus seems somewhat essentialist and deterministic, which has attracted criticism from sociolinguists, especially Duchêne and Heller (2007). But this does not mean that there is no link between language and culture, or that endangered languages have no cultural value. 'But neither is [language] reconstituted and reconstructed by every speaker anew in every generation. ... And much of culture (if we still accept the notion that there is such a thing) is transmitted through language' (Schiffman, 1996: 9).

Many recent writers, influenced by postmodernism, see identities not as fixed, formal realities, but rather as fluid, shaped while people compose and position themselves within the various social settings of their everyday lives (for example, Castells, 2004; Omoniyi and White, 2006). This may help to account for the paradox whereby many endangered language speakers claim a strong identification with their language, yet do not transmit it to their children. As Le Page and Tabouret-Keller (1985: 239–40) note, feelings of ethnic identity can survive total language loss. Dorian (1999: 31) comments, 'Because it is only one of an almost infinite variety of potential identity markers, [a language] is easily replaced by others that are just as effective. In this respect the ancestral language is functionally expendable'. Bankston and Henry (1998) note that a strong identification with a minority language may not always correlate positively with language maintenance, particularly when it comes to transmitting a low-status variety to children. In addition, in a multilingual environment, different languages may be used to express different aspects of personal identity, as they are used in different roles and domains (Friederike Lüpke, pers comm).

There is a trend for campaigners to focus their attention on language as a symbol of identity, rather than on the social and economic factors which contribute to language shift, or on maintenance of living languages through intergenerational transmission. For example, Bankston and Henry (2000) describe the 'commodification of ethnic culture' amongst Cajuns in Louisiana, where an increased emphasis on Acadian heritage coincides with acculturation and language shift; perhaps this attempt to make culture more visible is a reaction to the divorce of language and culture from speakers. Mohanty (2000: 56) suggests that collective identity can be consciously forged through re-examination of accepted cultural meanings and values. In the context of language shift such re-examination might challenge accepted ideologies such as 'majority language = progress', as has happened in Wales and the Basque Country in Spain.

Postmodern ideas on the constructed, fluid nature of identity are not well known among 'lay' people, and many take for granted received, essentialist views of language, culture and identity. Freeland and Patrick (2004: 8) assume that folk ideologies will challenge essentialist views of language and identity, and language boundaries, whereas my research findings indicate that people tend to have quite traditional views on these matters (Sallabank, 2006). As noted by May (2004) and Patrick (2004), distinguishing oneself by linguistic differentiation continues to be important for groups' and individuals' identity construction; and Nieldzielski and Preston (2003), like Mohanty (2000), stress that respondents' perceptions are valid factors in researching language. Such 'folk linguistic' ideologies are more likely to

affect linguistic outcomes than objective evidence for or against linguistic determinism.

Identification with a language, and strong emotional bonds to it, do not guarantee its maintenance or transmission in the face of other pressures. But it is hard to see how a minority language can be maintained without a focus on identity: it is difficult to rationalize on instrumental grounds alone. Campaigning therefore often leans heavily on links with traditional culture and identity. A careful line needs to be trodden, however, between this and alienating both younger generations and non-indigenous people (Myhill, 1999). In the Isle of Man, revival of the Manx language is motivated by a desire to 'hold on to something uniquely Manx', but at the same time, Manx is being repositioned to create an 'inclusive' identity, which both natives and incomers can identify with (Cain, 2008).

33.7 WHY WORRY ABOUT LANGUAGE ENDANGERMENT?

Most researchers in the field of language endangerment are predisposed to a favourable attitude towards maintaining linguistic diversity. Nevertheless, some commentators question this. Edwards (1985) takes a pessimistic view that language shift is natural and inevitable. Malik (2000), in a review of Nettle and Romaine (2000), claims that proponents of linguistic diversity are 'impossibly nostalgic': 'There is nothing noble or authentic about local ways of life; they are often simply degrading and backbreaking'. Like Cameron (2007), he claims that the 'belief that different peoples have unique ways of understanding the world … draws on the same philosophy that gave rise to ideas of racial difference'. As noted earlier, struggles for self-determination and linguistic rights are often connected; but so too are efforts to reduce disadvantage, and to improve minorities' educational achievement. Linguists tend to promote diversity rather than hegemony, and cannot be blamed for the misappropriation of nineteenth-century Romantic ideas by twentieth-century extremist groups.

De Swaan (2004) claims that languages 'do not die out but are abandoned by those who used to speak them', echoing Denison's (1977) view that speakers collude in 'language suicide'; however, as noted above, language 'choice' is not always free. Ladefoged (1992) claims that many people accept the loss of their language as the price of entering modern society, commenting 'Who am I to say he was wrong?' about a Dahalo speaker in Kenya who smiled when affirming that his son spoke only Swahili. In response, Dorian (1993) notes that some of the youngest members of endangered language communities have begun to berate their elders for choosing not to transmit the ancestral language and so allowing it to die.

Ladefoged (1992), Malik (2000) and de Swaan (2004) follow the common assumption that members of minority groups benefit materially from shifting to a dominant language. According to Nettle and Romaine (2000), this benefit does not necessarily materialize. On the other hand, campaigns for minority and linguistic rights can have tangible benefits. Thieberger (1990) examines seven reasons commonly advanced for the maintenance of Australian Aboriginal languages: preservation of linguistic resources, social cohesion, identity, diversity, language maintenance as part of cultural maintenance, individual well-being and social justice. Although Thieberger finds each to have merit, he argues that the appeal to morality and social justice provides the strongest justification: by allowing speakers to maintain a connection with their cultural past, a maintenance programme gives Aboriginal peoples a voice in the new Australia.

Fishman (1991) asserts that those who wish to reverse language shift 'should not be embarrassed about the fact that theirs is basically a value position ... because the position of their opponents is also no more than a value position' (ibid.: 19). As Wright (2004: 225) notes, 'The strongest argument for taking the necessary institutional decisions to support maintenance of a language has to be because its individual speakers wish to do so.'

Communicating with the public

This chapter has emphasized that language endangerment cannot be separated from other problems such as socioeconomic disadvantage or lack of political rights. But in publicizing their cause, campaigners (and linguists) frequently avoid such potentially controversial arguments and focus on more 'soft and furry', comfortable explanations such as parallels with the loss of ecological diversity. An actual correlation between linguistic and biological diversity observed by biological scientists (Sutherland, 2003) has been taken up enthusiastically by campaigners such as the organization Terralingua[17] and some researchers (for example, Haarmann, 1986; Skutnabb-Kangas, 2002). It has received considerable public attention – for example, in popular books such as Dalby (2002) and in the media.

Both field- and sociolinguists have criticized such strategies (for example, Hill, 2002; Dobrin, Austin and Nathan, 2007; Duchêne and Heller, 2007). However, as Dobrin et al. (2007: 60) comment, 'While analytically suspect in a number of respects, this "emotive and moralistic" discourse [Cameron, 2007: 269] has been – and continues to be – highly effective'. Public and scholarly interest in language endangerment has never been so high, with tangible results in terms of funding for documentation and the number of degree programmes and training courses available; the discipline of linguistics has also become more socially relevant (Dobrin et al., 2007: 60).

To what extent does it matter if some misconceptions circulate due to 'strategic simplification' (Heller, 2004: 286)? Do they propagate patronizing, exoticist views of indigenous peoples? Do they damage the survival of linguistic diversity in the long term? Hill (2002: 128–9) asks, 'Can endangered-language advocates modify their rhetoric in such a way as to balance between the two audiences, helping community activists to rally people in endangered-language communities to defend and reclaim their languages while simultaneously attracting resources from dominant communities?' Hill recommends the promotion of linguistic human rights as an 'appropriate stance in opposition to oppression'; however, this too has been criticized, especially the link between discourses of language rights and essentialist views of identity and linguistic boundaries (Freeland and Patrick, 2004).

33.8 CONCLUSION

The picture painted above may at times look gloomy. Grenoble and Whaley (2006: ix) note soberly that most language revitalization efforts to date have been failures, although 'there are enough success stories to warrant optimism'. Around the world, attitudes towards endangered languages are changing, at all levels from local to international. A degree of support for indigenous languages is now accepted policy in the European Union and in Canada, the USA, South Africa and New Zealand, and by international bodies such as the Council of Europe and UNESCO.

Through language revitalization measures, speakers gain in confidence and awareness, and are able to challenge ideologies of deficit. This is seen in the example of Mayan described by Barrett (2008), and by Newman, Trenchs-Parera and Ng (2008), who suggest that support for bilingualism and the easing of divisions in Catalunya are signs of increased 'linguistic cosmopolitanism', 'a stance that looks beyond parochial own-group communities and favors bridging linguistic boundaries'. As Newman et al. note, it is significant that minority languages can be valued when they take on such symbolic roles. Elsewhere too, indigenous languages are being 'rebranded' to create an 'inclusive' identity that all members of the community can express themselves through, from indigenous people to those most recently arrived.

NOTES

1 www.hrelp.org/, accessed 9 June 2008.
2 www.mpi.nl/DOBES/, accessed 9 June 2008.
3 www.neh.gov/grants/guidelines/del.html, accessed 9 June 2008.
4 www.esf.org/index.php?id=4632, accessed 9 June 2008.
5 www.ogmios.org, accessed 9 June 2008.
6 www.endangeredlanguagefund.org/, accessed 9 June 2008.
7 The original source is unclear.
8 For examples of training, see http://www.hrelp.org/events/workshops/eldp2008_6/ and http://www.linguistics.ucsb.edu/faculty/infield/, accessed 24 June 2008.
9 Grass-roots community efforts are particularly likely to be undocumented or not the subject of research.
10 http://www.openoffice.org/, accessed 30 June 2008.
11 http://www.rosettastone.com/, accessed 30 June 2008.
12 http://news.softpedia.com/news/The-Mapuche-Indians-Wage-Legal-War-Against-Microsoft-41037.html, accessed 18 May 2009. For discussion of the language sovereignty issue see http://blogs.usyd.edu.au/elac/2006/11/sovereignty_over_languages_and_1.html (accessed 18 May 2009).
13 Although this may cause problems if the older speaker favours linguistic purism: see Section 33.5 below.
14 Marcellesi's works are not well known among English-speaking linguists, as they are only available in French.
15 The author is currently employed in the Endangered Languages Academic Programme at SOAS (School of Oriented and African Studies), part of the Project, but is free to express her own opinions.
16 http://www.neh.gov/grants/guidelines/del.html, accessed 28 June 2008.
17 http://www.terralingua.org/, accessed 28 June 2008.

REFERENCES

Ahmad, M. (2008) 'What factors contribute to sign language endangerment?'. MA dissertation, School of Oriental and African Studies, London.

Aikhenvald, A. (2002) 'Language obsolescence: progress or decay? The emergence of new grammatical categories in "language death"', in D. Bradley and M. Bradley (eds), *Language Endangerment and Language Maintenance*. London: Routledge Curzon. pp. 144–55.

Amery, R. (2000) *Warrabarra Kaurna! Reclaiming an Australian Language*. Lisse: Swets and Zeitlinger.

Ashmore, R. D., Jussim, L. and Wilder, D. (eds) (2001) *Social Identity, Intergroup Conflict, and Conflict Reduction*. Oxford: Oxford University Press.

Baker, C. (1999) *Encyclopaedia of Bilingualism and Bilingual Education*. Clevedon, UK: Multilingual Matters.

Baker, C. (2001) *Foundations of Bilingual Education and Bilingualism*. Clevedon, UK: Multilingual Matters.

Bankston, C. L. III and Henry, J. (1998) 'The silence of the gators: Cajun ethnicity and intergenerational transmission of Louisiana French', *Journal of Multilingual and Multicultural Development*, 19: 1–23.

Bankston, C. L., III and Henry, J. (2000) 'Spectacles of ethnicity: festivals and the commodification of ethnic culture among Louisiana Cajuns', *Sociological Spectrum*, 20: 377–407.

Barrett, R. (2008) 'Linguistic differentiation and Mayan language revitalization in Guatemala', *Journal of Sociolinguistics*, 12(3): 275–305.

Bauman, R. (ed.) (2003) *Voices of Modernity: Language Ideologies and the Politics of Inequality. Studies in the Social and Cultural Foundations of Language*. Cambridge: Cambridge University Press.

Bennett, R. (2003) 'Saving a language with computers, tape recorders, and radio', in J. Reyhner, O. Trujillo, R. L. Carrasco and L. Lockard (eds), *Nurturing Native Languages*. Flagstaff, AZ: Northern Arizona University. pp. 59–77. http://jan.ucc.nau.edu/~jar/NNL/NNL_5.pdf. Accessed 28 June 2008.

Benton, R. and Benton, N. (2001) 'RLS in Aotearoa/New Zealand 1989–1999', in J. A. Fishman (ed.), *Can Threatened Languages be Saved? Reversing Language Shift, Revisited: A 21st Century Perspective*. Clevedon, UK: Multilingual Matters. pp. 423–50.

Bourdieu, P. (1977) *Outline of a Theory of Practice*. Cambridge: Cambridge University Press.

Bradley. D. and Bradley, M. (eds) (2002) *Language Endangerment and Language Maintenance*. London: Routledge Curzon.

Brewer, M. B. (2001) 'Intergroup identification and intergroup conflict: when does ingroup love become outgroup hate?', in R. D. Ashmore, L. Jussim and D. Wilder (eds), pp. 17–41. *Social Identity, Intergroup Conflict, and Conflict Reduction*. Oxford: Oxford University Press.

Cain, A. (2008) Paper presented at Workshop on Language Revitalisation, Centre for Language in Social Life, Lancaster University, 16 May 2008.

Calvet, J. -L. (2006) *Towards an Ecology of World Languages*. Cambridge: Polity.

Cameron, D. (1992) *Researching Language: Issues of Power and Method*. London: Routledge.

Cameron, D. (2007) 'Language endangerment and verbal hygiene: history, morality and politics', in A. Duchêne and

M. Heller (eds), *Discourses of Endangerment*. London: Continuum. pp. 268–87.

Cameron, D., Frazer, E., Harvey, P., Rampton, M. B. H. and Richardson, K. (1993) 'The relations between researcher and researched: ethics, advocacy and empowerment', in D. Graddol, J. Maybin and B. Stierer (eds), *Researching Language and Literacy in Social Context*. Clevedon, UK: The Open University/Multilingual Matters. pp.18–25.

Castells, M. (2004) *The Power of Identity: The Information Age: Economy, Society and Culture*. Oxford: Blackwell.

Cheng, C. (1996) 'Quantifying dialect mutual intelligibility', in C.-T. J. Huang, and Y.-H. A. Li (eds), *New Horizons in Chinese Linguistics*. Dordrecht: Kluwer. pp. 269–92.

Cotter, C. (1999) 'From folklore to "News at 6": maintaining language and reframing identity through the media', in M. Bucholz, A. C. Liang and L. A. Sutton (eds), *Reinventing Identities: The Gendered Self in Discourse*. New York: Oxford University Press. pp. 369–87.

Crasborn, O. and Zwitserlood, I. (2008) 'Just in time? The importance of creating sign language archives', paper presented at Sociolinguistics Symposium 17, Vrije Universiteit, Amsterdam, 3–5 April 2008.

Csató, É. Á. and Nathan, D. (2007) 'Multiliteracy, past and present, in the Karaim communities', *Language Documentation and Description* 4.

Crystal, D. (2000) *Language Death*. Cambridge: Cambridge University Press.

Daftary, F. (2000) *Insular Autonomy: A Framework for Conflict Settlement? A Comparative Study of Corsica and the Aaland Islands*. Flensburg: European Centre for Minority Issues. http://www.ecmi.de/download/working_paper_9.pdf. Accessed 27 June 2008.

Dalby, A. (2002) *Language in Danger*. London: Penguin.

Dauenhauer, N. M. and Dauenhauer, R. (1998) 'Technical, emotional, and ideological issues in reversing language shift: examples from Southeast Alaska', in L. A. Grenoble and L. J. Whaley (eds), *Endangered Languages: Language Loss and Community Response*. Cambridge: Cambridge University Press. pp. 57–98.

Denison, N. (1977) 'Language death or language suicide?', *International Journal of the Sociology of Language*, 12: 13–22.

de Swaan, A. (2004) 'Endangered languages, sociolinguistics, and linguistic sentimentalism', *European Review*, 12: 567–80. doi: 10.1017/S1062798704000481.

Dobrin, L., Austin, P. and Nathan, D. (2007) 'Dying to be counted: the commodification of endangered languages in documentary linguistics', in P. Austin, O. Bond and D. Nathan (eds), *Proceedings of Conference on Language Documentation and Linguistic Theory, 7–8 December 2007*. London: School of Oriental and African Studies. pp. 59–68.

Dorian, N. C. (1977) 'The problem of the semi-speakers in language death', *Linguistics*, 191: 23–32.

Dorian, N. C. (1981) *Language Death: The Life Cycle of a Scottish Gaelic Dialect*. Philadelphia: University of Pennsylvania Press.

Dorian, N. C. (1987) 'The value of maintenance efforts which are unlikely to succeed', *International Journal of the Sociology of Language*, 68: 57–67.

Dorian, N. C. (1993) 'A response to Ladefoged's other view of endangered languages', *Language*, 69: 575–9.

Dorian, N. C. (1994) 'Choices and values in language shift and its study', *International Journal of the Sociology of Language*, 110: 113–24.

Dorian, N. C. (1999) 'Linguistic and ethnographic fieldwork', in J. A. Fishman (ed.), *Handbook of Ethnic Identity*. Oxford: Oxford University Press. pp. 25–41.

Duchêne, A. and Heller, M. (eds) (2007) *Discourses of Endangerment*. London: Continuum.

Edwards, J. R. (1985) *Language, Society, and Identity*. Oxford: Basil Blackwell.

Edwards, V. and Newcombe, L. P. (2005) 'Language transmission in the family in Wales: an example of innovative language planning', *Language Problems and Language Planning*, 29: 135–50.

Fennell, D. (1981) 'Can a shrinking minority be saved? Lessons from the Irish experience', in E. Haugen, J. McClure and D. Thompson (eds), *Minority Languages Today: A Selection from the Papers Read at the First Conference on Minority Languages*. Edinburgh: Edinburgh University Press. pp. 32–9.

Fishman, J. A. (1965) 'Who speaks what language to whom and when', *La Linguistique*, 2: 67–88.

Fishman, J. A. (1989) *Language and Ethnicity in Minority Sociolinguistic Perspective*. Clevedon, UK: Multilingual Matters.

Fishman, J. A. (ed.) (1991) *Reversing Language Shift: Theoretical and Empirical Foundations of Assistance to Threatened Languages*. Clevedon, UK: Multilingual Matters.

Fishman, J. A. (ed.) (2001) *Can Threatened Languages be Saved? Reversing Language Shift, Revisited: A 21st Century Perspective*. Clevedon, UK: Multilingual Matters.

Freeland, J. and Patrick, D. (eds) (2004) *Language Rights and Language Survival*. Manchester: St Jerome Press.

Giles, H., Bourhis, R. and Taylor, D. M. (1977) 'Towards a theory of language in Ethnic Group Relations', in H. Giles (ed.), *Language, Ethnicity and Intergroup Relations*. London: Academic Press. pp. 307–48.

Gnerre, M. (2008) 'I heard it on the radio: indigenous language radio and political activism', paper presented at ELAP Workshop on Engagement and Activism in Endangered Languages Research, 2 May 2008, School of Oriental and African Studies, London.

Gordon, R. G., Jr. (ed.) (2005) *Ethnologue: Languages of the World*. 15th edn. Dallas, Tx.: SIL International. Online version: http://www.ethnologue.com/. Accessed 6 June 2008.

Gorter, D. (2006) 'Introduction: the study of the linguistic landscape as a new approach to multilingualism', *International Journal of Multilingualism*, 3: 1–6.

Grenoble, L. A. and Whaley, L. J. (eds) (1998) *Endangered Languages: Language Loss and Community Response*. Cambridge: Cambridge University Press.

Grenoble, L. A. and Whaley, L. J. (2006) *Saving Languages: An Introduction to Language Revitalization*. Cambridge: Cambridge University Press.

Grimes, B. F. (2001) 'Global language viability: causes, symptoms and cures for endangered languages', *Notes on Linguistics*, 4: 205–23.

Grinevald, C. (2003) 'Speakers and documentation of endangered languages', *Language Documentation and Description*, 1: 52–72. London: Hans Rausing Endangered Languages Project.

Gunther, W. (1989) 'Language conservancy or: Can the anciently established British minority languages survive?', in D. Gorter, J. F. Hoekstra, L. G. Jansma and J. Ytsma (eds), *Fourth International Conference on Minority Languages, Vol. II: Western and Eastern European Papers*. Clevedon, UK: Multilingual Matters. pp. 53–68.

Haarmann, H. (1986) *Language in Ethnicity: A View of Basic Ecological Relations*. Berlin: Mouton de Gruyter.

Hale, K., Yamamoto, A., Krauss, M., Ladefoged, P. and Watahomigie, L. (1992) 'Special issue on endangered languages', *Language*, 68: 1–42.

Hammarstrom, H. (2008) 'Counting languages in dialect continua using the criterion of mutual intelligibility', *Journal of Quantitative Linguistics*, 15: 34–45.

Harrison, D. (2007) *When Languages Die*. Oxford: Oxford University Press.

Heller, M. (2004) 'Analysis and stance regarding language and social justice', in J. Freeland and D. Patrick (eds), *Language Rights and Language Survival*. Manchester: St Jerome. pp. 283–6.

Hill, J. H. (2002) '"Expert Rhetorics" in advocacy for endangered languages: who Is listening, and what do they hear?', *Journal of Linguistic Anthropology*, 12(2): 119–33.

Hindley, R. (1990) *The Death of the Irish Language: A Qualified Obituary*. London: Routledge.

Hinton, L. (1997) 'Survival of endangered languages: The Californian Master–Apprentice program', *International Journal of the Sociology of Language*, 123: 177–91.

Hinton, L. (2003) 'How to teach when the teacher isn't fluent', in J. Reyhner, O. Trujillo, R. L. Carrasco and L. Lockard (eds), *Nurturing Native Languages*. Flagstaff, AZ: Northern Arizona University. pp. 79–92. http://jan.ucc.nau.edu/~jar/NNL/NNL_6.pdf. Accessed 28 June 2008.

Hinton, L. and Hale, K. (eds) (2002) *The Green Book of Language Revitalization in Practice*. San Diego: Academic Press.

Hornberger, N. (ed.) (2008) *Can Schools Save Indigenous Languages? Policy and Practice on Four Continents*. Basingstoke: Palgrave Macmillan.

Hornberger, N. H. and King, K. (1996) 'Language revitalization in the Andes: can the schools reverse language shift?', *Journal of Multilingual and Multicultural Development*, 17: 427–41.

Husband, C. and Saifullah-Khan, V. (1982) 'The viability of ethnolinguistic vitality: some creative doubts', *Journal of Multilingual and Multicultural Development*, 3: 195–205.

Irvine, J. T. and Gal, S. (2000) 'Language ideology and linguistic differentiation', in P. V. Kroskrity (ed.), *Regimes of Language: Ideologies, Politics and Identities*. Santa Fe, NM: School of American Research Press.

Jaffe, A. (1999) *Ideologies in Action: Language Politics on Corsica*. Berlin: Mouton de Gruyter.

Jaffe, A. (2005) 'L'éducation bilingue corse et la polynomie' ['Corsican bilingual education and polynomia'], *Marges Linguistiques*, 10: 282–300. http://www.revue-texto.net/marges/marges/Documents%20Site%201/00_ml102005/00_ml102005.pdf. Accessed 5 June 2008.

Kallen, J. (2005) 'The linguistic landscape in Ireland: tourism and national (re)presentation', paper presented at Association Internationale de Linguistique Appliquée, Madison, Wisconsin, 24–29 July 2005.

Komarova, N., and Niyogi, P. (2004) 'Optimizing the mutual intelligibility of linguistic agents in a shared worlds'. *Artificial Intelligence*, 154: 1–42.

Kelly-Holmes, H. (ed.) (2000) Special Issue on 'Minority Language Broadcasting', *Current Issues in Language and Society*, 7. http://www.multilingual-matters.net/cils/007/2/default.htm. Accessed 28 June 2008.

Keskitalo, I. (1981) 'The status of the Sámi language', in E. Haugen, J. McClure and D. Thompson (eds), *Minority Languages Today: A Selection from the Papers Read at the First Conference on Minority Languages*. Edinburgh: Edinburgh University Press. pp. 152–62.

Kloss, H. (1967) '"Abstand languages" and "Ausbau languages"', *Anthropological Linguistics*, 9: 29–71.

Krauss, M. (1992) 'The world's languages in crisis', *Language*, 68: 4–10.

Krauss, M. (1997) 'The indigenous languages of the North: a report on their present state', *Senri Ethnological Studies*, 44: 1–34.

Kroskrity, P. V. (ed.) (2000) *Regimes of Language: Ideologies, Polities, and Identities*. Santa Fe, NM: School of American Research Press.

Ladefoged, P. (1992) 'Another view of endangered languages', *Language*, 68: 809–11.

Laponce, J. (1987) *Languages and Their Territories*. Toronto, UK: University of Toronto Press.

Lee, T. S. and McLaughlin, D. (2001) 'Reversing Navajo language shift, revisited', in J. A. Fishman (ed.), *Can Threatened Languages be Saved?* Clevedon, UK: Multilingual Matters. pp. 23–43.

Le Page, R. B. and Tabouret-Keller, A. (1985) *Acts of Identity: Creole-Based Approaches to Language and Ethnicity*. Cambridge: Cambridge University Press.

Lord, N. (1996) 'Native tongues', *Sierra*, 81: 46–69.

Maffi, L. (2003) 'The "business" of language endangerment: saving languages or helping people keep them alive?', in H. Tonkin and T. G. Reagan (eds), *Language in the Twenty-First Century: Selected Papers of the Millennial Conferences of the Center for Research and Documentation on World Language Problems*. Amsterdam: John Benjamins. pp. 67–86.

Makoni, S., and Pennycook, A. (eds) (2006) *Disinventing and Reconstituting Languages*. Clevedon, UK: Multilingual Matters.

Malik, K. (2000) 'Let them die', *Prospect*, November. 2000: 16–17. Reproduced at http://www.kenanmalik.com/essays/die.html. Accessed 28 June 2008.

Marcellesi, J.-B. (1986) 'Actualité du processus de naissance de langues en domaine roman', *Cahiers de*

Linguistique Sociale, Vol. 9, *Sociolinguistique Romane.* Rouen: University of Rouen. pp. 21–9. Reproduced at http://membres.lycos.fr/bulot/cauchois/Marcel.htm. Accessed 28 June 2008.

Marcellesi, J.-B., Bulot, T., and Blanchet, P. (2003) *Sociolinguistique: Epistemologie, Langues Regionales, Polynomie.* Paris: l'Harmattan.

May, S. (2004) 'Rethinking linguistic human rights: answering questions of identity, essentialism and mobility', in J. Freeland and D. Patrick (eds), *Language Rights and Language Survival.* Manchester: St Jerome. pp. 35–54.

Mohanty, S. P. (2000) 'The epistemic status of cultural identity', in P. M. L. Moya and M. R. Hames-Garcia (eds), *Reclaiming Identity: Realist Theory and the Predicament of Postmodernism.* Berkeley, CA: University of California Press. pp. 29–66.

Moseley, C. (ed.) (2009) *UNESCO Atlas of the World's Languages in Danger of Disappearing.* UNESCO. Online edition at, http://www.unesco.org/culture/ich/index.php?pg=00206. Accessed 5 June 2009.

Moseley, C., Ostler, N. and Ouzzate, H. (eds) (2001) *Endangered Languages and the Media: Papers from the 5th Foundation for Endangered Languages Conference.* Bath: Foundation for Endangered Languages.

Mühlhäusler, P. (1990) '"Reducing" Pacific languages to writing', in J. E. Joseph and T.J. Taylor (eds), *Ideologies of language.* London: Routledge. pp. 189–205.

Mühlhäusler, P. (2000) 'Language planning and language ecology', *Current Issues in Language Planning,* 1(3): 306–67.

Muysken, P. (2008) 'Endangered language documentation and sociolinguistics: the case of Bolivia', plenary address at Sociolinguistics Symposium 17, Vrije Universiteit, Amsterdam, 3–5 April 2008.

Myhill, J. (1999) 'Identity, territoriality and minority language survival', *Journal of Multilingual and Multicultural Development,* 20: 34–50.

Nettle, D., and Romaine, S. (2000) *Vanishing Voices: The Extinction of the World's Languages.* New York: Oxford University Press.

Newman, M., Trenchs-Parera, M. and Ng, S. (2008) 'Normalizing bilingualism: the effects of the Catalonian linguistic normalization policy one generation after', *Journal of Sociolinguistics,* 12(3): 306–33.

Nicholson, R. (1990) 'Maori total immersion courses for adults in Aotearoa/New Zealand: a personal perspective', in J. Reyhner (ed.), *Effective Language Education Practices and Native Languages Survival.* Choctaw, OK: Native American Language Issues. pp. 107–20.

Nieldzielski, N. A. and Preston, D. R. (2003) *Folk Linguistics.* Berlin: Mouton de Gruyter.

Omoniyi, T., and White, G. (eds) (2006) *The Sociolinguistics of Identity.* London: Continuum.

Ó Riagáin, P. (1997) *Language Policy and Social Reproduction: Ireland 1893–1993.* Oxford: Oxford University Press.

Patrick, D. (2004) 'The politics of language rights in the eastern Canadian Arctic', in J. Freeland and D. Patrick (eds),

Language Rights and Language Survival. Manchester: St Jerome. pp. 171–90.

Rice, K. and Saxon, L. (2002) 'Issues of standardization and community in Aboriginal language lexicography', in W. Frawley, K. C. Hill and P. Munro (eds), *Making Dictionaries: Preserving Indigenous Languages of the Americas.* Berkeley, CA: University of California Press. pp. 125–54.

Ricento, T. (ed.) (2005) *An Introduction to Language policy.* Oxford: Blackwell.

Romaine, S. (2006) 'Planning for the survival of linguistic diversity', *Language Policy,* 5: 441–73.

Ruíz, R. (1984) 'Orientations in language planning', *NABE Journal,* 8: 15–34. Reprinted in S. L. McKay, and S. L. C. Wong, (eds) (1988) *Language Diversity: Problem or Resource?* New York: Newbury House.

Sallabank, J. (2006) 'Guernsey French, identity and language endangerment', in T. Omoniyi, and White, G. (eds), *The Sociolinguistics of Identity.* London: Continuum, pp. 131–56.

Sallabank, J. (2007) 'Endangered language maintenance and social networks', in P. Austin, O. Bond and D. Nathan (eds), *Proceedings of Conference on Language Documentation and Linguistic Theory, 7–8 December 2007.* London: School of Oriental and African Studies. pp. 197–208.

Schieffelin, B., Woolard, K. A. and Kroskrity, P. V. (eds) (1998) *Language Ideologies: Practice and Theory.* Oxford: Oxford University Press.

Schiffman, H. F. (1996) *Linguistic Culture and Language Policy.* London: Routledge.

Schiffman, H. F. (2002) 'Comment', *International Journal of the Sociology of Language,* 157: 141–50.

Schmidt, A. (1985) *Young people's Dyirbal: An Example of Language Death from Australia.* Cambridge: Cambridge University Press.

Skutnabb-Kangas, T. (2002) 'Language key to life on Earth', *Language Magazine,* April 2002: 22–4.

Sutherland, W. J. (2003) 'Parallel extinction risk and global distribution of languages and species', *Nature,* 423: 276–9.

Tang, C. and van Heuven, V. J. (2009) 'Mutual intelligibility of Chinese dialects experimentally tested', *Lingua* 119: 709–32.

Thieberger, N. (1990) 'Language maintenance: why bother?', *Multilingua,* 9: 333–58.

Thornton Media, Inc. (2008) 'Language tools for Indian country', http://www.ndnlanguage.com/story.html. Accessed 23 June 2008.

Trudgill, P. (2004) 'Glocalisation and the Ausbau sociolinguistics of modern Europe', in A. Duszak and U. Okulska (eds), *Speaking from the Margin: Global English from a European Perspective.* Frankfurt: Peter Lang.

UNESCO Ad Hoc Expert Group on Endangered Languages. (2003a) 'Language vitality and endangerment', http://www.unesco.org/culture/ich/doc/src/00120-EN.pdf. Accessed 27 June 2008.

UNESCO. (2003b) 'Safeguarding of endangered languages: recommendations for action plans', International Expert

Meeting, Paris, 10–12 March 2003. http://www.unesco.org/culture/ich/doc/src/00117-EN.pdf. Accessed 27 June 2008.

Urtéaga, E. (2005) 'La langue basque au début du XXIe siècle' ['The Basque language in the early 21st century'], *Marges Linguistiques*, 10: 175–89. http://www.revue-texto.net/marges/marges/Documents%20Site%201/00_ml102005/00_ml102005.pdf. Accessed 5 June 2008.

Walsh, M. (2005) 'Will Indigenous languages survive?', *Annual Review of Anthropology*, 34: 293–315.

Williamson, R. C. (1991) *Minority Languages and Bilingualism: Case Studies in Maintenance and Shift*. Norwood, NJ: Ablex.

Wright, S. (2004) *Language Policy and Language Planning: Nationalism and Globalisation*. Basingstoke: Palgrave Macmillan.

Wright, S. (2007) 'The right to speak one's own language: reflections on theory and practice', *Language Policy*, 6: 203–24.

34

Global Englishes

Alastair Pennycook

34.1 INTRODUCTION

It is not hard to make a case that English is intimately involved with processes of globalization. From its wide use in many domains across the world, or the massive efforts in both state and private educational sectors to provide access to the language, to its role in global media, international forums, business, finance, politics and diplomacy, it is evident not only that English is widely used across the globe but also that it is part of those processes we call globalization. What this means for English, other languages and cultures, and processes of global change, however, is much harder to determine. Much work over the past 20 years has been done under the label of world Englishes (WE), a term that has been employed with various meanings (Bolton, 2004). It may be used as an umbrella term to cover all varieties of English across the world (analysed from a diversity of perspectives), to refer more narrowly to new varieties of English that have developed, particularly in former British colonies, or more narrowly again to the particular framework developed by Braj Kachru and his colleagues to analyse such Englishes.

The focus of this chapter is considerably broader than this world Englishes focus: it looks critically not only at this Kachruvian school but also at linguistic imperialism and English as a lingua franca (ELF). Most important, it does so within a focus on globalization (hence **global** Englishes). In order to address such concerns, it is important first of all to establish what is meant by globalization. As with all socio-linguistic questions, mapping relations between language and society depends not only on robust understandings of language but also on strong conceptualizations of the social. I therefore sketch out some of the major concerns around globalization in an attempt to clarify what is at stake when we consider English globally. This will be followed by a sociology of global English, with a focus on the ways English is related to media, development, inequality, religion and other key concerns in a globalizing world. Then I shall turn to concerns about the language itself, as a threat to other languages, as a lingua franca, as a collection of varieties of English (hence global **Englishes**). The chapter concludes with a discussion of potential new ways forward for thinking about global Englishes.

34.2 GLOBALIZATION AND ENGLISH

Vast amounts have been written about globalization. Lacking space or reason to try to cover this burgeoning literature, I shall instead draw attention to certain themes that have implications for discussions of English. First, globalization is not only about economic processes but also about political, technological and cultural processes as well. Kumaravadivelu (2008: 32), sees globalization in terms of new 'interconnections and flows among nations, economies and peoples. It results in the transformation of contemporary social life in all its economic, political, cultural, technological, ecological, and individual dimensions'. To view all aspects of globalization as flowing from the role of international capital is to overlook several concerns. While globalization is of course interlinked with international capital, it is by no means reductively determined by it. Capitalism remains a driving force in the world, yet it is not clear that we live in an era of capitalism so much as corporatism (Graham, Luke and Luke, 2007; Pennycook, 2007), where a particular set of neo-liberal ideologies predominate, turning publicly-owned sectors into privately-run corporations and emphasizing a free market to which large corporations should have access. Although global inequalities of poverty, health and education remain primary concerns, it is more useful to see globalization as complexly related to these than as synonymous with their cause. International relations of trade, commerce, pollution, interaction and intervention are fundamentally inequitable, but it is not useful to reduce globalization only to a term that reflects such inequities.

Secondly, therefore, to suggest that globalization is **only** a process of US or Western domination of the world is to take a narrow and ultimately unproductive view of global relations. Likewise, to view culture and language in terms only of reflections of the economic is to miss the point that new technologies and communications are enabling immense and complex flows of people, signs, sounds and images across multiple borders in multiple directions. The very point about globalization is that it is global, and thus inevitably caught up in multiple influences. Indian and Philippine call centres, indigenous education conferences, global migrations of workers, Japanese animated cartoons, anti-globalization networks, fashion trends, salsa classes, gay and lesbian travel organizations, the ubiquity and similarity of urban graffiti – these are all part of globalization. Globalization may be better understood as a compression of time and space, an intensification of social, economic, cultural and political relations, a series of global linkages that render events in one location of potential and immediate importance in other, quite distant locations (Giddens, 1999). Education is a good example of this, with students moving in increasing numbers to take up educational possibilities elsewhere (Singh and Doherty, 2004), resulting in changing practices in the new 'educational contact zones', and new flows of knowledges across borders. This diversity of concerns can be captured in part by Appadurai's (1996) formulation of 'scapes' – ethnoscapes (the new mobility of tourists, migrants and refugees), technoscapes (new technologies), financescapes (flows of capital), mediascapes (global media) and ideoscapes (ideas and values) – and the various additions that have been made to them, including sacriscapes (religion) (Waters, 1995), eduscapes (global educational movements), and of interest to the theme of

this paper, global linguascapes (languages) (Pennycook, 2007).

Thirdly, globalization is both old and new: we need to understand both its historical precedents and its contemporary particularity. While Steger (2003) suggests that globalization can be mapped more or less against the entirety of human history, others, such as Robertson (2003), describe successive waves of globalization starting with the era of European expansionism. For Mignolo (2000: 236), although the scope and speed of current globalization is without precedent, it is 'the most recent configuration of a process that can be traced back to the 1500s, with the beginning of transatlantic exploration and the consolidation of Western hegemony'. Such an account of globalization, as intimately tied to colonial expansion, accords well with an overview of the spread of English: from a minor language isolated to an island off the north coast of Europe in the sixteenth century, it was the expansion of British colonialism, as people moved to colonize newly invaded territories (North America, Australia), and to work within newly colonized states (India, Nigeria), that led to its first wave of expansion in the eighteenth and nineteenth centuries. The subsequent emergence of the United States of America as a dominant global player in the twentieth century played a major role in the current dominance of English. Such perspectives, that render globalization the latest manifestation of European imperialism, have, however, been critiqued for failing to account for 'the novelty of the structures and logics of power that order the contemporary world. Empire is not a weak echo of modern imperialisms but a fundamentally new form of rule' (Hardt and Negri, 2000: 146).

Unlike the old imperialism(s), which were centred around the economic and political structures and exchanges of the nation-state (indeed, the two were in many ways mutually constitutive), globalization may also be seen to represent a fundamentally new set of relations. A view of globalization as the historical continuation of European imperialism also suffers from a Eurocentrism that overlooks the role of other empires (Ottoman, Chinese, Japanese, to name a few) and global forces. It is nevertheless not so hard to reconcile these two arguments: on the one hand, if we lose sight of the historical precedents of the current state of globalization, we lose a crucial understanding of how current global conditions have come into being; on the other, if we focus too much on continuity, we fail to see that the forces of globalization demand new ways of thinking, new solutions to new problems. Similarly with English, it is useful on the one hand to account for its current global position in terms of the shift from eighteenth- and nineteenth-century British colonialism to twentieth-century American imperialism. Yet it is also important, on the other hand, to acknowledge that the new conditions of twenty-first-century globalization require new ways of thinking about states, languages and social orders.

So finally, globalization demands that we think differently. The rapid and extensive changes brought about by globalization cannot be conceptualized through pre-globalization lenses. There is an important distinction between an understanding of globalization as a realist position that focuses on the state of the world under late capitalism, and an alternative position that focuses on the ways in which globalization undermines our modernist modes of thought. This way of thinking is, in part, captured by Radhakrishnan's (2007: 313) explanation of 'worldliness' as acknowledging 'that the very one-ness of the world can only be understood on the basis of an irreducible perspectival heterogeneity'. Not only does globalization thus invoke new forms of localization but also it changes them. As Edwards and Usher (2008: 24) explain, 'the integration of the globe reconfigures rather than supplants diversity, in the process introducing new forms of economic, social and cultural creolisation'. Central here is not only the concern as to whether globalization is a process of homogenization or heterogenization (increasing similarity or increasing diversity) (Pennycook, 2003; Kumaravadivelu, 2008), but also what new forms of language, culture and knowledge it brings about and what new ways of thinking about these it makes possible.

It is evident, therefore, that while we cannot deal with English without also dealing with globalization, we need to consider very carefully how we understand globalization in order to understand global Englishes. English is now embedded in many parts of the global system: one need only map it against a list of 'scapes' (finance, media, tourist, religion, knowledge production) to see its global significance. At the very least, we need to understand how English operates in an uneven world (cf. Radhakrishnan, 2003), how English is involved in global flows of culture and knowledge, and how English is used and appropriated by users of English round the world, from popular culture to unpopular politics, from international capital to local transaction, from diplomacy to peacekeeping, from religious proselytizing to secular resistance. Yet the very conditions of globalization and the role of global English also demand that we rethink what we mean by language, language spread, native speakers, or multilingualism. Indeed, globalization requires us to consider whether we should continue to think of languages as separate, distinguishable, countable entities. I shall return to these concerns

at the end of this chapter after looking in greater depth at the social, cultural and political roles played by English, and the changes that English has undergone.

34.3 ENGLISH IN AN UNEVEN WORLD

The first set of concerns about English and globalization are questions of the sociology of English and its relation to globalization. It is common in language studies and English language teaching to talk in terms of English as the 'language of international communication' rather than a language embedded in processes of globalization. English is all too often assumed to be a language that holds out the promise of social and economic development to all those who learn it, a language of equal opportunity, a language that the world needs in order to be able to communicate. Yet any critical analysis suggests that it is also an exclusionary class dialect, favouring particular people, countries, cultures, forms of knowledge and possibilities of development; it is a language which creates barriers as much as it presents possibilities. As Tollefson (2000: 8) warns, 'At a time when English is widely seen as a key to the economic success of nations and the economic wellbeing of individuals, the spread of English also contributes to significant social, political, and economic inequalities'.

Bruthiaux (2002: 292–3) argues convincingly that, for many of the world's poor, English language education is 'an outlandish irrelevance,' and 'talk of a role for English language education in facilitating the process of poverty reduction and a major allocation of public resources to that end is likely to prove misguided and wasteful'. Bringing a sophisticated economic analysis to the question of global English, Lysandrou and Lysandrou (2003: 230) argue that 'the embrace of the English language is to the detriment of the majorities of communities the world over insofar as it contributes to their systematic dispossession'.[1] Thus we need to distinguish very clearly between individually-oriented access arguments about escape from poverty, and class-oriented arguments about large-scale poverty reduction.

For those who already speak English, the economic value of the language translates directly into greater opportunities in education, business, and employment. For those who must learn English, however, particularly those who do not have access to high-quality English language education, the spread of English presents a formidable obstacle to education, employment, and other activities requiring English proficiency (Tollefson, 2000: 9).

As Ramanathan's (2005: 112) study of English and Vernacular medium education in India shows, English is a deeply divisive language, tied on the one hand to the denigration of vernacular languages, cultures, and ways of learning and teaching, and, on the other, dovetailing 'with the values and aspirations of the elite Indian middle class'. While English opens doors to some, it is simultaneously a barrier to learning, development and employment for others.

Some of the harshest critiques of the global role of English have come from Robert Phillipson (1992, 1994, 2003), whose views have attracted a great deal of debate. There is nothing in fact very controversial about Phillipson's definition of English linguistic imperialism in terms of the ways in which English is constantly promoted over other languages (1992: 47), or his concern with the role of institutions such as the British Council and their constant sponsorship of English language teaching, nor indeed with his focus on how the promotion of English has become embedded in various tenets of English language teaching, such as promoting native speaker teachers of English over their non-native speaker counterparts, or suggesting that the learning of English is better started as early as possible (a trend that is continuing worldwide, with English language teaching occurring more and more at the primary and even pre-primary levels). And despite major debates about the notion of language rights (see Wee, 2005; Brutt-Griffler, 2002a, 2002b), there is nothing particularly controversial either about broad support for languages other than English in the face of the dominance of English in education systems and other institutions worldwide. If this were all that was at stake in the notion of linguistic imperialism, the debate would only be about the detrimental effects of the promotion of English over other languages, and the extent of the threat that this poses to the use, and in some cases the existence, of other languages. These are clearly concerns we need to continue to take very seriously.

Phillipson is concerned with much more than this, however, since he also argues that English is deeply connected to particular forms of Western culture and knowledge. 'Linguistic imperialism', he suggests, 'dovetails with communicative, cultural, educational, and scientific imperialism in a rapidly evolving world in which corporate-led globalization is seeking to impose or induce a neo-imperial world order' (Phillipson, 2006: 357). This is a much stronger claim than one that suggests only that English is being promoted over other languages, since it links English on the one hand to particular forms of culture and knowledge, and on the other to a process of globalization that is always in favour of certain neo-imperial powers and is always in the direction of homogenization. At stake therefore in this vision of English linguistic imperialism is not only the dominance of English in relation to other languages but also the role English plays in much broader processes of the dominance of forms of global capital and the homogenization of world culture (Phillipson, 1999: 274).

This is, of course, a much larger claim and a much harder relationship to demonstrate beyond a general observation concerning the conjunction of the spread of English and certain economic and political formations. Yet for Phillipson (2008: 38), 'acceptance of the status of English, and its assumed neutrality implies uncritical adherence to the dominant world disorder, unless policies to counteract neolinguistic imperialism and to resist linguistic capital dispossession are in force'. While Phillipson thus quite appropriately locates English within inequitable relations of globalization, and shows that rather than an accidental process, the global spread of English has been very deliberate policy, his vision of globalization is also a narrow 'homogenization' perspective (Pennycook, 2003; Kumaravadivelu, 2008) that allows for little understanding of the complexity of global flows and resistances. This perspective cannot adequately account for the ways in which the spread of English has also been a result of an active desire for English (see Brutt-Griffler, 2002a), which in turn cannot be dismissed as a form of misguided subjection to global hegemony without also bringing in to play a heavy-handed notion of ideology that implies that the demand for English is only a superstructural reflection of neo-capital and English infrastructure.

While we ignore Phillipson's warnings at our peril, it is also crucial to understand the ways in which English is resisted and appropriated—how English users 'may find ways to negotiate, alter and oppose political structures, and reconstruct their languages, cultures and identities to their advantage. The intention is not to *reject* English, but to *reconstitute* it in more inclusive, ethical, and democratic terms' (Canagarajah, 1999: 2). One of the problems, as Bruthiaux (2008) points out, caused by the rhetoric of linguistic imperialism is that the particular understanding of language and globalization that it promotes occludes other critical approaches to English and globalization. By assuming a globalization-as-homogenization thesis, by linking English indelibly to forms of neoliberal capital, and by supporting nationalist counter-discourses, the linguistic imperialist position presents the same flattened world that it aims to critique. The equation of a linguistic imperialism thesis with a critical standpoint, and the frequent dismissal of this totalizing version of events on the grounds that it overstates the case, draws attention away from the necessity to evaluate the global spread of English critically and carefully.

We also need to consider with care the kinds of oppositional strategies that different critical frameworks engender: 'If inaction on language policy in Europe continues, at the national and supranational levels', Phillipson (2003: 192) warns, 'we may be heading for an American-English only Europe'. While the ways in which English has come to dominate exchanges in European contexts need to be considered carefully, the measures taken to oppose it also need to be considered with caution. Arguing for the need to safeguard diversity through the support of other European languages, particularly French, Hagège (2006: 37; my translation), for example, argues that 'to defend a culture is also to defend the language in which it is expressed'. To defend diversity in terms of bolstering national languages, however, is to operate with a view that the nation-state and its attendant languages is a guarantor of diversity, a view that runs counter to the broader image of diversity put forward both by more complex models of a plurilingual Europe (see the DYLAN project, for example) and by proponents of a creolist position, which valorizes mixing and hybridity over the purisms of national languages (Bernabé, Chamoiseau and Confiant, 1993).

More broadly, this concern over the threat to other languages posed by English has become part of the wider debate over linguistic human rights, and whether linguistic diversity can be guaranteed through international legislation (Skutnabb-Kangas, 2000). Widely debated in terms of its practicality, whether the focus should be on linguistic or cultural diversity, and how linguistic and minority rights are related (May, 2001; Wee, 2005), this 'willingness to use the language of human rights on the global level to frame local linguistic demands vis-à-vis global English' (Sonntag, 2003: 25) may also fall into the trap of continuing to promote the very ways of thinking about language and diversity that are part of the problem. A language rights perspective thus promotes the defence of linguistic diversity in terms of less powerful languages being accorded equal rights with dominant languages, and does so within a political perspective on human rights that promotes global solutions to local problems.

The point here is not that we should avoid questions of power in relation to English: any good sociolinguistic study has to make power central. What we need, however, is a focus on the workings of power at the local level, rather than assumptions about the effects of power based on totalizing analyses: good sociolinguistics also has to be local (Pennycook, 2010). If we look, for example, at the question of the motivations to learn English, it is important to move beyond assumptions that English is learned only in relation to pragmatic goals of social and economic development. As Piller and Takahashi (2006) observe, we need to understand the gender and sexual politics involved in English language learning, since English is marketed in relation to a particular set of images of sexual desire. Thus 'English emerges as a powerful tool to construct a gendered identity and to gain access to the romanticized West'. For young Japanese women, they argue, 'surrounded by the multiple discourses of English as a desirable and powerful language', this desire for English becomes 'increasingly gendered and romanticized' (Piller and Takahashi, 2006: 69).

In the context of the Philippines we get a very different story. With around eight million Filipino working overseas, from domestic workers in Singapore or Hong Kong to construction workers in Southeast Asia or the Middle East, and boat crews across the world, the Philippines has developed educational and linguistic policies to develop and encourage this export of workers. This policy of English for global competitiveness (Lorente and Tupas 2002) means that English has become an increasingly commodified language through the educational system, so that the export of workers with greater English linguistic capital can bring a greater economic return on the educational investment. As Tupas (2008: 98) points out, this 'commodification of English in the Philippines' should not be considered in terms of 'English as a monolithic language since, more importantly, it is the different English language proficiencies that are commodified in terms of the varying monetary, instrumental and symbolic values attached to them by the market'. Lorente's (2007) study of Filipino domestic workers in Singapore, and the 'scripts of servitude' that they learn to gain jobs, shows how these different forms of linguistic capital operate in a competitive job market where particular performances in English are valued in particular ways. Such studies allow us to see how this global language is always also a local language caught up in local economic and political relations.

For Phillipson and Skutnabb-Kangas (1996: 439; italics in original) English is part of *the homogenization of world culture* ... spearheaded by films, pop culture, CNN and fast-food chains'. More detailed analyses of popular culture, the complex global circuits of flow of culture and language, and the ways in which languages are borrowed, used, taken up and changed, however, suggest that we need more multifaceted investigations of these processes than such dismissals of mass cultural homogenization (Pennycook, 2007). As studies of hip-hop and language use

(Alim, Ibrahim and Pennycook, 2009), for example, have shown, while certain hubs of cultural production, such as the metropolitan centres of France and the USA, remain highly influential, the flows of popular culture and language are by no means simply from centre to periphery, but rather operate in highly complex and dynamic circuits of influence. While the flow back into the centres may be limited, the directions and take-up of cultural production are many and diverse. Once cultural formations such as hip-hop become localized, furthermore, the movement into local languages, and particularly the mixing of local and metropolitan languages, brings about new relations among languages and cultures. In addition, engagement with popular culture in diverse contexts is by no means a process of passive consumption; rather it is about the active construction of different possible worlds and identities.

Amongst many other domains in which English is tied in particular ways to forms of culture and knowledge, the relations between English and religion are important. As Karmani (2005: 262) observes, 'as the "war on terror" rages on military, political, and media fronts, a crucial much-forgotten battle is also being contested on the linguistic front: between "Islam and English" '. The promotion, use and teaching of English in such contexts cannot be understood without an appreciation of the control of oil, current concerns about terrorism, and the recent increase in global battles over religious affiliation. Attention has also been drawn recently to the connections between English language teaching and Christian missionary activity (Edge, 2003; Pennycook and Coutand-Marin, 2003). As Varghese and Johnston observe, the widespread use of English, and the opportunities this provides for missionary work dressed up as English language teaching (ELT), raises

> profound moral questions about the professional activities and purposes of teachers and organizations in our occupation. The status of ELT in missionary work is especially important in light of post-9/11 developments in world politics and the role of an American foreign and domestic policy driven increasingly by imperialist goals and guided by an evangelical Christian agenda (2007: 6).

As part of a comprehensive sociolinguistics of global English, therefore, we undoubtedly need closely studied accounts of the ways in which English is embedded in local economies of desire, and the ways in which demand for English is part of a larger picture of images of change, modernization, access and longing; it is tied to the languages, cultures, styles and aesthetics of popular culture, with its particular attractions for youth, rebellion and conformity; it is enmeshed within

local economies, and all the inclusions, exclusions and inequalities this may entail; it is bound up with changing modes of communication, from shifting Internet[2] uses to its role in text-messaging; it is increasingly entrenched in educational systems, bringing to the fore many concerns about knowledge, pedagogy and the curriculum. We need to understand the diversity of what English is and what it means in all these contexts, and we need to do so not with prior assumptions about globalization and its effects, but with critical studies of the local embeddedness of English.

34.4 THE CHANGING FACE OF WORLD ENGLISHES

Critiquing the linguistic imperialist take on the global spread of English for being in itself a 'new form of linguistic colonialism', Bhatt (2005: 33) argues that such a view overlooks 'the role various Englishes play in different social, economic, and political market-places' in contexts such as India. This perspective shifts the viewpoint in two significant ways. First it stresses the local contexts of English use: while English may be a global language, this also always implies local usage, which needs to be understood contextually. Secondly, it turns its focus away from sociologies of English and instead looks at the sociolinguistics of the language in terms of the effects that the global spread of English has wrought on English itself. This becomes an inherently pluralist endeavour, focusing on different Englishes in different contexts. While the WE agenda has dominated this focus since the 1980s, the more recent emergent focus on ELF has also engendered considerable current debate.

Rejecting the dominance of native speaker ('inner circle') varieties of English, the WE perspective has taken up a strong focus on heterogeny by looking at 'implications of pluricentricity ... the new and emerging norms of performance, and the bilingual's creativity as a manifestation of the contextual and formal hybridity of Englishes' (Kachru, 1997: 66). The WE paradigm has focused on the ways in which English has become locally adapted and institutionalized to create different varieties of English (different Englishes) around the world (B. Kachru, 1985, 1986, 1992; Y. Kachru and Nelson, 1996). This work has been very significant in a number of ways. It has opened up a large field of study of difference in terms of new Englishes and has made it possible to argue that different forms of English should be understood as local varieties rather than errors, interlanguages, dialects or misformations. The central focus has been on descriptions of those varieties of English that have developed in former British colonies where English has an internal role within the country (Singaporean, Indian, Philippine, Malaysian, Nigerian and Kenyan Englishes, amongst others).

Bhatt (2005: 26) talks of the

> evidence of local practices to demonstrate creativity and systematicity in the so-called English linguistic 'chaos.' The examination of currently evolving hybrid codes and discourses provides an understanding of how Indian English speakers and writers navigate sociolinguistically between their regional riches and the homogenized global norms.

From studies of the particular use of particles such as 'lah' in Singaporean and Malaysian English to the use of the invariant 'isn't it' across new varieties (for discussion, see Bhatt, 2005), from analyses of syllable-timed as opposed to stress-timed versions of English (the tendency in many new versions of English to use intonation patterns based on more even patterns of stress than the particular patterns of central varieties) to the regularization of structures such as 'discuss about' (by analogy with 'talk about', 'think about' and so on), and from the vocabulary of Hong Kong English (chop (personal seal or stamp), astronaut (someone whose family is based overseas but who works in Hong Kong, commuting back and forth), cage (partitioned bed space among Hong Kong urban poor), ABC (American- or Australian-born Chinese)) to the development of terms such as *prepone* in India (to move an appointment forward – back formation from postpone) (see Bolton, 2000, 2004; Kachru, 2005; Y. Kachru and Nelson, 2006) the case has been made that each of these constitutes a variety of English that should be considered on an equal footing with other varieties, such as American, British or Australian English.

The WE framework thus promotes a fundamentally pluralist vision of language and the world, opposing attempts to control, own and define English according to centrist, native-speaker norms. If the linguistic imperialism paradigm presents a critique of the homogenizing tendencies of English and globalization, then that of WE presents its counterpart, the heterogenizing possibilities offered by globalization. It is a celebration of diversity and the centrifugal forces of bi-multi-lingual English language use, attempting 'to alter and relocate the focus of our ongoing debate on this linguistic icon. The English language is generally discussed as a language that is in Asia, but not of Asia' (Kachru, 2005: 9). Many detailed accounts of how such 'outer circle' varieties of English differ at all levels – phonological, syntactic,

lexical, semantic, pragmatic – from inner-circle varieties have been produced (Baumgardner, 1993, for Pakistan, for example; Bautista, 2000, for the Philippines; Bolton, 2002, for Hong Kong; and so on) alongside the argument that such varieties need to be established as the local norms by which standards of correctness are judged.

The 'expanding circle' of all other English users (from China to Brazil) has received less attention, yet there are significant debates emerging over the status that should be accorded to local varieties in this expanding circle, and whether the sometimes derogatory terms such as 'Chinglish', 'Japlish' and so forth should be reclaimed to describe valid local English variants. At the heart of these debates is the question as to whether, or under what conditions, a linguistic item that differs from an inner-circle version of that item – the pluralization of supposedly non-pluralizable nouns, such as furnitures or researches, is a commonly cited example – should be accorded varietal rather than incorrect status. If nothing else, a major achievement of WE has been to encourage us to think in terms of divergent varieties within different circles, rather than along lines of correctness or incorrectness in relation to a putative and often undefined inner-circle standard.

While a WE perspective has been influential in making its case for a diversity of Englishes, it has been critiqued on a number of grounds. Leaving aside the political quietism that often has little to say about the role of English in an uneven world (Parakrama, 1995; Canagarajah, 1999), or the concern that by making hybridity its central focus it may fall into the trap of bad postcolonial theory where 'the notion of the "hybrid" can become as fixed a category as its essentialist nemesis' (Zuberi, 2001: 239–40), a major concern is how good it is as a form of sociolinguistics. Probably the best known and most often cited dimension of the WE paradigm is the model of concentric circles already alluded to: the inner circle refers to English in countries such as the UK, USA or Australia, where English is the native language of a large part of the population, and where the varieties of English spoken have often been considered the standard norms for the rest of the world; the outer circle describes English in those former colonies of Britain or the USA, such as Singapore, India, Malaysia, the Philippines or Nigeria, where English is widely used for internal purposes and where local norms of appropriacy may have developed; and the expanding circle refers to the rest, from China to Brazil, where English is used predominantly for communication outside the country, and where norms may still be considered to be those of the inner-circle countries.

Although only 'tentatively labelled' (Kachru, 1985: 12) in earlier versions, it has been claimed more recently that 'the circles model is valid in the senses of earlier historical and political contexts, the dynamic diachronic advance of English around the world, and the functions and standards to which its users relate English in its many current global incarnations' (B. Kachru and Nelson, 1996: 78). Yano (2001: 121) refers to this model as the 'standard framework of world Englishes studies', and of all current discussions around global Englishes, it is probably this model that is most widely referred to. While it has clearly therefore served some purposes in providing labels for different contexts of language use, it shares the concern of other domains of sociolinguistics (for extended discussion, see Williams, 1992) that if it is underpinned by questionable sociology, it must also be questionable as a sociolinguistic enterprise. Of serious concern here is the descriptive adequacy of the circles, the ascription of a variety along national lines within these circles, and the concomitant tendency to overlook further variety at the expense of establishing a nationally-based new variety.

As Bruthiaux (2003: 161) points out, the descriptive and analytic inconsistency of the concentric circle model gives it little explanatory power. This 'superficially appealing and convenient model conceals more than it reveals' since it attempts to compare varieties of English, different speaker types and geographical locations all at once. Its use of inconsistent criteria to categorize so-called varieties of English is confounded by a 'primarily nation-based model'. Holborow (1999: 59–60) points out that the concentric circle model fails 'to take adequate account of social factors and social differences within the circles'. Rajadurai (2005) suggests that even if the concentric model may have worked in the past, its over-reliance on historical and geographical frames of reference render it unable to deal with the current global spread of English.

The concentric model of English at the heart of the WE framework overlooks difference within regions and ascribes variety based on postcolonial political history: where a nation-state was created, so a variety emerged. By positing these new Englishes, it perpetuates the myth of national languages that the global spread of English allows us to start to rethink, and does so by focusing on a narrow selection of standardized forms in particular communities. As Parakrama (1995: 25–6) argues, 'The smoothing out of struggle within and without language is replicated in the homogenizing of the varieties of English on the basis of "upper-class" forms. Kachru is thus able to theorize on the nature of a monolithic Indian English'. While appearing, therefore, to work from an inclusionary political agenda in its attempt to have the new Englishes acknowledged as varieties of English, this approach to language is remorselessly exclusionary. Ultimately, concludes Bruthiaux, 'the Three Circles model is a 20th century construct that has outlived its usefulness' (2003: 161).

34.5 THE RISE OF LINGUA FRANCA ENGLISH

Phillipson (2003: 176) warns that the use of English across Europe is leading to 'a simplified, pidginized but unstable "Euro-English" that inhibits creativity and expressiveness, whether English is used as a mother tongue or as a foreign language, a language that is spoken with so much imprecision that communication difficulties and breakdowns multiply'. Others, however, have addressed the question of what happens to English when used as a lingua franca on a less deficit-oriented basis. Taking up many concerns common to the WE framework, studies of ELF have sought to identify features common to regional (particularly European and Asian) communication among diverse users of English. While there is a wide variety of work under this rubric, the attempts to describe a lexicogrammatical (Seidlhofer, 2001) or phonological (Jenkins, 2000) core of ELF have received wide attention. ELF researchers, explains Jenkins (2006b: 161), 'seek to identify frequently and systematically used forms that differ from inner circle forms without causing communication problems and override first language groupings'. The point, then, is to find, through analyses of corpora of English language use, how communication is achieved across regions. What regular forms that differ from native speaker norms appear not to impede – indeed may appear to improve – communication?

The ELF approach has been critiqued from the WE perspective on the grounds that it falls into the camp of those approaches to English that 'idealize a monolithic entity called "English" and neglect the inclusive and plural character of the worldwide phenomenon' (Kachru and Nelson, 2006: 2). Such a critique, however, as Jenkins (2006b) points out, is misguided, since it rests on the mistaken assumption that ELF is the same as English as an international language, which in turn may be associated with the notion of World Standard (Spoken) English proposed by authors such as Crystal (2003). While Crystal's notion is of a possibly emergent variety of common spoken English rather than any prescribed version, it differs from both the pluricentric focus of WE and from the lingua franca focus. Certainly the suggestion that ELF somehow promotes inner-circle norms is mistaken since 'ELF researchers specifically exclude mother tongue speakers from their data collection. Indeed, in its purest form, ELF is defined as a contact language used only among non–mother tongue speakers' (Jenkins, 2006b: 160). A plausible case can in fact be made that the ELF focus is trying to address precisely that gap left by the holes in the WE model: how to come to grips with a non-centrist understanding of English as an international language that is dependent neither on hegemonic versions of central English nor on nationally defined new Englishes, but rather attempts to account for the ever-changing negotiated spaces of current language use. The ELF model, it is argued, 'liberates L2 speakers from the imposition of native speaker norms as well as the cultural baggage of World Englishes models' (Rubdy and Saraceni, 2006: 8).

A major focus of debate is whether the description of ELF is also used as a basis for teaching, i.e. as a prescriptive rather than a descriptive tool. As Rani Rubdy and Mario Saraceni suggest,

> So long as the underlying tacit assumption is that once the Lingua Franca core is systematically codified, it can then be used as a model for teaching and learning this form of English in the classroom, the question that arises is whether one form of prescription is not being (unwittingly or even wittingly) replaced by another (2006: 10).

Certainly, some of the discussions about ELF do seem to suggest more than just a descriptive project. Expressing concerns with the trend in applied linguistic circles to adopt a *laissez-faire* attitude towards heterogenization, Jenkins (2006a: 35) suggests that 'if a policy of pluricentricity is pursued unchecked, there is a danger that mutual comprehension may be impeded, that accents will move further and further apart until a stage is reached where pronunciation presents a serious problem to lingua franca communication'. Yet the ELF protagonists vehemently reject accusations of prescriptivism, arguing that it is precisely 'the polymorphous nature of the English language' (Seidlhofer, 2006: 42) that is of interest, that they are 'trying to understand as far as possible emically, from participants' perspectives, what they do when they negotiate meaning in these encounters' (Seidlhofer, 2006: 44), or that an ELF approach 'closely approximates … Kachru's idea of a "polymodel" approach to the teaching of English' (Kirkpatrick, 2006: 81).

Whereas some ELF researchers therefore claim an interest only in description rather than prescription (to the extent that such a distinction is workable; see Harris, 1981), there are other reasons why the prescriptive label does not hold. Although Jenkins (2006a: 36) maintains a goal to 'safeguard mutual phonological intelligibility', she does not

do so by seeking 'to impose a monolithic pronunciation model on ELF users'. Rather, she suggests

> that anyone participating in international communication needs to be familiar with, and have in their linguistic repertoire for use, as and when appropriate, certain forms (phonological, lexicogrammatical, etc.) that are widely used and widely intelligible across groups of English speakers from different first language backgrounds. This is why accommodation is so highly valued in ELF research (Jenkins, 2006b: 161).

For other ELF researchers, meanwhile, the goal is not in any case to propose a model, but rather simply to account for the diversity of language uses that are tied neither to native nor to nativized varieties (Kirkpatrick, 2006) in order to capture how 'postcolonial speakers of English creatively negotiate the place of English in their lives' (Canagarajah, 2006: 200).

As Rubdy and Saraceni (2006: 13) put it,

> In the end, the validity of the English as an International Language/English as a lingua franca proposal will probably depend upon whether or not it chooses to embrace a polymodel approach to the teaching of English or a monolithic one, whether it leads to the establishing and promoting of a single (or a limited form of) Lingua Franca Core for common use among speakers in the Outer and Expanding Circles, possibly stripped of any cultural influences, or whether it will be flexible enough to manifest the cultural norms of all those who use it along with the rich tapestry of linguistic variation in which they are embedded.

Indeed, Canagarajah (2007: 91) prefers the term Lingua Franca English (LFE) with its suggestion that English emerges in its use as a lingua franca rather than being a language with prior existence that is pressed into service as a lingua franca (ELF). LFE, he suggests, 'does not exist as a system out there. It is constantly brought into being in each context of communication'.

34.6 CONCLUSION: NEW LANGUAGES FOR NEW TIMES

While there are often serious disagreements between proponents of different positions on global Englishes – (Kachru (2005), for example, dismisses both critical and conservative approaches to the global spread of English as 'victimology' while suggesting that English as a lingua franca is a misuse of the term) – it is nevertheless worth noting that all are in favour of diversity in one form or another. The critique of the homogenizing forces of linguistic imperialism is counterbalanced by an emphasis on language rights as a guarantor of diversity (Skutnabb-Kangas, 2000); the WE model places its hopes in a heterogeneous plurality of Englishes. Both treat a relation between language, culture and nation as the lynchpin of diversity. The ELF/LFE approaches, meanwhile, move either centripetally towards descriptions of English diversity or centrifugally towards an understanding of the possibilities of English use in diverse contexts, while suggesting a more open-ended relation between language, culture and nation.

At various points in this chapter we have encountered the critique that discussions of the global role of English have failed to engage with the injunction to think differently. Several of these approaches to global English – whether linguistic imperialism and language rights, or WE and some approaches to ELF – remain stuck within twentieth-century frameworks of language and diversity. As Canagarajah (2007: 98) points out,

> The hegemonic thrust of global English derives from the dominant assumptions of linguistics, informed by the modernist philosophical movement and intellectual culture in which they developed. To begin with, the field treats language as a thing in itself, an objective, identifiable product. The field also gives importance to form, treating language as a tightly knit structure, neglecting other processes and practices that always accompany communication.

Just as a language rights perspective maintains a twentieth-century model of international relations, so a WE perspective maintains a focus on national Englishes. Neither raises the question of whether we need to reconsider what languages are in more fundamental terms.

According to Bruthiaux (2003: 174),

> While the Three Circles model has provided us with a convenient shorthand for labeling contexts of English worldwide, the categories that the model created have also had the unfortunate side-effect of reifying the content of these categories and of encouraging the notion that Englishes are Englishes, regardless of circle.

It is also less than clear whether the WE focus on diversity is in fact so different from a lingua franca approach as its proponents claim. Thus, when Braj Kachru focuses on 'educated South Asian English' rather than 'Broken English' (2005: 39), he is surely open to the same critiques that he levels at the purveyors of ELF. As Canagarajah (1999: 180) observes, in Kachru's 'attempt to systematize the

periphery variants, he has to standardize the language himself, leaving out many eccentric, hybrid forms of local Englishes as too unsystematic. In this, the Kachruvian paradigm follows the logic of the prescriptive and elitist tendencies of the center linguists'. The question we need to face, therefore, is how we think about language and diversity under conditions of globalization and how we can get beyond those ways of thinking that have dominated modernist conceptions of language and diversity.

In much of this writing on global Englishes, then, there are several important factors missing. There is often a failure to engage more fully with diversity. We are still confronted, for example, by the inability to deal with pidgins and creoles, a concern noted a number of times by Mufwene, who suggests that 'the naming practices of new Englishes has to do more with the racial identity of those who speak them than with how these varieties developed and the extent of their structural deviations' (2001: 107). English-based creoles present a problem for much of the thinking of WE because of their origins, status and diversity, and yet their exclusion from discussion remains problematic. One framework that does seek to incorporate creoles alongside other postcolonial Englishes (PCEs) is Schneider's (2007: 32) Dynamic Model of the evolution of Postcolonial Englishes, which suggests that 'PCEs have emerged by undergoing a fundamentally uniform process which can be described as a progression of five characteristic stages: foundation, exonormative stabilization, nativization, endormative stabilization, and differentiation'. In this 'overarching and unifying perspective' that moves away from the 'static and individualizing typologies of earlier perspectives' we have the most comprehensive attempt yet to pull the diverse observations about Englishes into one framework in which differences between varieties of English are 'instantiations of characteristic phases of an underlyingly uniform process' (2007: 313).

Yet, while getting away from the nation-state as the unit of analysis, and favouring instead the speech community, this model incorporates all diversity into one model of uniformity. By arguing that 'the evolution of language follows principles of its own' and that we should therefore separate such investigation from broader social and political concerns (2007: 19), Schneider avoids exactly those concerns that need to remain central to any understanding of language change: global Englishes are deeply embedded in economic and political processes. Furthermore, we need to consider that none of these models of English spread will have much relevance for English users unless they also take into account the dynamics of English in an uneven world. Whether we are talking of WE or ELF, access to such models 'will still be largely determined by one's proximity to education and, for that matter, all other related symbolic goods in the social market' (Tupas, 2006: 180). Whatever we may make of the limitations of a linguistic imperialism framework, we nevertheless also need to be wary of simultaneously rejecting a focus on questions of power and inequality in relation to access and variety in global Englishes.

These discussions of global Englishes will also have little relevance unless they shift their ways of thinking about languages. LFE, suggests Canagarajah (2007: 94), 'is not a product located in the mind of the speaker; it is a social process constantly reconstructed in sensitivity to environmental factors'. The central concern that the debates between these rival conceptualizations leave uncontested is how we can understand diversity outside those very frameworks that are part of the problem. Neither a defence of national languages and cultures, nor a description of a core of ELF, nor even a focus on plural Englishes adequately addresses questions of diversity under new conditions of globalization. Rather than centrist descriptions of local Englishes, we need by contrast to move towards an understanding of the worldliness of English, whereby the very oneness of English can only be understood on the basis of local perspectives of difference (Pennycook, 2010; Radhakrishnan, 2007). This is not a question of pluralizing Englishes but of understanding the ways different language ideologies construct English locally. Questioning the ways in which we have come to think about languages within colonialism and modernity, and regarding the grand narratives of imperialism, language rights, linguae francae or world Englishes with suspicion, this perspective looks towards local, situated, contextual and contingent ways of understanding languages and language policies.

What this suggests is the need to think about English and globalization outside the nationalist frameworks that gave rise to twentieth-century models of the world. In dealing with English in an uneven world, we do need to understand its historical formation within forms of nationalism and imperialism, and its contemporary roles in the inequitable distribution of resources, in the promotion of certain ideas over others and in the threat it may pose to other languages, cultures and ways of being. And yet we need simultaneously to appreciate not only its appropriation and relocalization by diverse users but also its reconfiguration as something different. Perhaps it is time to question the very notions that underpin our assumptions about languages (Jacquemet, 2005; Makoni and Pennycook, 2007), to ask whether the ways we name and describe languages as separate entities and the ways we view bi- and multilingualism are based on twentieth-century epistemologies that can no longer be used to describe the use of languages in a globalizing world. If it is clear that the ways we think about language are inevitably products of particular historical contexts, then an age of globalization suggests that we need both to reflect on how and why we look at languages as separate, countable, describable entities in the way we do, and to consider that languages may be undergoing such forms of transition as to require new ways of conceptualization in terms of local activities, resources or practices.

NOTES

1   This does not imply, however, that the solution lies in opposing the spread of English, since it is 'the realm of economic policy, not that of language policy, that one should look to for redress' (Lysandrou and Lysandrou, 2003: 230).

2   Contrary to some suppositions, recent observations of language use on the Internet have suggested that while the total sum of English language use may be increasing, its proportional representation is decreasing as more languages are used (see Danet and Herring, 2007; Graddol, 2006).

REFERENCES

Alim, H. S., Ibrahim, A. and Pennycook, A. (eds) (2009) *Global Linguistic Flows: Hip Hop Cultures, Youth Identities, and the Politics of Language*. New York: Routledge.

Appadurai, A. (1996). *Modernity at Large: Cultural Dimensions of Globalization*. Minneapolis: University of Minnesota Press.

Baumgardner, R. (ed.) (1993) *The English Language in Pakistan*. Karachi: Oxford University Press.

Bautista, M. L. (2000) *Defining Standard Philippine English: Its Status and Grammatical Features*. Manila: De La Salle University Press.

Bernabé, J., Chamoiseau, P. and Confiant, R. (1993) *Éloge de la créolité*. Paris: Gallimard.

Bhatt, R. (2005) 'Expert discourses, local practices, and hybridity: the case of Indian Englishes', in A. S. Cangarajah (ed.), *Reclaiming the Local in Language Policy and Practice*. Mahwah, NJ: Erlbaum. pp. 25–54.

Bolton, K. (2000) 'The sociolinguistics of Hong Kong and the space for Hong Kong English', *World Englishes*, 19(3): 265–85.

Bolton, K. (ed.) (2002) *Hong Kong English: Autonomy and Creativity*. Hong Kong: Hong Kong University Press.

Bolton, K. (2004) 'World Englishes', in A. Davies and C. Elder (eds), *The Handbook of Applied Linguistics*. Oxford: Blackwell. pp. 369–96.

Bruthiaux, P. (2002) 'Hold your courses: language education, language choice, and economic development', *TESOL Quarterly*, 36(3): 275–96.

Bruthiaux, P. (2003) 'Squaring the circles: issues in modeling English worldwide', *International Journal of Applied Linguistics*, 13(2): 159–77.

Bruthiaux, P. (2008) 'Dimensions of globalization and applied linguistics', in P. Tan and R. Rubdy (eds), *Language as Commodity: Global Structures, Local Marketplaces*. London: Continuum. p. 1–30.

Brutt-Griffler, J. (2002a) *World English: A Study of its Development*. Clevedon, UK: Multilingual Matters.

Brutt-Griffler, J. (2002b) 'Class, ethnicity, and language rights: an analysis of British colonial policy in Lesotho and Sri Lanka and some implications for language policy', *Journal of Language, Identity and Education*, 1(3): 207–34.

Canagarajah, S. (1999) *Resisting Linguistic Imperialism in English Teaching*. Oxford: Oxford University Press.

Canagarajah, S. (2006) 'Interview', in Rubdy, R. and M. Saraceni (eds), *English in the World: Global Rules, Global Roles*. London: Continuum. pp. 200–12.

Canagarajah, S. (2007) 'The ecology of global English', *International Multilingual Research Journal*, 1(2): 89–100.

Crystal, D. (2003) *English as a Global Language*. 2nd edn. Cambridge: Cambridge University Press.

Danet, B., and Herring, S. C. (eds) (2007) *The Multilingual Internet: Language, Culture, and Communication Online*. New York: Oxford University Press.

DYLAN project: language dynamics and management of diversity. http://www.dylan-project.org/Dylan_en/home/home.php [last accessed 14 April 2009].

Edge, J. (2003) 'Imperial troopers and servants of the lord: a vision of TESOL for the 21st century', *TESOL Quarterly*, 37: 701–8.

Edwards, R. and Usher R. (2008) *Globalisation and Pedagogy: Space, Place and Identity*. 2nd edn. London: Routledge.

Giddens, A. (1999) *Runaway World: How Globalisation is Reshaping Our Lives*. London: Profile Books.

Gradoll, D. (2006) *English Next: Why Global English May Mean the End of "English as a Foreign Language"*. London: British Council.

Graham, P., Luke, C. and Luke, A. (2007) 'Globalization, corporatism, and critical language education', *International Multilingual Research Journal*, 1(1).

Hagège, C. (2006) *Combat pour le Français: au nom de la diversité des langues et des cultures*. Paris: Odile Jacob.

Hardt, M. and A. Negri. (2000) *Empire*. Cambridge, MA: Harvard University Press.

Harris, R. (1981) *The Language Myth*. London: Duckworth.

Holborow, M (1999) *The Politics of English: A Marxist View of Language*. London: Sage Publications.

Jacquemet, M. (2005) 'Transidiomatic practices, language and power in the age of globalization', *Language & Communication*, 25: 257–77.

Jenkins, J. (2000) *The Phonology of English as an International Language*. Oxford: Oxford University Press.

Jenkins, J. (2006a) 'Global intelligibility and local diversity: possibility or paradox?', in R. Rubdy and M. Saraceni (eds), *English in the World: Global Rules, Global Roles*. London: Continuum. pp. 32–9.

Jenkins, J. (2006b) 'Current perspectives on teaching world Englishes and English as a lingua franca', *TESOL Quarterly* 40(1): 157–81.

Kachru, B (1985) Standards, codification, and sociolinguistic realism: The English language in the Outer Circle. In R. Quirk and H.G. Widdowson (eds.) *English in the World: Teaching and Learning the Language and Literatures* Cambridge: Cambridge University Press. 11–30.

Kachru, B. (1997) 'World Englishes and English-using communities', *Annual Review of Applied Linguistics*, 17: 66–87.

Kachru, B. (2005) *Asian Englishes: Beyond the Canon*. Hong Kong: Hong Kong University Press.

Kachru, B and C Nelson (1996) World Englishes. In Sandra McKay and Nancy Hornberger (eds.) *Sociolinguistics in Language Teaching*. Cambridge: Cambridge University Press. 71–102.

Kachru, Y. and C. Nelson (2006) *World Englishes in Asian contexts*. Hong Kong: Hong Kong University Press.

Karmani, S. (2005) 'English, "terror", and Islam', *Applied Linguistics*, 26(2): 262–7.

Kirkpatrick, A. (2006) 'Which model of English: native-speaker, nativized or lingua franca?', in R. Rubdy and M. Saraceni (eds), *English in the World: Global Rules, Global Roles*. London: Continuum. pp. 71–83.

Kumaravadivelu, B. (2008) *Cultural Globalization and Language Education*. New Haven, CT: Yale University Press.

Lorente, B.P. and Tupas, T.R.F. (2002) 'Demythologizing English as an economic asset: the case of Filipina domestic workers in Singapore', *ACELT Journal*, 6(2): 20–32.

Lorente, B.P. (2007) 'Mapping English linguistic capital: the case of Filipino domestic workers in Singapore'. Unpublished PhD thesis, National University of Singapore.

Lysandrou, P. and Lysandrou,Y. (2003) 'Global English and proregression: understanding English language spread in the contemporary era', *Economy and Society*, 32(2): 207–33.

Makoni, S. and Pennycook, A. (eds) (2007) *Disinventing and Reconstituting Languages*. Clevedon, UK: Multilingual Matters.

May, S. (2001) *Language and Minority Rights: Ethnicity, Nationalism and the Politics of Language*. London: Longman.

Mignolo, W. (2000) *Local Histories/Global Designs: Coloniality, Subaltern Knowledges, and Border Thinking*. Princeton, NJ: Princeton University Press.

Mufwene, S. (2001) *The Ecology of Language Evolution*. Cambridge: Cambridge University Press.

Parakrama, A. (1995) *De-Hegemonizing Language Standards: Learning from (Post)Colonial Englishes about 'English'*. Basingstoke: MacMillan.

Pennycook, A. (2003) 'Beyond homogeny and heterogeny: English as a global and worldly language', in C. Mair (ed.), *The Cultural Politics of English*. Amsterdam: Rodopi. pp. 3–17.

Pennycook, A. (2007) *Global Englishes and Transcultural Flows*. London: Routledge.

Pennycook, A. (2010) *Language as a Local Practice*. London: Routledge.

Pennycook, A. and Coutand-Marin, S. (2003) 'Teaching English as a missionary language', *Discourse: Studies in the Cultural Politics of Education*, 17(3): 337–53.

Phillipson, R. (1992) *Linguistic Imperialism*. Oxford: Oxford University Press.

Phillipson, R. (1994), 'English language spread policy', *International Journal of the Sociology of Language*, 107: 7–24.

Phillipson, R. (1999) 'Voice in global English: unheard chords in Crystal loud and clear. Review of D. Crystal, *English as a Global Language*, Cambridge: Cambridge University Press', *Applied Linguistics*, 20(2): 265–76.

Phillipson, R. (2003) *English only Europe? Challenging Language Policy*. London: Routledge.

Phillipson (2006) 'Language policy and linguistic imperialism', in T. Ricento (ed.), *An Introduction to Language Policy: Theory and Method*. Oxford: Blackwell. pp. 346–61.

Phillipson, R. (2008) 'The linguistic imperialism of neoliberal empire', *Critical Inquiry in Language Studies*, 5(1): 1–43.

Phillipson, R. and Skutnabb-Kangas, T. (1996) 'English only worldwide or language ecology?', *TESOL Quarterly*, 30(3): 429–52.

Piller, I. and Takahashi, K. (2006) 'A passion for English: desire and the language market', in A Pavlenko (ed.), *Bilingual Minds: Emotional Experience, Expression and Respresentation*, Clevedon, UK: Multilingual Matters. pp. 59–83.

Radhakrishnan, R. (2003) *Theory in an Uneven World*. Oxford: Blackwell.

Radhakrishnan, R. (2007) 'Globality is not worldliness', in R. Radhakrishnan, Kishori Nayak, R. Shashidhar, Ravishankar Rao Parinitha and D. R. Shashidhara (eds), *Theory as Variation*. New Delhi: Pencraft International. pp. 313–28.

Rajadurai, J. (2005) 'Revisiting the concentric circles: conceptual and sociolinguistic considerations', *The Asian EFL Journal Quarterly* 7(4): 111–30.

Ramanathan, V. (2005) *The English-Vernacular Divide: Postcolonial Language Politics and Practice*. Clevedon, UK: Multilingual Matters.

Robertson, R. (2003) *Three Waves of Globalization: A History of a Developing Global Consciousness*. London: Zed Books.

Rubdy, R. and Saraceni, M. (2006) 'Introduction', in R. Rubdy and M. Saraceni (eds), *English in the World: Global Rules, Global Roles*. London: Continuum. pp. 5–16.

Schneider, E. (2007) *Postcolonial English: Varieties around the World*. Cambridge: Cambridge University Press.

Seidlhofer, B. (2001) 'Closing a conceptual gap: the case for a description of English as a lingua franca', *International Review of Applied Linguistics*, 11(2): 133–58.

Seidlhofer, B. (2006) English as a Lingua Franca in the expanding circle: What it isn't. In R. Rubdy and M. Saraceni (eds) *English in the World: Global Rules, Global Roles*. London: Continuum, 40–50.

Singh, P. and Doherty, C. (2004) 'Global cultural flows and pedagogic dilemmas: teaching in the global university contact zone', *TESOL Quarterly*, 38(1): 9–42.

Skutnabb-Kangas, T. (2000) *Linguistic Genocide in Education—or Worldwide Diversity and Human Rights?* Mahwah, NJ: Lawrence Erlbaum.

Sonntag, Selma (2003) *The Local Politics of Global English: Case Studies in Linguistic Globalization*. Lanham, MD: Lexington Books.

Steger, M. (2003) *Globalization: A Very Short Introduction*. Oxford: Oxford University Press.

Tollefson, J. (2000) 'Policy and ideology in the spread of English', in J. K. Hall and W. Eggington (eds), *The Sociopolitics of English Language Teaching*. Clevedon, UK: Multilingual Matters. pp. 7–21.

Tupas, R. (2006) 'Standard Englishes, pedagogical paradigms and conditions of (im)possibility', in R. Rubdy and M. Saraceni (eds), *English in the World: Global Rules, Global Roles*. London: Continuum. pp. 169–85.

Tupas, R. (2008) 'Anatomies of linguistic commodification: the case of English in the Philippines vis-à-vis other languages in the multilingual marketplace', in P. Tan and R. Rubdy (eds), *Language as Commodity: Global Structures, Local Marketplaces*. London: Continuum. pp. 89–105.

Varghese, M. and Johnston, B. (2007) 'Evangelical Christians and English language teaching', *TESOL Quarterly*, 41(1): 5–31.

Waters, M. (1995) *Globalisation*. London: Routledge.

Wee, L. (2005) 'Intra-language discrimination and linguistic human rights: the case of Singlish.', *Applied Linguistics*, 26(1): 48–69.

Williams, G. (1992) *Sociolinguistics: A Sociological Critique*. London: Routledge.

Zuberi, N. (2001) *Sounds English: Transnational Popular Music*. Urbana, IL: University of Illinois Press.

PART 6

Applications

35

Forensic Linguistics

Malcolm Coulthard, Tim Grant
and Krzysztof Kredens

35.1 INTRODUCTION

Forensic linguistics in the broadest sense is the application of linguistics to three principal domains: written legal texts, spoken legal practices and the provision of evidence for criminal and civil investigations and courtroom disputes (see www.tinyurl.com/forensic-linguist for a brief video presentation on the work of the forensic linguist). Naturally the division between spoken and written texts suggested in the above characterization is somewhat fluid. So, for example, the UK Police Caution and the equivalent United States Miranda warnings are provided as written texts to every police officer, but they are animated into spoken form by an arresting or interviewing officer, while, conversely, the spoken testimony of witnesses, for example in an *audiencia* within the Chilean inquisitorial system (Gibbons, 2001) or when being interviewed at the scene of a crime by a police officer, is often transformed and condensed into a written text mainly authored by the interviewer. These transformations of mode between written and spoken are clearly in themselves of great linguistic interest and they may also have legal implications and consequences.

Even more complicated transformations can occur in English courtrooms. Initial police-investigative interviews with suspects have been standardly tape-recorded for the past 25 years, but normally the legal professionals work most of the time, before and during the trial, with a written transcription of what was (heard by a non-present transcriber to have been) said. However, when a particular police interview is of crucial importance, the lawyer may decide that the jury should hear it in full – in such cases, to many lay people's surprise, the tape of the original interview is not played to the court, but, somewhat bizarrely, the police officer and the lawyer 'perform' the written text. The majority of the legal professionals on both sides are apparently unaware of the semantic changes that such a double conversion process can accidentally, and at times deliberately, introduce.

Nevertheless, the tripartite distinction between legal texts, legal discourse and the provision of evidence is a convenient one and will be largely followed in this chapter.

35.2 A BRIEF HISTORY OF FORENSIC LINGUISTICS

Although forensic linguistics is a relatively recent discipline, interest in how, and to what effect, language is used in legal and forensic contexts dates back to at least ancient Greece and Rome. In the fourth century BC, Aristotle produced a typology of rhetoric according to the occasions it served, distinguishing between political, ceremonial and forensic oratory; the latter he associated with the courtroom. In the first century AD, Gaius Aelius Gallus published, in Latin, a volume 'On the meaning of words referring to the law', (in modern terms, a monolingual dictionary of legal language), and over a century later, Sextus Pompeius Festus, a Roman grammarian, included in his encyclopaedic lexicon a considerable number of legal entries. If anything, those early works certainly indicated that law was to a large extent instituted through language, a diagnosis that was to be confirmed and acted upon vigorously many centuries later.

On a practical level, issues of language rights and language planning also have a long history. In England, the *Pleading in English Act* of 1362 was enacted to replace French with English in legal proceedings, and the Blasphemy Act of 1650 penalized acts of, *inter alia*, 'filthy and lascivious speaking', although rather than being aimed at suppressing bad language, it was in fact an attempt to silence a Protestant sect known as the Ranters (McEnery, 2005). A law with a significant impact on the linguistic situation in Spain was King Charles III's 1768 decree giving the Castillian dialect priority in administration and education.

Among the pioneering works in the twentieth century were Wróblewski's (1948) exposition of the differences between legal language and the language of the law, Philbrick's (1949) *Language and the Law: the Semantics of Forensic English*, essentially a textbook for lawyers, and Gowers (1953) chapter on the nature of legal language. In 1963, Mellinkoff published a seminal study, where he called for simplification and clarity of legalese. Five years later the phrase 'forensic linguistics' was coined by Svartvik (1968) in an analysis where he demonstrated considerable stylistic discrepancies across four confession statements allegedly made by Timothy Evans, a Welshman executed in 1950 for the murder of his baby daughter and pardoned posthumously 16 years later. Svartvik did not build on earlier scholarship, which was irrelevant for his purposes, but rather opened a new door. However, perhaps unfairly, it is his phrase that has come to function as superordinate to describe most activity where legal and linguistic interests converge, at least in the English-speaking world. To be sure, most texts in the last 40 years have been produced in English, though it would be wrong to overlook the francophone tradition of *jurilinguistique*, Polish *juryslingwistyka*, and German *Sprache und Recht* ('language and law') and *Rechtslinguistik* ('legal linguistics'), which can be traced back to early nineteenth-century Prussia. That said, the term 'forensic linguistics' has been adopted through direct translation by German (*Forensische Linguistik*) and Spanish and Portuguese (*lingüística forense*), amongst other languages.

When it comes to the provision of language-based evidence, it is safe to assume that linguists (or, in the early days, 'philologists') have assisted law-enforcement agencies, lawyers and courts of law ever since linguistics gained a visible presence, though it is not easy to trace what must have been isolated instances of such activity. The earliest well-documented casework comes from the 1970s and includes: Hannes Kniffka's contributions in the German legal system (Kniffka, 2007); Raven McDavid's involvement in a trademark dispute (McDavid (1977) in Butters, 2008); Michael Gregory's evidence on a disputed confession statement (Gregory, 2000); and Roger Shuy's evidence in a case of solicitation to murder (Shuy, 2005). Mention must be made also of the early days of forensic phonetics, i.e. a discipline drawing on acoustic and articulatory properties of speech: in 1960, tape-recorded evidence was deemed admissible by Poland's Supreme Court, which a few years later led to the creation by the Polish police of what must have been one of the first forensic phonetics laboratories in the world; similar developments soon followed in countries of the former Eastern bloc. In Canada and the USA, evidence based on 'voiceprints' was used as early as in 1966 (Tosi, 1979).[1]

Forensic linguistic casework and research have been advancing rapidly since the beginning of the 1980s (Danet, 1980; Kniffka, 1981; Levi and Walker, 1990; Coulthard, 1993; Solan, 1993; for forensic phonetics see, in particular, Hollien, 1990; Rose, 2003) and today the field is thriving, with more and more research into aspects of language and law, ever more books and papers published, and ever-growing numbers of linguists asked to act as expert witnesses all over the globe.

35.3 WRITTEN LEGAL TEXT

There has been substantial study of legal texts – statutes, contracts and wills – and much of this work has been motivated recently by the concerns of Plain Language campaigners. The laws of a country have universal application, and yet they are written in such a way that a large number of the citizens to whom they apply are unable to fully understand them. As well as statutes and criminal codes, written legal texts can comprise an agreement between either two laypersons or between a layperson and an organization or corporation. A good example might be a household insurance document. Figure 35.1 shows the main title page of such a document. This document, insuring a 'private dwelling house' in Leicester, UK for £5250.00, was signed on 9 July 1963.

Before considering the language variety of this document, the typography and layout clearly identify it as a legal contract. Although such devices have no legal effect, the emphatic gothic script

D U P L I C A T E

THE

EMPLOYERS'

LIABILITY ASSURANCE CORPORATION

LIMITED

HEAD OFFICE: HAMILTON HOUSE, VICTORIA EMBANKMENT, LONDON, EC4

Household Policy

BUILDINGS

Whereas the Insured named in the schedule hereto has by a signed proposal and declaration which proposal and declaration the Insured has agreed shall be the basis of this contract and be held as incorporated herein applied to the Company for insurance against the contingencies hereinafter specified

Now this policy witnesseth that in consideration of the Insured paying to the Company for this insurance the first premium mentioned in the said schedule

The Company hereby agrees subject to the conditions contained herein or endorsed or otherwise expressed hereon which conditions shall so far as the nature of them respectively will permit be deemed to be conditions precedent to the right of the Insured to recover hereunder that in the event of any of the said contingencies happening during the period of insurance set forth in the said schedule or in any subsequent period in respect of which the Insured shall pay to the Company and it shall accept the premium required for the renewal of this insurance the Company will by payment reinstatement or repair indemnify the Insured as hereinafter provided

Figure 35.1 Insurance document from UK, 1963

used to head each of the paragraphs indicates that this is a document to be taken seriously. After the headings, the first paragraph of the insurance policy reads thus:

Whereas the Insured named in the schedule hereto has by a signed proposal and declaration which proposal and declaration the Insured has agreed shall be the basis of this contract and be held as incorporated herein applied to the Company for insurance against the contingencies hereinafter specified.

The lack of punctuation is no transcription error. Indeed, as with international treaties and United Nations resolutions, this household insurance document is written as a single sentence. In this case the sentence is entirely unpunctuated, without even a terminal full stop. Structuring of the sentence is provided through paragraphing, and in some parts through changes in typeface and the provision of numbered lists, and this may assist the reader to some degree. The whole policy document is presented as a single sheet of paper, printed on both sides and designed to be folded in half and then in three, revealing a further title page with an instruction to the insured that:

> This Policy should be read carefully and returned for correction if any alteration is required therein.

There is no suggestion that correcting (or indeed adding) punctuation is the kind of alteration one might require of the drafters. Indeed the combined pragmatic effect of these features suggests that the document is not intended to be read by an ordinary reader, let alone corrected. Special training is required and expected of the readers of this text, and lay readers may well be unable to fully engage with it or even understand many of its implications.

As with any text designed for a specialist audience, we might expect it to contain lexical items which are rare; and sure enough we find items such as *proposal, contingency* and *indemnify*, and also archaisms such as *witnesseth*. It is not, however, these 'terms of art' which are the main cause of lexical difficulty in comprehension. The more substantial problem is the heavy use of rare functional items such as *whereas, herein, hereto, hereinbefore* and *hereunder*. One striking feature of many of these rare functional words is that they are self-referential. That is to say, they refer to other locations within the text rather than to the world outside. Legal texts need to maintain a constant meaning even while the social (and perhaps physical) circumstance of the world which they describe changes. One explanation for this self-referential language is that referring to the external world must be done extremely carefully. One way this is achieved is to gather together all the potentially-changing information about the world into one part of the document. This is referred to as the 'schedule'. In this insurance document there is a strongly-specified schedule, which includes the (witnessed) identity of the insured, the identity of the 'Mortgagees' and of course the address of the private dwelling house. This 'Scheduled' information is enclosed in a table and restricted to one sparsely filled page of the document. The distinction between internal textual information and scheduled real-world information thus explains some of the linguistic oddity.

Other features of this text which make it difficult to read have also been identified by other linguists (e.g. Tiersma, 1999). These include nominalization, multiple embedding of sub-clauses, and the use of redundant or near-redundant lists such as 'storm tempest and flood' (which are insured against) and 'rebellion, revolution and insurrection' (which are not). Tiersma identifies these features as originating in oral legal tradition and, in an insurance document, can be seen to

have a more functional role than for example in a 'will and testament'.

The 1960s insurance document can be usefully contrasted with a contemporary one signed in Leicestershire in 2008 (Figure 35.2). This document is clearly intended to appear to be consumer friendly. The Schedule providing the specific information is a separate single sheet and the Policy booklet is now 41 pages long, with the text referring to the Buildings cover using about twice as many words as that of the earlier policy. Whereas the older document provided general cover with rather generalized terms and exclusions, the modern document consists of four detailed pages of terms. A variety of documentary design devices, colour and the use of headings and indexes, are all intended to assist the reader; in addition, this document is, in the main, well-punctuated.

The biggest linguistic difference is the near complete absence of the rare, self-referential functional items. Replacing them are different types of references to other named and numbered sections. Some of these references are very explicit – for example 'see section 5.4' – but others are more hidden. Some of the words such as 'buildings' have special definitions beyond their ordinarily understood meaning and they appear in bold. The reader can, if they wish, look up these definitions at the end of the booklet. This device renders the surface-level text easier to read but produces a kind of hypertext document, the understanding of which involves processing rather complex legal language which has been removed to distant sections of the booklet. These underlying definitions and exclusions are perhaps at a linguistic midpoint between the complex 1960s text and the superficially accessible top-level text within the contemporary booklet. The exclusion on 'War' for example reads:

> Any consequence whatsoever resulting directly or indirectly from or in connection with any of the following regardless of any other contributing cause or event: war invasion act of foreign enemy hostilities or a warlike operation or operations (whether war be declared or not) civil war rebellion revolution insurrection civil commotion assuming the proportions or amounting to an uprising, military or usurped power.

This exclusion is only lightly punctuated – although it is a list, it contains no commas – and while one embedded clause is indicated by the use of brackets, earlier embedding is not, and so on.

Even in the top-level text there remain lists of near synonyms such as 'riot, civil unrest, strikes, and labour or political disturbances' (which are now insured) but within the 'General Conditions'

Buildings section

This section applies only if it is shown on the schedule.

Exclusions applying to the Buildings section
See also the General Exclusions on page 39.
£60 excess (but not for subsidence, heave and landslip, where the excess is £1,000.)

No excess applies to sections E and G.

The following exclusion applies to all sections, except G.

Loss of or damage to any appliance forming part of the buildings from that appliance failing to correctly recognise or respond to any date.

Damage by wet or dry rot arising from any cause, except as a direct result of a claim We have already paid, and where repair or preventative action was carried out by a tradesman We have approved.

Cover

Section A
The buildings

Loss of or damage to the **Buildings** caused by any of the following.

1. a. Fire, explosion, lightning or earthquake
   b. Smoke
   Exclusion applying to 1b:
   Loss or damage that happens gradually

2. Storm or flood
   Exclusions:
   Loss or damage by frost.
   Loss of or damage to fences, gates and hedges.

3. a. Riot, civil unrest, strikes, and labour or political disturbances
   b. Malicious acts

Exclusions applying to 3b:
Loss or damage that happens after the home has been left unoccupied or unfurnished for more than 60 days in a row.
Loss or damage caused by:
- *You; or*
- *paying guests or tenants.*

4. Being hit by:
   a. aircraft or other flying objects, or anything falling from them; or
   b. vehicles or animals.

5. a. Water escaping from water tanks, pipes, equipment or fixed heating systems.
   b. Water freezing in tanks, equipment or pipes.

Exclusions:
Loss or damage that happens after the home has been left unoccupied or unfurnished for more than 60 days in a row.
Loss or damage to solid floors caused by infill materials settling, swelling or shrinking as a result of water escaping in the home.
Subsidence, heave or landslip caused by water escaping from the home.

Figure 35.2 Insurance document from UK, 2008

and 'General Exclusions' these features of legal language are much more pronounced.

One final striking difference between the two documents is the more personal tone of the contemporary policy: rather than referring to 'The Company', the pronoun 'We' is used (in a bold typeface indicating it is a defined term). A lot of work has been done to help the contemporary text appear friendly to consumers, and comparison with the 1960s document reveals the reforms which have been effective in achieving this. However, the legal language of the document still persists and it is the 'small print' of the definitions and exclusions which will often contain the legal force which enables the insurer to avoid paying out.

Explanations for the persistence of legal language in these documents and in the written texts of statutes, wills and other legal texts can vary; one suggestion is that the conservatism of legal language creates professional protection for lawyers and their clerks. By this explanation, the move from the legal document of the 1960s to the consumer document of the twenty-first century might be interpreted as a social shift indicating a diminution in the power of the legal profession. Tiersma (1999) has a good discussion of this

history. A more benign explanation for the persistence of legalese in contemporary drafting lies in the nature of legal documents themselves; as we have seen, they have to be written to be context-free, time-travelling documents unaffected by shifts in the sands of meaning. It can be argued that this quest for sociolinguistic independence and the accompanying quest for precision require a document to be encapsulated in its own definitions and such documents will thus always be strange and require expert interpretation.

While failure to understand an insurance document can have financial consequences, failure to understand the Police Caution or the Miranda warnings can result in someone losing their liberty, and failure by jury members to understand some Pattern Jury Instructions could result in someone losing their life. Forensic linguists have interested themselves in such important texts. Cotterill (2000), Rock (2001, 2007) and Shuy (1997) have examined different aspects of the Police Caution and the Miranda warnings, pointed out significant linguistic/communicative problems and suggested, sadly so far to no avail, changes and improvements. The only recorded success in this area has been that of Gibbons (2001) working with the New South Wales police to improve their version of the caution. By contrast, Ainsworth (2010) depressingly traces the gradual erosion of the Miranda rights to a point where, despite the wording, 'You have the right to remain silent', it has become virtually impossible in practice for those arrested in the United States to claim their right to remain silent.

Some forensic linguists in the United States have moved beyond describing problems to intervention. Levi (1993) reports on a lexical analysis of a set of jury instructions concerned with imposing the death penalty, which she undertook as part of an expert report in an appeal against the imposition of the sentence. She was asked to express an opinion on the question 'How well could [the language of the jury instructions] have served its purpose in communicating clearly to the jury the legal concepts they needed to understand for sentencing in a capital case?'. The instructions in question were (highlighting added):

If you unanimously find from your consideration of all the evidence that there are no mitigating factors **sufficient** to **preclude** the imposition of a sentence of death then you should return a verdict imposing a sentence of death.

If, on the other hand, you do not unanimously find that there are no mitigating factors **sufficient** to **preclude** the imposition of a sentence of death then you should return a verdict that the sentence of death should not be imposed.

Levi produced a detailed argued case focusing on the inherent vagueness of *sufficient* and the rarity of *preclude* and concluded that there were grave doubts about the comprehensibility of the instructions. Dumas (2002) produced a similar damning and disturbing linguistic analysis of the Tennessee Pattern Instructions for the definition of 'reasonable doubt'. However, the most useful input to date has been by Tiersma (2010), a trained linguist and law professor, who acted as 'linguistic consultant' over a period of six years to two committees of judges and lawyers set up in 1997, following the perceived O. J. Simpson debacle, to redraft the Californian instructions so that they would 'accurately state the law using language ... understandable to jurors' (Kelso, 1996). The much more comprehensible Pattern Instructions became effective in 2006, so, if you are going to commit a crime in the States, make sure it is in California.

35.4 SPOKEN LEGAL DISCOURSE

Spoken legal discourse pervades the legal system from the moment of arrest and the first communication of rights (Rock, 2007) through police interview, interrogation and charge, to the announcement of the verdict at the end of the trial.

Since the Police and Criminal Evidence Act of 1984, all significant police interviews in England and Wales have had to be tape-recorded and this has, incidentally, provided a body of data for research. Within the UK in particular, but also internationally, there has been considerable research into techniques of police interviewing (e.g. Williamson, 1993; Milne and Bull, 1999: Heydon, 2005), much of it occasioned by a concern about coercive interviewing following a number of miscarriages of justice that came to light during the 1980s and early 1990s. Most of the research on interviewing has been carried out by psychologists and the techniques espoused are aimed at retrieving a maximum of useful and relevant information from interviewed suspects and witnesses, including vulnerable adults and children, without exposing them to coercive or suggestive pressures (e.g. Milne and Bull, 1999; Gudjonsson, 2003). So far, with some notable exceptions (Aldridge and Wood, 1998; Heydon, 2005), the practical impact of linguists in this area has been limited.

The psychological research has fed into a substantial project of police training and accreditation of interviewers, with hierarchal recognition of expertise and specialization into different policing areas (e.g. interviewing of children, fraud interviewing, etc.). The relative lack of impact of linguists is changing and they are becoming more involved with researching interviews in a way which can directly impact on police training. Heydon's (2005) work has led to her involvement in training in Australia. In the UK, the authors of this paper have delivered training courses to police forces on question types, the preparation of witness statements and how to manage interpreters in police interviews. If linguists are to involve themselves in this way, in police training and practices, they must rely on a well-researched understanding of the interview in its legal and sociolinguistic context, and they must also be prepared to engage with the practicalities.

One recent contribution to research into police interviewing, which takes a linguistic approach, is Stokoe and Edwards' (2008) examination of what they call 'Silly Questions' in police interviews. They cite such fine examples as:

• *Did Melvin give you permission to throw the hammer at his front door?* (90)
• *D'you 'ave permission to smash it basically?* (93)

Stokoe and Edwards take a conversation analysis approach and describe the turn-taking and conversation management which occurs around exchanges such as these. They make a number of observations, including the fact that interviewing officers distance themselves from such questions through the use of discourse markers, such as extended hesitations and false starts in the run-up to these questions, and also, on occasions, by prefacing such questions with explicit phrases such as 'For the record...' Such distancing relieves the interviewer of the embarrassment of asking such silly questions but also underlines the importance of understanding that 'the record' is a crucial, unspeaking participant in police interviews. The record in UK suspect interviews is always an electronic recording (either audio or video) but can, in other jurisdictions, be a transcript, notes or witness statement.

The purpose of such questions is clearly to establish the knowledge of the interviewee against a specific point of law, but there is a wider point of explanation for the silliness of these questions which also goes some way to explaining the silliness in the language of the insurance policies and the wider oddity of legal language. In police interviews, phrases such as *for the record* or *for the tape* go some way to making explicit the presence of the Court in the interview suite. *The record* can be usefully considered as the ear of the Court in the interview and acknowledgment of the existence of the Court in the room renders these questions rather less silly. Indeed, Haworth (2008) argues that some police officers' skill in questioning is such that the primary audience for their questions might be considered the Court, rather than the respondent in the room.

In the insurance documents it is less explicit, but here too the primary audience, in the sense of the audience that determines the lexis, syntax and overall structure of the document, is the Court. Insurance documents are not written principally to be understood by the consumer. Where a trade-off is necessary between ease of comprehension and legal precision, the texts are written first and foremost to be legally watertight. If a dispute should arise, the matter will be taken to Court. The police interview is not a private conversation between the interviewer and the suspect; rather, it is explicitly designed to be overheard by the Court. In lay–legal communication, the needs of the Court are always paramount, and this can be observed in as diverse contexts as the restraining orders applied to abusive partners and judges' instructions to juries.

Once an individual has been investigated and charged, they may end up in court, and the well-studied area of courtroom linguistics includes: work on the language of sexual assault and rape trials (Ehrlich (2001) and this volume); work focused on the input of different participants – lawyers, witnesses, experts (Cotterill, 2003;

Heffer, 2010); and work on specific processes like cross-examination or summing-up (Heffer, 2005, 2007). Finally, there is a body of work on prison language and the activities of offenders in prison; this includes interaction with prison staff (Mayr, 2003), with psychologists engaging in treatment programmes (Lea and Auburn, 2001) and the language varieties used by prisoners more generally (e.g. Looser, 2004).

Although procedurally different, the contexts mentioned above can each be associated with different linguistic issues, which in turn take on a fresh significance when one of the actors involved does not speak the language of the jurisdiction in question and requires the assistance of an interpreter. According to the provisions of Article 6 of the European Convention on Human Rights:

[e]veryone charged with a criminal offence has the following minimum rights: (a) to be informed promptly, in a language which he (sic) understands and in detail, of the nature and cause of the accusation against him; (...) (e) to have the free assistance of an interpreter if he cannot understand or speak the language used in court.

There are similar national regulations and, as a result, in many multilingual societies interpreters work in courts of law, police stations, probation offices, prisons, etc. Research in the area of legal interpreting focuses on communication issues and ways in which semantic misrepresentation arises in interpreter-mediated interaction in such settings, with most attention devoted to court interpreting. Hale (1999: 57) found that when Spanish/English interpreters translated lawyers' questions in courtroom proceedings, they tended to ignore discourse markers, which, she notes, 'are important in portraying a speaker's intentions and adding tone and force to their utterances'. Berk-Seligson (2002: 181) studied the impact of hedging devices on the evaluation of a Mexican-American witness by mock jurors. She got them to listen to two versions of his interpreted testimony – one with and another without hedges – and found that those who listened to the latter evaluated the witness more favourably on all of the four social/psychological traits tested (convincingness, competence, intelligence, trustworthiness). Filipović (2007) describes how differences between patterns of lexicalization of motion events in English and Spanish affected interpreted witness testimonies in a number of trials in California. If there is one concern that these studies have in common, it has to do with the fact that inadequate interpreting can have quite tangible repercussions for the administration of justice. Filipović's findings seem also to imply that because of certain typological differences between languages, it may be simply impossible to communicate successfully in one language the meanings formulated in another.

35.5 INVESTIGATIVE AND EVIDENTIAL LINGUISTICS

On some occasions the linguist is asked to provide investigative assistance or expert evidence for use in Court. Within the linguistics literature there has been considerable focus on the rules for admission of authorship identification evidence to criminal prosecutions, but the role of the linguist in providing evidence is broader than this. Much of the evidence provided by linguists does not involve authorship identification, and the assistance a linguist may offer is not restricted to only providing evidence for criminal prosecution. Investigative linguistics can be considered that portion of forensic linguistics which provides advice and opinions for investigative and evidential purposes. Under UK law, investigative advice and opinion is subject to disclosure, and so the linguist needs to be cognizant of the needs of the court when undertaking any investigative work.

Although it is not the only concern of investigative linguists, one of their main areas of interest is authorship analysis. Linguists are approached to comment on the authorship of many kinds of texts in cases where alleged infringements of the law appear to have been effectuated or accompanied by linguistic substance. Examples include extortion letters, suicide notes, plagiarized literary works or terrorist conspiracy documents, and, more and more, these incriminating texts are coming from digital sources such as the Internet or mobile phones. The linguist's task is carried out with two underlying assumptions: that every language user has a unique linguistic style, or 'idiolect', and that features characteristic of that style will recur with a relatively stable frequency. There seem to be good reasons to make the first of these assumptions, as it can easily be confirmed through simple impressionistic observation of variation in individual linguistic habits. For example, no two independently-produced student essays on the same topic will ever be identical. This is so because the biologically- and socially-conditioned uniqueness of individual mental experience means that members of the same speech community make different choices to lexicalize their meanings. The second assumption, though intuitively appealing, still requires more empirical confirmation, particularly when it comes to identifying individual patterns of language use across different situations, modes of production, etc.

The notion of idiolect has been around under different guises since at least the seventeenth century, when Blaise Pascal made a connection between personal characteristics and linguistic style in his *Pensées*. In 1753, Georges-Louis Buffon's often-cited aphorism 'Le style est l'homme même' encapsulated the interrelation of an individual's personality with his language style, and in 1817 Samuel Taylor Coleridge noted that '[e]very man's language varies according to the extent of his knowledge, the activity of his faculties, and the depth or quickness of his feelings' (1847: 489). In linguistics, idiolect was first deemed worthy of investigation by Hermann Paul in the late nineteenth century and got extensive treatment in Sapir (1927), though the first use of the term itself is attributed to Bloch (1948). Interestingly, if sociolinguistics seemed like a natural milieu for further investigations, it in fact failed to provide answers, choosing to focus almost exclusively on communities rather than individuals. A notable exception is the work of Barbara Johnstone, who posits that 'it is more enlightening to think of factors such as gender, ethnicity, and audience as resources that speakers use to create unique voices, than determinants of how they will talk' (1996: 56). From a forensic linguistic perspective this is an attractive suggestion as not much is known about the dynamics of how, say, lexical or syntactic choices are made by individuals.

Nevertheless, sociolinguistic findings about how particular linguistic forms are associated with certain social variables can be of great help in forensic linguistic casework, simply because, in addressing authorship issues, the linguist needs to ensure that potentially telling features are individual, i.e. idiolectal, and not dialectal, sociolectal, genderlectal, etc. A linguistic pattern found to recur regularly in the texts under investigation may also be genre-specific or the result of accommodation effects. Put simply, sociolinguistics can help reveal the sources of variation.

35.6 SINGLE TEXT PROBLEMS

When asking questions about the origins of a text a basic distinction can be made between single text problems and comparative questions (Grant, 2008). A single text problem occurs where comparison texts are unavailable or where an investigation is not yet narrowly focused on a small pool of suspects. These non-comparative problems do sometimes in fact concern more than one text, but where this is the case the set of texts can be combined to create a single group of texts which can be analysed together. In these situations, the linguist is essentially being asked whether they can determine anything about the writer from their written style and sometimes to elaborate potential meanings from unclear or ambiguous communications. Faced with such questions it is important to distinguish between psychological and linguistic considerations. Psychological commentary on a threatening letter might include an opinion on the dangerousness of the writer and the likelihood that they would carry out their threat. Providing such opinions is not the role of a linguist. The linguist might comment on the fact that a communication was intended to threaten (directly or indirectly) and on the possible dislocation between communicative intent and perceived meaning, or they may be asked to provide assistance in decoding a language variant to help the court come to its own view on intent, but they are in no position to comment on the intentions of the writer.

A recent example where a single text problem involved clarification of meaning was a case in which the task was to provide a transcription of an Internet Relay Chat (IRC) between two members of the London Afro-Caribbean community. The conversation appeared to contain a conspiracy to murder. Commissioned by the prosecution, the task was to provide a 'translation' and gloss of the conversation which contained a high level of abbreviations and word-forms typical of 'net-speak' (Crystal, 2006), and also a high number of dialect items narrowly specific to the particular community of the two interactants. One part of the chat included the offer:

ill get da fiend to duppy her den.

Interpreting *da* and *den* is fairly straightforward. These are accent stylizations typical of the more abbreviated forms of computer-mediated communication and 'fiend' is fairly common street slang for a drug addict. The verb form *to duppy* is, however, rarer in British English and crucial to the interpreted meaning. Analysis of the etymology of 'duppy' suggests an origin in Jamaican folklore where a duppy is a kind of ghost. A corpus-based approach (collecting data from community-relevant Internet sites) shows this original meaning has spilled over into the realm of video gaming where duppies are zombies and other 'undead' characters. Within the collected corpus, a few examples were found for the use of 'duppy' as a verb, and these did seem to indicate meanings associated with shooting and killing, but the danger of arguing from very few examples is that these might be considered rare or idiosyncratic uses. The combined etymological and corpus

analysis, however, allows the linguist to construct an argument that this turn within the IRC chat conversation is indeed an offer by one protagonist to get a drug addict to kill their victim. In expressing this opinion the linguist has to be extraordinarily careful to make clear that they have no comment on whether this is merely a conversation containing an unpleasant fantasy, or whether it constitutes a real plan to kill. The judgement of intent is not for the linguist.

On some occasions, when a linguist is faced with a single text, they will not be asked to explain meanings within that text but rather to identify sociolinguistic or, for spoken samples, sociophonetic features which might provide information about the author. In an unrelated case to that described above, the following paragraph was taken from a letter addressed to the British Prime Minister. It was sent on headed paper purporting to be from a UK police force and this passage concerns the death of Diana, Princess of Wales:

> *She was an innocent girl who tried to do her best in a world governed by old cruel farts. [...] Sir, the whole system stinks. Sometimes, I am ashamed to be white by the things others are allowed to say and do. Why did many stand by and allow Diana to be killed? Surely, this cannot be right? Many in this force are gutted by the things we have come to know and are told to keep quiet about. Sir, it is time to bring these shameful things out into the open. Please. Do'nt [sic] let our country go down the pan just to protect the interests of a few bad-minded people.*

There are a number of sociolinguistic clues in this letter which can help provide a profile for the writer. Perhaps the most striking sociolinguistic clues are the dialect items, *innocent girl*, *gutted*, *these shameful things* and *bad-minded people*. *Bad-minded people* can be revealed (by simple Internet searches) to be a feature of a Jamaican variety of English. Considerable caution is necessary, however, when drawing a conclusion based on this observation; this cannot be taken as evidence that the writer is Jamaican, but only that he is likely to have been exposed to Jamaican varieties of English. Recent work on lexical priming (Hoey, 2005) can help support such conclusions. Other than the difficulty with demarcating the linguistic and the psychological, there is a further difficulty in divorcing language from its content. In the above paragraph the writer claims to be a white policeman. In fact he turned out to be a black British man of Jamaican origin who had never served in the police.

Given the amount of work on language and gender a further question arises as to the gender of the writer. This throws into relief the methodological problem of any form of profiling (whether linguistic or psychological). Normal scientific method moves from observation of a large number of examples to a generalization. Profiling involves taking a single example and, by matching it to a well-founded generalization, drawing a conclusion about that instance. This reversal of 'normal' scientific method must be done with caution and is prone to error. The single instance could easily be a statistical outlier such that any generalization might be considered to not apply.

The most successful attempts to profile single texts into sociolinguistic categories do so using complex computational and statistical models and take into account a large number of linguistic variables. Argamon et al. (2003), for example, started with about a thousand language variables and, using machine learning techniques, built a classifier for gender discrimination tasks; also, in other work, they examined discrimination for age and first language of the non-native English writer (e.g. Koppel, Schler and Argamon, 2009). Such work might be used in intelligence and screening tasks but in the forensic context it is not certain enough to provide evidence to the courts.

As a matter of course, single-author concerns are different when the linguist works with spoken language. In such cases, determination of gender normally poses no problem and additional information can be derived. A sociolinguistic profile for a law enforcement agency could thus include such characteristics of the offender as his/her age, geographical provenance, social background, level of education or ethnicity. It must be stressed that profiles of this kind can never be treated as absolute, in the sense of always being true of the speaker in question. Speech is subject to various kinds of socio-stylistic variation as people are usually quite successful at manipulating their phonetic repertoire according to, for example, formality of situation or level of mutual familiarity. Free from such limitations is information on medical conditions, affective states and alcohol or drug intoxication, which can sometimes be obtained from speech samples.

Perhaps the most famous example of sociolinguistic profiling comes from the 'Yorkshire Ripper' case. In 1981, a lorry driver named Peter Sutcliffe was convicted of murdering 13 women in West Yorkshire and Manchester between 1975 and 1980. In the course of the police investigation, phoneticians Stanley Ellis and Jack Windsor Lewis were asked to comment on the accent of a man, who, in a tape-recorded message, said he was responsible for 11 of the murders. They pointed to the Southwick and Castletown areas of Sunderland and excluded accent disguise, and after a time also noted that the recording could be

a hoax. Unfortunately, their concern was not shared by the police, who eliminated men without a Sunderland accent from their list of suspects, including the real murderer, Sutcliffe, a native of Bradford. In 2005, the hoaxer was eventually identified; he was still a resident of a Sunderland suburb a mile from Castletown.

35.7 COMPARATIVE AUTHORSHIP PROBLEMS

In some authorship analysis cases considerable material is available against which anonymous or disputed texts can be compared. If there is sufficient material, such cases might be described as 'authorship recognition' cases rather than authorship identification (Hänlein, 1999). In these cases there may be a small pool of suspect authors and sample texts may have been collected from all and the task is then essentially one of classification. Alternatively, there may only be a single suspected author and in this case the linguist has to weigh the evidence of similarity and difference between texts of known authorship and disputed texts, and also weigh sociolinguistic explanations for any similarity or difference in order to reach a yes/no opinion on whether to exclude or include the suspect as a possible author of the disputed message(s). Much of the forensic linguistic work that goes to court is concerned with this type of author assignment. Growingly, such cases involve email, and instant and text messaging, and typically there is a suspicion that the named sender was not the actual sender. Cases include emails containing threatening, abusive or defamatory material, instant messaging interactions between children, mature adults posing as adolescents for grooming purposes, and text messages sent from the mobile phones of people suspected to have been dead at the time of sending. Although the details and therefore the analytic approach change from case to case, the basic strategy is the same: the forensic linguist creates a series of collections of data or 'corpora' – at least two and often more depending on the case and the question s/he is asked to address – and then sets out to discover the distinctive/idiolectal/idiosyncratic features of each of the corpora.

To exemplify: Jenny Nicholl disappeared on 30 June 2005 and her mobile phone, normally in frequent use, remained switched off – after nine days it was switched on very briefly to send two text messages to friends. It was switched on again five days later to send two messages in quick succession to her father and has never been used again. Police suspected that she had not authored the four messages. Coulthard was provided with the four suspect messages and 11 authenticated text messages sent by Jenny in the preceding months to the two friends.

In these cases providing an opinion is a two-stage process. The first stage is to decide if the language evidence is **compatible** with the person under consideration having produced the data. If at that stage the decision is positive, a second stage is to decide how distinctive are the features that are shared.

In the Jenny Nicholl case there were of course many identical choices, but analysis showed that certain texting abbreviations used in the authenticated messages like *im*, *m not*, *ive*, *cu* and *fone* were not instanced at all in the suspect messages, which used the alternatives *I am*, *aint*, *ave*, *cya* and *phone*, while for several other items where Jenny had one fixed choice the suspect messages displayed variations. In other words, Jenny had a set of encoding rules that differed from those instanced in the suspect texts and these systematic differences between the two corpora led Coulthard to conclude that the form of the suspect messages was not compatible with their having been produced by Jenny.

As a second step, a set of texts produced by the suspect were analysed and the analysis showed that his choices overlapped with, though were not identical to, those of the suspect messages; in other words, they were compatible. One explanation for this lack of total fit could be that he had tried to disguise his own style and/or to imitate that of Jenny which would be the Prosecution view. These differences could, of course, be evidence that he was not in fact the author, but simply shared a lot of the systematic choices with the real author. For example, Hollien (2002) reports a forensic phonetic case where he was convinced that a voice committing a crime was that of the accused, even though there were one or two very minor differences. Late in the day he discovered that the accused had a twin and that his voice matched the suspect samples even more closely. Fortuitously, in the Nicholl case, Coulthard had access to a series of emails written by one of the suspect's daughters and she turned out to share many of the same distinctive features: in other words, her style was also compatible. The degree of overlap with the suspect messages was less, but she needed to be included with him, on the basis of the linguistic analysis, in the group of possible authors, although he shared more features with the suspect texts and on linguistic grounds alone was a more likely author.

As regards spoken language, another interesting example is provided in Baldwin and French (1990), who describe the case of M, a Catholic man who, passing himself off as a member of a protestant paramilitary organization in Northern Ireland, threatened to kill the members of a family unless money was paid to him. After he was arrested, samples of his voice as well as recordings of the voice of the extortionist were made available to Professor John Baldwin, an expert phonetician, whom the prosecution expected to make a positive identification claim. With the converse being the case, Professor Baldwin was then approached by the defence lawyers, who invited him to make another recording of M's voice. This time, however, Baldwin's conclusion was that the extortionist and M **were** in fact the same person: the reason for such a turn of events being accent-switching, a sociolinguistic phenomenon triggered by, for example, the kind of attitude speakers assume towards their interlocutors. It transpired that when interrogated by the police, M was using an adopted accent apparently in order to distance himself from the officers. He was eventually sentenced to 10 years' imprisonment, though on evidence other than linguistic.

The forensic phonetician is normally required to compare incriminating spoken substance with speech samples known to have been delivered by the suspect (or the accused). In the process, a set of potentially individuating features is identified and segments are processed in respect of qualitative and quantitative characteristics. **Acoustic** analysis is concerned with such parameters as, *inter alia*, vowel formant trajectories, mean fundamental frequency, duration of the noise burst related to the release stage of plosives and duration of pauses. Relevant values are obtained in the course of computer-aided analysis and are made available for visual interpretation as, for example, spectrograms. The actual articulation of particular speech sounds as well as the phonological processes employed by a speaker are in turn central to **auditory** analysis. In the case of M, for example, the salient features chosen for analysis were 'the widespread use of the glottal stop ... the use of a back rounded diphthong in words like 'cold', 'go', etc. ... and the ... pronunciation of dental fricatives' (Baldwin and French, 1990: 105). Needless to say, auditory analysis is often concerned with sociolinguistic (or, to be precise, sociophonetic) sources of language variation.

35.8 UNIQUENESS OF UTTERANCE

Another concept on which the forensic linguist draws is uniqueness of utterance—the idea that fairly quickly in stringing words together any speaker/writer produces a unique string (Coulthard, 2004). Sometimes the authorship question involves already known authors and, in such cases, the forensic linguist is asked whether (parts of) a text claimed by author A is too similar to another text, produced by author B, to have been produced independently.

With growing frequency linguists are being asked to help academic colleagues in the detection or confirmation of student plagiarism. Any linguistically-based investigation of plagiarism is based consciously or unconsciously on the notion of idiolect. In other words, it is expected that any two writers writing on the same topic, even if intending to express very similar meanings, will, because of their differing linguistic histories, choose an overlapping, but by no means identical, set of lexico-grammatical items to do so. It follows from this that, in any comparison of two texts, the more similar the set of lexical items chosen, the greater the likelihood that one of the texts was derived, at least in part, from the other (or, alternatively, that both were derived from a third text), rather than composed independently.

Whereas (occasional) identical strings in two texts which are supposed to have different authors can be indicative of unacknowledged borrowing or plagiarism, it is harder to argue the case when the second text is (supposedly) produced by the same author on a different occasion but without recourse to the first. The example I want to use is from a famous English murder case, dating from 1978, where one piece of strongly-contested evidence was a record of a police interview with a suspect.

In this case, four men were accused, and subsequently convicted, solely on the basis of the confession of one of them, Patrick Molloy, of the murder of a 13-year-old newspaper delivery boy, Carl Bridgewater. There was no corroborating forensic evidence and Molloy later retracted his confession, but to no avail. He admitted that he did actually say (most of) the words recorded as his confession, but insisted that he was being told what to say, while he was dictating the confession, by a policeman who was standing behind him. In other words he said he spoke – but did not author – the confession.

The police, in order to reinforce the credibility of Molloy's confession, produced a contemporaneous handwritten record of an interview which they claimed had taken place immediately before the confession-dictation session and which contained substantially the same information expressed in words very similar to those of the confession. Molloy denied that this interview had ever taken place and counter-claimed that the interview record had been fabricated later on the basis of the by-then pre-existing confession. As is evident from a cursory glance at the two extracts below which are taken, respectively, from the statement which Molloy admitted making and the interview record which he claimed was falsified,

the similarities are enormous; I have highlighted them in bold.

Extract from Molloy's Statement

(20) I went downstairs and **the three of them were still in the room.** (21) **They all looked shocked and were shouting at each other.** (22) **I heard Jimmy say, "It went off by accident".** (23) I looked and **on the settee** I saw the body of the boy. (24) **He had been shot in the head.** (25) I was appalled and felt sick.

Extract from Disputed Interview with Molloy

P.   What were the others doing?
(20) **The three of them were still in the room.**
P.   What were they doing?
(21) **They all looked shocked and were shouting at each other.**
P.   Who said what?
(22) **I heard Jimmy say 'it went off by accident'.**
P.   Did you see the boy's body?
(23) Yes sir, he was **on the settee.**
P.   Did you see any injury to him?
(24) Yes sir, **he had been shot in the head.**
P.   What happened then?
(25) **I was appalled and felt sick.**

At the time of the trial there were no forensic linguists in Britain to question the authenticity of the interview record or challenge the prosecution claim that such similarity was exactly what one would expect when one has the same person telling the same story twice in quick succession. The four accused were convicted, Molloy died in prison, and the other three served 18 years. Following recent research on uniqueness of utterance, no linguist would now dispute that the massive similarity of the two texts demonstrates that they were not produced independently and, if needed, additional linguistic support for this observation is provided by the lack of cohesion between some of the invented questions and the surrounding text – see in particular the Q–A pairs 20–22.

35.9 DISPUTED MEANINGS

If authorship issues account for arguably the greatest proportion of linguists' activity associated with the provision of evidence, they have a strong contender in the disputed meanings which may arise in legislative acts, contracts, transcripts of speech, alleged slander or libel, trademark and copyright disputes, etc. In some countries courts are often disinclined to admit such evidence on the assumption that judges and jurors, as competent language users, have the capacity to understand and interpret the linguistic matter in question. This is exemplified by an English Court of Appeal ruling in a case of assault occasioning actual bodily harm (Stubbs, 1996), where the Lord Chief Justice rejected a linguistic opinion demonstrating how the language of a lower-court judge's summing-up may have influenced the decision of the jury, on the grounds that:

> ... what the meaning is of the language used by a learned Judge in the course of his directions to the jury is a matter for this Court to determine and is not a matter for any linguistic expert (Stubbs, 1996: 239).

However, people, including judges, may sometimes have contrasting intuitions about the meaning of a piece of language. In 2002, in Poland, a landlord who wanted to evict his tenants but was unable to do so for legal reasons, sent them a letter of which the following is an adequate translation:

> You should know that I will smoke you out of the house in an unprecedented way .... I declare that each tenant who has made the decision to stay in the house against my will, is themself fully responsible for their fate and the fate of their relatives. If someone's health or life is affected, it will be so at their own wish.

While the Court of the first instance found the landlord guilty of making a threat to harm or kill, the learned judges of the Appeal Court offered a different reading and overturned the verdict. Even so, the landlord subsequently resorted to a more subtle, semiotic, means of making his feelings known by sending the tenants a festive card with the picture of a Christmas tree from which were suspended hanged paper cut-out human figures. Incidentally, the case also illustrates all too clearly the problems raised in legal and linguistic discussions (see, for example, Ross (2004) and Butler (1997), respectively) of what actually constitutes a threat.

Instances of cases where meaning was at issue are abundant in the literature. Lentine and Shuy (1990), for example, report on their contribution to a trademark infringement case, in which the McDonald's Corporation won an injunction against *Quality Inns International* – a company which some time earlier had announced its plans for a new chain of economy hotels that it intended to call *McSleep Inns*. Having carried out an analysis of distributional patterns of the formative *Mc-*, Lentine and Shuy found that it was unlikely 'that one would immediately associate *Mc-* with McDonald's' (1990: 358). Shuy (1986) writes

about his involvement as an expert in another, criminal, case where a prominent politician and two other men were indicted for an insurance fraud. The main body of evidence was transcripts of clandestinely tape-recorded conversations, during which the defendants allegedly accepted bribes in return for help in securing a state contract for an insurance company. Following a pragmatic analysis, Shuy demonstrated that no speech act had occurred in the conversations that would corroborate the prosecution's version of events. The five defence attorneys used some of Shuy's findings in their summary arguments and the defendants were found not guilty.

Durant (1996) gives an account of semantic and pragmatic evidence he provided regarding the expression *economical with the truth* in a case of libel, while McMenamin (1993) provides an exhaustive analysis of the meaning of the term *accident*, as appearing in the insurance policy of a father whose 18-month-old child died of Sudden Infant Death Syndrome (SIDS). More recently, Butters (2007, 2008) has described his opinions in a number of trademark disputes in the United States.

Somewhat underreported are cases where linguists comment on naming practices. Many jurisdictions have laws preventing parents from giving names to their newborn children that could have potentially adverse consequences. In Poland, for example, officials have the right not to register a name that ridicules, is indecent, diminutivized, or makes it impossible to distinguish the sex of the child. Registrars also use the legally non-binding guidelines published by the Polish Language Council and in the more problematic cases seek its opinion directly. Although different disputed names pose different problems, the Council's opinions typically include references to etymology, cultural connotations, as well as phonetic and orthographic issues. A recent case involved the name Dąb ('oaktree') as a second given name for a male child. After a long legal battle at many judicial levels, Poland's Supreme Administrative Court finally rejected the contention that the name does not indicate the child's sex and can ridicule (noting that 'the word is synonymous with strength, honour and magnanimity'). The Court disagreed also with the Polish Language Council's opinion that, even if used as a second name, it can cause distress to the child.

Within the forensic linguistic community there has recently been a bitter dispute over 'Charlatanry'. This dispute was initiated by an article entitled *Charlatanry in forensic speech science* (Eriksson and Lacerda, 2007). The authors attacked the validity of a commercial computational system which purports to detect particular stresses in speech and goes on to claim that these phenomena are indicative of deception. The scientific criticisms contained within the article appear to be sound, but sadly the use of the word 'charlatanry', and the wider tone of the article, led to threats of libel action and the publisher withdrew the electronic version of the article from their website. The issues of charlatanry, 'junk science' (Chaski, 2001) and bad or good practice are very real concerns for forensic linguists who act as experts.

The United States federal jurisdiction is unusual in holding legal hearings to determine the validity of a forensic science before it can be admitted to the courts. Howald (2009) provides a discussion of some of the issues this process provokes for linguistic testimony. In other adversarial jurisdictions, the Court tends to hear opposing experts and come to a case-specific determination as to whether the evidence provided is more probative than prejudicial. In inquisitorial systems, the Court tends to appoint an expert who in certain circumstances can be challenged by parties to the case. Outside of the United States, the evaluation of the Court in determining the admission of expert evidence tends not to concentrate on the method but focuses on the expert. Experts in the UK are rather inclusively defined as having the qualifications and experience such that their knowledge can be said to be over and above that expected of the jury.

Following a series of miscarriages of justice in the UK, an attempt was made to remedy this situation through the creation of a Council for the Registration of Forensic Practitioners (CRFP). The CRFP set up an accreditation system and register where criteria were set for good science and good administrative processes such that practitioners' case files could be evaluated against these criteria. In September 2008, after considerable debate and work on devising criteria for linguistics, a forensic linguistics register was opened. Sadly, after 10 years in existence, in the spring of 2009 funding was withdrawn from the organization and the CRFP was closed. In the UK there are no plans for a direct successor organization. In the *Independent* newspaper, Sue Black, a Professor of Forensic Anthropology at the University of Dundee, commented:

> The UK is at risk of being at the mercy of 'forensic cowboys' – those who profess their expertise but may have little or no means of backing up their alleged credentials. The CSI factor has left us with hordes of eager but underqualified graduates, keen to scale the perimeter fence of forensic science, and we are about to take away the border guards (*Independent*, 22 March 2009).

The challenges of working as a forensic practitioner are considerable. Taking academic knowledge of linguistics and applying it to a context where an analysis has significant consequences is both challenging and rewarding. It is necessary but not sufficient to have real expertise in linguistics, and to be able to apply that expertise imaginatively to sets of data which can be small, selective and in a variety of ways imperfect. It is easy to be led to conclusions by adversarial bias, or by a real motivation to help victims of horrific crimes or to prevent potential miscarriages of justice. Charlatanry may be a real danger but there are insidious dangers to even the competent linguist.

Forensic linguistics is, however, not only restricted to the practice, i.e. the provision of evidence for investigative or legal processes; linguists also have much to contribute in studying and understanding these contexts. Through the academic study of language and the law, and language used in legal processes, linguists can help provide a greater understanding of these contexts and enhance the likelihood of justice being served.

NOTE

1 A recent resolution of the International Association for Forensic Phonetics and Acoustics refers to the methodology used in those early cases as 'without scientific foundation', and recommends that 'it should not be used in forensic casework' (www.iafpa.net/voiceprintsres.htm).

REFERENCES

Ainsworth, J. (2010) 'Curtailing coercion in police interrogation: the failed promise of *Miranda v. Arizona*', in M. Coulthard and A. Johnson (eds), *Handbook of Forensic Linguistics*. London: Routledge, 111–25.

Aldridge, M. and Wood, J. (1998) *Interviewing Children: A Guide for Child Care and Forensic Practitioners*. London: Wiley.

Argamon, S., Koppel, M., Fine, J. and Shimoni, A. R. (2003) Gender, genre and writing style in formal written texts. *Text*, 23(3).

Baldwin, J. and French, P. (1990) *Forensic Phonetics*. London: Printer Publishers.

Berk-Seligson, S. (2002). *The Bilingual Courtroom: Court Interpreters in the Judicial Process*. Chicago: University of Chicago Press.

Bloch, B. (1948) 'A set of postulates for phonemic analysis', *Language*, 2: 1–15.

Butler, J. (1997) *Excitable Speech: A Politics of the Performative*. London: Routledge.

Butters, R. (2007) 'Changing linguistic issues in US trademark litigation', in M. Turell, M. Spassova and J. Cicres (eds), *Proceedings of the Second European IAFL Conference on Forensic Linguistics/Language and the Law*, Barcelona: Universitat Pompeu Fabra, 29–42.

Butters, R. (2008) 'A linguistic look at trademark dilution', *Santa Clara Computer and High Technology Law Journal*, 24: 101–13.

Chaski, C. (2001) 'Empirical evaluations of language-based author identification techniques', *Journal of Forensic Linguistics: The International Journal of Speech Language and the Law*, 8(1).

Coleridge, S. T., Coleridge, H. N. and Coleridge, S. (1847). *Biographia Literaria, or, Biographical Sketches of my Literary Life and Opinions*. New York: Wiley and Putnam.

Cotterill, J. (2000) 'Reading the rights: a cautionary tale of comprehension and comprehensibility', *Forensic Linguistics: The International Journal of Speech Language and the Law*, 7(1): 4–25.

Cotterill, J. (2003) *Language and Power in Court*. London: Palgrave.

Coulthard, M. (1993) 'On beginning the study of forensic texts: corpus, concordance collocation', in M. Hoey (ed.), *Data Description and Discourse*. London: Harper Collins.

Coulthard, M. (2004) 'Author identification, idiolect and linguistic uniqueness', *Applied Linguistics*, 25(4): 431–447.

Crystal, D. (2006) *Language and the Internet*. Cambridge: Cambridge University Press.

Danet, B. (1980) '"Baby" or "Fetus"? Language and the construction of reality in a manslaughter trial', *Semiotica*, 32(3, 4): 187–219.

Dumas, B. (2002) 'Reasonable doubt about reasonable doubt: assessing jury instruction adequacy in a capital case', in J. Cotterill (ed.), *Language in the Legal Process*. London: Palgrave. pp. 246–59.

Durant, A. (1996) 'Allusions and other "innuendo meanings" in libel actions: the value of semantic and pragmatic evidence', *Forensic Linguistics*, 3(2): 195–210.

Ehrlich, S. (2001) *Representing Rape: Language and Sexual Consent*. London: Routledge.

Eriksson, A. and Lacerda, F. (2007) 'Charlantry in forensic speech science: a problem to be taken seriously', *International Journal of Speech Language and the Law*, 14(2): 169–93.

Filipovic, L. (2007) 'Language as a witness: insights from cognitive linguistics', *International Journal of Speech Language and the Law*, 14(2).

Gibbons (2001) 'Revising the language of New South Wales police procedures: applied linguistics in action', *Applied Linguistics*, 22(4): 439–469.

Gowers, E. (1953) *The Complete Plain Words*. London: Pelican.

Grant, T. D. (2008) 'Approaching questions in forensic authorship analysis', in J. Gibbons and M. T. Turell (eds), *Dimensions of Forensic Linguistics*. Amsterdam: John Benjamins.

Gregory, M. (2000) 'Doing forensic linguistics: endangered people in the community', in E. Ventola (ed.), *Discourse and Community. Doing Functional Linguistics*. Tubingen: Gunter Narr Verlag.

Gudjonsson, G. (2003) *The Psychology of Interrogations and Confessions*. London: Wiley.

Hale, S. (1999) 'Interpreters' treatment of discourse markers in courtroom questions', *Forensic Linguistics*, 6(1): 57–82.

Hänlein, H. (1988) *Studies in Authorship Recognition—A Corpus Based Approach*. Frankfurt am Main: Peter Lang.

Heffer, C. (2005) *The Language of Jury Trial: A Corpus-Aided Analysis of Legal-Lay Discourse*, Basingstoke/New York: Palgrave Macmillan.

Heffer ,C. (2007) 'Judgement in court: evaluating participants in courtroom discourse', in K. Kredens and S. Gozdz-Roszkowski (eds), *Language and the Law: International Outlooks*, Frankfurt am Mein: Peter Lang, 145–79.

Heffer C (2010) 'Narrative in the trial: Constructing crime stories in court' in M. Coulthard and A. Johnson (eds), *Routledge Handbook of Forensic Linguistics*, London, Routledge, 199–217.

Heydon, G. (2005) *The Language of Police Interviewing: a Critical Analysis*, Basingstoke: Palgrave Macmillan.

Hoey, M. (2005) *Lexical Priming: A New Theory of Words and Language*. Abingdon: Routledge.

Hollien, H. (1990) *The Acoustics of Crime: The New Science of Forensic Phonetics*. New York: Plenum.

Hollien, H. (2002) *Forensic Voice Identification*, London: Academic Press.

Howald, B. S. (2009) 'Authorship attribution under the rules of evidence: empirical approaches in the layperson legal system', *Speech, Language and the Law. The International Journal of Forensic Linguistics*, 15(2): 219–47.

Johnstone, B. (1996) *The Linguistic Individual: Self-Expression in Language and Linguistics*. New York: Oxford University Press.

Kniffka, H. (1981) 'Der Linguist als Gutachter bei Gericht. Ueberlegungen und Materialien zu einer "Angewandten Soziolinguistik"', in G. Peuser and S. Winter (eds), *Angewandte Sprachwissenschaft. Grundfragen—Bereiche—Methoden*. Bonn: Bouvier Verlag H. Grundmann. pp. 584–634.

Kelso, J.C. (1996) 'Final report of the blue ribbon commission on jury system improvement', *Hastings L.J.*, 47: 1433.

Kniffka, H. (2007) *Working in Language and Law. A German Perspective*. London: Palgrave Macmillan.

Koppel, M., Schler, J. and Argamon, S. (2009) 'Computational methods in authorship attribution', *Journal of the American Society for Information Science and Technology*, 60(1): 9–26.

Lea, S. and Auburn, T. (2001) 'The social construction of rape in the talk of a convicted rapist', *Feminism and Psychology*, 11(1): 11–33.

Lentine, G. and Shuy, R. W. (1990) 'Mc-: meaning in the marketplace', *American Speech*, 65(4): 349–66.

Levi, J. N. and Walker, A. G. (eds) (1990) *Language in the Judicial Process*. New York: Plenum Press.

Levi, J. N. (1993) 'Evaluating jury comprehension of the Illinois capital sentencing instructions', *American Speech*, 68, i, 20–49.

Looser, D. (2004) 'Lexicography on the inside: doing time in every New Zealand prison', *International Journal of Lexicography*, 17: 69–87.

Mayr, A. (2003) *Prison Discourse. Language as a Means of Control and Resistance*. London: Palgrave.

McEnery, T. (2005) *Swearing in English: Bad Language, Purity and Power from 1586 to the Present*. London: Routledge.

McMenamin, G. R. (1993) *Forensic Stylistics*. Amsterdam: Elsevier.

Mellinkoff, D. (1963) *The Language of the Law*. Boston, Toronto: Little, Brown and Company.

Milne, R. and Bull, R. (1999) *Investigative Interviewing: Psychology and Practice*. Chichester: John Wiley & Sons.

Philbrick, F. A. (1949) *Language and the Law: The Semantics of Forensic English*. New York: Macmillan.

Rock, F. (2001) 'The genesis of a witness statement', *Forensic Linguistics*, 8(2): 44–72.

Rock, F. (2007) *Communicating Rights: The Language of Arrest and Detention*. Basingstoke, London: Palgrave Macmillan.Shuy.

Rose, P. (2003) *Forensic Speaker Identification*. New York: Taylor & Francis.

Ross, S. D. (2004) *Deciding Communication Law: Key Cases in Context*. Philadelphia, PA: Lawrence Erlbaum.

Sapir, E. (1927) 'Speech as a personality trait', *American Journal of Sociology*, 32: 892–905.

Shuy, R. W. (1986) 'Some linguistic contributions to a criminal court case', in S. Fisher and A. Todd (eds), *Discourse and institutional Authority: Medicine, Education and Law*. Westport, CT: Ablex. pp. 234–49.

Shuy, R. (2005) *Creating Language Crimes: How Law Enforcement Uses (and Misuses) Language*. Oxford: Oxford University Press.

Solan, L. M. (1993) *The Language of Judges*. Chicago: University of Chicago Press.

Stokoe, E. and Edwards, D. (2008) '"Did you have permission to smash your neighbour's door?" Silly questions and their answers in police suspect interrogations', *Discourse and Society*, 10(1): 89–111.

Stubbs, M. (1996) *Text and Corpus Analysis—Computer-assisted Studies of Language and Culture*. Oxford: Blackwell.

Svartvik, J. (1968) *The Evans Statements: A Case for Forensic Linguistics*. Gothenburg: Gothenburg University Press.

Tiersma, P. M. (1999) *Legal Language*. Chicago: University of Chicago Press.

Tiersma (2010) 'Instructions to jurors: Redrafting California's jury instructions', in M. Coulthard and A. Johnson (eds), *Routledge Handbook of Forensic Linguistics*, London, Routledge, 251–64.

Tosi, O. (1979) *Voice Identification: Theory and Legal Applications*. Baltimore: University Park Press.

Williamson, T. A. (1993) 'From interrogation to investigative policing: strategic trends in police questioning', *Journal of Community and Applied Social Psychology*, 3: 89–99.

Wróblewski, B. (1948) *Język prawny i prawniczy*. Kraków: Polish Academy of Arts and Sciences.

36

Language Teaching and Language Assessment

Constant Leung

36.1 INTRODUCTION

In the past 40 years or so the fields of language teaching and assessment have taken account of the social dimensions in language and language use in a variety of ways. Sociolinguistics, with its central concern for achieving an understanding of the relationship between language and society, has contributed substantially to the 'socio-ising' of language teaching and assessment. Language teaching and language assessment can be, and sometimes are, conceptualized in terms of principles and theories that are context-independent. For instance, a grammar-based approach may be indifferent to the who, where, how and why questions of language use because of its focus on the formal system of a language, grammar. This view can be justified by an epistemological assumption that language is primarily an autonomous phenomenon unsullied by instances of language use. By extension, language teaching and assessment can therefore treat 'language' as a more or less stable body of objectified, formal and context-independent knowledge (see Bell, 1981: Ch. 5; Swann, 2002 for further elaboration). The contact with ideas from sociolinguistics has helped to create a more socially-informed conceptual and theoretical infrastructure for language teaching and assessment.

Many areas within sociolinguistics are potentially relevant to language education generally. An early example of an attempt to capture this broad connection is Pride (1979) which, *inter alia*, links the following areas of sociolinguistics to language teaching and learning: sociolinguistic surveys, children's sociolinguistic competence and dialect diversity, standard and non-standard language in relation to bilingualism and minority communities,

and the use of pidgin. Preston (1989) discusses the relevance of variationist accounts of language forms and language use for second language acquisition. Spolsky (1989: 3), in a discussion on conditions for second language learning, presents his focal questions in this classic sociolinguistic formulation: 'Who learns how much of what language under what conditions?'

This chapter will attempt to trace some of the key conceptual and theoretical connections between aspects of sociolinguistics and language teaching and assessment since the 1970s. Examples from curriculum development and classroom teaching will be used to illustrate, where appropriate, how ideas might have been applied in practice. It is notoriously difficult to periodize ideas and their influences. It is not suggested here that prior to the 1970s there had been no attempt to apply sociolinguistic (however defined) insight in language education. Indeed the opposite may be the case. For instance, Howatt (with Widdowson) (2004: 142) reported that in the British colonies of Malaya and Singapore in the 1900s there was recognition that the wholesale importation of grammar school English language and literature courses were inappropriate because the pupils were learners of English in a foreign language context. The value of using the 1970s as a reference point lies in the fact that it represents a moment when there was a decisive shift from primarily a grammar and structure orientation to a more socially-sensitive perspective in language teaching and assessment, particularly in English-speaking countries. More importantly, many of the arguments presented to advance the case for the embracing of the 'social' then are, perhaps in slightly different guises, still part of the ongoing debate now.

The main connections between sociolinguistics and language teaching and assessment will be traced historically through two lines of developments in this discussion. The first is the body of work broadly associated with ethnography of communication. In this respect, the work of Hymes (references in later sections) has influenced not only how language is conceptualized for language education but also how the social can be taken into account in complex linguistic and educational environments. The second line of development concerns systemic functional linguistics (SFL), with particular reference to the work of Halliday and his colleagues (references in later sections). The fundamental insight of SFL – that the use of language is itself a constitutive part of social action and that linguistic resources, e.g. lexis and grammar, themselves embody social meaning – has generated another body of work that connects language education to the social world. As Berns (1990) observes, both Hymes and Halliday share the view that social life shapes people's use of language, but they diverge in terms of how language is conceptualized and analysed.

For reasons of scope and space, I will not attempt a comprehensive survey of all the sociolinguistics output relevant to language teaching or education; instead, the main purpose is to develop an account that highlights some of the currents in sociolinguistics that have been fed into language teaching and assessment. In this discussion, the terms 'language teaching' and 'language assessment' are used broadly; examples will be drawn from the teaching of a language to students for whom it is not their mother tongue, e.g. English as a foreign language in Japan or English as an additional/second language in Australia for linguistic minority students, as well as the teaching of mother tongue. The context of teaching will be made explicit where appropriate. The term 'language assessment' will cover both language testing and other forms of assessment. The first half of this discussion will be taken up by a largely descriptive account of the points of contact between sociolinguistics and language teaching and assessment. In the second half, I will look at some recent work that may have a bearing on further developments in sociolinguistically-minded language teaching and assessment. The references used in this discussion have all appeared in the English language but they relate to research in different parts of the world.

36.2 LANGUAGE TEACHING

Communicative language teaching

The development of the concept of communicative language teaching (CLT) was generally associated

with a break with the grammar-focused approaches to language teaching that predominated in practice up to the 1960s and early 1970s. The emerging socially-oriented work of Austin (1962), Halliday (1973, 1975), Halliday, McIntosh and Strevens (1964) and Sauvignon (1972) (among others) in this period paved the way for a paradigm shift in language teaching. At a conceptual level, the work of Hymes (1972, 1977) on ethnography of communication and communicative competence was particularly influential[1]. His 1972 paper (it first appeared in 1966 as a conference paper) presented an ethnographically-oriented formulation of the notion of communicative competence. This paper explicitly addressed language education issues. It was partly a critical response to Chomsky's (1965) highly abstracted notion of (grammatical) competence, and partly a call for language educators to take account of the '*differential competence* within a *heterogeneous speech community*, both undoubtedly shaped by acculturation' (Hymes, 1972: 274, italics in original). The point here is that if one conceptualizes competence as a biologically-endowed facility essentially residing within individuals in homogeneous linguistic communities, as a Chomskyan position would suggest, then this concept would be of little value to language teaching. Hymes observed that, in actual communities, individuals varied in their competences in the use of language/s across different social settings (for further elaboration, see Hornberger, 1989), and that the differentials were associated with socio economic and socio cultural factors such as class and status.

For Hymes (1972: 277), a child learning to communicate through language has to acquire 'knowledge of sentences, not only as grammatical, but also as appropriate. He or she acquires competence as to when to speak, when not, and as to what to talk about with whom, when, in what manner'. In other words, there are social rules of use, a dimension of language use 'without which the rules of grammar would be useless' (Hymes, 1972: 278). This inclusion of the 'social' makes it necessary to raise questions of context of communication and aspects of socio cultural practice when working towards a theory of language in use. In this connection, Hymes (1972: 281, emphasis in original) suggests that four empirical questions must be raised:

Whether (and to what degree) something is formally **possible**:

Whether (and to what degree) something is **feasible** in virtue of the means of implementation available;

Whether (and to what degree) something is **appropriate** (adequate, happy, successful) in relation to a context in which it is used and evaluated;

Whether (and to what degree) something is in fact done, actually **performed**, and what its doing entails.

The pedagogical relevance of these questions to language teaching, and language education more generally, was quickly appreciated by language educators. A concept of competence that is built on a view of contextualized language use is potentially very helpful for teachers who are interested in framing their work in socially realistic ways. Canale and Swain (Canale, 1983, 1984; Canale and Swain, 1980a, 1980b; among others), building on the works of Hymes and others, propose that communicative competence comprises four components (areas of knowledge and skills):

1 *Grammatical competence.* This component is concerned with ' ...knowledge of lexical items and of rules of morphology, syntax, sentence-grammar semantics, and phonology' (Canale and Swain, 1980a: 29). A measure of knowledge and skill in this area will allow the language learner to make sense of and to produce language expressions representing literal meaning.
2 *Sociolinguistic competence.* '[It] addresses the extent to which utterances are produced and understood appropriately in different sociolinguistic contexts depending on contextual factors such as status of participants, purposes of the interaction, and norms or conventions of interaction... ' (Canale, 1983: 7). This component deals with what Hymes (1972, 1977) would call the rules of use, including what he (1972: 281) means by 'whether (and to what degree) something is in fact done'.
3 *Discourse competence.* For Canale (1983: 9), this competence is concerned with '[u]nity of a text [that] is achieved through cohesion in form and coherence in meaning. Cohesion deals with how utterances are linked structurally and facilitates interpretation of a text. For example, the use of cohesion devices such as pronoun, synonyms .... Coherence refers to the relationship among the different meanings in a text, where these meanings may be literal meanings, communicative functions and attitudes'. (Also see Halliday and Hasan (1976) on cohesion, and Widdowson (1978) on coherence.)
4 *Strategic competence.* This component is concerned with language learners' ability to achieve communication by 'mastery of verbal and non-verbal communication strategies that may be called into action for two main reasons: (a) to compensate for breakdowns in communication due to limiting conditions in actual communication (e.g. momentary inability to recall an idea or grammatical form) or due to insufficient competence in one or more of the other ... [component

competences] above; and (b) to enhance the effectiveness of communication (e.g. deliberately slow and soft speech for rhetorical effect)' (Canale, 1983: 11).

This formulation of communicative competence represented a considerable shift in the conceptual base of second/foreign language pedagogy which had been largely grammar-oriented.

The Canale and Swain framework very quickly became the central doctrine of the emerging CLT approach in the worldwide English Language Teaching (ELT) enterprise in the early 1980s (Brown, 2000). The strong influence of CLT was felt beyond the English language teaching and teacher training programmes (often with direct links to the Anglo-American academy) in different parts of the world and quasi-government institutions such as the British Council; second/foreign language educators in countries such as Germany made explicit reference to it in their deliberations (e.g. see Edmondson (2001) for an account). The development of the European Framework of Common Reference for Languages (Council of Europe, 2001) has drawn on CLT explicitly. More recently, elements of CLT have been incorporated in the discussions on content and language integrated learning (CLIL) which is gaining rapid popularity in Europe (see Klippel, 2008). Even a cursory glance at the current ELT textbooks and teacher training menus would show that the popularity of CLT has not diminished in 30 years. (For further discussions see Block (2003) and Leung (2005).)

Patterns of use of language/s

There are other bodies of sociolinguistic work that have made a contribution to language education. At a whole society level, work on patterns of language use such as 'who is speaking what to whom in what contexts' can assist language policymaking and educational resources allocation (e.g. Kaplan and Baldauf, 1997, Ch. 4; Ohannessian and Ansre, 1979; Whitely, 1979). The Linguistic Minority Project (1985), for instance, provided data on patterns of language use and language teaching among Asian and Eastern European minority groups in England. However, as Extra (2006) observes, more of this kind of survey work is urgently needed in places where linguistic diversity is increasing.

Another strand of sociolinguistic work examines patterns of language use in specific classroom contexts, a well-known example of which is *Functions of Language in the Classroom*, edited by Cazden, John and Hymes (1972). Hymes has this to say in the Introduction:

For language in the classroom, what we need to know goes far beyond how the grammar of

English is organized.... It has to do with the relationship between a grammar of English and the ways in which English is organized in use by teachers, by children, and by the communities from which they come; with the features of intonation, tone of voice, rhythm...; with the meanings of all those means of speech to those who use them and those who hear them, not in the narrow sense of ... naming things and stating relationships, but in the fuller sense, as conveying respect ... concern or indifference, intimacy..., seriousness or play...; with the appropriateness of one or another means of speech, or way of speaking, to one or another topic, person, situation; in short, with the relation of the structure of language to the structure of speaking
(Op. cit.: xiii).

The chapters in this volume address a number of prominent language education issues in the United States at that time (many of which are still current some 35 years later). The topics of discussion include the issues surrounding the use of African American Vernacular English (AAVE) (Fishman and Lueders-Salmon, 1972; and others), code-switching (Gumperz and Hernández-Chavez, 1972), classroom communication issues involving first nations (North American Indian) and other ethnolinguistic minority children (John, 1972; and others) as well as deaf children (Cicourel and Boese, 1972), and so on. In relation to this discussion, perhaps Philips' (1972) paper on participant structures in schools in Warm Springs Indian Reservation can be seen as a good example of the types of enquiries presented in these chapters. Philips looked at the Warm Springs Indian children's participation and verbal interaction (in a local variety of English) in Grade 1 and Grade 6 classrooms. It was observed that these Indian children showed a general tendency not to take up opportunities to respond to teacher questions in front of classmates, yet they would engage actively in self-directed group projects or tasks. The fieldwork data suggested that the children's levels of participation in the different activities were related to their community experience. It was suggested that in their home and community settings children tended to learn by silent observation or by sharing tasks (e.g. cleaning a room) with elders with little verbal interaction. Furthermore, the Indian children were not generally asked to tell what they knew or could do while learning; they showed their success in learning by producing an accomplished deed (e.g. a cooked meal). All of this clearly contrasted with the heavy reliance on verbal interaction in learning (and the checking and displaying of learning) processes in school.

This line of sociolinguistic enquiry has been reflected in work situated in other world locations. Here are some of the more recent examples. Lin (1999) studied the uses of English and Cantonese in English-medium secondary schools in Hong Kong. In these schools, teachers and students – a vast majority of whom were local ethnic Chinese Cantonese speakers – are meant to conduct all curriculum and school activities through English. However, in this study, Lin found that there were different practices in different classrooms and schools. For instance, in a school located in a middle- class/professional neighbourhood, both the teacher and the students of a Form 3 class (3rd year in secondary school) were comfortable with English as a medium for teaching and learning activities. In another school, located in an industrial area where the students came from families of manual labour or service occupations, the teacher of a Form 2 class (2nd year in secondary school) would speak first in English to ask questions, but then she would repeat or elaborate the questions in Cantonese to get responses from the students. The students would offer answers in Cantonese and she would then recast the answers in English. She had to do this because the students had limited English proficiency and they were not yet able to engage in grade-level work through English. (See Lin, 2001 for a further discussion.)

Ndayipfukamiye (2001) investigated the use of Kirundi and French in rural and urban Grade 5 (primary school) classrooms in Burundi. The students were taught the curriculum through the medium of Kirundi and learned French as a subject up to Grade 4. At Grade 5, curriculum teaching was switched to French-medium. Curriculum guidelines suggested that only French should be used from Grade 5, and that teachers should build on pupils' life experience for learning. But many children, particularly those in rural areas, would have little direct contact with French outside school, and the kind of background knowledge (encoded in French) needed to do the curriculum. A consequence of this situation was that teachers often resorted to code-switching to teach curriculum content. The following is an example of a teacher switching from French to Kirundi to connect with the students' experience:

Key:
Italics – French
Bold – Kirundi

T: *on dit qu'on prend ses feuilles pour faire des. pour faire les to-its.. vous avez été à l'intérieur?* **hanyuma hari ivyo bariko barwaganya vyitwa** *hein. donc eh ubu* **biriko birahera mugabo kera ugiye wasanga inzu zose zisakaje ivyatsi. ivyatsi. hamwe wasanga ari ubgatsi vyo mw ishamba. ahandi ugasanga ari ubgatsi?** (Op. cit.: 108, original transcription conventions)

Translation into English:
T: it is said that its leaves [the leaves of a tree] are used to cover roofs. Have you already been in the

countryside? **there is a practice that is being combated called thatched roofing** er. and so. **the practice is now receding but in the past all the houses were covered in thatch. Thatch. It was forest foliage and in other instances what could you find?**
(Loc. cit.)

Both Lin and Ndayipfukamiye point to the constraints of using a non-local or non-indigenous language as medium of instruction in two different contexts. Quite often, educational policies would promote the use of a non-local language as medium of instruction because it is believed that this would create a rich language environment leading to accelerated acquisition of the preferred language. These two studies represent classroom research that paints a very different story and highlights the importance of taking local social circumstances into account.

In ethnically and linguistically diverse schools in England where the official medium of the national curriculum is English, bilingual assistants are sometimes deployed to work with students whose English proficiency is not yet able to cope with classroom communication unaided. Martin-Jones and Saxena (2001) examined the ways bilingual classroom assistants were positioned and used in the classroom by class teachers. These assistants tend to come from the local neighbourhood and share a minority community language/s with the students. They are generally not formally trained as teachers. In the classroom, the differentials in professional status and authority are reflected in the ways the bilingual assistant's speaking turns are directed by the teacher and the minority community languages are subordinated to English. Figure 36.1 shows one of the moments when the class teacher gave an explicit signal to the bilingual assistant to begin to use Urdu to explain to the students what had been said in English.

The educational policy rhetoric in England in the past 30 years has been that all languages are to be respected and, where appropriate, they should be used in school to promote learning. But as this study shows, the prestige and the symbolic authority of English as the official curriculum language and the status of non-qualified bilingual assistants can in practice mean that minority community languages are often consigned to a subservient role in the classroom.

As part of a much larger study of language and interaction in a London secondary school, Rampton (2006) observed some Year 9 (13/14 year-old students) German lessons. Compared to other subject lessons, the teaching in the German lessons appeared to be designed to orchestrate whole-class activities. Whereas in the other subject lessons students were often involved in group or individual work, the German lessons were organized in a 'flow' of activities such as whole-class listening comprehension, hands-up survey of individual answers and choral repetition of drill sentences. It is suggested that these observed teacher-orchestrated language learning activities, which appeared to be representative of foreign language teaching in this school and resonated with reported data from elsewhere, share similarities with ritual events which can be characterized by, among other things, 'obscurity in propositional meaning', 'parallelism' and delivery that entails fluency and stylized intonation which are supported by prescribed proxemics, behaviours and attitudes. Clarity in language content meaning would not be a priority 'when they [students] were expected to respond to the third-person question "what is J__ doing according to her card" with, for example, an answer in the first-person – '**ich wache auf**' ((*'I wake up'*))' (Rampton, 2006: 180, original typography). Parallelism manifested itself in activities such as imitation drills and filling-in exercises where students were asked in insert a piece of information (e.g., time) into a slot in a sentence set up by the teacher. The extract of a teacher-orchestrated choral drill in Figure 36.2 can be seen as an example of an attempt at ritualistic delivery.

Rampton also found instances where students were not expected to provide personally truthful answers in some of the learning activities. For instance, a teacher said this to her students in connection with a task involving giving times for morning routines: 'you can give me any time, I don't really mind too much ... we're just practising this construction' (op. cit.: 178). These findings suggest an interesting contrast to the official foreign languages curriculum goals which include: '[d]eveloping the skills of listening, speaking, reading and writing in a range of situations and contexts' and '[u]sing imagination to express thoughts, ideas, experiences and feelings' (QCA, 2007: 166).

In a study on the vitality of African American Vernacular English, Labov (2008) suggests that AAVE is continuing to flourish and develop. For instance, he reports that the use of the commonly recognized invariant form *be* (same form for *is*, *am* or *are*) before noun phrases and adjectives has now been extended from identificatory meaning to signal habitual meaning, e.g.:

A: Do you know where I can find Nukey?
B: She be here [most of the time] but she ain't here now.
(Labov, 2008: 221)

Labov argues that the maintenance and development of AAVE are linked to residential (and the associated social and schooling) segregation of African Americans, which shows signs of

Key:
BA- bilingual assistant
CT – class teacher
L – learner
LL – learners
<E> – English
<U> – Urdu

1	CT:	<E>right. Do you know what this is called?
	L?:	wire
	L?:	+ wire
	CT:	+wire
5	LL:	wire
	CT:	and these clips on the end are called crocodile clips. ('cause they go){ } like a crocodile like that
	L?:	like a dog
	CT:	like a dog ([nauu]) crocodile clip
10	CT:	Mrs. A she'll tell you ..
	BA:	<U>**kyaa hai ye**<E>clip<U>**jo hai~**. Ye<E>wire<U>**hai...** What is this? This clip= This is a wire.
		Ye kyaa hai ye<E>wire<U>**hai aur jo iske uupar**<E>clip What's this? This is a wire. And look at the shape of
		<U>**hai uskii**<E>shape<U>**aage se dekho.**<E>crocodile the clip in front of it. Look from the front. Have you seen a
		<U>**dekhaa hai jo paanii mai~ hotaa hai. uske jaisii**<E>shape crocodile {which/it} is found in water? The shape looks like
15		<U>**hai ye dekho. uskaa muuh kaise khultaa hai**<E>crocodile that. ok here, see, it opens like a crocodile's mouth
		<U>**kaa aise. [wo:~a]** {making sound} Like this.
	L?:	**[wo: ~a]**
	BA:	**[wo: ~a]** {CT laughing?}
	L?:	**[wo:~a]**
20	BA:	<P>**e dekh aise..**<E>crocodile<U>**kii tarah wo:~a. hai** Look, like this. 'wo:~a' like a crocodile, isn't
		naã. kyoõ kii aise khultaa hai. ye hai<E>crocodile clip..= it? Because it opens like this. This is a crocodile clip.

Figure 36.1 Example of language switching using a bilingual classroom assistant. (Martin-Jones and Saxena, 2001:126–127; original transcription conventions).

continuing and spreading in many cities in the United States. Furthermore, it is suggested that the use of AAVE is associated with low decoding accuracy in reading. Residential segregation is itself part of an interlocking set of social and environmental factors such as unemployment, poverty, low(er) educational achievement (including low reading achievement) and other social problems.

Labov's paper is somewhat different from all the other studies cited earlier in this section which share a common methodological starting point, i.e. they start by focusing on a particular situation of language use; the ensuing investigation then attempts to describe and explain the circumstances and reasons that have led to the observed patterns of

use of language/s. Labov's 2008 paper looks at the use of AAVE by African Americans as a vernacular variety and accounts for its maintenance and development in terms of macro-social factors such as residential segregation and poverty. The commonality among all the papers is the role played by social and cultural factors in language use.

It is obvious that the kind of sociolinguistic enquiry exemplified by the studies cited in this discussion does not always deal with language pedagogy in a direct way, unlike the work on communicative competence and CLT. But this kind of sociolinguistic work provides important description and analysis that help to account for some of the complexities and intricacies in language use in

```
 1  MS W                            right
 2                                  if everybody can (      ) now (.)
 3                                  ICH |ESSE 'FRÜH|STÜCK
                                    ((trans: I eat breakfast))
 4  SINGLE PUPIL                    ich |esse 'früh|stück
 5  MS W                            ICH |ESSE 'FRÜH|STÜCK
 6                                  bitte 'alle zu`sammen
                                    ((trans: all together please))
 7  SEVERAL VOICES, BUT NOT HANIF   ((ragged chorus:))
                                    ich esse 'Früh|stück
 8  MS W                            ich |e::sse 'Früh|stück
 9  OTHER VOICES                    ((still ragged:))
                                  ⎡ ich |esse 'Früh|stück
10  HANIF                           ((quite quietly))
                                  ⎣ ich |e::sse 'Früh|st/ück
11  MS W                            ich |esse 'Früh|stück
12  SEVERAL                         ich ⎡esse 'Früh|stück
13  HANIF                              ⎣esse 'Früh|stück
14  BOY                             ((loud))
                                    (QUIET)
15  MS W                            BITTE
                                    ((trans: PLEASE!))
16                                  ((shouting very loud:))
                                    'ALLE 'ZU`SAMMEN
                                    ((trans: ALL TOGETHER))
17                                  ICH |ESSE 'FRÜH|STÜCK
18  OTHERS                          /ich |esse 'Früh|stück
19  HANIF                           ((sounding less than whole-
                                    hearted:))
                                    ich esse Frühstü:
20  ANON                            (        )
21  GUY                             it's `breakfast |time
22  BOY                             what⎡`is it
```

Figure 36.2 Teacher-orchestrated choral drill. (Rampton, 2006: 181).

classroom communication in specific contexts. Such accounts illuminate the socially-enacted underside of officially sponsored curriculum claims, and they can serve to signal the possibilities and the limits of possibilities of the espoused principles and goals.

Systemic functional grammar

Another strand of sociolinguistics that has impacted on language teaching is the work of Halliday and his associates. The idea of 'function' in language is understood in terms of the relationship between meaning and language expressions. This functional relationship ' ...reflects the fact that language has evolved in the service of particular human needs ... what is really significant is that this functional principle is carried over and built into the grammar, so that the internal organization of the grammatical system is also functional in character' (Halliday, 1975: 16). Halliday identified a number of social functions such as instrumental function (using language to satisfy material needs) and regulatory function (using language to control the behaviour of other people) and so on. In principle, there are infinite options in meaning (expressing social functions) and language can be seen as a 'meaning potential' (op. cit.: 16). Linguistically, the meaning options are expressed through three functional components (often referred to in the Hallidayan literature as metafunctions):

- Ideational – 'the speaker expresses his experience of the phenomena of the external world, and of the internal world of his own conscious-ness' (op. cit.: 17); thus, language is a means with which people talk about the world.

- Interpersonal – the 'function of language as a means whereby the speaker participates in … [a] speech situation' (op. cit.: 17); through this component individuals can adopt a role in relation to other participants, express their own views and values, and so on.
- Textual – an 'enabling function . . . the function that language has of creating text' (op. cit.: 17); this component is concerned with the deployment and organization of linguistic resources (in the broadest sense) to form a text (spoken or written) to make meaning in context (cf. discourse competence in the Canale and Swain framework).

These functional components are conceptual and analytical categories. In actual language communication, they are embedded in and realized by instances of speech or writing simultaneously. (For a fuller discussion of systemic functional grammar see, for example, Halliday and Matthiessen, 2000, 2004.)

The work of Schleppegrell, Achugar and Orteíza (2004) offers an example of this functional approach at work in a language-teaching context.

In school systems where linguistic minority students are expected to participate in a common curriculum with other students, many of them may find the ways in which content ideas are expressed through the school language difficult (the school language being their additional/second language). This kind of domain/subject-specific language is often referred to as register. In a United States context, Schleppegrell et al., using a functional grammar approach, examine how lexical and grammatical resources are used in history texts. Students need to be able to identify events and happenings (ideational function) when working with History texts; these tend to be encoded in action verbs of processes. However, history texts also contain other information. They therefore argue that it is important to help students understand that there are different types of verbs and that they serve different functions.

The verbs used in writing about history can be classified as action verbs such as *fight, defend, build, vote* and so forth; saying and thinking-feeling verbs such as *said, expressed, supposed, like, resent*, and so forth; and relating verbs such as *is, have, is called*, and so forth. This categorization helps students understand when authors are writing about events (action verbs), when they are giving opinions or telling what others have said (thinking-feeling and saying verbs), and when they are giving background information (relating verbs).

(Schleppegrell et al., 2004: 77)

In addition to looking at verbal processes, Schleppegrell and her colleagues also examine how actors and agents, i.e. participants, in historical events are represented. Participants can be difficult to identify in history texts. For instance, in a statement such as 'The slave trade peaked in the late eighteenth century', it is not clear who might have been involved, nor is it easy to see the activities in 'slave trade'. The use of abstract nouns or noun phrases (e.g. 'slave trade') may be efficient as a means of conveying complex historical events and processes, but the wording can obscure the intended meaning. Functional grammatical analysis can help make text meaning more transparent by unpacking the relationship between wording and meaning.

The work of the Language In The National Curriculum project (LINC, 1989–1992) in the UK (Carter, 1990, 1996, 1997; LINC, 1989–1992) also draws on the SFL perspective. This was a government-funded initiative to produce teacher development material that would support the teaching of English (mainstream school subject) within the statutory National Curriculum in England and Wales. For example, on the topic of teaching 'variations in written language' the following teaching activities are suggested:

- Preparation: the teacher prepares three groups of labels – showing writing purposes (printed on card, as shown in Figure 36.3), audiences and text types – cuts them up and puts them in three piles.
- In class: the teacher shuffles each of the three piles of cards and lays down each pile face down, then turns the top card of each pile face up. The random sequencing of the cards in each pile may show up in unpredictable combinations such as Complain, Unknown Person and Recipe. These combinations can be used to generate questions such as: Is this combination likely/possible? Is written language appropriate for this purpose? How would the writer organize the text? This kind of teaching activity quite clearly reflects a functional view of language use that relates form to purpose and context in a systematic way.

In broadly the same period, this functional view of language use has also underpinned the development of the genre theory approach to teaching literacy in schools in Australia. Cope and Kalantzis (1993: 67) state that:

…writing and speaking have distinctively different linguistic structures; and different ways of using language have different social effects. Literacy, and the types of transformation of oral language that come with literacy, open linguistic doors into certain realms of social action and social power. It follows that literacy teaching, if it is to provide

PURPOSES

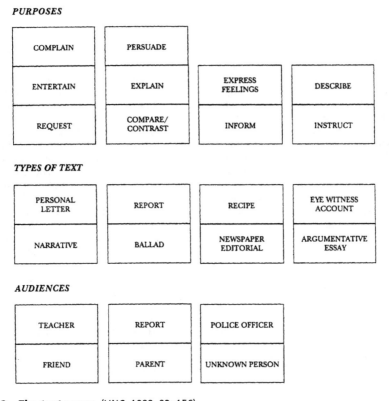

Figure 36.3   The text game. (LINC, 1989–92: 156).

students with equitable social access, needs to link the different social purposes of language in different contexts to predict patterns of discourse.

This approach recognizes that in society and in education some types of text carry more social and educational power than others; government committee reports, official curriculum documents and textbooks are examples of such powerful texts. These texts tend to conform to '[g]enres [which] are conventional structures which have evolved as pragmatic schemes for making certain types of meaning and to achieve distinctive social goals, in specific settings, by particular linguistic means' (op. cit.: 67). By looking at genre in this particular way, it is possible to help students understand 'how language works; who it works for; why it works' (op. cit.: 84) in a context-sensitive way. Veel (1997), for example, looks at a number of different science texts and relates their linguistic features to the purposes they are designed to serve. The following is an example:

Silicones are similar to hydrocarbons, but the 'backbones' of the molecules consist of silicon and oxygen atoms, instead of carbon atoms. Attached to the silicon atoms are side-chains of carbon and hydrogen.

Silicones have exceptional resistance to heat. They repel water, and are not affected by most chemicals... (Coghill and Wood, 1989: 117, cited in Veel, 1997: 166)

Veel argues that this text, like many school science texts, presents and represents science as a body of stable and 'true' facts or content for learning. In terms of sequencing and staging of information in secondary school science texts, Veel suggests that there are some clearly identifiable genres, for instance:

- procedure – this genre serves the social and educational purpose of enabling experiments and observations; the content is presented in three stages: aim-materials needed-steps
- causal explanation – this genre deals with why or how an abstract or a not readily observable process takes place; it has two stages: identification of phenomena-explanation sequence (comprising a number of phases), and so on.

Veel further suggests that school science texts tend to follow a knowledge trajectory that starts with the genres related to doing science (e.g. procedures for doing experiments) in the lower years of schooling. The 'doing science' phase is followed by explaining science (e.g. causal explanations), organizing scientific information (e.g. descriptive and taxonomic reports), and, in the senior years in school, challenging science (e.g. exposition of argument for or against an issue). Coffin (1997) has also observed this movement from the concrete (learning about events) to the abstract (arguing against a theory) in history. Paying attention to language use in particular subject areas can make reading and writing more transparent to teach and, at the same time, can help students become more aware of the close relationship between content meaning and language use.

36.3 LANGUAGE ASSESSMENT

In this section, 'language assessment' will be used as a superordinate term to encompass both psychometrically-oriented language testing and classroom-based teacher assessment of language. The relevant issues surrounding these two approaches and practices of language assessment will be discussed in turn. The focus here, in line with the perspective taken in the previous section on language teaching, will be on the conceptual links between sociolinguistics and language assessment.

A good deal of the conceptual and theoretical work in language testing in the past 20 years or so, particularly in relation to English as a foreign language, has been concerned with the notion of 'construct'. By construct is meant 'the ability [testers] want to measure' in an individual test-taker (Bachman and Palmer, 1996: 89). It is argued that, with a defined construct for a particular test, it becomes possible to develop test items (questions) which are designed to tap into target ability, as well as to evaluate the validity of the way that test scores are understood and interpreted. So, for instance, the construct for academic writing in a given subject at first-degree university level may comprise a knowledge of grammar, rhetorical organization and register appropriate to that subject. The notion of construct is thus directly connected to questions of what counts as language knowledge and what should be included in an ability to use language knowledge with reference to context and purpose. In other words, the issues here are to do with language modelling. It is at this point that language testing, a psychometrically-oriented enterprise, connects with sociolinguistics, or more precisely, with the notion of communicative competence.

The advent of the concept of communicative competence in language teaching has been accompanied by a search for a language model by language testers that would account for the complexity in language use (performance) in context. Bachman (1990) and Bachman and Palmer (1996), building on the work of Hymes, Canale and Swain, Sauvignon and others (see earlier references), put forward a multi-component hierarchical model of language competence which has become a strong point of reference in the language testing field since the early 1990s. The Bachman model (1990:87), as it has come to be known, divides the concept of competence into two sub-components: organizational competence and pragmatic competence. In turn organizational competence is made up, at the next level below, of grammatical competence (e.g. vocabulary and syntax) and textual competence (e.g. cohesion and rhetorical organization). Likewise, pragmatic competence comprises illocutionary competence (e.g. ideational and manipulative functions) and sociolinguistic competence (e.g. sensitivity to variety and register, and cultural references).

The lineage of this model of competence can be easily seen at level of grammatical competence, textual competence and sociolinguistic competence which correspond closely to the grammatical, discourse and sociolinguistic competences set out in the Canale and Swain model. Illocutionary competence is clearly related to the Hallidayan language functions mentioned earlier.

The detailed breakdown of these competences at the fourth tier into potentially discrete and identifiable language features reflects the concerns and the operational requirements of language testing. Put differently, language test developers are interested in being able to specify what language knowledge and/or language use are being sampled in any standardized test (for a discussion see North, 1993). And it is in the way language specification is accomplished in the Bachman model that one can see the links between language testing and sociolinguistics.

Bachman and Palmer (1996: 44) acknowledge that 'language use, by its very nature, is embedded in particularly situations', and that each instance is 'virtually unique'. However, they argue that 'it is possible ... to identify certain distinguishing characteristics of language use tasks and to use these characteristics to describe a language use domain' (op. cit.). Insofar as contemporary language testing tends to claim to be interested in test-takers' ability to use the target language in specific domains (e.g. a vocational training course for adult immigrants), and for specific tasks (e.g. to engage in laboratory experiments), and is not interested in their general language ability or competence, this argument connects with the concern for situatedness in the Hymesian notion of communicative competence well. If the job of a language test is to sample test-takers' performance in a given domain, the specificity of an identified domain allows a highly-focused selection of features of language to be included in a test. For instance, in an English language test developed for the purpose of hiring hotel telephone receptionists (located in Asia), the target language use domain is telephone room booking and the tasks include providing information on room occupancy (availability) and verifying credit card details and so on. Within these well-defined parameters, the grammatical competence to be sampled by the test is characterized as 'Vocabulary: general and specialized for hotel reservations… '; pragmatic functions are characterized as 'Functional: Ideational and manipulative… '; and in terms of sociolinguistic competence; 'Dialect: standard …. Cultural references: none' (Bachman and Palmer, 1996: 310–11).

The communicative competence approach in general has been very influential in language testing since the mid-1980s. The Bachman model in particular has made a substantial contribution to this enterprise. As Alderson and Banerjee (2002: 80) note in a state-of-the-art review, the Bachman model has been 'very useful as the basis for test construction… '. A glance at the literature in the field of language testing would support this view. Davies' (2008) detailed historical account of the conception and revision of the hugely popular International English Language Testing System (IELTS, English language tests) and provides some insights into how the concept of communicative competence and the Bachman model have been integral to its evolution. Almost invariably, all book-length academic discussions (e.g. McKay, 2006; McNamara, 1996; Weir, 1990) and practical guides and resource menus (e.g, Davidson and Lynch, 2002; Fulcher and Davidson, 2007) in the field contain substantial reference to the concept of communicative competence. Its impact is also felt in the politically significant Common European Framework of Reference for Languages (Council of Europe, 2001) which has been designed to inform language teaching and learning programmes, assessment and certification in European countries; 'communicative language competence', comprising linguistic, sociolinguistic and pragmatic components, forms an important part of its theoretical foundations.

Another area of language assessment that has made a connection with a strand of sociolinguistics is classroom-based formative assessment of student language use by teachers. Classroom-based formative assessment has gained a good deal of policy and professional support in recent years (for a discussion see Assessment Reform Group, 2002; Black and Wiliam, 1998a, 2006; Broadfoot and Black, 2004). A good deal of the current discussions on formative assessment is focused on exploring the learning-enabling potential of classroom interaction between teachers and students, and among students themselves. The discussion has gravitated around the well-known classroom interaction Initiation–Response–Evaluation (I–R–E) sequence. It is generally observed that the Initiation move by the teacher tends to take the form of closed or display-oriented questions, e.g. What is the population of Greenland? Such questions tend to lead to short responses by students which are, in turn, evaluated by the teacher in terms of correctness or accuracy. While this kind of exchange between the teacher and the student can be used to assess what a student knows, it does not necessarily lead to further learning. Black and others argue that formative assessment should make more educational use of teacher questions and teacher evaluation, or more appropriately, teacher feedback (Black and Wiliam, 1998b; Black et al., 2003; for a wider discussion see Alderson, 2007; van Lier, 1996). The use of open questions, increasing the wait time for a student answer, and providing student-oriented feedback that shows the next learning steps are all part of the exploration of making teacher assessment in the classroom more formatively oriented. The discussion by Leung and Mohan (2004) on the discourse of classroom-based formative assessment is an example of an attempt to extend this kind of exploration.

Working with data collected in multiethnic primary classrooms, which included students speaking English as an additional/second language, Leung and Mohan, drawing on aspects of the work on analysing casual conversations by Eggins and Slade (1997), itself a development built on Halliday (1994; for more recent discussion, see Halliday and Matthiessen, 2004), suggest that it would be useful to examine classroom language interaction in terms of three conversation moves: offer, continue and respond. For the purpose of analysing formative interaction: the 'open' move can be taken to include asking for and/or offering to give an answer; 'continue' can include reasons given for or against an answer; and 'respond' can include accepting or rejecting an answer on offer. The extract in Table 36.1 is an example of this analysis. A Year 4 class (9 year olds) in a primary school near London had been working on an early British history topic. The students were by now familiar with the theme. In this lesson their task was to read the text of a number of paragraphs and decide which sentence in each of the paragraphs was the most important (in relation to the theme). At the start of this task Andy (A), the teacher, explained the task and read the first paragraph with the class. He stressed that

Table 36.1

Offer answer	Give reasons for/against	Respond to offer
[Andy returns]		
13 A: Have you finished? What have you decided? What's the most important sentence?		
14 F: 'Some of the Britons fell back.'		
15		A: 'Some of the Britons fell back.' Or do you think there's a more important fact?
16		F: yes, yes.
17 A: What, who's it about?		
18 F: King Arthur		
19		A: King Arthur.
20	A: Do you think he's important?	
21	Chorus: Yes, yes.	
22	A: Right. Why is he important?	
23	F: Because he is king.	
24	A: No, what did he do that was so, that's become legendary?	
25	M&O: He ruled the kingdom.	
26	A: He ruled the kingdom. It doesn't say that here though. Why was he famous? What did he do that was so good?	
27	F: I know. 'He won overthe Anglo-Saxons' . . .	
28		A: Yes, he fought the Anglo-Saxons and he won.
29 A: Let's have a look at this one [reading] 'The Anglo Saxons pushed...'		
30		A: So you think that's the important part [to M, who nods 'yes']
31	A: Why's it more important than the other part that tells you where they. 'they took most of the east and the south and they called . . . England ' Why do you think it's more important that the Britons went to Wales . . . or the beginning of England?	
32	F: Because . . . it tells you how they did it, because where they pushed them.	

Source: From Leung and Mohan (2004: 351–2).

the students should work collaboratively in small groups to decide on the most important sentence. He then moved around the class to interact with students in small groups. The data extract shown in Table 36.1 begins when Andy came to the group where Farhana (F), Meena (M), Narinder, Sarfia, Saleh and Osman (O) were working together. These students were at various stages of learning English as an additional language.

Using the Eggins and Slade analytic schema it is quite easy to see that the teacher, Andy, asked questions but did not provide answers himself. When an incorrect answer was offered, he elicited

an alternative answer by asking a question (turn 15). At turn 18 when a correct answer was given, Andy asked further questions to elicit the reasons used by the students. In turns 24 and 26 his questions guided the students through a reasoning process. From the point of view of developing classroom-based formative assessment, this analytic approach shows the range and the directionality of teacher feedback, which can contribute to a fuller understanding of classroom interaction and how formative opportunities can be exploited.

Teacher assessment does not take place in a social vacuum. In a study of teacher assessment in nine primary schools in England, Rea-Dickins and Gardner (2000) collected data through a combination of questionnaires, interviews and classroom observations. Some of the sociolinguistically-oriented research questions in their study yielded findings that would otherwise be hidden from view. For instance, it is reported that in the schools with open plan classrooms where several classes may be in the same space, there was pooling of teachers and teaching assistants in some curriculum activities. This practice meant that individual teachers were not always 'in demand' (as they would be if they were with their classes in their own classrooms). One consequence of this was that it was possible for teachers to organize small group/one-to-one activities in which formative assessment could be carried out. This was reported by one of the teachers:

> When I say it's essential I wouldn't be able to do it without this level of staff .... And it's also the possibility of having small groups so that you can speak to the children individually. If you're a single teacher in a class, very often you get mobbed after five minutes .... The quality of assessment I do now is streets ahead of what I'd be able to do as a single class teacher ...'
> (Rea-Dickins and Gardner, 2000: 219)

36.4 SOCIOLINGUISTIC ISSUES IN LANGUAGE TEACHING AND ASSESSMENT: LOOKING AHEAD

This section reflects on some of the ideas and developments discussed above, and offers a view on the emerging issues that have a bearing on both sociolinguistics and language teaching and assessment. My comments will be selective to the extent that they are meant to highlight the conceptual and theoretical challenges posed by some of the current debates in the relevant fields, including applied linguistics, language education and literacy studies.

In the move away from grammar-oriented approaches to language teaching, the Hymesian-inspired notion of communicative competence offered language educators a dynamic and situated perspective on language and language use. Instead of generating teaching content out of some formal aspect of the target language system, e.g. grammatical structures, CLT would first identify what and how language is used in the target domain of use before drawing up teaching content. This language identification process is meant to be carried out through a needs analysis (e.g. Brindley, 1989; Yalden, 1983). However, as Dubin (1989) and Leung (2005) point out, this empirically-oriented approach to curriculum development has been more honoured in the breach than the observance. For example, Brown (2001: 43) offers a set of characteristics of CLT which includes the following:

- use of classroom activities and student tasks that would 'engage learners in the pragmatic, authentic, functional use of language for meaningful purposes'
- use of the teacher as 'a facilitator and guide.... Students are therefore encouraged to construct meaning through genuine linguistic interaction with others'.

This characterization reflects a common professional understanding of what passes for 'communicativeness'. However, this rendering of 'communicativeness' departs quite significantly from the original Hymesian aspirations. Instead of observing what goes on in actual communication in specific contexts, the concern now is to promote language communication in learning activities. Instead of finding out how participants use linguistic (and other semiotic) resources to communicate in specific real-world contexts, teachers are asked to use their 'expert' knowledge to assist students to achieve meaningful communication with others in classroom activities. The use of teacher expertise as a guide to 'genuine' interaction has also introduced teacher-determined norms that may be highly partial and idiosyncratic[2].

The migration of a research perspective from ethnography to language teaching has led to noticeable recontextualization, i.e. selective interpretation of the concept of communicative competence. It may well be that language teaching (however theorized) demands a relatively stable body of authoritative knowledge as a foundation, whereas a research enterprise such as ethnography would, among other things, encourage the discovery of new findings and a commitment to provisionality. From a language teacher's point of view, it may not be all that important to retain a research-oriented perspective in day-to-day classroom work. Conceptually though, the reduction of the notion of communication to classroom language use and the reliance on teacher expertise to facilitate 'genuine linguistic interaction' have combined to constrict and reify how and what language is used in actual communication practices, leading to an impoverished curriculum base. Gilmore (2007) provides a survey of some of the consequences of this impoverishment in terms of lexicogrammar and discourse pragmatics. For instance, it has been found that modal lexical items which have been found to occur frequently in recorded data of language use are often under-represented in well-known textbooks. Other documented instances of non- or under-representation reported by Gilmore (op. cit.: 100) include a study which found that there was 'almost no corre-spondence' between 'the language taught for meetings in 30 business English textbooks' and the language used in real-life business meetings.

In the field of language testing, the need to define target language ability has thrown up some complex questions about the components that make up such an ability. The operationalization of the concept of communicative competence for testing (see earlier discussion) has certainly helped throw light on this issue. Paradoxically, as Widdowson (2001, also see Harley et al., 1990) observes, a major conceptual and empirical prob-lem with the established models or frameworks of communicative competence is that little is known about how the component competences (e.g. grammatical and discourse competences) interact in actual stances of language use (test perform-ance). This observation clearly raises some com-plex psycholinguistic processing issues. But from the point of view of this discussion it also alerts us to the particular way in which sociolinguistic con-cerns have been absorbed in language testing, a primarily psychometric enterprise. As mentioned earlier, the notion of construct (the target language ability to be measured) in language testing is real-ized in terms of a target language use situation. However, the 'social' dimension of the target lan-guage use situation in language testing, as McNamara and Roever (2006: 32) point out, is generally portrayed in terms of test-takers' cognitive ability:

> The target language use situation is conceptual-ized in terms of components of communicative language ability, which, in turn, is understood as the ability to handle the target language use situ-ation. The situation or context is projected onto the learner as a demand for a relevant set of cogni-tive abilities; in turn these cognitive abilities are read onto the context. What we do not have is a theory of the social context in its own right...

Thus the social is converted into cognitive abili-ties, and the notion of the social context is trans-formed into a set of particular cognitive abilities identified in and attributed to a given situation.

In operationalizational terms, the disconnection with the 'social' can also be seen in a study carried out by Chalhoub-Deville (1997) in which she investigates the fit between language assessment frameworks that have been developed for local purposes and general paradigmatic theoretical models of communicative competence (e.g. the Bachman model mentioned earlier). These local assessment frameworks were derived from criteria used by raters to serve a purpose: for example, assessing student proficiencies in a language such as Arabic in a specific university. She has found

that while locally-developed assessment frame-works might focus on aspects of competence which are consistent with the general models, e.g. grammatical competence, they vary in terms of the emphasis they place on the different areas of grammar such as morpheme-inflectional markers and syntax. Chalhoub-Deville (1997: 14) con-cludes that 'theoretical models such as Bachman's ... do not provide all-inclusive representations of the proficiency construct. Instead these [local] frameworks emphasize specific aspects of that more general theoretical construct to reflect the characteristics of their specific contexts'.

The point made by Chalhoub-Deville is in fact related to a wider issue in language assessment concerned with the extent to which a single com-petence model should be used as a basis for the assessment in situations where there is considera-ble ethnic, linguistic and social diversity. For instance, Leung and Lewkowicz (2008) examined the validity issues that can arise when a 'common' language model is applied to students with differ-ent language backgrounds and learning trajecto-ries. They showed that when a long-term resident/native speaker-derived model of competent English language use is adopted to assess students from diverse linguistic minority communities in English-speaking schooling systems, factors such as age of arrival, home language backgrounds, curriculum content, and previous schooling and other social experience can all serve to bear on the ability to use language effectively in school con-texts. A failure to take these into account would invalidate assessment outcomes.

I will now turn to some more **basic** constitutive sociolinguistic issues that are related to language teaching and assessment. In contemporary condi-tions of increasing contact of people across national and language boundaries for a variety of reasons, the notions of an 'intercultural speaker' and 'intercultural communicative competence' tap into an important area of additional/second language learning. Byram, Nichols and Stevens (2001) suggest that an intercultural speaker is a person who can interpret different perspectives and has a willingness and ability to manage social interaction with others from a different cultural background. The notion of 'intercultural commu-nicative competence' broadens the Hymesian con-cept to include 'sociocultural competence' and 'social competence'. Sociocultural competence is concerned with the intercultural speaker having a certain degree of familiarity with language use in specific situations; this involves a knowledge of social processes and practices in different cultural contexts. Social competence is concerned with 'the will and the skill to interact with others' (Byram, 1997: 10). In a sense, intercultural com-petence here is about engaging in social interaction in situations where one has to actively make use of one's (probably always provisional) knowledge to actively make sense and to get on with others; whereas in the more conventional conceptualization of communicative competence, the concern is with making use of known conventions and rules. Kramsch (2005, 2006) has also pointed out that to communicate effectively in complex multilingual and multiethnic encounters, one needs more than a knowledge of what native speakers might do. For Kramsch (2006: 251), communication, particularly for college students studying additional languages, entails the immersion of 'whole persons with hearts, bodies, and minds, with memories, fantasies, loyalties, identities'. This doesn't obviate the need to have the sort of communicative competence mentioned earlier, but, in addition, Kramsch calls for a 'symbolic competence' which can enrich communication. This is about a capacity to make sense of complexity and ambiguity, to make sense of symbolic forms as aesthetics and so on[3].

In the established understanding of communicative competence, the starting point is 'what would people do in such and such a situation?'. Lee (2006) asks whether communicative competence is a condition of language teaching or its objective. This rhetorically-posed question is helpful because it foregrounds the fact that the language teaching-learning situation is itself a language-using situation, and a certain amount of communicative competence is needed, particularly on the part of learners, if engagement with learning activities is to be achieved. The following extract of a classroom conversation between a teacher (T) and a student (J) on 'crazy and goofy' inventions offers an illustration (Lee, 2006:361):

[Teacher eliciting and commenting on students' idea of 'goofy' inventions]

> T: =Wake you up, and I hope the machine would then actually get you to class (.) on time, hahaha ... what else, what's another (.) possible invention?
> J: A robot can (cook)
> T: I'm sorry?
> J: A robot can (cook) for me.
> (0.5)
> J: (Cook).
> T: Oh, a robot to <u>bring</u> a can of coke to you?
> J: Yeah.

In this conversation on imaginary inventions that would be useful in everyday life, J (the student), despite certain difficulties in pronouncing `cook', has clearly grasped the nature of the teacher's problem in understanding him and produced repairs (reiterating `cook'). When the repair efforts failed, J resorted to accommodation (consenting to the teacher's `coke'). Lee suggests that this is

the kind of communicative competence that should be taken into account.

This kind of competence is brought into view in instances of language use in actual social interaction. Understanding communicative competence in language teaching therefore requires a knowledge of what learners can readily do, a kind of existential competence, in learning situations. This connects with the next point.

Hall, Cheng and Carlson (2006: 226) suggest that the language knowledge of an individual is closely related to language use:

> ... language knowledge [is] comprised of dynamic constellations of linguistic resources, the shapes and meanings of which emerge from continual interaction between internal, domain-general cognitive constraints on the one hand and one's pragmatic pursuits in his or her everyday worlds on the other, that is through language use.

Thus, a person's communicative repertoire is not just 'learned' or 'acquired', but is constantly being shaped and reshaped by experience of use. This argument applies to both monolinguals and multilinguals. In this view, instead of attempting to specify communicative competence with reference to some external reference point (whether based on ethnographic observations or a generalized description of a target language use situation), one would seek to define competence in terms of 'the pragmatic variation in the use of language within and across social experiences in which individuals are engaged, variation that exists even within a single language code' (op. cit.: 230). This draws attention to language learning and using opportunities afforded to students when considering issues of competence. In other words, competence is, at least in part, a reflexive outcome of language learning experience.

Recent work in academic literacies, a field largely concerned with the use of language for academic writing in university settings, has also shown the need to be reflexive about the notion of competence in terms of dynamic interplay between locally-interpreted disciplinary practices and power relations. It is now reasonably well understood that there isn't a single common 'standard' in academic writing that would apply to all disciplines and university institutions (e.g. Ivanič, 1997; Lea and Street, 1998; Lillis, 1999, 2001; Lillis and Scott, 2007; Street, 2003, 2005). Lea and Street (1998) provide an illustrative case study of how different disciplines have different expectations and practices: a first-year university student wrote two essays, one for history and the other for anthropology. The student used the same format, emphasizing content and factual information. His history tutor evaluated his writing positively, but he was criticized by his anthropology tutor. The anthropology tutor was critical because, in his opinion, the essay lacked structure and argument. Lea and Street (1998: 165) offer this view:

> We suggest that the explanation for this divergence of opinion and response lies at a deeper level than the surface features of 'writing' ... the cause of the poor assessment of his essay can be traced ... to the student's lack of familiarity with the subject matter of anthropology, which was not his major ... and to his greater ease with history [his major] ... his experience with writing in history led him to break down and categorise some factual aspects of his knowledge in his anthropology essay, without attention to some of the implicit ways of writing knowledge in his anthropology, and in particular the need to abstract theory rather than attend to factual detail as evidence ...

In this case, the deeply-hidden epistemological differences between history and anthropology, as interpreted by the tutors concerned, appear to have triggered the tutors' different evaluations.

Alongside disciplinary differences there is also the question of power relations. Academic tutors are often conferred a good deal of power in relation to the judging of 'quality' in student work. Indeed many universities operate statutes that explicitly state that academic judgements cannot be challenged. Leung (2008) reports an example of this power at work in a mock gatekeeping moment.[4] In England, university applicants are required to write a personal statement as part of their application. Applicants can use the statement as an opportunity to 'sell' themselves. The following extract is taken from a practice personal statement written by a 17-year-old school student from a minority language background.

> I want to study a degree in Computer Science because I am interested in the role that computers play in society now and in the future. Now-a-days each and every organisation uses IT. Currently I am studying ICT, Mathematics, Physics and Urdu which I hope will help me to be successful in Computer Science degree. Apart from studying I also have some experience of fixing computer hardware wiring problems.
> What I find most interesting about the computer is that it is helping humans in many aspects of life. Where will computers go in the next 15 or 20 years? What will be the reaction of humans to the increasing use of them? My ambition is to be a computer engineer either in relation to hardware problems, software problems or both. Perhaps I will be able to be involved in solving hardware design difficulties or in devising better software

solutions in the areas of databases or spreadsheets....

(Leung, 2008: 157)

A university admissions tutor was asked to evaluate this statement in terms of the admissibility of this applicant to an English Language degree programme. He indicated that this statement would not persuade him to offer this applicant a place because:

> ... I am ... a bit wary of kind of massive, banal, generalisations.... OK this person is saying 'where will computers go in the next 15–20 years?.... What I find most interesting about the computer is that it is helping humans in many aspects of life' my reaction to both of those comments is... big deal... you know... say something a bit more precise about you and why you want to do this course and what is computers which interests you in a more specific sense...

(loc. cit.).

It is quite clear that the admissions tutor concerned had a preference for certain kinds of information. Irrespective of the reason/s lying behind such a preference, the point here is that the institutional authority conferred on tutors has afforded him the power to make judgements of student suitability. This power differential is an intrinsic part of the judgement and it should be brought into analysis.

36.5 CLOSING REMARKS

The contact with sociolinguistics has broadened and complexified many of the conceptual assumptions of language teaching and assessment. The concept of communicative competence in particular has been a major influence on theory and practice for the best part of 30 years. The conscious inclusion of the social dimension has undoubtedly generated innovative moves in curriculum conceptualization and assessment frameworks. The incorporation of sociolinguistic concepts is, of course, an ongoing recontextualization enterprise which can lead to some reframing of original ideas, – for instance, the pedagogic narrowing of 'communication' in terms of language use in classroom activities. Seen in this light, the **socio-ising** of language teaching and assessment is an uncertain affair. Much depends on how and how far conceptual and research-derived ideas are intellectually and practically integrated into professional practice. Looking beyond the immediate, and judging from the tenets of the work cited in the previous sections, there is every reason to believe that the broad concept of competence itself is undergoing some fundamental reconsideration in the light of changing political and sociocultural experiences, and communication practices. The protean nature of concepts and ideas in sociolinguistics is itself a source of both stimulation and destabilization. Some of the emergent thinking may impinge on language teaching and assessment in fundamental ways. If, for instance, the power exercised by participants in social interaction is a major constituent in situated communicative competence, how might this play out in teaching and assessment? And if communicative practices and social norms (in interaction) are increasingly negotiated in intercultural encounters, how far would we be able to describe, teach and assess sociolinguistic and strategic competences beyond broad generalizations? A good deal of challenging work lies ahead.

NOTES

1   For other contemporaneous work, see Habermas (1970) and Campbell and Wales (1970).

2   This norming process would depend on teachers' preferred models of formality, politeness, genre and so on in relation to learning tasks. In addition, teacher-determined norms may promote some language varieties (e.g. Standard English) and not others; recent debates in English as a lingua franca have added considerable complexity to this issue. See Jenkins (2006, 2007) for a discussion.

3   The issue of how to handle what people actually do/say in interaction has also been debated in the language- testing literature. From a language-testing perspective, the main concern is how to relate 'unique' individual actions in context to a consistent pattern of performance or trait. See Bachman (2007) for a discussion.

4   This study used Personal Statements produced by students in practice sessions to elicit an admissions tutor's views. In actual university admissions procedures, there is no requirement to state such views explicitly.

ACKNOWLEDGEMENTS

Figure 36.2 from Ben Rampton, *Language in Late Modernity: Interaction in an Urban School*, 2006, Cambridge University Press. Reprinted with permission.

Lee extracts (page 549) from Yo-Ann Lee, 'Towards respectification of communicative competence: condition of L2 instruction or its objective', *Applied Linguistics*, 2006, 27(3): 349–76, by permission of Oxford University Press.

REFERENCES

Alderson, C. and Banerjee, J. (2002) 'Language testing and assessment (Part II)', *Language Teaching*, 35: 79–113.

Alderson, J. C. (2007) 'The challenge of (diagnostic) testing: do we know what we are measuring?', in J. Fox, M. Wesche, D. Bayliss, et al. (eds), *Language testing reconsidered*. Ottawa: University of Ottawa Press. pp. 21–39.

Assessment Reform Group (2002) 'Assessment for learning: 10 principles', Retrieved 24 November 2006, from http://www.assessment-reform-group.org.uk/CIE3.pdf.

Austin, J. L. (1962) *How to do things with words*. London: Clarendon Press.

Bachman, L. (1990). *Fundamental considerations in language testing*. Oxford: Oxford University Press.

Bachman, L. F. (2007) 'What is the construct? The dialectic of abilities and contexts in defining constructs in language assessment', in J. Fox, M. Wesche, D. Bayliss, et al. (eds), *Language testing reconsidered*. Ottawa: Ottawa University Press. pp. 41–71.

Bachman, L. F. and Palmer, A. S. (1996) *Language testing in practice*. Oxford: Oxford University Press.

Bell, R. T. (1981) *An introduction to applied linguistics: approaches and methods in language teaching*. London: Batsford Academic and Educational Ltd.

Berns, M. (1990) *Contexts of competence: social and cultural considerations in communicative language teaching*. New York: Plenum Press.

Black, P. and Wiliam, D. (2006) Assessment for learning in the classroom. In J. Gardner (Ed.), *Assessment and learning* (pp. 9–25). London: Sage.

Black, P. and Wiliam, D. (1998a) 'Assessment and classroom learning', *Assessment in Education*, 5(1): 7–73.

Black, P. and Wiliam, D. (1998b) *Inside the black box*. London: King's College London.

Black, P., Harrison, C., Lee, C., Marshall, B. and Wiliam, D. (2003) *Assessment for learning: putting it into practice*. Maidenhead: Open University Press.

Block, D. (2003) *The social turn in second language acquisition*. Edinburgh: Edinburgh University Press.

Brindley, G. (1989) 'The role of needs analysis in adult ESL programme design', in R. K. Johnson (ed.), *The second language curriculum*. Cambridge: Cambridge University Press. pp. 63–78.

Broadfoot, P. and Black, P. (2004) 'Redefining assessment? The first ten years of *Assessment in Education*', *Assessment in Education*, 11(1): 7–27.

Brown, H. D. (2000) *Principles of language learning and teaching*. 4th edn. White Plains, NY: Pearson Education (Longman).

Brown, H. G. (2001) *Teaching by principles: an interactive approach to language pedagogy*. 2nd edn. White Plains, NY: Pearson Education.

Byram, M. (1997) *Teaching and assessing intercultural communicative competence*. Clevedon, UK: Multilingual Matters.

Byram, M., Nichols, D. A. and Stevens, D. (2001) *Developing intercultural competence in practice*. Clevedon, UK: Multilingual Matters.

Campbell, R. and Wales, R. (1970) 'The study of language acquisition', In J. Lyons (Ed.), *New horizons in linguisitcs* (pp. 242–260). Harmondsworth, Middlesex: Penguin Books.

Canale, M. (1983) 'From communicative competence to language pedagogy', in J. Richards and J. Schmidt (eds), *Language and communication*. London: Longman. pp. 2–27.

Canale, M. (1984) 'A communicative approach to language proficiency assessment in a minority setting', in C. Rivera (ed.), *Communicative competence approaches to language proficiency assessment: research and application*. Clevedon, UK: Multilingual Matters. pp. 107–22.

Canale, M. and Swain, M. (1980a) 'Theoretical bases of communicative approaches to second language teaching and testing', *Applied Linguistics*, 1(1): 1–47.

Canale, M. and Swain, M. (1980b) *A domain description for core FSL: communication skills*. Ontario: Ministry of Education.

Carter, R. (ed.) (1990) *Knowledge about language and the curriculum: the LINC Reader*. London: Hodder.

Carter, R. (1996) 'Politics and knowledge about language: the LINC Project', in R. Hasan and G. Williams (eds), *Literacy and society*. London: Longman. pp. 1–21.

Carter, R. (1997). *Investigating English discourse: language, literacy and literature*. London: Routledge. Chapter 3.

Cazden, B., John, V. P. and Hymes, D. (eds) (1972) *Functions of language in the classroom*. New York: Teachers College Press.

Chalhoub-Deville, M. (1997) 'Theoretical models, assessment frameworks and test construction', *Lanugage Testing*, 14(1): 3–22.

Chomsky, N. (1965) *Aspects of the theory of syntax*. Cambridge, MA: MIT Press.

Cicourel, A. V. and Boese, R. J. (1972) 'Sign language acquisition and the teaching of the deaf', in B. Cazden, V. P. John and D. Hymes (eds), *Functions of language in the classroom*. New York: Teachers College Press. pp. 32–62.

Coffin, C. (1997) 'Constructing and giving value to the past', in F. Christie and J. Martin (eds), *Genres and institutions: social processes in the workplace and the school*. London: Continuum. pp. 196–230.

Coghill, G. and Wood, P. (1989). *Spectrum Science 3*. Melbourne: Heinemann.

Cope, W. and Kalantzis, M. (1993) *The powers of literacy: a genre approach to teaching writing*. London: Falmer Press.

Council of Europe (2001) *Common European Framework of Reference for languages: learning, teaching, assessment*. Cambridge: Cambridge University Press.

Davidson, F. and Lynch, B. K. (2002) *Testcraft: a teacher's guide to writing and using language test specifications*. New Haven, ET: Yale University Press.

Davis, A. (2008) *Assessing Academic English: testing English proficiency 1950–1989 – the IELTS solution*. Cambridge: Cambridge University Press.

Dubin, F. (1989) 'Situating literacy within traditions of communicative competence', *Applied Linguistics*, 10(2): 171–81.

Edmondson, W. (2001) 'Conversational analysis and language teaching', in K. Brinker, A. Gerd, H. Wolfgang and S. F. Sager (eds), *Text – und Gesprächslinguistik/ Linguistics of Text and Conversation*. Berlin: de Gruyter.

Eggins, S. and Slade, D. (1997) *Analysing casual conversation*. London: Cassell.

Extra, G. (2006) 'Dealing with multilingualism in multicultural Europe: immigrant and minority languages at home and school', in C. Leung and J. Jenkins (eds), *Reconfiguring Europe: the contribution of applied linguistics*. London: Equinox. In association with the British Association for Applied Linguistics. pp. 21–40.

Fishman, J. A. and Lueders-Salmon, E. (1972) 'What has sociology of language to say to the teacher? On teaching the standard variety to speakers of dialectal or sociolectal varieties', in B. Cazden, V. P. John and D. Hymes (eds), *Functions of language in the classroom*. New York: Teachers College Press. pp. 67–83.

Fulcher, G. and Davidson, F. (2007) *Language testing and assessment: an advanced resource book*. London: Routledge.

Gilmore, A. (2007) 'Authentic materials and authenticity in foreign language learning', *Language Teaching*, 40: 97–118.

Gumperz, J. J. and Hernández-Chavez (1972) 'Bilingualism, bidialectalism, and classroom interaction', in C. B. Cazden, V. P. John and D. Hymes (eds), *Functions of language in the classroom*. New York: Teachers College Press. pp. 84–108.

Habermas, J. (1970) 'Towards a theory of communicative competence', *Inquiry*, 13, 360–375.

Hall, J. K., Cheng, A. and Carlson, M. T. (2006) 'Reconceptualizing multicompetence as a theory of lanugage knowledge', *Applied Linguistics*, 27(2): 220–40.

Halliday, M. (1994). *An introduction to functional grammar*. 2nd edn. London: Edward Arnold.

Halliday, M. A. K. (1973) *Explorations in the functions of language*. London: Edward Arnold.

Halliday, M. A. K. (1975) *Learning how to mean: explorations in the development of language*. London: Edward Arnold.

Halliday, M. A. K. (2004) *An introduction to functional grammar*. 3rd edn. Revised by C. M. I. M. Matthiessen. London: Arnold.

Halliday, M. A. K. and Hasan, R. (1976). *Cohesion in English*. London: Longman.

Halliday, M. A. K. and Matthiessen, C. M. I. M. (2000). *Construing experience through meaning: a language-based approach to cognition*. London: Continuum.

Halliday, M. A. K. and (revised by) Matthiessen, C. M. I. M. (2004) *An introduction to functional grammar* (3rd ed.). London: Arnold.

Halliday, M. A. K., McIntosh, A. and Strevens, P. (1964) *The linguistic sciences and language teaching*. London: Longman.

Harley, B., Allen, P., Cummins, J. and Swain, M. (1990) *The development of second language proficiency*. Cambridge: Cambridge University Press.

Hornberger, N. (1989) 'Tramites and transportes: the acquisition of second language communicative competence for one speech event in Puno, Peru', *Applied Linguistics*, 10(2): 214–30.

Howatt, A. P. R. with Widdowson, H. G. (2004) *A history of English language teaching*. 2nd edn. Oxford: Oxford University Press.

Hymes, D. (1972) 'On communicative competence', in J. B. Pride and J. Holmes (eds), *Sociolinguistics*. London: Penguin.

Hymes, D. (1977) *Foundations in sociolinguistics: an ethnographic approach*. London: Tavistock Publications.

Ivanič, R. (1997) *Writing and identity: the discoursal construction of identity in academic writing*. Amsterdam: John Benjamins.

Jenkins, J. (2006) 'Current perspectives on teaching world Englishes and English as a lingua franca', *TESOL Quarterly*, 40(1): 157–81.

Jenkins, J. (2007) *English as a lingua franca: attitude and identity*. Oxford: Oxford University Press.

John, V. P. (1972) 'Styles of learning – styles of of teaching: reflections on the education of Najavo children', in C. B. Cazden, V. P. John and D. Hymes (eds), *Functions of language in the classroom*. New York: Teachers College Press. pp. 331–43.

Kaplan, R. B. and Baldauf Jr, R. B. (1997) *Language planning: from practice to theory*. Clevedon, UK: Multilingual Matters.

Kramsch, C. (2005) 'Post 9/11: foreign languages between knowledge and power', *Applied Linguistics*, 26(4): 545–67.

Kramsch, C. (2006) 'From communicative competence to symbolic competence', *The Modern Language Journal*, 90(2): 249–52.

Labov, W. (2008) 'Unendangered dialects, endangered people', in K. King, N. Schilling-Estes, L. Wright Fogle, J. J. Lou and B. Soukup (eds), *Sustaining linguistic diversity: endangered and minority languages and language varieties (Georgetown University Round Table on Languages and Linguistics)*. Washington, DC: Georgetown University Press. pp. 219–328.

Language in the National Curriculum (1989–92) *LINC material available on CD ROM or DVD* http://www.phon.ucl.ac.uk/home/dick/ec/linc.htm: LINC Project.

Lea, M. and Street, B. (1998) 'Student writing in higher education: an academic literacies approach', *Studies in Higher Education*, 23(2): 157–72.

Lee, Y.-A. (2006) 'Towards respecification of communicative competence: condition of L2 instruction or its objective', *Applied Linguistics*, 27(3): 349–76.

Leung, C. (2005) 'Convivial communication: recontextualizing communicative competence', *International Journal of Applied Linguistics*, 15(2): 119–44.

Leung, C. (2008) 'Second language academic literacies: converging understandings', in B. Street and N. H. Hornberger (eds), *Encyclopedia of language and education*. Vol. 2. New York: Springer. pp. 143–61.

Leung, C. and Lewkowicz, J. (2008) 'Assessing second/additional language of diverse populations', in E. Shohamy and N. H. Hornberger (eds), *Encyclopedia of language and education*. Vol. 7. New York: Springer. pp. 301–17.

Leung, C. and Mohan, B. (2004) 'Teacher formative assessment and talk in classroom contexts – assessment as discourse and assessment of discourse', *Language Testing*, 20(3): 335–59.

Lillis, T. M. (1999) 'Whose common sense? Essayist literacy and the institutional practice of mystery', in C. Jones, J. Turner and B. Street (eds), *Student writing in university: cultural and epistemological issues*. Amsterdam: John Benjamins. pp. 127–47.

Lillis, T. M. (2001) *Student writing: access, regulation, desire*. London: Routledge.

Lillis, T. M. and Scott, M. (2007) 'Defining academic literacies research: issues of epistemology, ideology and strategy', *Journal of Applied Linguistics*, 4(1): 5–32.

Lin, A. M. Y. (1999) 'Doing-English-Lessons in the reproduction or transformation of social worlds?', *TESOL Quarterly*, 33(3): 393–412.

Lin, A. M. Y. (2001) 'Symbolic domination and bilingual classroom practices in Hong Kong', in M. Heller and M. Martin-Jones (eds), *Voices of authority: education and linguistic difference*. Westport, CT: Ablex Publishing. pp. 139–68.

Linguistic Minority Project (1985) *The other languages of England*. London: Routledge and Kegan Paul.

McKay, P. (2006) *Assessing young language learners*. Cambridge: Cambridge University Press.

McNamara, T. F. (1996) *Measuring second language performance*. London: Longman.

McNamara, T. and Roever, C. (2006) *Language testing: the social dimension*. Oxford: Blackwell Publishing.

Martin-Jones, M. and Saxena, M. (2001) 'Turn-taking and the positioning of bilingual participants in classroom discourse: insights from primary schools in England', in M. Heller and M. Martin-Jones (eds), *Voices of authority: education and linguistic difference*. Westport, CT: Ablex Publishing. pp. 117–38.

Ndayipfukamiye, L. (2001) 'The contradictions of teaching bilingually in postcolonial Burundi: from Nyakatsi to *Maisons en Étages*', in M. Heller and M. Martin-Jones (eds), *Voices of authority: education and linguistic difference*. Westport, CT: Ablex Publishing. pp. 101–16.

North, B. (1993) *The development of descriptors on scales of language proficiency*. Washington, DC: National Foreign Language Center.

Ohannessian, S. and Ansre, G. (1979) 'Some reflections on the educational use of sociolinguistc surveys', in J. B. Pride (ed.), *Sociolinguistic aspects of language learning and teaching*. Oxford: Oxford University Press. pp. 57–70.

Philips, S. U. (1972) 'Participant structures and communicative competence: Warm Springs children in community and classroom', in C. B. Cazden, V. P. John and D. Hymes (eds), *Functions of language in the classroom*. New York: Teachers College Press. pp. 370–94.

Preston, D. R. (1989). *Sociolinguistics and second language acquisition*. Oxford: Basil Blackwell.

Pride, J. B. (ed.) (1979) *Sociolinguistic aspects of language learning and teaching*. Oxford: Oxford University Press.

QCA; Qualifications and Curriculum Authority (2007) *The National Curriculum*. London: QCA.

Rampton, B. (2006) *Language in late modernity: interaction in an urban school*. Cambridge: Cambridge University Press.

Rea-Dickins, P. and Gardner, S. (2000) 'Snares and silver bullets: disentangling the construct of formative assessment', *Language Testing*, 17(2): 215–43.

Sauvignon, S. J. (1972) *Communicative competence: an experiment in foreign language teaching*. Philadelphia: Center for Curriculum Development.

Schleppegrell, M. J., Achugar, M. and Orteíza, T. (2004) 'The grammar of history: enhancing content-based instruction through a functional focus on language', *TESOL Quarterly*, 38(1): 67–93.

Spolsky, B. (1989) *Conditions for second language learning.* Oxford: Oxford University Press.

Street, B. (2003) 'What's "new" in New Literacy Studies? Critical approaches to literacy in theory and practice', *Current Issues in Comparative Education*, 5(2): 1–14.

Street, B. V. (2005) 'Introduction: New Literacy Studies and literacies across educational contexts', in B. V. Street (ed.), *Literacies across educational contexts: mediating learning and teaching.* Philadelphia: Caslon Pubishing. pp. 1–21.

Swann, M. (2002) 'Seven bad reasons for teaching grammar – and two good ones', in J. C. Richards and W. A. Renandya (eds), *Methodology in language teaching: an anthology of current practice.* Cambridge: Cambridge University Press. pp. 148–52.

van Lier, L. (1996). *Interaction in the language curriculum: awareness, autonomy and authenticity.* London: Longman.

Veel, R. (1997) 'Learning how to mean – scientifically speaking: apprenticeship into scientific discourse in the secondary school', in F. Christie and J. Martin (eds), *Genre and institutions: social processes in the workplace and school.* London: Continuum. pp. 161–95.

Weir, C. J. (1990) *Communicative language testing.* London: Prentice Hall.

Whitely, W. (1979) 'Sociolinguistic survey at the national level', in J. B. Pride (ed.), *Sociolinguistic aspects of language learning and teaching.* Oxford: Oxford University Press. pp. 44–56.

Widdowson, H. (1978) *Learning language as communication.* Oxford: Oxford University Press.

Widdowson, H. G. (2001) 'Communicative language testing: the art of the possible', in C. Elder, N. Brown, E. Iwashita, et al. (eds), *Experimenting with uncertainty: essays in honour of Alan Davies.* Cambridge: Cambridge University Press. pp. 12–21.

Yalden, J. (1983). *The communicative syllabus: evolution, design and implementation.* Oxford: Pergamon Press.

37

Guidelines for Non-Discriminatory Language Use

Marlis Hellinger

37.1 INTRODUCTION

The analysis of guidelines for non-discriminatory language use requires an understanding of how language may function as a vehicle for the expression of bias and discrimination. Language is not simply a neutral tool for the transmission of referential meaning: as an instrument of social practice it contributes to the communication, maintenance and change of ideologies, attitudes and stereotypes. Language is used to perform acts of inclusion and exclusion, and is therefore invested with the potential to protect or disrupt social relations.

Guidelines are designed to increase the awareness of the discriminatory power of language and to offer alternative wordings. Significantly, in their introductory sections to guidelines, authors tend to emphasize the social functions of language. For example, in the guidelines to non-discriminatory language published by the University of Salford, Greater Manchester, UK (http://policies.salford.ac.uk/; accessed 19 January 2009) it is pointed out that language is both a symptom of and a contributor to the unequal status of women, people with disability and people from various ethnic and racial backgrounds. Extra visibility in English (*authoress, female doctor*) or emphasis on difference (*the handicapped* vs *people with physical disabilities; an AIDS victim* vs *a person with AIDS*) may harm people's individuality in that such practices highlight traits such as gender or disability which may be irrelevant to the context. Expressions such as *the handicapped* or *AIDS victim* tend to depersonalize the referent(s) by defining the individual person in terms of a deviation from the norm or by invoking associations of

powerlessness and dependency. Stereotyping, derogatory or imposed labelling are identified as the major strategies of discriminatory language use, with 'language, sex, and gender' receiving the most extensive treatment.

'Language and gender' also constitutes the central theme of the non-discriminatory language guidelines issued by The University of Sydney, Australia (http://www.usyd.edu.au/staff/styleguide/; accessed Jan 19, 2009), focusing on such topics as sex, pregnancy, marital status, sexual preference and transgender status. In addition to gender, disability and ethnicity, the Sydney guidelines include a section on language and Australian indigenous people: care needs to be taken in choosing labels that are acceptable to Australian indigenous people, some of whom will object to terms such as *Aborigine(s)* or *Aboriginal person*, while others will accept them. The examples of Salford and Sydney demonstrate that guidelines typically address global (gender/disability) as well as local concerns of discrimination (the multiethnic and multilingual composition of Australian or British society).

The focus of this chapter is on guidelines for non-sexist language for the following reasons: sexist language practices have been identified in a large number of languages, which supports the hypothesis that linguistic sexism is a universal phenomenon of gender-related discrimination (Hellinger and Bussmann (eds), 2001–03). Linguistic sexism is of particular interest since it affects not only the level of lexical choices but also – depending on the type of language – involves issues of grammar and word-formation.

Linguistic sexism is an important area of language and gender research (cf. Hellinger and

Pauwels, 2007). Today, 'language and gender' presents itself as a particularly dynamic field where many voices contribute to theoretical debates and the solution of practical problems. Language and gender research has developed into an explicitly interdisciplinary field which benefits from sociolinguistics and discourse analysis as well as from sociology, psychology, cultural studies and sexuality studies. A large number of comprehensive resources are now available that attest to the diversity of issues being addressed in the field (e.g. Hall and Bucholtz (eds), 1995; Wodak (ed.), 1997; Kotthoff and Wodak (eds), 1997; Litosseliti and Sunderland (eds), 2002; Eckert and McConnell-Ginet, 2003; Holmes and Meyerhoff (eds), 2003; Mills, 2003; Lakoff, 2004; Lazar 2005 (ed.), Harrington et al. (eds), 2008; see also the journal *Gender and Language*; valuable language and gender links can be found on the homepage of IGALA, the *International Gender and Language Association* (http://www.lancs.ac.uk/fass/organisations/igala/index.htm).

The chapter is structured as follows: in Section 37.2, 'Theoretical background', I outline the structural and psycholinguistic foundations of linguistic sexism and language reform, including references to categories of linguistic gender and the relation between language and thought. This discussion is placed in the wider context of theories of gender.

Section 37.3, 'Language reform', focuses on the psycholinguistic effects of masculine/male generics. The major strategies of non-discriminatory usage, i.e. female visibility, symmetrical gender marking and avoidance of stereotyping, are outlined and illustrated by examples from various languages. Taking an explicitly cross-linguistic perspective, I demonstrate that manifestations of linguistic sexism present language-specific problems for language reform which require individual solutions rather than an adherence to the hegemonic model of English.

Section 37.4, 'The public discourse on non-discriminatory language policies', discusses the legal foundations of many guidelines at national as well as international level. It also addresses strategies of public resistance to language reform, which has often been linked to the related context of 'political correctness'.

Section 37.5, 'Evaluating the impact of guidelines for non-discriminatory language', focuses on the implementation and spread of reform measures. Illustrative examples are job advertising in German, alternatives to generic *he* in English, and changes in the use of address labels for women in English and German.

In Section, 37.6, 'Conclusion', the function of guidelines as agents in language change is related to various other factors which pertain to the sociocultural context of the respective speech community.

37.2 THEORETICAL BACKGROUND

Linguistic sexism refers to one type of discriminatory language, i.e. expressions that exclude, trivialize or insult mainly women. Manifestations of such practices are:

- Female invisibility: cf. English *mankind*, German *Studenten* (m) 'students', French *l'étudiant moyen* (m) 'the average student', Italian *i cittadini* (m) 'citizens', or Spanish *los niños* (m) 'the children', in cases that are supposed to include female referents.
- Asymmetrical gender-marking: cf. English *lady philosopher*, German *Frauenfussball* 'women's soccer', or French *une femme écrivain* (m) 'a woman writer', where explicit gender-marking is not used in parallel male-specific or neutral contexts.
- Stereotyping: cf. English *delegates and their wives*, German *Ärzte und Krankenschwestern* 'doctors (m) and nurses (f)', or French *le sexe faible* 'the weak sex', which portrays women and men in traditional gender roles.

Female invisibility may lead to ambiguities and potentially false interpretations, as in this example from a German newspaper:

> *Ehe zwischen zwei jungen Türken* (m) *endet in einer Tragödie.*
> 'Marriage between two young Turks (m) ends in a tragedy.'

The noun phrase *zwei junge Türken* contains the masculine plural noun *Türken* which in the context of the noun *Ehe* '(heterosexual) marriage' creates an awkward ambivalence. In many cases, additional contextual information is necessary to disambiguate expressions which contain masculine/male expressions.

Awareness and documentation of sexist practices emerged in the 1970s when Robin Lakoff's analysis of *Language and Woman's Place* (1975, 2004) in the USA, Dale Spender's *Man Made Language* (1980) in the UK, Luise Pusch's *Das Deutsche als Männersprache* (1984) in Germany, and Marina Yaguello's *Les Mots et les Femmes* (1978) gained popularity even outside academia, initiating extensive research in anglophone countries and elsewhere (for a historical overview see Hellinger and Pauwels, 2007: 652ff.).

Initiatives for language reform rest on the assumption that sexist practices are not only a reflection of conservative usage symbolizing gender relations in a particular culture but also they actively contribute towards the maintenance of gendered hierarchies and stereotypes. Whereas the first view interprets language as a symptom, the second attributes to language the potential of an agent in constructing or maintaining social inequality (cf. Cameron, 1992: 102ff., Miller and Swift, 1995).

37.2.1 *Categories of gender*

Although linguistic sexism has been described as a global phenomenon, guidelines for the elimination of sexist language are necessarily developed for one particular language. Guidelines must respond to language-specific structural properties as well as to current usage norms and the sociopolitical context. Therefore, the analysis of manifestations of gender and proposals for non-discriminatory usage requires that the concept of 'gender' be clarified. Four categories of gender will be differentiated in this chapter: grammatical, lexical, referential and social (cf. Hellinger and Pauwels, 2007: Ch. 3).

Grammatical gender

Grammatical gender is one phenomenon that structures the lexicon of so-called gender languages. It is an inherently morphosyntactic property of the noun which controls agreement between the noun's gender class (typically feminine, masculine, and often neuter) and some satellite element, frequently an article, adjective, pronoun, numeral or verbal form.

For example, in the highly-inflected Slavic languages, grammatical gender-marking is much more visible than in most Germanic languages, simply because more satellite elements have gender-variable forms. In the following example from Polish, agreement is established between the noun and three satellite elements, in each case a demonstrative pronoun, a numeral and an adjective (cf. Koniuszaniec and Błaszkowska, 2003: 261). By contrast, the English translational equivalents show no formal agreement of this kind:

ten jeden mały chłopiec (m)   'this one little boy'
ta jedna mała dziewczynka (f)   'this one little girl'
to jedno małe dziecko (n)   'this one little child'

Obviously, languages with grammatical gender like Polish, Russian or French are confronted with very different problems in searching for gender-inclusive alternatives than grammatically genderless languages like English, Turkish or Chinese. While neutralization rather than female visibility is the primary strategy in English for achieving gender-fair wording (e.g. *flight attendant* for *stewardess*), this strategy plays only a minor role in a language with grammatical gender, where female visibility is a well-established concept, as in German *Lehrerinnen und Lehrer* 'teachers (f) and teachers (m)' to replace the traditional masculine form *Lehrer* 'teachers (m)'. The dominance of English in discourses about linguistic sexism has often led to unfortunate interpretations suggesting that solutions for English might also be applied to other languages (cf. Section 37.4).

Lexical gender

Lexical gender constitutes part of the semantics of animate/personal nouns. In English, personal nouns such as *daughter* and *son* are lexically specified as [female] and [male], respectively. Such nouns may be classified as gender-specific, in contrast to nouns, such as *citizen* or *patient*, which are considered to be gender-neutral or gender-indefinite. A language has lexically-gendered nouns, irrespective of whether it also possesses grammatical gender; cf. the examples in Table 37.1 from English, Spanish (which has two grammatical gender classes) and Polish (which has three).

Lexical gender may or may not be marked on the noun itself. In English, most human nouns are not formally marked for lexical gender, with exceptions such as *widower* or *princess*, which show overt lexical gender-marking by suffixation. By contrast, lexical gender is marked extensively in German, since most personal feminine nouns are derived from corresponding masculine nouns by means of the fully productive suffix *-in*, as in *Bischöfin* 'female bishop', *Elektrikerin* 'female electrician', or *Soldatin* 'female soldier'.

Languages have competing processes of female-specific suffixation which may be an obstacle to promoting female visibility (cf. Section 37.3.2). Examples are

Table 37.1 Lexical gender

Language	Female-specific	Male-specific	Gender-indefinite
English	*daughter, girl*	*son*, boy	*citizen, patient*
Spanish	*hermana* (f) 'sister'	*hermano* (m) 'brother'	*individuo* (m) 'individual'
Polish	*kobieta* (f) 'woman'	*mężczyzna* (m) 'man'	*osoba* (f) 'person'

- French *-ice oratrice* 'speaker (f)', *-euse acheteuse* 'consumer (f)', *-ère conseillère* 'councillor (f)'
- Polish *-ka lekarka* 'doctor (f)', *-ini gospodyni* 'hostess', *-owa szefowa* 'boss (f)'.

Productivity of these processes may be variable, and apart from indicating the lexical property [female], the feminine terms may transport additional gendered messages, e.g. symbolizing the dependence of the female on the male, as in Polish *profesorowa* 'professor's wife'. Such language-specific features will have to be acknowledged when proposals for language reform are made. While the creation of female-specific nouns will lead to more female visibility, this strategy may, however, result in unwanted genderization in languages that not only lack grammatical gender but also productive female-specific word-formation rules. In these languages, female visibility can hardly be recommended as a general solution to androcentric practices.

Referential gender

Referential gender relates linguistic expressions to the non-linguistic world and identifies a referent as 'female', 'male' or 'gender-indefinite'. For example, personal nouns like German *Person* (f) or Polish *osoba* (f), both meaning 'person', are grammatically feminine, lexically gender-indefinite, and may be used to refer to males or females. In conservative language, so-called 'generic' masculine or male expressions, e.g. German *der Bürger* (m) 'the citizen', French *les hommes* (m) 'the men, people', or English *chairman*, may be used to refer to males, to people whose gender is unknown or unimportant in the context, and even to females. Even in cases which – presupposing a heterosexual cultural tradition – include both a female and a male referent, masculine expressions may be the default choice, cf. Spanish *los novios* (m) 'the couple'.

Social gender

Personal nouns have social or 'covert' gender if the choice of associated words can neither be explained by grammatical gender (agreement) nor by lexical or referential gender. Social/covert gender is a reflection of stereotypical assumptions about what are appropriate social roles for women and men, including expectations about who will be a typical member of the class of, say, *surgeon* or *receptionist*.

An illustration of social gender in English is the fact that many high-status professional terms such as *lawyer* or *scientist* will frequently be pronominalized by *he* in neutral contexts. By contrast, low-status occupational titles such as *school-*

teacher or *nurse* will often be followed by anaphoric *she*. In cases of conflict between such practices and actual reference, explicit gender-marking is an option, as in English *woman scientist* or *male nurse*. Typically, such marking tends to be asymmetrical, since expressions such as *man scientist* or *female nurse* are not normally used. Social gender provides an explanation for stereotypically gendered expressions such as French *les délégués* (m) *et leurs épouses* 'the delegates and their spouses', the message being that female participation is unimportant or marginal.

37.2.2 Linguistic relativity

Theories of linguistic relativity predict that the structural differences between languages correlate with cognitive differences observed in native speakers of the respective languages (e.g. Whorf, 1956; Hill, 1988: 14). In more popular wording, the hypothesis predicts that languages influence people's world-views or thinking. Frank and Treichler noted that 'in one form or another, this hypothesis underlies much current theoretical work in sociology, anthropology, criticism, and feminist theory' (Frank and Treichler (eds), 1989: 3).

While it has not been claimed that discriminatory language determines the way people experience the world, researchers in language and gender take the view that androcentric practices not only reflect normative ideologies but also are instrumental in maintaining and reproducing the status quo. Language reform will provide language users with alternative concepts of reality, thus contributing to changes in attitudes and social practices.

Since the 1980s, there has been a considerable resurgence of interest in *linguistic relativity* (cf. Hellinger, 1991; Boroditsky, 2003). Researchers tend to speak about Whorfian effects rather than linguistic relativity (see Lakoff, 1987: 333; Hill, 1988: 28), emphasizing that the non-linguistic effects induced by linguistic differences will not affect underlying universal cognitive processes which can be recovered under appropriate contextual conditions (Kay and Kempton, 1984: 77). For example, spatial and temporal distinctions are reinforced by particular language structures, making language a powerful tool in shaping native speakers' habitual thinking, but leaving room for potential learning. In another example it has been shown that the grammatical gender assigned to objects (e.g. table, window) does indeed influence people's mental representation of these objects: grammatically feminine objects are rated more similar to females, grammatically masculine objects more similar to males (Boroditsky, 2003). The ascription of female/male properties to these objects, i.e. people's thinking about these objects, appears to be influenced by grammatical gender.

In discussing discriminatory language, applied linguists and language planners are primarily concerned with intra-linguistic variation. The assumption is that the choice of either traditional wording or reformed expressions will affect speakers' cognition, producing psycholinguistic effects which can be interpreted in terms of linguistic relativity (cf. Section 37.3.1).

37.2.3 Gender theories

Currently, a tension between various lines of thought can be observed in the research on language and gender. One approach accepts 'gender' as a social category and thus acknowledges the fact that the binary opposition of 'female' and 'male' is still a fundamental principle of social structures and practices. Research traditions in this framework include sociolinguistic investigations of women's and men's language use which began in the 1960s (cf. Trudgill, 1974; Lakoff, 1975, 2004; O'Barr and Atkins, 1980; Milroy, 1987; Holmes, 1995; Coates 2004), but also more structure-oriented studies that analyse the representation of gender in the domains of morphology, syntax and semantics (e.g. Hellinger and Bussmann (eds), 2001–03).

A second approach distances itself from essentialist assumptions of gender and interprets gender as a result of variable social and interactive practices. Gender is no longer seen as a given social category; rather, multiple and sometimes precarious gender identities may be performed depending on various cultural and contextual factors (cf. Butler, 1990, 2004; Bing and Bergvall, 1996; Freed, 1996; Hornscheidt, 2002).

A third position incorporates elements of both theoretical approaches. On the one hand, concepts of 'female' and 'male' are still used, but the boundaries of these categories are seen as fuzzy and variable. In addition, 'female' and 'male' are interpreted as internally diverse rather than homogeneous categories. On the other hand, this position is deconstructionist in that it interprets language use as a set of symbolic practices that are instrumental in staging normative or alternative gender representations (cf. Motschenbacher, 2006: Ch. 2).

The issue of guidelines may be placed within the third framework. Guidelines necessarily deal with female and male reference. A major concern is the invisibility and derogation of female referents in language(s), asymmetrical practices in referring to females and males, and stereotypical assumptions about femininity and masculinity as these manifest themselves in language use.

Guidelines are actively involved in 'doing gender', demonstrating how alternative femininities and masculinities may be performed by employing reformed linguistic practices, e.g., by referring to female politicians not only by social title plus last name (German *Frau Merkel* 'Mrs Merkel') but also by last name only (*Merkel*), a practice which in German is stereotypically associated with male reference (see Section 37.3.2). Guidelines identify traditional linguistic practices as transporting stereotypically gendered messages, where 'gendered' not only means separating females from males but also placing both genders in hierarchical frameworks which function according to the ideology 'male as norm'.

37.3 LANGUAGE REFORM

Alternatives for discriminatory wording have been proposed by feminist linguistic activists as well as language planning agencies since the 1970s (cf. Pauwels, 1998, 2003). The first proposals for the elimination of sexist practices emerged from academia, popular examples including Miller and Swift (1980 [1995]) for English, Guentherodt, Hellinger, Pusch and Trömel-Plötz (1980) and Hellinger and Bierbach (1993) for German, Sabatini (1986) for Italian, Instituto de la Mujer (1989) for Spanish, and *Au féminin: Guide de féminisation des titres de fonction et des textes* (1991) for Canadian French.

Guidelines are often designed for specific domains of use, e.g. a university, a trade union, or a publishing house; examples are McGraw-Hill (1972), Scott, Foresman and Company (1974), American Psychological Association (1977, rev. 1994), NCTE (National Council of Teachers of English) (1975, rev. 1985, rev. 2002), and UNESCO (1987, rev. 1999). They are intended to offer practical solutions which language users can apply freely to their own purposes; e.g. the NCTE guidelines offer suggestions for writing papers, preparing textbooks, designing oral presentations and developing curricula. Of course, bias-free educational materials are no guarantee that classroom discourse will also be bias-free, and it is essential to appreciate the role of the teacher as a mediator between the text and the learner (cf. Sunderland et al., 2002).

As instruments of language planning, reform proposals symbolize the dissonance between traditional prescription and alternative usage. In offering gender-fair alternatives, guidelines challenge the political and social status quo which is characterized by the use of 'generic' masculine/male expressions to refer to both sexes (cf. Cameron, 1995; Romaine, 1999: 293).

At this point, a cautionary note seems appropriate on what sexism in language means. Linguistic sexism may not be easy to identify; cf. Mills' (2008) distinction between *overt* and *indirect* sexism. Seemingly straightforward instances of sexism such as *the girls in the office* (referring to adult women) may – under specific pragmatic conditions – not be interpreted as offensive. Thus, in the analysis of sexism in language, contextual features such as public–private, formal–informal, or the behavioural conventions (including language) in certain communities of practice will generally have to be considered.

37.3.1 The psycholinguistic effects of masculine/male generics

Convincing arguments supporting language reform derive from psycholinguistic evidence demonstrating that the generic potential of masculine/male expressions is a myth. Psycholinguistic documentation is available for English (e.g. MacKay and Fulkerson 1979; Gastil, 1990; Switzer, 1990; Prentice, 1994), German (Irmen and Köhncke, 1996; Braun et al., 1998; Rothmund and Scheele, 2004; Irmen and Linner, 2005) and French (Houdebine, 1989; Houdebine-Gravaud, 1998), while empirical research on other languages is rare; among the exceptions are Braun (2000) for Turkish, Engelberg (2002) for Finnish and Hornscheidt (2006) for Swedish. Currently, an International European Research Network is being developed in which (psycho)linguists, cognitive psychologists, neuroscientists and social psychologists from six EU member states will investigate the cognitive representation of the sexes in their languages and the impact of gendered language on behaviour (see EU Framework Programmes, Marie Curie Initial Training Network Language, Cognition, and Gender; http://cordis. europa.eu/fp7).

In experimental studies on English, the focus has generally been on pronouns (generic *he*) and instances of generic *man* (*mankind, chairman*), while studies on German – and other languages with grammatical gender – have tested the effects of masculine personal nouns. Typically, informants will perform tasks like the following:

- read a story and give the story's protagonist a name
- complete sentences that require the use of anaphoric gendered pronouns
- create a story around a referent, thus constructing the referent as female or male
- decide whether a given sentence can refer to females or males
- draw figures to illustrate a sentence or story

- estimate the percentage of females/males in a given group of referents
- react to texts, e.g. job advertisements, that contain 'generic' masculine/male expressions or alternatives.

Overwhelmingly, the results of these studies demonstrate that androcentric generics invoke significantly more male than female imagery, i.e. the concept 'female' is not generally available when androcentric expressions are processed by language users. More generally, the studies support the view that language 'shapes and reinforces selected cognitive tendencies, usually those in conformity with widely accepted cultural practices and beliefs' (Frank and Treichler (eds), 1989: 9).

It seems ironic that at their 2008 Convention in Rotterdam, the Netherlands, ZONTA International, an organization of professional women whose policy is to advance the status of women worldwide (http://www.zonta.org), insisted on the continued use of the title *chairman* for their – exclusively female – international leaders and executives.

A note of caution is necessary relating to some unpredictable psycholinguistic effects of reform proposals. In empirical research on German, it was found that masculine generics did indeed produce significantly more male-specific imagery, but the various gender-inclusive alternatives did not necessarily produce a gender-symmetrical imagery (cf. Hellinger and Pauwels, 2007: 672ff.). Only long nominal splitting, e.g. *Wähler und Wählerinnen* 'voters; literally voters (m) and voters (f)' seems to produce a roughly symmetrical imagery of female and male referents, while abbreviated splitting (*Wähler/innen* 'voters') and neutral expressions such as *die Wahlberechtigten* 'voters; literally those eligible to vote' produced asymmetries of various kinds. Unexpectedly, the so-called 'internal I', a recent form of abbreviated splitting (*WählerInnen* 'voters'), tended to evoke an overly female imagery. It appears that 'internal I' has the effect of politically correct symbol signalling a pro-feminist attitude (cf. Kargl et al., 1997; Stahlberg and Sczesny, 2001: 138).

Finally, adding a footnote to explain that the masculine expressions used in the text are intended to include women turned out to be totally ineffective. In fact, this practice created an even stronger male bias than the use of generic masculine forms (cf. Rothmund and Scheele, 2004: 8). From this evidence it may be concluded that in languages with grammatical gender the only way to significantly increase the availability of the concept 'female' seems to be the use of multiple female-specific expressions throughout a text. Of course, there is an urgent need for research not only on the psycholinguistic effects of reformed usage in other languages but also on potential changes of belief systems and language ideologies.

37.3.2 Strategies of change

Female visibility

Generally, gender-fair language is characterized by the following principles: avoidance of false generics; female visibility; symmetrical gender-marking; and avoidance of stereotyping. However, these principles must be applied with care, acknowledging that languages have different structural properties that require individual solutions. In English, the derivation of lexically female nouns by suffixation is no longer productive, leaving only a few examples that are still used today (*actress, usherette, heroine*). One recent formation is *proette* 'female golf professional'. Typically, forms such as *poetess, aviatrix* 'female pilot' or *jockette* 'female jockey' tend to carry negative connotations having undergone processes of semantic slippage. In some notorious cases these processes have resulted in asymmetrical pairs like *governor–governess* or *major–majorette* where the meaning of the lexically female term cannot be derived from the morphologically simpler term. Similar examples can be found in many other languages:

- French *couturier* (m) 'fashion designer' vs *couturière* 'seamstress'
- Polish *sekretarz* (m) '(Party) secretary' vs *sekretarka* (f) 'secretary in an office'.

In English, female visibility is primarily recommended for pronouns (*she or he* as an alternative for generic *he*), for compounds ending in *-woman* (*camerawoman, congresswoman*), and in cases of explicit gendered reference, as in *female and male lawyers* where the use of *lawyers* alone might be interpreted as excluding females (covert gender). The major strategy to avoid false generics is neutralization, which includes instances of singular *they* (*a lawyer should look after their clients*) and the use of plural forms (*Americans like their coffee black* as an alternative for *an American likes his coffee black*).

By contrast, in languages with grammatical gender, agreement rules require that articles, adjectives or verbal forms which accompany masculine nouns or pronouns must also appear in the masculine gender. Such forms are a powerful means of communicating the message 'male as norm'. Also, in constructions that coordinate a feminine and a masculine noun, related satellite forms typically respond to the preceding masculine form, making the feminine noun invisible in agreement, as in this sentence from Polish (cf. Koniuszaniec and Błaszkowska, 2003: 263):

Adam i Ewa s¹ szczęśliwi (m)
'Adam (m) and Ewa (f) are happy (m)'

Therefore, in gender languages, female visibility suggests itself as the primary strategy to avoid false generics. However, this strategy will only be successful if the language has fully productive morphological mechanisms for the generation of feminine personal nouns, such as the German suffix *-in*. Since the 1970s, existing feminine personal nouns have been used more consistently in German, especially for individual reference, and a large number of new feminine nouns have been created: e.g. *Bundeskanzlerin* 'female Chancellor', *Bischöfin* 'female bishop', *Soldatin* 'female soldier', *Bankerin* 'female banker', *Fundraiserin* 'female fundraiser', etc. In addition, numerous compounds ending in *-frau* '-woman' have been added to the German lexicon, e.g. *Torfrau* 'female goalkeeper', *Geschäftsfrau* 'businesswoman', *Fachfrau* 'female expert', *Feuerwehrfrau* 'female firefighter', *Kneipenfrau* 'woman working in a pub', etc. (cf. Hellinger, 1995).

However, a language may have competing derivational mechanisms for the generation of feminine nouns. In addition, these mechanisms may not be fully productive or may produce formations with additional shades of meaning. This is the situation in French where female visibility requires multiple solutions (cf. Burr, 2003; Schafroth, 2003; Elmiger, 2008).

In France, the *Circulaire relative à la féminisation des noms de métier, fonction, grade ou titre* (1986) ['Circular with respect to the feminization of the names of professions, functions, grades or titles'] was mainly concerned with two issues: providing the morphological mechanisms for the feminization of existing masculine terms, and the prescription of use of the new formations in official communication. Some mechanisms of derivation are given in Table 37.2

However, there exists uncertainty and uneasiness among language users as to whether or not a feminine form should be used, and if so which suffix is the best choice. Also, some forms have become unacceptable today: e.g. the suffix *-esse* (*poétesse* 'female poet') and compounds such as *femme-policier* 'female police officer' (Burr, 2003: 122f).

Schafroth (2003: 99f) notes a reluctance among speakers to accept feminine terms for prototypically male and/or prestigious professions. He points out that morphologically regular feminine forms such as *ambassadrice* 'female ambassador', *conseillère* 'female consultant, advisor', or *inspectrice* 'female inspector' are used mainly for

Table 37.2 Mechanisms of derivation

French		English
Masculine	*Feminine*	
Suffixation by zero (*e muet* 'silent *e*') or orthographic *e*		
un architecte	*une architecte*	'an architect'
principal	*principale*	'director'
chef	*cheffe*	'boss'
délégué	*déléguée*	'delegate'
professeur	*professeure*	'professor'
Additive suffixation		
beur	*beurette*	'second-generation North African living in France'
avocat	*avocate*	'lawyer'
animateur	*animatrice*	'entertainment officer'
Suppletive suffixation		
cocher	*cochère*	'driver'
écrivain	*écrivaine*	'writer'
vigneron	*vigneronne*	'wine farmer'
acheteur	*acheteuse*	'consumer'

socially less important jobs or for charity functions. Female agents in more prestigious functions would rather be denoted by the respective masculine terms (*ambassadeur, conseiller, inspecteur*). Significantly, Édith Cresson, French Prime Minister from 1991 to 1992, was usually referred to by masculine labels in newspapers and journals: *le premier ministre* (m) and *le chef* (m) *du gouvernement* 'the head of government'. The debate about female visibility in French received momentum when the female ministers in the Jospin government requested to be addressed by a feminine title (*Madame la ministre* instead of *Madame le ministre*). In spite of fierce protest from the Académie Française, the denomination of women by feminine titles was legalized by the Prime Minister in 1998 (cf. Burr, 2003: 128).

From a postmodern perspective an increase of female visibility in language has been criticized as contributing to binary, essentialist symbolizations of gender (Bing and Bergvall, 1996: 18; Hornscheidt, 1998, 2002; Motschenbacher, 2006: 39ff.). Such practices would inadvertently reinforce female–male differences rather than promote a deconstructionst approach to gender as learned behaviour. This criticism ignores the fact that the categories [female] and [male] are deeply embedded in most social practices, including language. Gender is a fundamental category not only of kinship terminologies, address and honorific systems, and non-personal animate nouns, but also – especially in languages with grammatical gender – structures even morphological and syntactic systems.

Symmetrical gender-marking

Symmetrical gender-marking avoids expressions in which females are marked differently from their male counterparts, as in English *Barack Obama and Hillary,* or *the men and the girls* where the reference is to female adults. Such practices often portray the female as the lesser, more trivial category. In the German address phrase *Herrn Paul Müller und Frau* 'to Mr Paul Müller and wife', the female is identified not by name but by marital status alone. Typically, the address systems of many languages are characterized by various gendered asymmetries. Neutral terms are often used for males while female/feminine labels tend to transport additional information about the referent's marital status; cf. English *Mr* vs *Mrs, Miss, Ms*; German *Herr* vs *Frau, Fräulein,* Italian *Signor* vs *Signora, Signorina,* Spanish *Señor* vs *Señora, Señorita*; French *Monsieur* vs *Madame, Mademoiselle*. This forces language users to make choices in addressing female but not male referents.

In expressions that explicitly name both sexes, men will frequently be identified by a functional or professional title, while women simply receive a general social label, as in this example from German:

Frau (f) *Merkel und der* (m) *CSU-Vorsitzende Stoiber*
'Mrs Merkel and CSU-leader Stoiber'

The use of last name alone to refer to women (*Merkel*) continues to be a loaded practice. In a study which analysed more than 1600 references to German politicians in four German newspapers, covering the period from October 2005 to January 2006, i.e. immediately before and after Angela Merkel's election as German Chancellor, the use of first and last names was found to be indicative of the paper's respective political and ideological profile (cf. Hellinger, 2006b). Conservative papers like the *Frankfurter Allgemeine Zeitung* avoid the use of last name only to refer to women, a practice which is common in more liberal papers like *Die Zeit*. The use of social title plus last name (*Frau Merkel*) emerges as a female-specific mechanism, since overwhelmingly female but very few male politicians are thus identified. In political discourse as elsewhere, an excessive emphasis on femininity where a corresponding emphasis on masculinity does not occur creates gendered asymmetries. It may be argued that the newspapers' labelling practices not only contribute to the symbolization of referents as gendered beings, but that underlying the choice of referential labels are opposing gender ideologies.

Similarly, instances of excessive and unnecessary female visibility, as in English *woman driver, lady philosopher* or *authoress*, Japanese *joseiki-sha* 'literally woman.reporter', or Indonesian *dokter perempuan* 'literally doctor.woman', may be interpreted as depicting female referents as an exception from the (male) norm. In gender languages, the combination of a feminine/female-specific noun with a masculine modifier creates similar asymmetries, cf. French *une femme ingénieur* 'literally a (f) woman (f) engineer (m)', *une jeune femme médicin* 'literally a (f) young woman (f) doctor (m)'; Ital. *la donna medico* 'literally the (f) woman (f) doctor (m)'. Compare also Italian *il iudice donna* 'literally the (m) lawyer (m) woman (f)', where a masculine noun is combined with a feminine/female-specific noun. In all these cases, guidelines will recommend symmetrical expressions, in particular avoidance of redundant female-specific identification in genderless languages, but the use of feminine occupational and functional labels in gender languages.

Avoidance of stereotyping

Stereotyping portrays women as sexualized beings by emphasizing their physical features, reproductive capacities and functions as caretakers (English *mothering, working mother, housewife*; French *le beau sexe, le deuxième sexe* 'the beautiful/second sex, women'). The secondary status of women is further symbolized through practices which identify women in terms of their relationship to men; examples are women's courtesy titles and the practice of women changing their name upon marriage (cf. Hellinger and Pauwels, 2007: 653).

Comparing a woman's achievements to those of men, as in *she was a second Einstein*, or *she has balls* (intended as a 'compliment') results in an elevated status for the woman, while the reverse, i.e. comparing a male to a female, as in *he is effeminate* or *he is a sissy*, has a demeaning effect. Examples where a man benefits from being compared to a famous woman (*he is a second Madonna; he is a male Jeanne d'Arc*) are rare. The same behaviour may be evaluated differently depending on whether it is performed by a male or female agent, cf. English *outspoken men* vs *hysterical women* or *ambitious men vs aggressive women*.

Among instances of stereotyping are expressions which portray women and men as representatives of traditional gender hierarchies, where women typically occupy the lower (paid) and less prestigious ranks. The following examples are from German:

Die ideale Beziehung: Sekretärinnen und ihre Chefs
  'The ideal relationship: Secretaries (f) and their bosses (m)'
Wo Krankenschwestern den Arzt ersetzen müssen
  'Where nurses (f) will have to replace the doctor (m)'
Professoren, Putzfrauen und Pförtner
  'professors (m), cleaning women (f) and janitors (m)'

Avoidance of stereotyping, especially in texts about categories of people rather than particular individuals, can easily be achieved by the choice of alternative lexical items, e.g., *parenting, child-rearing*, or *fussing* (if a pejorative sense is intended) for *mothering*, or *delicate, gentle, languid* and many others for *effeminate*.

37.4 THE PUBLIC DISCOURSE ON NON-DISCRIMINATORY LANGUAGE

37.4.1 Language politics

The UNESCO guidelines of 1987 are an early example of international language politics. Originally, the titles of both the French and the English edition made explicit reference to linguistic sexism (*Pour un Langage Non Sexiste; Guidelines on Non-Sexist Language*). In the 1999 edition, the title of the French version was modified to *Pour l'Égalité des Sexes dans le Langage*, emphasizing gender equality, while the new English title *Guidelines on Gender-Neutral Language* indicates that neutralization rather than female visibility is the preferred reform strategy in English (see Hellinger, 2004, 2006a).

Repeatedly (e.g. in 1987, 1989, 1991, 1995), UNESCO's General Conference has discussed the question of the elimination of sexist language from all UNESCO Basic Texts which must be produced in UNESCO's six working languages, i.e. English, French, Spanish, Russian, Arabic and Chinese. In 1994, the General Conference adopted a resolution stating its conviction that gender-neutral wording 'may alter attitudes and expectations that now constitute a barrier to achieving equality of opportunity for women and men' (UNESCO, 1994: 1). It is significant that the 1999 UNESCO guidelines make reference to global legislation: the Universal Declaration of Human Rights (1948), the Convention Against Discrimination in Education (1960) and the Convention on the Elimination of all Forms of Discrimination Against Women (1979); see http://www.un.org/womenwatch (since January 2008, see the website of the *UN Office of the High Commissioner for Human Rights* http://www2.ohchr.org/; accessed 20 January 2009).

On the national level, guidelines also tend to refer to larger legislative frameworks. For example, many German guidelines quote from the German constitution (GG *Grundgesetz*) which in Art. 3 para. 2 calls for equality of opportunity for women and men in all domains of life (work sphere, education, social and public services). The German Civil Code (BGB *Bürgerliches Gesetzbuch*) rules that – except in such special cases as prison personnel, the military or religious institutions – a job must not be advertised only for men or only for women. Similar references to legislative authorities can be found in guidelines for other languages, e.g. Austrian German (Kargl et al., 1997); Swiss German (Swiss Report, 1991; Schiedt and Kamber, 2004); Welsh (Awbery, Jones and Morris, 2002); and Dutch (Werkgroup, 1982).

In spite of the impressive rhetoric displayed by UNESCO's General Conference, the practical consequences of the reform measures were minimal, since non-discriminatory replacements for male/masculine generics were largely modelled on English. Only a small number of androcentric expressions were replaced by gender-inclusive or gender-indefinite alternatives For example:

- English *(chair)man, mankind* → *(chair)person, humanity*
- French *homme* → *la personne humaine, l'individu*
- Spanish *hombres* → *los seres humanos, las personas*

Not only is neutralization the favoured reform strategy but also it is claimed that the continued linguistic invisibility of women is no problem in the UNESCO languages with grammatical gender (French, Spanish, Russian and Arabic), since 'the generic use of the masculine form for post titles for both sexes is considered acceptable' (UNESCO, 1994: 4). In fact, a decision was made to the effect that all UNESCO documents must simply carry a footnote explaining that any person-denoting term is to be interpreted as referring equally to women and men. This decision ignores empirical evidence which has demonstrated, e.g. for German, that such a footnote is the least effective instrument to achieve a gender-inclusive imagery (cf. Section 37.3.1). It also ignores national guidelines which take a much more diversified approach to non-discriminatory language reform in that they acknowledge language-specific properties.

In Europe, the Committee of Ministers of the Council of Europe adopted the UNESCO recommendations on the use of non-sexist language in 1990 (Council of Europe, 1990), and in 2003 the European Parliament recalled that 'the sexism reflected in language is an obstacle to equality between men and women' (EU, 2003: 8). The use of non-discriminatory language in all EU documents was mandatory, 'since equality is one of the democratic values of the European Union' (EU, 2003: 30). Considering past legislation in EU member states, one should not be overly optimistic as to the practical consequences of such statements for language use outside EU institutions. For example, in 1990, the German Federal Government adopted the following solutions for legal language (*Rechtssprache*): it recommends female visibility in official language (*Amtssprache*), i.e. the language used in administrative communication, personal documents, educational material, etc., but supports the continued use of masculine generics in legislative language (*Vorschriftensprache*), i.e. the language used in decrees, laws, etc. (cf. Hellinger, 1995: 305ff.).

Similarly in France, at the Prime Minister's request the *Commission générale de terminologie et de néologie* (1998) produced a report on the feminization of job titles, functional labels and academic titles (cf. Burr, 2003: 128ff.). The Commission makes a fundamental distinction between *espace public* 'public sphere' and *espace privé* 'private sphere', for which different and sometimes contradictory recommendations were made. For example, since a woman's professional title or address label was considered part of the private sphere, it was left to the woman's decision whether or not she would request or use a feminized form. In statutory or legal texts, however, or in cases where a title did not refer to an individual but to the function itself, the use of generic masculines continued to be mandatory.

A considerably more progressive approach to changes in legal language was taken by the Swiss authorities (see Hellinger, 1995: 307ff.). Although the Swiss Report of 1991 also distinguishes between administrative language and legislative language, the guidelines are intended to apply to both varieties. Significantly, the implementation of non-sexist guidelines is interpreted as a measure of language policy far more important than, say, the much debated spelling reform. It is acknowledged that in everyday Swiss German more and more androcentric expressions are being replaced by forms of splitting, with the result that masculine personal nouns are increasingly losing their generic potential. There is an urgent need for more documentation of language policies in different countries, of language-specific recommendations, and of the implementation of reform measures in various domains of use.

37.4.2 *Voices of resistance*

Public responses to feminist language politics have frequently revealed openly hostile reactions, maintaining that reformed usage violates grammar, is cumbersome and unaesthetic and interferes with freedom of speech (cf. Ehrlich and King, 1994; Cameron, 1995: 132ff.). By contrast, supporters of reformed usage adhere to various degrees of linguistic relativity, suggesting that a change in behaviour, i.e. using more instances of non-sexist language, will enlarge the mental space of female imagery and weaken the male-as-norm ideology, thus contributing to social change.

The major strategies of resistance are the following (cf. Blaubergs, 1980; Hellinger, 1997):

1 It is denied that linguistic discrimination exists. Subscribing to the view that language is a neutral instrument of communication, it is claimed that androcentric expressions do not contribute to the linguistic marginalization of women, and that therefore change is unnecessary. This view is contradictory in that it cannot explain why only gender-inclusive but not androcentric expressions would violate the ideology of language as a neutral instrument of communication.

2 Change is unnecessary, since language is simply a reflection of reality. Language change will follow social change. This view not only ignores the fact that language is instrumental in shaping speakers' perceptions and interpretations of reality but also its potential as an instrument of social practice, and more specifically, of social protest.

3 Gender-inclusive formulations, especially instances of female visibility, are interpreted as an obstacle to emancipation, since they are interpreted as substituting the male norm by a female norm. This is a false argument since it distorts the fundamental aim of non-discriminatory guidelines: namely, the equal linguistic representation of both sexes. The replacement of generic masculine/male expressions by generic feminine/female expressions has never been part of proposals for gender-fair wording.

4 Reform measures are applied to cases which require no change, with the intended effect that the reform as such is ridiculed. In gender languages, this may produce examples such as German *die Grünen und Grüninnen* 'literally the Greens (m) and Greens (f), i.e. male and female members of the Green Party'. Of course, the formation *Grüninnen* is ungrammatical, since in German, nominalized adjectival plural forms such as *die Grünen* or *die Reichen* 'the rich' are not specified for grammatical gender. Another example is *Führerinnenschein* 'drivers' (f) licence'; German guidelines have not proposed changes to non-personal compounds which contain a masculine form, as in *Bürgersteig*, 'sidewalk, literally citizens' (m) walk' or *Raucherzimmer* 'smoking room, literally smokers' (m) room'. There are a few exceptions, as when the compound refers explicitly to an all-female membership, e.g. *Deutscher Juristinnenbund* 'German Association of Female Lawyers'. Another provocative although creative case is this example: *Frau Ministerin, wir haben eine(n) Vorschlag/Idee* 'Mrs Minister, we have a suggestion (m)/an idea (f)'. The strategy of splitting, i.e. making explicit reference to both a female and male referent, is here applied to non-personal abstract nouns, thus distorting and discrediting original recommendations.

5 Reform measures are interpreted as undemocratic since they are believed to violate the principle of freedom of speech. In the past, however, no such arguments have accompanied the prescription of masculine/male generics. In addition, the domain of non-discriminatory language politics is official language, while no proposals have been made – nor can be made – for private language.

6 It is claimed that the use of 'generic' masculine/male expressions is simply the result of tradition, based on social agreement. This argument is unfounded, since 'social agreement' really means prescription by influential authorities such as grammars, stylebooks and language academies. Again, the potential of language as an agent in social change is ignored.

7 On the stylistic level, reform measures are seen as offending the principle of linguistic economy. Frequent instances of (pro)nominal splitting are interpreted as cumbersome and unaesthetic. However, making a choice between stylistic elegance and non-discriminatory formulations is unnecessary in most cases, since guidelines generally recommend various strategies or 'creative

solutions', rather than the application of only one reform measure.

Among examples that illustrate how reform proposals can be applied creatively, resulting in texts that remain comprehensible and readable, is the gender-inclusive version of the Constitution of the German Federal State of Lower Saxony. A comparison between the original version of 1951, which consistently used generic masculine expressions, and the revised version of 1993 supports the hypothesis that repeated instances of splitting, but also the use of gender-indefinite wording and other devices, will considerably reduce the text's male bias, creating an awareness of female participation in all constitutional and legal matters (cf. Dietrich, 2000).

37.4.3 Political correctness

The arguments presented by opponents to gender-inclusive language reform are reminiscent of debates about 'politically correct speech'. Originally, political correctness denoted behaviour conforming to a political party's ideology (cf. Berman, 1992; Perry, 1992; Peterson, 1994; Wirthgen, 1999). In the 1980s, the term was applied by the American political left to the implementation of liberal ideas on American university campuses, which included recognition of ethnic, sexual, religious and cultural diversity. The term was later used by the political right in the USA to discredit leftist politics. Conservative criticism denounced 'politically correct' (PC) language as enforced orthodoxy, censorship, and thought control. While many terms have since found wide acceptance (*African-American* for *Black, Native American* for *Indian, Inuit* for *Eskimo, senior citizen* for *old age pensioner*, or *disabled* for *handicapped*), others like *physically challenged* have invited critical, and often ironic commentary, i.e. creations such as *vertically challenged* for *short* or *visually challenged* for *blind* (for an analysis of PC see Cameron, 1995: Ch. 4). In Germany, the use of terms like *Ausländer* or *Türken* has been criticized by some people as implying racist attitudes; however, alternative wordings such as *Menschen mit Migrationshintergrund* 'people with a migratory background' or *Mitbürger türkischer Herkunft* 'fellow citizens of Turkish heritage' have been criticized as euphemistic and overly considerate (on political correctness, especially from a discourse analytical perspective, see the special issue of *Discourse and Society*, Vol. 14, 2003).

'Politically correct' terminology is largely concerned with the lexical-semantic level. Typically, recommendations consist of lists of words which

are interpreted as (potentially) offensive, and suggestions of bias-free alternatives (cf. Beard and Cerf, 1994, 1995). For example, the *Dictionary of Cautionary Words and Phrases* (1989), published by the Multicultural Management Program, contains some 230 nouns and adjectives, plus some verbs and idiomatic expressions, which are characterized as demeaning or offensive; cf. these examples:

> *Ghetto*: Avoid use. Has become a stereotype for poor minority community.
> *Latin lover*: A stereotype alluding to Latino sexual prowess. Avoid use.
> *Oriental*: Unacceptable to some Asian-Americans. Use Asian-American or Asian(s).

Compared to such wordlists, guidelines for gender-fair usage have a much wider range of application. They involve complex systems of personal reference that include not only central lexical fields such as kinship terms, occupational terms, functional labels, or address systems but also domains of grammar (pronominalization, agreement) and word-formation (derivation and compounding).

37.5 EVALUATING THE IMPACT OF GUIDELINES FOR NON-DISCRIMINATORY LANGUAGE

To date, there is a lack of empirical data documenting the impact of guidelines in various domains of use. An evaluation of reform measures presents considerable problems, since the spread of non-discriminatory practices is never just the result of language policies alone. Among the non-linguistic factors influencing processes of language change are the historical, cultural and ideological contexts of the individual language. For example, does the country have a tradition of language politics and of public discourse about issues of language more generally, e.g. about spelling reform, linguistic 'purity', or interference from other languages ('anglicisms')? Is there a belief that the language should be saved from 'decay' by opposing any change? Has the country experienced a major feminist movement which has recognized the feminist critique of language as a site of social change? Does the country have influential key agents or popular role models who will motivate others to adopt alternative practices?

A decrease in the use of masculine/male generics has been observed in English and a number of Western languages (cf. Ehrlich and King, 1994; Rubin et al., 1994, Pauwels, 1998). However, this change may not really be symbolic of pro-feminist attitudes. There may be opportunism involved or simply experimentation with stylistic variability. At the same time, processes of change may not necessarily reflect the original intentions of language reformers. Below I present three examples of observed change which indicate that change spreads in non-linear fashion across contexts and domains of use.

37.5.1 Job advertising in German

Since 1980, the German Civil Code (Para. 611b BGB) has required that employers use non-discriminatory language in job advertising as one measure to achieve equal opportunities for women and men in the work sphere (cf. Hellinger and Pauwels, 2007: 670ff.). In 1998, in the process of adapting German national law to the guidelines of the European Union, the regulation was changed from optional to obligatory. Employers must not advertise a job or post only for men or only for women. Exceptions include domains such as the medical profession, prisons or the fashion industry, where only male or only female applicants are acceptable.

Since then, changes in advertising practices have resulted in a steady increase in gender-fair language. In a study of 1987, only 21% of the 6000 advertisements analysed adhered to gender-inclusive wording (Brockhoff, 1987), while 10 years later the percentage had risen to some 45% (Oldenburg, 1998). More recent studies (Greve et al., 2002; Hellinger, 2004: 286ff.) have documented an increase in gender-inclusive language to over 70%. However, variability within each corpus may be considerable, depending on the type of newspaper (e.g. national or local, print or online version), the paper's political affiliation, and the type of job advertised (manual or professional). For example, Hellinger's (2004) analysis of some 900 advertisements found that the national quality weekly *Die Zeit*, which advertises prestigious posts in the civil/public service, in universities, research centres and (inter)national companies, used gender-inclusive wording in well over 90% of advertisements, while regional newspapers such as *Hannoversche Allgemeine* or *Frankfurter Rundschau*, which offer a much wider range of jobs, still used some 30% of discriminatory language. One local newspaper, *Wiesbadener Kurier*, still contained an exceptional 50% of sexist advertisements even in 2003. This evidence suggests that not only is there an urgent need for the documentation of (non)sexist practices in more languages but also for more data from various domains of use within a language.

37.5.2 Alternatives to generic he in English

In English, the most widely promoted alternatives to generic *he* are instances of pronominal splitting (*he or she*), generic *she*, and singular *they* (for a discussion of other alternatives, see Pauwels, 1998). As a consequence, a decrease in the use of generic *he* has been observed in English since the 1980s (Cooper, 1984; Markovitz, 1984; Rubin et al., 1994). In more recent analyses of newspapers, academic texts and TV interviews, singular *they* has been found to be the preferred alternative when reference is to antecedents such as *person, anyone,* or *everyone* (Newman, 1997; Baranowski, 2002). Singular *they* has also emerged as the preferred choice in most forms of spoken language, including formal public speech (e.g., Pauwels, 2001, 2003). The use of generic *he* is becoming the exception rather than the rule in North American, Australian and New Zealand varieties of English, while in British English and the 'new' Englishes, generic *he* continues to dominate, e.g., in Singapore by nearly 90%, and the Philippines by some 70% (cf. Pauwels and Winter, 2004a, 2004b). Previous research has focused on educational domains such as high school classrooms, the university campus, the lecture hall, and faculty meetings as the main sites of change, while there is a lack of documentation in other contexts.

37.5.3 Address terms for women

Frau/Fräulein in German
Since 1937, German Ministers of the Interior have repeatedly dealt with the issue of asymmetrical address terms, i.e. *Herr* 'Mr' vs *Frau* 'Mrs', *Fräulein* 'Miss', the latter term expressing the meaning 'unmarried woman' but often additional connotations such as 'single', 'young', 'immature', or 'having no children'. In 1972, the use of *Fräulein* was officially banned from public communication by legislation, since it was no longer acceptable that adult women should be treated differently from adult men (cf. Hellinger, 2004: 284ff.)). While the label *Fräulein* has largely disappeared from official usage, it has survived in informal communication, mainly as a derogatory term.

In a study of the language practices among teenage speakers in East and West Germany (Reiss, 2007: 174), it was found that the use of *Fräulein* was associated with a large number of meanings, among them 'young', 'unmarried', 'still a virgin', 'still living with parents', and 'having no children'. Contexts in which informants would still use or hear the term included: addressing a female waiter, as a derogatory term for a kindergarten or primary teacher, or used by the informant's mother when angry.

In Austria, the history of gender-fair language dates back to the 1980s, an early influential text being Wodak et al. (1987). A decade later, a comprehensive treatment of the theoretical as well as practical problems of feminist language reform was published by the Austrian Ministry for Women (Kargl et al., 1997). A more recent concise example is 'Geschlechtergerechtes Formulieren' 'gender-fair formulating' (Wetschanow, 2002). Occasionally, more specific issues are addressed in ministerial circulars; thus in 2008, the Federal Ministry for Education, Science and Culture issued a statement concerning academic titles for women: while officially feminine forms are not recommended, a woman may choose to use *Mag.a* or *Dr.in* rather than the traditional masculine forms (see http://www.bmukk.gv.at/schulen/unterricht/ba/sprachliche_gleichbehandlung.xml; accessed 21 January 2009).

Similarly, in Switzerland, the public discourse on feminist language reform began in the 1980s. In 1988 the Swiss Federal Government set up an interdepartmental working group on non-sexist language which considered not only Swiss German but also French and Italian, the other two official languages of Switzerland (Swiss Report, 1991). One field of reform was legal language, where the Swiss Report recommended female visibility not only in administrative language but also in legislative language. Comparable recommendations by the German Bundestag (BRD Report, 1991) were much less progressive, supporting for legislative language the status quo, i.e. the continued use of generic masculine expressions, rather than more gender-fair solutions (see Hellinger, 1995: 306ff.). Among popular Swiss guidelines are Häberlin et al. (1992), Schweizerische Bundeskanzlei (1996) and Schiedt and Kamber (2004).

Today, most Swiss (inter)national organizations and institutions have their own guidelines, as, for example, Amnesty International Switzerland (see http://www.amnesty.ch; accessed 4 February 2009), or one of the numerous guidelines published by Swiss universities, e.g. the University of Bern (http://www.gleichstellung.uniber.ch; accessed 4 February 2009).

Mrs/Miss/Ms in English
While the disappearance of *Fräulein* in official German has created a symmetrical pair of address terms (*Frau/Herr*), thus simplifying the German address system, the reverse process can be observed in English. The new formation *Ms*, intended by reformers as a semantically neutral

title which is indifferent to the referent's marital status, has not replaced *Miss*. In addition, adoption of the term presents a mixed picture across varieties of English. Although the use of *Ms* has increased significantly among Australian women, users are not agreed upon the promoted interpretation of the term. Rather, the term has taken on a number of unintended meanings, from 'separated', 'divorced', 'living in a de facto relationship', to 'feminist' and 'lesbian' (cf. Pauwels, 2001: 142).

Studies on the adoption of non-sexist expressions include: Pauwels (2003) on Australian English; Baranowski (2002), Ehrlich and King (1994) and Romaine (2001) on American and British English; Holmes (2001) on New Zealand English; and Pauwels and Winter (2004a, 2004b) on postcolonial Englishes. Whereas most of these studies document an increase of non-discriminatory usage, acceptance varies considerably across the global varieties of English:

> The United States and Canada lead the way by a small margin from Australia and New Zealand. Britain lags quite a bit behind these countries. Least evidence of non-sexist language use is found in the postcolonial varieties of English in the Philippines, Singapore and Hong Kong [...] .
> (Hellinger and Pauwels, 2007: 673)

37.6 CONCLUSION

The empirical research on gender-related language practices as well as the analysis of discourses about gender-inclusive language support the hypothesis that word meanings are not pre-discursively given, nor can they be determined by prescriptive measures. Rather, word meanings are continuously being negotiated in a speech community. As one instrument of challenging hegemonic assumptions about what masculine/male expressions actually refers to, guidelines have provoked many voices of resistance. Conservative criticism has deliberately distorted reform proposals and ignored empirical evidence that has decomposed the myth of the generic potential of androcentric expressions. Frequently, opponents to non-discriminatory wording, and to female visibility in particular, have resorted to the 'language of war' (cf. German *der radikal-feministische Geschlechterkampf um Worte* 'the radical-feminist war of the sexes about words') demonstrating that the reform is anything but trivial. It may be concluded that an increase in gender-inclusive language is symbolic not only of women's active role in defining word meanings, but more generally, in ongoing political struggles over the equal participation of women in all public domains.

REFERENCES

American Psychological Association (1994) *Guidelines to Reduce Bias in Language*. (Originally *Guidelines for Non-Sexist Language in APA Journals*, 1977.)

Au féminin (1991) *Au féminin: guide de féminisation des titres de fonction et des textes*. (Guide de l'Office de la langue française.) Québec: Publications du Québec.

Awbery, Gwenllian, Jones, Kathryn and Morris, Delyth (2002) 'The politics of language and gender in Wales', in Marlis Hellinger and Hadumod Bussmann (eds), *Gender Across Language. The Linguistic Representation of Women and Men*. Amsterdam: John Benjamins. pp. 313–30.

Baranowski, Maciej (2002) 'Current usage of the epicene pronoun in written English', *Journal of Sociolinguistics*, 6: 378–97.

Beard, Henry and Cerf, Christopher (1994) *The Official Politically Correct Dictionary and Handbook*. New York: Random House.

Beard, Henry and Cerf, Christopher (1995) *The Official Sexually Correct Dictionary and Dating Guide*. New York: Villard Books.

Bergvall, Victoria L., Bing, Janet M. and Freed, Alice F. (eds) (1996) *Rethinking Language and Gender Research: Theory and Practice*. London: Longman.

Berman, Paul (1992) *Debating P.C.: The Controversy Over Political Correctness on College Campuses*. New York: Delta Publishing.

Bing, Janet M. and Bergvall, Victoria L. (1996) 'The question of questions: beyond binary thinking', in Victoria L. Bergvall, Janet M. Bing and Alice F. Freed (eds), *Rethinking Language and Gender Research: Theory and Practice*. London: Longman. pp. 1–30.

Blaubergs, Maija S. (1980) 'An analysis of classic arguments against changing sexist language', in Cheris Kramarae, (ed.), *The Voices and Words of Women and Men*. Oxford: Pergamon. pp. 135–47.

Boroditsky, Lera (2003) 'Linguistic relativity', in Lynn Nadel, (ed.), *Encyclopaedia of Cognitive Science*. London: Macmillan. pp. 917–22.

Braun, Friederike (2000) *Geschlecht im Türkischen. Untersuchungen zum sprachlichen Umgang mit einer sozialen Kategorie*. Wiesbaden: Harrassowitz.

Braun, Friederike, Gottburgsen, Anja, Sczesny, Sabine and Stahlberg, Dagmar (1998) 'Können Geophysiker Frauen sein? Generische Personenbezeichnungen im Deutschen', *Zeitschrift für Germanistische Linguistik*, 26: 265–83.

BRD Report (1991) *Maskuline und feminine Personenbezeichnungen in der Rechtssprache. Bericht der Arbeitsgruppe Rechtssprache vom 17. Januar 1990*. Deutscher Bundestag. Drucksache 12/1041.1991.

Brockhoff, Evamaria (1987) 'Wie fragt Mann nach Frauen?', *Die Zeit*, 2 January 1987.

Burr, Elisabeth (2003) 'Gender and language politics in France', in Marlis Hellinger and Hodumod Bussmann (eds), *Gender Across Languages. The Linguistic Representation of Women and Men*, Amsterdam: John Benjamins. pp. 119–39.

Butler, Judith (1990) *Gender Trouble: Feminism and the Subversion of Identity*. New York: Routledge.

Butler, Judith (2004) *Undoing gender*. New York: Routledge.

Cameron, Deborah (1992) *Feminism and Linguistic Theory*. 2nd edn. London: Macmillan.

Cameron, Deborah (1995) *Verbal Hygiene*. London: Routledge.

Coates, Jennifer (2004) *Women, Men and Language. A Sociolinguistic Account of Gender Differences in Language*. 3rd edn. Harlow: Longman.

Cooper, Robert L. (1984) 'The avoidance of androcentric generics', *International Journal of the Sociology of Language*, 59: 5–20.

Council of Europe (1990) *Recommendation No. R(90)4 on the Elimination of Sexism from Language*. http://portal.unesco.org; accessed 21 January 2009.

Dictionary of Cautionary Words and Phrases (1989) University of Columbia, MO: Multicultural management program.

Dietrich, Margot (2000) '"Gerechtigkeit gegenüber jedermann" – "Gerechtigkeit gegenüber allen Menschen". Sprachliche Gleichbehandlung am Beispiel der Verfassung des Landes Niedersachsen', in Karin M. Eichhoff-Cyrus, and Rudolf Hoberg, (eds), *Die deutsche Sprache zur Jahrtausendwende: Sprachkultur oder Sprachverfall?* Mannheim: Dudenverlag. pp. 192–223.

Eckert, P. and McConnell-Ginet, S. (2003) *Language and gender*. Cambridge: Cambridge University Press.

Ehrlich, Susan and King, Ruth (1994) 'Feminist meanings and the (de)politicization of the lexicon', *Language in Society*, 23: 59–76.

Eichhoff-Cyrus, Karin M. (ed.) (2004) *Adam, Eva und die Sprache. Beiträge zur Geschlechterforschung*. Mannheim: Dudenverlag.

Elmiger, Daniel (2008) *La féminisation de la langue en Français et en Allemand*. Paris: Honoré Champion.

Engelberg, Mila (2002) 'The communication of gender in Finnish', in Marlis Hellinger and Hadumod Bussmann (eds), *Gender Across Language. The Linguistic Representation of Women and Men*, Amsterdam: John Benjamins. pp. 109–32.

European Union (EU) (2003) European Parliament 1999–2004. Session document. Final A5-0053/2003.

Frank, Francine W. and Treichler, Paula A. (eds) (1989) *Language, Gender, and Professional Writing: Theoretical Approaches and Guidelines for Nonsexist Usage*. New York: MLA.

Freed, Alice F. (1996) 'Language and gender research in an experimental setting', in Victoria L. Bergvall, Janet M. Bing and Alice F. Freed (eds), *Rethinking Language and Gender Research: Theory and Practice*. London: Longman. pp. 54–76.

Gastil, John (1990) 'Generic pronouns and sexist language: the oxymoronic character of masculine generics', *Sex Roles*, 23: 629–43.

Greve, Melanie, Iding, Marion and Schmusch, Bärbel (2002) 'Geschlechtsspezifische Formulierungen in Stellenangeboten', *Linguistik Online,* 11(2) http://www.linguistik-online.org/11_02/greschmid.html.

Guentherodt, Ingrid, Hellinger, Marlis, Pusch, Luise F. and Trömel-Plötz, Senta (1980), 'Richtlinien zur Vermeidung sexistischen Sprachgebrauchs', *Linguistische Berichte,* 69: 15–21.

Häberlin, Susanna, Schmid, Rachel and Wyss, Eva Lia (1992) *Übung macht die Meisterin. Ratschläge für einen nicht-sexistischen Sprachgebrauch.* München: Frauenoffensive.

Hall, Kira and Bucholtz, Mary (eds) (1995) *Gender Articulated: Language and the Socially Constructed Self.* New York: Routledge.

Harrington, Kate, Litosseliti, Pia, Sauntson, Helen and Sunderland, Jane (eds) (2008) *Gender and Language Research Methodologies.* London: Palgrave Macmillan.

Hellinger, Marlis (1991) 'Feminist linguistics and linguistic relativity', *Working Papers on Language, Gender and Sexism,* 1(1): 25–37.

Hellinger, Marlis (1995) 'Language and gender', in Patrick Stevenson (ed.), *The German Language and the Real World.* Oxford: Clarendon. pp. 279–314.

Hellinger, Marlis (1997) 'The discourse of distortion: inclusive language policies and political correctness', in Friederike Braun and Ursula Pasero (eds), *Kommunikation von Geschlecht – Communication of Gender.* Pfaffenweiler: Centaurus. pp. 164–82.

Hellinger, Marlis (2004) 'Empfehlungen für einen geschlechtergerechten Sprachgebrauch im Deutschen', in Karin M. Eichhoff-Cyrus (ed.), *Adam, Eva und die Sprache: Beiträge zur Geschlechterforschung.* Mannheim: Dudenverlag. pp. 275–91.

Hellinger, Marlis (2006a) ‚Sexist language', in *Encyclopedia of Language and Linguistics.* 2nd edn. Vol. XI. Oxford: Elsevier. pp. 265–72.

Hellinger, Marlis (2006b) 'Why Merkel is not enough: on the representation of fe/male politicians in German newspapers'. Paper presented at IGALA 4, Valencia, Spain.

Hellinger, Marlis and Bierbach, Christine (1993) *Eine Sprache für beide Geschlechter. Richtlinien für einen nicht-sexistischen Sprachgebrauch.* Bonn: UNESCO.

Hellinger, Marlis and Bussmann, Hadumod (eds) (2001–03) *Gender Across Languages. The Linguistic Representation of Women and Men.* 3 Vols. Amsterdam: John Benjamins.

Hellinger, Marlis and Pauwels, Anne (2007) 'Language and sexism', in Marlis Hellinger and Anne Pauwels (eds), *Handbook of Language and Communication: Diversity and Change.* (= *Handbooks of Applied Linguistics*, Vol. 9). Berlin: Mouton de Gruyter. pp. 651–84.

Hill, Jane H. (1988) 'Language, culture, and world view', in Frederick J. Newmeyer, (ed.), *Linguistics: The Cambridge Survey.* Vol. IV. Cambridge: Cambridge University Press. pp. 14–36.

Holmes, Janet (1995) *Women, Men, and Politeness.* London: Longman.

Holmes, Janet (2001) 'A corpus-based view of gender in New Zealand English', in Marlis Hellinger and Hadumod Bussmann (eds), *Gender Across Languages. The Linguistic Representation of Women and Men.* Amsterdam: John Benjamins pp. 115–36.

Holmes, Janet and Meyerhoff, Miriam (eds) (2003) *The Handbook of Language and Gender.* Oxford: Blackwell.

Hornscheidt, Antje (1998) 'Grammatik als Ort von Geschlechterkonstruktion. Eine kritische Analyse', in Antje, Hornscheidt, Gabriele Jähnert, and Annette Schlichter, (eds), *Kritische Differenzen – geteilte Perspektiven. Zum Verhältnis von Feminismus und Postmoderne.* Opladen: Westdeutscher Verlag. pp. 140–73.

Hornscheidt, Antje (2002) 'Die Nicht-Rezeption poststrukturalistischer Gender- und Sprachtheorien der Feministischen Linguistik im deutschsprachigen Raum', in Tamara Faschingbauer (ed.), *Neue Ergebnisse der empirischen Genderforschung.* Hildesheim: Georg Olms. pp. 5–51.

Hornscheidt, Antje (2006) *Die Sprachliche Benennung von Personen aus konstruktivistischer Sicht: Genderspezifizierung und ihre Diskursive Verhandlung im Heutigen Schwedisch.* Berlin: Mouton de Gruyter.

Houdebine, Anne Marie (1989) 'La féminisation des noms de métiers en français contemporain', in Georges Kassaï, (ed.), *Contrastes. La différence sexuelle dans le langage.* Nice: ADEC. pp. 39–71.

Houdebine-Gravaud, Anne Marie (1998) *La féminisation des noms de métiers. En Français et dans d'autres langues.* Paris: l'Harmattan.

Instituto de la Mujer (1989) *Propuestas para evitar el sexismo en el lenguaje.* Madrid: Instituto de la Mujer.

Irmen, Lisa and Köhncke, Astrid (1996) 'Zur Psychologie des "generischen" Maskulinums', *Sprache und Kognition,* 15: 152–66.

Irmen, Lisa and Linner, Ute (2005) 'Die Repräsentation generisch maskuliner Personenbezeichnungen. Eine theoretische Integration bisheriger Befunde', *Zeitschrift für Psychologie,* 213: 167–75.

Kargl, Maria, Wetschanow, Karin, Wodak, Ruth and Perle, Néla (1997) *Kreatives Formulieren. Anleitungen zu geschlechtergerechtem Sprachgebrauch.* Wien: Frauenministerium.

Kay, Paul and Kempton, Willett (1984) 'What is the Sapir-Whorf hypothesis?', *American Anthropologist,* 86: 65–79.

Koniuszaniec, Gabriela and Błaszkowska, Hanka (2003) 'Language and gender in Polish', in M. Hellinger and H. Bussmann (eds), *Gender Across Languages. The Linguistic Representation of Women and Men.* Amsterdam: John Benjamins. pp. 259–285.

Kotthoff, Helga and Wodak, Ruth (eds) (1997) *Communicating Gender.* Amsterdam: Benjamins.

Lakoff, George (1987) *Women, Fire, and Dangerous Things.* Chicago: University of Chicago Press.

Lakoff, Robin Tolmach (1975) *Language and Woman's Place.* New York: Harper and Row.

Lakoff, Robin Tolmach (2004) *Language and Woman's Place.* Ed. Mary Bucholtz. Oxford: Oxford University Press.

Lazar, Michelle M. (ed.) (2005) *Feminist Critical Discourse Analysis: Studies in Gender, Power and Ideology in Discourse.* London: Palgrave Macmillan.

Litosseliti, Lia and Sunderland, Jane (eds) (2002) *Gender Identity and Discourse Analysis*. Amsterdam: John Benjamins.

McGraw-Hill (1972) *Guidelines for Equal Treatment of the Sexes in McGraw-Hill Book Company Publications*. Highstown, NJ: McGraw-Hill.

MacKay, Donald and Fulkerson, David (1979) 'On the comprehension and production of pronouns', *Journal of Verbal Learning and Verbal Behavior*, 18: 661–73.

Markovitz, Judith (1984) 'The impact of the sexist language controversy and regulation on language in university documents', *Psychology of Women Quarterly*, 8(4): 337–47.

Miller, Casey and Swift, Kate (1995) *The Handbook of Non-Sexist Writing*. 3rd edn. London: The Women's Press. (1st edn, 1980.)

Mills, Sara (2003) *Gender and Politeness*. Cambridge: Cambridge University Press.

Mills, Sara (2008) *Language and Sexism*. Cambridge: Cambridge University Press.

Milroy, Lesley (1987) *Language and Social Networks*. Blackwell: Oxford.

Motschenbacher, Heiko (2006) *"Women and Men like Different Things"? Doing gender als Strategie der Werbesprache*. Marburg: Tectum.

NCTE (1975) *Guidelines for Nonsexist Use of Language in NCTE Publications*. National Council of Teachers of English (rev. 1985; rev. 2002).

Newman, Michael (1997) *Epicene Pronouns: The Linguistics of a Prescriptive Problem*. New York: Garland Publishing.

O'Barr, William and Atkins, Bowman K. (1980) '"Women's language" or "powerless language"?', in Sally. McConnell-Ginet, Ruth Borker, and Nelly Furman (eds), *Women and Language in Literature and Society*. New York: Praeger. pp. 93–110.

Oldenburg, Antje (1998) 'Von Arzthelfern, Bauschlosserinnen und anderen Berufstätigen', *Muttersprache*, 108: 67–80.

Pauwels, Anne (1998) *Women Changing Language*. London: Longman.

Pauwels, Anne (2001) 'Spreading the feminist word: the case of the new courtesy title *Ms* in Australian English', in Marlis Hellinger and Hadumod Bussmann (eds), *Gender Across Languages. The Linguistic Representation of Women and Men*. Amsterdam: Benjamins. pp.137–51.

Pauwels, Anne (2003) 'Linguistic sexism and feminist linguistic activism', in Janet Holmes and Miriam Meyerhoff (eds), *The Handbook of Language and Gender*. Oxford: Blackwell. pp. 550–70.

Pauwels, Anne and Winter, Joanne (2004a) 'Generic pronouns and gender-inclusive language reform in the English of Singapore and the Philippines', *Australian Review of Applied Linguistics*, 27(2): 50–62.

Pauwels, Anne and Winter, Joanne (2004b) 'Gender-inclusive language reform in educational writing in Singapore and the Philippines: a corpus-based approach', *Asian Englishes. An International Journal of the Sociolinguistics of English in Asia/Pacific*, 7(1): 4–21.

Perry, Ruth (1992) 'A short history of the term "politically correct"', in Patricia Aufderheide (ed.), *Beyond PC: Toward a Politics of Understanding*. Saint Paul. pp. 71–79.

Peterson, Eric E. (1994) 'Nonsexist language reform and "Political Correctness"', *Women and Language*, 17: 6–10.

Prentice, Deborah A. (1994) 'Do language reforms change our way of thinking?', *Journal of Language and Social Psychology*, 13(1): 3–19.

Pusch, Luise F. (1984) *Das Deutsche als Männersprache*. Frankfurt am, Main: Suhrkamp.

Reiss, Kristina (2007) *Gender-Sprachbewusstsein bei Jugendlichen in Ost und West*. Königstein (Ts): Ulrike Helmer Verlag.

Romaine, Suzanne (1999) *Communicating Gender*. Mahwah, NJ: Lawrence Erlbaum.

Romaine, Suzanne (2001) 'A corpus-based view of gender in British and American English', in Marlis Hellinger and Hadumod Bussmann (eds), *Gender Across Languages. The Linguistic Representation of Women and Men*. Amsterdam: John Benjamins. pp. 153–75.

Rothmund, Jutta and Scheele, Brigitte (2004) 'Personenbezeichnungsmodelle auf dem Prüfstand. Lösungsmöglichkeiten für das Genus-Sexus-Problem auf Textebene', *Zeitschrift für Psychologie*, 212: 40–54.

Rubin, Donald I., Greene, Kathryn and Schneider, Deirdra (1994) 'Adopting gender-inclusive language reforms. Diachronic and synchronic variation', *Journal of Language and Social Psychology*, 13(2): 91–114.

Sabatini, Alma (1986) *Raccomandazioni per un uso non sessista della lingua Italiana*. Roma: Presidenza del Consiglio dei Ministri.

Schafroth, Elmar (2003) 'Gender in French: structural properties, incongruences and asymmetries', in Marlis Hellinger and Hadumod Bussmann (eds), *Gender Across Languages. The Linguistic Representation of Women and Men*. Amsterdam: John Benjamins. pp. 87–117.

Schiedt, Margret and Kamber, Isabel (2004) 'Sprachliche Gleichbehandlung in der Schweizer Gesetzgebung: Das Parlament macht's möglich', in Karin M. Eichhoff-Cyrus (ed.), *Adam, Eva und die Sprache: Beiträge zur Geschlechterforschung schong*. Mannheim: Dudenverlag. pp. 332–48.

Schweizerische Bundeskanzlei (1996) *Leitfaden zur sprachlichen gleichbehandlung im Deutschen*. Bern: Schweizerische Bundeskanzlei. (abbreviated version 2006)

Scott, Foresman and Company (1974) *Guidelines for Improving the Image of Women in Textbooks*. Glenview, IL: Scott, Foresman and Company.

Spender, Dale (1980) *Man Made Language*. London: Routledge and Kegan Paul.

Stahlberg, Dagmar and Sczesny, Sabine (2001) 'Effekte des generischen Maskulinums und alternativer Sprachformen auf den gedanklichen Einbezug von Frauen', *Psychologische Rundschau*, 52: 131–40.

Sunderland, Jane et al. (2002) 'From representation towards discursive practices: gender in the foreign language textbook revisited', in Lia Litosseliti and Jane Sunderland (eds), *Gender Identity, Discourse Analysis*. Amsterdam: John Benjamins. pp. 223–55.

Swiss Report (1991) *Sprachliche Gleichbehandlung von Frau und Mann in der Gesetzes- und Verwaltungssprache. Bericht einer interdepartementalen Arbeitsgruppe der Bundesverwaltung*. Bern: Schweizerische Bundeskanzlei.

Switzer, Jo Young (1990) 'The impact of generic word choices: an empirical investigation of age- and sex-related differences', *Sex Roles*, 22: 69–82.

Trudgill, Peter (1974) *The Social Differentiation of English in Norwich*. Cambridge: Cambridge University Press.

UNESCO (1987) *Guidelines on Non-Sexist Language. Pour un langage non sexiste*. (rev. 1999) Paris: UNESCO.

UNESCO (1994) UNESCO 145th Session. Item 5.7.1. Paris.

Werkgroup (1982) *Werkgroup Wijziging Beroepsnaming. Gevraagd*. Amsterdam: Uitgave Ministerie von Sociale Zaken en Werkgelegenheid en de Aktiegroup Man Vrouw Maatschappi.

Wetschanow, Karin (2002) *Geschlechtergerechtes Formulieren*. Wien: Bundesministerium für Bildung, Wissenschaft und Kultur.

Whorf, Benjamin Lee (1956) *Language, Thought and Reality*. Cambridge, MA: MIT Press.

Wirthgen, Andrea (1999) *Political correctness: die "korrigierte" Sprache und ihre Folgen*. Universität Duisburg-Essen. PDF file. (www.linse.uni-due.de)

Wodak, Ruth, Feistritzer, Gert, Moosmüller, Silvia and Doleschal, Ursula (1987) *Sprachliche Gleichbehandlung von Frau und Mann*. Wien: Bundesministerium für Arbeit und Soziales.

Wodak, Ruth (ed.) (1997) *Gender and Discourse*. London: Sage.

Yaguello, Marina (1978) *Les mots et les femmes*. Paris: Payot.

38

Language, Migration and Human Rights

Ingrid Piller and Kimie Takahashi

38.1 INTRODUCTION

We begin this chapter with the story of Robert Dziekanski, who arrived in Canada as a new immigrant from Poland in October 2007. The 40-year-old man, who had never flown before in his life, was to be met by his mother, who had migrated earlier and was his sponsor, at Vancouver International Airport. Exhausted from the intercontinental flight and without knowledge of English or of how to navigate the arrivals section of an international airport, Dziekanski spent almost 10 hours in the restricted arrivals area, presumably waiting to be met by his mother (a record of his movements during those 10 hours is available in a report released by the Canada Border Services Agency after his death (Kooner, 2007)). The immigration officer who conferred landed immigrant status on him described him as follows:

[V]isibly fatigued and somewhat disheveled showing signs of impatience consistent with behavior displayed after a long flight and frustrations due to lack of English language skills. At no time did he display any signs of behavior that would be cause for concern (2007: 2).

Eventually, Dziekanski became very agitated and the Royal Canadian Mounted Police (RCMP) were called in to deal with him. Not speaking any English, Dziekanski remained oblivious to the officers' approach – an obliviousness that was interpreted as resistance by the officers. The assumption of resistance led to their next action: he was shot from behind with a taser gun and pinned to the floor by four officers. Within minutes, Robert Dziekanski died.

The death of Robert Dziekanski, which was videoed by another traveller and made the rounds on *YouTube*, triggered national and international outrage. Of the range of issues and debates that were linked to Dziekanski's death (e.g. the excessive use of taser guns by the Canadian police or a supposed loss of confidence in the Canadian nation as a multicultural, democratic country), the issue that we want to focus on here is the degree to which Dziekanski's death is language-related. Dziekanski's most basic human right – the right to life – was violated because he found himself in a situation where, presumably, he became fundamentally disoriented due to his inability to communicate (we write 'presumably' because the report of the inquest into Dziekanski's death (CBC News, 2008) had not been released at the time of writing this chapter in February 2009), and because his disorientation was interpreted, by police officers, as posing a security threat. While the case clearly presents human rights issues that are not related to language and communication – most notably the use of excessive force – it is the inability to communicate in an unfamiliar context that exposed Dziekanski and made him a target of police violence in the first place. Dziekanski's case may be exceptional on two grounds: first, it resulted in his death rather than less grave consequences; and, secondly, it received international media attention and widespread condemnation. However, the circumstances of the case itself are common enough in today's world: millions of people are on the move across international borders – either voluntarily or involuntarily – and are often thrown into situations in which they cannot communicate effectively. International border checkpoints, such as the international arrivals sections of international airports, are mostly designed to restrict international freedom of movement and thus present specific communicative challenges to the traveller, the conventions of which are familiar only to a small minority of 'frequent flyers'. Even in contexts where the linguistic and communicative challenges of international people movements are recognized, lack of resources can still result in discrimination against transnational migrants. In Dziekanski's case, for instance, immigration officers recognized his lack of English but could not help him out by bringing in a Polish interpreter because of staffing shortages on the evening shift.

It is the aim of the present chapter to examine the interrelationship between language, transnational migration and human rights. We use the term 'transnational migration' as an umbrella term for all forms of human movements across international borders, both voluntary and involuntary, and irrespective of the purpose of the travel and the length of the anticipated stay. We begin by reviewing the role of language in contemporary human rights issues. We note that a significant body of research exists on 'linguistic human rights', i.e. the postulated right to the use of a specific language, usually the so-called 'mother tongue', and is sometimes framed in the discourse of human rights. However, while the use of a specific language is sometimes presented as a human right, investigations into the role of language – or communication more generally – as an overarching factor in human rights issues are relatively rare, particularly in transnational spaces. Existing debates, research and institutional practices often seem almost blind to the role of language and communication in the social inclusion – or rather exclusion – of migrants. There is thus a need for a language- and communication-focused approach to migrants' human rights as they cross international borders and settle outside their countries of origin.

In the following sections, we explore the lack of communication that results from the inability to use a particular language as a human rights issue in itself, before moving on to examine the role of language and communication in migrants' human rights and their social inclusion in two key transnational spaces – where language and differential migrant status powerfully mediate access to human rights – employment and health. Our reasons for choosing these particular spaces are two-fold: first, these are spaces where basic human rights and social inclusion are produced or denied; secondly, language crucially mediates migrants' access to these spaces – knowing the language of the host country enhances access to employment opportunities and health care. Conversely, lack of proficiency in the right language(s) usually invalidates other entry requirements, such as prior qualifications and experience.

We recognize that our focus on employment and health in this chapter means that we are not covering some equally important spaces, particularly education and the legal system. We have done so because the central language and human rights issue is around access, and in order to avoid repetition of the same issue in different contexts, we have used examples from these contexts in other sections of the chapter. In the final section, we will present an example of a language learning programme that aims at enhancing migrant access, the Australian Adult Migrant English Program (AMEP).

Throughout, we endeavor to illustrate our argument with international examples. At the same time, readers will notice a predominance of Australian examples. Apart from the fact that we are most familiar with the Australian context, there are good reasons to focus on the Australian experience when it comes to issues of language and the social inclusion of migrants. In contrast to most other countries that have received significant numbers of transnational migrants in recent history, particularly in Europe, Australia has defined itself as an immigrant nation for almost a century (Castles and Vasta, 2004; Jupp, 2007). Furthermore, in comparison to the USA, another country where immigration is part of the national imagery, Australia has consciously adopted and experimented with state intervention to facilitate social inclusion, including language programmes (Lo Bianco, 2008; Martin, 1998). Based on our overview of the AMEP and other relevant programmes, we will also sketch out a broader framework for the provision of language services to migrants, in particular translating and interpreting, and multilingual resources.

We begin with an overview of the existing literature and present a theoretical framework for research into the intersections of language, migration and human rights.

38.2 LANGUAGE AND HUMAN RIGHTS: A THEORETICAL FRAMEWORK

The Universal Declaration of Human Rights (United Nations, 1948) mentions 'language' only once, in Article 2, proscribing, inter alia, discrimination on the basis of language:

> Everyone is entitled to all the rights and freedoms set forth in this Declaration, without distinction of any kind, such as race, colour, sex, **language**, religion, political or other opinion, national or social origin, property, birth or other status [our emphasis].

The authors of the Declaration thus saw language and human rights as indirectly related; i.e. the linguistic profile of an individual or a community may lead to their human rights being denied. Language can powerfully mediate access to human rights, but the authors of the *Universal Declaration of Human Rights* did not conceive of language as mediating access to human rights, nor did they see a particular language or a particular proficiency level as a human right in itself.

Examples of the violation of human rights on the basis of language are numerous from around the world, of course, even if one does not consider migration as an additional complicating factor. There is the obvious human rights violation of the prohibition against speaking or using a particular minority language in public that can be found in many contexts across the world: for example, the prohibition against the public use of any language other than Amharic during the regimes of Emperor Haile Sellassie and Mengistu in Ethiopia (Hussein, 2008), or the prohibition against the public use of any language other than Persian during the Shah's regime in pre-revolutionary Iran (Dei and Asgharzadeh, 2003). Such obvious violations of the human rights of speakers of a particular language, by regimes that have become notorious for their high levels of human rights abuses, are probably unsurprising. What may be surprising is that discrimination against speakers of minority languages occurs even in liberal democracies that are committed to upholding the principles espoused in the *Universal Declaration of Human Rights*, and that are generally considered good world citizens. Consider equality before the law (Article 7) as a basic human right. For instance, Pousada (2008) describes how the mandatory use of English in the federal courts of Puerto Rico means that jury service is restricted to upper-class Puerto Ricans, who have the required levels of proficiency in English. Many defendants thus have their right to a fair trial, where they are tried by a jury of their own peers, violated. While there is nothing in the law that directly says that eligibility for jury service requires upper-class status, the fact that high levels of proficiency in standard English only occur amongst this group – as a direct result of educational privilege – means that language mediates against access to jury service for the vast majority of Spanish-speaking Puerto Ricans (see also Delanty, Wodak and Jones, 2008, for related European case studies).

Even where only one language is involved, not speaking the 'right variety' may result in the denial of a fair trial, as Eades (2000, 2006) shows in her meticulous analyses of Aboriginal defendants before Australian courts. While the ways in which Aboriginal defendants and non-Aboriginal legal counsel, magistrates and judges speak English seem, superficially, very similar, different discourse and pragmatic conventions often mean that Aboriginal defendants are effectively prohibited from giving evidence, from presenting their character in a clear and detailed way, and generally from engaging in the trial as a meaningful interaction. Their voices are being silenced because both parties are ignorant of each other's varieties and the linguistic and cultural expectations that prevail in court.

These examples show that the relationship between language and human rights is a complex one – it is not only about speakers of a particular language being discriminated against but also about which particular variety is valued in which particular context and which particular linguistic practices are associated with access to a particular human right. We thus see language as a practice or a resource that may enhance or restrict access to human rights – or social inclusion more generally. With Heller (2007: 2), we see language as 'a set of resources which circulate in unequal ways in social networks and discursive spaces, and whose meaning and value are socially constructed within the constraints of social organizational processes, under specific historical conditions'. Similarly, abstract human rights, as enshrined in the *Universal Declaration of Human Rights*, are instantiated in specific practices that are socially constructed in institutions. The valorization of a particular linguistic practice in a particular social space or a particular institution pertinent to human rights – such as the police and the courts, the healthcare system or the education system – automatically enhances or restricts access to human rights on the basis of having the right sort of linguistic proficiency. As Bourdieu (1991: 55) puts it: '[S]peakers lacking the legitimate competence are *de facto* excluded from the social domains in which this competence is required, or are condemned to silence'.

The best – and probably most universally pertinent – example of a linguistic practice that mediates access to human rights is literacy. In most contemporary societies, literacy mediates access to health care, consumer rights, further education or employment, to name but a few. However, we live in a world where basic literacy is a 'right still denied to nearly a fifth of the world's adult population' (UNESCO, 2005: 17). That means that some 771 million people aged 15 or above are excluded from the access to education, health services, career opportunities and full citizenship that literacy affords.

While we thus see the relationship between language and human rights as mediated, a movement for specifically linguistic human rights has been gaining ground in recent years that sees a much more direct relationship between language and human rights. In fact, it sees the right to use a particular language as a human right. The concept of 'linguistic human rights' originates in the work of Tove Skutnabb-Kangas (e.g. Skutnabb-Kangas, 2000, 2001, 2003; Skutnabb-Kangas and Phillipson, 1994, 1998), and finds its most comprehensive expression in the *Universal Declaration of Linguistic Rights* (Follow-up Committee, 1998). The concept of linguistic human rights is characterized by an understanding that sees language itself at the core of human rights issues and the imposition of a language other than the mother tongue, particularly through schooling, as a human rights violation. Linguistic human rights are thus conceptualized as both a collective and an individual right: minority groups are seen as having a right to their ancestral tongue, and individuals are seen as having a right to their mother tongue. While the concept of linguistic human rights has been enthusiastically embraced by some non-governmental organizations and international organizations, such as UNESCO, it has been controversial within sociolinguistics. One key criticism of the concept of linguistic human rights has been that the understanding of 'language' it is based upon – a bounded entity that is associated with a particular ethnic or national group – is in itself the product of a particular language ideology that brought the modern nation-state and its colonial relationship with internal (and sometimes external) minorities into being (Blommaert, 2001a; Duchêne and Heller, 2007). As Blommaert (2001a: 136) explains:

> [W]hat counts is not the existence and distribution of languages, but the availability, accessibility and distribution of specific linguistic-communicative skills such as competence in standard and literate varieties of the language. Granting a member of a minority group the right to speak his or her mother tongue in the public arena does not in itself empower him or her. People can be 'majority' members (e.g. they can speak the language of the ruling groups in society) yet they can be thoroughly disenfranchised because of a lack of access to status varieties of the so-called 'power language'.

Another central criticism of the concept of linguistic human rights hinges on the way in which languages are tied to territory in an essentialist fashion. The *Universal Declaration of Linguistic Rights* (Follow-up Committee, 1998), for instance, defines a 'language community' (to which community rights accrue in this framework) as follows:

> This Declaration considers as a *language community* any human society established historically in a particular territorial space, whether this space be recognized or not, which identifies itself as a people and has developed a common language as a natural means of communication and cultural

cohesion among its members. The term *language proper to a territory* refers to the language of the community historically established in such a space (italics in the original; pages not numbered).

Even if one were to cast the theoretical criticisms of the concept of linguistic human rights mentioned above aside, it is easy to see that the close nexus between language rights and territory make linguistic human rights a rather blunt instrument, once migration out of the traditional territory of the language community is added to the picture (Wee, 2007). In the next section, we discuss how transnational migration complicates the relationship between language and human rights.

38.3 LANGUAGE, HUMAN RIGHTS AND TRANSNATIONAL MIGRATION

In the examples we quoted above of language-mediated access to equality before the law, it was the rights of citizens – Puerto Ricans are US citizens and Aboriginal Australians are Australian citizens – that were at stake, and there is agreement in principle that a violation occurs if working-class Puerto Ricans cannot be tried by a jury of their peers or if Aboriginal Australians cannot give adequate evidence before a court. There is also a consensus that the state – i.e. the US and Australian states, respectively – have a duty to right those wrongs even if there is disagreement as to how equality before the law can best be achieved for these people in the most efficient and equitable manner.

However, now consider the following case. In 1992, Chika Honda arrived in Australia as a Japanese tourist on what was supposed to be a five-day trip. When heroin was discovered in her suitcase and that of four other members of her tour, she was first charged with and then convicted of drug smuggling and sentenced to up to 15 years in prison. She served 10 and a half of these in a Melbourne jail and was repatriated to Japan in 2003. Chika Honda has always maintained her innocence and has, after her release, attracted substantial support, both in Australia and Japan, for a retrial to have herself exonerated (Hyland, 2008). The argument that a miscarriage of justice may have occurred rests mostly on language issues and cultural misunderstandings. An entry on one of her support websites writes:

> They [the suspects/defendants] could not speak enough English to communicate with their Legal Aid lawyers, let alone give proper evidence in their own defence. Worse, police had found it hard to find interpreters to conduct interviews and

the result was a mess: meanings of questions and answers were so mangled in translation that, like a house built on quicksand, any trial relying on those interviews would be hopelessly compromised by its shaky foundations (http://www.usp.com.au/fpss/news-japan13b.html; last accessed on 08/02/2009).

In a detailed investigation of one aspect of the judiciary process – the cautions (i.e. the Australian equivalent of the Miranda warnings in the USA) being read to and interpreted for the five suspects when they were first detained at Melbourne Airport – Nakane (2007) identified six problems that disadvantaged the suspects before the law. To begin with, the provision of interpreters for non-English-speaking suspects is a legal requirement in Australia. However, the necessity to question five Japanese-speaking suspects at once meant that five interpreters were needed at the same time. Even in a city the size of Melbourne – and for a language such as Japanese, which is the most widely-learnt foreign language in Australia, the language of a significant immigrant community and the language of one of Australia's major trading partners – this proved to be difficult. Only one accredited interpreter was available, two interviews were interpreted by paraprofessionals (accredited to translator level) and the accreditation status of two interpreters was unknown (and no longer retrievable when the issue of interpreter qualifications became a topic of concern during the trial). In addition to the lack of qualifications of the interpreters, Nakane (2007) found that even professional accreditation did not guarantee that the interpreters could handle the challenges presented by interpreting the cautions in a police interview. These challenges included the following:

1 The police officers delivered the cautions in segments that were too long for the interpreters to interpret accurately.
2 The police officers made arbitrary decisions about turn boundaries, which resulted in omissions in the interpretations.
3 The importance of comprehension checks was underestimated, both by the police officers and by the interpreters.
4 The police officers showed no awareness that the transformation of a written text into interpreted dialogic speech might be difficult.
5 The police officers treated the cautions as 'rituals' rather than 'real' communication.

As a result of these shortcomings, some of the suspects failed to understand that they were under arrest and considered their situation less serious than it was, including failing to seek immediate assistance from their embassy. Case studies of

similar language and communication issues faced by transnational migrants in judiciary processes in Europe and North America can, for instance, be found in the work of Kamali (2008), Trinch (2006) and Trinch and Berk-Seligson (2002).

There can be little doubt that language – i.e. the suspects', and later defendants', lack of proficiency in English as well as the interpreters' lack of competence in the genre of the cautions and police interviews – meant that these tourists' human rights to equality before the law was violated. (See also Blommaert (2001b) for an extensive analysis of limited linguistic proficiency resulting in narrative inequalities in the asylum procedure in Belgium.) The example shows how transnational migration complicates considerations of the relationship between language and human rights in four ways:

1 A larger number of languages become involved and the language and communication needs of transnational migrants can be very diverse.
2 Meeting the needs of an increasingly linguistically-diverse population has resource implications.
3 The very act of migrating is likely to throw migrants into a wider range of contexts where their human rights may be compromised or – to put it differently – migration generates more situations where access to human rights is mediated by language proficiency and communicative competence.
4 The international human rights framework is set up in such a way that states are charged with protecting human rights. However, state protection is mediated by citizenship and non-citizens – i.e. the vast majority of transnational migrants – tend to fall between the cracks of human rights provisions.

In sum, transnational migration increases the complexity of access relationships exponentially by bringing a wider range of linguistic proficiencies into contact with a wider range of institutional practices, some of which are specifically designed to restrict the movement of international migration. Indeed, the human right to 'freedom of movement and residence' (Article 13) is restricted by the phrase 'within the borders of each State'. This restriction points to a significant limitation of 'universal' human rights: i.e. access to human rights is usually mediated by citizenship. Maher (2002: 19) points out that:

> [...] while the human rights regime is international, its greatest influence has been to establish standards for states' obligations vis-à-vis their own citizenries. Hence, even in Western states that are vocal champions of human rights, policymakers debate the extent to which they are responsible

for protecting the full range of human rights for noncitizen migrants, particularly migrants lacking state authorisation.

The extent to which the state is under an obligation to ensure equal access for non-citizens and the extent to which resources of the state should be diverted away from citizens is often a matter of fierce contestation and mediated by other state interests. Rottman, Fariss and Poe (2009), for instance, demonstrate, in a detailed analysis of the outcomes of applications for asylum before US asylum officers and immigration judges, that decision makers were – in addition to obvious and legislated humanitarian considerations – also guided by national economic, military and security interests. Of particular relevance for the concerns of this chapter is the finding that since the terrorist attacks of '9/11', Arabic speakers were less likely to have their asylum applications accepted than speakers of any other language:

> Most importantly, physical integrity rights, which are supposed to be a central concern in the decision to grant asylum, seem less important after 2001 in asylum officers' decisions and asylum applicants from Arabic-speaking countries were more likely to have had their claims denied after the terrorists – who had similar heritage – struck on September 11 of that year (Rottman et al., 2009: 29).

The question of the obligations of states towards non-citizens also ties in with the question of 'critical mass'. In the example above of the Japanese drug-smugglers detained in Australia, we pointed out that even speakers of Japanese, a major international language, the language of a powerful nation-state and one of the world's largest economies, and a language that is relatively widely-known in Australia, were disadvantaged linguistically in their encounter with the Australian legal system. It does not take much to imagine how speakers of smaller or lesser-known languages might fare. May (2005: 326) has asked 'when there is a *sufficient* number of these speakers to warrant language protection' (italics in original). This observation is not purely hypothetical as the following case shows. Since May 2007, twelve refugee families from the small West-African nation of Togo have been resettled in the regional town of Ballarat (about 88,000 inhabitants) in Victoria as part of Australia's Humanitarian Settlement Program (Piper, 2009). When the first 10 families were due to arrive, the local planning committee was not advised of the languages these new entrants would speak until shortly before their arrival. Finding out what language a person from Togo speaks is not simply a matter of googling it: with three official languages (Ewe, Kabiya, French), 39 other recognized languages and a literacy rate of less than 40 per cent, the linguistic repertoire of an individual Togolese is impossible to predict on the basis of country information. Mindful of the fact that speakers of any West African language would be few and far between in Ballarat, a selection criterion for the initial 10 families included proficiency in French. However, '[a]s it was often only the head of household who spoke French, [...], this led to problems communicating with other family members, in particular the women'. (Piper, 2009: 27). Another positive twist to the story is that it emerged that two Ewe speakers from Ghana happened to live in Ballarat and 'they were encouraged to train and register with language service provider(s)' (Piper, 2009: 27). Australia's humanitarian settlement programme is exemplary and – by international standards as far as refugee resettlement goes – comparatively well-resourced. However, despite this fact and considerable linguistic planning (the choice of French-speaking refugees for resettlement) and linguistic good luck (two Ewe-speaking residents in Ballarat), the challenges to the social inclusion – access to education, employment, health care, including torture and trauma counselling – of these 10 families are formidable on linguistic grounds alone.

Before we move on to explore the linguistic challenges faced by transnational migrants in two specific arenas of human rights, i.e. employment and health, we want to highlight one further aspect of communication in transnational contexts – that is, the inability to communicate as a human rights issue per se.

38.4 COMMUNICATION AS A HUMAN RIGHT

As we explained above, we see language as mediating access to human rights and we do not see that the idea of having a right to a particular language (as in the linguistic human rights concept) is tenable. However, while there cannot be a right to a particular language, communication itself is a human right and being placed in a situation where one cannot communicate is a human rights concern, particularly as it is closely linked to the gross human rights violations involved in slavery and human trafficking. Human trafficking itself has emerged as an increasing human rights concern linked to transnational migration, and so in this section we focus on coerced transnational migration. We start by looking back at the transatlantic slave trade. bell hooks (1994: 169) imagines the terror on the slave ships that brought Africans to the Americas as closely linked to language:

> When I imagine the terror of Africans on board slave ships, on auction blocks, inhabiting the unfamiliar architecture of plantations, I consider that this terror extended beyond fear of punishment, that it resided also in the anguish of hearing a language they could not comprehend. The very sound of English had to terrify. [...] How to remember, to invoke this terror? How to describe what it must have been like for Africans whose deepest bonds were historically forged in the place of shared speech to be transported abruptly to a world where the very sound of one's mother tongue had no meaning?

Terrors such as those imagined by bell hooks for the victims of the transatlantic slave trade are as real in the twenty-first century as they were 200 years ago. In early 2009, the plight of the Rohingya of Burma briefly made the news in some international media. The Rohingya are an indigenous Muslim minority in Burma, who are not recognized as Burmese citizens by the Burmese regime and who are subjected to grave human rights abuses (http://www.rohingya.org/; last accessed 01/03/2009). When a couple of boat loads of Rohingya refugees arrived in Thailand in December 2008, they were detained, beaten, and then put back on boats, and towed out to sea, where they were finally cast adrift. Interviews with some of the survivors who were later rescued off Aceh, more dead than alive (broadcast on Al Jazeera; http://www.youtube.com/watch?v=9p-WyHJb_T4; last accessed 01/03/2009), show that their utter incomprehension of what was being done to them was aggravating their situation. One of the survivors, interviewed on Al Jazeera TV, stated that it was only his belief that God 'comprehends' that had kept him alive. For the Rohingya, and many other victims of systematic human rights' abuses around the world, the inability to communicate (to understand the threats of the soldiers) is not only a human rights concern in an immediate situation – i.e. being subject to military brutality, but also one in the broader context of finding a voice – and therefore raising concern and potential support, in the wider media world. The human rights situation of the Rohingya, both inside and outside Burma, is catastrophic (http://www.amnesty.org/en/news-and-updates/news/myanmar-minority-group-peril-20090202; last accessed 01/03/2009). Yet, in a world where the plight of so many is competing for attention, they are hardly noticed on the international stage and are even ignored on the regional level (http://news.bbc.co.uk/2/hi/asia-pacific/7916254.stm; last accessed 01/03/2009). In January 2009, when the Rohingya refugee crisis hit a new high after the discovery of the boat off Aceh mentioned above, the only international media outlet that gained access to the survivors and considered their story newsworthy enough for broadcast was Al Jazeera. Even on Al Jazeera, the interviewees remained nameless and were identified only by their age ('20-year old'; '23-year old'). While this is a significant communicative aspect of any human rights discussion, we consider inequalities in media access outside the scope of this chapter and will not pursue them further here (see, for instance, Baker et al., 2008; Pavarala and Malik, 2007; Wodak and Van Dijk, 2000 for useful overviews).

The fact that lack of proficiency in the majority language can be a constituting factor in contemporary slavery was recently recognized in an Australian court trial in which the defendant was found guilty of holding slaves because 'while the women were not kept under lock and key, they could not run away as they had no money, no passport, *limited English* and were told to avoid immigration authorities' (AAP, 2006, our emphasis).

Humans are social creatures and being able to communicate with one's fellow humans is clearly a basic human right – even if it is one that has largely gone unnoticed by scholars and activists alike, perhaps because it usually goes hand in hand with more obvious human rights violations. In the examples of slaves and boat people quoted above, their inability to comprehend what was done to them – and to communicate – is an aspect of a much larger atrocity. In such cases, it is probably strategically ineffective to point to communication as a human right because it is likely to be perceived as a minor infringement compared to the fear for one's life, the brutality and the starvation. However, communication needs to be recognized as a human right to campaign effectively against cases such as the following, which occurred in Australia and the UK – countries committed to upholding human rights – in their endeavour to deal with asylum seekers who have made it into the country: 'unauthorized arrivals' in the bureaucratic terminology of Australia. For instance, Aladdin Sisalem, a Kuwait-born Palestinian who tried to reach Australia via Indonesia in order to seek asylum there, got stuck in an 'offshore processing centre' in Papua New Guinea. In July 2003, when Sisalem had been in the detention centre for about a year, the Australian authorities were preparing to close down the centre and all other inmates were resettled, either in Australia or New Zealand. However, Sisalem's case was not yet resolved at the time and he was left behind as the only inmate for another 10 months before he was finally granted an Australian visa (http://www.safecom.org.au/sisalem.htm; last accessed 2009–03–01). When he was finally released, he had this to say about the company he had kept for 10 months: 'Honey, a stray cat [...] was the only company I had since I was left alone in detention ten months ago' (Jackson, 2004). Even in cases where other detainees were present in detention centres, detainees from different language and national backgrounds may not necessarily have been able to communicate. The violation entailed in detention without communication is most powerfully symbolized by detainees sewing up their own lips in a desperate bid to draw attention to their plight (Cox and Minahan, 2004).

It is not only detention that may make it impossible to communicate with others around you, as can be seen in the UK's policy of regionalization, which is an attempt to disperse asylum seekers away from London. For instance, Suleiman Dialo, an asylum seeker from Guinea, was sent to Newcastle in 2000, while his claim for asylum was being assessed. One-and-a-half years later his application was refused and he was awaiting deportation back to Guinea when he committed suicide. In the book *Human Cargo*, the journalist Caroline Moorehead (Moorehead, 2006: 129) describes Dialo's case as follows:

> This is not a plaintive tale about a cruel bureaucracy condemning a vulnerable young man to death; rather, it is a story about the loneliness and fear which are common to asylum-seekers everywhere, made worse perhaps in Dialo's case by the fact that his native language was Fula, which is spoken across parts of West Africa, and that there were no other known Fula speakers in the whole of north-east England; that his French was very poor and that he spoke scarcely a sentence of English; and that, in all his childhood in Guinea, he had never learnt to read or write. Signposts, letters, instructions, telephone calls, the television and radio, ordinary, daily conversation – none of this meant much to him in England; and his sense of aloneness was both overwhelming and shocking to him. [...] 'He didn't ever really understand what was happening to him. [...] The world about him had shrunk to almost nothing.'

In sum, finding oneself in a situation where one cannot communicate is maybe not particularly uncommon for transnational migrants and particularly for refugees. Even so, it has yet to be recognized as a human rights issue. The only way to address some of the loneliness of refugees – as involuntary migrants – is to recognize the grave consequences of the inability to communicate in a situation that has many other characteristics of instability and exclusion and to consider family and community resettlement. Of the few countries in the world that have an official refugee resettlement programme – Australia, Canada, Finland, New Zealand, Norway, Sweden and the USA – the programmes of some of these countries (Australia, Canada, the USA) are large and flexible enough that those accepted for resettlement can, in most cases, find a community of their own language background if they so wish. However, others have had to be more deliberate in their attempt to avoid isolating newly-resettled refugees (Moorehead, 2006: 266–80). We will describe one such resettlement programme – of Dinka from the Sudan in the Finnish city of Oulu – in the next section, where it also serves to launch our discussion of the role of language in transnational migrants' access to employment.

38.5 EMPLOYMENT

In her discussion of community resettlement mentioned above, Moorehead (2006: 266–80) describes a community of 71 Dinka from Southern Sudan resettled in Oulu, a city of 123,000 inhabitants in Finland. The Finnish resettlement programme is generous and the Dinka felt blessed to be safe and to be assisted generously. At the same time, their dependence on welfare and their inability to find employment was a constant topic.

> As they know well, as they tell each other every day, of the 250 refugees who were resettled in Oulu before them – Iraqis and Iranians, Bosnians and Somalis, Afghans and Burmese – only two have found work, and both as interpreters for social workers. Among the 71 Sudanese are teachers, electricians, nurses, farmers and university students. Talking about their lives, they say that they had simply assumed that resettlement would bring education, and with education would come work and a future. Now, it seemed, they would learn Finnish but not much else. They had never imagined, never conceived it possible, that there might be a life without an occupation. "We watch television, we eat, we sleep," said Malish. "We visit people. And we sit. This is really useless for me. I had a dream. It was about how I would work, and learn things, and become someone. If I don't succeed in my dream, I don't know how my life will be. My dream is dead. [...]' (Moorehead, 2006: 274).

The experience of the Dinka in Oulu – the death of dreams and the waste of human potential – is not uncommon for transnational migrants across the world: many transnational migrants have a hard time finding employment, and particularly employment at their level. The experience of unemployment and underemployment tends to be more common for transnational migrants than for the native-born. In Australia, for instance, even during the period of low unemployment and labour and skills shortages that characterized much of the first decade of the twenty-first century, the unemployment rate of recent migrants (5.5%) was considerably higher than that of the Australian-born population (4.1%) (Australian Bureau of Statistics, 2008). Furthermore, these statistics only reflect unemployment – not underemployment. The experience of un- and underemployment affects different groups of migrants differently. Within the group of recent migrants to Australia, there are stark differences according to visa class: while the unemployment for skilled migrants is 4.7%, the one for family reunion migrants is 7.5%, and the one for humanitarian entrants (i.e. refugees accepted for resettlement from UNHCR camps) is not published (Australian Bureau of Statistics, 2008).

The *Report on the Labour Force Status and other Characteristics of Recent Migrants* (Australian Bureau of Statistics, 2008) also provides evidence for the role of proficiency in English in finding employment. Table 38.1 lists the unemployment rates for four levels of self-reported English proficiency. As can be seen, as proficiency in English goes down, the unemployment rate goes up.

Another indicator of the role of proficiency in English can be gleaned from the fact that, of recent migrants, those born in an English-speaking country were more likely to employed (88%) than those from non-English-speaking countries (76%) (Australian Bureau of Statistics, 2008). Finally, 35% of recent migrants reported that language difficulties were the main obstacle they experienced in finding work. In sum, numerous reports from around the world suggest that transnational migrants face significant social exclusion through their difficulties in finding employment or employment at their level – the human right to work (Article 23). In this section, we ask how language mediates access to employment for transnational migrants and focus on two aspects: namely,

lack of proficiency in the majority language and 'accent-ceiling'.

Limited proficiency in the majority language is one of the main barriers to employment faced by transnational migrants (see, for instance, Adib and Guerrier, 2003; Alcorso, 2003; Colic-Peisker, 2002, 2005; Dávila, 2008; Masterman-Smith and Pocock, 2008). A migrant fitter and turner in Australia, interviewed by Masterman-Smith and Pocock (2008), describes his experience:

I have tried to apply for many jobs in that field of fitter and turner but the requirements are with the English. They have to be like high standard of English [sic] … and this is the difficulty I have had in the past. I've been to (over 20) interviews with different companies regarding a job but I haven't been successful and I think the main problem would have been the English.

However, even if migrants acquire a functional or even advanced level of proficiency in the local language, they are often still discriminated against on the basis of their accent. For example, Dávila (2008) reports how the accent of Latino immigrant workers is constantly problematized by native speakers of English in US workplaces, sometimes causing enormous emotional stress. Although the migrants in her study were highly educated and spoke English well, they experienced downward occupational mobility. Furthermore, they felt they were constantly harassed for their accent, as described by a university graduate from the Dominican Republic:

My boss, she's the wife of the owner. She's always complaining around me because she can't understand me. She says 'I don't know what you are talking about!' Or, 'Say it again' (3 times). It's so rude. Because she doesn't try to understand me either. (Dávila, 2008: 365)

In spite of gaining fluency in English, migrants' accents seem perpetually to hinder their ability to attain the professional positions they seek. As we have pointed out elsewhere (Piller and Takahashi, in press), in a context where racism has largely become invisible and a majority of White people consider themselves and their societies to be non-racist or post-racist (Hill, 2008), linguistic discrimination can sometimes substitute for racial or ethnic discrimination. (See Krzyzanowski and Wodak (2008) for an insightful study of institutional and everyday racism in the Austrian context.) Racial and/or ethnic discrimination are often illegal and individual employers may genuinely feel themselves to be non-racists. Linguistic discrimination, however, is often a commonsense proposition, and it 'just so happens' that non-standard

Table 38.1 Self-reported English proficiency and unemployment rates (adapted from Australian Bureau of Statistics, 2008)

Self-reported level of proficiency in English	Unemployment rate
English spoken very well	7.0
English spoken well	8.7
English not spoken well	4.9
English not spoken	23.1

speakers – people 'whose English isn't good enough' – usually happen to be minority members, and, even more importantly for our discussion, transnational migrants. (See Lippi-Green (1997) for an excellent overview of linguistic discrimination in the USA.) 'English has a colour', as Creese and Kambere (2003) put it in their exploration of the settlement experiences of female migrants from Africa in Canada.

A good example of how language discrimination can work at the micro level of everyday workplace interactions comes from Barrett's (2006) workplace ethnography in a Mexican restaurant in Texas. To begin with, the researcher found that, in that restaurant, jobs that required interactions with customers (who are predominantly Anglo-Americans), such as wait staff and managers, were overwhelmingly taken up by Anglo-American staff. By contrast, backstage roles in the kitchen were predominantly filled with Spanish-speaking migrants from Mexico or Guatemala. In addition to the obvious segregation of roles on the basis of status as migrant or native-born, Anglo managers frequently gave directives to Spanish speakers in what they thought was Spanish but was really 'Mock Spanish' (Hill, 1999) – an invented language that sounds Spanish to English speakers. Unsurprisingly, Mock Spanish was mostly incomprehensible to the real Spanish speakers and directives delivered in Mock Spanish tended to be misinterpreted. However, when a directive failed, Anglo managers never considered their limited use of Spanish as the cause of miscommunication but 'almost always interpreted [the miscommunication] on the basis of racist stereotypes of Spanish speakers as lazy, indignant, uncooperative, illiterate, or unintelligent' (Barrett, 2006: 163–4). The researcher argues that because Mock Spanish does not serve as an effective communication mode, it mainly functions to achieve the racial subordination of Latino workers. Nevertheless, managers do not consider the restaurant as a racist place, and Anglo employees often regard their use of any Spanish as 'an index of egalitarian attitudes towards Latinos and by extension, general sympathy with minority groups' (p. 165).

The issue of accent as a discriminatory tool in the workplace is not only relevant to migrants who are racially marked but also among those who may be 'invisible' migrants (Farrell, 2008). For instance, Colic-Peisker (2005) found that, in Australia, migrants from the former Yugoslavia were not subjected to 'prejudicial gazes' in public spaces because of their European backgrounds. Being White in anglophone but multi-ethnic Australia meant being invisible as a migrant and could be an advantage in social interactions, as this Yugoslavia-born cab driver explains:

One day a mature lady entered my cab in South Perth and said: 'I always only call "Black and White Taxis" [a smaller taxi company in Perth] because "Swan Taxis" they're all strangers, Arabs, whoever. ... You cannot talk to them, they speak poor English'. I said, 'Well, my English is not the best either.' She gave me a look sideways and said: 'At least you're the right colour.' (Colic-Peisker, 2005: 620)

The search for employment and economic opportunities has always held first place among the many reasons why humans choose to migrate, and many migrants measure the success of their migration in economic terms (see, for example Ong, 1998). Likewise, receiving societies tend to measure successful settlement largely in economic terms. Indeed, employment can be considered key to social inclusion as economic well-being powerfully impacts all other dimensions of human life including health, as we will discuss in the next section. As we have seen in this section, while limited proficiency dramatically limits access to employment, increased fluency of non-native speakers in the local language does not automatically lead to access to careers consistent with qualifications and experience, as such access tends to be mediated by a range of factors including accent and race.

38.6 HEALTH

Being discriminated against in the workplace, as in the cases discussed in the previous section, makes migrants sick, as, for instance, Vahedi (1996) demonstrated in his study of Turkish blue-collar workers in Germany. As a general background remark, it is important to note that – despite popular images of healthy, happy 'guest workers' – the health of migrants has been found to be worse than that of the native-born population in a wide range of international contexts (Solé-Auró and Crimmins, 2008). This is true despite the fact that good health tends to be an access criterion for most forms of legal transnational migration and health screenings tend to be used to control migration at the entry level (e.g. Hilsdon, 2006; Wolffers, Verghis and Marin, 2003).

The relatively poorer health of migrants than of the native born is the result of a range of issues that may or may not be related to language and communication. Among the reasons that are not language- and communication-related are the fact that relatively more migrants are employed in workplaces where occupational health and safety violations are of concern. A prime example would be the abattoirs of the Western world, the harsh working conditions of which have been the focus of labour and immigrant rights activists from Sinclair's (1906) novel about the plight of Lithuanian workers in the stockyards of Chicago to Schlosser's (2002) documentation of the harsh conditions and frequent workplace injuries in contemporary meat-processing plants in rural America. Even under less gruelling conditions, workplace discrimination can make migrant workers sick, as demonstrated by Vahedi (1996). Furthermore, refugees are one group of transnational migrants who may suffer from a larger number of preexisting conditions, often resulting from torture and/or trauma. In sum, there are some significant aspects that make it more likely that migrants have higher health needs than the native-born population and there may be non-linguistic reasons, related to visa status or economic status, that may mediate their access to appropriate health care. However, there is also a range of linguistic reasons that mediate migrants' access to health care. These include lower health literacy and language difficulties in interactions in medical contexts. We provide examples for each in turn.

'Health literacy' refers to '[t]he ability to access, understand, evaluate and communicate information as a way to promote, maintain and improve health in a variety of settings across the life-course' (Rootman and Gordon-El-Bihbety, 2008: 11). The authors of a 2008 report into health literacy in Canada found that being a recent immigrant and having a mother tongue other than English or French had a strong negative impact on health literacy (Rootman and Gordon-El-Bihbety, 2008). Enhancing the health literacy of migrant populations needs significant effort, as Griffiths, Quan and Procter (2005) describe. They report on a project to improve access to mental health services for asylum seekers from Afghanistan living in rural Australia. This is a group with a high prevalence of depression and other mental health issues and, at the same time, a group unlikely to have much access to mental health services. The 'no more *mualagh*' project – *mualagh* is a Dari word for 'deep sad feeling like being suspended in the air' – aimed to enhance mental health outcomes for this population, and, at the same time:

> to pilot, evaluate and report on a model of developing multilingual information on depression and the safe use of antidepressant medication with isolated and vulnerable communities (Griffiths et al., 2005: 7).

The intervention model adopted by the research team from *Multicultural Mental Health Australia* was based on the assumptions that:

- healthcare workers needed to learn from Afghan consumers about their perspectives on mental health
- Afghan consumers needed to learn from each other about practical issues in coping with mental health issues
- Afghan consumers also needed to learn from healthcare workers about the role of health providers in Australia, general and specific aspects of the healthcare system and the availability and use of interpreters.

On the basis of these reciprocal engagements, the research team eventually produced three resources: (1) a factsheet in Dari about mental health aimed at Afghan consumers, (2) a factsheet about the specific needs and expectations of Afghan patients aimed at healthcare providers, and (3) an audiotape in Dari about mental health issues (the latter to address the relatively low literacy rate, even in the first language, among this population). Griffiths, Quan and Procter (2005) provided a useful checklist on how to develop health literacy materials for and with linguistically- and culturally-diverse populations. It is particularly the reciprocal nature of this project that made it effective in contrast to some other multilingual resources used internationally. (See, for instance, Collins and Slembrouck (2006) for a detailed analysis of the limited effectiveness of multilingual consultation manuals in a Belgium clinic.)

Even where second language speakers have access to appropriate healthcare services, the quality of the interaction may be such that they are not receiving adequate care. Roberts et al. (2005) analysed interactions between linguistically-diverse patients and GPs in 19 surgeries in the London area and found that 20% of all the recorded interactions contained misunderstandings. These misunderstandings resulted from four different linguistic areas: (1) pronunciation and word stress; (2) intonation and speech delivery; (3) grammar, vocabulary and lack of contextual information; and (4) style of presentation. Style of presentation problems included patients who said very little about what their problem was or patients who overloaded the interaction with numerous topics, which seemed unconnected to the GP. The authors recommend awareness-raising for GPs and training in identifying miscommunication resulting from different ways of using language.

38.7 ENHANCING ACCESS

In this chapter we have sketched out how language mediates access to human rights in some key transnational arenas. In this final section, we provide applied perspectives on the ways in which the language and communication needs of transnational migrants can be addressed. We start with a discussion of language-teaching options for migrants and then move on to a more holistic provision of multilingual services.

'Migrants need to learn the local language' is a commonsense proposition in many international contexts. States differ, though, in the degree to which they place the burden for language learning on the shoulders of migrants or take on some of that burden. Over recent decades, most states have assumed that it is the migrants' own responsibility to learn the new language and very few countries have adopted a national strategy for migrant language learning. Australia is probably the only country in the world that has had a national language learning programme for migrants for 60 years now (Lo Bianco, 2008; Martin, 1998). English tuition for non-English-speaking migrants to Australia has been provided through the Adult Migrant English Program (AMEP) since 1948. In contrast to most other countries around the world that have seen significant immigration, Australia has for a long time chosen to take a pragmatic approach to the language needs of non-English-speaking migrants. Instead of ignoring the language needs of migrants or making language learning an individual responsibility, Australia recognized, with the introduction of the AMEP, a federally-funded language learning programme, that a society must assist newcomers in learning a new language if it wants to avoid the development of groups permanently excluded from the mainstream. Free English tuition to new arrivals as a way to facilitate their social inclusion as well as their economic productivity was, for a long time, an internationally unique feature of Australian immigration policy.

The AMEP started out in the immediate aftermath of World War II as a relatively small English tuition programme on board ships during the long voyage from Europe to Australia and, on-shore, as a language programme in a large migrant reception centre of the time, Bonegilla in Victoria. From these humble beginnings, AMEP has developed into a nationwide programme that, at the beginning of the twenty-first century, provides English tuition to over 30,000 new migrants per year. The language-learning needs of adults and their workplaces resulted in a number of early innovations in language teaching that have since been adopted around the world. The AMEP developed the 'Australian Situational Method', which consisted of three focal points for instruction: namely, social phrases, grammatical structures and Australian culture. Delivery options were quickly expanded beyond the classroom and have

come to include workplace language training, home-tutor schemes and distance education provisions. Flexible delivery options and responsiveness to the changing language needs of changing migrant groups have become a hallmark of AMEP.

AMEP is nowadays delivered in about 250 locations around the country and, in order to ensure consistency across the country, AMEP adopted a national curriculum, the *Certificates in Written and Spoken English (CSWE),* in the early 1990s. The CSWE was specifically developed for AMEP and is based on a functional description of English. The CSWE recognizes four proficiency levels and a learner is deemed to have mastered functional English once they have successfully passed CSWE III. Only a limited number of learners exit the AMEP after completing CSWE III, as the language-learning entitlement of new migrants has been limited to 510 hours since the early 1990s. Humanitarian entrants who have experienced torture or trauma may be granted an additional 400 hours. While the purpose of the AMEP is to provide learners with access to English instruction, it is not the purpose of the AMEP to ensure that each learner achieves functional proficiency. Indeed, 510 and even 910 hours have been found to be insufficient for learners with no existing proficiency in English to reach CSWE Level III. Since the late 1990s, learner groups who not only had hardly any proficiency in English but also no or very limited education and literacy in their first language or languages have presented a particular challenge for the AMEP.

There can be no doubt that the AMEP is an excellent language-teaching programme and similar national programmes, which are starting to develop in other countries, are an important step to the social inclusion of migrants. At the same time, it needs to be recognized that, even under excellent language-learning conditions, not all adults will learn a new language to the high standards of proficiency needed to negotiate some of the complex contexts sketched out above – nor will they do so fast (Collier, 1989; Watts and Lake, 2004). There are many entrants who are likely to fall through the cracks – from temporary sojourners via rural residents to women with family obligations – and a national language-teaching strategy on its own is therefore insufficient to meet the language needs of non-speakers of the majority language.

A comprehensive language and communication strategy for linguistically- and culturally-diverse societies will therefore also need to comprise substantial multilingual provision in home languages. To begin with, comprehensive language strategies need to be based on the recognition of language communities and the provision of services in community languages. Programmes that aim at hiring community liaison officers in education, health care or the judicial system are a good start but it is also important to 'mainstream' bilingualism through considering proficiency in community languages as a selection criterion for employment in all these sectors. Secondly, the availability of materials and resources in community languages is important (Aspinall, 2007), and there are many exciting projects that have developed best-practice strategies on how to create and disseminate such materials (e.g. Griffiths et al., 2005 described above); applied sociolinguists have an important role to play in disseminating such practices and strategies and making them more widely recognized. At present, most analyses of the provision of services in community languages note a dire lack of such materials, even in contexts where the importance of such provision has been recognized or even mandated, as the following report by the UK Office of the Deputy Prime Minister (2005: 46) reports:

> One in seven people from ethnic minorities face language barriers when accessing and using public services, yet translated materials are often unavailable. A recent report on local authority compliance with the Race Relations Act, for example, found that only one in ten benefit departments had produced leaflets in ethnic minority languages. Translating leaflets does not always solve the problem, however, as they may be poor quality or inappropriate for people who cannot read their mother tongue or have a culture of oral communication.

As the quote points out, the provision of materials in home languages is not always feasible and the provision of materials in plain English – or a plain version of whatever the national language is – also needs to be an important part of the language strategy for linguistically- and culturally-diverse societies.

In this chapter, we have shown that transnational migration poses significant challenges for societies committed to upholding human rights and to achieving social inclusion of all groups in societies. Many of these challenges are related to language, which crucially mediates access to key sites where human rights and social inclusion are produced. For such societies, a coherent language strategy – which aims at both language learning and multilingual, multimodal and plain language provision – is crucial to achieving equal opportunities for all. Unfortunately, most such initiatives are fragmented, leading to frequent breaks and inconsistencies in provisions. Most transnational migrants around the world have experienced 'language issues' of one kind or another and, in the absence of the recognition of the importance

of language and communication and coherent language strategies, they often blame themselves for their social exclusion and internalize their communication difficulties (Garrett, Dickson, Young and Whelan, 2008; Shemirani and O'Connor, 2006). We need to recognize that in language and communication 'it takes two to tango' and adopt strategies that serve to share the communicative burden.

REFERENCES

AAP (2006, June 9) Sex slavery: first woman jailed. *Sydney Morning Herald.* Retrieved 16 February 2009 from: http://www.smh.com.au/news/national/sex-slavery-first-woman-jailed/2006/06/09/1149815296540.html

Adib, A. and Guerrier, Y. (2003) 'The interlocking of gender with nationality, race, ethnicity and class: the narratives of women in hotel work', *Gender, Work and Organization,* 10(4): 413–32.

Alcorso, C. (2003) 'Immigrant employees in hotels', *Labour and Industry,* 14(1): 17–40.

Aspinall, P. J. (2007) 'Language ability: a neglected dimension in the profiling of populations and health service users', *Health Education Journal,* 66(1): 90–106.

Australian Bureau of Statistics (2008) *Labour Force Status and other Characteristics of Recent Migrants.* Canberra: Australia Bureau of Statistics.

Baker, P., Gabrielatos, C., Khosravinik, M., Krzyzanowski, M., et al., (2008) 'A useful methodological synergy? Combining critical discourse analysis and corpus linguistics to examine discourses of refugees and asylum seekers in the UK press', *Discourse and Society,* 19(3): 273–306.

Barrett, R. (2006) 'Language ideology and racial inequality: competing functions of Spanish in an Anglo-owned Mexican restaurant', *Language in Society,* 35: 163–204.

Blommaert, J. (2001a) 'The Asmara Declaration as a sociolinguistic problem: reflections on scholarship and linguistic rights', *Journal of Sociolinguistics,* 5(1): 131–55.

Blommaert, J. (2001b) 'Investigating narrative inequality: African asylum seekers' stories in Belgium', *Discourse and Society,* 12(4): 413–49.

Bourdieu, P. (1991) *Language and Symbolic Power.* Cambridge: Polity Press.

Castles, S. and Vasta, E. (2004) 'Australia: new conflicts around old dilemmas', in W. Cornelius, T. Tsuda, P. Martin and J. Hollifield (eds), *Controlling Immigration: A Global Perspective.* Stanford, CA: Stanford University Press.

CBC News (2008, May 4) Inquiry examining Taser use, Dziekanski's death begins Monday. Retrieved 15 April 2009 from: http://www.cbc.ca/canada/british-columbia/story/2008/05/04/bc-dziekanski-taser-inquiry.html.

Colic-Peisker, V. (2002) 'The process of community and identity building among recently arrived Bosnian Muslim refugees in Western Australia', *Mots Pluriel:* 21.

Colic-Peisker, V. (2005) "At least you're the right colour": identity and social Inclusion of Bosnian refugees in

Australia', *Journal of Ethnic and Migration Studies*, 31(4): 615–38.

Collier, V. P. (1989) 'How long? A synthesis of research on academic achievement in a second language', *TESOL Quarterly*, 23(3): 509–31.

Collins, J. and Slembrouck, S. (2006) '"You don't know what they translate": language contact, institutional procedure, and literacy practice in neighborhood health clinics in urban Flanders', *Journal of Linguistic Anthropology*, 16(2): 249–68.

Cox, J. W. and Minahan, S. (2004) 'Unravelling Woomera: lip sewing, morphology and dystopia', *Journal of Organizational Change Management*, 17(3): 292–301.

Creese, G. and Kambere, E. N. (2003) 'What colour is your English?', *Canadian Review of Sociology and Anthropology*, 40(5): 565–73.

Dávila, L. T. (2008) 'Language and opportunity in the "land of opportunity": Latina immigrants' reflections on language learning and professional mobility', *Journal of Hispanic Higher Education*, 7(4): 356–70.

Dei, G. J. S. and Asgharzadeh, A. (2003) 'Language, education and development: case studies from the Southern contexts', *Language and Education*, 17(6): 421–49.

Delanty, G., Wodak, R. and Jones, P. (eds) (2008) *Migration, Identity, and Belonging*. Liverpool: University of Liverpool Press.

Duchêne, A. and Heller, M. (eds) (2007) *Discourses of Endangerment: Ideology and Interest in the Defence of Languages*. London: Continuum.

Eades, D. (2000) '"I don't think it's an answer to the question": silencing Aboriginal witnesses in court', *Language in Society*, 29: 161–95.

Eades, D. (2006) 'Lexical struggle in court: Aboriginal Australians versus the state', *Journal of Sociolinguistics*, 10(2): 153–80.

Farrell, E. (2008) 'Negotiating identity: discourses of migration and belonging'. Doctoral thesis, Macquarie University, Sydney.

Follow-up Committee (1998) *Universal Declaration of Linguistic Rights*. Barcelona: Institut d'Edicions de la Diputació de Barcelona.

Garrett, P. W., Dickson, H. G., Young, L. and Whelan, K. A. (2008) '"The happy migrant effect": perceptions of negative experiences of healthcare by patients with little or no English: a qualitative study across seven language groups', *Quality and Safety in Health Care*, 17(2): 101–3.

Griffiths, M., Quan, D. and Procter, N. G. (2005) *Beyond Words: Lessons on Translation, Trust and Meaning*. Canberra: Multicultural Mental Health Australia, Australian Department of Health and Ageing.

Heller, M. (2007) 'Bilingualism as ideology and practice', in M. Heller (ed.), *Bilingualism: A Social Approach*. Basingstoke, UK: Palgrave. pp. 1–22.

Hill, J. H. (1999) 'Language, race, and white public space', *American Anthropologist*, 100(3): 680–9.

Hill, J. H. (2008) *The Everyday Language of White Racism*. Malden, MA: Wiley-Blackwell.

Hilsdon, A.-M. (2006) 'Migration and human rights: the case of Filipino Muslim women in Sabah, Malaysia', *Women's Studies International Forum*, 29(4): 405–16.

Hooks, B. (1994) *Teaching to Transgress: Education as the Practice of Freedom*. New York: Routledge.

Hussein, J. W. (2008) 'The politics of language, power and pedagogy in ethiopia: addressing the past and present conditions of the Oromo language', *Australian Journal of Linguistics*, 28(1): 31–57.

Hyland, T. (2008, February 10) 'The ballad of Chika Honda', *The Age*. Retrieved 22 September 2008 from: http://www.theage.com.au/articles/2008/02/09/1202234230100.html?page=fullpage#contentSwap2.

Jackson, A. (1 June 2004) 'Aladdin Sisalem released from Manus Island', *The Age*. Retrieved 15 June 2009, from: http://www.theage.com.au/articles/2004/05/31/1085855499159.html.

Jupp, J. (2007) *From White Australia to Woomera: The Story of Australian Immigration*. Port Melbourne, VIC: Cambridge University Press.

Kamali, M. (2008) *Racial Discrimination: Institutional Patterns and Politics*. New York: Routledge.

Kooner, B. (2007) *RCMP Taser Incident at Vancouver International Airport*. Vancouver: Canada Border Services Agency.

Krzyzanowski, M. and Wodak, R. (2008) *The Politics of Exclusion: Debating Migration in Austria*. New Brunswick, NJ: Transaction Publishers.

Lippi-Green, R. (1997) *English with an Accent*. London: Routledge.

Lo Bianco, J. (ed.) (2008) *Encyclopedia of Language and Education*. Vol. 1, *Language Policy and Political Issues in Education*. New York: Springer.

Maher, K. H. (2002) 'Who has a right to rights? Citizenship's exclusions in an age of migration', in A. Brysk (ed.), *Globalization and Human Rights*. Berkeley, CA: University of California Press. pp. 19–43.

Martin, S. (1998) *New Life, New Language: The History of the Adult Migrant English Program*. Sydney: NCELTR Publications.

Masterman-Smith, H. and Pocock, B. (2008) *Living Low Paid: The Dark Side of Prosperous Australia*. Sydney: Allen and Unwin.

May, S. (2005) 'Language rights: moving the debate forward', *Journal of Sociolinguistics*, 9(3): 319–47.

Moorehead, C. (2006) *Human Cargo: A Journey Among Refugees*. London: Vintage.

Nakane, I. (2007) 'Problems in communicating the suspect's rights in interpreted police interviews', *Applied Linguistics*, 28(1): 87–112.

Office of the Deputy Prime Minister (2005) *Improving Services, Improving Lives: Evidence and Key Themes*. London: A Social Exclusion Unit Interim Report.

Ong, A. (1998) *Flexible Citizenship: The Cultural Logics of Transnationality*. Durham, NC: Duke University Press.

Pavarala, V. and Malik, K. K. (2007) *Other Voices: The Struggle for Community Radio in India*. Los Angeles: Sage.

Piller, I. and Takahashi, K. (in press, 2010) 'At the intersection of gender, language and transnationalism', in

N. Coupland (ed.), *The Handbook of Language and Globalization* 540–54. Oxford: Wiley-Blackwell.

Piper, M. (2009) *Regional Humanitarian Settlement Pilot*. Ballarat: Department of Immigration and Citizenship.

Pousada, A. (2008) 'The mandatory use of English in the Federal Court of Puerto Rico', *Centro Journal, 20*(1): 136–55.

Roberts, C., Moss, B., Wass, V., Sarangi, S. and Jones, R. (2005) 'Misunderstandings: a qualitative study of primary care consultations in multilingual settings, and educational implications', *Medical Education*, 39: 465–75.

Rootman, I. and Gordon-El-Bihbety, D. (2008) *A Vision for a Health Literate Canada: Report of the Expert Panel on Health Literacy*. Ontario, CA: Canadian Public Health Assocation.

Rottman, A. J., Fariss, C. J. and Poe, S. C. (2009) 'The path to asylum in the US and the determinants for who gets in and why', *International Migration Review*, 43(1): 3–34.

Schlosser, E. (2002) *Fast Food Nation: What the All-American Meal is Doing to the World*. London: Penguin.

Shemirani, F. S. and O'Connor, D. L. (2006) 'Aging in a foreign country: voices of Iranian women aging in Canada', *Journal of Women and Aging*, 18(2): 73–89.

Sinclair, U. (1906) *The Jungle*. New York: Doubleday.

Skutnabb-Kangas, T. (2000) *Linguistic Genocide in Education or Worldwide Diversity and Human Rights*. Mahwah, NJ: Lawrence Erlbaum.

Skutnabb-Kangas, T. (2001) 'The globalisation of (educational) language rights', *International Review of Education*, 47(3, 4): 201–19.

Skutnabb-Kangas, T. (2003) 'Linguistic diversity and biodiversity: the threat from killer languages', in C. Mair (ed.), *The Politics of English as a World Language: New Horizons in Postcolonial Cultural Studies*. Amsterdam: Rodopi. pp. 31–52.

Skutnabb-Kangas, T. and Phillipson, R. (eds) (1994) *Linguistic Human Rights: Overcoming Linguistic Discrimination*. Berlin: Mouton de Gruyter.

Skutnabb-Kangas, T. and Phillipson, R. (1998) 'Language in human rights', *The International Communication Gazette*, 60(1): 27–46.

Solé-Auró, A. and Crimmins, E. M. (2008) 'Health of immigrants in European countries', *International Migration Review*, 42(4): 861–76.

Trinch, S. (2006) 'Bilingualism and representation: locating Spanish–English contact in legal institutional memory', *Language in Society*, 35(4): 559–93.

Trinch, S. and S. Berk-Seligson (2002) 'Narrating in protective order interviews: a source of interactional trouble', *Language in Society*, 31(3): 383–418.

United Nations (1948) *Universal Declaration of Human Rights*.

UNESCO (2005) Literacy for life. Education for all: Global Monitoring Report 2006. Paris: UNESCO. http://www.unesco.org/education/GMR2006/full/headline.pdf;last accessed on February 06, 2009.

Vahedi, N. (1996) *Diskriminierung, gesundheitliche Beschwerden und Arbeitszufriedenheit: eine Studie zur Situation türkischer Industriearbeitnehmer in der Bundesrepublik Deutschland. [Discrimination, Health and Employment Satisfaction: A Study of the Situation of Turkish Workers in Germany.]* Ulm, Germany: Universitätsverlag Ulm.

Watts, D. L. E. and Lake, D. M. (2004) *Benchmarking Adult Rates of Second Language Acquisition and Integration: How Long and How Fast?* Final report 2004.

Wee, L. (2007) 'Linguistic human rights and mobility', *Journal of Multilingual and Multicultural Development*, 28(4): 325–38.

Wodak, R. and Van Dijk, T. A. (eds) (2000) *Racism at the Top: Parliamentary Discourses on Ethnic Issues in Six European States*. Klagenfurt, Austria: Drava-Verlag.

Wolffers, I., Verghis, S. and Marin, M. (2003) 'Migration, human rights, and health', *Lancet*, 362: 2019.

39

Literacy Studies

David Barton and Carmen Lee

39.1 A TEXTUALLY-MEDIATED SOCIAL WORLD

People today are constantly encountering written texts. Imagine the amount of reading and writing people might come across in a Western-style café such as Starbucks: walking towards the counter, they might go through the menu, which might appear in the form of colourful handwriting on a chalkboard; someone might order a cup of decaffeinated cappuccino and be given a receipt by the shop assistant, who then marks 'decaf' with a pen on a paper cup. Around the place, people might be doing different things while enjoying their coffee: a group of students might be sitting together and discussing a school project with a few reference books lying on the table; at another table, a couple might be talking about current affairs and referring to a newspaper in front of them; some other people might be surfing the Web or reading their email by connecting their laptop computers to the free wireless network in the café.

As another example, we can think about the range of literacy-related activities in a university lecture theatre: before the lecture begins, some students might be reviewing notes from the previous lecture, while others might be talking about their assignments. The lecturer then comes in and sets up a PowerPoint presentation on the screen, and talks about the bullet points on each slide based on a set of notes which he or she had written before the lecture. Students might be taking notes as they are listening to the lecturer – some might prefer writing notes on their laptop computers, while others might scribble handwritten notes in a notepad. At the same time, some students might not be paying attention to the lecture at all – they might be checking mobile phone messages under the desk or surfing the Web.

These two scenes demonstrate that reading and writing activities are tied up with the particular details of a situation and that literacy activities are particular to a specific community at a specific point in history. Using these everyday activities as a starting point provides a distinct view of literacy. The two scenes further illustrate several other points. The first point to be made is that literacy impinges on people in their daily lives, whether or not they regularly read books or do much writing. Literacy is embedded in these activities of ordinary life. It is not just a set of skills which are learnt or taught in school. They are carried out in a wide variety of settings or domains. As seen in the above examples, much of the literacy in a café may be quite unlike that encountered in a lecture theatre. In addition, several people can be involved in reading or in writing, and they may participate in various ways, each treating the written word differently. There are many ways of reading in a particular situation with a particular text. The various texts are recognized as distinct and are read in different ways – there are many ways of taking meaning from the text. Reading a menu, taking notes in a lecture and writing text messages on a mobile phone may all involve different participants acting in different ways.

The central argument of our approach to literacy is that we live in a **textually-mediated social world**, where texts are part of the glue of social life. Texts are central to social interaction and much spoken language is performed in the context of written language and takes into account this textual context. Understanding what people do with texts, including both page-based and screen-based texts, and what texts do to people is an essential part of understanding contemporary social change. Language and literacy are at the heart of much of current social change because it is language and literacy which structure knowledge and enable communication. The field of Literacy Studies, or New Literacy Studies, provides a powerful lens for examining the changing nature of texts and discourses in our contemporary society.

In the rest of the chapter, we provide an overview of this distinct approach to literacy. We first review various definitions of literacy and outline the central ideas in the social practice view of literacy. In particular, we describe the two major units of analysis in Literacy Studies – literacy practices and literacy events. We then consider ways of researching literacy by reviewing studies in different traditions and areas of interest in the field. We also discuss some recent issues in Literacy Studies, concentrating on the materiality of texts, the relationship between globalization and literacies, as well as the impact of new technologies on literacy practices. The chapter concludes by discussing the importance of studying both texts and practices and how we can combine methods of discourse analysis with the ethnographic approaches of literacy studies to understand the textually-mediated social world.

Defining literacy

Looking for a precise dictionary definition of a complex concept such as literacy may be an impossible task. We are using the term to cover new broader views of reading and writing, and that is how it is being used in several disciplines, and in phrases like emergent literacy, used in education. As already pointed out, it is extended in another way to mean competent and knowledgeable in specialized areas, with terms like computer literacy, economic literacy and political literacy. People talk of different **literacies**, so that different media can be discussed and, for example, film literacy can then be contrasted with print literacy. Other dictionary examples of the terms include emotional literacy, cultural illiteracy and a house being described as having an illiterate design.

In other languages of the world, there also exist words that are equivalent to 'literacy', 'illiteracy', or 'literate'. However, translation of these terms often brings confusions and contradictions. For example, the word 'literacy' does not easily translate into French, while there is no easy English equivalent of the French sense of *écriture* as *writings*, nor of *illetrisme* as *unlettered*. *Analphabetisme* is also used in French for illiterate and words equivalent to unalphabetized exist in other languages, including Spanish, Italian, Greek and Danish. Note that it is a partisan word: in its make-up there is the idea that an alphabetic writing system is necessary in order to be literate. In languages where the writing system is not based on an alphabet, such as Chinese and Japanese, literacy is often broadly associated with the ability to read and write, or knowledge of words; illiteracy in both Chinese and Japanese has negative connotations: *wen mang* in Chinese and *man mou* in Japanese both literally mean 'sentence-blindness'. Nevertheless, in English 'literacy' has become a unifying term across a range of disciplines for new views of reading and writing; there has been such a growth of study in the area that it is now referred to as 'Literacy Studies' or 'New Literacy Studies'.

39.2 A SOCIAL PRACTICE VIEW OF LITERACY

The field of Literacy Studies has come into being in the past 20 years. In many ways, Literacy Studies grew out of a dissatisfaction with conceptions of reading and writing which were prevalent in education in all areas, from early childhood reading to adult literacy programmes: these were conceptions of reading and writing which were based on oversimplistic psychological models. The critique has been made from a range of disciplinary vantage points and in a range of ways: it can be found in Baynham (1995), Barton (2007), Bloome and Green (1992), Gee (1996), Giroux (1983) and Willinsky (1990), as well as in the work of Heath (1983), Scribner and Cole (1981) and Street (1984), which have become classic studies in the field. Willinsky talked of the 'New Literacy' and Gee (1996) first referred to the 'New Literacy Studies'. The critique of earlier views of literacy, or 'autonomous' approaches to literacy (Street, 1984), has been well rehearsed in these publications, opposing psychological approaches to language which fail to take account of social phenomena and critiquing inadequate educational views of literacy which do not look beyond pedagogy and the classroom.

A key to new views of literacy is situating reading and writing in its social context. Literacy Studies starts from people's uses of literacy, not from their formal learning of literacy. It also starts from everyday life and from the everyday activities which people are involved in. It is important to stress that education has not been used as a starting point and by the time the discussion gets to schools and learning there will be a different view of what literacy is and what learning is.

The social approach to literacy starts out from three areas of inquiry: the social, the psychological and the historical. Barton (2007) has outlined the characteristics of such an integrated theory of literacy, grouped under a set of eight headings:

1　Literacy is a social activity and can best be described in terms of people's literacy practices which they draw upon in literacy events.
2　People have different literacies which they make use of, associated with different domains of life. Examining different cultures or historical periods reveals more literacies.
3　People's literacy practices are situated in broader social relations. This makes it necessary to describe the social settings of literacy events, including the ways in which social institutions support particular literacies.
4　Literacy is based upon a system of symbols. It is a symbolic system used for communication and as such exists in relation to other systems of information exchange. It is a way of representing the world to others.

A literacy event is also embedded in our mental life; it forms and is formed by our awareness, intentions and actions. Thus, we need a psychological view of literacy:

5　Literacy is a symbolic system used for representing the world to ourselves. Literacy is part of our thinking. It is part of the technology of thought.
6　We have awareness, attitudes and values with respect to literacy and these attitudes and values guide our actions.

Any literacy event has a history, both at the personal and at the cultural level:

7　Literacy has a history. Our individual life histories contain many literacy events from early childhood onwards which the present is built upon. We change and as children and adults are constantly learning about literacy.
8　A literacy event also has a social history. Current practices are created out of the past.

Detailed elaboration of these eight propositions can be found in Barton (2007). In the following, we focus on three major issues which we believe are essential in the understanding of a social view of literacy.

Units of analysis: literacy events and literacy practices

The first important point to be made about the social approach to literacy is that literacy is a social activity and can best be described in terms of people's literacy practices; these practices are drawn upon in literacy events which are mediated by written texts.

The two terms 'literacy practices' and 'literacy events' need to be explained. The first basic unit of analysis is that of event; there are all sorts of occasions in everyday life where the written word has a role. We can refer to these as 'literacy events'. Talking in terms of literacy events is necessary to describe how literacy is actually used in people's everyday lives. An obvious example of a literacy event is when an adult reads a story to a child at bedtime. The bedtime story is an interesting literacy event in that it is often a regular event with repeated patterns of interaction. The term is broader than this though and includes any activity which involves the written word; for some events, especially within education, the explicit purpose is learning, but for most literacy events this is not so. In their everyday lives, people can be involved in a wide range of literacy events. On a typical morning at work, for example, we might check our email, listen to phone messages, and write notes in our diary while talking to a colleague about a meeting agenda. These quite different literacy events are nested within each other with micro and macro events; they are chained together in sequences and they are networked across contexts. Even in less text-based jobs such as those of cleaners and security guards, people often have to keep records of their activities; they follow written instructions and deal with written issues of health and safety as well as records of their pay.

The notion of literacy event has its roots in the sociolinguistic idea of speech events, which goes back at least to the work of Dell Hymes (1962). It is used in relation to literacy by Anderson et al. (1980) in a study of young children at home. They define a literacy event as being an occasion when a person 'attempts to comprehend or produce graphic signs', either alone or with others. Heath develops this, referring to literacy events generally as being 'when talk revolves around a piece of writing' (1983: 386). Elsewhere, she defines literacy events as 'any occasion in which a piece of writing is integral to the nature of the participants' interactions and their interpretative processes' (Heath, 1982: 50). This is important in demonstrating that literacy has a role in so many communicative activities. In raising children at home and teaching them in school there are often regular repeated events involving the written word and it is useful to focus on these literacy events in order to understand more about how children learn to read and write.

The second central concept in Literacy Studies is 'literacy practices'. There are common patterns in using reading and writing in a particular situation where people bring their cultural knowledge to an activity. It is useful to refer to these ways of using literacy as literacy practices. The term practices is used in different disciplines, and several researchers have applied the term directly to literacy, including the studies by Scribner and Cole (1981) and by Street (1984) which have been mentioned already. Scribner and Cole see the idea as central and they discuss how practices can be seen as ways of using literacy which are carried from one particular situation to another similar situation (1981: 234–8). Another way of thinking about it is to start from more general notions of social practices and to view literacy practices as being the social practices associated with the written word. This can be done in order to see how social institutions and the power relations they support structure our uses of written language. For example, critical discourse analysts explore the notion of language as a set of social practices, in order to reveal how social institutions and power relations structure our uses of language, both spoken and written, as in Fairclough (2003) and Wodak and Meyer (2009).

Together, events and practices are the two basic units of analysis of the social activity of literacy. Literacy events are the particular activities where literacy has a role; they may be regular repeated activities. Literacy practices are the general cultural ways of utilizing literacy which people draw upon in a literacy event. Examples of literacy events and practices can be found in many areas in life. For example, writing a letter is a 'literacy event'. In deciding where and when to write the letter, how to write it, whether it should be typewritten or handwritten, whether it should be delivered by post or by email, along with the associated ways of writing, the letter writer makes use of various 'literacy practices'.

What counts as literate activity and what counts as a literacy event or a literacy practice is not straightforward; defining the limits and boundaries of these concepts is particularly difficult for those carrying out empirical research. First of all, in many situations text and talk are mixed up, especially with new technologies, and all activities are very multimodal with language and images intertwined. Nevertheless, often a good starting point for research into literacy practices is to identify and examine literacy events.

Domains of literacies

There are many ways of reading and writing, and thus there is not one set of literacy practices. An adult at home may engage in very different practices at the same time: this person may be helping a child with homework, looking up an entry in a diary, trying to fill out a tax form, reading food labels, and searching the Internet. To take a particular example from the *Local Literacies* research reported in Barton and Hamilton (1998), a man is involved in a range of different sorts of literacy: he writes shopping lists and telephone messages; he uses the local library; he reads and discusses the newspaper. At the library he participates in many different events and draws on a range of practices: as well as reading books he flicks quickly through the newspapers, sometimes renews books for friends he has recommended the books to, but claims never to read the notices in the library. He sometimes looks up old newspapers to read about himself and people he knows. In his home he has few books but he does have a collection of books on local history, which he seems to use regularly. Involving quite different practices from a different domain of life, he is asked to write the occasional letter of reference for former work colleagues in the fire service.

Where these different practices cluster into coherent groups, it is very useful to talk in terms of them as being different **literacies**. A literacy is a stable, coherent, identifiable configuration of practices such as *legal literacy,* or the literacy of specific workplaces. Literacies are identified culturally. Different literacies are associated with different domains of life such as home, school and work. There are different places in life where people act differently and use language differently. The social rules underlying people's actions in these three places are different. The physical space – the buildings and the layout of rooms – is typically different and time is broken up differently. These are different domains and they give rise to different social practices – meaning both the general ways of acting and how people individually act on particular occasions.

The starting point for detailed examination of literacy practices is to realize that literacy may be different in different domains and that school, for example, is but one domain of literacy activity. Other domains may be just as significant. The home is a particularly important domain in that it is the site for a wide range of activities and it is where children typically first encounter literacy events. The home is 'the centre from which individuals venture out into other domains' (Klassen, 1991: 43). Within a domain such as the home, one can look in more detail and examine a wide range of activities involving different literacies.

Having been precise about identifying distinct domains of activity, the reality is more fluid. When starting out, it may be useful to name home, school and work as separate domains with their own distinctive practices and discourse communities giving rise to particular literacies. In fact the home is a site, a physical location, for all sorts of activities. Different sorts of reading and writing from many sources, including school and work, are carried out in the home. The practices leak from one domain to the other and there is much overlap. Nevertheless, home and school remain separate domains where certain literacy practices are sustained, nurtured and legitimized while others are not. The same event might be valued very differently in the two domains and have very different meaning to the participants.

Literacy as communication

Literacy is part of communication and of reporting the world to others. The relationship of reading and writing to other forms of communication needs to be examined. First, there is the relation to spoken language. Ideas about written language have moved on considerably from viewing it as speech which is written down. Written language has different functions from spoken language and any choice between written and spoken usually has other implications beyond a simple choice of medium. Writing enables us to go much further than with spoken language. Writing results in **texts**, where we are able to fix things in space and time. Because it often is reproducible and open to inspection, written language can be a powerful form of language; we need to understand the ways in which writing extends the possibilities of language. It should be clear then that any view of literacy is part of a theory of language and it is necessary here to clarify the relation between written and spoken language.

Although they have different properties, written and spoken language are not easy to separate in actual use. In fact they are closely entwined, and in daily life people participate in literacy events where reading and writing are mixed in with spoken language and with other means of communication. Literacy events typically involve a written text and talk around the text and spoken language typically is supported by written texts. In many ways, written and spoken language are not separable in literacy events and some researchers would go so far as to blur any distinction between the written and the spoken and call all forms of public communication literate activities. Writing is based on speech in some very real ways: spoken language is the basis for most people's learning of written language, for instance, and the very form of written language gets its inspiration from spoken language. Still, it is important to stress that the roots of written language lie only partly with spoken language. Written language has a life of its own.

Other aspects of communication come into play with written language. Most significantly, it is visual; it is laid out in some way and displayed. The importance of the role of design, layout and other aspects of the physical context should be self-evident, and they form part of what is meant by writing. A social approach to literacy offers a different view of communication from traditional functional models which see it in terms of transmitters and receivers of messages, with writing and other technologies simply amplifying what spoken language can do. The point is that, with written language, we can do things we cannot do with spoken. It does not just amplify spoken language. It extends the functions of language, and enables us to do different things.

39.3 RESEARCHING LITERACY PRACTICES

The view of literacy as being part of social practices which are inferred from events and mediated by texts requires a certain methodology. In this section we first describe some methods that can be employed to research literacy practices, and outline some examples of studies which have done this.

Research methods

Researching literacy practices relies on a methodology of attention to detail which draws heavily on ethnographic approaches. It involves the examination of particular events in order to understand broader practices. Researchers integrate a variety of methods, including observation, interviews, the analysis of texts and the use of photography. Researchers have been innovative in developing methods which are ethical, responsive and collaborative. As with all research, there is a close link between theory and methodology and each informs and constrains the other.

Larger-scale empirical studies like *Local Literacies* (Barton and Hamilton, 1998) often involve researchers spending time in particular communities, using a multi-method approach to develop as complete a picture as possible of the detail of people's lives and the place of literacy practices within them, effectively carrying out an ethnography of literacy. Data collection in ethnography may include some or all of the following: observation of and participation in literacy events, which are documented using notes, audio recording and video recording; formal and informal interviews and conversations, which might again be recorded in a variety of ways; the collection of texts and artefacts created within the community, and of externally-produced documents about the community where these exist; the use of photographs both as data in themselves and as a spur for interview discussions (Hodge and Jones, 2000);

historical methods, including oral history interviews and working with archive material. It may involve methods such as questionnaires, used as one method among others to develop an overall picture. Researchers are constantly developing and pushing at the edges of research methods and now work with what is called virtual ethnography (Hine, 2005), using email, discussion forums, or chat rooms to interact with research participants and collect data.

Smaller-scale studies of literacy practices are also valuable. One of the best ways to conduct smaller-scale literacy research is to reflect on our own practices and the practices around us by focusing on a particular area of everyday life. This would start with the identification of a particular topic – a place, an activity, or a group. This could be something very familiar, or something completely new. This method is a good way for people to increase their understanding of literacy. In Lancaster, students have studied literacy practices as diverse as those involved in celebrating Chinese New Year, buying a lottery ticket, using a shared college kitchen or going to church (see also Barton, 2000). After identifying a topic, the next step is to observe elements of the visual or physical environment such as the participants and the activities in which they engage, as well as the objects around them. Getting down to detail is important here. Taking photographs is useful and can prove a very revealing part of the research. Having observed the visual environment, the focus shifts to identifying and documenting particular literacy events and the texts used within them. This might involve collecting or photocopying examples of texts. The next important step is to interview people engaged in the literacy events. Talking to the participants can help make their cultural knowledge clear and make sense of the observations.

As a methodology, Literacy Studies provides powerful ways of researching texts and practices. The concept of literacy events provides a starting point for analysing interactions, whereas the concept of literacy practices provides a way of bringing in broader structural aspects. Concentrating on specific domains of life, multi-method, collaborative and responsive methodologies provide ways of carrying out research that pay close attention to details. Juxtaposed with methods in discourse analysis, the ethnographic approaches of literacy research are also powerful in understanding language use in context.

Literacy studies in a range of contexts

To further illustrate the methodologies we described, we first provide an overview of some studies which have been carried out in the

UK. The *Local Literacies* research (Barton and Hamilton, 1998) studied the role of reading and writing in the local community of Lancaster, in England. The study identified key areas of everyday life where reading and writing were significant for people and it contrasted these vernacular literacies, which were often voluntary, self-generated and learned informally, with more dominant literacies which were often more formalized and defined in terms of the needs of institutions.

Further examples of local and community literacy research can be found in the later edited volume *Situated Literacies* (Barton, Hamilton and Ivanič, 2000), which brought together a number of studies of reading and writing in a variety of different local contexts, informed by the same theoretical perspective outlined above. Many of the studies in this collection show how qualitative methods and detailed local studies can deepen a theoretical understanding of literacy. For instance, a study of literacy in prisons by Anita Wilson demonstrated the role of literacies in the struggle against institutionalization and the importance of literacy in maintaining individual identity within a bureaucratic institution, and how people used literacy to construct a 'third space' between prison and outside (see also Wilson, 2007). This resistant use of literacy contrasts with work by Kathryn Jones with bilingual Welsh farmers at an auction market, where literacy inscribed the people's lives into a broader social order.

Literacy Studies research in the field of education has also provided significant insights. Extensive research in Further Education (FE) colleges in the UK takes our understanding forward in a distinct way: this *Literacies for Learning* research has identified the different literacies being drawn upon in these vocational colleges and helped disentangle the dynamics of the different literacies in educational contexts. Students are learning the reading and writing demands of the vocations they are training for – literacies for particular workplaces, such as catering, construction, or hairdressing. At the same time, there are particular ways of reading and writing which help students in their learning – the literacies for learning. These literacies for work and literacies for learning exist alongside other distinct forms of reading and writing associated with assessment and, increasingly, with accountability, as in the record-keeping they have to do. This work demonstrates the different literacies which students have to grapple with simultaneously, and identifies a phenomenon which is significant in other domains (see Ivanič et al., 2008).

Studies of the literacy practices of everyday life can provide data, methods and theories for educational practice. A study of adult learners by Barton et al. (2007) provides details of how and what people read and write in their everyday lives which can inform the educational curriculum. The theory of literacy as social practice offers educational practitioners a language to talk in when discussing literacy issues and can be used to develop a social practice pedagogy. For example, the range of studies of adult language, literacy and numeracy provision in England (e.g. Appleby and Barton, 2007; Tett, Hamilton and Hillier, 2006) enables us to move towards developing principles of a social practice pedagogy, i.e. ways of teaching adults which are based upon a social practice view of literacy. Other work in educational contexts has been concerned with the development of writing and identity in educational contexts (Ivanič, 1998, 2006), work applying a social practice view to understanding learning and people's lives in adult literacy education (Papen, 2005), and in the area of English for Speakers of Other Languages (ESOL) (Pitt, 2005).

Across the world, there has now been a broad range of studies across different domains of activity and it is possible to draw out common themes from the research. People have been carrying out research utilizing the theories and methodologies of literacy studies and complementing these with different frameworks, including discourse analysis, textual analysis, narrative analysis and aspects of social theory. They work in different contexts, including all areas of education, specific workplaces and particular communities, and may focus on childhood, teenagers, gender, multilingualism, new technologies or other issues. Many studies focus on the links between home communities and schools. Purcell-Gates (2007), for example, provides a useful set of case studies that cover home, school, young people, across cultures and immigrant experiences – ways in which literacy is multiple and is looking for 'new pedagogies for new literacies' (p. 179), meaning in this case new social practices from a range of cultures and not particularly new technologies. The studies in Street (2005) also cover many educational sites.

To give an example of a study outside of education, there is a tradition of South American research on the centrality of the written word in indigenous cultures and Wogan (2003) brings a social practice approach to this work. He sees the value of literacy studies being that it now provides

'A well established tradition of ethnographic research.[...] Twenty years ago, in the absence of such research, a study like mine would have not been conceived.[...] I focus on identity categories and state and church documentation.[...] Other studies do not fully explore the perspectives of ordinary non-elite groups'

(p. 66).

Community literacies have also been studied in Australia (Breen et al., 1994) and South Africa (Prinsloo and Breier, 1996). The personal letter-writing practices of Pacific islanders are examined in Besnier (1993). Wagner studied Arabic speakers in Morocco (1993). American studies such as those by Moss (1994), Perez (2004) and Reder (1987, 1994) have often been carried out on the literacies of minority communities. Other studies that share a similar starting point include Hull and Schultz (2001), and Gonzalez, Moll and Amanti (2005). Merrifield et al. (1996) studied two distinct communities, urban Appalachians and Californian immigrant Americans, exploring their literacies and learning in different contexts. In France, there is a growing body of research in the area of *l'Anthropologie de l'Écriture* (the Anthropology of Writing); although from a different theoretical tradition, studies within this approach share a great deal of similarities in methods and themes of research with the British tradition of Literacy Studies. For example, the concept of *actes d'écriture* (writing acts) that the French scholars work with (e.g. Fraenkel, 2007) broadens our notion of literacy events.

Such research tends to involve detailed studies of particular groups of people at particular sites: the references so far give a hint of their range and diversity. There has now been such a wealth of studies that it is possible to look across them and see common themes and repeated findings and at the same time to see how the meaning of reading and writing is tied to specific practices. This is all leading to new understandings of the nature of literacy.

Language and literacy in society

As mentioned earlier, nearly all everyday activities in the contemporary world are mediated by literacy and people act within a textually-mediated social world. It is this textually-mediated social world which Literacy Studies itself can continue to investigate, linking culture and cognition and analysing the dynamics of textually-mediated communities of practice. The critique this provides of dominant sociolinguistics research is similar to the critique which Dorothy Smith has made of sociology. She accuses sociology of being extraordinarily blind to

the phenomenon of textually mediated communication, action and social relations.[...] Our lives are infused with a process of inscription, producing written or printed traces or working from them.

(Smith, 1990: 209).

She continues

> The appearance of meaning as a text detaches meaning from the lived processes of its transitory construction, made and remade at each moment of people's talk. The vesting of meaning in such permanent or semi-permanent forms is routine and commonplace, and has transformed our relations to language, meaning and each other.
>
> (Smith, 1990: 210–11;
> see also Smith, 1999: 219–20).

By investigating practices, our approach to literacy complements other work in linguistics, especially in areas which focus on the analysis of texts. The study of everyday literacy practices pays close attention to the texts of everyday and personal life. It starts from people's social practices, noting that many of these involve texts of some sort, and that in carrying out many activities in life people use texts. There is a strand of work within Literacy Studies which has drawn inspiration from sociolinguistics, including Heath's work, mentioned above, as well as Baynham (1993), Blommaert (2008), Collins and Blot (2003), Gee (1996) and Tabouret-Keller et al. (1997). Such studies link Literacy Studies to sociolinguistic issues such as language choice, code-switching, and language and power. Barton (1998) has also discussed the potential inter-animation of Literacy Studies and sociolinguistics. A strength of Literacy Studies is that it combines a very strong empirical tradition with attention to theory, and that it can draw upon a broader range of areas of social theory than just critical theory. To address its social aims, the study of language needs to utilize theories about topics such as

- how the media works
- the relationship between local detail and global activity
- notions of self and identity
- social and technological change
- the shift from modern to postmodern.

An additional task is to link up, in a motivated way, research which starts with the analysis of texts with research which sets out from the analysis of practices. These have been quite different traditions of research: discourse analysis studies have analysed texts and much Literacy Studies research has been of practices. The difficulty is to link these up in a way which shows the mutual influences of the texts and the practices. Cruickshank (2006) is a good example of a study which mixes the ethnographic approaches of Literacy Studies with discourse analysis, focusing on a mixture of home, school, teenagers and

technology, and emphasizing the importance of networks, mediation and roles. Contributors to Cope and Kalantzis (2000) also linked up texts and practices, as did Ormerod and Ivanič (2000). Texts and practices come together where Williams (1998) and Leander and Prior (2004) talk of *textual practices*, referring to the processes of reading and writing; here textual practices are one element of social practices, complemented by the practices associated with the creation and use of texts. Scollon and Scollon's (2003) *Discourses in Place* explores the meaning-making process of public texts and considers the ways in which such a process is shaped by the physical world where the texts are situated.

Literacy Studies also broadens the notion of interaction by focusing on the importance of texts and examining the various roles that texts have in interaction. Sociolinguistic research on interaction has primarily been of spoken language and of face-to-face-interaction. In literacy research, the concept of literacy events provides a way of studying interaction between texts and talk. An example of such research is Pitkanen-Huhta (2003), which examines in detail the conventional structure of literacy events in EFL (English as a Foreign Language) classroom interaction in Finland.

However, there are other sorts of literacy event, where texts are present but are not read in a conventional sense; there are events where texts have symbolic functions; and there are various ways in which texts which may or may not be present are invoked. Events vary in the role of text: the text can be central, as in the act of reading instructions from a manual; the text can be symbolic, as when swearing on the Bible; and the text can be implicit, as when talking about texts which are not present. Consequently, within Literacy Studies, there has been a broadening of the notion of literacy event; the concept can be expanded from one which focuses on talk **around** a text, such as the mother and child story-time, to one that includes talk **about** a text, such as a discussion of a previously-read magazine, to an event not containing talk, such as browsing a web page. Similarly, there are many relations between events: events can be serial, coordinated and chained; they can be embedded or subordinated; they can be fuzzy. Such interrelationships between different events are also noted in a number of recent studies, such as Leander (2003), Barton and Hamilton (2005) and Kell (2005).

Alongside these broadening definitions there is evidence that the existence of texts in events changes things: interaction around a text is different. First, talk around texts is important in several ways. To give a range of examples, with children's book reading, there is evidence that talk around texts can be much richer for learning (Snow, 1983). Baynham (1993) has examined the way people go back and forth between text and talk, which he refers to as mode-switching. There is also research on the importance of bilingual talk around monolingual texts in the community and in the classroom (Martin-Jones and Jones, 2000). Secondly, even when there are no texts physically present in the event, texts can be the subject of the talk: people talk about texts. As the work of Maybin and Moss (1993) and Kathryn Jones (2000) demonstrates, much talk is about texts. Much of the 'language as spoken by ordinary people in their everyday lives', the focus of most sociolinguistics research, is in fact talk about texts. It can be revealing then to move to the position that most speech events in contemporary society are, in a broad sense, literacy events.

In addition to supplementing linguistics research with new theoretical and methodological perspectives, Literacy Studies offers new views about configurations or modes of language. Traditional formulations of sociolinguistics have focused primarily on spoken language (see Barton, 1998). A social practice approach to literacy expands existing views of speech and writing. In this approach, writing is more than just the spoken language written down. For example, a number of literacy scholars look into the physical presence of texts and trace how their functions and meanings change over time and contexts (see 'The materiality of texts' section). From another viewpoint, for some, written language is language made visible. Here the visual characteristics of language are investigated. The work of Kress and colleagues (e.g. Kress and van Leeuwen, 1996; Kress, 2003) has focused largely on the visual characteristics of texts. They prefer a narrow definition of literacy in order to distinguish writing from other semiotic systems such as the visual. Linking different semiotic systems, Kress and van Leeuwen (1996) have developed an analysis of visual images which develops out of language analysis. Kress and van Leeuwen (2001) also talk of multimodal meaning-making and their work, along with Hamilton (2000) and Stenglin and Iedema (2001), demonstrates the practical value of applying concepts developed in the study of language to visuals. This body of work not only provides new meanings of writing but also broadens the scope of language data.

There are parallels and overlaps among the different traditions of Literacy Studies that we have presented in this section. They all start from everyday life and what people read and write. They look at particular societies in detail, examining separate groups within a society and how they use literacy. They observe closely and they are willing to make use of a wide range of evidence.

Each study makes comparisons between groups in a society, teasing out differences, but they avoid making grand generalizations. Rather, they make points about the particular situations they have studied. They provide ideas for other people looking at specific situations. Equally importantly, they raise more general questions about what is meant by literacy, about the role of texts in people's lives, and about the fact that much of our current understanding of literacy is not obvious, thus leading to new definitions of literacy.

39.4 LITERACY STUDIES IN A CHANGING WORLD

One of the most obvious aspects of contemporary life is change. As society is changing, so language and the associated ways of using language are also changing. Understanding the future is about understanding literacies and texts and their shifting role in people's everyday lives. This section provides an overview of three recent directions of research within the field of Literacy Studies: the materiality of texts, the impact of new technologies, and the relationship between globalization and multilingual literacies.

The materiality of texts

In order to understand the changing nature of literacy practices in the contemporary world, we need first to understand some properties of texts which enable them to travel across contexts, and then to see how texts fare in the changing world. There is now greater understanding of texts and how they function, and how a written text is different from other artefacts. First, texts are things and this 'thingness' is important as we investigate and come to understand the virtual world and its relation to the physical world. Wenger (1998) identifies four characteristics of 'things' (or reifications in his terms):

- their succinctness and power to evoke meanings
- their portability across time, physical space and context
- their potential for physical persistence or durability
- their focusing effect, drawing attention to specific features or distinctions within social reality.

It is useful to think of texts in these terms and, in fact, when Wenger and others (such as Latour, 1987) focus on things, they are often talking primarily about language-laden texts (Barton and Hamilton, 2005). Texts are a special sort of reification and, compared with other objects, are generally strong on all four of these characteristics. The significance of the material existence of written language was apparent in the *Local Literacies* research, where such disparate things as the physical existence of books on shelves, the displays on notice-boards and texts on clothing were all acts of meaning-making. In addition, Ormerod and Ivanič (2000), studying children's homework projects, and Wilson (2007), studying prisoners' literacy practices, have drawn attention to the importance of the materiality of texts in very different situations. The physical nature of the text is one aspect of this materiality.

Another salient aspect of materiality is the existence of the range of cultural artefacts associated with literacy (see Graddol, 1994; Hall, 2000). (Of course, spoken language has a materiality; what is important is the changing materiality in different forms of language.) One significant aspect is that because of its materiality, written language has a different relationship to context from much spoken language, and often its importance is in how it is contextualized and recontextualized; which is particularly relevant within the sphere of education. Materiality has also been investigated from a different viewpoint by those interested in the book as an object, considering its importance as a material object and the contribution of materiality to processes of reading and understanding (as in Moylan and Stiles, 1996; Nunberg, 1999; Pahl, 2001).

Literacies and new technologies

The contemporary interest in materiality arises, and perhaps even originates, in studies of screen-based technologies where, compared with paper, the materiality of texts changes to a large extent (Baron, 2000; Haas, 1996; Kress, 2003; Snyder, 1998). The new configurations of language use, developing with technologies, render impossible the simplistic distinctions between written and spoken language. Understanding the language of Internet chat, for example, or mobile phone use, or text messaging is more complex than analysing the language and attempting to classify it on a scale from spoken to written. These are new forms of communication, with new forms of language and literacy practices. The practices around the texts and the technologies are an integral part of the language.

Theories have been developed to account for such changes in literacy practices under the influence of new media. These new views do not start with the acquisition of computer skills, but with the culture-specific literate activities associated with new technologies. Literacies of technology are seen as emerging social practices embedded in the larger cultural ecology (Hawisher and Selfe, 2000; Selfe and Hawisher, 2004). The development of new technologies also offers new affordances for textual representations and meaning-making (see, for example, Kress, 2003; Kress and van Leeuwen, 1996; 2001; Lee, 2007). Carrington (2005) also explores various new 'textual landscapes' in young people's lives, including SMS texting and computer games.

Some studies place more emphasis on the role of communication technologies in education (e.g. Freebody and Hornibrook, 2005; Knobel and Lankshear, 2007; Snyder and Prinsloo, 2007), while a growing number of literacy researchers are interested in particular types of computer-mediated communication in out-of-school contexts, such as writing personal emails (Yates, 2000), using chatrooms at home (Merchant, 2001), and private Instant Messaging (Jacobs, 2008; Lee, 2007; Lewis and Fabos 2005). In his studies of video gaming, Gee (2004, 2007) develops new ideas of learning in what he calls 'affinity spaces'.

More recently, a group of literacy researchers has started to explore newer forms of literacy in the second generation of the world wide web, or what is known as web 2.0. These new literacies are characterized by new practices involving collaborative writing, new notions of authorship and participation, and multimodality (Knobel and Lankshear, 2007). Examples of such technologies are blogging (Davies and Merchant 2007; Mortensen, 2008), online fan fiction (Thomas, 2007), and Flickr (Lee and Barton, to appear; Davies, 2006).

Studies of literacies in times of technological change provide strong evidence for the fact that literacy practices have a social history, and that new literacy practices are generated out of existing ones (Barton, 2007; Barton and Hamilton, 1998). These new literacies or digital literacies, as with other forms of literacy, are situated in different points in history (Sugimoto and Levin 2000; Yates, 2000). They present new possibilities and constraints for communication. Some of these changes increase literacy demands, while some reduce literacy demands. In general, these possibilities are all changing the basis of communication in human relationships. To account for such changes we need new definitions of language, and of speech and writing.

Globalization and multilingual literacies

In relation to globalization, the examination of literacy practices provides a way of interrogating the complex changes in specific sites, and tracing links between local and global practices, and documenting local forms of appropriation and resistance. Drawing on Actor Network Theory, Brandt and Clinton (2002) refer to literacy artefacts as a type of stable mobile which have a particularly important role to play in linking local and global practices because they serve to build and sustain long, stable connections and thus networks across time and space. Literacy artefacts, in other words, are particularly effective social agents in terms of making links across contexts. Papen (2007) explores the impact of globalization on reading and writing in times of social change in Namibia. The study shows the ways in which literacy practices are patterned in terms of power and equality, as well as the ways in which local people develop practices in the face of global issues such as the dominance of English and tourism. A more recent study by Blommaert (2008) also considers the relationship between grassroots literacies and globalization by analysing handwritten documents in Africa.

The global–local link is reinforced in studies in multilingual literacies. Work by Kathryn Jones (2000) with bilingual Welsh farmers at an auction market, where literacy inscribed the people's lives into a broader social order, showed how the local and the global are linked by textual activity. Jones focuses on the process of filling in a particular form, showing how the individual farmers are incorporated into the agricultural bureaucratic system through a complex process of locally-situated talk around texts and the interweaving of spoken Welsh with written English. In the USA, studies of literacies in multilingual settings are often related to improving the education of students from linguistically and culturally diverse backgrounds. The goal is to use ethnographic methods to understand better the different 'funds of knowledge' students bring from their homes and communities. Schools and teachers can then draw on this knowledge by relating school learning to home and community practices in more meaningful ways (Ferdman, Weber and Ramirez, 1994; Gonzalez, Moll and Amanti, 2005; Pérez, 2004).

A wide range of further studies in multilingual literacies are reported in Martin-Jones and Jones (2000). In one study, Blackledge (2000) shows how unequal relations of power between dominant-culture schools and minority-culture families dictated that Bangladeshi mothers of six-year-old children were unable to use their own literacies in the home-school learning context, constructing them as 'illiterate' despite the majority being literate in Bengali. Other studies of minority bilingual communities in Britain include Baynham (1993), Bhatt et al. (1996), Gregory (1996) and Saxena

(1994). Multilingual literacies have also been extended to screen-based settings. Globalization of the Internet presents opportunities for multilingual literacy practices in online spaces. Lee (2007), for example, explores the ways in which Hong Kong people deploy multilingual resources in instant messaging.

Other recent directions in the field include making links with work on communities of practice (Barton and Tusting, 2005). Another direction has been work on spelling and orthography as social practices (Johnson, 2005; Sebba, 2007). Research on literacy and creativity (Papen and Tusting, 2006) again shows the value of Literacy Studies, showing individual creativity in literacy practices and how people combine resources to act within social structuring.

39.5 CONCLUSIONS

The fact that people live and act in a textually-mediated world is the issue which makes the theoretical and methodological frameworks provided by Literacy Studies so essential for the more general study of language. Writing is not just speech written down, it is a different form of language and a distinct form of meaning-making. This is one of the original starting points of Literacy Studies as part of sociolinguistics (see Stubbs, 1980). Sociolinguistic research which sets out from face-to-face spoken language interaction has difficulty in addressing other aspects of social life which are mediated by written texts. The social view of literacy introduced in this chapter is especially important in understanding and analysing contemporary changes in language use and interaction, including areas such as globalization and new technologies. Whether it is change in technologies, education, the nature of learning, the relation of language to poverty and social exclusion, or language in the workplace, an analysis which starts from literacies is central to understanding language use in social life. Studies restricted to spoken language cannot adequately account for these crucial areas of contemporary language use.

The body of work within Literacy Studies also provides new methods of researching texts in contemporary social life. These include combining discourse analytic approaches of text analysis with ethnographic approaches of Literacy Studies and concentrating on the role of texts in specific domains of life. It is also essential to be explicit about such detailed, multi-method, collaborative and responsive methodologies. More broadly, Literacy Studies redefines the scope of linguistics and sociolinguistics and provides a paradigm which is essential in the study of contemporary language use and how it is changing in the textually-mediated social world we inhabit.

REFERENCES

Anderson, A. B., Teale, W. H. and Estrada, E. (1980) Low-income children's preschool literacy experiences: some naturalistic observations. *Q. Newsletter of the Laboratory of Comparative Human Cognition*, 2, 59–65.

Appleby, Y. and Barton, D. (2007) *Responding to People's Lives in Adult Literacy, Language and Numeracy Teaching*. Leicester: NIACE.

Baron, N. S. (2000) *Alphabet to Email: How Written Language Evolved and Where it's Heading*. London: Routledge.

Barton, D. (1998) 'Is literacy studies re-inventing sociolinguistics?' Paper presented at Sociolinguistics Symposium, London, March 1998.

Barton, D. (2000) 'Researching literacy practices: learning from activities with teachers and students', in D. Barton, M. Hamilton, and R. Ivanič (eds), *Situated Literacies: Reading and Writing in Context*. London: Routledge. pp. 167–79.

Barton, D. (2007) *Literacy: An Introduction to the Ecology of Written Language*. 2nd edn. Oxford: Blackwell.

Barton, D. and Hamilton, M. (1998) *Local Literacies*. London: Routledge.

Barton, D. and Hamilton, M. (2005) 'Literacy, reification and the dynamics of social interaction', in D. Barton and K. Tusting (eds), *Beyond Communities of Practice: Language, Power and Social Context*. Cambridge: Cambridge University Press. pp.14–35.

Barton, D. and Tusting, K. (eds) (2005) *Beyond Communities of Practice: Language, Power and Social Context*. Cambridge: Cambridge University Press.

Barton, D., Hamilton, M. and Ivanič, R. (2000) (eds) *Situated Literacies: Reading and Writing in Context*. London: Routledge.

Barton, D., Ivanic, R., Appleby, Y., Hodge, R. and Tusting, (2007) *Literacy, Lives and Learning*. London: Routledge.

Baynham, M. (1993) 'Code switching and mode switching: community interpreters and mediators of literacy', in B. V. Street. (ed.), *Cross-Cultural Approaches to Literacy*. Cambridge: Cambridge University Press. pp. 294–314.

Baynham, M. (1995) *Literacy Practices: Investigating Literacy in Social Contexts*. London: Longman.

Besnier, N. (1993) 'Literacy and feelings: the encoding of affect in Nukulaelae letters', in B. Street (ed.), *Cross-Cultural Approaches to Literacy*. Cambridge: Cambridge University Press. pp. 62–86.

Bhatt, A., Barton, D., Martin-Jones, M. and Saxena, M. (1996) *Multilingual Literacy Practices: Home, Community and School*. Lancaster University: Centre for Language in Social Life Working Papers No. 80.

Blackledge, A. (2000) 'Power relations and the social construction of "literacy" and "illiteracy": the experience of Bangladeshi women in Birmingham', in M. Martin-Jones and K. Jones (eds), *Multilingual Literacies: Reading and Writing Different Worlds*. Amsterdam: John Benjamins. pp. 55–70.

Blommaert, J. (2008) *Grassroots Literacy: Writing, Identity and Voice in Central Africa*. London: Routledge.

Bloome, D. and Green, J. L. (1992) 'Educational contexts of literacy', *Annual Review of Applied Linguistics*, 12: 49–70.

Brandt, D. and Clinton, K. (2002) 'Limits of the local: expanding perspectives on literacy as a social practice', *Journal of Literacy Research*, 34(3): 337–56.

Breen, M., Louden, W. Barratt-Pugh, C. et al. (1994) *Literacy in its Place: Literacy Practices in Urban and Rural Communities*. Western Australia: Edith Cowan University.

Carrington, V. (2005) 'The uncanny, digital texts and literacy', *Language and Education*, 19(6): 467–82.

Collins, J. and Blot, R. (2003) *Literacy and Literacies: Texts, Power and Identity*. Cambridge: Cambridge University Press.

Cope, B. and Kalantzis, M. (2000) 'Designs for social futures', in B. Cope and M. Kalantzis (eds), *Multiliteracies*. London: Routledge. pp. 203–34

Cruickshank, K. (2006) *Teenagers, Literacy and School: Researching in Multilingual Contexts*. London: Routledge.

Davies, J. (2006) 'Affinities and beyond!! Developing ways of seeing in online spaces', *E-Learning – Special Issue: Digital Interfaces*, 3(2): 217–34.

Davies, J. and Merchant, G. (2007) 'Looking from the inside out: academic blogging as new literacy', in M. Knobel, and C. Lankshear (eds), *A New Literacies Sampler*. New York: Peter Lang. pp.167–98.

Fairclough, N. (2003) *Analysing Discourse: Textual Analysis for Social Research*. New York: Routledge.

Ferdman, B. M., Weber, R.-M. and Ramirez, A. G. (eds) (1994) *Literacy Across Languages and Cultures*. Albany, NY: State University of New York Press.

Fraenkel, B. (2007) Actes d'écriture, quand écrire c'est faire. *Langage et Société*, 121–122: 101–2.

Freebody, P. and Hornibrook, M. (2005) The relationship of reading information and communication technology (ICT) to opportunity structure: an object of study? *Reading Research Quarterly*, 40: 371–6.

Gee, J. P. (1996) *Social Linguistics and Literacies*. 2nd edn. London: Routledge.

Gee, J. P. (2004) *Situated Language and Learning*. London: Routledge.

Gee, J. P. (2007) 'Pleasure, learning, video games, and life: the projective stance', in M. Knobel and C. Lankshear (eds), *A New Literacy Studies Sampler*. New York: Peter Lang. pp. 95–114.

Giroux, T. H. (1983) *Theory and Resistance in Education: A Pedagogy for the Opposition*. South Hadley, MA: Bergin and Garvey.

Gonzalez, N. E., Moll, L. and Amanti, C. (eds) (2005) *Funds of Knowledge: Theorizing Knowledge in Households, Communities and Classrooms*. Mahwah, NJ: Lawrence Erlbaum.

Graddol, D. (1994) 'What is a text?', in D. Graddol and O. Boyd-Barrett (eds), *Media Texts: Authors and Readers*. Cleveland, UK: Multilingual Matters. pp. 40–50.

Gregory, E. (1996) *Making Sense of a New World: Learning to Read in a Second Language*. London: Paul Chapman.

Haas, C. (ed.) (1996) *Writing Technology: Studies on the Materiality of Literacy*. Mahwah, NJ: Lawrence Erlbaum.

Hall, N. (2000) 'The materiality of letter writing: a nineteenth century perspective', in D. Barton, and N. Hall (eds), *Letter Writing as a Social Practice*. Amsterdam: John Benjamins. pp. 83–108.

Hamilton, M. (2000) 'Expanding the new Literacy Studies: using photographs to explore literacy as social practice', in D. Barton, M. Hamilton and R. Ivanič (eds), *Situated Literacies: Reading and Writing in Context*. London: Routledge. pp. 16–34.

Hamilton, M., Barton, D. and Ivanič, R. (eds) (1994) *Worlds of Literacy*. Clevedon, UK: Multilingual Matters.

Hawisher, G. and Selfe, C. (eds) (2000) *Global Literacies and the World-Wide Web*. London: Routledge.

Heath, S. B. (1982) 'What no bedtime story means: narrative skills at home and school', *Language and Society*, 11: 47–76.

Heath, S. B. (1983) *Ways with Words*. Cambridge: Cambridge University Press.

Hine, C. (2005) *Virtual Methods*. Oxford: Berg.

Hodge, R. and Jones, K. (2000) 'Photography in collaborative research on multilingual literacy practices: images and understandings of researcher and researched', in M. Martin-Jones and K. Jones (eds), *Multilingual Literacies: Reading and Writing Different Worlds*. Amsterdam: John Benjamins. pp. 299–318.

Hull, G. and Schultz, K. (eds) (2001) *School's Out! Bridging Out-Of-School Literacies with Classroom Practice*. New York: Teachers' College Press.

Hymes, D. (1962) 'The ethnography of speaking', in T. Gladwin and W. Sturtevant (eds), *Anthropology and Human Behaviour*. Washington, DC: Anthropological Society of Washington. pp. 13–53.

Ivanič, R. (1998) *Writing and Identity*. Amsterdam: John Benjamins.

Ivanič, R. (2006) 'Language, learning and identification', in R. Kiely, P. Rea-Dickens, H. Woodfield and G. Clibbon (eds), *Language, Culture and Identity in Applied Linguistics*. London: Equinox. pp. 7–29.

Ivanič, R., Edwards, R., Barton, D., et al. (2008) *Improving Learning in College: Rethinking Literacies across the curriculum*. London: Routledge.

Jacobs, G. E. (2008) 'People, purposes, and practices: insights from cross-disciplinary research into instant messaging', in J. Coiro, M. Knobel, C. Lankshear and D. J. Leu (eds), *Handbook of Research on New Literacies*. New York: Lawrence Erlbaum. pp. 467–90.

Johnson, S. (2005) *Spelling Trouble? Language, Ideology and the Reform of German Orthography*. Clevedon, UK: Multilingual Matters.

Jones, K. (2000) 'Becoming just another alphanumeric code: farmers' encounters with the literacy and discourse practices of agricultural bureaucracy at the livestock auction', in D. Barton, M. Hamilton and R. Ivanič (eds), *Situated Literacies: Reading and Writing in Context*. London: Routledge. pp. 70–90.

Kell, C. (2005) 'Texts, movements and participation', in A. Rogers (ed.), *Urban Literacy*. Hamburg: UNESCO Institute for Education.

Klassen, C. (1991) 'Bilingual written language use by low-education Latin American newcomers', in D. Barton and R. Ivanič (eds), *Writing in the Community*. Newbury Park, CA: Sage. pp. 38–57.

Knobel, M. and Lankshear, C. (2007) *A New Literacy Studies Sampler*. New York: Peter Lang.

Kress, G. (2003) *Literacy in the New Media Age*. London: Routledge.

Kress, G. and van Leeuwen, T. (1996) *Reading Images*. New York: Routledge.

Kress, G. and van Leeuwen, T. (2001) *Multimodal Discourse: the Modes and Media of Contemporary Communication*. London: Edward Arnold.

Latour, B. (1987) *Science in Action*. Cambridge, MA: Harvard University Press.

Leander, K. M. (2003) 'Writing travelers' tales on new literacyscapes', *Reading Research Quarterly*, 38(3): 392–7.

Leander, K. M. and Prior, P. (2004) 'Speaking and writing: how talk and text interact in situated practices', in C. Bazerman and P. Prior. (eds), *What Writing Does and How it Does it: An Introduction to Analyzing Texts and Textual Practices*. Mahwah, NJ: Lawrence Erlbaum.

Lee, C. K. M. (2007) Affordances and text-making practices in online instant messaging. *Written Communication*, 24(3): 223–49.

Lee, C. and Barton, D. (to appear) Constructing glocal identities through multilingual writing practices on Flickr.com. *International Multilingual Research Journal*, 4.

Lewis, C. and Fabos, B. (2005) 'Instant messaging, literacies, and social identities'. *Reading Research Quarterly*, 40(4), 470–501.

Martin-Jones, M. and Jones, K. (eds) (2000) *Multilingual Literacies*. Amsterdam: John Benjamins.

Maybin, J. and Moss, G. (1993) 'Talk about texts: reading as a social event', *Journal of Research In Reading*, 16: 138–47.

Merchant, G. (2001) 'Teenager in cyberspace: an investigation of language use and language change in internet chatrooms', *Journal of Research in Reading*, 24(3): 293–306.

Merrifield, J., Bingham, B. Hemphill, D. and Bennett de Marais, K. P. (1996). *Life at the Margins: Language and Technology in Everyday Life*. New York: Teachers College Press.

Mortensen, T. E. (2008) 'Of a divided mind: weblog literacy', in J. Coiro, M. Knobel, C. Lankshear and D. J. Leu (eds), *Handbook of Research on New Literacies*. New York: Lawrence Erlbaum. pp. 449–66.

Moss, B. J. (1994) *Literacy Across Communities*. Creshill, NJ: Hampton Press.

Moylan, M. and Stiles, L. (1996) *Reading Books: Essays on the Material Text and Literature in America*. Amherst, MA: University of Massachusetts Press.

Nunberg, G. (ed.) (1999) *The Future of the Book*. Berkeley, CA: University of California Press.

Ormerod, F. and Ivanič, R. (2000) 'Texts in practices: interpreting the physical characteristics of children's project work', in D. Barton, M. Hamilton and R. Ivanič (eds), *Situated Literacies*. London: Routledge. pp. 91–107.

Pahl, K. (2001) 'Texts as artefacts crossing sites: map making at home and school', *Reading: Literacy and Language*, 35(3): 120–5.

Papen, U. (2005) *Adult Literacy as Social Practice: More than Skills*. London: Routledge.

Papen, U. (2007) *Literacy and Globalization*. London: Routledge.

Papen, U. and Tusting, K. (2006) 'Literacies, collaboration and context', in J. Maybin and J. Swann (eds), *The Art of English: Everyday Creativity*. Basingstoke: Palgrave Macmillan.

Perez, B. (ed.) (2004) *Sociocultural Contexts of Language and Literacy*. Mahwah, NJ: Lawrence Erlbaum.

Pitkanen-Huhta, A. (2003) *Texts and Interaction: Literacy Practices in the EFL Classroom*. Jyväskylä: University of Jyväskylä.

Pitt, K. (2005) *Debates in ESOL Teaching and Learning: Cultures, Communities and Classrooms*. London: Routledge.

Prinsloo, M. and Breier, M. (eds) (1996) *The Social Uses of Literacy*. Amsterdam: John Benjamins.

Purcell-Gates, V. (ed.) (2007) *Cultural Practices of Literacy: Case Studies of Language, Literacy, Social Practice, and Power*. Mahwah, NJ: Lawrence Erlbaum.

Reder, S. (1987) 'Comparative aspects of functional literacy development: three ethnic American communities', in D. Wagner (ed.), *The Future of Literacy in a Changing World*. Oxford: Pergamon Press. pp. 250–70.

Reder, S. (1994) 'Practice-engagement theory: a sociocultural approach to literacy across languages and cultures', in B. Ferdman, R.-M. Weber and A. G. Ramirez (eds), *Literacy Across Languages and Cultures*. Albany, NY: State University of New York Press. pp. 37–74.

Saxena, M. (1994) 'Literacies among Panjabis in Southall', in M. Hamilton, D. Barton and R. Ivanič (eds), *Worlds of Literacy*. Clevedon, UK: Multilingual Matters. pp. 195–214.

Scribner, S. and Cole, M. (1981) *The Psychology of Literacy*. Cambridge, MA: Harvard University Press.

Scollon, R. and Scollon, S. W. (2003) *Discourses in Place: Language in the Material World*. London: Routledge.

Sebba, M. (2007) *Spelling and Society: The Culture and Politics of Orthography around the World*. Cambridge: Cambridge University Press.

Selfe, C. and Hawisher, G. (2004) *Literate Lives in the Information Age*. Mahwah, NJ: Lawrence Erlbaum.

Smith, D. (1990) *Texts, Facts and Femininity*. London: Routledge.

Smith, D. (1999) *Writing the Social: Critique, Theory and Investigations*. Toronto: University of Toronto Press.

Snow, C. (1983) 'Literacy and language: relationships during the preschool years', *Harvard Educational Review*, 55: 165–89.

Snyder, I. (ed.) (1998) *Page to Screen: Taking Literacy into the Electronic Era*. London: Routledge.

Snyder, I. and Prinsloo, M. (2007) 'Young people's engagement with digital literacies in marginal contexts in a globalised world', *Language and Education*, 21(3): 171–9.

Stenglin, M. and Iedema, R. (2001) 'How to analyse visual images: a guide for TESOL teachers', in A. Burns and C. Coffin (eds), *Analysing English in a Global Context*. London: Routledge. pp.194–208.

Street, B. V. (1984) *Literacy in Theory and Practice*. Cambridge: Cambridge University Press.

Street, B. V. (ed.) (2005) *Literacies Across Educational Contexts*. Philadelphia: Caslon.

Stubbs, M. (1980) *Language and Literacy*. London: Routledge and Kegan Paul.

Sugimoto, T. and Levin, J. A. (2000) 'Multiple literacies and multimedia: a comparison of Japanese and American uses of the Internet', in G. E. Hawisher and C. L. Selfe. (eds), *Global Literacies and the World-Wide Web*. London: Routledge. pp.133–53.

Tabouret-Keller, A., Le Page, R., Gardner-Chloros, P. and Varro, G. (eds) (1997) *Vernacular Literacy: A Re-Evaluation*. Oxford: Clarendon Press.

Tett, L., Hamilton, M. and Hillier, Y. (eds) (2006) *Adult literacy, Numeracy and Language: Policy, Practice and Research*. Milton Keynes: Open University Press.

Thomas, A. (2007) 'Blurring and Breaking through the boundaries of narrative, literacy, and identity in adolescent fan fiction', in M. Knobel and C. Lankshear (eds), *A New Literacy Studies Sampler*. New York: Peter Lang. pp. 95–114.

Wagner, D. A. (1993) *Literacy, Culture and Development: Becoming Literate in Morocco*. Cambridge, UK: Cambridge University Press.

Wenger, E. (1998) *Communities of Practice: Learning, Meaning and Identity*. Cambridge: Cambridge University Press.

Williams, G. (1998) 'Children entering literate worlds: perspectives from the study of textual practices', in F. Christie and R. Mission (eds), *Literacy and Schooling*. London: Routledge.

Willinsky, J. (1990) *The New Literacy*. London: Routledge.

Wilson, A. (2007) '"I go to get away from the cockroaches": educentricity and the politics of education in prisons', *Journal of Correctional Education*, 58(2): 185–203.

Wodak, R. and Meyer, M. (2009) *Methods for Critical Discourse Analysis*. 2nd edn. London: Sage.

Wogan, P. (2003) *Magical Writing in Salasaca: Literacy and Power in Highland Ecuador*. Boulder, CO: Westview Press.

Yates, S. (2000) 'Computer-mediated communication: the future of the letter?', in D. Barton and N. Hall (eds), *Letter Writing as a Social Practice*. Amsterdam: John Benjamins. pp. 233–52.

Name Index

Diagrams and tables are given in italics and the page numbers followed by n. denote endnotes.

Subject Index

Diagrams and tables are given in italics and the page numbers followed by n. denote endnotes.